OXFORD EC LAW LIBRARY

General Editor: F.G. Jacobs
formerly Advocate General, The Court of Justice
of the European Communities

EC EMPLOYMENT LAW

Third Edition

OXFORD EC LAW LIBRARY

The aim of this series is to publish important and original studies of the various branches of EC Law. Each work provides a clear, concise, and original critical exposition of the law in its social, economic, and political context, at a level which will interest the advanced student, the practitioner, the academic, and government and Community officials.

Other Titles in the Library

EC Employment Law

Third Edition

CATHERINE BARNARD

OXFORD
UNIVERSITY PRESS

OXFORD
UNIVERSITY PRESS

Great Clarendon Street, Oxford OX2 6DP

Oxford University Press is a department of the University of Oxford.
It furthers the University's objective of excellence in research, scholarship,
and education by publishing worldwide in

Oxford New York

Auckland Cape Town Dar es Salaam Hong Kong Karachi
Kuala Lumpur Madrid Melbourne Mexico City Nairobi
New Delhi Shanghai Taipei Toronto

With offices in

Argentina Austria Brazil Chile Czech Republic France Greece
Guatemala Hungary Italy Japan Poland Portugal Singapore
South Korea Switzerland Thailand Turkey Ukraine Vietnam

Oxford is a registered trade mark of Oxford University Press
in the UK and in certain other countries

Published in the United States
by Oxford University Press Inc., New York

British Library Cataloguing in Publication Data
Data available

Library of Congress Cataloging in Publication Data
Data available

Typeset by RefineCatch Limited, Bungay, Suffolk
Printed in Great Britain
on acid-free paper by
Biddles Ltd., King's Lynn

ISBN 0–19–928002–9   978–0–19–928002–5
ISBN 0–19–928003–7 (Pbk.)   978–0–19–928003–2 (Pbk.)

1 3 5 7 9 10 8 6 4 2

General Editor's Foreword

This new edition of a now well-established book on EC employment law is to be welcomed on many counts.

Employment law has had from the outset of the European Community a fundamental place in its very conception as well as a special role in the founding Treaties. It has maintained that important place throughout the Community's evolution, with both Community legislation and the case-law of the Court of Justice making substantial contributions to the protection of employees in the Member States. More recently, there have been far-reaching developments in the Community's social policy, with changes in priorities and an increasing role for 'soft law'.

In the founding Treaties, the free movement of workers throughout the Community, to be ensured without any discrimination on grounds of nationality, was a cardinal principle, which also informed far-reaching legislation on both employment rights and social security. The rights, not only of migrant workers, but of others moving within the Community, have an important role and an appropriate place in this book.

Equal pay for men and women, and equal treatment of men and women in employment, were also among the first and most significant contributions of Community law to the national laws of the Member States, and remain a vital part of the current law. The principles of equal pay and equal treatment have powerfully reinforced the rights of workers, sometimes in ways which might not have been expected—for example in their impact on retirement ages, on pensions, and on affirmative action. The author's discussion of these fundamental but complex concepts of equality and discrimination, and their various ramifications, succeeds in being both illuminating and highly practical.

But EC employment law now goes much further, and the scope of the book is correspondingly wide-ranging. It encompasses major items of legislation, such as the working time directive, the acquired rights directive, the collective redundancy directive, the insolvency directive, and many others. Inevitably, the law bears on health and safety, as well as on working conditions, and the protection of workers on the transfer of undertakings. Recently, the focus has shifted: and there have been fundamental political initiatives with implications for employment law: the Lisbon agenda and the Nice Treaty, and the still uncertain impact of the Charter of Fundamental Rights—or indeed the Constitutional Treaty. There are indeed few areas of EU activity where it is so important to take account of law and policy together. Throughout her work, the author combines legal analysis with an examination of the policy implications.

This book will not merely give its readers a knowledge of the reach, and much of the detail, of EC employment law. It will also give them a new understanding of the basic concepts and underlying policy aims; and it will make possible an informed and critical assessment of a subject of great social and economic importance.

Francis G. Jacobs

Preface to the Third Edition of EC Employment Law

Any book about the employment law of the European Union must consider the rules—both hard and soft—which regulate the relationship between individuals and their employer, and between worker representatives and employers. However, in order to understand EC employment law, the regulation in this field needs to be considered against the broader backcloth of employment policy (measures to protect and promote employment) and social policy. Traditionally, 'social' policy refers to measures which come under the broad umbrella of the welfare state, such as housing, health care, education, social security and social assistance. However, in the EU context, social policy has often been considered as broadly synonymous with employment law: the relevant Title in the Treaty (Title XI) is headed social policy and the relevant chapter (chapter 1) 'Social provisions' even though their content, especially in the early days, was broadly employment related. Thus, there is an inevitable bleeding and mixing of concepts. It is with the area of social policy concerned with employment law, both individual and collective, that this book is concerned, and not with social law and policy as more broadly understood.

Within the field of employment law—and policy—this book considers both the law-making process and the rules which result. It also analyses the (now extensive) case law of the European Court of Justice which has, at different times, been creative, imaginative and conservative. This book does not examine the individual employment laws of the Member States, nor does it consider the means by which European Community rules have been implemented by the Member States; these topics require their own consideration. It does, however, consider how aspects of Community law are informed by, and derived from, national employment laws.

Since the previous edition of this book was published in early 2000, the law has changed substantially. In particular, the Lisbon strategy, which determined that the EU should become the most competitive, knowledge-based economy in the world by 2010, was launched in March 2000, and relaunched in March 2005. This strategy marked a sea change in the Community's approach, shifting attention away from a concentration on hard law Directives to softer forms of policy co-ordination. As a result, I have restructured this book. It is now divided into six parts. The first Part is introductory, intended to give an overview of the development of social policy by the EU and the various approaches to rule-making. In particular, chapter 1 considers the Union's stumbling progress towards developing 'social policy', or more particularly 'employment law' at Community level. It considers the rationale for such a policy and the pressures which operate to constrain its development. Chapter 2 examines how these pressures shape the law-making process in the field of (hard) Community employment law, while chapter 3 considers the Employment Title, the Lisbon strategy and soft law-making in the social field.

The remainder of the book focuses on the substantive law. Part II looks at the position of migrants, particularly migrant workers, their rights (chapter 4) and the limits on their rights (chapter 5). Part III considers one of the major pillars of EC employment law: equality and non-discrimination. After an introduction (chapter 6) considering how the law has evolved in this field and an explanation of the key principles, chapter 7 examines equal pay, chapter 8 equal treatment, chapter 9 family friendly policies, and chapter 10 equal treatment in respect of social security and pensions. Part IV then looks at health and safety (chapter 11) and working conditions (chapter 12), while Part V considers employee rights on the restructuring of enterprises, in particular transfers of undertakings (chapter 13), and collective redundancies and employee rights on the insolvency of the employer (chapter 14). Finally, Part VI examines the more 'collective' aspect of labour law, worker representation, particularly through information and consultation (chapter 15), and freedom of association, collective bargaining, and industrial action (chapter 16).

Two issues have bedevilled anyone attempting to write in this area: Treaty renumbering and the Constitution. As to the first, the renumbering of the Treaties at Amsterdam was a particular problem in the social field because, in effect, it happened twice: once when the Social Policy Agreement (SPA) was incorporated into the Treaty of Rome and again when the whole Treaty was renumbered. Thus, the health and safety legal basis Article 118a became Article 118 and then Article 137. Confusingly, Article 3 SPA became Article 118a at Amsterdam and then Article 138. The destination tables reflect the second set of changes only. As a result, when talking historically, I have used the original old numbers followed by the numbers resulting from the second set of Amsterdam renumberings. When talking of the present situation, I have used the new numbers only. As for the Constitutional Treaty, I have taken the view that, following the French and Dutch 'no' votes, it is unlikely to be adopted, at least in its current form. I have therefore referred to it but not dwelt upon it. When talking about the European Union's Charter of Fundamental Rights 2000, I have usually used the numbers in the 2000 version of the Charter and not the numbers in Part II of the Constitutional Treaty.

Many people have been extremely generous with their time and patience in the completion of this project. The first two editions of this book benefited from the advice of Jon Clark, Nicholas Emiliou, Lorraine Fletcher, Rosa Greaves, Clive Lewis, Roy Lewis, Simon Steel, and Christine Warry. For this edition I have been very grateful for the comments and help of Katherine

Apps, Albertina Albors Llorens, Diamond Ashiagbor, Alan Dashwood, Michael Dougan, Andrew Fielding, Stephen Hardy, Bob Hepple, Tammy Hervey, Jeff Kenner, Clive Lewis, Louise Merrett, and Tonia Novitz. John Louth, Alex Flach, and Dédé Tété-Rosenthal at OUP have been enthusiastic and supportive. I am grateful for Elissa Connor's copy-editing skills. Domestically, I have been grateful for the distraction of two villainous, but gorgeous, small boys and the love and support of a bigger one.

Catherine Barnard
Trinity College
15 May 2006

Summary Table of Contents

Part I: Introduction

Part II: Migrant Workers

Part III: Equality Law

Part IV: Health and Safety and Working Conditions

Part V: Employee Rights on Restructuring Enterprises

Part VI: Collective Labour law

Contents

Part I: Introduction

1   The Evolution of EC 'Social' Policy

Part II: Migrant Workers

4 Free Movement of (Economically Active) Persons

Part III: Equality Law

6   Equality Law: An Introduction

Part IV: Health and Safety and Working Conditions

11 Health and Safety

Part V: Employee Rights on Restructuring Enterprises

13 Transfers of Undertakings

Part VI: Collective Labour Law

15 Worker Involvement in Decision-Making: Information, Consultation, and Worker Participation

Table of Cases from the European Court of Justice

References printed in **bold** *refer to the page number where a substantial discussion of the Case commences.*

Table of Cases from the Court of First Instance

Table of Cases from the European Court and Commission of Human Rights

Table of Cases from the EFTA Court

Table of Cases—National

Table of European Commission Decisions

Table of Acts, Agreements, and Conventions

References printed in **bold** *refer to the page number where a substantial discussion of the Act, Agreement, or Convention commences.*

Table of Decisions

*References printed in **bold** refer to the page number where a substantial discussion of the Decision commences.*

Table of EC Directives

References printed in **bold** *refer to the page number where a substantial discussion of the Directive commences.*

Table of Proposed Directives

Table of National Legislation

United States

Table of European Community Regulations

*References printed in **bold** refer to the page number where a substantial discussion of the Regulation commences.*

Table of Proposed European Community Regulations

Table of European Community Treaties

References printed in **bold** *refer to the page number where a substantial discussion of the Treaty commences.*

List of Tables

List of Figures

PART I

Introduction

1

The Evolution of EC 'Social' Policy

A. INTRODUCTION

Social policy has long been viewed as the poor relation in the integration process. The near total absence of any provision for social matters in the original European Economic Community Treaty eventually precipitated one of the most profound debates affecting the development of the European Union: should the Union have a social face and, if so, what form should it take and at what level should it be provided? The principal aim of this chapter is to trace the evolution of Community social policy[1] and to consider the forces and principles driving this development. It will be seen that the creation of a European social policy has been by no means linear: phases of great activity have been matched by lengthy phases of inertia. It will also be seen that while there is an identifiable body of EC law which can loosely be described as 'labour' or 'social' policy, its coverage is far from comprehensive, and it certainly does not represent a replication of national social policy on the EC stage. The justifications for establishing a European social policy have varied over time too, and the legislative techniques for achieving these objectives have also been the subject of a dramatic evolution. Chapter 1 focuses on the development of EC 'social' policy and the justification for its existence; chapters two and three examine the different legislative and governance techniques.

---

[1] For more detail, see, e.g., Nielsen and Szyszczak, *The Social Dimension of the European Community* (2nd edn), (Handelshøjskolens Forlag, Copenhagen, 1997); Collins, *The European Communities, The Social Policy of the First Phase* (London, 1975); Shanks, *The European Social Policy Today and Tomorrow* (Pergamon, Oxford, 1977); Teague, *The European Community, the Social Dimension, Labour Market Policies for 1992* (Kogan Page, London, 1989) esp. Ch. 4; Bercusson, *European Labour Law* (Butterworths, London, 1996); Kenner, *EU Employment Law: from Rome to Amsterdam and Beyond* (Hart Publishing, Oxford, 2003).

B. THE DEVELOPMENT OF EC SOCIAL POLICY BY THE COMMUNITY INSTITUTIONS

1. The Treaty of Rome

1.1. The Social Provisions

The basic thrust of the Treaty of Rome was economic: to create a common market consisting of free movement of products (goods and services) and production factors (labour and capital).[2] Although the Treaty of Rome did contain a Title on Social Policy, its provisions were largely exhortatory and conferred little by way of direct rights on citizens.[3] This was illustrated by Article 117 (new and amended Article 136), which provided the 'Member States agree upon the need to promote improved working conditions and an improved standard of living for workers, so as to make possible their harmonisation while the improvement is being maintained'. Similarly, Article 118 (new and amended Article 140) failed to provide legally enforceable rights. It entrusted the Commission with the task of promoting 'close cooperation between the Member States and [facilitating] the coordination of their action in all social policy fields', particularly in matters relating to employment, labour law and working conditions, basic and advanced vocational training, social security, prevention of occupational accidents and diseases, occupational hygiene, the right of association and collective bargaining between employers and workers. The limited scope of this Article was highlighted in *Germany, UK and Others* v. *Commission*[4] where the Court ruled that the Article gave the Commission only procedural powers to set up consultations within the subjects covered. It could not be used to impose on Member States results to be achieved, nor could it prevent Member States from taking measures at national level.

The other social provisions found in the Social Title were similarly limited in scope. Article 121 EEC (new but wholly revised Article 144) permitted the Council to assign to the Commission tasks in connection with the 'implementation of common measures', in particular as regards social security for migrant workers; Article 122 (new Article 145) required the Commission to include a separate chapter on 'social developments' in its annual report to the European Parliament,[5] and Article 128 (new and amended Article 150) required the Council to 'lay down general principles' for implementing a common vocational training policy. The only provision which might have

---

[2] Arts. 2 and 3.

[3] Hallstein, *Europe in the Making* (1972), 119, cited in Watson, 'The Community Social Charter' (1991) 28 *CMLRev.* 37, 39.

[4] Joined Cases 281/85, 283/85, 285/85, 287/85 *Germany, UK and Others* v. *Commission* [1987] ECR 3203.

[5] The Parliament may also request the Commission to draw up reports on any particular problems relating to social conditions.

contained some substance was Article 119 (new Article 141) on equal pay for men and women; and even that obligation was addressed to the Member States and not to individual employers.

1.2. The Influence of the Ohlin and Spaak Reports

This raises the question why a Title headed 'Social Policy' should contain so little of substance. The answer lay in part with the original objectives of the European *Economic* Community. The view was that economic integration—the removal of artificial obstacles to the free movement of labour, goods and capital—would in time ensure the optimum allocation of resources through-out the Community, the optimum rate of economic growth and thus an opti-mum social system,[6] which would lead, according to the Preamble, to the 'constant improvement of the living and working conditions of their peoples'. This approach was spelled out in Article 117 EEC which provided that Member States believed that an improvement in working conditions 'will *ensue* not only from the functioning of the Common Market . . . but also . . . from the approximation of provisions laid down by law, regulation or administrative action'.[7] This statement represented a victory for the classic neo-liberal market tradition: there was no need for a European-level social dimension because high social standards were 'rewards' for efficiency.[8]

The highly influential Spaak report,[9] drawn up by the foreign ministers prior to the signing of the Treaty of Rome, had also envisaged only limited action in the social field to ensure the functioning of the Common Market. It rejected the idea of trying to harmonize the fundamental conditions of the national economy—its natural resources, its level of productivity, the signifi-cance of public burdens—considering that any harmonization might be the result of, as opposed to a condition precedent to, the operation of the Common Market and the economic forces which it released. Spaak relied heavily on the earlier Ohlin report of ILO experts.[10] This report had argued for the trans-national harmonization of social policy in some areas, such as equal pay, but, invoking the economic theory of comparative advantage, rejected a general role for harmonization of social policy. It argued that differences in nominal wage costs between countries did not, in themselves, pose an obstacle to economic integration because what mattered was unit labour costs, taking into account the relationship between nominal costs and productivity.

---

[6] Shanks, 'Introductory Article: The Social Policy of the European Community' (1977) 14 *CMLRev.* 14.

[7] Emphasis added.

[8] See further Hervey, *European Social Law and Policy* (Longman, Harlow, 1998) 7.

[9] Rapport des Chefs de Délèlgations, Comité Intergouvernemental, 21 April 1956, 19–20, 60–1.

[10] International Labour Office, 'Social Aspects of European Economic Cooperation' (1956) 74 *International Labour Review* 99.

Because higher costs tended to accompany higher productivity, differences between countries were less than they seemed. This explained why there was no need for harmonization.

Ohlin also suggested that the system of national exchange rates, which could be expected to reflect general prices and productivity levels within states, would cancel out the apparent advantage of low-wage states, so avoiding a race to the bottom—the phenomenon of standards of social protection either being depressed in states with higher standards or at least prevented from rising, by increased competition from states with substantially lower social standards. Consequently, Ohlin argued that the market itself would ensure that conditions of competition were not distorted. The strength of this argument and its influence on the debate about the function of EC social policy is considered below.

Although opposed to general intervention in the social sphere, the Spaak committee did say that action should be taken to correct or eliminate the effect of specific distortions which advantage or disadvantage certain branches of activity. By way of example, the authors cited a list of areas including working conditions of labour such as the relationship between the salaries of men and women, working time, overtime and paid holidays, and different policies relating to credit. This suggested that the Community should act in these fields only.

However, later commentators suggested that the Spaak committee's views were not as clearly reflected in the final version of the Treaty as might have been the case,[11] perhaps because the relevant provisions were drafted only at the end of a crucial conversation between the French and German Prime Ministers.[12] At the time of the Treaty negotiations there were important differences in the scope and content of social legislation in force in the states concerned. France, in particular, had a number of rules which favoured workers, including legislation on equal pay for men and women, and rules permitting French workers longer paid holidays than in other states. French workers were also entitled to overtime pay after fewer hours of work at basic rates than elsewhere. This raised concerns that the additional costs borne by French industry would make French goods uncompetitive in the Common Market. Consequently, the French argued that an elimination of gross distortions of competition was not enough, and that it would be necessary to assimilate the entire labour and social legislation of the Member States, so as to achieve a parity of wages and social costs. The Germans, however, were strongly committed to keeping to a minimum government interference in the

---

[11] Kahn-Freund, 'Labour Law and Social Security', in Stein and Nicholson (eds), *American Enterprise in the European Common Market: A Legal Profile* (University of Michigan Law School, Ann Arbor, 1960) 300. See Barnard, 'The Economic Objectives of Article 119', in Hervey and O'Keeffe (eds), *Sex Equality Law in the European Union* (Wiley, Chichester, 1996).

[12] Kahn-Freund, above n. 11, citing Katzenstein, *Der Arbeitnehmer in der europäischen Wirtschaftsgemeinschaft* (1957) 31 *Betriebs-Berater* 1081.

area of wages and prices. The resulting compromise was reflected in the Treaty's social policy provisions. Articles 117 and 118 EEC (new and amended Articles 136 and 140) on the need to improve working conditions and co-operation between states, even if textually broad, were legally shallow, reflecting the German preference for laissez-faire.[13] Article 119 (new Article 141) on equal pay and Article 120 (new Article 142) on paid holiday schemes and the third protocol on 'Certain Provisions Relating to France' on working hours and overtime,[14] by contrast, were specific provisions designed to protect French industry.[15] This was the sort of intervention envisaged by Spaak and Ohlin.

Although the original EEC Treaty contained little by way of traditional social policy measures, it did contain more detailed provisions in respect of free movement of persons. According to the Spaak report,[16] free movement of labour was crucial to social prosperity. By allowing workers to move to find available work, they would go from areas where labour was cheap and plentiful to areas where there was demand. It was hoped that free circulation of labour would facilitate an equalization in the terms and conditions of competition.[17] To achieve this goal, Articles 48–66 (new Articles 39–55) were introduced into the Treaty to remove obstacles to the free movement of workers, and complemented by Article 123 (new Article 146) establishing the European Social Fund, designed to make the employment of workers easier and to increase their geographic and occupational mobility.[18] Article 51 (new Article 42) provided a basis for EC regulation in the social security field, based on a policy of co-ordination and not harmonization.

In conclusion, the absence of a clearly identifiable Community social policy can be explained by the fact that generally Member States believed that social policy, and labour law in particular, lay at the very heart of national

---

[13] Forman, 'The Equal Pay Principle under Community Law' (1982) 1 *LIEI*. 17.

[14] This provided that the Commission was to authorize France to take protective measures where the establishment of the Common Market did not result, by the end of the first stage, in the basic number of hours beyond which overtime was paid and the average rate of additional payment for overtime industry corresponding to the average obtaining in France in 1956. It does not seem that France has called upon this safeguard clause: Budiner, *Le Droit de la femme l'Égalité de salaire et la Convention No. 100 de l'organisation internationale du travail* (Librairie Générale de Droit et de Jurisprudence, Paris, 1975).

[15] According to the French Advocate General Dutheillet de Lamothe in Case 80/70 *Defrenne (No. 1) v. SABENA* [1971] ECR 445, 'It appears to be France which took the initiative, but the article [119] necessitated quite long negotiations'. However, the content of Art. 119 was strongly influenced by ILO Convention No. 100 on equal pay. See Hoskyns, *Integrating Gender* (Verso, London, 1996).

[16] Rapport des Chefs de Délégations, Comité Intergouvernemental, 21 April 1956, 19–20, 60–1.

[17] Ibid, 78.

[18] There was also a social dimension to the Common Agricultural Policy (Art. 39 (new Art. 33)) in the form of grants from the European Agricultural Guidance and Guarantee Fund (EAGGF).

sovereignty,[19] and viewed it as an important vehicle to preserve 'the integrity and political stability of their respective political regimes'.[20] Thus, at a time of unprecedented activity at national level with workers gaining new legal rights and welfare benefits, there was little pressure for harmonization at Community level. However, this decision to give precedence to economic over social objectives was to have serious ramifications for years to come. By decoupling two policies (economic policy and social policy) traditionally inter-linked at national level, and by giving primacy to economic policy, social policy has inevitably been downgraded. And, as decisions of the European Court of Justice have shown,[21] in the absence of an express constitutional imperative to take social matters into account, economic polices such as free trade and free competition, read in conjunction with the doctrines of supremacy and direct effect, risked seriously destabilizing national social systems.

That said, the Commission noted in its *First General Report on the Activities of the Community* in 1958[22] that 'it bears particular responsibilities in this field [of social policy] and intends to neglect no sphere in which it may prove possible to "promote close cooperation" '. With remarkable prescience, the Commission observed that '[i]t is convinced that in the future the Community will be judged by a large part of public opinion on the basis of its direct and indirect successes in the social field'.[23] The Commission also noted that the reference in the Preamble of the Treaty to 'both economic and *social* progress' and to 'constantly improving the living and working conditions of their peoples' made it clear that 'the objectives of a social character are placed on the same footing as those of an economic character',[24] albeit that 'the legal framework of the Community's action in the social field is less rigid'.[25] These words neatly encapsulate the tension originally surrounding social policy at European level: the desire, especially in the Commission, to develop an EU social policy but the absence of a clear legal basis on which to do so.

2. A Change of Direction

2.1. The 1970s and Legislative Activity

The non-intervention by the Community in the social field did not last. On the eve of the accession of three new Member States in 1973, the heads of

---

[19] Ross, 'Assessing the Delors' Era and Social Policy', in Leibfried and Pierson (eds), *European Social Policy: Between Fragmentation and Integration* (Brookings Institution, Washington DC, 1995) 360.

[20] Streeck, 'Neo-voluntarism: A New Social Policy Regime' (1995) 1 *ELJ*. 31.

[21] These decisions are considered below at nn. 201–8.

[22] 17 September 1958. The Social Affairs Council did not even meet between 1964 and 1966, see Hervey, above, n. 8, 16.

[23] Para. 103.   [24] Para. 102.   [25] Para. 103.

government meeting in Paris issued a communiqué, stating that the Member States:

. . . emphasised that vigorous action in the social sphere is to them just as important as achieving Economic and Monetary Union. They consider it absolutely necessary to secure an increasing share by both sides of industry in the Community's economic and social decisions.[26]

This change of approach can be explained in part by reference to the social unrest in Western Europe in 1968,[27] and in part by an economic recession in Europe following the twin oil shocks of the 1970s. The feeling was that the Community required a human face to persuade its citizens that the social consequences of growth were being effectively tackled and that the Community was more than a device enabling business to exploit the Common Market.[28] Failure by the EC to have taken action at this time might have jeopardized the whole process of economic integration. Thus, the early 1970s was the first time when it was realized that the growth-based, neo-liberal ideology of the European Economic Community was not actually delivering on its promises and that a social dimension was necessary to address the problems faced by the 'losers'—both individuals and companies—suffering from the consequences of European economic integration; and that social policy measures were now necessary to maintain and support the established social order.

In response, the Commission drew up an Action Programme[29] containing three objectives: the attainment of full and better employment in the Community, the improvement of living and working conditions, and increased involvement of management and labour in the economic and social decisions of the Community and of workers in the life of the undertaking. This Action Programme precipitated a phase of remarkable legislative activity. Directives were adopted in the field of sex discrimination,[30] and the whole field of sex equality assumed a new importance as a result of judgments by the Court in the *Defrenne* cases.[31] An action programme and a number of Directives were adopted in the field of health and safety and, in the face of rising unemployment, measures were taken to ease the impact of mass redundancies,[32] the transfer of undertakings,[33] and insolvent employers.[34] At the same time, the European Regional Development Fund[35] was introduced in order to address the problems of socio-economic convergence in the Community.

[26] EC Bull. 10/1972, paras. 6 and 19.
[27] Wise and Gibb, *Single Market to Social Europe* (Longman, Harlow, 1993) 144.
[28] Shanks, above, n. 1, 378.   [29] OJ [1974] C13/1.
[30] Dir. 75/117 on equal pay (OJ [1975] L45/19), Dir. 76/207 on equal treatment (OJ [1976] L39/40) and Dir. 79/7 on equal treatment in social security (OJ [1979] L6/24).
[31] Case 80/70 *Defrenne (No. 1)* v. *Belgian State* [1971] ECR 445, Case 43/75 *Defrenne (No. 2)* v. *SABENA* [1976] ECR 455 and Case 149/77 *Defrenne (No. 3)* v. *SABENA* [1978] ECR 1365. See further Ch. 6
[32] Dir. 75/129/EEC (OJ [1975] L48/29).   [33] Dir. 77/187/EEC (OJ [1977] L61/27).
[34] Dir. 80/987/EEC (OJ [1980] L283/23).   [35] Reg. 724/75 (OJ [1975] L73/8).

Although this legislation appeared quite extensive, it was in fact confined to certain areas of employment law, as strictly understood, and not to the broader social sphere as originally envisaged by the 1972 communiqué. Further, this legislation had to be adopted under the general Treaty bases, Articles 100 and 235 (new Articles 94 and 308), both requiring the unanimous agreement of all the Member States. This ensured the Member States retained control over the supranational regulation of employment rights.

2.2. The Early 1980s: Stagnation

By the start of the 1980s, enthusiasm for developing a European social policy began to wane. The new Conservative government in the UK, led by Margaret Thatcher, insisted on strict limits to the growth of Community social policy, and, in particular, it was fundamentally opposed to the notion that workers' participation had an essential role in the management of change, thereby stymieing the adoption of two important Directives: the Fifth Directive on Company Structure and the draft Vredling Directive on information and consultation of employees.[36] It strongly advocated deregulation of the labour markets in order to ensure maximum flexibility of the workforce, in line with the American model, and argued for the need to adapt to new technology and the necessity of reducing the burden of regulation on business in order to enable business to compete in a global market.[37] This view represented a strong form of the neo-liberal market tradition. Put simply, the Thatcherite view was that society comprised individuals, each of whom could compete within the marketplace: no further state intervention, especially in the social field was either necessary or desirable.[38] This philosophy ran into direct conflict with the regulatory stance adopted by the Commission. While the Commission recognized the need for a flexible and adaptable workforce, it did not equate flexibility with deregulation and it refused to renege on its commitment to safeguarding the rights of employees.[39] However, since at that stage, all social policy measures required unanimity in Council the UK was able to veto any proposals to which it objected.[40]

Such stagnation was not confined to the social field. Disillusion with the tenets of Community policy and wranglings over budgetary contributions brought the Community legislative process shuddering almost to a halt. The arrival of Jacques Delors as President of the Commission, and his proposal for

---

[36] These Directives are considered further in Ch. 15.

[37] See e.g. *Employment: the Challenge to the Nation*, Cmnd 9474.

[38] Hervey, above, n. 8, 7.

[39] See further Hepple, 'The Crisis in EEC Labour Law' (1987) 16 *ILJ*. 77, 81.

[40] Community legislation on sex equality and health and safety was, however, adopted in this period. This can be explained in part by the fact that UK legislation already guaranteed fairly substantial protection in these fields.

a Single Market to be completed by 1992, represented, at least in the medium term, an end to this period of inertia.

3. The Single Market and the Community Social Charter 1989

3.1. The Single European Act 1986

The Single European Act 1986 (SEA) and the Single Market programme breathed new life into the idea that liberalization of trade would lead to economies of scale and economic growth from which the greatest number of Community citizens would benefit. The Cecchini report on the costs of non-Europe emphasized the importance of the Single Market programme in terms of its implications for 'very substantial job creation'.[41] This was really the only recognition of the social consequences of the Single Market. Although the idea of adding a social dimension to the internal market programme had been discussed, particularly by the European Parliament, the Single European Act in fact made few concessions to those who had argued for greater social competence for the Community. The Community did, however, commit itself to strengthening economic and social cohesion (Article 130a (new Article 158)), with the aim of reducing disparities between the levels of development of the various regions and the backwardness of the least favoured regions, including rural areas, and to developing the 'dialogue between management and labour at European level', institutionalizing the so-called social dialogue (Article 118b (new and amended Article 139)). Otherwise, Article 8a (new Article 14), setting the deadline of 31 December 1992 for the completion of the internal market programme, was concerned only with the realization of the four freedoms (goods, workers, services, and capital) and made no mention of social policy.

For practical purposes, perhaps the most significant innovation for social policy introduced by the SEA was the extension of qualified majority voting to measures adopted in the field of health and safety of workers[42] by Article 118a (new and amended Article 137), although matters 'relating to the rights and interests of employed persons' (Article 100a(2) (new Article 95(2))) still required the unanimous agreement of Council. Article 118a(2) gave the Council the power to adopt minimum standards directives which allowed Member States to maintain or introduce 'more stringent measures for the protection of working conditions compatible with this Treaty'

---

[41] Cecchini, *The European Challenge: 1992, the Benefits of a Single Market* (Gower, Aldershot, 1988) XIX.

[42] This became the Art. 189c (new Art. 252) procedure after the Treaty on European Union and the Art. 251 procedure after Amsterdam.

(Article 118a(3)).[43] These provisions represented an important shift in thinking. First, they demonstrated that the Community would not harmonize all labour standards but merely set a floor of basic rights. Secondly, they viewed the 'protection' of labour as a value in its own right, and a value which the Community should have a role in preserving.

The true significance of Article 118a only became apparent as the British hostility to the EU's social policy became ever more firmly entrenched: Article 118a provided the Commission with a way of circumventing the UK's veto. Article 118a therefore offered the EU the opportunity to construct a larger 'social' Europe, providing a bulwark against the dismantling of national labour law,[44] at a time when certain Member States (notably the UK) were pursuing a deregulatory agenda. As a result, Article 118a provided the legal basis for the successful adoption of certain important Directives on Working Time,[45] on Pregnant Workers,[46] and on Young Workers.[47]

The lack of a true social dimension to the SEA did, however, prompt some concern that the ambitious Single Market programme would not succeed unless it had the support of the Community citizens. This concern was combined with the realization that the Single Market programme would also produce negative consequences for employees: as the European market opened up, uncompetitive firms would go out of business and large companies might relocate to areas of the Community where social costs were lower. In both cases unemployment would result. For these reasons Jacques Delors set out his plans for 'L'Espace Social Européen',[48] arguing that:

The creation of a vast economic area, based on the market and business cooperation, is inconceivable—I would say unattainable—without some harmonisation of social legislation. Our ultimate aim must be the creation of a European social area.[49]

Delors's vision coincided with growing pressure for the establishment of a people's Europe designed to give the 'individual citizen a clearer perception of the dimension and the existence of the Community'[50]—in other words a recognition that 'Europe exists for its citizens, and not the other way round'.[51]

[43] These provisions are considered further in Ch. 2.

[44] Poiares Maduro, 'Europe's Social Self: "The Sickness unto Death" ', in Shaw (ed.), *Social Law and Policy in an Evolving European Union* (Hart Publishing, Oxford, 2000).

[45] Council Dir. 93/104/EC (OJ [1993] L307/18).

[46] Council Dir. 92/85/EEC (OJ [1992] L348/1).

[47] Council Dir. 94/33/EC (OJ [1994] L216/12).

[48] This is not a new concept: the French government had been talking in these terms since 1981. See further, Vandamme, 'De la Politique Social a l'Espace Social Européen (1983) *Revue du Marché Commun* 562. Mitterand had issued a memorandum to Council on the creation of a European Social Area.

[49] EC Bull. 2/1986, 12.

[50] The Adonnino Report, *A People's Europe: Reports from the ad hoc Committee*, Bull. Supp. 7/1985, 14. See also Commission, *Towards a People's Europe*, European File 3/86.

[51] President of the Council, 14 July 1993, cited in Commission, *A Citizen's Europe* (Brussels, 1993) 9.

These statements demonstrated a growing recognition that social and economic conditions were not in fact divisible and that economic efficiency had to be balanced by welfare objectives to 'humanize' the market, for reasons of fairness and distributive justice.[52] This is sometimes described as the market-correcting or the social justice approach to social policy. As Hervey points out, this model is based on notions of solidarity, a position which views social welfare as a collective activity rather than the responsibility of individuals, and social citizenship, the normative claim that egalitarian provision of welfare needs is superior to individual neo-liberal provision.[53]

3.2. The Community Social Charter 1989 and the Social Charter Action Programme

The social dimension of the internal market took more concrete form with the signing of the Community Charter of Fundamental Social Rights, by all the Member States except Britain, during the Strasbourg summit in 1989. Although the European Parliament was most anxious that the Charter be incorporated into Community law by means of a binding instrument,[54] in the event it was adopted merely as, in the words of the Preamble, a 'solemn proclamation of fundamental social rights'. It therefore had no free standing legal effect[55] (albeit it has been invoked by the European Court of Justice as an interpretative tool).[56] The absence of legal effect, combined with concerns about its content,[57] attracted adverse comment in some quarters. Vogel-Polsky described it variously as a 'bitter failure' and putting 'non-decision into a concrete form';[58] and Metall called it 'a non-binding wish list' full of 'rubber formulations' and loopholes that were 'not worth the paper on which it was printed'.[59] Silvia explained the Charter's failings by reference first, to British intransigence within the Council, combined with a willingness on the part of the other EC governments to take advantage of the UK's position; and second, to the failure by the European Trade Union movement either to raise

---

[52] Hervey, above, n. 8, 10.   [53] Ibid.

[54] See OJ [1991] C96/61 and OJ [1989] C120/5.

[55] Cf. Riley, 'The European Social Charter and Community Law' (1989) 14 *ELRev*. 80 and the reply by Gould, 'The European Social Charter and Community Law. A Comment' (1989) 14 *ELRev*. 80. AG Jacobs confirmed that the Charter was not legally binding: Case C–67/96 *Albany International BV* v. *Stichting Bedrijfspensioenfonds Textielindustrie* [1999] ECR I–5751, para. 137.

[56] See, e.g. Joined Cases C–397/01 to C–403/01 *Pfeiffer* v. *Deutches Rotes Kreuz* [2004] ECR I–000, para. 91.

[57] See esp. Bercusson, 'The European Community's Charter of Fundamental Social Rights of Workers' (1990) 53 *MLR* 624, Watson, 'The Community Social Charter' (1991) 28 *CMLRev*. 37, Silvia, 'The Social Charter of the European Community: A Defeat for European Labor' (1990–91) 44 *Industrial and Labour Relations Review* 626.

[58] 'What Future is there for a Social Europe Following the Strasbourg Summit?' (1990) 19 *ILJ*. 65.

[59] German Metal Workers' Union, quoted in Silvia, above, n. 57.

convincingly the spectre of social unrest if it was dissatisfied or to promise electoral benefits to ministers if they adopted more radical social policy proposals.[60]

In one sense the Charter is not a radical document: its Preamble still contains an endorsement of the old philosophies, that the completion of the internal market is the 'most effective means of creating employment and ensuring maximum well being in the Community', earlier references to combating *un*employment having been removed. Earlier drafts of the Charter had also talked of improvements in the social field for *citizens*. The final version specified that the Charter gave rights only to *workers*.[61] This suggests that the concept of a European social area had been abandoned for the present; and that the social aspect of the internal market had been substituted in its place.

On the other hand, the Charter does contain 26 rights which Member States have the responsibility to guarantee and it does recognize that the 'same importance' be attached to the social aspects as to the economic aspects of the European Community which must be 'developed in a balanced manner'.

The rights contained in the Social Charter 1989 were to be implemented through the Social Charter Action Programme[62] and any measures adopted were to be based on the EC Treaty and therefore binding on the UK. The Action Programme put forward by the Commission, when its power, prestige and entrepreneurialism may have been at its highest point, proposed that 47 different instruments be submitted by 1 January 1993. However, of these 47 proposals there were only 17 Directives,[63] of which 10 dealt with narrow health and safety matters, such as safety of the workplace,[64] safety of work equipment,[65] safety of VDUs,[66] and manual handling of loads.[67] This contrasted unfavourably with the proposals for almost 300 Directives submitted as part of the White Paper for Completing the Internal Market.[68] Nevertheless, the Action Programme led to the enactment of important pieces of social legislation aimed at protecting individual workers, including Directives on proof of the employment contract,[69] posted workers,[70] and, taking advantage of the new legal basis, Article 118a, the Commission also managed to secure

---

[60] Ibid., 640. See also Jacobs, 'Social Europe in Delay' (1990) 6 *IJCLLIR* 26, 35.
[61] See Bercusson, above, n. 57, 626.
[62] COM(89) 568 final Brussels, 29 November 1989.
[63] Social Europe 1/90, Commission of the European Communities (Brussels, 1990) contains the full text of the Social Charter, the Action Programme, background material and comments. Reports on the progress of the implementation of the Action Programme can be found in COM(91) 511 final, summarized in ISEC/B1/92, and Szyszczak (1992) 21 *ILJ*. 149, ISEC/B25/93 COM(93) 668 final.
[64] Council Dir. 89/654/EEC (OJ [1989] L393/1).
[65] Council Dir. 89/655/EEC (OJ [1989] L393/13).
[66] Council Dir. 90/270/EEC (OJ [1991] L156/14).
[67] Council Dir. 90/269/EEC (OJ [1990] L156/9).
[68] COM(85) 310 final.   [69] Council Dir. 91/533/EEC (OJ [1991] L288/32).
[70] Council Dir. 96/71/EC (OJ [1997] L18/1).

the adoption of Directives on pregnant workers,[71] working time,[72] and young workers.[73] The Action Programme also led to the enactment of some soft law measures, such as the Commission Recommendation on Sexual Harassment,[74] which softened up the legislature towards enacting a hard law measure in the field sometime later.[75]

Although the Directives adopted under the Social Charter Action Programme focused principally on individual rights, the Social Charter itself contained a strong endorsement of collective rights, including freedom of association,[76] the right to negotiate and conclude collective agreements,[77] possibly resulting in 'contractual relations', and the right to resort to collective action in the event of a conflict of interests, including the right to strike.[78] These rights have not, however, been reflected in any legislation, although the role of collective bargaining was given a considerable boost by the Treaty on European Union.[79]

The Social Charter Action Programme and the resulting Directives represented the high point for what is referred to as Community social policy but what, in reality, amounts to employment law—and an eclectic body of employment law at that. As Freedland has pointed out, it was concerned with equal pay and equal treatment between men and women, rather than with discrimination in employment generally; with collective dismissals and acquired rights on transfer of undertakings, rather than with the termination of employment more generally; with particulars of the terms of the contract rather than the terms themselves; with consultation of worker representatives on certain issues rather than with collective representation and workers' organizations as a whole; and with working time and health and safety rather than with the quality of working conditions more generally.[80]

4. The Treaty on European Union

4.1. Introduction

By the early 1990s, the Community had to come to terms with three main trends in economic and industrial relations, common across virtually all

---

[71] Council Dir. 92/85/EEC (OJ [1992] L348/1).

[72] Council Dir. 93/104/EC (OJ [1993] L307/18).

[73] Council Dir. 94/33/EC (OJ [1994] L216/12).

[74] Commission Recommendation 92/131/EEC on the protection and dignity of men and women at work (OJ [1992] L49/1).

[75] The prohibition against sexual harassment is now contained in Dir. 2002/73 (OJ [2002] L269/15) amending Dir. 76/207 (Art. 2(2)(a) of the Consolidated Directive 2006/54).

[76] Art. 11.   [77] Art. 12.   [78] Art. 13.   [79] See below n. 96 and Ch. 2.

[80] Freedland, 'Employment Policy', in *European Community Labour Law: Principles and Perspectives. Liber Amicorum Lord Wedderburn of Charlton*, eds. Davies, Lyon-Caen, Sciarra and Simitis (Clarendon, Oxford, 1996), 278–9.

Member States.[81] The first concerned the structural transformation of the economy, involving the internationalization of corporate structures and the sectoral redistribution of the labour force away from agriculture and traditional industries to services, particularly private services. The second trend concerned the economic crises leading to major recessions in the early 1980s and again in the early 1990s. These were accompanied by relatively high levels of unemployment and, with some exceptions, relatively low levels of inflation. At the same time there were increasing problems of industrial adjustment, mismatches between the supply and demand for skills, and as Rhodes points out, a more general failure of west European welfare states to respond to the challenges of post-industrial economic development.[82] The third trend was the change in the political climate in the 1980s, reflected in a general move to the right in national government policy-making together with a shift in the economic balance of power away from employees and trade unions and towards employers and managers. Employment relations were characterized by greater flexibility in recruitment, deployment and rewards, and the decentralization of decision-making, mainly through collective bargaining but also increasingly through the exercise of managerial prerogative.

The conclusion of the Treaty on European Union, with its significant amendments to the Treaty of Rome,[83] represented the Community's response to these changes. The desire to combat unemployment and encourage non-inflationary growth were now placed at the forefront of the Community's agenda. Article 2 EC said that the Community's tasks would be to promote throughout the Community 'sustainable and non-inflationary growth respecting . . . a high level of employment and of social protection, the raising of the standard of living and quality of life, and economic and social cohesion and solidarity among Member States'. In order to achieve these objectives the Community was given some additional activities, listed in Article 3, which talked of 'a policy in the social sphere comprising a European Social Fund', 'the strengthening of economic and social cohesion' and 'a contribution to education and training of quality'.[84] The Edinburgh European Council helped to provide the financial support necessary to achieve these objectives. Agreement was reached to increase the Community's own resources from

---

[81] See Barnard, Clark and Lewis, *The Exercise of Individual Employment Rights in the Member States* (Department of Employment, 1995).

[82] Rhodes, 'Employment Policy: Between Efficacy and Experimentation' in Wallace, Wallace and Pollack (eds), *Policy Making in the European Union* (OUP, Oxford, 2005) 281.

[83] See generally, Lo Faro, 'EC Social Policy and 1993: The Dark Side of European Integration' (1992) 14 *Comparative Labour Law Journal* 1, esp. 27ff.

[84] Art. 3(j), (k) and (q), respectively.

1.2 per cent of GDP in 1993 to 1.27 per cent by 1999[85] in order to precipitate a 'big bang effect'[86] to achieve growth.

These new tasks and activities were reflected in the relabelling of the social policy Title as 'Social policy, education, vocational training and youth'. Articles 123–128 on the European Social Fund were combined (Articles 123–125 (new Articles 146–148)) and Articles 126 and 127 (new Articles 149 and 150) formed a new chapter covering education, vocational training and youth, where the Community was given new, but closely circumscribed, competence. The question of competence was brought into sharp focus by the inclusion of Article 3b (new Article 5) into the Treaty where, for the first time, the Treaty recognized the doctrine of attribution of powers, the principle of subsidiarity (with the presumption that Member States should act, unless the action could be better achieved by the Community), and proportionality.[87]

4.2. The Social Chapter

For our purposes the most significant change introduced by the Maastricht Treaty concerned social policy. It was originally proposed that Articles 117–122 EEC be amended to expand the EC's social competence but this idea met with stubborn resistance from the UK. In order to secure the UK's agreement to the Treaty on European Union as a whole, it was agreed to remove these changes from the main body of the Treaty and place them in a separate Protocol and Agreement (the Social Policy Agreement (SPA) and the Social Policy Protocol (SPP)), together referred to as the Social Chapter) which would not apply to the UK. In what was the first clear example of a two-speed Europe,[88] the UK secured an opt-out from the Social Chapter as well as from the provisions on EMU.

At the time, there was much debate about the legal status of this opt-out. The prevailing view[89] was that the Protocol was an agreement by the 12

---

[85] This proposal represents a weaker version of the Delors II package (COM(92) 2000) which proposed an increase in the EC total resources to 1.37 per cent of GNP, discussed in Shackleton, 'Keynote Article: the Delors II Budget Package' (1993) 31 *JCMS*. 11.

[86] Kenner, 'Economic and Social Cohesion: The Rocky Road Ahead' [1994] *LIEI*. 1.

[87] These principles are considered further in Ch. 2.

[88] See generally, Towers, 'Two Speed Ahead: Social Europe and the UK after Maastricht' (1992) 23 *IRJ*. 83; Shaw, 'Twin-track Social Europe—The Inside Track', in O'Keeffe and Twomey (eds), *Legal Issues of the Maastricht Treaty* (Wiley, Chichester, 1994) 295. Such 'flexibility' was consititutionalized at Amsterdam. Ehlermann, 'Differentiation Flexibility, Closer Cooperation: the New "Provisions of the Amsterdam Treaty" ' (1998) 4 *ELJ*. 246, 247. Shaw, 'The Treaty of Amsterdam: Challenges of Flexibility and Legitimacy' (1998) 4 *ELJ*. 63, 66. Weatherill, ' "If I'd Wanted You to Understand I would have Explained it Better": What is the Purpose of the Provisions on Closer Cooperation Introduced by the Treaty of Amsterdam?', in O'Keeffe and Twomey (eds), *Legal Issues of the Amsterdam Treaty* (Hart, Oxford, 1999).

[89] Watson, 'Social Policy After Maastricht' (1993) 31 *CMLRev*. 481, 488, *Maastricht and Social Policy—Part Two*, EIRR 239, 19, Whiteford, 'Social Policy after Maastricht' (1993) 18 *ELRev*. 202.

Member States that only 11 were to be bound by the new social provisions.[90] According to Article 311 EC, protocols annexed to the Treaty form an integral part of the Treaty. The Protocol on social policy was therefore part of the Maastricht Treaty and thus part of Community law. Similarly, since the Protocol provided that the agreement on social policy was annexed to the Protocol, which in turn was annexed to the Treaty, the Agreement also formed part of Community law. Nevertheless, this view was not without its critics[91] who argued variously that the Social Chapter constituted an intergovernmental agreement or that the Agreement on social policy was not part of the Protocol on social policy but was an independent arrangement made between the 11.[92] The debate was effectively settled in favour of the Social Chapter being part of Community law when the Court was prepared to rule in *UEAPME*[93] on the legality of the Parental Leave Directive adopted under the Social Chapter.

As far as substance is concerned, the SPA was significant for three reasons. First, it both broadened the scope of Community competence in the social field as well as increasing the areas in which measures could be taken by qualified majority vote (as part of the co-operation procedure).[94] Thus, measures concerning working conditions, information and consultation of workers, equality between men and women with regard to labour market opportunities and treatment at work, and the integration of those excluded from the labour market could be adopted by qualified majority vote.[95] In addition, the Council of Ministers could adopt, by unanimity, measures in the area of social security and social protection of workers, protection of workers when their employment contract is terminated, representation and collective defence of the interests of workers and employers, including co-determination and conditions of employment for legally resident third country nationals (Article 2(3) (new Article 137(3))). However, Article 2(6) (new Article 137(5)) expressly provided that '[t]he provisions of this Article shall not apply to pay, the right of association, the right to strike or the right to impose lock-outs'.

---

[90] The Social Protocol opens with the statement that 'THE HIGH CONTRACTING PARTIES [the twelve], NOTING that eleven Member State . . . wish to continue along the path laid down in the 1989 Social Charter; that they have adopted among themselves an agreement to this end'.

[91] Weiss, 'The Significance of Maastricht for European Social Policy' (1992) 8 *IJCLLIR* 3; Barnard, 'A Social Policy for Europe: Politicians 1 Lawyers 0' (1992) 8 *IJCLLIR* 15; Vogel-Polsky, *Evaluation of the Social Provisions of the Treaty on European Union*, Report prepared for the Committee on Social Affairs, Employment and the Working Environment of the European Parliament, DOC EN\CM\202155, cited in Watson, above, n. 89, 481, 491. See also the submissions made in *R v. Secretary of State for Foreign and Commonwealth Affairs, ex parte Lord Rees Mogg* [1993] 3 CMLR 101.

[92] Cf. Watson, above n. 89, 481, 491–4 and Whiteford, above, n. 89, 203–4.

[93] Case T–135/96 *UEAPME v. Council* [1998] ECR II–2335, considered further in Ch. 2.

[94] As amended to take account of the UK's absence (44 votes out of a possible 66 needed). Now the Co-decision procedure is applied (see further Ch. 2).

[95] Art. 2(1) and (2) SPA (new Art. 137(1) and (2)).

The second reason for the SPA's significance lay in the greater role it envisaged for the Social Partners (representatives of management and labour): not only would they be consulted both on the possible direction of Community action and on the content of the envisaged proposal,[96] but they could, if they chose, also negotiate collective agreements[97] which could be given *erga omnes* effects by a Council 'decision'.[98] The details of this collective approach to legislation or 'law by collective agreement' are considered in chapter 2. For the present it is sufficient to note two points. First, these new provisions were the direct result of the 'Val Duchesse' social dialogue between the intersectoral (cross-industry) Social Partners (UNICE and CEEP on the employers' side and ETUC on the workers' side) which started in 1985.[99] On 31 October 1991 these Social Partners reached an agreement which, to the surprise of its proponents,[100] was inserted almost *verbatim* into Articles 3 and 4 SPA (new Articles 138 and 139). Thus, for the first time in the social field *private* agents could make public policy.[101] Second, this bipartite social dialogue highlights the multi-faceted and paradoxical nature of the principle of subsidiarity. Although the Social Partners are negotiating (a form of 'horizontal' subsidiarity), they are doing so at European level at a time when decentralized collective bargaining is the trend in many states.[102]

The third reason for the SPA's significance was more intangible but nevertheless significant: the inclusion of a more substantial provisions on social policy helped to rebalance the disequilibrium inherent in the original Treaty of Rome between the economic and social dimension of the (newly named) European Union. This reorientation of the Treaty was reinforced by the inclusion in Article 17(1) of the title of 'Union citizen' for those holding the nationality of one of the Member States. While many were disappointed by the paucity of rights expressly conferred on Union citizens,[103] Article 17(2)

---

[96] Art. 3(2) and (3) (new Art. 138(1) and (2)).

[97] Art. 4(1) (new Art. 139(1)). See generally Bercusson, 'Maastricht—a Fundamental Change in European Labour Law' (1992) 23 *IRJ*. 177 and 'The Dynamic of European Labour Law after Maastricht' (1994) 23 *ILJ*. 1.

[98] Art. 4(2) (new Art. 139(2)). The term 'decision' is not used in the sense of Art. 249 (old Art. 189) but has been interpreted to mean any legally binding act, in particular, Directives.

[99] This is considered further in Ch. 16.   [100] Rhodes, above n. 82, 289.

[101] Obradovic, 'Accountability of Interest Groups in the Union Law-Making Process', in Craig and Harlow (eds), *Lawmaking in the European Union* (Kluwer, Deventer, 1998) 355.

[102] E.g., in the UK, most leading firms have abandoned industry-wide agreements and moved towards single employer bargaining. Edwards *et al.*, 'Great Britain: From Partial Collectivism to Neoliberalism to Where?', in Ferner and Hyman (eds), *Changing Industrial Relations in Europe* (Blackwell, Oxford, 1998).

[103] See M. Everson, 'The legacy of the Market Citizen' in Shaw and Moore (eds), *New Legal Dynamics of European Union* (OUP, Oxford, 1995); J. Weiler, 'European Citizenship and Human Rights' in Winter, Curtin, Kellermann and de Witte (eds), *Reforming the Treaty on European Union* (Kluwer/Asser Institute, 1996), esp. 65, cited in J. Shaw, *Citizenship of the Union: Towards Post-National Membership*, specialized course delivered at the Academy of European Law, Florence, July 1995.

does allow Union citizens to enjoy rights (but also duties) drawn from across the Treaty, including most obviously the social provisions, while Article 18(1) EC grants EU citizens the right to move to other Member States and reside there subject to the limitations and conditions laid down in the Treaty

4.3. Economic and Monetary Union

From an economic perspective, the establishment of a timetable for the creation of economic and monetary union (EMU) was by far the most significant component of the Treaty on European Union. While, at first sight, the provisions of EMU had no direct impact on either national or European social policy, its indirect effect was potentially vast. On the positive side, the creation of a single currency would lead to currency stability which in turn would be good for the economy and for jobs. On the negative side, the constraints imposed by EMU on national government expenditure meant that this would inevitably have an effect on the ability of national governments to control their own social policy. In particular, the budgetary restrictions imposed by the convergence criteria of the euro and the Stability and Growth Pact[104] prevent any systematic policy of public investment, and the existence of the single currency and its management by the European Central Bank prevent national governments from pulling any monetary or interest rate levers to promote national competitiveness.[105] Furthermore, the absence of any employment criteria among the convergence criteria for accession to the EMU highlighted the continued dissonance between the economic and social aspects of the European Union.

The introduction of EMU was significant for another reason: the new method of governance it put in place to ensure that Member States conducted their economic policies in accordance with both the objectives of Community law based on broad economic guidelines laid down by the European Council to steer Member State policies, combined with multilateral surveillance. Using this new type of soft law,[106] which combined an intergovernmental approach dominated by the Council and the Commission, political monitoring at the highest level, clear procedures and iterative processes,[107] the EU was able to link EU and national action while leaving states with a considerable discretion how to manage their own policies. This methodology

---

[104] This is considered further in Ch. 3.

[105] Hatzopoulos, 'A (More) Social Europe: A Political Crossroad or a Legal One-Way? Dialogues between Luxembourg and Lisbon' (2005) 42 *CMLRev.* 1599, 1600.

[106] Hodson and Meyer, 'The Open Method as a New Mode of Governance: the Case of Soft Economic Policy Coordination' (2001) 39 *JCMS.* 719 and 'Soft Law and Sanctions: Economic Policy Coordination and Reform of the Stability and Growth Pact' (2004) 11 *JEPP.* 798.

[107] Borrás and Jacobsson, 'The Open Method of Coordination and New Governance Patterns in the EU' (2004) 11 *JEPP.* 185, 188.

subsequently provided the template for Community action in other areas, notably employment, in the Amsterdam Treaty.[108]

5. From Maastricht to Amsterdam

With the Social Charter Action Programme nearing its natural conclusion and now armed with the new Social Chapter, the Commission began to examine the future direction of Community social policy in the light of the changing trends in economic and industrial relations, focusing especially on the serious levels of unemployment and the implications of EMU. Its response was to issue a White Paper on Growth, Competitiveness and Employment,[109] and a Green Paper on European Social Policy,[110] leading to a White Paper on Social Policy, putting forward specific proposals.[111] The striking feature of these three documents is the emphasis placed on social goals, such as the promotion of high levels of employment and the elimination of social exclusion, and the move away from harmonization of social rights to a greater reliance on convergence, technocratic support and soft law.[112]

The Growth White Paper, issued by DGXV (now DG Internal Market) saw the issues of growth, competitiveness and employment as interrelated and said that the 1992 programme, while successful in its own terms, had generated 'jobless growth'. To address the EU's problem of high levels of unemployment, it put forward a package of proposals with a potent mix of deregulation (making labour markets more flexible), infrastructure investment (especially developing trans-European networks), and active labour market measures (such as the investment in training). As we shall see, this prescription has underpinned the Union's recent concentration on raising the levels of employment.

Meanwhile, the Green and White Papers on Social Policy, issued by DGV (now DG Empl, the Employment, Social Affairs and Equal Opportunities Directorate General) concentrated more on consensus building, based on shared values to create a European social model. The Commission said that the SPA provided a new basis for Union action which it intended to use 'to ensure a dynamic social dimension of the Union'.[113] However, recognizing

---

[108] Presidency Conclusions, Extraordinary European Council Meeting on Employment, Luxembourg, 20 and 21 November 1997, para. 3 said that the Employment Guidelines would draw 'directly on the experience built up in the multilateral surveillance of economic policies'.

[109] Bull. Supp. 6/93.

[110] COM(93) 551, 17 November 1993 and ECOSOC's response 94/C148/10. See Kuper, 'The Green and White Papers of the European Union: The Apparent Goal of Reduced Social Benefits' (1994) 4 *Journal of European Social Policy* 129, and Kenner, 'European Social Policy—New Directions' (1994) 10 *IJCLLIR*. 56.

[111] COM(94) 333, 27 July 1994.

[112] Cullen and Campbell, 'The Future of Social Policy-Making in the EU', in Craig and Harlow (eds), above, n. 101, 263.

[113] COM(94) 333, 13.

that the UK would not be bound by any measure adopted on such a basis, the Commission noted the 'strong desire of all Member States to proceed as twelve wherever possible' and hoped that 'Union social policy action will in future once again be founded on a single legal framework'.[114] This was achieved when the Labour government came to power in the UK in May 1997. One of the first steps taken by the new government was to agree to sign-up to—or opt back into—the Social Chapter.[115] This raised the question of how the UK would be bound by the legislation which had already been adopted under the Social Chapter. In fact, during the five years of the UK opt-out only four Directives had been adopted under the Social Chapter,[116] (on European Works Councils,[117] Parental Leave,[118] Part-time Work,[119] and Burden of Proof).[120] Thus, despite the 11 Member States' avowed intention of continuing 'along the path laid down in the 1989 Social Charter'[121] they did so with little enthusiasm in the absence of the UK. In fact, the extension of these four measures to the UK did not prove difficult: they were re-adopted under the legal bases provided for by the EC Treaty and the UK was set new deadlines by which to implement the measures.

6. The Amsterdam Treaty

6.1. The Social Title

With the UK's decision to opt back into the Social Chapter, the Amsterdam IGC agreed to amend the chapter on social policy, incorporating both Articles 117–121 of the EC Treaty and the SPA, which was included in the EC Treaty, in a new section entitled 'The Union and the Citizen'.[122] The IGC also agreed three substantive changes to the text of the new Chapter on Social Provisions.

---

[114] COM(94) 333, 13. See also the Commission's Communication concerning the application of the SPA: COM(93) 600.

[115] See Barnard, 'The United Kingdom, the "Social Chapter" and the Amsterdam Treaty' (1997) 26 *ILJ.* 275. The UK also signed up to the Social Charter 1989 at the same time.

[116] McGlynn, 'An Exercise in Futility: The Practical Effects of the Social Policy Opt-out' (1998) 49 *NILQ.* 60.

[117] Council Dir. 94/95/EC (OJ [1994] L254/64), as amended by Council Dir. 97/74/EC (OJ [1998] L10/22); consolidated legislation (OJ [1998] L10/20).

[118] Council Dir. 96/34/EC (OJ [1996] L145/4), as amended by Council Dir. 97/75 (OJ [1998] L10/24).

[119] Council Dir. 97/81/EC (OJ [1998] L14/9), as amended by Council Dir. 98/23/EC (OJ [1998] L131/10; consolidated legislation (OJ [1998] L131/13).

[120] Council Dir. 97/80/EC (OJ [1997] L14/16), as amended by Council Dir. 98/52/EC (OJ [1998] L205/66).

[121] Opening words of the Preamble to the SPP.

[122] The social provisions were then renumbered twice: the first time to reflect the incorporation of the SPA into the Treaty and then the whole Social Chapter was renumbered again as part of the global renumbering which occurred at Amsterdam. This is reflected in the equivalence tables.

First, Article 117 (new Article 136) was significantly revised to include, among other things, an express reference to 'fundamental social rights such as those set out in the European Charter signed at Turin on 18 October 1961 and in the 1989 Community Charter of Fundamental Social Rights'. While the (11) Member States had, in the SPA agreed at Maastricht, referred to their wish to 'implement the 1989 Social Charter on the basis of the *aquis communautaire*', the reference to the 1961 Social Charter adopted by the Council of Europe is new, although the Court had already referred to it as a source of fundamental rights in various cases.[123] The importance of Article 117 (new Article 136) had already been emphasized by the Court in *Sloman*[124] where it said that the objectives of Article 117, although in the nature of a programme, constituted an important aid for the interpretation of other provisions of the Treaty and of secondary legislation on the social field.

The second change can be found in Article 137, which replaces the co-operation procedure with the co-decision procedure found in Article 251. Further, the use of the Article 251 procedure was extended to enable the Council to 'adopt measures designed to encourage co-operation between Member States through initiatives aimed at improving knowledge, developing exchanges of information and best practices, promoting innovative approaches and evaluating experiences in order to combat social exclusion'.

The third change concerned the importance of equality between men and women. The significance of this principle was reinforced by its inclusion in Article 2 EC as one of the tasks of the Community and as one of the activities of the Community in Article 3. Article 3 mainstreams gender equality. It provides that '[i]n all the activities referred to in this Article, the Community shall aim to eliminate inequalities, and to promote equality, between men and women'. Perhaps more importantly, Article 119 (new Article 141) on equal pay was amended for the first time since 1957. In particular, Article 141(3) finally provides an express legal basis for the Council to adopt measures, again in accordance with the Article 251 co-decision procedure, 'to ensure the application of the principle of equal opportunities and equal treatment of men and women in matters of employment and occupation, including the principle of equal pay for equal work or work of equal value'. There is, however, some overlap between Article 141(3) and Article 137(1) which allows for Community action in the field of 'equality between men and women with regard to labour market opportunities and treatment at work'.[125] The other

---

[123] Case 149/77 *Defrenne (No. 3)* [1978] ECR 1365, para. 28; Case 126/86 *Zaera v. Instituto Nacional de la Securidad Social* [1987] ECR 3697, para. 14.

[124] Joined Cases C–72/91 and C–73/91 *Sloman Neptun v. Bodo Ziesemer* [1993] ECR I–887, para. 26.

[125] Given that the legislative procedures are the same under each Article, the overlap is not perhaps of great significance.

striking change to Article 119 can be found in the paragraph 4 which recognizes the principle of positive action, first introduced by Article 6(3) SPA.[126] The importance of these developments will be considered in chapter 6.

6.2. The Employment Title

The other significant development at Amsterdam was the inclusion of a new Title on Employment,[127] introduced largely as a result of pressure from France and the Scandinavian countries. A new task for the Community of 'a high level of employment and of social protection' was added to Article 2 EC and the objective of a 'high level of employment' was mainstreamed (ie 'taken into consideration in the formulation and implementation of Community policies and activities')[128] by Article 127(2). Article 125, the key provision of the new Title, provides that:

Member States and the Community shall, in accordance with the Title, work towards developing a co-ordinated strategy for employment and particularly for promoting a skilled, trained and adaptable workforce and labour markets responsive to economic change with a view to achieving the objectives defined in Article 2 of the Treaty on European Union and in Article 2 of this Treaty.

Although it appears from Article 125 that action is to be jointly conducted by Member States and the Community, the principal actors are, according to the Treaty, the Member States. Article 126 requires the Member States to co-ordinate their policies for the promotion of employment (which is to be regarded as an issue of 'common concern')[129] within the Council, in a way consistent with the broad economic guidelines laid down within the framework of EMU, which are issued annually by the Council as part of the process of ensuring economic stability and convergence.[130] The European Council must also draw up guidelines according to Article 128 which the Member States are obliged to take into account in their employment policies. Under Article 129 the Council may adopt incentive measures designed to encourage co-operation between Member States.[131]

This annual cycle of policy formation, policy implementation and policy monitoring was formally launched at Luxembourg in November 1997 and became known as the European Employment Strategy (EES). The EES highlighted a shift in emphasis in the EU from measures protecting those in employment to addressing the high levels of unemployment in Europe.

---

[126] See Betten and Shrubsall, 'The Concept of Positive Sex Discrimination in Community Law—Before and After the Treaty of Amsterdam' (1998) 14 *IJCLLIR*. 65.

[127] For a full consideration of this subject, see Ashiagbor, *The European Employment Strategy* (OUP, Oxford, 2006).

[128] Art. 127(2).   [129] Art. 126(2).   [130] Ibid., Art. 126(1).

[131] The decision-making mechanism under the Employment Title is considered in more detail in Ch. 3.

This was a direct response to the growing crisis faced by many west European states of 'welfare without work':[132] expensive social welfare programmes unsupported by high levels of employment which risked putting euroland countries in breach of the budgetary commitments laid down by EMU. Furthermore, as we saw above, traditional national tools for addressing high levels of unemployment—monetary and fiscal policy—could no longer be used as a result of the constraints imposed by the Growth and Stability Pact. Thus the EES replaced the focus on demand side policies with the adoption of *supply* side policies, stimulating productivity through the creation of a favourable business environment, shorn of much red tape, and improving the quality of the workforce.[133]

The inclusion of the Employment Title amounted to a recognition by the euroland states—largely overlooked at Maastricht—of the increased inter-dependencies between EC economic policy and national social policy. As Trubek and Trubek put it,[134] so long as national markets are relatively closed and national budgets relatively independent, social policy is basically a domestic concern. But once nations create a common currency and join in a Single Market, then social policy in one country becomes relevant to other nations. Thus, the constraints and interdependencies generated by EMU pointed to the need for some form of transnational policy co-ordination in the field of employment: the Employment Title was the EU's response.

For Szyszczak, the Amsterdam Treaty represented the culmination and implementation of the Commission's attempts during the 1990s, through its soft law discourse on social policy, to create a better mix between economic and social policies.[135] However, given the acute political sensitivities involved (the Member States have long viewed job creation as lying at the heart of national sovereignty), a new method of policy-making was needed to be developed which would stimulate job creation without threatening national social, employment and economic policies. This new approach, found in Articles 125–129, is modelled in part on the strategy which had been adopted in respect of EMU,[136] based on the Commission proposing (non-binding) guidelines which the Member States are obliged to take into account in their national action plans (NAPs), now renamed national reform programmes (NRPs). Thus, in terms of regulatory technique, this new approach focused less on providing rights for individual employees and more on the co-ordination of employment policies, focusing in particular on active labour market policies such as training, work practice, and lifelong learning. At

---

[132] Rhodes, above, n. 82, 281.   [133] Hatzopoulos, above, n. 105, 1600.
[134] 'Hard and Soft Law in the Construction of Social Europe: the Role of the Open Method of Coordination' (2005) 11 *ELJ*. 343, 345.
[135] 'The New Paradigm for Social Policy: A Virtuous Circle' (2001) 38 *CMLRev*. 1125, 1134.
[136] See further Ch. 3.

Lisbon this new method of governance was given a name: the Open Method of Co-ordination (OMC).

7. The Lisbon Strategy

At the Lisbon summit in March 2000[137] the Union set itself a new and ambitious strategic goal 'to become the most competitive and dynamic knowledge-based economy in the world capable of sustainable economic growth with more and better jobs and greater social cohesion'.[138] The strategy has three, mutually interdependent limbs: an economic limb (making the EU more competitive while sustaining a stable economy), an environmental limb (especially sustainable development), and a social limb (modernizing the European social model, investing in people and combating social exclusion). This strategy is designed to enable the Union to regain 'the conditions for *full employment*' (not just a high level of employment as laid down by Article 2 EC), and 'strengthening regional cohesion in the European Union'. This is to be achieved by 'improving existing processes, introducing a new open method of coordination at all levels coupled with a stronger guiding and coordinating role for the European Council'.[139] The Presidency Conclusions describe the Open Method of Co-ordination as the means of spreading best practice and achieving greater convergence towards the EU's main goals by helping Member States develop their own policies.[140] Implementation of OMC involves tools such as indicators and benchmarks as well as the exchange of experiences, peer reviews and the dissemination of good practice. In particular, the Lisbon and subsequently Stockholm European Council set the EU the objective of reaching an overall employment rate of 70 per cent by 2010, an employment rate of over 60 per cent for women and employment rate among older men and women (55–64) of 50 per cent.[141] However, in its 2005 mid-term review of the Lisbon strategy, the Brussels European Council recognized that there

---

[137] Presidency Conclusions, 24 March 2000.   [138] Para. 5.

[139] Para. 7. The Commission's social policy agenda goes further. The Commission says that it does not 'seek to harmonise social policies. It seeks to work towards common European objectives and increase coordination of social policies in the context of the internal market and the single currency' (COM(2000)379, 7).

[140] Lisbon European Council, 23 and 24 March 2000, para. 37. See also the definition of OMC offered in the Final report of Working Group XI on Social Europe: 'It is a new form of coordination of national policies consisting of the Member States, at their own initiative or at the initiative of the Commission, defining collectively, within the respect of national and regional diversities, objectives and indicators in a specific area, and allowing those Member States, on the basis of national reports, to improve their knowledge, to develop exchanges of information, views, expertise and practices, and to promote, further to agreed objectives, innovative approaches which could possibly lead to guidelines or recommendations.'

[141] Stockholm European Council, 23 and 24 March 2001, para. 9.

were significant delays in reaching these targets, and in the Lisbon relaunch
no reference is made to the 2010 deadline.

Given the importance of these developments, they are considered in detail
in chapter three. For the purposes of this chapter, the events at Lisbon were
significant for four reasons. First, as Hatzopoulos points out,[142] the Lisbon
strategy was the next 'big' project for the EU, after the completion of the
internal market (1992), EMU (1999), and enlargement (2003–5), but,
unlike the previous projects, the Lisbon Strategy had a determinedly social
aspect.

Secondly, the principal emphasis of Community social policy has changed
from employment protection (giving rights to those already in work) to
employment creation (getting those out of work into employment). Thus
employment is seen as the key to citizenship, 'guaranteeing equal opportunities for all' and enabling the 'full participation of citizens in economic,
cultural and social life and realising their potential'.[143]

Thirdly, the regulatory techniques used to achieve these objectives have
shifted from an exclusive focus on traditional command and control regulation adopted under the classic Community Method based on harmonization
towards a new mode of governance which is based on co-ordination of
action by the states, as opposed to harmonization, under the direction of the
European Union (particularly the European Council, the Council of Ministers
and the Commission).[144] To give a concrete example, in the field of equal
opportunities, the emphasis is no longer exclusively on the enactment of
equality Directives, although this is still taking place,[145] but Member States
are now required also to look at issues ranging from the organization of work,
childcare, tax and benefit structures to school curricula and careers advice.[146]
Thus, in areas where law has proved to be a rather blunt instrument to bring
about social change, the Union has focused on different regulatory techniques
to achieve its objectives. With the advent of enlargement—and the arrival
of 10 new Member States with very diverse legal and industrial relations
traditions—the change in approach has proved particularly significant.

Fourthly, the Lisbon approach was intended to improve the legitimacy of
governance within the European Union by involving a wider range of social
actors, including not only the Social Partners but also civil society more
generally.

---

[142] Above, n. 105, 1628 and 1630.

[143] Dir. 2000/78 establishing a general framework for equal treatment in employment and
occupation (OJ [2000] L303/16), ninth preambular paragraph.

[144] Despite the novelty of this approach, the Treaty of Rome had always envisaged
co-ordination as the principal regulatory approach, as Art. 118 EEC (now Art. 140) made clear.

[145] See, esp. Chs. 6–10.

[146] Szyszczak, 'The New Paradigm for Social Policy: A Virtuous Circle' (2001) 38 *CMLRev.*
1125, 1144.

8. The Nice Treaty

8.1. Changes to the Social Title

Article 137 EC was amended again by the Treaty of Nice. Most of the changes were cosmetic and involved a restructuring and tidying up of the Article. However, one substantive change was made: in line with the increasing focus on OMC methodology, greater prominence was given to this approach. While Article 137(1) listed the fields in which the Community must 'support and complement the activities of the Member States', with two new areas specified—social inclusion and the modernization of social protection systems—Article 137(2) then details how this might be achieved. Part (a) provides that the Council may 'adopt measures designed to encourage co-operation between Member States . . . excluding any harmonisation of the laws and regulations of the Member States'; the power to adopt Directives only appears in part (b). In addition, the Treaty of Nice amended Article 144 to empower the Council to establish a Social Protection Committee with advisory status to promote cooperation on social protection between Member states and with the Commission. It, too, is to use OMC techniques including 'promoting exchanges of information, experience and good practice'.

8.2. The Charter of Fundamental Rights

From the perspective of this book, by far the most significant development at Nice was the adoption of the Community Charter of Fundamental Rights. This Charter was the product of a long gestation period[147] but eventually, in 1999, the European Council launched an innovative, deliberative process by which an EU charter of fundamental rights of the EU would be agreed.[148] As the European Council explained, 'Protection of fundamental rights is a founding principle of the Union and an indispensable prerequisite for her legitimacy'. The final Charter, agreed at Nice, contained, in a single document, the fundamental rights and freedoms and basic procedural rights guaranteed by the European Convention on Human Rights as well as some of the economic and social rights contained in the European Social Charter and the Community Social Charter 1989.[149] It also contained a mixture of rights

---

[147] See, e.g., *For a Europe of Civic and Social Rights*, Report by the Comité des Sages chaired by Maria de Lourdes Pintasilgo, Brussels, October 1995–February 1996, Commission, DGV; *Affirming Fundamental Rights in the European Union: Time to Act*, Report of the Expert Group on Fundamental Rights, Brussels, February 1999.

[148] De Búrca, 'The Drafting of the European Union Charter of Fundamental Rights' (2001) 26 *ELRev.* 126.

[149] For a discussion of the significance of having both first generation (civil and political) and second generation (economic and social) rights in the same document, despite the fluidity of these terms, see De Búrca, 'The Future of Social Rights Protection in Europe', in De Búrca and De Witte (eds), *Social Rights in Europe* (OUP, Oxford, 2005).

(essentially a catalogue of individual, negative rights) and principles (which allow for the progressive realisation of rights).

The principal provisions relating to 'social matters' can be found in Title III entitled 'Equality'[150] and Title IV, 'Solidarity',[151] although two key rights, the right to freedom of association and of assembly and the freedom to choose an occupation and right to engage in work, are found in Title II 'Freedoms' and the prohibition of slavery and forced labour is found in Title I, 'Dignity'. The provisions in these Titles are essentially about rights in the classic sense of the word but, especially in the solidarity section, the rights are carefully delimited by reference to national and Community law. For example, controversial Article 28 (Article II–88 of the Constitution) provides that:

> Workers and their employers, or their respective organisations, have, *in accordance with Union law and national laws and practices*, the right to negotiate and conclude collective agreements at the appropriate levels and, in cases of conflicts of interest, to take collective action to defend their interests, *including strike action*.[152]

This provision does not grant a right to strike because the Charter contains 'General Provisions Governing the Interpretation and Application of the Charter'. These so-called 'horizontal provisions' provisions include Article II–111(2)[153] which says that '[t]his Charter does not extend the field of application of Union law beyond the powers of the Union or establish any new power or task for the Union, or modify powers and tasks defined in other parts of the Constitution' and Article II–112(2)[154] which provides that '[r]ights recognised by this Charter for which provision is made in other Parts of the Constitution shall be exercised under the conditions and within the limits defined by these relevant parts'. In particular, Article 137(5) (III–210(6) of the Constitutional Treaty) expressly excludes Community competence in respect of strike action under Article III–210.[155] Thus, the Charter does not empower the Community to create a right to strike, nor does it require the Member States to create a right to strike. In this way the Charter preserves national autonomy.[156] The

---

[150] Art. 20 lays down the principle of equality before the law; Art. 21 contains a non-exhaustive list of prohibited grounds of discrimination; Art. 22 talks of cultural, religious, linguistic diversity and Art. 23 concerns equality between men and women.

[151] E.g., Art. 27 concerns information and consultation within the undertaking; Art. 28 the right of collective bargaining and collective action; Art. 30 on protection in the event of unjustified dismissal and Art. 31 fair and just working conditions including, in Art. 31(2), 'the right to limitation of maximum working hours, to daily and weekly rest periods and to an annual period of paid leave'; and Art. 33 family and professional life.

[152] Emphasis added.

[153] Prior to the Constitutional Treaty, the relevant Article was Art. II–51(2), albeit rather differently worded.

[154] Art. 52(2) of the Charter.

[155] For criticism, see Weiss, 'The Politics of the EU Charter of Fundamental Rights', in Hepple (ed.), *Social and Labour Rights in a Global Context* (CUP, Cambridge, 2002).

[156] See below n. 159, 30, subject to the Court respecting that autonomy: cf. Case C–71/02 *Karner* [2004] ECR I–000. See also Case C–109/01 *Akrich* [2003] ECR I–9607.

provision could, however, be used to ensure that where strike action taken in a Member State interferes with the free movement of goods or services, this interference—which is potentially unlawful—is balanced against the fundamental right to strike.[157]

The Solidarity Title also contains a number of principles which are not intended to be justiciable.[158] Hepple[159] subdivides the 'principles' category into (1) those rights which the EU/Member States must 'respect' (i.e. EU and Member States must refrain from any action which would undermine the rights) and those rights which they must recognize (i.e. EU and Member States must protect these rights including preventing action by third parties who might interfere with the rights); and (2) those rights which the EU and Member States are under a duty to 'ensure'. This latter category imposes a positive obligation and requires real resources. Article II–94 (Article 34 of the Charter) on social security and social assistance is confined to 'recognise and respect'. It provides that 'The Union recognises and respects the entitlement to social security benefits and social services providing protection in cases such as maternity, illness, industrial accidents, dependency or old age, and in the case of loss of employment' in accordance with Union and national laws and practices. By contrast, Article II–83 (Article 23 of the Charter) requires equality between men and women to be 'ensured'.

However, the distinction between 'rights' and 'principles' is not always so clear.[160] Lord Goldsmith, the UK's representative involved in drafting the Charter, tried to explain the difference. He suggested that in order to give effect to the Cologne European Council decision to include social and economic rights in a single Charter together with traditional civil and political rights,[161]

---

[157] For an example of this balancing exercise, see Case C–112/00 *Schmidberger* [2003] ECR I–5659 and also Art. 2 of Reg. 2679/98 (OJ [1998] L337/8). This is considered further in Ch. 16.

[158] Art. II–112(5), formerly Art. II–52(5), provides: 'The provisions of this Charter which contain principles may be implemented by legislative and executive acts taken by Institutions, bodies, offices and agencies of the Union, and by acts of the Member States when they are *implementing* Union law, in the exercise of their respective powers. They shall be judicially cognisable only in the interpretation of such acts and in the ruling on their legality'. Thus, ostensibly, the Charter does not apply to the Member States when they are derogating from EC Law: cf. Case C–260/89 *ERT* [1991] ECR I–2925. Yet the Praesidium explanations (drawn up as a way of providing guidance in the interpretation of the Charter and to which due regard has to be given by the courts of the Union and of the Member States (Article II–112(7))) refer to both Case 5/88 *Wachauf* [1989] ECR 2609 (which concerns implementation) and *ERT* (which concerns derogations) by way of explanation for the rule. See generally, Arnold, 'From Charter to Constitution and beyond: Fundamental Rights in the New European Union' [2003] *Public Law* 774, 780.

[159] *Rights at Work: Global, European and British Perspectives* (Sweet & Maxwell, London, 2005) 35.

[160] This was recognized by the House of Lords Select Committee on the European Union, 'The Future Status of the EU Charter of Fundamental Rights', 6th Report, 2002–2003 Session, http://www.publications.parliament.uk/pa/ld200203/ldselect/ldeucom/48/4801.htm, para. 86. See e.g. Art. II–87 on workers' 'right' to information and consultation which, in the Article itself, is drafted in terms of workers or their representatives being 'guaranteed' information and consultation in good time.

[161] For a discussion of the distinction between the two groups of 'rights', see Kenner, 'Economic and Social Rights in the EU Legal order: the Mirage of Indivisibility' in Hervey and Kenner (eds),

'these [social and economic] "rights" essentially take the form of principles' which are tied to national law or, where it exists, Community law.[162] The principles do not provide any mandate to the Community institutions to try to implement these rights outside their own competence, or impose on Member States some obligation to recognize the principle differently from how they currently do under national law.[163] It means that the Union shall not 'violate the principle by a side wind in some other legislation within its competence'.[164]

Not only is there confusion about the distinction between rights and principles but there is also the dissonance between existing Community law and the Charter. For example, the list of prohibited grounds of discrimination contained in Article II–81 is more extensive than those listed in Article 13 EC.[165] In addition, Article II–90 provides that 'Every worker has the right to protection against unjustified dismissal in accordance with Union law and national laws and practices'. Yet, there is no Union law on unfair dismissal. Some are critical of the omissions from the Charter: there is, for example, no right to fair remuneration, a right found in both the Council of Europe and the Community's Social Charter.[166] Others offer a more fundamental critique of the notion of rights. For example, Hepple argues that rights tend to be individualistic and individualize what may well be, in the social field, a collective problem.[167] Rights also put considerable power in the hands of the courts, particularly the Court of Justice, which, as we shall see, has at times shown itself unaware of the broader social issues. Rights, he argues, also need to be accompanied by positive duties on the part of states to achieve particular social goals.

The Charter was intended to have legal effect through its incorporation in the Treaty establishing a Constitution for Europe. So long as that Treaty remains unratified, the Charter, though drafted to be legally binding, retains soft law status. Nevertheless, it has been cited by a number of Advocates General,[168] the Court of First Instance,[169] the European Court of Human Rights,[170] and national courts.[171] The role of the Charter can be seen in

---

Economic and Social Rights under the EU Charter of Fundamental Rights (Hart Publishing, Oxford, 2003) 3.

[162] 'A Charter of Rights, Freedoms and Principles' (2001) 38 *CMLRev.* 1201, 1212.

[163] Ibid., 1213.   [164] Ibid.

[165] E.g. Art. II–81 includes genetic features, language, political or other opinion, membership of a national minority, property, and birth.

[166] Kenner, above n. 161, 17.   [167] 'The Future of Labour Law' (1995) 24 *ILJ.* 303.

[168] See, e.g. AG Jacobs' Opinion in Case C–50/00 *Unión de Pequeños Agricultores* v. *Council of the European Union* [2002] ECR I–6677; AG Geelhoed's Opinion in Case C–224/98 *D'Hoop* v. *Office National d'Emploi* [2002] ECR I–6191.

[169] E.g. Case T–177/01 *Jégo Quéré et Cie SA* v. *European Commission* [2002] ECR II–2365, Case T–54/99 *Max Mobil Telekommunikation Service GmbH* v. *European Commission* [2002] ECR II–313.

[170] *Godwin* v. *UK* (2002) 35 EHRR 18.

[171] *R (on the application of Robertson)* v. *Wakefield MDC* (2002) QB 1052, 170.

Advocate General Tizzano's Opinion in *BECTU*,[172] a case concerning the entitlement to paid annual leave, where he said:

in proceedings concerned with the nature of a fundamental right, the relevant statements of the Charter cannot be ignored; in particular, we cannot ignore its clear purpose of serving, where its provisions so allow, as a substantive point of reference for all those involved—Member States, institutions, natural and legal persons—in the Community context. Accordingly, I consider that the Charter provides us with the most reliable and definitive confirmation of the fact that the right to paid annual leave constitutes a fundamental right.

Thus, the Charter is gradually assuming a harder edge but it is not until it is cited by the Court of Justice that this can be said with any certainty. Even in the absence of legal enforceability, it might be envisaged that OMC methodologies such as benchmarks and indicators—techniques so intrinsically associated with the EES and the Lisbon strategy—could be deployed to assess compliance with the Charter.[173] This will be buttressed by the establishment of an EU Agency for Fundamental Rights.[174]

Perhaps the Charter's greatest importance will prove to lie in the fact that, in the social field at least, it will help provide some counterweight to the neo-liberal orientation of the Treaty, providing the Court with a firmer foundation to reconcile social and economic rights. For the other Community institutions and the Member States, the Charter will provide a stark reminder of the EU's social rights agenda at a time when aspects of the EES have a deregulatory edge[175] and states, deprived of the traditional tools for managing their economies, might look to removing social rights as a way of gaining a competitive advantage.

9. The Constitutional Treaty

In the field of social policy, as narrowly defined, the Constitutional Treaty would have had little direct impact on its provisions. Some minor tweaking was proposed (for example, reference to management and labour became references to the Social Partners, European Community became European Union) but otherwise the inclusion of the Title on social policy into Part

---

[172] Case C–173/99 *BECTU v. Secretary of State for Trade and Industry* [2001] ECR I–4881, para. 28.

[173] Bernard, 'A "New Governance Approach to Economic, Social and Cultural Rights in the EU' in Hervey and Kenner (eds), above n. 161.; De Schutter, 'The Implementation of the EU Charter of Fundamental Rights through the Open Method of Coordination' in De Schutter and Deakin (eds), *Social Rights and Market Forces* (Bruylant, Louvain-La-Neuve, 2005).

[174] Proposal for a Council Reg. establishing a European Union Agency for Fundamental Rights COM(2005) 280. See also the Commission's Communication on a Fundamental Rights Agency COM(2004) 693.

[175] Hepple, *Rights at Work* (Sweet & Maxwell, London, 2005) 36–7.

Three of the Treaty meant that these provisions were not subject to careful scrutiny by the Convention.[176] However, as we shall see in subsequent chapters, the proposed inclusion of the Charter of Fundamental Rights into the Treaty would have made a significant impact in the field of social policy more generally. In addition, the recognition of pluralism, non-discrimination, tolerance, justice, solidarity and equality between women and men as values of the EU in Article I–2 would have sent a strong message to the Court of Justice. More noteworthy, is the description in Article I–3(3) of the objectives of the EU: 'The Union shall work for the sustainable development of Europe based on balanced economic growth and price stability, a highly competitive social market economy,[177] aiming at full employment and social progress, and a high level of protection and improvement of the quality of the environment.' This emphasized the links between the social and economic provisions of the Treaty, a link which the Amsterdam Treaty had begun to identify.

At the time of writing, the fate of the Constitution remains uncertain: 'no' votes in France and the Netherlands have resulted in a 'period of reflection'. This book will proceed on the assumption that the Constitutional Treaty will not come into force;[178] but reference will be made to its provisions where necessary.

C. THE ROLE OF THE EUROPEAN COURT OF JUSTICE

1. Introduction

Any historical review of the development of EC social policy would not be complete without reference to the important role played by the European Court of Justice. We have already seen how the Court reinvigorated Article 141 on equal pay in the *Defrenne* cases by saying that it was directly effective. This highlights what Davies identifies as the Court's preoccupation, especially strong in the early years, of ensuring that those parts of Community law which were intended to govern relations between and among legal persons in day-to-day life did in fact give rise to legal rights and obligations within

---

[176] Indeed, originally there was no working group at all on 'Social Europe': Joerges and Rödl, ' "Social Market Economy" as Europe's Social Model?' EUI Working Paper Law No. 2004/8, 21.

[177] For a discussion of this term, see Joerges and Rödl, above n. 176, 19 who argue that 'this concept contained an ordoliberal basis which was complemented by social and societal policies, whose aims and instruments were supposed to reply on market mechanisms'. According to Working Group XI on Social Europe (CONV 516/1/03 REV 1, para. 17, the objectives should refer to 'social market economy' to underline the link between the economic and social development and the efforts made to ensure greater coherence between economic and social policies.

[178] On the future, see Kenner, 'The Constitution that never was: is there anything worth salvaging from the wreckage?' (2005) 36 *IRJ*. 541.

the judicial system of the Member States.[179] The social policy cases, with their direct impact on individuals, therefore presented the Court with the opportunity to develop important principles, such as the direct effect of Directives,[180] while at the same time stengthening the protection given to individuals.

At the same time the Court showed itself willing to bolster the substantive protection provided by the social legislation, often as a result of a flourishing judicial dialogue with the national courts.[181] For example, it ruled that the Equal Treatment Directive 76/207 (now Consolidated Directive 2006/54)[182] prohibited discrimination against transsexuals[183] and women on the grounds of their pregnancy,[184] but allowed 'soft quotas';[185] it recognized that Directive 2001/23 on transfers of undertakings could apply to contracting-out,[186] even in the public sector;[187] and, perhaps most controversially, it ruled in *Barber*[188] that Article 141 required equality in respect of occupational pension age, despite the derogation to Directive 86/378/EEC for equal treatment in respect of occupational pensions.

In more recent years, the Court has developed a second, linked area of interest—ensuring that the procedural and remedial laws of the Member States governing the enforcement of causes of action derived from Community law are effective. Once again the Court has used the social cases as the principal vehicle to develop these ideas. For example, in *Johnston*[189] the Court said that the requirement of judicial control stipulated by Article 6 of the Equal Treatment Directive 76/207 reflected a general principle of law, while in *Von Colson*[190] the Court said that the Equal Treatment Directive required that the sanction chosen by the Member State had to be such as to guarantee real and

---

[179] Davies, 'The European Court of Justice, National Courts, and the Member States', in Davies *et al.* above, n. 80.

[180] Case 152/84 *Marshall* v. *Southampton Area Health Authority (No. 1)* [1986] ECR 723; Case C–188/89 *Foster* v. *British Gas* [1990] ECR I–3313.

[181] See the essays in S. Sciarra (ed.), *Labour Law in the Courts* (Hart Publishing, Oxford, 2001) Chs. 2 and 3.

[182] OJ [2006] L204/23.

[183] Case C–13/94 *P.* v. *S.* [1996] ECR I–2143, but not homosexuals (see Case C–249/96 *Grant* v. *S. W. Trains* [1998] ECR I–621).

[184] Case C–177/88 *Dekker* v. *Stichting Vormungscentrum voor Jong Volwassenen* [1990] ECR I–3941, Case C–32/93 *Webb* v. *EMO Air Cargo* [1994] ECR I–3567.

[185] Cf. Case C–450/93 *Kalanke* v. *Freie Hansestadt Bremen* [1995] ECR I–3051 with Case C–409/95 *Marschall* v. *Land Nordrhein-Westfalen* [1997] ECR I–6363.

[186] Case C–209/91 *Rask and Christensen* v. *ISS Kantineservice* [1992] ECR I–5755. Cf. Case C–13/95 *Süzen* v. *Zehnacker Gebäudereinigung GmbH Krankenhausservice* [1997] ECR I–1259.

[187] Case C–29/91 *Dr Sophie Redmond* v. *Bartol* [1992] ECR I–3189.

[188] Case C–262/88 *Barber* v. *Guardian Royal Exchange* [1990] ECR I–1889.

[189] Case 222/84 *Johnston* v. *RUC* [1986] ECR 1651.

[190] Case 14/83 *Von Colson and Kamann* v. *Land Nordrhein-Westfalen* [1984] ECR 1509.

effective judicial protection.[191] In *Marshall (No. 2)*[192] the Court accepted that a limit on the total amount of compensation a tribunal could award a complainant and the absence of any power to award interest amounted to a breach of Article 6 of Directive 76/207 which required the award of full compensation.

This desire to make Community law effective in the national systems culminated in the Court's decision on state liability in *Francovich (No. 1)*, a case concerning the Italian government's failure to implement Directive 80/987/EEC on employees' rights on their employer's insolvency.[193] The Court ruled that in order to ensure the full effectiveness of Community law, and as part of the state's duty under Article 5 to take all appropriate measures to fulfil its Community law obligations, the state was liable for 'loss and damage caused to individuals as a result of breaches of Community Law'.[194]

Taken together, these developments have prompted some commentators to observe that the European Court of Justice has been instrumental in enforcing the social rights as part of the process of creating European social citizenship.[195] Others are more critical. Some ask whether, given the limited law-making powers in the social field, it was legitimate for the Court to expand both its own power and that of the Community into this area. Others argue that the Court, by giving a voice to individual litigants and pressure groups may well have increased the participative element of democracy in the Union as a whole.[196] If this perspective is adopted, then the Court's own legitimacy has been eroded by some poorly reasoned judgments and a lack of consistency. For example in *Süzen*[197] the Court threatened the complex edifice of worker protection on contracting out, and in *ex parte Sutton*,[198] in the context of Directive 79/7, the Court undermined the effectiveness of its earlier ruling in *Marshall (No. 2)* on the value of compensation. Others point out that, when giving its decisions, the Court disregards the broader policy agenda being developed elsewhere in the EU. Therefore, in cases such as

---

[191] Para. 23.

[192] The UK removed these limitations by passing SI 2798/1993 Sex Discrimination and Equal Pay (Remedial) Regulations 1993. It also extended this protection to race relations—Race Relations (Remedies) Act 1994. See also Case C–180/95 *Draehmpaehl* v. *Urania Immobilienservice ohG* [1997] ECR I–2195; cf. Case C–66/95 *R* v. *Secretary of State for Social Security, ex parte Sutton* [1997] ECR I–2163; cf. Case C–246/96 *Magorrian* v. *Eastern Health and Social Services Board* [1997] ECR I–7153.

[193] Joined Cases C–6 and 9/90 *Francovich (No. 1)* v. *Italian Republic* [1991] ECR I–5357. See also Ch. 7.

[194] Para. 35.

[195] See, e.g. Ball, 'The Making of a transnational capitalist society: The European Court of Justice, social policy, and individual rights under the European Community's legal order' (1996) 37 *Harvard International Law Journal* 307, 314; Bleijenbergh, de Bruijn and Bussemaker, 'European Social Citizenship and Gender: The Part-Time Work Directive (2004) 10 *EJIR*. 309, 311.

[196] See Fredman, 'Social Law in the European Union: The Impact of the Lawmaking Process', in Craig and Harlow (eds), *Lawmaking in the European Union* (Kluwer, Deventer, 1998) 402.

[197] Case C–13/95 [1997] ECR I–1259, considered further in Ch. 13.

[198] Case C–66/95 [1997] ECR I–2163.

Abdoulaye[199] where the Court's judgment merely reinforced traditional assumptions about the role of men and women in relation to family responsibilities, the Court demonstrated little awareness of the developing policy agenda of reconciling work and family life.

But, perhaps most critical for the purpose of the discussion in this chapter, is the challenge the Court's decisions have posed to the integrity of the national system of labour and social protection and it is this issue that the next section will focus on.[200]

2. Social Policy in the Face of the Internal Market

2.1. The Internal Market without a Social Face

We have already seen how the advent of EMU has constrained Member States from using economic tools to address problems of high unemployment and low levels of growth. Single Market rules and European competition policy also seemed to threaten key pillars of national social systems when interpreted by the Court of Justice without taking into account social policy. For example, in *Macrotron*[201] the Court held that the German Federal Employment Office was not entitled to maintain its statutory monopoly over employment placement services. The Court said it was abusing its dominant position contrary to Articles 82 and 86 because the statutory service could not meet demand and tolerated private head-hunters, even though their activities were illegal. However, the Court made no reference to the social interest behind the existing legislation: that private employment agencies might be tempted to concentrate on the most attractive job seekers, leaving aside the weaker prospects.[202]

Similarly, in *Porto di Genoa*[203] the Court said that Article 86 precluded national rules which conferred on an undertaking established in that state

---

[199] Case C–281/98 *Abdoulaye* v. *Renault* [2000] ECR I–4139, considered further in Ch. 9.

[200] See generally Wedderburn, 'Workers' Rights: Fact or Fake' (1991) 13 *Dublin University Law Journal* 1; Davies, 'Market Integration and Social Policy in the Court of Justice' (1995) 24 *ILJ*. 49; and Lyon-Caen, 'Droit Social et droit de la concurrence. Observations sur une rencontre', in *Orientations Sociales du Droit Contemperain: Ecrits en l'honneur de Pr. Jean Savatier* (PUF, Paris, 1992).

[201] Case C–41/90 *Höfner and Elser* v. *Macroton* [1991] ECR I–1979; see also Case C–55/96 *Non-Contentious Proceedings brought by Job Centre Coop arl* [1997] ECR I–7140. See generally, Ricci, 'Il controverso rapporto fra principi comunitari della concorrenza e normative nazionali del lavoro il caso *Job Centre II*' (1998) 2 *Diritto delle relazioni industriali* 145.

[202] Sciarra, 'Part II: *Job Centre*: An Illustrative Example of Strategic Litigation', in Sciarra (ed.), *Labour Law in the Courts: National Judges and the European Court of Justice* (Hart Publishing, Oxford, 2001) 245.

[203] Case C–179/90 *Merci Convenzionali Porto di Genova* v. *Siderurgica Gabrielli* [1991] ECR I–5889. See also Case C–163/96 *Criminal Proceedings against Silvano Raso* [1998] ECR I–533; Decision of the Commission 97/744/EC Re *Italian Ports Employment Policy: The Community* v. *Italy* [1998] 4 CMLR 73.

(but not individual dockers)[204] the exclusive right to organize dock work and required it to have recourse to a dock work company formed exclusively of national workers. Although the facts of *Porto di Genoa* were exceptional (the company was abusing its monopoly to demand payment for unrequested services, to offer selective reductions in prices and by refusing to have recourse to modern technology), the most striking feature of the Court's judgment, as Deakin points out,[205] was the almost complete disregard shown for social arguments which could have been made in favour of the dock labour monopoly. In particular, no reference was made to the need to combat casualization of labour.[206]

The potentially damaging scope of the state aid rules to the integrity of national social legislation was highlighted by the Court's decision in *Commission v. France*.[207] The Commission decided that the financial participation of the French Fonds National de l'Emploi (FNE), a state body, in paying for measures included in the social plan drawn up by a company faced with large scale redundancies, constituted a state aid contrary to Article 87(1) and therefore had to be notified to the Commission.[208] The Commission did, however, conclude that, in the event, the aid was not illegitimate, since it fell under an exception provided by Article 87(3)(c), (which allows aid where it is made 'to facilitate the development of certain economic activities or of certain economic areas, where such aid does not adversely affect trading conditions to an extent contrary to the common interest'). The French government challenged the Commission's initial finding that the payment by FNE came under Article 87 at all, because, if correct, it meant that France would have to notify all similar payments in future to the Commission. The Commission would then have the power to nullify them if the payments did not, in its view (subject to review by the Court), fall under the relevant derogation.

The pre-existing case law on state aid drew a distinction between measures of general application, which were not aid, and subsidies payable to particular undertakings, which were. According to Advocate General Jacobs:

. . . measures taken within the framework of employment policy are usually not state aid. However, where public funds are used to reduce the salary costs of undertakings,

---

[204] Case C–22/98 *Criminal Proceedings against Bew, Verweire, Smeg and Adia Interim* [1999] ECR I–5665.
[205] Deakin, 'Labour Law as Market Regulation: the Economic Foundations of European Social Policy', above, n. 80, 75.
[206] For a recent example: Kubosova, 'Dock Workers Strike against EU Port Bill', *euobserver.com*, 11 January 2006.
[207] Case C–241/94 *French Republic v. Commission* [1996] ECR I–4551. See also Case C–256/97 *Proceedings relating to DMT* [1999] ECR I–3913. See Barnard and Deakin, 'European Community Social Policy: Progression or Regression?' (1998/1999) 2 *IRJ*. 117.
[208] See also Case 203/82 *Commission v. Italy* [1983] ECR 2525: legislation reducing employer's sickness insurance contributions by different amounts in respect of male and female employees indirectly benefited certain sectors with more female employees and was declared contrary to Art. 87.

either directly (for example by recruitment premiums) or indirectly (for example by reductions in fiscal or social charges), the distinction between state aid and general measure becomes less clear. The existence of discretion serves to identify those financial measures promoting employment which are liable to distort competition and affect trade between Member States.

The Court followed this lead and concluded that since the French legislation gave the administration some discretion in the amounts of subsidy which it could grant to a particular employer, this constituted a state aid. It therefore had to be notified and approved.

By contrast, in *Kirsammer-Hack*[209] and *Viscido*[210] the Court found that national measures aimed at job creation were compatible with the rules on state aid. In the first case the Court found that the exemption of small business from national unfair dismissal law did not constitute a state aid and in the second the Court ruled that a law exempting the Italian post office from the requirement that employees had to be appointed on indefinite contracts only also did not constitute a state aid.

Subsequently, the Commission issued a Regulation on the application of Articles 87 and 88 EC to state aid for employment.[211] Consistent with the social inclusion objectives of the Luxembourg European Employment Strategy and the Lisbon strategy, the Commission permits states to provide aid for the creation of employment, for the recruitment of disadvantaged and disabled workers or to cover the additional costs of employing disabled workers, provided the conditions laid down in the Regulation were satisfied. In these circumstances, the aid does not need to be notified to the Commission. The Court rejected Belgium's challenge to this Regulation in *Belgium* v. *Commission*.[212] In particular, the Court noted that the Commission is required to ensure that Articles 87 and 88 are applied consistently with other provisions of the Treaty, including Article 127 (considered above) which requires the Community to contribute to a high level of employment. The Court concluded that 'the Commission is required to ensure the necessary consistency between its aid policy and Community action relating to employment'.[213]

---

[209] Case C–189/91 *Kirsammer Hack* v. *Sidal* [1993] ECR I–6185. See also Joined Cases C–72/91 and C–73/91 *Sloman* [1993] ECR I–887, where the Court held that only benefits granted directly or indirectly out of state resources were to be regarded as an aid. Consequently, a German system allowing employment contracts for seamen not to be subject to German law did not constitute a state aid. Cf. Commission Decision 2000/128/EC (OJ [2000] L42/1) concerning aid granted by Italy to promote employment. See Biondi and Rubini, 'EC State Aid Law and its Impact on National Social Policies' in Dougan and Spaventa (eds), *Social Welfare and EU Law* (Hart Publishing, Oxford, 2005).
[210] Joined Cases C–52/97, C–53/97 and C–54/97 *Viscido* v. *Ente Poste Italiane* [1998] ECR I–2629.
[211] Commission Reg. 2204/2002 (OJ [2002] L349/126) adopted under the powers laid down by Council Reg. 994/98 on the application of Arts. [87] and [88] of the Treaty establishing the European Community to certain categories of horizontal state aid (OJ [1998] L142/1).
[212] Case C–110/03 *Belgium* v. *Commission* [2005] ECR I–000.   [213] Para. 66.

2.2. Striking a Balance between the Internal Market and (National) Social Policy

(a) The Role of Public Interest Requirements[214]

The cases considered so far demonstrate the effect the EC market integration rules—described as fundamental freedoms (mainly free movement and competition rules)—have had on national social rights. The neo-liberal conception of the European Economic Constitution has promoted deregulatory consequences at national level with negative effects on social rights.[215] The absence of any fully developed social dimension in the original EEC Treaty exacerbated the asymmetry between the economic and social imperatives. However, even without the Charter of Fundamental Rights, the Court does have the tools—such as public interest requirements—to strike a better balance between free trade and national rights and has at times shown itself willing to give precedence to national social rights, especially where the values protected by national law are shared by a large number of the Member States.[216] For example, when interpreting Article 28 on the free movement of goods, the Court has found that national measures designed to ensure worker protection—such as legislation prohibiting employment of workers on Sunday[217] or prohibiting night work in bakeries[218]—while potentially a restriction on trade, were compatible with Community law. In *Rush Portuguesa*[219] the Court ruled that host states were entitled to apply their labour laws to the employees of subcontractors from another Member State while the employees were working on the host state's territory and this did not infringe Article 49.[220] This case gave the green light to the enactment of the Directive 96/71 on Posted Workers.[221] The Directive is intended to promote the transnational provision of services, which requires a 'climate of fair competition and measures guaranteeing respect for the rights of workers'.[222] In essence, it allows host states

---

[214] Paras. 64–5.

[215] Poiares Maduro, 'Balancing Economic Freedoms and Social Rights' in Alston *et al.* (eds), *The EU and Human Rights* (OUP, Oxford, 1999) 451.

[216] Ibid. and expanded more fully in Poiares Maduro, *We the Court: The European Court of Justice and the European Economic Constitution* (Hart Publishing, Oxford, 1998).

[217] Case C–312/8 *Union départementale des syndicats CGT de l'Aisne v. Conforama* [1991] ECR I–977 and Case C–332/89 *Criminal Proceedings against Marchandise* [1991] ECR I–1027. Cf. Case C–398/95 *SETTG v. Ypourgos Ergasias* [1997] ECR I–3091 where the Court said that a restriction to the free movement of services could not be justified on the grounds of 'maintaining industrial peace as a means of bringing a collective dispute to an end and thereby preventing any adverse effects on an economic sector and consequently on the economy of the state'.

[218] Case 155/80 *Oebel* [1981] ECR 1993. See, generally, Poiares Maduro, *We, the Court, The European Court of Justice and the European Economic Constitution* (Hart Publishing, Oxford, 1998) 61–78.

[219] Case C–113/89 *Rush Portugesa Ltda v. Office Nationale d'Immigration* [1990] ECR 1417.

[220] Para. 18. This is considered further in Ch. 5.

[221] Dir. 96/71/EC (OJ [1996] L18/1). See Davies, 'Posted Workers: Single Market or Protection of National Labour Law Systems' (1997) 34 *CMLRev.* 571.

[222] Preambular, para. 5.

to apply to posted workers certain key labour law rules, in particular relating to minimum wages, working time and equal treatment, even in the case of short-term postings. However, since the Directive has the effect of requiring the out-of-state service provider to adapt its terms and conditions of employment each time it posts workers to another Member State, some argue that it interferes with, rather than promotes, the provision of services.[223]

It may be for this reason that the Court has retreated somewhat from its bold but unreasoned approach in *Rush Portuguesa* and brought subsequent cases into line with its post-*Gebhard/Säger*[224] jurisprudence.[225] Therefore, in its more recent decisions it has looked to see whether the host state's rule laying down particular social standards in principle breaches Article 49 and then examines whether the measure can be justified on the grounds of worker protection[226] (especially the interests of the posted workers)[227] and whether the steps taken are proportionate.[228]

These recent decisions on posted workers help to explain the approach adopted (but not always articulated) in the earlier cases: that where the national legislation is, in principle, in breach of a fundamental freedom, the Member States can rely on the (judicially developed) 'mandatory' or 'public interest' requirements of worker protection which take precedence over free movement, provided that the national measures are proportionate.

In other cases the Court has simply interpreted the relevant EU provision in a way that permits the realization of the social objective. For example, in *Beentjes*[229] the Court said that it was compatible with the EC rules on public procurement[230] to exclude a company tendering for a contract on the grounds

---

[223] See e.g. P. Davies, 'The Posted Workers Directive and the EC Treaty' (2002) 31 *ILJ*. 298, 300.

[224] Case C–55/94 [1995] ECR I–4165 and Case C–76/90 [1991] ECR I–4221 respectively, considered in Barnard, *The Substantive Law of the European Union* (OUP, Oxford, 2004) Ch. 10.

[225] See e.g. Case C–43/93 *Vander Elst* [1994] ECR I–3803 and Case C–272/94 *Criminal Proceedings against Michel Guiot and Climatec SA* [1996] ECR I–1905.

[226] Joined Cases C–49, 50, 52, 54, 68, and 71/98 *Finalarte Sociedade de Construçâo Civil Lda* [2001] ECR I–7831, paras. 41–9, for a careful scrutiny of the worker protection justification and that the national measures did actually confer a genuine benefit on the posted worker. See also Case C–164/99 *Portugaia Construçôes Lda* [2002] ECR I–787, paras. 28–9.

[227] Joined Cases C–49, 50, 52, 54, 68, and 71/98 *Finalarte* [2001] ECR I–7831, para. 41.

[228] See e.g. Joined Cases C–369 and 376/96 *Criminal Proceedings against Jean-Claude Arblade and Arblade & Fils SARL and against Bernard Leloup and others* [1999] ECR I–8453.

[229] Case 31/87 *Beentjes* v. *Minister van Landbouw en Visserij* [1988] ECR 4635. This was followed in Case C–225/98 *Commission* v. *France* [2000] ECR I–7445 (criteria linked to the campaign against unemployment). See Boris, 'A Social Policy Agenda in European Public Procurement Law and Policy' (1998) 14 *IJCLLIR*. 137. Tobler, 'Encore: "Women's Clauses" in Public procurement under Community Law' (2000) 25 *ELRev*. 618. See also Commission, *Interpretative communication on the Community law applicable to public procurement and the possibilities for integrating social considerations into public procurement*, COM(2001) 566.

[230] Council Directive 71/305/EEC on the award of public works contracts (OJ [1971] SE (II)/682). The current rules are found in Dir. 2004/18/EC (OJ [2004] L134/114 which takes account of the *Beentjes* line of case law. See in particular Recital 46: 'In order to guarantee equal treatment, the criteria for the award of the contract should enable tenders to be compared and

that it was not in a position to employ the long-term unemployed provided that the requirement (to employ the long-term unemployed) did not discriminate against tenderers from other Member States of the Community.[231]

(b) The Principle of Solidarity

In more recent cases the Court has developed a new principle to help balance the EC competition rules with the needs of the national welfare state: the principle of solidarity.[232] Advocate General Fennelly defined solidarity in his opinion in *Sodemare*[233] as the 'inherently uncommercial act of involuntary subsidization of one social group by another'.[234] In the national system it has meant that national taxpayers pay their taxes to help look after their fellow nationals who need assistance. This sense of solidarity is derived in part from a shared nationality, in part from a shared sense of identity.

The Court started using the principle of solidarity in the early 1990s to protect certain social welfare schemes from the ravages of EC competition law:[235] the Court says that where the activity is based on national solidarity, it is not an economic activity and therefore the body concerned cannot be classed as an undertaking to which Articles 81 and 82 apply. This principle, when applied, indicates a certain supremacy for social protection over the Single Market.

The principle was first recognized in this context in *Poucet and Pistre*[236] where the Court held that certain French bodies administering the sickness and maternity insurance scheme for self-employed persons engaged in

---

assessed objectively. If these conditions are fulfilled, economic and qualitative criteria for the award of the contract, such as meeting environmental requirements, may enable the contracting authority to meet the needs of the public concerned, as expressed in the specifications of the contract. Under the same conditions, a contracting authority may use criteria aiming to meet *social requirements*, in response in particular to the needs—defined in the specifications of the contract—of particularly disadvantaged groups of people to which those receiving/using the works, supplies or services which are the object of the contract belong'. Art. 26 provides: 'Contracting authorities may lay down special conditions relating to the performance of a contract, provided that these are compatible with Community law and are indicated in the contract notice or in the specifications. The conditions governing the performance of a contract may, in particular, concern social and environmental considerations.'

[231] The Court said that an additional specific condition of this kind had to be mentioned in the contract notice (para. 36).

[232] Hervey, 'Social Solidarity: a Buttress against Internal Market law?', in Shaw (ed.), *Social Law and Policy in an Evolving European Union*, (Hart Publishing, Oxford, 2000). See more generally, De Búrca (ed.), *EU Law and the Welfare State: In Search of Solidarity* (OUP, Oxford, 2005).

[233] Case C–70/95 *Sodemare SA, Anni Azzurri Holding SpA and Anni Azzurri Rezzato Srl* v. *Regione Lombardia* [1997] ECR I–3395.

[234] Para. 29.

[235] For a fuller consideration of these developments, see Barnard, 'Solidarity and New Governance in the Field of Social Policy?' in De Búrca and Scott (eds), *New Governance and Constitutionalism in Europe and the US* (Hart Publishing, Oxford, 2006).

[236] Joined Cases C–159/91 and C–160/91 *Poucet and Pistre* v. *AGF and Cancava* [1993] ECR I–637.

non-agricultural occupations and the basic pension scheme for skilled trades, were not to be classified as undertakings for the purpose of competition law. The schemes provided a basic pension.[237] Affiliation was compulsory. The pension scheme was a non-funded scheme: it operated on a redistributive basis with active members' contributions being directly used to finance the pensions of retired members; and the schemes had a social objective in that they were intended to provide cover for the beneficiaries against the risks of sickness or old age regardless of the individuals' financial status and state of health at the time of affiliation. The principle of solidarity was embodied in the *redistributive* nature of the pension scheme: contributions paid by active workers served to finance the pensions of retired workers. It was also reflected by the grant of pension rights where no contributions had been made and of pension rights that were not proportional to the contributions paid. Finally, there was solidarity between the various social security schemes, with those in surplus contributing to the financing of those with structural difficulties. The Court said:

It follows that the social security schemes, as described, are based on a system of compulsory contribution, which is indispensable for the application of the principle of solidarity and the financial equilibrium of those schemes.

. . . [O]rganisations involved in the management of the public social security system fulfil an exclusively social function. That activity is based on the principle of national solidarity and is entirely non-profit-making. The benefits paid are statutory benefits bearing no relation to the amount of the contribution. Accordingly, that activity is not an economic activity . . .

However, in *FFSA* (also known as *Coreva*)[238] the Court 'clarified' its case law. The case concerned a French supplementary retirement scheme for self-employed farmers.[239] The Court noted that in *FFSA* membership of the scheme was optional, that the scheme operated in accordance with the principle of capitalization, rather than on a redistributive basis as in *Poucet*, and that the benefits to which it conferred entitlement depended solely on the amount of contributions paid by the recipients and the financial results of the investments made by the managing organization. It concluded that the managing body therefore carries on an economic activity in competition with life assurance companies and so the Community competition rules, in particular Article 81, applied. On the question of solidarity the Court said that 'the

---

[237] These are helpfully summarized by Advocate General Jacobs in his Opinion in Case C–67/96 *Albany* [1999] ECR I–5751, para. 317.

[238] Case C–244/94 *Fédération Française des Sociétés d'Assurances* [1995] ECR I–4013 discussed by Laigre, 'L'intrusion du droit communautaire de la concurrence dans le champ de la protection sociale' [1996] *Droit Social* 82.

[239] Case C–67/96 *Albany v. Stichting Bedrijfspensioenfonds Textielindustrie* [1999] ECR I–5751, para. 325. This case is considered in more detail in Ch. 16.

principle of solidarity is extremely limited in scope' and noted that while the scheme had solidaristic elements that was not sufficient to take the scheme outside Article 81.

The Court reached much the same conclusion in *Albany*,[240] another case involving a capitalization scheme. It said that a pension fund charged with the management of a supplementary pension scheme set up by a collective agreement to which affiliation was compulsory by the public authorities for all workers in that sector, was an undertaking within the meaning of Article 81. However, it did say that the solidarity elements[241] justified the exclusive right of the fund to manage the supplementary scheme under Article 86(2) and so there was no breach of Articles 82 and 86(1) respectively.

Although the Court's initial enthusiasm for the principle of solidarity seemed to have rather cooled after *FFSA*, the principle was successfully invoked in *Sodemare*[242] to allow Italy to insist that only non-profit-making private operators could participate in the running of its social welfare system. The Italian rules did not breach Articles 43 and 48 on freedom of establishment because, as the Court noted, the system of social welfare, whose implementation is in principle entrusted to the public authorities, is based on the principle of solidarity, as reflected by the fact that it is designed as a matter of priority to assist those who are in a state of need.[243] Thus, in *Sodemare* the Court used the principle of solidarity to reinforce its view that Community law is not just about unrestricted access for all economic operators to the market in other Member States.[244]

Since *Sodemare* the Court has carefully examined the facts of the individual cases to consider whether there is a sufficient degree of solidarity to justify a finding that the activity is not economic, so falling outside the scope of Community law, or insufficient solidarity and so Community law applies. For

---

[240] Case C–67/96 [1999] ECR I–5751, para. 87.

[241] The solidarity was reflected by the obligation to accept all workers without a prior medical examination, the continuing accrual of pension rights despite exemption from contributions in the event of incapacity for work, the discharge by the fund of arrears of contributions due from an employer in the event of the latter's insolvency and by the indexing of the amount of the pensions in order to maintain their value. The principle of solidarity was also apparent from the absence of any equivalence, for individuals, between the contribution paid, which is an average contribution not linked to risks, and pension rights, which are determined by reference to an average salary. Such solidarity makes compulsory affiliation to the supplementary pension scheme essential. Otherwise, if 'good' risks left the scheme, the ensuing downward spiral would jeopardize its financial equilibrium (para. 75). This would increase the cost of pensions for workers, particularly those in small and medium-sized undertakings with older employees engaged in dangerous activities, to which the fund could no longer offer pensions at an acceptable cost (para. 108).

[242] Case C–70/95 *Sodemare* v. *Regione Lombardia* [1997] ECR I–3395.   [243] Para. 29.

[244] In the context of free movement of goods, cf. Case C–267/91 *Criminal proceedings against Keck and Mithouard* [1993] ECR I–6097.

example, in *AOK*[245] the Court found that the sickness funds in the German statutory health insurance scheme were involved in the management of the social security system where they fulfilled 'an exclusively social function which is founded on the principle of national solidarity and is entirely non-profit-making'.[246] Since the funds were obliged by law to offer their members essentially identical benefits, irrespective of contributions, that they were bound together in a type of community founded on the basis of solidarity which enabled an equalization of costs and risks between them, and they did not compete with one another or private institutions,[247] the Court considered they fell on the *Poucet and Pistre* side of the line and so their activity could not be regarded as economic in nature. On the other hand, in *Wouters*[248] the Court said that because a professional regulatory body such as the Bar of the Netherlands was neither fulfilling a social function based on the principle of solidarity nor exercising powers which were typically those of a public authority, it did engage in an economic activity and so was subject to Community law.

(c) Conclusions

Our review of the Court's case law suggests that where domestic labour market and more general social regulation collides with European Single Market (de)regulation the Court has shown itself to be least sure-footed. The outcomes of the cases are unpredictable, the standards applied are unclear and national labour protection is undermined. On the other hand, the Court has equipped itself with tools to fend off such attacks, whether through the principle of solidarity or public interest justification, if it cares to use them. The inclusion of a more pronounced social dimension to the European Union since Maastricht, together with the Charters of Fundamental Rights (both of

---

[245] Joined Cases C–264/01, C–306/01, C–354/01 and C–355/01 *AOK Bundesverband, Bundesverband der Betriebskrankenkassen (BKK), Bundesverband der Innungskrankenkassen, Bundesverband der landwirtschaftlichen Krankenkassen, Verband der Angestelltenkrankenkassen eV, Verband der Arbeiter-Ersatzkassen, Bundesknappschaft and See-Krankenkasse* v. *Ichthyol-Gesellschaft Cordes, Hermani & Co. (C–264/01), Mundipharma GmbH (C–306/01), Gödecke GmbH (C–354/01) and Intersan, Institut für pharmazeutische und klinische Forschung GmbH (C–355/01)* [2004] ECR I–000. See also Case C–218/00 *Cisal di Battistello Venanzio & C.Sas* v. *Istituto nazionale per l'assicurazione contro gli infortuni sul lavoro* [2002] ECR I–691 concerning compulsory insurance against accidents at work and occupational diseases; Case C–355/00 *Freskot AE* v. *Elliniko Dimosio* [2003] ECR I–5263; Case T–319/99 *FENIN* v. *Commission* [2003] ECR II–357 concerning the bodies which run the Spanish national health system); Joined Cases C–266/04 to C–270/04 *Nazairdis* v. *Caisse nationale de l'orgaisation autonome d'assurance viellesse des travailleurs non salariés des professions industrielles et commerciales (Organic)* [2005] ECR I–000, para. 54 (old age insurance schemes for self-employed persons in the craft sector). See Sciarra, 'Market Freedom and Fundamental Social Rights', in Hepple (ed.), *Social and Labour Rights in a Global Context* (CUP, Cambridge, 2002).

[246] Para. 51.   [247] Paras. 51–3.

[248] Case C–309/99 *Wouters, Savelbergh, Price Waterhouse Belastingadviseurs BV* v. *Algemene Raad van de Nederlandse Orde van Advocaten* [2002] ECR I–1577, para. 58. See also Case C–55/96 *Job Centre Coop. Arl* [1997] ECR I–7119.

1989 and 2000) have helped to rebalance the competing interests. There are signs that the Court has begun to recognize this. In *Albany*[249] it said:

[I]t is important to bear in mind that, under [Article 3(1)(g) and (j)] of the EC Treaty, the activities of the Community are to include not only a 'system ensuring that competition in the internal market is not distorted' but also 'a policy in the social sphere'. Article 2 of the EC Treaty provides that a particular task of the Community is 'to promote throughout the Community a harmonious and balanced development of economic activities' and 'a high level of employment and of social protection'.

More recently, it noted in *Deutsche Post*[250] that the economic aim pursued by Article 141 of the Treaty, namely the elimination of distortions of competition between undertakings established in different Member States, was secondary to the social aim pursued by the same provision, which constitutes the expression of a fundamental human right.[251] Thus the gradual evolution of some social—or rather employment—policy at EU level has meant that the Court has now found itself on firmer footing to reconcile the social imperatives of the EU and its Member States with the more natural economic, deregulatory orientation of the EC Treaty.

2.3. The Citizenship Case Law

The Court's greater confidence in protecting social rights may also be explained in part by the formal creation of the title Union citizen by the Maastricht Treaty. EU citizens enjoy EC-created social rights which they can enforce against their own states. They can also enjoy rights under Article 18(1) EC against other states when they exercise their rights of free movement. Article 18(1) EC grants EU citizens the right to move to other Member States and reside there subject to the limitations and conditions laid down in the Treaty. These limitations include not only the express derogations of public policy, public security, and public health but also, in the case of those migrants who are not economically active, the requirements laid down in what were the 1990 Residence Directives,[252] now the Citizens' Rights Directive 2004/38,[253] of having sufficient resources and medical insurance. In an important and recent line of case law, the Court of Justice has made clear that

---

[249] Case C–67/96 [1999] ECR I–000, para. 54.
[250] Joined Cases C–270/97 and C–271/97 *Deutsche Post AG v. Elisabeth Sievers and Brunhilde Schrage* [2000] ECR I–929.
[251] Para. 57.
[252] Council Dirs.: 90/364/EEC (OJ [1990] L180/26) on the rights of residence for persons of sufficient means (the 'playboy Directive'), 90/365/EEC on the rights of residence for employees and self-employed who have ceased their occupational activity (OJ [1990] L180/28) and 90/366/EEC (OJ [1990] L180/30) on the rights of residence for students (now Dir. 93/96 (OJ [1993] L317/59).
[253] OJ [2004] L158/77.

Article 18(1) is directly effective,[254] that, in the name of Union citizenship, the derogations and limitations must be narrowly construed and applied proportionately,[255] that an interpretation of a case through the prism of citizenship may cast doubt on existing orthodox case law,[256] and perhaps, most dramatically, the solidarity principle justifies imposing obligations on the host state to look after migrant citizens. These principles can be seen in operation in *Grzelczyk*.[257]

Grzelczyk was a French student studying at a Belgian university. Having supported himself financially during the first three years of study, he applied to the Belgian authorities for a minimex (a guarantee of minimum income) to fund his fourth and final year. He was turned down on the grounds that he was neither Belgian nor a worker under Regulations 1612/68. When considering Grzelczyk's position as a Union citizen the Court began with its now oft-repeated statement that:[258]

Union citizenship is destined to be the fundamental status of nationals of the Member States, enabling those who find themselves in the same situation to enjoy the same treatment in law irrespective of their nationality, subject to such exceptions as are expressly provided for.

It continued that 'a citizen of the European Union, lawfully resident in the territory of a host Member State, can rely on Article [12] of the Treaty [non-discrimination on the grounds of nationality] in all situations which fall within the scope ratione materiae of Community law',[259] including 'those situations involving the exercise of the fundamental freedoms guaranteed by the Treaty and those involving the exercise of the right to move and reside freely in another Member State, as conferred by Article 18 of the Treaty.'[260]

The Court then considered the limits laid down in the Residence Directives, in particular the limits imposed by Article 1 of the Students' Directive 93/96 which required migrant students to have sufficient resources when exercising the rights of free movement. The Court said that while a Member State could decide that a student having recourse to social assistance no longer fulfilled the conditions of his right of residence and so could withdraw his residence permit or decide not to renew it,[261] such actions could not be the automatic consequence of a migrant student having recourse to the host State's social assistance system.[262] The Court continued that beneficiaries of the right of residence could not become an 'unreasonable' burden on the public finances of the host State.[263] Therefore, the Belgian authorities had to provide some

---

[254] Case C–413/99 *Baumbast and R v. Secretary of State for the Home Department* [2002] ECR I–7091.
[255] Ibid.   [256] Case C–138/02 *Collins* [2004] ECR I–2703.
[257] Case C–184/99 *Rudy Grzelczyk v. Centre public d'aide sociale d'Ottignies-Louvain-la-Neuve* [2001] ECR I–6193.
[258] Para. 31.   [259] Para. 32.   [260] Para. 33.
[261] Para. 42.   [262] Para. 43.   [263] Para. 44.

temporary support (the minimex) to the migrant citizen, as they would to nationals, given that there existed 'a certain degree of financial solidarity' between nationals of a host Member State and nationals of other Member States.[264] In other words, due to this 'certain degree of financial solidarity' between the Belgian taxpayer and the French migrant student, derived from their common (EU) citizenship, the student could enjoy the social benefit but only for so long as the student did not become an unreasonable burden on public finances. In *Bidar*[265] the Court built on the ruling in *Grzelczyk* to justify finding that the UK was obliged to treat legally resident migrants equally with nationals in respect of access to maintenance grants and loans. However, the Court said that the UK would be justified in imposing a three-year residence requirement before the individual could claim maintenance grants and loans.

The solidarity principle also helps to explain *Baumbast*.[266] Baumbast was a German national who had been working in the UK and continued residing there with his family once his work in the EU had ceased. While he had sufficient resources for himself and his family, his German medical insurance did not cover emergency treatment in the UK, as required by Directive 90/364 on persons of independent means.[267] For this reason the British authorities refused to renew his residence permit. The Court said that he could rely on his directly effective right to reside under Article 18(1) but this right had to be read subject to the limitations laid down in the Residence Directives.[268] It then qualified this remark by adding that the limitations and conditions referred in Article 18(1) had to be applied 'in compliance with the limits imposed by Community law and in accordance with the general principles of that law, in particular the principle of proportionality'.[269] It concluded that, given neither Baumbast nor his family had become a financial burden on the state, it would amount to a disproportionate interference with the exercise of the right of residence if he were denied residence on the ground that his sickness insurance did not cover the emergency treatment given in the host Member State.[270] When viewed through the lens of solidarity, it could be argued that there was a sufficient degree of solidarity between Baumbast and the British

---

[264] Ibid.

[265] Case C–209/03 R *(on the application of Danny Bidar)* v. *London Borough of Ealing, Secretary of State for Education and Skills* [2005] ECR I–000.

[266] Case C–413/99 *Baumbast and R* v. *Secretary of State for the Home Department* [2002] ECR I–7091. See also the reference in para. 44 of *Grzelczyk* to Dirs. 90/364 and 90/365 which, like Dir. 93/96, 'accepts a certain degree of financial solidarity'. See also Advocate General Geelhoed's comments in *Bidar*, para. 31: 'The notion of 'unreasonable burden' is apparently flexible and, according to the Court, implies that Directive 93/96 accepts a degree of financial solidarity between the Member States in assisting each other's nationals residing lawfully in their territory. As the same principle is at the basis of the conditions imposed by Directive 90/354, there is no reason to presume that this same financial solidarity does not apply in that context too.'

[267] Para. 88. See also Case T–66/75 *Hedwig Kuchlenz-Winter* v. *Commission* [1997] ECR II–637, paras. 46–7.

[268] Para. 90.   [269] Para. 91.   [270] Para. 93.

taxpayer to justify him (and his family) receiving emergency medical treatment on the NHS.

The reliance on the solidarity principle to justify imposing additional financial obligations on the host state in respect of EU migrants is a remarkable development. It raises the question of whether solidarity can be invoked by all EU migrants, including those who have recently arrived in the host state, especially those seeking education.[271] *Bidar* suggests that the answer is no: that only those who enjoy a certain degree of integration in the host state can expect equal treatment in respect of certain benefits like maintenance grants and loans. In paragraph 56 the Court referred to the need for Member States to show 'a certain degree of financial solidarity with nationals of other Member States' in the organisation and application of their social assistance systems. It then continued that:

In the case of assistance covering the maintenance costs of students, it is thus legitimate for a Member State to grant such assistance only to students who have demonstrated a *certain degree of integration* into the society of that State.[272]

The Court then makes clear that length of residence is a key indicator of integration:[273]

... the existence of a certain degree of integration may be regarded as established by a finding that the student in question has resided in the host state for a certain length of time.

Thus, *Bidar* emphasizes a 'quantitative' approach:[274] the longer migrants reside in the Member State, the more integrated they are in that state and the greater the number of benefits they receive on equal terms with nationals. The corollary of this is that in respect of newly arrived migrants there is insufficient solidarity between them and the host state taxpayer to justify requiring full equal treatment in respect of social welfare benefits. This was the view taken by Advocate General Ruiz-Jarabo Colomer in *Collins*.[275] Collins,

---

[271] See Advocate General Geelhoed's opinion in Case C–413/01 *Franca Ninni-Orasche v. Bundesminister für Wissenschaft, Verkehr und Kunst* [2003] ECR I–13187 where he referred to the need for a minimum degree of financial solidarity towards those residents who are students but holding the nationality of another Member State and concluded that a resident like Mrs Ninni-Orasche with a 'demonstrable and structural link to Austrian society' could not be treated in Austria 'as any other national of a third country' (para. 96). See Dougan and Spaventa, 'New Model of Social Solidarity in the EU', in Dougan and Spaventa (eds), *Social Welfare and EU Law* (Hart Publishing, Oxford, 2005).

[272] Para. 73. Emphasis added.

[273] Para. 59. See also AG Geelhoed's remarks in Case C–413/01 *Ninni-Orasche v. Bundesminister für Wissenschaft* [2003] ECR I–13187, paras. 90–1. For an emphasis on the contextual approach which takes account of length of residence and degree of integration, see AG Ruiz-Jarabo Colomer's opinion, in Case C–138/02 *Brian Francis Collins v. Secretary of State for Work and Pensions* [2004] ECR I–2703, paras. 65–7.

[274] This idea is developed further in Barnard (2005) 42 *CMLRev.* 1465.

[275] Case C–138/02 *Collins* [2004] ECR I–2703.

who was Irish, arrived in the United Kingdom and promptly applied for a job-seeker's allowance (JSA) which was refused on the grounds that he was not habitually resident in the UK. The Advocate General distinguished the facts of *Grzelczyk*[276] (and the Court's reference to solidarity) and concluded that Community law did not require the benefit to be provided to a citizen of the Union who entered the territory of a Member State with the purpose of seeking employment while lacking any connection with the state or link with the domestic employment market.[277] The Court decided the case on a different basis but reached the same conclusion.

D. THE NATURE AND PURPOSE OF EC SOCIAL POLICY

1. The European Social Model

It is clear from the description above that the evolution of EC social policy has been spasmodic with the resulting rules representing a patchwork of European social regulation rather than a fully fledged social policy with welfare institutions and cradle-to-grave protection.[278] It makes no provision for what is generally agreed to be the central core of social policy: social insurance, public assistance, health and welfare services, education and housing policy.[279] There is also no evidence of the creation of a European welfare state to replace the national welfare states: the EU has neither the competence nor the budget for it.[280] However, the existing body of EC regulation is often referred to as 'European social policy', not least by the EC Treaty itself,[281] and various institutions talk of the European Social Model.[282] For example, in its White Paper on Social Policy[283] the Commission said that the 'European Social Model' is based around certain shared values:

These include democracy and individual rights, free collective bargaining, the market economy, equality of opportunity for all and social welfare and solidarity. These values

---

[276] Para. 66.   [277] Para. 76.

[278] This section develops the arguments in Barnard, 'EC "Social" Policy', in Craig and de Búrca (eds), *The Evolution of EU Law* (OUP, Oxford, 1999).

[279] Majone, 'The European Community: Between Social Policy and Regulation' (1993) 31 *JCMS*. 153, 158. However, the EC Treaty does contain a chapter on education vocational training and youth and Titles on culture, public health and consumer protection. The cases on health testing of staff at the institutions also demonstrate some awareness of the wider dimension of social policy. See e.g. Case C–404/92 P *Commission* v. *X* [1994] ECR I–4737.

[280] Teague, 'Deliberative Governance and EU Social Policy' (2001) 7 *EJIR*. 7, 21.

[281] Title XI is headed 'Social Policy, Education, Vocational Training and Youth'. Ch. 1, which contains Arts. 136–45, is entitled 'Social Provisions'. See also the Commission's 'White Paper on Social Policy', COM(94) 333.

[282] See Adnett and Hardy, *The European Social Model: Modernisation or Evolution* (Edward Elgar, Cheltenham, 2005). This issue is considered further in Ch. 3.

[283] COM(94) 333, para. 3.

... are held together by the conviction that economic and social progress must go hand in hand. Competitiveness and solidarity have both been taken into account in building a successful Europe for the future.

Six years later, at the Nice European Council, the heads of state said:[284]

The European social model has developed over the last forty years through a substantial Community acquis ... It now includes essential texts in numerous areas: free movement of workers, gender equality at work, health and safety of workers, working and employment conditions and, more recently, the fight against all forms of discrimination.

The Council continued that this social model also includes the agreements between the Social Partners in the law-making process, the Luxembourg EES and the open method of co-ordination on the subject of social exclusion and greater co-operation in the field of social protection.[285]

The Final Report of the Constitutional Treaty's Working Group XI on Social Europe offered its own view.[286] It said that 'the European social model is based on good economic performance, competitiveness, a high level of social protection and education and social dialogue'. It also noted that the European social model allows for a diversity of approaches in order to achieve shared European values and objectives and that this diversity should be treated as an asset and a source of strength.[287]

The common features of these descriptions are first, that there is no single concept of a European social model, that it is based on some shared values but a diversity of means for achieving this, and that the success of this social model is tied up with good economic performance; second, the European social model is based on *high* standards (such as a high level of social protection) and quality,[288] rather than a low quality, low skilled workforce; and third, all the institutions mention an eclectic range of policies grouped together under the broad banner of European social policy. Finally, and perhaps most importantly, all of the EU institutions recognize that there is such a thing as European Union social model which builds on but is, in many respects, separate from the social model found in the Member States. This raises the fundamental question as to why the EU, a transnational body with limited competence, has a European social model that it wishes to call its own. This question has bedevilled the Community since its inception.

---

[284] Para. 12.   [285] Para. 11.   [286] CONV 516/1/03.   [287] Para. 17.
[288] See, e.g. Commission Communication, 'Employment and Social Policies: a framework for investing in quality' (COM(2001) 313, 5).

2. Market Making vs Market Correcting

2.1. Introduction

Traditionally, at national level, social policy is viewed as serving a social just-ice/social cohesion or a *market-correcting*[289] function. In Marshall's words, social policy involves the use of 'political power to supersede, supplement or modify operations of the economic system in order to achieve results which the economic system would not achieve on its own, . . . guided by values other than those determined by market forces'.[290] These values include the need to redistribute income and resources in order to promote social inclusion and cohesion, thereby ensuring political stability. As we shall see, elements of this logic, given renewed vigour by the advent of European Union citizenship, can be detected in the development of EC social legislation.

On the other hand, as Streeck has observed, 'Economic governance through fragmented sovereignty and international relations is more suited to *market making* by way of negative integration and efficiency enhancing regu-lation than to institution building and redistributive intervention, or market distortion'.[291] Thus Streeck argues that the Treaty of Rome charged the Community with:

developing *a new kind of social policy*, one concerned with *market making rather than market correcting*, aimed at creating an integrated European labour market and enabl-ing it to function efficiently, rather than with correcting its outcomes in line with political standards of social justice.[292]

In other words, the existing body of EC employment-related social policy represents regulation in support of a free or common market to ensure, in the words of Article 96, that the conditions of competition are not distorted. This has been the most influential of the justifications for social policy. The market-making thesis comprises two limbs: first, the creation of a 'European-wide labour market',[293] by removing obstacles to the mobility of workers,[294] and secondly, removing distortions to competition by, on the one hand, seeking to harmonise costs on firms and, on the other, preventing social dumping by firms and a race to the bottom by States.

The clearest example of the market-making thesis can be found with the inclusion of Article 141 on equal pay in the Treaty. As we have seen, much of the debate between the French and German governments prior to the signing of the Treaty of Rome[295] revolved around economic interests (concerns about

---

[289] Streeck, 'From Market Making to State Building? Reflections on the Political Economy of European Social Policy', in Leibfried and Pierson (eds), above, n. 19, 399.
[290] Marshall, *Social Policy* (Hutchinson, London, 1975) 15.
[291] Streeck, above, n. 289, 34.   [292] Streeck, above, n. 289.
[293] Streeck, above, n. 289, 397.   [294] Considered further in Ch. 4.
[295] See above, n. 13.

loss of competitiveness on the part of France) rather than the social interests of the workers in the EC (although the drafting of Article 141 was inspired by ILO Convention No. 100).[296] The French were particularly concerned about discriminatory pay rates resulting from collective agreements in Italy. At that time France had one of the smallest differentials between the salaries of male and female employees (7 per cent compared with 20–40 per cent in the Netherlands and in Italy).[297] This risked placing those parts of French industry employing a very large female workforce, such as textiles and electrical construction, in a weaker competitive position than identical or similar industries in other Member States employing a largely female workforce at much lower salaries.[298]

Consequently, Article 119 (new Article 141) was included in the Treaty to impose parity of costs on the Member States and to prevent such destructive competition.[299] This point was noted, albeit somewhat obliquely, by the French Advocate General Dutheillet de Lamothe in *Defrenne (No. 1)*,[300] the first case to consider the application of Article 141. Advancing the market-making thesis, he said that although Article 141 had a social objective it also had an economic objective,

for in creating an obstacle to any attempt at 'social dumping' by means of the use of female labour less well paid than male labour, it helped to achieve one of the fundamental objectives of the common market, the establishment of a system ensuring that 'competition is not distorted'.

He continued that 'This explains why Article [141] of the Treaty is of a different character from the articles which precede it in the chapter of the Treaty devoted to social provisions'.

---

[296] Hoskyns, *Integrating Gender: Women, Law and Politics in the European Union* (Verso, London, 1996) Ch. 3.
[297] Budiner, *Le Droit de la femme a l'Egalité de salaire et la Convention No. 100 de l'organisation internationale du travail* (Librairie Générale de Droit et de Jurisprudence, Paris, 1975), citing Sullerot, *L'emploi des femmes et ses problèmes dans les Etats Membres de la Communauté Européene* (CEC, 1972) 177. See generally Barnard, above, n. 11.
[298] Budiner, above, n. 297, citing Jean-Jacques Ribas, 'L'Egalité des salaires feminins et masculins dans la Communauté Economique européene' (novembre 1966), Droit Social, para. 1, and Clair, 'L'article 119 du Traité de Rome. Le Principe de l'Egalisation des salaires masculins et feminins dans la CEE' (mars 1968), *Droit Social*, 150. In addition, France had ratified ILO Convention No. 100 by Law No. 52–1309 of 10 December 1952 (Journal Officiel, 11 décembre 1952). By 1957 the Convention had also been ratified by Belgium, France, Germany and Italy, but not by Luxembourg and the Netherlands. (Luxembourg ratified the Convention in 1967 and the Netherlands in 1971.)
[299] See further Ch. 6.
[300] Case 80/70 [1971] ECR 445. In Case 69/80 *Worringham and Humphreys* v. *Lloyds Bank* [1981] ECR 767 Advocate General Warner again referred back to Advocate General Dutheillet de Lamothe's statement in *Defrenne (No. 1)* that the first purpose of Art. 119 was to 'avoid a situation in which undertakings established in Member States with advanced legislation on the equal treatment of men and women suffer a competitive disadvantage as compared with undertakings established in Member States that have not eliminated discrimination against female workers as regards pay'.

It would therefore seem that the social provisions of the Treaty 'respond above all to the fear that unless employment costs are harmonised, economic integration will lead to competition to the detriment of countries whose social legislation is more advanced'.[301] However, the Court, pursuing in Streeck's words its own 'distinctive integrationist agenda',[302] has recognized the market-correcting, as well as market-making, dimension of the 'social' provisions. In its landmark judgment in *Defrenne (No. 2)*[303] the Court said:

Article [141] pursues a double aim. *First*, . . . the aim of Article [141] is to avoid a situation in which undertakings established in states which have actually implemented the principle of equal pay suffer a competitive disadvantage in intra-Community competition as compared with undertakings established in states which have not yet eliminated discrimination against women workers as regards pay.

Having recognized the economic purpose of Article 141, the Court then continued:

Second, this provision forms part of the social objectives of the Community, which is not merely an economic union, but is at the same time intended, by common action to ensure social progress and seek the constant improvement of living and working conditions of their peoples . . . This double aim, which is at once economic and social, shows that the principle of equal pay forms part of the foundations of the Community.

The Court again recognized the dual purpose of the Community's social provisions in *Commission* v. *UK*.[304] It said that in the Directives on Collective Redundancies and Acquired Rights[305] 'the Community legislature intended both to ensure comparable protection for workers' rights in the different Member States and to harmonise the costs which such protective rules entail for Community undertakings'.[306] Further, the legislation of the 1970s cannot be explained solely in terms of harmonization of costs. Measures such as those on sex equality, transfers of undertakings, collective redundancies, and insolvency suggested a project of market correcting as well as market making for Community social policy.[307]

It therefore seems that the Community has seen social policy in terms of a dichotomy combining a market-led conception of employment regulation, with some recognition of the market-correcting or social function of such

---

[301] Author's translation of Valticos, *Droit international du travail*, para. 180, cited in Budiner, above, n. 297, 3.

[302] Streeck, above, n. 289, 39.

[303] Case 43/75 [1976] ECR 455. This was emphasized in Case C–50/96 *Deutsche Telekom* v. *Schröder* [2000] ECR I–743, paras. 53–5.

[304] Case C–382/92 *Commission* v. *UK* [1994] ECR I–2435 and Case C–383/92 [1994] ECR I–2479.

[305] Originally Directives 75/129/EEC (OJ [1975] L48/29) and 77/187/EEC (OJ [1977] L61/27), respectively considered in detail in Chs. 13 and 14.

[306] Para. 15.   [307] Streeck, above, n. 289, 399.

regulation. This prompts Freedland to suggest that the evolution of EC employment law has always depended on the possibility of legitimating it in economic policy terms as well as social policy terms. He argues that this is a possibility which is made all the more attainable by the fact that the proponents of economic policy have felt the need to lay claim to a social legitimation.[308]

2.2. The Market-Making Thesis Examined

The effect of the EC rules on free movement of goods, persons, services and capital is to place the different national systems into competition because those individuals or companies not satisfied with the political/legal/social environment in which they find themselves are free to move to another Member State which has a regime which suits them better.[309] This freedom for individuals/capital to move has the effect of forcing the national systems to compete to produce the best rules to attract (or retain) valuable assets (capital and labour). This is known as competitive federalism or regulatory competition.[310]

For competitive federalism to function, two conditions need to be satisfied. First, the *federal* (central) authorities must lay down and enforce the rules giving goods, persons and capital freedom to exit one Member State and enter another. Second, the *states* (the decentralized authorities) must remain free to regulate the production of goods and the qualifications of people according to their own standards, enabling regulators to respond to the competition. The outcome of this process of regulatory competition should be to produce optimal, efficient and innovative legislation (a race to the top) because state officials vie with one another to create increasingly attractive economic circumstances for their citizens, knowing that their re-election depends upon their success.[311]

Yet, in order to ensure successful regulatory competition, certain conditions must be satisfied.[312] For example, there must be full mobility of people and resources at little or no cost; migrants must have full knowledge of each jurisdiction's revenue and expenditure patterns; and there must be a wide choice of destination jurisdictions to enable the citizens to be able to make

---

[308] Freedland, above, n. 80, 287.

[309] Some of this section is taken from Barnard, *The Substantive Law of the European Union: The Four Freedoms* (OUP, Oxford, 2004).

[310] This is based on Tiebout's famous 'pure theory' of fiscal federalism: Tiebout, 'A pure theory of local expenditure' (1956) 64/5 *Journal of Political Economy* 416. For further details see Barnard and Deakin, 'Market Access and Regulatory Competition', in Barnard and Scott (eds), *The Law of the Single European Market: Unpacking the Premises* (Hart Publishing, Oxford, 2002).

[311] Tarullo, 'Federalism Issues in the United States', in Castro, Méhaut and Rubery, *International Integration and Labour Market Organisation* (Academic Press, London, 1992) 101.

[312] For the literature on the economics of federalism, see Tiebout, above, n. 310; Easterbrook, 'Antitrust and the Economics of Federalism' (1983) 26 *Journal of Law and Economics* 23, 34.

meaningful decisions about migration. In reality these conditions are never met. For individuals the likelihood of exit is slim because they are unlikely to leave their own jurisdiction for linguistic, cultural, financial, or personal reasons; and capital (direct investment in business operations) is unlikely to leave unless a variety of factors (market proximity, transport costs, infrastructure levels, labour costs and productivity levels) justify the move. Even if these conditions could be met, state legislation is often insufficiently responsive to the needs of its consumers.[313] This creates the risk that the type of regulatory competition which emerges is undesirable: it does not lead to a race to the top but a race to the bottom.[314]

The following example demonstrates this. The UK knows that in practice workers are less mobile than capital and so it decides to gain a competitive advantage by reducing employment protection. While such a strategy might have short-term benefits (e.g. job creation or at least job retention) it undermines longer-term interests of the citizenry as a whole (e.g. lower quality jobs and inferior working environment). Nevertheless, faced with such deregulation by the UK, Poland—which risks losing capital and thus jobs to the UK—relaxes its own standards. The UK responds by lowering its standards still further and a race to the bottom ensues where the UK and Poland are competing on the basis of low standards.

While there is much controversy about the likelihood of EU states actually engaging in a full blown race to the bottom,[315] there is a perception that so long as states remain free to regulate or, more likely deregulate, their social standards it may happen. These concerns were brought into sharp focus by the highly publicized Hoover affair. Hoover decided to close its factory in

---

[313] Sun and Pelkmans, 'Regulatory Competition in the Single Market' (1995) 33 *JCMS* 67, 84.

[314] This is sometimes referred to as the Delaware effect: Cary, 'Federalism and Corporate Law: Reflections Upon Delaware' (1974) 83 *Yale Law Journal* 663.

[315] Barnard, 'Social Dumping Revisited: Lessons from Delaware' (2000) 25 *ELRev.* 57. However, despite the rhetoric there is in fact little evidence of the states being engaged in an active policy of deregulation of labour standards for the purpose of gaining a competitive edge, a point noted by the OECD which said 'there is no compelling evidence that "social dumping" has occurred so far in OECD countries' (OECD, 'Labour Standards and Economic Integration', in *Employment Outlook 1994* (OECD, 1994) 138). Schonfield has added 'The dangers of "social dumping" have been exaggerated with only isolated examples of competitive undercutting of pay and conditions by firms exploiting labour cost differences between countries' (reported by Taylor, 'Wage Bargaining diversification under EU Single Market', *Financial Times*, 7 April 1997). On the other hand, he noted that there was evidence from Germany that companies are increasingly using the possibility of relocation as a bargaining counter to achieve changes in working practices at home. (See e.g. the concessions made by German workers at Bosch and Daimler Benz because of threats of locating to new plants abroad (see 'Can Europe compete?', *Financial Times*, 28 February 1994).) See also the campaign by the British trade unions Amicus and TGWU to encourage British consumers to boycott Peugeot cars when faced with the news that Peugeot was to close its plant in Coventry in the UK and would be making its new car in Slovakia: Mackintosh and Taylor, 'Unions launch battle for Ryton with campaign to boycott Peugeot', *Financial Times*, 8 June 2006, 3.

Longvic, near Dijon, with the loss of 600 out of 700 jobs, and to transfer its activities to the Cambuslang plant, near Glasgow in Scotland, resulting in the recruitment of 400 workers on 24-month fixed-term contracts.[316] This followed the conclusion of a collective agreement between management and the British Amalgamated Engineering and Electrical Union (AEEU) providing for improved flexibility of labour, new working patterns, a no-strike deal, and a pay freeze. At the same time Rockwell Graphic systems announced that 110 jobs were to be lost out of 272 at its Nantes plant with production being relocated to Preston in England. The French blamed the deregulatory agenda adopted by the British Conservative government between 1979 and 1997. Martine Aubry, the French Minister for labour, and the French Prime Minster both said that Hoover's decision constituted 'social dumping'.[317]

Social dumping is the term used to describe a variety of practices by both Member States and employers. In essence it concerns behaviour designed to give a competitive advantage to companies due to low labour standards[318] rather than productivity. Companies that move in response to a deliberate lowering of standards by the state are said to be engaged in social dumping. This in turn might precipitate a race to the bottom, with Member States competing to deregulate to attract capital or at least to retain existing capital.[319] Social dumping inevitably leads to calls for transnational social legislation to prevent this race to the bottom. In its White Paper on Social Policy[320] the Commission relied on this rhetoric to justify the enactment of Community social legislation:

the establishment of a framework of basic minimum standards, which the Commission started some years ago, provides a bulwark against using low social standards as an instrument of unfair economic competition and protection against reducing social standards to gain competitiveness, and is also an expression of the political will to maintain the momentum of social progress.[321]

---

[316] See *EIRR* 230, 16.

[317] *EIRR* 230, 16. John Major, the then British Prime Minister, is reported as saying in response 'France can complain all it likes. If investors and business choose to come to Britain rather than pay the costs of socialism in France, let them call it "social dumping". I call it dumping socialism' (*Financial Times*, 6 March 1993). Such concerns also underpinned much of the criticism levelled at the Commission's first draft of the services Dir. (COM(2004) 2). Trade unions feared that it would allow a firm to establish itself in State A (with lower labour standards) and then provide services in State B (with higher standards but with which the firm's workforce would not have to comply). In order to combat this perception, the Presidency Conclusions of the Brussels European Council of 22–23 March 2005, para. 2 expressly said that 'The internal market of services has to be fully operational while preserving the European social model'. This Directive is considered further in Ch. 5.

[318] See also Hepple, 'New Approaches to International Labour Regulation' (1997) 26 *ILJ*. 353, 355 and, more generally, *Labour Laws and Global Trade* (Hart Publishing, Oxford, 2005).

[319] See also the Commission's Green Paper on European Social Policy (COM(93)551, 7) which describes social dumping as 'the gaining of unfair competitive advantage within the Community through unacceptably low social standards'.

[320] COM(94) 333, 27 July 1994.

[321] Ibid., Introduction, para. 19. See also COM(94) 333, Ch. III, para. 1 and the Commission's Green Paper on European Social Policy (COM(93) 551, 46) where it said that '. . . a commitment

However, some argue that such legislation would be inefficient[322] and would have the effect of killing the poorer states with kindness,[323] depriving them of their comparative advantage—their cheaper workforce—and their vehicle for improvement.[324] In other words by requiring the southern and eastern European states to apply the full gamut of EC social legislation serves to reinforce the already advantageous position enjoyed by the Northern European states.

3. The New Approach: Active Labour Market Policies

Others argue that the debate about social dumping in the EU misses the point: the challenge to northern European employers/producers comes not from within the EU but from outside, especially from South East Asia and China. This has forced the EU to think hard about what sort of European social model it wishes to have: one based on low wages and low skills or one based on higher wages and skills. As we have already seen, the Community institutions have opted for the high skills model. Thus, the focus of the European Union's attention dating from around the time of the Amsterdam Treaty is on flexibility for firms combined with security for workers—so-called 'flexicurity'. This theme can be found in a number of Commission documents,[325] together with the Employment Guidelines. Attempts to reconcile the two lie in an 'improved organisation of work' which, although unable 'of itself to solve the unemployment problem', may nevertheless 'make a valuable contribution, first, to the competitiveness of European firms, and secondly, to the improvement of the quality of working life and the employability of the workforce'.[326] More specifically, 'the flexible firm could offer a sound basis for fundamental organisational renewal built on high skill, high productivity, high quality, good environmental management—and good wages'.[327] In other words, the

---

to high social standards and to the promotion of social progress forms an integral part of the [TEU]. A "negative" competitiveness between Member States would lead to social dumping, to the undermining of the consensus making process . . . and to danger for the acceptability of the Union.'

[322] See e.g. Fischel, 'The "Race to the Bottom" revisited—Reflections on Recent Developments in Delaware's Corporation Law' (1982) 31 *Northwestern University Law Review* 913.

[323] *The Economist*, 23 June 1990, 17.

[324] Kiernan and Beim, 'On the Economic Realities of the European Social Charter and the Social Dimension of EC 1992' (1992) 2 *Duke Journal of Comparative and International Labour Law* 149.

[325] See, e.g. Commission's Green Paper, *Partnership for a New Organisation of Work* COM(97) 127 final; *Modernising and Improving Social Protection in the European Union* COM(97) 102 final. See also Commission Communication, 'A Concerted Action for Modernising Social Protection' COM(99) 347 and 'Council Conclusions on the strengthening of cooperation for modernising and improving social protection' (OJ [2000] C8/7) and *Modernising the Organisation of Work*, COM(98) 592.

[326] Ibid., para. 4.   [327] Ibid., para. 24.

EU is breaking away from the rather sterile market-making/market-correcting dichotomy to see social rights no longer as merely a beneficial consequence of growth but as an integral part of realizing that growth.[328] This view is supported by Sen's capability approach[329] which has been translated by lawyers to mean that:

Social rights are the foundation of a market order which is based on extensive mobilisation of resources and the widest division of labour which are compatible with a given society's initial endowments in terms of human and physical resources.[330]

Deakin and Browne illustrate the value of the capability approach by using the example of laws prohibiting the dismissal of a pregnant woman.[331] While a conventional economic analysis would view the introduction of such a law as imposing costs on employer who might be discouraged from employing women of child-bearing age who would then eventually become deskilled, a capability approach would view the situation rather differently. In addition to remedying the injustice which would otherwise affect individuals who are dismissed for being pregnant, such a law has the potential to alter incentive structures to encourage women employees to seek out, and employers to provide training for, jobs involving relation-specific skills. Deakin and Browne conclude that pregnancy protection laws can be seen as a form of institutional support for individual capabilities: they provide the conditions under which the freedom for women workers to enter the labour market becomes more than merely formal; it becomes a substantive freedom. Thus, relying on Sen's capability arguments, they argue that social rights have a value not just in themselves, a fact which the Court has recognized in cases such as *Deutsche Post* and *Albany*, but in terms of their pro-competitive effect, in the sense of encouraging enterprises to invest in human capital and avoiding the destructive social effects of low wage competition.[332]

Although social rights, particularly when viewed in terms of their capacity to enhance capability, have a value in the new approach to EC social policy, the core of the approach lies with the idea of encouraging active economic participation in the labour market[333] by ensuring that employees possess the new skills that are required in a knowledge-based society. Thus, much

[328] See the Commission Communication, 'Modernising and Improving Social Protection in the EU' COM(97) 102 and the follow-up 'A Concerted Strategy for Modernising Social Protection' COM(99) 347. This theme is considered further in Ch. 3.

[329] See, e.g., *Commodities and Capabilities* (North-Holland, Deventer, 1985) and *Development as Freedom* (OUP, Oxford, 1999).

[330] Deakin and Browne, 'Social Rights and Market Order: Adapting the Capability Approach' in Kenner and Hervey (eds), above, n. 161, 42. More generally, see Deakin and Wilkinson, *The Law of the Labour Market: Industrialization, Employment, and Legal Evolution* (OUP, Oxford, 2005) and Deakin, 'The "Capability" Concept and the Evolution of European Social Policy', in Dougan and Spaventa, *Social Welfare and EU Law* (Hart Publishing, Oxford, 2005).

[331] Ibid., 35–6.   [332] Ibid., 42.

[333] 'The New Paradigm for Social Policy: A Virtuous Circle?' (2001) 38 *CMLRev*. 1125, 1125.

emphasis is placed on training workers and providing them with incentives to enable them to acquire sufficient skills both to enter the workforce and then to adapt themselves to the changing demands of the workplace in years to come. In this way employers will gain the flexibility necessary to enable them to compete; individuals will attain higher standards of living; and national welfare systems will be able to afford to continue providing high levels of protection to those in need which are funded by contributions made by those in employment. Given the importance of this 'third way' to the success of the EU economy, it is considered in more detail in chapter 3.

4. The Legislative Impact

The choice of thesis that shapes EC social policy has implications for regulation. If a pure *market-correcting* vision of social policy were accepted, this would point to the need for a comprehensive social policy at EU level, replacing national diversity with uniformity, and imposing EU homogeneity on long standing national policy regimes and institutional arrangements. By contrast, if a pure *market-making* conception of EC social policy prevailed, this would suggest that the EU should enact social policy only where there is a risk that conditions of competition are distorted or where there is a transnational interest at stake (e.g. the regulation of transnational companies where national regulation would prove ineffective unless co-ordinated). This model would envisage significantly less EU level legislation in terms of volume but nevertheless when such legislation is enacted it would need to be set at the highest level to ensure that standards in the highest regulated state were not undercut.

Neither outcome is palatable to the Member States with their diverse industrial relations traditions and strong desire to preserve their national social systems. Nor would such uniformity be desirable or optimal: uniformity would replace diversity and the freedom to experiment would be removed. As we shall see in chapter 2, the legislative approach actually adopted conforms to neither stereotype: most EU legislation sets minimum standards (to avoid the worst excesses of race to the bottom, imagined or real), giving Member States the freedom to improve upon those standards in their own system, thereby preserving some regulatory diversity. The question of whether the Community should act in a particular field and why (the subsidiarity question) has received only cursory attention by the courts, thereby avoiding difficult judgments about the nature of EC social policy. Furthermore, a capabilities approach would endorse the adoption of such legislation recognizing its value as an input into the Union's competitiveness.

If, however, the goal of European social policy is, in fact, about active labour market polices then a traditional legislative approach cannot provide the answer. As Kilpatrick points out, states have always had employment polices aimed at activities such as vocational training and income replacement in periods of employment or underemployment.[334] Such policies have never typically been associated with a hard law 'command and control model' but have relied instead on spending money and the creation of guidelines and indicators in attempts to steer national policies.[335] It should therefore come as no surprise that employment policies at EU level rely on the same kind of tools as used at national level. Traditional legislation is not a suitable tool to achieve the objectives of full employment. Moreover, the EU has limited direct control over national employment policies. It has therefore developed a different regulatory technique, the so-called Open Method of Co-ordination (OMC), which commits Member States to work together towards common goals (such as full employment) without seeking to harmonize their diverse policy regimes and institutional arrangements. Some commentators see this as the 'third way' for EC social policy between 'regulatory competition and harmonization, an alternative to both intergovernmentalism and supranationalism, which may open up a sustainable path between a fragmented Europe and a European super state'.[336] Whether OMC is capable on delivering on such promise will be considered in chapter 3.

E. CONCLUSIONS

It would seem that the development of the Community's 'social' policy has in the past been constrained—perhaps fatally[337]—by the need to operate within both an economic and social framework. This has led, on the one hand, to some inconsistent decisions by the Court concerning the interface between

---

[334] 'New EU Employment Governance and Constitutionalism' in De Búrca and Scott (eds), *Law and New Governance in the EU and US* (Hart Publishing, Oxford, 2006).

[335] Ibid.

[336] Zeitlin, 'Introduction: The Open Method of Coordination in Question' in Zeitlin and Pochet with Magnusson (eds), *The Open Method of Coordination in Action: The European Employment and Social Inclusion Strategies* (PIE Peter Lang, 2005).

[337] See, e.g., the problems generated by the Commission in the case of atypical workers noted by Deakin and Wilkinson ('Rights vs Efficiency? The Economic Case for Transnational Labour Standards' (1994) 23 *ILJ*. 289, 302–3). In the Explanatory Memorandum accompanying its proposals for a draft Directive on atypical work the Commission said that 'relative cost differences resulting from different kinds of rules on different types of employment relationships, . . . may provide comparative advantages which constitute veritable distortions of competition' (COM(90) 228). However, the Commission's arguments were weakened by its attempts to suggest that while harmonization of indirect wage costs resulting from social security taxation and employment regulation should take place, harmonization of direct costs (rules governing wages and salaries) was unnecessary because 'differences in productivity levels attenuate these differences in unit labour costs to a considerable degree'. Such a distinction has little merit from either an economic or a legal standpoint and it had the effect of rejecting the very argument put forward in 1957 for the adoption of Art. 141.

Community law on market integration and national law and, on the other, to a patchwork of Community social legislation aimed at both harmonization and minimum standards. Of course, national social policy faces similar dilemmas but the dichotomy is brought into sharper focus in the Community context due to its original economic objectives and to the lack of the under-pinnings of a welfare state. On the other hand, the absence of any 'social' policy in the EU would have caused a serious legitimacy crisis. The piecemeal European social model which has been created, however awkwardly through a mix of legislation (both hard and soft) and judicial decisions, provides the bridge between the economic aspect of the Treaty (job creation) and the social dimension of the Treaty (politics of social inclusion, solidarity and citizen-ship) and a step towards the creation of a European 'civil society'.[338] This has gone some way to rebutting allegations of the EU's 'social deficit'.

The Amsterdam Treaty and Lisbon strategy have brought about a seismic shift in EC social policy as it moves from being focused solely on a rights based agenda, where the EU legislates for employment rights, towards employment policies with a new method of governance based on guidelines, benchmarking, targets, National Reform Programmes, and recommenda-tions. While much has been written about the newness of the governance techniques adopted in this area, it is important to view these developments in context. OMC does not mean throwing the legislative baby out with the bath-water; rather OMC and legislation serve different functions. While OMC tools are particularly suited to the area of employment or labour market *policy* (i.e. job creation and combating unemployment), legislation (hard law) is more suited for the creation of employment *rights* intended to protect workers. What is new is that employment policy has now become an EU objective and not just a national one, that social justice at EU level is no longer conceived of simply in terms of creating ad hoc rights for those who are already economic-ally active (workers) but extends to removing obstacles to labour market par-ticipation for socially excluded groups;[339] and that there is greater and more deliberate synergy between the classic Community method and new govern-ance tools, notably OMC. Chapter 2 examines the traditional legislative route for the creation of employment rights while chapter 3 examines the creation of employment policy through the EES and the Lisbon Strategy. As we shall see, stereotypes about the governance tools used to achieve the different results soon break down with hard law in the employment rights field being characterized by diversity and soft law in the employment policy field being buttressed by some hard(ish) rules, leading to the emergence of an increasingly sophisticated, hybrid regime. The question remains: does it work?

---

[338] See Opinion of the Economic and Social Committee, 'The Role and Contribution of Civil Society Organisations in the Building of Europe' (OJ [1999] L329/30), 32.
[339] Ibid.

2

(Hard) Law-making in the Field of Social Policy

A. INTRODUCTION

While the EC Treaty laid down substantive rights in the field of equal pay, the main body of EC employment law has taken the form of secondary legislation, primarily Directives. Most of this hard law has been adopted via the classic Community method[1] where the Commission proposes legislative measures and the Council and European Parliament adopt them.[2] Such traditional top-down, command and control regulation results, according to the stereotype, in mandates that are 'relatively specific and uniform, hierarchically determined, static and substantive'.[3] When compared with the Open Method of Co-ordination (considered in chapter 3) which uses 'soft law' techniques including (non-binding) objectives and guidelines, the legislation to be discussed in this chapter certainly does have a 'hard' edge, creating obligations on states and, once implemented, on employers which are enforceable in national courts. However, the very different legal, social and industrial relations cultures in the Member States have forced the European Union to be experimental and flexible in the social field, even when adopting 'hard' law. This chapter begins by examining the traditional route to legislation and considers the way in which the EU has attempted to reconcile the goal of setting common Community standards with the need to accommodate diversity at national level. It then considers the innovative method of law-making introduced by the Treaty on European Union—of legislating by collective agreement, primarily by the cross-industry (interprofessional or intersectoral) Social Partners but also by the sectoral Social Partners.

---

[1] Scott and Trubek, 'Mind the Gap: Law and New Approaches to Governance in the European Union' (2002) 8 *ELJ*. 1.

[2] Governance White Paper COM(2001) 428, 8.

[3] Mosher, 'Open Method of Coordination: Functional and Political Origins' (2000) 13 *ECSA Review* 6, 6.

B. ADOPTING COMMUNITY SOCIAL LEGISLATION

1. Introduction

In order for the Community to legislate in a particular field it must have the competence to act. The Community must also consider whether it is the most appropriate body to act (the subsidiarity question) and, if it is, whether the action it takes is proportionate. In the social field, a further question needs to be considered: what form should that action take: hard law or soft; and are there other ways of reconciling flexibility with uniformity? We shall consider these issues in turn.

2. Competence

2.1. The Nature of Competence

The European Community enjoys no general competence to enact legislation: it has only specific competences or enumerated powers given to it by the Member States in the Treaties. As Article 5(1) makes clear, 'The Community shall act within the limits of the powers conferred on it by this Treaty and of the objectives assigned to it therein'.[4] These powers may be specific, as in the case of Article 137 concerning measures in the field of, *inter alia*, health and safety and working conditions, or more general, as in the case of Articles 94, 95 and 308 concerning measures for the attainment of the common market and internal market.[5] Where the Community has *per se* exclusive competence, Member States cannot act in the field, irrespective of whether the Community itself has acted.[6] The corollary of this is where the Member States have not conferred power to act on the Community, the Member States retain legal competence.

---

[4] See Dashwood, 'The Limits of European Community Powers' (1996) 21 *ELRev.* 113 and Barnard, *The Substantive Law of the EU: The Four Freedoms* (OUP, Oxford, 2004) Ch. 18.

[5] Art. 94 (measures which directly affect the establishment or functioning of the Common Market) was used to adopt the three Directives in the late 1970s on restructuring of enterprises (Dir. 75/129 (OJ [1975] L48/29) on collective redundancies (now Dir. 98/59 (OJ [1998] L225/16), Dir. 77/187 on transfers of undertakings (OJ [1977] L61/126 now replaced by 2001/23 (OJ [2001] L82/16) and Dir. 80/987 (OJ [1980] L283/23). Dir. 75/117 on equal pay (OJ [1975] L45/19) was also adopted on the basis of Art. 94. Dir. 76/207 on equal treatment in respect of access to employment (OJ [1976] L39/40) and Dir. 79/7 on equal treatment in matters of social security (OJ [1979] L6/24) were adopted on the basis of Art. 308 (action by the Community to attain one of the objectives of the Community where the Treaty has not provided the necessary powers). Dirs. 86/378 (OJ [1986] L225/40) and 86/613 (OJ [1986] L359/56) on equality in occupational social security and of the self-employed respectively were both based on Arts. 94 and 308. Both legal bases require unanimous voting in Council.

[6] See e.g. in the context of Art. 133 *Opinion 1/75* [1975] ECR 1355 and Case 41/76 *Donckerwolke* v. *Procureur de la République* [1976] ECR 1921. See also AG Ruiz-Jarabo Colomer Opinion in Case C–110/03 *Belgium* v. *Commission* [2005] ECR I–000, para. 67.

Between these two extremes lie areas where the Community and the Member States are concurrently competent. This means that until the Community acts in these fields the Member States may act, provided they do so within the limits set by the Treaty relating to, for example, free movement of goods and persons under Articles 28, 39, 43, and 49, non-discrimination on the grounds of nationality under Article 12, and the obligation of co-operation with the Community under Article 10. Thus, in the social field, in the absence of Community action, Member States remain free to legislate provided that their social legislation does not, for example, discriminate against other EU nationals. In other words, concurrence still implies the supremacy of Community norms. However, if, by reason of the scale and effects of the measure,[7] the Community decides it should act, it can convert a field of concurrent competence into a field of exclusive competence for the Community.[8] This effect is described in American constitutional law as the doctrine of 'preemption'.[9]

While the attribution of competence to the Community has great significance, both internally and externally,[10] the original EEC Treaty did not identify those areas which fall within the exclusive competence of either the Community or the Member States, or those areas which fall within the concurrent competence of the Member States and the Community.[11] We know, because the EC Treaty now tells us, that in the field of social policy the Community has no competence, at least under Article 137,[12] in respect of pay, the right to strike or the right to impose lock-outs (Article 137(5)). Otherwise, it has been left to the Court to determine the scope and nature of competence and, in those areas where there has been no judicial decision, educated guess work. Therefore, there is probably concurrent competence in

---

[7] The principle of subsidiarity contained in Art. 5(2) is considered below.

[8] If the Community acts again in this field the principle of subsidiarity now does not apply.

[9] See, e.g. Weatherill, 'Beyond Preemption? Shared Competence and Constitutional Change in the European Community', in O'Keeffe and Twomey (eds), *Legal Issues of the Maastricht Treaty*, (Chancery, Chichester, 1994); Cross, 'Preemption of Member State Law in the European Economic Community: a Framework for Analysis' (1992) 29 *CMLRev.* 447; Soares, 'Preemption, Conflicts of Powers and Subsidiarity' (1998) 23 *ELRev.* 109. It is at least arguable that the Community can never have exclusive competence in the field of employment law under Art. 137(1) since the Community is allowed only to 'support and complement' Member State activities. See also House of Lords Select Committee on the European Union, 'The Future of Europe: "Social Europe" ', Session 2002–03, 14th Report, 9.

[10] Where the Community has internal competence it also has authority to enter into international commitments necessary to attain this objective, even in the absence of express provision to that effect: Joined Cases 3, 4 and 6/76 *Kramer and Others* [1976] ECR 1279 and *Opinion 2/91* [1993] ECR I–1061, considered below at n. 15.

[11] Cf. the Constitutional Treaty Arts. I–11 to I–17.

[12] See Brinkman, 'Lawmaking under the Social Chapter of Maastricht', in Craig and Harlow (eds), *Lawmaking in the EU* (Kluwer, Deventer, 1998) 244, who suggests that this does not preclude other legal bases from being used, a view confirmed by Final Report of Working Group XI on Social Europe CONV 516/1/03, para. 28 and Case C–14/04 *Abdelkader Dellas and Others* v. *Premier ministre and Others* [2006] ECR I–000, para. 39.

respect of both Article 95(2) concerning 'the rights and interests of employed persons' introduced into the Treaty by the Single European Act (SEA) and the areas listed in Article 137. The predecessor provision to Article 137, Article 118a, was also included in the Treaty of Rome by the SEA. Prior to the Social Policy Agreement being incorporated into the EC Treaty, Article 118a was the only express legal basis included in the social Title of the Treaty of Rome. Given that a number of important pieces of Community legislation were adopted under Article 118a (as it then was) it deserves some attention in its own right before we consider Article 137 in detail.

2.2. Article 118a

(a) The Scope of the Competence

Article 118a(1) provided that 'Member States shall pay particular attention to encouraging improvements, especially in the working environment, as regards health and safety of workers'. Article 118a(2) then added that the Council, acting by a qualified majority vote,[13] was to adopt directives laying down '*minimum requirements* for gradual implementation' (emphasis added) to help achieve the objective laid down in Article 118a(1). According to Article 118a(3), Member States were free to maintain or introduce 'more stringent measures for the protection of working conditions'.[14]

The nature of the Community's competence in respect of social policy was considered by the Court in Opinion 2/91[15] concerning ILO Convention No. 170 on safety in the use of chemicals at work. During the negotiations leading up to the agreement of this Convention, the Commission argued that the subject-matter of the Convention fell within the exclusive competence of the Community. This was disputed by some Member States and the matter was considered by the Court under Article 300(6).[16] The Court began by noting that the area covered by the Convention fell within the Title on Social Policy. Referring to Article 118a, it said that the Community 'enjoys an internal legislative competence in the area of social policy'.[17] It continued that since the subject-matter of Convention No. 170 coincided with that of several Directives adopted under Article 118a,[18] the Convention fell within the Community's area of competence. The Court then distinguished between two situations. On the one hand, it said that in the areas where the Community has laid down only minimum requirements and those standards were

---

[13] At Maastricht this was amended to the co-operation procedure contained in Art. 252.

[14] See further Case C–14/04 *Abdelkader Dellas and Others* v. *Premier ministre and Others* [2006] ECR I–000, para. 51, considered further in Ch. 12.

[15] [1993] ECR I–1061. See Emiliou, 'Towards a Clearer Demarcation Line? The Division of External Relations Power between the Community and the Member States' (1994) 19 *ELRev*. 76.

[16] Under this provision, the EP, Council, Commission or a Member State can obtain the opinion of the ECJ as to whether an agreement envisaged is compatible with the provisions of the Treaty.

[17] Para. 40.   [18] See further Ch. 11.

inferior to those set by the ILO, the Member States had competence under Article 118a(3) to adopt more stringent measures.[19] On the other hand, the Court said that in those areas where the Community had harmonized rules, for example, relating to classification, packaging and labelling of dangerous substances and preparations,[20] the Community alone had competence.

The ILO Convention also contained provisions about implementation, making express reference to consultation with the Social Partners. The Court said that insofar as it had been established that the substantive provisions of the Convention came within the Community's sphere of competence, the Community was also competent to undertake commitments for putting those provisions into effect. It recognized that 'as Community law stands at present, social policy and in particular co-operation between the two sides of industry are matters which fall predominantly within the competence of the Member States'[21] but, pointing to Article 118b [new Article 139] which provided that the Commission shall endeavour to develop a dialogue between management and labour at European level,[22] it said these matters had not been 'withdrawn entirely from the competence of the Community'. It added that where the subject-matter of an agreement fell in part within the competence of the Community and in part within the competence of the Member States, there had to be a close association between the two, particularly because, unlike the Member States, the Community had only observer status at the ILO and so could not itself conclude an ILO Convention.[23]

(b) The Legislative Procedure

The legal basis of a measure not only confers the Community with the power to act but it also sets out the legislative procedure by which the measure must be adopted, be it simple consultation with the European Parliament and unanimous voting (as is the case with Article 95(2) concerning 'the rights and interests of employed persons', introduced by the Single European Act (SEA) which appears to refer back to the procedure in Article 94),[24] the co-operation procedure under Article 252 (abolished by the Amsterdam Treaty, with the exception of the Title on EMU[25]) or now, more usually, the

---

[19] Para. 18. The Court dismissed the argument made by the Commission that it could be difficult to determine whether one specific measure was more favourable to a worker than another. The Court said that such difficulties could not constitute a basis for exclusive competence.

[20] Dir. 67/548/EEC (OJ/SE [1967] 234), as amended and Dir. 88/379/EEC (OJ [1988] L187/14).

[21] Para. 30.

[22] Para. 31. Cf. Case C–67/96 *Albany International BV* v. *Stichting Bedrijfspensioenfonds Textielindustrie* [1999] ECR I–5751, considered further in Ch. 16.

[23] Paras. 36–7.

[24] This is due to the fact that Art. 95(2) derogates from Art. 95(1) and so by implication refers back to Art. 94. Art. 94 was due to be abolished by the Constitution.

[25] Dashwood, 'European Community Legislative Procedures after Amsterdam' (1999) 1 *CYELS*. 25, 33.

co-decision procedure under Article 251. When Article 118a was introduced by the SEA, the choice of legal basis became a political football: the Commission, in an attempt to circumvent the UK's veto, made extensive use of Article 118a (in preference to say, Article 100a(2) [new Article 95(2)] on the rights and interest of employed persons) since Article 118a provided for qualified majority, as opposed to unanimous, voting.

The Commission's strategy was eventually challenged in *UK v. Council (Working Time)*.[26] The Working Time Directive 93/104/EC[27] (now Directive 2003/88) was adopted under Article 118a, with the UK abstaining in the final vote. The UK then challenged the choice of legal basis under Article 230 arguing, *inter alia*, that since the organization of working time envisaged by the Directive was intended to achieve both job creation and social policy objectives, recourse should have been had to Article 100 EC (new Article 94) or to Article 235 (new Article 308), both requiring unanimity in Council. It also argued that on a proper interpretation, Article 118a (new Article 137) had to be read in conjunction with Article 100a(2) (new Article 95(2)) concerning the rights and interests of employed persons and required a unanimous vote.

The Court rejected these arguments. It said that since Article 118a appeared in the section dealing with social provisions it related only to measures concerning the health and safety of workers.[28] The Court reasoned that it therefore constituted a more specific rule than Articles 100 and 100a (new Articles 94 and 95 respectively), an interpretation confirmed by the fact that the provisions of these general legal bases were to apply 'save where otherwise provided in this Treaty'.[29]

The UK also argued that the link between health and safety (as narrowly understood under English law) and working time was too tenuous. However, the Advocate General pointed out that under Danish law the term 'working environment' (*arbejdsmiljø*) in Article 118a(1) was a very broad one, not limited to classic measures relating to safety and health at work in the strict sense, but included 'measures concerning working hours, psychological factors, the way work is performed, training in hygiene and safety, and the protection of young workers and worker representation with regard to security against dismissal or any other attempt to undermine their working conditions'.[30] The Court, without referring to the Danish origins of Article 118a, also favoured a broad approach to health and safety. It pointed

---

[26] Case C–84/94 *UK v. Council (Working Time)* [1996] ECR I–5755. See generally, *The ECJ's Working Time Judgment: The Social Market Vindicated*, CELS Occasional Paper No. 2, 1997; Waddington, 'Towards a Healthier and More Secure European Social Policy' (1997) 4 *Maastricht Journal of European and Comparative Law* 83.

[27] OJ [1993] L307/18. See Ch. 12 for further details of the Directive.   [28] Para. 12.

[29] Ibid. An approach favouring a specific basis in preference to a general legal basis is consistent with the Court's earlier jurisprudence, esp. the *Tariff Preference* case (Case 45/86 *Commission v. Council* [1987] ECR I–1493) concerning Arts. 133 and 308.

[30] Para. 42.

to the World Health Organization's definition of health as 'a state of complete psychic, mental and social well being that does not merely consist of an absence of disease or infirmity'.[31] As a result it was able to conclude that 'where *the principal aim* of the measure in question is the protection of the health and safety of workers, Article 118a must be used, albeit such a measure may have ancillary effects on the establishment and functioning of the internal market'.[32]

The Court then examined whether the Directive was correctly based on Article 118a. Noting that the Directive was a social policy measure and not a general measure relating to job creation and reducing unemployment, the Court said that health and safety was the essential objective of the Directive,[33] albeit that it might affect employment as well, and therefore the Directive was properly adopted on the basis of Article 118a. The Court did, however, annul Article 5(2) of the Directive which provided that the minimum weekly rest period 'shall in principle include Sunday'. The Court said that the 'Council has failed to explain why Sunday as a weekly rest day, is more closely connected with health and safety of workers than any other day of the week'.[34] As a result, the provision 'which is severable from the other provisions of the Directive', had to be annulled.[35]

The outcome of the decision is unsurprising and served to reinforce Article 118a as an autonomous legal basis for social policy measures, thereby preserving the rather fragile 'social' policy which was being constructed by the Community, with the Commission at the helm. In this respect, the judgment can be seen as political and this helps to explain why, on the one hand, the Court was content with relying on 'self-justifying proclamations' in the Preamble as the basis of making the link between working time and health and safety,[36] and, on the other, why the Court failed to give a thorough examination either to the scientific evidence produced or to consider the impact of the numerous exceptions and derogations to the Directive on the overall health and safety objective.[37]

2.3. Article 137

(a) The Competence

The SPA substantially amended Article 118a in respect of the then 11 Member States and extended the areas to which qualified majority voting (in the

---

[31]　Para. 15.

[32]　Para. 22. This approach confirms that adopted by the Court in e.g. the *Waste Directive* case (Case C–155/91 *Commission* v. *Council* [1993] ECR I–939) and Case C–271/94 *Parliament* v. *Council* [1996] ECR I–1705).

[33]　Para. 30.　　　　[34]　Para. 37.　　　　[35]　Ibid.

[36]　Kenner, 'A Distinctive Legal Base for Social Policy? The Court of Justice Answers a "Delicate Question" ' (1997) 22 *ELRev.* 579, 584.

[37]　Ellis (1997) 34 *CMLRev.* 1049, 1057. See further Ch. 12.

co-operation procedure) applied. It also introduced express new areas of competence to which unanimous voting applied. These changes were incorporated into the EC Treaty at Amsterdam, revised slightly and then amended at Nice. Thus, according to Article 137(1) and (2), the Community now has competence to adopt, by the Article 251 co-decision procedure (which includes *qualified majority voting*), after consulting the Economic and Social Committee and the Committee of the Regions, minimum standards Directives, supporting and complementing the activities of the Member States, concerning:

- improvements in particular of the working environment to protect workers' health and safety;
- working conditions;
- the information and consultation of workers;
- the integration of persons excluded from the labour market without prejudice to Article 150;
- equality between men and women with regard to labour market opportunities and treatment at work.

The Council also has the power to adopt minimum standards Directives by *unanimous* vote, again after consulting the European Parliament and the relevant Committees, in the fields of:

- social security and social protection of workers;
- protection of workers where their employment contract is terminated;
- representation and collective defence of the interests of workers and employers, including co-determination, subject to paragraph 5 (which provides that the 'provisions of this Article shall not apply to pay, the right of association, the right to strike and the right to impose lock-outs');
- conditions of employment for third country nationals legally residing in Community territory.[38]

In all cases, the Directives must avoid imposing administrative, financial and legal constraints which would hold back the creation and development of small and medium sized enterprises (Article 137(2)(b)).[39] The importance of this provision (or at least its predecessor in Article 118a(2), paragraph 2) was recognized by the Court in *Kirsammer-Hack*[40] where, in the context of

---

[38] According to Art. 137(2), the Council, acting unanimously on a proposal from the Commission, and after consulting the European Parliament, can decide to render the co-decision procedure applicable to the areas currently decided by unanimity with the exception of the fields of social security and social protection of workers.

[39] This does not, mean, however, according to the first declaration appended to the SPA, that when laying down minimum requirements for the protection of health and safety there is an intention to discriminate 'in a manner unjustified by the circumstances' against employees in small and medium enterprises.

[40] Case C–189/91 *Kirsammer-Hack v. Sidal* [1993] ECR I–6185.

national legislation exempting part-time workers from the protection against unfair dismissal, the Court ruled that such legislation formed part of a series of measures 'intended to alleviate the constraints burdening small businesses which play an essential role in economic development and the creation of employment within the Community'.[41] The Court also indicated that these undertakings could be 'the subject of special economic measures'.[42] Thus, the Court suggested that the national law, albeit indirectly discriminatory on the grounds of sex, could be justified on the grounds of the 'need to alleviate the constraints weighing on small businesses'.[43]

Even when faced with the revised competence under Article 137, the Court has remained consistent and applied its pre-existing case law on legal basis. This can be seen in *Belgium* v. *Commission*[44] concerning the Commission's adoption of a Regulation essentially authorizing state aid for the purposes of encouraging employment of disadvantaged and disabled workers. The Commission's powers derived from a Council Regulation which in its turn was based on the state aid provision of the Treaty. Belgium argued that the authority granted to the Commission to adopt such measures ceased to exist as regards matters covered by Article 137. The Court disagreed, arguing that even though the Council and Commission Regulations had an impact on the promotion of employment, their main purpose was to determine which aid was compatible with the Common Market and to exempt it from the obligation of notification. Thus, they implemented Article 87(3) which states that certain aid, conducive to objectives in the public interest, may be found to be compatible with the Common Market in so far as its objectives justify the distortion of competition,[45] and not Article 137.

(b) Minimum Standards

As with (old) Article 118a(2) and (3), when the Council adopts a measure setting minimum requirements under Article 137(2), Member States remain free to maintain or introduce more stringent protective measures compatible with the Treaty.[46] In the *Working Time* case[47] the Court said that the phrase 'minimum requirements' in Article 118a(2) (new Article 137(2)) did not limit Community action 'to the lowest common denominator, or even the lowest level of protection established by the Member States'.[48] It meant that Member States were free to adopt more stringent measures than those resulting from Community law,[49] high as that might be.[50] The Advocate General

---

[41] Para. 33.   [42] Para. 34.   [43] Second concluding paragraph.
[44] Case C–110/03 *Belgium* v. *Commission* [2005] ECR I–000 considered further in Ch. 1.
[45] Para. 80.   [46] Art. 137(4), second indent.
[47] Case C–84/94 *UK* v. *Council* [1996] ECR I–5755.   [48] Para. 56.
[49] See also *Opinion 2/91* [1993] ECR I–1061, para. 16, and Case C–2/97 *Società Italiana Petroli SpA* v. *Borsana* [1998] ECR I–8597.
[50] Para. 56. As Szyszczak notes in 'The New Parameters of European Labour Law', in O'Keeffe and Twomey (eds), *Legal Issues of the Amsterdam Treaty* (Hart Publishing, Oxford, 1999), such

also strongly rejected the contention that 'the Community cannot take action except on the basis of the lowest common denominator, or at the lowest possible level'. He said that this was diametrically opposed to the very conception of Community law where Community action has never been geared towards levelling down, in particular because Article 2 refers to 'harmonious development', and to a 'high degree of convergence', 'to a high level of employment and of social protection'.[51] The function of minimum standards Directives is considered further below.[52]

(c) Changes introduced by the Treaty of Nice

Not only did the Nice Treaty reorganize Article 137 but it also added two further fields of Community activity:

- the combating of social exclusion;
- the modernization of social protection systems without prejudice to point (c) (i.e. social security and social protection of workers).

However, harmonization is expressly excluded in respect of these grounds.[53] Instead, according to Article 137(2)(a), the Council:

may adopt measures designed to encourage cooperation between Member States through initiatives aimed at improving knowledge, developing exchanges of information and best practices, promoting innovative approaches and evaluating experiences, excluding any harmonisation of the laws and regulations of the Member States;

Indeed, given the promotion of these OMC methodologies to Article 137(2)*(a)*, and the possibility of adopting directives placed in Article 137(2)*(b)* (reversing the order prescribed by the Amsterdam Treaty), OMC seems to be the preferred way forward in respect of all the fields of social activity and not just social exclusion and the modernization of social protection systems.

In an attempt to ring-fence social security from the incursion of European Community law still further, the Treaty of Nice also adds that the provisions adopted pursuant to Article 137 'shall not affect the right of Member States to define the fundamental principles of their social security systems and must not significantly affect the financial equilibrium thereof'.[54]

---

high principles do not always rule the day in practice. E.g. the UK was responsible for watering down the content of the Pregnant Workers' Directive 92/85/EEC (OJ [1992] L348/1) to such an extent that the Italian government abstained, claiming that the level of protection was too low for it to accept.

[51] Para. 54.   [52] See text attached nn. 84–5.   [53] Art. 137(2)(b).
[54] Art. 137(4) first indent.

3. Subsidiarity and Proportionality

If the Community does have (non-exclusive) competence to legislate, it must then consider the application of the principle of subsidiarity.[55] Article 5(2) requires that Community action should be taken 'only if and insofar as the objectives of the proposed action cannot be sufficiently achieved by the Member States and can therefore, by reason of the scale and effects of the proposed action, be better achieved by the Community'.[56] This is a decentralized or bottom-up approach to subsidiarity where the presumption is that it is the Member States that should act. Article 5(3) then adds that 'any action taken by the Community shall not go beyond what is necessary to achieve the objectives of this Treaty' (the principle of proportionality). Read together, Article 5(2) and (3) mean that in areas such as social policy the Community can take action only if the tests of effectiveness and scale are satisfied and any measure taken is proportionate. The Commission has phrased this rather differently.[57] It says that three questions must be answered:

- What is the Community dimension of the problem?
- What is the most effective solution given the means available to the Community and the Member States?
- What is the real added value of common action compared with isolated action by the Member States?[58]

It continues that 'the intensity of the action should leave the Member States all possible room for manoeuvre in its implementation. Subsidiarity requires Community legislation to be limited to what is essential'.

At Amsterdam the Member States added a Protocol on the application of

---

[55] AG Ruiz-Jarabo Colomer Opinion in Case C–110/03 *Belgium v. Commission* [2005] ECR I–000, para. 67.

[56] See generally, Toth, 'A Legal Analysis of Subsidiarity', in O'Keeffe and Twomey (eds), *Legal Issues of the Maastricht Treaty* (Chancery, London, 1994). See also the essays by Steiner and Emiliou in the same volume; Emiliou, 'Subsidiarity: An Effective Barrier Against "the Enterprises of Ambition" ' (1992) 17 *ELRev.* 383; Toth, 'The Principle of Subsidiarity in the Maastricht Treaty' (1992) 29 *CMLRev.* 1079. The Constitutional Treaty made provision for a procedure allowing national parliaments to register formal objections to a Commission proposal ('the yellow light procedure'), because it fails to respect the principle of subsidiarity. The principle means, in effect, that action should only be taken at the level of the Union, rather than at national level, where there is demonstrable added value in doing so. Under the procedure envisaged by the Treaty, if a third of national parliaments objected to a proposal, the Commission would be bound to review it (see Art. I–11(3) and the Protocol).

[57] *Commission Report to the European Council on the adaptation of Community legislation to the subsidiarity principle* COM(93) 545 final, 1. See also SEC(92) 1990, 27 October 1992.

[58] See also the Commission White Paper COM(94) 333, 11. The Preamble to the Community Social Charter 1989 makes clear that the implementation of social rights must respect the principle of subsidiarity, i.e. 'responsibility for the initiatives to be taken … lies with the Member States or their constituent parts and, *within the limits of its powers*, with the European Community' (emphasis added).

the principles of subsidiarity and proportionality[59] which provides guidelines as to whether the conditions laid down in Article 5(2) EC are fulfilled:

- the issue under consideration has transnational aspects which cannot be satisfactorily regulated by action by Member States;
- action by Member States alone or lack of Community action would conflict with the requirements of the Treaty (such as the need to correct distortions of competition or avoid disguised restrictions on trade or strengthen economic and social cohesion) or would otherwise significantly damage Member States' interests;
- action at Community level would produce clear benefits by reason of its scale or effects compared with action at the level of the Member States.

The application of the principle of subsidiarity to employment issues raises particularly difficult questions. First, what is the most effective level? Is it EC level, national level, or perhaps regional, district, sectoral, enterprise, or plant level? Secondly, who should make the decisions—the EC institutions, national or regional authorities, the Social Partners or the individual manager? Thirdly, what type of measures should be taken—normative measures such as directly applicable regulations, Directives which confer some discretion on Member States as to their manner of implementation, soft law measures such as recommendations and opinions, collective agreements, or now OMC? And if Directives are the chosen method, to what extent should they be exhaustive harmonization measures or merely minimum harmonization?[60]

The subsidiarity question also raises a further, particularly contested issue: what is the appropriate extent of the Community action? Different views exist as to precisely when the Community should act in the social field.[61] The first view advocates a positive and active role for the Community, regarding the Community as having a duty of care for the social well-being of its citizens as much as the furtherance of their collective economic interests within the framework of a single integrated market. This would justify wide-ranging action by the Community. The second view sees the Community as being primarily concerned with economic matters and therefore as being competent to act in the social field only to the extent necessary to prevent distortions of competition arising out of divergences in production costs between Member

---

[59] This Protocol takes account of the Inter-institutional Agreement of 25 October 1993 between the European Parliament, the Council and the Commission on procedures for implementing the principle of subsidiarity and confirms the conclusions of the Birmingham European Council on 16 October 1992 and the overall approach to the application of the subsidiarity principle agreed by the European Council meeting in Edinburgh on 11–12 December 1992 will continue to guide the action of the Union's institutions as well as the development of the application of the principle of subsidiarity.

[60] For a discussion of the differences between these terms, see C Barnard, *The Substantive Law of the EU: the Four Freedoms* (OUP, Oxford, 2004) Ch. 18.

[61] Watson, 'The Community Social Charter' (1991) 28 *CMLRev*. 37, 40.

States due to differences in national social standards, levels of health and safety protection and other similar matters. The third view claims that the Community should act in the social field only where it can add value: i.e. where there is a transnational element to the problem. The fourth view says that the Community should not act since there is no firm evidence on the incidence of differing social standards upon production costs. This last view is not supported by the legislation adopted to date but elements of the first three views have influenced Community action.

The question of subsidiarity was broached, albeit rather hesitantly, by the UK in *Working Time* [62] where the UK alleged that Directive 93/104 (now Directive 2003/88) infringed the principles of subsidiarity and proportionality. Advocate General Léger dismissed the UK's arguments. Distinguishing between subsidiarity and proportionality, he said:

The two principles operate in turn, at two different levels of Community action. 'The first (subsidiarity) determines whether Community action is to be set in motion, whereas the second (proportionality) defines its scope. Hence the question of competence is dissociated from that of exercise.'[63] In other words, the principle of subsidiarity comes into play before the Community takes action, whilst the principle of proportionality comes into play after such action has been taken.[64]

He then said that in so far as harmonization is an objective of the Directive, it was difficult to criticize the measures adopted by the Council. He said it would be illusory to expect the Member States alone to achieve the harmonization envisaged since it necessarily involved supranational action.[65]

The Court also rejected the argument of non-compliance with the principle of subsidiarity, saying:

Once the Council has found that it is necessary to improve the existing level of protection as regards the health and safety of workers and to harmonise the conditions in this area while maintaining the improvements made, achievement of that objective through the imposition of minimum requirements necessarily presupposes Community wide action.[66]

Thus, the Court was prepared to accept without question the Council's assertion that harmonization was necessary. Starting from this premise, the Court was able to conclude that harmonization 'necessarily presupposes Community wide action', thereby reinforcing a centralized, top-down approach to subsidiarity.

The Court then examined the application of the principle of proportionality, looking to see whether the means which the Community institution employed were suitable for the purpose of achieving the desired objective and

---

[62] Case C–84/94 *UK v. Council* [1996] ECR I–5755.

[63] Citing Lenaerts and Van Ypersele, 'Le principle de subsidiarité et son contexte: étude de l'article 3B du traité CE' (1994) 1–2 *Cahiers de droit Européen* 3, para. 100.

[64] Para. 126.   [65] Paras. 130–1.   [66] Para. 47.

whether they went beyond what was necessary to achieve it. Rejecting the plea,[67] the Court said:

As to the judicial review of these conditions, however, the Council must be allowed a wide discretion in an area which, as here, involves the legislature in making social policy choices and requires it to carry out complex assessments. Judicial review of the exercise of that discretion must therefore be limited to examining whether it has been vitiated by a manifest error or misuse of powers, or whether the institution concerned has manifestly exceeded the limits of its discretion.[68]

It therefore seems that the Court has clipped the wings of Article 5(2) and (3) and restricted judicial review to the rare case of manifest abuse.

4. The Form of Legislation: Diversity and Flexibility

4.1. Introduction

The principle of subsidiarity applies not only to the level at which legislation is enacted but also to the form which it takes. This is particularly significant in the labour law context where the national systems are characterized by their wide diversity. Prior to the enlargement of the EU, three main systems of legal regulation of industrial relations could be found in the EU:[69] the Romano-Germanic system, the Anglo-Irish system and the Nordic system.

The hallmark of the Romano-Germanic system, found in countries such as Belgium, France, Germany, Greece, Italy, Luxembourg, and the Netherlands, is that the state has a central and active role in industrial relations and workers' rights are provided by both constitutional provision and comprehensive labour market regulation. In addition, in states such as Belgium, France, and Germany, collective agreements can be extended to all workers and employers. Trade union density also tends to be lower in these countries than elsewhere, and falling—in France, for example, trade union membership declined from around 20 per cent in the mid-1970s to below 10 per cent today (see Table 2.1). The Romano-Germanic system is also characterized by comprehensive legislation governing various areas of working conditions such as the length of the working day, rest periods, and employee representation. Since the Community was numerically dominated by those Member States from the highly regulated Romano-Germanic tradition, in the past this has provided the model for much EC legislation on employment rights.

---

[67] Para. 57, citing Case C–426/93 *Germany* v. *Council* [1995] ECR I–3723, para. 42.

[68] Para. 58.

[69] The following discussion draws on Commission, *Comparative Study on Rules Governing Working Conditions in the Member States—a Synopsis* SEC(89) 1137, 30 June 1989, 10 and Due, Madsen and Jensen, 'The Social Dimension: Convergence or Diversification of IR in the Single European Market' (1991) 22 *IRJ*. 85, 90–1. See also Fitzpatrick, 'Community Social Law After Maastricht' (1992) 21 *ILJ*. 199, 209–13.

Table 2.1 Union Density Rates

- over 90% in Romania
- 80%–89% in Belgium, Denmark, Finland, and Sweden
- 70%–79% in Italy and Norway
- 60%–69% in Cyprus and Malta
- 50%–59% in Luxembourg
- 40%–49% in Austria and Slovenia
- 30%–39% in Hungary, Ireland, and Portugal
- 20%–29% in Bulgaria, Germany, Greece, the Netherlands, Slovakia, and the UK
- 10%–19% in Estonia, Latvia, Poland, and Spain
- 0–10% in France[73]

Source: European Industrial Relations Observatory, Trade Union Membership 1993–2003 (2004)[74]

The main feature of the Anglo-Irish system has been the traditionally limited role played by the state in industrial relations (sometimes known as voluntarism or collective laissez-faire). For example, collective agreements apply solely to the parties involved; they are not legally binding,[70] nor can they be extended to the entire workforce by administrative act.[71] Neither the individual nor the collective relationship is subject to extensive legal regulation, especially when compared with the Romano-Germanic system, despite a trend towards legislative intervention over the last four decades. Consequently, the Anglo-Irish system is characterized by the lack of comprehensive coverage of either collective agreements or legislation and it is the contract of employment which forms the cornerstone of the employment relationship.

In the Nordic system the state also assumes a relatively limited role in industrial relations. However, the functional equivalent to legislative frameworks is provided by a series of corporatist labour market collective agreements, including a permanent basic agreement which is seldom challenged or amended. The state participates only when asked to do so by the parties, and there is very limited general legislative regulation. However, as a result of high levels of unionization which is characteristic of the Nordic system, the vast majority of workers are covered by collective agreements (see Table 2.1). The Nordic model is attracting considerable interest in the EU at present,[72] since it

---

[70] Trade Union and Labour Relations (Consolidation) Act 1992, s. 179.

[71] Although Schedule II of the Employment Protection Act 1975, now repealed, did offer a form of *erga omnes* effect in the UK.

[72] Anderson and O'Brien, 'Beyond the Social Model', *euobserver*, 7 April 2006 and the reply by Sundaram, *euobserver.com*, 26 April 2006.

[73] No figures for union density were provided in the 2004 study. The figure used here is from the EIRO's 1997 study.

[74] http://www.eiro.eurofound.ie/2004/03/update/tn0403105u.html

combines high levels of unionization, high public spending and high tax rates with a knowledge economy and flexicurity—aspirations of the Lisbon strategy. But, as we shall see in chapter 5, this model is also under threat from the opening up of the services market.

However, as Rhodes points out, the different systems of labour market regulation belie a more complex reality.[75] While employers in Germany, the Netherlands, Belgium and the Nordic countries are heavily constrained by hiring, dismissal and contract regulation, they enjoy more in-firm flexibility due to high levels of skills and consensual workplace rule setting. By contrast, employers in the UK and Ireland enjoy higher levels of internal and external flexibility but have a less skilled workforce which constrains adjustment capacities. Employers in southern states (Italy, Greece, Portugal, and Spain) experience the worst of both worlds: they have enjoyed neither flexibility nor consensus due to tightly constraining, state legislated labour regulations and this is combined with adversarial industrial relations. Enlargement has added a further model to the mix: state intervention, akin to that of the southern countries, is combined with weak levels of unionization (see Table 2.1) and firm-level representation of the Anglo-Irish group.[76]

4.2. The EU's Response: the Need for Flexibility

Many commentators make much of the diversity[77] of industrial relations systems in the Member States and the dangers of simply identifying what is successful in one state and bolting it onto the structures in other states where different political and industrial relations cultures exist.[78] On the other hand, other commentators have advised caution in suggesting that characteristics of employee relations policies are necessarily predetermined to be culturally specific.[79] Nevertheless, the different national approaches to the regulation of labour standards have forced the Community to be creative and flexible about

---

[75] Rhodes, 'Employment Policy: Between Efficacy and Experimentation' in Wallace, Wallace and Pollack (eds), *Policy Making in the European Union* (OUP, Oxford, 2005) 281.

[76] Ibid. See also Mailand and Due, 'Social Dialogue in Central and Eastern Europe: Present State and Future Development' (2004) 10 *EJIR*. 179.

[77] See e.g. Hyman, 'Industrial Relations in Europe: Theory and Practice' (1995) 1 *EJIR*. 17, 35, but cf. Marginson and Sisson, 'European Collective Bargaining: A Virtual Prospect?' (1998) 36 *JCMS*. 505, 509, and Hansen, Madsen and Jensen, 'The Complex Reality of Convergence and Diversification in European Industrial Relations Systems' (1997) 3 *EJIR*. 357.

[78] For his seminal analysis, see Kahn-Freund, 'On the Uses and Misuses of Comparative Law' (1974) 37 *MLR*. 1. For a practical example of the problems experienced with comparative work, see the Supiot report, *Transformation of Labour and Future of Labour Law in Europe*, June 1998, published as *Beyond Employment: Changes in Work and the Future of Labour Law in Europe* (OUP, Oxford, 2001).

[79] Bridgeford and Stirling, 'Britain in a Social Europe: Industrial Relations and 1992' (1991) 22 *IRJ* 263, 263.

its legislation.[80] This flexibility takes a number of forms which we shall now consider.[81]

(a) The Use of Directives

First, there has been flexibility in the forms of legislative instrument. Regulations, seen by many as the epitome of uniformity, have never been used to set EC employment standards. The principal regulatory vehicle has been Directives which, by their very nature, allow for a degree of flexibility in the way in which EC norms manifest themselves in the Member States. This flexibility is increased in three ways: first, by the use of framework Directives which lay down certain core standards but the detail of their operation is left to be determined by the Member States and/or the Social Partners;[82] secondly, through the use of Directives aimed at partial harmonization;[83] and thirdly, through the use of Directives setting minimum standards which Member States are free to improve upon.[84]

This practice of adopting minimum standards Directives was endorsed by the Council Resolution on Certain Aspects for a European Union Social Policy.[85] It points out:

Minimum standards constitute an appropriate instrument for achieving economic and social convergence gradually while respecting the economic capabilities of the individual Member States. They also meet the expectations of workers in the European Union and calm fears about social dismantling and social dumping in the Union.[86]

The Resolution continues that the Council is convinced that a 'comprehensive legislative programme' is not necessary but rather it requires 'agreement on specific fields of action in order to build up the core of minimum social standards gradually in a pragmatic and flexible manner'.[87] The resolution then provides a framework for Community social legislation. Community legislative acts must:[88]

---

[80] See generally, Falkner *et al*, *Complying with Europe: EU Harmonisation and Soft Law in the Member States* (CUP, Cambridge, 2005).

[81] This section draws on Barnard, 'Flexibility and Social Policy', in De Búrca and Scott (eds), *Flexible Governance in the EU* (Hart Publishing, Oxford, 2000).

[82] See e.g. the Framework Directive on Health and Safety 89/391 (OJ [1989] L183/9), considered further in Ch. 11 and the Parental Leave Dir. 96/34/EC (OJ [1996] L145/4) considered further in Ch. 9.

[83] Dir. 2001/23/EC on transfers of undertakings (OJ [2001] L82/16 and Dir. 98/59/EC on collective redundancies (OJ [1998] L225/16) provide a good example of this. While these Directives provide a core of rights, such as the right for the transferor's employees to enjoy the same terms and conditions when transferred to the transferee, the detail of those rights and key definitions, e.g. the meaning of terms 'dismissal' and 'worker representatives', are left to be determined by national law. See further Chs. 13 and 14.

[84] See Art. 137(4).

[85] Council Resolution of 6 December 1994 on certain aspects for a European Union Social Policy: a contribution to economic and social convergence in the Union (OJ [1994] C368/6).

[86] Para. 10.   [87] Para. 11.   [88] Para. 17.

- take account of the situation in all Member States when each individual measure is adopted and neither overstretch any one Member State nor force it to dismantle social rights;
- avoid going into undue detail but concentrate on basic, binding principles and leave the development and transposition to the Member States individually[89] and, where this is in accordance with national traditions, to the two sides of industry;[90]
- be flexible enough and confine themselves to provisions which can be incorporated into the various national systems;
- include clauses which allow the two sides of industry room for manoeuvre on collective agreements;
- contain review clauses so that they can be corrected in the light of practical experience.

Stressing the diversity of the national systems, the Resolution says that 'unification of national systems in general by means of rigorous approximation of laws [is] an unsuitable direction to follow as it would also reduce the chances of the disadvantaged regions in the competition for location'.[91] The Resolution advocates instead 'gradual convergence of systems—with due regard for economic strength of the Member State—by means of alignment of national goals'.[92]

From the perspective of the market-making/market-correcting debate considered in chapter 1, minimum standards Directives help to square a particularly difficult circle: the Directives occupy the field in respect of the minimum standards but above those minima they promote a space for states to experiment and develop diverse national solutions. The minima thus represent a 'floor of rights', allowing Member States to improve upon their provisions but generally preventing 'downwards' derogation.[93] Thus, minimum standards Directives operate to induce individual states to enter into a 'race to the top' when they would otherwise have had an incentive to

---

[89] See also Art. 6 of the Protocol on the application of the principles of subsidiarity and proportionality.

[90] See also the Commission's Green Paper, *Partnership for a New Organisation of Work* (COM(97) 127) which talks of 'the likely development of labour law and industrial relations from rigid and compulsory systems of statutory regulations to more open and flexible legal frameworks' (para. 44). This raises 'fundamental questions concerning the balance of regulatory powers between public authorities (legislation) and the social partners (collective bargaining) and between the social partners and individual employees (individual employment contracts) which may well mean greater scope for derogations from legislative standards through not just collective agreements but also individual contracts of employment (para. 43).

[91] Para. 18.   [92] Para. 19.

[93] Most of the social Directives are minimum harmonization Directives and some Directives also contain a 'Non-reducing clause': see e.g. Art. 16 of Council Dir. 94/33/EC (OJ [1994] L216/12) '. . . as long as the minimum requirements provided for by this Directive are complied with, the implementation of this Directive shall not constitute valid grounds for reducing the general level of protection afforded to young people'.

compete on the basis of the withdrawal of protective standards (the 'race to the bottom').

(b) The Use of Soft Law Measures

Another consequence of this desire for flexibility in the form of legislative instruments has been the increasing use of soft law measures. Most of the EC legislation adopted under the 1974 and 1989 Action Programmes was legally binding, hard law.[94] By contrast, the Medium Term Action Programme 1995–1997[95] its successor programme for 1998–2000[96] and the Social Policy Agenda 2000–2005[97] and 2005 and beyond[98] were characterized by their heavy reliance on soft law measures[99] which are persuasive rather than coercive in nature.[100] This shift had already been flagged up by the conclusions of the Edinburgh Council on the implementation of Article 5 on the principle of subsidiarity[101] which said that 'Non-binding measures such as recommendations should be preferred where appropriate. Consideration should also be given where appropriate to the use of voluntary codes of conduct'.[102] The Commission endorsed this view, suggesting that recourse to the most binding instruments should be had only as a last resort.[103]

Soft law measures have also formed the principal legislative vehicle under the new Employment Title.[104] Presidency Conclusions, Commission Communications, annual reports, and even the Employment Guidelines[105] all come in to the category of soft law: they are no more than methods of

---

[94] See generally Beveridge and Nott, 'A Hard Look at Soft Law', in Craig and Harlow (eds), *Lawmaking in the European Union* (Kluwer, Deventer, 1998); Senden, *Soft Law in European Community Law* (Hart Publishing, Oxford, 2004).

[95] COM(95) 134 final.   [96] COM(98) 259.   [97] COM(2000) 379.

[98] COM(2005) 33.

[99] See e.g. the Council Resolution on the promotion of equal opportunities through action by the Structural Funds (94/C 231/01 (OJ [1994] C231/1); Council Recommendation on the balanced participation of men and women in the decision-making process (96/C694/EC (OJ [1996] C319/11). and Resolution of the Council and of the Representatives of the governments of the Member States 94/C 368/02 on equal participation by women in an employment intensive economic growth strategy in the EU (OJ [1994] C368/2) considered in more detail in Ch. 6.

[100] See also Snyder, 'Soft Law and Institutional Practice in the European Community', EUI Working Paper, Law No. 93/5, Klabbers, 'Informal Instruments before the European Court of Justice' (1994) 31 *CMLRev*. 997 and Kenner, 'EC Labour Law: The Softly, Softly Approach' (1995) 11 *IJCLLIR*. 307.

[101] EC Bull. 12/1992, 25–26, Council Conclusions II, Guidelines, 3rd para., point 3.

[102] See generally Sciarra, 'Social Values and the Multiple Sources of European Social Law' (1995) 1 *ELJ*. 60, esp. 78–9 and Whiteford, 'W(h)ither Social Policy', in Shaw and More (eds), *New Legal Dynamics of European Union* (Clarendon, Oxford, 1995).

[103] SEC(92) 1990 final. Cram, *Policy Making in the EU: Conceptual Lenses and the Integration Process* (Routledge, London, 1997) describes the Commission as a 'purposeful opportunist' in that it uses soft law measures among others to 'soften-up' the Member States, paving the way for the Commission's preferred course of action should a 'policy window' open up.

[104] Considered in detail in Ch. 3.

[105] See e.g. Council Resolution of 15 December 1997 on the 1998 Employment Guidelines (OJ [1998] C30/1). Cf. Council Dec. 2000/228/EC on guidelines for Member States' Employment Policies for the Year 2000 (OJ [2000] L72/15).

Community guidance or rules which create an expectation that the conduct of Member States will be in conformity with them (the Open Method of Co-ordination (OMC)), but without any accompanying legal obligation.[106] This, Kenner notes, has certain advantages. The flexibility of soft law allows the Community institutions to stimulate European integration by building on and around existing Treaty objectives without directly creating legal obligations. They are a kind of informal law-making by exhortation.[107] OMC is considered in detail in chapter 3.

(c) 'Internal Flexibility'

Flexibility is not confined to the form of the legislative instruments. Increasingly flexibility manifests itself within the Directive which can be described as 'internal flexibility'. Two examples illustrate this. First, Article 13 of the European Works Councils Directive 94/95/EC[108] provides that where an agreement which covered the entire workforce was already in existence by 22 September 1996,[109] the date by which the Directive should have been implemented, the substantive obligations contained in the Directive did not apply. 386 such agreements were signed by the September 1996 deadline,[110] including 58 signed by British companies at a time when the UK had secured an opt-out from the Social Chapter.[111] In a similar vein, Article 5 of the Framework Directive 2002/14[112] for informing and consulting employees provides that where information and consultation agreements between management and labour already exist they can contain provisions different to those laid down in the Directive provided that they respect the general principles laid down in Article 1 which include an obligation on the two sides working together in a 'spirit of cooperation'.

The second example of internal flexibility can be found in provisions allowing Member States more time to implement certain more controversial Directives. For example, according to Article 17(1)(b) of the Young Workers Directive 94/33/EC the UK 'may refrain from implementing' certain provisions on working time and night work for a period of four years.[113] The Working Time Directive 2003/88[114] (originally 93/104/EC[115]) also provides

---

[106] Kenner, 'The EC Employment Title and the "Third Way": Making Soft Law Work' (1999) 15 *IJCLLIR*. 33, 57–8.

[107] Ibid.

[108] OJ [1994] L254/64, as amended by Council Dir. 97/74/EEC (OJ [1998] L10/22).

[109] 15 December 1999 for the UK: Art. 3(1) of Dir. 97/74/EC (OJ [1998] L10/22).

[110] See Marginson, Gilman, Jacobi, and Krieger, *Negotiating European Works Councils: an Analysis of Agreements under Article 13*, European Foundation of Living and Working Conditions, EF9839. A particularly high incidence of such agreements can be found in Norway, see Knudsen and Bruun, 'European Works Councils in the Nordic Countries: An Opportunity and a Challenge for Trade Unionism' (1998) 4 *EJIR*. 131.

[111] See Ch. 1 for further details.   [112] OJ [2002] L80/29 considered further in Ch. 13.

[113] OJ [1994] L216/12. See also the transitional provisions in Art. 10 of Dir. 2002/14.

[114] OJ [2003] L299/9.   [115] OJ [1993] L307/18.

for the possibility of an individual opt-out from Article 6 on the maximum 48-hour working week (subject to review before 2003)[116] and permitted the states to delay the implementation of the four weeks' paid annual leave contained in Article 7.[117] These provisions were also introduced largely for the benefit of the UK where the legacy of collective laissez-faire meant that the state has traditionally abstained from regulating key aspects of the employment relationship, notably pay and working time, leaving these issues to be negotiated collectively. These two Directives (on Working Time and Young Workers) therefore represented a cultural clash between the Romano-Germanic countries, with their history of centralized regulation of issues such as working time, and the abstentionist Anglo-Saxon tradition. The Working Time Directive does, however, envisage a substantial role for the Social Partners. The Directive provided that not only could the 'social partners' implement the Directive,[118] but 'collective agreements or agreements between the two sides of industry' could be used in setting certain standards, such as the duration and terms on which a rest break can be taken,[119] and derogating from those standards.[120] Thus, the Working Time Directive provides a further example of internal flexibility by introducing a new set of actors. It creates a space in which the Social Partners can negotiate for better standards and—contrary to the Continental legal tradition[121]—for worse. This is one example of 'controlled' or 'negotiated' flexibility'.[122]

(d) Negotiated Flexibility

The possibility introduced by the Maastricht Social Chapter for negotiated European-level collective agreements concluded by the European Social Partners provides a further example of this phenomenon.[123] Once negotiated, these agreements can be extended to cover all workers by means of a 'decision'.[124] These agreements take controlled flexibility one stage further: it is the interprofessional (or sectoral) European-level Social Partners who are negotiating a framework collective agreement which in turn provides space for the national (interprofessional or sectoral) or subnational (enterprise or

---

[116] Art. 18(1)(b)(i), now Article 22(1) of Dir. 2003/88.

[117] Art. 18(1)(b)(ii), now Article 22(2) of Dir. 2003/88.

[118] The details of this procedure are considered further below, nn. 155–68.   [119] Art. 4.

[120] Art. 17. This is most unusual: collective agreements usually improve upon statutory protection.

[121] Wedderburn, 'Collective Bargaining at European Level: the Inderogability Problem' (1992) 21 *ILJ*. 245.

[122] This is also described as 'centrally-coordinated' regulation (Ferner and Hyman, *Changing Industrial Relations in Europe* (Blackwell, Oxford, 1998) xvi. See also 5(2) of Dir. 2001/23 (OJ [2001] L82/16) noted by Davies (1998) 27 *ILJ*. 365, 369.

[123] See further the text attached to nn. 155–68, below. The background to the adoption of this procedure is considered further in Ch. 16.

[124] This has been interpreted to mean any legally binding instrument, including a Directive. See further below, nn. 174–84.

plant) level social partners to act. This process also demonstrates a form of subsidiarity—not just in the vertical sense envisaged by Article 5 (Member State or Community level) but in the horizontal or multi-layered sense that different tasks can be assigned to different actors.[125] As the Council Resolution on certain aspects for a European Union Social Policy explains, the Social Partners are 'as a rule closer to social reality and to social problems'.[126] This raises the fundamental question, who are the Social Partners? Are they truly representative? This will be considered in the next section. For the present it is sufficient to note that the Community now has a twin-track approach to legislation: on the one hand legislative, following the usual channels, and on the other, collective based on collective bargaining between the Social Partners.[127] This latter approach has been described by Streeck as 'neo-voluntarism', putting the will of those affected by a rule, and the 'voluntary' agreements negotiated between them, above the will or potential will of the legislature.[128]

5. Conclusions

The discussion so far demonstrates the lengths the Community legislature has gone to—over many years—to ensure that the social legislation adopted is flexible and adaptable. Far from employing a detailed regulatory approach, which both the market-making and market-correcting theses might support, the Community has generally adopted legislation which provides a steer to the Member States or the Social Partners to negotiate solutions suitable to their own national systems, with the minima laid down by the Directive as a back up. This prompts some commentators to describe Community social legislation as a form of 'reflexive harmonisation', by analogy with the idea of reflexive law.[129] The essence of reflexive law is the acknowledgement that regulatory

---

[125] Sciarra, 'Collective Agreements in the Hierarchy of European Community Sources', in Davies *et al.* (eds), *European Community Labour Law: Principles and Perspectives* (OUP, Oxford, 1996) 203.

[126] OJ [1994] C368/6, II.3. See also e.g. Recital 9 of the Parental Leave Dir. 96/34/EEC (OJ [1996] L145/4).

[127] Bercusson, 'The Dynamic of European Labour Law after Maastricht' (1994) 23 *ILJ*. 1. Shaw, 'Twin-track Social Europe—the Inside Track' in O'Keeffe and Twomey (eds), *Legal Issues of the Maastricht Treaty* (Wiley Chancery, Chichester, 1994).

[128] Streeck, 'Competitive Solidarity: Rethinking the 'European Social Model' *MPIfG Working Paper* 99/8 and Streeck, 'Neo-voluntarism: A New European Social Policy Regime' (1995) 1 *ELJ*. 31. See also Jensen, 'Neo-functionalist Theories and the Development of European Social and Labour Market Policy' (2000) 38 *JCMS*. 71, 90. See Bernard, 'Privatisation of European Social Law: Reflections around the *UEAPME* Case', in Shaw (ed.), *Social Law and Policy in an Evolving European Union* (Hart Publishing, Oxford, 2000) who argues that this may promote 'privatisation' of European social law.

[129] See generally, G.Teubner, *Law as an Autopoietic System* (Oxford, Blackwell, 1993); R. Rogowski and T. Wilthagen (eds), *Reflexive Labour Law* (Kluwer, Deventer, 1994).

interventions are most likely to be successful when they seek to achieve their ends not by direct prescription, but by inducing 'second-order effects' on the part of social actors.[130] In other words, reflexive law aims to 'couple' external regulation with self-regulatory processes:[131] the law underpins and encourages autonomous processes of adjustment, in particular by supporting mechanisms of group representation and participation, rather than by intervening to impose particular distributive outcomes.[132] We see this with Directives which allow Member States to act above the minimum standards or allow other actors such as trade unions and employers to make qualified exceptions to limits on working time or similar labour standards.

Reflexive law also implies an important difference in the way in which the law responds to market failures: it does not seek to 'perfect' the market, in the sense of reproducing the outcome which parties would have arrived at in the absence of transaction costs because it is understood that information problems facing courts and legislatures make the process of identifying an optimal bargaining solution extremely hazardous.[133] Rather, reflexive law concentrates on the value of the process of discovery or adaptation instead of focusing on the achievement of optimal states or distribution. This is done by giving states a number of options for implementation as well as by allowing for the possibility that existing, self-regulatory mechanisms can be used to comply with EU-wide standards. In these ways, far from suppressing regulatory innovation, harmonization aims to stimulate it.

Of course, not all Community law conforms to this ideal: some Directives—particularly the older Directives adopted under the traditional route to legislation—more closely mirror the traditional command and control model than others. On the other hand, the Directives adopted under the collective route to legislation do approach the reflexive law stereotype. In the next section we consider the legislative process applied under the two routes.

C. THE LEGISLATIVE PROCESS

1. Introduction

Whether Community social legislation is to be adopted via the legislative or the collective route the Commission retains the power of initiative for submitting proposals (see Figure 2.1). Before doing so it must consult the Social Partners on the possible direction of Community action.[134]

---

[130] See Barnard and Deakin, ' "Negative" and "Positive" Harmonisation of Labor Law in the European Union' (2002) 8 *Columbia Journal of European Law* 389.
[131] Ibid., 408.   [132] Ibid.   [133] Ibid., 409.
[134] Art. 138(2). For further details of this process, see Brinkman, above, n. 12.

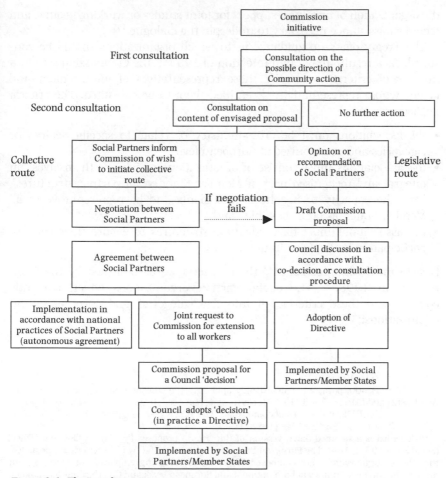

Figure 2.1 The Legislative Process
Source: COM(93) 600, 43 with updates

2. Consultation of Management and Labour

Article 138(1) provides that the Commission has the task of promoting the consultation of management and labour at Community level. It must also take any relevant measures to facilitate their dialogue by ensuring balanced support for the parties. This provision was intended to replace the weaker obligation 'to endeavour to develop the dialogue' contained in the original Article 118b. The Commission considers that it can be more active under Article 138(1) than under Article 118b by providing three types of support:

the organization of meetings, support for joint studies or working groups, and technical assistance necessary to underpin the dialogue.[135]

The Treaty offers no guidance as to which organizations should be consulted. As a result, in a Communication of 1993[136] the Commission set out a number of criteria to identify those representatives of management and labour whose representativity,[137] entitled them to be consulted. The criteria applied are:

• the associations must be cross-industry or relate to specific sectors or categories and be organized at European level;
• the associations must consist of organizations which are themselves 'an integral and recognised part of Member State social partner structures', have the capacity to negotiate agreements and be representative of all Member States 'as far as possible'; and
• the associations must have adequate structures to ensure their effective participation in the consultation process.[138]

Despite much disagreement,[139] these criteria were confirmed by the Commission in 1998.[140] The Social Partner organizations which currently comply with these criteria fall into five categories and cover about 50 organizations:[141]

---

[135] COM(93) 600, para. 12.

[136] COM(93) 600, para. 24. This list only applies to the consultation stage provided for by Art. 138(2) and (3), see Case T–135/96 *Union Européenne de l'Artisanat et des Petites et Moyennes Entreprises' (UEAPME)* v. *Council and Commission* [1998] ECR II–2335, para. 77.

[137] See Case T–135/96 *UEAPME* [1998] ECR II–2335, para. 72.

[138] This list is a slimmed down version of the criteria proposed by ETUC, CEEP, and UNICE (*Social Europe* 95/2, 164). The European Parliament proposed that two further criteria be added: that eligible organizations are composed of groups representing employers or workers with membership that is voluntary at both national and European level; and that they have a mandate from their members to represent them in the context of the Community social dialogue and can demonstrate their representativeness: Report A3–0269/94, PE 207.928—fin, cited in COM(96) 448, para. 62. ECOSOC proposed that the criteria should also include the capacity to negotiate for and bind national structures: Opinion 94/C397/17, paras. 2.1.12 and 2.1.15 (OJ [1994] C397/43).

[139] See e.g. the responses to the Commission's Communication concerning the Development of the Social Dialogue at Community Level: COM(96) 448.

[140] COM(98) 322.

[141] Annex II of Commission's Communication COM(93) 600. An updated list of those organizations satisfying the criteria is found in Annex I of COM(98) 322 and a further revised list is found in Annex I of COM(2002) 341. The ICL-IST, the Institute of Labour Sciences at the Catholic University of Louvain, carried out research for the Commission in order to enable it to assess the representativeness of the European Social Partner organizations. The IST continues to conduct various studies on the representativeness of organizations at cross-industry and sectoral level, as well as transversal analyses, in order to keep the Commission updated. Report of ICL-IST on the representativeness of European social partner organizations: http://europa.eu.int/comm/employment_social/soc-dial/social/index_en.htm

- general cross industry organizations (the trade union body ETUC,[142] the employers' organization UNICE,[143] and the public sector employers' association CEEP);[144]
- cross-industry organizations representing certain categories of workers or undertakings (UEAPME,[145] CEC,[146] and Eurocadres);
- specific organizations (the association of European Chambers of Commerce and Industry, EUROCHAMBRES);
- sectoral organizations representing employers such as the Community of European Railways (CCFE), and the Association of European Airlines (AEA);
- European trade union organizations such as European Transport Workers' Federation (ETF).

Consultation for the purposes of legislation occurs at two stages. First, *before submitting proposals* in the social policy field, the Commission must consult management and labour about the possible direction of Community action.[147] If, after such consultation, due to last no longer than six weeks,[148] the Commission considers that Community action is advisable, the second stage of consultation is triggered. This requires the Commission to consult management and labour *on the content of the envisaged proposal.*[149] The Social Partners then have a choice. One possibility is for them to forward to the Commission an opinion or a recommendation within six weeks.[150] Any measure proposed will then follow the usual legislative route outlined below. The other possibility, provided by Article 138(4), is for management and labour to inform the Commission of their wish to initiate the process to negotiate Community-level agreements provided for in Article 139.

---

[142] European Trade Union Confederation.

[143] Union of Industrial and Employers' Confederations of Europe.

[144] European Centre of Enterprises with Public Participation and of Enterprises of General Economic Interest.

[145] Union Européenne de l'Artisanat et des Petites et Moyennes Entreprises.

[146] Conféderation Européene des Cadres (higher white-collar employees and managerial employees).

[147] Art. 138(2). It also proposes to continue to consult all European or national organizations which might be affected by the Community's social policy. This confirms previous practice (COM(93) 600, para. 22).

[148] COM(93) 600, 19. Despite some criticisms that the six-week time limit was too short, the Commission has decided to maintain it so as not to put the effectiveness of the process at risk, but may apply it flexibly depending on the nature and complexity of the subject-matter (COM(98) 322, 9).

[149] Art. 138(3).

[150] Ibid. It seems that there is no obligation on the Commission to take into account the recommendation or opinion issued by management and labour.

3. The Legislative Route

If management and labour do not inform the Commission of their wish to negotiate collectively, the measure follows the legislative route. Depending on the subject-matter,[151] a Directive will be adopted either by the Article 251 co-decision procedure or by unanimous vote. Once adopted, Article 137(3) provides the Member States with the possibility of entrusting the Social Partners, at their joint request, with the implementation of any Directives. This possibility had already been introduced in Directives since the early 1990s.[152] This is a further example of 'internal' flexibility: it allows the general language of the Directive to be adapted to local conditions, especially at company or plant level. However, the buck stops with the Member States. According to Article 137(3), second indent, Member States must take 'any necessary measure enabling it at any time to be in a position to guarantee the results imposed by that directive'. This may include, as in Belgium, the passing of a Royal Decree which gives *erga omnes* effect to a collective agreement.[153] Thus, despite the autonomy of the Social Partners, Member States do retain the ultimate responsibility of ensuring that all workers are afforded the full protection of the Directive, especially in the case where the workers are not union members, where the sector is not covered by a collective agreement or where the agreement does not fully guarantee the principle laid down in the Directive.[154]

4. The Collective Route

4.1. Negotiation

The collective route constitutes the second limb of this twin-track approach to Community social legislation. The Social Partners at Community level negotiate agreements which are then extended to all workers by Council

---

[151] See the text attached to n. 38, above.

[152] See e.g. Dir. 91/533/EC on conditions applicable to the contract of employment (OJ [1991] L288/32), Dir. 92/56 on collective redundancies (OJ [1992] L255/63) and the Working Time Dir. 93/104/EC (OJ [1993] L307/18). This corresponds to the implementation requirements of the ILO (Convention Nos 100, 101, 106, 111, 171, 172) and the Council of Europe (Art. 35(1) of the European Social Charter).

[153] In a case decided before the Social Chapter, the Court considered that Belgium had adequately implemented the Directive on collective dismissals when a collective agreement had been extended *erga omnes* by legislative instruments, see Case 215/83 *Commission* v. *Belgium* [1985] ECR 1039, discussed in Adinolfi, 'The Implementation of Social Policy Directives through Collective Agreements?' (1988) 25 *CMLRev.* 291. Art. 137(3) was introduced to meet the Court's earlier criticisms of implementation of Directives by collective agreements: see e.g. Case 1/81 *Commission* v. *Italy* [1982] ECR 2133, considered further in Ch. 14.

[154] Case C–187/98 *Commission* v. *Greece* [1999] ECR I–7713, para. 47. See also Case 143/83 *Commission* v. *Denmark* [1985] ECR 427, para. 8.

'decision'. The collective route is triggered when, at the second stage of the consultation process,[155] the Social Partners inform the Commission that they would like to negotiate Community-level agreements. If they do this they have nine months,[156] or longer with the agreement of the Commission,[157] to enter into 'a dialogue at Community level [which] may lead to *contractual relations, including agreements*'.[158] There is no indication as to what constitutes an agreement, nor what is considered a suitable subject-matter of the agreement.[159] The Commission's Communication simply says that the question of whether an agreement between Social Partners constitutes a sufficient basis for the Commission to suspend its legislative action will have to be examined on a case by case basis.[160]

The Commission is also not clear about who should negotiate. In its first Communication the Commission said that 'the social partners concerned will be those that agree to negotiate with each other'.[161] Such agreement is entirely in the hands of the different organizations. Subsequently, the Commission said that the Social Partners can develop 'their own dialogue and negotiating structures'.[162] It continued:

. . . it is up to the social partners who sits at the negotiating table and it is up to them to come to the necessary compromises. The respect of the right of any social partner to choose its negotiating counterpart is a key element of the autonomy of the social partners.[163]

The Commission has said that where Article 139(1) is applied it must assess the validity of an agreement in the light of its content which requires an assessment of whether those affected by an agreement have been represented. It therefore says that the question of representativeness must be examined on a case by case basis, as the conditions will vary depending on the subject-matter under negotiation. The Commission therefore examines whether those involved in the negotiation have a genuine interest in the matter and can demonstrate significant representation in the domain concerned.[164] To date, in the interests of efficient bargaining, negotiation over agreements which apply generally to all employment relationships[165] has been conducted only

---

[155] COM(93) 600, para. 29, although ECOSOC has suggested that it might occur after the first stage of consultation.

[156] Art. 138(4).   [157] Ibid.

[158] Emphasis added. 'Contractual relations' is a translation of the French term *relations contractuelles* which means relations based on agreement. It has been suggested that the addition of the phrase 'including agreements' serves only to emphasize that legally binding contracts are only one potential outcome. Hepple, *European Social Dialogue—Alibi or Opportunity* (IER, London, 1993) 23.

[159] The Commission has, however, made clear that certain matters are not appropriate for negotiations such as the Burden of Proof in Sex Discrimination cases (COM(93) 600, para. 67.)

[160] COM(93) 600, para. 30.   [161] COM(93) 600, para. 31.   [162] COM(98) 322, 12.

[163] Ibid.   [164] COM(96) 448, para. 71.

[165] Sectoral agreements have also been negotiated by European sectoral organizations. These are considered further below.

by the established general cross-industry organizations (ETUC, UNICE, CEEP)[166] 'based on principles of autonomy and mutual recognition of the negotiation parties'.[167] Although the Commission has said that these three organizations fulfil its own criteria of representativeness,[168] as we shall see, the question of representativity has become a running sore which has threatened the legitimacy of the collective route to social legislation.

4.2. Implementation

(a) Via National or Subnational Collective Agreements: Autonomous Agreements

Once an EC-wide collective agreement is reached, Article 139(2) provides two methods for its implementation. First, an agreement can be implemented 'in accordance with the procedures and practices specific to management and labour and the Member States'—so-called autonomous agreements. The second declaration appended to the SPA explains that this means 'developing, by collective bargaining according to the rules of each Member State, the content of the agreements'. However, the declaration continues that this does not imply any obligation on the Member States 'to apply the agreements directly or to work out rules for their transposition, nor any obligation to amend national legislation in force to facilitate their implementation'. In other words, in the case of an EC-level agreement, there is no obligation to bargain on these matters at national level nor to ensure that it applies to all workers. As Hepple has argued, these provisions attach the social dialogue to the existing structures of collective bargaining and labour law in the Member States. These structures were never intended to take on a new hierarchy of EC-level obligations and, in many cases, are under compelling pressures to decentralize and become more flexible.[169]

The Telework Agreement of July 2002[170] was the first agreement to be implemented via this route. This agreement defines the scope of telework and establishes a general European framework for teleworkers' conditions of employment. It aims to ensure that teleworkers are afforded a general level of protection equivalent to employees working on the employer's premises. The same approach was adopted in the Social Partners' framework agreement on

---

[166] These three cross-sector organizations have long enjoyed a favoured position through the social dialogue steering group and have therefore developed a 'substantial body of experience' COM(93) 600, para. 25, confirmed in COM(96) 448 and COM(98) 322.

[167] COM(98) 322, 13. See Case T–135/96 *UEAPME* [1998] ECR II–2335, para. 79, 'it is the representatives of management and labour concerned, and not the Commission which have charge of the negotiation stage properly so-called'.

[168] COM(96) 26 final, para. 14.   [169] Hepple, above, n. 158, 31.

[170] http://www.eiro.eurofound.eu.int/2002/07/feature/eu0207204f.html, considered in Ch. 9.

work-related stress[171] whose aim is to increase awareness and understanding of work-related stress among employers, workers and their representatives and draw their attention to signals that could indicate that workers are suffering from stress.

A framework agreement on action for the lifelong development of competences and qualifications has also been adopted but the Social Partners decided to implement this not via national or subnational collective agreements but (for the first time) via the open method of co-ordination. The Social Partners agreed to monitor progress of the four agreed priorities[172] on an annual basis and evaluate the impact on both companies and workers though annual reports presented at the Tripartite Social Summit taking place (usually) in March of each year before the Spring summits. This evaluation can, if necessary, lead to updating of the priorities identified.[173]

In its 2004 Communication on the European Social dialogue, the Commission noted that it has a particular role to play if the autonomous agreement was the result of an Article 138 consultation because the Social Partners' decision to negotiate an agreement temporarily suspends the legislative process at Community level. The Commission also says that it will undertake its own monitoring of the agreement to assess the extent to which the agreement has actually contributed to the achievement of the Community's objectives and, where it considers the agreement wanting, it will consider proposing a legislative act. It also threatens to exercise its own right of initiative at any point, including during the implementation period, should it conclude that either management or labour are delaying the pursuit of Community objectives.

(b) Via a 'Decision' of the Council

The alternative method for implementation envisaged by Article 139(2) is for management and labour jointly to request the Commission to propose that the Council adopt a 'decision' implementing the agreement in respect of matters covered by Article 137.[174] This would give *erga omnes* effect, extending the collective agreement to all workers. The Council then follows the procedure set

---

[171] http://europa.eu.int/comm/employment_social/news/2004/oct/stress_agreement_en.pdf, considered in Ch.11. For a sectoral example of an autonomous agreement, see the Agreement on the European licence for drivers carrying out a cross-border interoperability service (2004). The Commission Communication 'Partnership for change in an enlarged Europe—Enhancing the contribution of European social dialogue' (COM(2004) 557) which, in Annex 2, also details other possible outcomes of the European social dialogue such as Process Oriented texts (frameworks of action, guidelines and codes of conduct, policy orientations), Joint Opinions and tools and procedural texts.

[172] (1) To identify and anticipate competences and qualifications needs, (2) to recognize and validate competences and qualifications, (3) to inform, support, and provide guidance, and (4) to mobilize resources.

[173] EIRO, *Industrial relations developments in Europe 2004*, (OPEC, Luxembourg, 2005) 5–6.

[174] The Social Partners are not obliged to do this. They could confine themselves to negotiating a single agreement producing effects *inter partes*, see Case T–135/96 *UEAPME* [1998] ECR II–2335, para. 45.

out in Article 137 (qualified majority vote except where the agreement contains one or more provisions relating to one of the areas for which unanimity is required in which case it must act unanimously).[175] The Social Partners had requested that in order to respect the autonomy of the Social Partners the Commission's proposal should follow the Social Partners' agreement 'as concluded' by them[176] but this requirement was deleted from the final version of the SPA. While this appears to give the Commission the discretion to amend the agreement in its proposal to the Council, the Commission has never done so. In practice, the agreement has been annexed to the proposal to the Council, and the Commission considers that the Council has no opportunity to amend the agreement.[177] This seems to have been acknowledged by the Council: according to its legal service, while the Commission and Council could introduce rules for implementation or amend those agreed by management and labour, neither could amend the essence of the agreement.[178]

In making its proposals for a 'decision' by the Council, the Commission resumes control of the procedure.[179] In its capacity as guardian of the Treaties, the Commission considers the mandate of the social partners[180] and the 'legality' of each clause in the collective agreement in relation to Community law, and the provisions regarding SMEs set out in Article 137(2)(b).[181] The Council, when taking its 'decision' must verify whether the Commission has fulfilled these obligations, otherwise it runs the risk of ratifying a procedural irregularity capable of vitiating the measure ultimately adopted by it.[182]

The use of the term 'decision' as the legal form by which the agreement is implemented is misleading. In Article 249 a 'Decision' is defined as being 'binding in its entirety upon those to whom it is addressed'. Decisions are individual in nature and are addressed to undertakings, individuals or Member States; they are not usually normative in the sense of creating generally applicable Community law. Therefore, the Commission has said that in this context the term 'decision' refers to one of the binding legislative instruments listed in Article 249 (Regulations, Directives, and Decisions) and that the Commission will choose the most appropriate measure.[183] In the case of the

---

[175] Art. 139(2), second indent.

[176] The October 1991 agreement had provided 'on a proposal from the Commission, with regard to the agreements *as they have been concluded*' (emphasis added): *Social Europe* 2/95, 149.

[177] COM(93) 600, para. 38.

[178] Opinion of 31 March 1994, Council Doc 6116/94, cited in Brinkman, above, n. 12.

[179] Case T–135/96 *UEAPME* [1998] ECR II–2335, para. 84.

[180] Confirmed by Case T–135/96 *UEAPME* [1998] ECR II–2335, para. 85.

[181] COM(93) 600, para. 39. This assumption of power was contested by ECOSOC (Opinion 94/C 397/17 (OJ [1994] C397/40), cited in Bercusson, 'Democratic Legitimacy and European Labour Law' (1999) 28 *ILJ*. 153, 162) on the grounds that the Commission has no discretion whether a collective agreement should be put to the Council.

[182] Case T–135/96 *UEAPME* [1998] ECR II–2335, para. 87.

[183] COM(96) 26 final, 7. See generally Bercusson and Van Dijk, 'The Implementation of the Protocol and Agreement on Social Policy of the Treaty on European Union' (1995) 11 *IJCLLIR*. 3.

Parental Leave Collective Agreement the Commission said that the content of the agreement and its framework nature suggested that a Directive was the most appropriate legal form, based on what is now Article 137(1)(i) (equal opportunities for men and women on the labour market). It therefore seems that 'decision' in the context of Article 139(2) has a more general meaning. This is reflected in the German and Danish texts which use 'decide' as a verb rather than in the technical sense of a 'Decision'.[184]

The European Parliament has no formal role in this collectively negotiated legislation. For this reason, its attitude towards the corporatist pattern of interest representation is ambiguous. On the one hand, it sees the collective approach to legislating as a step towards greater involvement of citizens in policy formation.[185] It also recognizes that the lack of parliamentary involvement is common in those Member States where collective agreements are given *erga omnes* effect, usually by an *administrative* act.[186] Nevertheless, the absence of European Parliamentary involvement has prompted concerns by some MEPs about the possible 'democratic deficit' of a process where the Social Partners dictate social legislation from behind closed doors.[187] Despite the wording of the Treaty, the Commission says that the Parliament will have the opportunity to see any proposed decision and deliver an opinion where necessary.[188] The Constitutional Treaty made this official: Article III–106(2) provides that 'The European parliament shall be informed' of agreements concluded at Union level.

D. THE COLLECTIVE ROUTE TO LEGISLATION IN PRACTICE

1. Introduction

When the collective route to legislation was introduced at Maastricht it was hoped that, by using the Social Partners as legislators, this would not only improve the legitimacy of EC legislation but would also make the resulting

---

[184] Hepple, above, n. 158, 31 (*Beschluß v. Entscheidung*).

[185] Obradovic, 'Accountability of Interest Groups in the Union Lawmaking Process', in Craig and Harlow (eds), above, n. 12, 363–4.

[186] See the agreement between management and labour of 31 October 1991, *Social Europe* 2/95, 148, cited in Szyszczak, above, n. 50.

[187] See A3–0091/94 *Resolution on the New Social Dimension of the Treaty on European Union* (OJ [1994] C77/30). See also Case T–135/96 *UEAPME* [1998] ECR II–2335, para. 89, considered below, and Betten, 'The Democratic Deficit of Participatory Democracy in Community Social Policy' (1998) 23 *ELRev.* 20. Parliament asked the Commission and the Council to conclude an institutional agreement in order to ensure the consultation and opinion of Parliament before the Council refuses to implement an agreement.

[188] COM(93) 600, para. 40.

legislation sufficiently flexible to accommodate the diversity of European industrial relations. However, the first attempt to use the collective route was unsuccessful. It had been intended to break the deadlock over the proposals for a European Works Council.[189] On 8 February 1994, in accordance with Article 138(3), the Commission initiated the second phase of the consultation process. By the deadline for the second phase of consultation, 30 March 1994, the Social Partners sent their views on the consultation document. However, the Social Partners failed to reach agreement on setting in motion the procedure provided for in Article 139.[190] Because the Commission considered that a Community initiative on the information and consultation of workers was still warranted, it adopted a further proposal,[191] this time on the legislative footing of Article 137(2). The measure, Directive 94/45, was adopted on 22 September 1994. The collective approach was, however, successful in the (less controversial) case of parental leave and it is this Directive that we shall now consider as an example of the collective route to legislation.

2. Negotiating the Parental Leave Directive

The Parental Leave agreement was reached against a background of further institutional failure. The Commission's proposal for a Council Directive on parental leave and leave for family reasons[192] had been discussed in the Council of Ministers on various occasions between 1985 and 1994 but the unanimity required by Article 94, the Directive's proposed legal basis, was not obtained. As a result, the Commission decided to initiate the procedure under Article 138. Seventeen employers' and workers' organizations informed the Commission of their views at the end of the first consultation period but it was the three established partners, UNICE, CEEP, and the ETUC, which, on 5 July 1995, announced their intention of starting negotiations, with the assistance of an active conciliator appointed by the parties. A framework agreement laying down minimum requirements designed to facilitate the reconciliation of parental and professional responsibilities for working parents[193] was concluded by the Social Partners on 14 December 1995.

The matter was then placed in the hands of the Commission which proposed that the measure be adopted by a Directive. The Explanatory Memorandum accompanying the Proposal for a Council Directive on the framework agreement on parental leave concluded by UNICE, CEEP and the ETUC[194] carefully details the Commission's application of its own 1993 Communication on how

---

[189] See e.g. COM(90) 581 final (OJ [1991] C39/10). For further details see Ch. 15.
[190] For details of the Social Partners 'talks about talks', see Gold and Hall, 'Statutory European Works Councils: the Final Countdown?' (1994) 25 *IRJ* 177, 179–82.
[191] COM(94) 134 final.   [192] COM(83) 686 final.   [193] Clause 1(1).
[194] COM(96) 26 final. This Directive is considered in detail in Ch. 9.

the process would work.[195] First, the Commission considered the representative status of the contracting parties and their mandate.[196] It said that since UNICE, CEEP, and ETUC had committed themselves to an 'autonomous and voluntary process' (the Val Duchesse dialogue) since 1985 they satisfied the criteria defined in the Commission's Communication,[197] and so they were representative.[198] Second, the Commission considered the 'legality' of the clauses of the agreement. It found that none of the clauses contravened Community law even though the collective agreement contained a clause imposing obligations on the Member States to implement the Commission decision.[199]

The Commission's proposal for a Directive on parental leave contained two articles. The first provided that the parental leave agreement annexed to the Directive was made binding. The original proposal also contained two additional clauses concerning the principle of non-discrimination and sanctions but they were dropped from the final version. The collective agreement itself was placed in a separate annex. The Commission kept the Parliament informed about the various phases of consultation of the Social Partners and also forwarded the proposal to the Parliament and the Economic and Social Committee so that they could deliver their opinion to the Commission and Council. The Directive was adopted on 3 June 1996.

A similar approach was followed in the case of Part-time Work and Fixed-term Work.[200] It was also applied in respect of the sectoral agreements that have been negotiated, including the agreement on the organization of working time by seafarers which was negotiated under the collective route by the European Community Shipowners' Association (ECSA) and the Federation of Transport Workers' Unions (FST)[201] and extended by Directive 99/63/EC[202] to all seafarers on board every commercial seagoing ship registered in the territory of a Member State, and again in the agreement between the Association of European Airlines (AEA), European Region Airlines Association (ERA), International Air Carrier Association (IACA), European Cockpit Association

---

[195] COM(93) 600. See now the Commission's drafting checklist for new generation Social Partner texts: Commission Communication 'Partnership for change in an enlarged Europe—Enhancing the contribution of European social dialogue' (COM(2004) 557), Annex 3.

[196] COM(96) 26 final.   [197] COM(93) 600, para. 24, considered above, n. 135.

[198] The Commission forwarded the framework agreement to all of the organizations which it had previously consulted or informed.

[199] The Commission said that it followed from the second declaration annexed to the SPA that collective agreements were likely to create obligations for the Member States.

[200] Council Dir. 97/81/EC (OJ [1998] L14/9 as amended by Council Dir. 98/23/EC (OJ [1998] L131/10 and Council Dir. 99/70/EC (OJ [1999] L175/43), respectively. See Lo Faro, *Regulating Social Europe: Reality and Myth of Collective Bargaining in the EC Legal Order* (Hart Publishing, Oxford, 2000) Ch. 5; Falkner *et al*, *Complying with Europe: EU Harmonisation and Soft Law in the Member States* (CUP, Cambridge, 2005) Ch. 9.

[201] A European Industry Committee with ETUC affiliation: COM(98) 322, Annex 1.

[202] OJ [1999] L167/33.

(ECA), and European Transport Workers' Federation (ETF) on the working time of mobile workers in civil aviation.[203]

3. A Challenge to the Legitimacy of the Collective Route

The successful outcome of the negotiations on parental leave was hailed by some as the birth of Euro-corporatism.[204] However, UEAPME, CEC, and EUROCOMMERCE criticized the monopoly created by the established Social Partners. This led UEAPME, representing small and medium-sized employers, to bring judicial review proceedings seeking annulment of the Parental Leave agreement and/or Directive 96/34,[205] with respect to its application to small and medium-sized undertakings. The grounds of review advanced by UEAPME were breach of the principle of equality, breach of Articles 2(2), 3(3) and 4 SPA (new Articles 137(2), 138(3) and 139), the principles of subsidiarity and proportionality, and the principle of *patere legem quam ipse fecisti*.

However, before the Court of First Instance (CFI) could consider the substantive grounds of challenge it had to examine whether UEAPME, a 'non-privileged applicant' (NPA), had *locus standi* to bring the claim. A literal reading of Article 230 EC suggested that UEAPME had no locus because natural or legal persons (NPAs) can 'institute proceedings against a decision addressed to that person or against a decision which, although in the form of a regulation or a decision addressed to another person, is of direct and individual concern to the former'. Thus, since the measure was a Directive and not a Decision or a Decision in the form of a Regulation it seemed as though UEAPME did not have *locus standi*. However, the CFI reached a different conclusion. Taking into account its character and legal effects, rather than its form,[206] the CFI agreed that Directive 96/34 was not a 'decision' but a general legislative measure.[207] Yet, the Court went on to find

---

[203] Council Dir. 2000/79/EC OJ [2000] L302/57.

[204] Falkner, 'The Maastricht Protocol on Social Policy: Theory and Practice' (1996) 6 *JESP*. 1, and *EU Social Policy in the 1990s: Towards a Corporatist Policy Community* (Routledge, London, 1998).

[205] Case T–135/96 *UEAPME* [1998] ECR II–2335. In Case T–55/98 *Union européenne de l'artisanat et des petites et moyennes entreprises (UEAPME)* v. *Council*, UEAPME started but then withdrew a challenge to the Directive on Part-time Work. The action was removed from the Court's register on 14 January 1999. For an early example of an unsuccessful claim of this sort, see Case 66/76 *CFDT* v. *Council* [1977] ECR 305. CFDT, the second largest trade union confederation, complained that it had not been included among the representative organizations designated to draw up lists of candidates for a consultative committee. The Court dismissed the application because the ECSC Treaty did not empower claimants like CFDT to file such an application.

[206] See Case C–298/89 *Gibraltar* v. *EU Council* [1993] ECR I–3605.

[207] Case T–135/96 *UEAPME*, paras. 63–7.

that, notwithstanding the legislative character of Directive 96/34, it might nevertheless be of direct and individual concern to UEAPME.[208]

The case therefore turned on the question of individual concern. The Court noted that such individual concern would be present where a measure affected an applicant in a special way 'by reason of certain attributes peculiar to them or by reason of circumstances which differentiate them from all other persons'.[209] UEAPME claimed that this was the case, by reference to the consultation procedures set out in Article 138, as implemented by the Commission: it argued that, as it had been represented in the 'informal' consultation (as we have seen, it was explicitly listed in the Commission's Communication), its exclusion from the formal negotiation stage was unlawful. The CFI did not agree. It said that the consultation stage was separate from the negotiation stage, and there was no general right of those consulted to take part in the negotiations under Articles 138(4) and 139 or an individual right to participate in negotiation of the framework agreement.[210]

However, the CFI found that this in itself did not render the action inadmissible. The question was whether 'any right of the applicant has been infringed as the result of any failure on the part of either the Council or the Commission to fulfil their obligations under the [collective] procedure'.[211] The CFI said that the Commission and Council were obliged, in carrying out their roles under Articles 138(4) and 139, to act in conformity with the principles governing their action in the field of social policy.[212] In particular, the Commission was obliged by Article 138(1) to promote consultation of management and labour and facilitate dialogue by ensuring balanced support for the parties. This obligation was interpreted by the CFI as imposing a duty on the Commission, when resuming control of the collective procedure at the joint request of the social partners under Article 139(2), to examine the representativity of the signatories to agreements proposed for implementation at the Community level under Articles 138(4) and 139, and a duty on the Council to verify whether the Commission had fulfilled this task. Both institutions had to ascertain whether 'having regard to the content of the agreement in question, the signatories, taken together are sufficiently representative'.

The CFI noted that the Council and Commission's duty to examine the representativity of the signatories to agreements was particularly important in the case of the collective procedure from which, as we have seen, the European Parliament is excluded. It said that participation of the European Parliament in the Community legislative process reflects at Community

---

[208] Applying (para. 69) Case C–358/89 *Extramet Industrie v. Council* [1991] ECR I–2501; Case C–309/89 *Codorniu v. Council* [1994] ECR I–1853.
[209] Ibid., para. 69; Case 25/62 *Plaumann v. Commission* [1963] ECR 95; Case C–309/89 *Codorniu* [1994] ECR I–1853.
[210] Para. 82.　　　[211] Para. 83.　　　[212] Para. 85.

level 'the fundamental democratic principle that the people must share in the exercise of power through a representative assembly'.[213] The Court pointed out that, in respect of measures adopted by the Council under the legislative route provided by Article 137, the democratic legitimacy derives from the European Parliament's participation.[214] By contrast, in respect of measures adopted under the collective route (Articles 138(4) and 139) the European Parliament is absent. In this case, the 'principle of democracy on which the Union is founded requires ... that the participation of the people be otherwise ensured, in this instance through the parties representative of management and labour who concluded the agreement which is endowed by the Council ... with a legislative foundation at Community level'.[215]

Thus, the autonomy of the social dialogue is subject to the scrutiny of the Commission, the Council and ultimately the Court. The Court continued that where that degree of representativity was lacking the Commission and Council had to refuse to implement the agreement at Community level.[216] In such a case, the representatives of management and labour which were initially consulted by the Commission under Articles 138(2) and (3) but which were not parties to the agreement, and 'whose particular representation—again in relation to the content of the agreement—is necessary in order to raise the collective representativity[217] of the signatories to the required level, have the right to prevent the Commission and the Council from implementing the agreement at Community level by means of legislative instrument'.[218] Thus, even after a European collective agreement has been concluded it can be challenged by those organizations excluded from it on the grounds of the absence of sufficient collective representativity.

The CFI went on to find that, in respect of the Framework Agreement on Parental Leave, the Commission and Council did indeed take sufficient account of the representativity of the parties.[219] Since the Agreement applied to all employment relationships, the signatories, in order to satisfy the requirement of sufficient collective representativity, had to be qualified to represent all categories of undertakings and workers at Community level.

---

[213] Citing, *inter alia*, Cases C–300/89 *Commission v. Council* [1991] ECR I–2867, para. 20; Case 138/79 *Roquette Frères v. Council* [1980] ECR 333, para. 33.

[214] Para. 88.   [215] Para. 89.   [216] Para. 90.

[217] Bercusson, above, n. 181, argues that this is an inadequate translation of the original French 'une representativité *cumulée* suffisante'. He prefers the translation found earlier in para. 90 'the signatories, *taken together*, are sufficiently representative'. This interpretation might include collective organizations which in themselves are not sufficiently representative but, when taken together, attain that status.

[218] Para. 90.

[219] See Commission, *The European social dialogue, a force for innovation and change*, COM(2002) 341 on the Commission's continued awareness of the profound governance issues raised by the bipartite social dialogue and the need to keep representativity under review.

Since the signatories (ETUC, UNICE and CEEP) were *general* cross-industry organizations with a general mandate,[220] as distinct from cross-industry organizations representing *certain* categories of workers and undertakings with a specific mandate (the sub-group in which UEAPME was placed), they were sufficiently representative.[221] The CFI also considered that the particular constituency which UEAPME claimed to represent—small and medium-sized undertakings—was adequately represented by UNICE which was a signatory party to the agreement. The fact that UEAPME represented more small and medium-sized undertakings than UNICE, and that CEEP represented only the interests of undertakings governed by public law, was not sufficient to require UEAPME's participation. UEAPME had failed to show that it was sufficiently different, in terms of its representativity, from all other organizations consulted by the Commission which were not part of the formal negotiation procedure.[222] Thus UEAPME was not individually concerned by Directive 96/34 by reason of certain attributes which were peculiar to it or by reason of a factual situation which differentiated it from all other persons and so the CFI found the action inadmissible.[223]

The judgment in the *UEAPME* case raises general issues concerning the nature of governance and democratic processes in the EU.[224] As we have seen, it has been argued that the social dialogue, and the collective route to legislation in particular, help to legitimise the EU in the eyes of its citizens because it enhances democracy, not by conferring ever wider powers on the European Parliament—quite the converse—but because, as the Court notes,[225] it provides an alternative type of representative democracy.[226] This is based, not on representatives elected by their constituencies on a territorial basis, but on representatives of management and labour selected on a functional basis. The CFI has therefore effectively condoned the 'established' Social Partners of UNICE, CEEP, and the ETUC, thereby ensuring continuity of the social dialogue process begun under the Delors Presidency at the Val Duchesse talks of 1985. However, the CFI did not take the opportunity to undertake a wider consideration of the representativity of the established Social Partners,

---

[220] This is a delicate question. In the ETUC, decisions to approve agreements may be taken by majority vote; in the case of UNICE negotiations are undertaken only where there is unanimous agreement. Thus, consultation is as wide and as inclusive as possible.

[221] Paras. 95 and 96.   [222] Para. 111.

[223] The appeal of Case C–316/98 *UEAPME* [1998] ECR II–2335 to the Court was removed from the Court's register on 2 February 1999.

[224] See Armstrong, 'Governance and the Single Market', in *The Evolution of EU Law*, Craig and de Búrca (eds), (OUP, Oxford, 1999); Armstrong, *The Problems and Paradoxes of EU Regulatory Reform* (Kogan Page, London, 1999). Bernard, *Multi-level Governance in the European Union* (Kluwer, The Hague, 2002).

[225] Case T–135/96 *UEAPME* [1998] ECR II–2335, para. 89.

[226] See the work of Bernard, above, n. 128.

especially in respect of those who are not members of a trade union at all.[227] Instead, it confined itself to imposing a minimal review requirement on the Commission and Council.

But are the Social Partners truly representative?[228] Bercusson argues that they are representative of the *interests* of their members, rather than the actual number of those members,[229] from whom they have a mandate to negotiate.[230] As far as the cross-industry (intersectoral) Social Partners are concerned, the ETUC changed its statutes in 1995 to mandate the ETUC to negotiate by qualified majority decisions[231] with a view to strengthening and intensifying the bargaining capacity of the European-level association. In UNICE a similar change occurred. If required, UNICE can receive a mandate to negotiate but, unlike the ETUC, a consensus of all members is still required in the Council of Presidents for all decisions referring to the social chapter. As Keller and Sörries point out, this internal rule can constrain UNICE's ability to enter into negotiations and to ratify more far-reaching agreements because it takes only one vetoing member to undermine any agreement. This also has the effect of neutralizing the shift to qualified majority voting elsewhere. As far as representativity is concerned, UNICE is the most representative of all categories of private undertakings, although this is questioned by UEAPME.[232] However, in contrast with ETUC, UNICE has no sectoral organization but only national umbrella associations as members. According to UNICE, these sectoral interests are already represented within its national member federations which have sectoral members themselves, albeit that UNICE has started to develop an informal network of sectoral business associations on a voluntary basis to keep its members informed. CEEP covers only public enterprises. This leaves other public employers, notably the civil service

---

[227] That said, in many systems, trade unions are accustomed to negotiating on behalf of members and non-members alike.

[228] See the Social Partners' Study of 1993, Doc No. V/6141/93/E. The main findings of the study can be found in COM(93) 600, Annex 3. The Commission is currently conducting studies on the representativeness of the European Social Partner organizations: http://europa.eu.int/comm/ dg05/soc-dial/social/index_en.htm

[229] Bercusson, 'Democratic Legitimacy and European Labour Law' (1999) 28 *ILJ*. 153, 159. See also Wedderburn, 'Collective Bargaining or Legal Enactment: the 1999 Act and Union Recognition' (2000) 29 *ILJ*. 1, 6. Franssen and Jacobs, 'The Question of Representativity in the European Social Dialogue' (1998) 35 *CMLRev*. 1295, 1309 argue that 'it is essential to judge the representativeness of the totality of the signatory parties, not the representativity of one single organisation'.

[230] This reflects the Parliament's proposed criteria for reprensentativity listed in COM(96) 448, para. 62, discussed above, n. 138. The following draws on Keller and Sörries 'The New Social Dialogue: Old Wine in New Bottles?' (1999) 9 *JESP*. 110.

[231] Art. 13 of the Constitution. On the problems that might arise if one large national trade union confederation voted against the agreement, see Bercusson, above, n. 181, 161.

[232] However, since the *UEAPME* case, UNICE and UEAPME have concluded a co-operation agreement (12 November 1998 cited in Bercusson, above, n. 181, 160) outlining 'the modalities of cooperation . . . in social dialogue and negotiation meetings'.

without representation.[233] The ETUC, by contrast, does represent the over-whelming majority of trade unions but some national trade union organizations are still not affiliated to the ETUC. Other European organizations, such as CESI and CEC, also wish to be involved.[234]

Thus, while the picture is complicated, the established interprofessional Social Partners do seem to be more representative than the other organizations. But the representativity of the established Social Partners is likely to become more problematic as (if?) law-making in the social field expands under the new Social Policy Title. For instance, it is difficult to see how UNICE, CEEP, and the ETUC could represent the various concerns of those who might be affected by action to promote 'the integration of persons excluded from the labour market' (Article 137(1)(h)), a social policy matter covering issues far wider than those of classic labour law agreements which are traditionally the subject of social dialogue. Even in the more traditional labour law areas, as trade union membership continues to decline across the Member States (see Table 2.1 above), the extent to which trade unions actually represent 'the people', especially women, is questionable. There is a risk, as Betten suggests, that the social dialogue actually leads to a predominance of an interest group in creating rules.[235]

Given the problems of viewing the legitimacy of the social dialogue as being derived from representative democracy, other commentators have argued that the legitimacy of the social dialogue actually comes from the participatory model of democracy. At the heart of this model lies the idea that decisions are taken as close to the citizens as possible on subject matter of interest and relevance to the citizens. As Fredman puts it, the social dialogue is uniquely suited to the development of social policy because it is based on an intimate knowledge by the bargainers of the factual basis of issues discussed, and leads to a synthesis which is all the more effective because it carries with it the commitment of the two sides of industry.[236] Yet, this model is also problematic: as Fredman argues, there is the fundamental inequality of bargaining power between the two sides of the process and the use of bargaining could well entrench such inequalities leading to an unjustifiable concentration of power in the hands of management representatives legitimized under the cloak of Social Dialogue.[237] This prompts Obradovic to suggest that[238]

[233] Franssen and Jacobs, above, n. 229, 1299. See Szyszczak, 'The New Parameters of European Labour Law', in O'Keeffe and Twomey (eds), *Legal Issues of the Amsterdam Treaty* (Hart Publishing, Oxford, 1999).

[234] COM(93) 600, Annex III.

[235] Betten, 'The Democratic Deficit of Participatory Democracy in Community Social Policy' (1998) 23 *ELRev.* 20.

[236] Fredman, 'Social Law in the European Union: the Impact of the Lawmaking Process', in Craig and Harlow (eds), above, n. 12, 386, 410.

[237] Ibid.

[238] Above, n. 185, citing Hirst, *Representative Democracy and its Limits* (Polity Press, Cambridge, 1990) 12.

corporatism should supplement, but not supplant, representative democracy, by facilitating consultation and co-ordination between social interests and public bodies.

However, Bercusson doubts the validity of viewing the collective route to legislation through a public law lens. He argues that although in *UEAPME* the CFI opted for 'the EU constitutional law paradigm of democratic legitimacy' in its analysis of the social dialogue, the social dialogue should not be seen as a legislative process at all. With its roots in private law and industrial relations, he advocates that 'European labour law cannot afford to abandon national labour law systems'.[239] However, as Fredman notes, the nature of the sanctions available to the parties especially the unions in respect of European level collective bargaining is far weaker than at domestic level due to the absence of any economic pressure such as industrial action.[240] The only pressure to reach an agreement, especially on the employer's side, is the prospect that without an agreement the legislative initiative will return to the Community legislator which will lead, at least for employers, to inferior results (less flexibility and fewer derogations).[241] This has been described as 'bargaining in the shadow of the law'.[242] For these very reasons, the union representatives prefer the use of the law, with collective bargaining being used to top up the minimum standards provided by the law[243] since this may well produce superior results for their members.

4. Sectoral Dialogue

It therefore seems that the issues raised by *UEAPME* are to be resolved by the EU's legislative, rather than judicial, institutions. Szyszczak notes that the Commission has begun to address some of the problems of representativity by means of developing a sectoral strategy.[244] In its Communication on Adapting and Promoting the Social Dialogue at Community Level,[245] the Commission announced that it would set up a new framework for the

---

[239] Bercusson, 'Democratic Legitimacy and European Labour Law' (1999) 28 *ILJ*. 153, 165.

[240] Fredman, above, n. 236, 408.

[241] Fredman, above, n. 236, 409, Keller and Sörries, above, n. 230, 115, and Cullen and Campbell, 'The Future of Social Policy Making in the European Union', in *Lawmaking in the European Union* (Kluwer, The Hague, 1998) 272, citing Ross, *Jacques Delors and European Integration*, (Cambridge, Polity Press, 1995) 150–51.

[242] Bercusson, 'Maastricht: a Fundamental Change in European Labour Law' (1992) 23 *IRJ*. 177, 185.

[243] Fredman, above, n. 236, 409. They fear that the social dialogue will enable employers to 'avoid the unwelcome attentions of the European Commission and European Parliament and to engage in what will in effect be a social monologue with trade unions weakened by recession and structural changes in the economy'.

[244] Szyszczak, above, n. 50, and Bercusson, above, n. 181, 165.   [245] COM(98) 332.

sectoral social dialogue. This led to a Decision[246] on the establishment of new sectoral dialogue committees[247] which constitute the main forum for sectoral social dialogue (consultation, joint action, and negotiations). The committees are to be set up in all sectors which 'submit a joint request and are sufficiently well organized with a meaningful European presence in line with the established criteria of representativeness'.[248] The committees are consulted on developments at Community level having social implications and must develop and promote the social dialogue at sectoral level.[249] A maximum of 50 people, representing the two sides of industry equally, can take part in the meetings of the Committees.[250] Although each committee, together with the Commission, is to establish its own rules of procedure[251] the Decision does specify that the committee must meet at least once a year[252] (the 'high-level plenary meeting'),[253] and that the meeting is to be chaired by a representative of the employers' or employees' delegations or, at their joint request, by a representative of the Commission.[254] Where the Commission informs the Committee that a matter discussed is confidential, members of the committee are bound not to disclose any information acquired at the meetings of the secretariat.[255] Finally, the Decision provides that the Commission and the Social Partners are to review the functioning of the sectoral committee regularly.[256]

At present the social dialogue is being developed in at least 30 sectors at European level.[257] While much of this dialogue has involved identifying relevant problem areas for the social dialogue and trying out common vocabulary, agreements on the reduction of working time in agriculture and on the organization of working time (maritime transport[258] civil aviation,[259] and railways[260]) have been negotiated. In its Communication on Adapting and

---

[246] Commission Decision 98/500/EC on the establishment of Sectoral Dialogue Committees promoting the Dialogue between the Social Partners at European level (OJ [1998] L225/27). On the future of the sectoral dialogue see Keller and Sörries, 'The Sectoral Social Dialogue and European Social Policy: More Fantasy, Fewer Facts' (1998) 4 *EJIR*. 331, and 'Sectoral Social Dialogues: New Opportunities or Impasses?' (1999) 30 *IRJ*. 330.

[247] Replacing existing Joint Committees on Maritime Transport, Civil Aviation, Inland Navigation, Road Transport, Railways, Telecoms, Agriculture, Sea Fishing, and Post.

[248] COM(98) 332, 8 and Art. 1 of the Commission Decision 98/500/EC (OJ [1998] L225/27).

[249] Art. 2.   [250] Art. 3.   [251] Art. 5(1).   [252] Art. 5(3).

[253] There is to be reimbursement for a maximum of 15 representatives on each side.

[254] Art. 5(2).   [255] Art. 6.   [256] Art. 5(4).

[257] http://europa.eu.int/comm/employment_social/social_dialogue/sectoral_en.htm

[258] Council Dir. concerning the Agreement on the Organization of Working Time of Seafarers concluded by ECSA and FST (OJ [1999] L167/33, corrected OJ [1999] L244/64).

[259] Dir. 2000/79 on the organization of mobile staff in civil aviation (OJ [2000] L302/57).

[260] On 18 September 1996 the Social Partners meeting in the Joint Committee on Rail Transport reached agreements on including all railway workers, whether mobile or non-mobile under Dir. 93/104. See also Co. Dir. 2005/47 on the Agreement of 27 January 2004 between the Community of European Railways (CER) and the European Transport Workers' Federation (ETF) on certain aspects of the working conditions of mobile workers engaged in interoperable cross-border services in the railway sector (OJ [2005] L195/15).

Promoting the Social Dialogue[261] the Commission noted that there was nothing in the SPA (as it then was) 'that limits possible sectoral negotiations thereunder, either as a complement to cross-industry agreements or establishing independent agreements limited to their sector concerned'. However, a potential problem may arise if the sectoral organizations were to negotiate a collective agreement in an area already covered by the intersectoral partners and then pass it on to the Commission for a Council Decision.

E. CONCLUSIONS

This chapter has focused on the 'hard' rules adopted by the European Community. As we have seen, in the social field, the hard rules are not as 'hard' as would first appear. By concentrating on Directives, especially framework Directives, the EU has allowed Member States to adapt EU requirements to national situations. The use of opt-outs and delayed implementation has allowed Member States to move at different speeds while ensuring that they keep moving in the same direction. Most radically, the collective route to legislation has allowed the Social Partners to negotiate collective agreements which become hard law. Thus social legislation has never conformed to the hard law stereotype.

Nevertheless, despite the flexibility already incorporated into the Directives, traditional legislation was not seen as a suitable vehicle for responding to the structural problems presented by increasingly high levels of unemployment, an ageing population, and a rising number of people excluded from the labour market. Nor did the EU have clear competence to address all of these problems. This led the Portuguese Presidency of the Council of Ministers in 2000 to look round for alternatives. Drawing inspiration from the OECD, and the Treaty-based procedures found in the Titles on Economic and Monetary Policy and Employment,[262] the Lisbon Presidency developed a new approach, the Open Method of Co-ordination. The Employment Title, the Lisbon Strategy and OMC form the subject of chapter three.

---

[261] COM(98) 322, 14.
[262] Rodrigues, 'The Open Method of Coordination as a New Governance Tool' *Europa Europe* 2–3 (special issue, 'L'evoluzione della governance europea', ed. Mario Telò). Rome: Fondazione Istituto Gramsci available on the OMC website at Wisconsin: http://www.eucenter.wisc.edu/OMC/index.htm. Maria João Rodrigues was special adviser to the Portuguese Prime Minister at the time of Lisbon and co-ordinator of the Lisbon European Council.

3

The Employment Title and the Lisbon Strategy: (Soft) Law-making in the Field of Social Policy

A. INTRODUCTION

So far this book has focused on the development of employment rights and the legislative processes (either traditional or collective) used to adopt these rights. In essence such legislation has broadly drawn on the classic Community method to produce binding rules enforceable by national courts. The Treaty of Amsterdam, which introduced the Employment Title into the Treaty, marked a sea change, moving away from giving rights to those in work in favour of addressing the high levels of unemployment across the European Union. This new focus was accompanied by a more voluntarist, intergovernmental form of governance based on the co-ordination of policy, the use of non-binding, flexible instruments and new techniques such as benchmarking.[1] This new approach was given a formal title by the Lisbon European Council—the Open Method of Co-ordination (OMC). OMC was to be one of the central means for achieving the Lisbon objective of making the EU the most competitive and dynamic knowledge-based economy in the world by 2010. The aim of this chapter is consider how the EU has set about trying to realize the Lisbon goals, and the interplay between the Lisbon strategy, the European Employment Strategy (EES), and the EU's economic strategy. However, we begin by examining the economic and social environment which led to the decision to focus on job creation rather than employment rights.

---

[1] Benchmarking has been a tool for EU employment policy since the Commission's 1993 White Paper on 'Growth, Competitiveness and Employment'. The first significant reference to benchmarking was the Commission's Communication 'Benchmarking the Competitiveness of European Industry' (COM(96) 463). See also Commission 'Benchmarking: Implementation of an Instrument Available to Economic Actors and Public Authorities' (COM(97) 153).

B. THE ECONOMIC AND SOCIAL CONTEXT PRIOR TO AMSTERDAM

1. Levels of Unemployment in Europe in the mid-1990s

By the mid-1990s the European Union was becoming increasingly concerned about the high levels of unemployment in Europe, drawing comparisons with the US where the rate of unemployment was lower than the European average, and the rate of job creation higher.[2] For example, in 1996 the unemployment rate stood at around 5 per cent in the US compared with the average unemployment rate in the EU15 of virtually 11 per cent.[3] Between 1971 and 1994 civilian employment increased by 55 per cent in the US, but by only 11 per cent in the EU.[4] In the US only 9.7 per cent of those unemployed had been out of work for 12 months or more in 1995, while in the EU this ratio varied between 17 per cent in Austria and more than 60 per cent in Belgium and Italy. Women and older male workers, unskilled workers, and young workers with low levels of schooling were disproportionately affected.[5] Long-term structural unemployment and marked regional unemployment imbalances were also endemic in parts of the Union.[6]

The Employment Rates Report argued that as many individuals as possible should have an attachment to the world of work and to contribute to, as well as participate in, active society, and to enjoy the benefits of progress and prosperity. The contribution of employment towards social cohesion and personal dignity was also emphasized in the Amsterdam European Council's Resolution on Growth and Employment:[7]

This approach, coupled with stability based policies, provides the basis for an economy founded on principles of inclusion, solidarity, justice and a sustainable environment,

---

[2] Scharpf, *Governing in Europe: Effective and Democratic?* (OUP, Oxford, 1999) 123.

[3] OECD Employment Outlook, Table A and *Employment in Europe* (OPEC, Luxembourg, 1997) 117. Some commentators prefer to use the employment rate, defined as the proportion of the working age population in employment, as a more effective indicator of the performance of an economy since it measures how the economy is able to provide jobs for all those who are able to work. It focuses attention both on employment, and on the employment potential of the non-employed, including both 'economically inactive' people and the unemployed. The EU also compared unfavourably with the US by this standard. In the late 1970s, the EU's employment rate was 64%, while that of the US was 62%. (The measure of unemployment may be misleading since in the US the figures exclude a number of economically inactive, especially the large prison population.) By 1997, however, the EU rate had dropped to 60.5%, while that of the US had increased to 74%, a spread of almost 14 percentage points (COM(99) 572, Employment Rates Report 1998: Employment Performance in the European Union).

[4] OECD, *Labour Force Statistics 1971–1996*, Paris, 1997.

[5] Scharpf, above, n. 2, 124, citing OECD, *Employment Outlook*, July 1996.

[6] Lisbon strategy, para. 4.

[7] 97/C 236/02. See also Resolution of the European Council on the European Employment Pact, paras. 1, 3 and 4, June 1999.

and capable of benefiting all its citizens. Economic efficiency and social inclusion are complementary aspects of the more cohesive society that we all seek.

At the economic level, three arguments were made for lowering unemployment. First, by making productive use of unused labour stock this would lead to a significant reduction on the burdens experienced by national social security systems. As the Commission's Communication on 'Community Policies in Support of Employment' pointed out, if the performance of the three best Member States or of the US were taken as a benchmark, an additional 30 million or more people could be employed, raising EU employment from 150 million to 180 million, substantially improving public finances and making pension systems more sustainable.[8] This highlights the second argument: that an ageing population[9] needs to be supported by higher employment. Third, high levels of employment are also important to close the gender gap. In 1997 the gap between male and female employment rates was 20 per cent, although it had declined from 26 per cent in 1990.

2. Methods of Addressing Unemployment in Europe Pre-Amsterdam: the Essen Council

While there was much agreement as to the need to increase the employment rate, there was much less agreement as to how to bring it about. In the mid-1990s, there was an active debate about whether centralized expenditure should be used to stimulate demand, and thus employment, through investments in infrastructure and public works.[10] While this approach received some impetus from the 1993 White Paper on *Growth, Competitiveness and Employment*,[11] the Member States refused to countenance a significant increase in the Commission's budget. However, the importance of this White Paper lay in the policy mix it proposed based on the centralized co-ordination of employment policies and its combination of a deregulatory agenda with active labour market measures.

This policy mix was essentially endorsed by the Essen summit in 1994 which identified five job creation priorities:[12]

- greater investment in vocational training, especially for young people and for lifelong learning;

[8] COM(99) 127.
[9] In 1985, life expectancy for men aged 60 was 17.5 years, and the employment rate of men aged 55–64 was 54%. Ten years later, life expectancy for men aged 60 had increased to 19 years, but employment rates for the 55–64 age group had fallen to 47%.
[10] Barnard and Deakin, 'A Year of Living Dangerously? EC Social Policy Rights, Employment Policy and EMU' (1998) 2 *IRJ European Annual Review* 117.
[11] EC Bull. Supp. 6/93.   [12] Bull. 12/94.

- an increase in the employment-intensiveness of growth through more flexible organization of work, moderation of wage settlements, and support for job creation in growing sectors such as environmental and social services;
- a reduction in non-wage labour costs;
- a move from a passive to an active labour market policy, eliminating disincentives, providing suitable income support measures, and reviewing the effectiveness of instruments of labour-market policy;
- improved measures to help people hit particularly hard by unemployment, especially unqualified school leavers, the long-term unemployed, unemployed women, and older job seekers.

A number of the areas for intervention identified by the Essen Council were clearly deregulatory in character,[13] stressing the reduction of the 'tax wedge' of indirect labour costs and the need for greater flexibility in the utilization of labour. Others, however, assumed a more pro-active role for the state and were based on an agenda of restructuring public expenditure in favour of more active employment market policies (e.g. subsidies for training) and the need to strengthen structural policy objectives relating to those excluded from the labour market (women, young people, and the long-term unemployed).[14] From a procedural perspective, the approach agreed at Essen was also of longer-term interest. The Council laid down a monitoring procedure under which the Member States were required to report back on the steps they had taken. A benchmarking exercise was conducted to promote best practice, focusing on long-term unemployment, youth unemployment, and equal opportunities. Essen provided the template for the European Employment Strategy, and the Essen priorities were replicated in what became the employment guidelines. Most significantly, Essen showed to the Member States that it was possible to co-ordinate their activities at *European* level to achieve *national* objectives of reducing unemployment.

The Essen policy agenda was taken further by the Florence Council of 1996 which endorsed a 'Confidence Pact' on employment put forward by the Commission, and by the Dublin Council of 1997 which issued a 'Declaration on Employment'. Together these steps paved the way for the adoption of the Employment Title at Amsterdam.

---

[13] See Deakin and Reed, 'Between Social Policy and EMU : The New Employment Title of the EC Treaty', in Shaw (ed.), *Social Law and Policy in an Evolving European Union* (Hart Publishing, Oxford, 2000).

[14] Szyszczak, 'The New Paradigm for Social Policy: A Virtuous Circle' (2001) 38 *CMLRev.* 1125, 1136.

C. THE EMPLOYMENT TITLE

1. The Treaty Provisions

1.1. The Co-ordination of Policy

Despite the fact that there had been little evaluation of the success of the Essen strategy,[15] its approach was a defining feature of the new Employment Title introduced by the Amsterdam Treaty.[16] According to Article 125, the key provision of the new Title:

Member States and the Community shall, in accordance with the Title, work towards developing a *coordinated strategy* for employment and particularly for promoting a skilled, trained and adaptable workforce and labour markets responsive to economic change.[17]

Article 126 makes clear that the principal actors are the Member States. They are required to co-ordinate their policies for the promotion of employment (which is to be regarded as an issue of 'common concern')[18] within the Council, but in a way consistent with the broad economic guidelines (BEPG) laid down within the framework of EMU. This point is reiterated in Article 128(2). Thus, the Treaty appears to mandate the supremacy of the BEPGs over employment policy, a view which is supported by the harder sanctions available for the failure to comply with the chapter on Economic Policy.[19] However, in an important recognition of the diversity of social policy, the states must have regard to 'national practices related to the responsibilities of management and labour'.[20]

The (subsidiary) role of the Community is laid down by Article 127 which calls on the Community to 'contribute to a high level of employment by encouraging cooperation between Member States and *by supporting* and, if necessary, complementing their action' after respecting 'the competence of the Member States'.[21] This provision is reminiscent of the circumscribed competence of the Community in the fields of education and vocational

---

[15] Pochet, 'The New Employment Chapter of the Amsterdam Treaty' (1999) 9 *JESP*. 271, 275.

[16] See also Biagi, 'The Implementation of the Amsterdam Treaty with Regard to Employment: Coordination or Convergence?' (1998) 14 *IJCLLIR*. 325.

[17] Emphasis added.

[18] Art. 126(2). Sciarra notes the parallel track of co-ordination and co-operation in the Employment Title ('The Employment Title in the Amsterdam Treaty: A Multilanguage Legal Discourse' in O'Keeffe and Twomey (eds), *Legal Issues of the Amsterdam Treaty* (Hart Publishing, Oxford, 1999).

[19] Ball, 'The European Employment Strategy: The Will but Not the Way?' (2001) 30 *ILJ*. 353, 360 although she notes that the Cologne and subsequent European Councils have stressed the equal importance of both aspects of EU law and policy.

[20] Art. 126(2). The Cologne summit expressly recognized the 'autonomy of the social partners in collective bargaining'.

[21] Emphasis added.

training (Articles 149 and 150), culture (Article 151), and public health (Article 152) where the Community is ostensibly given competence but has limited options as to how to exercise it. Together these provisions provide a good example of what Kenner describes as 'Third Way' thinking: the principal themes are those of shared responsibility between and within the Community and the Member States, and a decentralizing conception of subsidiarity in which the 'the Community enables and the Member States deliver'.[22]

1.2. The Review Process

(a) Drawing up of the Guidelines

The role of the Community is in fact less subsidiary than would first appear when the process laid down in Article 128 for monitoring and reporting on Member States' activities is considered (see Figure 3.1).

Each year the Council and Commission are to make a joint report on employment in the Community.[23] This is then considered at a European Council meeting which draws up its conclusions.[24] On the basis of these conclusions the Council, acting by qualified majority on a proposal from the Commission (after consulting the European Parliament, the Economic and Social Committee, the Committee of the Regions and the Employment Committee (EMCO)), draws up employment guidelines which the Member States 'shall take into account in their employment policies'.[25] These guidelines must also be consistent with the broad economic guidelines issued in relation to EMU.[26]

(b) The Role of EMCO

The newly created Employment Committee (EMCO)[27] which the Council has to consult, consists of two nominees from each Member State and two from the Commission,[28] selected from among 'senior officials or experts possessing outstanding competence in the field of employment and labour market policy in the Member States'.[29] It has an 'advisory status' to promote co-ordination between Member States on employment and labour market policies.[30] Its tasks are to monitor employment policies both within the Member States and the Commission, and to formulate opinions at the request of the Commission or

---

[22] Kenner, 'The EC Employment Title and the "Third Way": Making Soft Law Work' (1999) 15 *IJCLLIR*. 33, 48.
[23] Art. 128(4).   [24] Art. 128(1).   [25] Art. 128(2).
[26] Art. 99. See e.g. Council Recommendation 99/570/EC (OJ [1999] L217/34).
[27] Council Decision 2000/98/EC establishing the Employment Committee (OJ [2000] L29/21). This replaces the Employment and Labour Market Committee established by Decision 97/16/EC (OJ [1997] L6/32).
[28] Art. 130.   [29] Art. 2 of Decision 2000/98.   [30] Art. 130 EC.

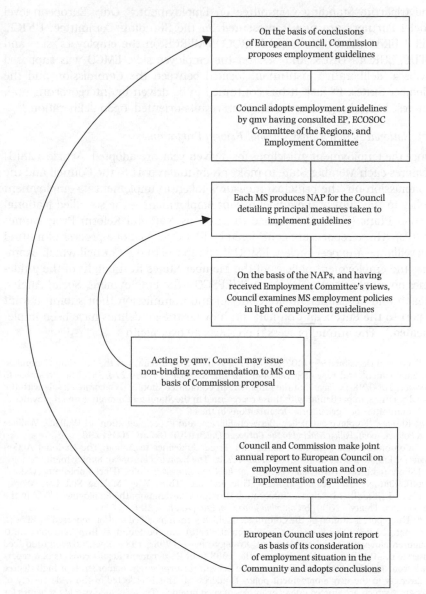

On the basis of conclusions of European Council, Commission proposes employment guidelines

Council adopts employment guidelines by qmv having consulted EP, ECOSOC Committee of the Regions, and Employment Committee

Each MS produces NAP for the Council detailing principal measures taken to implement guidelines

On the basis of the NAPs, and having received Employment Committee's views, Council examines MS employment policies in light of employment guidelines

Acting by qmv, Council may issue non-binding recommendation to MS on basis of Commission proposal

Council and Commission make joint annual report to European Council on employment situation and on implementation of guidelines

European Council uses joint report as basis of its consideration of employment situation in the Community and adopts conclusions

Figure 3.1 The Application of the Monitoring Procedure under the Employment Title

the Council or on its own initiative. It must also contribute to the preparation of the employment guidelines.[31] In fulfilling its mandate, the Employment Committee is obliged to consult the Social Partners[32] who are represented on

---

[31] Ibid.   [32] Art. 2 of Decision 2000/98.

the tripartite Standing Committee on Employment.[33] Only European-level Social Partners are now represented on the Standing Committee: UNICE, CEEP, UEAPME, COPA,[34] and EUROCOMMERCE on the employers' side and ETUC, EUROCADRES, and CEC on the employee side. EMCO was supposed to be a 'deliberative institution' located between the Commission and the Member States. In fact, it has continued to be driven by intergovernmental, interest-based bargaining rather than results-oriented, open deliberation.[35]

(c) National Action Plans/National Reform Programmes

Once the employment guidelines for a given year are adopted, Article 128(3) requires each Member State to make an annual report to the Council and the Commission on 'the principal measures taken to implement its employment policy in the light of the guidelines for employment'—the so-called National Action Plans (NAPs)[36] renamed in 2005 as National Reform Programmes (NRPs). These reports are considered by EMCO as part of a process of mutual surveillance and peer review. EMCO then reports to the Council which examines the employment policies of the Member States in the light of the guidelines on employment. The Council (EPSCO—the Employment, Social Affairs, Health and Consumer Affairs Council) and Commission then submit a joint report to the European Council[37] on how far the guidelines have been implemented.[38] The annual process then starts all over again.

---

[33] Council Decision 1999/207/EC (OJ [1999] L72/33) on reform of the Standing Committee on Employment and repealing Decision 70/352/EEC (OJ [1970] L273/25). The Preamble to Decision 2000/98/EC says that the Employment Committee should 'collaborate closely with the social partners, in particular with those represented in the Standing Committee on Employment'.

[34] Committee of Agricultural Organizations in the EC.

[35] Rhodes, 'Employment Policy: Between Efficacy and Experimentation' in Wallace, Wallace and Pollack (eds), *Policy Making in the European Union* (OUP, Oxford, 2005) 298.

[36] Communication from the Commission 'From Guidelines to Action: The National Action Plans for Employment', COM(98) 316. Szyszczak, 'The Evolving European Employment Strategy' in J.Shaw (ed.), *Social Law and Policy in an Evolving European Union* (Hart Publishing, Oxford, 2000); Kenner, 'The EC Employment Title and the 'Third Way: Making Soft Law Work?' (1999) 15 *IJCLLIR*. 33; Sciarra, 'Integration through Coordination: the Employment Title in the Amsterdam Treaty' (2000) 6 *Columbia Journal of European Law* 209.

[37] The report is drafted by the Commission which is then modified and/or endorsed by EPSCO.

[38] Art. 128(5). The first Joint Employment Report can be found at http://europa.eu.int/comm/employment_social/employment_strategy/report_1998/jer98_en.pdf. As Deakin and Reed observe, n. 40 below, for the most part, the 1998 Joint Employment Report consists of a report back from Member States on their practices which, unsurprisingly, demonstrate a high degree of diversity in the way employment policy is addressed. This is reflected in the wide variety of measures which are singled out as examples of good practice. These include subsidy schemes for the integration of the unemployed (Danish youth unemployment policies, the UK's New Deal for young people and the Irish back-to-work allowance), various schemes of state subsidies for self-employment in Portugal, Germany, Finland, and France, the 1997 Spanish agreement of the Social Partners on employment stability (aimed in part at enhancing competitiveness by reducing the share of temporary employment), and an Austrian package of vocational training and support measures for raising the employment rate of women. Although the value of the exercise was regarded as one of 'peer review' and exchange of 'best practice', in reality the lack of evidence has made it difficult to assess whether these policies should be adopted as reference models for

(d) The Recommendation Procedure

When making its examination of the NAPs/NRPs, the Council may, acting by qualified majority on a recommendation from the Commission, 'make recommendations to Member States'.[39] This recommendation procedure is the main innovation in the new Employment Title: if the employment guidelines are not being observed by a Member State, a recommendation can be issued which is, in effect, a warning for failure to comply with the guidelines.[40] A similar procedure can be found in monitoring the compliance with EMU. However, under EMU, a Member State which fails to observe warnings issued by the Council in relation to excessive levels of national debt and excessive budget deficits may be subject to a fine;[41] under the Employment Title the recommendation is without sanction. This recommendation process is supposed to form part of the 'naming and shaming' process. In practice, recommendations have been issued annually against all Member States since 1999 and the Member States have been involved in drafting the recommendation to be used against them, largely through their representatives in EMCO, with the result that the Commission's draft recommendations are considerably watered down and oversensitive suggestions and wording are removed.

Member States prepare their NAPs/NRPs in response to these recommendations. These Programmes are subsequently 'peer reviewed' in the 'Cambridge' process—a closed two-day meeting of the Employment Committee. The peer review is followed by bilateral meetings between representatives of government and the Commission.[42]

(e) Incentive Measures

Not only can the Council issue recommendations, it can also act to 'adopt incentive measures designed to encourage co-operation between Member States and to support their action in the field of employment through initiatives aimed at developing exchanges of information and best practices, providing comparative analysis and advice as well as promoting innovative approaches and evaluating experiences, in particular by recourse to pilot projects' (Article 129). However, these limited measures 'shall not include harmonisation of the laws and regulations of the Member States'.

Two Declarations issued at the time of the adoption of the Amsterdam Treaty further limit the utility of Article 129.[43] The first sets limits to the

other Member States' (*JER* 1998, 30). This suggests that the process of monitoring and vetting employment policy initiatives within Member States is a very long way short of achieving any kind of centralized convergence.

[39] Art. 128(4).

[40] Deakin and Read, 'Between Social Policy and EMU: the New Employment Title of the EC Treaty' in Shaw (ed.), *Social Law and Policy in an Evolving European Union* (Hart Publishing, Oxford, 2000). The first recommendations were issued in 2000: Council Recommendation 2000/164/EC (OJ [2000] L52/32).

[41] Art. 104(1).   [42] Rhodes, above, n. 35, 295.   [43] Deakin and Read, above, n. 40.

validity, duration, and financing of measures under this Article and the second says that incentive measures may not be supported from the structural funds expenditure but from other areas of the Community budget where resources are insignificant compared to those available to the Social Fund. These restrictions were included at the insistence of the German and British governments and illustrate again how the Member States resisted any significant expansion in the powers of the central Community organs to act as initiators of expenditure aimed at boosting job creation. Article 129 has, however, led to the launch of the peer-review procedure. Under this procedure, states hosted reviews of their own programmes and visited programmes presented by other Member States. Initial assessments indicated that little learning was achieved, what was learnt was not passed on to the relevant decision makers, and there was little transfer of ideas.[44] In 2005 peer review was incorporated into the Mutual Learning Programme.[45]

(f) Assessment

Deakin and Reed suggest that the institutional framework put in place by the Employment Title is facilitative rather than prescriptive.[46] Member States continue to have immediate control over their own employment policies which may well be highly diverse in terms of their approach and effects. Harmonizing laws are ruled out and, in their place, is a process of benchmarking, peer review, and multilateral surveillance.

This soft policy co-ordination apes the business oriented model of 'management by objective' aimed at delivering targets within a given timeframe. While targets are laudable, businesses and government differ. Businesses need to concentrate on one principal objective: the bottom line for their shareholders. By contrast, governments have multiple objectives to reconcile and there is a risk that, by focusing on the objectives in one field, this may have unintended consequences in another. These unintended consequences are magnified in a necessarily more wooden, rules based environment such as EU level policy co-ordination, where Member States do not want/trust the Commission to operate more discretionary rules.[47]

Academic commentators have also been critical of the Employment Title. For example, De la Porte et al., question the effectiveness of the benchmarking methodology.[48] They note that it is difficult to reach agreement on common objectives and guidelines and, even once a benchmark is agreed, the means to

---

[44] Casey and Gold, 'Peer Review of Labour Market Programmes in the European Union: What Can Countries Really Learn from One Another?' (2005) 12 *JESP*. 23.

[45] http://www.peerreview-employment.org/MutualLearningProgramme.

[46] See above, n. 40.

[47] These comments are based on conversations with a Commission official to whom I am most grateful.

[48] De la Porte, Pochet, Room, 'Social Benchmarking, Policy Making and New Governance in the EU' (2001) 11 *JESP*. 291.

pursue it may not be. Targets can also prove hostages to fortune; often they depend on external factors (e.g. energy prices) over which governments have no control. Szyszczak doubts the legitimacy of the benchmarking exercise: its prioritization of some Community policies over others and its choice of indicators and the creation of league tables—so central to the naming and shaming process—is not an outcome envisaged by the EC Treaty.[49] More fundamentally, Goetschy and Pochet[50] question the need for a joint approach, given that unemployment had already been reduced in a number of states using different methods. They also said that the choice of a 'diplomatic' type process involving Ecofin (the Economic and Finance Council), EPSCO (the Social Affairs Council) and the European Council was risky in terms of the consistency of diagnosis and solutions. This process favours consensual solutions (such as vocational training) over possibly more suitable but also more controversial solutions (such as reducing labour costs or reducing working time).

2. The Luxembourg Process

2.1. The Luxembourg Guidelines

Despite these concerns, the European Council decided to put the relevant provisions on monitoring employment policy into effect before the Treaty of Amsterdam came into force. At an Extraordinary meeting of the European Council in Luxembourg in November 1997, the first guidelines outlining policy areas for 1998 were agreed by the Member States and adopted by the Council of Ministers.[51] Developing the fields of action identified at Essen, the (19) guidelines centred on four main 'pillars' (see Table 3.1)[52] which were intended to address 'the jobs gap, the skills gap, the participation gap and the gender gap'.[53] So what were these pillars and what did they do?

First, the *employability* pillar focused on the prevention of long-term and youth unemployment by means of vocational education and training[54] and active labour market policies including the placement of young workers in work experience schemes and subsidies to employers offering training.

---

[49] Above, n. 14, 1146.

[50] Goetschy and Pochet, 'The Treaty of Amsterdam: a New Approach to Social Affairs' (1997) 3 *Transfer* 607.

[51] Council Resolution of 15 December 1997 on the 1998 Employment Guidelines (OJ [1998] C30/1). See further Ashiagbor, *The European Employment Strategy: Labour Market Regulation and New Governance* (OUP, Oxford, 2005) 74–85, on the influence of the OECD's Jobs Strategy on the EU's EES.

[52] See Barnard and Deakin, above, n. 10, 117.

[53] 'An interview with Padraig Flynn' (1998) 288 *European Industrial Relations Review* 20.

[54] See Resolution of the Council and Representatives of the Governments of the Member States on the employment and social dimension of the information society (OJ [2000] C8/1).

Table 3.1 The Luxembourg Process: Employment Guidelines 1998

Pillars	Guidelines	Examples of activities and targets
I. Improving employability	Tackling youth unemployment	Within a period not exceeding five years: —every unemployed young person is offered a new start before reaching six months of unemployment (e.g. training, retraining, work practice —unemployed adults to be offered a 'fresh start' before reaching 12 months of unemployment
	Transition from passive measures to active measures	To increase the numbers of unemployed who are offered training, each MS will fix a target of the average of the three most successful states and at least 20%
	Encouraging a partnership approach	Social Partners to conclude agreements to increase the possibilities for training, work experience, traineeships and equivalent MS and Social Partners to develop possibilities for lifelong training
	Easing the transition from school to work	MS to improve the quality of school to reduce substantially the number of young people who drop out from school early MS to ensure that they equip young people with greater ability to adapt to technological and economic changes
II. Developing entrepreneurship	Making it easier to start up and run businesses	Reduce significantly the overhead costs and administrative burdens for businesses, especially SMEs, particularly in relation to hiring workers Encourage the development of self-employment by removing obstacles (e.g. tax and social security) to setting up as self-employed or running small businesses
	Exploiting the opportunities for job creation	MS must investigate measures to exploit fully the possibilities for job creation at local level, especially concerning new activities not yet satisfied by the market

	Making the taxation system more employment friendly and reversing the long-term trend towards higher taxes and charges on labour[1]	MS to set a target for gradually reducing the overall tax burden and for reducing the fiscal pressure on labour and non-wage labour costs MS to examine the advisability of reducing the rate of VAT on labour intensive services not exposed to cross-border competition[2]
III. Encouraging adaptability in businesses and their employees	Modernizing work organization	Social Partners to negotiate agreements to modernize work, including flexible working arrangements (e.g. annualized hours, reduction of working hours, reduction of working time, development of part-time work, lifelong training and career breaks) striking a balance between flexibility and security MS to look at the possibility of incorporating in its law more adaptable types of contracts
	Support adaptability in enterprises	Examine obstacles, especially tax obstacles, to investment in human resources
IV. Strengthening policies for equal opportunities	Tackling gender gaps	MS to reduce the gap in unemployment rates between women and men by actively supporting the increased employment of women and acting to reverse the under-representation of women in certain economic sectors and over-representation in others
	Reconciling work and family life	MS to implement the Directives on Parental Leave and Part-time Work MS to raise levels of access to care services where some needs are not met
	Facilitating return to work	MS to examine the means of gradually eliminating the obstacles to return to work for women and men
	Promoting the integration of people with disabilities into working life	MS to give special attention to the problems people with disabilities may encounter in participating in working life

MS=Member State.

[1] These increased from 35% in 1980 to more than 42% in 1995.

[2] See Dir. 1999/85/EC (OJ [1999] L277/34) on the possibility of applying a reduced VAT rate on labour-intensive services on an experimental basis.

Secondly, the *entrepreneurship* pillar attempted to make the process of business start-ups more straightforward, and incorporated steps to revise regulations affecting small businesses. Thirdly, the *adaptability* pillar encouraged negotiation over the improvement of productivity through the reorganization of working practices and production processes. The reduction and re-negotiation of working time, the flexible implementation of labour standards, and information and consultation over training issues also came under this heading. Finally, the *equal opportunities* pillar concerned raising awareness of issues relating to gender equality in terms of equal access to work, family friendly policies, and the needs of people with disabilities.[55]

Some of the benchmarks set by the 1998 guidelines were detailed and specific. For example, the second guideline under the first pillar (employability) said that in order to increase significantly the number of persons benefiting from active measures (training) to improve their employability, Member States must fix a target 'of gradually achieving the average of the three most successful Member States, and at least 20%'. However, in most areas the guidelines lacked any quantitative target; their wording was vague and aspirational. For example, the fourth guideline under the equal opportunities pillar merely provides that the Member States will give 'special attention to the problems people with disabilities may encounter in participating in working life'.

The need for quantitative targets and indicators was noted in the 1999 guidelines which required Member States to develop reliable flow data on employment and unemployment, and to ensure that adequate and comparable data systems and procedures were available. Member States were also invited to 'set themselves national targets which could be quantified wherever possible and appropriate'.

2.2. The Guidelines 1999–2001

The substance of the 1999[56] and 2000[57] guidelines largely repeated those of 1998, albeit that they placed greater emphasis on the need to exploit the job-creation potential of the services sector (especially information and communication technologies), on partnership—particularly with the Social Partners—at all levels (European, national, sectoral, local, and enterprise) and on promoting a labour market open to all, especially the disabled and ethnic minorities. The 1999 guidelines also devoted more attention to the problems faced by women in gaining access to the employment market, in career development and in reconciling professional and family life. They therefore spelt out in some detail the types of policies required to address this problem (e.g. design, implement, and promote family friendly polices, including affordable,

[55] See generally the Commission's 'EQUAL' programme.
[56] Council Resolution on the 1999 Employment Guidelines (OJ [1999] C69/2).
[57] Council Dec. 2000/228/EC (OJ [2000] L72/15).

accessible and high quality care services for children and other dependants, as well as parental leave and other schemes) as well as requiring Member States to adopt a gender mainstreaming approach to implementing the guidelines across all four pillars.[58]

The 2001 guidelines were drafted against the backdrop of the Lisbon strategy which had been launched in March 2000 (considered below). To the four pillars were added five 'horizontal objectives', contained in a so-called 'chapeau', designed to reorientate the EES towards the Lisbon strategy:

- Enhancing job opportunities and providing adequate incentives for all those willing to take up gainful employment with the aim of moving towards full employment. Member States should set national targets towards the realization of the Lisbon targets.
- Developing comprehensive and coherent strategies for lifelong learning with responsibility shared among public authorities, enterprises, the Social Partners, and individuals, with relevant contribution from civil society. Member States must set national targets for an increase in investment in human resources as well as in participation in further education and training (whether formal or informal) and monitor regularly progress towards such targets.
- Developing a comprehensive partnership between the Member States and the Social Partners for the implementation, monitoring, and follow-up of the Employment Strategy. The Social Partners are also invited to develop their own process of implementing the guidelines for which they have the key responsibility.
- Balanced translation of all four pillars and the horizontal objectives by the Member States 'so as to respect the integrated nature and equal value of the guidelines' while allowing Member States to focus, in particular, on certain dimensions of the strategy to meet the particular needs of their labour market situation.
- Developing common indicators by the Commission, the Member States and the Social Partners to evaluate adequately progress under all four pillars and to underpin the setting of benchmarks and the identification of good practice.

The 2001 guidelines also updated the existing guidelines (e.g. 'easing the transition from school to work' became 'developing skills for the new labour market in the context of lifelong learning') as well as introducing new ones (e.g. 'active policies to develop job matching and to prevent and combat emerging bottlenecks'). Some more specific targets were also introduced (e.g. Member States should aim at halving the number of 18- to 24-year-olds

---

[58] See further Chs. 6 and 9.

with only lower-secondary education who are not in further education and training) as well as requiring Member States to set targets or at least to think about setting targets (e.g. the Member States and the social partners will 'consider setting a national target, in accordance with the national situation, for increasing the availability of care services for children and other dependants').

2.3. The 2002 Review and the 2003 Guidelines

At the Barcelona Spring Council in March 2002, the heads of state declared that 'The Luxembourg Employment Strategy has proved its worth' but noted that the Strategy had to be simplified with fewer guidelines and had to be aligned with the Lisbon deadline of 2010. The strategy also had to be stream-lined with the other policy co-ordination processes, with synchronized calendars for the adoption of the broad economic policy guidelines (see below) and the employment guidelines, and that both sets of guidelines, together with the third policy co-ordination instrument, the internal market strategy, had to operate in a consistent way with a new, three-year perspective.[59] The Council gave the Social Partners a greater role in, and responsibility for, the implementation and monitoring of the guidelines. The Council's view was borne out by the Commission in its own 2002 review of the Luxembourg process,[60] which focused on the need to simplify the guidelines and streamline the various instruments of co-ordination.

As a result, the timetable of the EES was brought into line with the BEPGs, a three-year policy cycle was introduced and the structure of the 2003 employment guidelines[61] was overhauled. The four pillars were dismantled in favour of three 'overrarching and interrelated objectives' of 'full employment, quality and productivity at work, and social cohesion and inclusion',[62] thus reflecting the Lisbon agenda's goals. These objectives were then fleshed out by 10 'result oriented' guidelines, the so-called 'ten commandments', (as compared with the 20 or so guidelines under the previous regime) (see Table 3.2).

Nevertheless, the 2003 guidelines reflected the content of the original four pillars and accompanying guidelines. Thus, there is emphasis on the need to

---

[59] Council Dec. 2003/578/EC (OJ [2003] L127/13, preambular para. 6. See also Commission Communication, Streamlining the Annual Economic and Employment Policy Coordination Cycles (COM(2002) 487.

[60] Commission Communication, 'Taking Stock of Five Years of the European Employment Strategy', COM(2002) 416.

[61] Council Decision 2003/578/EC (OJ [2003] L197/13. See the influence of the Commission's Communication; 'The future of the European Employment Strategy (EES) "A strategy for full employment and better jobs for all" ' (COM(2003) 6).

[62] Annex, p. 17.

Table 3.2 The Employment Guidelines 2003

The Overarching and Interrelated Objectives

- Full employment (i.e. achieving the Lisbon targets)
- Improving quality and productivity at work
- Strengthening social cohesion and inclusion

In pursuing the three objectives, Member States shall implement policies which take account of the 10 specific guidelines which are priorities for action. In so doing they must adopt a gender mainstreaming approach across each of the priorities.

10 Priorities

Guidelines	Examples of activities, targets and benchmarks
1. Active and preventative measures for the unemployed and inactive	All jobseekers to benefit from an early identification of their needs and from service such as personalized action plans Offer jobseekers access to effective and efficient means to enhance their employability with the new target of 25% of the long-term unemployed participating in an active measure in the form of training, work practice, etc by 2010 with the aim of achieving the average of the three most advanced Member States Modernize and strengthen labour market institutions, especially employment services Ensure regular evaluation of the effectiveness and efficiency of labour market programmes and review them
2. Job creation and entrepreneurship	Simplifying and reducing administrative and regulatory burdens for business start ups and for the hiring of staff, facilitating access to capital (see also BEPGs, guideline 11) Promoting education and training in entrepreneurial and management skills and providing support, including through training, to make entrepreneurship a career option for all
3. Address change and promote adaptability and mobility in the labour market	MS to review and reform overly restrictive elements in employment legislation that affect labour dynamics and the employment of those groups facing difficult access to the labour market MS to promote diversity of contractual and working arrangements, favouring career progression, a better work/life balance and between flexibility and security

Continued

Table 3.2 Continued

Guidelines	Examples of activities, targets and benchmarks
	Access for workers to training, especially low-skilled workers
	Better working conditions, including health and safety
	The design and dissemination of innovative and sustainable forms of work organization
	The anticipation and positive management of economic change and restructuring
4. Promote development of human capital and lifelong learning	MS to implement lifelong learning strategies: —by 2010 at least 85% of 22-year-olds in the EU should have completed upper secondary education —the EU average level of participation in lifelong learning should be at least 12.5% of the adult working age population
5. Increase labour supply and promote active ageing	Increase labour market participation by using the potential of all groups of the population Promote active ageing, notably by fostering working conditions conducive to job retention and eliminating incentives for early exit from the labour market. By 2010 policies will aim to achieve an increase by five years at EU level of the effective average exit age from the labour market (estimated at 59.9 in 2001) Give full consideration to the additional labour supply resulting from immigration
6. Gender equality	Policies will aim to achieve by 2010 a substantial reduction in the gender pay gap in each MS through a multi-faceted approach addressing the underlying factors of the gender pay gap Particular attention will be given to reconciling work and private life, notably through the care facilities for children and other dependants To provide childcare by 2010 to at least 90% of children between 3 and the mandatory school age and at least 33% of children under 3
7. Promote the integration of, and combat the discrimination against, people at a disadvantage in the labour market	By 2010 there should be no more than 10% of children leaving school early A significant reduction in each MS in the unemployment gaps for people at a disadvantage (e.g. early school leavers, low-skilled workers, people with disabilities, immigrants, and ethnic minorities A significant reduction in each MS in the unemployment gaps between non-EU and EU nationals, according to national targets

8. Make work pay through incentives to enhance work attractiveness	MS to reform financial incentives to make work attractive and encourage men and women to seek, take up and remain in work While preserving an adequate level of social protection, MS to review replacement rates and benefit duration, ensure effective benefit management, notably with respect to the link with effective job search Policies will aim at achieving by 2010 a significant reduction in high marginal effective tax rates and, where appropriate, in the tax burden on low-paid workers
9. Transform undeclared work into regular employment	MS should develop and implement broad actions and measures to eliminate undeclared work MS should undertake the necessary efforts at national and EU level to measure the extent of the problem and progress achieved at national level
10. Address regional employment disparities	MS to promote favourable conditions for private sector activity and investment in regions lagging behind MS to ensure that public support in regions lagging behind is focused on investment in human and knowledge capital, as well as adequate infrastructure (see also BEPGs, guidelines 18 and 19)

MS=Member State.

encourage people into training and to update their skills, on the need to reduce burdens on business and to modernize work organization, but no reference to underemployability (setting out active policies to develop job matching and to combat emerging bottlenecks in the new European labour markets).[63] There was also new emphasis on addressing regional disparities together with the need for economic migration from third countries, given the ageing and related skills gaps.

The 2003 guidelines contained a greater number of specific targets (see Table 3.3), some very specific (e.g. 25 per cent of the long-term unemployed participating in an active measure in the form of training, work practice, etc by 2010 with the aim of achieving the average of the three most advanced Member States; by 2010 at least 85 per cent of 22-year-olds in the EU should have completed upper secondary education; the EU average level of participation in lifelong learning should be at least 12.5 per cent of the adult working age population), some vague (e.g. a 'significant reduction' in each Member State in the unemployment gaps for people at a disadvantage and a 'significant

[63] Rhodes, above n. 35, 297.

Table 3.3 Targets and Benchmarks set by the 2003 EES

Targets and benchmarks set in the framework of the European Employment Strategy 2003

- that every unemployed person is offered a new start before reaching six months of unemployment in the case of young people and 12 months in the case of adults in the form of training, retraining, work practice, a job or other employability measure, combined where appropriate with on-going job search assistance;
- that 25% of long-term unemployment should participate by 2010 in an active measure in the form of training, retraining, work practice, or other employability measure, with the aim of achieving the average of the three most advanced Member States;
- that jobseekers throughout the EU are able to consult all job vacancies advertised through Member States' employment services;
- an increase by five years, at EU level, of the effective average exit age from the labour market by 2010 (compared to 59.9 in 2001);
- the provision of childcare by 2010 to at least 90% of children between three years old and the mandatory school age and at least 33% of children under three years of age;
- an EU average rate of no more than 10% early school leavers;
- at least 85% of 22-year-olds in the EU should have completed upper secondary education by 2010;
- that the EU average level of participation in lifelong learning should be at least 12.5% of the adult working-age population (25–64 age group).

reduction' in each Member State in the unemployment gaps between non-EU and EU nationals, according to national targets).[64] The 2003 guidelines also reduced the number of indicators from 99 in 2002 (35 key indicators and 64 context indicators) to 64 (39 key indicators and 25 context indicators).

The other striking feature of the 2003 employment guidelines was the greater emphasis they placed on 'good governance and partnership' in employment policies. A wide range of actors are to be involved: parliamentary bodies, both at European, national and sub-national level, the Social Partners at national and European level, and other relevant actors, including 'operational services' which should 'deliver the employment policies in an efficient and effective way'. Member States are required to ensure transparency and cost-effectiveness in spending to implement the employment guidelines, while complying with the need for sound public finances in line with the broad economic policy guidelines. Reference is also expressly made to the potential contribution of the Community structural funds, especially the European Social

---

[64] For examples of what the targets could have looked like, see Commission's Communication 'The future of the European Employment Strategy (EES) "A strategy for full employment and better jobs for all" ' (COM(2003) 6, annex).

Fund, to support the delivery of policies and to strengthen the institutional capacity in the field of employment.

2.4. The 2004 and 2005 Guidelines

Because the 2003 employment guidelines were intended to form part of a three-year policy cycle, they were applied without alteration during 2004.[65] However, following the intervention of the European Employment Taskforce, headed by Wim Kok, which carried out a detailed examination of employment-related policy challenges during 2003,[66] the emphasis for 2004 was on more forceful recommendations and a more effective peer review, rather than more changes to the guidelines.[67]

Yet, despite the desire to apply the 2003 guidelines for three years, the relaunch of the Lisbon strategy in 2005 (considered below) precipitated yet another overhaul of the guidelines. This followed a second report by Wim Kok on how to revitalize the Lisbon strategy.[68] As Table 3.5 (page 163 below) shows, the 2005 guidelines (confirmed in 2006) are also based around three overarching objectives which mirror those in the 2003 guidelines. From this point of view, the new guidelines read like a softer version of the original 1998 guidelines.

2.5. Assessment

The tension, long recognized, between deregulation as a means of achieving the flexibility necessary to help fight against unemployment, and the need for social rights[69] can be seen very clearly in the Luxembourg strategy. The deregulatory aspects of the Employment Strategy can most obviously be seen in the entrepreneurship pillar and in aspects of the employability and adaptability pillars. On the other hand, the emphasis on social rights can be found in the equal opportunities pillar as well as in social policy more generally. The Treaty of Amsterdam does not itself contain an obviously deregulatory agenda. Not only did the Treaty incorporate the SPA into the new Social Title in the EC Treaty, but Article 2 talks of 'a high level of employment *and* social protection' (emphasis added) and 'equality between men and women', as well as 'sustainable and non-inflationary growth, a high degree of competitiveness and convergence of economic performance'.

---

[65] Council Dec. 2004/740/EC (OJ [2004] L326/45).

[66] *Jobs, Jobs, Jobs. Creating More Employment in Europe*, November 2003.

[67] Council Dec. 2004/740/EC (OJ [2004] L326/45), second preambular para.

[68] Kok, *Facing the Challenge: The Lisbon Strategy for Growth and Employment. Report from the High Level Group chaired by Wim Kok* (OPEC, Luxembourg, 2004). See also Presidency Conclusions, Brussels, 25–26 March 2004, para. 36.

[69] See also Sciarra, 'The "Making" of EU Labour Law and the "Future" of Labour Lawyers' in Barnard *et al.* (eds), *The Future of Labour Law: Liber Amicorum Sir Bob Hepple QC* (Hart Publishing, Oxford, 2004).

Read together, the Treaty of Amsterdam and the Luxembourg strategy demonstrate the Community's attempts to find a 'third way' between the 'Anglo-Saxon' model of deregulation, low unemployment and fewer welfare benefits, and the European model of job protection, high unemployment, and generous welfare provision. This third way was to create a new European employment model which would balance social protection, competitiveness, and welfare provision with sound finance.[70] The aim is to achieve competitiveness through creating highly productive workplaces, rather than combating unemployment through the creation of low-paid, low-productivity 'entry jobs'.[71] Thus, the new emphasis is on flexibility for firms combined with security for workers.

'Flexicurity' is the theme found in the Commission's Green Paper, *Partnership for a New Organisation of Work*,[72] the Commission's Communications, *Modernising and Improving Social Protection in the European Union*[73] and *Modernising the Organisation of Work*,[74] and the 1998 Employment Guidelines under the Adaptability Pillar. Attempts to reconcile flexibility with security lie in an 'improved organisation of work' which, although unable 'of itself to solve the unemployment problem', may nevertheless 'make a valuable contribution, first, to the competitiveness of European firms, and secondly, to the improvement of the quality of working life and the employability of the workforce'.[75] More specifically, 'the flexible firm could offer a sound basis for fundamental organisational renewal built on high skill, high productivity, high quality, good environmental management—and good wages'.[76]

The flexibility envisaged by the Community can take a variety of forms:[77] *numerical* flexibility, allowing the firm to modulate the numbers employed; *working time* flexibility which permits the firm to raise or lower hours through overtime or through variations to normal hours; *financial* flexibility which links remuneration directly to output; and *functional* flexibility which refers to the multi-skilling of workers permitting them to move between tasks and adapt their working practices to new technical or organizational requirements. Thus, workers themselves need to become more flexible but this will only be achieved if they feel secure in their jobs. As the Commission says in its Communication:

---

[70] Pierson, Forster and Jones, 'The Politics of Europe: (Un)employment Ambivalence' (1997) 1 *Industrial Relations Journal European Annual Review* 5, 15. See also Kenner, 'The EC Employment Title and the "Third Way": Making Soft Law Work' (1999) 15 *IJCLLIR*. 33.

[71] Deakin and Reed, above, n. 40.   [72] COM(97) 127 final.

[73] COM(97) 102 final. See also Commission Communication: A Concerted Action for Modernising Social Protection COM(99) 347 and Council Conclusions on the strengthening of cooperation for modernizing and improving social protection (OJ [2000] C8/7).

[74] COM(98) 592.   [75] Ibid., para. 4.   [76] Ibid., para. 24.

[77] See Deakin and Reed, above, n. 40. More generally, see the Supiot report, *Beyond Employment: Changes in Work and the Future of Labour Law in Europe* (OUP, Oxford, 2001) Ch. 2.

Flexibility internal to the enterprise not only promotes corporate productivity but also the quality of working life ... Security for workers can also give benefits to the enterprise in the form of a more stable, versatile and motivated workforce.[78]

Thus, the EU is beginning to see social policy as an input into the productive process[79] and not a burden on it.[80] As the Commission said in its White Paper on Social Policy 'the pursuit of high social standards should not be seen as a cost but also as a key element in the competitive formula';[81] and in the Medium Term Social Action Programme it talks of encouraging 'high labour standards as part of competitive Europe'.[82] This is the virtuous circle of 'flexicurity': workers receive more employment protection but in return they are prepared to be more adaptable and this leads to greater productivity. However, some commentators are sceptical of claims that there is a genuine *quid pro quo*. For example, Ball, writing about the original EES guidelines, notes that the main thrust of the employability pillar is to place an onus on individuals to enhance their own value by learning new and higher skills, without any correlative obligation on employers to offer security of employment.[83]

It could therefore be argued that, through the EES, the EU is developing a new type of social citizenship, a citizenship which is no longer based merely on an eclectic range of social rights and social security[84] but one which requires an active involvement in the market.[85] For individuals—all individuals, young and old—this mean equipping themselves with the necessary skills to make themselves more employable and then going out to find a job or moving between jobs as and when the need so arises. Yet while having a job is seen as an important means for integrating the socially excluded, the focus on employment risks creating another group of the social excluded—those who cannot work or, for family reasons, do not wish to work.

---

[78] COM(98) 592, 3.

[79] See Deakin and Wilkinson, 'Rights vs Efficiency: the Economic Case for Transnational Labour Standards' (1994) 23 *ILJ*. 289, 295–6. See the Commission Communication, 'Modernising and Improving Social Protection in the EU' COM(97) 102 and the follow-up 'A Concerted Strategy for Modernising Social Protection' COM(99) 347.

[80] See e.g. the views of Addison and Siebert, 'The Social Charter: Whatever Next?' (1992) 30 *BJIR*. 495.

[81] COM(94) 333, introduction, para. 5. This is wholly consistent with the 'essential objective' expressed in the Preamble to the EC Treaty of 'the constant improvement of the living and working conditions of their peoples'.

[82] Social Europe 1/95, 9, 18, 19. See also now the UK government's *Fairness at Work* White Paper, Cm. 3968 (HMSO, London, 1998).

[83] Ball, above, n. 19, 369.

[84] Cf. the Supiot report, *Beyond Employment: Changes in Work and the Future of Labour Law in Europe* (OUP, Oxford, 2001) 228.

[85] The language of 'active citizenship' is used by the Commission in its Communication in European policies concerning youth: COM(2005) 206, 8.

D. ECONOMIC AND MONETARY UNION (EMU)

The Vienna European Council in December 1998 proclaimed the birth of the euro to be 'a milestone in the process of European integration. The single currency will strengthen Europe's capacity to foster employment growth and stability'.[86] It argued that the creation of the single currency reinforced the need for economic policy co-ordination which has led to the development of instruments to co-ordinate macroeconomic policies in order to maintain sustainable growth and productivity, which in turn translates to the maintenance of higher levels of employment, instruments to improve the effectiveness of national employment policies and instruments to accelerate reform in product, service and capital markets.[87] These sentiments were repeated in the Ecofin Council's 2005 Report on improving the implementation of the Stability and Growth Pact: 'it contributes to achieving macroeconomic stability in the EU and plays a key role in securing low inflation and low interest rates, which are essential contributions for delivering sustainable economic growth and job creation'.[88]

The procedures for the implementation of EMU derive initially from the convergence criteria laid down in the Maastricht Treaty.[89] These require the Member States participating in the third stage of EMU (full monetary union) to maintain retail price inflation within certain limits, restrict national debt to 60 per cent of gross domestic product (GDP), and confine budget deficits to no more than 3 per cent of GDP. The provisions governing excessive levels of national debt and excessive budget deficits (now contained in Article 104 of the EC Treaty and Protocol 5 on the Excessive Deficit procedure)[90] continue beyond the launch of EMU, according to the Stability and Growth Pact[91] which set up a monitoring and reporting process[92] which can (but has not to date[93]) result in sanctions being applied to a Member State. These include requiring the Member State to make a non-interest-bearing deposit 'of an appropriate size' with the Community until the budget deficit in question has been cleared, and, in the last resort, the levying of a fine on the Member State.[94]

In addition, Article 99(2) EC allows the Council to issue 'broad economic

---

[86] Para. 7. See also Cologne European Council, 4 June 1999, para. 5.   [87] Para. 9.

[88] Annex I of the Presidency Conclusions of the Brussels European Council 22 and 23 March 2005 which endorsed Ecofin's report.

[89] See generally, Deakin and Reed, above, n. 40.

[90] See also Co. Reg. 3605/93 on the application of the Protocol on the excessive deficit procedure annexed to the Treaty establishing the European Community (OJ [1993] L332/7).

[91] Considered below at n. 99.

[92] This process still remains separate, even under the Lisbon relaunch: SEC (2005) 193, 3.

[93] Buti and Pench, 'Why do large countries flout the Stability Pact? And what can be done about it?' (2004) 42 JCMS. 1025

[94] Art. 104(11) and Reg. 1467/97, Arts. 12 and 13.

policy guidelines' (BEPGs) for the conduct of economic policy by the Member States, since economic policies are now matters of 'common concern' for the Member States.[95] Once drafted, these guidelines are considered by the European Council[96] and then adopted by the Council in the form of a Recommendation.[97] Member States must report to the Commission on developments in the field of economic policy; the Commission then reports to the Council. The Council monitors economic developments in the States and the Community. It also ensures the consistency of the economic policies with the broad economic guidelines.[98] If this 'multilateral surveillance procedure' reveals that the economic policies of a Member State are not consistent with the broad economic guidelines or 'risk jeopardising the attainment of the proper functioning of economic and monetary union', the Council has the power, under Article 99(4) acting on a qualified majority on the basis of a recommendation from the Commission, to make a recommendation to the Member State concerned.

These Treaty-based procedures are supplemented by the Stability and Growth Pact,[99] agreed by the Member States at the Amsterdam European Council, which is contained in two Regulations[100] and a Council Resolution.[101] Regulation 1466/97 on the strengthening of the surveillance of the budgetary procedures and the surveillance and co-ordination of economic policies focuses on prevention.[102] It aims to prevent budget deficits going above the 3 per cent reference value and it also puts in place an 'early warning system' designed to alert the Council to the possibility that a Member State participating in the third stage of EMU may be running up an excessive deficit. By contrast, Regulation 1467/97 on speeding up and clarifying the implementation of the excessive deficit procedure[103] serves a dissuasive or corrective function. It concerns the situation where, in the event of the 3 per cent reference value being breached, Member States must take immediate corrective action. If necessary, the Regulation allows for sanctions to be imposed.[104] In the light of the Commission's successful challenge to Ecofin's decision to suspend the excessive deficit procedure against France and Germany, even though their net borrowing exceeded 4 per cent of GDP, the SGP was reformed to provide

---

[95] Art. 99(1), first para.
[96] Art. 99(2), second para.   [97] Art. 99(2), third para.   [98] Art. 99(3).
[99] See generally, Hahn, 'The Stability Pact for European Monetary Union' (1998) 35 *CMLRev.* 77.
[100] Council Regulation 1466/97 (OJ [1997] L209/1) and Council Regulation 1467/97 (OJ [1997] L209/7).
[101] Resolution 97/C236/01 (OJ [1997] C236/1).
[102] This is now accompanied by the *Code of Conduct on the Content and Format of the Stability and Convergence Programmes*, endorsed by the Ecofin Council on 11 October 2005. It incorporates the essential elements of Co. Reg. 1466/97 into guidelines to assist the Member States in drawing up their programmes. It also aims at facilitating the examination of the programmes by the Commission, the Economic and Financial Committee, and the Council.
[103] [1997] OJ L209/6.   [104] Art. 12.

greater flexibility or rather, as the Ecofin Council report of 20 March 2005 put it, 'effectiveness', based on a greater emphasis on economic developments and an increased focus on safeguarding the sustainability of public finances.[105] This led to the two Regulations being amended[106] and the inclusion of the Ecofin report itself in the SGP.[107]

The Regulations are supplemented by a Council *Resolution* on the Stability and Growth Pact.[108] This contains a political commitment by all the parties involved in the SGP (the Member States, the Commission, and the Council) to the 'strict and timely'[109] implementation of the budget surveillance process,[110] and that effective peer pressure is exerted on a Member State failing to live up to its commitments. The Resolution is significant for employment policy, in that it 'underlines the importance of safeguarding sound government finances as a means to strengthening the conditions for price stability and for strong sustainable growth conducive to employment creation'.[111] In other words, creating a stable economic and monetary base and thus a climate of low inflation and interest rates will foster an attractive and sustainable environment suitable for the maintenance of existing jobs and the creation of new jobs. However, various commentators have noted that the rules establishing the SGP would seem to privilege 'stability' over 'growth'—certainly to the extent that Member States can no longer spend their way into employment creation.[112]

This dilemma is heightened further by the Resolution on Growth and Employment[113] issued alongside the Resolution on the Stability and Growth Pact. This states:

it should be a priority aim to develop a skilled, trained and adaptable workforce and to make labour markets responsive to economic change. Structural reforms need to be comprehensive in scope, as opposed to limited or occasional measures, so as to address in a coherent manner the complex issue of incentives in creating and taking up a job.[114]

It also calls for more 'employment-friendly' tax and social protection systems aimed at 'improving the functioning of the labour market'.[115] Thus labour markets have got to be made more competitive and workers need to be

---

[105] Presidency Conclusions, Brussels European Council, 22 and 23 March 2005, Annex II 'Improving the Implementation of the Stability and Growth Pact'.

[106] Reg. 1466/97 was amended by Co. Reg. 1055/2005 (OJ [2005] L174/1); Reg. 1467/97 was amended by Co. Reg. 1056/2005 (OJ [2005] L174/5). For a full discussion of the amendments, see Louis, 'The Review of the Stability and Growth Pact' (2006) 43 *CMLRev.* 85.

[107] See the second recital in the Preamble to Reg. 1055/2005 and the Conclusions of the Brussels European Council 22–23 March 2005, para. 3.

[108] Resolution 97/C 236/01 (OJ [1997] C236/1). This was not changed by the 2005 revisions.

[109] Para. I.

[110] http://europa.eu.int/comm/economy_finance/about/activities/sgp/sgp_en.htm

[111] Para. I.   [112] See e.g. Ashiagbor, above, n. 51, 261.

[113] Resolution 97/C 236/02 (OJ [1997] C236/3).

[114] Ibid., para. 1.   [115] Ibid., para. 4.

more skilled. But herein lies the rub: while the Resolution on Growth and Employment (and the Employment Guidelines) call for active labour market measures, the constraints on public expenditure envisaged by the Stability and Growth Pact may jeopardize the attainment of these objectives.[116] While the BEPG response to this is to restructure public expenditure to support investment in tangible and intangible capital,[117] this is easier said than done when national budgets risk breaching the SGP limits.[118] In the rhetoric, economic and social policies are described as 'mutually reinforcing';[119] in practice many see employment policy as subordinate to macroeconomic policy,[120] with EMU dictating a neo-liberal agenda based on 'flexibilisation of the labour market, in particular flexibility in wage setting systems and downward wage flexibility' to make the labour market economically responsive and more competitive, combined with a very strict fiscal policy, restrictions on public expenditure and 'modernisation' of social protection systems.[121]

The potential tension between economic and social policy objectives can be seen in the BEPGs themselves. For example, the 1997 BEPGs,[122] agreed shortly after the Amsterdam Treaty was concluded, proposed that 'real wage developments should be below the increase in productivity in order to strengthen the profitability of employment-creating investment',[123] and that wages need to 'better take into account differences [in] qualification and regions'.[124] This clearly has immediate and tangible implications for workers.

In order to address this tension, successive European Councils have called for a 'greater synergy'[125] between the BEPGs and the Employment Guidelines (EGs). The so-called 'European Employment Pact', prepared by the German Presidency and presented to the Cologne Council in June 1999,[126] was intended to help realize this by improving the interaction between fiscal, wage and monetary policies. The Pact's first limb comprised the effective implementation of the employment strategy (in essence the Luxembourg process). The second limb, which had been developed at the Cardiff Summit in December 1998, concerned microeconomic reform. It involved comprehensive structural reform and modernization to improve the innovative capacity and efficiency of the labour market and the markets in goods, services, and capital. The third limb, added at the Cologne European Council, concerned macroeconomic dialogue between the ECB, the Social Partners, the Council, and the Commission aimed at preserving non-inflationary growth. Specifically,

---

[116] See further Ball, above n. 19, 361–2.　　　[117] See e.g. BEPGs 2000 OJ [2000] L210/1.
[118] See also the threat posed to the realization of employment policies by EC competition law: Ball, above n. 19, 363–6.
[119] Resolution 97/C236/02 (OJ [1997] C236/3), para. 1.　　　[120] Ball, above, n.19.
[121] Ashiagbor, above, n. 51, 263.
[122] Council Recommendation 97/479/EC ([1997] OJ L 209/12).
[123] Para. 2, third indent.　　　[124] Para. 6(i).　　　[125] COM(99) 127, 3.
[126] Cologne European Council Presidency Conclusions, 3 and 4 June 1999, para. 7.

Cologne was intended to focus attention on the co-ordination of economic policy and to improve the interaction between fiscal policy, monetary policy and wage developments. Minimum social standards have a role, but only to the extent that they can maintain the conditions of economic growth and competitiveness.[127] A more radical realignment of the BEPGs and the EGs occurred in 2005 when they were incorporated into a single set of 'integrated guidelines'. This development is considered below (see Table 3.4 on p. 161).

The macroeconomic dialogue under the Cologne process and the need for macroeconomic policies to promote stability while stimulating growth and employment also lay at the heart of the Lisbon strategy. It is this strategy which forms the core of the Union's economic and social agenda today.[128]

E. THE LISBON STRATEGY

1. Introduction

Europe is caught between a rock and a hard place.[129] On the one hand it is competing with the tiger economies in Asia. With wages a fraction of those in Europe, China and India compete in the low skill end of the market and in the high value added goods market. Meanwhile, the US dominates high-tech manufacturing. The EU, with its ageing population, high level of welfare spending and relatively low employment rate, must carve out a role for itself. Since competing with China and the others in terms of wages and social conditions is not an option, the EU has to take on the US and Japan for the top end of the market, equipping itself to compete in a knowledge-based economy. This was the idea behind the Lisbon strategy. On 23–24 March 2000 the European Council held a special meeting in Lisbon to agree a 'new strategic goal' for the Union in order to 'strengthen employment, economic reform and social cohesion as part of a knowledge-based economy'.[130] This strategic goal was for the Union to become 'the most competitive and dynamic knowledge based economy in the world, capable of sustainable economic growth with more and better jobs and greater social cohesion'.[131] The section which follows will consider the aim of the strategy, the means used to pursue it, the actors involved and the strategy's relaunch in 2005.

---

[127] Ashiagbor, above, n. 51, 271, and Annex I, Resolution of the European Council on the European Employment Pact 11.

[128] Lisbon Presidency Conclusions, 23 and 24 March 2000, paras. 22–3.

[129] See *Facing the Challenge: The Lisbon Strategy for Growth and Employment. Report from the High Level group chaired by Wim Kok* (November 2004) 12.

[130] Lisbon Presidency Conclusions, 23 and 24 March 2000.   [131] Para. 5.

2. The Strategy

2.1. Overview of the Strategy

The heads of state agreed that achieving the Lisbon goal required an overall strategy aimed at:

* preparing the transition to a knowledge-based economy and society by better policies for the information society and R&D, as well as stepping up the process of structural reform for competitiveness and innovation and by completing the internal market;
* modernizing the European social model, investing in people, and combating social exclusion;
* sustaining the healthy economic outlook and favourable growth prospects by applying an appropriate macroeconomic policy mix.[132]

As originally conceived, Lisbon was about harnessing the internal market strategy, the broad economic policy guidelines and the employment guidelines[133] to enable the Union to regain 'the conditions for *full employment*', not just a high level of employment as envisaged by Article 2 of the EC Treaty. Subsequently, the 2001 Göteborg European Council incorporated the environment as a further pillar to the strategy. Today the EU talks of the three dimensions of the Lisbon strategy: economic, social and environmental.[134] For our purposes we shall focus primarily on the social pillar of the Lisbon strategy, where the emphasis is on modernizing the European social model.

2.2. Modernizing the European Social Model

(a) The European Social Model

The Lisbon strategy requires the 'European social model' to be modernized. But what is meant by the 'European social model'?[135] Does it mean the social models of the individual Member States or the European Union's own social model? This question is never clearly answered and both understandings can be detected in the pronouncements by the EU's institutions on this matter. The Commission, in its Social Policy Agenda, says that a key feature of the European social model is the combination of 'good social conditions with high productivity and high quality goods and services'.[136] The Nice Council's Social Policy Agenda added social welfare into this pot. It said:[137]

The European social model, characterised in particular by systems that offer a high

---

[132] Ibid.   [133] Brussels Presidency Conclusions, 20 and 21 March 2003, para. 17.
[134] Luxembourg Presidency Conclusions, 22 and 23 March 2005, para. 5.
[135] This issue is considered in more detail in Ch. 1.
[136] COM(2000) 379, 7.   [137] Para. 10.

level of social protection, by the importance of the social dialogue and by services of general interest covering activities vital for social cohesion, is today based, beyond the diversity of the Member States' social systems, on a common core of values.

These pronouncements have tended to define the EU's social model in terms of *national* social models but the Nice Council also considered the *EU* dimension:[138]

The European social model has developed over the last forty years through a substantial Community acquis . . . It now includes essential texts in numerous areas: free movement of workers, gender equality at work, health and safety of workers, working and employment conditions and, more recently, the fight against all forms of discrimination.

It also includes the agreements between the Social Partners in the law-making process, the Luxembourg EES and the Open Method of Co-ordination on the subject of social exclusion and greater cooperation in the field of social protection. Thus the 'European social model' is somewhat amorphous and ill defined. Nevertheless, it needs to be modernized.

(b) Its Modernization

How, then, is this modernization to occur? According to the Lisbon Conclusions, it will come about by 'investing in people and building an active welfare state.'[139] Inspiration is drawn from the very successful Nordic model,[140] which combines open markets and job flexibility with all the support employers need to restructure their workforce to meet changing demands. The Nordic approach is endorsed by strong trade unions because of the tripartite pact between employers, trade unions and the state, and a generous system of social welfare to cushion the effect of change. High levels of public expenditure also produce highly educated school leavers and graduates and a good health service.[141] This has led to steady economic growth for over 50 years, low levels of inflation and relatively low levels of unemployment (between 5 and 6 per cent).

The Lisbon strategy therefore identifies four elements to this process of modernization:

* education and training
* more and better jobs
* modernizing social protection
* promoting social inclusion

---

[138] Para. 12.   [139] Para. 24.   [140] See further Ch. 2.

[141] Toynbee, 'The most successful society the world has ever known: The Nordic model mixes welfare and economic success, but Sweden's Social Democrats are at a risk from a loss of confidence', *The Guardian*, 25 October 2005, 33; Watt, 'Europe's leaders look north, but has Sweden really got the best of both worlds? The next EU summit will highlight the Nordic model of steady growth and social protection as a solution to economic slumber', *The Guardian*, 5 January 2006, 20. Cf. Synon 'Copying the Swedes is the road to ruin', *Daily Mail*, 3 March 2006, 14.

In respect of modernizing social protection, the Council does not intend to dismantle social welfare systems which must 'underpin the transformation to the knowledge based economy'. Instead, the emphasis is on ensuring that 'work pays' (i.e. to ensure that social benefits do no discourage employment) and in maintaining the long-term sustainability of benefits in the face of an ageing population.[142] However, the targets are limited (strengthening co-operation between Member States by exchanging experiences and best practice and mandating the High Level Working Party on Social Protection (now the Social Protection Committee—see below)[143] to prepare a study on the future evolution of social protection, especially concerning pensions.[144]

More concrete action is mandated in respect of promoting social inclusion for people living below the poverty line. The Council expressly envisages that OMC is to be used,[145] with objectives defined to evaluate the impact of social policies applied in Member States and indicators defined as common references, in the fight against social exclusion and the eradication of poverty.[146] A Social Protection Committee was set up[147] to serve as a vehicle for exchanges of information, experience and good practice between the Commission and the Member States[148] and to work on four main issues: to make work pay and provide secure income, to make pensions safe and pension systems sustainable, to promote social inclusion and to ensure high quality and sustainable health care.[149] It has contributed actively to the application of OMC in the areas of social inclusion and pensions.

However, as the Council notes, the best safeguard against social exclusion is a job and in order to find work, efforts need to be made to improve skills. Therefore, the first two elements of the process of the modernization of the European social model (education and training and more and better jobs) are crucial and it is these two elements that we shall focus on.

(c) Education and Training

The Lisbon European Council recognized that '[p]eople are Europe's main asset'[150] and that 'Europe's education and training systems need to adapt both to the demands of the knowledge society and to the need for an improved level and quality of employment'.[151] With this aim in mind, it laid down a number of targets to be achieved by the Member States, including halving the number of 18–24-year-olds with only lower-secondary level education who are not in

---

[142] Para. 31.
[143] Co. Dec. 2004/689/EC (OJ [2004] L314/8).   [144] Ibid.   [145] Para. 32.
[146] Feira European Council Conclusions, 19/20 July 2000, para. 35.
[147] Council Dec. 2000/436 (OJ [2000] L172/26). The Treaty of Nice introduced a new legal basis into the EC Treaty (Art. 144) providing for the establishment of a Social Protection Committee. Dec. 2004/689/EC (OJ [2005] L314/8) essentially provided for the re-establishment of the Committee in line with the new legal basis.
[148] Art. 1(2).   [149] Fourth preambular para. This is considered further in Ch. 12.
[150] Para. 24.   [151] Para. 25.

further education, and linking all schools and training centres to the internet which should be accessible to all.[152] It also proposed a common European format for curricula vitae, to be used on a voluntary basis to facilitate mobility by helping the assessment of knowledge acquired.

The need for better education and training has long been a favourite theme for the Commission. For example, in its White Paper on Growth, Competitiveness and Employment 1993,[153] the Commission called for a significant increase in investment in human capital and greater and more effective efforts in vocational training. This implied increasing skill levels, especially in the new technologies, and promoting lifelong learning.[154] In its subsequent action plan the European Council identified seven areas for particular attention by the Member States, including improving education and training systems, especially continuing training; and specific measures concerning young people without adequate training. The European Social Fund (see below) was to be used to help implement a guarantee to provide access to recognized education or training for all young people under 18.

Maastricht's new Chapter on Education, Vocational Training and Youth confirmed the Community's growing competence in this field.[155] A new DG was established, DG XXII (now DG Education and Culture), to take responsibility for this area. Prior to this, the development of a Community education and vocational training strategy[156] was hampered as a result of an insecure legal basis provided by the original EC Treaty.[157] Nevertheless, the Community's competence for education is still heavily circumscribed by the principle of subsidiarity and respect for cultural and linguistic diversity.[158] Article 150 provides that the 'Community shall implement a vocational training policy which shall support and supplement the action of the Member States, while fully respecting the action of the Member States for the content and origination of vocational training'.[159] Once again the

---

[152] Para. 26.

[153] Bull. Supp. 6/93, endorsed at the Brussels European Council of December 1993.

[154] See also the Commission's White Paper on Education and Training COM(95) 590 and the Green Paper on Innovation COM(95) 688 final.

[155] Arts. 126–127 (new Arts. 149–150) of the EC Treaty. See Shaw, 'From the Margins to the Centre': Education and Training Law and Policy', in Craig and De Búrca (eds), *The Evolution of EU Law* (OUP, Oxford, 1999).

[156] See generally, Commission, *Education and Training in the European Community: Guidelines for the Medium Term* COM(91) 397.

[157] The original Art. 128 EEC empowered the Council of Ministers only to 'lay down general principles for implementing a common vocational training policy capable of contributing to the harmonious development both of the national economies and the common market'. These principles were elaborated by Council Decision 63/266 (OJ SE [1963] 64/25).

[158] Art. 149(1).

[159] See Barnard, 'The Maastricht Agreement and Education: One Step Forward and Two Steps Back?' (1992) 4 *Education and the Law* 123; Johnson, 'From Vocational Training to Education: the Development of a No-frontiers Education Policy for Europe' (1999) 11 *Education and the Law* 199; M. Dougan, 'Fees, Grants, Loans and Dole Cheques: Who Covers the Costs of Migrant Education within the EU' (2005) 42 *CMLRev.* 943.

principle of subsidiarity is emphasized, with the Community playing only a supportive role. The Community does have the 'carrot' of funding, possibly leading to some convergence in training policy, but harmonization is expressly excluded.

The developments in the field of training and employment once again serve to highlight the shift in emphasis from the enactment of employment *law* (the body of rules directly concerned with the employment relationship) to the creation of employment *policy* (measures directly concerned with the creation and maintenance of employment, including measures concerned with training).[160] As Freedland observes, vocational training policy seems to lie within a relatively highly consensual area of convergence between economic policy and social policy (particularly if dressed up as education policy):[161] it has always been potentially difficult to deny the generally ameliorative nature of vocational training policy. Therefore vocational training has seemed a good area for Community development and the strengthening of the power base of the Community institutions, and of the Commission in particular. On the other hand, while it may seem overridingly important to ensure that vocational training is provided for all groups in society, especially to the young, this may result in an under-awareness of, or under-concern with, the potential of vocational training arrangements to erode labour standards. Freedland therefore argues that there is a danger that an educational policy in favour of ever greater flexibility and adaptability in vocational training might be conducive to an over-ready endorsement of all forms and types of flexibility as a matter of employment policy.

(d) More and Better Jobs

More Jobs

The Lisbon strategy looked to the Luxembourg process, as amended by the mid-term review,[162] to give substance to the goal of 'more and better jobs'. However, it recognized that the Luxembourg process needed to be better targeted (see Table 3.2 above), focusing on four issues:

• improving employability and reducing the skills gap;
• giving a higher priority to lifelong learning, with progress towards the goals needing to be benchmarked;
• increasing employment in services;
• furthering all aspects of equal opportunities, including reducing occu-

---

[160] See Freedland, 'Employment Policy', in Davies, Lyon-Caen, Sciarra and Simitis (eds), *European Community Labour Law: Principles and Perspectives. Liber Amicorum Lord Wedderburn of Charlton* (Clarendon, Oxford, 1996) 97.

[161] Freedland, 'Vocational Training in EC Law and Policy—Education, Employment or Welfare' (1996) 25 *ILJ*. 110, 118–19.

[162] See Barcelona European Council, 15–16 March 2002, para. 30.

pational segregation, making it easier to reconcile work and family life, in particular by setting a new benchmark for improved childcare provision.[163]

The heads of state then agreed at Lisbon to set employment rate targets for what would amount to 'full employment', something they had not managed at Luxembourg.[164] The targets were ambitious: of 'raising the employment rate from an average of 61% today to as close as possible to 70% by 2010 and to increase the number of women in employment from an average of 51% today to more than 60% by 2010'.[165] An additional target was added by the Stockholm European Council, namely increasing the average EU employment rate among older men and women (55–64) to 50 per cent by 2010.[166] These targets made for convenient round numbers (70 per cent/ 60 per cent/ 50 per cent) but have proved overoptimistic.

Better Jobs

While the Lisbon strategy focused on 'more' jobs, the question of 'better' jobs was left to be fleshed out by the Commission in its Social Policy Agenda adopted in June 2000. It said that 'growth is not an end in itself but essentially a means of achieving a better standard of living for all. Social policy underpins economic policy and employment has not only economic but also a social value'.[167] Against this backcloth, said the Commission, is the 'promotion of quality as the driving force for a thriving economy . . . quality of work, quality in industrial relations and quality of social policy'.[168] Quality of *work* includes better jobs and more ways of combining working life with personal life. It is based on 'high skills, fair labour standards and decent levels of occupational health and safety'.[169] Quality of *social policy* implies a high level of social protection, good social services, real opportunities for all and the guarantee of fundamental and social rights.[170] Quality of *industrial relations* is determined by the capacity to build consensus on both diagnosis and ways and means of taking forward the adaptation and modernisation agenda.[171] The heads of state meeting at Nice in December 2000 agreed that '[q]uality of training, quality in work, quality of industrial relations and quality of social policy as a whole are essential factors if the European Union is to achieve the goals it has set itself regarding competitiveness and full employment'.[172] Thus,

---

[163] Lisbon European Council, para. 29.

[164] Cf. Commission Communication, 'Proposal for Guidelines for member States Employment Policies 1998', COM(97) 497, Section I where the Commission proposed a target of increasing the employment rate from 60.4% to 65% thereby creating at least 12 million new jobs.

[165] Para. 30. Intermediate targets were also set: of 67% overall and 57% for women: Stockholm European Council, 23 and 24 March 2001, para. 9.

[166] Stockholm European Council, 23 and 24 March 2001, para. 9.

[167] COM(2000) 379, 13.   [168] Ibid.   [169] Ibid.   [170] Ibid.

[171] COM(2000) 379, 14.

[172] European Council's Social Policy Agenda, Annex I to the Nice Presidency Conclusions, para. 26.

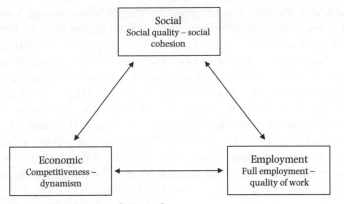

Figure 3.2 The Social Policy Agenda Triangle
Source: COM(2000) 379, 6 and COM(2001) 313, 17

quality is seen as a 'key element' linking competitiveness and social cohesion which the Commission depicts in a diagram illustrating the virtuous circle linking economic, social and employment policies in a mutually reinforcing manner (see Figure 3.2).

At the Council's request,[173] the Commission issued a Communication entitled 'Employment and Social Policies: a Framework for investing in quality'[174] defining quality in work broadly, taking into account:[175]

- the objective characteristics related to employment, both the wider work environment (eg working conditions, training, career prospects, health insurance coverage, etc) and specific job characteristics (eg pay, hours of work, skill requirements, job content);
- worker characteristics—the characteristics the employee brings to the job;
- the match between worker characteristics and job requirements; and
- the subjective evaluation (job satisfaction) of these characteristics by the individual worker.

The Commission then applied OMC methodology (see below) to the question of quality, focusing on 10 main elements of quality within two broad dimensions (1) the characteristics of the job itself (objective and intrinsic characteristics, including: job satisfaction, remuneration, non-pay rewards, working

[173] See both the Nice European Council's Conclusions under the heading 'More and better Jobs, point (c) and the Stockholm European Council's conclusions, para. 26.
[174] COM(2001) 313.
[175] See also the definition of quality as one of the three overarching and interrelated objectives in the 2003 Employment Guidelines Co. Dec. 2005/601/EC (OJ [2005] L205/28): 'Quality is a multi-dimensional concept addressing both job characteristics and the wider labour market. It encompasses intrinsic quality at work, skills, lifelong learning and career development, gender equality, health and safety at work, flexibility and security, inclusion and access to the labour market, work organisations and work-life balance, social dialogue and worker involvement, diversity and non-discrimination, and overall work performance'.

time, skills and training and prospects for career advancement, job content, match between jobs characteristics and worker characteristics); and (2) the work and the wider labour market context (gender equality, health and safety, flexibility and security, access to jobs, work/life balance, social dialogue and worker involvement, diversity and non-discrimination). The Commission then identified 10 dimensions of job quality[176] and the Employment Committee agreed a list of indicators on quality of work under the 10 dimensions. Thus, under gender equality the key indicator concerned the ratio of women's hourly earnings index to men's for paid employees at work; for health and safety it was the evolution of the incidence rate, defined as the number of accidents at work per 100,000 persons in employment. The Commission's efforts to improve quality were reviewed in 2003.[177]

3. The Means

3.1. Introduction

According to the Presidency Conclusions, implementing the Lisbon strategy was to be achieved in part by improving the existing processes (i.e. through the Broad Economic Policy Guidelines together with the Luxembourg, Cardiff and Cologne processes, now synchronized in terms of calendars)[178] and in part through the 'new' approach, the so-called Open Method of Co-ordination[179] (OMC) together with corporate social responsibility (CSR). In its social policy Agenda, the Commission went further and emphasized that OMC was just one of a number of means by which the strategy would be realized,[180] a view endorsed by the Nice European Council.[181] The other methods were: legislation, adopted via the legislative or collective routes,[182] developing or adapting standards, social dialogue and the structural funds, especially the European Social Funds. Thus, using Daintith's distinction,[183] the Commission envisages a mix of not only government by *imperium* (attaining objectives by commands—both hard and soft—backed by sanctions) and *dominium* (attaining

---

[176] (1) Intrinsic job quality, (2) Skills, lifelong learning and career development, (3) gender equality, (4) health and safety at work, (5) flexibility and security, (6) inclusion and access to the labour market, (7) work organization and work/life balance, (8) social dialogue and worker involvement, (9) diversity and non-discrimination, and (10) overall work performance.

[177] Commission Communication, 'Improving Quality in Work: a Review of Recent Progress' (COM(2003) 728 final).

[178] Barcelona Presidency Conclusions, 15 and 16 March 2001, para. 49.

[179] Paras. 7 and 37.

[180] COM(2000) 379, para. 3.3

[181] Nice Presidency Conclusions, 7–9 December 2000, para. 28.

[182] See further Ch. 2.

[183] Daintith, 'The Techniques of Government', in Jowell and Oliver (eds), *The Changing Constitution*, 3rd edn (OUP, Oxford, 1994) 209.

objectives through the use of government wealth) but also governance by private actors (such as the social partners and corporations).

In this section we shall examine the different means of achieving the Lisbon strategy, beginning with OMC.

3.2. OMC

(a) What is it?

The Open Method of Co-ordination is described as a 'means of spreading best practice and achieving greater convergence towards the main EU goals[184] through common targets and guidelines for Member States, sometimes backed up by national action plans'.[185] It relies on regular monitoring of progress to meet those targets, allowing Member States to compare their efforts and learn from the experience of others.[186] In the specific context of the Lisbon strategy, the European Council explained that OMC means:[187]

- fixing guidelines for the Union combined with specific timetables for achieving the goals which they set in the short, medium and long terms;
- establishing, where appropriate, quantitative and qualitative indicators and benchmarks against the best in the world and tailored to the needs of different Member States and sectors as a means of comparing best practice;
- translating these European guidelines into national and regional policies by setting specific targets and adopting measures, taking into account national and regional differences;
- periodic monitoring, evaluation, and peer review organized as mutual learning processes.

Thus, the Lisbon European Council confirmed the EES (and the BEPG) methodology, gave it a new title and extended it to other areas (notably social inclusion, pension reform (since 2001), information society/eEurope, enterprise promotion research and innovation, education and training). However, there is no single 'OMC' methodology. As Belgian minister Frank Vandenbroucke vividly put it,[188] open co-ordination is not some kind of 'fixed recipe' that can be applied to whichever issue, but is instead 'a kind of cookbook that contains various recipes, lighter and heavier ones'.[189] OMC for policy areas such as the

---

[184] COM(2002) 629, para. 14.

[185] The European Governance White Paper (COM(2001) 428, 21).

[186] Ibid.   [187] Ibid.

[188] He played a key part in launching the social inclusion and pensions processes during his country's presidency of the Council in 2001.

[189] Cited in Zeitlin, 'Introduction: The Open Method of Coordination in Question' in Zeitlin and Pochet with Magnusson (eds), *The Open Method of Coordination in Action: The European Employment and Social Inclusion Strategies*' (PIE/Peter Lang, Brussels, 2005). See also Final report of Working Group XI on Social Europe, CONV 516/1/03, para. 39: 'An empirical approach has

EES, BEPG, and social inclusion is of the 'heaviest' variety and the most fully institutionalized. In the case of the EES and the BEPG, it is also Treaty based and backed up by soft law sanctions.[190] In these three contexts, OMC can be broken down into five component parts: (1) agreeing common objectives for the Union; (2) establishing common indictors as a means of comparing best practice and measuring progress; (3) translating the EU objectives into national/regional policies through the development of National Action Plans/ National Reform Programmes; (4) publishing reports analysing and assessing the National Action Plans; (5) establishing a Community Action Programme to promote policy co-operation and transactional exchange of learning and good practice.[191]

In other areas, a 'lighter' approach is used involving only certain elements of the broader methodology such as scoreboards, peer review, and exchange of good practices. For example, in the field of education and training, benchmarking is the principal policy instrument,[192] referring to concrete targets for which it is possible to measure progress.[193] The basic model looks as follows:[194]

	Present levels			Progress		Benchmarks	
Indicator	Average (EU)	Average of 3 best performing (EU)	USA and Japan (where available)	Up till 2004	Up till 2010	For 2004	For 2010

Thus, if the indicator is the reduction in the number of early school leavers (the drop out rate), then the present levels are an EU average of 19.4 per cent while the average of the three best performing countries in the EU is 10.3 per cent. The Commission asked the Council to adopt the benchmark of halving the rate of early school leavers with reference to the rate recorded in

been used to develop and adapt this method to the specific characteristics of each field of action. The method is therefore applied in different ways to different areas, with an ad hoc procedure being worked out each time. That is why we sometimes speak of open methods of coordination, in the plural.'

[190] For a helpful catalogue of the differences between the OMC processes, see Borrás and Jacobsson, 'The Open Method of Coordination and New Governance Patterns in the EU' (2004) 11 JEPP 185, 193–194 and Zeitlin, 'Introduction: The Open Method of Coordination in Question' in Zeitlin and Pochet with Magnusson (eds), The Open Method of Coordination in Action: The European Employment and Social Inclusion Strategies (PIE/Peter Lang, Brussels, 2005).
[191] http://europa.eu.int/comm/employment_social/social_inclusion/index_en.htm
[192] Communication from the Commission, 'European Benchmarks in Education and training: follow-up to the Lisbon European Council' (COM(2002) 629).
[193] Para. 20.   [194] Para. 16.

the year 2000 to achieve an EU-average rate of 10 per cent or less which the Council incorporated into the specific employment guideline number 7 in 2003.[195] By contrast, in respect of the indicator 'Public expenditure on education as a percentage of GDP' (EU average 5 per cent, average of three best performing countries (EU) 7.4 per cent, USA 5 per cent, Japan 3.5 per cent) the Commission did not recommend a specific benchmark because the data was provisional and incomplete. Instead, it suggested that Member States should recognize their responsibility for ensuring that total expenditure on education and training, both public and private, responds appropriately to the Lisbon requirements; and should do so on the basis of transparent, publicly acknowledged benchmarks, while respecting the requirements of the Stability and Growth Pact.

(b) Perspectives on OMC

Borrás and Jacobssen argue that OMC perches on the fence between the Community method and the international method. It coaxes Member States into co-ordinating their national public actions within a collectively decided framework, spreads widely into different policy areas, and cuts across the national-EU borders using persuasion but not coercion.[196] Rhodes describes it as heterarchical, adopting a 'new' problem-solving logic based on deliberation and policy learning.[197] Most commentators agree that it should increase democracy in the EU through the enhanced role for deliberation among policy makers and participation of a broad range of actors at different levels.[198]

Advocates of OMC therefore argue that it offers a 'third way' for European social policy between regulatory competition (with the risk of a race to the bottom) and harmonization (with the risk of ill-suited uniformity). According to the Commission,[199] OMC has greater visibility, encourages a strategic and integrated approach, puts a particular issue in the mainstream, mobilizes all relevant actors and encourages mutual learning. It can also be used in areas which are not so easily susceptible to regulation either because of the subject-matter (e.g. employment policy) or because of a lack of clear Community competence (e.g. education). It can sit alongside a legislative approach, in areas such as employment and social policy, or it can stand alone, adding 'value' at a European level where there is little scope for legislative solutions (e.g. work at a European level defining future objectives for national education systems).[200]

---

[195] See above, Table 3.2.   [196] Above n. 190, 187.   [197] Rhodes, above, n. 35, 292.
[198] Although, for a sceptical view based on a case study taken from the Occupational Health and Safety sector, see Smismans, 'New Modes of Governance and the Participatory Myth', *European Governance Papers* (EUROGOV) No. N–06–01.
[199] http://europa.eu.int/comm/employment_social/social_inclusion/index_en.htm
[200] Governance White Paper, COM(2001) 428, 22.

On the other hand, detractors of OMC criticize the process on a number of levels: in terms of its legality in that it allows the EU to encroach into policy areas largely reserved for the Member States;[201] in terms of its governance techniques in that it is more opaque and unaccountable[202] than the classic Community method;[203] in terms of substance, in that the supremacy of the BEPGs constrain the free development of a social policy; and in terms of its outcomes, in that it is still dependent on Member State action. If or when states do not fulfil their commitments, the credibility of the process is undermined.[204]

Others point out that OMC has led to a proliferation of national and Community reporting obligations[205] which may not translate into action, and an obsession with placings in league tables to the detriment of the quality of outcomes.[206] This has led some to suggest that OMC in its present form amounts to little more than 'the European emperor's newest clothes, an exercise in symbolic politics where national governments repackage existing policies to demonstrate their apparent compliance with EU objectives'.[207]

These widely differing views about OMC also preoccupied the Convention on the Future of Europe. The Social Europe Working Group was divided on the issue, as was the Convention Praesidium.[208] In the event OMC was not referred to expressly by name in the final Constitution, albeit that Part III of the Treaty provided for the application of key features of OMC to a number of areas including social policy. For example, Article III–213, which closely followed the wording of Article 140 EC, contains the addition that the Commission shall act in close contact with the Member States 'in particular in initiatives aiming at the establishment of guidelines and indicators, the organisation of exchange of best practice, and the preparation of the necessary

---

[201] Szyszczak, 'The New Paradigm for Social Policy: A Virtuous Circle' (2001) 38 *CMLRev.* 1125.

[202] De la Porte and Nanz, 'The OMC—a deliberative-democratic mode of governance? The cases of employment and pensions' (2004) 11 *JEPP* 267. As Hepple puts it (*Rights at Work* (Sweet & Maxwell, London, 2005) 32, the employment guidelines are phrased in 'the mumbo-jumbo of modern management speak'.

[203] Cf. the principles of good governance set out in the Commission's *White Paper on Governance* (COM(2001) 428).

[204] This problem was noted by the Spring European Council in Brussels in 2004 where the Presidency Conclusions state that 'the critical issue now is the need for better implementation of commitments already made . . . There must be speedier translation of agreements and policy making at EU level into concrete measures': Presidency Conclusions, Brussels, 25 and 26 March 2004, para. 10.

[205] Commission, 'Working Together for Growth and Jobs. Next steps in implementing the revised Lisbon strategy' SEC(2005) 622/2, 5.

[206] Arrowsmith, Sisson and Marginson, 'What can benchmarking offer the open method of coordination?' (2004) 11 *JEPP.* 311, 321.

[207] Zeitlin, above n. 189. See also Scharpf, 'Notes Towards a Theory of Multilevel Governing in Europe', MPIfg Discussion Paper 2000/5.

[208] Ibid.

elements for periodic monitoring and evaluation'.[209] In a nod towards concerns about the lack of democratic oversight of the procedure, Article III–213 adds that 'The European Parliament shall be kept fully informed'. Part I of the Constitutional Treaty contained a new provision entitled 'The coordination of economic and employment policies'. Specifically, paragraph 1 provides that 'The *Member States* shall coordinate their economic policies within the Union'[210] while paragraph 2 provides that the 'The *Union* shall take measures to ensure coordination of the employment polices of the Member States, in particular by defining guidelines for these policies' and paragraph 3 says that 'The Union may take initiatives to ensure the coordination of Member States' social policies'. Article I–17 lists areas of supporting, co-ordinating or complementary action which include education, youth and vocational training.

3.3. Corporate Social Responsibility

While OMC was the principal 'new' mechanism introduced at Lisbon, the European Council at Lisbon also made a 'special appeal' to companies' corporate sense of social responsibility (CSR) regarding best practices on lifelong learning, work organization, equal opportunities, social inclusion, and sustainable development.[211] This led to a Green Paper on Promoting a European Framework for CSR, followed by a Council Resolution,[212] a follow-up Communication from the Commission,[213] and a further Council Resolution. CSR involves companies voluntarily taking on commitments which go beyond common regulatory and conventional requirements, 'to raise the standards of social development, environmental protection and respect for fundamental rights and embrace open governance, reconciling interests of various stakeholders in an overall approach of quality and sustainability'.[214] Implementation of CSR can be 'facilitated by the participation of workers and their representatives in a dialogue that promotes exchanges and constant adaptation'.[215] In this respect business is being encouraged to ape government, especially with the appeal to business to be more participatory and accountable in its decision-making.

From the perspective of this chapter, the CSR envisaged by the Commission is primarily internal to the enterprise: it relates to quality employment, life-

---

[209] Declaration 18 confirms that policies described within this Article 'fall essentially within the competence of the Member States'. Measures to provide encouragement and promote co-ordination to be taken at Union level shall be of 'a complementary nature'. They shall 'serve to strengthen cooperation between member States and not to harmonise social systems'.

[210] Emphasis added.   [211] Para. 39.

[212] Council Resolution on the follow-up to the Green Paper on corporate social responsibility 2002/C 86/03, [2002] OJ C86/3), para. 10.

[213] Commission Communication, *Corporate Social Responsibility: A Business Contribution to Sustainable Development* (COM(2002) 347).

[214] COM(2001) 366, 3 and 6.   [215] Ibid.

long learning, information, consultation and participation of workers, equal opportunities, integration of people with disabilities, anticipation of industrial change and restructuring. Social dialogue is seen as a powerful instrument to address employment-related issues.[216]

CSR 'fits' with OMC in that both are examples of new forms of governance which do not rely on top down command and control-style regulation. CSR is about 'responsible self-regulation'.[217] Indeed, if a sufficient number of companies embrace CSR, the carrot is that it might become the alternative to traditional forms of regulation in the social field. As Anna Diamantopoulou, former Social Affairs Commissioner, pointed out,[218] globalization and advances in communications technology are making it increasingly hard 'for legislators to address social problems with the necessary flexibility and lightness of touch'. She adds that in many cases CSR and partnership will come to be seen as the 'preferred solution'.

3.4. The Structural Funds

(a) What are They?

The Luxembourg process and the incentive measures under Article 129 comprise two limbs of the 'European employment strategy'.[219] The third limb is the role played by the structural funds, as emphasized by the Lisbon Presidency Conclusions[220] and the Commission's Social Policy Agenda.[221] As we have seen, much of the concern about high levels of unemployment is that it undermines economic and social cohesion, concepts which have now found express recognition in the Treaty. Title XVII[222] on economic and social cohesion was added by the Single European Act 1986; Article 2 EC, as amended by the Maastricht Treaty, identifies 'economic and social cohesion and solidarity between Member States' as one of the tasks of the Community and Article 3(k) lists 'strengthening of economic and social cohesion' as one of the activities of the Community.

The Community is to support the achievement of these cohesion objectives through the use of the structural funds.[223] The most important in terms of unemployment is the European Social Fund (ESF),[224] set up by the original

---

[216] COM(2002) 347, 19.

[217] Hunt, 'The European Union: Promoting a Framework for Corporate Social responsibility?' in Macmillan, *International Corporate Law Annual* (Hart Publishing, Oxford, 2003) 137.

[218] Cited in Hunt, ibid., 137.

[219] See generally Goetschy, 'The European Employment Strategy: Genesis and Development' (1999) 5 *EJIR*. 117.

[220] Para. 33.   [221] COM (2000) 379, para. 3.3

[222] Arts. 158–62. See also point 10 of the Community Social Charter 1989.

[223] Art. 158.

[224] See generally http://europa.eu.int/comm/employment_social/esf2000/index-en.htm. The ESF was one of the four structural funds. The other three funds are the European Regional Development Fund introduced in 1975, whose aim is to help redress 'the main regional

Treaty of Rome in response to the problem of declining industries, especially coal and steel. The original Article 3(i) talked of 'the creation of a European Social Fund in order to improve employment opportunities of workers and to contribute to the raising of their standard of living'. Subsequently Article 3(i) (now Article 3(j)), amended by the Maastricht Treaty, talks of 'a policy in the social sphere comprising a European Social Fund'. Substantive provisions concerning the ESF can be found in Articles 146–148 EC. Article 146 now provides that:

In order to improve employment opportunities for workers in the internal market and to contribute thereby to raising the standard of living, a European Social Fund is hereby established . . .; it shall aim to render the employment of workers easier and to increase their geographical and occupational mobility within the Community, *and to facilitate their adaptation to industrial changes and to changes in production systems, in particular through vocational training and retraining.*[225]

The structural funds were reformed in 1988, 1993, and 1999.[226] Based on the principles underpinning the 1988 and 1993 reforms, especially transparency and effectiveness,[227] the 1999 Regulations reduced the number of objectives of the structural funds to three. The ESF[228] was to be used primarily to achieve Objective 3 (training systems and employment promotion).[229] The funds are subject to a further major reform for the 2007–2013 period in order to make the Community's structural actions more targeted on the EU's strategic priorities (principally the Lisbon strategy). The three priority objectives of the 2000–2006 programme are to be replaced by three new objectives.[230] The first is *convergence*, speeding up the economic convergence of the less developed regions by, for example, improving conditions for growth and employment and by investing in human and physical capital and encouraging adaptability to economic and social change. The European Regional and Development Fund (ERDF) will be used to strengthen infrastructures; the ESF will be used to improve human resources to increase employment prospects.

imbalances in the Community through participation in the development and structural adjustment of regions whose development is lagging behind and in the conversion of declining industrial regions'; EAGGF (guidance section), whose aim is to help those excluded by restructuring of the agricultural sector; and FIFG (Financial Instrument of Fisheries Guidance) on fisheries. The Maastricht Treaty provided for the inclusion of a Cohesion Fund, this time to assist those Member States likely to be disproportionately affected by the advent of EMU (Spain, Greece, Portugal, and Ireland). The Cohesion Fund is designed to provide a financial contribution to projects in the field of the environment and Trans European Networks (TENs) in the area of transport infrastructure.

[225] The section in italics was added by the Treaty on European Union.
[226] Reg. 1260/1999 (OJ [1999] L161/1) replacing Reg. 2052/88 (OJ [1988] L185/9) and Co-ordination Reg. 4253/88 (OJ [1988] L374/1). See also Commission Communication concerning the Structural Funds (1999/C 267/02) (OJ [1999] C267/2).
[227] Preambular para. 25 of Reg. 1260/1999 (OJ [1999] L161/1).
[228] Reg. 1262/1999 (OJ [1999] L161/48) replacing Reg. 4255/88 (OJ [1988] L374/21).
[229] Art. 1 of Reg. 1260/1999 (OJ [1999] L161/1).
[230] Ibid., 4–6 and the helpful summary in Commission, *Inforegio*, Factsheet 2004.

The second is *regional competitiveness and employment*, which will apply to the rest of the EU not covered by the convergence objective: the ERDF will be used to strengthen regional competitiveness and attractiveness while the ESF will assist workers and companies, on the basis of the EES, to adapt to change and encourage the development of job markets that give priority to social inclusion. The third objective is *European territorial cooperation*, whose aim is to strengthen co-operation in cross-border areas in order to promote stronger integration of the territory of the Union in all its dimensions. Together these funds will have a budget of 336.1 billion euros (approximately one third of the Community budget).

The Commission has also issued three Guidelines for Cohesion Policy[231] which are intended to ensure that the reformed funds operate to secure the Lisbon goals and give effect to the EES priorities[232]: (1) improving the attractiveness of the Member States, regions and cities by improving accessibility, ensuring adequate quality and level of services, and preserving their environmental potential; (2) encouraging innovation, entrepreneurship and the growth of the knowledge economy; and (3) creating more and better jobs by attracting more people into employment or entrepreneurial activity, improving adaptability of workers and enterprises and increasing investment in human capital.[233] The link between the ESF and the EES is made in Article 2 of the draft ESF Regulation entitled 'Mission': 'The ESF shall strengthen economic and social cohesion by supporting Member States' policies aiming to achieve full employment, improve quality and productivity at work and promote social inclusion and the reduction of regional employment disparities'. It continues that 'In particular, the ESF shall support action in line with the guidelines and recommendations adopted under the European Employment Strategy'. In this respect there is a greater sense of co-ordination between the Community instruments.

(b) Justification for Expenditure of the Structural Funds

So the aim of the structural funds is to use government (both national and EU) wealth to secure redistributive objectives. Using Daintith's distinction, this is government by *dominium*. At national level cohesion policies are based on the fact that citizens of the state feel a certain solidarity—or cohesion— towards one another based on shared identity.[234] This 'cohesion' justifies the

---

[231] Commission Communication, 'Cohesion Policy in Support of growth and Jobs: Community Strategic Guidelines, 2007–2013', COM(2005) 299.
[232] Art. 23 of the draft general Co. Reg. COM(2004) 492.   [233] COM(2005) 299, 12.
[234] These ideas emerge in para. 1 of the Preamble to Council Recommendation 92/441/EEC (OJ [1992] L245/46) on common criteria concerning sufficient resources and social assistance in social protection systems which says: 'Whereas reinforcing social cohesion within the Community requires the encouragement of solidarity with regard to the least privileged and most vulnerable people'. See also the Preamble to Council Recommendation 92/442/EEC (OJ [1992] L245/49).

redistribution of resources, financed through taxation, which is necessitated by social policy. By contrast, at Community level the justification for such policies was initially expressed in terms of economic integration: that disadvantages experienced by regions on the periphery of the EU must be corrected to enable them to have an equal opportunity[235] to compete in the single internal market.[236] Ross is more pragmatic. He argues that the well-constructed regional development policies, designed to redistribute wealth from richer to poorer regions, have become 'the most significant instruments for pre-empting any "race to the bottom" in labour standards and labour-market regulation'.[237]

More recently, the justification for the existence of such funds has focused primarily on the need to combat high levels of unemployment[238] and secondarily on the promotion of a 'European' identity through citizenship of the Union. Thus, 'national' justifications have begun to influence the Community debate, although there is still much less of a sense of transnational solidarity (solidarity between the nationals of the Member States (and even less within the 25 or more states of an expanded Europe)) than national solidarity (solidarity between nationals within a Member State).[239] This makes a major expansion of the EC structural funds politically unacceptable.[240]

3.5. Legislation and Social Dialogue

The remaining tools to achieve the Lisbon objectives are legislation and the social dialogue. The first two chapters of this book have already highlighted the patchwork of legislation adopted in the social field. In some areas, hard law plays an important role in helping to steer a broader policy agenda. Thus a Directive prohibiting age discrimination not only provides a concrete tool to help those who are discriminated against on the grounds of age but it also sends out a strong signal that a policy of active ageing is a genuine commitment. In this way legislation provides the cornerstone for a broader range of policy initiatives.

Furthermore, legislation, social dialogue and OMC, far from being mutually exclusive, can be mutually enhancing. As the Commission noted in its Governance White Paper,[241] 'legislation is often only part of a broader

---

[235] COM(92) 84.

[236] Hervey, *European Social Law and Policy* (Longman, Harlow, 1998) 176–7.

[237] Ross, 'Assessing the Delors Era and Social Policy' in Leibfried and Pierson (eds), *European Social Policy: Between Fragmentation and Integration* (Brookings Institution, Washington DC, 1995). Scott and Mansell, 'European Regional Development: Confusing Quantity with Quality' (1993) 18 *ELRev.* 87.

[238] See e.g. Council Reg. 1260/1999 (OJ [1999] L161/1), discussed below, and the accompanying Commission Communication (99/C 267/02).

[239] Hervey, above, n. 236, 193. Compare the Court's case law on citizenship and solidarity discussed in Ch. 1.

[240] See the Commission's 'Agenda 2000' report.   [241] COM(2001) 428, 20.

solution combining formal rules with other non-binding tools such as recommendations, guidelines, or even self-regulation within a commonly agreed framework'.[242] Thus, the effectiveness of the Race Discrimination Directive 2000/43 has been enhanced by a wider range of supporting policy tools (such as networks of experts and an action plan), while the Member States are encouraged to promote dialogue with the social partners with a view to fostering equal treatment.[243]

Yet despite the Commission's commitment to use legislation to achieve the goals laid down in the European Social Policy Agenda, in fact the legislative cupboard is rather bare. In its 2005 Communication on the European Social Agenda,[244] the Commission proposed the updating of the Directives 2001/23 on transfers of undertakings and 98/59 on collective redundancies, the revision of Directive 94/45 on European Works Councils, the consolidation of the various provisions on worker information and consultation, and the amendment of the regulations on the co-ordination of social security. The only area in which new (unspecified) measures were to be considered was in the field of diversity and non-discrimination. Its proposed Green Paper on labour law will result only in a range of measures to 'modernise and simplify the current rules'. Thus, despite the protestations about the value of legislation, there is in fact a disequilibrium: OMC processes are in the ascendancy, replacing traditional rights at work with programmes which may well be destructive of national social rights. With the potential removal of national social rights under the impetus of the EES, especially under what were the entrepreneurship, employability, and adaptability pillars of the EES, there are currently no concrete plans to restore those rights at EU level. Instead, the Commission puts its trust in the social dialogue which it proposes to promote at cross-industry and- sectoral levels, especially by strengthening its logistic and technical support.[245] This in turn raises the question of the importance of the Social Partners as key actors in the Lisbon process.

---

[242] See also COM(2001) 428, 21 'In some areas, such as employment and social policy or immigration policy, [OMC] sits alongside the programme-based and legislative approach; in others [such as education], it adds value at a European level where there is little scope for legislative solutions'.

[243] OJ [2000] L180/22. See de Búrca, 'EU Race Discrimination Law: a Hybrid Model' in de Búrca and Scott (eds), Law and New Governance in the EU and US (Hart Publishing, Oxford, 2006) and Ch. 6 of this book for further details.

[244] COM(2005) 33.

[245] Commission Communication, 'Partnership for change in an enlarged Europe—Enhancing the contribution of European social dialogue' COM(2004) 557.

4. The Actors

4.1. Introduction

We have already seen how a wide range of actors are to be harnessed to the yoke of reform. According to the Lisbon summit, the European Council is to take a 'pre-eminent guiding and coordinating role to ensure overall coherence', in particular through an additional meeting of the European Council, taking place in the spring, concerned solely with economic *and* social questions;[246] and the Council and the Commission must draw up reports, benchmarking best practice. For the Commission, soft co-ordination has not necessarily been a good thing: it has reinforced its think-tank role, at the expense of its role in hard policy (as we saw there are few legislative initiatives in the pipeline), and this makes the Commission look weaker than the other institutions.[247]

At national level, the Member States, regional and local authorities, companies through CSR, NGOs, and civil society more generally[248] all have a role to play. But prominent among all of these actors are the Social Partners, at European, national, and subnational levels.[249]

4.2. The Social Partners

As we saw in chapter 2, the role of the Social Partners was formally recognized by the Maastricht Treaty when they were given the power to adopt collective agreements which could be given legislative effect. The Luxembourg EES also envisaged a major role for the Social Partners. The first set of employment guidelines made specific appeals to the interprofessional and sectoral Social Partners, at European and national level, to take new initiatives, especially under the adaptability and employability pillars.[250] The Lisbon summit also emphasized the need for the Social Partners to be more closely involved in 'drawing up, implementing and following up the appropriate guidelines',[251] focusing particularly on modernizing work organization[252] and

---

[246] Paras. 35 and 36.   [247] Discussion with Commission official.
[248] Luxembourg Presidency Conclusions, 22 and 23 March 2005, para. 6.
[249] See, e.g., Commission Communication, *Social Policy Agenda* (COM(2000) 379, 14 and the Nice Presidency Conclusions, 7–9 December 2000, para. 27, the Commission's White Paper *European Governance* (COM(2001) 428, 14 and Commission, *The European social dialogue, a force for innovation and change* (COM(2002) 341, 7).
[250] On the use of this language, see Terry and Towers, 'Editorial' *Industrial Relations Journal Annual European Review* (Blackwell, Oxford, 1997).
[251] Presidency Conclusions, Lisbon European Council, 23 and 24 March 2000, para. 28, a view reiterated by the Conclusions to the Feira European Council, 19–20 June 2000, para. 34. See, in particular, Horizontal objective C in Council Decision 2001/63/EC on Guidelines for Member States' Employment Policies for the year 2001 (OJ [2001] L22/18).
[252] Presidency Conclusions of Feira European Council, 19 and 20 June 2000, para. 34. See in particular the Adaptability pillar of the 2001 Employment Guidelines: Council Decision

equal opportunities. They were also to have a significant role in respect of life-long learning,[253] and they were to be actively involved in this OMC, especially benchmarking best practices, 'using variable forms of partnership'.[254]

The Commission also envisages that the Social Partners will have a particular role in respect of modernizing and improving social protection systems and promoting social inclusion[255] and quality in industrial relations.[256] At Nice the European Council recognized that in modernizing and deepening the European social model 'all due importance' had to be given to the social dialogue.[257] The Commission took up this theme again in its Communication, *The European social dialogue, a force for innovation and change*,[258] where it noted that the Social Partners are 'best placed to take up the fundamental challenge of [the Lisbon] strategy: the positive management of change which can reconcile the flexibility essential to businesses with the security needed by employees, particularly in the event of major restructuring.[259] This was followed up by the Commission's Communication, *Partnership for Change in an enlarged Europe—Enhancing the contribution of European social dialogue*[260] where the Commission called on the European and national Social Partners to take part in a genuine partnership for change by stepping up their efforts to achieve the Lisbon agenda.

The Social Partners are taking these calls seriously. They made a Joint Contribution to the Laeken summit in December 2001 and followed this up with the adoption of their first joint multi-annual work programme for 2003–2005 at the social dialogue summit in November 2002.[261] In addition to this (bipartite) involvement of the Social Partners, formal (tripartite) concertation with the Social Partners occurs, originally in the Standing Committee on Employment,[262] which the Employment Committee (EMCO),[263] set up under Article 130 of the Employment Title, was obliged to consult,[264] and now directly with EMCO. The Employment Committee must also work in co-operation with the Social Protection Committee which, in turn, must

2001/63/EC OJ [2001] L22/18. See also the Commission's comments on the importance of the Social Partners in the process of structural change in its Communication, Promoting Core Labour Standards and improving social governance in the context of globalization COM(2001) 416 final.

[253] Presidency Conclusions of Feira European Council, 19 and 20 June 2000, para. 33 and Annex I of the Nice Presidency Conclusions, paras. 15 and 11.

[254] Presidency Conclusions, Lisbon European Council, 23 and 24 March 2000, para. 38.

[255] COM(2000) 379, 20.   [256] COM(2000) 379, 23.

[257] Nice Presidency Conclusions, Annex I, para. 26.   [258] COM(2002) 341.

[259] Ibid., 6.   [260] COM(2004) 557.

[261] The main forum for the bipartite social dialogue at European level is the Social Dialogue Committee for the interprofessional Social Partners with its three technical working groups in macroeconomic issues, employment/labour market issues and education and training issues.

[262] Council Decision 1999/207/EC (OJ [1999] L72/33), repealing Decision 70/532/EEC. This Committee was abolished by Co. Dec. 2003/174 (OJ [2003] L70/31).

[263] Art. 5 of Council Decision 2000/98/EC (OJ [2000] L29/21).   [264] See further Ch. 2.

'establish appropriate contacts with the social partners'.[265] Both the Employment Committee and the Social Protection Committee are instructed to favour 'contributions from the social partners'.[266] At the political level, these issues are discussed in meetings with the Informal Council on Employment and Social Affairs that customarily take place at the beginning of each presidency.

The recently established Tripartite Social Summit for Growth and Employment,[267] enables the troika (the Council presidency and the two subsequent presidencies), the Commission and the Social Partners to meet to ensure greater consistency in tripartite concertation in four areas (macroeconomics, employment, social protection, education and training).[268] In respect of the macroeconomic dialogue, Article 1(6) of the Council Decision 2000/604 on the statutes and composition of the Economic Policy Committee says:[269]

The Committee shall provide the framework within which the macroeconomic dialogue involving representatives of the Committee (including the European Central Bank), the Economic and Financial Committee, the Employment Committee, the Commission and social partners shall take place at technical level.

This has led the Commission to note that the EMU process and economic convergence have 'progressively made visible the importance of the role of the Social Partners, not only in influencing the local competitiveness and employment conditions, but also as a major player in the achievement of growth and an employment-friendly overall policy mix in the Euro zone and in the Community'.[270] The role of the Social Partners was highlighted at the Cologne summit in June 1999 where the European Council noted that, for a consistent policy mix to be implemented successfully, it was helpful to have a fruitful

---

[265] Art. 1(4) of Council Decision 2000/436/EC setting up a Social Protection Committee OJ [2000] L 172/26.

[266] Nice Presidency Conclusions, Annex I, 9.

[267] Established by Council Decision 2003/174/EC (OJ [2003] L70/31). See also Art. I–47 of the Constitutional Treaty.

[268] Art. 1 of the Decision provides 'The task of the Summit shall be to ensure, in compliance with the Treaty and with due regard for the powers of the institutions and bodies of the Community, that there is a continuous concertation between the Council, the Commission and the social partners. It will enable the social partners at European level to contribute, in the context of their social dialogue, to the various components of the integrated economic and social strategy, including the sustainable development dimension as launched at the Lisbon European Council in March 2000 and supplemented by the Göteborg European Council in June 2001. For that purpose, it shall draw on the upstream work of and discussions between the Council, the Commission and the social partners in the different concertation forums on economic, social and employment matters.'

[269] Council Decision 2000/604/EC on the composition and the statutes of the Economic Policy Committee (OJ [2000] L257/28).

[270] Commission Communication, 'Adapting and Promoting the Social Dialogue at Community Level' COM(98) 322, 4.

macroeconomic dialogue between Social Partners, fiscal and employment policy makers and monetary policy makers within existing institutions.[271]

However, the Social Partners' involvement in such a dialogue may come at a price. The 1999 (and subsequent) guidelines provide that 'For wage developments to contribute to an employment-friendly mix, the Social Partners should continue to pursue a responsible course and conclude wage agreements in Member States in line with the general principles set out in previous Broad Economic Policy Guidelines', namely:[272]

- nominal wage increases must be consistent with price stability;
- real wage increases in relation to labour productivity growth should take into account the need to strengthen and maintain the profitability of investment;
- wage agreements should take into account differentials in productivity levels according to qualifications, regions, and sectors.

As Deakin and Reed point out, the suggestion in the Council Resolution on growth and employment that the Social Partners should 'fully face their responsibilities within their respective sphere of activity',[273] coupled with the direction in the broad economic guidelines that real wage levels should be pegged below increases in productivity so as to provide incentives for investment, indicates a role in suppressing wage growth which sits unhappily with the traditional role of trade unions.

Nevertheless, the importance of social dialogue as a mechanism for promoting the appropriate conditions for growth should not underestimated; it is reflected in experiences at Member State level. Italy, Spain, and France, for example, have a long tradition of successful tripartite bargaining between government and the Social Partners over labour costs, flexibilization, and wage growth.[274] On the other hand, experience to date of social partner involvement in the various Lisbon processes has been patchy. De la Porte and Nanz note a lack of commitment to the strategy on the union side and a

---

[271] Cologne European Council Presidency Conclusions, 3 and 4 June 1999. See also Recommendation 97/249, para. 2(iii) which calls on the Commission to promote social dialogue at Community level 'notably on macroeconomic policy issues'; the Commission Communication of 20 May 1998 on *Adapting and Promoting the Social Dialogue at Community Level* also notes that: 'the incorporation of a new Employment Title in the Amsterdam Treaty and the application of these arrangements has changed the nature of the tripartite dialogue' (COM(98) 322, at 10).

[272] Council Recommendation 99/570/EC (OJ [1999] L217/34).

[273] Resolution 97/C 236/02, para. 13. Above, n. 40.

[274] See Treu, 'European Collective Bargaining Levels and the Competences of the Social Partners', in Davies, Lyon-Caen, Sciarra and Simitis (eds), *European Community Labour Law: Principles and Perspectives. Liber Amicorum Lord Wedderburn of Charlton* (Clarendon, Oxford, 1996) 179. For a detailed analysis of the various types of social pacts, see Avdagic, Rhodes and Visser, 'The Emergence and Evolution of Social Pacts: A Provisional Framework for Comparative Analysis' *European Governance Papers* (EUROGOV) No. N–0501.

reluctance to become involved on the employers' side.[275] Even in respect of the NAPs, the involvement of the Social Partners has varied significantly from state to state.[276]

4.3. The Missing Actors

Notable by their absence from the discussion so far is the European Court of Justice and the European Parliament. To date, the European Court of Justice has no specific role in OMC, due to the strong political logic of the methodology, although it may eventually have to rule on the legality of some of the procedural issues involved in the OMC process, as it was prepared to do in *Commission* v. *Council (SGP)*.[277] There, in the context of the excessive deficit procedure, the Court ruled that the Council could not depart from the rules laid down by the Treaty and in the SGP. However, unlike soft law adopted under the classic Community method—such as the recommendation on sexual harassment, which is subject to judicial interpretation[278] and once hardened into hard law, judicial enforceability—the soft law of the EES derives its regulatory strength from government powers or capacities.[279] As Kilpatrick puts it, OMC does not constitute a hard law opportunity manqué, rather soft law in this regard is shorthand for 'different from law (in its classical conception)', not 'less than law'.[280]

If this interpretation is correct, then the role for the Court of Justice will always be residual. This then focuses attention on political accountability. Yet the European and national parliaments have also been marginalized in the OMC process. According to Article 128(2) EC the European Parliament is to be consulted in the drawing up of the employment guidelines (although it is not involved in any other OMC process) but experience over the first five years of the EES showed that the European Parliament's role was marginal, in part due to the lack of time in the EES timetable for it to prepare its opinion.[281] The involvement of the Social Partners was hoped to fill this legitimacy gap but, as

---

[275] 'The OMC—a deliberative-democratic mode of governance? The cases of employment and pension' (2004) 11 *JEPP*. 267, 279.

[276] EIRO, 'Participation of Social Partners in the NAPs of the Employment Strategy (2002), http:// www.eiro.eurofound.ie.

[277] Case C–27/04 [2004] ECR I–000.

[278] See Case 322/88 *Grimaldi* v. *Fonds des Maladies Professionnelles* [1989] ECR 4407 where the Court said in the context of a Recommendation on compensation for persons with occupational diseases, that national courts were bound to take Recommendations into account in order to decide disputes before them, in particular where they clarify the interpretation of national rules adopted in order to implement them or when they are designed to supplement binding Community measures.

[279] Borrás and Jacobsson, 'The Open Method of Coordination and New Governance Patterns in the EU' (2004) 11 *JEPP*. 185, 188 and 199.

[280] 'New EU Employment Governance and Constitutionalism' in De Búrca and Scott (eds), *Law and New Governance in the EU and US* (Hart Publishing, Oxford, 2006).

[281] The 2003 reforms have helped to overcome this problem: Rhodes, above n. 35, 295.

we have seen, the commitment on paper to the participation of the Social Partners, has often not manifested itself in practice. This has led some commentators to suggest that, on the one hand, the involvement of such a wide range of actors has actually blurred responsibility for economic and social policy, and, on the other, the absence of effective involvement by the Social Partners, the lack of involvement the European Parliament and the absence of judicial review, has meant that the EES and Lisbon strategies, far from being open, heterarchical, and deliberative, are more closed, elitist, and less democratic than the classic Community method.[282]

F. RELAUNCH OF THE LISBON STRATEGY

1. Introduction

The Employment in Europe Report 2004 made clear that the EU is still 'far short' of the Lisbon objectives and targets.[283] The overall employment rate in the EU25 stagnated at slightly below 63 per cent in 2003. The marginal increase in the employment rate, only 0.1 per cent in 2003, was much lower than the annual increases observed in the late 1990s, with the result that the 2003 employment rates overall fell short of the Lisbon target by 7 per cent, and the employment rate of women and older people fell short by 5 per cent and 10 per cent respectively. By the end of 2004, unemployment reached a peak of 9 per cent.[284]

Even before this report, alarm bells had begun to ring that the EU was not on course to achieve its Lisbon objectives.[285] These concerns were articulated more clearly at the Brussels Spring Council in 2004 where the heads of state noted that 'the pace of reform needs to be significantly stepped up if the 2010 targets are to be achieved'.[286] This was confirmed by Wim Kok's 2004 Report[287] which pressed the Member States and Social Partners to give 'urgent attention' to four particular structural challenges (adaptability of workers and enterprises to changing economic conditions and labour market demands, attracting more people into and remaining in the labour market and making

---

[282] Syrpis, 'Legitimising European Governance: Taking Subsidiarity Seriously within the Open Method of Coordination' *EUI Working Papers*, Law 2002/10. See the calls in the Final report of Working Group XI on Social Europe, CONV 516/1/03, para. 44 for the 'incorporation of the open method of coordination in the Treaty [which] would improve its transparency and democratic character, and clarify its procedure by designating the actors and their respective roles'.

[283] Commission, *Employment in Europe 2004: Recent Trends and Prospects* (Luxembourg. OPEC, 2004), 10.

[284] Presidency Conclusions, Brussels European Council, 23–24 March 2005, para. 7.

[285] See e.g. Presidency Conclusions, Thessaloniki 19 and 20 June 2003, para. 48.

[286] Presidency Conclusions, Brussels, 25 and 26 March 2004, para. 7.

[287] *Facing the Challenge: The Lisbon Strategy for Growth and Employment. Report from the High Level Group chaired by Wim Kok* (OOPEC, Luxembourg, 2004).

work a real option for all, improving the quality of employment, and investing in human capital). More significantly, the Kok report emphasized the need to improve governance of the EES in order to encourage a broader ownership of the Lisbon strategy, not only in national governments but among civil society.

The Commission's own diagnosis of the failure of the Lisbon strategy to deliver was based on the fact that 'The overall Lisbon goals were right but the implementation was poor'.[288] Part of the problem seems to have been too many objectives and lack of focus.[289] More fundamentally, the problems also lay with the methodology: OMC was proving too unwieldy.[290] As the Commission points out, the Lisbon strategy contained 28 main objectives, 120 sub-objectives, 117 different indicators, and a reporting system which led 25 Member States to produce up to 300 annual reports: 'Nobody reads all of them'.[291] As a result, the Commission proposed a new programme entitled 'Working together for Growth and Jobs'[292] in which it identified 'new actions at European and national level which will help to see our Lisbon vision achieved', without attempting to rewrite the Lisbon strategy (or indeed the ambitious Lisbon targets).[293] This document was endorsed by the Spring European Council in Brussels in March 2005.[294]

2. Relaunching the Lisbon Process

2.1. The Substance

According to the Brussels European Council 2005, the relaunch of the Lisbon process has two objectives: first, a refocusing on growth and jobs and second, effective ownership by improving governance procedures at both the European and national levels. The first objective is subdivided into three priorities: (1) knowledge and innovation as the engines for a sustainable growth. This focuses particulary on research and development to develop new goods and services; (2) making Europe more attractive to invest and work in. This focuses in particular on completing the internal market and making the EU's regulatory environment more business friendly. At the same time, it calls on business, in its turn, to develop its sense of CSR; (3) growth and employment making for social cohesion. This priority revisits familiar territory: the objectives of

---

[288] IP/05/130, 2 February 2005.
[289] Commission Communication, 'Working Together for Growth and Jobs. A New Start for the Lisbon Strategy' COM(2005) 24.
[290] Kok report, above n. 287, 42: 'The open method of coordination has fallen far short of expectations'.
[291] http://europa.eu.int/growthandjobs/index_en.htm
[292] Communication to the Spring European Council, 'Working Together for Growth and Jobs—a new Start for the Lisbon Strategy' (COM(2005) 24).
[293] COM(2005) 24, 7.
[294] Presidency Conclusions of the Brussels European Council, 22–23 March 2005, para. 8.

full employment, job quality, labour productivity, and social cohesion are to be reflected in clear and measurable priorities: making work a real option for everyone, attracting more people into the labour market, improving adaptability, investing in human capital, modernizing social protection, promoting equal opportunities *inter alia* between men and women, and fostering social inclusion.[295]

In respect of each of these three priority areas, the Commission highlights specific areas of action. For example, as concerns the third strand, growth and employment for social cohesion, this involves attracting more people into employment and modernizing social protection systems, improving the adaptabiliy of workers and enterprises and the flexibility of labour markets, and investing more in human capital through better education and skills.[296] None of this is particularly new and its success is in reality dependent on good economic growth in the Europe over the next five years. The more dramatic changes have occurred in respect of governnance.

2.2. Improving Governance

(a) The Basic Rules

The second objective of the Lisbon relaunch is to improve the governance of the different strands of the Lisbon strategy. In particular, the Commission was concerned that responsibilities had been muddled between the Union and the Member States, with 'too many overlapping and bureaucratic reporting procedures and not enough political ownership'.[297] This new approach, based on a three-year cycle which started in 2005, comprises the following steps (see Figure 3.3).[298]

First, the Commission presents a strategic report covering the economic policy and the employment guidelines (an in-depth review every three years) which will be examined by the various Council configurations and discussed at the spring European Council.[299] The European Council then establishes political guidelines for the economic, social and environmental strands of the strategy.[300] In accordance with the procedures laid down in Articles 99 and 128 EC, and on the basis of the European Council conclusions, the relevant formations of the Council then adopt a package of 'integrated guidelines' consisting of both the broad economic policy guidelines (BEPGs), adopted by Ecofin, and employment guidelines (EGs), adopted by EPSCO based on a proposal by the Commission, thereby integrating macroeconomic,

---

[295] Para. 31.   [296] COM(2005) 24, 9.   [297] COM(2005) 24, 10.

[298] See Brussels European Council Presidency Conclusions, 22–23 March 2005, para. 39 and the greater detail in SEC(2005) 193.

[299] Brussels European Council Presidency Conclusions, 22–23 March 2005, para. 39(a).

[300] Ibid.

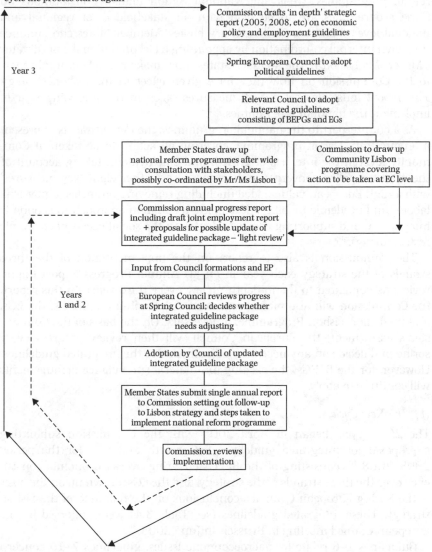

At the end of the third year of the
cycle the process starts again

Commission drafts 'in depth' strategic
report (2005, 2008, etc) on economic
policy and employment guidelines

Year 3

Spring European Council to adopt
political guidelines

Relevant Council to adopt
integrated guidelines
consisting of BEPGs and EGs

Member States draw up
national reform programmes after wide
consultation with stakeholders,
possibly co-ordinated by Mr/Ms Lisbon

Commission to draw up
Community Lisbon
programme covering
action to be taken at EC level

Commission annual progress report
including draft joint employment report
+ proposals for possible update of
integrated guideline package – 'light review'

Input from Council formations and EP

Years
1 and 2

European Council reviews progress
at Spring Council; decides whether
integrated guideline package
needs adjusting

Adoption by Council of updated
integrated guideline package

Member States submit single annual report
to Commission setting out follow-up
to Lisbon strategy and steps taken to
implement national reform programme

Commission reviews
implementation

Figure 3.3 Governance under the Lisbon Relaunch

microeconomic, and employment policies into one instrument.[301] Both
the Commission and the Member States then respond to these 'integrated

[301] Ibid., para. (b). See also Commission, *Delivering on Growth and Jobs: A New and Integrated
Economic and Emploment Co-ordination Cycle in the EU*, SEC (2005) 193.

guidelines'.[302] In the case of the *Member States*, they are to draw up 'national reform programmes' (replacing National Action Plans). Consultations on these programmes are to be held with all stakeholders at regional and national level, including parliamentary bodies. Member States can enhance their own internal co-ordination by appointing a Lisbon national co-ordinator ('Mr' or 'Ms Lisbon'). The Member States must make a single annual report to the Commission on how they have given effect to the Lisbon strategy. This report must also set out all measures taken in the preceding year to implement the national programmes.[303]

As a counterpart to the national programmes, the *Commission* is to present a 'Community Lisbon programme' covering all action to be taken at Community level in the interests of growth and employment, taking account of the need for policy convergence. It proposed a further eight 'key measures' with a high European value-added (including removing obstacles to physical, labour, and academic mobility; developing a common approach to economic integration; and supporting efforts to deal with the social effects of economic restructuring).[304]

The Commission is also to report on the implementation of the three strands of the strategy each year in an EU Annual Progress Report ('light' review as compared to the in-depth review every third year). In this report, the Commission will also make proposals for amending the BEPGs, the EGs, and the Union Lisbon Programme, if necessary. On the basis of the Commission's assessment, the European Council will then review progress every spring and decide on any necessary adjustments to the integrated guidelines. However, for the BEPGs, the existing multilateral surveillance arrangements will continue to apply.

(b) The New Cycle

The 2005 cycle began in April 2005 with the Commission submitting a proposal for integrated guidelines for growth and jobs for the period 2005–2008,[305] consisting of the BEPGs ensuring overall economic consistency over the three strands of the strategy, and the EGs, drawn up on the basis of the Spring European Council's conclusions on the relaunch of the Lisbon strategy. These integrated guidelines (see Table 3.4) were endorsed by the European Council meeting in Brussels in June 2005.[306]

Guidelines 1–6 relate to macroeconomic issues, guidelines 7–16 concern microeconomic issues, and guidelines 17–24 concern employment issues.

---

[302] See Brussels European Council Presidency Conclusions, 22–23 March 2005, para. 39 (c).
[303] See Brussels European Council Presidency Conclusions, 22–23 March 2005, para. 39 (d).
[304] http://europa.eu.int/rapid/pressReleasesAction.do?reference=IP/05/973&format=HTML&aged=0%3Cuage=EN&guiLanguage=en
[305] COM(2005) 141.
[306] Brussels European Council Presidency Conclusions, 16–17 June 2005, Annex II.

Table 3.4 Integrated Guidelines for Growth and Jobs 2005–2008, Annex II, Brussels European Council Presidency Conclusions, 16–17 June 2005

Integrated guidelines for growth and JOBS 2005–2008

1. Guarantee the economic stability for sustainable growth
2. Safeguard economic and budgetary sustainability, a prerequisite for more jobs
3. Promote an efficient allocation of resources, which is geared to growth and jobs
4. Ensure that the development of salaries contributes to macroeconomic stability and growth
5. Strengthen the consistency of macroeconomic, structural, and employment policies
6. Contribute to the dynamism and smooth operation of EMU
7. Increase and improve investments in research and development, in particular in the private sector, with a view to establishing a European area of knowledge
8. Facilitate all forms of innovation
9. Facilitate the spread and effective use of ICTs and build a fully inclusive information society
10. Strengthen the competitive advantages of its industrial base
11. Encourage the sustainable use of resources and strengthen the synergies between environmental protection and growth
12. Extend and deepen the internal market
13. Ensure open and competitive markets inside and outside Europe, reap the rewards of globalization
14. Create a more competitive business environment and encourage private initiative by improving regulations
15. Promote a more entrepreneurial culture and create a supportive environment for SMEs
16. Expand, improve, and connect European infrastructures and complete priority cross-border projects
17. Implement employment policies aimed at achieving full employment, improving quality and productivity at work, and strengthening social and territorial cohesion
18. Promote a lifecycle approach to work
19. Ensure inclusive labour markets, enhance work attractiveness, and make work pay for job seekers, including disadvantaged people and the inactive
20. Improve matching of labour market needs
21. Promote flexibility combined with employment security and reduce labour market segmentation, having due regard to the role of Social Partners
22. Ensure employment-friendly labour costs developments and wage-setting mechanisms
23. Expand and improve investment in human capital
24. Adapt education and training systems in response to new skill requirements

These guidelines were then fleshed out by a Commission Recommendation on the BEPG in respect of macro- and microeconomic issues and by a Council Decision in respect of the Employment Guidelines.[307]

As can be seen from Table 3.5, the 2005 Employment Guidelines are based around three express overarching objectives which mirror those expressed in the 2003 guidelines (see Table 3.2 above), albeit amended to reflect the need for territorial as well as social cohesion. In addition, the 2005 guidelines list a number of other objectives to supplement gender mainstreaming, such as implementing the European Youth Pact[308] and reducing employment gaps for people at a disadvantage. Like their 2003 counterparts, the 2005 guidelines also emphasise the need for good governance using a wide range of actors and tools to achieve their objectives. The 2005 guidelines then take Guidelines 17–24 of the new integrated guidelines (see Table 3.4) and expand them by reference to a number of activities which draw on the activities listed in previous sets of guidelines, albeit with a greater emphasis on a 'new inter-generational approach'. Guideline 17 contains the overall objective of the EES (full employment, productivity and quality of work, and social and terri-torial cohesion), while the subheadings (I–III) highlight the EU's priorities. This time, however, there are no targets or benchmarks attached. The only targets and benchmarks found are those contained in the 2003 guidelines (see Table 3.3) which have been consolidated and placed in a separate annex.[309]

Based on these guidelines, the Member States drew up their first *National Reform Programmes*.[310] The Commission also drew up a *Community* Lisbon programme,[311] based around the three priority areas for action identified by the March 2005 Brussels European Council. In respect of the third priority area, 'growth and employment making for social cohesion', or as the Commission calls it, 'creating more and better jobs', its action programme is almost entirely aspirational: for example, the Community is 'committed to improving the anticipation and management of economic restructuring', it wants to 'remove obstacles to labour mobility' to facilitate 'occupational and geographic mobility' and the Commission is to work towards a 'common framework for managing economic migration' in order to 'tap the world's human capital and mine its wealth of knowledge'.[312]

The Commission then assessed the policies and progress identified by the Member States and, on the basis of this assessment, adopted its annual

---

[307] Co. Dec. 2005/600/EC (OJ [2005] L205/21).
[308] COM(2005) 206, considered further in Ch. 12.
[309] Co. Dec. 2005/600/EC, above, n. 307, 27.
[310] With guidance from the Commission: SEC (2005) 622/2. Their reports can be found at http://europa.eu.int/growthandjobs/pdf/nrp_2005_en.pdf
[311] Commission Communication, *Common Actions for Growth and Employment: The Community Lisbon Action Programme* COM(2005) 330.
[312] COM (2005) 330, 9.

Table 3.5 The 2005 Employment Guidelines

The Objectives

- Full employment (i.e. achieving the Lisbon targets)
- Improving quality and productivity at work
- Strengthening social cohesion and *territorial* inclusion

Member States, in co-operation with the Social Partners, must adopt a gender mainstreaming approach in all action taken. Particular attention should be paid to the situation of young people, implementing the European Youth Pact, to promoting access to employment throughout working life, reducing employment gaps for people at a disadvantage, as well as between TCNs and EU citizens.

Guidelines	Activities
17. Implement employment policies aiming at achieving full employment, improving quality and productivity at work and strengthening social and territorial cohesion Policies should contribute to achieving an average employment rate for the EU of 70% overall, of at least 60% for women and of 50% for older workers by 2010 and to reduce unemployment and inactivity. MS should consider setting national employment rate targets	Attract and retain more people in employment, increase labour supply and modernize social protection systems Improve adaptability of workers and enterprises Increase investment in human capital through better education and skills
I. *Attract and retain more people in employment, increase labour supply and modernize social protection systems*	
18. Promote a lifecycle approach to work through:	—a renewed endeavour to build employment pathways for young people and reduce youth unemployment, as called for in the European Youth Pact; —resolute action to increase female participation and reduce gender gaps in employment, unemployment and pay; —better reconciliation of work and private life and the provision of accessible and affordable childcare facilities and care for other dependants;

Continued

Table 3.5 Continued

Guidelines	Activities
	—support for active ageing, including appropriate working conditions, improved (occupational) health status and adequate incentives to work and discouragement of early retirement; —modern social protection systems, including pensions and healthcare, ensuring their social adequacy, financial sustainability and responsiveness to changing needs, so as to support participation and better retention in employment and longer working lives. See also integrated guideline no. 2
19. Ensure inclusive labour markets, enhance work attractiveness, and make work pay for job seekers, including disadvantaged people, and the inactive through:	—active and preventive labour market measures including early identification of needs, job search assistance, guidance and training as part of personalized action plans, provision of necessary social services to support the inclusion of those furthest away from the labour market and contribution to the eradication of poverty; —continual review of the incentives and disincentives resulting from the tax and benefit systems, including the management and conditionality of benefits and a significant reduction of high marginal effective tax rates, notably for those with low incomes, whilst ensuring adequate levels of social protection; —development of new sources of jobs in services for individuals and businesses, notably at local level.
20. Improve matching of labour market needs through:	—the modernization and strengthening of labour market institutions, notably employment services, also with a view to ensuring greater transparency of employment and training opportunities at national and European level; —removing obstacles to mobility for workers across Europe within the framework of the Treaties;

—better anticipation of skill needs, labour market shortages and bottlenecks;
—appropriate management of economic migration.

II. *Improve adaptability of workers and enterprises*

21. Promote flexibility combined with employment security and reduce labour market segmentation, having due regard to the social partners, through:

—the adaptation of employment legislation, reviewing where necessary the different contractual and working time arrangements;
—addressing the issue of undeclared work;
—better anticipation and positive management of change, including economic restructuring, notably changes linked to trade opening, so as to minimize their social costs and facilitate adaptation;
—the promotion and dissemination of innovative and adaptable forms of work organization, with a view to improving quality and productivity at work, including health and safety;
—support for transitions in occupational status, including training, self-employment, business creation and geographic mobility.

See also integrated guideline no. 5

22. Ensure employment-friendly labour cost developments and wage-setting mechanisms by:

—encouraging social partners within their own areas of responsibility to set the right framework for wage bargaining in order to reflect productivity and labour market challenges at all relevant levels and to avoid gender pay gaps;
—reviewing the impact on employment of non-wage labour costs and where appropriate adjust their structure and level, especially to reduce the tax burden on the low-paid.

See also integrated guideline no. 4

III. *Increase investment in human capital through better education and skills*

23. Expand and improve investment in human capital through:

—inclusive education and training policies and action to facilitate significantly access to initial vocational, secondary and higher education, including apprenticeships and entrepreneurship training;

Continued

Table 3.5 Continued

Guidelines	Activities
	—significantly reducing the number of early school leavers;
	—efficient lifelong learning strategies open to all in schools, businesses, public authorities and households according to European agreements, including appropriate incentives and cost-sharing mechanisms, with a view to enhancing participation in continuous and workplace training throughout the lifecycle, especially for the low-skilled and older workers.
	See also integrated guideline no.7
24. Adopt education and training systems in response to new competence requirements by:	—raising and ensuring the attractiveness, openness and quality standards of education and training, broadening the supply of education and training opportunities and ensuring flexible learning pathways and enlarging possibilities for mobility for students and trainees; —easing and diversifying access for all to education and training and to knowledge by means of working time organization, family support services, vocational guidance and, if appropriate, new forms of cost sharing; —responding to new occupational needs, key competences and future skill requirements by improving the definition and transparency of qualifications, their effective recognition and the validation of non-formal and informal learning.

progress report, "Time to Move up a Gear"[313] in January 2006, which has three main elements. First, it provides an analysis of the 25 National Reform Programmes; second, it identifies the strengths in different national programmes with a view to promoting the exchange of good ideas; and third, it highlights areas where there are shortcomings and proposes concrete action

[313] http://europa.eu.int/growthandjobs/pdf/2006_annual_report_full_en.pdf

at EU and national level to deal with them. Four priority action areas are identified: investment in education, research and innovation; freeing up SMEs; guaranteeing a secure and sustainable energy supply; and employment policies to get people into work. This last policy area contains a mix of the general ('Member States should adopt a 'lifecycle approach to employment', with people of all ages offered the support they need, with emphasis on 'active ageing', with more training for those over 45, financial incentives for prolonging working lives, and use of part-time work) and the specific (every young person who has left school or university should be offered a job, apprenticeship or additional training within six months of becoming unemployed by the end of 2007, and within 100 days by 2010).

Integral to the Commission Communication is the Annex which provides a more detailed picture within the three broad strands of the integrated guidelines: macroeconomic, microeconomic, and employment. The latter section also constitutes the draft joint employment report 2005/2006 of the Commission, in accordance with Article 128 EC. The Commission concludes that the Integrated Guidelines, including the agreed benchmarks and targets should remain unchanged.[314] The Employment and Social Affairs Council (EPSCO) meeting in early March endorsed the Commission report,[315] and the Brussels Spring European Council 23–24 March 2006 agreed that the integrated guidelines for jobs and growth remain valid and that focus should be on increasing employment opportunities for specific groups (the young, women, older workers, persons with disabilities, and legal migrants and minorities).[316] In July 2006, the Council decided to maintain the 2005 Guidelines.[317]

G. CONCLUSIONS

The revisions to the Lisbon strategy provide a sense of *déjà vu*. The 2005 Employment Guidelines do not differ so radically from 2003 guidelines which in turn reflected the content of the original 1998 guidelines. To an extent there is now a closer synergy now between the BEPGs and the EGs. For example, the detail of Integrated Guideline 4 (ensuring that the development of salaries contributes to macroeconimc stability and growth) expressly cross refers to Integrated Guideline 22 (ensuring employment friendly labour costs developments and wage setting mechanisms). Nevertheless, as we saw with the 1997 BEPGs which contained a similar provision, the requirement in Integrated Guideline 4 for Member States to promote nominal wage increases

---

[314] Annex, para. 6.
[315] http://www.ue.eu.int/ueDocs/cms_Data/docs/pressData/en/lsa/88755.pdf
[316] Para. 34.
[317] Council Dec. 2006/544/EC (OJ [2006] L215/26).

and labour costs consistent with price stability and the trend in productivity, means that the BEPGs still take precedence and the basic tension between economic and social policy objectives remain.

Much ink has been spilt on developing a complex web of pacts, strategies, and processes. One presidency adds its own priorities to the already high pile of priorities agreed by its predecessors until eventually the term 'priority' loses its meaning. While the Council and Commission are broadly in agreement as to the problems and what needs to be done to fix them, the EU is dependent on the Member States co-operating and delivering substantively on their commitments and not just on paper. In fact, this 'voluminous churning of paper' has produced scant results,[318] in part because the Lisbon goal is both immensely (unrealistically?) ambitious and amorphous. While the Lisbon relaunch has helped to simplify, the simplification is relative: the resulting documents and processes are still opaque and remote to the casual, but interested, observer—and the basic policy cocktail remains the same.

For states which have to implement these policies, and for commentators who need to observe and explain them, the Lisbon strategy in its various forms is like nailing blancmange to a wall. There is no obvious way of grasping what is actually required, just a sense that (lots of big) 'things have got to be done'. It would be unfair to say that the Lisbon relaunch has the feeling of deckchairs being reorganized on the Titanic, but achieving the Lisbon goals does require the turning round of a large and unwieldy steamship.

* * *

As we know, some of the techniques deployed in the Lisbon strategy have been extended to the substantive areas of employment law which form the major preoccupation of this book. We begin by considering the rules on free movement of workers (Part II) and equality (Part III), both rights which have been found in the Treaty since its inception in 1957, before moving on to consider health and safety and working conditions (Part IV) and the rules on employees' rights when enterprises are restructured (Part V). We conclude by looking at the collective dimension to EC employment law, notably worker representation and collective action (Part VI).

---

[318] Gillingham, *Design for a New Europe* (CUP, Cambridge, 2006) 10.

PART II

Migrant Workers

4

Free Movement of (Economically Active) Persons

A. INTRODUCTION

One strand of the Lisbon relaunch was to encourage the cross-border mobility of persons. Three provisions included in the original Treaty of Rome (Articles 39, 43, and 49) aimed to achieve just that. Article 39 gives workers—employed persons—the right to move freely to seek and take up employment in another Member State on the same terms as nationals. Article 43 allows the self-employed to do the same while Articles 49 and 50 permit individuals to provide services in another Member State. The focus of this chapter will primarily be on the position of workers and the free movement rights they enjoy; specific issues concerning the establishment of natural persons (i.e. the self-employed) and some reference to the provision of services—always in an employment context—will also be made. The next chapter will focus on the limits to an individual's rights to free movement.

The principle of free movement was introduced to enable workers from states with high levels of unemployment to move to states where employment levels were high. There they could find a job, probably benefit from higher wages than in their home state and provide the skills needed by the host state. Furthermore, the principle of non-discrimination meant that employers selected candidates based on merit and not nationality. At least, this was the theory. In practice, workers often preferred to stay (unemployed) in a state they were familiar with, in the company of family and friends. The Community addressed this problem by adopting a series of measures giving rights not only to workers but also to their families in an attempt to encourage them to move. The legislature's approach has been reinforced by the Court which has been instrumental in helping secure this objective, first by removing obstacles which impeded free movement and then on finding ways to ensure that workers and their families became integrated into the host state. And with these developments came a change in perspective. Workers were no longer simply viewed as factors of production needed to fulfil the objectives of the common market. Now they were seen as EU citizens with rights enforceable against the host state. This perspective was reinforced by the inclusion of the provisions on Citizenship into the EC Treaty by Maastricht[1]

---

[1] These are considered in Ch. 1.

and now the adoption of the Citizens' Rights Directive (CRD) 2004/38.[2] This chapter begins by examining who is a worker, as well as a self-employed person and a service provider, before considering the rights enjoyed by workers and their family members. In particular we focus on the Citizens' Rights Directive[3] which consolidates a number of earlier Directives while also giving new rights to EU citizens and their families.

B. THE WORKER, THE SELF-EMPLOYED PERSON, AND THE SERVICE PROVIDER

1. Worker

Although there is no definition of the term 'worker' in the Treaty, the Court has insisted that it be given a broad Community meaning, based on objective criteria to ensure uniform interpretation across the Member States.[4] In essence, a worker is engaged in a relationship based on subordination where the individual is under the control of the employer. As the Court put it in *Lawrie-Blum*,[5] the essential feature of an employment relationship is that '. . . for a certain period of time a person performs services for and under the direction of another person in return for which he receives remuneration'. The national court must decide whether a relationship of subordination exists;[6] both the sphere of employment[7] and the nature of the legal relationship between employer and employee (whether or not it involves public law status or a private law contract)[8] are immaterial. On the facts of *Lawrie-Blum* the Court found that a trainee teacher was a worker for the purpose of Article 39(1).

The 'worker' must also be engaged in a 'genuine and effective' economic activity within the meaning of Article 2 EC. While most activities satisfy

---

[2] OJ [2004] L158/77.   [3] OJ [2004] L158/77.
[4] See Case 75/63 *Unger* v. *Bestuur* [1964] ECR 1977, Case 53/81 *Levin* v. *Stratssecretaris van Justitie* [1982] ECR 1035; paras. 11–12; Case 139/85 *Kempf* v. *Staatssecretaris van Justitie* [1986] ECR 1741, para. 15; Case 66/85 *Lawrie-Blum* v. *Land Baden-Württemberg* [1986] ECR 2121, para. 16.
[5] Case 66/85 [1986] ECR 2121, paras. 16–17. Parts of this chapter are taken from Chs. 10 and 11 of Barnard, *The Substantive Law of the EU: The Four Freedoms* (OUP, Oxford, 2004).
[6] Case C–337/97 *Meeusen* v. *Hoofddirectie van de Informatie Beheer Groep* [1999] ECR I–3289, para. 15. According to Case C–107/94 *Asscher* v. *Staatssecretaris van Financiën* [1996] ECR I–3089, para. 26, due to the absence of subordination the director of a company of which he is the sole shareholder is not a worker, but in *Meeusen* the Court said that result could not be automatically transposed to his spouse.
[7] Case 36/74 *Walrave and Koch* [1974] ECR 1405, para. 21.
[8] Case 152/73 *Sotgiu* v. *Deutsche Bundespost* [1974] ECR 153, para. 5.

this requirement[9]—including playing professional football,[10] doing an apprenticeship,[11] and being a prostitute[12]—this may not always be the case. For example, in *Bettray*[13] the Court found that paid activity provided by the state as part of a drug rehabilitation programme did not represent a genuine and effective economic activity since the work, which was designed for those who could not take up work under 'normal' conditions, was tailored to an individual's needs and was intended to reintegrate them into the employment market. On the other hand, in *Steymann*[14] an individual who did work in a religious community could be considered a worker. The case concerned a plumber who worked for a Bhagwan community as part of its commercial activities. The Court considered that since the community looked after his material needs and paid him pocket money this might constitute an indirect *quid pro quo* for genuine and effective work and so Steymann could be considered a worker.

The economic activity must also not be on 'such a small scale as to be purely marginal and ancillary'.[15] Although this hurdle can raise particular difficulties for part-time workers, the Court has generally found that they can be workers. For example, in *Levin*[16] the Court said that a British woman working part-time as a chambermaid in the Netherlands could be a worker even though she earned less than a subsistence wage because part-time work constituted an effective means of improving an individual's living conditions.[17] In *Kempf*[18] the Court also found that the work of a part-time music teacher was not on 'such a small scale as to be purely marginal and ancillary', even though his income was supplemented by social security benefits. The Court said that once a finding of effective and genuine employment had been established, it was irrelevant whether the individual subsisted on his earnings or whether his pay was used to add to other family income[19] or was supplemented by public funds.[20]

However, in *Raulin*[21] the Court was less sure. It said that an 'oproepkracht' (an on-call worker) who was not actually guaranteed any work or obliged to

[9] See e.g. Case 13/76 *Dona v. Mantero* [1976] ECR 1333, para. 12.

[10] Case C–415/93 *Union Royale Belge de Société de Football Association v. Bosman* [1995] ECR I–4921, para. 73.

[11] Case C–188/00 *Kurz, née Yüce v. Land Baden-Württemberg* [2002] ECR I–10691, decided in the context of the EEC-Turkey Association Agreement.

[12] Case C–268/99 *Aldona Malgorzata Jany and Others v. Staatssecretaris van Justitie* [2001] ECR I–8615, para. 33.

[13] Case 344/87 *Bettray v. Staatssecretaris van Justitie* [1989] ECR 1621, para. 17. Cf. Case C–1/97 *Birden v. Stadtgemeinde Bremen* [1998] ECR I–7747, decided in the context of the EEC-Turkey Association Agreement.

[14] Case 196/87 *Steymann v. Staatssecretaris van Justitie* [1988] ECR 6159, para. 14.

[15] See e.g. Case C–357/89 *Raulin v. Minister van Onderwijs en Wetenschappen* [1992] ECR I–1027, para. 10.

[16] Case 53/81 [1982] ECR 1035, para. 17.   [17] Para. 15.

[18] Case 139/85 [1986] ECR 1741.   [19] Case 53/81 *Levin* [1982] ECR 1035.

[20] Para. 14.   [21] Case C–357/89 [1992] ECR I–1027.

take up any work offered and often worked only a very few days per week or hours per day could be a 'worker' but that it was a matter for the national court to decide, taking into account the irregular nature and limited duration of the services.

The Court has extended the definition of 'worker' to include those seeking work.[22] While the period allowed for work seekers to remain in the host State depends on the rules of that state, they must be allowed at least three months to look for work,[23] although if they are dependent on social security they may be asked to leave.[24] In the UK migrants can have six months to look for work[25] which the Court found in *Antonissen*[26] to be compatible with Community law. If, after the six-month period, the work seekers can show that they have genuine chances of being employed, they cannot be required to leave the host state. For this reason the Court said in *Commission v. Belgium*[27] that a Belgian law requiring a work seeker to leave the state automatically on the expiry of the three-month period breached Article 39. Article 14(4)(b) of Directive 2004/38 confirms this line of case, making clear that work seekers cannot be expelled for as long as they can 'provide evidence that they are continuing to seek employment and that they have a genuine chance of being engaged'. No time limit is specified.

2. The Self-Employed

Article 43 provides that 'restrictions on the freedom of establishment of nationals in the territory of another Member State shall be prohibited'.[28] In practice this means that the self-employed have the right to establish themselves in another Member State. The Treaty does not define 'self-employed' but in *Jany*[29] the Court explained that, unlike workers, the self-employed work outside a relationship of subordination, they bear the risk for the success or failure of their employment and they are paid directly and in full.[30] The case concerned Czech and Polish women working as prostitutes in the

---

[22] Case C–85/96 *Martínez Sala v. Freistaat Bayern* [1998] ECR I–2691, para. 32. Art. 39(3) also envisages that the worker has already found a job before leaving for the host state.

[23] In certain circumstances work seekers are entitled to social security benefits for three months under Art. 69, Reg. 1408/71.

[24] Declaration of Council accompanying Dir. 68/360 and Reg. 1612/68 (OJ [1968] SE 485).

[25] Statement of Changes to the Immigration Rules (HC 169).

[26] Case C–292/89 *R v. IAT, ex parte Antonissen* [1991] ECR I–745, para. 21. see also Case C–138/02 *Brian Francis Collins v. Secretary of State for Work and Pensions* [2004] ECR I–2703.

[27] Case C–344/95 *Commission v. Belgium* [1997] ECR I–1035, para. 18.

[28] Art. 43 is largely replicated in Art. III–22 of the Draft Constitution.

[29] Case C–268/99 *Aldona Malgorzata Jany and Others v. Staatssecretaris van Justitie* [2001] ECR I–8615, noted by C. Hillion (2003) 40 *CMLRev.* 465.

[30] Paras. 34 and 70–1.

Netherlands.[31] They paid rent to the owner of the premises and received a monthly income which they declared to the tax authorities. The Court considered them to be self-employed. The fact that prostitution was considered by some to be immoral did not alter the Court's conclusions: recognizing the margin of discretion allowed to the Member States in these sensitive areas, the Court said that it would not substitute its own assessment for that of the Member States where an allegedly immoral activity was practised legally.[32]

Jany suggests that Article 43 permits individuals to engage in a wide range of economic activities and still be considered self-employed. As the Court put it in *ex parte Barkoci and Malik*,[33] a self-employed person could conduct 'activities of an industrial or commercial character, activities of craftsmen, or activities of the professions of a Member State'.[34] As *Gebhard* made clear:

... the concept of establishment within the meaning of the Treaty is therefore a very broad one, allowing a Community national to participate, on a stable and continuous basis, in the economic life of a Member State other than his state of origin and to profit therefrom, so contributing to social and economic penetration within the Community in the sphere of activities as self-employed persons.[35]

Finally, Directive 2004/38 has recognized that Union citizens who are no longer workers or self-employed retain these statuses if:[36]

- they are temporarily unable to work as the result of an illness or accident;
- they are in duly recorded involuntary unemployment after having been employed for more than one year and have registered as a job seeker with the relevant employment office;
- they are in duly recorded *in*voluntary unemployment after completing a fixed-term employment contract of less than a year or after having become involuntarily unemployed during the first 12 months and have registered as a job seeker with the relevant employment office, in which case they will retain worker status for a period not less than six months; or
- they embark on vocational training (but if the person is involuntarily unemployed, retaining worker status requires that the training be related to their previous occupation).

---

[31] The case was decided under the Europe Agreements but in this regard the Court said that the principles were the same as those under Art. 43 (para. 38).

[32] Para. 56. However, the Court could not resist adding: 'Far from being prohibited in all Member States, prostitution is tolerated, even regulated, by most of those States, notably the Member State concerned in this case [the Netherlands]' (para. 57).

[33] Case C–257/99 *R v. Secretary of State for the Home Department, ex parte Barkoci and Malik* [2001] ECR I–6557, para. 50. This was in the context of Art. 45(3) of the Association Agreement which has wording 'similar or identical to' Art. 43.

[34] See also Case C–55/94 *Gebhard* [1995] ECR I–4165, para. 23, 'all types of self-employed activity'.

[35] Para. 25.   [36] Art. 7(3).

3. The Service Provider

Articles 49 and 50 lay down the principle of freedom to provide services on a temporary basis by a person established in one Member State to a recipient established in another. Article 50 defines services and applies the principle of equal treatment to the service provider.[37] Thus, the structure of Articles 49 and 50 do not differ very much from the Treaty provisions on workers and establishment. The first paragraph of Article 49 provides that:

restrictions on freedom to provide services within the Community shall be prohibited in respect of nationals of Member States who are established in a state of the Community other than that of the person for whom the services are intended.

It therefore envisages the situation where the service provider established in State A holding the nationality of one of the Member States (but not necessarily that of State A) enters State B to provide services and then leaves State B once the activity is completed.[38]

Article 49 can be used to challenge rules laid down by both the host state (State B) and the home state (State A) which obstruct the provision of services. Most cases concern barriers raised by the host state (State B). For example, in *Van Binsbergen*[39] a Dutch national challenged a Dutch rule requiring legal representatives to be established in the Netherlands before they could represent a person in the Dutch courts. Kortmann was representing Van Binsbergen before a Dutch social security court. During the proceedings he moved from the Netherlands to Belgium and was then told that he could no longer represent his client. The Court found that the Dutch rule in principle breached Article 49.

An increasing number of cases concern obstacles to the provision of services created by the home state, State A. Perhaps the most remarkable decision in this line of case law is *Carpenter*[40] where a Filipino woman married to a British citizen successfully challenged British immigration rules which were going to result in her deportation on the grounds that this would be 'detrimental to family life' and, therefore, to the conditions under which he exercised the freedom to provide services.[41] Mr Carpenter ran a business selling advertising space in medical and scientific journals. Although the business was established in the UK, where the publishers of the journals were

---

[37] See also General Programme for the Abolition of Restrictions of Freedom to provide services (OJ [1961] SE Second series IX/3).

[38] The case law has also made it clear that Arts. 49 and 50 apply to the recipients of services. This is not relevant for the purposes of this book but is considered in more detail in Barnard, *The Substantive Law of the EU: The Four Freedoms* (OUP, Oxford, 2004), Ch. 13.

[39] Case 33/74 *J.H.M. van Binsbergen v. Bestuur van de Bedrijfsvereniging voor de Metaalnijverheid* [1974] ECR 1299.

[40] Case C–60/00 *Carpenter v. Secretary of State for the Home Department* [2002] ECR I–6279.

[41] Para. 39.

based, much of his work was conducted with advertisers established in other Member States. The Court found that such services fell within Article 49, 'both in so far as the provider travels for that purpose to the Member State of the recipient and in so far as he provides cross-border services without leaving the Member State in which he is established'.[42] The Court said 'That freedom could not be fully effective if Mr Carpenter were to be deterred from exercising it by obstacles raised in his country of origin to the entry and residence of his spouse'.[43]

4. Citizen of the Union

If a person is not considered a worker, self-employed person, or a service provider, they can still be a Union citizen under Article 17(1) with the right to move and reside freely within the territory of the Member States, subject to the limitations and conditions laid down in the Treaty and by the measures adopted to give it effect.[44] As we saw in chapter one, the rights of citizens are evolving, but it is clear from *Collins*[45] that citizenship of the Union has the capacity to reshape the contours of the economic freedoms. The Court said that, as a work seeker, the rights Collins enjoyed under Article 39 and Regulation 1612/68 were limited to equal treatment in respect of access to employment; he did not enjoy equal treatment in respect of social (financial) advantages. However, the Court then said that 'in view of the establishment of citizenship of the Union', it was no longer possible to exclude from the scope of Article 39 benefits of a 'financial nature intended to facilitate access to employment in the labour market of a Member State'. Therefore, while the orthodox case law would deny Collins even the chance of claiming a benefit, the orthodox case law, as interpreted through the lens of citizenship, would not.[46]

---

[42] Para. 29.   [43] Para. 39.

[44] Joined cases C–482/01 and C–493/01 *Orfanopoulos v. Land Baden-Württemberg* [2004] ECR I–5257, para. 53.

[45] Case C–138/02 *Brian Francis Collins v. Secretary of State for Work and Pensions* [2004] ECR I–2703.

[46] O. Golynker, 'Jobseekers' Rights in the European Union: Challenges of Changing the Paradigm of Social Solidarity' (2005) 30 *ELRev*. 111, 115 '*Collins* proved that the Court of Justice is determined to ensure that Art. 17 is destined to be a genuine constitutional tool of interpretation of all Community provisions concerning the right to free movement of persons and residence'.

C. THE RIGHTS CONFERRED ON WORKERS

1. Introduction

1.1. The Treaty Provisions

Article 39(1) provides that workers should enjoy the right of free movement which, according to Article 39(2), includes the abolition of any discrimination based on nationality between workers of the Member States, as regards employment, remuneration and other conditions of work and employment.[47] Article 39(3) then adds that free movement comprises the right to:

* accept offers of employment actually made,
* move freely within the territory of the Member States for this purpose,
* stay in the Member State for the purpose of the employment, and
* remain in the Member State after having been employed.[48]

In addition, the Court has recognized that workers have the right, derived directly from the Treaty, to leave their state of origin, to enter the territory of another Member State, and to reside and pursue an economic activity there.[49] Implicit in Article 39, and explicit in Article 43,[50] is that the Treaty provisions can be invoked only by those nationals who move from one Member State to another. As the Court said in *Saunders*,[51] the free movement provisions cannot be applied to situations which are 'wholly internal to a Member State'. Therefore, a British woman could not use Community law to challenge an undertaking given to a criminal court in England that she return to Northern Ireland and that she did not visit England or Wales for three years. As the Court said, Community law does not apply to activities which have no factor linking them with any of the situations governed by Community law[52] and which are confined in all aspects within a single Member State.[53]

A purely hypothetical prospect of employment in another Member State will not suffice. In *Moser*[54] a German national was denied access to a teacher training course in Germany because he was a member of the Communist party. He argued that the refusal to admit him to the course prevented him from applying for teaching posts in schools in other Member States. The Court

---

[47] Art. 39(2).   [48] Art. 39(3).

[49] Case C–363/89 *Roux* v. *Belgium* [1991] ECR I–273, para. 9; Case C–18/95 *Terhoeve* v. *Inspecteur van de Belastingdienst Particulieren* [1999] ECR I–345, para. 38.

[50] Art. 43 refers to 'the freedom of establishment of nationals of a Member State in the territory of *another* Member State'.

[51] Case 175/78 *R* v. *Saunders* [1979] ECR 1129, para. 11.   [52] Ibid.

[53] See e.g. Case C–18/95 *Terhoeve* v. *Inspecteur van de Belastingdienst Particulieren* [1999] ECR I–345, para. 26; Joined Cases C–64–65/96 *Land Nordrhein-Westfalen* v. *Kari Uecker and Vera Jacquet* v. *Land Nordrhein-Westfalen* [1997] ECR I–3171, para. 16.

[54] Case 180/83 *Moser* [1984] ECR 2539, para. 15.

said that this 'hypothetical' possibility did not establish a sufficient connection with Community law to justify the application of Article 39.[55]

These cases demonstrate that nationals cannot invoke the free movement provisions against their own Member State if they have not exercised their rights of free movement in some way.[56] Migrant workers who can take advantage of their Community law rights may therefore enjoy more favourable treatment than nationals who cannot, a situation referred to as 'reverse discrimination'.[57] This rule has been much criticized and some commentators have advocated its abolition, particularly following the introduction of 'citizenship of the Union'.[58] While the Court has been dismissive of any such suggestion[59] in recent cases, of which *Carpenter* is a notable example, the Court has been prepared to find a sufficient link to trigger the application of Community law, however tenuous that link may be.[60]

1.2. Direct Effect

The rights contained in Articles 39, 43 and 49 are directly effective. In respect of Article 39 this was first acknowledged by the Court in *French Merchant Seamen*[61] and confirmed in *Van Duyn*[62] where the Court ruled that, despite the derogations to the principle of free movement contained in Article 39(3), the provisions of Articles 39(1) and (2) imposed a sufficiently precise obligation to confer direct effect. The Court also ruled that Articles 43 and 49 were directly effective in *Reyners*[63] and *Van Binsbergen*[64] respectively. Applicants can rely on the direct effect of Articles 39, 43, and 49[65] against both the host state (the more usual situation)[66] and the home state,[67] provided the situation is not wholly internal.

---

[55] Para. 18.   [56] Although cf. Joined Cases C–321–4/94 *Pistre* [1997] ECR I–2343.

[57] 'Reverse discrimination arises when a national of a Member State is disadvantaged because he or she may not rely on a protective provision of Community law when a national of another Member State in otherwise identical circumstances may rely on that same provision' (D. Pickup, 'Reverse Discrimination and Freedom of Movement for Workers' (1986) 23 *CMLRev.* 135, 137).

[58] See N. Nic Shuibhne, 'Free Movement of Persons and the Wholly Internal Rule: Time to Move On?' (2002) 39 *CMLRev.* 731.

[59] Joined Cases C–64–65/96 *Uecker and Jacquet* [1997] ECR I–3171, para. 23.

[60] Joined Cases C–51/96 & C–191/97 *Deliège* [2000] ECR I–2549; Case C–60/00 *Carpenter* [2002] ECR I–6279.

[61] Case 167/73 *Commission* v. *France* [1974] ECR 359, para. 41.

[62] Case 41/74 [1974] ECR 1337, para. 8.   [63] Case 2/74 [1974] ECR 631, para. 32.

[64] Case 33/74 *Johannes Hervicus Maria van Binsbergen* v. *Bestuur van de Bedrijfsvereniging voor de Metaalnijverheid* [1974] ECR 1299, para. 27.

[65] The applicants can be the workers, self-employed or service providers themselves or employers applying on their behalf: Case C–350/96 *Clean Car* [1998] ECR I–2521, para. 24.

[66] E.g., Case 41/74 *van Duyn* [1974] ECR 1337.

[67] This arises in cases concerning impediments to the 'export' of the worker, self-employed person or company and service: e.g. Case C–384/93 *Alpine Investments* [1995] ECR I–1141, para. 30; Case C–107/94 *Asscher* [1996] ECR I–3089, para. 32; C–18/95 *Terhoeve* [1999] ECR I–345, para. 39; but also in cases about returners: e.g. Case C–19/92 *Kraus* [1993] ECR I–1663, para. 15.

While in principle Treaty provisions can have both vertical and horizontal direct effect (and so can be relied on by an individual against both the state and a private body),[68] for many years it was not clear whether Articles 39, 43, and 49 had vertical and horizontal direct effect or only vertical direct effect. In *Walrave and Koch*[69] the Court suggested that the Treaty provisions had both: it said 'the rule on non-discrimination applies in judging *all legal relationships* in so far as these relationships, by reason either of the place they are entered into or the place where they take effect, can be located within the territory of the Community'. The Court also said that in addition to public authorities the ban on discrimination 'extends likewise to rules of any other nature aimed at collectively regulating gainful employment and services'.[70] Yet subsequent cases concerned action taken by public authorities[71] or professional regulatory bodies (e.g. the Bar Council,[72] the Italian football association,[73] or the International Cycling Union[74]) which suggested an extended form of vertical direct effect only.

However, in *Clean Car*[75] the Court provided a strong hint that the free movement of *workers* provisions had both vertical and horizontal direct effect, and this was subsequently confirmed in *Angonese*.[76] Applicants applying for jobs in a private bank had to produce a certificate of bilingualism issued by the local authority. The Court noted that since working conditions were governed not only by laws but also by agreements and other acts adopted by private persons, there would be inequality in the application of Article 39 if it applied only to acts of a public authority.[77] Drawing on the long-established case law interpreting Article 141 on equal pay,[78] the Court then ruled that the prohibition of discrimination in Article 39 applied both to agreements intended to regulate paid labour collectively and to contracts between individuals.[79] Therefore Article 39 had horizontal direct effect and so applied to private persons.[80] It is not clear whether this ruling can be extended to Articles 43 on establishment and 49/50 on services.

---

[68] See e.g. Case 43/75 *Defrenne v. Sabena* [1976] ECR 455 concerning Art. 141 on equal pay but not goods (see Ch. 5).

[69] Case 36/74 [1974] ECR 1405, dispositif, emphasis added.   [70] Para. 17.

[71] See e.g. the Home Office in Case 41/74 *Van Duyn* [1974] ECR 1337 and local authorities in Case 197/84 *Steinhauser v. Ville de Biarritz* [1985] ECR 1819 and Case C–168/91 *Konstantinidis v. Stadt Altensteig-Standesamt* [1993] ECR I–1191.

[72] Case 71/76 *Thieffry v. Conseil de l'ordre des avocats de la cour de Paris* [1977] ECR 765; Case C–309/99 *Wouters* [2002] ECR I–1577, para. 120.

[73] Case 13/76 *Donà* [1976] ECR 1333.

[74] Case 36/74 *Walrave and Koch* [1974] ECR 1405.

[75] Case C–350/96 [1998] ECR I–2521, itself confirming the hint in Case C–415/93 *Bosman* [1995] ECR I–4921, para. 86.

[76] Case C–281/98 [2000] ECR I–4139.   [77] Para. 33.

[78] Esp. Case 43/75 *Defrenne v. Sabena* [1976] ECR 455, considered in Chs. 6 and 7.

[79] Para. 34.   [80] Para. 36.

1.3. The Secondary Legislation

(a) Introduction

The details of the rights laid down by Article 39 were expanded by three secondary measures: Directive 68/360 on the rights of entry and residence, Regulation 1612/68 on the free movement of workers[81] and Regulation 1251/70 on the right to remain. Directive 68/360,[82] Regulation 1251/70,[83] and two Community directives on establishment and services,[84] including the provisions on family rights laid down in Articles 10 and 11 of Regulation 1612/68, have been replaced by a single Directive on Citizens' Rights, Directive 2004/38.[85] This Directive applies to all citizens, not just to the economically active, who benefit from the principle of equal treatment. At the heart of the Directive lies the basic idea that the rights enjoyed by the migrant increase the longer a person is resident. There are three different degrees of integration: (1) rights for those wishing to enter for up to three months, (2) rights for those residing for up to five years, and (3) rights for those residing for more than five years ('the right of permanent residence'). While this Directive will have a significant effect on the non-economically active and their family members, most of the existing secondary legislation, as interpreted by the Court, will continue to apply to workers. Therefore, the existing legislation is discussed here together with reference to the changes introduced by Directive 2004/38 where appropriate.

(b) The Personal Scope of the Citizens' Rights Directive 2004/38

   The Rules

The Directive applies to Union citizens, defined, as with Article 17(1) of the Treaty, as 'any person having the nationality of a Member State'[86] who 'move to or reside in a Member State other than that of which they are a national'.[87] It also applies to their family members who 'accompany or join them'.[88] The definition of family members is drafted more broadly than in the original Regulation 1612/68. It covers, according to Article 2(2):[89]

(a) spouse;
(b) the partner with whom the Union citizen has contracted a registered partnership, on the basis of the legislation of a Member State, if the legislation of the host Member State treats registered partnerships as equivalent to marriage and in accordance with the conditions laid down in the relevant legislation of the host Member State;

---

[81] OJ [1968] L257/2.   [82] OJ [1968] SE (II) L257/13/485.
[83] This was repealed by Commission Reg. 635/2006 (OJ [2006] L112/9).
[84] Dir. 73/148 (OJ [1973] L172/14) and Dir. 75/34 (OJ [1975] L14/10).
[85] COM(2003)199 final amending COM(2001)257 final.
[86] Art. 2(1).   [87] Art. 3(1).   [88] Ibid.   [89] Art. 2(2).

(c) the direct descendants who are under the age of 21 or are dependants and those of the spouse or partner as defined in (b);

(d) the dependent direct relatives in the ascending line and those of the spouse or partner as defined in (b).

These five categories of family members (spouse, registered partner recognized in the home and host state, dependent ascendants, descendants under 21, and dependent descendants) must, in principle, be admitted to the host state.[90] In addition, the host Member State must 'facilitate entry and residence' of:[91]

(a) any other family members, irrespective of their nationality, not falling under the definition in point 2 of Article 2 who, in the country from which they have come, are dependants or members of the household of the Union citizen having the primary right of residence, or where serious health grounds strictly require the personal care of the family member by the Union citizen;

(b) the partner with whom the Union citizen has a durable relationship, duly attested.

We shall now consider the meaning of these various terms, particularly in the light of the Court's case law under (the now repealed) Article 10 of Regulation 1612/68.

Spouses and Partners

The Court has defined a 'spouse' in a conventional manner. In *Diatta*[92] the Court considered the situation of a couple who were married but separated. The case concerned a Senegalese woman married to a French national who lived and worked in Belgium. Eventually she separated from her husband and lived in separate accommodation with the intention of divorcing. The authorities then refused to renew her residence permit on the ground that she was no longer a family member of an EC national and did not live with her husband.

The Court ruled that Article 10 did not require members of a migrant's family to live permanently together. It reasoned that if cohabitation of spouses was a mandatory condition for a residence permit, the worker could cause his spouse to be expelled from the Member State at any moment, simply by throwing her out of the house. Therefore, it would seem that separated couples must be allowed to remain in the host state. This decision is compatible with the Court's approach in *Commission* v. *Germany*[93] that Regulation 1612/68 must be interpreted in the light of the requirement of

---

[90] Art. 3(1).   [91] Art. 3(2).   [92] Case 267/83 *Diatta* v. *Land Berlin* [1985] ECR 567.
[93] Case 249/86 [1989] ECR 1263, para. 10.

the respect for family life set out in Article 8 of the European Convention of Human Rights. However, a divorced spouse may well not be in such a favourable position: in *Diatta*[94] the Court said that a 'marital relationship cannot be regarded as dissolved so long as it has not been terminated by the competent authority'.[95] This would suggest that on the completion of all the formal stages of divorce proceedings and a decree absolute has been granted, the spouse's dependent right of residence in the Member State would cease. However, as we shall see, Article 13 of Directive 2004/38 does give certain legal protection to divorcees.[96]

The term 'spouse' also does not include cohabitees. This was shown in *Reed*[97] where the Court ruled that an English woman wishing to join her cohabitee in the Netherlands could not rely on Article 10 of Regulation 1612/68 because she was not a spouse. However, on the facts of the case Reed was successful because under *Dutch* law foreigners in a stable relationship with a Dutch national were entitled to reside in the Netherlands. If Ms Reed was not allowed to remain in the Netherlands, it would therefore be discriminatory, contrary to Articles 12 and 39 EC and Article 7(2) of Regulation 1612/68.

The Citizens' Rights Directive follows the approach adopted in *Reed* and gives rights to 'the partner with whom the Union citizen has contracted a registered partnership, on the basis of legislation of a Member State' provided that 'the legislation of the host Member State treats registered partnerships as equivalent to marriage and in accordance with the conditions laid down in any such legislation'.[98] While unmarried heterosexual couples may be able to benefit from this provision, the most immediate beneficiaries will be homosexual couples. Therefore a British man who has entered into a civil partnership under the British Civil Partnership Act 2004 with a Brazilian man, would be able to go, with his Brazilian partner, to Sweden and live there since Swedish law recognizes the rights of homosexual couples. Unmarried heterosexual couples whose relationship is not formally recognized by law are more likely to rely on Article 3(2)(b) in order to persuade the host state to admit the Union citizen's partner.

Dependants

Directive 2004/38 gives rights to the Union citizen's direct descendants under the age of 21 and dependent descendants, as well as to those of the spouse or partner. It also gives rights to the dependent ascendants (e.g. parents, grandparents) of the Union citizen and the Union citizen's spouse or partner. In *Lebon*[99] the Court made clear that dependency is a question of fact. It said that a dependant is 'a member of the family who is supported by the

---

[94] Case 267/83 [1985] ECR 567.
[95] Para. 20.   [96] See below, text attached to n. 288.
[97] Case 59/85 [1986] ECR 1283.   [98] Art. 2(2)(b).
[99] Case 316/85 [1987] ECR 2811.

worker',[100] adding that there was no need to determine the reasons why the dependant needed the worker's support or to enquire whether the dependants could support themselves by working.[101] In respect of the Union citizen's other family members who are dependants or members of his household (e.g. aunts, uncles, cousins), the state must 'facilitate their entry and residence'. The same applies to those whose 'serious health grounds strictly require the personal care of the family member of the Union citizen'.

2. Rights of Departure, Entry, and Residence

2.1. The Right to Depart the Home State

Provisions which preclude or deter nationals of a Member State from leaving their state of origin interfere with freedom of movement, even if they apply to all workers.[102] Directive 2004/38 reinforces the Treaty right to depart from a Member State—not necessarily the state of origin—where workers and their families currently live.[103] According to the Directive, Union citizens and their family members[104] may leave the Member State by producing a valid identity card or passport, specifying the person's nationality, which the Member State is obliged to issue or renew.[105] The passport[106] must be valid for all Member States and for any states through which the holder must pass when travelling between Member States.[107] Expiry of the identity card or passport on the basis of which the person entered the host state and was issued with a registration certificate of card (see below) is not to constitute a ground for expulsion from the host state.[108]

2.2. The Right to Enter the Host State

Host states must allow workers and their families to enter their territory on the production of an identity card or passport.[109] No visa or other entry

---

[100] Para. 22.   [101] Ibid.

[102] Case C–10/90 *Masgio* v. *Bundesknappschaft* [1991] ECR I–1119, paras. 18–19; Case C–415/93 *Bosman* [1995] ECR I–4921, para. 104; Case C–18/95 *Terhoeve* [1999] ECR I–345, paras. 37–8; Case C–190/98 *Graf* v. *Filzmoser Maschinenbau GmbH* [2000] ECR I–493, para. 22; Case C–232/01 *Hans van Lent* [2003] ECR I–11525, para. 21.

[103] Art. 4(1).   [104] As defined in Art. 2 of Dir. 2004/38.   [105] Art. 4(3).

[106] If the passport is the only document with which the person may lawfully leave the country, it must be valid for at least five years: Art. 4(4).

[107] Art. 4(4). Having produced a passport or identity card, the Member State may not demand from the worker an exit visa or similar document (Art. 4(2)).

[108] Art. 15(2).

[109] Art. 5(1). Art. 5(4) provides that where an EU citizen or family member does not have the necessary travel documents (or visas), the Member State must: give them every reasonable opportunity to obtain the documents; have the documents brought to them within a reasonable period of time; or to corroborate or prove by other means that they are covered by the right to freedom of movement and residence.

formality can be demanded from Union citizens[110] but it can be demanded from a member of the worker's family who is not an EC national.[111] Spouses of third country nationals (TCNs) can be refused entry if they do not have valid passport/identity cards,[112] and where necessary a visa, but in *MRAX*[113] the Court said that such a refusal would be disproportionate if TCN spouses were able to prove their identity and marital ties and there was no evidence that they represented a risk to public policy, security, or health.

3. The Right of Residence in the Host State

3.1. Right of Residence for up to Three Months

If Union citizens (whether workers or otherwise) can produce a valid identity card or passport, and they wish only to stay for up to three months, Member States must grant them the right of residence.[114] The same applies to their family members, including third country nationals, on production of a valid passport.[115] The host state may, however, require the person concerned to report his/her presence in the territory within a reasonable and non-discriminatory period of time. Failure to comply with this requirement may make the person concerned liable to proportionate and non-discriminatory sanctions.[116]

3.2. Right of Residence between Three Months and Five Years

All Union citizens have the right of residence on the territory of another Member State for more than three months if they are a worker or self-employed person.[117] The same right also applies to their family members who are not nationals.[118] The host state can require Union citizens to register with the relevant authorities.[119] The deadline for registration may not be less than three months from the date of arrival.[120] A registration certificate must then be issued[121] on production of a valid identity card or passport, a confirmation of engagement from the employer or certificate of

---

[110] Art. 5(1), second para.

[111] Art. 3(2). Case 157/79 *R v. Pieck* [1980] ECR 2171, para. 10. The list of third countries whose nationals need visas when crossing the external border of the Member States is determined by Council Reg. 539/2001 (OJ [2001] L81/1).

[112] Case C–459/99 *Mouvement contre le racisme l'antisémeitisme et la xénophobie ASBL (MRAX) v. Belgium* [2002] ECR I–6591, para. 57. Cf. Case C–109/01 *Akrich* [2003] ECR I–9607.

[113] Case C–459/99 [2002] ECR I–6591, para. 61.

[114] Art. 6(1).   [115] Art. 6(2).   [116] Art. 5(5).

[117] The same right also applies to those with sufficient resources and medical insurance and also to students. However, the rights of these groups fall outside the scope of this chapter.

[118] Art. 7(2).   [119] Art. 8(1).   [120] Art. 8(2).   [121] Ibid.

employment or proof that they are self-employed.[122] Failure to comply with the registration requirement may render the person concerned liable to 'proportionate and non-discriminatory sanctions'. In this regard the Directive confirms the Court's case law. For example, in *Watson and Belmann*[123] the Court found that an Italian law providing for migrants to be deported if they failed to register with the Italian authorities within three days of entering Italy was unlawful.[124]

A migrant worker can start working before completing the formalities to obtain a residence permit[125] because the right of residence is a fundamental right derived from the Treaty and is not dependent upon the possession of a residence permit.[126] Residence permits have only probative value,[127] as *Martínez Sala*[128] shows. A Spanish national living in Germany since 1956 held various residence permits which had expired and a series of documents saying that she had applied for an extension of her permit. She then had a baby and applied for a child allowance but her application was rejected on the grounds that she did not have either German nationality or a residence entitlement or a residence permit. The Court said that it was discriminatory to require a national of another Member State to produce a document to obtain the benefit (the residence permit) when its own nationals were not required to do the same.[129]

Union citizens retain the right of residence so long as they remain workers/self-employed person,[130] which, according to Article 7(3), includes the situation where the individual cannot work because they are temporarily incapacitated through illness or accident) or because of *involuntary* unemployment,[131] or they are work seekers. In this case, Union citizens and their family members cannot be expelled for as long as the Union citizen can provide evidence that they are continuing to seek employment and they have a genuine chance of being engaged.[132]

---

[122] Art. 8(3). Additional documents are required for family members who are themselves Union citizens (Art. 8(5)). The rules on administrative formalities for family members who are not nationals of a Member State are contained in Art. 9. They are to be issued with residence cards (Art. 10) which must be valid for five years (Art. 11).

[123] Case 118/75 *Watson and Belmann* [1976] ECR 1185.

[124] See also Case C–265/88 *Messner* [1989] ECR 4209. In respect of a TCN spouse of a migrant worker, see Case C–459/99 *MRAX* [2002] ECR I–6591, para. 78.

[125] See n. 126 below.

[126] Case 118/75 *Watson and Belmann* [1976] ECR 1185, paras. 15–16.

[127] To this effect, see Case 48/75 *Royer* [1976] ECR 497, para. 50. The same rule also applies to a TCN spouse of a migrant worker: Case C–459/99 *MRAX* [2002] ECR I–6591, para. 74.

[128] Case C–85/96 [1998] ECR I–2691.

[129] For an extension of this principle to the member of a Turkish worker's family legally residing in a Member State, see Case C–262/96 *Sürül v. Bundesanstalt für Arbeit* [1999] ECR I–2685.

[130] Art. 14(4)(a).

[131] By implication, a residence permit can be withdrawn from a migrant who is voluntarily unemployed.

[132] Art. 14(4)(b).

3.3. Right of Permanent Residence

Union citizens and their family members, including third country nationals,[133] who have resided legally for a continuous period of five years in the host state have the right of permanent residence there.[134] This right is not dependent on the Union citizen being a worker/self-employed person or having sufficient resources/medical insurance.[135] Continuity of residence is not affected by temporary absences not exceeding a total of six months a year, or by absences of a longer duration for compulsory military service, or by one absence of a maximum of 12 consecutive months for important reasons such as pregnancy and childbirth, serious illness, study or vocational training, or a posting in another Member State or a third country.[136] On the other hand, continuity of residence is broken by any expulsion decision duly enforced against the person concerned.[137]

Once acquired, the right of permanent residence is lost, according to Article 16(4), only through absence from the host Member State for a period exceeding two consecutive years. Proof of five years' residence is given by the Member State issuing, as soon as possible, a 'document certifying permanent residence',[138] having verified the Union citizen's duration of residence. Article 21 provides that continuity of residence is attested by any means of proof in use in the host Member State.

4. Access to Employment and the Right to Equal Treatment

4.1. Introduction

Article 24(1) lays down a general right of equal treatment 'within the scope of the Treaty' for all Union citizens residing on the basis of Directive 2004/38 in the territory of the host state. The Article continues that the benefit of this right is to be extended to family members who are not nationals of a Member State but who have the right of residence or permanent residence. Although the basic principle is of equal treatment, the principle is subject to a number of limitations. First, Article 24(1) expressly makes the principle of equal treatment '[s]ubject to such specific provisions as are expressly provided for in the Treaty and secondary law'. Therefore, it is possible to derogate from the principle of equal treatment on the grounds, *inter alia*, of public policy, public security, public health, and employment in the public service (see chapter 5).

Second, Article 24(2) provides for a phased enjoyment of the principle

---

[133] Art. 16(2).   [134] Art. 16(1).   [135] Ibid.   [136] Art. 16(3).   [137] Art. 21.
[138] Art. 19. A renewable permanent residence *card* is issued to the family members who are not nationals of a Member State (Art. 20).

of equal treatment in respect of social assistance and maintenance aid for students. The justification for this is that the longer citizens reside in the host state, the more integrated they are, the more they are entitled to the full range of social benefits. In respect of social assistance, the host state is not obliged to confer entitlement to it during the first three months of residence or, in the case of a work seeker, the period during which Union citizens can provide evidence that they are continuing to seek employment and that they have a genuine chance of being engaged. In respect of maintenance aid for studies, including vocational training, the host state is not obliged to give grants or student loans to Union citizens or their family members until they have acquired permanent residence. The only exception to this rule is where the Union citizen is a worker, self-employed person, a person who retains such status and members of their families. This is considered further below.

Against this background, we now need to consider the specific provisions governing workers. Although Directive 2004/38 lays down the general principle of equal treatment for all Union citizens the detailed manifestation of this principle for workers is still spelt out in Regulation 1612/68[139] and it is likely that the Court will continue to refer to this Regulation when considering workers' cases. Regulation 1612/68 was designed both to facilitate the free movement of workers and their families as well as ensuring their integration into the community of the host state. When enacting the Regulation the Council

. . . took into account, first, the importance for the worker, from a human point of view of having his entire family with him and, secondly, the importance, from all points of view, of the integration of the worker and his family into the host Member State without any difference in treatment in relation to nationals of that State.[140]

The consideration of this Regulation falls into two parts: first, the right of *access* to a post on non-discriminatory terms (Title I), and second, the right to equal treatment while doing that job, i.e. non-discrimination in respect of *exercise* of Community rights, (Title II).

4.2. Equal Treatment in respect of Access to Employment

Article 1 of Regulation 1612/68 reiterates the substance of Article 39: any national of a Member State 'has the right to take up an activity as an

---

[139] OJ SE [1968] L257/2, amended by Reg. (EEC) No. 312/76 (OJ [1976] L3/2) and Council Reg. (EEC) No. 2434/92 (OJ [1992] L25/1). Measures previously existed which protected the national labour market: Reg. 15/1961 allowed a migrant worker to take a job in another Member State if, after three weeks, no national was available to take the job. This was changed by Reg. 38/1964 and Dir. 64/240.

[140] Case C–249/86 *Commission v. Germany* [1989] ECR 1263, para. 11.

employed person, and to pursue such activity, within the territory of another Member State', enjoying the same priority as a national. The worker may conclude and perform contracts of employment in accordance with the laws of the host state.[141] Any provisions which discriminate against foreign nationals or hinder foreign nationals from obtaining work are not permissible.[142]

(a) Direct Discrimination

The prohibition against discrimination applies to both directly and indirectly discriminatory measures. Measures are directly discriminatory where the migrant worker is treated less favourably than the national worker. This was the case with the Italian law in *Commission* v. *Italy*[143] which provided that private security work could be carried out only by Italian security firms employing only Italian nationals. The '3+2 rule' in *Bosman*,[144] according to which football clubs could play no more than three foreign players and two 'acclimatised' players in any match, was also directly discriminatory. The Court, referring to the principle of non-discrimination contained in Article 39(2) and Article 4 of Regulation 1612/68, said that the principle applied to clauses contained in the regulations of sporting associations which restricted the rights of nationals of other Member States to take part, as professional players, in football matches. It continued that it was irrelevant that the clauses did not concern the employment of such players, on which there was no restriction, but the extent to which their clubs could field them in official matches. It said that in so far as participation in official matches was the essential purpose of a professional player's life, a rule which restricted that participation obviously also restricted the chances of employment of the player concerned. Such directly discriminatory measures breach both Article 39 (and the Regulation) and can be saved only by reference to one of the express derogations laid down by the Treaty or the secondary legislation.

Regulation 1612/68 itself identifies and seeks to eliminate other directly discriminatory barriers on access to employment. For example, Article 4(1) provides that national provisions which restrict, by number or percentage, the employment of foreign nationals in any undertaking do not apply to nationals of the other Member States. Therefore in *Commission* v. *France*[145]

---

[141] Art. 2.

[142] Art. 3(1). Some examples listed in Art. 3(2) are: prescribing a special recruitment procedure for foreign nationals, restricting the advertising of vacancies in the press, and imposing additional requirements on applicants from other Member States of subjecting eligibility for employment to conditions of registration with employment offices.

[143] Case C–283/99 *Commission* v. *Italy* [2001] ECR I–4363.

[144] Case C–415/93 [1995] ECR I–4921. See also Case 13/76 *Dona and Mantero* [1976] ECR 1333.

[145] Case 167/73 *Commission* v. *France (French Merchant Seamen)* [1974] ECR 359. See also the '3+2 rule' in Case C–415/93 *Bosman* [1995] ECR I–4921.

the Court said that a French rule requiring a ratio of three French to one non-French seaman on a merchant ship contravened Article 4(1). Article 4(2) provides that if there is a requirement that an undertaking is subject to a minimum percentage of national workers being employed, nationals of the other Member States are counted as national workers. Article 6 provides that the engagement and recruitment of a worker must not depend on medical, vocational or other criteria which are discriminatory on the grounds of nationality. However, it does permit the employer to require the migrant worker to take a vocational test when offering employment.

(b) Indirect Discrimination

Indirect discrimination involves the elimination of requirements which, while apparently nationality-neutral on their face, have a greater impact or impose a greater burden on nationals of other Member States or have the effect of hindering the free movement of persons.[146] Thus, indirect discrimination focuses on the effect of a measure. This is recognized by Article 3(1) of Regulation 1612/68[147] which says that provisions laid down by national law will not apply where, 'though applicable irrespective of nationality, their exclusive or principal aim *or effect* is to keep nationals of other Member States away from employment offered'.[148] The Court also made this clear in *O'Flynn*:[149]

[C]onditions imposed by national law must be regarded as indirectly discriminatory where, although applicable irrespective of nationality, they affect essentially migrant workers . . . or the great majority of those affected are migrant workers, . . . where they are indistinctly applicable but can be more easily satisfied by national workers than by migrant workers . . . or where there is a risk that they may operate to the particular detriment of migrant workers . . .

Indirectly discriminatory measures also breach Article 39 and the Regulation unless saved by one of the express derogations or objectively justified.[150] As the Court continued in *O'Flynn*:[151]

It is otherwise only if those provisions are justified by objective considerations independent of the nationality of the workers concerned, and if they are proportionate to the legitimate aim pursued by national law.

From this we can see that, unless objectively justified and proportionate

---

[146] See e.g. Case C–175/88 *Biehl* v. *Admininstration des Contributions* [1990] ECR I–1779; Case C–111/91 *Commission* v. *Luxembourg* [1993] ECR I–817.
[147] OJ SE [1968] L257/2/475.   [148] Emphasis added.
[149] Case C–237/94 *O'Flynn* v. *Adjudication Officer* [1996] ECR I–2617, para. 18.
[150] See e.g. Case C–15/96 *Kalliope Schöning-Kougebetopoulou* v. *Freie und Hansestadt Hamburg* [1998] ECR I–47. See also Case C–187/96 *Commission* v. *Greece* [1998] ECR I–1095; Case C–350/96 *Clean Car Autoservice* v. *Landeshauptmann von Wien* [1998] ECR I–2521.
[151] Para. 19.

to its aim, the provision of national law must be regarded as indirectly discriminatory and contrary to Community law if it is *intrinsically liable* to affect migrant workers more than national workers and if there is *a risk* that it will place migrant workers at a particular disadvantage.[152] The Court added that it was not necessary to find that the measure did in practice affect a substantially higher proportion of migrant workers. It was sufficient that it was liable to have such an effect.[153]

Service requirements are often found to be indirectly discriminatory. This can be seen in *Scholz*[154] where a German woman applied for a job in Italy but the selection board refused to take into account her previous employment in Germany. The Court found this constituted unjustified indirect discrimination.[155] Language requirements are also indirectly discriminatory but they can usually be justified. This is expressly recognized by Article 3(1), paragraph 2 of Regulation 1612/68 which provides that the principle of equal treatment does not apply in respect of 'conditions relating to linguistic knowledge required by reason of the nature of the post to be filled'. This provision was successfully relied on by the Irish government in *Groener*[156] concerning a Dutch woman who was refused a permanent post at the design college in Dublin where she had been teaching because she did not speak Gaelic. Even though she did not need to use Gaelic for her work, the Court upheld the language requirement because it formed part of government policy to promote the use of the Irish language as a means of expressing national culture and identity.[157] It said that since education was important for the implementation of such a policy, with teachers playing an essential role, the requirement for teachers to have an adequate knowledge of the Irish language was compatible with Article 3(1), provided that the level of knowledge was not disproportionate to the objective pursued.[158] However, the Court did add that the Irish government could not require that the linguistic knowledge be acquired in Ireland.[159] *Angonese*[160] emphasized this point.

Angonese concerned a requirement imposed by a bank operating in Bolzano (the Italian and German speaking province of Italy), that admission to its recruitment competition was conditional on possession of a certificate of bilingualism. Because this certificate could be obtained only in Bolzano,

---

[152] Para. 20. The fact that nationals may also be affected by the rule does not prevent the rule from being indirectly discriminatory, provided that the majority of those affected were non-nationals: Case C–281/98 *Roman Angonese v. Cassa di Risparmio di Bolzano* [2000] ECR I–4139, para. 41.

[153] Para. 21. Cf. the position in respect of Art. 90 where actual disparate impact must be shown: Case 132/88 *Commission v. Greece* [1990] ECR I–1567.

[154] Case C–419/92 *Scholz v. Opera Universitaria di Cagliari and Cinzia Porcedda* [1994] ECR I–505.

[155] Para. 11.   [156] Case 379/87 *Groener v. Minister for Education* [1989] ECR 3967.

[157] Paras. 18–19.   [158] Para. 21.   [159] Para. 23.

[160] Case C–281/98 [2000] ECR I–4139.

Angonese, an Italian national who had studied in Austria, was not able
to compete for a post working in the bank on the grounds that he lacked
the Bolzano certificate, even though he submitted other evidence of his
bilingualism.

The Court found the rule to be indirectly discriminatory[161] even though
the requirement affected Italian nationals resident in other parts of Italy as
well as nationals from other Member States. It said that since the majority
of residents of the province of Bolzano were Italian nationals the obligation
to obtain the certificate put nationals of other Member States at a disadvantage compared with residents of the province, making it difficult, if not
impossible, for them to get jobs in Bolzano.[162] On the question of justification, the Court said that while the bank could justify requiring job applicants to have a certain level of linguistic knowledge (e.g. a diploma),
the fact that it was impossible to show proof of this knowledge by any
other means—in particular by equivalent qualifications from other Member
States—was disproportionate[163] and so the bank's requirement breached
Article 39.

(c) Non-discrimination and Measures which Substantially Impede Market Access

Non-discriminatory national measures which (substantially) impede access to
the market also breach Article 39 and the Regulation unless objectively justified. This can be seen in *Bosman*.[164] Not only did Bosman object to the 3+2
rule but he also complained that the rules laid down by sporting associations
under which a professional footballer who was a national of one Member
State could not, on the expiry of his contract with a club, be employed by
another, unless the latter club had paid to the former a transfer, training, or
development fee. The rules were not discriminatory, because they also applied
to transfers between clubs belonging to different national associations within
the same Member State and were similar to those governing transfers between
clubs belonging to the same national association. Nevertheless, the Court
found that the rules 'directly affect[ed] players' access to the employment
market in other Member States'[165] and therefore constituted an unjustified
'obstacle to the freedom of movement of workers'.[166] They therefore breached
Article 39.

---

[161] The Court reasoned that 'in order for a measure to be treated as being discriminatory
on grounds of nationality, it is not necessary for the measure to have the effect of putting at
an advantage all the workers of one nationality or of putting at a disadvantage only workers
who are nationals of other Member States, but not workers of the nationality in question'
(para. 41).

[162] Para. 39.   [163] Para. 44.

[164] Case C–415/93 [1995] ECR I–4921.   [165] Para. 103.

[166] Para. 104. See Johnson and O'Keefe, 'From Discrimination to Obstacles to Free Movement:
Recent Developments concerning the Free Movement of Workers 1989–1994' (1994) 31
CMLRev. 1313.

On the other hand, if the effect of the national legislation is, as in *Graf*,[167] 'too uncertain and indirect . . . to be capable of being regarded as liable to hinder free movement for workers', then the measure does not breach Article 39 or the Regulation.[168] The facts of *Graf* were unusual. Graf, a German national, had worked for his Austrian employer for four years until he resigned to take up employment in Germany. Under Austrian law, a worker who had worked for the same employer for more than three years was entitled to unfair dismissal compensation provided that he was dismissed (and did not just resign). Graf argued that this rule contravened Article 39 because the effect of the Austrian rule was that he lost the chance of being dismissed and so was unable to claim compensation for unfair dismissal.

The Court disagreed: the Austrian law was genuinely non-discriminatory and did not preclude or deter a worker from ending his contract of employment in order to take a job with another employer. The Court explained that the entitlement to unfair dismissal compensation was not dependent on the worker's choosing whether or not to stay with his current employer but on a future and hypothetical event (being unfairly dismissed). The Court concluded that such an event was too uncertain and indirect a possibility for legislation to be capable of being regarded as liable to hinder free movement for workers.[169] Thus, the Court considered that the event was too remote to be considered liable to affect free movement.[170] Putting it another way, measures which do not substantially hinder access to the market fall outside Article 39.

Sometimes the Court abandons the discrimination analysis altogether and examines instead whether the national measure constitutes an 'obstacle to freedom of movement for workers' (the language used in *Bosman* and confirmed in *Terhoeve*)[171] or is 'liable to hamper or to render less attractive' the exercise of the rights to free movement (*Kraus*).[172] Whichever form of words is used, if the Court finds there is an obstacle or impediment,[173] it then examines whether the rule can be objectively justified. If, on the other hand, the Court finds there is no obstacle to free movement then the measure is lawful. Therefore, in *Burbaud*[174] the Court said that the requirement of passing an exam in order to take up a post in the public service could

---

[167] Case C–190/98 [2002] ECR I–493.   [168] Paras. 24–5.   [169] Para. 25.
[170] Cf. Case C–159/90 *SPUC v. Grogan* [1991] ECR I–4685, para. 24; Case C–168/91 *Konstantinidis* [1993] ECR I–1191, para. 15.
[171] Case C–18/95 *Terhoeve* [1999] ECR I–345, para. 41; Case C–385/00 *F.W.L. de Groot v. Staatssecretaris van Financiën* [2002] ECR I–11819, para. 95.
[172] Case C–19/92 *Kraus v. Land Baden-Württemberg* [1993] ECR I–1663, para. 32; Case C–431/01 *Mertens v. Belgium* [2002] ECR I–7073, para. 37.
[173] Occasionally it finds no obstacle: Case C–33/99 *Fahmi and Cerdeiro-Pinedo Amado v. Bestuur van de Sociale Verzekeringsbank* [2001] ECR I–2415, para. 43.
[174] Case C–285/01 *Isabel Burbaud v. Ministère de l'Emploi et de la Solidarité* [2003] ECR I–000.

not 'in itself be regarded as an obstacle' to free movement.[175] The national rule was therefore compatible with Community law. This was also the effect of the rule in *Graf*, considered above, although the language used was different.

(d) Justification

As we have seen in *O'Flynn*, indirectly discriminatory measures and non-discriminatory measures which substantially impede market access in principle breach Article 39. However, if the defendant Member State can objectively justify the measure and the steps taken are proportionate then the measure is lawful.[176] This can be seen in *Bosman*. The justifications raised were that in view of the considerable social importance of sporting activities and in particular football in the Community, the aims of maintaining a balance between the clubs by preserving a certain degree of equality and uncertainty as to results, and of encouraging the recruitment and training of young players, had to be accepted as legitimate. However, while the Court in principle accepted the justification, it supported Bosman's contention that the application of the transfer rules was not an adequate means of maintaining financial and competitive balance in the world of football. Those rules neither precluded the richest clubs from securing the services of the best players nor prevented the availability of financial resources from being a decisive factor in competitive sport, thus considerably altering the balance between clubs.

The Court also accepted that the prospect of receiving transfer, development or training fees was likely to encourage football clubs to seek new talent and train young players. However, it said that since it was impossible to predict the sporting future of young players with any certainty and because only a limited number of such players went on to play professionally, those fees were by nature contingent and uncertain and were, in any event, unrelated to the actual cost borne by clubs of training both future professional players and those who would never play professionally. The prospect of receiving such fees could not therefore be either a decisive factor in encouraging recruitment and training of young players or an adequate means of financing such activities, particularly in the case of smaller clubs.

---

[175] Para. 96. To emphasize the point, the Court said that inasmuch as all new jobs are subject to a recruitment procedure, the requirement of passing a recruitment competition could not 'in itself be liable to dissuade candidates who have already sat a similar competition in another Member State from exercising their right to freedom of movement as workers' (para. 97).

[176] This issue is considered in more detail in Ch. 5.

4.3. Equal Treatment during the Employment Relationship

(a) Equal Treatment in Respect of the Terms and Conditions of Employment

Title II of the Regulation 1612/68 concerns the exercise of employment (as opposed to access to employment in Title I). Article 7(1) states that a migrant worker must not be treated:

... differently from national workers in respect of any conditions of employment and work, in particular as regards remuneration, dismissal, and should he become unemployed, reinstatement or reemployment.[177]

Most of the case law concerns indirectly discriminatory measures. For example, in *Allué and Coonan*[178] an Italian law limited the duration of contracts of employment of foreign language assistants, without imposing the same limitation on other workers. Since only 25 per cent of foreign language assistants were Italian nationals, the law essentially concerned nationals of other Member States. It was indirectly discriminatory[179] and could not be justified.

Service requirements may also be indirectly discriminatory. For example, in *Ugliola*[180] German law provided that a period spent performing military service in Germany had to be taken into account by an employer when calculating periods of service for the purposes of pay or other benefits but this requirement did not apply to military service carried out in other Member States. The Court found the rule to be indirectly discriminatory since it had a greater impact on non-Germans working in Germany who were more likely to have done their military service in their state of origin. Similarly, in *Schöning-Kougebetopoulou*[181] the Court found that a collective agreement (BAT) providing for promotion on grounds of seniority but which took no account of service performed in another Member State 'manifestly' worked to the detriment of migrant workers and so breached Article 39.

Subsequently, in *Köbler*[182] the Court departed from the discrimination model in favour of the hindrance/obstacle approach in a case concerning a special length-of-service increment granted by Austria to professors who had worked

---

[177] Art. 7(1) only applies to payments made by virtue of statutory or contracted obligations incumbent on the employer as a condition of employment; see Case C–315/94 *Peter de Vos v. Stadt Bielefeld* [1996] ECR I–1417.

[178] Case 33/88 *Allué and Coonan v. Università degli studi di Venezia* [1989] ECR 1591. See also Case 41/84 *Pinna v. Caisse d'allocations familiales de la Savoie* [1986] ECR 1 and Case C–272/92 *Spotti v. Freistaat Bayern* [1993] ECR I–5185. The Court extended this ruling to nationals of a non-EU state (e.g. Poland) in the context of Art. 37(1) of the Europe Agreement: Case C–162/00 *Land-Nordrhein-Westfalen v. Beata Pokrzeptowicz-Meyer* [2002] ECR I–1049, para. 44.

[179] Para. 12.

[180] Case 15/69 *Württembergische Milchverwertung Südmilch AG v. Ugliola* [1969] ECR 363.

[181] Case C–15/96 [1998] ECR I–47. See also Case C–187/96 *Commission v. Greece* [1998] ECR I–1095; Case C–195/98 *Österreichischer Gewerkschaftsbund, Gewerkschaft öffentlicher Dienst v. Republik Österreich* [2000] ECR I–10497; Case C–27/91 *URSSAF v. Le Manoir* [1991] ECR I–5531 and Case C–419/92 *Scholz* [1994] ECR I–505.

[182] Case C–224/01 *Gerhard Köbler v. Republik Österreich* [2003] ECR I–10239.

in an Austrian university for at least 15 years. It said that such a regime was clearly 'likely to impede freedom of movement for workers'[183] because first, the regime operated to the detriment of migrant workers who were nationals of other Member States and secondly, it deterred freedom of movement for workers established in Austria by discouraging them from leaving the country to work in other Member States if this period of experience was not taken into account on their return to Austria.[184] The measure was therefore 'likely to constitute an obstacle to freedom of movement for workers'.[185]

Residence requirements are also likely to be indirectly discriminatory. So, in *Clean Car*[186] the Court found that an Austrian rule requiring business managers to be resident in Austria before they could work in Vienna breached Article 39. It noted that the rule was liable to operate mainly to the detriment of nationals of other Member States since the majority of non-residents were foreigners.[187]

If the measure is indirectly discriminatory, then the burden shifts to the Member State to justify the restriction and to show that the steps taken are proportionate. Generally the Court takes a rigorous approach to justifications put forward by Member States. In *Clean Car*[188] Austria sought to justify the residence requirement on the grounds that the manager needed to be in a position to act effectively in the business, to be served with a notice of any fines imposed and to have those fines enforced against him. The Court rejected such justifications, ruling that the residence requirement was either inappropriate to achieve the aim pursued or went beyond what was necessary for that purpose.[189] It also noted that other less restrictive measures were available to achieve those objectives, such as serving a notice of the fines at the registered office of the company employing the manager. Austria could also ensure that the fines would be paid by requiring a guarantee in advance.

The Court adopted a similarly rigorous approach to justification of seniority requirements. In *Schöning-Kougebetopoulou*[190] the German government justified its rule on the grounds that it rewarded loyalty to the employer and motivated the employee by the prospect of improvement in his financial situation. The German government explained that the BAT covered not only the majority of German public institutions but also undertakings performing public interest tasks. For this very reason, the Court said that to take into account periods of employment completed with one of those institutions in determining seniority for the purposes of promotion could not, given the multiplicity of employers, be justified by the desire to reward employee loyalty. The system afforded

---

[183] Para. 72.   [184] Paras. 73–4.   [185] Para. 77.
[186] Case C–350/96 [1998] ECR I–2521. See also Case C–472/99 *Clean Car Autoservice GmbH* v. *Stadt Wien and Republik Österreich* [2001] ECR I–9687 on the issue of costs following the Court's earlier judgment.
[187] Para. 29.   [188] Case C–350/96 [1998] ECR I–2521.
[189] Para. 34.   [190] Case C–15/96 [1998] ECR I–47.

employees covered by the BAT considerable mobility within a group of legally separate employers and therefore the discrimination could not be justified.

Where, as in *Schöning-Kougebetopoulou*, the Court finds that a clause from a collective agreement or contract discriminates against workers from other Member States, Article 7(4) of Regulation 1612/68 provides that such clauses are null and void in so far as they lay down or authorize discriminatory conditions. Until the parties amend the agreement to eliminate the discrimination, the migrant workers enjoy the same rules as those which apply to nationals.[191]

(b) Equal Treatment in Respect of Social and Tax Advantages

Tax Advantages

Article 7(2)[192] provides that a worker will enjoy the same social and tax advantages as national workers. As far as taxation is concerned,[193] most of the cases concern the situation of national rules which treat residents differently from non-residents. As we have already seen, discrimination on the grounds of residence can indirectly discriminate against migrants.[194] However, this presupposes that the circumstances of residents and non-residents are comparable. In *Schumacker*[195] the Court recognized that this might not always be the case since there are objective differences between the two situations:[196] usually the state of residence grants taxpayers all the tax allowances relating to their personal and family circumstances because the state of residence is in the best position to assess the taxpayers' ability to pay tax since their personal and financial interests are centred there;[197] the same will not apply to non-residents. This distinction is recognized by international tax law and may justify the two situations being treated differently.

However, if, on the facts of the case, the situations of the resident and non-resident taxpayer can be considered comparable, then it would be discriminatory to treat the two situations differently. This is particularly so in

---

[191] Case C–15/96 *Kalliope Schöning-Kougebetopoulou* [1998] ECR I–47, para. 33, applying by analogy the Art. 141 case law on equal pay: e.g. Case C–184/89 *Nimz v. Freie und Hansestadt Hamburg* [1991] ECR I–297, para. 18; Case C–33/89 *Kowalska v. Freie und Hansestadt Hamburg* [1990] ECR I–2591, para. 20. This is considered further in Ch. 7.

[192] For a detailed examination of this provision see O'Keefe, 'Equal Rights for Migrants: the Concept of Social Advantages in Article 7(2), Reg. 1612/68' (1985) 5 *YEL*. 92.

[193] It has always been clear that direct taxation falls within the competence of the Member States. As the Court pointed out in Case C–246/89 *Commission v. UK* [1991] ECR I–4585, the powers retained by the Member States in respect of taxation, however, must be exercised consistently with Community law.

[194] Case C–175/88 *Biehl v. Administration des contributions du grand-duché de Luxembourg* [1990] ECR I–1779, para. 14.

[195] Case C–279/93 *Finanzamt Köln-Altstadt v. Schumacker* [1995] ECR I–225.

[196] See also Art. 58(1) EC.   [197] Para. 32.

the case of frontier workers such as Mr Schumacker,[198] a Belgian national who lived in Belgium with his family but worked in Germany. Because he was a non-resident worker his wages were subject to German income tax on a limited basis. This meant that he was denied certain benefits which were available to resident taxpayers. The Court ruled that a non-resident taxpayer who received all or almost all of his income in the state of employment was objectively in the same situation as a resident in that state who did the same work there. The discrimination arose because the non-resident taxpayer did not have his personal and family circumstances taken into account either in his state of residence (where he received no income) or in his state of employment (where he was not resident).[199] Consequently, his overall tax burden was greater than that of the resident taxpayer.[200]

If discrimination can be shown, then the Court must consider whether it can be justified. In *Bachmann*[201] the Court recognized the 'need to preserve the cohesion of the tax system' as one such justification. The case concerned a Belgian law according to which the cost of life insurance premiums could not be deducted from taxable income where the premiums were paid in other Member States. This was because Belgium tax law gave the individual the choice of either having tax deducted on the premiums and then paying tax on future benefits or not having tax deducted on the premiums and then not paying tax on future benefits. If it deducted premiums paid in Germany, it would have no way of being able to tax future benefits also payable in Germany. For this reason the Belgian rules were justified because there was a 'direct link' between the right to deduct contributions and the taxation of sums payable by insurers under pension and life assurance contracts; and that preserving that link was necessary to safeguard the cohesion of the tax system.[202] Since *Bachmann* Member States have regularly invoked fiscal cohesion as a justification for its tax policies—but always without success.[203] The Court has insisted that the cohesion justification requires a direct link between the discriminatory tax rule and the compensating tax advantage.

The other justification commonly raised is the effectiveness of fiscal supervision. Although first recognized in *Cassis* in 1979,[204] Member States

---

[198] Case C–279/93 [1995] ECR I–225. See also Case C–87/99 *Zurstrassen* v. *Administration des contributions directes* [2000] ECR I–3337. See generally Wathelet, 'The Influence of Free Movement of Persons, Services and Capital on National Direct Taxation: Trends in the Case Law of the European Court of Justice' (2001) 20 *YEL*. 1.

[199] Para. 38.   [200] Para. 28.

[201] Case C–204/90 *Bachmann* v. *Belgian State* [1992] ECR I–249, para. 21, and Case C–300/90 *Commission* v. *Belgium* [1992] ECR I–305, para. 14.

[202] Paras. 21–3.

[203] See e.g. Case C–80/94 *Wielockx* v. *Inspecteur der Directe Belastingen* [1995] ECR I–2493; Case C–107/94 *Asscher* v. *Staatssecretaris van Financiën* [1996] ECR I–3089; Case C–264/96 *Imperial Chemical Industries* v. *Colmer* [1998] ECR I–4695.

[204] Case 120/78 *Rewe Zentrale* v. *Bundesmonopolverwaltung für Branntwein* ('*Cassis de Dijon*') [1979] ECR 649.

have had little success in actually relying on it since.[205] For instance, in *Schumacker* Germany said that administrative difficulties prevented the state of employment (Germany) from determining the income received by non-residents in their state of residence (Belgium). The Court rejected this argument, reasoning that this difficulty could be overcome through the application of Directive 77/799[206] on mutual assistance in the field of direct taxation.[207]

Social Advantages

Article 7(2) requires social advantages to be provided on a non-discriminatory basis. In *Even*[208] the Court defined 'social advantages' broadly to include all benefits:[209]

. . . which, whether or not linked to a contract of employment, are generally granted to national workers primarily because of their objective status as workers *or by virtue of the mere fact of their residence on the national territory* and the extension of which to workers who are nationals of other Member States therefore seems suitable to *facilitate their mobility* within the Community.

The concept of social advantage embraces benefits granted as of right[210] or on a discretionary basis[211] and those granted after employment has terminated (e.g. a pension).[212] It also covers benefits not directly linked to employment such as language rights,[213] death benefits,[214] rights for a dependent child to obtain finance for studies,[215] and rights to bring in unmarried companions.[216] These benefits do not necessarily 'facilitate mobility', as the *Even* formula requires, but do assist in the process of integrating the migrant worker into the society of the host state.[217]

The decision in *Even*, with its reference to 'residence on the national territory', showed that Article 7(2) applied not just to benefits granted by the host

---

[205]   See e.g. Case C–254/97 *Baxter and others* v. *Premier Ministre and others* [1999] ECR I–4809; Case C–55/98 *Skatteministeriet* v. *Bent Vestergaard* [1999] ECR I–7641.

[206]   [1977] OJ L336/15.   [207]   Para. 45.

[208]   Case 207/78 *Criminal Proceedings against Even* [1979] ECR 2019.

[209]   Para. 22, emphasis added.

[210]   See e.g. Case C–111/91 *Commission* v. *Luxembourg*; Case C–85/96 *Martínez Sala* [1998] ECR I–2691, para. 28.

[211]   Case 65/81 *Reina* v. *Landeskreditbank Baden-Württemberg* [1982] ECR 33, para. 17.

[212]   See e.g. Case C–57/96 *Meints* v. *Minister van Landbouw, Natuurbeheer en Visserij* [1997] ECR I–6689, para. 36 (payment to agricultural workers whose employment contracts are terminated); Case C–35/97 *Commission* v. *France* [1998] ECR I–5325 (supplementary retirement pension points).

[213]   Case 137/84 *Criminal proceedings against Mutsch* [1985] ECR 2681, para. 18 (criminal proceedings in the defendant's own language).

[214]   Case C–237/94 *O'Flynn* v. *Adjudication Officer* [1996] ECR I–2617 (social security payments to help cover the cost of burying a family member).

[215]   Case C–3/90 *Bernini* v. *Minister van Onderwijs en Wetenschappen* [1992] ECR I–1071; Case C–337/97 *Meeusen* [1999] ECR I–3289, para. 15

[216]   Case 59/85 *Netherlands* v. *Reed* [1986] ECR 1283, para. 28.

[217]   Ellis, 'Social Advantages: A New Lease of Life' (2003) 40 *CMLRev.* 639, 648.

state to its workers[218] but also to its residents.[219] This meant that both migrant workers *and* their families who were legally resident could enjoy the social advantages offered by the home state.[220] The Court justified this development on the grounds that Article 7(2) was essential not only to encourage free movement of workers as well as their families (without whom the worker would be discouraged from moving)[221] but also to encourage their integration into the environment of the host state.[222] As the Court said in *Baumbast*,[223] the aim of Regulation 1612/68 on free movement of persons was 'for such freedom to be guaranteed in compliance with the principles of liberty and dignity, the best possible conditions for the integration of the Community worker's family in the society of the host Member State'.

In *Christini*[224] and *Castelli*[225] the Court confirmed that family members enjoyed equal treatment in respect of social advantages. In *Christini* the French railways had a scheme which offered a fare reduction for people with large families. Christini, an Italian mother resident in France and the widow of an Italian who had worked in France, was refused the fare reduction on the grounds of her nationality and SNCF justified this on the grounds that Article 7(2) applied only to advantages connected with the contract of employment. The Court disagreed, arguing that in view of the equality of treatment that Article 7(2) was designed to achieve, its substantive area of application had to be delineated to include all social and tax advantages, regardless of any connection with an employment contract, including fare reductions for large families. It added that Article 7(2) applied to those lawfully entitled to remain in the host state, irrespective of whether the 'trigger' for the rights—the worker—was alive.

The Court adopted a similarly broad approach in *Castelli* concerning an Italian woman who lived in Belgium with her son but who never worked. She was refused a pension on the grounds that she was not Belgian and that no reciprocal agreement existed between Belgium and Italy. Nevertheless, the

---

[218] This includes those who are not resident in the territory of the providing state: Case C–57 *Meints* [1997] ECR I–6689, para. 50; Case C–337/97 *Meeusen* [1999] ECR I–3289, para. 21.

[219] AG Jacobs in Case C–43/99 *Leclerce and Deaconescu* v. *Caisse nationale des prestations familiales* [2001] ECR I–4265, para. 96. Peers, ' "Social Advantages" and Discrimination in Employment: Case Law Confirmed and Clarified' (1997) 22 *ELRev.* 157, 164.

[220] Cf. the early decision in Case 76/72 *Michel S.* v. *Fonds national de reclassement social des handicapés* [1973] ECR 457, para. 9, where the Court limited social advantages to workers.

[221] See e.g. Case 94/84 *ONEM* v. *Deak* [1985] ECR 1873.

[222] See also Joined Cases 389 and 390/87 *Echternach and Moritz* v. *Minister van Onderwijs en Wetenschappen* [1989] ECR 723; Case C–308/93 *Bestuur van de Sociale Verzekeringsbank* v. *Cabanis-Issarte* [1996] ECR I–2097.

[223] Case C–413/99 *Baumbast and R* v. *Secretary of State for the Home Department* [2002] ECR I–7091, para. 50.

[224] Case 32/75 *Fiorini (née Christini)* v. *SNCF* [1975] ECR 1085. See also Case C–278/94 *Commission* v. *Belgium* [1996] ECR I–4307 (tideover benefits); Case C–185/96 *Commission* v. *Greece* [1998] ECR I–6601 (attribution of large family status).

[225] Case 261/83 *Castelli* v. *ONPTS* [1984] ECR 3199.

Court found that the concept of social advantage in Article 7(2) included a pension, reasoning that the concept of equal treatment in Article 7(1) of Regulation 1612/68 was also intended to prevent discrimination against a worker's dependent relatives.[226]

This line of case law has been endorsed by the Citizens' Rights Directive 2004/38.[227] This provides that EU citizens *and* family members with the right of residence and the right of permanent residence will enjoy equal treatment with the nationals of the host state in areas covered by the Treaty.[228] However, it appears that even workers and their family members can be deprived of the right to 'social assistance', a term which is not defined in the Directive, during the first three months of residence or for a longer period in the case of work seekers (Article 24/2), although compare Article 14(1) which suggests merely that they cannot be 'an unreasonable burden' on the host state's social assistance system. This limitation does not appear in Article 7(2) although in *Lebon*[229] the Court did rule that certain groups (e.g. work seekers and non-dependent family members) did not enjoy the benefit of Article 7(2).[230] *Collins*,[231] considered in chapter 1, appears to have reversed this ruling.

However, there are some limits to the scope of Article 7(2), as the facts of *Even* itself demonstrates.[232] The case concerned Belgian regulations providing that a retirement pension could begin, if requested, up to five years prior to the normal pension age of 65, albeit with a 5 per cent reduction for early payment per year. This reduction was not made in the case of Belgians who had served in the Allied Forces during World War II and had received an invalidity pension granted by a World War II allied country. Mr Even, a French national living in Belgium, in receipt of an invalidity pension from the French government, wished to receive the full Belgian state pension. The Court said that the relevant Belgian legislation could not be considered an advantage granted to a national worker because it benefited those who had given wartime service to their own country and 'its essential objective is to give those nationals an advantage by reason of the hardships suffered for that country'.[233] *Even* can perhaps be explained on the basis of the sensitive issues at stake: the Court did not want to face a future claim made by a migrant who was a former World War II soldier but who did not serve with the Allied Forces.

---

[226] Ibid., concerning dependent relatives in the ascending line; in Case 94/84 *Deak* [1985] ECR 1873 the Court extended the benefit to dependent descendants, even though the descendant was a TCN.

[227] COM(2003)199 final.   [228] Art. 21.

[229] Case 316/85 *Centre public d'aide sociale de Courcelles (CPAS)* v. *Lebon* [1987] ECR 2811 and Case C–3/90 *Bernini* [1992] ECR I–1071

[230] See further M. Dougan, 'The Workseeker as Citizen' (2001) 4 *CYELS* 93.

[231] Case C–138/02 *Brian Francis Collins* v. *Secretary of State for Work and Pensions* [2004] ECR I–2703.

[232] Case 207/78 [1979] ECR 2019. See also Case C–315/94 *De Vos* [1996] ECR I–1417. Cf. Case 15/69 *Ugliola* [1970] ECR 363.

[233] Para. 23.

In *Leclere*[234] the Court gave a more detailed statement of the limits of Article 7(2). Leclere and his wife were Belgian. He was a frontier worker who lived in Belgium but worked in Luxembourg. After having an accident in Luxembourg the authorities there paid him an invalidity pension but when his wife subsequently had a child he was refused a childbirth allowance by the Luxembourg authorities on the grounds that he was not a worker. The Court upheld this decision. It said that as a former worker Leclere retained his status as worker in respect of the invalidity pension linked with his previous employment and so was protected against any discrimination affecting rights acquired during the former employment. On the other hand, since he was not currently engaged in an employment relationship, he could not claim *new* rights which had no links with his former occupation.[235]

If the benefit does constitute a social advantage, then it must be provided on a non-discriminatory basis. While most of the cases considered so far concern direct discrimination, the Court has also used Article 7(2) to prohibit unjustified indirect discrimination.[236] For example, in *O'Flynn*[237] an Irish national resident in the UK applied to the British authorities for a payment to cover the costs of his son's funeral in Ireland. His application was refused on the grounds that the burial should have taken place in the UK. This requirement was found to be indirectly discriminatory and contrary to Article 7(2). However, the Court did say that the UK could limit the allowance to a lump sum or reasonable amount fixed by reference to the normal cost of a burial in the UK.

(c) Equal Treatment and Vocational Training

Article 7(3) provides that a worker shall 'have access to training in vocational schools and retraining centres' under the same conditions as national workers. In *Gravier*[238] the Court defined 'vocational training' broadly to include any form of education which prepares for a qualification or which provides the necessary training or skills for a particular profession, trade, or employment. In *Blaizot*[239] the Court confirmed that vocational training could be received at universities, except in the case of courses intended for students 'wishing to improve their general knowledge rather than prepare themselves for a particular occupation'.[240]

---

[234] Case C–43/99 [2001] ECR I–4265.   [235] Para. 59.
[236] See e.g. Case C–299/01 *Commission v. Luxembourg* [2002] ECR I–5899. See also Case C–111/91 *Commission v. Luxembourg* [1993] ECR I–817.
[237] Case C–237/94 [1996] ECR I–2617.
[238] Case 293/83 *Gravier v. Ville de Liège* [1985] ECR 593, para. 30. For background see Lenaerts, 'Education in European Community Law after "Maastricht" ' (1994) 31 *CMLRev*. 7; Shaw, 'From the Margins to the Centre: Education and Training Law and Policy', in Craig and de Búrca (eds), *The Evolution of EU Law* (OUP, Oxford, 1999).
[239] Case 24/86 *Blaizot v. Université de Liège and Others* [1988] ECR 379.
[240] Paras. 19–20.

Access to training is one thing, payment for that training is another. In *Gravier* the Court said that since access to training was likely to promote free movement of persons by enabling them to obtain a qualification in the Member State where they intended to work,[241] the conditions of access to vocational training fell within the scope of the Treaty. Therefore, if a host state charged a registration fee to migrant students but not to its own students, it breached Article 12 EC.[242]

Gravier concerned fees and not maintenance grants. Maintenance grants can constitute 'social advantages' within the meaning of Article 7(2),[243] as *Matteucci*[244] shows. The case concerned the daughter of an Italian worker in Belgium who was educated in Belgium and then taught rhythmics. She applied for a scholarship, which was available on a bilateral (Belgium–Germany) basis, to study singing in Berlin but her application was rejected on the ground that she was not Belgian. The Court said that this was contrary to Article 7(2): a bilateral agreement reserving scholarships for nationals of the two Member States which were the parties to the agreement could not prevent the application of the principle of equality under Community law.

Mateucci's case was a strong one: she had lived and worked in Belgium all her life. But the case law on Article 7(2) is open to exploitation by those who do short-term casual work in another Member State and then claim entitlement to social advantages in the form of a grant for further study in the host state. The Court had to deal with this problem in two important cases, *Lair*[245] and *Brown*.[246] *Lair* concerned a French woman who had moved to Germany where she worked on a series of part-time contracts. Having decided to study for a languages degree at the University of Hanover she sought a maintenance grant. The Court recognized that people who had previously pursued an effective and genuine activity in the host state could still be considered workers and so could receive a maintenance grant under Article 7(2) but on condition that there was a link between the previous occupational activity[247] and the studies.[248] However, in the case of a migrant worker becoming involuntarily unemployed no link between the studies and the occupational

---

[241] Para. 24.   [242] Para. 26.

[243] Case C–3/90 *Bernini* [1992] ECR I–1071, para. 23, where the Court ruled that descendants of workers could rely on Art. 7(2) to obtain study finance under the same conditions as children of national workers. This also applies to non-resident children of migrant workers (Case C–337/97 *Meeusen* [1999] ECR I–3289, para. 25) but not to workers who have returned to their states of origin (Case C–33/99 *Fahini* [2001] ECR I–2415, para. 46).

[244] Case 235/87 *Matteucci v. Communauté française de Belgique* [1988] ECR 5589.

[245] Case 39/86 *Lair v. Universität Hannover* [1988] ECR 3161. See also Case C–357/90 *Raulin* [1992] ECR I–1027, para. 21.

[246] Case 197/86 *Brown v. Secretary of State for Scotland* [1988] ECR 3205.

[247] The host state cannot make the right to the same social advantages conditional upon a minimum period of prior occupational activity (Case 39/86 *Lair* [1988] ECR 3161, para. 44).

[248] If no link exists between the study and the previous occupational activities, the person does not retain the status of a migrant worker (Case C–357/89 *Raulin* [1992] ECR I–1027).

activity was required before a maintenance grant was awarded. This line of case law has been incorporated in Article 7(3)(d) of the Citizens' Rights Directive 2004/38 which confirms that a Union citizen retains the status of worker or self-employed person if 'he/she embarks on vocational training. Unless he/she is involuntarily unemployed, the retention of the status of worker shall require the training to be related to the previous employment.' The status of worker means that the individual is entitled to equal treatment in respect of maintenance grants under Article 24(2) of the Citizens' Rights Directive 2004/38. For those who are not economically active, they will enjoy equal treatment in respect of students' maintenance only when they are permanent residents (i.e. after five years' residence).

Brown concerned a student with dual French and British nationality who lived in France for many years but had a place at Cambridge University to read engineering. He was sponsored by Ferranti and worked for the company in the UK for eight months before starting his course. He then claimed that he was a worker and so was entitled to a grant from the British government under Article 7(2). However, the Court refused to recognize him as a worker, viewing his work for Ferranti as merely ancillary to his studies,[249] and so he could not claim a grant under Article 7(2). Nor could he rely on the general prohibition of discrimination in Article 12 to obtain a maintenance grant. The Court said that at that stage of development of Community law the assistance given to students for maintenance and training fell outside the scope of the EC Treaty for the purposes of Article 12 EC.[250] This latter aspect of the ruling in *Brown* has been reversed by *Bidar*[251] where the Court ruled that social assistance for a student 'whether in the form of a subsidised loan or a grant, intended to cover his maintenance costs'[252] fell within the scope of application of the Treaty. As a result, Bidar was therefore entitled to have the principle of non-discrimination on the grounds of nationality applied to him.[253]

(d) Equal Treatment and Other Benefits

Equality is not confined to tax and social advantages and vocational training. Article 8(1) provides that migrant workers must also enjoy equality of treatment with nationals in respect of trade union membership and the exercise of rights related to trade union membership, 'including the right to vote and to

---

[249] Para. 27.
[250] Para. 18. This view was confirmed by Art. 3 of the Students' Dir. 93/96 which provided that the Directive does not establish any right to payment of maintenance grants by the host state for students who benefit from the right of residence.
[251] Case C–209/03 R *(on the application of Danny Bidar)* v. *London Borough of Ealing, Secretary of State for Education and Skills* [2005] ECR I–000, considered further in Ch. 1.
[252] Para. 42.
[253] See Dougan, 'Fees, Grants, Loans and Dole Cheques: Who Covers the Costs of Migrant Education within the EU' (2005) *CMLRev.* 943.

be eligible for the administration or management posts of a trade union'.[254] Workers, however, may be excluded from taking part in the management of bodies governed by public law and from holding office governed by public law.[255]

Finally, Article 9 provides that workers must enjoy all the rights and benefits accorded to national workers in matters of housing, including ownership, and the right to put their names on housing lists in the region where they are employed. Therefore in *Commission v. Greece*[256] the Court found a Greek rule restricting a foreigner's right to own property in Greece breached the free movement rules since access to housing and ownership of property was the corollary of free movement.[257] Originally, Article 10(3) of Regulation 1612/68 provided that workers must have available for their family 'housing considered as normal for national workers in the region where he is employed'. According to *Diatta*,[258] the purpose of Article 10(3) is both to implement public policy and to protect public security by preventing immigrants from living in precarious conditions.[259] In *Commission v. Germany*[260] German law required family members of EC migrant workers to have appropriate housing not only upon their arrival but also for the duration of their residence. The Court said that the German law went too far and that Article 10(3) applied solely when the worker and his family were reunited. Once the family had been brought together the position of the migrant worker was no different from that of a national. This rule has now been abolished and not replaced by Directive 2004/38.

(e) Equal Treatment and the Right to Work for Family Members

Article 23 of Directive 2004/38 permits the Union citizen's family members who have the right of residence or the right of permanent residence to take up employment or self-employment in the host state (but not in any other state).[261] This provision broadly replicates Article 11 of Regulation 1612/68. Both Article 23 and the original Article 11 make clear that the right to work applies irrespective of the nationality of the family member.[262] Article 24(1) of Directive 2004/38 provides that these family members must also enjoy equal treatment in respect of their own employment.

---

[254] See further A. Evans, 'Development of European Community Law regarding the Trade Union Rights and Related Rights of Migrant Workers' (1979) 28 *ICLQ* 354. See also Case C–213/90 *Association de Soutien aux Travailleurs Immigrés* v. *Chambre des Employés Privés* [1991] ECR I–3507 and Case C–118/92 *Commission v. Luxembourg* [1994] ECR I–1891. In respect of Art. 10 of the EEC–Turkey Agreement which is interpreted in the same way as Art. 8 of Reg. 1612/68, cf. Case C–171/01 *Wählergruppe, 'Gemeinsam Zajedno/Birlikte Alternative und Grüne Gewerkschafter Innen/UG' and others* [2003] ECR I–4301.

[255] Art. 8.   [256] Case 305/87 *Commission v. Greece* [1989] ECR 1461.

[257] Para. 18.   [258] Case 267/83 [1985] ECR 567.

[259] Ibid., para. 10.   [260] Case 249/86 [1989] ECR 1263.

[261] Case C–10/05 *Mattern v. Ministre du travail et de l'Emploi* [2006] ECR I–000.

[262] Case 131/85 *Gül v. Regierungspräsident Düsseldorf* [1986] ECR 1573.

(f) Equal Treatment and Schooling

With a view to encouraging the integration of migrant children into the society of the host state,[263] Article 12 of Regulation 1612/68 requires the children of an EU national who is or has been employed in another Member State to be admitted to that state's general educational, apprenticeship or vocational training courses.[264] Member States are obliged to encourage these children to attend such courses and, if necessary, make special efforts to ensure that the children can take advantage of educational and training facilities on an equal footing with nationals.[265]

The reference to 'children' includes not only school age children but also those over the age of 21 who are no longer dependent on the working parent. In *Gaal*[266] the Court refused to make a link between the limitations imposed in the original Article 10 (identification of family members) and the rights contained in Article 12. It said that the principle of equal treatment required that the children of migrant workers should be able to continue their studies in order to be able to complete their education successfully.

Article 12 says that admission for migrant workers' children to education and training must be on the same conditions as for nationals. The reference to 'same conditions' is broadly construed. In the early case of *Casagrande*[267] the Court ruled that the term 'conditions' extended to 'general measures intended to facilitate educational attendance', including a grant for maintenance and training. Therefore, it was unlawful for the German authorities to refuse a monthly maintenance grant payable to school age children to the daughter of an Italian working in Germany. The right to a maintenance grant applies even where the children decide to receive their education in their state of origin. For this reason the Court ruled in *Di Leo*[268] that the German authorities could not refuse a grant to the daughter of an Italian migrant worker employed in Germany for 25 years on the grounds that she wished to study medicine in her state of origin (Italy).[269]

The importance of the right to education was emphasized in *Baumbast*[270] which concerned a German national who had been working in the UK. Relying on his rights under Regulation 1612/68 he had brought his Colombian

---

[263] Case 9/74 *Casagrande* v. *Landeshauptstadt München* [1974] ECR 773, para. 7.

[264] These are to be read disjunctively: Joined Cases 389 and 390/87 *Echternach and Moritz* [1989] ECR 723.

[265] Case 9/74 *Casagrande* [1974] ECR 773, para. 8. Council Dir. 77/486/EEC (OJ [1977] L199/139) on the education of migrant workers' children requires that free tuition is available, including the teaching of the official language of the host state (Art. 2) and that the host state must promote the teaching of the children's mother tongue and culture (Art. 3). This applies equally to children with a disability: Case 76/72 *Michel S.* [1973] ECR 457, paras. 15–16.

[266] Case C–7/94 *Landesamt für Ausbildungsförderung Nordrhein-Westfalen* v. *Gaal* [1995] ECR I–1031.

[267] Case 9/74 [1974] ECR 773.

[268] Case C–308/89 *Di Leo* v. *Land Berlin* [1990] ECR I–4185.

[269] Para. 12.   [270] Case C–413/99 [2002] ECR I–7091.

wife and children with him to the UK but when he ceased working the British authorities refused to renew his residence permit or those of his family with the result that the children could not complete their education in the UK. The Court found that this breached Article 39 because, as the Court explained, to prevent a child of an EU citizen from continuing his education in the host state might 'dissuade that citizen from exercising the rights to freedom of movement laid down in Article 39 EC and would therefore create an obstacle to the effective exercise of the freedom thus guaranteed by the EC Treaty'.[271] For much the same reason in R.[272] the children of an American woman and her French husband who worked in the UK were entitled to carry on their education in the UK, even though the parents were divorced and the children were living with their mother (a non-EU national).[273]

If the children of migrants can continue receiving their education in the host state, then in order to be able to enjoy that right they need someone to look after them. This was confirmed in *Baumbast* and *R*. Reading Article 12 in the light of the requirement of the respect for family life under Article 8 ECHR, the Court said the right conferred by Article 12 'necessarily implies' that that child has the right to be accompanied by the person who is his primary carer and who is entitled to reside with the child during his studies,[274] notwithstanding that the carers might not have independent rights under EC law.[275]

5. The Right to Permanent Residence in the Host Member State

Regulation 1251/70[276] gave effect to Article 39(3)(d) on the right to remain in a Member State after having been employed there but has now been repealed.[277] Article 17 of Directive 2004/38 maintains the existing acquis but changes the language from the 'right to remain' to the 'right of permanent residence'. It provides that workers (and the self-employed) have the right to remain in the host state and retain the right of permanent residence in three situations:

- retirement at the pension age or through early retirement, provided they have been employed for the last 12 months[278] and resided in the host state continuously for more than three years;

---

[271] Para. 50.   [272] Case C–413/99 [2002] ECR I–7091.   [273] Paras. 60–2.
[274] Para. 73.
[275] Para. 71. See also Art. 12(3) of Dir. 2004/38 considered below, n. 292.
[276] OJ SE [1970] L142/24, 402.   [277] Commission Reg. 635/2006 (OJ [2006] L112/9).
[278] Periods of involuntary unemployment duly recorded by the relevant employment office, periods not worked for reasons not of the person's own making and absences from work or cessation of work due to illness or accident are to be regarded as periods of employment: Art. 17(1).

- incapacity, provided they have resided for more than two years in the host state[279] and have ceased to work due to some permanent incapacity; or
- frontier workers, provided after three years of continuous employment and residence in State A, they work as employees in State B, while retaining their residence in State A to which they return each day or at least once a week.

The conditions as to length of residence and employment do not apply if the worker's spouse is a national of the host state or has lost the nationality of the host state through marriage.[280] Thus, the provisions of Article 17 of Directive 2004/38 are more favourable to migrant workers and the self-employed than the rights given to Union citizens more generally (where five years' residence is required).

According to Article 3 of Regulation 1251/70 and, now, Article 17 of Directive 2004/38, the worker's family is entitled to remain/enjoy permanent residence in the host state in one of two situations. First, if the worker/self-employed person is entitled to remain then the family members residing with him have the right of permanent residence, irrespective of nationality. Secondly, if the worker/self-employed person dies during his working life before having acquired the right to permanent residence, but (a) the worker/self-employed person has resided continuously in the host state for two years at the time of death, or (b) the death resulted from an accident at work or occupational disease, or (c) the surviving spouse lost the nationality of the host state through marriage to the worker/self-employed person, then the family members have the right to remain. In *Givane*[281] the Court showed that it will interpret these requirements strictly.

Givane, a Portuguese national, worked in the UK as a chef for three years before going to India for 10 months. He then returned to the UK with his Indian wife and three children but died less than two years later. The Court upheld the British authorities' decision refusing Givane's family indefinite leave to remain on the grounds that Givane had not satisfied the requirements of Article 3 of Regulaiton 1251/70 which required him to have resided in the UK for the two years immediately preceding his death.[282] Such a literal reading of the requirement stands in stark contrast to the generous approach to the interpretation of Regulation 1612/68 based on the right to family life in cases such as *Baumbast*.[283] More striking still is the fact that the Court

---

[279] If the incapacity is due to an occupational accident or disease entitling the worker to a pension for which an institution of the state is entirely or partially responsible, then no condition to length of residence is imposed.

[280] Art. 2(2).

[281] Case C–257/00 *Nani Givane and others* v. *Secretary of State for the Home Department* [2003] ECR I–345.

[282] Para. 46.

[283] See also Case C–60/00 *Mary Carpenter* v. *Secretary of State for the Home Department* [2002] ECR I–6279, para. 38; Case C–459/99 *MRAX* [2002] ECR I–6591, paras. 53–61.

uses the integration argument to justify *excluding* Givane's family from the UK. It said that the two-year requirement was intended to establish a significant connection between the Member State and the worker and his family and 'to ensure a certain level of their integration in the society of that state'.[284]

The Citizens' Rights Directive 2004/38 also gives family members the right to retain their residence in the host state on the death or departure of the EU citizen (Article 12) or in the event of divorce, annulment or marriage or termination of registered partnership (Article 13). In the case of the death or departure of the Union citizen, family members who are not EU citizens retain the right of residence provided that they have been residing in the host state as family members for at least a year before the citizens' death.[285] This condition is not applied to family members who are EU nationals[286] since they have a residence entitlement in their own right.[287] In the case of divorce or equivalent, TCN family members do not lose the right of residence where:

- prior to the divorce or equivalent, the marriage or registered partnership lasted at least three years including one year in the host Member State; or
- by agreement between the spouses or partners or by court order, the TCN spouse or partner has custody of the Union citizen's children; or
- this is warranted by particularly difficult circumstances, such as having been a victim of domestic violence while the marriage or registered partnership was subsisting; or
- by agreement between the spouses or partners or by court order, the TCN spouse or partner has the right of access to a minor child, provided that the court has ruled that such access must be in the host state and for as long as is required.[288]

These conditions do not apply to family members who are nationals of a Member State.[289] This provision was included to provide 'certain legal safeguards to people whose right of residence is dependent on a family relationship by marriage and who could therefore be open to blackmail with threats of divorce'.[290]

Before acquiring the right of *permanent* residence, the family members must be workers, self-employed, students, have independent means, or be family members of a person in one of these categories. In the case of TCN family members, they will acquire the right of permanent residence after residing legally for a period of five consecutive years in the host Member State.[291]

Finally, if EU citizens leave the host state (as opposed to dying) their non-EU children retain their right of residence, as will the parent with actual custody

---

[284] Para. 46.   [285] Art. 12(2).   [286] Art. 12(1).   [287] COM(2001) 257, 14.
[288] Art. 13(2).   [289] Art. 13(1).   [290] COM(2001) 257, 15.   [291] Art. 18.

of the children, irrespective of nationality, if the children reside in the host state and are enrolled at an educational establishment, for the purposes of studying there, until the completion of their studies.[292]

D. SOCIAL SECURITY: REGULATION 1408/71 AND REGULATION 883/2004

1. Introduction

So far we have concentrated on the approach adopted by Regulation 1612/68 and Directive 2004/38 to encourage workers and their families to move. One factor that has influenced workers' decisions to migrate are concerns about social security: in the absence of a common European Community-wide social security system the risk remains that workers leaving one state might lose their entitlement to any benefits which had accrued while they worked in that state when they enter another state. This problem was recognized by those drafting the Treaty of Rome. Article 42 provides that the Council must adopt such measures in the field of social security, now in accordance with the co-decision procedure in Article 251 but subject to unanimous voting, as are necessary to provide freedom of movement of workers.[293] The result was the (infamous) and much amended Regulation 1408/71.[294] The most important amendment was contained in Regulation 1390/81[295] which extended the scope of Regulation 1408/71 to the self-employed. Regulation 1408/71 is due to be replaced, for most purposes, by Regulation 883/2004[296] which was designed to modernize and shorten the co-ordination instrument. This Regulation will only come into force when an implementing Regulation is adopted. Until then Regulation 1408/71 will continue to apply in full. This chapter will refer to both sets of rules.

Regulations 1408/71 and 883/2004 are not intended to harmonize the diverse national legislation on social security.[297] Instead, from its foundation

---

[292] Art. 12(3) reflecting the decisions in Joined Cases 389/87 and 390/87 *Echternach and Moritz* [1989] ECR I–723, Case C–413/99 *Baumbast and R* v. *Secretary of State for the Home Department* [2002] ECR I–7091.

[293] Enacting such legislation was clearly seen as a priority: Regs. 3/58 (JO [1958] 561) and 4/58 (JO [1958] 597) came into force on 1 January 1959. These were revised and replaced on 1 October 1972 by Regs. 1408/71 and 574/72 (OJ [1971] L149/2 and OJ [1972] L74/1) containing substantive and procedural provisions respectively.

[294] OJ [1971] L149/2.

[295] OJ [1981] L143/1. It does not apply to periods prior to 1 July 1982.

[296] OJ [2004] L166/1.

[297] On the question of harmonization, see Van Langendonck, 'Social Security Legislation in the EEC' (1973) 2 *ILJ* 17, 23–27.

the EU has focused on the *co-ordination* of the national legislation,[298] ensuring that those wishing to exercise their rights of free movement do not suffer detriment in terms of their social security benefits. This area of law is already highly complex. The complexity is exacerbated by the fact that some social assistance benefits are now also covered by the requirement that migrant workers and their families enjoy equal treatment in respect of social advantages under Article 7(2) of Regulation 1612/68.

It is beyond the scope of this book to provide a detailed analysis of each substantive provision of the Regulations.[299] Instead, this section is intended to offer an overview of the personal scope of the Regulation 1408/71, and the type of benefits it covers, especially as they affect workers who are moving between states. In particular, it focuses on the principles underpinning the Community approach to social security. The Court interprets questions referred to it[300] in the light of these principles, read in conjunction with the guidance provided by the Preamble to the Regulation,[301] and it is to these principles which we now turn.

2. The Principles of Co-ordination

2.1. Introduction

As we have seen, in the field of social security, the EU has focused on the *co-ordination* of the diverse national legislation:[302] the national legislative systems remain distinct. The Court emphasized this in *Pinna*:[303]

---

[298] Cf. Art. 137(3) gives the Community the power to issue minimum standards Directives on 'social security and social protection of workers'. This new Treaty base is not qualified by the need that the Directives relate to co-ordination only, although the requirement of unanimous voting will limit its utility.

[299] For a more detailed analysis, see Watson, *Social Security Law in the European Communities* (Mansell, London, 1980); White, *EC Social Security Law* (Longman, Harlow, 1999); Hervey, *European Social Law and Policy* (Longman, Harlow, 1999); Luckhaus, 'European Social Security Law', in Wikely, Ogus and Barendt's *The Law of Social Security* (Butterworths, London, 2002). See also Watson, 'Social Security for Migrants', in Wyatt and Dashwood (eds), *European Community Law*, 3rd edn, (Sweet and Maxwell, London, 1993).

[300] For a survey of the ECJ's case law on social security see reviews by: Knorpel (1981) 18 *CMLRev*. 579, (1982) 19 *CMLRev*. 105, (1983) 20 *CMLRev*. 97, (1984) 21 *CMLRev*. 241, (1985) 22 *CMLRev*. 43, (1986) 23 *CMLRev*. 359; Morgan (1987) 24 *CMLRev*. 483, (1988) 25 *CMLRev*. 391; Monroe (1990) 27 *CMLRev*. 547; Eichenhofer (1993) 30 *CMLRev*. 1021; Moore, 'Freedom of Movement and Migrant Workers' Social Security' (1998) 35 *CMLRev*. 409–57.

[301] See e.g. Case 63/76 *Inzirello v. Caisse d'allocations familiales de l'arondissement de Lyon* [1976] ECR 2057; Case 50/75 *Caisse de pension des Employées Privés v. Massonet* [1975] ECR 1473, para. 9.

[302] Cf. Art. 137(3) gives the Community the power to issue minimum standards Directives on 'social security and social protection of workers'. This new Treaty base is not qualified by the need that the Directives relate to co-ordination only, although the requirement of unanimous voting will limit its utility.

[303] Case 41/84 *Pinna v. Caisse d'allocations familiales de la Savoie* [1986] ECR 1, 24–5.

... Article [42] of the Treaty provides for the coordination, not the harmonisation, of the legislation of the Member States. As a result, Article [42] leaves in being differences between the Member States' social security systems and, consequently, in the rights of persons working in the Member States. It follows that substantive and procedural differences between the social security systems of individual Member States, and hence in the rights of persons working in the Member States, are unaffected by Article [42] of the Treaty.

Therefore, individual Member States remain responsible for determining the detailed rules concerning the right or duty to be insured[304] as well as the financing of the schemes,[305] the conditions for affiliation[306] and entitlement to benefits and the actual level and scheme of benefits.[307] However, any features of those systems which have adverse effects on workers crossing national frontiers must be rectified.[308] This can be seen in *Terhoeve*[309] where the Court ruled that national legislation requiring an employed person working in another Member State to pay higher social security contributions than if he continued to reside in the same Member State constituted an obstacle to the free movement of workers contrary to Article 39. The Court added that such a heavier contributions burden could not be justified either by the fact that it stemmed from legislation whose objective was to simplify and co-ordinate the levying of income tax and social security contributions or by difficulties of a technical nature preventing other methods of collection or by certain income tax advantages. Therefore, the individual was entitled to pay the same level of contributions as paid by a worker who had continued to reside in the Member State.

Regulation 1408/71—and now Regulation 883/2004—is constructed on the basis of four co-ordinating principles: non-discrimination, the single state rule, aggregation, and exportability. These principles are designed to displace the *territorial* basis of social security rights, whereby entitlements are provided on condition that contributions have been made in that territory, and to substitute in its place a *personal* right. This ensures that rights follow the individual.[310]

---

[304] Case C–120/95 *Decker* v. *Caisse de maladie des Employés Privés* [1998] ECR I–1831 and Case C–158/96 *Kohll* v. *Union des Caisses de maladie* [1998] ECR I–1931.

[305] See e.g. Case 238/82 *Duphar* v. *Netherlands State* [1984] ECR 523, Case C–70/95 *Sodemare* v. *Regione Lombardia* [1997] ECR I–3395.

[306] Joined Cases C–88/95, C–102/95 and C–103/95 *Martínez Losado* v. *INEM* [1997] ECR I–895.

[307] See e.g. Case 266/78 *Brunori* [1979] ECR 2705, Watson (1981) 6 *ELRev*. 41 and Case 110/79 *Coonan* v. *Insurance Officer* [1980] ECR 1445. See Watson (1980) 5 *ELRev*. 220, (1984) 9 *ELRev*. 428.

[308] See Case 100/63 *Van der Veen* v. *Bestuur der Sociale Verzekeringsbank* [1964] ECR 565, 574. This does not imply alteration of schemes but rather Reg. 1408/71, being directly applicable, operates by conferring additional rights which Member States will apply by virtue of the Regulation and not by changing their own schemes.

[309] Case C–18/95 *Terhoeve* v. *Inspecteur van de Belastingdienst Particulieren* [1999] ECR I–345.

[310] Luckhaus, 'The Role of the "Economic" and the "Social" in Social Security and Community Law', in Weich (ed.), *National and European Law on the Threshold to the Single Market* (Peter Lang, Berlin, 1993).

These principles have as their overriding goal the idea that migrant workers and their families should suffer no disadvantage as a result of moving within the Community—the so-called *Petroni*[311] principle, which is considered below.[312]

2.2. Non-discrimination

The first and most important principle is equality of treatment—or non-discrimination—on the ground of nationality.[313] A further manifestation of the principle laid down by Article 12 EC,[314] the principle of equality is spelt out in Article 3(1) of Regulation 1408/71 and Articles 4 and 5 of Regulation 883/2004.[315]

The principle of non-discrimination outlaws both direct discrimination (less favourable treatment on the grounds of nationality) and indirect discrimination (the application of a requirement or condition to all applicants which in fact disadvantages a greater number of migrants).[316] Both types of discrimination can be seen in *Toia*.[317] An Italian woman was denied a benefit paid by the French social security system to French women over 65, with insufficient means, and who had brought up five children of French nationality. The Court ruled that the French authorities were correct not to rely on the fact that the mother did not have French nationality in assessing her eligibility for the benefit since this would have constituted direct discrimination. However, it declared that the condition that the children had to be French was indirectly discriminatory and breached Article 3 of Regulation 1408/71 unless it could be justified by objective reasons on grounds other than nationality. This was not the case on the facts.[318]

It seems that the principle of non-discrimination in the context of social security, unlike the more general rules on the free movement of persons, also prevents reverse discrimination—that is discrimination by national authorities against their own nationals and in favour of migrants. In *Kenny*[319] the Court ruled that:

... it is for the national legislation to lay down the conditions for the acquisition, retention, loss or suspension of the right to social security benefits so long as those

---

[311] Case 24/75 *Petroni v. Office des Pensions pour Travailleurs Salariés* [1964] ECR 565, 574.

[312] This principle is affirmed in the Preamble to Reg. 883/2004.

[313] See e.g. Case 1/78 *Kenny v. Insurance Officer* [1978] ECR 1489 and Case 110/79 *Coonan* [1980] ECR 1445.

[314] See further section 4 above.

[315] See also the Preamble to Reg. 883/2004 at (5) 'It is necessary, within the framework of such coordination, to guarantee within the Community equality of treatment under the different national legislation for the persons concerned.'

[316] Case C–27/91 *Ursaff* [1991] ECR I–5531, para. 10.

[317] Case 237/78 *CRAM v. Toia* [1979] ECR 2645.

[318] See also Case 33/88 *Allué and Coonan v. Università Venezia* [1989] ECR 1591.

[319] Case 1/78 *Kenny* [1978] ECR 1489. See also Wyatt, 'Social Security Benefits and Discrimination by a Member State against its own Nationals' (1978) 3 *ELRev.* 488.

conditions apply without discrimination to the *nationals of the Member State concerned* and to those of other Member States.[320]

It has been argued that since freedom of movement includes the right *not* to migrate, as well as the right to do so, reverse discrimination in the administration of social security rules should be regarded as incompatible with the Treaty.

Finally, the application of the principle of non-discrimination may result in migrant workers receiving inferior benefits to those they would have received had they not exercised their rights of free movement, since benefits in the host Member State may be lower than those provided by the state of origin. As discussed below, the Court has developed the principle of 'no disadvantage' to help address such situations.

2.3. Single State Rule

The second co-ordinating principle is that only one national system of legislation can apply to the migrant worker at any one time (the single state rule).[321] While the Regulation lays down detailed choice of law rules, the basic position, according to Article 13 of Regulation 1408/71 (Article 11 of Regulation 883/2004), is that the system applicable is that of the country where the worker or the self-employed person works (*lex laboris*), irrespective of their place of residence or the place of residence of their employer.[322]

It is also the state of employment which is the 'competent state' for administering the social security benefits. The main exception is laid down in Article 14(1)(a) (workers) and Article 14a(1)(a) (self-employed) (Article 12(1) and 12(2) of Regulation 883/2004 respectively) which provided that where a self-employed person or a worker normally works for a company in one Member State (A) but is posted to another Member State (B) for up to a year (two years in Regulation 883/2004) but continues to work for the same company, the worker remains subject to the legislation of State A.[323] In

---

[320] Para. 16, emphasis added. Cf. Case C–153/91 *Petit* v. *Office National des Pensions* [1992] ECR I–4973.

[321] Art. 13(1). This, of course, says nothing about the content of the rules applied.

[322] Art. 13(2)(a) (Art. 11(3)(b) of Reg. 883/2004). In Case 302/84 *Ten Holder* v. *Nieuwe Algemene Bedrijfsvereniging* [1986] ECR 1821, the Court said that a worker who has ceased to carry on an activity in the territory of a Member State and who has not gone to work in another Member State continues to be subject to the legislation of the Member State in which s/he was last employed, regardless of the length of time which has elapsed since the termination of the activity in question and the end of the employment relationship. This principle was reversed by Art. 13(2)(f) (added by Art. 1(2) of Reg. 2195/91 (OJ [1991] L206/2)). This provided that a person to whom the legislation of a Member State ceases to be applicable, without the legislation of another Member State becoming applicable to him 'shall be subject to the legislation of the Member State in whose territory he resides'.

[323] See generally Case C–18/95 *Terhoeve* [1999] ECR I–345. This can be extended for a further 12 months: Arts. 14(1)(b) (workers) and 14a(1)(b) (self-employed). In both cases this is subject to the consent of the Member State where the work is being done. The definition of 'employed' and

Manpower[324] the Court held that the equivalent provision to Article 14(1) in Regulation No. 3 applied to 'a worker who is engaged by an undertaking pursuing its activity in a Member State, is paid by that undertaking, is answerable to it for misconduct, is able to be dismissed by it and who on behalf of that undertaking performs work temporarily in another undertaking in another Member State', even where the employer was an employment agency specializing in short-term placements.[325]

The application of the single state rule ensures that the worker is either not simultaneously insured in two Member States and therefore has to pay double the contributions or is not insured at all. It therefore avoids 'any plurality or purposeless confusion of contributions and liabilities which would result from the simultaneous or alternate application of several legislative systems'.[326] However, while Article 13 (Article 11 of Regulation 883/2004) suggests that the single state rule is exclusive,[327] in some of its early case law the Court did not rule out the possibility of the concurrent application of other systems, providing that workers were entitled to additional benefits for any additional contributions they are required to make.[328]

2.4. The Principle of Aggregation

The third principle of co-ordination, the principle of aggregation, ensures that the host Member State takes account of periods of insurance completed

---

'self-employed' should be understood to refer to activities which are regarded as such for the purposes of the social security legislation of the Member State in whose territory those activities are pursued: Case C–340/94 *De Jaeck* v. *Staatssecretaris van Financiën* [1997] ECR I–461.

[324] Case 35/70 *Manpower* v. *Caisse primaire d'assurance maladie de Strasbourg* [1970] ECR 1251. See also Case C–202/97 *Fitzwilliam Executive Search Ltd* v. *Bestuur van het Landelijk Instituut Sociale Verzekeringen* [2000] ECR I–883. For the employment rights of posted workers see Council Dir. 96/71/EC (OJ [1996] L18/1), discussed further in Ch. 5.

[325] There are two further important exceptions: (i) where a worker is normally employed in several Member States, Art. 14(2)(b) provides that s/he is subject to legislation of Member State where s/he resides if s/he does some work there; if not, then s/he will be subject to the social security legislation of the country where the employer's registered office is situated, see Case 13/73 *Angenieux* v. *Hackenberg* [1973] ECR 935; (ii) where a person is self-employed in several Member States, Art. 14a(2) provides that s/he is subject to the legislation of the Member State where s/he resides if s/he does some work there; if not, then s/he is subject to legislation of the country where s/he pursues his or her main activity. (For principal activity see Art. 12a(5)(d) Reg. 574/72).

[326] Case 19/67 *Soziale Verzekeringsbank* v. *Van der Vecht* [1967] ECR 345. See also Case 50/75 *Massonet* [1975] ECR 1473, para. 15.

[327] Case 19/67 *Van der Vecht* [1967] ECR 345.

[328] In Case 92/63 *Nonnenmacher* v. *Sociale Verzekeringsbank* [1964] ECR 281, concerning old Reg. 3, the Court said that while the single state rule is intended to avoid placing migrant workers in an unfavourable legal position as regards social security the Regulation is 'not opposed to legislation by Member States designed to bring about additional protection by way of social security for the benefit of migrant workers'. However, Reg. 3 did not make clear the principle of exclusivity; the case law under Reg. 1408/71 (e.g. Case 302/84 *Ten Holder* v. *Direction de la Nieuwe Algemene Bedrijfsvereniging* [1986] ECR 1821) is much more clear about the exclusive effect of the single state rule.

in other Member States when calculating whether the claimant has satisfied the necessary qualifying period of work, residence, or period of contributions in order to be entitled to receive the benefit. Consequently, rights in the process of being acquired must be preserved. In Regulation 1408/71 the principle of aggregation relates to, for example, sickness and maternity,[329] invalidity,[330] death grants,[331] and family benefits and family allowances.[332] Under Article 6 of Regulation 883/2004 there is a presumption that the principle of aggregation applies unless otherwise provided.[333]

2.5. The Principle of Exportability

The fourth principle, the principle of exportability or deterritoriality, preserves rights which have already been acquired. Long-term benefits, such as pensions, must be paid to the migrant by the Member State of origin, irrespective of where that person now resides[334] in the EU. Article 10(1) of Regulation 1408/71 (Article 7 of Regulation 883/2004) provides:

... invalidity, old-age or survivors' cash benefits, pensions for accidents at work or occupational diseases and death grants acquired under the legislation of one or more Member States shall not be subject to any reduction, modification, suspension, withdrawal or confiscation by reason of the fact that the recipient resides in the territory of a Member State other than that in which the institution responsible for payment is situated.

As the Court explained in *Smieja*,[335] the aim of Article 10(1) is to guarantee the party concerned the right to have the benefit of such payments, even after taking up residence in a different Member State, including the individual's country of origin. If a person's rights are derived from the legislation of several Member States, payment is made according to the provisions of the Regulation, including the principle of non-discrimination on the grounds of nationality contained in Article 3 (Articles 4 and 5 of Regulation 883/ 2004).

However, the newly introduced Article 10a provides that, notwithstanding the provisions of Article 10, special non-contributory benefits[336] may be

---

[329] Art. 18(1) provides that the host Member State must 'take account of periods of insurance ... completed under the legislation of any other Member State as if they were periods completed under the legislation which it administers'.

[330] Art. 38.   [331] Art. 64.   [332] Art. 72.

[333] As in the case of Art. 24 (with respect to pensions); Art. 45 (with respect to invalidity payments); Art. 51 (pensions and survivors pensions); Art. 61 (unemployment benefits).

[334] 'Residence' according to Art. 1(7)(b) means 'habitual residence'. Therefore, Art. 10(1) does not apply to temporary residence.

[335] Case 51/73 *Sociale Verzekeringsbank* v. *Smieja* [1973] ECR 1213. See also Case 92/81 *Carraciolo* [1982] ECR 2213.

[336] See below, n. 377.

limited to persons resident in the territory of the state granting the benefit.[337] This inclusion of the new category of special non-contributory benefits disrupts the 'purity' of the co-ordination system of Regulation 1408/71, and appears to undermine the underlying principle of freedom of movement.[338]

2.6. Other Principles

The principles outlined above provide the four main pillars of co-ordination. Commentators have, however, identified three additional principles. The first is known as pro-raterization, the equitable distribution of the cost of the benefit between the Member States where the claimant has been insured. Each Member State pays in proportion to the length of time the claimant has been insured in that Member State. This is particularly important where pensions are paid over a long period.[339]

The second additional principle prevents the overlapping of benefits. Article 12(1) provides that Regulation 1408/71 (Article 10 of Regulation 883/2004) can 'neither confer nor maintain the right to several benefits of the same kind for one and the same period of compulsory insurance'.[340] Nevertheless, the application of the single state principle, laid down by Article 13 (Article 11 of Regulation 883/2004), Article 12 (Article 10 of Regulation 883/2004) may result in claimants receiving less from the competent state than they would have received had they not moved. Consequently, as an application of the third additional principle—that workers should not suffer disadvantage as a result of exercising their rights of free movement—the Court has ruled that claimants should be entitled to receive the difference between the sum payable by the competent institution and the sum which would have been paid by the more generous state. This difference is payable by the more generous state.[341] Indeed, cases such as *Nonnenmacher*[342] suggest that not only should Community social security rules not put the migrant worker at a disadvantage, they should improve his or her position.[343]

---

[337] Art. 7 of Reg. 883/2004 is expressly excluded for non-contributory cash benefits under Art. 70(3). The Treaty provisions on citizenship probably do not disrupt this: Case C–406/04 *De Cuyper* [2006] ECR I–000.

[338] See Case C–132/96 *Stinco and Panfilo v. INPS* [1998] ECR I–5225, para. 16, in which the Court held that, as a derogation provision, Art. 10a must be interpreted strictly.

[339] Pro-raterization applies particularly in respect of long-term benefits, i.e. invalidity, old-age, and death benefits by virtue of Arts. 40 and 46, and to a limited extent to occupational diseases (Art. 60). It does not apply to sickness and maternity benefits (Art. 18).

[340] This principle does not apply to benefits in respect of invalidity, old age, death (pensions) or occupational disease (Art. 2(1)).

[341] The competent state is the state where the person is insured (Art. 1(q)) which, according to Art. 13, is the state where the person works, see Case 128/88 *De Felice v. INASTI* [1989] ECR 923.

[342] Case 92/63 [1964] ECR 281.

[343] See also Case 24/75 *Petroni* [1975] ECR 1149.

3. The Personal Scope of the Regulation[344]

Article 2(1) provides that the Regulation applies to 'employed or self-employed persons who are or have been subject to the legislation of one or more Member States[345] and who are nationals of one of the Member States . . . as well as to the members of their families[346] and their survivors'. Students have been added to the personal scope by Regulation 307/99.[347] Article 1(a)(i) of Regulation 1408/71 defines the employed and self-employed to whom the Regulation applies as '. . . any person who is *insured*, compulsorily or on an optional continued basis, for one or more of the contingencies covered by branches of a social security scheme for employed or self-employed persons' (emphasis added).[348] Since this definition refers to people insured under the national legislation rather than by reference to Articles 39 and 43, it would seem that the reference to 'employed persons' is not synonymous with the definition of 'workers' developed by the Court in the context of Article 39. In *Hoekstra*[349] the Court ruled that the term 'worker' has a Community meaning. It refers to 'all those who, as such and under whatever description, are covered by the different national systems of social security'. The Court then confirmed that the Regulation applies not only to workers in employment but also to 'the worker who, having left his job, is capable of taking another'.[350]

The Court has also given a broad interpretation to the term self-employed. In *Van Roosmalen*[351] the Court was asked to consider whether a Roman Catholic priest who served as a missionary in the Belgian Congo was a self-employed person within the meaning of Regulation 1408/71. It said that

[344] See generally, Lasok, 'Employed and Self-Employed Persons in EEC Social Security Law' (1982) 4 *JSWL*. 323.

[345] As a consequence of this wording, the Regulation applies to an employed or self-employed person who has only ever pursued his or her occupation in the country of origin, see Case 75/63 *Hoeckstra v. Bedrijfsvereniging Detailhandel* [1964] ECR 805.

[346] Defined in Art. 1(i) as any person defined or recognized as a member of the family or designated as a member of the household by the legislation under which benefits are provided. See also Case 139/82 *Piscitello v. INPS* [1983] ECR 1427. Members of the family are included irrespective of their nationality: Case 40/76 *Kermanschek v. Bundenstalt für Arbeit* [1976] ECR 1669.

[347] OJ [1999] L38/1.

[348] Stateless persons and refugees residing within the territory of one of the Member States are also covered by the Regulation but not by this book.

[349] Case 75/63 [1964] ECR 177.

[350] Ibid., 185. See also Case 99/80 *Galinsky v. Insurance Officer* [1981] ECR 941 where a person compulsorily insured as an employed person is a worker and Case 143/79 *Walsh v. Insurance Officer* [1980] ECR 1639 where a person entitled under legislation of a Member State to benefits covered by Reg. 1408/71 by virtue of contributions previously paid does not lose his status as a 'worker' within the meaning of Regulation 1408/71 by reason only of the fact that at the time when the contingency occurred he was no longer paying contributions and was not bound to do so. Part-time workers are also covered irrespective of the number of hours worked, see Case 2/89 *Bestuur van de Sociale Verzekeringsbank v. Kits van Heijningen* [1990] ECR 1753.

[351] Case 300/84 *Van Roosmalen v. Bestuur van de Bedrijfsvereniging* [1986] ECR 3095.

the expression 'self-employed person' applies to 'persons who are pursuing or have pursued, otherwise than under a contract of employment or by way of self-employment in a trade or profession, an occupation in respect of which they receive income permitting them to meet all or some of their needs, even if that income is supplied by third parties [parishioners] benefiting from the services of a missionary priest'.

In Regulation 883/2004 the definition of employed and self-employed person has been replaced. It now goes beyond those Community nationals insured as employed/ self-employed/ students to cover all Union citizens insured in whatever capacity, as well as to members of their family and to their survivors.[352]

As we have already seen, Regulation 1408/71 applies not only to the employed and self-employed, who are nationals of one of the Member States, but also to their families and survivors who do not need to be nationals. However, while there was no nationality requirement for the application of the Regulation to the family members or survivors they had only derived rights (i.e. those rights acquired through the person's status as a member of the worker's family) which meant they could not benefit from some provisions of the Regulation, such as the entitlement to claim unemployment benefit (Articles 67–71). This was the situation in *Kermaschek*[353] and subsequent judgments.[354] However, in *Cabanis-Issarte*[355] the Court changed its mind and ruled that members of the worker's family had personal rights to protection under the Regulation.

Under the applicable national law, Cabanis-Issarte, a French national resident in the Netherlands, was required to pay higher voluntary contributions to supplement a period of compulsory insurance towards her state old-age pension, than would have been payable by a Dutch national in her situation. The Court distinguished *Kermaschek* on the grounds that the benefit at issue there was unemployment benefit, a benefit which is provided for workers and not for family members.[356] *Cabanis-Issarte* concerned the application of the non-discrimination principle in Article 3(1) which applies to 'persons resident in the territory of one of the Member States', without distinguishing between workers, family members or surviving spouses.[357] Article 3(1) applied to Mrs Cabanis-Issarte. Any derogation from the equal treatment principle set out in Article 3(1) had therefore to be objectively justified.[358] The Court then

---

[352] For a full discussion of this development, see Pennings, 'Inclusion and Exclusion of Persons and Benefits in the New Coordination Regulation' in Dougan and Spaventa (eds), *Social Welfare and EU Law* (Hart Publishing, Oxford, 2005) 244–47.

[353] Case 40/76 [1976] ECR 1669.

[354] See e.g. Case 157/84 *Frascogna v. Caisse des dépôts et consignations* [1985] ECR 1739, Case 94/84 *ONEM v. Deak* [1985] ECR 1873, Case C–310/91 *Schmid v. Belgian State* [1993] ECR I–3011.

[355] Case C–308/93 *Bestuur van de Sociale Verzekeringsbank v. Cabanis-Issarte* [1996] ECR I–2097.

[356] Para. 23.   [357] Para. 26.   [358] Ibid.

reconsidered the established jurisprudence on family members, pointing out that:

the distinction between rights in person and derived rights ... may undermine the fundamental Community law requirement that its rules should be applied uniformly, by making their applicability to individuals depend on whether the national law relating to the benefits in question treats the rights concerned as rights in person or derived rights, in the light of the specific features of the domestic social security scheme.[359]

The Court said that such a distinction might undermine the spirit and purpose of the co-ordination rules, by introducing a disincentive to free movement of workers, if they might be concerned for the social security protection of their spouses, in the event of the migrant worker predeceasing his or her spouse.

The ruling in *Cabanis-Issarte* produces consistent treatment for family members who are citizens of the EU with that granted to family members of a worker from a third country with which the Community has concluded a Co-operation Agreement.[360] The Court also seems to recognize that the solution found appropriate in many of the earlier cases—application of the 'social advantages' non-discrimination provision in Article 7(2) of Regulation 1612/68—will not always provide a solution consistent with promoting free movement of persons.[361] In view of the fundamental change of approach introduced, the Court limited the temporal scope of the judgment to claims relating to periods subsequent to the date of the judgment.[362]

Regulation 1408/71 also applies to survivors[363] of the employed or self-employed who have been subject to the legislation of the Member States, irrespective of the nationality of the employed or self-employed person, where the survivors are nationals of one of the Member States, and to civil servants or people who have been treated as civil servants according to the laws of the Member States. Most significantly, the Regulation does not apply to the non-employed (i.e. those who are not capable of taking another job), since the focus of this Regulation is to buttress the rules on free movement of *workers*. However, as we saw above, the position has now changed under Regulation 883/2004 which applies to anyone insured, whether or not in an employed/self-employed/student capacity.

Third country nationals (TCNs) were previously excluded from Regulation 1408/71 unless they were stateless persons/ refugees and their situation was

---

[359] Para. 31.

[360] Case C–18/90 *Office national de l'emploi* v. *Kziber* [1991] ECR 199; Case C–103/94 *Krid* v. *Caisse nationale d'assurance vieillesse* [1995] ECR I–719; see Moore, 'Case C–308/93 *Cabanis-Issarte*' (1997) 34 *CMLRev.* 727–39, 731.

[361] Moore, above, n. 360, 735–39. See Barnard and Hervey, 'European Union Employment and Social Policy Survey 1996 and 1997' (1997) 17 *YEL.* 435.

[362] Paras. 46–8.

[363] Defined in Art. 1(g) as any person defined or recognized as a survivor by the legislation under which the benefits are granted.

not wholly internal to one Member State;[364] though their country of origin might have an agreement with the Community conferring certain social security rights (as with Turkey).[365] However, TCNs were brought within the personal scope of Regulation 1408/71 by Regulation 859/2003,[366] again provided their situation was not wholly internal to one Member State, and without full retroactive effects. Under the new regime of Regulation 883/2004, TCNs will continue to be governed by 1408/71 and 859/2003 unless and until the legislature determines otherwise.

4. The Material Scope of the Regulation

4.1. Introduction

Community legislation makes a distinction between social security, social assistance and mixed benefits.[367] Originally social security was based on ideas of social insurance against the occurrence of risks facing those in work—sickness, unemployment and accidents at work. In addition, such insurance covered the 'risks' in life which were likely to occur—the birth of children, retirement and the needs of survivors on the death of the breadwinner. Having paid insurance contributions (in the UK through national insurance) the individual would become entitled to the benefit on the occurrence of the particular risk, without the application of any means test. By contrast, social assistance looked to need, and was more likely to be discretionary, requiring a decision of some authority on the suitability of the applicant for support. The distinction became blurred, first, because entitlement to social assistance has tended to become a matter of right rather than discretion, and second, because the burden of funding social insurance has resulted in moves to require a test of means even for some insurance-based benefits.[368] More recently, a third type of benefit has emerged: mixed benefits which display aspects of both social insurance and social assistance. The face of social insurance is presented by the recognition of a social risk (for example, of suffering an injury or illness which results in permanent disability), and the benefit might be paid as of right to those meeting tightly defined conditions of entitlement without any means test. On the other hand, the benefit is not dependent on the payment of contributions, and for many recipients, the benefit represents their means of subsistence.[369]

---

[364] Cases C–95–98 and 180/99 *Khalil* v. *Bundesanstalt für Arbeit* [2001] ECR I–7413.
[365] See Art. 39 of the EC–Turkey Association Agreement (OJ [1977] L361/29) and Decision 3/80 of the Association Council (OJ [1983] L110/60).
[366] OJ [2003] L124/1.   [367] White, above, n. 299, 5–6.
[368] White, above, n. 299, 6.   [369] Ibid.

Regulation 1408/71 applies to all legislation[370] relating to *social security* benefits. Article 4(1) (Article 3(1) of Regulation 883/2004) provides that the following exhaustive[371] list of branches of social security[372] are covered by the Regulation:

- sickness and maternity benefits;[373]
- invalidity benefits;
- old-age benefits;
- survivors' benefits;
- benefits in respect of accidents at work or occupational diseases;
- death grants;
- unemployment benefits;
- family benefits.

The Regulation applies irrespective of whether the benefits are derived from general or special social security schemes, whether contributory or non-contributory.[374] In *Hughes* and *Newton*,[375] two important decisions concerning the UK benefits, family credit and mobility allowance, the Court recognized that non-contributory benefits of a mixed type—combining elements of both social security and social assistance—were also caught by Regulation 1408/71.[376] These decisions precipitated an amendment to Regulation 1408/71 which introduced new Article 4(2)(a).[377] This provides:

special non-contributory benefits which are provided under legislation or schemes other than those referred to in paragraph 1[378] or excluded by virtue of

---

[370] Legislation is defined by Art. 1(j) to include statutes, regulations and other provisions and all other implementing measures, present or future, relating to the branches and schemes of social security. See also Case 61/65 *Vassen-Goebbels* v. *Beambtenfonds voor het Mijnbedrijf* [1966] ECR 377.

[371] Case 249/83 *Hoeckx* v. *Openbaar Centrum voor Maatschappelijk Welzijn Kalmthout* [1985] ECR 973.

[372] This is based on ILO Convention No. 102 of 1952. According to Art. 5, it is for the Member States to specify the schemes which are caught by Art. 4. Such declarations are only indicative in scope and are not legislative in character (Case 100/63 *Van der Veen* [1964] ECR 565) but they are conclusive proof that the benefits are considered social security benefits (Case 35/77 *Beerens* v. *Rijksdienst voor Arbeidsvoorziening* [1977] ECR 2249 and Case 237/78 *Toia* [1979] ECR 2645).

[373] Reg. 883/2004 adds paternity benefits and pre-retirement benefits.

[374] Art. 4(2) of Reg. 1408/71; Art. 3(2) of Reg. 883/2004.

[375] Case C–78/91 *Hughes* v. *Chief Adjudication Officer* [1991] ECR I–4839 and Case C–356/89 *Newton* v. *Chief Adjudication Officer* [1991] ECR I–3107.

[376] For a comprehensive list of the relevant cases see *Social Europe* 3/92, 21. They include allowances for handicapped people (Case 63/76 *Inzirello* [1976] ECR 2057), guaranteed income for old people in Belgium (Case 1/72 *Frilli* v. *Belgian State* [1972] ECR 457 and Case 261/83 *Castelli* v. *ONTFS* [1984] ECR 3199), benefits of a remedial nature (Case 14/72 *Heinze* v. *Landesversicherungsanstalt* [1972] ECR 1105). See also Wyatt (1975–76) 1 *ELRev.* 127 and Watson (1985) 10 *ELRev.* 335.

[377] Reg. 1247/92 (OJ [1992] L136/1).

[378] The 'traditional risks' of sickness, maternity, invalidity, old-age, death (including survivors' benefits), accidents at work and industrial diseases, unemployment and family benefits.

paragraph 4[379] where such benefits are intended either to provide supplementary, substitute or ancillary cover against the risks covered by the branches of social security referred to in paragraph 1 (a) to (h), or solely as specific protection for the disabled.

This formally brought these mixed benefits within the material scope of the Regulation but Article 10a provided that they were non-exportable. This reduced the protection provided by the Regulation.

The Regulation does not apply, according to Article 4(4) (Article 3(5) of Regulation 883/2004), to *social assistance* and medical assistance, to benefit schemes for victims of war or its consequences[380] or to special schemes for civil servants.[381] Such cases of social assistance may, however, be caught by the principle of equal treatment in Article 7(2) of Regulation 1612/68 which, as the Court pointed out in *Inzirillo*, [382] 'must be defined in such a way as to include *every* social and tax advantage, whether or not linked to a contract of employment' (emphasis added), such as an allowance for handicapped adults which is awarded by a Member State to its own nationals.[383]

Regulation 1408/71 provides no criteria for distinguishing between social security schemes, which fall within the material scope of Regulation 1408/71 and thus may be exportable, social assistance which is not and the new special non-contributory benefits. Distinguishing between the three categories of benefit has been a matter for the Court which examines 'the factors relating to each benefit, in particular its purpose and the conditions of its grant'.[384] It does not depend on whether a benefit is classified as a social security benefit by national legislation.[385]

Social security is used to describe 'legislation which confers on the beneficiaries a legally defined position which involves no individual and discretionary assessment of need or personal circumstances'.[386] Social assistance, on the other hand, describes legislation designed to provide benefits to those in need, where eligibility is not dependent on periods of employment, affiliation or insurance, but there is some element of individual assessment

---

[379] Art. 4 (4) provides that Reg. 1408/71 'shall not apply to social and medical assistance, to benefit schemes for victims of war or its consequences, or to special schemes for civil servants and persons treated as such'.

[380] See Case 9/78 *Directeur Régional de la Securité Sociale de Nancy* v. *Gillard* [1978] ECR 1661.

[381] It also seems not to apply to occupational social security schemes. This is certainly the view that the Commission has taken in its Communication to the Council on suplementary social security schemes (SEC(91) 1332 final).

[382] Case 63/76 [1976] ECR 2057.

[383] Case 63/76 *Inzirillo* [1976] ECR 2057, para. 21. See Wyatt 'The Social Security of Migrant Workers and their Families' (1977) 14 *CMLRev.* 411.

[384] Case 249/83 *Hoeckx* [1985] ECR 973. The Court ruled that a Member State's designation that a benefit is social assistance is not conclusive. See also Case 9/78 *Gillard* [1978] ECR 1661, para. 12.

[385] Case C–78/91 *Hughes* [1992] ECR I–4839, para. 14.

[386] Case 79/76 *Fossi* v. *Bundesknappschaft* [1977] ECR 667, para. 6. See also Case 249/83 *Hoeckx* [1985] ECR 973, para. 12, and Case 139/82 *Piscitello* [1983] ECR 1427.

(means-testing).[387] In *Piscitello*[388] the Court found a *pensione sociale* to be a measure of social security because no provision was made for individual assessment and the legislation conferred a legally defined status on recipients entitling them to a benefit analogous to an old-age pension.[389] On the other hand, in *Hoeckx*[390] the Belgian minimex (minimum means of subsistence) was considered to be a measure of social assistance. It was a benefit providing assistance to those without means, irrespective of periods of work or contributions or affiliation to any social security body. Need was the criterion for entitlement.

It used to be thought that social security benefits were granted on the occurrence of a specific risk.[391] Therefore, for the benefit to be considered as social security the legislation at issue must, in any event, satisfy one of the rights specified in Article 4(1) (Article 3(1) of Regulation 883/2004).[392] More recently, the Court has relaxed the requirement, recognizing that Regulation 1408/71 applies to benefits where a *link* exists between the benefit and one of the contingencies listed in Article 4(1).[393] The Court has therefore ruled that Regulation 1408/71 covers preventative health care,[394] assistance for vocational training,[395] benefits for the disabled,[396] and certain measures of national recognition relating to acts of war or reparation for suffering or injury caused by the national socialist regime, supplementing or implementing the general provisions on social insurance.[397]

At times it is also difficult to distinguish between social assistance (which is totally excluded from the Regulation) and special non-contributory benefits referred to in Article 4(2a). Entitlement to the latter, by definition, does not arise through membership or contribution to a social security or insurance scheme, and, in some cases, some elements of means-testing may attach to the grant of special non-contributory benefits. These difficulties arose in

---

[387] Case 139/82 *Piscitello* [1983] ECR 1427, para. 11. See also Council Recommendation of 24 June 1992 on common criteria concerning sufficient resources and social assistance in social protection: 92/441/EEC (OJ [1992] L245/46).

[388] Case 139/82 [1983] ECR 1427.

[389] The benefit was paid by reference to lack of means and did not prescribe any requirements as to periods of employment, affiliation or insurance. This might indicate social assistance.

[390] Case 249/83 [1985] ECR 973.

[391] Case 33/65 *Dekker* [1965] ECR 901.

[392] The Court is moving in the same direction in the context of Directive 79/7, see further Ch. 10, and Joined Cases C–63/91 and 64/91 *Jackson and Cresswell* v. *Chief Adjudication Officer* [1992] ECR I–4737.

[393] Case C–249/83 *Hoeckx* [1985] ECR 973.

[394] Case 14/72 *Heinze* [1972] ECR 1127 and Case 818/79 *Allgemeine Ortskrankasse Mittelfranken* v. *Landesversicherungsanstalt Schleswig-Holstein* [1980] ECR 2729.

[395] Case 375/85 *Camapana* v. *Bundesanstalt für Arbeit* [1987] ECR 2387.

[396] Case 39/74 *Costa* v. *Belgium* [1974] ECR 1251 and Case 63/76 *Inzirello* [1976] ECR 2057.

[397] Case 79/76 *Fossi* [1977] ECR 667, Case 144/78 *Tinelli* [1979] ECR 757, Case 9/78 *Gillard* [1978] ECR 1661, Case 207/78 *Ministère public* v. *Even* [1979] ECR 2019 and Case 70/80 *Vigier* [1981] ECR 229.

respect of disability benefits in *Snares*[398] and *Partridge*.[399] Mr Snares worked in the UK until the age of 39, when he suffered a serious accident which left him with severely impaired mobility. He received a Disability Living Allowance (DLA), a UK social security benefit which is non-contributory, not linked to incapacity for work and non-means tested. In November 1993, Mr Snares moved from the UK to Tenerife, where his mother lived, so that she could care for him. The relevant British legislation provides that DLA was only available to claimants who were resident in the UK.[400] Accordingly, the UK social security authorities decided that Mr Snares' entitlement to DLA would cease, relying on Article 4(2a) and Article 10a. Snares challenged this decision, on the grounds that the effect of the amendment was to remove from the scope of Article 4(1) a benefit which would have been granted irrespective of the place of residence. The question of the validity of the amending Regulation thus arose and was referred to the Court.

The Court noted that the principle of exportability, as found in Article 10(1) of the Regulation, is subject to the express exemption 'save as otherwise provided in this Regulation'. For example, the exportability of unemployment benefits is restricted in Article 69 of the Regulation (Article 64 of Regulation 883/2004) to a period of three months. The validity of this particular restriction was tested in *Testa*,[401] where the Court held that it was not contrary to Article 51. Likewise, the Court said that derogations from the principle of exportability applicable to special non-contributory benefits, such as DLA, were lawful.[402] In practice, for Mr Snares, the applicability of Articles 4(2a) and 10a of the Regulation to his situation meant that his benefit entitlement would be significantly reduced if he moved to Tenerife, a fact likely to deter free movement. His position was aggravated by the fact that the Spanish authorities could, in accordance with Directive 90/365/EEC[403] (now Article 7(1)(b) of Directive 2004/38), refuse to grant Mr Snares a right of residence, as he would not be in receipt of sufficient benefits from his 'home state' to avoid becoming a burden on the social security system of the host state. Thus, in making detailed provision for the system of co-ordination of social security benefits under the Regulation 1408/71, the Court has confirmed that the EU legislature may lawfully enact measures which have the effect of *reducing* the mobility of persons within the EU. This conclusion was supported by the

---

[398] Case C–20/96 *Snares* v. *Chief Adjudication Officer* [1997] ECR I–6057.

[399] Case C–297/96 *Partridge* v. *The Adjudication Officer* [1998] ECR I–3467. See also Case C–154/05 *Kersbergen-Lap* [2006] ECR I–000.

[400] Social Security Contributions and Benefits Act 1992, s. 71 (6); Disability Living Allowance Regulations, Reg. 2(1) and (2). See Barnard and Hervey, 'European Union Employment and Social Policy Survey 1998' (1998) 18 *YEL* 613, 644–9.

[401] Joined Cases 41/79, 121/79 and 796/79 *Testa and Others* v. *Bundesanstalt für Arbeit* [1980] ECR 1979.

[402] Case C–20/96 *Snares* [1997] ECR I–6057, paras. 44–51, 54.

[403] OJ [1990] L180/28.

Court's rulings in *Partridge*,[404] concerning attendance allowance, and also by the ruling in *Swaddling*,[405] concerning income support. *Swaddling* confirms that the principles established in *Snares* and *Partridge* applied not only in the case of disability benefits, but also to the more general category of 'benefits ... intended either to provide supplementary, substitute or ancillary cover against the risks covered by the branches of social security referred to in paragraph 1 (a) to (h)' of Article 4 of Regulation 1408/71.

Robin Swaddling was a UK national. He worked in France from 1980 to 1988, but paid UK national insurance contributions. In 1988 he worked for six months in the UK; then he held fixed term jobs in France until 1994. In 1994 he was made redundant when his employer's business failed. In January 1995, Swaddling returned to the UK. He applied for income support. The UK Regulations governing entitlement to income support provided that the applicable amount of the benefit was nil where the claimant was a 'person from abroad'.[406] A 'person from abroad' is defined as someone 'not habitually resident in the UK', except in the case of a 'worker' in the terms of Regulation 1612/68/EEC. In practice, habitual residence for these terms was defined as an intention to remain in the UK *plus* at least eight weeks' actual residence. Thus a 'person from abroad' could not claim income support for the first eight weeks of their residence in the UK. Mr Swaddling was refused income support on the grounds that he did not meet the habitual residence test.

The Court followed its Advocate General by maintaining that income support was a 'special non-contributory benefit' in terms of Article 4(2a) of the Regulation.[407] Such benefits were only for persons resident in the territory of the state granting the benefit. Residence was a Community law concept, referring to the habitual centre of a person's interests.[408] However, the length of actual residence 'cannot be regarded as an intrinsic element of the concept of residence within the meaning of Article 10a'.[409] The habitual residence test, as applied to income support by the UK authorities, was inconsistent with Regulation 1408/71.[410] Thus the Court concluded that there was no need to consider Article 39 EC. The co-ordination provisions of Regulation 1408/71 were applicable.

The conclusions of the Court in cases such as *Swaddling*, *Snares*, and *Partridge* sit uneasily with the Court's ruling in *Martínez Sala*[411] in which the Court apparently regarded the primary Treaty rights of citizenship as prior to the provisions of regulatory co-ordination of social security law as set out in Regulation 1408/71. Ms Martínez Sala was a Spanish national who had lived

---

[404] Case C–297/96 [1998] ECR I–3467.
[405] Case C–90/97 *Swaddling v. The Adjudication Officer* [1999] ECR I–1075.
[406] Social Security Contributions and Benefits Act 1992; Income Support (General) Regulations 1987, s. 21.
[407] Ibid., para. 24.   [408] Ibid., para. 29.   [409] Ibid., para. 30.
[410] Ibid., para. 33.
[411] Case C–85/96 *Martínez Sala v. Freistaat Bayern* [1998] ECR I–2691.

in German since 1968. She worked from 1976 to 1986 and for a brief period in 1989. After that, she was in receipt of social assistance benefits from the German authorities. In 1984, her residence permit expired. Thereafter, she was given a series of documents simply certifying that she had applied for an extension of her residence permit. A further residence permit was granted for one year in 1994, and extended for one year on its expiry. In January 1993, Ms Martínez Sala gave birth to a child. She applied for a child-raising allowance (*Erzeihungsgeld*), but her application was rejected on the grounds that she was neither a German national nor in possession of a valid residence permit.

The national court referred to the Court various questions on the interpretation of Regulation 1408/71 and Regulation 1612/68. In terms of the material scope of these provisions, the Court held that the child raising allowance constituted both a 'family benefit' in the sense of Article 4(1) of Regulation 1408/71,[412] and a 'social advantage' in the sense of Article 7(2) of Regulation 1612/68. The more difficult question concerned the personal scope of these provisions. On the question of whether Ms Martínez Sala was a 'worker' in the sense of Article 39 EC and Regulation 1612/68, the Court referred to its earlier case law to the effect that 'worker' was a Community law concept in this context,[413] and held that this was a question for the national court to decide. The question of whether Ms Martínez Sala was an 'employed person' in the sense of Regulation 1408/71 was more difficult. The German government argued that, for the purposes of entitlement to family benefits, only a person compulsorily insured against unemployment constitutes an 'employed person'. In this respect, the German government relied on the Court's earlier ruling in *Stöber and Pereira*[414] and on the provisions in the Annex to Regulation 1408/71 covering German family benefits. However, the Court pointed out that the provisions of the Annex could not apply to Ms Martínez Sala, and hence held that her status was to be determined (by the national court) solely on the basis of Article 1(a) of Regulation 1408/71.

The Court then considered whether the residence requirement in respect of the child-raising allowance was contrary to Community law. The Court had no difficulty in finding that, should the national court find that Ms Martínez Sala fell within the personal scope of Community law, the residence requirement would be discriminatory on grounds of nationality in breach of Article 6 EC. As Ms Martínez Sala was lawfully resident in Germany, there was no need to consider the Commission's argument to the effect that Article 18 EC

---

[412] Following Joined Cases C–245/94 and C–312/94 *Hoever and Zachow* v. *Land Nordrhein Westfalen* [1996] ECR I–4895.

[413] See e.g. Case 66/85 *Lawrie-Blum* v. *Land Baden-Württemberg* [1986] ECR 2121, Case 39/86 *Lair* v. *Universität Hannover* [1988] ECR 3161, and Case C–292/89 *The Queen* v. *Immigration Appeal Tribunal, ex parte Antonissen* [1991] ECR I–745, considered in section B above.

[414] Joined Cases C–4 and 5/95 *Stöber and Piosa Pereira* v. *Bundesanstalt für Arbeit* [1997] ECR I–511.

granted a new right of residence to citizens of the EU. Ms Martínez Sala could rely on Article 12 EC,

... in all situations which fall within the scope *ratione materiae* of Community law, including the situation where a Member State delays or refuses to grant to that claimant a benefit that is provided to all persons lawfully resident in the territory of that state on the ground that the claimant is not in possession of a document which nationals of that same state are not required to have ...

Nothing would justify that discrimination on grounds of nationality in a case such as this.[415]

In *Hosse*[416] the Court also demonstrated a certain robustness of approach, this time in the context of the interpretation of the Regulation. Mr Hosse, a German, was a frontier worker employed in Austria as a teacher in the Province of Salzburg. He paid taxes and social security contributions in Austria and was affiliated to sickness insurance in Austria. He resided in Germany, near the Austrian frontier, with his daughter Silvia, who was severely disabled. He applied for a care allowance under a law of the Province of Salzburg for Silvia but his application was refused on the ground that Silvia should have had her main residence in the Province of Salzburg in order to receive the care allowance.

The Court of Justice said that although the care allowance was mentioned in the annex to the Regulation listing special non-contributory benefits, that mention on its own was not sufficient to exclude the allowance from the scope of the Regulation. Derogating provisions of the Regulation which excluded certain specific benefits from the scope of the Regulation had to be interpreted strictly. Those derogations could apply only to benefits which satisfied cumulatively the conditions for exclusion it lays down (i.e. benefits which are both special and non-contributory and are laid down by legislation whose application is limited to part of the territory of a Member State).

The Court then found that the care allowance did not constitute a special non-contributory benefit but a sickness benefit within the meaning of the Regulation (it was a benefit which is granted objectively on the basis of a legally defined position and is intended to improve the state of health and life of persons reliant on care, its essential purpose being to supplement sickness insurance benefits). Finally, the Court added that that the entitlement to care allowance under the law of the Province of Salzburg was Silvia Hosse's own right, not a right derived from her father. However, that did not prevent her from being able to benefit from that entitlement even though she resided in

---

[415] See further Barnard and Hervey, 'European Union Employment and Social Policy Survey 1998' (1998) *YEL.* 613, 644–9.

[416] Case C–286/03 *Hosse v. Land Salzburg* [2006] ECR I–000. See also Case C–215/99 *Jauch v. Pensionsversicherungsanstalt der Arbeiter* [2001] ECR I–1901; Case C–43/99 *Leclere v. Caisse nationale des prestations familiales* [2001] ECR I–4265; Case C–160/02 *Skalka v. Sozialversicherungsanstalt der gewerblichen Wirtschaft* [2004] ECR I–5613.

Germany, if she satisfied the other conditions of grant under the Regulation. The Court points out that the intention of the Regulation was that the grant of sickness benefits should not be conditional on the residence of the members of the worker's family in the Member State of the place of employment, so as not to deter Community workers from exercising their right to freedom of movement. It would therefore be contrary to the Regulation to deprive the daughter of a worker of a benefit she would be entitled to if she were resident in that Member State.

4.2. Specific Benefits

The content of Article 4(1)—Article 3 of Regulation 833/2004—is fleshed out by eight chapters containing detailed provisions about various categories of benefit. For the purposes of this book, the application of the principles outlined above will be considered in respect of two benefits most closely related to those in employment: the so-called 'short-term' benefits—sickness and maternity benefits and unemployment benefits.

(a) Sickness and Maternity Benefits for Migrant Workers

Chapter 1 of Title III deals with sickness[417] and maternity benefits. The Regulations are particularly detailed because the basic rule that the competent state is the state where the worker is employed may present difficulties if the worker and his or her family are resident elsewhere. Two situations shall be considered. First, if a migrant worker residing and working in Member State A, becomes ill in Member State A and claims in Member State A (the competent state)[418] he or she will, under the principle of equality, receive the same benefits as nationals under the same terms as nationals.[419] According to Article 18 (Article 17 of Regulation 883/2004), the principle of aggregation applies where entitlement is conditioned on the completion of a period of insurance, so that the competent institution (in State A) takes into account any periods of insurance, employment or residence completed under the legislation of any other Member State as if they were periods completed under the legislation which it administers.[420]

The second situation is where the migrant worker habitually resides in Member State B and becomes ill there but works in Member State A, the competent state.[421] For practical reasons Article 19 provides that *benefits in*

---

[417] This includes insurance to pay for the costs of long-term care: Case C–160/96 *Molenaar v. Allgemeine Ortskrankenkasse Baden-Würtemberg* [1998] ECR I–843.

[418] The competent state (Art. 1(q)) is the state where the person is insured which, according to Art. 13, is the state where the person works. The competent institution (Art. 1(o)) is the social security institution with which the worker is insured.

[419] Case 1/78 *Kenny* [1978] ECR 1489.   [420] Art. 18(1).

[421] The same rules apply to a worker's family (Art. 19(2)).

kind (health services) are to be provided in the country of residence (State B), even if the recipient is affiliated to another Member State's social security system. These benefits in kind are provided on behalf of the competent institution in State A by the institution in the place of residence (State B), 'in accordance with the provisions of the legislation administered by that institution as though he were insured with it'. By contrast, cash benefits[422] are provided by the competent institution in State A but may be provided by the institution of the place of residence on behalf of the competent institution if they so agree. The Court has said that *benefits in kind* include health and welfare services as well as cash payments to reimburse the cost of those services for which the claimant has already been charged.[423] *Cash benefits*, on the other hand, are benefits to compensate for loss of earnings.[424] These rules apply to those who are habitually resident, namely, those who habitually reside in State B but who are temporarily working and living in State A, and those who have left State A to become habitually resident in State B but who remain subject to State A's legislation.[425]

(b) Unemployment Benefits[426]

As we have seen, the Community is keen to encourage people to move between Member States to look for work and this has been facilitated by Regulation 1408/71. The need to invoke the Regulation may apply in three circumstances. First, if the migrant worker resides, *last* worked and was insured in state A where he becomes unemployed and claims in State A (the competent state) the principle of aggregation applies. Thus, if its legislation makes entitlement conditional on periods of *insurance*, the competent institution in Member State A must take into account periods of insurance in any other Member State which would have counted as periods of insurance had they been completed under its own legislation; or, if its legislation makes entitlement conditional on periods of employment, periods of employment or insurance in any other Member State must be taken into account as though they were periods of employment under its own legislation.[427]

The principle of aggregation is limited to the country in which the person claiming 'lastly' completed periods of insurance or unemployment. Thus, as White points out, a British national living and working in the Germany who becomes unemployed in Germany cannot return to the UK to seek Job Seekers' Allowance (JSA) on the basis of contributions to the German scheme

---

[422] This includes a benefit such as a care allowance (Case C–160/96 *Molenaar* [1998] ECR I–843).

[423] Wyatt and Dashwood, above, n. 299, 338.

[424] See Case 61/65 *Vaassen* [1966] ECR 261.

[425] Case C–215/90 *Chief Adjudication Officer v. Twomey* [1992] ECR I–1823.

[426] Ch. 6 of Title III (Arts. 67–71). See also Wikeley, 'Migrant Workers and Unemployment Benefit in the European Community' (1988) 10 *JSWL.* 300.

[427] Art. 67. See also Wyatt and Dashwood, above, n. 299, 346.

because he or she will not have lastly completed a period of insurance in the UK.[428] Two situations will be considered.

First, if State A bases its calculation of benefit on the amount of previous earnings, Article 68 (Article 62 of Regulation 883/2004) provides that account must be taken of the earnings of the unemployed person during his or her last employment in the territory of State A. If this employment lasted less than four weeks the figure to be used is the normal earnings in State A for employment equivalent or similar to the individual's last employment in the Member State from which he has come. In addition, Article 68(2) provides that Member States whose legislation provides that the amount of benefits varies with the number of members of the family, shall take account of the members of the family of the person concerned who are residing in the territory of another state as if they were residing in the territory of the competent state.

The second situation is where the worker becomes unemployed in State A (competent state) and goes to look for work in State B where he or she has never been employed. It will be recalled that in *ex parte Antonissen* a work seeker enjoys some, if not all, the rights of a worker for at least three months.[429] Those people looking for work enjoy a limited right of exportability of unemployment benefit under Articles 69 and 70 of Regulation 1408/71 (Article 64 of Regulation 883/2004). These provisions entitle work seekers to receive unemployment benefit during their stay provided they satisfy certain conditions: before leaving the competent State, Member State A, they must be registered with the employment services there; they must have remained available for work in Member State A for at least four weeks after becoming unemployed (unless waived under Article 69(1)(a)) in order to exhaust all the employment possibilities in Member State A, and they must register, within seven days of ceasing to be available to the employment services of State A, with the employment services of Member State B. They are then entitled to benefits paid by the authorities of State B, payable on behalf of State A and at State A's rates but reimbursed by the state of last employment, State A, unless State A waives this.[430] These benefits must be reimbursed by the authorities of the state where the unemployed person last worked (Member State A), unless the paying state, Member State B, waives this.[431] The unemployed are entitled to receive benefits for three months[432] from the date when they leave Member

---

[428] White, above, n. 299, 86.

[429] Case C–292/89 *ex parte Antonissen* [1991] ECR I–745, cf Case C–138/02 *Collins* [2004] ECR I–000.

[430] Art. 70.   [431] Art. 70(1) and (3).

[432] Host Member States are entitled to insist on the three-month limit: Case C–272/90 *Van Noorden v. ASSEDIC* [1991] ECR I–2543 and Case C–62/91 *Gray v. Adjudication Officer* [1992] ECR I–2737. The Commission proposed an amendment to Art. 69 to address the situation of those most affected by the operation of Art. 69 wanting to return to a country with which they have close links (OJ [1980] C169/22). However, the three-month limit may be extended in 'exceptional cases', see Art. 69(2), Case 139/78 *Coccioli v. Bundesanstalt für Arbeit* [1979] ECR

State A, provided they do not receive benefits for longer than they would be entitled to if they had stayed in State A.[433] If they return to the competent State (State A) within three months they maintain their entitlement in that State.[434] Failure to do so leads to the loss of all entitlement to benefit.[435] However, under 883/2004, forfeiture becomes optional for Member States, rather than compulsory as a matter of Community law.

Article 69 can be invoked for only *one* period of three months between two periods of employment.[436] Therefore, X, who is British and has lost his job in the UK, can leave the UK and go to France to look for work. At the end of the three-month period X cannot leave France and go to look for employment in Spain without first having worked. Alternatively, X can go to France for two months and to Spain for the remaining month. According to Article 70, the unemployment benefits are provided by the institution of State B. Therefore, if Y went to France for one month and then returned to the UK he also could not seek a further authorization to go abroad again for the balance of the three months. These rules do not apply if the unemployed person has never been employed or never treated as an unemployed person under national law.[437]

The third situation covered by the Regulations is where the worker who, during his or her last employment was employed in State A (the competent state) before becoming unemployed, but was resident in State B. Article 71 deals with this situation.[438] As far as frontier workers are concerned, if they are 'partially or intermittently' unemployed they must remain available to the employment services in the competent state (State A) and claim unemployment benefit there, as though they were residing there.[439] By contrast, 'wholly unemployed' frontier workers are entitled to benefits in the state of residence, as though they had been subject to that state's legislation while working there.[440] As far as other workers are concerned, wholly unemployed workers can choose whether unemployment benefits are paid in the country of last employment (State A) or in the country of residence (State B).[441] Partially or

991 and Case 41/79 *Testa* v. *Bundesanstalt für Arbeit* [1980] ECR 1979. Cf. Case 24/75 *Petroni* [1975] ECR 1149. The Commission's 1998 (COM (1998) 779) proposal had tried to extend this from three months to six months, but the MS rejected it.

[433] Art. 69(1)(c).   [434] Art. 69(2).

[435] The compatibility of this regime with the Treaty provisions on citizenship was considered by the Court in Case C–406/04 *De Cuyper* v. *Office national de l'emploi* where AG Geelhoed and the Court said that the citizenship rules could not be used to undermine the provisions of Reg. 1408/71.

[436] Art. 69(3).

[437] See Case 66/77 *Kuyken* v. *Rijksdienst voor Arbeidsvoorziening* [1977] ECR 2311.

[438] These provisions as derogations to the basic rule must be interpreted strictly, see Case 76/76 *Di Paolo* v. *Office del'Emploi* [1977] 315.

[439] Art. 71(1)(a)(i).

[440] Art. 71(1)(a)(ii). Case C–131/95 *Huijbrechts* v. *Commissie voor de Behandeling van Administratieve Geschillen* [1997] ECR I–1409.

[441] Art. 71(1)(b).

intermittently unemployed workers, by contrast, who remain available for work in the territory of the competent state (State A) receive unemployment benefits in accordance with the provisions of the legislation of the competent state as though they resided there. If the individual has the right to receive benefit in the competent state (State A) the individual's rights to benefit in the state of residence (State B) is suspended under Article 71(2).

4.3. Conclusions

This discussion on social security is intended to give a taste of just how significant Regulation 1408/71 and, soon, Regulation 883/2004 is to the free movement of workers. As a regulatory tool, its approach differs from that of, say, the Citizens' Rights Directive which is based on the traditional command and control approach to harmonization. In the next section we consider yet another regulatory approach in respect of qualifications, this time based on mutual recognition. This applies primarily in the context of freedom of establishment and freedom to provide services. In the absence of such a measure, national rules on qualifications, while applied in a non-discriminatory fashion, would have significantly impeded free movement.

E. QUALIFICATIONS

1. Introduction

The refusal by a host state to recognize qualifications acquired in other EU states has represented a serious practical obstacle to freedom of establishment. Although Article 47 allows the Council to adopt Directives for the mutual recognition of diplomas, for many years the requirement of unanimity in Council[442] slowed the process. As a result the Court was left with the task of reconciling the host state's legitimate need for qualified people to do certain jobs with the fundamental principle of freedom of movement.

2. Where there is no Community Legislation

At first the Court gave effect to the non-discrimination principle contained in Article 43. It said that if Community law had not laid down provisions to secure the objective of freedom of establishment, the Member States and legally recognized professional bodies[443] retained the jurisdiction to adopt the

---

[442] Now the Art. 251 procedure generally applies.
[443] Case 71/76 *Thieffry v. Conseil de l'ordre des avocats à la cour de Paris* [1977] ECR 765.

234 EC Employment Law

necessary measures,[444] provided that they complied with the obligations of co-operation laid down by Article 10[445] and the principle of non-discrimination.[446] This point was made in *Patrick*[447] where a British architect applied for authorization to practise in France but his application was rejected on the ground that there was neither a diplomatic convention between the UK and France concerning the mutual recognition of certificates nor was there an EC Directive on recognition of architectural qualifications.[448] However, the Court said that the need for Directives had 'become superfluous with regard to implementing the rule on nationality since this is henceforth sanctioned by the Treaty itself with direct effect'.[449] Therefore the French authorities could not, on the grounds of nationality, deny Patrick the right to establish himself nor could they require him to satisfy additional conditions (such as being authorized to practise) which were not applicable to nationals.

In *Thieffry*[450] the Court began to shift its focus from the principle of non-discrimination to one of mutual recognition. The case concerned a Belgian advocate who held a Belgian diploma of Doctor of Laws which had been recognized by a French university as equivalent to the French *licenciate*'s degree in law. He subsequently obtained a French *avocat*'s certificate, having passed a French exam. However, he was refused admission to the Paris bar on the grounds that he lacked a French degree. The Court held that this requirement constituted an unjustified restriction on the freedom of establishment because Thieffry held a diploma recognized as an equivalent qualification by the competent authority in France and had passed the French bar exams.

The importance of the principle of mutual recognition was made clear in *Vlassopoulou*.[451] Vlassopoulou, a Greek lawyer, worked in Germany advising on Greek and EC law. Her application to join the local German bar was rejected on the grounds that she had not pursued her university studies in Germany, had not sat the two German state exams and had not completed the preparatory stage, although she did hold a German doctorate. The Court, relying not on the non-discrimination model but on one based on hindrance of access to the market, ruled that :[452]

---

[444] Case 292/86 *Gullung* [1988] ECR 111.

[445] Case 222/86 *UNECTEF v. Heylens* [1987] ECR 4097, para. 10.

[446] Case C–61/89 *Criminal proceedings against Marc Gaston Bouchoucha* [1990] ECR I–3569.

[447] Case 11/77 *Patrick* v. *Ministre des affaires culturelles* [1977] ECR 1199.

[448] However, see now the Council Dir. 85/384/EEC (OJ [1988] L223/15) on the mutual recognition of formal qualifications in architecture.

[449] Para. 13.   [450] Case 71/76 [1977] ECR 765.

[451] Case C–340/89 [1991] ECR I–2357, noted J. Lonbay (1991) 16 *ELRev.* 507. See also N. Hopkins, 'Recognition of Teaching Qualifications; Community Law in the English Context' (1996) 21 *ELRev.* 435. This approach was approved in respect of a Community national with a Turkish dental qualification who had practised in a Member State but lacked the qualifications required by Council Dir. 78/686/EEC, see Case C–319/92 *Haim I* [1994] ECR I–425.

[452] Para. 15, emphasis added. See also Case C–19/92 *Kraus* [1993] ECR I–1663, para. 32.

... national requirements concerning qualifications may have the effect of *hindering nationals of the other Member States in the exercise* of their right of establishment guaranteed to them by Article [43]. That could be the case if the national rules in question took no account of the knowledge and qualifications already acquired by the person concerned in another Member State.

Thus, by focusing on the obstacles to free movement created by qualification requirements, the Court was able to elaborate on the principle of mutual recognition. It said that the host state had to compare a migrant's qualifications and abilities with those required by the national system to see if the applicant had the appropriate skills to join the equivalent profession. If the comparison revealed that the holder had the knowledge and qualifications which were, if not identical, then at least equivalent to the national diploma, then the host state was obliged to recognize the diploma. If, on the other hand, the comparison revealed that the applicant only partially fulfilled the necessary qualifications, then the host Member State could require the applicant to demonstrate that she had acquired the relevant knowledge and qualifications which then had to be taken into account.[453] The Court added that to ensure that the Member States complied with the obligations inherent in the principle of mutual recognition, the decision-making body had to give reasons for its decisions which also had to be reviewable by the courts to verify compatibility with Community law.[454]

Vlassopoulou effectively pre-empted the 'diabolically complex and completely unnecessary'[455] Council Directive 89/48/EEC on mutual recognition of higher education diplomas and the complementary Directive 92/51/EEC,[456] now replaced by Directive 2005/36.[457] Nevertheless, the Community proceeded with the adoption of these two 'horizontal' Directives to complement and gradually replace the existing vertical directives.

3. Where there is Community Legislation

3.1. Introduction

(a) The Vertical Approach

In its first wave of harmonization legislation the Council adopted a vertical approach, harmonizing the diverse national rules profession by profession.

---

[453] Paras. 17–21.

[454] C–104/91 *Colegio Oficial de Agentes de la Propriedad Inmobiliaria* v. *José Luis Aguirre Borrell and others* [1992] ECR I–3003, para. 16.

[455] Lonbay, above n. 451, 516.

[456] The principles still apply where the Directives do not: Case C–164/94 *Georgios Aranitis* v. *Land Berlin* [1996] ECR I–135.

[457] OJ [2005] L255/22.

This led to Directives on doctors, nurses, dentists, and vets[458] as well as a number of Directives concerning a range of industries such as manufacturing and processing, small craft, food and retail,[459] the activities of intermediaries and the building industry.[460] These Directives lay down minimum standards on training. The advantage of these Directives is that once the individual has completed the training and acquired the qualification then recognition is automatic:[461] the host state must accept the equivalence of the qualifications and cannot require the individual to comply with requirements other than those laid down by the relevant Directives.[462] These Directives have now been consolidated into a single Directive, 2005/36 which is due to be implemented by 20 October 2007.

The process of negotiating these individual, vertical Directives was interminably slow (the Directive on architects[463] alone took 17 years to agree) and they were also limited in scope (for example, the Directive on Lawyers' Services[464] applied only to services and not to establishment).[465] Consequently, the single market programme heralded a new approach: horizontal harmonization based on the principle of mutual recognition derived from the Court's rulings in *Cassis de Dijon*[466] and *Vlassopoulou*.[467] The result of this initiative was Directive 89/48[468] on the mutual recognition of higher education diploma—the first 'general system' or horizontal directive.

---

[458] See Dirs. 75/362/EEC (OJ [1975] L167/1) and 75/363/EEC (OJ [1975] L167/14) on doctors, 77/452/EEC (OJ [1977] L176/1) on nurses responsible for general care, 78/686/EEC (OJ [1978] L233/1) on dentists, 78/1026/EEC (OJ [1978] L362/1) on vets, 80/154/EEC (OJ [1980] L33/1) on midwives, 85/432/EEC (OJ [1985] L253/34) on pharmacists, 86/457/EEC (OJ [1986] L267/26) on general practitioners, and 87/540/EC (OJ [1987] L322/20) on carriers of goods by waterway. Council Dirs. 75/362/EEC, 75/363/EEC and 86/457/EEC.

[459] See e.g. Dirs. 64/427/EEC (OJ SE [1963–4] 148), 75/369/EEC (OJ [1995] L167/29) and 68/367 (OJ [1968] L175/25).

[460] Dir. 64/224/EEC (OJ [1963–4] LSE/26).

[461] Case C–154/93 *Abdullah Tawil-Albertini* v. *Ministre des Affaires Sociales* [1994] ECR I–451, para. 11.

[462] Case C–238/98 *Hocsman* v. *Ministre de l'Emploi et de la Solidarité* [2000] ECR I–6623, para. 33.

[463] Council Dir. 85/384/EEC (OJ [1985] L223/85) and Communication 2002/C 214/03 considered in Case C–310/90 *Nationale Raad van de Orde der Architecten* v. *Egle* [1992] ECR I–177; Case C–447/93 *Dreessen* v. *Conseil national de l'ordre des architectes* [1994] ECR I–4087. See also Council Recommendation 85/386/EEC concerning the holders of a diploma in architecture awarded in a third country (OJ [1985] L223/28).

[464] Council Dir. 77/249/EEC (OJ [1977] L78/17). See Case 427/85 *Commission* v. *Germany (Re Lawyer's Services)* [1988] ECR 1123; Case C–294/89 *Commission* v. *France* [1991] ECR 3591.

[465] However, see now EP and Council Dir. 98/5/EC (OJ [1998] L77/36) to facilitate practice of the profession of lawyer on a permanent basis in a Member State other than that in which the qualification was obtained which is considered below.

[466] Case 120/78 *Rewe-Zentral* v. *Bundesmonopolverwaltung für Branntwein* [1979] ECR 649.

[467] Case C–340/89 [1991] ECR I–2357.

[468] OJ [1989] L19/16 as amended.

(b) The Horizontal Approach

Directive 89/48 was the first 'general system' or horizontal directive. It applied to any Member State national wishing to pursue a regulated profession as an employed or self-employed person in a host Member State,[469] unless the profession is covered by a specific sectoral directive.[470] A regulated profession involves the pursuit of a 'regulated professional activity'[471] which is defined as an activity subject directly or indirectly to the possession of a diploma.[472] A diploma is defined as a certificate or other formal qualification which:[473]

- has been awarded by a competent authority[474] in a Member State;
- shows that the holder has successfully completed a post-secondary course of at least three years' duration, or equivalent part-time, at a university or establishment of higher education, and, where appropriate, has successfully completed the professional training required in addition to the post-secondary course;[475] and
- shows that the holder has the professional qualifications required to take up or pursue a regulated profession in that Member State.

Therefore, a solicitor awarded the title by the Law Society, having completed a three-year university degree followed by a vocational training course (the legal practice course) and who has done a two-year training contract, holds a 'diploma' for the purpose of the Directive.

Article 3 lays down the basic principle of automatic recognition by the host state. It provides that where the taking up and pursuit of a regulated profession in a host state is subject to the possession of a diploma, the competent authority may not, on the grounds of inadequate qualifications, refuse to authorize a national of another Member State to take up or pursue that profession on the same terms as apply to its own nationals, provided either that the applicant holds a diploma (as defined above) or has pursued that profession for at least two years during the previous 10 years in a state

---

[469] Art. 2, para. 1. It does not apply to a wholly internal situation: Joined Cases C–225–7/95 *Anestis Kapasakalis* [1998] ECR I–4239.

[470] Ibid., para. 2.   [471] Art. 1(c).

[472] Art. 1(d). See e.g. Case C–285/01 *Burbaud v. Ministère de l'Emploi et de la Solidarité* [2003] ECR I–8219 for an example of what constitutes a diploma.

[473] Art. 1(a).

[474] Competent authorities are designated by Member States in accordance with Art. 9(1).

[475] This education and training must have been received mainly in the Community, or the holder must have three years' professional experience certified by the Member State which recognized a third country diploma, certificate or other evidence of formal qualifications. However, Council Rec. 89/49/EEC, concerning nationals of Member States who hold a diploma conferred by a third state (OJ [1989] L19/24), recommends that governments should allow nationals of Member States who hold diplomas, certificates or other evidence of formal qualifications awarded in third states—whose position is comparable to those in Art. 3—to take up and pursue regulated professions within the Community by recognizing these diplomas.

that does not regulate that profession and possesses evidence of one or more formal qualifications. In addition, Community nationals who fulfil the conditions for taking up a regulated profession in their territory can use the professional title of the host Member State corresponding to that profession.[476]

Article 4 contains the exceptions to the basic principle of mutual recognition laid down in Article 3. Article 4(1)(a) concerns differences between the home and host state in respect of the *duration* of training. It provides that where the applicant's education and training are at least one year shorter than that required by the host state, the host state may require the applicant to produce evidence of professional experience. This may neither exceed the shortfall in supervised practice nor be more than twice the duration of the shortfall in education and training required by the host state. In any event the host state cannot require professional experience of more than four years.

Article 4(1)(b) concerns the situation where the *substance* of the training differs significantly between the home and host states (for example, in professions requiring detailed knowledge of local law). In this case the Member State may require compensatory measures[477] i.e. the applicant must take an aptitude test or complete a period of adaptation not exceeding three years when:

- the matters covered by the applicant's training and education differ substantially from those covered by the diploma required by the host state; or
- where the profession regulated in the host state comprises activities which are not pursued in the state from which the applicant originates, provided the difference corresponds to specific education and training and covers matter which differ substantially from those covered by the evidence of the formal qualifications adduced by the applicant; or
- the profession regulated in the host state comprises regulated professional activities which are not in the profession in the state of origin.

Usually it is for the individual to choose between the aptitude test or adaptation period but, in the case of the legal profession or other professions which depend on the precise knowledge of national law, the host state decides which of the two alternatives should apply.

In *Colegio de Ingenieros*[478] the Court noted that compensatory measures had to be restricted to those cases where they were proportionate to the objective pursued because, due to the time and effort involved, they could be a 'highly dissuasive factor for a national of a Member State exercising his right under the Directive'. For this reason the Court ruled that the Directive did permit the

---

[476] Art. 7(1).

[477] But only if the state has legislated to this effect: Case C–142/04 *Aslanidou* v. *Ypourgas Ygeias & Pronoias* [2005] ECR I–000, para. 35. See also Case C–141/04 *Peros* v. *Techniko Epimelitirio* [2005] ECR I–000.

[478] Case C–330/03 *Colegio de Ingenieros de Caminos, Canales y Puertos* v. *Adminstración del Estado* [2006] ECR I–000, para. 24.

'partial' taking up of a regulated profession, dispensing the migrant professional from having to comply with the compensatory measures and allowing him to take up immediately professional activities for which he was already qualified. This meant that in principle an Italian engineer qualified only in hydraulics could take up the more general profession of civil engineer in Spain. Although this might lead to some confusion on the part of the consumer, the Court said this could be overcome by requiring migrants to mention the names and locations of the bodies or examining board which awarded them their academic titles and/or require the migrant to use their titles in the original language form as well as the translation.[479]

The system of mutual recognition has been extended by the second general system Directive 92/51/EEC,[480] to professions for which the level of training is lower. Directive 92/51 closely follows the pattern of Directive 89/48/EEC. It distinguishes between 'certificates' and 'diplomas'. Certificates show that the holder, after having followed a course of secondary education, has completed a course of education and training provided at an educational or training establishment or on the job.[481] Diplomas show that the holder has completed either a post-secondary course of at least one year's duration and the necessary professional training or one of the education or training courses listed in an annex to the Directive.[482] These certificates and diplomas are to be recognized by the host state[483] but, as with Directive 89/48, compensatory measures may be required from a migrant whose education and training differ significantly in terms of substance or duration from that provided in the host state.[484]

The third general system Directive 99/42/EC[485] extended the mutual recognition approach to the industrial and professional sectors previously covered by earlier vertical directives. This Directive also gives recognition not only to formal qualifications but also to experience and skills. These horizontal Directives differ markedly from their sectoral forebears: they apply to all professions satisfying the criteria laid down by the directive rather than to a single profession;[486] recognition is based on the principle of mutual trust without prior co-ordination of the preparatory and educational courses for the various professions;[487] and recognition is granted to the 'end product'—to

---

[479] Para. 25.

[480] OJ [1992] L209/25 as amended. Council Res. of 18 June 1992 (OJ [1992] C187/1) accompanying Dir. 92/51 EEC invites the Member States to allow EC nationals who have been awarded diplomas, certificates, or other qualifications by third countries to take up and pursue professions in the Community by recognizing these diplomas and certificates in their territories.

[481] Art. 1(1)(b).   [482] Art. 1(1)(a).

[483] Arts. 3 and 5 respectively. No additional requirements (e.g. of reciprocity) can be added by the Member State: Case C–142/01 *Commission v. Italy (ski monitor)* [2002] ECR I–4541.

[484] Art. 4.

[485] OJ [1999] L201/77. See also the proposal for a single Directive replacing the two general system Directives: COM(2002) 119.

[486] Bull. EC 6/1988, 11.   [487] Ibid.

fully qualified professionals who have already received any professional train-ing.[488] Although this approach has avoided some of the problems associated with the negotiation of sectoral specific Directives, the gain has come at a price. The general system Directives do not guarantee recognition; they merely require the host state authorities to consider the migrant's qualifica-tions and, if the qualifications prove to be lacking in terms of duration and content, the Member State can impose additional requirements. However, in an attempt to reorganize, rationalize, and standardize the principles which apply across both the vertical and horizontal Directives, the Parliament and Council have adopted a single Directive, Directive 2005/36/EC[489] on the recognition of professional qualifications whose aim is 'to introduce a more flexible and automatic procedure based on common platforms established by professional associations at European level, stemming from increased co-operation between the public and private sectors.'[490] It is a complicated Directive, running to 120 pages including Annexes, which is not due to be implemented until 20 October 2007. The section that follows gives an outline of some of the key principles underpinning the new Directive.

3.2. Directive 2005/36

(a) The Basic Rules

The Directive applies to all nationals of a Member State wishing to pursue a 'regulated profession' in a Member State other than that in which they obtained their professional qualifications on either a self-employed or employed basis.[491] A regulated profession involves the pursuit of a 'profes-sional activity'[492] access to which is subject to the possession of specific pro-fessional qualifications[493] which, in turn, are defined as qualifications attested by evidence of formal qualifications, an attestation of competence and/or professional experience.[494] The basic rule is found in Article 4(1):

The recognition of professional qualifications by the host Member State allows the beneficiary to gain access in that Member State to the same profession as that for which he is qualified in the home state and to pursue it in the host Member State under the same conditions as its nationals.

The Directive then distinguishes between those providing services (Title II) and those wishing to establish themselves (Title III).

(b) Free Provision of Services

Any Member State national legally established in a Member State (State A) may provide services on a temporary and occasional basis in another Member State (State B) under their original professional title without having to apply

---

[488] Bull. EC 6/1988, 11.   [489] OJ [2005] L255/22.   [490] IP/02/393.
[491] Art. 2(1).   [492] Art. 1(c).   [493] Art. 3(1)(a).   [494] Art. 3(1)(b).

for recognition of their qualifications. However, if service providers relocate outside of their Member State of establishment (State A) in order to provide services, but on a temporary and occasional basis,[495] they must also provide evidence of two years' professional experience if the profession in question is not regulated in State A.[496] Conversely, if the profession is regulated then the two years' practice cannot be required.[497]

The Directive lays down a number of administrative provisions, including the possibility for the host state, State B, to require the service provider to make a declaration prior to providing any services on its territory, and renew it annually, including the details of any insurance cover or other means of personal or collective protection with regard to professional liability.[498] State B can also require that the first application be accompanied by certain documents listed in Article 7(2), such as proof of the nationality of the service provider, of their legal establishment, and of their professional qualifications. State B can also require that where the service is provided under the professional title of the Member State of establishment or under the formal qualification of the service provider, State B's competent authorities can require service providers to furnish the recipient of the service with certain information, particularly with regard to insurance coverage against the financial risks connected with any challenge to their professional liability.[499]

(c) Freedom of Establishment

The Directive also makes provision for a professional to become established in another Member State in order to conduct a professional activity there on a stable basis. The Directive composes the three existing systems of recognition:

- General system for the recognition of professional qualifications (Chapter I)
- System of automatic recognition of qualifications attested by professional experience (Chapter II)
- System of automatic recognition of qualifications for specific professions (Chapter III).

We shall consider these in turn.[500]

The General System for the Recognition of Professional Qualifications

This 'general' system applies as a fallback to all the professions not covered by specific rules of recognition and to certain situations where the migrant professional does not meet the conditions set out in other recognition schemes. As with Directives 89/48 and 92/51, this general system is based on the principle of mutual recognition. It envisages two possible situations.

---

[495] Art. 5(2).   [496] Art. 5(1)   [497] Ibid.   [498] Art. 7(1).   [499] Art. 9.

[500] SCADPlus contains a helpful explanation of the Dir: http://europa.eu/scadplus/leg/en/cha/c11065.htm on which this section draws.

First, when access to or pursuit of a profession in the host state (State B) is regulated (i.e. subject to possession of specific professional qualifications),[501] the competent authority in State B must allow access to and pursuit of the profession under the same conditions as for nationals, provided that the applicant holds a training qualification obtained in another Member State (State A) which attests to a level of training at least equivalent to the level immediately below that required in the host Member State.[502] Second, where, in the applicant's Member State access to a profession is not subject to possession of specific professional qualifications, the applicant should, in order to be able to gain access to the profession in a host Member State which does regulate that profession, provide proof of two years of full-time professional experience over the preceding 10 years on top of the qualification.[503]

However, the host Member State can make recognition of qualifications subject to the applicant's completing a compensation measure (aptitude test or adaptation period of up to three years) if:[504]

- the training is one year shorter than that required by the host Member State; or
- the training received covers substantially different matters to those covered by the evidence of formal training required in the host Member State; or
- the profession as defined in the host Member State comprises one or more regulated professional activities which do not exist in the corresponding profession in the applicant's home Member State, and that difference consists of specific training which covers substantially different matters from those covered by the completed by the migrant.

The host Member State must, in principle, offer the applicant the choice between an adaptation period and an aptitude test[505] but it can derogate from this requirement in specific cases (for example those professions requiring a precise knowledge of law)[506] or with the Commission's permission.[507] The Directive also introduces the concept of 'common platforms', drawn up by representative professional associations, which are suitable for compensating for substantial differences which have been identified between the training requirements existing in the various Member States for a given profession.[508] If such a platform is likely to make the mutual recognition of qualifications easier, the Commission can submit it to the Member States and adopt an implementing measure.[509] In these circumstances, the host state must waive the imposition of compensatory measures on applicants who meet the platform's conditions.

Thus Chapter I of the Directive offers a qualified version of mutual recognition: mutual recognition applies subject to the application of compensatory

---

[501] Art. 3(1)(a).   [502] Art. 13(1).   [503] Art. 13(2).   [504] Art. 14(1).
[505] Art. 14(2), first para.   [506] Art. 14(3).   [507] Art. 14(2), paras. 2 and 3.
[508] Art. 15(1).   [509] Art. 15(2).

measures if there are substantial differences between the training acquired by the migrant and the training required in the host Member State.

System of Automatic Recognition of Qualifications Attested by Professional Experience

Chapter II contains the second approach to mutual recognition: the industrial, craft and commercial activities listed in the Directive[510] are subject to the automatic recognition of qualifications attested by professional experience provided that conditions concerning the duration and form of professional experience (in a self-employed or employed capacity) are satisfied.[511] Previous training is also taken into consideration and may reduce the amount of professional experience required. All previous training should, however, be proven by a certificate recognized by the Member State or judged by a competent professional body to be fully valid. Thus, Chapter II of the Directive offers an unqualified version of mutual recognition.

System of Automatic Recognition of Qualifications for Specific Professions

Chapter III deals with the specific professions. As with the previous sectoral Directives, each Member State must automatically recognize certificates of training, on the basis of co-ordination of the minimum training conditions, covering the professions of doctors, nurses responsible for general care, dental practitioners, specialized dental practitioners, veterinary surgeons, midwives, pharmacists, and architects.[512] Thus Chapter III contains an approach of unqualified mutual recognition combined with partial harmonization (of the training requirements).[513]

Common Provisions

Chapter IV contains the procedure for submitting a request for mutual recognition of professional qualifications.[514] It also permits the migrant professional to use the title conferred on them by the home state as well as the professional title of the corresponding host Member State.[515] If a profession is regulated in the host Member State by an association or organization, the

---

[510] I.e. those sectors previously covered by the former 'transitional' Directives (Dirs. 64/222/EEC, 64/427/EEC, 68/364/EEC, 68/366/EEC, 68/368/EEC, 70/523/EEC, 75/368/EEC, 75/369/EEC, 82/470/EEC, and 82/489/EEC, already consolidated by Dir. 1999/42/EC).

[511] Arts. 17–19.

[512] The Directive also recognizes the principle of automatic recognition for medical and dental specializations common to at least two Member States under existing law but limits future additions to Dir. 2005/36 to those that are common to at least two fifths of the Member States.

[513] Chalmers *et al.*, *European Union Law* (CUP, Cambridge, 2006) 722.

[514] Arts. 50–1.   [515] Art. 52(1).

migrant must also be able to become a member of that organization or association in order to be able to use the title.[516]

Title IV contains detailed rules for pursuing the profession, including the
possibility for the host state to require migrants to have the knowledge of
languages necessary for practising the profession. It also requires close collaboration between the competent authorities in the host Member State and
the home Member State,[517] by, for example, requiring each Member State to
designate a co-ordinator to facilitate the uniform application of the Directive[518] and to designate contact points which must provide citizens with information on the recognition of professional qualifications and to assist them
in enforcing their rights, particularly through contact with the competent
authorities to rule on requests for recognition.[519]

3.3. Non-application of Horizontal Directives

If the activity does not fall within the scope of (one of) the general system
Directives, then, as *Bobadilla*[520] demonstrates, the principles laid down in
Gebhard and *Vlassopoulou* continue to apply. Bobadilla, a Spanish national,
undertook a postgraduate course in fine arts restoration in the UK with financial help from the leading Spanish museum, the Prado. Although she then
worked in the Prado on a temporary contract, she was refused a permanent
job on the grounds that her British qualification had not been recognized as
equivalent to a Spanish degree. The Court said that if the national court
found that the profession was not regulated within the meaning of the two
horizontal Directives, the Prado had to investigate whether Bobadilla's diploma and professional experience were regarded as equivalent to the qualification required. The Court added that the Prado was 'ideally placed' to assess
Bobadilla's actual knowledge and abilities, given that it had helped to fund
her course and had already employed her.[521]

In the absence of harmonization the host Member State remains competent
to define the exercise of those activities,[522] including the power to impose
criminal penalties on a national of another Member State for the illegal
pursuit of a regulated profession,[523] provided that it respects Article 43. In
practice this means that any requirement imposed by the host state is liable to
hinder or make less attractive the exercise of the right of establishment and so

---

[516] Art. 52(2).   [517] Art. 56(1).   [518] Art. 56(4).   [519] Art. 57.
[520] Case C–234/97 *Fernández de Bobadilla* v. *Museo Nacional del Prado* [1999] ECR I–4773
was in fact decided under Art. 39 on free movement of workers, not Art. 43 on establishment.
See also Case C–108/96 *Criminal proceedings against MacQuen and others* [2001] ECR I–837,
paras. 24–6.
[521] Para. 35.
[522] Case C–108/96 *MacQuen* [2001] ECR I–837, para. 24.
[523] Case C–104/91 *Borrell* [1992] ECR I–3003, para. 19.

will breach Article 43 unless it can be justified.[524] In *Bouchoucha*[525] the Court said that the French authorities could prevent a French national with a British qualification in osteopathy from practising on public health grounds because the qualification enjoyed no mutual recognition in the Community and the activity was confined to doctors in France. For much the same reason the Court ruled in *MacQuen*[526] that a Belgian law restricting the conduct of eye examinations to ophthalmologists, to the exclusion of opticians who were not qualified medical doctors, could be justified on the grounds of public health.

3.4. Qualifications Obtained in Third Countries

A particular problem has arisen in respect of Community nationals who, after acquiring professional qualifications in a third country, return to work in Member State A which does recognize their qualification before going to work in State B which does not. Does Community law require the authorities in State B to apply the Directives or the *Vlassopoulou* principles? At first the answer seemed to be no. In *Tawil-Albertini*[527] a French national obtained Lebanese dentistry qualifications which were subsequently recognized by the Belgian authorities. Relying on this fact and on the provisions of Dentists' Directive 78/686/EEC, he applied to the French Ministry to practise in France. His application was refused and this decision was upheld by the Court which said that the recognition by one Member State of qualifications awarded by non-Member States did not bind the other Member States.[528]

In *Haim*[529] the Court qualified *Tawil-Albertini*. Haim was an Italian national who had acquired Turkish dentistry qualifications which had been recognized by the Belgian authorities. Haim was not, however, allowed to practise in Germany on the grounds that he had not completed the two-year preparatory training required by German law. This time the Court said that, while the German authorities had not breached the Directive (since the *Directive* did not require Germany to recognize Turkish qualifications recognized by Belgium) they had breached Article 43 by failing to do a *Vlassopoulou*-type comparison, examining whether and to what extent the *experience* already acquired in another Member State corresponded to that required by German law.[530]

---

[524] Case C–108/96 *MacQuen* [2001] ECR I–837, paras. 24–6.

[525] Case C–61/89 [1990] ECR I–3551. See also J. Lonbay, 'Picking over the Bones: Rights of Establishment Reviewed' (1992) 17 *ELRev.* 507, 509.

[526] Case C–108/96 [2001] ECR I–837. See also Case C–294/00 *Deutsche Paracelsus Schulen für Naturheilverfahren GmbH v. Kurt Gräbner* (Heilpratikers) [2002] ECR I–6515.

[527] Case C–154/93 [1994] ECR I–451.

[528] Para. 13.

[529] Case C–319/92 [1994] ECR I–425.

[530] Para. 29. Haim then sued the German Association of Dental Practitioners of Social Security Schemes for *Factortame III* damages for the loss suffered by being denied the possibility of practising as a dentist for the scheme: Case C–424/97 *Haim II* [2000] ECR I–5123.

In *Hocsman*[531] the Court went one stage further. It required State B to take account of all of the *formal qualifications* acquired elsewhere as well as practical experience when making the *Vlassopoulou* comparison. Hocsman, an Argentinian, acquired Spanish nationality in 1986 and then became a French citizen in 1998. His Argentinian medical diploma was recognized by the authorities in Spain where he was authorized to practise as a specialist in urology in 1986. He was, however, refused permission to practise in France due to the fact he held an Argentinian diploma. Clarifying its earlier case law,[532] the Court said that the French authorities had to take into consideration:

all the diplomas, certificates and other evidence of formal qualifications of the person concerned and his relevant experience, by comparing the specialised knowledge and abilities so certified and that experience with the knowledge and qualifications required by the national rules.[533]

F. CONCLUSIONS

Free movement of persons, one of the fundamental *economic* freedoms, has increasingly been interpreted by the Court within the framework of human rights. In particular, the Court's decisions on social advantages under Article 7(2) of Regulation 1612/68 go far beyond what is necessary to ensure the mobility of workers. The ever expanding rights given to the worker's family members provided the testing ground for the Court's subsequent more ambitious jurisprudence giving rights to EU citizens who are not economically active. This perspective is now reinforced by the Citizens' Rights Directive 2004/38. The human rights orientation which underpins much of the Court's case law on workers is less visible in respect of freedom of establishment. In this area we see a greater preoccupation with ensuring that individuals gain access to the host state's market and do not suffer impediments once on that market. Directive 2005/36 on professional qualifications has helped to realize this.

In the next chapter we move to consider the limitations on the rights to free movement as laid down by the Treaty and justifications developed by Community law. We also take posted workers, as a case study, where the tensions between market access and workers' rights are brought into particularly sharp focus.

---

[531] Case C–238/98 [2000] ECR I–6623.   [532] Para. 30.   [533] Para. 35.

5

Limitations on Freedom of Movement

A. INTRODUCTION

In chapter 4 we considered the rights given to workers and their families by Community law. In this chapter we look at the limits to those rights as laid down first by the Treaty, in the form of express derogations, and second, by the case law in the form of objective justifications/public interest requirements. We also look at the limits to the limits on free movement, notably the general principles of law, especially proportionality and fundamental rights, and the implications of the decision in *Viking*. Finally, we consider the issue of 'posted workers' as an example of the public interest justification of workers' protection being used by host states to justify imposing their terms and conditions of employment on posted workers while they are employed in the host state, and the legislative implementation of this principle. We begin by examining the express derogations.

B. EXPRESS DEROGATIONS

1. Introduction

We turn now to examine the express powers given to the host state by Community law to prevent or restrict migrants from enjoying the rights to free movement in full. For many years the express derogations laid down by the Treaty were the main focus of attention. They fall into two categories: general derogations (public policy, public security and public health) and specific derogations (employment in the public service). The *general* derogations apply to justify a decision to refuse entry as well as justifying any discriminatory measure or other conduct which prevents or impedes access to the market or exercise of the freedom. With these general derogations, Member States can preserve their sovereign right to control those who are entering their territory and residing there. The *specific* derogation applies only to the initial refusal of access to employment.[1]

---

[1] See further below nn. 94–144. The first part of this chapter draws on Barnard, *The Substantive law of the EU: The Four Freedoms* (OUP, Oxford, 2004) Ch. 14.

2. Public Policy, Public Security, Public Health

2.1. Introduction

Article 39(3) allows Member States to derogate from the principle of free movement of workers on the grounds of public policy, public security and public health. Articles 46 and 55 contain the same derogations for establishment and services. The list of derogations is exhaustive;[2] derogations to fundamental freedoms are interpreted strictly so that their scope cannot be determined unilaterally by a Member State without being subject to control by the Community institutions.[3] In *Orfanopoulos*[4] the Court said that 'a particularly restrictive interpretation of the derogations from that freedom is required by virtue of a person's status as a citizen of the Union'. Derogations do not apply where Community Directives provide for exhaustive harmonization of the field,[5] and they are read subject to the general principles of law, in particular proportionality[6] and fundamental human rights.[7] Derogations also cannot be used to serve economic purposes.[8] Therefore, a Member State cannot rely on a derogation to justify excluding foreign nationals from its labour market simply because unemployment is high in the state and there is a political need to preserve jobs for nationals.[9]

The bare bones of the general derogations were originally fleshed out by the

---

[2] Case C–17/62 *Federación de Distribuidores Cinematográficos* v. *Estado Español et Unión de Productores de Cine y Televisión* [1993] ECR I–2239, para. 20 (cultural policy is not one of the justifications set out in Art. 46); Case C–388/01 *Commission* v. *Italy* [2003] ECR I–721, para. 20 (cohesion of the tax system not one of the justifications under Art. 46). For this reason, the Court has developed the concept of objective justification/public interest requirements to allow Member States/employers to justify rules which are indirectly discriminatory or non-discriminatory but which hinder access to the market.

[3] See, e.g., Case 41/74 *Van Duyn* v. *Home Office* [1974] ECR 1337, para. 18; Case C–348/96 *Criminal Proceedings against Calfa* [1999] ECR I–11, para. 23; Case C–114/97 *Commission* v. *Spain* [1998] ECR I–6717, para. 34.

[4] Joined cases C–482/01 and C–493/01 *Orfanopoulos* v. *Land Baden-Württemberg* [2004] ECR I–000, para. 53.

[5] Case C–421/98 *Commission* v. *Spain (architects)* [2000] ECR I–10375, paras. 41–2.

[6] Case C–100/01 *Ministre de l'Intérieur* v. *Olazabal* [2002] ECR I–10981, para. 43; Case C–108/96 *MacQuen* v. *Grandvision Belgium* [2001] ECR I–837, para. 31; Case C–3/88 *Commission* v. *Italy* [1989] ECR I–4035, para. 15; Case C–348/96 *Criminal Proceedings against Donatella Calfa* [1999] ECR I–11, para. 23.

[7] See Case C–260/89 *ERT* v. *DEP* [1991] ECR I–2925, para. 43 where the Court said that the application of the derogations in Arts. 46 and 55 had to be appraised in the light of the general principle of freedom of expression in Art. 10 of the European Convention of Human Rights. For an example of its application in the UK, see *B* v. *Secretary of State for the Home Department* [2000] 2 CMLR 1086.

[8] See, e.g., Case 352/85 *Bond* v. *The Netherlands* [1988] ECR 2085, para. 34. See also Art. 2(2) of Dir. 64/221 now replaced by Art. 27(1) of Dir. 2004/38.

[9] Cf. the limitations on free movement of workers contained in some of the Accession Agreements.

provisions of Directive 64/221[10] which applied to all three categories of free movement of persons as well to spouses and members of their families.[11] This Directive was repealed when the Citizens' Rights Directive 2004/38 (CRD) came into force.[12] However, because Directive 2004/38 drew on Articles of Directive 64/221, as interpreted by the Court, this chapter examines both the provision of Directive 64/221 and its case law, as well as the provisions of Directive 2004/38.

2.2. Public Policy and Public Security

Member States have a certain margin of discretion to determine what constitutes public policy in the light of their national needs.[13] For example, in *Van Duyn*[14] the Court said that the particular circumstances in which a Member State could rely on the concept of public policy might 'vary from one country to another and from one period to another'. It was therefore 'necessary to allow the competent national authorities an area of discretion within the limits imposed by the Treaty'. Similarly, in *Jany*[15] the Court said that 'Community law does not impose on Member States a uniform scale of values as regard the assessment of conduct which may be considered to be contrary to public policy'. Yet this margin of discretion is limited by the provisions of the Directive.

(a) Personal Conduct

The starting point for determining what constitutes public policy and public security was Article 3(1) of Directive 64/221,[16] now Article 27(2), which says that measures taken on the grounds of public policy or public security must be 'based exclusively on the *personal conduct* of the individual concerned'.[17]

---

[10] OJ SE [1964] 850/64/117. See also Commission Communication to the Council and the European Parliament on the Special Measures concerning the movement and residence of citizens of the Union which are justified on the grounds of public policy, public security or public health 1999: COM(99) 372.

[11] Art. 1.   [12] OJ [2004] L158/77.

[13] Case 41/74 *Van Duyn* [1974] ECR 1337; Joined Cases 115 & 116/81 *Adoui and Cornuaille* v. *Belgian State* [1982] ECR 1665, para. 8; and Case 36/75 *Rutili* v. *Ministre de l'intérieur* [1975] ECR 1219.

[14] Case 41/74 *Van Duyn* v. *Home Office* [1974] ECR 1337, para. 18.

[15] Case C–268/99 *Aldona Malgorzata Jany* v. *Staatssecretaris van Justitie* [2001] ECR I–8615, para. 60.

[16] This provision is directly effective: Case 41/74 *Van Duyn* [1974] ECR 1337, para. 15.

[17] Emphasis added. See also F. Wooldridge, 'Free Movement of EEC Nationals: The Limitation Based on Public Policy and Public Security' (1977) 2 *ELRev*. 190. While the category of public policy and public security is usually considered from the perspective of personal conduct, the Annex to Dir. 64/221 also listed diseases and disabilities which might threaten public security or public policy. It identifies drug addiction, profound mental disturbance and manifest conditions of psychotic disturbance with agitation, delirium, hallucinations or confusion as falling within this category. This list is not contained in Directive 2004/38 on Citizens' Rights.

The corollary of this is, as the Court pointed out in *Bonsignore*,[18] that extraneous matters unrelated to the individual concerned may not be taken into account. Bonsignore was convicted of a firearms offence and for causing the death of his brother by negligence when handling a pistol for which he had no licence. A deportation order was made against him for reasons of a 'general preventive nature'. In other words, faced with a resurgence of violence among immigrant communities,[19] the court wanted to make an example of Bonsignore to deter others. The Court of Justice said that in these circumstances the deportation would contravene the Directive; deportation could be ordered but only in the case of breaches of the peace and public security actually caused by the individual defendant himself.[20]

The question of what constitutes personal conduct was considered in detail in *Van Duyn*.[21] Mrs Van Duyn was refused entry into the UK to work as a secretary for the Church of Scientology. Although membership of this church was not prohibited by the British authorities, its activities were considered to be 'socially harmful'.[22] The Court said that the personal conduct did not need to be unlawful before a Member State could invoke the public policy exception. It was sufficient that the conduct be deemed 'socially harmful' and that the state had taken administrative measures to counteract these particular activities.[23]

The Court was also asked to decide in *Van Duyn* whether membership of a particular organization could constitute personal conduct. It ruled that a person's *past* association could not, in general, justify a decision refusing him the right to move freely; but a person's *present* association with an organization could constitute personal conduct, because present association reflected voluntary participation in the activities of an organization, as well as an identification with its aims and designs.[24]

More controversially, the Court also suggested in *Van Duyn* that the host state could refuse a national of another Member State the benefit of the rules on the free movement of persons, even though the state did not place a similar

---

[18] Case 67/74 *Bonsignore* v. *Oberstadtdirektor of the City of Cologne* [1975] ECR 297.

[19] AG Mayras doubted the basis for such an order. He expressed himself to be 'rather sceptical' of the deterrent effect of a deportation order. He feared it masked xenophobia ([1975] ECR 297, 315).

[20] Paras. 6–7.   [21] Case 41/74 [1974] ECR 1337.

[22] On 25 July 1968 the Minister of Health said in the House of Commons that 'Scientology is a pseudo-philosophical cult . . . [It] is socially harmful. It alienates members of families from each other and attributes squalid and disgraceful motives to all who oppose it. . . . There is no power under existing law to prohibit the practice of Scientology; but the government have concluded that it is so objectionable that it would be right to take all steps within their power to curb its growth.' These steps included preventing foreign nationals from entering to study or work there. As AG Mayras noted, the UK's lack of power to take measures against the church is 'one consequence of a particularly liberal form of government'.

[23] Para. 19.   [24] Para. 17.

restriction on its own nationals.[25] Therefore, the UK could refuse to allow a Dutch national to enter the UK to work for the Church of Scientology on public policy grounds while permitting, albeit with disapproval, a British national to do the very same job. The Court justified this decision by reference to the principle of international law[26] that Member States have no authority to refuse entry or to expel their own nationals from the territory of their own state[27] but can do the same to migrants.

However, this aspect of the ruling in *Van Duyn* sits uncomfortably with the general principle of non-discrimination on the grounds of nationality and subsequent case law has implicitly reversed this part of the judgment. It is now clear that Member States must apply the doctrine of non-discrimination in so far as it is consistent with the principles of international law. Therefore, if equivalent conduct on the part of the state's own nationals is not subject to 'repressive measures or other genuine and effective measures intended to combat such conduct',[28] it cannot be a cause for expelling migrants. This can be seen in *Adoui and Cornuaille*[29] where two French prostitutes[30] were refused permission to reside in Belgium on public policy grounds, despite the fact that prostitution was not prohibited by Belgium legislation.[31] The Court said that Member States were not entitled to base the exercise of their discretion on 'assessments of certain conduct which would have the effect of applying an arbitrary distinction to the detriment of nationals of other Member States'.[32] Therefore, Member States must be consistent in their conduct towards nationals and migrants. As the Court put it succinctly in *Jany*,[33] conduct by migrants (prostitution) which a Member State (the Netherlands) accepts on the part of its own nationals could not be regarded as constituting a genuine threat to public order.

The concept of personal conduct adopted in *Van Duyn* was further narrowed

---

[25] Para. 21. See Mancini who described this aspect of the ruling as a 'false step' in 'The Free Movement of Workers in the Case Law of the European Court of Justice' in Curtin and O'Keeffe (eds), *Constitutional Adjudication in EC and National Law: Essays for the Hon. Mr. Justice T.F. O'Higgins* (Butterworths, Dublin, 1992) 75. For further consideration of the 'double penalty' rule, see Guild, 'Security of Residence and Expulsion of Foreigners: European Community Law' in Guild and Minderhoud, *Security of Residence and Expulsion: Protection of Aliens in Europe* (Kluwer, The Hague, 2000) 68–9.

[26] Para. 22.

[27] See further Case C–171/96 *Pereira Roque v. Governor of Jersey* [1998] ECR I–4607, paras. 49–50; Case C–348/96 *Calfa* [1999] ECR I–11, para. 20.

[28] Joined Cases 115 and 116/81 *Adoui and Cornuaille v. Belgian State* [1982] ECR 1665, para. 8.

[29] Ibid.

[30] Or, as the Court delicately put it, Adoui worked at a bar that was 'suspect from the point of view of morals'.

[31] Para. 6, although certain incidental activities, such as the exploitation of prostitution by third parties and various forms of incitement to debauchery, were unlawful.

[32] Para. 7.

[33] Case C–268/99 *Jany* [2001] ECR I–8615, para. 61. This case concerned the Association Agreements with Poland and the Czech Republic.

in *Bouchereau*.[34] The Court said that the public policy exception could be invoked to justify restrictions on the free movement of workers only if 'there was a genuine and sufficiently serious threat affecting one of the fundamental interests of society'.[35] Therefore, a simple infringement of the social order by breaching the law (possessing drugs) would not be enough to justify steps taken on public policy grounds. For similar reasons, in *Adoui*[36] the Court said that being a prostitute did not constitute sufficiently serious personal conduct to justify applying the derogations.

This line of case law, starting with *Van Duyn*,[37] has been incorporated into Article 27(2) of the Citizens' Rights Directive 2004/38:

> The personal conduct of the individual concerned must represent a genuine, present and sufficiently serious threat affecting one of the fundamental interests of society. Justifications that are isolated from the particulars of the case or that rely on consider- ations of general prevention shall not be accepted.

Article 3(2) of Directive 64/221 and Article 27(2) of Directive 2004/38 provide that previous criminal convictions will not themselves constitute reasons for taking measures on the grounds of public policy.[38] This issue was also considered in *Bouchereau*[39] where a French national working in England, was convicted of unlawful possession of drugs. Six months earlier he had pleaded guilty to a similar offence and had been given a 12-month con- ditional discharge. The magistrate now wished to deport him on the grounds of public policy. The Court decided that the existence of a criminal conviction could be taken into account only in so far as the circumstances which led to that conviction were evidence of 'personal conduct constituting a *present threat* to the requirements of public policy' by showing a propensity to commit the similar acts again.[40] This was a matter for the national court to decide.

The importance of showing that the individual constituted a present threat to public policy was emphasized in *Calfa*.[41] Greece had expelled Calfa for life on the grounds that she had been convicted of obtaining and being in possession of drugs for personal use. The Court ruled that an expulsion order could be made against a Community national but only if, besides her having commit- ted an offence under national drugs laws, her personal conduct created a genuine and sufficiently serious threat affecting one of the fundamental

---

[34] Case 30/77 [1977] ECR 1999.

[35] Para. 35, emphasis added. This test has also been applied in the context of the EU and Turkey Association Council Decision: Case C–340/97 *Nazli* [2000] ECR I–957, paras. 56–61. This test is also used to define public policy more generally when it is not related to individual conduct: Case C–355/98 *Commission v. Belgium* [2000] ECR I–1221, para. 28.

[36] Joined Cases 115 and 116/81 [1982] ECR 1665.

[37] On the importance of this case, see Case C–503/03 *Commission v. Spain*, judgment of 31 January 2006.

[38] Art. 27(3) lays down details about information sharing by Member States in this regard.

[39] Case 30/77 [1977] ECR 1999.   [40] Paras. 28–9.

[41] Case C–348/96 [1999] ECR I–11.

interests of society.[42] Under Greek law foreign nationals convicted under the drugs law were automatically expelled for life.[43] The Court said that because no account was taken of the personal conduct of the offender, or of the danger which she represented to the requirements of public policy, Greek law therefore breached Directive 64/221.[44]

(b) Measures which can be Taken against the Migrant

Expulsion or Exclusion

The most draconian measure that can be taken against an individual is exclusion (the refusal to allow an individual to enter the country), as in *Van Duyn*, or expulsion (the removal of an individual who has already entered the state), as in *Calfa*.[45] As the Court said in *Watson and Belmann*,[46] deportation 'negates the very right conferred and guaranteed by the Treaty'.[47] It can also have a significant effect on the individual's life, particularly their family life if the migrant is a long-time resident. For this reason Directive 2004/38 introduces specific protection against expulsion. Article 28(1) provides that when deciding whether to deport an individual on the grounds of public policy or public security, the host state must take into account length of residency, age, health, family and economic situation, social and cultural integration into the host state, and enduring ties with their country of origin.[48] Citizens and their family members who have permanent residence (i.e. more than 5 years) cannot be deported, save on *serious* grounds of public policy *or* public security.[49] Minors[50] and citizens who have resided in the host state for the previous 10 years cannot be deported except if the decision is

---

[42] Para. 25.

[43] See also Joined cases C–482/01 and C–493/01 *Orfanopoulos v. Land Baden-Württemberg* [2004] ECR I–000, para. 53.

[44] Paras. 27–8. In Joined Cases C–482/01 and C–493/01 *Orfanopoulos* [2004] ECR I–000, para. 82, the Court added that national courts, when reviewing the lawfulness of an expulsion order, had to take into account. Factual matters which occurred after the final decision of the competent authorities which could point to the cessation or the substantial diminution of the present threat.

[45] See Barav, 'Court Recommendation to Deport and the Free Movement of Workers in EEC Law' (1981) 6 *ELRev.* 139. If expulsion/deportation is ordered, the state which issued the identity card or passport must allow the holder to re-enter its territory, even if the document is no longer valid or the nationality of its holder is in dispute (Art. 27(4) of Dir. 2004/38). See also Case C–459/99 *MRAX v. Belgium* [2002] ECR I–6591 on the position of TCNs.

[46] Case 118/75 [1976] ECR 1185; Case 157/79 *R v. Pieck* [1980] ECR 2171, paras. 18–19; Case C–265/88 *Criminal Proceedings against Messner* [1989] ECR I–297, paras. 14–15. See also Case C–329/97 *Ergat* [2000] ECR I–1487 in respect of Turkish workers.

[47] Para. 20.

[48] See also Joined cases C–482/01 and C–493/01 *Orfanopoulos v. Land Baden-Württemberg* [2004] ECR I–000, para. 99. At para. 98 the Court also recognizes the right to family life which must be weighed in the balance.

[49] Art. 28(2).

[50] Except if the expulsion is necessary for the best interests of the child as provided for in the UN Convention on the Rights of the Child 1989.

based on 'imperative grounds of public security' (not public policy), as defined by Member States.[51]

Thus, whether deportation (as opposed to some lesser measure) can be justified turns largely on the question of proportionality. Deportation cannot be automatic,[52] nor can there be a presumption that the migrant should be expelled.[53] Deportation for 'technical' infringements of the host state's law is not permissible. Therefore, in *Watson and Belmann* the Court said that deportation of a migrant for failing to have reported to the police, within three days of entering the country, the place where she was staying was 'so disproportionate to the gravity of the infringement that it becomes an obstacle to the free movement of persons'.[54] In much the same vein Article 15(2) of Directive 2004/38 provides that the expiry of an identity card or passport is not to constitute a ground for expulsion from the host Member State.

Article 33 adds that expulsion orders cannot be issued by the host Member State as a penalty or legal consequence of a custodial penalty unless they comply with the general principles laid down in Article 27, protection against expulsion under Article 28 and the rules concerning public health under Article 29.[55] Furthermore, if an expulsion order is enforced more than two years after it was issued, the Member State must check whether the individual is currently and genuinely a threat to public policy or public security and must assess whether there has been any material change in the circumstances since the expulsion order was issued.[56]

Other Measures

The national system can, of course, impose other, less severe, sanctions on the migrant. For example, in *Pieck*[57] the Court said the host state could fine or imprison a migrant for breaching national laws on immigration formalities, provided that the penalties were comparable to those for equivalent offences committed by nationals. In *Rutili*[58] the Court said that restricting a person's right of residence to a limited area in the country was also possible under Article 12 EC (non discrimination on the grounds of nationality)[59] (but not under Article 39(3)),[60] provided that the Member State could impose similar restrictions on its own nationals.[61] Therefore, the French Minister could

---

[51] Art. 28(3).   [52] Case C–408/03 *Commission* v. *Belgium* [2005] ECR I–000.
[53] Joined Cases C–482/01 and C–493/01 *Orfanopoulos* v. *Land Baden-Württemberg* [2004] ECR I–000, para. 92.
[54] Case 118/75 *Watson and Belmann* [1976] ECR 1185, para. 21. See also Case C–215/03 *Oulane* v. *Minister voor Vreemdelingenzaken en Integratie* [2005] ECR I–000, paras. 38 and 40.
[55] Art. 33(1).   [56] Art. 33(2).
[57] Case 157/79 *R* v. *Pieck* [1980] ECR 2171, paras. 18–19.
[58] Case 36/75 [1975] ECR 1219.   [59] Para. 49.
[60] The Court made clear that Art. 39(3) applied to prohibitions on residence only in respect of the whole territory and not by reference to its internal subdivisions (paras. 46–8).
[61] Para. 50. See also Art. 22 of Dir. 2004/38 'The right of residence and the right of permanent residence shall cover the whole territory of the Member State. Member States may impose

prohibit Rutili, an Italian national who had spent all his life in France, from living in certain regions of France due to his political and trade union activities. Yet, despite the ruling in *Rutili*, the Court diluted the principle of non-discrimination in *Olazabal*.[62]

Olazabal, a Spanish national of Basque origin, was a member of ETA, 'an armed and organised group whose activity constitute[d] a threat to public order'.[63] As a result of his involvement in the kidnapping of a Spanish industrialist he was sentenced to 18 months' imprisonment in France followed by a four-year ban on his residing in the vicinity of the Spanish border. He argued that the residence ban was discriminatory since nationals could not be subject to any such limitation. The Court rejected his arguments. It said that because Community law allowed migrants to be subject to the ultimate sanction (deportation) they could therefore be subject to less severe measures—such as facing restrictions on their right of residence—without it being necessary for identical measures to be applied to nationals.[64]

Thus, by examining the facts of *Olazabal* through the lens of proportionality rather than non-discrimination the Court reached an entirely different conclusion to the one in *Rutili*. It distinguished the two cases on factual grounds: Rutili was, to all intents and purposes, French; Olazabal was a migrant worker. Furthermore, there was some suspicion in *Rutili* that the action taken against him was on the grounds of his trade union activities which itself would have contravened Article 8 of Regulation 1612/68. By contrast Olazabal was a terrorist and could have been deported for that reason.[65] He was therefore benefiting by not having such a draconian step taken against him.

The Court also clarified the criteria laid down in *Rutili*. It said that a Member State could—under Article 39(3)—limit a worker's right of residence to a part of the national territory provided that:[66]

- such action was justified by reasons of public order or public security based on his individual conduct;
- those reasons were so serious that otherwise he would have been prohibited from residing in, or banished from, the whole of the national territory; and
- the conduct which the Member State concerned wished to prevent gave rise, in the case of its own nationals, to punitive measures or other genuine and effective measures.

territorial restrictions on the right of residence and the right of permanent residence only where the same restrictions apply to their own nationals.'

[62] Case C–100/01 *Ministre de l'Intérieur v. Olazabal* [2002] ECR I–10981, para. 45.
[63] Para. 35.   [64] Para. 41.   [65] Paras. 34–6.   [66] Para. 45.

(c) The Right to Reapply

In *Adoui*[67] the Court made clear that excluded or expelled individuals had to have the chance to reapply. This point was more recently confirmed in *Shingara*[68] where the Court said that, because a decision excluding migrants from entering a Member State was a derogation from the fundamental principle of freedom of movement, it could not be of unlimited duration.[69] Therefore a Community national expelled from a Member State could apply for a fresh residence permit.[70] If that application was made after a reasonable time, the competent administrative authority in the host state had to consider whether there had now been a material change in the circumstances which had justified the first decision ordering expulsion.[71]

The Citizens' Rights Directive 2004/38 confirms that Member States cannot issue orders excluding individuals covered by the Directive from their territory for life.[72] Individuals must be able to submit an application to lift an exclusion order after a reasonable period and, in any event, after three years from enforcement of the final exclusion order. Individuals must also establish a material change in the circumstances which justified the decision ordering their exclusion in the first place. Member States must reach a decision within six months. During this time the applicant remains excluded.

3. Public Health

The Annex to Directive 64/221 provided an exhaustive list of diseases or disabilities which could trigger action against an individual on public health grounds: those subject to quarantine listed in International Health Regulation No. 2 of the World Health Organization of 25 May 1951; tuberculosis (TB); syphilis; and other infectious or contagious diseases or contagious parasitic diseases if they are subject to provisions for protection of nationals of the host country. Migrants who are HIV positive or who suffer from AIDS found themselves in a particularly invidious position.[73] Some Member States have tried to deny them admission,[74] although there is no express provision for this

---

[67] Joined Cases 115 and 116/81 [1982] ECR 1665, para. 12; Case C–348/96 *Calfa* [1999] ECR I–11, para. 27.

[68] Joined Cases C–65/95 and C–111/95 *R v. Secretary of State for the Home Department, ex parte Mann Singh Shingara (C–65/95) and ex parte Abbas Radiom* [1997] ECR I–3343.

[69] Para. 40. See also Case C–235/99 *R v. Secretary of State for the Home Department, ex parte Kondova* [2001] ECR I–6427, para. 90; Case C–63/99 *R v. Secretary of State for the Home Department, ex parte Gloszczuk* [2001] ECR I–6369, para. 85.

[70] Para. 39.   [71] Ibid.   [72] Art. 32.

[73] See Van Overbeek, 'AIDS/HIV Infection and the Free Movement of Persons within the Community' (1990) 27 *CMLRev.* 791.

[74] Ibid., 792. Guild notes that in Bavaria there was an attempt to use HVI/AIDS as a public health ground for expulsion but it was quickly stopped as illegal under the Directive: Guild, 'Security of Residence and Expulsion of Foreigners: European Community Law' in Guild and

in the Directive.[75] However, in its 1999 Communication the Commission rejected the use of any measures which could lead to 'social exclusion, discrimination or stigmatisation of persons with HIV/AIDS'.[76] More generally, the Commission observed that the public health grounds were 'somewhat outdated'. It concluded that 'restrictions of free movement can no longer be considered a necessary and effective means of solving public health problems'. Nevertheless, the public health derogation contained in Directive 64/221 is largely repeated in Article 29(1) of the Citizens' Rights Directive in respect of those medical conditions which are still current. It provides that:

The only diseases justifying measures restricting freedom of movement shall be the diseases with epidemic potential as defined by the relevant instruments of the World Health Organisation and other infectious diseases or contagious parasitic diseases if they are the subject of protection provisions applying to nationals of the host Member State.

Unlike the public policy and public security derogations, which can be invoked in respect of the migrant's initial entry to the territory or at any time during the first five years of the migrant's stay, the public health derogation can be invoked only to justify the initial refusal of entry or deportation within three months from the date of arrival. Thus, once recognized, the right of residence cannot be contested on health grounds. In exceptional cases the host state can require those entitled to the right of residence to undergo a medical examination, free of charge, to certify that they are not suffering from any of the conditions listed in Article 29(1).

4. Procedural Requirements

4.1. General Provisions

Directive 64/221 laid down minimum procedural requirements to protect migrants faced with a decision refusing renewal of a residence permit or

---

Minderhoud, *Security of Residence and Expulsion: Protection of Aliens in Europe* (Kluwer, The Hague, 2000) 64.

[75] In this context, the Community's treatment of its own staff or job applicants with HIV is instructive. The Court has ruled that the requirement that every person undergo a medical examination did not infringe Art. 8 of the ECHR provided that the individual consents: Case C–404/92P *X v. Commission* [1994] ECR I–4737, para.17. The Court has examined the conclusions of the Council as the Ministers of Health which said that employees who are HIV positive but who do not show any symptoms of AIDS should be looked on as normal employees fit for work (OJ [1989] C28/2). The Court said that the administration must treat these conclusions as rules of practice, otherwise the principle of equal treatment would be infringed, see Case T–10/93 *A v. EC Commission* [1994] ECR II–179, IA–119, II–387.

[76] See above, 'Special measures concerning the movement and residence of citizens of the Union which are justified on the grounds of public policy, public security, or public health' COM(99) 372, 12.

ordering expulsion on the grounds of public policy, public security and public health. These requirements were much criticized because they were minimal but complex. They also generated a large volume of case law. Directive 2004/38 has improved upon and simplified the procedural protection. It requires that migrants facing any decision taken against them on the grounds of public policy, public security, and public health must be informed in writing in such a way that they are able to comprehend its content and the implications for them.[77] They must also be told 'precisely and in full' of the grounds on which the decision in their case is based, unless this is contrary to the interests of the security of the state.[78] This provision is intended to enable the migrant to be able to prepare an effective defence.[79] The notification must also specify the court or administrative authority with which the person concerned may lodge an appeal, the time limit for the appeal and, where applicable, the time allowed for the person to leave the territory. Except in 'duly substantiated' cases of urgency, the period provided for leaving the country must not be less than one month from the date of notification.[80]

4.2. Remedies

(a) The New Rules

The Directive then provides for the availability of certain remedies. In the original Directive 64/221, Article 8 required the individual to have the same legal remedies as nationals. Where no legal remedies were available (or the remedies were inadequate in some way), then Article 9 required that the individual had to be able to exercise his right of defence before a 'competent authority' which could not be the same as that which adopted the measure restricting his freedom.[81] While the original drafts of the Citizens' Rights Directive broadly followed the distinction between the Article 8 and Article 9 remedies contained in Directive 64/221, the final version of the Directive abandoned this approach. Instead, Article 31(1) provides that:

The persons concerned shall have access to judicial and, where appropriate, administrative redress procedures in the host Member State to appeal against or seek review of any decision taken against them on the grounds of public policy, public security or public health.

In addition, Article 31(3) provides that the 'redress procedures shall allow for an examination of the legality of the decision, as well as of the facts and circumstances on which the proposed measure is based. They shall ensure

---

[77] Art. 30(1). See also Joined Cases 115 and 116/81 *Adoui and Cornuaille* [1982] ECR 1665, para. 13.
[78] Art. 30(2).
[79] Case 36/75 *Rutili* [1975] ECR 1219, para. 39; Joined Cases 115 and 116/81 *Adoui and Cornuaille* [1982] ECR 1665, para. 13.
[80] Art. 30(3).   [81] Case 36/75 *Rutili* [1975] ECR 1219, para. 35.

that the decision is not disproportionate, particularly in view of the requirements laid down in Article 28 [concerning protection against expulsion]'.

Despite the fact that the content of Article 31 differs from that of Articles 8 and 9, it is likely that the Court will draw on its pre-existing case law to interpret the provision. For this reason, we shall now examine the salient features of the Court's jurisprudence.

(b) Access to Judicial Redress: Appeal and Review

While Article 31(1) of Directive 2004/38 talks of 'access to judicial . . . procedures in the host Member State to appeal against or seek review of any decision', Article 8 of Directive 64/221 gave the migrant the same legal remedies as nationals in respect of acts of the administration, when the migrant was faced by a decision concerning entry, or the refusal to issue or renew a residence permit, or a decision ordering expulsion from the territory. Consistent with the principle of national procedural autonomy, the Court said that Article 8 did not govern the ways in which remedies were to be made available (for instance by stipulating the courts from which such remedies could be sought)[82] and this is likely to be extended to Article 31. However, the Court said in *ex parte Shingara*[83] that Member States could not execute a decision ordering expulsion before the migrant was able to avail himself of the Article 8 remedy.

In *ex parte Shingara*[84] the Court was also asked whether the requirement on Member States to provide 'the same legal remedies' referred to (a) specific remedies available in respect of decisions concerning entry by *nationals* of the state concerned (*in casu* an appeal to an immigration adjudicator) or (b) only to remedies available in respect of acts of the administration generally (*in casu*, an application for judicial review, a less substantial remedy than an appeal). The Court said that no account could be taken of the remedies available to *nationals* concerning the right of entry because the two situations were not comparable. As we have already seen,[85] with nationals the right of entry is a consequence of the status of being a national; by contrast, with migrants Member States have the discretion whether to invoke the public policy derogation. Therefore, since an appeal to an immigration adjudicator was ruled out, migrants were left with the same remedies as those available against acts of the administration generally and the Court said that this satisfied the obligation under Article 8. Given that Article 31 expressly provides for appeal or review in the alternative, it is likely that *Shingara* will continue to apply.

---

[82] Case 48/75 *Royer* [1976] ECR 497, para. 60

[83] Joined Cases C–65/95 and C–111/95 *The Queen v. Secretary of State for the Home Department, ex parte Singh Shingara and Abbas Radiom* [1997] ECR I–3343, para. 24.

[84] Joined Cases C–65/95 and C–111/95 *The Queen v. Secretary of State for the Home Department, ex parte Singh Shingara and Abbas Radiom* [1997] ECR I–3343, para. 24.

[85] See text attached to n. 27 above.

In *Pecastaing*[86] the Court said that the 'same remedies' would include suspension of the acts challenged, if this remedy was available to nationals. However, it added that Article 8 did not oblige the host state to allow the migrant to remain in its territory throughout the entire proceedings, so long as he was able to obtain a fair hearing and to present his defence in full.[87] This is now confirmed in Article 31(4) which allows Member States to exclude the individual from their territory pending the redress procedure but adds that 'Member States may not prevent the individual from submitting his/her defence in person, except where his/her appearance may cause serious troubles to public policy or public security or when the appeal or judicial review concerns a denial of entry or residence'.

(c) Administrative Redress

Article 31 envisages that administrative redress must be available where appropriate *in addition* to judicial redress. This is a marked change from Article 9 of Directive 64/221 which applied where there were no legal remedies or where the legal remedies were inadequate in some way. So, for example, Article 9(1) said that where:

- there was no right of appeal to a court of law; or
- the appeal was only in respect of the legal validity of the decision; or
- the appeal did not have suspensory effect

then the authority making the final decision (refusing renewal of a residence permit or ordering expulsion of the holder of a residence permit) could not, save in cases of urgency, take a decision until a 'competent authority',[88] which differed from the decision maker, had given its view.[89] Therefore, the competent authority had to give its opinion—based on an exhaustive examination of all the facts and circumstances of the case, including the

---

[86] Case 98/79 *Pecastaing v. Belgium State* [1980] ECR 691, para. 12.

[87] Case 98/79 [1980] ECR 691, para. 13.; Case C–357/98 *ex parte Yiadom* [2000] ECR I–9265, para. 35. On interim orders see Art. 31(2).

[88] Art. 9 did not define the term 'competent authority'. In Case 131/79 *ex parte Santillo* [1980] ECR 1585 the Court recognized that a recommendation for deportation made by a criminal court at the time of conviction could constitute an opinion given by a competent authority, provided that the court has taken account of Art. 3(2) of Dir. 64/221, now Art. 27(2) of the CRD (that the mere existence of criminal convictions did not automatically constitute grounds for deportation). However, the Court has made clear that the competent authority does not have to be judicial in nature: all that Art. 9 requires is for the authority to perform its duties in absolute independence; that it is not directly or indirectly subject to any control by the administrative body empowered to take the measures provided for in the Directive; and that the authority follow a procedure which enables the person concerned, on the terms laid down by the Directive, effectively to present his defence and that all the factors to be taken into account by the administration are placed before it.

[89] Art. 9(1). See also Case 48/75 *Royer* [1976] ECR 497, para. 61.

expediency of the proposed measure[90]—*before* the decision maker finally decided to expel or not to renew the residence permit.[91]

Some of the more general rules developed by the Court in the context of its case law under Article 9(1) are likely to be applied equally to administrative redress under Article 31 including the requirement that while Member States can decide on the procedure by which a person appears before the competent authority, the individual must enjoy 'the same rights of defence and assistance or representation as the domestic law of that country provides for',[92] and must be informed of the authority's decision.[93]

5. Employment in the Public Service

5.1. Introduction

It has been traditional for Member States, as part of the exercise of their sovereignty,[94] to reserve certain public service jobs to their own nationals.[95] Article 39(4) provides that the principles of free movement of workers and non-discrimination on the ground of nationality do not apply to 'employment in the public service'. Articles 45 and 55 contain an equivalent provision in respect of establishment and services, albeit drafted in rather different terms. Article 45 says that 'The provisions of this chapter shall not apply ... to activities which in that state are connected, even occasionally, with the exercise of official authority'. The justification for this 'public service' derogation is that particular posts presume a 'special relationship of allegiance to the state' and a 'reciprocity of rights and duties which form the foundation of the bond of nationality'.[96]

Because Articles 39(4), 45, and 55 represent further exceptions to fundamental freedoms they are also narrowly construed,[97] with their scope limited to what is 'strictly necessary for safeguarding the interests of the state which that provision allows the Member States to protect'.[98] Therefore, in

---

[90] Joined Cases 115 and 116/81 *Adoui and Cornuaille* [1982] ECR 1665, para. 15.

[91] Case C–175/94 *R* v. *Secretary of State for the Home Department, ex parte John Gallagher* [1995] ECR I–4253, para. 20.

[92] Art. 9(1); Joined Cases C–297/88 and C–197/89 *Dzodzi* v. *Belgium* [1990] ECR I–3763, para. 62.

[93] Ibid.; Case C–175/94 *R* v. *Secretary of State for the Home Department, ex parte Gallagher* [1995] ECR I–4253.

[94] See AG Mancini in Case 307/84 *Commission* v. *France* [1986] ECR 1725, para. 2.

[95] For further details see Morris, Fredman and Hayes, 'Free Movement and the Public Sector' (1990) 19 *ILJ*. 20; Lenz, 'The Public Service in Article 48(4) EEC with Special Reference to the Law in England and in the Federal Republic of Germany' [1989] 15 *LIEI*. 75.

[96] Case 149/79 *Commission* v. *Belgium* [1980] ECR I–3881, para. 10. See also Handoll, 'Article 48(4) and Non-National Access to Public Employment' (1988) 13 *ELRev*. 223.

[97] Case 152/73 *Sotgiu* v. *Deutsche Bundespost* [1979] ECR 153, para. 4.

[98] Case 225/85 *Commission* v. *Italy* [1987] ECR 2725.

Sotgiu[99] the Court said that Article 39(4) applied only to conditions of access to employment; it did not authorize discriminatory conditions of employment once access had been granted. This meant that the German postal service could not rely on Article 39(4) to justify its refusal to pay Sotgiu, an Italian national, a separation allowance granted to German workers, on the grounds that he was employed in the public service. The Court said that the fact that Sotgiu had been admitted to the service denied the existence of those interests which justified the derogation.

5.2. Article 39(4): 'Employment in the Public Service'

The Court has insisted on a Community definition of the phrase 'employment in the public service'.[100] In *Commission* v. *Belgium*[101] it explained that the jobs envisaged by Article 39(4) 'involve direct or indirect participation in the exercise of powers conferred by public law and duties designed to safeguard the interests of the state or of other public authorities'. The Court continued that these jobs are 'characteristic of specific activities of public service in so far as [they are] invested with the exercise of public power *and* the responsibility for safeguarding the general interests of the state'.[102] It is not clear whether these requirements are to be read cumulatively or disjunctively.[103] A cumulative reading is consistent with the view that Article 39(4) must be interpreted restrictively; but support can be found in *Commission* v. *Italy*[104] that the requirements are to be read disjunctively.

The other question facing the Court is whether the phrase 'public service' requires an institutional or a functional approach. The *institutional* or organic approach, which is supported by the wording of Article 39(4), views the institution and its personnel as a whole, regardless of the specific functions carried out by individuals within the organization. This approach would allow a Member State to reserve all jobs in a particular organization, such as the civil service, to nationals even where some of those jobs are of a purely administrative or technical nature and involve no tasks designed to safeguard the interests of the state. This approach has been favoured by states keen to reserve as many posts as possible for their own nationals.[105] By contrast, the *functional* approach looks at the work involved in a particular post to see if it involves direct or indirect participation in the exercise of powers conferred by pubic law and duties designed to safeguard the interests of the state. The functional approach would allow Member States to reserve only certain posts to nationals.

---

[99] Case 152/73 [1979] ECR 153, para. 4.
[100] See, e.g., Case C–473/93 *Commission* v. *Luxembourg* [1996] ECR I–3207, para. 26.
[101] Case 149/79 [1982] ECR 1845, para. 7.   [102] Emphasis added.
[103] Cf. Lenz, above, n. 95, 99–100, Morris *et al.*, above, n., 23.
[104] Case 225/85 [1987] ECR 2725, paras. 9–10.
[105] See the Belgian government's arguments in Case 149/79 *Commission* v. *Belgium* [1980] ECR 3881.

Consistent with the view that derogations are narrowly construed, the Court actually adopts the functional approach.[106] On a case by case basis, it examines the tasks and responsibilities inherent in the post[107] to see if they fulfil 'the very strict conditions'[108] of Article 39(4) rather than considering the nature of the legal relationship between the employee and the employing administration or the individual's job description.[109] This approach has led the Court finding that most jobs do not benefit from the Article 39(4) derogation. For example, it has said that the jobs of a teacher in a state school,[110] a state nurse,[111] a foreign language assistant in a university,[112] various posts on the state railways,[113] a local government employee,[114] a seaman,[115] a job in research which did not involve sensitive research work,[116] and a post in the lower echelons of the civil service did not constitute employment in the public service.[117] On the other hand, in the rather odd case of *Commission v. Belgium*[118] the Court found that local authority posts for architects, supervisors[119] and night watchmen did fall within the Article 39(4) exception. Less controversially, it said in *Commission v. Italy*[120] that those involved in advising the state on scientific and technical questions were employed in the 'public service'.

While it is difficult to draw any clear principles from the case law, it would seem that senior government jobs can be confined to nationals only, even though this may mean that Article 39(4) represents a barrier to promotion for non-nationals.[121] However, where the exercise of public law powers is purely marginal and ancillary to the principal function of the posts, then such jobs generally fall outside Article 39(4). This is the view taken by the Commission in its Communication designed to eliminate restrictions in areas of the public sector[122] where it listed jobs in the public sector to which, in normal circumstances, Article 39(4) does not apply. These include jobs in public

---

[106] Case C–473/93 *Commission v. Luxembourg* [1996] ECR I–3207, para. 27.

[107] Case 149/79 *Commission v. Belgium* [1982] ECR 1845, para. 8; Case C–473/93 *Commission v. Luxembourg* [1996] ECR I–3207, para. 27.

[108] Case C–473/93 *Commission v. Luxembourg* [1996] ECR I–3263, para. 33.

[109] Case 152/73 *Sotgiu* [1974] ECR 153.

[110] Case 66/85 *Lawrie-Blum* [1986] ECR 2121. Case C–4/91 *Bleis v. Ministère de l'education nationale* [1991] ECR I–5627.

[111] Case 307/84 *Commission v. France* [1986] ECR 1725.

[112] Case 33/88 *Allué and Coonan* [1989] ECR 1591.

[113] Case 149/79 *Commission v. Belgium* [1982] ECR 1845.

[114] Case 149/79 *Commission v. Belgium* [1980] ECR 3881 and [1982] ECR 1845 (plumbers, carpenters, electricians, gardeners).

[115] Case C–37/93 *Commission v. Belgium* [1993] ECR I–6295.

[116] Case 225/85 *Commission v. Italy* [1987] ECR 2625.

[117] Case 66/85 *Lawrie-Blum* [1986] ECR 2121.

[118] Case 149/79 *Commission v. Belgium* [1982] ECR 1845, para. 8.

[119] Namely head technical office supervisor, principal supervisor, works supervisor, and stock controller.

[120] Case 225/85 *Commission v. Italy* [1987] ECR 2625, para.9.

[121] Case 225/85 *Commission v. Italy* [1987] ECR 2625, para.10.   [122] 88/C 72/02.

health care services, employment in state educational institutions, jobs in research for non-military purposes in public establishments, and jobs in public bodies responsible for administering public, commercial services, including public transport, gas or electricity distribution, air or maritime navigation, post and telecommunications, and broadcasting. On the other hand, the Commission suggested that Article 39(4) would apply to the police and other forces of order, the armed forces, the judiciary, tax authorities, and the diplomatic service.[123]

The Commission's approach was reflected in the Court's decisions in *Anker*[124] and the *Spanish Merchant Navy* case,[125] both decided on the same day. In *Anker* the Court upheld in principle a German law requiring the post of master of a fishing vessel flying the German flag to be German. Because the job entailed duties connected to the maintenance of safety and to the exercise of police powers, particularly in the case of danger on board together with powers of investigation, coercion, and punishment, the Court said that the post entailed direct participation in the exercise of powers conferred by public law for the purposes of safeguarding the general interest of the state.[126] It added that even though masters were employed by private bodies this did not take the matter outside the scope of Article 39(4) because the individuals were acting as 'representatives of public authority in the service of the general interests of the state'.[127]

However, the Court emphasized that, to benefit from the Article 39(4) derogation, the powers had to be exercised on a regular basis and did not represent only a 'very minor part of their activities'.[128] It therefore found that the post of master of small-scale deep-sea fishing vessels, which involved skippering small boats with a small crew and participating in fishing and processing fish products, did not benefit from the Article 39(4) derogation.[129] In the *Spanish Merchant Navy* case[130] the Court followed *Anker*, and found that the posts of master and chief mate in the Spanish merchant navy were also posts in which exercise of the duty of representing the flag state was in practice only occasional.[131]

The Commission followed up its Communication on Article 39(4) with enforcement proceedings against defaulting Member States. Greece was condemned for maintaining posts for its nationals in education, health care, the

---

[123] OJ [1988] C72/2, Watson (1989) 14 *ELRev.* 415. And even in respect of these sectors, the Commission has since tightened up its approach: COM(2002) 694, 19.
[124] Case C–47/02 *Albert Anker, Klaas Ras, Albertus Snoek v. Bundesrepublik Deutschland* [2003] ECR I–10447.
[125] Case C–405/01 *Colegio de Oficiales de la Marina Mercante Española v. Administración del Estado* [2003] ECR I–10391.
[126] Para. 61.   [127] Para. 62.   [128] Para. 63.   [129] Para. 64.
[130] Case C–47/02 *Colegio de Oficiales de la Marina Mercante Española v. Administración del Estado* [2003] ECR I–10391.
[131] Para. 45.

utilities, public transport, post and telecommunications, radio and television broadcasting, the Athens opera, and municipal and local orchestras;[132] and Luxembourg was condemned for restricting posts in the public sectors of research, education, health, inland transport, post, telecommunications, and in the utilities to its own nationals.[133] In the field of education, the Luxembourg government argued that teachers had to be Luxembourg nationals in order to 'transmit traditional values' and that, in view of the size of the country and its specific demographic situation, the nationality requirement was an essential condition for preserving Luxembourg's national identity. While recognizing that the preservation of the Member States' national identities was a legitimate aim, the Court said that Luxembourg government's response was disproportionate. It argued that Luxembourg's interest could be effectively safeguarded otherwise than by a general exclusion of nationals from other Member States, in particular by imposing conditions relating to training, experience, and knowledge of the language.[134]

5.3. The Exercise of 'Official Authority'

In respect of establishment, Article 45 contains an equivalent derogation to Article 39(4); Article 55 extends this to services. Article 45 talks of the 'exercise of official authority' which more clearly suggests a functional approach than the Article 39(4) equivalent 'employment in the public service'. Since the Court applied the functional test to Article 39(4), and since the objectives of Article 45 are similar to those of Article 39(4), it is likely that the jurisprudence on Article 39(4) will apply equally to Article 45.[135]

The nature of what constitutes official authority was considered in *Reyners*[136] where the Court examined whether the profession of *avocat* could be confined to nationals on the grounds that *avocats* were connected with the public service of administration of justice. The Court said that Article 45 had to be narrowly construed: it applied only to those activities which had a 'direct and specific connection with official authority'.[137] It continued that Article 45 would justify the exclusion of a whole profession only where those activities were linked to that profession in such a way that freedom of establishment would require the host Member State to allow the exercise by non-nationals, even occasionally, of functions related to official authority.[138] This would not be the case with the legal profession where contacts with the courts, although regular and organic, did not constitute the exercise of official

---

[132] Case C–290/94 *Commission v. Greece* [1996] ECR I–3285.
[133] Case C–473/93 *Commission v. Luxembourg* [1996] ECR I–3263. See also Case C–173/94 *Commission v. Belgium* [1996] ECR I–3265.
[134] Case C–473/93 *Commission v. Luxembourg* [1996] ECR I–3263, paras. 32–5.
[135] Cf. Case C–283/99 *Commission v. Italy* [2001] ECR I–4363, para. 25.
[136] Case 2/74 [1974] ECR 631.   [137] Para. 45.   [138] Para. 46.

authority because it was possible to separate tasks involving the exercise of official authority from the professional activity taken as a whole.[139]

In subsequent cases the Court has also rejected arguments based on Article 45. For example, it found that the job of road traffic accident expert, whose reports were not binding on the courts,[140] did not involve the exercise of official authority, nor did the technical job of designing, programming and operating data processing systems,[141] nor did the job of transport consultant.[142] In *Commission v. Belgium (security guards)*[143] the Court said that the activities of security firms, security systems firms and internal security services were not normally directly and specifically connected with the exercise of official authority. As the Court said in *Commission v. Spain*,[144] merely making a contribution to the maintenance of public security, which any individual may be called upon to do, did not constitute exercise of official authority.

C. JUSTIFICATIONS

1. The General Approach

1.1. Justifications

The (general) express derogations are available in respect of any breach of Community law (refusal of entry as well as directly, indirectly and non-discriminatory measures). However, indirectly discriminatory and non-discriminatory measures which hinder free movement can also be saved by a broader category of objective justifications/public interest requirements. In *O'Flynn*[145] we saw that the language of objective justification was used in the context of free movement of workers. In respect of establishment and services, the Court tends to talk about justifications in the 'public' or 'general interest' or 'imperative requirements'.[146] It is likely that the term 'objective justification' is the functional equivalent to the 'public interest' requirements.[147] At the heart of this approach is the idea that there exist certain

---

[139] Para. 51.   [140] Case C–306/89 *Commission v. Greece* [1991] ECR I–5863, para. 7.
[141] Case C–3/88 *Commission v. Italy* [1989] ECR I–4035, para. 13.
[142] Case C–263/99 *Commission v. Italy* [2001] ECR I–4195.
[143] Case C–355/98 *Commission v. Belgium* [2000] ECR I–1221, para. 26; Case C–283/99 *Commission v. Italy* [2001] ECR I–4363, para. 20.
[144] Case C–114/97 *Commission v. Spain* [1998] ECR I–6717, para. 37.
[145] Case C–237/94 *O'Flynn v. Adjudication Officer* [1996] ECR I–2617, para. 18. This is considered further in Ch. 4.
[146] Case C–76/90 *Säger v. Dennemeyer & Co. Ltd* [1991] ECR I–4221, para. 15; Case C–55/94 *Gebhard* [1996] ECR I–4165, para. 37.
[147] This view is supported by the workers' case, Case C–195/98 *Österreicher Gewerkschaftsbund v. Republik Österreich* [2000] ECR I–10497, para. 45, where the Court reported that the Austrian government contends that the restrictions on free movement are 'justified by overriding reasons of public interest and are consistent with the principle of proportionality'.

national interests which are worthy of protection[148] and which should take precedence over the free movement provisions.

In *Gebhard*,[149] a case on establishment, the Court elaborated on the requirements necessary for the national rule to satisfy the test of justification. It said that national measures liable to hinder or make less attractive the exercise of fundamental freedoms guaranteed by the Treaty had to fulfil four conditions in order not to breach Article 43. They had to:

- be applied in a non-discriminatory manner;
- be justified by imperative requirements in the general interest;
- be suitable for securing the attainment of the objective which they pursued; and
- not go beyond what was necessary to attain it.[150]

The operative part of the judgment in *Gebhard* makes clear that this test also applies to the free movement of workers and services.[151]

In *Säger*[152] the Court added an additional requirement in the context of services:[153]

. . . the freedom to provide services may be limited only by rules which are justified by imperative reasons relating to the public interest and which apply to all persons or undertakings pursuing an activity in the State of destination, *in so far as that interest is not protected by the rules to which the person providing the services is subject in the Member State in which he is established.*

This additional requirement, requiring account to be taken of the extent to which that interest is already protected in the home state, is a reflection of the principle of home state control or 'country of origin'. The importance of this principle can be seen in *Guiot*.[154] The Court said that a national law requiring an employer providing a service in the host Member State to pay employer's contributions to the social security fund of the host Member State, in addition to the contributions paid to the social security fund in the state in which the employer was established, placed an additional financial burden on the employer which was liable to restrict the freedom to provide services. It then considered whether the national legislation could be justified by the public interest relating to the 'social protection of workers in the construction industry'.[155] Then, reflecting the country of origin principle, the Court said that if the workers enjoyed the same protection, or essentially similar protection, by virtue of employer's contributions already paid by the employer in the

---

[148] See AG Tesauro in Case C–118/96 *Safir* [1998] ECR I–1897, para. 29.
[149] Case C–55/94 [1995] ECR I–4165.   [150] Para. 37.   [151] Para. 6.
[152] Case C–76/90 [1991] ECR I–4221.   [153] Para. 15, emphasis added.
[154] Case C–272/94 *Criminal proceedings against Guiot* [1996] ECR I–1905.
[155] Para. 16.

Member State of establishment,[156] which was a matter for the national court to decide,[157] then the justification was not made out.

In the services case, *Gouda*,[158] the Court listed the public interest grounds which it had already recognized. For our purposes the most important are:

- professional rules intended to protect the recipients of a service;[159]
- protection of workers.[160] This is sometimes referred to as reasons of social welfare;[161]
- consumer protection.[162]

Other justifications have also been recognized by the Court:

- the coherence of a scheme of taxation;[163]
- the effectiveness of fiscal supervision;[164]
- preserving the financial balance of a social security scheme;[165]
- guaranteeing the quality of skilled trade work and protecting those who have commissioned such work;[166]

---

[156] Para. 17. See also Joined Cases C–369/96 and C–376 *Arblade* [1999] ECR I–8453, para. 80, concerning 'timbres-intempéries' and 'timbres-fidélité'. The Court also said that the host state could not require the service provider to draw up social or labour documents such as labour rules, a special staff register and an individual account for each worker in the form prescribed by the rules of the host state where the social protection of workers is already safeguarded by the home state. The host state also could not require the service provider to keep social documents, such as a staff register, for five years after the service provider has ceased to employ the workers in the host state at the address of an agent in the host state.

[157] On the facts the Court observed that the Belgian and Luxembourg contributions at issue in practice covered the same risks and had a similar, if not identical purpose (para. 19).

[158] Case C–288/89 [1991] ECR I–4007.

[159] Joined Cases 110 and 111/78 *Ministère public v. Willy van Wesemael and others* [1979] ECR 35, para. 28. In Case C–3/95 *Reisebüro Broede v. Sandker* [1996] ECR I–6511, para. 38, the Court spelled out this justification more fully: 'the application of professional rules to lawyers, in particular those relating to organization, qualifications, professional ethics, supervision and liability, ensures that the ultimate consumers of legal services and the sound administration of justice are provided with the necessary guarantees in relation to integrity and experience'.

[160] Case 279/80 *Webb* [1981] ECR 3305, para. 19; Joined Cases 62–63/81 *Seco v. EVI* [1982] ECR 223, para. 14; Case C–113/89 *Rush Portuguesa* [1990] ECR I–1417, para. 18. Subsequently in Case C–272/94 *Guiot* [1996] ECR I–1905, para. 16, the Court stressed the importance of the social protection of workers in the construction industry; Case C–79/01 *Payroll Data Services (Italy)* [2002] ECR I–8923, para. 31.

[161] Case C–445/03 *Commission v. Luxembourg* [2004] ECR I–10191, para. 28.

[162] Case 220/83 *Commission v. France* [1986] ECR 3663, para. 20; Case 252/83 *Commission v. Denmark* [1986] ECR 3713, para. 20; Case 205/84 *Commission v. Germany* [1986] ECR 3755, para. 30; Case 206/84 *Commission v. Ireland* [1986] ECR 3817, para. 20; Case C–180/89 *Commission v. Italy (Tourist Guides)* [1991] ECR I–709, para. 20.

[163] Case C–204/90 *Bachmann* [1992] ECR I–249; Case C–300/90 *Commission v. Belgium* [1992] ECR I–305; Case C–294/97 *Eurowings Luftverkehrs AG v. Finanzamt Dortmund-Unna* [1999] ECR I–7447, para. 19. However, this has been marginalized in more recent case law: see e.g. Case C–264/96 *ICI v. Colomer* [1998] ECR I–4695, para. 29, possibly being confined to the sphere of pensions and insurance policies (N. Travers (1999) 24 *ELRev.* 403, 408).

[164] Case C–55/98 *Skatteministeriet v. Bent Vestergaard* [1999] ECR I–7641, para. 23.

[165] Case C–158/96 *Kohll* [1998] ECR I–1931, para. 41.

[166] Case C–58/98 *Josef Corsten* [2000] ECR I–7919, para. 38.

- ensuring the balance between sports clubs;[167]
- prevention of social dumping[168] or unfair competition;[169]
- prevention of abuse of free movement of services;[170]
- avoiding disturbances on the labour market.[171]

The Court has not extended the list indefinitely[172] and is particularly sceptical of national justifications with a hint of economic protectionism. For example, in *SETTG*[173] the Court said that a Greek law requiring all tourist guides to have a particular employment relationship with their employer (which effectively prevented self-employed tourist guides from other Member States from providing services in Greece) could not be justified on the grounds of 'maintaining industrial peace as a means of bringing a collective dispute to an end and thereby preventing any adverse effects on an economic sector and consequently on the economy of the state'. The Court said that such a justification had to be regarded as an 'economic aim' which could not constitute a reason relating to the general interest that justified a restriction on the freedom of establishment'.[174] Despite this, the Court has allowed some largely economic justifications—ensuring the coherence of a scheme of taxation, the effectiveness of fiscal supervision, the preservation of the financial balance of a social security scheme and controlling control costs and preventing wastage of financial, technical and human resources[175]—to be successfully invoked by the Member States. Hatzopoulos explains this different treatment on the grounds that these latter objectives serve a 'structural' purpose and so are regarded more leniently than those which do not.[176]

Outside these 'structural' cases, the Court will look to see if the expressed aim is genuinely economic or whether, viewed objectively, the rules actually serve another, legitimate objective. This can be seen in *Finalarte*[177] and *Portugaia Construções*[178] which both concerned the German law (AEntG)[179] whose aim was, according to the accompanying explanatory memorandum, to protect the German construction industry from competition in the

---

[167] Case C–415/93 *Bosman* [1995] ECR I–4921, para. 106; Case C–176/96 *Lehtonen v. FRSB* [2000] ECR I–2681, para. 54.
[168] Case C–244/04 *Commission v. Germany* [2006] ECR I–000, para. 61.
[169] Case C–60/03 *Wolff & Müller v. Pereira Félix* [2004] ECR I–9553, para. 41.
[170] Case C–244/04 *Commission v. Germany* [2006] ECR I–000, para. 38.
[171] Case C–445/03 *Commission v. Luxembourg* [2004] ECR I–10191, para. 38.
[172] E.g. Case C–18/95 *Terhoeve* [1999] ECR I–345, para. 45 where the Court held that considerations of a purely administrative nature could not make lawful a restriction on the free movement of persons.
[173] Case 398/95 *SETTG v. Ypourgos Ergasias* [1997] ECR I–3091.   [174] Para. 23.
[175] Case C–157/99 *Geraets-Smits and Peerbooms* [2001] ECR I–5473, paras. 78–9.
[176] Hatzopoulos (2000) 37 *CMLRev.* 43, 79.
[177] Joined Cases C–49, 50, 52, 54, 68 and 71/98 *Finalarte Sociedade de Construção Civil Lda* [2001] ECR I–7831.
[178] Case C–164/99 *Portugaia Construções Lda* [2002] ECR I–787.
[179] The detail of this law is considered in n. 227 below.

European internal market, and thus from foreign providers of services, and reducing unemployment to avoid social tensions'.[180] In particular the law was aimed at combating the 'allegedly unfair practice of European businesses engaged in low-pay competition'[181] i.e. 'social dumping'.[182] The expressed aims of the legislation therefore seemed to be wholly economic. However, the Court said that while the political debates might indicate the intention of the legislature, it was not conclusive.[183] It was for the national court to check whether, viewed objectively, the rules in fact conferred a genuine benefit on the workers which significantly added to their social protection.[184]

1.2. Proportionality

Once the Member State has identified a public interest requirement which the Court has accepted, a court (theoretically the national court but often the Court of Justice) will determine whether the steps taken by the Member State to realize that objective were proportionate. The Court offers various formulations of this test[185] but, essentially proportionality raises two questions: first, whether the measures are suitable for securing the attainment of the objective and, secondly, whether they go beyond what is necessary in order to attain it.[186] As Straetmans observes,[187] the first question requires only a marginal control of the aptitude or suitability of the national legislation to obtain the aim pursued. By contrast, the second question requires courts to determine whether the interest pursued cannot be satisfied by other, less restrictive means.

1.3. Fundamental Human Rights

A Member State can invoke reasons of public interest to justify a national measure only if that measure is compatible with fundamental rights.[188] This

---

[180] Case C–164/99 *Portugaia Construções Lda* [2002] ECR I–787.
[181] *Finalarte*, para. 38.
[182] See AG Mischo's Opinion in Case C–164/99 *Portugaia Construções Lda* [2002] ECR I–787, para. 15.
[183] Para. 40.   [184] Para. 42.
[185] See e.g. Case C–288/89 *Gouda* [1991] ECR I–4007, para. 15: 'the application of national provisions to providers of services established in other Member States must be such as to *guarantee* the achievement of the intended aim and must not go beyond that which is necessary in order to achieve that objective. In other words, it must not be possible to obtain the same result by less restrictive rules' (emphasis added); Case C–157/99 *B.S.M Geraets-Smits v. Stichting Ziekenfonds VGZ and H.T.M. Peerbooms v. Stichting CZ Groep Zorgverzekeringen* [2001] ECR I–5473, para. 75: 'to make sure that the measures do not exceed what is objectively necessary for that purpose and that the same result cannot be achieved by less restrictive rules'.
[186] See e.g. Case C–67/98 *Questore do Verona v. Diego Zenatti* [1999] ECR I7289, para. 29.
[187] G. Straetmans (2000) 37 *CMLRev.* 991, 1002.
[188] Case C–260/89 *ERT* [1991] ECR I–2925, para. 43, and Case C–368/95 *Vereinigte Familiapress Zeitungsverlags- und vertriebs GmbH v. Heinrich Bauer Verlag* [1997] ECR I–3689, para. 24; Case C–413/99 *Baumbast and R v. Secretary of State for the Home Department* [2002] ECR I–7091, para. 72.

can be seen in *Carpenter*[189] where the UK proposed to deport Mrs Carpenter, a Filipino national, who, having overstayed her entry permit to the UK, married a British national. Faced with the threat of deportation, Mrs Carpenter argued that this would restrict her husband's ability to carry on business as a service provider in other Member States since she looked after his children while he was away.[190] The Court said that a Member State could 'invoke reasons of public interest to justify a national measure which is likely to obstruct the exercise of the freedom to provide services only if that measure is compatible with the fundamental rights whose observance the Court ensures'.[191] On the question of fundamental rights, the Court said that the decision to deport Mrs Carpenter constituted:

an interference with the exercise by Mr Carpenter of his right to respect for his family life within the meaning of Article 8 of the [ECHR] . . . which is among the fundamental rights which, according to the Court's settled case-law, restated by the Preamble to the Single European Act and by Article 6(2) EU, are protected in Community law.[192]

Drawing on the case law of the European Court of Human Rights, the Court then said that even though no right of an alien to enter or to reside in a particular country was guaranteed by the Convention, 'the removal of a person from a country where close members of his family are living may amount to an infringement of the right to respect for family life as guaranteed by Article 8(1) of the Convention'. It continued that such an interference would infringe the Convention if it did not meet the requirements of Article 8(2), namely that the deportation had to be in accordance with the law, motivated by one or more of the legitimate aims under Article 8(2) and 'necessary in a democratic society' (justified by a pressing social need and proportionate).[193] The Court concluded that a decision to deport Mrs Carpenter did not 'strike a fair balance' between the competing interests of the right of Mr Carpenter to respect for his family life on the one hand and the maintenance of public order and public safety, on the other.[194] Even though Mrs Carpenter had infringed UK immigration laws by overstaying she did not constitute a danger to public order and safety. Therefore, the decision to deport her was not proportionate.

---

[189] Case C–60/00 *Mary Carpenter v. Secretary of State for the Home Department* [2002] ECR I–6279, paras. 40–1.

[190] Para. 17.

[191] Para. 40, citing Case C–260/89 *ERT* [1991] ECR I–2925, para. 43, and Case C–368/95 *Familiapress* [1997] ECR I–3689, para. 24.

[192] Para. 41. See also Case C–63/99 *R v. Secretary of State for the Home Department, ex parte Gloszczuk* [2001] ECR I–6369, para. 85; Case C–235/99 *R v. Secretary of State for the Home Department, ex parte Kondova* [2001] ECR I–6427, para. 90; Case C–413/99 *Baumbast* [2002] ECR I–7091, para. 72; Case C–109/01 *Secretary of State for the Home Department v. Akrich* [2003] ECR I–9607, paras. 58–9.

[193] Para. 42, citing *Boultif v. Switzerland*, No. 54273/00, paras. 39, 41 and 46, ECHR 2001-IX.

[194] Para. 43.

2. The *Viking* Case

Viking[195] provides an interesting case study of how the different principles outlined above interrelate in the context of a major social policy issue: the reflagging of a ship to cut labour costs.

Viking Line, a Finnish company and one of the largest passenger ferry operators in the world, wanted to reflag its vessel, the *Rosella* which traded the loss-making route between Helsinki and Tallinn in Estonia, under the Estonian flag so that it could man the ship with an Estonian crew to be paid considerably less than the existing Finnish crew.[196] The International Transport Workers' Federation (ITF), which had been running a Flag of Convenience (FOC) campaign trying to stop ship owners from taking such action, told its affiliates in the jurisdictions which the *Rosella* visited, to boycott the *Rosella* and to take other solidarity industrial action against both the *Rosella* and other Viking vessels. The Finnish Seaman's Union (FSU) threatened strike action. Viking therefore sought an injunction in the English High Court (ITF had its base in London and so jurisdiction was established pursuant to the Brussels Regulation 44/2001[197]), restraining the ITF and the FSU from breaching, *inter alia*, Articles 43 and 49 EC.

In the High Court, Gloster J ruled that reflagging of a vessel in a Member State involved the exercise of establishment;[198] and that the ITF/FSU's proposed actions amounted to a restriction on the freedom of establishment under Article 43.[199] Applying *Gebhard*[200] and *Guiot*,[201] the judge ruled that 'Any measure which places an additional financial burden on a person so as to make the exercise of a free movement right more difficult constitutes a restriction on that free movement right'. She also thought that Article 43 applied to organizations like ITF/FSU which intended to create 'obstacles resulting from the exercise of their legal autonomy by associations or organisation not governed by public law'.[202] Indeed, she went so far as to say that the ruling in *Angonese*,[203] that Article 39 had full horizontal direct effect, was not confined to workers' cases and applied equally to Article 43.[204]

The judge then ruled that the FOC policy was directly discriminatory: it prevented the owner of a Finish vessel from reflagging so as to employ a crew of another Member State, and compelled the owner to retain its Finnish crew. Even if the policy was not directly discriminatory, it was, she said, indirectly

---

[195] *Viking Line ABP v. The International transport Workers' Federation, the Finnish Seaman's Union* [2005] EWHC 1222 (QBD) and [2005] EWCA Civ 1299 (Court of Appeal).

[196] For a full description of the facts, see Waller LJ in the Court of Appeal [2005] EWCA Civ 1299.

[197] OJ [2001] L12/1.   [198] Para. 106.   [199] Para. 99.

[200] Case C–55/94 [1995] ECR I–4165.

[201] Case C–272/94 *Criminal proceedings against Guiot* [1996] ECR I–1905.

[202] Case C–415/93 *Bosman* [1995] ECR I–4921, paras. 82–4.

[203] Case C–281/98 [2000] ECR I–4139, considered in Ch. 4.   [204] Para. 115.

discriminatory. She then considered whether the directly discriminatory conduct could be saved by reference to one of the express derogations, namely public policy which included fundamental rights. She said:[205]

It is clear that the exercise of fundamental rights may fall within the scope of the public policy justification; ... The right to take industrial action can, for present purposes, be characterised as part of the fundamental right of freedom of expression and of freedom of association and to take collective action.

However, since, as we have seen in *Carpenter*, the express derogations must also be appraised by reference to fundamental rights, Gloster J went on to find that the exercise of these fundamental rights could not, without more, authorize or justify discrimination on the grounds of nationality—or sex.[206] Thus, she said it was not compatible with Article 14 ECHR (prohibition against discrimination)[207] that workers have a fundamental right to strike to prevent women from being employed on ferry boats. In the same way, the exercise or enjoyment of the right to take industrial action to prevent the reflagging of a vessel could also be characterized as breach of a fundamental right (i.e. non-discrimination on grounds of nationality).[208] She therefore concluded that fundamental rights could not be invoked to justify discrimination on the grounds of nationality.

Gloster J then considered whether the FOC rule, if considered to be *indirectly* discriminatory, could be objectively justified. While acknowledging that the protection of workers was an acceptable public interest justification,[209] she required more of the social purpose of the justification. The first purpose offered, safeguarding the job opportunities of the FSU's members, was rejected by the judge on the grounds that Viking had given an undertaking that if it reflagged the Rosella none of its crew would be made redundant; they would be transferred elsewhere in the group.[210]

She also rejected the second purpose put forward by the unions, safeguarding the level of terms and condition of employment and the living standards of all seafarers working on vessels trading in the Baltic and Nordic area, regardless of their nationality, on the grounds first, that the primary purpose of the proposed action was to protect *Finnish* jobs; second that it would be

---

[205] Para. 123.
[206] Para. 124. See also AG Jacobs' Opinion in Case C–67/96 *Albany International BV* v. *Stichting Bedrijfspensioenfonds Textielindustrie* [1999] ECR I–5751 where he said that while management and labour are in principle free to enter into such agreements as they see fit, they must, like any other economic actor, respect the limitations imposed by Community law, such as sex equality and free movement of workers. He continues that this could be seen as an application of the general rule that the exercise of a fundamental right may be restricted provided that the restriction in fact corresponds to objectives of general interest pursued by the Community and does not constitute in relation to the aim pursued a disproportionate and intolerable interference, impairing the very substance of the rights guaranteed.
[207] This is considered further in Ch. 6.   [208] Para. 126.   [209] See n. 160, above.
[210] Paras. 133–4.

disproportionate to insist that Finnish terms and conditions be applied to all workers on board the *Rosella* even though the vessel was reflagged in Estonia; and lastly, if the vessel was reflagged in Estonia, the crew would be protected by an ITF-affiliated Estonian trade union and Estonian collective bargaining. If due regard was given to the principle of mutual recognition, the judge said that it did not seem proportionate that the FSU and ITF should be entitled to insist that the interests of workers on board the *Rosella* be protected by the FSU, as opposed to an ITF-affiliated trade union established in another Member State.[211] Thus the judge concluded that the unions' anticipated actions would not be objectively justified or were not appropriate or proportionate to secure the unions' purposes. As a result, she ordered interim relief in favour of Viking to restrain the unions from taking industrial action to deter Viking from (1) reflagging the *Rosella* and (2) if it did reflag, requiring Viking to continue paying its crew at Finnish rates negotiated with the FSU.

Gloster J's decision on interim relief was reversed by the Court of Appeal[212] which referred the case to the Court of Justice to rule on the issues considered by the judge at first instance. Before making the reference, Waller LJ, giving judgment on behalf of the court, expressed grave concerns about the view that Articles 43 and 49 applied to trade union acts.[213] While recognizing that there should not be a blanket exclusion of trade union activities from the free movement provisions, he thought the control mechanism should be the Social Policy Title of the Treaty i.e. 'if an activity plainly does not pursue a social object within Title XI, the free movement Articles will apply, whereas if it does they should not'.[214] He also suggested that if there was direct discrimination, the unions would be unlikely to justify any restriction but he thought it more likely that some indirect discrimination or other restriction would be found which, he recognized, might be justified by reference to fundamental rights. For these reasons, the Court of Appeal set aside Gloster J's decision and refused interim measures because, as Waller LJ said, granting the injunction to Viking would be close to giving Viking the remedy which should only be available to it after a full trial of the action.[215]

The unions see *Viking* as a case about unfair competition where ship owners used the rules on freedom of establishment to cut costs and lower labour standards. Mr Zitting, chairman of the FSU, is quoted by Gloster J as saying that 'this is a fight against social dumping'[216] and that social dumping is 'the idea that you replace an employee with a cheaper one coming from somewhere else'.[217] This debate about social dumping is also pertinent

---

[211] Para. 138.
[212] [2005] EWCA Civ 1299; [2006] IRLR 58. The reference is Case C–483/05. See Davies (2006) 35 *ILJ.* 75 and Novitz, 'The Right to Strike and Reflagging in the European Union: Free Movement and Human Rights' (2006) *LMCLQ* forthcoming.
[213] Para. 62.   [214] Para. 44.   [215] Para. 64.   [216] Para. 119.
[217] Para. 137.

in respect of free movement of services and it is to this issue that we now turn.

D. POSTED WORKERS

1. Introduction

As a result of the Treaty rules on the provision of services and the EC Directives on public procurement, transnational subcontracting has burgeoned. Consequently, companies established in one state, having been awarded a contract in another Member State (the host state), have relocated their employees to the host Member State to fulfil the contract. For the successful tendering company and, ultimately, for the home state from which they come, the company's success in winning the contract means more revenue and more employment. For the host state, securing the services of a cheaper out-of-state service provider means better value for money for the public purse. However, to the host state's labour unions such 'contracting-out' has raised the spectre of 'social dumping'[218]—that service providers take advantage of cheaper labour standards in their own states to win a contract in the host state,[219] to the detriment of employment in the host state. The potential problems facing the host state in this situation were highlighted by the case of *Rush Portuguesa*.[220]

2. The Case Law

2.1. *Rush Portuguesa*

Rush Portuguesa, a Portuguese company, entered into a subcontract with a French company to carry out rail construction work in France. It used its own third country national workforce,[221] contravening French rules which provided that only the French Office d'Immigration could recruit non-Community workers. The Court ruled that Articles 49 and 50:[222]

---

[218] See further Ch. 1.

[219] This point was also noted by the Commission which talked of the risk that 'in addition to disadvantages for workers this will give rise to distortions of competition between undertakings' (Social Charter Action Programme, s. 4).

[220] Case C–113/89 *Rush Portuguesa v. Office national d'immigration* [1990] ECR I–1417.

[221] The workforce was actually Portuguese but at the time the transitional arrangements for Portuguese accession to the EC were in place which meant that the rules on freedom to provide services were in force but not those relating to the free movement of workers. Therefore, Portuguese workers did not enjoy the rights of free movement and so for our purposes the Portuguese workers constitute third country nationals (see para. 4 of the judgment).

[222] Para. 12, emphasis added.

preclude a Member State from prohibiting a person providing services established in another Member State from moving freely on its territory *with all his staff* and preclude that Member State from making the movement of staff in question subject to restrictions such as a condition as to engagement *in situ* or an obligation to obtain a work permit.

The Court said the imposition of such conditions discriminated against guest service providers in relation to their competitors established in the host country who were able to use their own staff without restrictions. In *Vander Elst* [223] the Court went one stage further: it confirmed that Articles 49 and 50 precluded the host state (France) from obliging guest service providers which lawfully and habitually employed nationals of non-Member States (in this case Moroccan workers legally resident in Belgium, holding Belgian work permits, covered by the Belgian social security scheme and paid in Belgium) to obtain and pay for *work permits* for those workers, with the imposition of an administrative fine as the penalty for infringement, on condition that the workers did not seek access to the labour market in the host state and returned to their country of origin or residence after completion of their work. [224]

Thus, in these cases the Court appeared to be taking an important step to opening up the market in services and allowing companies from countries with cheaper labour costs, primarily the southern and eastern European states, to profit from their comparative advantage to win contracts in other states (primarily the northern states with higher labour costs) and to take their own workforce with them to do the job. The reason why they can afford to win contracts is that the conditions of employment of temporary staff are usually governed by the labour law rules applicable in the country where the company is established and where the individual habitually carries out his work (see the principles of the Rome Convention considered below). The only limitation by the case law is that the service provider's workforce (i.e. the posted workers) must return to the country of origin after completing the task: they cannot join the labour market of the host state. [225]

Germany was particularly concerned about the threat posed by the Treaty provision on services to its labour law system and it was especially anxious to preserve the local system of wage setting and collectively negotiated, levy-based 'social funds' in the German construction industry [226] from the threats

---

[223] Case C–43/93 *Vander Elst* v. *Office des Migrations Internationales* [1994] ECR I–3803.

[224] However, the Court did accept that the host state was entitled to insist on TCNs having a short-stay visa permitting them to remain in France for as long as necessary to carry out the work (para.19), a so-called '*Vander Elst* visa' which was subsequently adopted by Germany. The Court suggested that the prior checks connected with the visa procedure were unlawful in Case C–244/04 *Commission* v. *Germany* [2006] ECR I–000, para.18.

[225] Case C–445/03 *Commission* v. *Luxembourg* [2004] ECR I–10191, para. 38.

[226] See Streeck, 'Neo-voluntarism: A New Social Policy Regime' (1995) 1 *ELJ*. 31, 42, and Simitis, 'Dismantling or Strengthening Labour Law: the Case of the European Court of Justice' (1996) 2 *ELJ*. 156, 163.

posed by cheap migrant labour.[227] In recognition of these concerns, the Court ruled in *Rush Portuguesa* that:[228]

Community law does not preclude Member States from extending their legislation, or collective labour agreements entered into by both sides of industry, to any person who is employed, even temporarily, within their territory, no matter in which country the employer is established; nor does Community law prohibit Member States from enforcing those rules by appropriate means.[229]

Thus, in one (unreasoned) paragraph the Court put a stop to a threat of social dumping[230] by allowing the host state to extend its labour laws and conditions to the staff employed by service providers working in its country and, in so doing, gave the green light to the enactment of the Directive 96/71 on Posted Workers.[231] The Directive, which is considered in detail below, is intended to promote the transnational provision of services, which requires a 'climate of fair competition and measures guaranteeing respect for the rights of workers'.[232] In essence, the Directive allows host states to apply to posted workers certain key labour law rules, in particular relating to minimum wages, working time and equal treatment, even in the case of short-term postings. However, since the Directive has the effect of requiring the out-of-state service provider to adapt its terms and conditions of employment each time it posts

---

[227] In Germany the *Arbeitnehmer-Entsendungsgestez* (AEntG) was approved by Parliament on 26 February 1996 (see May 1996 *EIRR* 268, 15). The legislation stipulates that all employers based outside the country and sending one or more employees to work in Germany must abide by provisions laid out in the relevant collective agreement, relating to minimum pay and certain conditions of employment, such as minimum holiday pay. These employers must also make payments into the relevant social security funds unless they are already paying into social security funds in their own country or have already done so. Employers with headquarters outside Germany but which are sending employees to work in the country must register in writing with the relevant local authorities in Germany before work commences. Employers must supply the name of the employee concerned, the commencement and expected duration of the employment and the location of the site where the work is to be carried out. These provisions are valid from the first day of employment in Germany. Employers who contravene this legislation are liable to fines of up to €50,000 (£43,800). The Ministry of Labour and customs offices are to be responsible for ensuring that employers comply with this law. As EIRR points out, this legislation puts Germany on a par with other EU countries, most notably France, which has national legislation on minimum pay and conditions for posted workers. In answer to written question E–2507/97, the Commission said that the German law was in accordance with Community law, provided that the inspections carried out to ensure the compliance with the minimum wage were not discriminatory or disproportionate.

[228] Para. 18.

[229] Citing Joined Cases 62/81 and 63/81 *Seco SA and Another* [1982] ECR 223.

[230] This was the overriding public interest subsequently offered by the Court to explain *Rush Portuguesa* in Case C–244/04 *Commission v. Germany* [2006] ECR I–000, para. 61.

[231] Dir. 96/71/EC (OJ [1996] L18/1). See P. Davies, 'Posted Workers: Single Market or Protection of National Labour Law Systems' (1997) 34 *CMLRev.* 571.

[232] Preambular, para. 5 cited by the Court in Case C–60/03 *Wolff & Müller v. Pereira Félix* [2004] ECR I–9553, para. 42.

workers to another Member State, some argue that it interferes with, rather than promotes, the provision of services.[233]

2.2. The Subsequent Case law

The existence of the Posted Workers Directive may have helped to shape some of the subsequent decisions of the Court, albeit that most of the cases discussed below were decided before the deadline for the implementation of the Directive had expired. In these cases the Court has retreated somewhat from its bold but unreasoned approach in *Rush Portuguesa*, and brought subsequent cases into line with its *Gebhard/*[234] *Säger*[235] jurisprudence. Therefore, in its more recent decisions, the Court has looked to see (1) whether the requirements imposed by the host state on the service provider restrict the freedom to provide services (the answer is usually yes). It then examines (2) whether the measure can be justified on the grounds of, for example, worker protection,[236] especially the interests of the posted workers,[237] (again the answer is usually yes); (3) whether the same interest is already protected in the state of establishment (this is usually left to the national court to decide); and finally (4) whether the steps taken are proportionate.[238] While the proportionality question should be considered by the national court, sometimes the Court of Justice provides the answer itself.

This four-stage approach can be seen in *Mazzoleni*.[239] ISA, a French company, provided security guards who worked on a part-time basis for brief periods at a shopping mall in Belgium. In the course of an inspection by the Belgian labour inspectorate, it was found that the monthly wage of ISA workers was less than the minimum wage in Belgium, albeit that their remuneration package as a whole, including tax and social security contributions) was similar to, if not more favourable than, remuneration under Belgian law. The Court said that (1) while Belgian law in principle breached Article 49, because by subjecting service providers to all conditions required for establishment, it deprived the provisions on services of practical effectiveness, (2) the requirement to pay the host state's minimum wage could be justified on the grounds of worker protection.

[233] See e.g. P. Davies, 'The Posted Workers Directive and the EC Treaty' (2002) 31 *ILJ*. 298, 300.
[234] Case C–55/94 [1995] ECR I–4165.
[235] Case C–76/90 [1991] ECR I–4221, considered in Ch. 4.
[236] Joined Cases C–49, 50, 52, 54, 68 and 71/98 *Finalarte Sociedade de Construção Civil Lda* [2001] ECR I–7831, paras. 41–9, for a careful scrutiny of the worker protection justification and that the national measures did actually confer a genuine benefit on the posted worker. See also Case C–164/99 *Portugaia Construções Lda* [2002] ECR I–787, paras. 28–9.
[237] Joined Cases C–49, 50, 52, 54, 68 and 71/98 *Finalarte* [2001] ECR I–7831, para. 41.
[238] See e.g. Joined Cases C–369 and 376/96 *Criminal Proceedings against Jean-Claude Arblade and Arblade & Fils SARL and against Bernard Leloup and others* [1999] ECR I–8453.
[239] Case C–165/98 *Criminal proceedings against André Mazzoleni and Inter Surveillance Assistance SARL* [2001] ECR I–2189.

However, the Court suggested the application of the Belgian rules might be disproportionate.[240] It said that (3) the Belgian objective of worker protection would be attained if all the workers concerned enjoyed an equivalent position overall in relation to remuneration, taxation, and social security contributions in the host Member State and in the Member State of establishment.[241] It continued that (4) the application of Belgian law on minimum wages to service providers established in a frontier region of a Member State could result, first, in an additional, disproportionate administrative burden including, in certain cases, the calculation, hour-by-hour, of the appropriate remuneration for each employee according to whether he has, in the course of his work, crossed the frontier of another Member State and, second, in the payment of different levels of wages to employees who were all attached to the same operational base and carried out identical work. That last consequence might, in its turn, result in tension between employees and even threaten the cohesion of the collective labour agreements that are applicable in the Member State of establishment.[242]

Thus, *Mazzoleni* suggests that the host state is justified in requiring that, in appropriate circumstances, the service provider pay its workforce minimum wages laid down by the host state's law or, as in *Arblade*,[243] collective agreement, provided that the provisions of the collective agreement are sufficiently precise and accessible and they do not render it impossible or excessively difficult in practice for the employer to determine his obligations. In *Wolff*[244] the Court added the host state is also justified in extending to service providers measures intended to 'reinforce the procedural arrangements enabling a posted worker usefully to assert his right to a minimum rate of pay'. In a similar vein, the Court said in *Finalarte*[245] that the host state can require the service provider to give the posted workers 30 days worked, or 36 working days, of paid leave per year, even though this amount exceeds the four weeks' paid leave laid down by the Working Time Directive 2003/88.[246]

In addition, the Court has said in *Commission v. Germany*[247] that it is compatible with the Treaty provisions on services for the host state to insist that the service provider furnishes a 'simple prior declaration certifying that the situation of the workers concerned is lawful', particularly in the light of the

[240] Para. 34.   [241] Para. 35.   [242] Para. 36.
[243] Joined Cases C–369/96 and C–376/96 [1999] ECR I–8453.
[244] Case C–60/03 *Wolff & Müller v. Pereira Félix* [2004] ECR I–9553, paras. 36 and 41.
[245] Joined Cases C–49/98, C–50/98, C–52/98 to C–54/98 and C–68/98 to C–71/98 *Finalarte Sociedade de Construção Civil Lda* (C–49/98), *Portugaia Construções Lda* (C–70/98) and *Engil Sociedade de Construção Civil SA* (C–71/98) v. *Urlaubs- und Lohnausgleichskasse der Bauwirtschaft and Urlaubs- und Lohnausgleichskasse der Bauwirtschaft v. Amilcar Oliveira Rocha* (C–50/98), *Tudor Stone Ltd* (C–52/98), *Tecnamb-Tecnologia do Ambiente Lda* (C–53/98), *Turiprata Construções Civil Lda* (C–54/98), *Duarte dos Santos Sousa* (C–68/98) *and Santos & Kewitz Construções Lda* (C–69/98) [2001] ECR I–7831, para. 58.
[246] Considered further in Ch.12.
[247] Case C–244/04 *Commission v. Germany* [2006] ECR I–000.

requirements of residence, work visas and social security cover in the Member States where the provider employs them. In *Commission v. Luxembourg*[248] the Court also said that the host state could require the service provider to report beforehand to the local authorities on the presence of one or more posted workers, the anticipated duration of their presence and the provision or provisions of services justifying the deployment.[249] In *Arblade*[250] the Court said that the host Member State could insist that the service provider keep social and labour documents available on site or in an accessible and clearly-identified place in the host state, where such a measure was necessary to enable it effectively to monitor compliance with the host state's legislation. In *Finalarte*[251] the Court added that businesses established outside the Member State could be required to provide more information than businesses established in the host state to the extent that this difference in treatment could be attributed to objective differences between those businesses and businesses established in the host state.

On the other hand, the Court has said that host state laws requiring the posted worker to have been employed by the service provider for at least 6 months in the case of Luxembourg[252] (a year in the case of Germany)[253] were not lawful. A requirement for the posted workers to have individual work permits which were only granted where the labour market situation so allowed was also not compatible with the EC law.[254] The Court has also said that a requirement for the service provider to provide, for the purposes of obtaining a work permit, a bank guarantee to cover costs in the event of repatriation of the worker at the end of his deployment was not permitted,[255] nor was a requirement that the work be licensed.[256]

3. The Posted Workers Directive 96/71/EC

3.1. Personal and Material Scope of the Directive

(a) Directive 96/71/EC

Directive 96/71 on the posting of workers in the framework of the provision of services,[257] based on Articles 47(2) and 55, is intended to promote the

---

[248] Case C–445/03 [2004] ECR I–10191.   [249] Para. 31.
[250] Joined Cases C–369/96 and C–376/96 [1999] ECR I–8453.
[251] Joined Cases C–49/98, C–50/98, C–52/98 to C–54/98 and C–68/98 to C–71/98 [2001] ECR I–7831.
[252] Case C–445/03 *Commission v. Luxembourg* [2004] ECR I–10191, paras. 32–3.
[253] Case C–244/04 *Commission v. Germany* [2006] ECR I–000.
[254] Case C–445/03 *Commission v. Luxembourg* [2004] ECR I–10191, paras. 42–3. See also the earlier case of Case C–43/93 *Vander Elst* [1994] ECR I–3803 considered above.
[255] Ibid., para. 47.   [256] Ibid., para. 30.
[257] OJ [1996] L18/1. See also COM(93) 225 final—SYN 346.

transnational provision of services in a 'climate of fair competition' while 'guaranteeing respect for the rights of workers'.[258] As Vladimir Špidla, EU Employment, Social Affairs and Equal Opportunities Commissioner bluntly put it, 'This Directive is a key instrument both to ensure freedom to provide services and to prevent social dumping'.[259] It aims to co-ordinate the legislation in the Member States and to lay down and give detail of the hard core of mandatory EC rules which *must* be respected by undertakings assigning their employees to work in another Member State. In this way, the Directive goes further than *Rush Portuguesa* which merely permitted (as opposed to requiring) Member States to extend certain rules to employees posted to their territory and did not specify which rules could be extended.

The Directive applies to undertakings established in a Member State[260] which, in the framework of the transnational provision of services, post workers to the territory of another Member State (the host state).[261] The posting of workers can take one of three forms:[262]

- posting under a contract concluded between the undertaking making the posting and the party for whom the services are intended (this was the situation in *Rush Portuguesa*);
- posting to an establishment or an undertaking owned by the group (this category, referred to as intra-firm or intra-group mobility,[263] has been included to prevent an undertaking from opening a subsidiary in another Member State purely to place some of its workers there to carry out temporary assignments, and thereby to avoid the scope of the Directive);
- posting by a temporary employment or placement agency (temp agency) to a user undertaking established or operating in the territory of another Member State, provided there is an employment relationship between the temp agency and the worker during the period of posting.[264]

In all three cases the key feature is the employment relationship existing between the posted worker and the service providing undertaking which is established in a Member State other than that where the service is provided.

A posted worker means a worker, as defined by the law of the host state, who for a limited period, carries out his work in the territory of a Member State other than the state in which he normally works.[265] According to

---

[258] Preambular, para. 5.   [259] IP/06/423.
[260] Art. 1(1). Art. 1(4) provides that undertakings established in non-Member States must not be given more favourable treatment than undertakings established in a Member State.
[261] Art. 1(1).   [262] Art. 1(3).   [263] Arts. 1 and 2.
[264] Art. 3(9) provides that Member States may provide that workers employed by temp agencies must guarantee to temps the terms and conditions which apply to temporary workers in the Member State where the work is carried out.
[265] Art. 2(1) and (2). For the position on social security see Art. 14 of Reg. 1408/71 (OJ [1971] L149/2) as amended, discussed in Ch. 4. See also Case C–202/97 *Fitzwilliam Executive Search Ltd* v. *Bestuur van het Landelijk Instituut Sociale Verzekeringen* [2000] ECR I–883.

Article 3, whatever the law applicable to the employment relationship, the undertakings identified above, *must* guarantee posted workers the host state's terms and conditions of employment in respect of:

- maximum work periods and minimum rest periods;
- minimum paid holidays;
- minimum rates of pay,[266] as defined by the host state's law and/or practice, including overtime. This does not apply to supplementary occupational retirement pension schemes;
- the conditions of hiring out of workers, in particular the supply of workers by temp agencies;
- health, safety, and hygiene at work;
- protective measures with regard to the terms and conditions of employment of pregnant women or women who have recently given birth, of children and young people;
- equality of treatment between men and women and other provisions on non-discrimination.

Social security is not covered: Regulation 1408/71, soon to be replaced by Regulation 883/2004, applies instead.[267]

These mandatory rules listed in Article 3 can be laid down by law, regulation or administrative provision.[268] In the case of building work, including all work relating to the construction, repair, upkeep, alteration, or demolition of buildings,[269] the terms and conditions can be laid down by law, regulation or administrative provision and/or by collective agreements or arbitration awards which have been declared 'universally applicable',[270] that is, they must be observed by all undertakings in the geographical area and in the profession or industry concerned. In countries such as the UK, Sweden, and Denmark, where no such system exists, Member States may, if they so decide, base themselves on collective agreements or arbitration awards which are generally applicable to all similar undertakings in the geographical area and in the profession or industry concerned, and/or collective agreements which have been concluded by the most representative employers' and labour organizations at national level,[271] and which are applied throughout the national

---

[266] Allowances specific to the posting shall be considered to be part of the minimum wage, unless they are paid in reimbursement of expenditure actually incurred on account of the posting, such as expenditure on travel, board and lodging (Art. 3(7), para. 2).

[267] This is considered in Ch. 4.   [268] Art. 3(1).

[269] Esp. excavation, earth-moving, actual building work, assembly and dismantling of pre-fabricated elements, fitting out or installation, alterations, renovation, repairs, dismantling, demolition, maintenance, upkeep, painting and cleaning work, improvements (Annex).

[270] Art. 3(1), explained in Art. 3(8).

[271] According to the Commission, this means that Member States can include agreements or awards which are complied with by the great majority of 'national-level undertakings'. The key factor is the extent to which the national-level undertakings are real potential competitors to the service provider.

territory, provided that their application ensures equality of treatment in the matters listed in the bullet point above between undertakings in a similar position.[272]

Given this is a minimum standards Directive, the provisions outlined above also permit the application of (other) terms and conditions of employment which are more favourable to workers.[273] Article 3(10) allows Member States, on a basis of equality of treatment, to apply to national undertakings and to undertakings of other Member States terms and conditions of employment on matters other than those referred to in the bullet points above in the case of public policy provisions,[274] and terms and conditions of employment laid down in collective agreements or arbitration awards concerning activities other than those relating to building.[275] The higher standards are subject to compliance with Article 49 as interpreted by the Court (considered above).

The importance of these provisions, especially those concerning collective agreements, is highlighted by another case referred to the Court of Justice, *Laval un Partneri*.[276] The reference itself goes to the heart of the Swedish model of industrial relations, based as it is on voluntary collective agreements without *erga omnes* procedures:[277] is it compatible with rules of the EC Treaty on the freedom to provide services and with the provisions of Directive 96/71/EC for trade unions to attempt, by means of industrial action in the form of a blockade, to force a foreign (Estonian) service provider to sign a collective agreement in respect of terms and conditions of employment, if the situation in the host country (Sweden) is such that the legislation intended to implement Directive 96/71 has no express provisions concerning the application of terms and conditions of employment in collective agreements?

The dispute once again goes to the heart of the 'social dumping' debate.[278] A

---

[272] Equality of treatment shall be deemed to exist where national undertakings in a similar position are subject, in the place in question or in the sector concerned, to the same obligations as posting undertakings as regards the matters listed in the bullet points above and are required to fulfill such obligations with the same effects.

[273] Art. 3(7).

[274] At the time of the adoption of the Directive, the Council and the Commission stated (Statement 10) that the expression 'public policy provisions' should be construed as covering those mandatory rules form which there can be no derogation and which, by their nature and objective, meet the imperative requirements of the public interest. These may include, in particular, the prohibition of forced labour or the involvement of public authorities in monitoring compliance with legislation on working conditions: COM(2003) 458, 13. The Commission refers to the Court's case law on public policy, considered above, nn. 13–44, to help define the meaning of the term.

[275] Art. 4(2) requires the Commission and the competent public authorities to cooperate in order to examine any difficulties which might arise in the application of Art. 3(1).

[276] Case C–341/05 *Laval un Partneri Ltd v. Svenska Byggnadsarbetareförbundet*. An application for the case to be heard by the accelerated procedure was refused: Order of 15 November 2005. See Eklund, 'The *Laval* Case' (2006) 35 *ILJ*. 202.

[277] See further Ch. 2.

[278] For a full description of the dispute, form which the following draws, see Woolfson and Sommers, 'Labour Mobility in Construction: European Implications of the Laval un Partneri Dispute with Swedish Labour' (2006) 12 *EJIR*. 49.

Latvian company, Laval, won a contract to refurbish and extend a school in the Stockholm suburb of Vaxholm. Laval was not a signatory to the Swedish Construction Federation collective agreements with Byggnads, the major Swedish construction trade union. Laval used its own Latvian workers to fulfil the contract. These workers earned about 40 per cent less per hour than comparable Swedish workers. Byggnads wanted Laval to apply the Swedish national agreement but, after some prevarication, Laval decided against doing so. This led to a union picket at the school site and a blockade by construction workers, and sympathy industrial action was taken by the electricians' unions who boycotted Swedish companies operating at the site. Laval brought proceedings in the Swedish labour court, claiming that the industrial action and blockade were illegal, as was the sympathy strike. In an interim ruling, the court said that actions like this, aimed at pushing through an add-on to the leading collective agreement within the industry, could not be seen as going against good labour market practices.[279] Subsequently, the 10 million strong International Federation of Building and Wood Workers launched a solidarity campaign and the trade unions intensified their boycott. However, the Internal Market Commissioner, Charlie McCreevy, spoke out against Scandinavian collective agreements and said they breached EC law on free movement.[280] His remarks caused consternation in some quarters, in particular in the European Parliament where Martin Schulz MEP demanded that Mr Barroso 'disown this unacceptable attack on a social model that is universally recognised as being one of the most successful in the world'.[281] But for Laval, McCreevy's interventions came too late: it announced its withdrawal from Sweden[282] and its Swedish subsidiary filed for bankruptcy.

(b) The Relationship between the Directive and the Rome Convention

The Rome Convention of 19 June 1980[283] on rules concerning the law applicable to contractual obligations, which came into force on 1 April 1991, lays down choice-of-law rules for application in contractual disputes.[284] The

---

[279] Woolfson and Sommers, above, n. 278, 56.

[280] Küchler, 'McCreevy locks horns with Swedish unions', *euobserver.com*, 10 October 2005.

[281] Mahoney, 'Barroso and McCreevy called to account in Swedish social model row', *euobserver.com*, 13 October 2005. His appearance is reported by Kubosova, 'Scandidnavian model must comply with EU rules, says McCreevy', *euobserver.com*, 26 October 2005.

[282] Ibid., 57.

[283] OJ [1980] L266/1. See also the Report by Giuliano and Lagarde (OJ [1980] C282/1).

[284] The ECJ now has jurisdiction to interpret the Rome Convention. In December 1988 two Protocols on Interpretation were signed in Brussels. 'The First Protocol on the interpretation by the Court of Justice of the European Communities of the Convention' defines the scope of the jurisdiction of the ECJ and the conditions under which that jurisdiction is to be exercised. In particular, references are optional, not compulsory. 'The Second Protocol conferring on the Court of Justice of the European Communities certain powers to interpret the Convention' gives the ECJ power to deal with references under the First Protocol. The first Protocol only came into force when the second Protocol came into force (which was 5 May 2004). No cases have yet been referred to the ECJ under these Protocols. Prior to these Protocols coming into force, the Court

basic rule, laid down in Article 3, is that a contract is governed by the law chosen by the parties. However, Article 6(2) provides that:

... a contract of employment shall, in the absence of choice in accordance with Article 3, be governed:

(a) by the law of the country in which the employee habitually carries out his work in performance of the contract, even if he is temporarily employed in another country; or
(b) if the employee does not habitually carry out his work in any one country, by the law of the country in which the place of business through which he was engaged is situated;

unless it appears from the circumstances as a whole that the contract is more closely connected with another country in which case the contract shall be governed by the law of that country.

According to Article 6(1) of the Convention, the choice of law made by the parties must not have the result of depriving the employee of the protection afforded to him by the mandatory rules of the law which would be applicable under Article 6(2) in the absence of choice. Article 7(1) provides that, under certain conditions, effect may be given concurrently with the law declared applicable, to the mandatory rules of the law of another country, in particular those of a Member State within whose territory the worker is temporarily posted. These mandatory rules are not defined by the Convention. Directive 96/71 designates at Community-level mandatory rules within the meaning of Article 7(1) of the Rome Convention in transnational posting situations. The Directive does not seek to amend the law applicable to the employment contract but it lays down certain mandatory rules to be complied with during the period of posting to another Member States, 'whatever the law applicable to the employment relationship'.[285]

3.2. Access to Information and Administrative Co-operation

An important strand of the legislation is the 'one-stop shop' or single point of contact approach for service providers to find out about the requirements laid down by national law and/or collective agreement. So, in order to implement this Directive, Member States must, in accordance with national legislation or practice, designate one or more liaison offices or one or more competent national bodies.[286] They must also make provision for co-operation between

has referred to the Rome Convention and indicated that it was desirable to interpret what is now Art. 19 of the Brussels Regulation in such a way as to confer jurisdiction on the courts of the country whose substantive law governed the contract of employment: Case 133/81 *Ivenel v. Schwab* [1982] ECR 1891.

[285] COM(2003) 458, 6.
[286] Art. 4(1). Member States must notify the other Member States and the Commission of the liaison offices and/or competent bodies.

the public authorities which, in accordance with national legislation, are responsible for monitoring the terms and conditions of employment. This co-operation must, in particular, consist of replying (free of charge) to reasoned requests about information on transnational supply of workers, including manifest abuses[287] or possible cases of unlawful transnational activities.[288] The Commission and the public authorities must co-operate, especially in respect of any difficulties which might arise in the application of Article 3(10).[289]

3.3. Remedies

Article 5(1) of Directive 96/71 requires the Member States to 'take appropriate measures in the event of failure to comply with this Directive'. They must ensure that 'adequate procedures are available to workers and/or their representatives for the enforcement of the obligations under this Directive.[290] According to *Wolff*,[291] the Member States have a wide margin of appreciation in determining the form and detailed rules governing these adequate procedures. Article 6 provides that in order to enforce the right to the terms and conditions guaranteed by Article 3, judicial proceedings may be instituted in the Member State in whose territory the worker is or was posted, without prejudice, where applicable, to the right, under existing international conventions on jurisdiction, to institute proceedings in another Member State.[292] This provision adds to the rules laid down in the Brussels I Regulation.[293] Under the Regulation, the general principle is that persons domiciled in a contracting state must, whatever their nationality, be sued in the courts of that state.[294] However, in respect of employment contracts, Articles 18–21 of the Regulation lay down special rules. They provide that if the employer is domiciled in a Member State, the employee may sue the employer either:

- in the Member State of the employer's domicile;[295] or
- in the courts of the place where the employee *habitually* carries out his

---

[287] It can also be inferred from Case 113/89 *Rush Portuguesa* [1990] ECR I–1417 that the provisions on the freedom to provide services must not be abused to achieve some other purpose (para. 17).

[288] Art. 4(2). On the importance of this cooperation, see Joined Cases C–369 and 376/96 *Criminal Proceedings against Jean-Claude Arblade and Arblade & Fils SARL and against Bernard Leloup and others* [1999] ECR I–8453.

[289] Art. 4(2).   [290] Art. 5(2).

[291] Case C–60/03 *Wolff & Müller* v. *Pereira Félix* [2004] ECR I–9553, para. 30.

[292] Art. 6.

[293] Council Reg. 44/2001 (OJ [2001] L12/1) which came into force on 1 March 2002. Initially, it applied to all EU Member States except Denmark to which the old regime, the Brussels Convention of 27 September 1968, applied. Denmark has now opted into the Reg: Dec. 2006/325/EC (OJ [2006] L120/22). The EFTA states are covered by the Lugano Convention.

[294] Art. 2(1).   [295] Art. 19(1).

work[296] (or the place where he last did so).[297] If the employee does not carry out his work in any one country then jurisdiction is conferred on the courts of the place where the business which engaged the employee is situated.[298]

Article 6 of Directive 96/71 therefore adds to the Brussels Regulation by allowing the posted worker to bring proceedings in the courts of the host state even though he is employed there only *temporarily*.[299]

3.4. Exceptions and Derogations to the Directive

The provisions of the Directive do not apply to merchant navy undertakings as regards seagoing personnel.[300] As was argued by Counsel in *Viking*,[301] the reason for this exclusion was to avoid the absurdity of vessels having to satisfy the labour conditions applicable in each port they visited. He used this to justify his argument that an Estonian crew should not be subject to Finnish terms and conditions of employment, as the unions had argued.

In addition to this total exclusion, Article 3 lists four potential derogations. First, Article 3(1) provides that the rules relating to minimum rates of pay and paid holidays do not apply to skilled or specialist workers employed by an undertaking involved in a contract for supplying goods, where the workers are engaged in the initial assembly or installation of goods which is an integral part of the contract and the period of posting does not exceed eight days.[302]

---

[296] See Case C–383/95 *Rutten v. Cross Medical Ltd* [1997] ECR I–57. See also Case C–125/92 *Geels* [1993] ECR I–4075 where the Court had to consider the application of the principles laid down by the Brussels Convention before its amendment. Geels, a Dutch national domiciled in France, sued his employer Mulox, a limited company established under English law in London, in the French, courts for terminating his contract of employment. Geels had set up his office in France but marketed Mulox products in Germany, Belgium, the Netherlands, and Scandinavia. The Court pointed out that employment contracts differed from other contracts by virtue of the 'lasting bond which brings the worker to some extent within the organisational framework of the business' and consequently the link between the place where the activities are pursued which determines the application of mandatory rules and collective agreements. The Court therefore recognized that, given the peculiarities of contracts of employment, it was the courts of the place where the work was carried out which were best suited to resolving disputes in which one or more obligations under the contract of employment gave rise. The Court also added that the provisions of the Convention should be interpreted so as to take account of the need to ensure adequate protection for the socially weaker contracting party, namely the employee. Such adequate protection was better assured if the cases relating to contracts of employment fell within the jurisdiction of the courts in the place where the employee discharged his obligations to the employer to carry out the work agreed. The Court said that it was in this place that the employee could, at less cost, apply to the tribunals or defend himself before them. Consequently, the place of performance of the relevant obligation was the place where the employee carried out the activities agreed with the employer.
[297] Art. 19(2)(a).　　[298] Art. 19(2)(b).
[299] This is a provision governing a specific matter as permitted by Art. 67 of Reg. 44/2001.
[300] Art. 1(2).　　[301] [2005] EWCA 1299, para. 58.
[302] Art. 3(6) provides that the length of the posting shall be calculated on the basis of a reference period of one year from the beginning of the posting. In calculating the one-year period,

Second, Article 3(3) provides that Member States may, after consulting employers and labour, in accordance with the traditions and practices of each Member State, decide not to apply the provision relating to pay in the case of all posted workers, with the exception of those employed by a temp agency, where the posting does not exceed one month. Third, Article 3(4) provides that Member States may, in accordance with national laws or practices, provide that exemptions may be made from the provisions relating to pay in the case of all posted workers with the exception of those employed by a temp agency, and from a decision of a Member State within the meaning of Article 3(3), by means of a collective agreement,[303] where the posting does not exceed one month.[304] Fourth, Article 3(5) provides that Member States may provide for exemptions to be granted from the provisions relating to pay and holidays in the case of all posted workers, with the exception of those employed by a temp agency, on the grounds that the amount of work to be done is not significant.[305]

It is not clear how much use will be made of these derogations since, following the social dumping thesis, it is usually not in the host state's interest to exempt service providers from the domestic rules. This is the position taken by the UK, which has not taken advantage of any derogations.

3.5. Assessment

The Posted Workers' Directive does not try to harmonize the rules of the Member States categorized as mandatory. It merely identifies those employment conditions which the guest undertaking must respect. Thus, the Directive is based on co-ordination rather than harmonization, although the disparity between the rules of the different Member States in these core areas will be reduced as the Community passes further legislation in the social field. Significantly, those working conditions which this Directive identifies as important largely correspond to the areas in which Community legislation has already been passed or proposed.

Will the Directive fulfil its objectives? If the Directive is intended to facilitate the provision of services, it could be argued that the imposition of additional burdens on service providers hinders, rather than facilitates, the provision of services, albeit that the Court approved this interference in *Rush Portuguesa*. If, on the other hand, the Directive is intended to harmonize costs and stop social dumping the setting of only minimum standards suggests this is unlikely. For example, it is sufficient that the guest provider of services pays only the

---

account shall be taken of any previous periods for which the post has been filled by a posted worker. This provision does not apply to the building activities described above, see Art. 3(2).

[303] As defined in Art. 3(8).   [304] Art. 3(4).

[305] Art. 3(5). Member States must lay down the criteria to determine whether the work is considered non-significant.

minimum wage rates. Most companies established in the host state will pay workers at rates above the minimum level. Therefore, the guest service provider still retains a competitive advantage, albeit one whose significance has been reduced. If, however, the objective is worker protection then the Directive may well have succeeded. In the UK, the government has decided to extend all rights required by the Directive to posted workers.

4. Other Related Measures: the Services Directive

4.1. Background

The European Commission initially proposed two further Directives on the cross border provision of services.[306] The first covered the right of businesses established in the EU to provide services in another Member State using non-Community staff who are lawfully established in the EU. The second proposal covers self-employed workers from non-Community countries who are lawfully established in the EU. The two proposals primarily provide for the introduction of an 'EC service provision card' which would be issued by the Member State where the Community business or self-employed person is established. This would ensure compliance with the rules governing the free movement of services (the principal place of work must continue to be the place where the business is established). These proposals were, however, withdrawn in 2004. In their place—and of far greater political significance—is the proposed Services Directive.[307]

4.2. The 'Bolkestein' Directive

A Directive on freedom to provide and receive services was a central tenet of the economic reforms envisaged by the Lisbon strategy. Launched by the European Council in March 2000,[308] it had the objective of opening up the market in services, which accounts for over two thirds of Europe's GDP. According to one study, the economic benefits from a free market in services would amount to 37 billion euros, real wages would rise by 0.4 per cent, while the price of services would drop by more than 7 per cent.[309]

The proposed services Directive aimed at providing a legal framework that would eliminate the obstacles to (1) the freedom of establishment for service providers, and (2) the free movement of services between the Member States.

---

[306] COM(99) 3 final – 2. See also Case C–445/03 *Commission v. Luxembourg* [2004] ECR I–10191, para. 25.

[307] COM(2004) 2 final/3.   [308] See further Ch. 3.

[309] 'The Services Directive and the European Constitution', *euobserver. com*, 21 March 2005.

In order to eliminate the first type of obstacles—those connected with the freedom of *establishment*—the initial Bolkestein proposal provided for:[310]

- administrative simplification measures, particularly involving the establishment of single points of contact, at which service providers can complete, by electronic means, the administrative procedures relevant to their activities;
- certain principles which authorization schemes applicable to service activities must respect, in particular relating to the conditions and procedures for the granting of an authorization;
- the prohibition of certain particularly restrictive legal requirements that may still be in force in certain Member States and the obligation to assess the compatibility of certain other legal requirements with the conditions laid down in the Directive, particularly as regards proportionality.

In order to eliminate the obstacles to the free movement of *services*, the proposal provided for:

- the application of the country of origin principle, according to which a service provider was subject only to the law of the country in which it was established and Member States could not restrict services from a provider established in another Member State. This principle was accompanied by derogations which were either general, or temporary or which could be applied on a case-by-case basis;
- the right of recipients to use services from other Member States without being hindered by restrictive measures imposed by their country or by discriminatory behaviour on the part of public authorities or private operators, together with a mechanism to provide assistance to recipients who use a service provided by an operator established in another Member State;
- in the case of posting of workers, the proposed Directive provided that Directive 96/71 applied and, so Article 17 of the original proposal contained a derogation from the country of origin principle where those rules were concerned. However, in order to facilitate the free movement of services and the application of Directive 96/71 the original draft clarified the allocation of tasks between the country of origin and the Member State of posting, and the administrative supervisory procedure.[311] Specific provision

---

[310] COM(2004) 2 final/3, 3–4.

[311] Art. 24. This provided: 'Where a provider posts a worker to another Member State in order to provide a service, the Member State of posting shall carry out in its territory the checks, inspections and investigations necessary to ensure compliance with the employment and working conditions applicable under Directive 96/71/EC and shall take, in accordance with Community law, measures in respect of a service provider who fails to comply with those conditions.

However, the Member State of posting may not make the provider or the posted worker subject to any of the following obligations, as regards the matters referred to in point (5) of Article 17:
(a) to obtain authorisation from, or to be registered with, its own competent authorities, or to satisfy any other equivalent requirement;

was also made for the posting of TCNs.[312] In particular, the proposed Directive wished to scrap certain administrative obligations concerning the posting of workers, accompanied by measures to reinforce administrative co-operation between states.

In some quarters, two aspects of the Bolkestein proposal caused particular consternation: the country of origin principle and the rules on posted workers. Opponents of the Directive feared that it would lead to social dumping thereby undermining the European social model.[313] There was particular concern in France about the proposed Directive, where the 'Polish plumber' had for many French people assumed 'bogeyman status as low cost, low standard, Eastern European Labour'.[314] Some attributed the French 'no' vote in the referendum on the Constitutional Treaty in 2005 to French hostility to

---

(b) to make a declaration, other than declarations relating to an activity referred to in the Annex to Directive 96/71/EC which may be maintained until 31 December 2008;
(c) to have a representative in its territory;
(d) to hold and keep employment documents in its territory or in accordance with the conditions applicable in its territory.

    2. In the circumstances referred to in paragraph 1, the Member State of origin shall ensure that the provider takes all measures necessary to be able to communicate the following information, both to its competent authorities and to those of the Member State of posting, within two years of the end of the posting:
(a) the identity of the posted worker;
(b) his position and the nature of the tasks attributed to him,
(c) the contact details of the recipient,
(d) the place of posting,
(e) the start and end dates for the posting,
(f) the employment and working conditions applied to the posted worker;
    In the circumstances referred to in paragraph 1, the Member State of origin shall assist the Member State of posting to ensure compliance with the employment and working conditions applicable under Directive 96/71/EC and shall, on its own initiative, communicate to the Member State of posting the information specified in the first subparagraph where the Member State of origin is aware of specific facts which indicate possible irregularities on the part of the provider in relation to employment and working conditions.'

    [312] Art. 25.
    [313] See the remarks made by Evelyne Gebhardt, Socialist MEP, with responsibility for steering the Services Directive through the EP. Writing in *Parliament Magazine* and reported in *EUPolitix. com*, 4 October 2004, 1, she said the Bolkestein proposal 'constitutes a threat to consumer protection, the European social model and public services'. The Prime Minister and then president of the European Council, Jean-Claude Juncker, said (http://www.eu2005.lu, 24 March 2005) that any new draft of the Directive's text will 'take into account the double imperative of the opening of the services market as well as respect for the European social model in accordance with the motto: Yes to the liberalisation of services, no to social dumping. Those who wish the services directive to be fashioned in such a way that employees lose all their rights, thereby bringing unhealthy pressure to bear on the level of salaries and diminishing employees' rights through the opening up of markets, are sadly mistaken'.
    [314] Waterfield, 'Polish workers protest against French bosses', *EUPolitix.com*, 4 October 2005, 1. France was not alone. The Swedish trade minister, Thomas Ostros, was reported as saying 'There cannot be a service directive, unless there is also a protection against social dumping': Küchler, 'McCreevy locks horns with Swedish unions', *euobserver.com*, 10 October 2005.

the proposed Services Directive,[315] or at least to their perception of the excessive economic liberalism which they saw the Services Directive as representing, and its implications for the French social model. This led to fierce lobbying
and protests outside the European Parliament building in Strasbourg.[316]

4.3. The McCreevy Package

Eventually, the European Parliament, at first reading, put forward a watered
down measure,[317] and the Commission then drafted a revised proposal.[318]
This 'McCreevy' draft was narrower in scope than its Bolkestein predecessor
and shorn of both the country of origin principle[319] (but not the derogations
which went with it) and the social provisions.[320] At the same time, the Commission issued a Communication on the Posted Workers' Directive[321] aimed at
strengthening the position of service providers wishing to use their own
workforce to fulfil contracts in other Member States. In his speech to the
European Parliament,[322] McCreevy said that the decision to remove all interaction between the Services Proposal and labour law was one of the most
important elements in creating a more positive atmosphere around this new
draft. He continued that 'This has allowed us to move on from allegations of
lowering of social standards and threats to the European social model', adding that 'While this perception was wrong it did not go away and poisoned the
debate'.

The Communication on Posted Workers[323] draws on the provisions of
Article 24 of the Bolkestein Directive and the case law of the Court. Essentially, it rules out three types of requirements often imposed by host states and
permits another two. Those requirements which are prohibited are:

- the obligation for a service provider to have a permanent representative on
  the territory of the host Member State: the appointment of a person from

---

[315] Editorial Comments, 'The Services Directive Proposal: Striking a balance between the promotion of the internal market and preserving the European social model' (2006) 43 *CMLRev.*
307, 308.
[316] At much the same time—in early January 2006—dockers protested violently outside the
European Parliament about EU proposed directive to liberalize port services: COM(2004) 654.
The European Parliament rejected the proposal at first reading and the Commission subsequently
withdrew the proposal (OJ [2006] C64/3).
[317] A6–0409/2005 FINAL.   [318] COM(2006) 160.
[319] Only a year before, Commission President Barroso is quoted as saying that 'The directive
just wouldn't work without' the country of origin principle: 'The Services Directive and the
European Constitution', *euobserver. com*, 21 March 2005.
[320] Arts. 24 and 25 of the original proposal were removed.
[321] 'Guidance on the posting of workers in the framework of the provision of services':
COM(2006) 159. This is accompanied by a report SEC(2006) 439. It also issued a Communication, *Social services of general interest in the European Union* COM(2006) 177. It is beyond the scope
of this work to consider this.
[322] SPEECH/06/220, 4 April 2006.   [323] COM(2006) 159.

among the posted workers, such as the site foreman, to act as a link between the foreign company and the labour inspectorate is sufficient;

- no prior authorization can be required as a general rule by the host country for the posting of workers,[324] but service companies may have to obtain a specific authorisation in certain sectors (e.g. temporary employment agents) when rendering services in another Member State provided this requirement is justified, proportionate, and account is taken of the controls already carried out in the home state;
- The host state cannot impose administrative formalities or additional conditions on posted workers from third countries when they are lawfully employed by a service provider established in another Member State, without prejudice to the right of the host state to check that these conditions are complied with in the state where the service provider is established.[325]

Those requirements which are permitted are:

- the possibility for host states to ask for a *declaration* (which is less restrictive than a prior authorization) from the service provider by the time the work starts which contains information on the workers who have been posted, the type of service they will provide, where and how long the work will take.[326] In respect of TCNs, the declaration can specify that they are in a 'lawful situation' in the home state (i.e. the state in which the service provider is established), including in respect of visa requirements, and that they are legally employed in the home states;[327]
- the host state can require service providers to keep social documents such as time-sheets or documents related to health and safety conditions at the place of work. However, the host state cannot require a second set of documents if the documents required under the legislation of the Member State of establishment, taken as a whole, already provide sufficient information to allow the host state to carry out the checks required.

In addition, the Communication makes clear that the national authorities of the countries of origin have to cooperate loyally with the authorities in the host Member States and to provide them all the required information, in order to enable these authorities to perform their controlling duties and fight illegal practices. Liaison offices and the monitoring authorities have to be sufficiently equipped and resourced in order to be able to reply correctly and swiftly to any kind of demand. Appropriate measures must be in place to sanction foreign

---

[324] Relying on Case C–43/93 *Vander Elst* [1994] ECR I–3803.

[325] See the discussion of Case C–244/04 *Commission v. Germany* [2006] ECR I–000 and Case C–445/03 *Commission v. Luxembourg* [2004] ECR I–10191 above, n. 247.

[326] See the discussion of Case C–244/04 *Commission v. Germany* [2006] ECR I–000 and Case C–445/03 *Commission v. Luxembourg* [2004] ECR I–10191 above, n. 247.

[327] See the discussion of Case C–43/93 *Vander Elst* [1994] ECR I–3803 above.

service providers when the correct terms and conditions of employment as set out in the Directive are not complied with.

E. CONCLUSIONS

While the rights of free movement of persons have been the cornerstone of the EC Treaty since its inception, in fact remarkably few people actually took advantage of these provisions;[328] and the derogations and justifications gave the Member States an important tool to exclude those they did not wish to see admitted and to apply their own rules if they were justified. However, the world now is a very different place and while workers still might not want to relocate permanently to another Member State, they are much more willing to go for short periods when posted by their employers. The renaissance of the Treaty provisions on services in the last 15 or so years has helped to open up the market in services. When terms and conditions of employment did not differ so substantially between the original 12 Member States, the free market did not pose a significant threat to the integrity of national social orders. But as the EU began to expand, first to the south (Portugal, Spain, and Greece) and, more importantly to the east, the tensions between the free market and the preservation of national social models began to resurface. The *Viking* and *Laval* cases have brought these tensions into sharp focus and, indirectly, they have influenced public perception of the proposed services Directive. The Court, inevitably, has become caught up in this debate. It will have to decide *Viking* and *Laval*, and other cases like them, but it has already started to pin its colours to the mast. With its (uncritical) recognition of 'social dumping' as a public interest requirement in *Commission* v. *Germany*, it has disregarded the bigger social picture of the benefits to the eastern European workers of having access to a much wider market for their services.

* * *

According to the Posted Workers' Directive, one of the areas in which the out-of-state service provider must respect the host state's terms and conditions of employment concerns 'equality of treatment between men and women and other provisions on non-discrimination'. This is one area of law where the Community has now developed a substantial body of acquis. It is to this subject that we now turn.

---

[328] According to the Veil report to the Commission on free movement of persons (which preceded the Accession of the 10 New states in June 2004), about 18 million, of the 370 million, people living in the EU, have moved from their country of origin. About one third come from other Member States.

PART III

Equality Law

6

Equality Law: An Introduction

A. INTRODUCTION

The quest for equality—and in particular sex equality—has been the central and most highly developed pillar of the European Union's social policy. It lies at the core of the European social model and it has served as a catalyst for change in the Member States.[1] The pursuit of *sex* equality has been in the Community's sight since the signing of the Treaty of Rome in 1957. The pursuit of equality on other grounds—in particular race, ethnic origin, sexual orientation, religion, belief, age, and disability—is of much more recent vintage. Indeed, it took concrete form only in the Treaty of Amsterdam in 1997, four decades later, which included Article 13 as a legal basis for legislation to prohibit discrimination on these grounds.

It is not entirely clear why sex equality[2] has maintained such a unique hold on the attentions of EC legislators and litigators for so long.[3] It is true that women represent more than a third of the workforce, are more likely to occupy 'atypical' jobs, especially part-time jobs, and are particularly affected by long-term unemployment. Perhaps, as Ellis suggests, the attainment of sex equality served political and economic goals: on an economic level, it was important to prevent competitive distortions in a now quite highly integrated market; and on a political level, sex equality provided a relatively innocuous, even high-sounding platform, by which the Community could demonstrate its commitment to social progress.[4] Less cynically, it could be argued that sex equality has provided the EU with a readily accessible human face.[5]

The aim of this chapter is to outline the development of equality law in the EU as well as placing these developments in context. We begin by considering the evolution of the Union's approach to the realization of equal treatment

---

[1] White Paper on Social Policy COM(94) 333, 41.

[2] For a comprehensive discussion of this subject, see Ellis, *EU Anti-discrimination Law* (OUP, Oxford, 2005) and Bell, *Anti-discrimination Law and the European Union* (OUP, Oxford, 2002). For a general, positive review, see Prechal, 'Equality of Treatment, Non-discrimination and Social Policy: Achievements in Three Themes' (2004) 41 *CMLRev.* 533.

[3] See Kilpatrick, 'Gender Equality: A Fundamental Dialogue' in Sciarra (ed.), *Labour Law in the Courts: National Judges and the ECJ* (Hart Publishing, Oxford, 2001).

[4] Ellis, above n. 2, 22.

[5] Kilpatrick, 'Emancipation through law or the Emasculation of Law? The Nation State, the EU, and Gender Equality at Work' in Conaghan *et al. Labour Law in an Era of Globalization* (OUP, Oxford, 2002).

and then examine the meaning of equality, both theoretically and in practice, in the EC's legal order. Inevitably, because Community law on sex equality has been around for almost fifty years, many of the key concepts have been developed in respect of this strand and this is reflected in this chapter. The following chapters then consider the detailed application of the law: Chapter 7 considers equal pay for men and women; chapter 8 equal treatment across the strands; chapter 9 examines various aspects of so-called 'family friendly' policies, while chapter 10 considers the thorny question of equality in respect of social security and, in particular, pensions.

B. THE DEVELOPMENT OF EC LAW AND POLICY ON EQUALITY

1. Sex Equality

1.1. Introduction

Article 119 EC (now Article 141) established the principle that men and women should receive equal pay for equal work. Article 119 was introduced into the Treaty of Rome largely to serve the economic purpose of 'correcting or eliminating the effect of specific distortions which advantage or disadvantage certain branches of activity'.[6] France insisted on the inclusion of Article 119 because it feared that, in the absence of Community regulation, its worker protection legislation, including its laws on equal pay, would put it at a competitive disadvantage in a common market due to the additional costs borne by French industry.[7] Thus, the original rationale for including a provision on sex equality in the EEC Treaty was a negative one: to stop social dumping.[8] The social and moral justification for sex equality was largely overlooked. Yet, within 20 years the Community had adopted three Directives on equality, and the Court had started to recognize that the principle of equality

---

[6] The Spaak Report, 61 (author's translation). Comité Intergouvernemental Crée par la conférence de Messine, Rapport des Chefs de Délégations aux Ministères des Affaires Etrangères of 21 April 1956. The Committee, comprising of the heads of delegations, was established at the Messina conference in June 1955 under the chairmanship of M Paul Henri Spaak, then Belgian foreign minister. See generally Barnard, 'EC Sex Equality Law: A Balance Sheet', in Alston (ed.), *The EU and Human Rights* (OUP, Oxford, 1999) on which this section draws.

[7] See Kahn-Freund, 'Labour Law and Social Security', in Stein and Nicholson (eds), *American Enterprise in the European Common Market: A Legal Profile* (University of Michigan Press, Ann Arbor, Mich., 1960) 300, discussed in Barnard, 'The Economic Objectives of Article 119', in Hervey and O'Keeffe (eds), *Sex Equality Law in the European Union* (Wiley, Chichester, 1996); More, 'The Principle of Equal Treatment: From Market Unifier to Fundamental Right', in Craig and De Búrca (eds), *The Evolution of EU Law* (OUP, Oxford, 1999). See also the influence of ILO Convention 100: Hoskyns, *Integrating Gender* (Verso, London, 1996) Ch. 4.

[8] See further Ch. 1.

was a fundamental right which served a social as well as an economic function. This was first identified in the landmark judgment in *Defrenne (No. 2)*,[9] a case brought against the backcloth of serious industrial unrest by women in Belgium about the absence of equal pay.[10] The Court famously observed:

Article [141] pursues a double aim. *First,* . . . the aim of Article [141] is to avoid a situation in which undertakings established in states which have actually implemented the principle of equal pay suffer a competitive disadvantage in intra-Community competition as compared with undertakings established in states which have not yet eliminated discrimination against women workers as regards pay. *Second,* this provision forms part of the social objectives of the Community, which is not merely an economic union, but is at the same time intended, by common action to ensure social progress and seek the constant improvement of living and working conditions of their peoples . . . This double aim, which is at once economic and social, shows that the principle of equal pay forms part of the foundations of the Community.

In *Defrenne (No. 3)*[11] the Court took the social dimension of equality one stage further and elevated the principle to the status of a fundamental right. It said 'respect for fundamental personal human rights is one of the general principles of Community law . . . there can be no doubt that the elimination of discrimination based on sex forms part of those fundamental rights.' As we shall see, despite such statements, the yoke of the economic justification for Community sex equality legislation has far from been cast off. While the EU has never followed the neo-liberal route which opposes all anti-discrimination legislation in principle, considering that the market will achieve the optimal outcome without there being any need for the legislature to interfere with freedom of contract,[12] in the early 1970s it viewed equal opportunities as acceptable so long as they did not interfere significantly with the operation of the Single Market. Then, the late 1990s saw a shift in approach with the European employment strategy where the European Union saw discrimination laws as promoting efficiency by more rapidly eliminating discriminators, by inducing potential productivity and by reducing the inefficiencies associated with statistical discrimination.[13] In other words, equality—together with other social rights—came to be seen as inputs into growth.[14] The view that equality was socially and economically important was reinforced by the

[9] Case 43/75 *Defrenne (No. 2)* v. *SABENA* [1976] ECR 455.
[10] Hoskyns, *Integrating Gender* (Verso, London, 1996), 65–75.
[11] Case 149/77 *Defrenne (No. 3)* v. *SABENA* [1978] ECR 1365, 1378.
[12] See, e.g., Becker, *The Economics of Discrimination*, 2nd edn (Univ. of Chicago Press, Chicago, 1971). Cf. Hepple, 'The Principle of Equal Treatment in Article 119 EC and the Possibilities for Reform', in Dashwood and O'Leary (eds), *The Principle of Equal Treatment in EC Law* (Sweet & Maxwell, London, 1997) 141.
[13] Donohue, 'Prohibiting Sex Discrimination in the Workplace: An Economic Perspective' (1989) 56 *U.Chicago L.Rev.* 1337.
[14] This was recognized at a relatively early stage by the European Commission in its White Paper on Social Policy where it said that the 'adaptability and creativity of women is a strength which should be harnessed to the drive for growth and competitiveness in the EU' (COM(94) 333, 41).

prominent position of equality both in the Charter of Fundamental Rights adopted at Nice in December 2000 and the Constitutional Treaty. This changing perspective fed into rulings of the Court of Justice. In *Deutsche Post*[15] the Court said that in view of the case law recognizing that equality was a fundamental right:

. . . it must be concluded that the economic aim pursued by Article [141] of the Treaty, namely the elimination of distortions of competition between undertakings established in different Member States, is *secondary* to the social aim pursued by the same provision, which constitutes the expression of a fundamental human right.[16]

1.2. The Development of EU Law and Policy on Sex Equality

(a) Legislation

Hard Law

Following the inclusion of the original Article 119 into the EEC Treaty of 1957, little happened in the field of sex equality until the Social Action Programme 1974 which followed the Paris Communiqué in 1972. This said that the Community aspired to create a 'situation in which equality between men and women obtains in the labour market throughout the Community, through the improvement of economic and psychological conditions, and of the social and educational infrastructure'.[17] Three important Directives were adopted as a result:

- Directive 75/117/EEC[18] on equal pay for male and female workers, enshrining the principle of 'equal pay for equal work' laid down in Article 141, and introducing the concept of 'equal pay for work of equal value'. This has been supplemented by two codes of practice intended to give practical advice on measures to ensure the effective implementation of equal pay.[19]
- Directive 76/207/EEC[20] on equal treatment with regard to access to employment, vocational training, promotion and working conditions, aimed at eliminating all discrimination, both direct and indirect, in the world of

---

[15] Joined Cases C–270/97 and C–271/97 *Deutsche Post v. Sievers and Schrage* [2000] ECR I–929, para. 57.

[16] Emphasis added. See also Joined Cases C–234/96 and C–235/96 *Deutsche Telekom AG v. Vick and Conze* [2000] ECR I–799, para. 57.

[17] See Council Resolution of 21 January 1974 concerning a Social Action Programme OJ [1974] L14/10.

[18] OJ [1975] L45/19.   [19] COM(94) 6; COM(96)336 final.

[20] Council Dir. 76/207/EEC (OJ [1976] L39/40). The Directive was based on Art. 235 (new Art. 308). Member States had 30 months to implement the Directive from the date of notification. In addition, they had four years to revise discriminatory laws designed to protect one group whose justification is no longer well founded (Art. 9(1)).

work and providing an opportunity for positive measures. This Directive has now been amended by Directive 2002/73.[21]

- Directive 79/7/EEC[22] on the progressive implementation of equal treatment with regard to statutory social security schemes.

There followed five Action Programmes aimed specifically at equal opportunities for men and women.[23]

In the 1980s, at a time of stagnation in Community social policy, two specific Directives were adopted on sex equality:

- Directive 86/378/EEC[24] on the implementation of equal treatment in occupational schemes of social security. The Directive was amended by Directive 96/97/EC[25] in the light of the *Barber*[26] judgment.
- Directive 86/613/EEC[27] on equal treatment for men and women carrying out a self-employed activity, including agriculture.

The Directives considered so far were all adopted under Articles 100 and/or 235 EC (new Articles 94 and 308) requiring unanimous voting.[28] The 1989 Social Action Programme,[29] implementing the Community Social Charter 1989, led to the enactment of Directive 92/85/EC[30] improving the health and safety of workers who are pregnant or have recently given birth. This Directive was based on the recently adopted Article 118a EC (new Article 137) which required qualified majority voting.

Two further Directives were adopted under the Social Policy Agreement (SPA) annexed to the Treaty on European Union from which the UK initially secured an opt-out:

- Directive 96/34/EC on reconciling family and working life (parental leave).[31] This was the first Directive adopted as a result of an agreement concluded by the Social Partners.[32]

---

[21] OJ [2002] L269/15.   [22] OJ [1979] L6/24. This is considered in detail in Ch. 10.
[23] Action Programme 1982–5 OJ [1982] C186/3, EC Bull. 5–1982, point 2.1.48 and EC Bull. 7/8–1982, point 2.1.67; Equal Opportunities for Women Medium-term Community Programme 1986–1990, EC Bull. Supp. 3/86 and EC Bull. 6–1986, point 2.1.116; Third Medium-term Action Programme COM(90) 449 final; Fourth Medium Term Action Programme (1996–2000) Council Decision 95/593/EC (OJ [1995] L335/37); Fifth Action Programme (2001–2006) Council Decision, 2001/95 (OJ [2001] L17/22).
[24] OJ [1986] L225/40.   [25] OJ [1997] L46/20.
[26] Case 262/88 *Barber* v. *Guardian Royal Exchange* [1990] ECR I–1889. This is considered in detail in Ch. 10.
[27] OJ [1997] L359/56.
[28] E.g., Dir. 75/117 was adopted under Art. 100 (new Art. 94), Dir. 76/207 under Art. 235 (new Art. 308) and Dir. 86/378 under both Arts. 100 and 235 (new Arts. 94 and 308).
[29] COM(89) 568.   [30] OJ [1992] L245/23.
[31] OJ [1996] L145/4, amended by Dir. 97/75/EC (OJ [1998] L10/24), consolidated OJ [1998] L10/11.
[32] See Ch. 2. See also the Directives on Part-time Work 97/81/EC (OJ [1998] L14/9), as amended by Directive 97/81/EC (OJ [1998] L131/10), consolidated in OJ [1998] L131/13 and Fixed Term Work 99/70/EC (OJ [1999] L175/43), considered in Ch. 9.

- Directive 97/80/EC[33] on the burden of proof in cases of discrimination based on sex.

When the UK signed up to the Social Chapter in 1997 these two measures were readopted under Article 94 EC and were applied to the UK.[34] In addition, two other Directives adopted in this period, the Part-time Work Directive 97/81[35] and the Fixed Term Work Directive 99/70,[36] although not specifically part of the equality agenda, modelled themselves on the equality Directives, and inevitably helped women, who dominate the part-time and (to a lesser extent) the fixed term workforce.

Seven of the sex equality Directives (the Equal Pay Directive 75/117, the Equal Treatment Directive 76/207 as amended by Directive 2002/73, the Burden of Proof Directive 97/80 as amended by Directive 98/52 and Directive 86/378/EEC on equal treatment in occupational schemes of social security as amended by Directive 96/97/EC) have been recast into a single consolidated Directive 2006/54/EC which repeals the earlier Directives from 15 August 2009, albeit that the Directive itself must be implemented a year earlier.[37]

The common feature of all of the hard law Directives outlined above is that they are based on the 'human rights' model.[38] Fredman explains this model in the following terms. She says that since the function of human rights is to protect the individual against interference by the state, the rights are vested in the individual who must bring a claim before the courts (which are seen as the primary means of enforcing rights) and remedies are available only if the individual victim can prove the right has been breached. Remedies are retrospective, individual, and based on proof of breach, or 'fault'. She adds, 'Corresponding to this paradigm is also a particular view of equality as a negative duty, restraining the state or private individuals from discriminating against individuals'.

While this model offers a number of benefits—the language of fundamental rights has symbolic value, it provides litigants with an avenue of recourse, and it helps shape employer behaviour and establish a culture of compliance—the disadvantages are also well known. Litigation is stressful for those involved, particularly if the employment relationship is ongoing, it is expensive and it depends on the courts understanding, and being responsive to, the issues involved. It also overlooks the fact that, particularly with gender, breaches of rights operate in a 'collective and institutional way'.[39] As Fredman points out, the human rights approach fails to see that gender inequality is often not

[33] OJ [1998] L14/6, amended by Directive 98/52/EC (OJ [1998] L205/66).
[34] The Social Partners were also consulted with regard to combating sexual harassment at work: COM(96) 373 (first round consultation) and SEC(97) 373 (second round consultation). UNICE pulled out of their negotiations in September 1997.
[35] OJ [1998] L14/9, as amended by Dir. 97/81/EC (OJ [1998] L131/10).
[36] OJ [1999] L175/43.   [37] OJ [2006] L204/23.
[38] 'Changing the Norm: Positive Duties in Equal Treatment Legislation' (2005) 12 *MJ*. 369, 370.
[39] Ibid., 371.

individualized; it 'affects individuals as a result of their group membership and inequality is frequently a consequence of institutional arrangements for which no single actor is 'to blame'. When viewed through this lens, it is clear that the courts do not have the competence to intervene to seek to resolve wider social issues; and that the responsibility more often lies with the state. Yet, as Fredman argues, the human rights model assumes that the state is a potential threat to liberty, rather than a potential force for enhancing freedom through the provision of social goods. She therefore advocates a 'proactive model' where the initiative lies with policy makers, implementers and employers to identify and address the institutional and structural causes for inequality.[40] It is in this context that some of the other Community developments are worth examining.

Soft Law and the Open Method of Co-ordination (OMC)

From the mid-1980s the Community started adopting a variety of soft law measures covering a range of areas[41] including the integration of equal opportunities into the Structural Funds,[42] balanced participation by men and women in decision making[43] and in family and working life,[44] women in vocational training in general[45] and science in particular,[46] and equal participation by women in an employment-intensive growth strategy in the EU.[47] Although these texts are not legally binding, they form part of the 'softening up process' paving the way for the Commission's preferred course of action should a 'policy window' open up[48] and, more importantly, they steer the Community institutions and the Member States to take positive steps to address inequality through policy, and not just legal, means. They also provide an opportunity for decision makers to see a problem in the round rather than through the prism of legal categorization. Thus, policy is more responsive to the problems experienced by those facing multiple levels of

---

[40] Ibid., 373.
[41] See e.g. Council Resolution on the promotion of equal opportunities for women OJ [1986] L203/2.
[42] 94/C 231/01 OJ [1994] C231/1. See also Council Res. of 2 December 1996 on mainstreaming equal opportunities for men and women into the structural funds (OJ [1996] C386/1).
[43] Council Res. of 27 March 1995 (OJ [1995] L168/3) and Council Rec. 96/694/EC (OJ [1996] L319/11).
[44] OJ [2000] C218/5.
[45] Commission Rec. of 24 November 1987 on vocational training for women (OJ [1987] L342/35). More recently see, e.g., Council Res. on Social and Human Capital Building in the knowledge society: learning, work, social cohesion and gender (OJ [2003] C175/3) and Council Res. on Equal Access to and Participation of Women and men in the knowledge society for growth and innovation (OJ [2003] C317/6).
[46] Council Resolution of 20 May 1999 (OJ [1999] C201/1).   [47] 94/C 368/02.
[48] Cram, *Policy Making in the EU: Conceptual Lenses ands the Integration Process* (Routledge, London, 1997). On the role of soft law measures, see Ch. 2.

discrimination such as an ethnic minority, single mother.[49] Funding for some of these policy initiatives has been made available through the European Social Fund, especially its EQUAL programme.[50]

The Commission has now brought some of these soft-law initiatives under the broader umbrella of 'mainstreaming'.[51] As the Commission explains:

Gender mainstreaming is the integration of the gender perspective into every stage of policy processes—design, implementation, monitoring and evaluation—with a view to promoting equality between women and men. It means assessing how policies impact on the life and position of both women and men—and taking responsibility to re-address them if necessary.

The mainstreaming agenda spans issues as diverse as gender balance in decision making,[52] women and science,[53] development co-operation,[54] and gender-based violence and trafficking in women.[55]

The importance of mainstreaming was emphasized in the Commission's Framework Strategy on Gender Equality (2001–2005)[56] and Article 29 of the Consolidated Directive 2006/54. As the Commission explained, this integrated approach marks an important change from the previous Community action, mainly based on compartmental activities and programmes funded under different specific budget headings. The Framework Strategy aims at 'coordinating all the different initiatives and programmes under a single umbrella built around clear assessment criteria, monitoring tools, the setting

---

[49] Schiek, 'Broadening the Scope and the Norms of EU Gender Equality law: Towards a Multi-Dimensional Conception of Equality Law' (2005) 12 *MJ*. 427.

[50] http://ec.europa.eu/comm/employment_social/equal/index_en.cfm

[51] http://ec.europa.eu/comm/employment_social/gender_equality/gender_mainstreaming/general_overview_en.html

[52] According to the Commission, the number of EU countries where women have reached the highest political office can be counted on a single hand. Across Europe, just one in five government ministers is a woman, while the ratio is only slightly better among members of national parliaments. In business, women represent only 3% of presidents of boards in top companies: http://europa.eu.int/comm/employment_social/gender_equality/gender_mainstreaming/balancedparticipation/balanced_participation_en.html. See, e.g., Commission Dec. relating to Gender Balance within the Committees and Expert groups (OJ [2000] L154/34).

[53] Council Res. of 27 November 2003 on equal access to and participation of women and men in the knowledge society for growth and innovation (OJ [2003] C317/6.

[54] See, in particular, Co. Reg. (EC) No. 2836/98 on integrating gender issues in development cooperation (OJ [1998] L354/5) and EP and Co. Reg. 806/2004 on promoting gender equality in development co-operation (OJ [2004] L143/40) together with the Commission's Communication (COM(2001) 295).

[55] See, e.g., Council Res. on initiatives to combat trafficking in human beings, in particular women (OJ [2003] C260/4) and Council Framework Dec. 2002/629/JHA (OJ [2002] L203/1) on combating trafficking in human beings.

[56] COM(2000) 335 implemented by Council Dec. 2001/51 (OJ [2001] L17/22. The Council Decision envisages intervention in five areas: economic life, equal participation and representation, social rights, civil life, and gender roles and stereotypes. Funding can be applied for by a range of national and subnational bodies and NGOs involved in promoting gender equality. Under three strands (awareness raising, analysis and evaluation, and strengthening capacity). This is to be extended: COM(2004) 551.

of benchmarks, gender proofing and evaluation'.[57] Thus, OMC techniques are now being applied to gender equality.[58] The Framework Strategy has been followed up by the Roadmap for Equality (2006–2010) between women and men[59] which identified six priority areas for action:

• Achieving equal economic independence for women and men;
• Enhancing reconciliation of work, private and family life;
• Promoting equal participation of men and women in decision making;
• Eradicating gender-based violence and trafficking;
• Eliminating gender stereotypes in society;
• Promoting gender equality outside the EU.

One particular strand of the mainstreaming agenda concerns raising the employment rate for women which currently stands at 55.1 per cent (compared to 70.9 per cent for men) to 60 per cent by 2010 in line with the Lisbon strategy.[60] In this respect, the mainstreaming agenda dovetails with the European Employment Strategy (EES). The promotion of equal opportunities formed one of the four key pillars of the EES initiated in Luxembourg in November 1997.[61] Initially, the guidelines under the equal opportunities pillar focused on specific measures to strengthen gender equality such as the need to tackle gender gaps, especially in respect of unemployment rates and, according to the 1999 guidelines, pay inequalities, since women are paid 15 per cent less than men. Other measures included helping to reconcile work and family life, particularly through policies on career breaks, parental leave and part time work and adequate provision of good quality childcare, facilitating return to work after a period of absence.[62] Subsequently, the 2001 guidelines[63] placed emphasis on a gender mainstreaming approach in implementing the guidelines across all four pillars by developing and reinforcing consultative systems with gender equality bodies, applying procedures for gender impact assessment under each guideline; and developing indicators to measure progress in gender equality in relation to each guideline.

Gender equality and promoting the integration of, and combating discrimination against, people at a disadvantage in the labour market were identified as specific guidelines in the revised guidelines of 2003[64] which were set for three years (although in fact revised in 2005). Combating discrimination, both on the grounds of sex and on other grounds, expressly formed part of the

---

[57] COM(2000) 335, para. 2.1.
[58] See e.g., the annual reports from the Commission on equality between women and men such as COM(2006) 71. OMC is considered in detail in Ch. 3.
[59] COM(2006) 92.   [60] This strategy is considered in detail in Ch. 3.
[61] See further Ch. 1.
[62] See, e.g., the original (1998) Employment Guidelines OJ [1998] C30/1.
[63] Council Dec. 2001/63 (OJ [2001] L22/18). Gender mainstreaming had in fact been a feature of the Employment Guidelines since 1999 (OJ [1999] C69/2).
[64] Council Dec. 2003/578/EC (OJ [2003] L197/13).

quality agenda according to which 'Quality at work can help increase labour productivity and the synergies between both should be fully exploited.'[65] The 2005–8 guidelines[66] emphasize that 'equal opportunities and combating discrimination are essential for progress' and that '[g]ender mainstreaming and the promotion of gender equality should be ensured in all action taken'.[67]

While the pro-active model has much to commend it, it is of course dependent on the Community institutions and the Member States actually being pro-active rather than merely talking about being pro-active. As Pollack and Hafner-Burton show,[68] the success of gender mainstreaming in the EU has depended very much on the commitment of the various actors to its aims. Sanctions are therefore necessary to ensure that, in the absence of voluntary compliance, remedies are available in default.

Hervey points out that 'where we seek to resolve complex social problems, such as inequality of women and men, a notion of 'mixity' or 'hybridity' of old governance [hard law equality Directives] and new governance [soft law resolutions and OMC techniques such as indicators and benchmarking] probably holds the key to the realization of our goals'.[69] As lawyers, our task is to analyse the 'old governance' measures (principally Directives), but against a backcloth of an appreciation of the new governance agenda, and it is a consideration of these Directives that will predominantly form the subject-matter of the next five chapters.

(b) Treaty of Amsterdam

The Treaty of Amsterdam explicitly introduced equality between men and women as one of the tasks of the Community (Article 2) and one of its activities (Article 3). In addition, it introduced a new article, Article 13[70] allowing the Council, to take action on various grounds including sex. The Amsterdam Treaty also amended the equal pay provision, Article 141, for the first time. Article 141(1) extended the principle of equal pay for equal work to include 'work of equal value', thereby bringing the Treaty into line with the Court's case law.[71] The new Article 141(3) finally provided an express legal basis for the Council to adopt measures, in accordance with the Article 251 co-decision procedure, 'to ensure the application of the principle of equal opportunities and equal treatment of men and women in matters of employment and occupation, including the principle of equal pay for equal work or

[65] The second 'overarching and interrelated objective' on p.17.
[66] Council Dec. 2005/600 (OJ [2005] L205/21.   [67] P. 23.
[68] 'Mainstreaming Gender in the European Union' (2000) 7 *JEPP.* 432.
[69] 'Thirty Years of EU Sex Equality law: Looking Backwards, Looking Forwards' (2005) 12 *MJ.* 307, 322.
[70] Ex Art. 6a.
[71] Art. 1 of Dir. 75/117/EEC already made provision for this. In Case 96/80 *Jenkins* v. *Kingsgate* [1981] ECR 911 the Court said that Art. 1 'is principally designed to facilitate the practical application of the principle of equal pay outlined in Article 1[141] of the Treaty [and] in no way alters the content or scope of that principle as defined in the Treaty'.

work of equal value'. Finally, a new Article 141(4) allows Member States to adopt or maintain positive action measures for the under-represented sex in respect of professional careers.

The first measure adopted under Article 141(3) was the Equal Treatment Directive 2002/73[72] amending the Equal Treatment Directive 76/207.[73] This Directive was introduced to ensure coherence of key principles in the field of sex discrimination with the Article 13 Directives (see below) and to incorporate some of the decisions of the Court. Most significantly, in its proposal for the 2002 Directive, the Commission noted that the 'provision for equal opportunities in the framework of the Treaty has been greatly enhanced since the entry into force of the Treaty of Amsterdam'.[74] The Commission continued:

Originally regarded as a means of preventing distortion of competition, equal treatment between men and women is now an explicit objective of the Community enshrined in Article 2 of the Treaty. . . . These Treaty developments constitute an explicit embodiment of the Court's statement that the elimination of discrimination based on sex forms part of fundamental rights.

In 2004 the Council adopted, under Article 13, Directive 2004/113 which, following the pattern of the Race Directive 2000/43, extends the principle of equal treatment between men and women to access to and supply of goods and services.[75]

(c) Institutional Support

Institutional support for the realization of sex equality has also been provided: there are special committees concerned with women's issues in the European Parliament, including the Committee on Women's Rights and Equal Opportunities, an 'Equality between men and women' Unit within DGEmpl of the European Commission,[76] assisted by a Group of Experts on Gender, Social Inclusion and Employment, and an Advisory Committee on Equal Opportunities for men and women.[77] In addition, the Fundamental Rights, Anti-Discrimination and Equal Opportunities Working Party of Members of the Commission, set up in 1995, examines and monitors the integration of the gender dimension into all relevant policies and programmes. Its work is supported by the Inter-Service Group on Gender Equality which brings together representatives of all Commission services to develop gender mainstreaming activities. In addition, the high level group on gender mainstreaming is an

---

[72] OJ [2002] L269/15.
[73] The Consolidated Directive was also adopted under this legal basis.
[74] Para. 7.   [75] OJ [2004] L373/37.
[76] On a more independent basis the Centre for Research on Women (CREW) has been established, as has the European Network of Women (ENOW) and the Women's Lobby. See further Szyszczak, 'L'Espace Social Européen, Reality, Dreams or Nightmare' [1990] *German Yearbook of International Law*, 284, 298.
[77] Established by Commission Decision 82/43/EEC (OJ [1982] L20/35), as amended by Decision 95/420/EEC (OJ [1995] 249/43).

informal group of representatives responsible for gender mainstreaming at national level in the Member States which meets to exchange information on best practices and experience 'to support and improve the synergy among national policies on gender equality and strategies for mainstreaming at national level'.[78] At its instigation, the Commission adopted a communication on incorporating equal opportunities for women and men into all Community policies and activities.[79] However, perhaps the most visible demonstration of institutional commitment to sex equality is the establishment of a European Institute for Gender Equality whose tasks will be reviewing all existing EU gender equality law, increasing awareness of gender inequality and ensuring that gender equality is considered in all policies.[80]

2. Equality in Other Fields

2.1. Race

The European Council,[81] the Council, Commission[82] and Parliament[83] had long been concerned about racism and xenophobia but, prior to the introduction of Article 13 into the EC Treaty at Amsterdam in 1997, doubted the Community's competence to act. The Community institutions therefore limited their activities to issuing non legally binding declarations and resolutions.[84]

[78] http://europa.eu.int/comm/employment_social/gender_equality/gender_mainstreaming/ gender/high_level_group_en.html

[79] COM(96) 67 and the Commission's Progress Report COM(98) 122. See also the Commission's Guide to 'Gender Impact Assessment', http://europa.eu.int/comm/dg05/equ-opp/ index_en.htm. The Commission has also begun to put its own house in order: Commission Decision 2000/407/EC (OJ [2000] L154/34) relating to gender balance within the committees and expert groups established by it.

[80] IP/06/263 and COM(2005)81.

[81] See e.g. Conclusions of Meetings of the European Council in Cannes in June 1995, Madrid in December 1995, Florence in June 1996 and Dublin in December 1996.

[82] See also COM(94) 333, 52, and COM(98) 183 'An Action Plan against Racism'.

[83] See also the Parliament's resolutions of 27 October 1994 (OJ [1995] C126/75) and 27 April 1995 (OJ [1995] C126/75).

[84] For a full list see Annex II of the Commission's Communication on certain Community measures to combat discrimination (COM(99) 564). See also Gearty, 'The Internal and External "Other" in the Union Legal Order: Racism, Religious Intolerance and Xenophobia in Europe, in Alston (ed.), The EU and Human Rights (OUP, Oxford, 1999) and Hervey, 'Putting Europe's House in Order: Racism, Race Discrimination and Xenophobia after the Treaty of Amsterdam', in O'Keeffe and Twomey (eds), Legal Issues of the Amsterdam Treaty (Hart Publishing, Oxford, 1999). Some anti-racist provisions have been included in other legally binding instruments. For example, Art. 12 of Dir. 89/552 (OJ [1989] L2/98), 23 provides that television advertising must not include any discrimination on grounds of race, sex or nationality nor offend any religious or political beliefs, and Art. 22 provides that Member States shall ensure that broadcasts do not contain any incitement to racial hatred on the grounds of race, sex, religion, or nationality. See also the Commission's Communication on racism, xenophobia and anti-semitism (COM(95) 653 final) where the Commission promised to propose the insertion of anti-discrimination clauses in new legislation.

For example, the Council Resolution on the Fight Against Racism and Xenophobia of 29 May 1990,[85] encouraged Member States to take action, including ratifying international conventions on racism, enacting national laws restraining discriminatory acts, providing recourse to the legal system, and developing an effective policy of education[86] and information. The 1995 Resolution on the fight against racism and xenophobia in the fields of employment and social affairs produced by the Council and the representatives of the Member States' governments[87] condemned racism, xenophobia, and anti-semitism, flagrant breaches of individual rights, and religious intolerance, particularly in the fields of employment and social affairs. It also recognized the great importance of implementing, in the field of social policy, policies based on the principles of non-discrimination and equal opportunities at Union and Member State level.[88] As a result, a European Union Monitoring Centre on Racism and Xenophobia (EUMC) was set up.[89]

Thus, unlike gender equality where hard law preceded soft, in the context of race, much soft law work had been done, preparing the ground prior to the adoption of the (hard law) Directive 2000/43[90] under Article 13.[91] Yet, as the Commission noted in its explanatory memorandum,[92] 'at the end of the century, racial discrimination is still not eradicated from everyday life in Europe'. It continued:

It is widely acknowledged that legal measures are of paramount importance for combating racism and intolerance. The law not only protects victims and gives them a remedy, but also demonstrates society's firm opposition to racism and the genuine commitment of the authorities to curb discrimination. The enforcement of anti-racist laws can have a significant effect on the shaping of attitudes.

The Directive lays down 'broad objectives to ensure that discrimination is prohibited and that the victims of discrimination enjoy a basic minimum entitlement to redress'. In so doing the Directive aims to reinforce the 'fundamental values on which the Union in founded—liberty, democracy, the

---

[85] OJ [1990] C157/4.

[86] See also the Resolution of the Council and the representatives of Member States' governments of 23 October 1995 on the response of educational systems to the problems of racism and xenophobia OJ [1995] C312/1.

[87] Resolution 95/110 of 5 Oct. 1995 (OJ [1995] C296/13).

[88] See also third pillar measures such as Joint Action 96/443/JHA (OJ [1996] L185/5) concerning action to combat racism and xenophobia.

[89] Council Regulation1035/97 (OJ [1997] L151/2). This agency is due to become a general human rights agency. See further Ch. 1.

[90] OJ [2000] L180/22.

[91] The Tampere European Council (October 1999) urged the Commission to bring forward proposals for a Race Directive under Art. 13, in part due to concern about the rise of the far right in countries such as Austria (Douglas-Scott, *Constitutional Law of the European Union* (Longman, Harlow, 2002) 435 and in part because of concerns about levels of discrimination in some of the Accession states, especially in respect of the Roma.

[92] COM(99) 566, 2.

respect for human rights and fundamental freedoms and the rule of law—and contribute to the development of the Union as an area of freedom, security and justice. And it will help to strengthen economic and social cohesion'.[93]

The Race Directive was the first measure adopted under the new powers given to the Community by the Amsterdam Treaty. Article 13[94] allows the Council, acting unanimously on a proposal from the Commission, to take action to combat discrimination based not only on sex, racial or ethnic origin, but also on religion or belief, disability, age, or sexual orientation.[95] Close on the heels of the Race Directive the Community adopted the 'horizontal' or 'framework' labour market Directive 2000/78[96] prohibiting discrimination on all the other grounds listed in Article 13 except sex; a Communication on certain Community measures to combat discrimination;[97] and an Action Plan to combat discrimination 2001–2006 (which became Decision 2000/750).[98]

2.2. The Scope of the Directives

The Framework Directive prohibited discrimination on wide grounds (sexual orientation, religion or belief, disability, and age) but in narrow circumstances (matters relating to employment and vocational training). By contrast the Race Directive prohibited discrimination on narrow grounds (race and ethnic origin but not colour or nationality) but in broad circumstances (employment, vocational training as well as social protection, including social security and healthcare, social advantages, education, access to and supply of goods and services which are available to the public, including housing). However, both Directives share, with the sex equality Directives, a symmetrical approach to equality. Thus homosexuals must be treated in the same way as heterosexuals and vice versa. This means that more favourable treatment of the disadvantaged group will always breach the principle of equality. The exception to the rule of symmetry is disability: disabled persons can demand equal treatment with non-disabled but not vice versa and, in this way, the non-disabled cannot complain of more favourable treatment enjoyed by the disabled. As Ellis puts it,[99] this formulation can be seen 'to reflect a different underlying philosophy for the disability provisions from the rest of anti-discrimination legislation; they are more clearly directed to relieving the disadvantage experienced by the disabled section of society than to protecting a fundamental human right possessed by everyone'.

---

[93]   COM(99) 566, 4.   [94]   Ex Art. 6a.
[95]   Art. 13 was amended at Nice to allow for incentive measures to be adopted under qualified majority voting but excluding any harmonization of the Member States' legislation.
[96]   The proposal is at COM(99) 565. Now Council Dir. 2000/78/EC (OJ [2000] L303/16).
[97]   COM(99) 564.
[98]   The proposal is at COM(99) 567. Now Council Dec. 2000/750/EC (OJ [2000] L303/23).
[99]   Above, n. 2, 91.

2.3. A Common Approach: Social Inclusion

The two Article 13 Directives, like the sex equality directives, broadly adopt the classic, human rights model to combating discrimination: individual and rights based.[100] However, as with sex discrimination, the legislative approach is complemented by an action plan[101] to prevent and combat discrimination which envisages action under three strands: analysis and evaluation, capacity building and awareness raising.[102] In addition, the weight of the EES is being deployed to combat discrimination.[103] Thus, those who are socially excluded, especially the disabled, older workers, and ethnic minorities, can become included through employment because 'employment is the best guarantee against social exclusion',[104] and the Article 13 Directives provide those excluded with a vehicle to challenge that exclusion. The link between social exclusion and employment policy was expressly noted in the Preambles to the Article 13 Directives. The Race Directive refers to the 2000 Employment Guidelines which 'stress the need to foster conditions for a socially inclusive labour market by formulating a coherent set of policies aimed at combating discrimination against groups such as ethnic minorities'[105] while the Framework Directive adds that 'Employment and occupation are key elements in guaranteeing equal opportunities for all and contribute strongly to the full participation of citizens in economic, cultural and social life and to realising their potential'.[106]

2.4. Institutional Support

Institutional support for the elimination of discrimination is provided at a number of levels. For example, the Race Directive, like the Sex Directive 2002/73 (but not the horizontal Directive), requires Member States to designate a body or bodies for the promotion of equal treatment.[107] At Community level there is an anti-discrimination unit in DGEmpl which has regular contact with civil society and the NGOs.[108] In particular, under the Community Action Programme to combat discrimination, the European Commission

---

[100] This is recognized by the Commission, 'Equality and non-discrimination in an enlarged European Union' (COM(2004) 379, 6. See also McInerney, 'Bases for Action against Race Discrimination in EU Law' (2002) 27 *ELRev.* 72.

[101] Co. Dec. 2000/750 (OJ [2000] L303/23). See de Búrca, 'EU Race Discrimination Law: a Hybrid Model' in de Búrca and Scott (eds), *Law and New Governance in the EU and US* (Hart Publishing, Oxford, 2006).

[102] On the future of this approach, see Commission, Green Paper, *Equality and Non-discrimination in an enlarged European Union*, COM(2004) 379.

[103] Bell, 'Combating Racial Discrimination through the Employment Strategy' (2003–4) 6 *CYELS.* 55.

[104] Barcelona European Council, Presidency Conclusions, Bull. EU 3/2001, para. 22.

[105] 8th Premabular para. of Dir. 2000/43. See also the 8th Preambular para. of Dir. 2000/78.

[106] 9th Preambular para.   [107] Art. 13.

[108] http://ec.europa.eu/comm/employment_social/fundamental_rights/civil/civ_en.htm

itself funds four European umbrella NGO networks representing and defending the rights of people exposed to discrimination—one per ground of discrimination: AGE (The European Older People's Platform); ILGA Europe (International Lesbian and Gay Association—Europe); ENAR (European Network Against Racism); and EDF (European Disability Forum). The European Parliament has a committee on Civil liberties, justice and home affairs which deals with all issues of discrimination on grounds other than sex. The Union's work will be buttressed by the establishment of an EU Agency for Fundamental Rights[109] and by the designation of 2007 as the European Year of equal Opportunities for all.[110]

3. Equality under the Constitutional Treaty

From its lowly days as a one-Article provision in the European Economic Community Treaty in 1957, equality has become, by the time the Constitutional Treaty was agreed in 2004, a significant constitutional principle. The Constitutional Treaty—which will not enter into force until ratified by all 25 Member States—places much emphasis on the principle of equality. Non-discrimination and equality between men and women are identified as Union values in Article I–2 and as Union objectives in Article I–3.[111] In addition, Article I–45 requires the Union, in all its activities to observe the 'principle of the equality of its citizens'. Article III–116 adds that in all the activities referred to in Part II, 'the Union shall aim to eliminate inequalities, and to promote equality, between women and men'. Article III–118 goes further and contains the important horizontal statement on mainstreaming. This provides that:

In defining and implementing the policies and activities referred to in this part, the Union shall aim to combat discrimination based on sex, racial or ethnic origin, religion or belief, disability, age or sexual orientation.

Equality also forms one of the Titles of the Charter of Fundamental Rights found in Part II of the Constitution which, according to Article I–9(1), the Union must recognize. Title II opens with the classic assertion that 'Everyone

---

[109] Proposal for a Council Regulation establishing a European Union Agency for Fundamental Rights COM(2005) 280. See also the Commission's Communication on a Fundamental Rights Agency COM(2004) 693.

[110] IP/06/712. The year aims to make the Europeans aware of their right not to be discriminated against, to promote equal opportunities in areas from work to healthcare, and to show how diversity makes the EU stronger. The year will have four themes: rights, representation, recognition, and respect.

[111] The objectives must be taken into account in respect of the policies and activities referred to in Part III: Art. III–115. For a full discussion, see Bell, 'Equality and the European Union Constitution' (2004) 33 *ILJ*. 242.

is equal before the law'.[112] Article II–81(1) (Article 21(1) of the Charter) then contains a specific, but non-exhaustive, list of the grounds of discrimination which are prohibited 'sex, race, colour, ethnic or social origin, genetic features, language, religion or belief, political or any other opinion, membership of a national minority, property, birth, disability, age or sexual orientation'. This list differs in certain key respects from the (shorter) list of prohibited grounds in Article 13. However, while Article 13 provides the legal power for the Community to act, Article II–81(1) (Article 21(1) of the Charter) addresses discrimination by the institutions and bodies of the Union themselves, and by Member States when they are implementing Union law.[113] Article II–83(1) (Article 23(1) of the Charter) requires equality between men and women in 'all areas, including employment, work and pay'. Article II–83(2) (Article 23(2) of the Charter) contains the positive action provision. It specifies that the principle of equality 'shall not prevent the maintenance or adoption of measures providing for specific advantages in favour of the under-represented sex'.[114]

C. THE MEANING OF EQUALITY IN THE EU CONTEXT

1. Introduction

It is clear that the attainment of the principle of equality has a central role to play in the EU. But what is actually meant by 'equality'?[115] In fact, it is a term which cannot stand alone because it needs an answer to the question 'equal to what?' Aristotle famously explained, albeit in the context of a very different, highly stratified society, that '[e]quality in morals' meant 'things that are alike should be treated alike',[116] an understanding often described as formal equality. But who is alike? The very nature of human beings is that they are all unique—and different. It is a moral judgement as to who is alike. This leads Westen to conclude that the concept of equality is tautological. He says

[112] Art. II–80 (Art. 20 of the Charter). The numbering in the original Charter, adopted at Nice in 2000, is different from that in the Constitutional Treaty. There are also minor textual difference between the original version of the Charter and the version incorporated into the Constitutional Treaty. Since the discussion of the Charter occurs within the section on the Constitutional Treaty, the Constitution's numbers will be used.

[113] Art. II–111. See also the Praesidium explanation accompanying the article which must be given 'due regard by the Courts of the Union and of the Member States' (Art. II–112(7)).

[114] For a full discussion, see Costello, 'Gender Equalities and the Charter of Fundamental Rights of the European Union' in Hervey and Kenner (eds), *Economic and Social Rights under the EU Charter of Fundamental Rights* (Hart Publishing, Oxford, 2003).

[115] This section draws on Barnard, 'The Principle of Equality in the Community Context. *P, Grant, Kalanke* and *Marschall*: Four Uneasy Bedfellows?' (1998) 57 *CLJ*. 352.

[116] Aristotle, *Ethica Nicomachea* V.3.1131a–1131b (Ross, trans., 1925), cited in Westen, 'The Empty Idea of Equality' (1982) 95 *Harvard Law Review* 537, 543.

equality 'tells us to treat like people alike; but when we ask who "like people" are, we are told they are "people who should be treated alike" '. He therefore argues that equality is an empty vessel with no substantive moral content of its own. Without moral standards, equality remains meaningless, 'a formula that has nothing to say about how we should act'.[117]

Since equality provides no internal guidance as to the relevance of particular characteristics of individuals or groups, the principle of non-discrimination helps to fill this vacuum. At Community level this can be seen in Article 141 which provides for 'Equal pay without discrimination on the grounds of sex'.[118] The original Article 2(1) of Directive 76/207 said that the 'principle of equal treatment' means 'there shall be no discrimination whatsoever on grounds of sex either directly or indirectly', with the added steer that the Directive is intended to 'promote equal opportunity for men and women'.[119] Thus, it is the legislature which has defined the principle of non-discrimination, prohibiting, as Article 2(1) (Article 14(1) of Directive 2006/14) makes clear, both direct and indirect discrimination. Further, it is the legislature, and not the court, which has taken the policy decision and identified which people should be treated alike. In the section below we shall examine the meaning of the terms direct and indirect discrimination as well as considering the values under-pinning the Community's approach to equality. However, before that we shall consider the Community's other approach to equality—as a general principle of law. In this 'Constitutional' context, the Court takes the view that equality requires consistent treatment ('equality as consistency')—or in the Aristotelian formulation 'like must be treated with like'.[120] Equality in this context is shorn of the detailed elaboration of the principles of direct and indirect discrimination which seem to apply only to the more programmatic field of non-discrimination law, which aims at overcoming specific inequalities between groups.

2. Equality as a General Principle of Law

2.1. Introduction

As we have already seen, since *Defrenne (No. 3)* the Court has recognized equality as a general principle of law.[121] In developing general principles of

---

[117] Westen, above, n. 116, 547. Cf. Somek, 'A Constitution for Anti-discrimination: Exploring the Vanguard Moment of Community Law' (1999) 5 *ELJ*. 243.

[118] Art. 1 of Dir. 75/117 explains that the principle of equal pay outlined in Art. [141] means 'the elimination of all discrimination on grounds of sex'.

[119] Art. 2(4).

[120] I am grateful to Dagmar Schiek for discussion on this point. See also McCrudden, 'Equality and Non-Discrimination' in Feldman, *English Public Law* (OUP, Oxford, 2004).

[121] See also Case 152/84 *Marshall v. Southampton and South West Hampshire Area Health Authority (Teaching) (No. 1)* [1986] ECR 723, para. 36; Case 151/84 *Roberts v. Tate & Lyle Industries Ltd*

law the Court has often drawn inspiration from the European Convention on Human Rights. The principal non-discrimination provision in the ECHR is found in Article 14 which contains a non-exhaustive list of grounds on which discrimination is prohibited. It provides:

The enjoyment of the rights and freedoms set forth in this Convention shall be secured without discrimination on any ground such as sex, race, colour, language, religion, political or other opinion, national or social origin, association with a national minority, property, birth or other status.

However, in fact, the case law of the ECHR has had less impact in the field of EC equality law than in respect of other social policy areas, in part because Article 14 is not directly enforceable in its own right[122] (it needs to be read in conjunction with another Article in the Convention or its protocols),[123] in part because it can be invoked only in respect of state action and in part because the EC's rules are consciously stricter than those applied by the European Court of Human Rights.[124]

The 'Constitutional' use of the general principle of equality (or non-discrimination) can be found in three contexts: (1) as a ground for challenging the validity of Community acts of a general legislative nature as well as specific acts in respect of the EU's own staff; (2) as a value against which other Community measures are interpreted; and (3) as a ground to challenge the Acts of the Member States when acting in the sphere of Community Law. We shall consider these situations in turn.

2.2. The Use of the Principle of Equality to Challenge the Validity of Community Acts

General principles of law can be invoked to challenge the validity of *Community* legislative acts on the ground that they breach the principle of equality. In this context, the principle of equal treatment requires that 'comparable situations must not be treated differently and that different situations must not be

---

[1986] ECR 703, para. 35, and Case C–132/92 *Birds Eye Walls Ltd* v. *Roberts* [1993] ECR I–5579, para. 17; Case C–408/92 *Smith* v. *Avdel Systems* [1994] ECR I–4435, para. 25; and Case C–167/97 *R* v. *Secretary of State for Employment, ex parte Seymour-Smith and Perez* [1999] ECR I–623, para. 75; Joined Cases C–270/97 and C–271/97 *Deutsche Post* [2000] ECR I–929, para. 57; Case C–25/01 *Rinke* v. *Ärztekammer Hamburg* [2003] ECR I–8349, para. 25; Case C–256/01 *Allonby* v. *Accrington & Rosendale College* [2004] ECR I–000, para. 65. See also Docksey, 'The Principle of Equality between Women and Men as a Fundamental Right Under Community Law' (1991) 20 *ILJ*. 258 and Tridimas, *The General Principles of EU Law* (OUP, Oxford, 2006).

[122] *National Union of Belgian Police* v. *Belgium* [1979] 1 EHRR 578.

[123] Cf. Protocol 12, agreed and opened for signature by Member States of the Council of Europe in November 2000 which, once signed by 10 states, will establish a free-standing right to equality on the same grounds as those set out in Art. 14.

[124] See S. Fredman, 'Equality Issues' in B.S. Markesinis (ed), *The Impact of the Human Rights Bill on English Law* (OUP, Oxford, 1998) 111–32 at pp. 115–18.

treated in the same way unless such treatment is objectively justified.[125] Usually, the Court finds that the two situations are not comparable, or that the differences can be objectively justified. Therefore, in the *Alliance* case[126] the Court found that the distinction drawn by the challenged Directive between those substances which had already been approved when the Directive was adopted which were automatically added to the positive list, and those which had not already been approved which had to go through an onerous approval process, did not breach the principle of equality because the two situations were not comparable.

The principle of equal treatment can also mean non-discrimination on a prohibited ground. In this context, employees of the Community institutions have used the principle to challenge discriminatory rules and practices, and they have enjoyed somewhat more success than other applicants wishing to challenge a Community legislative act for breaching the principle of equality more generally. Thus, in *Razzouk and Beydoun*[127] the Court said the Community's staff regulations which distinguished between the treatment of widows and widowers for the purpose of a survivor's pension breached the principle of equal treatment on the grounds of sex.[128] In *Rinke*[129] the validity of two Directives on training for doctors was challenged on the grounds that the provision requiring part-time training in general medicine to include a certain number of full-time training periods was indirectly discriminatory against women. The Court said that 'compliance with the prohibition of indirect discrimination on grounds of sex is a condition governing the legality of all measures adopted by the Community institutions'.[130] However, on the facts the Court found that the training requirements could be objectively justified.

In *Prais*,[131] another staff case, this time concerning a potential applicant, the Court appeared to recognize the right to freedom of religion under Article 9 ECHR but said that it was not absolute. This meant that while the Community institutions should avoid having recruitment tests on dates which might be unsuitable for religious reasons and seek to avoid fixing such dates for tests, fundamental rights did not impose on the Community institutions a duty to avoid a conflict with a religious requirement of which they had not previously been informed.[132] The Court adopted a similarly cautious approach in *D v. Council*,[133] a case concerning the EU's refusal to pay a household

---

[125] Joined Cases C–184/02 and C–223/02 *Spain and Finland v. Parliament and Council* [2004] ECR I–7789, para. 64.

[126] Joined Cases C–154/04 and C–155/04 *R v. Secretary of State for Health, ex parte Alliance for Natural Health* [2005] ECR I–000, para. 116.

[127] Joined Cases 75 and 117/82 *Razzouk and Beydoun v. Commission* [1984] ECR 1509.

[128] Paras. 17–18. See also Case 212/74 *Airola v. Commission* [1975] ECR 221. For a successful challenge to an indirectly discriminatory measure, see Case 20/71 *Sabbatini v. European Parliament* [1972] ECR 345.

[129] Case C–25/01 *Rinke v. Ärztekammer Hamburg* [2003] ECR I–8349.

[130] Para. 28.   [131] Case 30/75 *Prais v. Council* [1976] ECR 1589.

[132] Para. 18.   [133] Case C–125/99P [2001] ECR I–4319.

allowance, which would have been payable to a married employee, to a homo-sexual employee who was in a stable partnership registered under Swedish law. While the Court appeared to recognize that the principle of non-discrimination extended to sexual orientation,[134] it found that the principle had not been breached on the facts of the case. The Court said that the principle of equal treatment could apply only to persons in comparable situations, and so it was necessary to consider whether the situation of an official who had registered a partnership between persons of the same sex was comparable to that of a married official.[135] The Court then noted that because there was a wide range of laws in the Member States on recognition of partnerships between persons of the same sex or of the opposite sex and because of the absence of any general assimilation of marriage and other forms of statutory union,[136] it concluded that the situation of an official who had registered a partnership in Sweden was not comparable, for the purposes of applying the Staff Regulations, to that of a married official.[137]

These cases demonstrate that the European Court of Justice's approach to the principle of equality is still evolving. By contrast, the US Supreme Court has adopted a sophisticated framework for analysing such cases, with strict scrutiny requiring a compelling state interest to be shown for measures which discriminate on the grounds of race, alien status (citizenship), national origin, and religion and political opinion; heightened scrutiny for discrimination on the grounds of sex and illegitimacy; and only rational basis review[138] for ordinary grounds of discrimination such as the distinction between the permitted activities of opthalmologists and opticians.[139]

2.3. Equality as a Vehicle for Interpretation

The Court of Justice has also used the general principles of law to interpret potentially ambiguous provisions of Community law. The significance of this can be seen in *P* v. *S.*[140] The case concerned the dismissal of a male to

---

[134] At para. 47 the Court said 'as regards infringement of the principle of equal treatment of officials irrespective of their sexual orientation, it is clear that it is not the sex of the partner which determines whether the household allowance is granted, but the legal nature of the ties between the official and the partner'.

[135] Para. 48.   [136] Para. 50.   [137] Para. 51.

[138] See *City of Cleburne, Texas* v. *Cleburne Living Center, Inc.* 473 US 432, 440 'The general rule is that legislation is presumed to be valid, and will be sustained if the classification drawn by the statute is *rationally related to a legitimate state interest.* . . . When social or economic legislation is at issue, the Equal Protection Clause allows the States wide latitude'.

[139] *Wiliamson* v. *Lee Optical of Oklahoma Inc* 348 US 483 (1955). The European Court of Human Rights has also adopted an approach which distinguishes between sensitive grounds such as sex, race, religion, nationality, and sexual orientation where differences in treatment by the state must be for 'very weighty reasons' and ordinary grounds which are easier to justify: Ellis, above n. 2, 321. See also the House of Lords' Decision in *R* v. *Secretary of State for Work and Pensions, ex parte Carson* [2005] UKHL 37.

[140] Case C–13/94 [1996] ECR I–2143.

female transsexual on the grounds of her gender reassignment. The question referred to the Court of Justice was whether the word 'sex' in the phrase there should be 'no discrimination whatsoever on the grounds of sex' in the Equal Treatment Directive 76/207 was broad enough to include 'change of sex'. Drawing on the general principle of equality, the Court said that the Equal Treatment Directive was 'simply the expression, in the relevant field, of the principle of equality, which is one of the fundamental principles of Community law'.[141] This enabled the Court to conclude that the scope of the Directive could not be confined simply to discrimination based on the fact that a person is of one or other sex and so would also apply to discrimination based on gender reassignment.[142]

This was a quite remarkable decision. It seems that a strong opinion on the part of the Advocate General was highly influential. He declared:

I am well aware that I am asking the Court to make a 'courageous' decision. I am asking it to do so, however, in the profound conviction that what is at stake is a universal fundamental value, indelibly etched in modern legal traditions and in the constitutions of the more advanced countries: the irrelevance of a person's sex with regard to the rules regulating relations in society. . . . I consider that it would be a great pity to miss this opportunity of leaving a mark of undeniable civil substance, by taking a decision which is bold but fair and legally correct, inasmuch as it is undeniably based on and consonant with the great value of equality.[143]

The guiding hand of the principle of equality—and another impassioned opinion by the Advocate General, this time Ruiz-Jarabo Colomer[144]—seems also to have helped a transsexual couple in *KB*.[145] The case concerned a decision by the NHS Pensions Agency not to award a widower's pension to KB's transsexual partner on the grounds that they were not married. KB was a woman who lived with R. R had been born a woman but, following gender reassignment, had become a man. Under English law, a birth certificate could not be amended to reflect this change in gender. This meant that the couple could not marry under English law because the Matrimonial Causes Act 1973 required marriage to take place between a man and a woman; according to their birth certificates KB and R were both female. As a result, R was not entitled to a survivor's pension, should KB predecease R, because under the NHS pension scheme a survivor's pension could be paid only to a spouse and R was not—and could never be—a spouse.

The Court began by finding that there was no discrimination on the grounds of sex because, for the purposes of awarding the survivor's pension,

---

[141] Para. 17.   [142] Para. 20.   [143] Para. 24.

[144] Case C–117/01 *KB* v. *National Health Service Pensions Agency* [2004] ECR I–000, AG's Opinon esp. paras. 79–80.

[145] Case C–117/01 *KB* v. *National Health Service Pensions Agency* [2004] ECR I–000 discussed by Cantor (2004) 41 *CMLRev.* 1113. See also Case C–423/04 *Richards* v. *Secretary of State for Work and Pensions* [2006] ECR I–000.

it was irrelevant whether the claimant was a man or a woman.[146] However, the Court then changed tack.[147] It noted that there was inequality in treatment, not in respect of the right to the pension itself, but in respect of one of the conditions for the grant of that right: the capacity to marry.[148] As the Court explained, while a heterosexual couple always had the option of getting married (and thus benefiting from the survivor's pension), a couple such as KB and R, where one of the partners had undergone gender reassignment, could never marry. The Court of Justice then noted that the European Court of Human Rights had already condemned the UK for not allowing transsexuals to marry a person of the sex to which they once belonged.[149] This enabled the Court of Justice to conclude that British legislation which, in breach of the ECHR, prevented a couple such as KB and R from being able to marry and thus to benefit from part of KB's pay, had to be 'regarded as being, in principle, incompatible with the requirements of Article 141 EC'.[150] However, the Court then added that since it was for the Member States to determine the conditions under which legal recognition was given to the change of gender of a person in R's situation, it was for the national court to determine whether a person in KB's situation could rely on Article 141 to gain recognition of her right to nominate her partner as a beneficiary of a survivor's pension.

2.4. The Use of the Principle of Equality to Challenge the Acts of the Member States when acting in the Sphere of Community Law

So far we have concentrated on the Court of Justice's approach to reviewing the validity of *Community* acts and interpreting of Community acts in the light of the principle of equality. However, the Court of Justice has not limited itself to using general principles in this way. It has also said that when *Member States* are acting within the sphere of Community law (i.e. when they are implementing Community law[151] and when they are derogating from Community law[152]), their actions must also be compatible with fundamental rights, including equality. In future, as a result of the remarkable decision in *Mangold*,[153]

---

[146] Para. 29.   [147] Para. 30.

[148] Ibid. Cf. Joined Cases C–122/99P and C–125/99P *D* v. *Council* [2001] ECR I–4319, para. 47, considered at n. 133 above (the refusal by the EU Council to pay a household allowance payable to married couples to an employee in a stable homosexual partnership registered under Swedish law), the Court said '. . . as regards infringement if the principle of equal treatment of officials irrespective of their sexual orientation, it is clear that it is not the sex of the partner which determines whether the household allowance is granted, but the legal nature of ties between the official and the partner'.

[149] *Goodwin* v. *UK* (2002) 13 BHRC 120 and *I* v. *UK* [2002] 2 FCR 613.   [150] Para. 34.

[151] Case 5/88 *Wachauf* [1989] ECR 2609, para. 19 and Case C–2/92 *Bostock* [1994] ECR I–995, para. 16.

[152] Case C–260/89 *ERT* [1991] ECR 2925.

[153] Case C–144/04 *Mangold* v. *Helm* [2005] ECR I–000. Cf. Case C–212/04 *Adeneler* v. *ELOG* [2006] ECR I–000.

the validity of *national* acts in the sphere of Community law may also be subject to challenge on the grounds of the principle of equality.

Mangold concerned the German law implementing the Fixed Term Work Directive 99/70.[154] According to this law, a fixed term employment contract could be concluded only where there were objective grounds for so doing. However, until December 2006 (when the age discrimination provisions of the Framework Directive 2000/78[155] came into force) the need for objective justification did not apply to fixed term contracts for workers aged over 52. The Court of Justice upheld Mangold's challenge to this rule that it was discriminatory on the grounds of age. Even though the age discrimination provisions of the Directive had not yet come into force, the Court said the source of the principle of non-discrimination found in the Framework Directive was various international instruments and the constitutional traditions common in the Member States.[156] It continued: 'The principle of non-discrimination on grounds of age must thus be regarded as a general principle of Community law'[157] and the observance of this general principle could not be made conditional on the expiry of the transposition date of the Framework Directive.

Most striking of all, the Court indicated that general principles of law could be directly effective and enforceable in the national courts. The Court said that:

In those circumstances it is the responsibility of the national court, hearing a dispute involving the principle of non-discrimination in respect of age, to provide, in a case within its jurisdiction, the legal protection which individuals derive from the rules of Community law and to ensure that those rules are fully effective, setting aside any provision of national law which may conflict with that law.[158]

Thus, national courts had to provide a genuine and effective remedy to enforce a general principle of Community law which applied in a horizontal situation.[159]

3. Non-discrimination on Prohibited Grounds

3.1. Introduction

So far, we have focused on the 'Constitutional' use of equality as a general principle of law. In essence, it requires like situations to be treated with like unless there are objectively justified reasons why not. We turn now to consider how the law has fleshed out the equality principle in order to address specific long-standing entrenched inequalities between groups of persons (e.g. men/women, black/white, able-bodied/disabled). In this context, the law dis-

---

[154] OJ [1999] L175/43.   [155] OJ [2000] L303/16.   [156] Para. 74.
[157] Para. 75.   [158] Para. 77.
[159] See also AG Tizzano's opinion, para. 99ff. Cf. AG Geelhoed's Opinion in Case C–13/05 *Chacón Navas v. Eurest Colectividades SA* [2006] ECR I–000.

tinguishes between direct discrimination and indirect discrimination. Only indirectly discriminatory measures can be objectively justified.

3.2. Direct Discrimination

(a) The Principle

Direct or 'overt' discrimination involves one prohibited group being treated less favourably than another: in the case of *Macarthys*[160] this meant that the woman received less pay than the man doing the same job. As the Consolidated Directive 2006/54 puts it, direct discrimination is where 'one person is treated less favourably on the grounds of sex than another is, has been or would be treated in a comparable situation'.[161] Equivalent rules apply in respect of the other strands. The motive or intention to discriminate is not a necessary element of direct discrimination:[162] it is enough that that the adverse treatment is grounded upon, or caused by, a prohibited classification.[163] In English law this causation-based approach is reflected in the so-called 'but for' test recognized by the House of Lords in *James* v. *Eastleigh Borough Council*.[164] According to this test, 'but for' the person's sex/race, etc they would have enjoyed the more favourable treatment experienced by the comparator. Directly discriminatory measures are unlawful unless they can be saved by an express derogation. No such derogations can be found in respect of Article 141 but express derogations are found in the Equal Treatment Directives (see Figure 6.1).

(b) Can Direct Discrimination be Justified?

As mentioned above, the open–ended 'objective justification' applies only to *indirect* discrimination.[165] Can it ever apply to direct discrimination? The

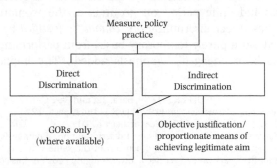

Figure 6.1 Discrimination: Overview

---

[160] Case 129/79 *Macarthys* v. *Smith* [1980] ECR 1275.   [161] Art. 2(1)(a).

[162] Case 69/80 *Worringham* v. *Lloyds Bank* [1981] ECR 767. See also AG Lenz in Case C–127/92 *Enderby* [1993] ECR I–5535, 5558.

[163] Ellis, above n. 2, 103.   [164] [1990] 3 WLR 55.

[165] The detail of objective justification is considered below. Cf. section C of Ch. 5.

orthodox answer—found in the Consolidated Directive and in the Article 13 Directives in respect of all strands, except age—is no.[166] Direct discrimination can be saved only by reference to the derogations expressly provided for by the legislation.

However, as we shall see further in the next chapter, the absence of any such derogations in Article 141 has generated particular difficulties. For example, in *Roberts*[167] the employer paid a former male employee a bridging pension between the ages of 60 and 65 but not a former female employee who received the equivalent from the state. The woman therefore received less pay from her employer than a man. Ostensibly she suffered direct discrimination but there were no derogations available for the employer. This prompted the Commission in *Roberts*[168] to follow the Continental view that direct discrimination could be objectively justified 'since the very concept of discrimination, whether direct or indirect, involves a difference in treatment which is unjustified'. The Advocate General, while noting that direct and indirect discrimination could not always be distinguished with clarity,[169] said that the Court had not ruled that direct discrimination could never be justified by objective factors,[170] making it arbitrary to permit the possibility of justifying a clear inequality of treatment dependent on whether that inequality was direct or indirect. On the other hand, in *Grant*[171] Advocate General Elmer reasserted the orthodox position. He said: 'direct discrimination cannot be justified by reference to objective circumstances'.

Although the Court did not expressly rule on this point in *Roberts*, in *Smith*[172] it did contemplate taking objective justification into account in the context of not applying the equality principle to pension benefits payable immediately post the *Barber* judgment.[173] Similarly, in *Webb*[174] the Court ruled in the context of the Equal Treatment Directive that the termination of a contract for an indefinite period on grounds of the woman's pregnancy, which constitutes direct discrimination *'cannot be justified* by the fact that she is prevented, on a purely temporary basis, from performing the work for which she has been engaged' (emphasis added). The implication of this

---

[166]   Case C–262/88 *Barber* [1990] ECR I–1889, para. 32, and Case C–177/88 *Dekker v. Stichting Vormingscentrum voor Junge Volwassen Plus* [1990] ECR I–3941, para. 12.

[167]   Case C–132/92 [1993] ECR I–5579. See further Ch. 10.   [168]   Ibid.

[169]   E.g. while *Roberts* looked like a case of direct discrimination, if emphasis were laid on the fact that the employer calculates the bridging pension in the same way but the result of such calculation is that for five years women receive a lower bridging pension, this constitutes indirect discrimination.

[170]   See e.g. Case C–217/91 *Spain v. Commission* [1993] ECR I–3923, para. 37: 'The principle of equal treatment viewed as a general principle of Community law requires that similar situations shall not be treated differently and that different situations shall not be treated in the same manner unless such differentiation is objectively justified'.

[171]   Case C–249/96 *Grant v. South West Trains* [1998] ECR I–621, para. 38.

[172]   Case C–408/92 [1994] ECR I–4435.   [173]   Paras. 30 and 31.

[174]   Case C–32/93 *Webb v. EMO Air Cargo* [1994] ECR I–3567.

statement is that termination of a fixed term contract on the grounds of pregnancy could be justified.[175] Although subsequent case law has removed this possibility in respect of pregnancy,[176] it does mark a further stage in the erosion of the clear distinction between direct and indirect discrimination. Does this matter? For most commentators, the answer is yes because, as Deakin and Morris put it, the application of the equality principle would become highly contingent, being dependent, in effect, on the courts' assessment of the justification defence in individual cases.[177]

Ellis has argued that those advocating that direct discrimination should be capable of being objectively justified misunderstand the structural elements of discrimination. Since discrimination means detrimental treatment which is grounded on sex, it consists of two elements—harm (adverse treatment) and causation (the grounding of that treatment in a prohibited classification).[178] The concept of justification is used in relation to indirect discrimination, where the root cause of the detrimental treatment is not clear and the defendant is seeking to show that its cause is unrelated to sex. The Court recognized this point in *Jørgensen*:[179]

Thus, once it is established that a measure adversely affects a much higher percentage of women than men, or vice versa, that measure will be presumed to constitute indirect discrimination on grounds of sex and it will be for the employer or the person who drafted the measure to prove the contrary.

Thus, if the adverse consequence to one group can be shown to be 'attributable to an acceptable and discrimination-neutral factor, then there is no discrimination'.[180] By contrast, in *direct* discrimination cases, where it is proved that the detrimental treatment is grounded upon the plaintiff's sex, cause has been established and there is no room to argue about justification.

Ellis also makes the practical point that the introduction of a concept of justification into direct discrimination would have the effect of extending the range of defences open to the employer in an open-ended manner contrary to the intentions of the drafters of the legislation,[181] and would seriously undermine discrimination law as it now stands.

---

[175] The justification will not include the financial loss which an employer who appointed a pregnant woman would suffer during her maternity leave (Case C–207/98 *Mahlburg* [2000] ECR I–549, para. 29).

[176] Case C–109/00 *Tele Danmark A/S v. Kontorfunktionaerernes Forbund I Danmark* [2001] ECR I–6993.

[177] Deakin and Morris, *Labour Law* (Hart Publishing, Oxford, 2005) para. 6.19. See also Bowers and Moran, 'Justification in Direct Sex Discrimination Law: Breaking the Taboo' (2002) 31 *ILJ*. 307 and the responses (2003) 32 *ILJ*. 115 and (2003) 32 *ILJ*. 185

[178] Above n. 2, 112.

[179] Case C–226/98 *Jørgensen v. Foreningen af Speciallæger and Sygesikringens Forhandlingsudvalg* [2000] ECR I–2447, para. 30.

[180] Ellis, above, n. 2, 112.

[181] See Ellis, 'The Definition of Discrimination in European Community Sex Equality Law' (1994) 19 *ELRev*. 563.

3.3. Indirect Discrimination

(a) The Definition of Indirect Discrimination

The notion of indirect discrimination is designed to target those measures which are discriminatory in *effect*. Talking in the context of sex discrimination, indirect discrimination arises when the application of a gender-neutral criterion or practice[182] in fact disadvantages a much higher percentage of women that men, unless that difference can be justified by objective factors unrelated to any discrimination on the grounds of sex.[183]

The Court's approach to indirect discrimination is neatly summed up in *Kachelmann*[184] where it said:

> . . . it is well settled that where national rules, although worded in neutral terms, work to the disadvantage of a much higher percentage of women than men, they discriminate indirectly against women, unless that difference in treatment is justified by objective factors unrelated to any discrimination on grounds of sex.

Thus, for a measure to be indirectly discriminatory *the Court* has required that (1) the apparently neutral rule or practice[185] (2) actually disadvantages (3) a considerably[186] higher percentage of women than men and (4) cannot be objectively justified by factors other than sex. The Court's approach has been used, but adapted, by the legislature. The first legislative definition was found in the Burden of Proof Directive 97/80[187] which provided that:

> . . . indirect discrimination shall exist where an apparently neutral provision, criterion or practice *disadvantages a substantially higher proportion* of the members of one sex, unless that provision, criterion or practice is appropriate and necessary and can be justified by objective factors unrelated to sex.[188]

The reference to '*disadvantages a substantially higher proportion*' emphasized the need for some statistical analysis. By contrast, the amended Equal Treatment Directive (and Article 2(1)(b) the Consolidated Directive) and the Article 13 Directives offer a somewhat different formulation. They provide that in the case of indirect discrimination:

> . . . an apparently neutral provision, criterion or practice *would put* persons of one sex at a *particular disadvantage* compared with persons of the other sex, unless that provision, criterion or practice is objectively justified by a legitimate aim, and the means of achieving that aim are appropriate and necessary.

---

[182] Case 170/84 *Bilka-Kaufhaus* [1986] ECR 1607; Case C–127/92 *Enderby* [1993] ECR I–5535.

[183] Case 171/88 *Rinner-Kühn* v. *FWW Spezial-Gebäudereinignung* [1989] ECR 2743.

[184] Cf. Case C–322/98 *Kachelmann* v. *Bankhaus Hermann Lampe KG* [2000] ECR I–7505, para. 23.

[185] Case C–127/92 *Enderby* v. *Frenchay Health Authority* [1993] ECR I–5535.

[186] Case C–236/98 *Jämställdhetsombudsmannen* v. *Örebro läns landsting* [2000] ECR I–2189, para. 50.

[187] OJ [1998] L14/6, amended by Directive 98/52/EC (OJ [1998] L205/66).

[188] Art. 2(2), emphasis added.

There are three important points of difference in this definition. First, there is a shift from showing actual disparate impact (as required by the ECJ and the Burden of Proof Directive) to potential disparate impact. Second, the emphasis on statistical analysis (as strongly required by the ECJ, less strongly by the Burden of Proof Directive) is reduced, if not removed altogether. Thirdly, the language of justification is differently formulated. For the purposes of this chapter, we shall work with the definition contained in the Article 13 Directives and the Consolidated Directive but with reference to the other definitions where appropriate.

(b) 'Provision, Criterion or Practice'

The first requirement—that there be a provision, criterion or practice—is derived from *Enderby*[189] where the Court talked freely of 'measure' and 'practice' without distinguishing between the terms. The phrase is deliberately broad and catches both legal and non-legal requirements. Cases do not usually fail at this hurdle.[190]

(c) '. . . Would Put Persons of One Sex at a Particular Disadvantage'

Introduction

It will be recalled that the Revised Equal Treatment Directive, the Consolidated Directive and the Article 13 Directives define indirect discrimination in terms of the potential *disadvantage* experienced by the protected group, language which is derived from the test of indirect discrimination laid down in *O'Flynn*.[191] This compares with the requirement of 'substantially higher proportion' in the Burden of Proof Directive and 'considerably larger' or 'considerably smaller' used by the Court—both requiring actual disparate impact. To what extent does this change of words make a difference?

First, the shift from actual to potential disparate impact recognises that in some areas common sense would dictate that there may well be disparate impact but it is difficult to obtain statistical proof (particularly in those countries which prohibit the collection of data on sensitive issues such as race). Second—and related to the first—the absence of references to 'significantly larger' or 'smaller' seems to rule out the mandatory use of statistics to show disparate impact. As the Commission says in its explanatory memorandum, the new test for indirect discrimination may be proven on the basis of statistical evidence or by any other means that demonstrate that a provision would be intrinsically disadvantageous for the person or persons concerned. This point is confirmed in the preamble to the sex Directive 2002/73:

---

[189] Case C–127/92 [1993] ECR I–5535.
[190] See, eg. in the UK context *British Airways* v. *Starmer* [2005] IRLR 863: an ad hoc decision of an employer constituted a provision, criterion or practice.
[191] Case C–237/94 *O'Flynn* v. *Adjudication Officer* [1996] ECR I–2617, para. 18, considered in Ch. 4. COM(99) 565.

'[National] rules may provide in particular for indirect discrimination to be established by any means including on the basis of statistical evidence'.[192] This view is shared by the British government which says[193] that 'Employment Tribunals will still need to consider whether a provision, criterion or practice causes disadvantage to a particular group of people. Statistics could be helpful in establishing evidence of particular disadvantage, although the new test makes clear that such evidence could also come from experts or other witnesses.'[194] So the new test does not altogether do away with the need to identify advantaged and disadvantaged groups and thus a need to construct a pool from which these groups are drawn. For this reason we shall now examine some of the older case law examining these requirements, but always bearing in mind that the new approach is intended to encourage national courts and the ECJ to take a more flexible approach.

Selecting the Pool

It is important to identify the group or groups of workers that are to be used for the purposes of comparing the treatment of men and women. Indirect discrimination is detected by showing that the impact of a practice on women—as a group—is greater than the effect on men. It is often critical to identify which groups of workers are to be used for that comparison. Generally, in the case of discrimination alleged against an *employer*, the pool is drawn from the undertaking where workers perform or performed comparable work.[195] However, when discriminatory *legislation* is at issue, then the pool is generally the workforce as a whole or at least workers throughout the country satisfying the requirements of the particular rule. Thus, in *Allonby*[196] the Court was asked to consider whether the requirement of being an 'employee' (a narrower concept in English law than 'worker' as defined by Community law) engaged as a teacher in a specified category of educational institution (which included Allonby's college) in order to be a member of the Teachers' Superannuation Scheme (TSS) (a condition deriving from state rules) was indirectly discriminatory against women. The Court took as the pool teachers across the country who were workers within the meaning of Article 141(1) and who fulfilled all the conditions of membership of the pension scheme except that of being employed under a contract of employment.[197]

The choice of the pool is usually a matter for the national court or tribunal but it is an issue that has bedevilled indirect discrimination case law. The

---

[192] Para. 10.
[193] *Equality   and   Diversity: Updating   the   Sex   Discrimination   Act*:   http://www. womenandequalityunit. gov.uk/publications/consultation.pdf
[194] Para. 23.
[195] See, e.g., Case C–256/01 *Allonby v. Accrington & Rosendale College* [2004] ECR I–000, para. 74.
[196] Ibid.   [197] Para. 75.

British case of *Rutherford*[198] provides a very good example of just how difficult it is to determine the correct pool. Rutherford, aged 67, was dismissed but he was prevented from bringing a claim for unfair dismissal/redundancy because the British statute precluded claims brought by those over 65. This, he argued, was indirectly discriminatory against men. The Industrial Tribunal agreed and said that 8 per cent of men over 65 were economically active (in employment or available to work) which was considerably higher than the 3 per cent of women. However, the Employment Appeal Tribunal allowed the appeal on the basis that a 5 per cent difference was not considerably higher and remitted the case to the tribunal. The Employment Tribunal took the new pool of those aged between 55 and 74 (i.e. those for whom retirement had real meaning) and concluded that the relevant measures disadvantaged a substantially higher proportion of men than women. However, the EAT again allowed the Secretary of State's appeal and said that the appropriate pool was those aged between 16 and 79 with one year's continuous service. In applying these statistics 98.88 per cent of men could comply as compared with 99.01 per cent of women. Therefore, there was no disparate impact. This approach was upheld by Court of Appeal. The House of Lords was also divided on this issue[199] and gave five different speeches from which it is not easy to extract 'a single easily stated principle'.[200] They did, however, all agree that there was no indirect discrimination, either because there was no discrimination at all or because the disparate impact was too small.

This case demonstrates that, in widening the pool, Rutherford's claim was undermined because, while there were more men than women in the category of older workers, the proportions of the sexes in the workforce as a whole was almost identical. At the other end of the spectrum, if the pool is too small then this might also undermine the individual's claim. This can be seen in the controversial decision of the British Court of Appeal in *Coker v. Lord Chancellor*.[201] The Lord Chancellor appointed his friend, Gary Hart, a partner in a City law firm, to be his special adviser. The post was never advertised and it was accepted that the Lord Chancellor did not look outside his personal acquaintances for the appointment. Jane Coker, a solicitor, unsuccessfully complained of indirect discrimination. The Court of Appeal said that if a requirement excluded almost the entirety of the pool (on the facts, the members of the pool were reduced to a single man—Hart) it could not constitute indirect discrimination; it could only have a discriminatory effect if a significant proportion of the pool were able to satisfy the requirement. However, as Pannick points out, the principle of disparate impact is not intended to make individuals' rights dependent on the arbitrary factors of where they work, and the number of men and women who do particular jobs there.[202]

---

[198] *Secretary of State for Trade and Industry v. Rutherford (No.2)* [2004] IRLR 892.
[199] [2006] UKHL 19.   [200] Lord Walker, para. 70.   [201] [2002] IRLR 80.
[202] *Sex Discrimination Law* (OUP, Oxford, 1985) 47.

Determining Disparate Impact

Once the pool has been established the Court then needs to determine whether the rule has a disparate impact on (i.e. puts at a particular disadvantage) the protected group. How can this be shown? Taking as our starting point *Seymour-Smith*[203] where, in a case concerning the issue of whether a two-year service requirement[204] prior to bringing a claim for unfair dismissal in the UK was indirectly discriminatory against women contrary to Article 141, the parties presented the Court with four ways of considering the question of disparate impact[205] (the case arose before the new approach was adopted by the legislature). The first was a rule-of-thumb of the kind adopted in the US Equal Employment Opportunity Commission (EEOC) Uniform Guidelines on Employee Selection Procedures.[206] These state that a selection rate for any race, sex or ethnic group which is less than four-fifths (80 per cent) of the group with the highest rate will generally be regarded as evidence of adverse impact. Smaller differences in selection rates may nevertheless constitute adverse impact where they are 'significant' in both statistical and practical terms or where a user's actions have discouraged applicants disproportionately. This rule has the advantage of being relatively easy to apply.

The second option was an impressionistic or 'eyeball' approach which asks, as the original British Sex Discrimination Act 1975 did, whether the difference in impact is 'considerable'. In *Seymour-Smith* the UK government argued for this approach, attaching to the word 'considerable' the meaning of a 'large disparity'. The advantage of this approach is that it does not rely solely on numbers, which may be an unreliable guide since they depend upon the size and male/female composition of the employer's workforce or (in the case of a legislative measure) the national labour force.

A third approach, for which the applicants argued in *Seymour-Smith*, is to ask whether there is an inherent risk that a measure adopted by a Member State will have a disparate impact as between men and women.[207] This approach has the advantage of allowing the tribunal to use its general knowledge and to look outside the pool for comparison to take account of social facts, such as the fact that 10 times as many women as men are likely to be

---

[203] Case C–167/97 [1999] ECR I–623.

[204] The two-year service requirement has now been reduced to one year by SI 1999/1436, Unfair Dismissal and Statement of Reasons for Dismissal (Variation of Qualifying Period) Order 1999.

[205] This is taken from Barnard and Hepple, 'Indirect discrimination: interpreting *Seymour-Smith*' (1999) 58 *CLJ*. 399.

[206] *Federal Register*, Vol. 43, No. 166, 25 August 1978.

[207] [1999] IRLR 253, 258. This accords with the important decision of the Court of Appeal in *London Underground Ltd* v. *Edwards* [1998] IRLR 364 upholding a tribunal finding that a rostering system requiring an early morning start had an adverse impact on women with family responsibilities, even though only one of 21 women train drivers positively complained about the arrangements.

single parents and responsible for a child. The language used in *O'Flynn* and the Equal Treatment Directives would support this approach.[208]

The fourth approach, for which the European Commission argued in *Seymour-Smith*, was to adopt a 'statistically significant' test, whereby a provision is indirectly discriminatory where it affects a significantly different number of members of one sex.[209] This test was said to enable the national court to determine whether a difference in impact is due to a mere chance or whether it reflects a social fact or structural phenomenon.

The Court did not consider the first of these options (the four-fifths rule), and failed to give any clear guidelines as to whether the second, third, or fourth options was to be preferred. Instead, the Court suggested that there were two ways of judging disparate impact. The first, found at paragraph 60, was to consider whether a 'considerably smaller proportion of women than men' was able to satisfy the two-year requirement (i.e. the second or third option).[210] It then went on to adopt a test of statistical significance (the fourth option).[211] It said that in 1985, the year in which the requirement of two years' employment was introduced, 77.4 per cent of men and 68.9 per cent of women fulfilled that condition.[212] According to the Court, such statistics did not appear, on the face of it, to show that a considerably smaller percentage of women than men was able to fulfil the requirement imposed by the disputed rule.[213] The Court seems to be equating statistical significance with a 'considerable' difference, since, where the sample is relatively small, a difference of less than 10 per cent is insufficient to prove indirect sex discrimination.[214]

At paragraph 61 it then proposed a second, alternative test for disparate impact. It said that there would be evidence of apparent sex discrimination 'if the statistical evidence revealed a lesser but persistent and relatively constant disparity over a long period between men and women who satisfy the requirement of two years' employment'. The Court did not have the evidence to propose an answer to the paragraph 61 test.[215]

What is clear from this decision is that the Court attached considerable weight to the need to produce statistics to show indirect discrimination. However, these statistics must be valid: i.e. they must cover enough individuals,

---

[208] See also Case C–25/01 *Rinke v. Ärztekammer Hamburg* [2003] ECR I–8349, para. 35 where, after considering the statistics produced, the Advocate General said 'That fact [the percentage of women working part-time is much higher than that of men working on a part-time basis], which can be explained in particular by the unequal division of domestic tasks between women and men, shows that a much higher percentage of women than men wishing to train in general medicine have difficulties in working full-time during part of their training.'

[209] Para. 57.   [210] Para. 60.   [211] Para. 62.   [212] Para. 63.   [213] Para. 64.

[214] For criticisms of this approach see Barnard and Hepple, above, n. 205.

[215] When the case returned to the House of Lords the majority considered that the para. 61 test, but not the para. 60 test, had been satisfied. Therefore, there was evidence of indirect discrimination but that it was not unlawful because it could be objectively justified.

they must not illustrate purely fortuitous or short-term phenomena, and appear, in general, to be significant.[216] In *Jørgensen* the statistics failed to satisfy these requirements. The case concerned a reorganization of medical practices based on turnover which, Jørgensen argued, was indirectly discriminatory against women. The Court noted that the application affected only 22 specialized medical practitioners, of whom 14 were women, out of a total of 1,680, of whom 302 were women. The Court concluded that 'It seems doubtful that such data could be treated as significant.'[217]

Assuming the statistics are significant, what can they show? They can show how many people (the qualifiers) *can* comply with the requirement (the so-called 'success rates' approach) or how many people (the non-qualifiers) *cannot* comply with the requirement (the so-called 'failure rates' approach). The first focuses on the proportion of men and women who are able to benefit. The second considers the proportion of men and women within the group who cannot obtain the benefit to determine whether the proportion of women in the disadvantaged group is greater than the proportion of men and, in particular, whether the proportion of women in the disadvantaged group is higher than the proportion of women in the workforce generally, which might indicate that the practice does adversely affect women more than men.

The difference between these approaches was highlighted by Lord Nicholls in the House of Lords in *Barry* v. *Midland Bank*.[218] He took the example of an employer whose workforce of 1,000 employees comprised an equal number of men and women. In his example, 10 per cent of the staff (100 people) worked part time and of these 90 per cent were women. If the employer offered a pension or redundancy scheme that favoured full-time workers would this be indirectly discriminatory? If the success rates question was asked (how many men and women can comply with the requirement to work full time?) the answer would be 98 per cent of men (490/500) and 82 per cent of women (410/500) could comply with the requirement. A difference of 16 per cent would probably satisfy the paragraph 60 test of whether a 'considerably smaller proportion of women than men' could satisfy the two-year requirement (although not the EEOC rule of thumb guidelines).

However, if the failure rates question was asked (how many men and women cannot satisfy the requirement of working full time?) the figures are much more stark: 2 per cent of men (10/500) compared with 18 per cent of women (90/500) would be disadvantaged, a ratio of 1:9. Putting it another way, of those who were non-qualifiers 10 per cent were men and 90 per cent were women. Some have argued that the language of 'disadvantage' used

---

[216] Case C–226/98 *Jørgensen* v. *Foreningen af Speciallæger and Sygesikringens Forhandlingsudvalg* [2000] ECR I–2447, para. 33.
[217] Para. 33.   [218] [1999] IRLR 581.

in the Burden of Proof Directive, the Consolidated Directive and the Article 13 Directives favours the failure rates approach. However, such arguments have not found favour with the British courts.[219]

In *Seymour-Smith* the Court seemed to accept an amalgam of the 'can' and 'cannot' comply tests. It said that the best approach to comparing statistics was to consider:

[o]n the one hand, the respective proportions of men in the workforce *able* to satisfy the requirement of two years' employment under the disputed rule and of those *unable* to do so, and on the other, to compare those proportions as regards women in the workforce.[220]

However, the later part of the judgment focused, especially in paragraph 60, on the success rates 'can' comply test.[221] More recently, the British House of Lords in *Rutherford* has also preferred the success rates test.

Seymour-Smith also considered the question of when the discrimination should be judged. The statistics in this case showed that over the period 1985 to 1993 the proportion of men and women who had two years' or more service with their current employer ranged for men, from a minimum of 72.5 per cent to a maximum of 78.4 per cent, and for women from a minimum of 63.8 per cent to a maximum of 74.1 per cent. Throughout the period 1985 to 1991 the ratio of the proportion of men qualified to the proportion of women qualified was about 10:9 reducing to about 20:19 in 1993. Therefore, the disparate impact appears to have diminished over time. This makes it crucial to determine the moment in time at which the disparate impact test is to be applied, not least because the objective justification which existed at one time may not exist at another. The Court failed to give an unequivocal answer to this question, preferring to throw it back to the national court, stating that 'the point in time at which the legality of a rule of the kind at issue in this case is to be assessed by the national court may depend on various circumstances, both factual and legal'.[222] It was suggested that if the legislator was alleged to have acted *ultra vires* (as in these judicial review proceedings), then this was in principle the time when the rule was adopted[223] but in cases of application of the rule to an individual, it was the time of application which is relevant.

Intention

In its earliest case law, the Court required discriminatory intention by the employer before the indirect discrimination was declared unlawful. For

---

[219] *Secretary of State for Trade and Industry* v. *Rutherford (No. 2)* [2003] IRLR 858 and [2004] IRLR 892; although cf. Lord Nicholls in the House of Lords [2006] UKHL 19.

[220] Para. 59 (emphasis added).

[221] See also Case C–236/98 *Jämställdhetsombudsmannen* v. *Örebro läns landsting* [2000] ECR I–2189, paras. 50–1.

[222] Para. 46.   [223] Para. 47 and implicit in para. 63.

example, in *Jenkins*,[224] a case where part time workers received a lower hourly rate than full time workers, the Court required national courts to look at the employer's intention[225] to see whether discrimination had occurred. Confining indirect discrimination to intentional acts only would have significantly limited its effectiveness. However, in *Bilka-Kaufhaus*[226] the Court recognized that the prohibition on discrimination also included *unintentional* indirect discrimination, that is, it covers those situations where the employer does not intend to discriminate but the effects of any policy are discriminatory.[227]

(d) '. . . Unless that Provision, Criterion or Practice is Justified by a Legitimate Aim, and the Means of Achieving that Aim are Appropriate and Necessary'

As we saw in *Jämo*,[228] the Court of Justice has long recognized that indirect discrimination can be objectively justified on grounds other than sex. Thus, once the applicant has established that the measure is indirectly discriminatory the burden shifts to the defendant to show that the measure is justified, by objective factors unrelated to sex, and the steps taken are proportionate. The Court's approach was replicated in the Burden of Proof Directive which provided that indirect discriminatory practices could be 'justified by objective factors unrelated to sex, provided that the practices were 'appropriate and necessary'.[229] The new approach, which requires the practice to be 'justified by a legitimate aim, and the means of achieving that aim are appropriate and necessary', follows the classic formulation in *Bilka-Kaufhaus*:[230] that the measures chosen must 'correspond to a real need on the part of the undertaking, are appropriate with a view to achieving the objectives pursued and are necessary to that end'. The new approach drops the requirement that the justification must be 'on grounds other than sex', prompting some to suggest that a legitimate aim could be sex, race etc related. Others argue that the strong trend in the case law that the justification must not be connected to the protected ground rules out any such suggestion.

Given the importance of objective justification, especially in the context of equal pay, it will be considered in more detail in the next chapter.

---

[224] Case 96/80 [1981] ECR 911.

[225] Para. 14. The employer, who had previously paid men and women at different rates, changed his system so that he paid part-time workers, the majority of whom were women, less than full-time workers. There was a concern that the employer had replaced a directly discriminatory system by an intentionally indirectly discriminatory system.

[226] Case 170/84 [1986] ECR 1607; Case 171/88 *Rinner-Kühn* [1989] ECR 2743.

[227] The culpability of the employer should be reflected in the remedy.

[228] Case C–236/98 *Jämställdhetsombudsmannen* v. *Örebro läns landsting* [2000] ECR I–2189, para. 50.

[229] Case 96/80 *Jenkins* [1981] ECR 911, para. 114. See Hervey, 'Justification of Indirect Sex Discrimination in Employment: European Community Law and United Kingdom Law Compared' (1991) 40 *ICLQ* 807 and *Justifications for Sex Discrimination in Employment* (Butterworths, London, 1993) Ch. 8; Vick, 'Disparate Effects and Objective justifications in Sex Discrimination Law' (2001) 5 *International Journal of Discrimination and the Law* 3.

[230] Case 170/84 [1986] ECR 1607, para. 36.

3.4. Conclusions

In the 1970s sex equality Directives, the principles of direct and indirect discrimination were the main pillars of protection for individuals. In the 'younger' Directives, the legislature deemed other conduct to be discriminatory including harassment and instructions to discriminate. The inclusion of these concepts, which are discussed in detail in the next two chapters, together with the prohibition of victimization and the duty of reasonable accommodation in respect of disability, is a reminder that equality law is not simply about formal equality but also about protecting a person's dignity at work. We shall now turn to consider the values underpinning Community equality law.

D. FORMAL AND SUBSTANTIVE EQUALITY

1. The Formal Equality Model

At one level, equality is about protecting the dignity and autonomy of the *individual*. This is perhaps the most prevalent view of equality: people should be treated according to their own merits and characteristics; irrelevant factors such as gender or race should not be taken into account. So decisions taken on the basis of stereotypes undermine a person's dignity and autonomy and thus the principle of equality.[231] This perspective most closely maps on to what is described as the formal equality model which requires, for example, women to be treated like men and ethnic minorities like whites. In law, this perspective is embodied in the concept of direct discrimination. The strength of this approach is that it assumes that men and women/ethnic minorities and whites, etc are equal and so should be paid the same and treated in the same way, irrespective of any dissimilarities they posses. As Ellis puts it, this is frequently referred to as the 'merit' principle: individuals ought to be rewarded according to their merit and not according to stereotypical assumptions made about them on account of the group to which they belong.[232]

This approach also characterizes what Deakin and Morris describe as 'equality within the market order'. According to this concept, the principal aim is to do what is necessary to ensure free and equal competition in the labour market, but to regulate outcomes in terms of the distribution of economic and social resources as little as possible.[233] This approach is particularly resonant in the EU, with its origins in the creation of a common, now single, market.

---

[231] Values such as these are did influence the Court of Justice in Case C–13/94 *P v. S* [1996] ECR I–2143, para. 22 where it said that to tolerate discrimination on the grounds of gender reassignment would be 'tantamount, as regards such a person, to a failure to respect the dignity and freedom to which he or she is entitled, and which the Court has a duty to safeguard'.

[232] Ellis, above n. 2, 5.   [233] *Labour Law* (Hart Publishing, Oxford, 2005) 581.

There are three main criticisms of the formal equality approach. First, hidden behind the apparent neutrality is a reality which is white, straight, and male. For women, it disregards the context in which many find themselves, balancing work with domestic and caring responsibilities.[234] This can be seen in *Hofman*[235] where the Court made clear that Directive 76/207 was not 'designed to settle questions concerning the organisation of the family or to alter the division of responsibility between parents'[236] and in *Helmig*[237] the Court ruled that there was no discrimination when part timers, who were predominantly women, did not receive overtime rates for hours worked over their normal contractual hours but less than the full-time hours, even though the social consequences for part timers to work one hour's overtime is likely to be more disruptive than for full timers.[238] These decisions serve to highlight the fact that while the Court will require non-discrimination in the world of work, it has been reluctant to look at the effects of its decisions in the domestic sphere. The creation of an artificial distinction between the world of work and the family further prejudices the many women who are not 'well-assimilated' to the male norm and denies them *de facto* equality.[239]

Second, the concept of formal equality embodies a notion of procedural justice which does not guarantee any particular outcome. So there is no violation of the principle if an employer treats white and black workers equally badly. A claim to equal treatment can be satisfied by depriving both the persons compared of a particular benefit (levelling down) as well as by conferring the benefit on them both (levelling up).[240]

Third, the formal equality model is also dependent on a comparator: it is impossible for a woman to achieve equal pay for work of equal value if there

---

[234] See further Mackinnon, *Feminism Unmodified—Discourses on Life and Law* (Harvard University Press, Cambridge, Mass., 1987) 32–45; Mackinnon, 'Reflections on Sex Equality under Law' (1991) 100 *Yale Law Journal* 1281; on the British Sex Discrimination Act 1975, see Lacey, 'Legislation against Sex Discrimination—Questions from a Feminist Perspective' (1987) 14 *Journal of Law and Society* 411. See generally Mancini and O'Leary, 'The New Frontiers of Sex Equality Law in the European Union' (1999) 24 *ELRev.* 331

[235] Case 184/83 *Hofman* v. *Barmer Ersatzkasse* [1984] ECR 3047. See Hervey and Shaw, 'Women, Work and Care: Women's Dual Role and Double Burden in EC Sex Equality Law' (1998) 8 *Journal of European Social Policy Law* 43.

[236] See also Case 170/84 *Bilka-Kaufhaus* v. *Weber von Hartz* [1986] ECR 1607 where the Court stopped short of imposing a positive requirement on companies to organize their occupational pension schemes in such a way as to accommodate the needs of their employees, and Case C–297/93 *Grau-Hupka* v. *Stadtgemeinde Bremen* [1994] ECR I–5535 where the Court said that since Community law on equal treatment did not oblige Member States to take into account in calculating the statutory pension years spent bringing up children, the national rules also did not breach Art. 141.

[237] Case C–399/92 *Stadt Lengerich* v. *Helmig* [1994] ECR I–5727. On the serious consequences of this decision, see the House of Lords' decision in *Barry* v. *Midland Bank* [1999] IRLR 581. However cf. Case C–285/02 *Elsner-Lakeberg* v. *Land Nordrhein-Westfalen* [2004] ECR I–000.

[238] See Rubinstein [1995] IRLR 183. These cases are considered further in Ch. 9.

[239] See Cullen, 'The Subsidiary Woman' (1994) 16 *JSWL* 407, 408.

[240] E.g., Case C–408/92 *Smith* v. *Avdel* [1994] ECR I–4435 (raising of pension age for women to the same as that for men satisfies principle of equal treatment).

is no male comparator in her establishment or an establishment of the same employer with common terms and conditions of employment.[241] Further, the choice of comparators can be determinative of the claim. So where a travel concession was denied to the lesbian partner of a female employee, in *Grant*, the ECJ made the comparison with the way in which the male partner of a gay employee would have been treated. Since the gay man would have been treated in the same way, there was no discrimination.[242] Had the comparator been a male employee with a female partner, she would have received the travel concession and this would have revealed a breach of the principle of equal treatment.[243]

The need for a comparator is particularly unrealistic when a male comparator has to be sought in claims of unequal treatment on grounds of pregnancy or childbirth.[244] Consequently the limited, formal notion of equality adopted by the law can assist only the minority who are able to conform to the male stereotype but cannot reach or correct underlying structural impediments.[245] Thus, as Fredman puts it, the formal equality model reinforces the liberal ideas of 'the primacy of the neutrality of law, the rights of the individual as individual, and the freedom of the market'.[246] Further, she argues, equal treatment of individuals who are not socially equal perpetuates inequalities.[247] This prompts some to advocate the need for steps to remedy *group* disadvantage.

2. The Substantive Equality Model

Women, ethnic minorities, homosexuals, and the disabled have suffered from a history of *group* disadvantage which requires more radical, group-based action to remedy. Thus, unlike the individualist perspective where a person's sex/race, etc is considered an *irrelevant* factor, the group based disadvantage perspective considers these factors to be *relevant* and requires decisions to be taken based on the real situation of the protected group.[248] Some commentators describe this as 'substantive equality', one aimed at achieving equality of

---

[241] Equal Pay Act 1970, s. 1(6). EC law appears to be slightly wider allowing a comparison with those in the same (public) service: *Scullard* v. *Knowles* [1996] IRLR 344, E.A.T.; cf. *Lawrence* v. *Regent Office Care Ltd.* [1999] IRLR 148, E.A.T.

[242] Case C–249/96 *Grant* v. *South West Trains* [1998] IRLR 165.

[243] See C. Barnard, 'The Principle of Equality in the Community Context: *P*, *Grant*, *Kalanke* and *Marschall*: Four Uneasy Bedfellows?' (1998) 57 *CLJ*. 352–373 at 364–6.

[244] See S. Fredman, *Women and the Law* (Clarendon Press, Oxford, 1997) 179–224.

[245] Fredman, 'European Community Discrimination Law' (1992) 21 *ILJ* 119, 121.

[246] Fredman, *Women and the Law* (Clarendon Press, Oxford, 1997) 383.

[247] Fredman, 'Reversing Discrimination' (1997) 113 *LQR* 575.

[248] Fenwick and Hervey, 'Sex Equality in the Single Market: New Directions for the European Court of Justice' (1995) 32 *CMLRev*. 443, 445.

outcome or results.[249] Writing in the context of sex discrimination, Fredman[250] explains that equality of results can itself be used in three different senses. The first focuses on the impact of apparently equal treatment on the individual. The second is concerned with the results on a group (e.g. women, ethnic minorities, etc), and the third demands an outcome which is equal, for example equal pay for women doing work of equal value with that of men or equal representation of women and men in the same grade.

The concept of indirect discrimination is results-oriented in the first sense, in that the treatment must be detrimental to an individual, but it also involves equality of results in the second sense (i.e. that an apparently neutral practice has an unjustifiable adverse disparate impact upon the group to which the individual belongs). However, the concept of indirect discrimination is not redistributive in the third sense. If there is no exclusionary practice or criterion, or if no significant disparate impact can be shown, or if there is an objective business or administrative justification for the practice, then there is no breach.

An approach which is more results-oriented in a redistributive sense is to define equality in terms of 'fair' (sometimes referred to as 'full') participation of groups in the workforce. This aims to overcome under-representation of disadvantaged groups in the workplace and to ensure their fair share in the distribution of benefits. This may involve special measures to overcome disadvantage. Thus in Northern Ireland, 'affirmative action' designed 'to secure fair participation in employment by members of the Protestant, or members of the Roman Catholic, community in Northern Ireland'[251] has been a cornerstone of the legislation against religious discrimination since the Fair Employment Act 1989. A similar redistributive approach is taken by the Canadian Employment Equity Act 1995, which utilizes the concept of 'employment equity' to indicate that equality 'means more than treating persons in the same way but requires special measures and the accommodation of differences'.[252] In the EU Article 141(4) talks of 'full equality in practice' yet the precise scope of this is far from clear.[253]

---

[249] In Case C–136/95 *Caisse Nationale d'Assurance Vieillesse des Travailleurs Salariés (CNAVTS)* v. *Évelyne Thibault* [1998] ECR I–2011 the Court claimed that the result pursued by the Directive was substantive, not formal, equality (para. 26).

[250] Fredman, 'A Critical Review of the Concept of Equality in U.K. Anti-Discrimination Law', Independent Review of the Enforcement of U.K. Anti-Discrimination Legislation, Working Paper No. 3, (Cambridge Centre for Public Law and Judge Institute of Management Studies, November 1999), paras. 3.7–3.19. This section is taken from Barnard and Hepple, 'Substantive Equality' (2000) 59 *CLJ* 562.

[251] FETO, Art.4(1); based on the White Paper, Northern Ireland Office, *Fair Employment in Northern Ireland* (HMSO, London, 1988, Cm. 3890). The FETO does not define 'fair participation'. The Fair Employment Commission (now merged in the Equality Commission for Northern Ireland), which administered the legislation, adopted an interpretation which involves redressing imbalances and under-representation between the two communities in Northern Ireland. The aims are to secure greater fairness in the distribution of jobs and opportunities and to reduce the relative segregation of the two communities at work.

[252] Employment Equity Act 1995 [Can.], s. 2.   [253] Considered further in Ch. 8.

Positive action—and more radically positive discrimination—provide perhaps the best example of measures intended to achieve substantive equality, often at the price of formal equality. The original Article 2(4) of Directive 76/207 permitted positive action and it was relied on by the Court in *Marschall*[254] to uphold the state's law which gave preference to a woman in a tie-break situation, subject to a saving clause operating in favour of the man. The Court said that this national rule was compatible with (the original) Article 2(4) because:

even where male and female candidates are equally qualified, male candidates tend to be promoted in preference to female candidates particularly because of prejudices and stereotypes concerning the role and capacities of women in working life and the fear, for example, that women will interrupt their careers more frequently, that owing to household and family duties they will be less flexible in their working hours, or that they will be absent from work more frequently because of pregnancy, childbirth and breastfeeding.[255] For these reasons, the mere fact that a male candidate and a female candidate are equally qualified does not mean that they have the same chances.[256]

This case is not an isolated example. On a number of occasions the Court has said, as in *Thibault*,[257] that 'the result pursued by the Directive [76/207] is substantive, not formal, equality'. This change in approach from *Hofman* and *Helmig* to *Marschall* and *Thibault* may in turn reflect something of a change in the European Union's self-perception from being a European *Economic* Community to a Union based on solidarity[258] and social inclusion[259] where attempts need to be made to accommodate those—particularly women with

---

[254] Case C–409/95 *Marschall v. Land Nordrhein-Westfalen* [1997] ECR I–6363. Cf. Case C–450/93 *Kalanke v. Stadt Bremen* [1995] ECR I–3051. These cases are considered in detail in Ch. 8.

[255] See also the views of the Federal Labour Court when the *Kalanke* case returned to it (No. 226), Urteil of 5 March 1996–1 AZR 590/92 (A). It said that it was impossible to distinguish between opportunity and result, especially in the case of engagement and promotion because the selection itself was influenced by circumstances, expectations, and prejudices that typically diminish the chances of women.

[256] Paras. 29 and 30.

[257] Case C–136/94 [1998] ECRI–2011, repeated in Case C–207/98 *Mahlburg v. Land Mecklenburg-Vorpommern* [2000] ECR I–549, para. 26; Case C–284/02 *Land Brandenburg v. Sass* [2004] ECR I–11143, para. 34. See also Case 109/88 *Handels- og Kontorfunktionærernes Forbund i Danmark v. Dansk Arbejdsgiverforening, acting on behalf of Danfoss (Danfoss)* [1989] ECR 3199 where the Court ruled that a criterion rewarding employees' mobility—their adaptability to variable hours and places of work—may work to the disadvantage of female employees who, because of household and family duties, are not as able as men to organize their working time with such flexibility. Similarly, the criterion of training may work to the disadvantage of women in so far as they have had less opportunity than men for training or have taken less advantage of that opportunity. In both cases the employer may only justify the remuneration of such adaptability or training by showing it is of importance for the performance of specific tasks entrusted to the employee.

[258] Barnard, 'The Future of Equality Law: Equality and beyond?' in Barnard *et al.*, *The Future of Labour Law* (Hart Publishing, Oxford, 2004).

[259] Collins, 'Human Rights; Employment Discrimination, Equality and Social Inclusion' (2003) 66 *MLR* 16. See also Hepple, 'Race and Law in Fortress Europe' (2004) 67 *MLR* 1.

caring responsibilities—who have so far been excluded from the labour market.

3. The EU Model of Equality: Equal Opportunities

Falling somewhere between formal and substantive equality lies the notion of equality of opportunity. Fredman points out that 'using the graphic metaphor of competitors in a race, [this approach] asserts that true equality cannot be achieved if individuals begin the race from different starting points. An equal opportunities approach therefore aims to equalise the starting point . . .'.[260] The EU has expressly endorsed the equal opportunities approach.[261] But what does it mean? The *procedural* view of equal opportunities involves the removal of obstacles or barriers, such as word-of-mouth recruitment or non-job-related selection criteria. This opens up more opportunities but does 'not guarantee that more women or minorities will in fact be in a position to take advantage of those opportunities' because their capacities have been limited by the effects of social disadvantage.[262]

A more substantive approach to equality of opportunity would require a range of other special measures to compensate for disadvantages. These measures might include positive action (see above) and positive duties being imposed on employers to 'promote equality of opportunity'.[263] Elements of this positive duty can also be detected in Article 1a of the Equal Treatment Amendment Directive 2002/73 (Article 29 of the Consolidated Directive) which provides that 'Member States shall actively take into account the objective of equality between men and women when formulating and implementing laws, regulations, administrative provisions, policies and activities'. Measures which tackle inequality in the labour market, such as specific rights for part-time workers and workers on fixed-term contracts (predominantly women) may also be substantive in nature, but as we shall see in chapter 9 they have been framed in EC Directives and UK law in terms of a principle of formal equality.

---

[260] Fredman, Working Paper (n. 250 above), para.3.12.
[261] See Art. 2(4) of Dir. 76/207 and Art. 1 of the Consolidated Dir. 2006/54 and Case C–450/93 *Kalanke v. Freie und Hansestadt Bremen* [1995] ECR I–3051, para. 23.
[262] Fredman, Working Paper (n. 250 above), para.3.13.
[263] FETO, Art. 5 provides that a person of any religious belief has equality of employment opportunity with a person of any other religious belief if he or she 'has the same opportunity . . . as that other person has or would have . . . due allowance being made for any material difference in their suitability'. Art.5(4) sets out the kinds of opportunity encompassed by the duty. Section 75 of the Northern Ireland Act 1998 requires public authorities in carrying out their functions relating to Northern Ireland to 'have due regard to promote equality of opportunity' between a wide range of groups.

7

Equal Pay

A. INTRODUCTION

Article 141 on equal pay is the cornerstone of the EC Treaty's employment law provisions. The basic principle is laid down in Article 141(1):

Each Member State shall ensure that the principle of equal pay for male and female workers for equal work or work of equal value[1] is applied.

The significance of Article 141 first became apparent in the case of *Defrenne (No. 2)*.[2] Defrenne was an air hostess employed by Sabena Airlines. Although she did identical work to a male cabin steward she was paid less than him, contrary she claimed, to Article 141. The Court, recognizing that the principle of equal pay forms part of the 'foundations of the Community', decided, despite strong objections from the Member States, that Article 141 was both horizontally and vertically directly effective, and could thus give rise to 'individual rights which the courts may protect'.[3] However, realizing the number of potential claims arising from this decision which might seriously affect the solvency of many companies, the Court ruled that, in the interests of legal certainty, the direct effect of Article 141 could not be relied on to support the claims of people in respect of periods of employment prior to the date of the judgment (8 April 1976), except in the case of workers who had already brought legal proceedings.

This litigation captures the Court's dynamic approach towards Article 141. On the one hand, the Court sees Article 141 as a key pillar of Community social policy and so fights to make it meaningful to victims of discrimination; on the other, it recognizes that changes in legal understanding can have profound consequences for individuals, particularly employers, who had no reason to believe that they were acting unlawfully. This has become a major issue in respect of addressing discrimination arising in the field of occupational pensions. This issue is considered separately in chapter 10. In this

---

[1] Reference to 'work of equal value' was added by the Treaty of Amsterdam.

[2] Case 43/75 *Defrenne v. Sabena (No. 2)* [1976] ECR 455. For the background to this case, see Hoskyns, *Integrating Gender* (Verso, London, 1996) 65–75.

[3] Para. 24. See also Case C–28/93 *Van den Akker v. Stichting Shell Pensioenfonds* [1994] ECR I–4527, para. 21.

chapter we focus on the meaning of equal pay primarily in the context of an ongoing employment relationship.

B. THE SCOPE OF ARTICLE 141

Article 141 applies to 'workers' who receive 'pay'. We begin by considering the meaning of these key terms.

1. Workers

The criterion on which Article 141(1) EC is based is the comparability of the work done by workers of each sex.[4] Yet unlike the field of free movement of workers where there is a voluminous case law on the meaning of the 'worker',[5] it was not until the 2004 decision of *Allonby*[6] that the Court grappled with the meaning of 'worker' in the context of equal pay. It began by noting that there was no single definition of worker in Community law: the definition varied according to the area in which the definition was applied.[7] However, as with the definition of 'worker' under Article 39 EC, the Court began by noting that 'worker' used in Article 141(1) EC had a broad, Community meaning.[8] Then, drawing on its Article 39 case law, the Court said:[9]

For the purposes of that provision [Article 141(1)], there must be considered as a worker a person who, for a certain period of time, performs services for and under the direction of another person in return for which he receives remuneration.

Then, referring to the definition of pay found in Article 141(2) EC (see below), the Court added that 'It is clear from that definition that the authors of the Treaty did not intend that the term "worker", within the meaning of Article 141(1) EC, should include independent providers of services who are not in a relationship of subordination with the person who receives the services'.[10] However, the Court added the caveat that formal classification of a self-employed person under national law did not exclude the possibility that a person had to be classified as a worker within the meaning of Article 141(1) EC if his independence was 'merely notional, thereby disguising an employment relationship within the meaning of that article.'

    [4] Case 149/77 *Defrenne (No. 3)* [1978] ECR 1365, para. 22.
    [5] See further Ch. 4.
    [6] Case C–256/01 *Allonby* v. *Accrington & Rosendale College* [2004] ECR I–000.
    [7] Case C–85/96 *Martínez Sala* [1998] ECR I–2691, para. 31.   [8] Para. 66.
    [9] Case 66/85 *Lawrie-Blum* [1986] ECR 2121, para. 17, and Case C–85/96 *Martínez Sala* [1998] ECR I–2691, para. 32.
    [10] Para. 68. See also, in the context of free movement of workers, Case C–337/97 *Meeusen* [1999] ECR I–3289, para. 15.

Allonby concerned teachers who used to be employed directly by a further education (FE) college on fixed term contracts. Once their contracts expired they were engaged on a self-employed basis by an agency, ELS. Allonby worked on specific assignments agreed by her with ELS at the FE college. The college agreed with ELS the fee it would pay for each lecturer. ELS then agreed with Allonby the fee she was to receive for each assignment and set the conditions under which its lecturers were to work. The effect of these changes was to reduce Allonby's pay. The question for the Court was whether the lecturers were genuinely self-employed. It said that it was necessary 'in particular to consider the extent of any limitation on their freedom to choose their timetable, and the place and content of their work'. It continued: 'The fact that no obligation is imposed on them to accept an assignment is of no consequence in that context'.[11]

2. The Meaning of 'Pay'

2.1. What Remuneration Constitutes 'Pay'?

Article 141(2) defines 'pay' broadly. It refers to the 'ordinary basic minimum wage or salary', which would include pay received as piece rates[12] or time rates, 'and any other consideration, whether in cash or in kind, which the worker receives directly or indirectly in respect of his[/her] employment from his[/her] employer'.[13] The Court has added that pay can be 'immediate or future' provided that the worker receives it, albeit indirectly,[14] in respect of his employment from his employer'.[15] Thus, in *Garland*[16] the Court found that concessionary travel facilities granted voluntarily to ex-employees fell within the scope of Article 141. The Court has also said that the legal nature of the facilities is not important: they can be granted under a contract of employment, a collective agreement,[17] as a result of legislative provisions,[18]

---

[11] Citing Case C–357/89 *Raulin* [1992] ECR I–1027, paras. 9 and 10.

[12] See also Case C–400/93 *Specialarbejderforbundet i Danmark* v. *Dansk Industri* [1995] ECR I–1275.

[13] This definition is repeated in Art. 2(1)(e) of the Consolidated Directive.

[14] Since Art. 141 also applies to money received indirectly from an employer, it would cover occupational pensions paid out of a trust fund, administered by trustees who are technically independent of the employer: see Case C–262/88 *Barber* v. *Guardian Royal Exchange* [1990] ECR I–1889. Joined Cases C–270 and C–271/97 *Deutsche Post AG* v. *Sievers and Schrage* [2000] ECR I–929; Joined Cases C–234 and C–235/96 *Deutsche Telekom AG* v. *Vick and Conze* [2000] ECR I–799; and Case C–50/96 *Deutsche Telekom AG* v. *Schröder* [2000] ECR I–743.

[15] Case 80/70 *Defrenne (No. 1)* v. *Belgian State* [1971] ECR 445.

[16] Case 12/81 *Garland* v. *British Railways Board* [1982] ECR 359.

[17] Case C–281/97 *Krüger* v. *Kreiskrankenhaus Ebersberg* [1999] ECR I–5127, para. 17.

[18] See Cases 43/75 *Defrenne (No. 2)* [1976] ECR 455, para. 40, and C–262/88 *Barber* v. *Guardian Royal Exchange* [1990] ECR I–1889.

or made *ex gratia*[19] by the employer,[20] provided always that they are
granted to the worker by reason of the employment relationship between the
worker and the employer in respect of employment.[21] This is the decisive
criterion.[22]

Therefore, the Court has ruled that all employer-based payments constitute
pay, such as sick pay,[23] redundancy payments resulting from voluntary or
compulsory redundancy,[24] unfair dismissal compensation,[25] occupational
pensions,[26] survivors' benefits,[27] bridging pensions,[28] additional statutory
redundancy payments,[29] maternity benefits paid under legislation or collective agreements,[30] special bonus payments made by the employer[31] (including

---

[19] *Ex gratia* payments are 'advantages which an employer grants to workers although he is not
required to do so by contract' (Case C–262/88 *Barber* [1990] ECR I–1889, para. 19, and Case
12/81 *Garland* v. *British Rail Engineering* [1982] ECR 359).

[20] Case C–360/90 *Arbeiterwohlfahrt der Stadt Berlin e.V* v. *Bötel* [1992] ECR I–3589.

[21] Cf. the position with additional voluntary contributions which are not granted in respect of
employment: see Case C–200/91 *Coloroll* v. *Russell* [1994] ECR I–4389.

[22] Case C–366/99 *Griesmar* v. *Ministre de l'Économie, des Finances et de l'Industrie* [2001] ECR
I–9383, para. 28.

[23] Case 171/88 *Rinner-Kühn* v. *FWW Spezial-Gebäudereinigung GmbH & Co. KG* [1989] ECR
2743.

[24] Case C–262/88 *Barber* [1990] ECR I–1889 concerned *compulsory* redundancy. Case 19/81
Burton v. *British Rail* [1982] ECR 555 concerned *voluntary* redundancy where the Court sug-
gested that the Equal Treatment Dir. 76/207 did not apply to discriminatory age conditions. The
Court seems *sotto voce* to have overruled this decision (see Curtin, 'Scalping the Community
Legislator: Occupational Pensions after *Barber*' (1990) 27 *CMLRev.* 475, 482) and it seems likely
that Art. 141 would apply to both.

[25] Case C–167/97 *Seymour-Smith* [1999] ECR I–623. In Case C–249/97 *Gruber* v. *Silhouette
International Schmied GmbH & Co. KG* [1999] ECR I–5295, the Court said that 'termination
payments' constitute pay.

[26] Case 170/84 *Bilka-Kaufhaus* v. *Weber von Hartz* [1986] ECR 1607 and Case C–50/99 *Podesta*
v. *CRICA* [2000] ECR I–4039 (supplementary pensions); Case C–262/88 *Barber* [1990] ECR
I–1889 (contracted-out pensions).

[27] Case C–109/91 *Ten Oever* [1993] ECR I–4879; Case C–147/95 *DEI* v. *Efthimios Evrenopoulos*
[1997] ECR I–2057.

[28] Case C–132/92 *Roberts* v. *Birds Eye Walls* [1993] ECR I–5579. See also Case C–19/02 *Hlozek*
v. *Roche Austria Gesellschaft mbH* [2004] ECR I–000, para. 51.

[29] Case C–173/91 *Commission* v. *Belgium* [1993] ECR I–673.

[30] C–342/93 *Gillespie* v. *Northern Health and Social Services Boards* [1996] ECR I–475. The
Court did, however, rule that neither Art. 141 nor Art. 1 of Dir. 75/117 required that women
should continue to receive full pay during maternity leave, nor did those provisions lay down
any specific criteria for determining the amount of benefit to be paid to them during that period.
See also Case C–218/98 *Abdoulaye* v. *Régie nationale des usines Renault SA.* [1999] ECR I–5723,
para. 14.

[31] Case 58/81 *Commission* v. *Luxembourg* [1982] ECR 2175 where a special 'head of household' allowance was deemed to be pay. Individual pay supplements to basic pay (Case 109/88
Handels- og Kontorfunktionærernes Forbund I Danmark v. *Dansk Arbejdsgiverforening, acting on behalf
of Danfoss (Danfoss)* [1989] ECR 3199) and increments based on seniority (Case 184/89 *Nimz* v.
Freie und Hansestadt Hamburg [1991] ECR 297) are considered to be pay. So, presumably, would
shift premia, overtime and all forms of merit and performance pay constitute 'pay' within Art.
141 (COM(94) 6 final).

an end-of-year bonus[32] and an 'inconvenient hours' supplement[33]), payment for extra hours,[34] concessionary train fares,[35] family and marriage allowances granted by collective agreement,[36] and a severance grant payable on the termination of an employment relationship[37] all constitute pay. Similarly, compensation in the form of paid leave or overtime pay for participation in training courses given by an employer to Staff Committee members[38] and rules governing the automatic reclassification to a higher salary grade can constitute pay.[39]

2.2. Remuneration Considered to be Social Security Payments

Payments do not constitute pay principally where they are considered to be social security payments[40] and so fall under Directive 79/7. In *Beune*[41] the Court provided some guidance as to how to identify whether a payment formed part of a state social security scheme (to which Directive 79/7 would apply) or part of the employment relationship (to which Article 141 would apply). The case concerned a pension scheme governed directly by statute. The Court said that Article 141 did not cover social security schemes or benefits, such as retirement pensions, directly governed by statute which were obligatorily applicable to general categories of employees, where no element of negotiation within the undertaking or occupational sector was involved.[42] It said that although these schemes were funded by the contributions of workers, employers and possibly the public authorities, the funding was determined not so much by the employment relationship between the employer and the worker as by considerations of social policy. Since Article 141 did not apply to these payments, they fell within the scope of Directive 79/7 on equal treatment.

In subsequent cases the Court has identified three conditions necessary for retirement pensions to fall within the scope of Article 141. These were neatly

---

[32] Case C–281/97 *Krüger* v. *Kreiskrankenhaus Ebersberg* [1999] ECR I–5127; Case C–333/97 *Lewen* v. *Lothar Denda* [2000] ECR I–7243 a Christmas bonus paid on a voluntary basis as an incentive for future work or loyalty to the undertaking constituted pay (para. 22).
[33] Case C–236/98 *Jämställdhetsombudsmannen* v. *Örebo läns landsting* [2000] ECR I–2189, para. 42.
[34] Case C–285/02 *Elsner-Lakeberg* v. *Land Nordrhein-Westfalen* [2004] ECR I–000, para. 16.
[35] Case C–249/96 *Grant* v. *South West Trains* [1998] ECR I–621.
[36] Case C–187/98 *Commission* v. *Greece* [1999] ECR I–7713.
[37] Case C–33/89 *Kowalska* v. *Freie und Hansestadt Hamburg* [1990] ECR I–2591. Such payments are deemed to be deferred pay.
[38] Case C–360/90 *Bötel* [1992] ECR I–3589.
[39] Case C–184/89 *Nimz* [1991] ECR I–297.
[40] Case 80/70 *Defrenne (No. 1)* [1971] ECR 445. This is considered further in Ch. 10.
[41] Case C–7/93 *Bestuur van het Algemeen Burgerlijk Pensioenfonds* v. *Beune* [1994] ECR I–4471.
[42] This language is actually taken from Case C–366/99 *Griesmar* v. *Ministre de l'Économie, des Finances et de l'Industrie* [2001] ECR I–9383, para. 27.

summarized in *Schönheit*[43] where the Court said that a scheme, although established by law, fell within Article 141 if (1) it concerned only a particular category of workers,[44] (2) it was directly related to the period of service completed, and (3) its amount was calculated by reference to the individual's final salary.[45] Where these conditions are satisfied a pension paid by a public sector employer is comparable to a pension paid by a private employer to his former employees; in other words it is equivalent to an occupational pension.[46] This definition has now been broadly incorporated into Article 7(2) of the Consolidated Directive 2006/54.

2.3. The Relationship between 'Pay' and Equal Treatment

As the definition of pay becomes broader it might be thought that the role for the Equal Treatment Directive 76/207 will diminish (except in relation to non-financial conditions of employment such as the provision of training), especially since Article 141 has both vertical and horizontal direct effect. It might also be thought that the advent of the Consolidated Directive would further erode the distinction between pay and other conditions of employment since both are now brought under one and the same prohibition on discrimination. However, in *Gillespie*,[47] a case decided before the Consolidated Directive, the Court emphasized that there was still a clear distinction between equal pay matters governed by Article 141 and equal treatment in respect of working conditions covered by Directive 76/207. The Court also emphasized this distinction in *Wippel*,[48] a case concerning a casual worker employed on a 'work on demand' contract. The Court said that where a contract affects the pursuit of an occupational activity by scheduling working time according to need, the contract laid down rules concerning working conditions and so fell within the Equal Treatment Directive 76/207 (and also the Part-time Work Directive 97/81) but not Article 141.[49] The Court added that the fact that

---

[43] Joined Cases C–4/02 and C–5/02 *Schönheit v. Stadt Frankfurt am Main* [2003] ECR I–12575. For a careful analysis of whether a particular scheme satisfies these requirements, see Case C–50/99 *Podesta v. CRICA* [2000] ECR I–4039.

[44] The particular category of workers is 'distinguished from employees grouped within an undertaking or group of undertakings in a particular sector of the economy, or in a trade or inter-trade sector, only by reason of the specific features governing their employment relationship with the state or with other public employers or bodies'. This is wide enough to cover a group comprising all public servants: Case C–366/99 *Griesmar v. Ministre de l'Économie, des Finances et de l'Industrie* [2001] ECR I–9383, para. 31.

[45] Para. 58. See also Case C–366/99 *Griesmar* [2001] ECR I–9383, paras. 28–34; Case C–351/00 *Niemi* [2002] ECR I–7007, paras. 47–52.

[46] Joined Cases C–4/02 and C–5/02 *Schönheit v. Stadt Frankfurt am Main* [2003] ECR I–12575, para. 65.

[47] Case C–342/93 [1996] ECR I–475, para. 24. See also Case C–281/97 *Krüger* [1999] ECR I–5127, para. 14.

[48] Case C–313/02 *Nicole Wippel v. Peek & Cloppenburg GmbH & Co. KG* [2005] ECR I–000.

[49] Para. 32.

the contract had financial consequences for the worker concerned was 'not sufficient to bring such conditions within the scope of Article 141 EC or of Directive 75/117, those provisions being based on the close connection which exists between the nature of the work done and the amount of the worker's pay.'[50]

C. THE SCOPE OF THE COMPARISON

1. Introduction

Article 141 talks about equal pay for male and female workers for equal work or work of equal value. Thus, the model originally envisaged by Article 141 is (usually) a woman claiming equal pay against her *employer* using a man engaged in like work or work of equal value as a comparator. Therefore, in order to determine whether the woman is entitled to equal pay, there must be (1) a comparator of the opposite sex who is, or has been, (2) engaged in equal work or work of equal value. In its case law the Court has added an additional requirement: (3) that the comparator has to be employed in the same establishment or service. In this section we shall focus on the application of Article 141 to cases where an employer is the defendant whose pay practices are being challenged. It will be suggested below that the Court adopts a rather different approach when the defendant is the state and discriminatory legislation is at issue.

2. Discriminatory Practices by Employers

2.1. Identifying the Comparator

(a) Real Comparator Similarly Situated

To bring an equal pay claim under Article 141, the applicant needs to point to a comparator of the opposite sex, who is paid better for doing equal work or work of equal value. The Court has said that the comparator does not need to be employed at the same time as the applicant[51] but he must be a real, identifiable person and not a 'hypothetical worker'.[52] This requirement prevents a

---

[50] Para. 33. See also Case C–476/99 *Lommers* v. *Minister van Landbouw* [2002] ECR I–2891, para. 27: provision of workplace nurseries is a working condition under Dir. 76/207 and does not constitute 'pay' under Art. 141; the measure does not constitute pay just because the cost of the nursery places is partly borne by the employer.

[51] Case 129/79 *Macarthys* [1980] ECR 1275, considered below n. 96.

[52] Case 129/79 *Macarthys* [1980] ECR 1275. This argument was based on the distinction the Court had drawn between direct and indirect discrimination. If the comparator were to be a hypothetical male this would be classed as indirect, disguised discrimination which would

woman from arguing that she was the victim of discrimination because, had she been a man, she would have received a higher salary. In *Macarthys* the Court explained that such claims should be excluded on the grounds that it would necessitate comparative studies of entire branches of industry which would require further Community legislation.

While hypothetical comparators do present considerable problems of proof, the requirement for an actual comparator limits the effectiveness of the equality legislation in sectors—such as cleaning and catering—dominated by women. However, with the 2002 amendments to the Equal Treatment Directive (now consolidated by Directive 2006/54) bringing pay and treatment under the same 'roof', it has been argued that key principles relating to equal treatment, in particular the possibility of using a hypothetical comparator, should now apply to equal pay claims as well. The UK government has hotly contested this, pointing to Preambular paragraph 16 of Directive 2002/73,[53] to suggest that the two regimes remain distinct.[54] Some support for the UK's view can be found in the Consolidated Directive which, in Article 4, suggests that the equal pay provisions are distinct.

Not only must the comparator be real, he must also be in an 'identical' situation with the woman.[55] In *Roberts*[56] the employer paid the man a bridging pension between the ages of 60 and 65 but paid Mrs Roberts only a reduced bridging pension on the grounds that she received a state pension at the age of 60 but her male comparator did not. The Court ruled that no discrimination occurred since the 'difference as regards the objective premise, which necessarily entails that the amount of the bridging pension is not the same for men and women, cannot be considered discriminatory'. Similarly, in *Abdoulaye*[57] the Court said that it was not contrary to Article 141 for women but not men to receive a maternity bonus intended to offset the occupational

require comparative studies of entire industries. At that stage Art. 141 was only directly effective in respect of direct discrimination. Since the law has now changed this approach may require reassessment. See also Case C–200/91 *Coloroll Pension Trustees Ltd* v. *Russell* [1994] ECR I–4389.

[53] This says 'The principle of equal pay for men and women is already firmly established by Article 141 of the Treaty and Council Directive 75/117/EEC of 10 February 1975 on the approximation of the laws of the Member States relating to the application of the principle of equal pay for men and women and is consistently upheld by the case-law of the Court of Justice; the principle constitutes an essential and indispensable part of the acquis communautaire concerning sex discrimination.' This paragraph has been removed from the Consolidated Directive.

[54] http://www.womenandequalityunit.gov.uk/publications/etadgovtresponse.pdf, paras. 18.2–18.4.

[55] Case C–132/92 *Roberts* [1993] ECR I–5579. See also Case C–342/93 *Gillespie and Others* v. *Northern Health and Social Services Board and Others* [1996] ECR I–475; Case C–249/97 *Gruber* [1999] ECR I–5295; Case C–309/97 *Wiener Gebietskrankenkasse* [1999] ECR I–2865; and Case C–333/97 *Lewen* v. *Lothar Denda* [2000] ECR I–7243, para. 38. Such differences in circumstances (such as the hours worked) may, however, constitute an objective justification: Case C–236/98 *Jämo* [2000] ECR I–2189, para. 61.

[56] Case C–19/02 *Roberts* v. *Birds Eye Walls* [1993] ECR I–5579. In a similar vein, see also Case C–19/02 *Hlozek* [2004] ECR I–000.

[57] Case C–218/98 *Abdoulaye* v. *Régre Nationale des Usines Renault SA* [1999] ECR I–5723.

disadvantages inherent in maternity leave, since the two situations were not comparable.[58]

There have been some concerns in the past that, in selecting a comparator group, particularly in the context of equal value claims, the applicant 'cherry-picks'—carves a group of women and a group of men out of larger groups—to facilitate an equal pay claim. In *Dansk Industri*[59] the Court sought to put a stop to this. It said that the two groups had to encompass all the workers who could be considered to be in a comparable situation, taking into account factors such as the nature of the work, training requirements, and working conditions. The group also had to comprise a relatively large number of workers and that any differences could not be due to purely fortuitous or short-term factors or to differences in the individual output of the workers concerned.

(b) Hard Cases

In most cases the selection of the comparator is straightforward. However, as *Grant* demonstrates,[60] this is not always the case. It will be recalled from the previous chapter that Lisa Grant, a lesbian, was denied benefits (concessionary train fares) for her female partner. One of her claims was that she was (directly) discriminated against on the grounds of sex since her (heterosexual) male colleague had received those benefits for his female partner. The Court, however, chose a homosexual male as the comparator. Grant lost her case since both (homosexual) men and women would have been treated equally (albeit equally badly).[61] Had the Court chosen a heterosexual male comparator, as Grant had argued, there would have been discrimination on the grounds of sex.[62] In *P* v. *S*,[63] by contrast, a case decided under the Equal Treatment Directive, a male to female transsexual was dismissed on the grounds of her sex change. The comparator selected by the Court was a person of the sex to which P was deemed to have belonged prior to the gender reassignment (i.e. a male). Discrimination was found. As the Advocate General recognized, had the Court selected a female to male transsexual as a comparator, as the UK government had argued for, the result might have been different.

---

[58] Cf. Case C–366/99 *Griesmar* v. *Ministre de l'Économie, des Finances et de l'Industrie* [2001] ECR I–9383, considered in Ch. 9.

[59] Case C–400/93 [1995] ECR I–1275.

[60] Case C–249/86 *Grant* v. *South West Trains* [1998] ECR I–621.

[61] This is sometimes referred to as 'equal misery': C. Denys 'Homosexuality: a non-issue in Community law' (1999) 24 *ELRev.* 419, 422. See also Joined Cases C–122/99P and C–125/99P *D and Kingdom of Sweden* v. *Council* [2001] ECR I–4319.

[62] Cf. *Baehr* v. *Lewin* 852 P.2d 44 (Hawaii 1993). See further Barnard, 'Some are More Equal than Others: the Case of *Grant* v. *South-West Trains*' (1999) 1 *Cambridge Yearbook of European Law*, 147; Bell, 'Shifting Conceptions of Sexual Discrimination at the Court of Justice': from *P* v. *S* to *Grant* v. *SWT* (1999) 5 *ELJ.* 63; Carey, 'From Obloquy to Equality: In the Shadow of Abnormal Situations' (2001) 20 *YEL.* 79.

[63] Case C–13/94 [1996] ECR I–2143.

2.2. Type of Work Undertaken by the Comparator

(a) Equal Pay for the Same Work

The chosen comparator must be engaged in 'equal work' or 'work of equal value'. 'Equal work' embraces the concept of equal pay for the same[64] or similar work (also known as 'like work'). Various factors need to be taken into account, such as:

• the nature of the work actually entrusted to the individual employees;
• the training requirements for carrying out those tasks;
• the working conditions in which the activities are actually carried out.[65]

The importance of weighing up a number of factors in determining 'like work' was highlighted in *Wiener Gebietskrankenkasse*[66] where the Court ruled that where the same activities were performed over a considerable length of time by persons the bases of whose qualification to exercise their profession were different, this did not constitute 'same work'. Therefore, graduate psychologists, most of whom were women, could not claim equal pay with medical doctors who were paid 50 per cent more, even though both groups worked as psychotherapists and the patients were charged the same irrespective of whether they were treated by a psychologist or a doctor.

An individual can bring a 'like work' claim even if the work of the applicant and her comparator is not performed contemporaneously. Thus, in *Macarthys*,[67] the complainant successfully claimed that she had been discriminated against on the grounds of her sex. She worked as a warehouse manageress earning £50 a week. Her predecessor, a man, had earned £60 a week. According to the Court, an assessment of whether the work was equal was 'entirely qualitative in character in that it is exclusively concerned with the nature of the services in question'. The Court said that the scope of Article 141 could not be restricted by the introduction of a 'requirement of contemporaneity'.

(b) Equal Pay for Work of Equal Value

The principle of equal pay for work of equal value, originally found in Article 1 of Directive 75/117 and now in the amended Article 141(1), is intended to redress the undervaluing of jobs undertaken primarily by women (such as cleaning) where they are found to be as demanding as different jobs more usually undertaken by men (such as maintenance work or gardening).

---

[64] Art. 1 of Dir. 75/117 and Art. 4. of the Consolidated Directive.
[65] Case C–381/99 *Brunnhofer v. Bank der österreichischen Postsparkasse AG* [2001] ECR I–4961, para. 48.
[66] Case C–309/97 *Angestelltenbetriebsrat der Wiener Gebietskrankenkasse v. Wiener Gebietskrankenkasse* [1999] ECR I–2865.
[67] Case 129/79 [1980] ECR 1275.

A job classification or job evaluation scheme,[68] while not obligatory,[69] offers one method of determining whether a man and woman's work is of equal value. This is recognized by Article 4(2) of the Consolidated Directive which provides that:

. . ., where a job classification system is used for determining pay, it shall be based on the same criteria for both men and women and so drawn up so as to exclude any discrimination on grounds of sex.

The contents of a job classification system were discussed in *Rummler*.[70] A German printing firm adopted a grading scheme which classified jobs according to the previous knowledge required, concentration, effort, exertion, and responsibility. Grade II jobs involved slight to medium muscular effort; Grade III jobs medium to high muscular effort, and Grade IV jobs involved on occasion high levels of muscular exertion. Mrs Rummler's job was classified as Grade III. She argued that it should have been classified as Grade IV because it involved lifting packages of 20 kg which, *for her*, was heavy physical work. She therefore asked that account be taken of her own (subjective) characteristics.

The Court said that the nature of the work had to be considered objectively. It recognized that a criterion which took account of an objectively measurable level of physical strength needed to do the job was compatible with Article 1(2) provided that the work, by its very nature, did actually require physical exertion. However, the Court said that when calculating the amount of physical exertion needed, a criterion based solely on the values of one sex, for example, the average strength of a woman, brought with it the threat of discrimination since it might result in work requiring use of greater physical strength being paid in the same way as work requiring less physical strength.

The Court did, however, accept that even though a strength criterion might generally favour male employees, the classification system was not discriminatory on this ground alone. Instead, the Court said that the scheme had to be considered overall and, in order for it to accord with the principles of the Directive, it had to be designed to include, if the nature of the work permitted, work in which other criteria were taken into account for which female employees might show 'particular aptitude'. Thus, as the United Kingdom government suggested, a system based on the criterion of muscular effort was only discriminatory if it excluded from consideration the activation of small

---

[68] Job classification is a non-analytical process used to categorize jobs. Job evaluation, used in the UK and Ireland, is a more analytical approach to assess the relative demands of a job. The analytical approach involves breaking the jobs down into their component elements for the process of comparison whereas the non-analytical approach considers the relative worth of the job based on a whole job comparison. While analytical schemes are more objective the whole process is still subject to judgments made by evaluators which reflect their own background, experience and attitudes (COM(94) 6 final).

[69] Case 61/81 *Commission v. UK* [1982] ECR 2601.

[70] Case 237/85 *Rummler v. Dato-Druck* [1986] ECR 2101.

groups of muscles which typifies manual dexterity, where women tend to score highly. The Court concluded that it was the task of national courts to decide in individual cases whether the job classification scheme in its entirety permitted fair account to be taken of all the criteria on the basis of which pay was determined.

A job classification system initiated by the employer is not the only method for determining whether work is of equal value. In *Commission* v. *United Kingdom*[71] the Court said that the individual should have the right to initiate an equal value claim in the national court, notwithstanding objections from her employer, since Article 6 of Directive 75/117 (now essentially Article 17 of the Consolidated Directive 2006/54) required Member States to endow an authority with the requisite jurisdiction to decide whether different jobs were of equal value, even though national courts might have difficulty in applying such an abstract concept.

(c) Equal Pay for Work of Greater Value

Murphy[72] confirms that Article 141(1) also covers the (unusual) situation where the woman is doing work of greater value than the man, is being paid less than the man, and wishes to be paid the same as the man. The case concerned female factory workers who dismantled, oiled, and reassembled telephones. They wished to be paid the same rate as a male worker employed in the same factory as a stores labourer and engaged in cleaning, collecting, and delivering equipment. The equality officer considered the women's work, taken as a whole, was of a higher value than the man's. The Court said that since the principle of equal pay forbade women engaged in work of equal value to men from being paid less than men on the grounds of sex, *a fortiori* it prohibited a difference in pay where the woman is engaged in work of higher value.[73] To adopt a contrary interpretation, said the Court, would be 'tantamount to rendering the principle of equal pay ineffective and nugatory' since an employer could circumvent the principle by assigning additional duties to women who could then be paid a lower wage.[74]

2.3. Same Establishment or Service

Under English law, the ability of the British statute, the Equal Pay Act 1970, to combat low pay in occupationally segregated sectors, such as cleaning and catering, has been curtailed by the requirement that the comparator be

---

[71] Case 61/81 [1982] ECR 2601. The Member States have adopted different mechanisms for resolving whether, in the light of the nature and demands of the different jobs, the work is of equal value. In Belgium, France, Italy, and Luxembourg, disputes may be resolved by labour inspectorates, while under Irish legislation any dispute on the subject of equal pay can be referred to one of three equality officers (COM(94) 6 final).

[72] Case 157/86 *Murphy* v. *Bord Telecomm Eireann* [1988] ECR 673.

[73] Para. 9.   [74] Para. 10.

employed in the 'same employment' as the woman. Section 1(6) explains that 'same employment' means that the woman and the man have to employed (1) by the same employer or any associated employer[75] and (2) at the same establishment or at establishments at which common terms and conditions of employment are observed. This requirement prevents a woman from making comparisons with colleagues in other establishments belonging to the same employer but with different terms and conditions or with comparators working for different employers in the same industry. It also prevents female workers, in a sector predominated by women, from making cross-industry comparisons.

However, no such requirement is expressly mentioned in Article 141 or in the original Equal Pay Directive 75/117. Nevertheless, the Court alluded to some similar restriction in *Defrenne (No. 2)*[76] where it said:

21 Among the forms of direct discrimination which may be identified solely by reference to the criteria laid down by Article [141] must be included in particular those which have their origin in legislative provisions or in collective labour agreements and which may be detected on the basis of a purely legal analysis of the situation.

22 This applies even more in cases where men and women receive unequal pay for equal work carried out in the same establishment or service, whether public or private.

These paragraphs appeared to suggest that while envisaging some limits to the selection of comparator, these limits were not as tightly drawn as those prescribed by English law.[77] Thus, it would seem that under EC law, the comparator is not confined to those working in the 'same establishment' but also covers those working in the same 'service' (para. 22). Paragraph 21 suggests that it is sufficient for the comparator to be covered by the same legislative provisions or collective agreements.

Although the language in *Defrenne (No. 2)* is not especially clear, it was relied on by the Scottish Court of Session in *South Ayrshire Council* v. *Morton*[78] to allow primary school head teachers (75 per cent of whom were women) to bring an equal pay claim using as a comparator secondary school head teachers (75 per cent of whom were men) employed by a different local education authority but whose salary scale was set by the same negotiating body under the aegis of the Secretary of State. The court allowed comparison across authorities because, under paragraph 21 of *Defrenne (No. 2)*, a comparison could be made where the discrimination arises from common legislation or collective bargaining.

---

[75] Two employers are treated as associated if one is a company of which the other (directly or indirectly) has control or if both are companies of which a third person (directly or indirectly) has control: s.1(6)(c).

[76] Case 43/75 [1976] ECR 455.

[77] In Case 143/83 *Commission* v. *Denmark* [1985] ECR 427 the Advocate General also expressed doubts about the validity of the single workplace rule which might defeat the purpose of the principle of equal pay.

[78] [2001] IRLR 28.

However, it was not until *Lawrence* [79] in 2002 that the Court of Justice had the chance to (re)consider the significance of its earlier remarks in *Defrenne (No. 2)*. *Lawrence* arose out of a long dispute concerning the pay rates of 'female catering assistants' (dinner ladies). Following the introduction of equal pay for work of equal value into UK law in 1983, [80] a job evaluation scheme was carried out by the employer, North Yorkshire County Council, in 1987 which rated the work of dinner ladies and cleaners as being of equal value to that of men performing jobs such as gardening, refuse collection, and sewage treatment. As a result of this exercise, the women's work was more highly paid.

The following year, the Local Government Act (LGA) 1988 required 'defined activities', including school catering and cleaning, to be subject to compulsory competitive tendering (CCT). However, when selecting a contractor, local authorities could not consider 'non-commercial matters' such as wages and conditions or gender equality. In order to compete with external contractors, who were tendering on the basis of significantly lower contract costs, North Yorkshire County Council (NYCC) therefore cut the dinner ladies' pay. In *Ratcliffe* v. *North Yorkshire County Council* [81] the dinner ladies successfully argued that they were entitled to be paid the same as male NYCC employees whose work had been rated as equivalent to theirs under the 1987 job evaluation scheme (i.e. road sweepers and dustbin men). [82]

However, while *Ratcliffe* was ongoing, NYCC had to engage in a further round of CCT. The catering and cleaning contracts were won by three external contractors which employed (some of) the dinner ladies but on inferior terms and conditions. The dinner ladies then brought equal pay claims against the contractors, using as comparators the road sweepers and dustbin men still employed by NYCC, whose work had been rated as equivalent to theirs under the 1987 job evaluation scheme. However, as we saw above, under the British Equal Pay Act, the fact that the women and their comparators were employed by different employers (the dinner ladies were now employed by private companies while their comparators worked for NYCC) was fatal to their claim. Did Article 141 contain equivalent limitations?

The Court of Justice said that there was nothing in the wording of Article 141(1) EC to suggest that it could be applied only to situations in which men and women work for the same employer. [83] However, it continued:

---

[79] Case C–320/00 *Lawrence* v. *Regent Office Care Ltd* [2002] ECR I–7325.

[80] As a result of successful infringement proceedings before the ECJ: Case 61/81 *Commission* v. *UK* [1982] ECR 2601.

[81] [1995] IRLR 439. For full details of the background, see Barnard, Deakin and Kilpatrick, 'Equality, Non-discrimination and the Labour Market in the UK' (2002) 18 *IJCLLIR* 129.

[82] The House of Lords said that NYCC's need to cut wages to compete effectively with external contractors, though the genuine reason for the pay cuts, was not a 'material factor which is not the difference of sex' as required by the Equal Pay Act 1970, s. 1(3).

[83] Para. 17.

where . . . the differences identified in the pay conditions of workers performing equal work or work of equal value *cannot be attributed to a single source*, there is no body which is responsible for the inequality and which could restore equal treatment. Such a situation does not come within the scope of Article 141(1) EC. The work and the pay of those workers cannot therefore be compared on the basis of that provision. [Emphasis added]

Thus, the Court said that there could only be a cross-employer comparison where the differences in pay could be attributed to a single source. That was not the case in *Lawrence* as there was no one body responsible for the inequality which could restore equal treatment.

So what is meant by single source? The paradigm case would be where the applicant and her comparator work for the same legal person or group of persons or for public authorities operating under joint control[84] or where their pay is covered by the same collective agreement or legislative provisions,[85] i.e. common terms and conditions (para. 21 of *Defrenne*). This is particularly important in the public sector where, as in *Morton*, comparators are drawn from different public authorities who operate under the same government department. However, in the absence of such a single source, the equal pay claim will fail. This was confirmed in *Allonby*.[86] Allonby was employed by an FE college on a series of part-time, one-year contracts. Because of its worries about the effects of the Part-time Work Directive[87] the college decided not to renew the existing contracts of part-time lecturers and instead use the services of an agency, ELS, which provided the same lecturers to the college, including Allonby. ELS engaged the lecturers under self-employed contracts. The effect of these changes was to reduce Allonby's overall pay. She brought an equal pay claim against the college, using a male full-time lecturer who had a permanent, full-time contract with the college as her comparator.

The Court of Justice said that Article 141 would not permit such a claim. It explained that while Article 141(1) could be invoked 'in particular in cases of discrimination arising directly from legislative provisions or collective labour agreements, as well as in cases in which work is carried out in the same establishment or service, whether private or public', where the differences in pay could not be attributed to a single source, there was 'no body which is responsible for the inequality and which could restore equal treatment' and so the situation did not come within the scope of Article 141(1) EC. The Court concluded that even though the level of pay received by Ms Allonby was influenced by the amount which the college paid ELS, this was not a sufficient basis for concluding that the college and ELS constituted a single source to which the differences identified in Ms Allonby's conditions of pay and those of the male worker paid by the college could be attributed.

---

[84] Cf. *Robertson* v. *DEFRA* [2005] IRLR 363.
[85] AG Geelhoed's Opinion in *Lawrence*, para. 54.
[86] Case C–256/01 *Allonby* v. *Accrington & Rosendale College* [2004] ECR I–000.
[87] See further Ch. 9.

As Fredman points out,[88] the fault-oriented model of equal pay introduced in *Lawrence* and applied with such damaging effect in *Allonby*, overlooks the widely recognized fact that inequality of pay is frequently a consequence of institutional arrangements for which no single actor is 'to blame'. Because the Court could not find fault on the part of either the college or ELS—even though the Advocate General acknowledged that the institutional arrangements had been deliberately manipulated to secure savings for the college and to avoid the consequences of the Part-time Work Directive—the loss fell on those who were least at fault—the part-time lecturers, the majority of whom were women.[89] Thus, the triangulation of the managerial function (with the college having control over the worker but ELS having control over their remuneration) successfully drew the teeth of the (fundamental) principle of equal pay and this was condoned by a Court unable 'to see beyond the formal boundaries of the employing enterprise'.[90] The effect of *Allonby* is that those workers working alongside each other in the same establishment but with contracts of employment with different legal entities could not enjoy equal pay.[91]

As Deakin and Morris point out, the *Lawrence* and *Allonby* reference to 'single source' represents an unjustified gloss on the wording of Article 141 which makes no reference to the employment unit as the sole basis for comparison.[92] Although there may be practical difficulties in allowing comparisons across employment boundaries, such difficulties did not arise in these two cases: *Lawrence* was a case of a unified job evaluation scheme, *Allonby* involved work in a single establishment where there was a contract between the college and the agency. In both cases comparisons were made with former co-workers.[93] Nevertheless, the requirement was inserted into Article 4 of the draft Consolidated Directive but removed from the final version.

D. THE PROHIBITION OF DISCRIMINATION ON THE GROUNDS OF SEX

1. Introduction

In the description above of the three criteria necessary to bring an equal pay claim (comparator, engaged in equal work/work of equal value, in the same establishment or service) there is no reference to the principle of discrimination. Yet, Article 141, does envisage a role for the discrimination principle. Talking in the specific context of piece and time rates, it says:

[88] Fredman, 'Marginalising Equal Pay Laws' (2004) 33 *ILJ*. 281, 281.
[89] Ibid.   [90] Ibid.
[91] Deakin and Morris, *Labour Law*, (Hart Publishing, Oxford, 2005) para. 6.80.
[92] Ibid.   [93] Ibid.

Equal Pay *without discrimination based* on sex means:

(a) that pay for the same work at piece rates shall be calculated on the basis of the same unit of measurement;
(b) that pay for work at time rates shall be the same for the same job.[94]

Similarly, in the original Equal Pay Directive 75/117 and in the Consolidated Directive, the principle of non-discrimination is central. Article 4 of the Consolidated Directive provides:

For the same work or for work to which equal value is attributed, *direct and indirect discrimination on grounds of sex* with regard to all aspects and conditions of remuneration shall be eliminated.[95]

In this section we consider the meaning of the term non-discrimination on the grounds of sex before considering the problems associated with applying the principle in the specific context of equal pay.

2. Non-discrimination

2.1. The Principle of Non-discrimination

In cases where discrimination is raised, the Court draws the conventional distinction between *direct* and *indirect* discrimination which was considered in detail in chapter 6. In essence, direct discrimination involves one sex being treated less favourably than the other. In the case of *Macarthys*[96] this meant that the woman received less pay than the man doing the same job. In *Moufflin*[97] French law provided that female civil servants with husbands suffering from a disability or an incurable illness were entitled to a retirement pension with immediate effect; male civil servants in an equivalent situation were not. In both cases the Court found the rule to be directly discriminatory contrary to Article 141.

Indirect discrimination means, according to Article 2(1)(b) the Consolidated Directive:[98]

Where an apparently neutral provision, criterion or practice *would put* persons of one sex at a *particular disadvantage* compared with persons of the other sex, unless that provision, criterion or practice is objectively justified by a legitimate aim and the means of achieving that aim are appropriate and necessary.

As we saw in chapter 6, the Court's approach to proving indirect discrimination has generally been more strict than the new legislative route.

---

[94] Emphasis added. The wording of Art. 141 is based on Art. 2(1) of ILO Convention 100, 1951 (UNTS, Vol. 165, 303).
[95] Emphasis added. [96] Case 129/79 *Macarthys v. Smith* [1980] ECR 1275.
[97] Case C–206/00 *Mouflin v. Recteur de l'académie de Reims* [2001] ECR I–10201.
[98] Art. 2(1)(b).

Nevertheless, both the legislative and judicial routes allow the defendant to justify the differential treatment for objective reasons unrelated to sex.

2.2. On the Grounds of Sex

The discrimination (either direct or indirect) must be 'on the grounds of sex'. This raises the question as to what constitutes 'sex': does it mean merely gender or is the term broader than that? Although this question is considered in more detail in the next chapter, for the purpose of equal pay we can observe the following. At first, it seemed that the Court would construe the concept of 'sex' broadly. For example, in *Liefting*[99] it recognized that 'gender-plus' (e.g. gender and marriage) discrimination was caught by Article 141. In that case employer contributions to a pension scheme discriminated against female civil servants married to (male) civil servants. Although there was no allegation that women were being discriminated against generally, the Court found that discrimination against this particular category of female civil servants was nevertheless caught by Article 141.[100] However, as we have already seen, in *Grant*[101] the Court was not prepared to allow the definition of sex in Article 141 to include sexual orientation.[102]

Discrimination for reasons other than sex is compatible with Community law. Sometimes this notion is dealt with through the defence of 'objective justification *on grounds other than sex*' (see below). In other cases this question forms an integral part of the assessment of whether the different treatment can be 'explained by the operation of factors which are unconnected with any discrimination on grounds of sex'.[103] For example, in *Danfoss*[104] the Court said that a criterion for awarding a pay increase based on the quality of work done by the employee is 'undoubtedly wholly neutral from the point of view of sex'.[105]

---

[99] Case 23/83 *Liefting v. Academisch Ziekenhuis bij de Universiteit van Amsterdam* [1984] ECR 3225.

[100] See also Case C–7/93 *Bestuur van het Algemeen Burgerlijk Pensioenfonds v. Beune* [1994] ECR I–4471 (discrimination against married men) and Case C–128/93 *Fisscher v. Voorhuis Hengelo and Stichting Bedrijfspensioenfonds voor de Detailhandel* [1994] ECR I–4583 (discrimination against married women). In *Beune* the Court ruled that married men placed at a disadvantage by discrimination must be treated in the same way and have the same rules applied to them as married women.

[101] Case C–249/96 [1998] ECR I–621.

[102] Case C–249/96 [1998] ECR I–621. Cf. the decision of the European Court of Human Rights concerning Art. 8 of the European Convention in *Smith and Grady v. United Kingdom* [1999] IRLR 734.

[103] Case 129/79 *Macarthys* [1980] ECR 1275, para. 12.

[104] Case 109/88 [1989] ECR I–3199.

[105] Although it did say that if the application of such a wholly neutral criterion systematically works to the disadvantage of women, then the only explanation is that the employer has misapplied the criterion and so cannot objectively justify its application.

The Court reiterated the point in the complex case of *Dansk Industri*[106] where it had to consider a collective agreement in a Danish ceramics factory under which the majority of workers opted to be paid largely on a piecework basis. Their pay consisted of a fixed element, paid as a basic hourly wage, and a variable element, paid by reference to the number of items produced. In April 1990 a comparison was made between the average hourly wage of three sub-groups of workers.[107] The workers' union argued that the difference in pay between the predominantly female blue-pattern painters and the male automatic machine operators breached the requirement under Article 141 of equal pay for work of equal value.

The Court said that while the principle of equal pay applied to piecework pay systems the mere finding that there was a difference in the average pay of two groups of workers, calculated on the basis of the total individual pay of all the workers belonging to the group, did not suffice to establish discrimination, since that difference might have been due to differences in the individual output of the workers constituting the two groups, rather than to a difference between the units of measurement applicable to the two groups. Further, the Court said that it was for the national court to decide whether a pay differential relied on by a worker belonging to a group consisting predominantly of women as evidence of sex discrimination against that worker compared with a worker belonging to a group consisting predominantly of men was due to a difference between the units of measurement, which would contravene Article 141, or to a difference in output, which would not.

2.3. Material Scope

The prohibition of discrimination applies to acts of employers, both in respect of the terms of the contract of employment and to unilateral acts.[108] It also applies to the terms of collective agreements: Article 4 of Directive 75/117/EEC (Article 23(b) of the Consolidated Directive) obliged Member States to take the necessary measures to ensure that provisions appearing in collective agreements, wage scales, wage agreements, or individual contracts of employment, which are contrary to the principle of equal pay, are declared null and void or can be amended.[109] Subsequently, in *Kowalska*,[110] the Court confirmed that

---

[106] Case C–400/93 [1995] ECR I–1275.

[107] This found that the average hourly pay of the automatic machine operators (an all-male group of 26 turners) was Danish Krone (DKR) 103.93, including a fixed element of DKR 71.69, the pay of the blue-pattern painters (155 women and 1 man) was DKR 91, including a fixed element of DKR 57, and the pay of the ornamental plate painters (an all-female group of 51) was DKR 116.20, including a fixed element of DKR 35.85.

[108] Case C–333/97 *Lewen* [1999] ECR I–7243, para. 26.

[109] See generally Lester and Rose, 'Equal Value Claims and Sex Bias in Collective Bargaining' (1991) 20 *ILJ*. 163.

[110] Case C–33/89 [1990] ECR I–2591. See also Case 109/88 *Danfoss* [1989] ECR 3199; Case C–281/97 *Krüger* [1999] ECR I–5127.

Article 141 also applied to terms contained in collective agreements. Therefore, a provision in a collective agreement excluding part-time workers from the payment of a severance grant on termination of their employment infringed Article 141 unless it could be objectively justified.

A similar situation arose in *Nimz*.[111] This case concerned a collective agreement which provided that the full period of service of employees working for at least three-quarters of normal working time was to be taken into account when reclassifying salary grades, whereas only one-half of the period of service was taken into account in the case of employees whose working hours were between one-half and three-quarters of normal working time. This latter group comprised a considerably smaller percentage of men than women. The Court ruled that Article 141 precluded such indirectly discriminatory agreements unless the employer could prove that such provisions were objectively justified.[112]

3. The Problem with Applying the Principle of Non-discrimination in Equal Pay Cases

Even though the principle of non-discrimination is well established in the case law on Article 141, it is not always easy to see how non-discrimination principles actually fit with those of equal pay, particularly where work of equal value is at stake. This is because the equal pay model is intended to eliminate pay practices which have, over time, worked to depress the pay of certain jobs typically carried out by women. This is not a straightforward case of direct or indirect discrimination on the grounds of sex; the equal pay legislation appears to go beyond the non-discrimination model.

This raises the question of how the requirement to show the three equal pay criteria (comparator, engaged in equal work/work of equal value, in the same establishment or service) can be reconciled with the need to show discrimination. One view is that the claimant needs to show both the three criteria and an element of discrimination. This was the approach adopted by the Court in *JämO*.[113] Two midwives claimed equal pay, arguing that they were engaged in work of equal value with a (male) clinical technician. The Court said that if the national court found that they were engaged on work of equal value, it (the ECJ) found that midwives were paid less. It continued:[114]

---

[111] Case C–184/89 [1991] ECR I–297.
[112] Ibid.; see also Cases 143/83 *Commission v. Denmark* [1985] ECR 427 and C–127/92 *Enderby* [1993] ECR I–5535.
[113] Case C–236/98 *Jämställdhetsombudsmannen v. Örebro läns landsting* [2000] ECR I–2189.
[114] Para. 50.

It follows that, in order to establish whether it is contrary to Article [141] of the Treaty and to Directive 75/117 for the midwives to be paid less, the national court must verify whether the statistics available indicate that a considerably higher percentage of women than men work as midwives. If so, there is indirect sex discrimination, unless the measure in point is justified by objective factors unrelated to any discrimination based on sex.[115]

Another view is that once the three criteria outlined above have been shown, it is sufficient to raise the presumption that the difference in pay is due to discrimination on the grounds of sex.[116] In other words, all the claimants needs to show is that a man and a woman are factually doing the same work but paid differently: this alone is sufficient to trigger the application of Article 141. This is the approach adopted by the British Equal Pay Act 1970 itself which makes no reference to the concept of discrimination.[117] Under the Equal Pay Act model all the complainants have to establish are the three conditions outlined above and then the burden shifts to the employer to show objective reasons for the pay differential unrelated to sex (the so-called genuine material factor defence). Thus, all pay differentials between men and women can be objectively justified (and no account is taken of whether those differentials are directly or indirectly discriminatory).

This 'Equal Pay' model appears to have influenced the Court in *Enderby*.[118] The case concerned a female speech therapist, doing a job predominantly carried out by women, who claimed equal pay with pharmacists and clinical psychologists, jobs predominantly carried out by men.[119] Instead of raising questions of direct and indirect discrimination, the Court merely said:[120]

... if the pay of speech therapists is significantly lower than that of pharmacists and if the former are almost exclusively women while the latter are predominantly men, there is a prima facie case of sex discrimination, at least where the two jobs in question are of equal value and the statistics describing that situation are valid.

In this case the burden shifted to the employer to show that the difference was based on objectively justified factors unrelated to any discrimination on the

---

[115] Case C–196/02 *Nikoloudi* v. *Organismos Tilepikinonion Ellados AE* [2005] ECR I–000, where the Court said 'It must be considered first of all whether equal work, or work of equal value exists' (para. 26). It then said 'If that is the case . . . the alleged difference in treatment must then be considered in order to determine whether it is directly based on sex' (para. 30).

[116] Lord Nicholls in *Glasgow* v. *Marshall* [2000] IRLR 272 said the scheme of the British Equal Pay Act was that a rebuttable presumption arose once a gender-based comparison shows that a woman doing like work/work rated as equivalent/work of equal value to that of a man was being treated less favourably than a man. The variation between his and her contract was presumed to be due to sex. In order to discharge the burden, the employer had to satisfy the tribunal of several matters: (1) the preferred reason is not a sham or pretence; (2) the less favourable treatment is due to this reason (the factor relied on is the cause of the disparity); (3) the reason is not the 'difference of sex' whether due to direct or indirect discrimination; and (4) the factor is a 'material one' between the woman and the man's case.

[117] Cf. Lord Browne-Wilkinson's approach in *Strathclyde* v. *Wallace* [1998] IRLR 146.

[118] Case C–127/92 [1993] ECR I–5535.   [119] Para. 3.   [120] Para. 16.

grounds of sex.[121] This approach has the advantage of allowing the employer to justify any pay differential without undermining the fundamental distinction (considered in the previous chapter) between direct discrimination which can only be saved by express derogations—there are no such derogations provided for in Article 141—and indirect discrimination which can be objectively justified.

Two other cases appear to follow the *Enderby* approach: *Elsner-Lakeberg*[122] and *Brunnhofer*.[123] In *Elsner-Lakeberg* the Court said:[124]

Article 141 and Article 1 of Directive 75/117, means that, for the same work or for work to which equal value is attributed, *all discrimination* on grounds of sex with regard to the aspects and conditions of remuneration is prohibited unless that different treatment is *justified by an objective* unrelated to sex.

Although the case concerned a measure which discriminated against part-time workers and so was indirectly discriminatory, the Court nevertheless suggested that *all* discrimination could be objectively justified. A more stark example of this 'equal pay' model can be seen in *Brunnhofer*. Ms Brunnhofer was paid less than a male colleague recruited after her, even though they were both employed in the same salary group. Assuming that the difference in pay was on the ground of sex (the facts were disputed on this point), the discrimination at issue here was direct and so, according to a conventional analysis, could not be objectively justified. However, the Court, making no reference to the principle of discrimination, merely said:[125]

. . . the fundamental principle laid down in Article [141] of the Treaty . . . precludes unequal pay as between men and women for the same job or work of equal value, whatever the mechanism which produces such inequality . . ., unless the difference in pay is justified by objective factors unrelated to any discrimination linked to the difference in sex.

One possible way of squaring this circle would be to say that most equal value claims concern indirect discrimination. *Enderby*[126] could be explained on this basis: the Court assumed that speech therapists were predominantly women and pharmacists predominantly men so that rules paying speech therapists less were indirectly discriminatory unless they could be objectively justified.

These issues are much less acute when the defendant is not an employer but the *state* and the challenge is to *legislation* which infringes the principle of equal pay. In these cases the Court places much less emphasis on establishing

---

[121] Para. 18.
[122] Case C–285/02 *Elsner-Lakeberg v. Land Nordrhein-Westfalen* [2004] ECR I–000.
[123] Case C–381/99 *Brunnhofer v. Bank der österreichischen Postsparkasse AG* [2001] ECR I–4961.
[124] Para. 12, emphasis added.   [125] Para. 30.
[126] Case C–127/92 [1993] ECR I–5535.

the three equal pay criteria and focuses instead on the need to prove discrimination.

The different approaches can be seen in respect of the two limbs of challenge in *Allonby*,[127] one against an employer, the other against the state. In her first claim, Allonby, a teacher employer by an agency, tried to bring an equal pay claim against her day-to-day employer (the FE college), using one of her former male colleagues as a comparator. Although this claim was ultimately unsuccessful (because there was no single source to address the inequality),[128] the case shows how the Court set about the task of determining equal pay: by focusing on the three conditions outlined above[129] and not on the question of any discrimination. However, in respect of Allonby's second claim, this time brought against the state (the Department for Education), that her exclusion from the Teachers' Superannuation Scheme (an exclusion based on *legislation*) was contrary to Article 141—she was more successful. The Court did not apply the traditional, three equal pay criteria. Instead it concentrated on the question of discrimination.[130]

We shall now examine in more detail the application of the principle of non-discrimination to legislative rules.

4. Discriminatory Legislative Rules

Article 3 of the Equal Pay Directive 75/117/EEC confirms that Member States are required to abolish all discrimination arising from laws, regulations, or administrative provisions which are contrary to the principle of equal pay; and this is repeated in Article 23(a) of the Consolidated Directive. Once again, both direct and indirect discrimination is prohibited. *Commission* v. *Greece*[131] was a case of direct discrimination: collective agreements and arbitration awards provided for the grant of family and marriage allowances exclusively to married men workers. The Court said this contravened Article 141.

Rinner-Kühn[132] concerned indirect discrimination. There the Court found that a German law obliging an employer to pay sick pay only to those employees who worked more than 10 hours a week or 45 hours a month discriminated against female workers and contravened Article 141 unless it could be objectively justified.[133] Similarly, in *Seymour-Smith*,[134] considered in detail in the previous chapter, the Court suggested that a rule requiring employees to work for two years before they acquired the right to claim unfair

---

[127] Case C–256/01 *Allonby* v. *Accrington & Rosendale College* [2004] ECR I–000.
[128] See above, text attached to nn. 89–90.   [129] Para. 42.   [130] Para. 81.
[131] Case C–187/98 *Commission* v. *Greece* [1999] ECR I–7713.
[132] Case 171/88 [1989] ECR 2743.   [133] See below, text attached to nn. 139–205.
[134] Case C–167/97 [1999] ECR I–623.

dismissal, might discriminate indirectly against women, where the statistics revealed a 'persistent and relatively constant disparity over a long period between men and women'[135] who were able to satisfy the requirement of two years' employment.

In these cases the focus is on statistics for the numbers of male and female workers at national level.[136] However, as the Court pointed out in *Allonby*, where state legislation is the source of the discrimination the consequences are binding not only on the public authority but also on individual employers. In this situation Article 141 does not require the woman to be compared with a man who is, or has been, employed by the same employer and who has received higher pay for equal work or work of equal value.[137]

E. JUSTIFICATIONS

1. Introduction

The possibility for the employer or the state to justify unequal pay for objective factors unrelated to sex is of great importance. This possibility is certainly available where indirect discrimination is alleged; increasingly, the Court is referring to the possibility of objective justification where the discrimination is direct[138] and more generally when, in cases such as *Enderby*, the Court applies the 'Equal Pay' model without considering issues of discrimination. The Court first recognized the possibility of objective justification in *Bilka-Kaufhaus*[139] where the Court said that the measures chosen must 'correspond to a real need on the part of the undertaking, are appropriate with a view to achieving the objectives pursued and are necessary to that end'. We begin by considering the factors that can be put forward to justify unequal pay (personal factors, market forces, and collective bargaining) before considering the different approaches the Court adopts to those factors depending on the nature of the rule (and the defendant) being challenged. We conclude with an examination of proportionality.

2. The Factors

2.1. Personal Factors

Common personal factors invoked by employers to justify paying one person more than another include seniority, training, productivity, the quality of the

---

[135] Para. 61.   [136] Case C–256/01 *Allonby* [2004] ECR I–000, para. 74.
[137] Para. 84.   [138] Case C–381/99 *Brunnhofer* [2001] ECR I–4961.
[139] Case 170/84 [1986] ECR 1607, para. 36.

work done, the difference between permanently established workers and secondees, and so-called 'red circling'.[140] Personal factors might also include the nature of the work done and the conditions in which it is carried out, including differences in the hours worked.[141]

The Court will check that the personal factor put forward is relevant. Thus in *Brunnhofer*[142] the Court said that if a male and female employee engaged on like work or work of equal value were appointed on different rates of pay, with the woman being paid less, the employer could not *later* justify that difference on the ground that the man's work was superior or that the woman's work has steadily deteriorated after her appointment.[143]

The Court has also been willing to scrutinize the justifications put forward to check that they do not themselves contain some form of unjustified discrimination. Its approach to personal factors, such as seniority, provides a good example. At first, the Court accepted a length of service justification without criticism. In *Danfoss*[144] the Court said that a criterion which rewarded length of service, while operating to the prejudice of women in so far as women have entered the labour market more recently than men or more frequently take a career break, did not require justification.[145] It reasoned that since length of service went hand in hand with experience, and since experience generally enabled employees to perform their duties better, the employer was free to reward length of service without having to establish the importance service had in the performance of specific tasks entrusted to the employee.

However, *Nimz*[146] suggests that the Court was prepared to offer a more nuanced view, at least in the context of part-time work. Once again it recognized that experience went hand in hand with length of service but this time it added that 'the objectivity of such a criterion depends on all the circumstances in a particular case, and in particular on the relationship between the nature of the work performed and the experience gained from the performance of the work upon completion of a certain number of working hours'.[147] This was a matter for the national court to determine.[148]

Gerster[149] and *Kording*[150] also concerned the application of length of service rules for the purposes of promotion and accreditation. In *Gerster* part-time workers had their service counted at either zero (for part-time work at less than half time), two-thirds (for part-time work at one-half to two-thirds time), or full-time (for part-time work over two-thirds time). As the Advocate General pointed out, such a system totally lacked the internal coherence

---

[140] *Snoxell v. Vauxhall Motors Ltd* [1977] IRLR 123, 125 (Philips J): Red circling occurs where 'it is necessary to protect the wages of an employee, or a group of employees, moved from a better paid type of work to a worse paid type of work, perhaps because the first type is no longer undertaken'.
[141] Case C–236/98 *JämO* [2000] ECR I–2189.   [142] Case C–381/99 [2001] ECR I–4961.
[143] Para. 79.   [144] Case 109/88 [1989] ECR I–3199.   [145] Para. 24.
[146] Case C–184/89 [1991] ECR I–297.   [147] Para. 14.   [148] Ibid.
[149] Case C–1/95 [1997] ECR I–5253.   [150] Case C–100/95 [1997] ECR I–5289.

necessitated by the requirement of objective justification. While not going as far as its Advocate General, the Court pointed out, as it had previously held in *Nimz*, that:[151]

> it is impossible to identify objective criteria . . . on the basis of an alleged special link between length of service and acquisition of a certain level of knowledge and experience, since such a claim amounts to no more than a generalisation concerning certain categories of worker.

Rather, it said, an individual assessment had to be made by the national court, on the basis of all the circumstances of the individual case, and the nature of the work and the experience acquired through time by the particular employee.

The Court is going to be forced to address the issue of seniority, outside the context of part-time work, in *Cadman*.[152] Mrs Cadman earned about £35,000 pa while her male comparators earned between £39,000 and £44,000 pa. These differences derived from their greater length of service since the pay scale was broadly service related and she argued that this was indirectly discriminatory against women. Advocate General Poiares Maduro neatly encapsulated the dilemma facing the Court. He said that if it is admitted that length of service is a valid proxy for rewarding experience and efficiency, then it will be impossible for an employee to challenge a pay system that relies on length of service even if such a system in fact works to the disadvantage of women. Conversely, if it is found that an employer must justify any difference in treatment which arises out of the use of length of service as a criterion in the pay system, it may prove difficult for the employer to give precise and detailed evidence of the extent to which efficiency and productivity increase with seniority.[153]

He recognized that *Danfoss* was probably no longer good law and said that an employer would have to justify recourse to the criterion of seniority in a pay system.[154] He then offered a nuanced approach to justification, drawing a distinction between justifying the pay system and justifying its application in individual cases.[155] He said that if the pay system has been consistently structured so as to take into account job specifications and the undertaking's business needs[156] then there will be no grounds for finding that Article 141

---

[151] Para. 39.   [152] Case C–17/05 *Cadman v. Health and Safety Executive.*
[153] Para. 1.   [154] Para. 47.   [155] Para. 64.
[156] At para. 63 the AG gives greater detail. He says: 'First, a degree of transparency as to how the length-of-service criterion is applied in the pay system is necessary, so that judicial scrutiny can take place. In particular, it should be clear how much weight is placed, in the determination of pay, on length of service—conceived either as a way of measuring experience or as a means of rewarding loyalty—as compared with other criteria such as merit and qualifications. In addition, the employer should explain why experience will be valuable for a specific job, and why it is rewarded proportionally. In this respect, while an analysis will have to be carried out by the national court, there can be no doubt, for example, that experience will be more valuable—and therefore legitimately rewarded—in the case of posts involving responsibility and management tasks than in the case of repetitive tasks, in respect of which the length-of-service criterion can

EC has been infringed, unless the employee can show that misapplication of the system leads to indirect discrimination. Furthermore, if the employer can objectively justify using seniority in the pay system then the employer will not need to justify why a specific employee is paid more than another. However, if the employer fails to prove that use of the criterion of length of service in the pay system is proportionate, or if it is impossible to verify that that is the case because the pay system is not sufficiently transparent, the employer will then have to justify the differences in pay in relation to the specific situation of the employee challenging the pay system.

The Court is also suspicious of justifications based on mobility and training. In *Danfoss*[157] it recognized that a criterion for awarding a pay increase to reward employees' adaptability to variable hours and places of work could work to the disadvantage of female employees who, because of household and family duties, were not as able as men to organize their working time with such flexibility.[158] Similarly, the criterion of training may work to the disadvantage of women in so far as they have had less opportunity than men for training or have taken less advantage of that opportunity.[159] In both cases the employer may only justify the remuneration of such adaptability or training by showing it is of importance for the performance of specific tasks entrusted to the employee.[160]

2.2. Market Forces/Labour Market Factors

The Court has also allowed objective justifications to take account of economic factors relating to the needs and objectives of the undertaking[161] and of the state.[162] Thus, when the *state* is defending its indirectly discriminatory legislation, the Court has recognized that the encouragement of recruitment constitutes a legitimate aim of social policy.[163] When *employers* are seeking to

---

account for only a small proportion of pay. This criterion may be of particular relevance in the training phase but become less relevant once the employee has acquired sufficient command of his or her job. Finally, the way length of service is accounted for must also minimise the negative impact of the criterion on women. It seems to me, for example, that a system which excludes periods of maternity or paternity leave, although it is prima facie neutral, would result in indirect discrimination against women.'

[157] Case 109/88 [1989] ECR I–3199.   [158] Para. 21.
[159] Para. 23.
[160] Paras. 22–3. Cf. Case C–309/97 *Angestelltenbetriebsrat der Wiener Gebietskrankenkasse* v. *Wiener Gebietskrankenkasse* [1999] ECR I–2865, para. 19.
[161] Case 96/80 *Jenkins* [1981] ECR 911.
[162] Case C–189/91 *Kirsammer-Hack* v. *Sidal* [1993] ECR I–6185, paras. 33–4: measures which excluded part-time workers from the calculation of the threshold of five employees (if the employer employed less than five employees the rules on unfair dismissal did not apply) could be objectively justified by reference to the need 'to alleviate the constraints burdening small businesses which play an essential role in economic development and the creation of employment in the Community'.
[163] Case C–167/97 *Seymour-Smith and Perez* [1999] ECR I–623, para. 71.

justify their practices, the Court has permitted them to justify paying full-time workers more than part-time workers in order to encourage full-time work,[164] and paying certain jobs more in order to attract candidates when the market indicates that such workers are in short supply.[165] However, the Court does not permit employers to pay part-time workers less simply because they are part-time,[166] or job-sharers less solely on the grounds that avoidance of such discrimination would involve increased costs.[167] In a similar vein, it also impermissible for a state to argue that public utilities should not bear excessive costs.[168]

While the Court will not usually accept economic justifications put forward by *employers* that it costs too much to secure equal pay,[169] it tends to be more deferential to a state's arguments based on budgets when the state is defending its own legislative choices, provided the state's argument is carefully tailored. Thus in *Jørgensen*[170] the Court said that although budgetary considerations might underlie a Member State's choice of social policy and influence the nature or scope of the social protection measures which it wishes to adopt, they did not in themselves constitute an aim pursued by that policy and could not therefore justify discrimination against one of the sexes.[171] As the Court explained in *Kutz-Bauer*, if budgetary considerations could justify a difference in treatment, the scope of the fundamental principle of equality could vary in time and place according to the state of the public

---

[164] See e.g. Case C–170/84 *Bilka-Kaufhaus* [1984] ECR 1607 where Bilka-Kaufhaus argued that the employment of full-time workers entailed lower ancillary costs and permitted the use of staff throughout opening hours. In general part-time workers refused to work in the late afternoons and on Saturdays. However, see now the Part-time Work Dir. 97/81 (OJ [1998] L14/9), considered in Ch. 9.

[165] Case C–127/92 *Enderby* [1993] ECR I–5535. If the national court can determine precisely what proportion of the increase in pay is attributable to market forces, it must necessarily accept that the pay differential is objectively justified to the extent of that proportion.

[166] Case C–196/02 *Nikoloudi v. Organismos Tilepikinonion Ellados AE* [2005] ECR I–000, para. 51. See also Joined Cases C–4/02 and C–5/02 *Schönheit v. Stadt Frankfurt am Main* [2003] ECR I–12575, para. 97 where the Court ruled that part-timers could not be paid less to stop them being placed at an advantage compared to full-timers. See now the Part-time Work Dir. 97/81 (OJ [1998] L14/9).

[167] Case C–243/95 *Hill* [1998] ECR I–3739, para. 40. In Case C–226/98 *Jørgensen v. Foreningen af Speciallæger and Sygesikringens Forhandlingsudvalg* [2000] ECR I–2447, para. 42, the Court said that budgetary considerations could not in themselves justify discrimination on grounds of sex. However, measures intended to ensure sound management of public expenditure on specialized medical care and to guarantee people's access to such care could be justified if they met a legitimate objective of social policy, were appropriate and necessary.

[168] Case C–196/02 *Nikoloudi v. Organismos Tilepikinonion Ellados AE* [2005] ECR I–000, paras. 51–2.

[169] Case C–226/98 *Jørgensen* [2000] ECR I–2447, para. 39; Case C–243/95 *Kathleen Hill and Ann Stapleton v. Revenue Commissioners* [1998] ECR I–3739, para. 40.

[170] Case C–226/98 *Jørgensen* [2000] ECR I–2447, para. 30.

[171] Case C–343/92 *De Weerd and Others* [1994] ECR I–571, para. 35.

finances of Member States.[172] However, in *Jørgensen*[173] the Court went on to recognize that reasons relating to the need to ensure sound management of public expenditure on specialized medical care and to guarantee people's access to such care were legitimate and could justify measures of social policy.

The Court has also made clear that generalizations about certain categories of workers—such as the belief that part-time workers are not as integrated in, or as dependent upon the undertaking employing them as full-time workers—do not constitute objectively justified grounds.[174] This point was reinforced in *Hill* where the Court sent out a strong message that it required concrete evidence before accepting any justification. Therefore, the Irish government's argument that its reward system maintained staff motivation, commitment, and morale was 'no more than a general assertion unsupported by objective criteria'. Similarly, in *Kutz-Bauer*[175] the Court said that mere generalizations about the capacity of a specific measure to encourage recruitment were not enough to show that the aim of the disputed provisions was unrelated to any discrimination on the grounds of sex or to provide evidence on the basis of which it could be reasonably considered that the means chosen were or could be suitable for achieving that aim.

2.3. Collective Bargaining

The Court has also examined the validity of the justification that the discrimination was the result of separate structures of collective bargaining. In *Enderby*[176] the Court ruled that the fact that collective bargaining had led to the rates of pay of two jobs of equal value (speech therapy carried out almost exclusively by women and pharmacy performed predominantly by men) was not sufficient objective justification for the difference in pay between the two jobs. The Court reached this conclusion despite the fact that the collective bargaining was carried out by the same parties, and, taken separately, had in itself no discriminatory effect.

However, in *Dansk Industri*[177] the Court seems to have relaxed its view. It said that the national court could take into account the fact that the elements of pay were determined by separate collective bargaining in its assessment as to whether the differences between the two groups of workers were due to objective factors unrelated to sex.

---

[172] Case C–187/00 [2003] ECR I–000, para. 60.
[173] Case C–226/98 *Jørgensen* [2000] ECR I–2447, para. 30.
[174] Case 171/88 *Rinner-Kühn* [1989] ECR 2743.
[175] Case C–187/00 *Kutz-Bauer v. Freie und Hansestadt Hamburg* [2003] ECR I–000, para. 58.
[176] Case C–127/92 [1993] ECR I–5535.
[177] Case C–400/93 *Specialarbejderforbundet i Danmark v. Dansk Industri* [1995] ECR I–1275.

3. Different Levels of Scrutiny

3.1. Introduction

The (strict) *Bilka* test for objective justification was developed in the context of indirectly discriminatory conduct by *employers*. That test was broadly reflected in the Burden of Proof Directive[178] and now the Consolidated Directive. It provides that an indirectly discriminatory measure is unlawful unless the measure is 'objectively justified by a legitimate aim, and the means of achieving that aim are appropriate and necessary'.[179] However, despite the fact that these two Directives lay down only the one test for objective justification, the Court of Justice seems to apply at least three tests for objective justification depending on the circumstances: the strict *Bilka* test for indirectly discriminatory conduct by employers, recently affirmed in *Hill*,[180] the weaker *Seymour-Smith*[181] test for indirectly discriminatory employment legislation, and the very dilute test for social security legislation in *Nolte/Megner*.[182]

3.2. The Sliding Scale of Objective Justification

In the context of indirectly discriminatory *legislation*, the Court initially formulated a test similar to that in *Bilka*. In *Rinner-Kühn*,[183] a case concerning indirectly discriminatory employment legislation, the Court ruled that the Member State could justify such legislation provided that it could show that the means chosen met a necessary aim of its social policy and that the legislation was suitable for attaining that aim. In *De Weerd*[184] the Court applied *Rinner-Kühn* in the context of social security.

More recently, however, the Court has shown signs of diluting this test, at least in the context of social security cases. *Nolte*[185] and *Megner*[186] concerned German social security law under which individuals working less than 15 hours per week and whose income did not exceed one seventh of the monthly reference wage[187] were termed 'minor' or 'marginal' part-time workers. Since these workers were not subject to the statutory old-age insurance scheme covering invalidity and sickness benefit, they did not have to pay contributions. They were also exempt from paying contributions for unemployment

---

[178] Dir. 97/80 ([1998] OJ L14/6).   [179] Art. 2(1)(b).
[180] Case C–243/95 [1998] ECR I–3739 (job sharers returning to full-time work).
[181] Case C–167/97 [1999] ECR I–623.
[182] Case C–317/93 *Nolte v. Landesversicherungsanstalt Hannover* [1996] ECR I–4625. For a full discussion, see O'Leary, *Employment Law at the European Court of Justice: Judicial Structures, Policies and Processes* (Hart Publishing, Oxford, 2002), Ch. 4.
[183] Case 171/88 [1989] ECR 2743.   [184] Case C–343/92 [1994] ECR I–571.
[185] Case C–317/93 *Nolte v. Landesversicherungsanstalt Hannover* [1996] ECR I–4625.
[186] Case C–444/93 *Megner*[1995] ECR I–4741.
[187] The average monthly salary of persons insured under the statutory old-age insurance scheme during the previous calendar year.

benefit. Although the legislation affected considerably more women that men, the German government argued that the exclusion of people in minor employment corresponded to a structural principle of the German social security scheme, that there was a social demand for minor employment and that if it subjected marginal workers to compulsory insurance there would be an increase in unlawful employment and an increase in avoidance techniques (for instance false self-employment).

The Court began by citing *De Weerd*[188] and repeated the standard *Rinner-Kühn* test for objective justification. It said that social policy was a matter for the Member States which had a broad margin of discretion and could choose the measures capable of achieving the aim of their social and employment policy. It then said:

> It should be noted that the social and employment policy aim relied on by the German government is objectively unrelated to any discrimination on the grounds of sex and that, in exercising its competence, the national legislature was *reasonably entitled* to consider that the legislation in question was necessary in order to achieve that aim.[189]

The Court reached similar conclusions in *Laperre*[190] and *Van Damme*.[191] The test of 'reasonableness' applied here is weaker than the more rigorous test envisaged by *Rinner-Kühn* and the subsequent cases. It is also striking that the Court itself decided in *Megner* that 'the legislation in question was necessary to achieve a social policy aim unrelated to any discrimination on the grounds of sex',[192] even though in *Lewark* the Court said that drawing such conclusions was a task for the national court. The Court reached this conclusion in *Megner* without citing any evidence, nor considering whether the social policy aim in question could be achieved by other means.[193] The Court also accepted that, with the exception of mere budgetary considerations,[194] almost any other social policy reason (provided it met the proportionality test) would justify indirect discrimination in state social security schemes.[195]

---

[188] Case C–343/92 [1994] ECR I–571.   [189] Para. 30, emphasis added.

[190] Case C–8/94 *Laperre* v. *Bestuurcommissie beroepszaken in de provincie Zuid-Holland* [1996] ECR I–273.

[191] Case C–280/94 *Posthuma-van Damme* v. *Bestuur van de Bedrijfsvereniging voor Detailhandel* [1996] ECR I–179.

[192] It decided similarly in Case C–317/93 *Nolte* [1996] ECR I–4625 and Case C–8/84 *Laperre* [1996] ECR I–273.

[193] Cf. the British House of Lords' ruling in *R* v. *Secretary of State for Employment, ex parte EOC* [1994] IRLR 176 that the Secretary of State had failed to show that discriminatory service thresholds could be objectively justified.

[194] Case C–343/92 *De Weerd* [1994] ECR I–571.

[195] Case C–280/94 *Posthuma-van Damme* [1996] ECR I–179 and Case C–8/94 *Laperre* [1996] ECR I–273. See also Case C–25/01 *Rinke* v. *Ärztekammer Hamburg* [2003] ECR I–8349, para. 39 where the Court applied the relaxed test of justification when faced by a challenge to the validity of Community legislation (considered further at n. 200 below).

In *Seymour-Smith*[196] the Court was asked to choose between the *Rinner-Kühn* and *Nolte/Megner* tests when the state sought to justify indirectly discriminatory *employment* legislation. The answer was inconclusive. The Court's initial observations favoured the *Rinner-Kühn* test. It said:

It must also be ascertained, in the light of all the relevant factors and taking into account the possibility of achieving the social policy aim [encouragement of recruitment][197] in question by other means, whether such an aim appears to be unrelated to any discrimination based on sex and whether the disputed rule, as a means to its achievement, is capable of advancing that aim.[198]

The UK government, introducing the language of reasonableness, maintained that a Member State should merely have to show that it was reasonably entitled to consider that the measure would advance a social policy aim. The Court recalled that in *Nolte/Megner* it had observed that, in choosing the measures capable of achieving the aims of their social and employment policy, the Member States have a broad margin of discretion. It added:

75. However, although social policy is essentially a matter for the Member States under Community law as it stands, the fact remains that the broad margin of discretion available to the Member States in that connection cannot have the effect of frustrating the implementation of a fundamental principle of Community law such as that of equal pay for men and women.
76. Mere generalisations concerning the capacity of a specific measure to encourage recruitment are not enough to show that the aim of the disputed rule is unrelated to any discrimination based on sex nor to provide evidence on the basis of which it could reasonably be considered that the means chosen were suitable for achieving that aim.

The Court then reformulated the test for justification in its answer to the national court in terms of the *Nolte/Megner* test:

77. Accordingly, the answer to the fifth question must be that if a considerably smaller percentage of women than men is capable of fulfilling the requirement of two years' employment imposed by the disputed rule, it is for the Member State, as the author of the allegedly discriminatory rule, to show that the said rule reflects a legitimate aim of its social policy, that that aim is unrelated to any discrimination based on sex, and that it could reasonably consider that the means chosen were suitable for attaining that aim.

It is still not clear which test is being applied: judges favouring a more rigorous approach to equality got their way in paragraphs 75 and 76; those favouring a more market-oriented concept, winning through in paragraph 77.[199]

---

[196] Case C–167/97 [1999] ECR I–623.
[197] The Court accepted that this was a legitimate aim of social policy (para. 71).
[198] Para. 72.
[199] For a further example of a relaxed approach to indirectly discriminatory state legislation, see Case C–322/98 *Kachelmann* v. *Bankhaus Hermann Lampe KG* [2000] ECR I–7505, para. 34.

So far we have been concentrating on indirectly discriminatory *state* legislation. However, in *Rinke*[200] the Court extended the same flexible approach to indirectly discriminatory *Community* legislation. At issue was a provision in Directive 86/457[201] requiring doctors to undertake certain periods of full-time training during part-time training in general medical practice. Although 'such a requirement does in fact place women at a particular disadvantage as compared with men',[202] the Court considered that:

It was reasonable for the legislature to take the view that that requirement enables doctors to acquire the experience necessary, by following patients' pathological conditions as they may evolve over time, and to obtain sufficient experience in the various situations likely to arise more particularly in general medical practice.

The existence of a sliding scale of tests is supported by the Court's decision in *Krüger*.[203] The case concerned the exclusion of those employed in 'minor' employment, as defined in *Nolte/Megner*, from an end of year bonus paid by the *employer* under a collective agreement. The Court, noting that the case concerned a situation 'which is different from . . . *Nolte* and *Megner*',[204] said:

In this case, it is not a question of either a measure adopted by the national legislature in the context of its discretionary power or a basic principle of the German social security system, but of the exclusion of persons in minor employment from the benefit of a collective agreement which provides for the grant of a special annual bonus, the result of this being that, in respect of pay, those persons are treated differently from those governed by that collective agreement.

This confirms that employers cannot rely on the more lenient test of justification available to the state. The Court itself then went on to find that the exclusion was indirectly discriminatory and, by implication, could not be objectively justified.[205]

4. Proportionality

While proportionality has always been an integral part of the test for objective justification, in the more recent cases the Court has sought to re-emphasize its importance. We have already seen the Court's reference in *Kutz-Bauer* and *Seymour-Smith* to the fact that mere generalizations are not sufficient to show either that the discrimination was not based on sex or that the steps taken were proportionate. In *Steinicke*[206] the Court underlined this point. In order to benefit from a law permitting public servants approaching retirement to work

---

[200] Case C–25/02 *Rinke v. Ärztekammer Hamburg* [2003] ECR I–8349.
[201] OJ [1986] L267/26.   [202] Para. 35.
[203] Case C–281/97 *Krüger v. Kreiskrankenhaus Ebersberg* [1999] ECR I–5127.
[204] Para. 29.   [205] Para. 30.
[206] Case C–77/02 *Steinicke v. Bundesanstalt für Arbeit* [2003] ECR I–9027.

part time, an individual employee was required to have worked full time for three of the five years immediately preceding the period of part-time work. Ms Steinicke, a part-time worker who could not satisfy the requirement of having worked full time for three of the five years, argued that the scheme was indirectly discriminatory contrary to Article 5(1) of Directive 76/207 (Article 14 of the Consolidated Directive). The Court agreed[207] and also found that the national law was not a proportionate means of achieving the objective. It noted that the national rules excluded from access to the part-time working scheme the very group of people (public servants working part-time) who made a considerable contribution to the unblocking of the employment market.[208] It continued:

As a result, a provision of national law which poses the risk that workers may be discouraged from accepting part-time work for older employees cannot *a priori* be considered to be an apt or suitable means of attaining the objective of unblocking the employment market.

F. ENFORCEMENT OF EQUALITY RIGHTS

1. Direct Effect

In *Defrenne (No. 2)*[209] the Court ruled that Article 141 was directly effective and could thus give rise to individual rights which the courts had to protect.[210] This means that the prohibition of discrimination applies 'not only to the actions of public authorities, but also extends to all agreements which are intended to regulate paid labour collectively, as well as contracts between individuals'.[211] Thus, Article 141 has both vertical *and* horizontal direct effect. At first the Court suggested that Article 141 was not directly effective in the context of 'indirect or disguised discrimination' which requires the elaboration by the Community and national legislative bodies of criteria of assessment',[212] but in *Bilka-Kaufhaus*[213] the Court said that individuals could rely on Article 141 to secure the elimination of indirect discrimination. It now seems that although the Court continues to pay lipservice to this potential limit on the direct effect of Article 141,[214] the limitation is, in reality, redundant for

---

[207] Para. 57.   [208] Para. 65.   [209] Case 43/75 [1976] ECR 455.

[210] On the background to the direct effect of Article 141, see AG Lamothe's opinion in Case 80/60 *Defrenne (No. 1)* [1971] ECR 445, 456.

[211] See also Case C–28/93 *Van den Akker* [1994] ECR I–4527, para. 21; Case C–320/00 *Lawrence* [2002] ECR I–7325, para. 13.

[212] Case 43/75 *Defrenne (No. 2)* [1996] ECR 455, para. 19, and Case 129/79 *Macarthys* [1980] ECR 1275, para. 15.

[213] Case 170/84 [1986] ECR 1607.

[214] See e.g. Case C–262/88 *Barber* [1990] ECR I–1889, para. 37.

the Court has found Article 141 to be directly effective in areas of great complexity, including occupational pensions and survivors' benefits.[215]

Since Article 1 of Directive 75/117 was essentially designed 'to facilitate the practical application of the principle of equal pay laid down in Article [141]' and in no way altered the scope or content of that principle,[216] exceptionally it had both vertical and horizontal direct effect. It is likely that the same approach will apply to Article 4 of the Consolidated Directive.

2. Burden of Proof

The Court has ruled that in principle the burden of proving the existence of sex discrimination lies with the complainant.[217] It has, however, recognized that adjustments to national rules on the burden of proof may be necessary to ensure the effective implementation of the principle of equality. This can be seen in *Danfoss*.[218] In that case the employer's pay structure provided the same basic wage to all employees but paid additional individual supplements on the basis of mobility, training, and seniority. This resulted in the average wage paid to men being 6.86 per cent higher than that paid to women. This system was so lacking in transparency that female employees could only establish differences between their pay and that received by their male colleagues by reference to average pay. Consequently, the Court concluded that the applicants would be deprived of any effective means of enforcing the principle of equal pay before the national courts if the effect of producing such evidence was not to impose upon employers the burden of proving that their pay practices were not in fact discriminatory.

Similarly, in *Enderby* the Court concluded that if the pay of speech therapists was significantly lower than that of pharmacists, and the speech therapists were almost exclusively women while the pharmacists were predominantly men, there was a prima facie case of discrimination, at least where the two jobs were of equal value and the statistics describing the situation were valid. As a result it was for the employers to show that there were objective reasons for the difference in pay and for the national court to assess whether it could take those statistics into account and to assess whether

---

[215] Case C–262/88 *Barber* [1990] ECR I–1889 and Case 109/91 *Ten Oever* [1993] ECR I–5535, respectively.
[216] Case 96/80 *Jenkins v. Kingsgate* 1981] ECR 911; Case C–381/99 *Brunnhofer* [2001] ECR I–4961, para. 29.
[217] Case C–127/92 *Enderby* [1993] ECR I–5535.
[218] Case 109/88 [1989] ECR I–3199. See further Case 318/86 *Commission v. France* [1988] ECR 3559; Case 248/83 *Commission v. Germany* [1985] ECR 1459, Case C–127/92 *Enderby* [1993] ECR I–5535.

they covered enough individuals, whether they illustrated purely fortuitous or short-term phenomena, and whether in general they appeared to be significant.[219]

However, in *Dansk Industri*[220] the Court sounded a note of caution. It said that in a piecework pay scheme a prima facie case of discrimination did not arise solely because significant statistics disclose appreciable differences between the average pay of two groups of workers, since those statistics might be due to differences in individual output of the workers in the two groups. However, where the individual pay consisted of both a fixed and a variable element, and it was not possible to identify the factors which determined the rates or units of measurement used to calculate the variable element in the pay, the employer might have to bear the burden of proving that the differences found were not due to sex discrimination. Again, it was for the national court to decide whether the conditions for shifting the burden of proof were satisfied.

This case law, allowing a reversal of the burden of proof,[221] helped to unblock a Directive on the Burden of Proof proposed under Articles 94 and 308,[222] but which had not made progress in Council. Eventually the Commission initiated the procedure under Article 3 of the SPA (new Article 138),[223] which led to the adoption (via the legislative route)[224] of Directive 97/80 on the burden of proof.[225] The Directive, now incorporated into the Consolidated Directive, is a minimum standards measure[226] which applies to the situations in the Consolidated Directive, together with Article 141, and, in so far as discrimination based on sex is concerned, the Directives on Pregnant Workers' and Parental Leave.[227] It also applies to any civil or administrative procedure concerning the public or private sector which provides for means of redress under national law pursuant to Article 141 and the Equality Directives.[228] The central provision is Article 4 of the Burden of Proof Directive, now

---

[219] See also Case C–400/93 *Dansk Industri* [1995] ECR I–1275; Case C–236/98 *Örebro läns landsting* [2000] ECR I–2189, para. 53.

[220] Case C–400/93 [1995] ECR I–1275.

[221] According to Ellis, *EU Anti-discrimination Law* (OUP, Oxford, 2005) 99 the Court meant the legal as distinct from the evidential burden of proof.

[222] The Commission's original proposal can be found at OJ [1988] C176/5.

[223] The first round of consultations was launched on 5 July 1995. The Social Partners' opinions differed. Some did not consider any action in the area to be justified, since a series of national legal instruments and the Court's case law had already achieved the desired aim. Others thought that action should be taken at European level while respecting the principle of subsidiarity. As far as the proper level and nature of the action to be taken, some organizations preferred a binding Community measure and others a less rigid approach, such as a recommendation.

[224] See further Ch. 2.

[225] OJ [1998] L14/16, amended by Council Directive 98/52 (OJ [1998] L205/66). See Lanquetin, 'Discriminations à raison du sexe' (1998) 7/8 *Droit Social* 688.

[226] Art. 19(2).   [227] Art. 20(4)(a).

[228] Art. 20(4)(b). It does not apply to out-of-court procedures of a voluntary nature or provided for in national law.

Article 19(1) of the Consolidated Directive. This provides that Member States shall take such measures as are necessary, in accordance with their national judicial systems, to ensure that:

when persons who consider themselves wronged because the principle of equal treatment has not been applied to them establish, before a court or other competent authority, facts from which it may be presumed that there has been direct or indirect discrimination, it shall be for the respondent to prove that there has been no breach of the principle of equal treatment.[229]

Although the reversal of the burden of proof is unpopular with employers, it is now firmly entrenched in the Community acquis. The principle also applies to the Article 13 Directives.

3. Judicial Remedies

3.1. Effectiveness of the Remedy

It is a long-established principle of Community law that under the duty of co-operation laid down in Article 10 EC, the Member States must ensure the legal protection which individuals derive from the direct effect of Community law.[230] In the absence of Community rules governing a matter, it is for the domestic legal system of each Member State to designate the courts having jurisdiction and to lay down detailed procedural rules governing actions for safeguarding rights for individuals (the principle of procedural autonomy). However, such rules must not be less favourable than those governing similar domestic actions (the principle of equivalence) nor render virtually impossible or excessively difficult the exercise of rights conferred by Community law (the principle of effective judicial protection).[231]

The question of the adequacy of national remedies has been of central importance to the procedural protection conferred by the Equality Directives. Originally, Article 6 of the Equal Pay Directive 75/117/EEC required Member

---

[229] Art. 19(1). Art. 19(2) says that para. 1 does not prevent Member States from introducing rules of evidence which are more favourable to claimants; Art. 19(3) says that Member States do not need to apply para. 1 to proceedings in which it is for the court or competent body to investigate the facts of the case; and Art. 19(5) says that the rules on the reversal of the burden of proof will not apply to criminal procedures unless otherwise provided by the Member States.

[230] According to Case C–187/98 *Commission* v. *Greece* [1999] ECR I–7713, para. 45, a Member State cannot plead practical, administrative or financial difficulties to justify non-compliance with the obligations and time limits laid down by the Directive.

[231] See e.g. Case 33/76 *Rewe-Zentralfinanz eG* v. *Landwirtschaftskammer für das Saarland* [1976] ECR 1989, para. 5. See generally Craufurd-Smith, 'Remedies for Breaches of EC Law in National Courts: Legal Variation and Selection', in Craig and De Búrca (eds), *The Evolution of EU Law* (OUP, Oxford, 1999).

States to ensure that the principle of equal pay was applied,[232] and that effective means were available to ensure that the principle is observed. This provision has been repealed by the Consolidated Directive. In addition, Article 2 of Directive 75/117 required Member States to allow those who consider themselves wronged by the failure to apply the principle of equal pay to pursue their claims by judicial process. This has now been replaced by Article 17 of the Consolidated Directive, which requires Member States to ensure that, after possible recourse to other competent authorities including conciliation procedures, judicial and/or administrative procedures:

for the enforcement of obligations under this Directive are available to all persons who consider themselves wronged by failure to apply the principle of equal treatment to them, even after the relationship in which the discrimination is alleged to have occurred has ended.

In addition, Article 18 of the Consolidated Directive requires Member States to introduce into their legal systems such measures as are necessary:

to ensure real and effective compensation or reparation as the Member States so determine for the loss and damage sustained by a person injured as a result of discrimination on grounds of sex, in a way which is dissuasive and proportionate to the damage suffered.

Since these provisions are largely based on the case law decided under the Equal Treatment Directive 76/207 they will be discussed in more detail in the next chapter. In this chapter we shall focus on the issues specific to equal pay.

The Court has required that the amount of *each* individual benefit paid be non-discriminatory[233] and that access to the benefits (such as membership of an occupational pension scheme) must be non-discriminatory.[234] The pensions case law has thrown up two other major remedies issues:[235] (1) claims for arrears of pay where national law only allows arrears to be recovered for a limited period; and (2) time limits for bringing a claim (e.g. six months from the end of employment). The first issue is considered in this chapter, the second in chapter 10.

In respect of the first issue, an individual may wish to claim for arrears in respect of periods which predate the period for which recovery is permitted

---

[232] According to the Court, Member States may leave the implementation of the principle of equal pay to representatives of management and labour but this does not discharge Member States from the obligation of ensuring that all workers are afforded the full protection of the Directive, especially where the workers are not union members, where the sector is not covered by a collective agreement, or where the agreement does not fully guarantee the principle of equal pay: Case 143/83 *Commission v. Denmark* [1985] ECR 427.

[233] Case C–262/88 *Barber* [1990] ECR I–1889 The same principle of transparency was applied to Directives 76/207 and 86/613 in Case C–226/98 *Jørgensen* [2000] ECR I–2447, paras. 27 and 36.

[234] Case 170/84 *Bilka-Kaufhaus* [1986] ECR 1607. See further Ch. 10.

[235] See further Ch. 10.

under national law.[236] In this context, the Court has had to strike a balance between, on the one hand, legal certainty (and the cost to an individual pension scheme, government or employer) and, on the other, the principle of effective judicial protection. In two social security cases, *Johnson*[237] and *Steenhorst Neerings*,[238] the Court held that a restriction on backdating was valid under Community law. However, in the context of equal pay this might have the effect of denying the individual the benefit of the entitlement. The interplay of these two issues can be seen in the cases of *Magorrian*[239] and *Levez*.[240]

In *Magorrian* the applicants began employment as full-time workers and then became part-time workers when they had children. When they retired they were not entitled to the more favourable pension benefits available to full-time workers and so they brought a claim under Article 141 in 1992. In response, it was argued that, under the relevant statute, no award for arrears of pay could be made relating to a period earlier than two years before the date on which the proceedings had been instituted (i.e. 1990). However, the Court said the fact that the right to be admitted to a scheme might have effect from a date no earlier than two years before the institution of proceedings would deprive the applicants of the additional benefits under the scheme to which they were entitled to be affiliated, since those benefits could be calculated only by reference to periods of service completed by them two years prior to the commencement of proceedings. The Court then distinguished *Magorrian* from *Johnson*. It said that in *Magorrian* the claim was not for the retroactive award of certain additional benefits but for recognition of entitlement to full membership of an occupational scheme (which would lead to payment in the future of benefits based on that membership). The rules at issue in *Johnson* merely limited the period, prior to the commencement of proceedings, in respect of which backdated benefits could be obtained. In *Magorrian* the rule at issue prevented the entire record of service completed by those concerned after 8 April 1976 (the date of the judgment in *Defrenne (No. 2)*) until 1990 (two years prior to the start of proceedings) from being taken into account for the purposes of calculating the additional benefits which would be payable even after the date of the claim. Consequently, the Court said that the two-year rule rendered any action by individuals relying on Community law impossible in practice.

---

[236] These issues will be examined further in respect of social security claims under Directive 79/7, considered in Ch. 10.

[237] Case C–410/92 *Johnson* v. *Chief Adjudication Officer* [1994] ECR I–5483.

[238] Case C–338/91 *Steenhorst-Neerings* v. *Bestuur van de Bedrijfsvereniging* [1993] ECR I–5475.

[239] Case C–246/96 *Magorrian and Cunningham* v. *Eastern Health and Social Services Board and Department of Health and Social Services* [1997] ECR I–7153. See also Case C–78/98 *Preston* v. *Wolverhampton Health Care NHS Trust* [2000] ECR I–3201 which is considered in detail in Ch. 10.

[240] Case C–326/96 *Levez* v. *TH Jennings (Harlow Pools) Ltd* [1998] ECR I–7835.

The Court also emphasized the principle of effectiveness in *Levez*.[241] In February 1991 Mrs Levez was appointed manager of a betting shop owned by Jennings at a salary of £10,800 per annum. The employer falsely declared to her that this had been her male predecessor's salary. In fact, Mrs Levez's salary did not reach that of the predecessor (£11,400 per annum) until April 1992. Mrs Levez did not find this out until September 1993, whereupon she brought a claim for equal pay. The UK Industrial Tribunal which heard the case that Mrs Levez was entitled to a salary of £11,400 from the date on which she had taken up the job, and ordered Jennings to pay her arrears. Jennings appealed this decision, arguing that, in view of the national law concerning damages for failure to comply with the equal pay principle, the Industrial Tribunal had no power to award arrears of remuneration in respect of a time earlier than two years before the date on which the proceedings were instituted before the tribunal.[242] Thus, as Mrs Levez's application to the Industrial Tribunal was dated 17 September 1993, arrears could not be awarded in respect of the period before 17 September 1991.

The Court, having reviewed its jurisprudence on effective judicial protection, concluded that in principle it was compatible with Community law for national rules to prescribe reasonable limitation periods for bringing proceedings, in the interests of legal certainty. Therefore, a national procedural rule, such as that at issue in *Levez*, would not in itself be incompatible with Community law.[243] However, the Court went on to consider the circumstances of Mrs Levez's case, and in particular the fact that the employer had concealed from Mrs Levez the pay of her predecessor. The Court pointed out that in such circumstances, an employee would have no means of determining whether she was being discriminated against. Thus the employer would effectively be able to deprive the employee of the entitlement to enforce the principle of equal pay before the courts.[244] To allow an employer, in such a situation, to rely on a procedural rule of national law, would make it virtually impossible or excessively difficult for the employee to obtain arrears of remuneration in respect of sex discrimination in pay. In these circumstances, the Court said, there existed no justification for the application of the national rules in terms of legal certainty or the proper conduct of proceedings.[245]

Levez also raised the issue as to what the principle of equivalence actually meant in practice. It was argued by the employer and the United Kingdom

---

[241] Case C–326/96 [1998] ECR I–7835.   [242] UK Equal Pay Act 1970, s. 2(5).
[243] Para. 20.
[244] Cf. the Court's approach in respect of transparency and the burden of proof in Case 109/88 *Danfoss* [1989] ECR 3199.
[245] Paras. 31–4. In *Levez (No. 2)* [1999] IRLR 764 the British EAT ruled that the two-year limitation on arrears of remuneration in EPA 1970, s. 2(5) breached Community law in that it was less favourable than those governing similar claims, such as for unlawful deduction from wages and unlawful discrimination on the grounds of race. It ruled that the six-year limit in the Limitation Act 1980 would apply.

government that Mrs Levez did have an adequate remedy in national law, in that she could bring proceedings not before the Industrial Tribunal, but before the county court on the basis of breach of contract pursuant to the UK Equal Pay Act 1970 and the tort of deceit committed by the employer. The national court asked the Court what would constitute a 'similar domestic action', in the context of the principle of equivalence, in the case of an equal pay claim, where national law made different provision for equal pay than that made for other employment rights. The Court essentially said that it was for the national court to determine this issue. Where the alternative remedy in the county court was likely to entail procedural rules or other conditions which were less favourable than those appertaining before an Industrial Tribunal, then the principle of equivalence would be breached. In making this determination, the national court would need to take into account matters such as the relative costs and delays involved in each proceedings.[246]

The Court in *Levez* showed some sensitivity to the practicalities of bringing an equal pay claim.[247] The reality of such claims is often that the employer is in a much stronger position than the employee, in terms of holding relevant information on comparative pay of men and women employees. In the absence of any duties of transparency, the remedial effect of equal pay law would be significantly reduced if an employer, particularly a deliberately deceitful employer, could hide behind technical procedural rules to escape an equal pay claim. What seems certain is that the Court is not going anywhere near so far as to impose on employers a duty to disclose sufficient information to allow women employees to ensure that they are paid equally with male comparators. Although to do so would no doubt improve the position of those seeking to bring an equal pay claim, it would also go a long way beyond the requirements of Article 141 and, in the absence of legislation requiring such disclosure, would constitute too great an infringement of national procedural autonomy.

3.2. Levelling Up or Down?

It might be expected that the realization of equality necessarily equates with a levelling up of entitlement. In *Defrenne (No. 2)*[248] the Court accepted this. It said that in view of the connection between Article 141 and the harmonization of working conditions while the improvement is being maintained,[249] it

---

[246] See further on this issue Hervey and Rostant, 'After *Francovich*: State Liability and British Employment Law' (1996) 25 *ILJ* 259. See also Case C–78/98 *Preston* v. *Wolverhampton Health Care NHS Trust* [2000] ECR I–3201, considered further in Ch. 10.

[247] See further Barnard and Hervey, 'European Union Employment and Social Policy Survey 1998' (1998) 18 *Yearbook of European Law* 613, 638–40.

[248] Case 43/75 [1976] ECR 455. See also Case C–102/88 *Ruzius Wilbrink* [1989] ECR 4311.

[249] See Art. 117 (new Art. 136) and Case 126/86 *Zaera* [1987] ECR 3697.

was not possible to comply with Article 141 in other ways than by raising the lowest salaries.[250] This point was reinforced by *Kutz-Bauer*[251] where the Court said that national courts were required to set aside discrimination, using all the means at their disposal, and 'in particular by applying those provisions for the benefit of the class placed at a disadvantage, and are not required to await the setting aside of the provisions by the legislature, by collective negotiation or otherwise'.[252]

Thus Community law envisages levelling up by national courts once a finding of discrimination has been made. However, if an employer subsequently decides to level down, this is compatible with Community law. This is because, under Community law there is no background requirement of distributive justice (since formal equality is satisfied whether the two parties are treated equally well or equally badly). This can be seen in *Smith*[253] where the Court said that where the employer had decided to achieve equality by levelling down of entitlement (so that women received their pension at 65, the age at which the men had received it, rather than men receiving their pension at 60, as women had previously), this was compatible with Community law.

3.3. Proportionate Value?

The Court has not yet decided the question of how equal in value the men and women's work must be to receive equal pay. Since the Court has insisted that 'equal work be remunerated with equal pay'[254] this suggests that only work of exactly equal value should receive equal pay. The Court has also not yet considered the question of whether Article 141 should secure a woman proportionate pay, that is, a proportionate increase in pay when her work is valued. For example, her work is valued at 60 per cent of the man's, yet she receives only 40 per cent of his pay, can she rely on Community law to receive the additional 20 per cent?[255] There are straws in the wind to suggest that the Court might consider such a claim. For example, in *Rummler*[256] the Court said that it followed from the principle that equal work must be remunerated with equal pay that work performed must be remunerated according to its nature. This case, when read in conjunction with Article 136 and the Directive on

---

[250] See also Case C–102/88 *Ruzius Wilbrink* [1989] ECR I–4311 where the Court stated that part-timers are entitled to have the same system applied to them as other workers in proportion to their working hours, and the application of this in the case of collective agreements: Case 33/89 *Kowalska* [1990] ECR I–2591.

[251] Case C–187/00 [2003] ECR I–000, para. 75.

[252] Case C–184/89 *Nimz* [1991] ECR I–297, para. 21.

[253] Case C–408/92 [1994] ECR I–4435.   [254] Case 237/85 *Rummler* [1986] ECR 2101.

[255] See perhaps Case C–127/92 *Enderby* [1993] ECR I–5535. See further Rubinstein, 'The Equal Treatment Directive and UK Law', in McCrudden (ed.), *Women, Employment and European Equality Law* (Eclipse, London, 1987).

[256] Case 237/85 [1986] ECR 2101.

Part-time Workers,[257] might suggest that part-time workers should receive a proportionate share of full-time earnings.[258]

Enderby[259] lends some support to this view. When considering the market forces justification for paying one group of (predominantly male) workers more than another (predominantly female) group, the Court said that if the national court has been able to determine precisely what proportion of the increase in pay is attributable to market forces, 'it must necessarily accept that the pay differential is objectively justified to the extent of that proportion'.[260] The Court then added that 'When national authorities have to apply Community law, they must apply the principle of proportionality'.[261] This sentence has prompted some commentators to suggest that Community law might provide a basis for a proportionate pay claim.

G. CONCLUSIONS

Although the principle of equal pay has been enshrined in the EC Treaty since 1957, women are still paid less than men for the same work or for work of equal value. The pay gap is greater in the private sector (25 per cent) than the public sector (9 per cent).[262] The pay gap is due to a variety of factors. First, women are segregated both in terms of occupation and establishment. Predominantly female occupations attract consistently lower rates of pay than do male occupations. This is particularly the case where women work part time, as the facts of *Enderby* highlight. In that case the majority of the speech therapists were women working part time while the majority of pharmacists were men working full time. Speech therapists earned up to 60 per cent less than pharmacists.

The second explanation for the difference in pay is that even where men and women do the same kind of work in the same organizations women tend to attract lower pay because they are concentrated in lower paying specialisms, they occupy lower status jobs and the method of remuneration impacts differently on men and women (by, for example, rewarding seniority or flexibility). Further, women's skills are often undervalued. This is exacerbated by the fact that, while much of the unfavourable stereotyping of women and their abilities has been swept away, many girls and young women are still

---

[257] Dir. 97/81/EC (OJ [1997] L14/9), as amended by Council Dir. 98/23/EC (OJ [1998] L131/10) and consolidated OJ [1998] L131/13.
[258] See also Case C–102/88 *Ruzius Wilbrink* [1989] ECR 4311.
[259] Case C–127/92 [1993] ECR I–5535.
[260] Para. 21.   [261] Ibid.
[262] Commission, *Towards a Community Framework Strategy on Gender Equality (2001–5)* COM(2000) 335, 21.

following traditional routes in education and training, and being paid less than men as a result.[263]

Once again, this highlights the limits of the law, especially a complex law such as the one on equal pay, in achieving full equality. The law, dependent as it is on individual enforcement, cannot really address the heart of structural inequalities. Decisions such as *Lawrence* and *Allonby* serve only to underline the limits of the law. On the other hand, law can trigger social change and the inclusion, in the second paragraph of Article 21(4) of the Consolidated Directive 2006/54, of the possible obligation on employers to provide information to employees and their representatives about pay and pay differentials is a small but important step. Such transparency may reveal that there is a problem of a gender pay gap. The Directive also suggests that employers must put forward possible measures of how to improve it.

[263] Women and Work Commission, *Shaping a Fairer Future*, February 2006, vii.

8

Equal Treatment

A. INTRODUCTION

As we have already seen, the European Union has enjoyed a long history of prohibiting discrimination on the grounds of sex in the context of employment, most notably through the Equal Pay Directive 75/117 and the Equal Treatment Directive 76/207. The inclusion of Article 13 in the EC Treaty at Amsterdam gave the Community the power to prohibit discrimination on other grounds, notably race and ethnic origin, sexual orientation, religion and belief, age, and disability. Two Directives were subsequently adopted, one on race and ethnic origin,[1] the other, so-called 'horizontal' or 'framework' Directive, covering the remaining grounds.[2] These built on the experience gained in the field of sex equality. This process of learning was extended in turn back into the sex equality field when Directive 2002/73 was adopted (under Article 141(3)) amending the Equal Treatment Directive 76/207, to bring it into line with the employment aspects of the Article 13 Directives, and to reflect developments in the case law; while Directive 2004/113 followed the pattern of the Race Directive 2000/43 and extended the principle of equal treatment between men and women to access to and supply of goods and services[3] (but not to other areas such as housing and education).[4] The aim of this chapter is to consider these developments against the backcloth of the broader debate on equality in the EU.

B. THE PROHIBITED GROUNDS OF DISCRIMINATION

1. Introduction

The list of grounds on which discrimination is prohibited by the Community Directives—sex, sex change, marital status, race, ethnic origin, religion or belief, sexual orientation, age, and disability—largely mirrors those found in

---

[1] Dir. 2000/43/EC.   [2] Dir. 2000/78/EC.   [3] OJ [2004] L373/37.
[4] Art. 3(3) expressly provides that 'This Directive shall not apply to the content of media and advertising nor to education'.

major international instruments[5] and other domestic Charters such as section 15(1) of the Canadian Charter of Fundamental Rights. The conventional
argument for the prohibition of discrimination on grounds of sex, race, and
ethnic origin is that these characteristics are immutable, clearly identifiable to
employers and are (usually) irrelevant to an individual's ability to do a job.
By taking these characteristics into account when making employment
decisions, employers narrow any pool of applicants, often based on stereotypical assumptions associated with the particular ground, with the result
that the employer is not selecting the best candidate on merit and suitability
alone.

In respect of the other prohibited grounds of discrimination—sexual orientation, religion or belief, age, and disability—they do not share all the characteristics associated with sex and race. For example, sexual orientation and
disability may not be clearly identifiable to an employer, and religion or belief
is not necessarily immutable. Age and disability may actually impact on an
individual's ability to do a job. However, what these groups do have in common is the risk that the individuals are excluded from the possibility of participating fully in working life based on stereotypical assumptions rather than
an assessment of the individual's personal characteristics.[6] These social
inclusion arguments underpin the European Employment Strategy. This
vision is articulated clearly in one of the so-called '10 commandments' in the
2003 guidelines.[7] Guideline 7 is headed 'Promote the integration of and
combat the discrimination against people at a disadvantage in the labour
market'. It then identifies early school leavers, low-skilled workers, people
with disabilities, immigrants, and ethnic minorities as those facing 'particular
difficulties'. Member States are urged to develop their employability, increase
job opportunities and prevent all forms of discrimination against them. The
law's response is therefore to deem certain characteristics to be irrelevant and
make it unlawful for decisions to be taken about individuals on these prohibited
bases. The differences between the strands are then reflected in adaptations to
the basic non-discrimination model.

2. Sex, Gender Reassignment, Marital and Family Status

The prohibition of discrimination on the grounds of sex is the longest standing prohibited ground. The term 'sex' is not defined in the Directive. However,
its meaning is neither obvious nor uncontentious. In general the courts have

---

[5] E.g. Art. 2 Universal Declaration of Human Rights; Art. 2(2) International Covenant of
Economic, Social and Cultural Rights; Art. 2(1) International Covenant of Civil and Political
Rights. Discrimination against smokers is, however, permitted: euobserver.com, 7 Aug 2006.

[6] Collins, 'Discrimination, Equality and Social Inclusion' (2003) 66 *MLR*. 16.

[7] Co. Dec. 2003/578/EC (OJ [2000] L 197/13).

taken the view that 'sex' refers to the biological or birth sex of the individual. The term 'sex' is *not* therefore understood legally as 'gender', that is to say, as a socially constructed category. However, in *P v. S*,[8] Advocate General Tesauro did recognize that the biological understanding of sex may well include a sociological understanding. He said:[9]

Sex is important as a convention, a social parameter. The discrimination of which women are frequently the victims is not of course due to their physical characteristics, but rather to their role, to the image which society has of women. Hence the rationale for less favourable treatment is the social role which women are supposed to play and certainly not their physical characteristics.

For these very reasons—both biological and sociological—the differences between the sexes might apparently justify different treatment. However, the law requires men and women to be treated in the same way, as the strong language of the original Article 2(1) of the Equal Treatment Directive 76/207 makes clear. It provided that 'there shall be no discrimination *whatsoever* on grounds of sex either directly or indirectly by reference in particular to marital or family status'.[10] The biological differences between the sexes are accommodated in the various, narrowly tailored derogations, relating in particular to pregnancy and maternity.[11] The historical and social differences between the sexes (notably the woman's caring function) are addressed—to a limited extent at least—by the prohibition against indirect discrimination and the provision for positive action.

Most famously, in *P v. S*[12] the Court ruled that 'sex' included change of sex or gender reassignment: a characteristic which is also irrelevant to the individual's ability to do a job. This point was recognized by Advocate General Tesauro in *P v. S*:[13]

the unfavourable treatment suffered by transsexuals is most often linked to a negative image, a moral judgment which has nothing to do with their abilities in the sphere of employment.

Therefore, a male to female transsexual dismissed on the grounds of her sex change had a remedy in EC law. The Court reasoned that since the right not to be discriminated against on grounds of sex was one of the fundamental human rights whose observance the Court had a duty to ensure, the scope of the Directive could not be confined simply to discrimination based on the fact that a person was of one sex or another.[14] It then said that in view of the purpose and the nature of the rights which it sought to safeguard, the scope

---

[8] Case C–13/94 [1996] ECR I–2143.   [9] Para. 20.
[10] Emphasis added. Art. 14(1) of the Consolidated Dir. is less explicit.
[11] See below nn. 140–151.   [12] Case C–13/94 [1996] ECR I–2143.   [13] Para. 20.
[14] Paras. 18–19. The Court reached this conclusion even though Advocate General Tesauro pointed out that it was indisputable that the *wording* of the principle of equal treatment laid down by the Directive referred to the traditional man/woman dichotomy.

of the Directive applied to discrimination arising from the gender reassignment of the person concerned, since 'such discrimination is based, essentially if not exclusively, on the sex of the person concerned'.[15]

In *Grant*,[16] however, the Court drew the line at extending the concept of 'sex' to include sexual orientation. The Court explained its reluctance to extend the definition of 'sex' to include sexual orientation by referring to the fact that the Amsterdam Treaty gave the Council the power under Article 13 'to take appropriate action to eliminate various forms of discrimination, including discrimination based on sexual orientation',[17] and so deferred to the legislature to act, which it has now done. The Framework Directive does prohibit discrimination on the grounds of sexual orientation and, according to Article 3(1)(c) the principle of non-discrimination applies to 'employment and working conditions, including dismissals and pay'.

Article 2(1) of the original Equal Treatment Directive 76/207 also prohibited discrimination on the grounds of marital and family status. This precludes discrimination against those who are married and presumably, those who are unmarried, as well as those who do or do not have children, irrespective of their marital status.[18] Again, these grounds are irrelevant to an individual's ability to do a job but not immutable. This provision has not been included in the Consolidated Directive.

3. Race and Ethnic Origin

The Directive itself does not define the key terms racial and ethnic origin.[19] The *Shorter Oxford English Dictionary*[20] defines race as a 'group or set, especially of people having a common feature or features'. The Preamble adds that the 'European Union rejects theories which attempt to determine the existence of separate human races. The use of the term "racial origin" in this Directive does not imply an acceptance of such theories.'

The British House of Lords has considered the meaning of the phrase 'ethnic origin' in *Mandla* v. *Lee*[21] in the context of a question whether Sikhs

---

[15] Paras. 20–21. See now the 3rd preambular para of Dir. 2006/54. Wintemute, 'Sexual Orientation Discrimination', in McCrudden and Chambers (eds), *Individual Rights and the Law in Britain* (Clarendon, Oxford, 1995).

[16] Case C–249/96 [1998] ECR I–621. Cf. the decision of the European Court of Human Rights concerning Art. 8 of the European Convention in *Smith and Grady* v. *United Kingdom* [1999] IRLR 734.

[17] Para. 48.

[18] The phrase 'family status' may also embrace those with other caring responsibilities including looking after elderly relatives. Presumably, 'marital status' could also apply to those who are no longer married, either because of death or divorce, or those who are unmarried.

[19] For a more detailed discussion, see Brennan, 'The Race Directive: Recycling Racial Inequality' (2002–3) 5 *CYELS*. 311, 320–5.

[20] OUP, Oxford, 2002, 5th edn.　　　　　[21] [1983] IRLR 209.

formed an ethnic group. Lord Fraser said an 'ethnic group' must regard itself, and be regarded by others, as a distinct community by virtue of certain characteristics. He then said that some of these characteristics are essential; others are not essential but one or more of them will commonly be found and will help to distinguish the group from the surrounding community. The essential conditions are: (1) a long shared history, of which the group is conscious as distinguishing it from other groups, and the memory of which it keeps alive; (2) a cultural tradition of its own, including family and social customs and manners, often but not necessarily associated with religious observance. He then listed those characteristics which are relevant: (3) either a common geographical origin, or descent from a small number of common ancestors; (4) a common language, not necessarily peculiar to the group; (5) a common literature peculiar to the group; (6) a common religion different from that of neighbouring groups or from the general community surrounding it; (7) being a minority or being an oppressed or a dominant group within a larger community, for example a conquered people (say, the inhabitants of England shortly after the Norman conquest) and their conquerors might both be ethnic groups. He concluded that Sikhs did form part of an ethnic group because they are a distinctive and self-conscious community, with a history dating back to the fifteenth century, with a written language, a common religion and a common origin: they were at one time politically supreme in the Punjab.

The British courts have subsequently applied this test to find that members of the 'traveller' community (formally known as gypsies) were an ethnic group because of their shared history and common geographic origin, common customs, and a shared language and culture of folktales and music.[22] The courts have also found that Jewish people formed an ethnic group.[23] However, Rastafarians did not form part of an ethnic group (60 years did not amount to a long shared history)[24] nor did Muslims because of the many different nationalities and languages spoken by them.[25] The impact of these rulings has now been reduced by the advent of religion and belief becoming a protected ground.

Finally, unlike the British statute, the Directive says nothing about colour. This is surprising because the principal trigger for racially discriminatory behaviour is frequently colour: discriminators will seldom know the victim's ethnic or national origin and sometimes not the racial group but 'colour' is a visibly different characteristic.[26]

---

[22] *CRE v. Dutton* [1989] QB 783.   [23] *Seide v. Gillette Industries Ltd* [1980] IRLR 427.
[24] *Crown Suppliers v. Dawkins* [1993] ICR 517.
[25] *J H Walkers Ltd v. Hussain* [1996] IRLR 11.
[26] Commission for Racial Equality quoted by Rubinstein, 'New Discrimination Regulations: An EOR Guide' (2003) 119 *EOR* 20, 21.

4. Religion or Belief

There has been significantly less soft law activity in the field of religion and belief in comparison with the other grounds. However, the rise of Islamophobia, even predating the attacks on 11 September 2001, and various research projects at national level provided significant evidence of religious discrimination taking place in employment.[27] It was therefore not surprising that the horizontal Directive prohibits discrimination on the grounds of religion or belief. Once again, these grounds are not defined.

In the UK the implementing regulations merely specify that the phrase means 'any religion, religious belief, or similar philosophical belief'.[28] The guidance issued by the government gives further explanation.[29] It begins by explaining the term 'religion'. It says that the reference to 'religion' is a broad one, and is in line with the freedom of religion guaranteed by Article 9 ECHR. It includes those religions widely recognized, such as Christianity, Islam, Hinduism, Judaism, Buddhism, Sikhism, Rastafarianism, Baha'is, Zoroastrians, and Jains. Equally, branches or sects within a religion can be considered as a religion or religious belief, such as Catholics or Protestants within the Christian church.[30] The European Court of Human Rights has recognized other collective religions including Druidism, the Church of Scientology, and the Divine Light Zentrum. The guidance adds that the main limitation on what constitutes a 'religion' for the purposes of Article 9 ECHR, is that it must have a clear structure and belief system.[31]

As far as religious belief is concerned,[32] the guidance points out that it may go further than simply a belief about adherence to a religion or its central articles of faith to include other beliefs founded in a religion, if they 'attain a certain level of cogency, seriousness, cohesion and importance, provided the beliefs are worthy of respect in a democratic society and are not incompatible with human dignity.'[33] Finally, the guidance explains that the reference to 'similar philosophical belief' does not include any philosophical or political belief unless it is similar to a religious belief. Thus, the belief in question should be 'a profound belief affecting a person's way of life, or perception of the world'. It suggests that atheism and humanism satisfy this test; support

---

[27] See, e.g., Weller et al., Religious Discrimination in England and Wales, Home Office Research Study No. 220, February 2001, cited in Vickers, 'Freedom of Religion and the Workplace: The Draft Employment Equality (Religion or Belief) Regulations 2003' (2003) 32 ILJ. 23, 25.

[28] SI 2003/1660 The Employment Equality (Religion or Belief) Regulations 2003. The ACAS guide provides a useful list of the religions that are likely to be covered: http://www.acas.org.uk/publications/pdf/religion.pdf. For a German perspective, see Thüsing, 'Following the US Example: European Employment Discrimination Law and the Impact of Council Directives 2000/43 and 2000/78' (2003) 19 IJCLLIR. 187, 199–202.

[29] http://www.dti.gov.uk/er/equality/so_rb_longexplan.pdf   [30] Para. 11.

[31] X v. UK (1977) 11 DR 55.   [32] Para. 12.

[33] Citing the judgment of the European Court of Human Rights in Campbell and Cosans v. UK (1982) 4 EHRR 293 at 304.

for a political party and support for a football team do not.[34] It also suggests that non-belief is protected.

The guidance draws a distinction between holding a religion or belief and its manifestation. The notes explain that, following the distinction drawn in Article 9 ECHR, the definition of 'religion or belief' does not include the 'manifestation' of, or conduct based on or expressing a religion or belief.

As with the other grounds of discrimination, religion and belief may be immutable and are generally irrelevant to an individual's ability to do a particular task. Where an individual's religion is relevant to his or her ability to do a task (e.g. refusal by a Muslim to handle meat), this is dealt with through a narrowly tailored exception. Unlike other grounds of discrimination, an individual's religion or belief may not be visible (except in the case of those religions which do require particular clothing or conduct).

5. Sexual Orientation

The decision in *Grant* v. *South West Trains*,[35] where the Court ruled that the word 'sex' in Article 141 could not be construed to include sexual orientation, together with rulings by the European Court of Human Rights recognizing that discrimination on the grounds of sexual orientation infringed an individual's right to family life,[36] put pressure on the Community legislature to prohibit discrimination on the grounds of sexual orientation. The horizontal Directive adopted under Article 13 did just that.

Once again sexual orientation is not defined. However, the explanatory memorandum makes clear that a 'dividing line should be drawn between sexual orientation which is covered by this proposal, and sexual behaviour, which is not'.[37] The memo continues that the proposal does not affect marital status and therefore does not impinge upon entitlements to benefits for married couples. In the UK sexual orientation is defined to mean orientation towards persons of the same sex (lesbians and gays), the opposite sex (heterosexuals), and the same and opposite sex (bisexuals).

At first glance, sexual orientation shares certain common features with the other prohibited grounds: it is immutable and irrelevant to an individual's ability to do a particular task. However, it differs from other grounds in that sexual orientation is usually not visible to a third party and may be intensely personal.[38] To that extent it shares certain common features with religion and belief. Many gay and lesbian employees do not come 'out' in the workplace,

---

[34] Para. 13.   [35] Case C–249/86 *Grant* v. *South West Trains* [1998] ECR I–621.
[36] See, e.g. *Smith and Grady* v. *United Kingdom* [1999] IRLR 734.
[37] COM(99)565.
[38] Oliver, 'Sexual Orientation Discrimination: Perceptions, Definitions and Genuine Occupational Requirements' (2004) 33 *ILJ*. 1.

often for fear of discrimination. The immutability of sexual orientation is also controversial. As Oliver points out, sexual orientation is not as fixed as would first appear: sexual orientation will often change over time as people try out different sexual experiences.

6. Age

The Community had begun to address the needs of older people through soft law measures. For example, the Community Social Charter 1989 provided that 'every worker of the European Community must, at the time of retirement, be able to enjoy resources affording him or her a decent standard of living'. It added that any person who has reached retirement age but who is not entitled to a pension must be entitled to sufficient resources and to medical and social assistance specifically suited to his needs. The Commission issued a Communication on the elderly[39] and drafted an Action Programme providing for pilot projects, exchanges of experience and improved information between groups representing the elderly. In addition, the Council and Representatives of the governments of the Member States adopted a Resolution on the employment of older workers[40] based on the principles that increased efforts are needed to adjust the conditions in which workers in the latter part of their working lives work and are vocationally trained, and that older workers must benefit from adequate resources and from measures to prevent their exclusion from the labour market.

The need to address the problems of an ageing population have become a central feature of the European Employment Strategy. A policy based on 'active ageing' was first highlighted in 1999 guidelines.[41] By the time of the 2005 revisions,[42] a 'new intergenerational approach' had become an overriding objective of Member State employment policies. Specifically, guideline 18 headed 'Promote a lifecycle approach to work', says that there is a need to provide 'support for active ageing, including appropriate working conditions, improved (occupational) health status and adequate incentives to work and discouragement of early retirement'.

This soft law has hardened with the inclusion of age as a prohibited ground

[39] Council Recommendation of 10 December 1982 on the principles of a Community policy with regard to retirement age (OJ [1982] L357/27) and Sergeant, *Age Discrimination in Employment* (IER, London, 1999).

[40] Resolution of the Council and of the Representatives of the governments of the Member States meeting within the Council on the employment of older workers OJ [1995] C228/1. See also the Resolution of the European Parliament of 24 February 1994 on measures for the elderly in the EC (OJ [1994] C77/24).

[41] Co. Res. of 22 February 1999 (OJ [1999] C69/2), para. 4.

[42] Council Dec. 2005/600 (OJ [2005] L205/21). See also Art. II–85 (Art. 25 of the Charter) which talks of the rights of the elderly.

in the Directive. The Directive also provides a valuable vehicle to ensure a change in attitude towards the employment of older workers. As the UK put it in its consultation paper on the implementation of the Directive, 'We want to move away from a culture that retires people without regard to the contribution they can still make to the labour market'.[43] Once again, age is not defined in the Directive. This generates its own problems. The soft law measures focus on the age discrimination experienced by older people yet young people also experience age discrimination: the Directive does not distinguish between the two situations and the interests of the two groups may well conflict at times. Further, while age is visible and immutable, in that an individual cannot change their age, age differs from the other grounds of discrimination in that age is a process not a fixed status. Thus, while most people will never experience life as a person of the opposite sex, everyone will have experience of being both young and old. This raises the question of whether older people should be able to demand all the opportunities now enjoyed by younger people, given that they themselves were once young and could have taken advantage of those opportunities (the 'good innings' argument). The converse is also true. This difference between age and the other grounds is reflected in the broader, but opaque, derogations available in the framework directive together with the possibility that direct discrimination can be objectively justified.

7. Disability

The Community Social Charter 1989 provided that all disabled persons, whatever the origin and nature of their disablement, must be entitled to additional concrete measures aimed at improving their social and professional integration. These measures must concern vocational training,[44] ergonomics, accessibility, mobility, means of transport,[45] and housing. The Council also adopted a Recommendation on the Employment of Disabled People in the Community.[46] The Preamble asserts that 'disabled people have the same right as all other workers to *equal* opportunity in training and employment'. The text of the Recommendation then talks in terms of '*fair* opportunities for

[43] DTI, *Equality and Diversity: Coming of Age. Consultation on the Draft Employment Equality (Age) Regulations 2006*, July 2005, para. 6.3.1. See also Fredman, below, n. 227, and also Case C–144/04 *Mangold v. Helm* [2006] ECR I–000, discussed in Ch. 6 where non-discrimination on the grounds of age was considered a general principle of law.

[44] See also Resolution 90/703 of the Council and Ministers for Education Meeting with the Council of 31 May 1990, concerning the integration of children and young people with disabilities into ordinary systems of education OJ [1990] C162/2.

[45] See e.g. the proposal for a Council Directive on Transport for Workers with Reduced Mobility designed to improve disabled workers' mobility and to provide them with safe transport to work, COM(90) 588 (OJ [1992] C15/21). This proposal was subsequently withdrawn by the Commission: COM(2001) 763.

[46] Council Recommendation 86/379/EEC of 24 July 1986 (OJ [1986] L225/43).

disabled people'.[47] The Recommendation provides that Member States should establish policies designed, first, to eliminate negative discrimination by, for example, reviewing laws and regulations to ensure that they are not contrary to the principle of fair opportunity, and taking measures to avoid dismissals linked to disability; and, secondly, to encourage 'positive action' for disabled people. This second head of policy describes positive action as the fixing by Member States, where appropriate and after consultation, 'of realistic percentage *targets* for the employment of disabled people in public or private enterprises having a minimum number of employees'.[48] This is very similar to the definition of positive *discrimination* which the Commission and some of the Member States will not countenance in the context of sex equality.[49] The Annex to the Recommendation contains guidelines for positive action to promote the employment and vocational training of disabled people, including policies relating to sheltered employment, vocational rehabilitation and training and providing incentives to employers to assist with the special costs incurred to an employer of employing a disabled worker.[50]

The Council also issued a Resolution on equal employment opportunities for people with disabilities.[51] The Resolution reflected the shift from a welfare approach, which had underpinned the Recommendation, to a human rights-based approach which focused on prevention and removal of barriers that denied equality of access to people with disabilities to, *inter alia*, the labour market.[52] The Resolution underlined that disability employment policies should be strengthened within the National Action Plans (now National Reform Programmes);[53] that full use should be made of the European structural funds, in particular the Social Fund, to promote equal employment opportunities; and that the Commission and the Member States should promote the principle of mainstreaming.[54]

Given this broad sweep of soft law measures it was inevitable that discrimination on the grounds of disability would be prohibited by the Framework Directive. Once again, disability is not defined in the Directive although there are extensive international and national definitions which would help provide meaning to the term. The British statute, the Disability Discrimination Act 1995, adopts a 'medical' approach to the definition of disability. Section (1) defines disability as 'a physical or mental impairment which has a substantial

---

[47] Art. 1.   [48] Art. 2(b). The minimum *might* be set at between 15 and 50.
[49] See below, text attached to nn. 336–337. See also Art. II-86 (Art. 26 of the Charter) on integration of persons with disabilities.
[50] Considerable help has been given from the European Social Fund.
[51] Council Resolution 99/702 (OJ [1999] C186/3). See also the Resolution of the Council and Representatives of the governments meeting within Council of 20 December 1996 on equality of opportunity for people with disabilities (OJ [1997] C12/1).
[52] COM(99)565, 4. See also COM(99) 565, para. 2.   [53] See further Ch. 9.
[54] See also DGV, 'Mainstreaming Disability within EU Employment and Social Policy', http://europa.eu.int/comm/dg05/soc-rot/disable/dresden/workpaper_en.pdf

and long-term adverse effect on [the] . . . ability to carry out normal day-to-day activities'. The Schedule further explains the precise meaning of the terms used in the Act. This definition of disability can be contrasted with a more social constructed view of disability. As Wells explains, while 'the medical model sees disability as a functional impairment, the social model sees disability as a particular relationship between the impaired individual and society'.[55] In *Chacón Navas*[55A] the (Full) Court of Justice favoured the medical definition of disability. It ruled that 'disability', a term which had to be given a Community meaning, referred to a limitation that resulted in particular from 'physical, mental or psychological impairments' which hindered the person's participation in professional life, and would probably 'last for a long time'.[55B] It also made clear that sickness and disability were different and that a person dismissed for sickness was not protected by the disability provisions of the Framework Directive.

Disability differs from the other grounds of discrimination for a number of reasons. First, it may or may not be immutable (in the case of some disabilities, an individual is born with them or the condition develops later in life and they will never improve; in respect of others the individual may well recover). Second, the disability may be visible (e.g. a wheelchair user) or it may not (e.g. a person suffering from a mental disability). Third, the disability may prevent an individual's ability to do a job (e.g. a person with a learning disability would not be able to become a surgeon), or it may not (e.g. a wheelchair user could perform an office-based job), or it may affect an individual's ability to do a job but a certain amount of assistance would overcome that difficulty (e.g. a person with arthritis could work perfectly well as a secretary with the help of an adapted keyboard). The key issue with disability is that there are all kinds of disabilities and one rule does not fit all situations.[56]

C. THE MATERIAL SCOPE

1. Sex

1.1. Field of Application

In its original version, Directive 76/207 applied the principle of equal treatment to access to employment, including promotion (Article 3), vocational training (Article 4) and working conditions, including dismissal (Article 5).

---

[55] 'The Impact of the Framework Employment Directive on UK Disability Discrimination Law' (2003) 32 *ILJ*. 253.
[55A] Case C–13/05 *Chacón Navas v. Eurest Colectividades SA* [2006] ECR I–000.
[55B] Paras. 43 and 45.
[56] For a full discussion of the Directive's provisions relating to disability, see Whittle, 'The Framework Directive for equal treatment in employment and occupation: an analysis from a disability rights perspective' (2002) 27 *ELRev.* 303.

The material scope of the Directive has, however, been expanded by the amendments made by Directive 2002/73 bringing the Equal Treatment Directive into line with the Framework Directive. These amendments can now be found in Article 3 of the revised Equal Treatment Directive and have been incorporated into Article 13 of the Consolidated Directive. This provides that application of the principle of equal treatment means that 'there shall be no direct or indirect discrimination on the grounds of sex in the public or private sectors, including public bodies',[57] in relation to:

(a) conditions for access to employment, to self-employment, or to occupation, including selection criteria and recruitment conditions, whatever the branch of activity and at all levels of the professional hierarchy, including promotion;
(b) access to all types and to all levels of vocational guidance, vocational training, advanced vocational training, and retraining, including practical work experience;
(c) employment and working conditions, including dismissals, as well as pay. Originally, the Directive 2002/73 version of this provision contained the addition 'as provided for in Directive 75/117/EEC'. The Consolidated Directive refers to Article 141 EC.
(d) membership of, and involvement in, an organization of workers or employers, or any organization whose members carry on a particular profession, including the benefits provided for by such organizations.

For our purposes, paragraph (c) is of most interest. The reference to 'pay', albeit mirroring the equivalent provision in the Race and Framework Directives, has raised the question as to the extent to which the equal treatment and the equal pay regimes have become merged, despite the Court's careful attempts to distinguish their different fields of application. If so, this opens up the possibility that principles which have hitherto been applied only to equal treatment cases now apply equally to pay cases.[58] Most notable among those is the possibility that directly discriminatory pay policies can be saved by reference to the express derogations found in the equal treatment Directive and the possibility that pay claims can be brought using a hypothetical comparator. However, there is no indication in either the Preamble or the travaux préparatoires that this was the intention behind either the amendment Directive or the Consolidated Directive.

The reference to 'working conditions' has already been the subject of litigation. In *Meyers* the Court refused to confine 'working conditions' to those conditions set out in a contract of employment or applied by the employer in

---

[57] This confirms Case 248/83 *Commission v. Germany* [1985] ECR 1459.
[58] The Commission takes the view that the exclusion of pay by Art. 137(5) refers only to Directives adopted under Art. 137 and so does not apply to Directives adopted under other legal bases: COM(99) 565.

respect of a worker's employment. It said that a benefit such as family credit constituted a working condition within the meaning of the original Article 5 of Directive 76/207 (Article 14(1)(c) of the Consolidated Directive).[59] This is consistent with its earlier case law. In *Burton*[60] the Court said that the phrase 'working conditions, including the conditions governing dismissal' had to be 'widely construed so as to include termination of the employment relationship between a worker and his employer, even as part of a voluntary redundancy scheme'. This idea was developed further in *Marshall (No. 1)*[61] where the Court made it clear that compulsory retirement fell within the scope of the original Article 5.[62] It was therefore unlawful for any employer to have different retirement ages for men and women.

1.2. Social Security

Social security remains largely excluded from the scope of the equal treatment principle. Article 1(2) of Directive 76/207 (but not the Consolidated Directive) provided that 'with a view to ensuring the progressive implementation of the principle of equal treatment in matters of social security, the Council ... will adopt provisions defining its substance, its scope and the arrangements of its application' (now Directive 79/7 considered in Ch. 10). The Court has consistently held that Article 1(2), as a derogation from a fundamental principle, must be narrowly construed.[63] Therefore, in *Jackson*[64] the Court said that a benefit could not be excluded from the scope of the Directive simply because it was formally part of the social security system; it might fall within the scope of the Directive if its subject-matter was access to employment, including vocational training and working conditions.[65] In *Meyers*[66] the Court considered that family credit, a social security benefit 'designed to encourage workers who are poorly paid to continue working and to meet family expenses'[67] did fall within the scope of Directive 76/207. It said that family credit, which was necessarily linked to an employment

---

[59] Case C–116/94 [1995] ECR I–2131. Working conditions also covers the provision of workplace nurseries: Case C–476/99 *Lommers v. Mininster van Landbouw* [2002] ECR I–2891, para. 26.
[60] Case 19/81 [1982] ECR 555.　　[61] Case 152/84 [1986] ECR 723.
[62] See also Case C–13/94 *P v. S* [1996] ECR I–2143. The conditions determining whether an employee was entitled, where they are unfairly dismissed, to obtain reinstatement or re-engagement are also covered by the Equal Treatment Directive (and not Art. 141), see Case C–167/97 *Seymour-Smith* [1999] ECR I–623; Case C–236/98 *Örebro läns landsting* [2000] ECR I–2189, para. 60, where the Court ruled that the reduction in working time related to working conditions (and not pay under Art. 119 (new Art. 141)).
[63] Case 151/84 *Roberts* [1986] ECR 703 and Case 152/84 *Marshall (No. 1)* [1986] ECR 723.
[64] Case C–63–4/91 *Jackson v. Chief Adjudication Officer* [1992] ECR I–4737.
[65] The fact that the Court in Case C–78/91 *Hughes v. Chief Adjudication Officer* [1992] ECR I–4839 found that family credit fell within Reg. 1408/71 and also did not prevent the benefit from falling within the scope of Dir. 76/207. See further Ch. 4.
[66] Case C–116/94 *Meyers v. Adjudication Officer* [1995] ECR I–2131.
[67] See the judgment in Case C–78/91 *Hughes* [1992] ECR I–4839.

relationship, was concerned with access to employment under Article 3 of Directive 76/207 (Article 14(1)(a) of the Consolidated Directive), since the prospect of receiving family credit might encourage an unemployed worker to accept work.

2. Race and Ethnic Origin

The Race Directive is the most ambitious equal treatment measure going well beyond the sphere of employment. It applies the principles of non-discrimination to 'all persons, as regards both the public and private sectors, including public bodies', in relation not only to[68] the four areas outlined above ((a)–(d)) for sex but also, more controversially,[69] to:

(e) social protection including social security and healthcare;
(f) social advantages;[70]
(g) education;
(h) access to and supply of goods and services which are available to the public, including housing.

The Goods and Services Directive 2004/113 has extended the material scope of the Sex Directive to cover 'all persons who provide goods and services, which are available to the public irrespective of the person concerned as regards both the public and private sectors, including public bodies, and which are offered outside the area of private and family life and the transactions carried out in this context'.[71]

The Commission justified the broad material scope of the Race Directive in order 'to make a serious contribution to curbing racism and xenophobia in Europe'.[72] It said that 'social protection systems play a fundamental role in ensuring social cohesion, and in maintaining political stability and economic progress across the Union'.[73] It also recognized that 'discrimination in access to benefits and other forms of support from the social protection system [and

---

[68] Art. 3(1). Art. 11(2) requires Member States to encourage the two sides of the industry to conclude at the appropriate level, including at undertaking level, agreements laying down anti-discrimination rules in these fields which fall within the scope of collective bargaining. These agreements must respect the minimum requirements laid down by this Directive and the relevant national implementing measures.

[69] For a discussion on the scope of the Art. 13 legal basis, see Whittle, 'Disability Discrimination and the Amsterdam Treaty' (1998) 23 *ELRev.* 50, 53.

[70] See further Ch. 4.

[71] Art. 3(1). The Directive expressly does not apply to the content of media and advertising nor to education (Art. 3(3)). Special provision is made in Art. 5 concerning actuarial factors.

[72] COM(99) 566, 5. The Directive does not apply to difference of treatment based on national-ity and is without prejudice to provisions and conditions relating to entry and residence of TCNs and to any treatment which arises from the legal status of TCNs and stateless persons.

[73] Ibid.

social advantages] contributes to and compounds the marginalization of individuals from ethnic minority and immigrant backgrounds';[74] and that high quality education was a prerequisite for successful integration into society.

Article 3(2) lists the areas excluded from the Directive: it does not cover difference of treatment based on nationality. Nationality discrimination, at least against those holding the nationality of one of the Member states is covered by Article 39 EC. In addition, the Directive is 'without prejudice to provisions and conditions relating to the entry into and residence of third country nationals and stateless persons on the territory of Member States, and to any treatment which arises from the legal status of the third country nationals and stateless persons'.

3. Framework Directive

The material scope of the Directive is narrower than that of the Race Directive. According to Article 3, the principle of equal treatment applies only to employment issues (i.e. the four areas outlined above ((a)–(d)) for sex). The Directive then envisages three exclusions from its scope, two mandatory, one permissive: first, as with the Race Directive, the Framework Directive does not cover differences of treatment based on nationality, and is without prejudice to provisions and conditions relating to the entry into and residence of TCNs and stateless persons in the territory of Member States, and to any treatment which arises form the legal status of TCNs and stateless persons.[75] Second, the Directive does not apply to payments of any kind made by state schemes or similar, including state social security or social protection schemes.[76] And third, Member States *may* provide that the Directive does not apply to the armed forces, but only in so far as it relates to discrimination on the grounds of disability and age.[77]

D. PROHIBITION OF DISCRIMINATION

The directives prohibit four types of discrimination:

- Direct discrimination
- Indirect discrimination
- Harassment
- Instruction to discriminate

We shall consider each in turn.

---

[74] Ibid.   [75] Art. 3(2).   [76] Art. 3(3).   [77] Art. 3(4).

1. Direct Discrimination

1.1. The Basic Rule

Article 2(2)(a) of the Race Directive provides that direct discrimination 'shall be taken to occur where one person is treated less favourably than another is, has been or would be treated in a comparable situation on grounds of racial or ethnic origin'. The other Directives contain an equivalent provision. The Directives therefore envisage a symmetrical approach to equality: the complainant needs to point to a comparator in a comparable situation who is better treated. The comparator can be either actual or potential.

The language of 'on grounds of sex [race etc]' used in the Directives is broader than the wording sometimes used in discrimination legislation of 'on the grounds of her sex [race etc]'. While the latter wording prohibits discrimination against a person because of his or her sex, race, etc, the former wording is wide enough to cover not only less favourable treatment on the grounds of the victim's sex (race, etc) but also because of the victim's association with a person of a particular race or false assumptions about the claimant's race, sexual orientation, disability etc. The protection based on false assumptions is of particular importance in the field of sexual orientation. As Oliver points out, sexual orientation discrimination and harassment are often based on stereotypical assumptions about a person's sexuality drawn from the way in which that person is perceived as projecting him/herself, whether through clothing, speech or other characteristics (men seen as acting 'gay' and women 'butch'), irrespective of their actual orientation. In *Coleman* v. *Attridge Law* a reference has been made to the ECJ on the question whether discrimination against a mother on the grounds of her son's disability is covered by the Directive. The argument is that she is suffering from discrimination by association.

1.2. Sex Discrimination

The principal drawback with the requirement of a comparator in the context of sex equality is that, as we saw in chapter 6, it takes the male as the norm and assumes that a woman is like a man and should be placed is the same position as a man. In some contexts, notably pregnancy, this makes no sense. Comparisons adopted by some courts between a pregnant woman and a sick man are artificial, inaccurate, and misleading. This point was recognized in both *Dekker*[78] and *Webb*.[79] In *Dekker* a woman was refused a job on the grounds that she was pregnant; another woman was appointed and there were no male candidates. Nevertheless, the Court found that discrimination

---

[78] Case C–177/88 [1990] ECR I–3941. This issue is considered in detail in Ch. 9.
[79] Case C–32/93 [1994] ECR I–3567, para. 24.

had occurred. It reasoned that since employment can only be refused because of pregnancy to a woman, such a refusal constituted discrimination on the grounds of sex. In *Webb* the Court confirmed that 'there can be no question of comparing the situation of a [pregnant] woman ... with that of a man similarly incapable for medical or other reason'.

Thus, the Court has recognized that discrimination on the grounds of pregnancy is *per se* unlawful: a male comparator is not needed when a woman has clearly been disadvantaged by the use of a sex-specific criterion, such as pregnancy (the asymmetrical approach). This approach was confirmed by Article 2(7) of Directive 76/207, now Article 2(2)(c) of the Consolidated Directive:

Less favourable treatment of a woman related to pregnancy or maternity leave within the meaning of Directive 92/85/EEC shall constitute discrimination within the meaning of this Directive.

Outside of the field of pregnancy, the Court has taken a narrow and literal view of the concept of direct discrimination: it appears that the discrimination must be overt and explicit on the face of the measure.[80] This can be seen in *Schnorbus*.[81] Julia Schnorbus applied to the Hessian Ministry of Justice for her practical legal training. Her application was rejected because, due to the number of applicants, preference was given to those applicants who had completed compulsory military or civilian service. Since only men could do military or civilian service, it might be thought that, following *Dekker*, more favourable treatment on the grounds of having done military or civilian service would constitute direct discrimination. Yet, the Court did not go down this route, arguing that the priority given to those having done military or civilian service could not be regarded as being directly based on the sex of the persons concerned.[82] Nevertheless, the Court did recognize that the rule was indirectly discriminatory but could be justified.

2. Indirect Discrimination

2.1. Sex, Race and Ethnic Origin, Religion or Belief, Age, Sexual Orientation

As we saw in chapter 6, the case law has long given guidance on the principle of indirect discrimination on the grounds of sex. For example, in *Rinke*[83] the

---

[80] For a recent example of this, see Case C–207/04 *Vergani v. Agenzia delle Entrate* [2005] ECR I–000, para. 35 (national law granted to workers over 50 (for women) and 55 (for men) a favourable taxation rate as an incentive for them to take voluntary redundancy. This provision was directly discriminatory on the grounds of sex.

[81] Case C–79/99 *Schnorbus v. Land Hessen* [2000] ECR I–10997.   [82] Para. 32.

[83] Case C–25/01 *Rinke v. Ärztekammer Hamburg* [2003] ECR I–8349, para. 33.

Court defined indirect discrimination as a provision which, although worded in neutral terms, 'works to the disadvantage of a much higher percentage of women than men, unless that difference in treatment is justified by objective factors unrelated to any discrimination on grounds of sex'.[84]

The amended Equal Treatment Directive and the Consolidated Directive both provide that 'the apparently neutral provision, criterion or practice *would put* persons of one sex at a *particular disadvantage* compared *with persons of the other sex*, unless that provision, criterion or practice is objectively justified by a legitimate aim, and the means of achieving that aim are appropriate and necessary'. Equivalent definitions can be found in the Article 13 Directives, albeit with slight differences. For example, Article 2(2)(b) of the Race Directive says indirect discrimination shall be taken to occur 'where an apparently neutral provision, criterion or practice would put persons of a racial or ethnic origin at a particular disadvantage compared *with other persons*, unless that provision, criterion or practice is objectively justified by a legitimate aim and the means of achieving that aim are appropriate and necessary'.[85] Thus, in respect of the Article 13 Directives (but not the revised Equal Treatment Directive) a comparison needs to be made between persons of a particular group (e.g. racial group) with 'other persons' (i.e. with any other person), and a particular disadvantage can be established if any detriment is proven.

2.2. Disability and the Duty of Reasonable Accommodation

Special rules apply to indirect discrimination on the grounds of disability. Article 1(2)(b) defines indirect discrimination in the same terms as for the other grounds (an apparently neutral provision, criterion or practice which would put persons having a particular disability at a particular disadvantage compared with other persons). It continues that such a measure is unlawful unless *either* (i) that provision, criterion or practice is objectively justified by a legitimate aim and the means of achieving that aim are appropriate and necessary, *or* (ii) 'the employer or any person or organisation to whom this Directive applies, is obliged, under national legislation, to take appropriate measures in line with the principles contained in Article 5 in order to eliminate disadvantages entailed by such provision, criterion or practice'. Article 5 refers to the duty of 'reasonable accommodation'.[86] This means that:

---

[84] Case C–226/98 *Jørgensen* [2000] ECR I–2447, para. 29.

[85] Art. 2(2)(b), drawing on Case C–237/94 *O'Flynn v. Adjudication Officer* [1996] ECR I–2617, para. 18. The surprising feature of this definition is the emphasis on the effect on the individual rather than its impact on the group.

[86] This provision supplements the employer's obligation to adapt the workplace to disabled workers, as provided by framework Directive on health and safety 89/391/EEC (OJ [1989] L 183/1), considered in Ch. 11.

. . . employers shall take appropriate measures,[87] where needed in a particular case, to enable a person with a disability to have access to, participate in, or advance in employment, or to undergo training, unless such measures would impose a disproportionate burden on the employer. This burden shall not be disproportionate[88] when it is sufficiently remedied by measures existing within the framework of the disability policy of the Member State concerned.

Thus, the obligation of reasonable accommodation is limited in two respects. First, it only pertains to what is reasonable. Secondly, it is limited if it would give rise to undue hardship.

The duty of reasonable accommodation is a core element of the new human rights-based approach to the elimination of discrimination against people with a disability, and a key feature of recent national legislation. The concept stems from the realization that the achievement of equal treatment can only become a reality where some reasonable allowance is made for disability in order to enable the abilities of the individual concerned to be put to work. However, as the Commission makes clear,[89] the duty of reasonable accommodation does not create any obligations with respect to individuals who, even with reasonable accommodation, cannot perform the essential functions of any given job.

Whittle provides a helpful example as to how the limitations in (i) and (ii) interrelate.[90] If an employer says that it is an advantage that the employee be able to drive, such a rule would place blind people at a particular disadvantage when compared to other persons and so would constitute an indirectly discriminatory rule. However, the employer could objectively justify this requirement. The second 'unless' clause (clause (ii)) provides the employer another opportunity to retain the driving requirement. If the employer is obliged to provide the blind person with 'reasonable accommodation' (e.g. swapping some of the blind person's tasks with a sighted colleague or providing a taxi on the necessary occasions) then, by virtue of the second 'unless' clause, the job requirement for a driving licence will be allowed to remain.

---

[87] See Recital 20 which explains that 'appropriate measures' means effective and practical measures to adapt the workplace to the disability, e.g. adapting premises and equipment, patterns of working time, the distribution of tasks or the provision of training or the integration of resources.

[88] See Recital 21: to determine whether the measures give rise to a disproportionate burden, account should be taken in particular of the financial and other costs entailed, the scale and the financial resources of the organisation or undertaking and the possibility of obtaining public funding or other assistance.

[89] COM(99) 565.

[90] Whittle, 'The Framework Directive for equal treatment in employment and occupation: an analysis form a disability rights perspective' (2002) 27 *ELRev.* 303, 310.

2.3. Justification/Proportionate Means of Achieving a Legitimate Aim

It has long been established in the Court's case law on sex discrimination that a measure which is prima facie indirectly discriminatory is unlawful unless it is objectively justified on grounds other than sex and the steps taken are proportionate. *Schnorbus*[91] provides an example of how objective justification operates. It will be recalled that Julia Schnorbus unsuccessfully applied to the Hessian Ministry of Justice for her practical legal training but due to the high level of applications, preference was given to those (men) who had completed compulsory military or civilian service. Although the Court found the rule indirectly discriminatory, it said that it could be justified: the national rule took into account the fact that doing military or civilian service delayed male applicants' education. The national rule was therefore objective in nature and prompted solely by the desire to counterbalance to some extent the effects of that delay.[92]

While the Article 13 Directives, the Revised Equal Treatment Directive and now the Consolidated Directive all permit indirectly discriminatory measures to be justified, the language through which this is achieved is slightly different from the case law. Each Directive refers to the measure being 'objectively justified by a legitimate aim and the means of achieving that aim are appropriate and necessary'. Unlike the Burden of Proof Directive which expressly prohibits the objective aim being sex based, the new Directives do not contain an equivalent prohibition, thereby opening up the possibility that the justification could relate to the prohibited ground.

3. Instruction to Discriminate

According to Article 2(4) of revised Directive 76/207, 'An instruction to discriminate against persons on grounds of sex shall be deemed to be discrimination within the meaning of this Directive'. Equivalent provisions can be found in the Article 13 Directives[93] and Article 2(2)(b) of the Consolidated Directive.

---

[91] Case C–79/99 *Schnorbus* v. *Land Hessen* [2000] ECR I–10997.
[92] Para. 44.   [93] Art. 2(4) of Dirs. 2000/43 and 2000/78.

4. Harassment

4.1. Sex

(a) Recommendation and Code

Despite the considerable weight of evidence concerning the serious consequences of sexual harassment, a Commission report found that in most countries there was no effective legal remedy against sexual harassment.[94] It therefore proposed that a specific Directive be passed with the aim of protecting workers from the risk of sexual harassment[95] but this suggestion was initially not followed. Instead, the Council passed a non-legally binding Resolution on the protection of the dignity of women and men at work.[96] This was followed by a Commission Recommendation and a Code of Conduct[97] which was approved by a Council Declaration.[98]

The Council Resolution contained a detailed definition of sexual harassment: it is 'conduct of a sexual nature, or other conduct based on sex affecting the dignity of women and men at work, including conduct of superiors and colleagues'. This conduct is deemed to constitute an 'intolerable violation of the dignity of workers or trainees' and is unacceptable if:

(a) such conduct is unwanted, unreasonable and offensive to the recipient;
(b) a person's rejection of or submission to such conduct on the part of employers or workers (including superiors or colleagues) is used explicitly or implicitly as a basis for a decision which affects that person's access to vocational training, access to employment, promotion, salary, or any other employment decisions; and/or
(c) such conduct creates an intimidating, hostile, or humiliating work environment for the recipient.[99]

[94] Rubinstein, *The Dignity of Women at Work: a Report on the Problem of Sexual Harassment in the Member States of the European Communities*, (OPEC, Luxembourg, October 1987).

[95] In June 1986 the European Parliament passed a resolution on violence against women which also called for a specific Directive on sexual harassment (OJ [1986] C176/79). The Social Partners started to negotiate an agreement on the prevention of sexual harassment at work with a view to concluding a Directive. UNICE pulled out of the negotiations: COM(96) 373 and SEC(97) 568.

[96] Resolution of 29 May 1990 (OJ [1990] C157/3).

[97] Commission Recommendation 92/131/EEC of 27 November 1991 on the protection and dignity of men and women at work (OJ [1992] L49/1). See Case 322/88 *Grimaldi* v. *Fonds des Maladies Professionnelles* [1989] ECR 4407 where the Court said in the context of a Recommendation on compensation for persons with occupational diseases, that national courts are bound to take Recommendations into account in order to decide disputes before them, in particular where they clarify the interpretation of national rules adopted in order to implement them or when they are designed to supplement binding Community measures, such as the Equal Treatment Directive.

[98] Council Declaration of 19 December 1991 on the Implementation of the Commission Recommendation on the Protection of the Dignity of Women and Men at Work including the Code of Practice to Combat Sexual Harassment (92/C 27/01).

[99] Art. 1 of the Council's Resolution on the Dignity of Women and Men at Work (OJ [1990] C157/3). For further definitions see the American EEOC's Guidelines on Sexual Harassment,

Thus, the definition of what constitutes sexual harassment is subjective not objective: account is taken of the effect of the conduct upon the particular individual concerned rather than examining the effect of equivalent conduct on a 'reasonable person'. The motive of the perpetrator is largely irrelevant.

The Code suggests that conduct constituting sexual harassment may take the form of physical conduct of a sexual nature, ranging from unnecessary touching to assault, verbal conduct of a sexual nature, including unwelcome sexual advances, suggestive remarks and innuendoes, non-verbal conduct of a sexual nature, including the display of pornographic or sexually explicit pictures, leering, whistling or making sexually suggestive gestures, and sex-based conduct, such as sex-based comments about appearance or dress. The essence of the definition is that the conduct is unwanted by the recipient. In the words of the Code, 'sexual attention becomes sexual harassment *if it is persisted in once it has been made clear that it is regarded by the recipient as offensive,* although one incident of harassment may constitute sexual harassment if sufficiently serious' (emphasis added).[100] The definition of sexual harassment also distinguishes between conduct which damages the employee's working environment creating a 'hostile work environment'[101] (Article 1(c)), and conduct which is used as a basis for employment decisions affecting the victim (Article 1(b)).

(b) The Directive

These soft law measures 'softened up' the legislature to introduce a hard law, free-standing wrong of harassment in the amendments to the Equal Treatment Directive which deem harassment to constitute discrimination, now incorporated into Article 2(2)(a) of the Consolidated Directive. The Directive recognizes two forms of harassment: harassment and sexual harassment. Article 2(2) of the Equal Treatment Directive (Article 2(1)(c) of the Consolidated Directive) defines *harassment* as the situation 'where unwanted conduct *related to the sex* of a person occurs with the purpose or effect of violating the dignity of a person, and of creating an intimidating, hostile, degrading, humiliating or offensive environment'. The language of 'related to the sex' (as opposed to the more traditional 'on the grounds of sex') catches a wider range of conduct, argues for a lower threshold of proof,[102] and can be satisfied

---

980, 29 CFR, s. 1604. 11(f) and the discussion in Ellis, *EU Anti-discrimination Law* (OUP, Oxford, 2005), 215ff.

[100] See, in the British context, *Bracebridge Engineering* v. *Darby* [1990] IRLR 3 where the EAT accepted that a single serious sexual assault constituted unlawful sexual discrimination.

[101] In *Meritor Savings Bank* v. *Vinson* 477 US 57, 65 the US Supreme Court distinguished between hostile work environment and *quid pro quo* claims. Both are cognizable under Title VII though a hostile environment claim requires harassment that is severe or perverse. In *Burlington Industries* v. *Ellerth*, 26 June 1998, the Supreme Court doubted the utility of these terms and it is not proposed to adopt this distinction here.

[102] Rubinstein, 'Amending the Sex Discrimination Act' (2005) 140 *EOR* 20.

without reference to how someone of the opposite sex was or would have been treated. By contrast, whether there has been unwanted conduct towards a woman 'on the ground of her sex' can be determined only by reference to the treatment of a man.[103]

Article 2(2) of the Equal Treatment Directive (Article 2(1)(d) of the Consolidated Directive) defines *sexual harassment* as the situation 'where any form of unwanted verbal, non-verbal or physical conduct of a sexual nature occurs, with the purpose or effect of violating the dignity of a person, in particular when creating an intimidating, hostile, degrading, humiliating or offensive environment'. Thus, sexual harassment is a distinct concept covering situations where the behaviour is sexual in nature, rather than on the grounds of a person's sex. The Code of Conduct would help provide examples of the type of conduct prohibited by the Directive.

Article 2(3) of the Equal Treatment Directive then contains the prohibition:

Harassment and sexual harassment within the meaning of this Directive shall be deemed to be discrimination on the grounds of sex and therefore prohibited. A person's rejection of, or submission to, such conduct may not be used as a basis for a decision affecting that person.

The last sentence is replaced in Article 2(2)(a) of the Consolidated Directive with the phrase discrimination includes 'any less favourable treatment based on a person's rejecton of or submission to such conduct'.

Article 2(5) of the Equal Treatment Directive (Article 26 of the Consolidated Directive) then requires Member States to encourage employers and those responsible for access to vocational training 'to take measures to prevent all forms of discrimination on grounds of sex, in particular harassment and sexual harassment at the workplace'. Here the Code may serve a useful function as guidance for employers as to good practice. For example, the Code recommends that employers, both in the public and private sectors should issue a policy statement, preferably linked to a broader policy promoting equal opportunities, which expressly states that all employees have a right to be treated with dignity, that sexual harassment will not be permitted, and that all employees have a right to complain about any sexual harassment. Furthermore, the policy should state that employees' complaints will be taken seriously, will be dealt with expeditiously, and that they will not suffer victimization or retaliation as a result of making the complaint. The Code further recommends that the policy statement should leave no doubt as to what is considered inappropriate behaviour and it should also specify that appropriate disciplinary measures will be taken against employees found guilty of sexual harassment. This statement must be communicated to all concerned to ensure maximum awareness.

---

[103] Ibid., 21.

The Code also expects that provision be made for both informal and formal means of resolving disputes. Employers should designate a specially trained officer to provide advice and assistance to employees subjected to sexual harassment and identify to whom a victim can make a complaint. Developing this idea, the European Parliament adopted a resolution calling for Member States to adopt legislation obliging employers to appoint an in-house confidential counsellor to deal with cases of sexual harassment.[104] Normally, formal proceedings should be commenced only after an unsuccessful informal approach to the alleged harasser has been made. This informal approach should make clear that particular behaviour is not welcome. Any investigations must be independent, objective, and handled with sensitivity, with due respect for the rights of both the complainant and the alleged harasser. Employers should monitor and review these procedures to ensure they are working effectively. Finally, the Code emphasizes that both trade unions and employees have a key role to play: trade unions by encouraging employers to develop policies on sexual harassment and advising their members of their rights not to be sexually harassed and supporting them when complaints arise; employees by discouraging any form of reprehensible behaviour and making it clear that it is unacceptable.

4.2. The Article 13 Directives

The Article 13 Directives also introduce the innovation that 'Harassment shall be deemed to be discrimination' when, in the case of Article 2(3) of the Race Directive, 'unwanted conduct related to racial or ethnic origin takes place with the purpose *or* effect of violating the dignity of a person *and* of creating an intimidating, hostile, degrading, humiliating or offensive environment'.[105] While the definition of harassment is broadly drawn so as to include conduct which has the purpose or effect of violating the victim's dignity, its scope is reduced by the fact that not only must the individual's dignity be violated but also the conduct must create a hostile environment. Therefore, as Rubinstein points out, a one-off incident of racial abuse might be said to violate the recipient's dignity without its creating a hostile working environment. This phrase implies something of greater breadth and duration than a one-off incident.[106] The Directives permit the concept of harassment being defined in accordance with national laws or practice of the Member States.[107]

---

[104] B3–1735/91 OJ [1994] C61/246.
[105] Emphasis added.
[106] 'New Discrimination Regulations: An EOR Guide' (2003) 118 *EOR* 17.
[107] Art. 2(3) of both Directives.

E. DEROGATIONS

1. Sex

1.1. Introduction

The original version of the Equal Treatment Directive 76/207 contained three express exceptions to the principle of equal treatment: first, where the sex of the worker constituted a determining factor (Article 2(2)); secondly, where women needed to be protected, particularly as regards pregnancy and maternity (Article 2(3)); and, thirdly, where the state has implemented 'positive action' programmes (Article 2(4)). These exceptions, being derogations from an individual right laid down in the Directive, had to be interpreted strictly,[108] had to be regularly reviewed,[109] and were subject to the principle of proportionality.[110] Although the Member States retained a reasonable margin of discretion as to the detailed arrangements for the implementation of these exceptions,[111] the list of exceptions was exhaustive. The Court made this clear in *Johnston*[112] where it said that the principle of equal treatment could not be subject to, for example, any general reservation as regards measures taken on the grounds of public safety.

The amendments to the Equal Treatment Directive introduced by Directive 2002/73 have somewhat changed Directive 76/207's approach, to bring Directive 76/207 into line with the Article 13 Directives. The first derogation has been replaced by an apparently more open-ended derogation:

Member States may provide, as regards access to employment including the training leading thereto, that a difference of treatment which is based on a characteristic related to sex shall not constitute discrimination where, by reason of the nature of the particular occupational activities concerned or of the context in which they are carried out, such a characteristic constitutes a *genuine and determining* occupational requirement, provided that its objective is legitimate and the requirement is proportionate.

This provision (Article 2(6) of Directive 76/207, Article 14(2) of the Consolidated Directive) allows sex-based criteria to be used provided that reliance on sex (1) constitutes a genuine and determining occupational requirement (so-called 'GOR'); (2) that the objective is legitimate; and (3) the requirement is proportionate.

The second derogation has been expanded. According to Article 2(7) of the Equal Treatment Directive, the Directive is without prejudice to:

---

[108] See e.g. Case C–450/93 *Kalanke v. Freie und Hansestadt Bremen* [1995] ECR I–3051.
[109] See also Arts. 3(2)(c), 5(2)(c), 9(1)–(2). See also Case 222/84 *Johnston v. Chief Constable of the RUC* [1986] ECR 1651.
[110] Ibid., para. 36.
[111] See e.g. Case 184/83 *Hofmann* [1984] ECR 3047, para. 27.
[112] Case 222/84 [1986] ECR 1651.

- provisions concerning the protection of women, particularly as regards pregnancy and maternity (Article 28(1) of the Consolidated Directive);
- provisions of the Parental Leave Directive 96/34 and the Pregnant Workers Directive 92/85 (Article 28(2) of the Consolidated Directive);
- national provisions giving distinct rights to paternity or adoption leave (Article 16 of the Consolidated Directive).

The third derogation has been recast. Article 2(8) now provides that '*Member States* may maintain or adopt measures within the meaning of Article 141(4) of the Treaty with a view to ensuring full equality in practice between men and women' (Article 3 of the Consolidated Directive). The wording suggests that this is no longer a derogation but an important way of realizing equality provided that the Member States take advantage of the provision. If this is the case, a position which is considered below, the rules outlined above which apply to derogations, no longer apply to Article 2(8).

In the section that follows we shall consider the first two derogations as originally drafted. The case law decided under these derogations is likely to offer guidance as to the scope of the new provisions. Positive action—since it is now no longer a true derogation—will be considered separately.

1.2. Sex of the Worker Constitutes a Determining Factor

According to the original Article 2(2), Member States have the option not to apply the principle of equal treatment to 'those occupational activities and, where appropriate, the training leading thereto, for which, by reason of their nature or the context in which they are carried out, the sex of the worker constitutes the determining factor'. Article 2(2) does not oblige Member States to exclude certain occupational activities from the scope of the Directive, nor does it require Member States to exercise the power of derogation in a particular manner.[113]

Certain clearly defined occupations such as singing, acting, dancing, and artistic or fashion modelling fall under Article 2(2).[114] The Court has also accepted that certain kinds of employment in private households might fall within Article 2(2)[115] but has ruled that a general exclusion of the application of the principle of equal treatment to employment in a private household or in undertakings with no more than five employees went beyond the objective which could be lawfully pursued under Article 2(2).[116] On the other hand, the Court has found that it was lawful to limit access by men to the post of

---

[113] Case 248/83 *Commission* v. *Germany* [1985] ECR 1459.

[114] Commission survey on the implementation of Art. 2(2) cited in Case 248/83 *Commission* v. *Germany* [1985] ECR 1459.

[115] Case 165/82 *Commission* v. *UK* [1983] ECR 3431.

[116] Ibid. See also Case E–1/02 *EFTA Surveillance Authority* v. *The Kingdom of Norway*, judgment of the Court 24 January 2003, para. 46.

midwife in view of the 'personal sensitivities' which may play 'an important role in relations between midwife and patient'.[117] Similar reasoning can explain the Court's acceptance that it was lawful to reserve posts primarily for men in male prisons and for women in female prisons.[118]

More surprisingly, however, the Court accepted in *Johnston*[119] that certain policing activities in Northern Ireland might be such that the sex of the police officers constituted a determining factor. In that case the Chief Constable of the RUC decided not to renew the contract of Mrs Johnston and other women, and not to give them training in the handling of firearms. The Court unquestioningly accepted that the justification for this policy was that 'in a situation characterised by serious internal disturbances the carrying of firearms by policewomen might create additional risks of their being assassinated and might therefore be contrary to the requirements of public safety'.[120] The Court did, however, insist that Member States had to assess the activities periodically in order to decide whether, in the light of social developments, the derogation from the general scheme of the Directive should be maintained.[121] The Court also recognized that it was for the national court to ensure that the principle of proportionality be maintained.

The Court re-emphasized the limited nature of the Article 2(2) derogation in *Commission* v. *France (prison warders)*.[122] It said that the exceptions provided for in Article 2(2) could relate only to specific activities and that they had to be sufficiently transparent to permit effective supervision by the Commission. Therefore a system of separate recruitment according to sex fell outside Article 2(2).

Despite the caveats in *Johnston* and *Commission* v. *France*, the Court again adopted a respectful approach to state policy in *Sirdar*.[123] Mrs Sirdar had been in the British army since 1983 and had served as a chef in a commando regiment since 1990. When she was made redundant she was invited to apply for a job as a chef in the Royal Marines provided that she satisfied a selection board and a commando training course. The invitation was subsequently withdrawn when the authorities realized that she was a woman, because women were excluded from this regiment. The existence of this policy was justified by the state on the grounds that the presence of women was incompatible with the requirement of 'interoperability'—the need for every Marine, irrespective of his specialization, to be capable of fighting in a commando unit.

Having ruled that Community law in principle applies to the case, since

[117] Ibid.   [118] Case 318/86 *Commission* v. *France* [1988] ECR 3559.
[119] Case 222/84 [1986] ECR 1651.   [120] Para. 36.
[121] See also Art. 9(2) and the requirement to notify the Commission of the results of the assessment and see Case 248/83 *Commission* v. *Germany* [1985] ECR 1459, para. 37.
[122] Case 318/86 [1988] ECR 3559.
[123] Case C–273/97 *Sirdar* v. *Secretary of State for Defence* [1999] ECR I–7403.

there was no general exception from Community law covering all measures taken for reasons of public security,[124] the Court considered the application of Article 2(2) derogation to see whether the measures have 'the purpose of guaranteeing public security and whether they are appropriate and necessary to achieve that aim'.[125] The Court said that it was clear that 'the organisation of the Royal Marines differs fundamentally from that of other units in the British armed forces, of which they are the "point of the arrow head" '.[126] They were a small force and were intended to be the first line of attack. The Court noted that it had also been established that, within this corps, chefs were required to serve as front-line commandos, that all members of the corps were engaged and trained for that purpose, and that there were no exceptions to this rule at the time of recruitment.[127] The Advocate General added that the evidence given by the Royal Marines showed the 'negative effects' which the presence of any female element might have on the operational cohesion of a commando unit, 'resulting from the foreseeable preoccupation of infanteers to protect women, quite apart from the latter's (as yet untested) physical suitability for difficult offensive operations involving hand-to-hand combat for which the marines are trained'.[128] Therefore the Court concluded that, 'In such circumstances, the competent authorities were entitled, in the exercise of their discretion as to whether to maintain the exclusion in question in the light of social developments, and without abusing the principle of proportionality, to come to the view that the specific conditions for deployment of the assault units of which the Royal Marines are composed, and in particular the rule of interoperability to which they are subject, justified their composition remaining exclusively male'.[129]

In the light of *Johnston* the outcome of this case is unsurprising. It does, however, reveal how easy it is for a Member State (condoned by the Court) to use the derogations as a shield for gender stereotyping and untested assumptions about male soldiers' attitudes to women. However, the limited nature of the exclusion of women in *Sirdar* was emphasized by the Court in *Kreil*.[130] It reiterated the point already made in *Johnston* and *Sirdar* that the principle of proportionality had to be observed in determining the scope of any derogation. Proportionality requires that 'derogations remain within the limits of what is appropriate and necessary in order to achieve the aim in view'.[131] The Court then ruled that the German law which excluded women from *all* military posts involving the use of arms and which allowed women access only to medical services and military music services could not be regarded as a derogating measure justified by the specific nature of the posts in question or

---

[124] Para. 19.   [125] Para. 28.   [126] Para. 30.   [127] Ibid.
[128] Para. 33.   [129] Para. 31.
[130] Case C–285/98 *Kreil v. Bundesrepublik Deutschland* [2000] ECR I–69. See Langer (2000) 37 *CMLRev.* 1433.
[131] Para. 23.

by the particular context in which the activities in question were carried out.[132]

However, the Court's deference to Member State policy was repeated again in *Dory*.[133] Mr Dory objected to being called up for compulsory military service, arguing, in the light of *Kreil*, that the German law on military service was contrary to Community law, in particular because women were not required to do military service. The Court accepted the German argument without criticism that compulsory military service was 'the expression of such a choice of military organisation to which Community law is consequently not applicable'.[134] The fact that, unlike women, the careers of men called up for military service were delayed was not enough to bring the matter within the scope of Community law. The Court added that:

The existence of adverse consequences for access to employment cannot, without encroaching on the competences of the Member States, have the effect of compelling the Member State in question either to extend the obligation of military service to women, thus imposing on them the same disadvantages with regard to access to employment, or to abolish compulsory military service.

As Anagnostaras points out,[135] *Sidar*, *Kreil* and *Dory* show that the Court draws a distinction between, on the one hand, the army as a profession and, on the other, military service as a civilian obligation aimed at protecting external security. It is only in the context of the former that Community sex equality law applies. Outside the professional army, it is for each country to decide on the necessity of military service and to determine which people will be affected by it.

The Commission summarized the Court's case law under Article 2(2) in the following terms:[136]

The main conclusion which can be drawn from this jurisprudence is that the 'certain degree of discretion' enjoyed by Member States to exclude some occupational activities from the scope of the Directive is subject to strict scrutiny. First, the exclusion can only concern specific posts. Secondly, Member States are under the obligation to reassess periodically the legitimacy of the exclusion, so that it may be authorised at a certain date, but become illegal subsequently.[137]

---

[132] Para. 27

[133] Case C–186/01 *Dory v. Federal Republic of Germany* [2003] ECR I–2479.

[134] Para. 39. See Trybus (2003) 40 *CMLRev.* 1269.

[135] 'Sex Equality and Compulsory Military Service: the Limits of National Sovereignty over Matters of Army Organisation' (2003) 28 *ELRev.* 713, 718.

[136] COM(2000) 334, para. 24.

[137] The example the Commission gives is that of the situation of midwives. In 1983, the Court ruled that 'at the present time personal sensitivities may play an important role in relations between midwife and patient' so that the United Kingdom had not exceeded the limits of the power granted to the Member States by the Directive in excluding men from that profession and the training leading thereto. However, even at that time, the United Kingdom stated that it intended to progressively fully open up the profession of midwives to men. More than 15 years later, that profession is fully open to men in all the Member States.

The Commission clearly had this case law in mind when drafting the new Article 2(6) (Article 14(2) of the Consolidated Directive) whose scope is unlikely to differ significantly from the original Article 2(2). The Commission said: 'In accordance with the above case law, where a difference of treatment, which relates to a genuine occupational qualification exists, it is not to be considered as discrimination.'[138] Emphasizing the exceptional nature of the derogation, the Commission said that 'the term "genuine occupational qualification" (now "requirement") should be construed narrowly to cover only those occupational requirements where a particular sex is necessary for the performance of the activities concerned.'[139]

1.3. Protection of Women, particularly as regards Pregnancy and Maternity

Article 2(7) (formerly Article 2(3) of Directive 76/207 and now Article 28(1) of the Consolidated Directive) permits a derogation from the principle of equal treatment to protect women 'particularly as regards pregnancy and maternity'. In *Johnston*[140] the Court made clear that this provision was intended 'to protect a woman's biological condition and the special relationship which exists between a woman and her child'. The significance of this observation can be seen in *Hofmann*.[141] The case concerned a father who took unpaid paternity leave to look after his new-born child while the mother, having completed the initial obligatory period of maternity leave, returned to work. When the father's claim for the state maternity allowance, which was payable to mothers, was refused, he claimed direct discrimination. However, the Court accepted that Article 2(3) permitted Member States to introduce provisions which were designed to protect both 'a woman's biological condition during pregnancy and thereafter until such time as her physiological and mental functions have returned to normal after childbirth' and 'to protect the special relationship between a woman and her child over the period which follows between pregnancy and childbirth,[142] by preventing that relationship from being disturbed by the multiple burdens which would result from the simultaneous pursuit of employment'.[143] Thus, the Court

---

[138] COM(2000) 334, para. 27.   [139] Ibid.   [140] Case 222/84 [1986] ECR 1651.
[141] Case 184/83 [1984] ECR 3047. This case is considered further in Ch. 9.
[142] See also Case C–394/96 *Brown* v. *Rentokil* [1998] ECR I–4185.
[143] Both requirements need not be present: in Case 163/82 *Commission* v. *Italy* [1983] ECR 3273 the Court found that an Italian law which gave a woman but not her husband the entitlement to the equivalent of maternity leave when they adopted a child under six years old was justified 'by the legitimate concern to assimilate as far as possible the conditions of entry of the child into the adoptive family to those of the arrival of a new born child in the family during the very delicate initial period'. Although Art. 2(3) was not cited the thinking is very similar to the requirement of safeguarding the 'special relationship' between mother and child.

ruled that Directive 76/207 did not require Member States to grant leave to fathers, even where the parents had decided differently.[144]

While the derogation can be used to justify the special protection of women where their condition requires it, it cannot be used to justify a total exclusion of women from a post of indefinite duration just because they are pregnant at the start of the employment[145] or to exclude women from an occupation, such as the police force, because public opinion demands that women be given greater protection than men, even though the risks are not specific to women.[146] It also cannot be used to exclude women from certain types of employment solely because they are on average smaller and less strong than average men, while men with similar features are accepted for that employment.[147] Women also cannot be excluded from certain types of employment, such as night work[148] or mining and diving[149] where, with the exception of pregnancy and its aftermath,[150] the risks are common to men and women.[151]

2. Race and Ethnic Origin

As with sex, direct discrimination on the grounds of race or ethnic origin can be saved only by reference to an express defence, the 'genuine and determining

---

[144] Cf. the Directive on Parental Leave 96/34 discussed in Ch. 9.

[145] Case C–207/98 *Mahlburg* v. *Land Mecklenburg-Vorpommern* [2000] ECR I–549, para. 25.

[146] Case 222/84 *Johnston* [1986] ECR 1651 and Case C–285/98 *Kreil* [2000] ECR I–69, para. 30. The Commission discussed the implications of the *Johnston* decision in its Communication on Protective Legislation for Women (COM(87) 105 final); Council Conclusions of 26 May 1987 on Protective Legislation for Women in the Member States of the European Community (OJ [1987] C178/04). It examined all national protective provisions, especially in the light of the Arts. 3(2)(c) and 5(2)(c) of the original Equal Treatment Directive which require Member States to revise all protective legislation which is no longer justified. It found that 'a mosaic of extremely varied and highly specific regulations exist, the reasons for which are not clearly defined' and concluded that protective legislation which does not relate to pregnancy or maternity should be made to apply equally to both sexes or be repealed.

[147] Case C–203/03 *Commission* v. *Austria* [2005] ECR I–000, para. 46.

[148] Case C–345/89 *Stoeckel* [1991] ECR I–4047. See also Case C–13/93 *Office national de l'emploi* v. *Minne* [1994] ECR I–371 where discriminatory derogations from the prohibition of nightwork contravened Art. 5 of Dir. 76/207/EEC.

[149] Case C–203/03 *Commission* v. *Austria* [2005] ECR I–000, para. 47.

[150] Case C–421/92 *Habermann-Beltermann* v. *Arbeiterwohlfahrt* [1994] ECR I–1657, para. 18; and Art. 7 of Dir. 92/85 (OJ [1992] L348/1) on pregnant workers.

[151] The French law at issue, Art. L213–1 of the French *Code du travail* preventing women from working at night, was based on ILO Convention No. 89. A new, non-discriminatory Convention has now been passed (No. 171) which the ILO hopes all Member States will ratify. See EIRR 219, April 1992. France was condemned for maintaining Art. L213–1 in force, see Case C–197/96 *Commission* v. *France* [1997] ECR I–1489. The Commission is now proposing a fine of 142,425 euros per day on France for non-implementation of the Court's earlier judgment (23 April 1999). Italy has also been condemned for retaining national rules prohibiting nightwork for women, see Case C–207/96 *Commission* v. *Italy* [1997] ECR I–6869.

occupational requirement' (GOR).[152] In its explanatory memorandum, the Commission gave examples of such GORs: where a person of a particular racial or ethnic origin is required for reasons of authenticity in a dramatic performance or where the holder of a particular job provides persons of a particular ethnic group with personal services promoting their welfare and those services can most effectively be provided by a person of that ethnic group. The Commission does, however, note that these GORs will be highly exceptional.

3. The Framework Directive

3.1. Introduction

The Framework Directive contains a general exclusion, a GOR and then some specific provisions for the affected grounds. The general exclusion is found in Article 2(5). This provides:

> This Directive shall be without prejudice to measures laid down by national law which, in a democratic society, are necessary for public security, for the maintenance of public order and the prevention of criminal offences, for the protection of health and for the protection of the rights and freedoms of others.

This provision was included in the Directive at the last minute and is intended to prevent members of harmful cults, paedophiles and people with dangerous physical or mental illnesses from gaining the protection of the Directive.[153]

The GOR is found in Article 4(1):

> Notwithstanding Article 2(1) and (2), Member States may provide that a difference of treatment which is based on a characteristic related to any of the grounds referred to in Article 1 shall not constitute discrimination where, by reason of the nature of the particular occupational activities concerned or of the context in which they are carried out, such a characteristic constitutes a *genuine and determining occupational requirement*, provided that the objective is legitimate and the requirement is proportionate.[154]

However, due to the different issues affecting the various strands, the derogations are more tailored for the framework Directive than in respect of sex and race and ethnic origin. We shall therefore consider the different strands in turn

3.2. Religion or Belief

(a) Ethos-based Organizations

In addition to the general GOR in Article 4(1) which would be available to all employers wishing to employ someone of a particular religion (e.g. a

---

[152] Art. 4.   [153] Ellis, above n. 99, 291.   [154] Emphasis added.

hospital wishing to employ a Christian chaplain), Article 4(2) makes special provision for 'entreprises de tendences', that is organizations which promote certain religious values where the jobs need to be performed by employees who share the relevant religious belief. According to Article 4(2), Member States may provide that, 'in the case of occupational activities within churches and other public or private organisations the ethos of which is based on religion or belief, a difference of treatment based on a person's religion or belief shall not constitute discrimination where, by reason of the nature of these activities or of the context in which they are carried out, a person's religion or belief constitute a *genuine, legitimate and justified occupational requirement*, having regard to an organisation's ethos'.[155] Thus a faith school would be allowed to insist under Article 4(2) that its teachers were a member of that particular faith provided that a person's religion or belief constitute 'a genuine, legitimate and justified occupational requirement' (the requirement of 'determining' does not apply under Article 4(2)). However, the same school might not be able to insist that a member of its ground or works' staff also be an adherent to that particular faith since such individuals do not have the same contact with children and are not responsible for their spiritual life.

(b) Special Provisions Relating to Northern Ireland

The political difficulties in Northern Ireland are well known and the peace process is at a delicate stage. In order not to undermine the careful negotiations which have already taken place, Article 15 of the Framework Directive makes two special provisions, one concerning the police and the other concerning teachers. In respect of preserving the Patten reforms to the police service which require an equal number of Catholic and Protestant recruits, Article 15(1) provides that in order to tackle the under-representation of 'one of the major religious communities' in the police service in Northern Ireland, differences in treatment regarding recruitment into that service, including its support staff 'shall not constitute discrimination in so far as those differences in treatment are expressly authorised by national legislation'. In respect of teachers, Article 15(2) provides 'In order to maintain a balance of opportunity in employment for teachers in Northern Ireland while furthering the reconciliation of historical divisions between the major religious communities there' the religion and belief provisions of the Directive do not apply to the recruitment of teachers in schools insofar as this is expressly authorized by national legislation.

---

[155] Emphasis added.

3.3. Age

In addition to the general GOR in Article 4(1), Article 6(1) contains a further derogation from the principle of equal treatment in respect of age discrimination. This says that Member States may provide that differences of treatment on grounds of age shall not constitute discrimination—either direct *or* indirect—if, within the context of national law, 'they are objectively and reasonably justified by a legitimate aim, including legitimate employment policy, labour market and vocational training objectives, and if the means of achieving that aim are appropriate and necessary'. The provision then goes on to provide (a non-exhaustive) list of measure of what might constitute differences of treatment:

- the setting of special conditions on access to employment and vocational training, employment and occupation, including dismissal and remuneration conditions, for young people, older workers, and persons with caring responsibilities in order to promote their vocational integration or ensure their protection;
- the fixing of minimum conditions of age, professional experience, or seniority in service for access to employment or to certain advantages linked to employment;
- the fixing of a maximum age for recruitment which is based on the training requirements of the post in question or the need for a reasonable period of employment before retirement.

Thus, Article 6(1) gives Member States the option of allowing employers to objectively justify not only indirect discrimination on the grounds of age but also direct discrimination. This constitutes an important departure from the basic model (see Figure 6.1 in chapter 6) but has been introduced to reflect the fact that age may genuinely be a relevant factor for certain aspects of employment and vocational training.[156] Article 6(1) therefore means that employers can lay down a retirement age, length of service criteria and, for jobs such as those in medicine involving a lengthy period of training, a maximum age for recruitment, provided always that the employer can show, on a case by case basis and on the production of evidence and not general assertions,[157] that the age criteria are objectively justifiable and the means of achieving the aim are appropriate and necessary. The possibility of objectively justifying direct discrimination also means that it is unlikely that the Article 4(1) GOR will be much invoked in the context of age discrimination.

In addition, Article 6(2) of the Framework Directive permits Member States to provide that the fixing for occupational social security schemes of ages for admission or entitlement to retirement or invalidity benefits and the use, in the context of such schemes, of age criteria in actuarial calculations, does not

---

[156] DTI, above, n.43, para. 4.1.10.   [157] Ibid., para. 4.1.14.

constitute discrimination on the grounds of age, provided this does not result in discrimination on the grounds of sex.

4. Conflicts between the Grounds

With the extension of the scope of the non-discrimination principle, there will inevitably come a time when the different grounds of protection come into conflict. The derogations provide some guidance as to hierarchy. Thus Article 4(2) of Directive 2000/78 allows ethos-based organizations to discriminate against those who do not share their ethos. It also seems to permit such orgnaizations to discriminate against those who once shared their ethos but through their conduct no longer adhere to it: ethos-based organizations can require 'individuals working for them to act in good faith and with loyalty to the organisation's ethos'. Therefore, the dismissal of a Catholic teacher employed in a Catholic school who gets divorced may be compatible with the Directive. However, this example demonstrates the potential conflict which arises between the different strands of protection: the dismissal of such a teacher might also contravene Directive 76/207's prohibition against discrimination on the grounds of marital status. Thus, the question is raised whether ethos-based organizations can discriminate against people who are protected on other grounds such as women and gays. Article 4(2) suggests that the answer is no: it provides that 'This difference of treatment . . . should not justify discrimination on another ground'. However, the same restriction does not apply in the case of non-ethos-based employers considered in Article 4(1).

F. POSITIVE ACTION

1. Sex

1.1. Introduction to the Issues

Article 2(4) of the original version of the Equal Treatment Directive provided that the Directive was 'without prejudice to measures which promote equal opportunity for men and women, in particular by removing existing inequalities which affect women's opportunities'. The importance of positive action as a way of securing women more senior positions in the labour market was recognized by a Commission report on occupational segregation.[158] The report concluded, first, that despite rising female participation in the workforce,

---

[158] Rubery and Fagan, *Occupational Segregation of Women and Men in the European Community*, Commission of the European Communities, V/5409/93-EN.

occupational segregation remains a central characteristic of all European labour markets; and, secondly, that although women have made entry into high level jobs, they have also increased their shares of lower level service and clerical work. The authors argued that positive action programmes, particularly those implemented in a favourable labour market context, have a role to play in reducing this segregation.

Positive action is a management approach intended to identify and remedy situations which lead to or perpetuate inequalities in the workplace. It is intended to put women in the position to be able to compete equally with men but does not interfere with the selection process. Thus, positive action aims to complement legislation on equal treatment and includes any measure contributing to the elimination of inequalities in practice. It focuses on balancing family and professional responsibilities, in particular looking at the development of childcare structures, the arrangement of working hours and the reintegration of women who have taken career breaks into the workplace.[159] Positive discrimination, by contrast, consists of setting recruitment targets or quotas and discriminating in favour of women at the point of selection in order to meet these targets. Although ostensibly contravening the principle of formal equality,[160] such discrimination can be justified in that it compensates for past discrimination, providing an immediate remedy to a long-standing problem.[161]

The Community has favoured positive action over positive discrimination. The Council's Recommendation on the Promotion of Positive Action for Women[162] recommends that Member States adopt a positive action policy 'designed to eliminate existing inequalities affecting women in working life and to promote a better balance between the sexes in employment'. The policy is intended, first, to eliminate the prejudicial effects on women which arise from existing attitudes, behaviour and structures based on the idea of a traditional division of roles in society for men and women; and, secondly, to encourage the participation of women in sectors where they are currently under-represented and at higher levels of responsibility in order to achieve better use of human resources.[163] Article 4 contains a list of the steps that Member States might take, including encouraging women to participate in vocational and continuous training,[164] encouraging women candidates in

---

[159] See also Advocate General Tesauro's Opinion in Case C–450/93 *Kalanke* [1995] ECR I–3051 and COM(96) 88.

[160] See Fredman, *Women and the Law* (Clarendon, Oxford, 1997), 380–3.

[161] But see Parekh, 'A Case for Positive Discrimination', in Hepple and Szyszczak (eds), *Discrimination: The Limits of the Law* (Mansell, London, 1992). See also Chs. 16–21 from the same book. For some lively discussion on the positive discrimination debate, see the essays by Kennedy and Delgado, in Donohue (ed.), *Foundations of Employment Discrimination Law* (OUP, New York, 1997).

[162] Recommendation 84/635/EEC (OJ [1984] L331/34).   [163] Art. 1.

[164] See further the Commission Recommendation 87/567/EEC of 24 November 1987 on Vocational Training for Women (OJ [1987] C342/5); the Council Resolution of 16 December on the Reintegration and Late Integration of Women into Working Life (OJ [1988] C333/01).

making applications, adapting working conditions, and adjusting working time. Article 8 emphasizes that the public sector should promote equal opportunities to serve as an example.[165]

The Commission published an extensive guide to positive action,[166] listing the organizational advantages of a positive action programme and the means by which to put it into place. Nevertheless, a report produced for the Commission found that 'despite almost a decade of the active promotion of positive action for women progress is slow . . . Many organisations do not appear to have a policy for equality of opportunity. Even less appear to have a programme of practical actions.'[167] As a result, the various Community action programmes contain a continued commitment to positive action,[168] including support for programmes such as NOW (New Opportunities for Women) aimed at promoting opportunities for women in the field of employment and training.[169]

1.2. The Role of the Court of Justice

(a) The Early Days

Given the sensitivities surrounding positive action it was inevitable that the Court would eventually become drawn into the debate, not least because some of the German *Länder* have quite extensive positive action programmes in their public sectors. In some of its earlier case law the Court took a very narrow view of what was permissible. For example, in *Commission v. France*[170] it said that the Article 2(4) exception was specifically and exclusively designed to allow measures which, although discriminatory in appearance, were in fact intended to eliminate or reduce actual instances of inequalities which might exist in the reality of social life. It ruled out, however, 'a generalised preservation of special rights for women in collective agreements'. This led one commentator to suggest that special measures—perhaps even positively discriminatory ones—would be excused by Article 2(4) to the extent that they compensated for specific instances of pre-existing inequality, albeit that Article 2(4) would not justify positive discrimination in favour of women in employment generally.[171]

---

[165] The Commission itself introduced a positive action programme on 8 March 1988.

[166] *Positive Action. Equal Opportunities for Women in Employment. A Guide*, Commission of the European Communities (1988) CB–48–87–525-EN-C.

[167] *An Evaluation Study of Positive Action in Favour of Women*, ER Consultants (1990), Commission V/587/91-EN, 39. For the Commission's own assessment, see its report to Council COM(88) 370 final.

[168] See e.g. II.2 Third Action Programme and Commission Document Implementation of the Third Action Programme on Equal Opportunities 1991–5, Development of Positive Action Measures, Strategy Document and Work Programme 1992–5.

[169] See further Ch. 1.

[170] Case 318/86 [1988] ECR I–6315. See also Case 111/86 *Delauche v. Commission* [1987] ECR 5345.

[171] Ellis, above, n. 99, 246.

(b) Kalanke *and* Marschall

The decision in *Kalanke*[172] cast doubt on any such broad reading of Article 2(4). The case concerned the Bremen law on positive discrimination which, in the case of a tie-break situation, gave priority to an equally qualified woman over a man if women were under-represented in the workforce.[173] Relying on this provision, the State of Bremen promoted Ms Glißman to the post of section manager in the parks department in preference to Mr Kalanke. He argued that he had been discriminated against on the grounds of sex, contrary to Article 2(1) of the Directive 76/207 (now Article 14 of the Consolidated Directive); Bremen relied on the Article 2(4) derogation.

The Court explained that Article 2(4) did permit national measures relating to access to employment, including promotion, which gave a specific advantage to women, with a view to improving their ability to compete on the labour market and to pursue their career on an equal footing with men.[174] However, it said that measures which, at the decision stage, departed from the principle of individual merit contravened Article 2(4). It continued that national rules which guaranteed women 'absolute and unconditional priority for appointment or promotion' went beyond promoting equal opportunities and overstepped the limits of the exception in Article 2(4) of the Directive.[175] Consequently, the Bremen system 'substitutes for equality of opportunity as envisaged in Article 2(4) the result which is only to be arrived at by providing such equality of opportunity'.[176]

Advocate General Tesauro's Opinion was equally narrow. He said: '[G]iving equal opportunities can only mean putting people in a position to attain equal results and hence restoring conditions of equality between members of the two sexes as regards starting points'.[177] This means removing existing barriers to achieve such a result. He then reasoned that since the man and woman in *Kalanke* had equivalent qualifications they must have had, and continued to have, equal opportunities: 'they are therefore on an equal footing at the starting block'.[178] Consequently, by favouring the woman, he said this created a

---

[172] Case C–450/93 [1995] ECR I–3051.

[173] Under-representation exists where women 'do not make up at least half the staff in the individual pay, remuneration and salary brackets in the relevant personnel group within a department'.

[174] Para. 19, referring to the Preamble of the Recommendation on Positive Action (84/635/EEC OJ [1984] L331/34).

[175] Para. 22. See also Case C–407/98 *Abrahamsson* v. *Fogelqvist* [2000] ECR I–5539 where the Court ruled that a national rule which gave automatic priority to a person of the under-represented sex who had adequate qualifications but qualifications which were inferior to those of the person who would otherwise have been appointed, albeit that the difference in qualifications was not important, breached Art. 2(4) of the Directive and Art. 141(4) EC. This outcome was not affected by the limited number of posts to which the rule applied or the level of the appointment.

[176] Para. 23.   [177] Para. 13.   [178] Ibid.

position of equality of results which exceeded the scope of Article 2(4). He said:[179]

In the final analysis, must each individual's right not to be discriminated against on grounds of sex—which the Court itself has held is a fundamental right the observance of which it ensures—yield to the rights of the disadvantaged group, in this case women, in order to compensate for the discrimination suffered by that group in the past?

Put this way the answer was, inevitably, no. He said that positive discrimination brought about a quantitative increase in female employment but it also most affected the principle of equality as between individuals. He concluded:

I am convinced that women do not merit the attainment of numerical—and hence only formal—equality—moreover at the cost of an incontestable violation of a fundamental value of every civil society: equal rights, equal treatment for all. Formal numerical equality is an objective which may salve some consciences, but it will remain illusory and devoid of all substance unless it goes together with measures which are genuinely destined to achieve equality . . . [W]hat is necessary above all is a substantial change in the economic, social and cultural model which is at the root of the inequalities.[180]

The judgment (and the opinion) were much criticized for their excessive reliance on the formal non-discrimination model, their focus on the individual, their failure both to show any sensitivity towards the position of women,[181] and to respect the principle of subsidiarity, and the absence of any attempt to weigh up any policy arguments. It also cast doubt on the legality of a variety of different forms of positive action. As a result, the Commission issued a Communication on *Kalanke*.[182] It took the view that the Court only condemned the special feature of the Bremen law which *automatically* gave women the absolute and unconditional right to appointment or promotion over men. Therefore, it considered that only those quota systems which were completely rigid and did not leave any possibility to take account of individual circumstances were unlawful. It therefore proposed an amendment to Article 2(4) of Directive 76/207/EEC to the effect that:

This Directive shall be without prejudice to measures to promote equal opportunity for men and women in particular by removing existing inequalities which affect the opportunities of the underrepresented sex in the areas referred to in Article 1(1). Possible measures shall include the giving of preference, as regards access to employment or promotion, to a member of the underrepresented sex, provided that such measures do not preclude the assessment of the particular circumstances of the individual case.

---

[179] Para. 7.   [180] Para. 28.

[181] See e.g. Schiek 'Positive Action in Community Law' (1996) 25 *ILJ*. 239; Prechal (1996) 33 *CMLRev*. 1245; Fredman, above, n. 160, 392; Peters, 'The Many Meanings of Equality and Positive Action in Favour of Women under European Community Law—A Conceptual Analysis' (1996) 2 *ELJ* 177.

[182] COM(96) 88.

The Commission's approach was reflected in the Court's decision in the subsequent case of *Marschall*.[183] Mr Marschall, a teacher, applied for promotion. The District Authority informed him that it intended to appoint a female candidate on the basis of the state law which provided for priority to an equally qualified woman where women were under-represented. However, unlike *Kalanke*,[184] the state law contained a saving clause (*Öffnungsklausel*): priority was given to the woman 'unless reasons specific to an individual [male] candidate tilt the balance in his favour'. Advocate General Jacobs thought that the saving clause did not alter the discriminatory nature of the rule in general. He agreed with Advocate General Tesauro in *Kalanke* that the measures permitted by Article 2(4) were those designed to remove the obstacles preventing women from pursuing the same results on equal terms. He said Article 2(4) did not permit measures designed 'to confer the results on them [women] directly, or, in any event, to grant them priority in attaining those results simply because they are women'. He said that the reasoning in *Kalanke* suggested that the rule in *Marschall* was also unlawful: if an absolute rule giving preference to women on the grounds of sex was unlawful, then a conditional rule which gave preference to men on the basis of admittedly discriminatory criteria *a fortiori* had to be unlawful.[185]

The Court disagreed. While recognizing that a rule which automatically gave priority to women when they were equally qualified to men involved discrimination on grounds of sex, it distinguished *Marschall* from *Kalanke* on the basis of the saving clause. Having noted the 'prejudices and stereotypes concerning the role and capacities of women in working life',[186] it said that:[187]

It follows that a national rule in terms of which, subject to the application of the saving clause, female candidates for promotion who are equally as qualified as the male candidates are to be treated preferentially in sectors where they are under-represented may fall within the scope of Article 2(4) if such a rule may counteract the prejudicial effects on female candidates of the attitudes and behaviour described above and thus reduce actual instances of inequality which may exist in the real world.

The Court then added a proviso. The state rule did not breach Article 2(4) provided that the national rule contained a saving clause. This means that:

... in each individual case the rule provides for male candidates who are equally as qualified as the female candidates a guarantee that the candidatures will be the subject of an objective assessment which will take account of all criteria specific to the individual candidates and will override the priority accorded to female candidates where

---

[183] Case C–409/95 [1997] ECR I–6363.
[184] The Bremen law at issue in *Kalanke* did not contain a saving clause. The Federal Labour Court, however, read exceptions into the Bremen law in accordance with the *Grundgesetz*. While this was mentioned to the Court (see para. 9), the questions referred made no reference to these exceptions. It therefore seems that the Court answered the question in *Kalanke* on the basis of the absence of such a clause.
[185] Para. 36.   [186] Paras. 29 and 30.   [187] Para. 31.

one or more of those criteria tilts the balance in favour of the male candidate. In this respect it should be remembered that those criteria must not be such as to discriminate against the female candidates'.[188]

It that said that it was for the national court to determine whether those conditions were fulfilled.

Marschall therefore suggests that so-called soft quotas (quotas with a saving clause) fall within Article 2(4), as an exception to the equal treatment principle, provided that the state law contains a proviso.[189] The ruling in *Marschall* therefore confines *Kalanke* to the (unusual) situation of an unqualified ('hard') quota rule. However, the qualification introduced by the Court to the types of saving clause permitted, and the limitations on the criteria which may be applied to tilt the balance (back) in favour of the man, in effect restricts the operation of such saving clauses. The criteria applied must be based on the individual concerned and 'not such as to discriminate against *female candidates*',[190] that is, they must be non-discriminatory in a general sense. Therefore, the criteria applied to bring the saving clause into operation may not be based on generalizations about men, such as, for instance, their need to bring home a 'household wage' (an indirectly discriminatory requirement), or the fact that the man is a sole breadwinner[191] (again an indirectly discriminatory assumption), or reasons of seniority (also potentially indirectly discriminatory).[192] This was Advocate General Jacobs' concern about the use of such a proviso. He said that such a saving clause would have 'the result that the post will be offered to the male candidate on the basis of criteria which are accepted as discriminatory'.[193]

The Commission summarized the *Kalanke* and *Marschall* line of case law in the following terms:[194]

- the possibility to adopt positive action measures is to be regarded as an exception to the principle of equal treatment;
- the exception is specifically and exclusively designed to allow for measures which, although discriminatory in appearance, are in fact intended to eliminate or reduce actual instances of inequality which may exist in the reality of social life;

---

[188] Para. 33.

[189] On the different types of quota, see Schiek, 'Sex Equality Law after *Kalanke* and *Marschall*' (1998) 4 *ELJ.* 148.

[190] Para. 33, emphasis added.

[191] It was suggested by the national court that this might be precisely one such criterion applied in the assessment. Mr Kalanke had argued that he should have been promoted on social grounds since he had to maintain three dependants (wife and two children) whereas Ms Glißman had no such obligation.

[192] On the question of seniority, see Ch. 7. For an analysis of the proviso, see Charpentier, 'The European Court of Justice and the Rhetoric of Affirmative Action' (1998) 4 *ELJ.* 167.

[193] Barnard and Hervey, 'Softening the Approach to Quotas: Positive Action after *Marschall*' (1998) 20 *JSWL.* 333.

[194] COM(2000) 334, para. 29.

- automatic priority to women, as regards access to employment or promotion, in sectors where they are under-represented cannot be justified;
- conversely, such a priority is justified if it is not automatic and if the national measure in question guarantees equally qualified male candidates that their situation will be the subject of an objective assessment which takes into account all criteria specific to the candidates, whatever their gender.

(c) The Effect of Article 141(4) EC

Marschall is a delicate compromise by the Court, echoing a compromise adopted by the US Supreme Court in *Johnson* v. *Santa Clara*[195] 10 years earlier. In *Johnson* the US Supreme Court upheld an affirmative plan under Title VII of the Civil Rights Act 1964 which 'sought to take a moderate, gradual approach to eliminating the imbalance in its workforce, one which establishes realistic guidance for employment decisions, and which visits minimal intrusion on the legitimate expectations of other employees'. The Court of Justice also shows an understanding of the real situation of women—that the private sphere cannot be divorced from the public—and that concepts such as equality of opportunity and equality of results are not mutually exclusive. There is much to suggest that the Court is adopting a more substantive approach to equality in *Marschall*[196] and the new Article 141(4), introduced by the Amsterdam Treaty, amending Article 6(3) of the SPA, may have provided some guidance. Article 141(4) provides:

With a view to ensuring *full equality in practice between men and women* in working life, the principle of equal treatment shall not prevent any Member State from maintaining or adopting measures providing for specific advantage, in order to make it easier for the *underrepresented sex* to pursue a vocational activity or to prevent or compensate for disadvantages in their professional careers.[197]

This is a stronger and more generalized formulation than its forebear in the SPA and appears to go further than Article 2(4) of Directive 76/207 by permitting a wider range of measures—possibly even positively discriminatory measures.[198] The Article 141(4) approach has now replaced Article 2(4) in the revised Equal Treatment Directive. Article 2(8) (Article 3 of the Consolidated Directive) provides:

Member States may maintain or adopt measures within the meaning of Article 141(4) of the Treaty with a view to ensuring full equality in practice between men and women.

---

[195] 107 S.Ct 1442, 480 US 616 (1987).
[196] Cabral, 'A Step Closer to Substantive Equality' (1998) 23 *ELRev.* 481; 486. See also Case C–407/98 *Abrahamsson* v. *Fogelqvist* [2000] ECR I–5539, para. 48.
[197] Emphasis added.   [198] See Ellis, above, n. 153, 259.

This provision 'makes obsolete' the Commission's former proposal to amend Directive 76/207 in the light of *Kalanke*.[199] The question remains whether Article 141(4) EC and Article 2(8) of Directive 76/207 (Article 3 of the Consolidated Directive) continue to be viewed as 'exceptions' to the principle of equality (as the Commission seems to think—see below), in which case the usual rules apply (exceptions are narrowly construed, are subject to the principle of proportionality and need to be reviewed over time), or whether these provisions are free standing and form an integral step to achieving equality of opportunity (as the prominent position of Article 3 in the Consolidated Directive indicates) in which case the usual rules do not apply. Certainly, the Norwegian government, in its submissions in the *EFTA* case,[200] favoured the broad approach advocating an interpretation of the original Article 2(4) (Article 141(4) does not form part of EFTA law) that views affirmative action measures aimed at gender equality in practice, 'not as constituting discrimination but rather as an intrinsic dimension of the very prohibition thereof'. The EFTA Court, apparently rather reluctantly, referred to the 'homogeneity objective underlying the EEA Agreement' which meant that it could not 'accept the invitation to redefine the concept of discrimination on grounds of gender in the way the defendant has suggested'.[201]

The Court of Justice's case law does not provide a clear answer as to whether Article 141(4) EC goes further than and differs from Article 2(4). In *Griesmar*[202] the Court merely noted that national measures covered by Article 141(4) (in its original form as Article 6(3) of the SPA) had to 'contribute to helping women conduct their professional life on an equal footing with men'. On the facts the Court suggested that the measure at issue—a service credit provided to female (but not male) civil servants in respect of each of their children for the purposes of calculating a pension—did not offset the disadvantages to which the careers of female civil servants were exposed by helping those women in their professional life.[203] It continued that the measure was limited to granting female civil servants who were mothers a service credit at the date of their retirement, without providing a remedy for the problems which they might encounter in the course of their professional career.[204]

In *Briheche*[205] the Court considered the arguments under Article 2(4) and Article 141(4) separately. It first examined whether a national rule, which removed the maximum age at which individuals could take public exams if they wanted to work in the public sector for widows—but not for widowers—

[199] COM(2000) 334, para. 12.
[200] Case E–1/02 *EFTA Surveillance Authority* v. *Kingdom of Norway* [2003] IRLR 318.
[201] Para. 45. See Tobler (2004) 41 *CMLRev.* 245.
[202] Case C–366/99 *Griesmar* v. *Ministre de l'Économie, des Finances et de l'Industrie* [2001] ECR I–9383, para. 46.
[203] Para. 64.   [204] Para. 65.
[205] Case C–319/03 *Serge Briheche* v. *Ministre de l'Interieur, Ministre de l'Education nationale and Ministre de la Justice* [2004] ECR I–8807.

who had not remarried could be saved by Article 2(4). Because the rule gave automatic and unconditional priority to women, the Court found that it 'could not be allowed under Article 2(4)'.[206] However, the Court then went on to consider whether the national provision was 'nevertheless allowed under Article 141(4).[207] On the facts, it found the national rule to be unjustified because it was disproportionate.[208] However, the interesting point in this case is that the Court's approach suggested that the two Articles were not co-extensive.[209]

(d) Beyond Kalanke *and* Marschall

In other cases the Court does not engage directly with the detail of Article 141(4) but the Court may refer to it to support its findings. In reality, the case law seems to ebb and flow, with the Court appearing to allow different degrees of flexibility in the national rule, depending on the circumstances.[210] The broader approach to positive action can be seen in the multi-faceted case of *Badeck*.[211] The Court ruled that Articles 2(1) and 2(4) of Directive 76/207/EEC did not preclude:

- national rules which allocated at least half of all training places in the public service to women, where women were under-represented, unless despite appropriate measures for drawing the attention of women to the training places available, there were not enough applications from women;
- national rules where male and female candidates have equal qualifications, but guarantees that qualified women who satisfy all the conditions required or laid down were called to interview, in sectors in which they were under-represented,
- national rules relating to the composition of employees' representative bodies and administrative and supervisory bodies, that recommended that the legislative provisions adopted for their implementation take into account the objective that at least half the members of those bodies had to be women.

These aspects of the ruling are unsurprising. Two important issues did, however, arise in the case.

The first concerned the legality of the so-called 'flexible result quota' ('*flexible Ergebnisquote*'). According to this rule, in sectors of the public service where women are under-represented, priority is given to female candidates, where male and female candidates for selection have equal quali-

---

[206] Para. 28.
[207] See also Case C–407/98 *Abrahamsson v. Folgequist* [2000] ECR I–5539, para. 54.
[208] Para. 31.
[209] Ibid. See also Case C–407/98 *Abrahamsson v. Folgequist* [2000] ECR I–5539, para. 40.
[210] Tobler (2004) 41 *CMLRev.* 245, 255 citing para. 41 of Case E–1/02 *EFTA Surveillance Authority v. Kingdom of Norway* [2003] IRLR 318.
[211] Case C–158/97 *Badeck v. Hessicher Ministerpräsident und Landesanwalt beim Staatsgerichtshof des Landes Hessen* [2000] ECR I–1875.

fications, where this proves necessary for complying with the binding targets in the women's advancement plan, if no reasons of 'greater legal weight' are put forward.[212] The Court said that this priority rule was not 'absolute and unconditional' in the *Kalanke* sense and so was compatible with Articles 2(1) and 2(4) of Directive 76/207. Following *Marschall* this outcome is not surprising.

Of more interest is the Court's (cursory) discussion of the criteria by which the initial selection of candidates occurred, before the flexible quota was applied.[213] For example, capabilities and experience acquired by carrying out work in the home were to be taken into account in so far as they were of importance for the suitability, performance, and capability of candidates. By contrast seniority, age, and the date of last promotion were to be taken into account only in so far as they were of importance to the job. The family status or income of the partner was immaterial. Further, part-time work, leave, and delays in completing training as a result of looking after children or other dependants could not have a negative effect on the selection process. As the Court simply noted:

Such criteria, although formulated in terms which are neutral as regards sex and thus capable of benefiting men too, in general favour women. They are manifestly intended to lead to an equality which is substantive rather than formal, by reducing the inequalities which may occur in practice in social life. Their legitimacy is not challenged in the main proceedings.

Thus, the Court seems to allow some (indirect) discrimination against men in the application of the selection criteria. Only if a female candidate and a male candidate could not be distinguished on the basis of their qualifications could the woman be chosen according to the flexible quota. However, as the Court emphasized in *Abrahamsson*,[214] the application of such criteria had to be transparent and amenable to review in order to 'obviate any arbitrary assessment of the qualifications of the candidates'.

The second interesting aspect of *Badeck* concerned the rule which pre-scribed binding targets for women for *temporary* posts in the academic service and for academic assistants where women were equally qualified to the men. These targets required that the minimum percentage of women be at least equal to the percentage of women among graduates, holders of higher degrees, and students in each discipline. The *Land* Attorney noted that this

---

[212] These reasons of 'greater legal weight' concern five rules of law, described as 'social aspects' which make no reference to sex, whereby preferential treatment is given, first, to former employees in the public service who have left the service because of family commitments; sec-ondly, to individuals who worked on a part-time basis for family reasons and now wish to resume full-time employment; thirdly, to former temporary soldiers; fourthly, to seriously disabled people; and fifthly, to the long-term unemployed.

[213] Paras. 31–2.

[214] Case C–407/98 *Abrahamsson v. Folgequist* [2000] ECR I–5539, para. 49.

minimum quota system came very close to equality as to results which had been rejected in *Kalanke*. Nevertheless, the Court said that this rule was compatible with Community law. It pointed out that this system did not fix an absolute ceiling but only a ceiling by reference to the number of persons who had received appropriate training. It said that this amounted to using an actual fact as a quantitative criterion for giving preference to women.

This aspect of *Badeck* can be contrasted with *Abrahamsson*[215] which concerned a Swedish rule which applied in the public sector, allowing the appointment of women in preference to men where they were under-represented, provided that the difference between the respective merits of the two candidates was not so great as to give rise to a breach of the requirement of objectivity in making public appointments. Folgequist, a woman, was appointed to a chair in hydrospheric sciences even though Abrahamsson, a man, was superior 'from the scientific point of view'. As the Court noted, unlike the rules at issue *Kalanke*, *Marschall* and *Badeck*, the Swedish measure allowed preference to be given to those who were 'sufficiently qualified' but not equally qualified.[216] For this reason, it said that the Swedish measure giving automatic preference to a person of the under-represented sex with merely sufficient qualifications failed to satisfy the requirements of Article 2(4) of the Directive and Article 141(4) EC.

Concern that posts would be awarded to female applicants with inadequate qualifications if there was an insufficient number of qualified women candidates also underpinned the *EFTA* case.[217] Norwegian law allowed for academic posts to be advertised as being open only to members of the under-represented sex. Based on this law, 10 post-doctoral posts and 12 permanent posts were earmarked for women only by the University of Oslo. This decision was challenged by the EFTA Surveillance Authority (the equivalent to the Commission). The Norwegian government argued that its legislation fell under Article 2(4) of the Equal Treatment Directive 76/207. However, the EFTA Court considered that the Norwegian legislation went further than the Swedish rule in *Abrahamsson* (where a selection procedure, involving an assessment of all candidates was foreseen, at least in principle). Since the ECJ found that the Swedish rule breached the equal treatment principle, *a fortiori* the Norwegian rule also fell foul of that principle:[218] the national rule, as applied by the University of Oslo, gave absolute and unconditional priority to women. There was no provision for flexibility and the outcome was determined automatically in favour of a female candidate.

Abrahamsson and the *EFTA* case can be contrasted with *Lommers*[219] which adopted a more generous approach to positive action in a similar vein to

[215] Case C–407/98 *Abrahamsson v. Folgequist* [2000] ECR I–5539.   [216] Para. 45.
[217] Case E–1/02 *EFTA Surveillance Authority v. Kingdom of Norway* [2003] IRLR 318, para. 45.
[218] Para. 51.
[219] Case C–476/99 *Lommers v. Mininster van Landbouw* [2002] ECR I–2891.

Marschall. A male employee challenged the policy of the Dutch Ministry of Agriculture to provide subsidised nursery places 'only to female employees . . . save in the case of an emergency'. The Court of Justice ruled that this was compatible with Community law. Because women were significantly under-represented in the Ministry of Agriculture, both in terms of their number and their occupation of higher grades, the Court said that a measure which formed part of the

> . . . restricted concept of equality of opportunity in so far as it is not places of employment which are reserved for women but enjoyment of certain working conditions designed to facilitate their pursuit of, and progression in, their career, falls in principle into the category of measures designed to eliminate the causes of women's reduced opportunities for access to employment and careers and are intended to improve their ability to compete on the labour market and to pursue a career on an equal footing with men.[220]

Having recognized that Article 2(4) was potentially satisfied, the Court then considered the question of proportionality.[221] It recognized that the number of nursery places was limited, that not all women got the places they wanted and that places were open to single fathers who had responsibility for children.[222] The Court therefore concluded that the Dutch measure was proportionate.[223]

The striking feature about *Lommers* is the shift in emphasis away from viewing Article 2(4) as a derogation to the principle of equal treatment which must be narrowly construed, to subjecting measures taken under Article 2(4) to a (relatively relaxed) proportionality analysis. This was also emphasized by the Court in the *EFTA* case.[224]

2. The Article 13 Directives

The Article 13 Directives contain an equivalent positive action provision, albeit that the reference to the workplace has been dropped. For example, Article 5 of the Race Directive provides:

> With a view to ensuring full equality in practice, the principle of equal treatment shall not prevent any Member State from maintaining or adopting specific measures to prevent or compensate for disadvantages linked to racial or ethnic origin.

In its explanatory memorandum, the Commission notes that the need for positive action has already been addressed by the European Court of Justice in *Kalanke* and *Marschall*. It then says that the wording is based on Article

---

[220] Para. 38. Similar sentiments underpinned AG Alber's reasoning in Case C–218/98 *Abdoulaye* v. *Régre Nationale des Usines Renault SA* [1999] ECR I–5723, paras. 57–8.
[221] Paras. 42–3.   [222] Para. 46.   [223] Para. 48.
[224] Case E–1/02 *EFTA Surveillance Authority* v. *Kingdom of Norway* [2003] IRLR 318, para. 43.

141(4) EC and that as positive action measures are in derogation from the principle of equality 'they should be interpreted strictly, in the light of the current case law on sex discrimination'.

However, in respect of two strands, age and disability, positive action raises particular issues. First, in respect of age, since direct age discrimination can be objectively justified, the need for a specific provision concerning positive action is significantly reduced. Second, in respect of disability, since the prohibition of discrimination is asymmetrical, positively discriminatory measures could be taken in favour of the disabled and the able bodied would not have legal grounds for complaint. Furthermore, Article 7(2) contains the following provision:

With regard to disabled persons, the principle of equal treatment shall be without prejudice to the right of Member States to maintain or adopt provisions on the protection of health and safety at work or to measures aimed at creating or maintaining provisions or facilities for safeguarding or promoting their integration into the working environment.

The first part of Article 7(2) suggests the opposite of positive action: apparently allowing Member States to restrict opportunities for disabled people on the grounds of health and safety. On the other hand, the second limb of Article 7(2) is seemingly broader than the general positive action provision in that it does not require the measures taken to 'compensate for previous disadvantages'.

G. POSITIVE DUTY TO PROMOTE EQUALITY

The standard non-discrimination model contained in the various directives plays a valuable role in sending out a signal about conduct which is considered unacceptable and in providing individuals with a means of redress. But, by its very nature, such an approach is dependent on individuals taking action which may lead to ad hoc, ad personam solutions rather than more general structural change. In this respect the Revised Equal Treatment Directive contained an important innovation: it imposed a duty on Member States 'actively [to] take into account the objective of equality between men and women when formulating and implementing laws, regulations, administrative provisions, policies and activities' (Article 1(1a), Article 29 of the Consolidated Directive). In addition, Member States must take the necessary measures to ensure that they abolish any laws, regulations, or administrative provisions contrary to the principle of equal treatment and to ensure that any discriminatory provisions contained in collective agreements,[225] individual

---

[225] The Directive covers all collective agreements, irrespective of whether they have legal effects or not because they have important *de facto* consequences for employment relationships: see Case 165/82 *Commission v. UK* [1982] ECR 3431.

contracts of employment, staff and other internal rules of undertakings, or in rules governing the independent occupations or professions and workers' and employers' organizations are or shall be declared null and void or are amended.[226]

Thus the Directive imposes positive duties on the state to be pro-active in the elimination of discrimination and promoting equality. As Fredman points out, such duties go beyond compensating identified victims and aim at restructuring institutions. The duty bearer is not the person at fault for creating the problem but is, nevertheless, responsible for identifying the problem and for participating in its eradication.[227] So far, the Community legislature has not introduced equivalent duties in respect of the other strands.

This 'mainstreaming' of equality is another important feature of Community policy. As we saw in chapter 6, the Community institutions have already applied it to their own policies in respect of sex[228] and now require Member States to consider gender equality in respect of their employment policies. Gender mainstreaming has been a key aspect of the employment guidelines since 2001.[229] In the chapeau to 2005 guidelines, the Council says that 'Equal opportunities and combating discrimination are essential for progress. Gender mainstreaming and the promotion of gender equality should be ensured in all action taken'.[230]

H. DIRECTIVE 86/613 ON EQUAL TREATMENT OF THE SELF-EMPLOYED

Directive 86/613[231] applies the principle of equal treatment both to self-employed workers who are defined as 'all those persons pursuing a gainful activity for their own account, under the conditions laid down by national law, including farmers and members of the liberal professions',[232] and to their

---

[226] Art. 3(2)(a) and (b) of Dir. 76/207, Art. 23(a) and (b) of the Consolidated Directive.

[227] 'The Age of Equality' in Fredman and Spencer (eds), *Age as an Equality Issue. Legal and Policy Perspectives* (Hart Publishing, Oxford, 2003) 62.

[228] Commission, *Incorporating Equal Opportunities for Men and Women into all Community Policies and Activities*, COM(96) 67. This is considered further in Ch. 6.

[229] Co. Dec. 2001/63/EC (OJ [2001] L22/18, para. 16: 'Therefore, the Member States will adopt a gender-mainstreaming approach in implementing the Guidelines across all four pillars:
—developing and reinforcing consultative systems with gender equality bodies;
—applying procedures for gender impact assessment under each guideline;
—developing indicators to measure progress in gender equality in relation to each guideline.'

[230] Council Dec. 2005/600 (OJ [2005] L205/21).

[231] Council Directive 86/613/EEC, based on Arts. 94 and 308 on the application of the principle of equal treatment between men and women engaged in an activity, including agriculture, in a self-employed capacity, and on the protection of self-employed women during pregnancy and motherhood (OJ [1986] L359/56).

[232] Art. 2(a).

spouses, not being employees or partners, who habitually participate in the activities of the self-employed worker and perform the same tasks or ancillary tasks.[233] The principle of equal treatment is applied to miscellaneous aspects of self-employed working life. First, it applies to all the self-employed, 'especially in respect of the establishment, equipment or extension of a business or the launching or extension of any other form of self-employed activity, including financial activities'.[234] Secondly, it applies to spouses who form a company, requiring that the conditions imposed on spouses when forming a company be no more restrictive than the conditions imposed on unmarried persons.[235]

The remaining provisions are characterized by their generality, more akin to a Recommendation or a Resolution than to a Directive, since they outline a programme of action for Member States. Thus, Article 7 says that if the Member State provides for a contributory social security scheme for the self-employed, a spouse who participates in the activities of the self-employed worker should be able to join the contributory scheme *voluntarily*.[236] It also provides that Member States should encourage the recognition of the work performed by spouses in these circumstances. Article 8 requires Member States to examine the conditions under which a female self-employed worker and the wife of a self-employed worker who interrupt their occupation on the grounds of pregnancy or motherhood may have access to services supplying temporary replacements or existing national social services or be entitled to cash benefits under a social security scheme.[237] Finally, Article 9 obliges Member States to allow those who consider that they have been discriminated against to pursue their claims by judicial process.

Although this Directive was designed to address the problems of self-employed women, particularly those working in agriculture who had complained of a lack of a clearly defined occupational status, of a precarious position in respect of social security entitlements, and of a lack of protection in respect of pregnancy and maternity,[238] its substance is weak and uninspired.[239] The Council was intending to review the Directive before 1 July 1993 but no action has so far been taken.

---

[233] Art. 2(b).   [234] Art. 4.

[235] Art. 5. If Art. 5 necessitates a change in domestic legislation on matrimonial rights and obligations, Member States had until 30 June 1991 to comply with this provision of the Directive.

[236] This provision would only be of assistance to those spouses who are earning a sufficient income to enable them to make such contributions.

[237] Art. 8.   [238] COM(84)57 final/2.   [239] See, further, Ellis, above, n. 99, 268–70.

I. REMEDIES

1. Introduction

The remedies provision of the original Equal Treatment Directive 76/207 inspired much litigation raising issues which not only profoundly affected national social policy but also raised points of fundamental constitutional importance. Some of the issues raised by the Court's case law on sex equality have been incorporated into the Article 13 Directives and have now been included in the Consolidated Directive. In the section that follows we shall therefore focus on the Court's case law in the field of sex discrimination.

2. Sex

2.1. Direct Effect and Beyond

It is well established that provisions of a Directive which are unconditional and sufficiently precise and which have not been implemented correctly or at all, can have vertical direct effect.[240] This means that an individual may, after the expiry of the period prescribed for implementation, rely on such provisions directly against the Member State in default.[241] This prevents Member States from taking advantage of their own failure to comply with Community law to deny rights to individuals.[242] The same argument does not apply to private individuals: as the Court explained in *Marshall (No. 1)*,[243] since the binding nature of a Directive exists only in relation to 'each Member State to which it is addressed . . . it follows that a Directive may not of itself impose obligations on an individual and that a provision of a Directive may not be relied upon as such against such a person'.[244] Consequently, clear and unambiguous provisions of an unimplemented or incorrectly implemented Directive cannot have horizontal direct effect. On the facts of the case, Helen Marshall was able to rely on the principle of equal treatment laid down in Article 2(1) (Article 14(1) of the Consolidated Directive), as applied to conditions governing dismissal referred to in Article 3(1)(c) (Article 14(1)(c) of the Consolidated Directive), which were directly effective, to complain against her

---

[240] Case 152/84 *Marshall (No. 1)* [1986] ECR 723.

[241] Case 148/78 *Pubblico Ministero* v. *Ratti* [1979] ECR 1629 and Case 8/81 *Becker* v. *Finanzamt Munster-Innenstadt* [1982] ECR 53. See generally De Witte, 'Direct Effect, Supremacy, and the Nature of the Legal Order', in Craig and de Búrca (eds), *The Evolution of EU Law* (OUP, Oxford, 1999); Prechal, *Directives in EC Law* (OUP, Oxford, 2006).

[242] Case 152/84 *Marshall (No. 1)* v. *Southampton Area Health Authority* [1986] ECR 723, para. 47. Cf. Case C–144/04 *Mangold* v. *Helm* [2005] ECR I–000 considered in Ch. 6.

[243] Case 152/84 *Marshall (No. 1)* [1986] ECR 723.

[244] Ibid., para. 48.

state employer of a discriminatory dismissal. Similarly, in *Johnston*[245] the Court said that Article 2(1) was directly effective when applied to conditions governing access to jobs, vocational training, and advanced vocational training referred to in Articles 3(1)(a) and (b) (Article 14(1)(a) and (b) of the Consolidated Directive) and could be invoked against the Royal Ulster Constabulary.

Early cases suggested that the terms of Article 6 of Directive 76/207 (Article 17 of the Consolidated Directive) on remedies were not, however, sufficiently unconditional or precise to be directly effective.[246] There was merely an obligation to interpret national law in the light of the wording and purpose of the Directive.[247] In *Marshall (No. 2)*,[248] however, the Court said that the combined provisions of Articles 3(1)(c) and 6 of Directive 76/207 conferred rights on a victim of a discriminatory dismissal which that person had to be able to rely upon before the national courts as against the state and authorities which were an emanation of the state.

The Court has taken three steps to address the hardship caused by the distinction between horizontal and vertical direct effect. First, it has given a broad definition to the term 'state'. In *Marshall (No. 1)*[249] the Court said a person can rely on a Directive against the state regardless of the capacity in which the state is acting, whether as an employer or as a public authority, such as Southampton and South West Hampshire Area Health Authority. Subsequently, in *Foster*[250] the Court defined 'state' as 'organisations or bodies which were subject to the authority and control of the state or had special powers beyond those which result from the normal rules applicable to relations between individuals'. Therefore, Mrs Foster could rely on Article 3(1)(c) of Directive 76/207 against British Gas, at that time a nationalized company, to claim damages for a discriminatory dismissal.[251] The directly effective provisions of the Equal Treatment Directive have also been relied on against constitutionally independent authorities responsible for maintaining law and order,[252] public authorities providing public health services,[253] and a nationalized industry responsible for providing energy.[254] The case of *Dekker*,[255]

---

[245] Case 222/84 [1986] 1651.

[246] Case 14/83 *Von Colson and Kamann v. Land Nordrhein Westfalen* [1984] ECR 1891, para. 27; Case 79/83 *Harz v. Deutsche Tradax* [1984] ECR 1921, para. 27. However, in Case 222/84 *Johnston* [1986] ECR 1651 Art. 6 seemed to have direct effect in so far as it overrode the national rule that denied the plaintiff access to the Court.

[247] Case 14/83 *Von Colson* [1984] ECR 1891, para. 26.

[248] Case C–271/91 *Marshall v. Southampton and South West Hampshire Area Health Authority (Teaching) (No. 2)* [1993] ECR I–4367.

[249] Case 152/84 [1986] ECR 723, para. 49.

[250] Case C–188/89 *Foster v. British Gas* [1990] ECR I–3313, para. 18.

[251] *Foster v. British Gas* [1991] IRLR 268 (House of Lords).

[252] Case 222/84 *Johnston* [1986] ECR 1651.

[253] Case 152/84 *Marshall (No. 1)* [1986] ECR 723.

[254] Case C–188/89 *Foster* [1990] ECR I–3313.   [255] Case C–177/88 [1990] ECR I–3941.

however, concerned a private employer who was nevertheless held bound to comply with the provisions of the Directive which had not been fully implemented by the Dutch government.[256]

Secondly, in *Von Colson, Marleasing*,[257] and *Pfeiffer*[258] the Court imposed a broad obligation on all state institutions, especially the national courts, arising from both the Directive and Article 10 EC, to interpret national law, as far as possible, in conformity with the requirements of Community law, subject to the general principles of law, especially the principles of legal certainty and non-retroactivity.[259] Therefore, in *Von Colson* the national court was obliged to interpret the national rules on compensation in the light of Directive 76/207. The *Von Colson* approach may well explain the Court's decision in *Dekker*.[260]

The third step taken by the Court was to introduce the principle of state liability in *Francovich*,[261] saying that Community law requires the Member States to make good damage caused to individuals through failure to transpose a Directive. Subsequently, in *Brasserie du Pêcheur and Factortame (No. 3)*[262] and *British Telecommunications*[263] (cases concerning breaches of Treaty provisions involving wide discretion and an incorrectly implemented Directive respectively) the Court made clear that the principle of state liability was inherent in the system of the Treaty. It did not merely apply in a situation where the provisions of Community law were directly effective: direct effect was only a 'minimum guarantee' and could not ensure in every case that individuals enjoyed their Community law rights. The Court then established a threefold test for liability: first, the rule of law infringed must be intended to confer rights on individuals; secondly, the breach must be sufficiently serious;

---

[256] It has been argued that this case is in reality an application of the *Marleasing/Von Colson* 'interpretation' mechanism, see Banks, 'Equal Pay and Equal Treatment for Men and Women in Community Law', *Social Europe* 3/91, Ch. 2. A similar point was raised in Case C–421/92 *Habermann-Beltermann* [1994] ECR I–1657. See also Case C–180/95 *Nils Draehmpaehl* v. *Urania Immobilienservice ohG* [1997] ECR I–2195, and Ward, 'New Frontiers in Private Enforcement of EC Directives' (1998) 23 *ELRev*. 65.

[257] The is also known as the doctrine of indirect effects: see Cases 14/83 *Von Colson and Kamann* v. *Land Nordrhein Westfalen* [1984] ECR 1891 and C–106/89 *Marleasing SA* v. *La Comercial Internacional de Alimentacion* [1990] ECR I–4135; and confirmed in Case C–185/97 *Coote* v. *Granada Hospitality Ltd* [1998] ECR I–5199. In Case C–54/96 *Dorsch Consult* [1997] ECR I–4961 the Court said that this minimum guarantee could not justify a Member State absolving itself from taking, in due time, implementing measures sufficient to meet the purpose of each Directive.

[258] Joined Cases C–397/01 to C–403/01 *Bernhard Pfeiffer (C–397/01), Wilhelm Roith (C–398/01), Albert Suß (C–399/01), Michael Winter (C–400/01), Klaus Nestvogel (C–401/01), Roswitha Zeller (C–402/01) and Matthias Dobele (C–403/01)* v. *Deutsches Rotes Kreuz, Kreisverband Waldshut eV* [2004] ECR I–000 considered in detail in Ch. 12.

[259] Case 14/86 *Pretore di Salò* v. *X* [1987] ECR 2545; Case C–168/95 *Criminal Proceedings against Arcaro* [1996] ECR I–4705.

[260] Case C–177/88 [1990] ECR I–3941.

[261] Joined Cases C–6 and C–9/90 *Francovich and Bonifaci* v. *Italian State* [1991] ECR I–5357 considered further in Ch. 13.

[262] Joined Cases C–46/93 *Brasserie du Pêcheur* v. *Bundesrepublik Deutschland* and C–48/95 *R* v. *Secretary of State for Transport, ex parte Factortame (No. 3)* [1996] ECR I–1029.

[263] Case C–392/93 *R* v. *HM Treasury, ex part British Telecommunications* [1996] ECR I–1631.

and, thirdly, there must be a direct causal link between the breach of the obligation resting on the state and the damage suffered by the injured parties. If the state totally failed to transpose a Directive the Court ruled in *Dillenkofer*[264] that the breach was *per se* sufficiently serious.

2.2. Effectiveness of the Remedy

It is a long established principle of Community law that under the duty of co-operation laid down in Article 10 EC the Member States must ensure the legal protection which individuals derive from the direct effect of Community law. In the absence of Community rules governing a matter, it is for the domestic legal system of each Member State to designate the courts having jurisdiction and to lay down detailed procedural rules governing actions for safeguarding rights for individuals (the principle of procedural autonomy). However, such rules must not be less favourable than those governing similar domestic actions (the principle of non-discrimination) or render virtually impossible or excessively difficult the exercise of rights conferred by Community law (the principle of effective judicial protection).[265]

The question of the adequacy of national remedies has been of central importance to the procedural protection conferred by the Equality Directives. The original (and only) remedies provision in the Equal Treatment Directive 76/207 was found in Article 6 which required Member States 'to introduce into their national legal systems such measures as are necessary to enable all persons who consider themselves wronged by failure to apply to them the principle of equal treatment . . . to pursue their claims by judicial process after possible recourse to other competent authorities'.[266] This provision, with some amendment, is found in Article 17(1) of the Consolidated Directive.

The Court has, however, circumscribed the Member States' discretion as to the remedies available for sex discrimination. First, as the Court ruled in *Johnston*,[267] Member States cannot exclude judicial control altogether. In *Johnston* the Secretary of State issued a certificate under section 53(2) of the Sex Discrimination Order declaring that the decisions taken by the Chief Constable of the Royal Ulster Constabulary were made for the purpose of safeguarding national security and protecting public safety and public order.

---

[264] Joined Cases C–178, C–179, C–188, C–189 and C–190/94 *Dillenkofer and Others* v. *Bundesrepublik Deutschland* [1996] ECR I–4845.

[265] See e.g. Case 33/76 *Rewe-Zentralfinanz eG* v. *Landwirtschaftskammer für das Saarland* [1976] ECR 1989, para. 5. See generally Craufurd-Smith, 'Remedies for Breaches of EC Law in National Courts: Legal Variation and Selection', in Craig and De Búrca (eds), *The Evolution of EU Law* (OUP, Oxford, 1999).

[266] For an example of a system which 'undeniably satisfies the requirement of adequate and effective judicial protection' see the Austrian law at issue in Case C–380/01 *Schneider* v. *Bundesminister für Justiz* [2004] ECR I–000, paras. 27–8.

[267] Case 222/84 [1986] ECR 1651.

Such a declaration constituted conclusive evidence that the conditions for derogating from the principle of equal treatment had been fulfilled and therefore excluded the exercise of any power of review by the courts. The Court held that such a provision deprived an individual of the possibility of asserting the rights conferred by the Equal Treatment Directive by judicial process and was therefore contrary to Article 6 of the Directive. The Court added that Article 6 'reflects a general principle of law which underlies the constitutional traditions common to the Member States, including Articles 6 and 13 of the European Convention on Human Rights'.[268]

The second area in which the Court has limited Member States' discretion concerns the actual remedy itself. The Court has insisted that any sanction provided for by the national system must be such as to 'guarantee real and effective judicial protection . . . it must also have a real deterrent effect on the employer'.[269] Therefore, if the Member State chooses to penalize the discrimination by the award of compensation that compensation must be adequate in relation to the damage sustained.[270] In both *Von Colson* and *Harz*[271] the compensation was limited to a purely nominal amount: the reimbursement of the travelling expenses incurred. The Court considered that this would not satisfy the requirements of Article 6.[272] Similarly, the Court held in *Marshall (No. 2)*[273] that the imposition of an upper limit on the amount of compensation received and the exclusion of an award of interest did not constitute proper implementation of Article 6. It reasoned that such limits restricted the amount of compensation '*a priori* to a level which is not necessarily consistent with the requirement of ensuring real equality of opportunity through adequate reparation for the loss and damage sustained

---

[268] See also Case C–185/97 *Coote* [1998] ECR I–5199 where the Court said the requirement laid down by Art. 6 that recourse be available to the courts reflects a general principle of law which underlies the constitutional traditions common to the Member States and which is also enshrined in Art. 6 of the European Convention for the Protection of Human Rights and Fundamental Freedoms of 4 November 1950. It added that by virtue of Art. 6 of the Directive, interpreted in the light of the general principle, all persons have the right to obtain an effective remedy in a competent court against measures which they consider to interfere with the equal treatment for men and women laid down in the Directive.

[269] Case 14/83 *Von Colson* [1984] ECR 1891, para. 23.

[270] Ibid., Case C–271/91 *Marshall (No. 2) v. Southampton and South West Hampshire Area Health Authority (Teaching) (No. 2)* [1993] ECR I–4367, para. 26; McCrudden, 'The Effectiveness of European Equality Law: National Mechanisms for Enforcing Gender Equality Law in the Light of European Requirements' (1993) 13 *OJLS* 320. See also Fitzpatrick, 'Towards Strategic Litigation? Innovations in Sex Equality Litigation Procedures in the Member States of the European Community' (1992) 8 *IJCLLIR* 8.

[271] Case 79/83 [1984] ECR 1921. See also Case C–180/95 *Draehmpaehl* [1997] ECR I–2195, and Fitzpatrick, 'The Effectiveness of Equality Law Remedies: A European Community Law Perspective', in Hepple and Szyszczak, *Discrimination: Limits of Law* (London, Mansell, 1992).

[272] See further Curtin, 'Effective Sanctions and the Equal Treatment Directive: the *Von Colson* and *Harz* Cases' (1985) 22 *CMLRev*. 505.

[273] Case C–271/91 [1993] ECR I–4367. See Art. 18, second sentence in the Consolidated Dir. 2006/54.

as a result of discriminatory dismissal'.[274] In addition, the Court said that excluding an award of interest to compensate for the loss sustained by the recipient of the compensation, as a result of the effluxion of time, until the capital sum awarded is actually paid, breached Article 6.

The Court adopted a similarly broad, purposive interpretation of Article 6 in *Draehmpaehl*,[275] a case concerning the measure of damages for an individual involved in a discriminatory recruitment process. Having noted that the Directive precluded provisions of domestic law making reparation of damage suffered as a result of discrimination on the grounds of sex subject to the requirement of fault,[276] the Court then considered the question of the adequacy of compensation. It drew a distinction between, on the one hand, less qualified applicants who would not have got the job, even if there had been no discrimination in the recruitment process, and on the other, those applicants who would have got the job but for the discrimination.

As far as the latter group was concerned, the Court, basing its ruling on the principle of non-discrimination, said that the Directive precluded provisions of domestic law which, unlike other provisions of domestic civil and labour law, prescribed an upper limit of three months' salary for the amount of compensation which could be claimed. As far as the former category was concerned, the Court said that although reparation had to be adequate in relation to the damage sustained, the reparation could take into account the fact that even if there had been no discrimination in the process some applicants would not have obtained the position because the applicant appointed had superior qualifications. It said, therefore, that given that the only damage suffered by less qualified applicants was that resulting from the failure, because of the sex discrimination, to take their applications into consideration, it was not unreasonable for a Member State to lay down a statutory presumption that the damage suffered could not exceed a ceiling of three months' salary. However, the burden of proof rested with the employer, who had all the applications submitted, to show that the applicant would not have obtained the vacant position even if there had been no discrimination.

The amendments to the Equal Treatment Directive and their incorporation into the Consolidated Directive seek to reflect the Court's case law. Article 6(1)/Article 17(1) now provides that 'Member States shall ensure that, after possible recourse to other competent authorities,[277] including where they

---

[274] English law now complies with the *Marshall (No. 2)* decision as a result of SI 1993/2798 The Sex Discrimination and Equal Pay (Remedies) Regulations 1993.

[275] Case C–180/95 [1997] ECR I–2195 (noted Steindorff (1997) 34 *CMLRev.* 1259). *Marshall (No. 2)* was not, however, referred to. Cf. the Court's robust approach to remedies with its attitude in Case C–66/95 *R* v. *Secretary of State for Social Security, ex parte Sutton* [1997] ECR I–2163, considered in Ch. 10.

[276] See also Case C–177/88 *Dekker* [1990] ECR I–3941, para. 22.

[277] Introduced by Art. 17(1) of the Consolidated Directive.

deem it appropriate conciliation procedures, judicial procedures for the enforcement of obligations under this Directive are available to all persons who consider themselves wronged by failure to apply the principle of equal treatment to them, even after the relationship in which the discrimination is alleged to have occurred has ended'. Article 6(2)/Article 18 continues that: 'Member States shall introduce into their national legal systems such measures as are necessary to ensure real and effective compensation or reparation as the Member States so determine for the loss and damage sustained by a person injured as a result of discrimination [on grounds of sex],[278] in a way which is dissuasive and proportionate to the damage suffered' (*Von Colson* and *Harz*). It continues that 'Such compensation or reparation may not be restricted by the fixing of a prior upper limit' (*Marshall (No. 2)*), 'except in cases where the employer can prove that the only damage suffered by an applicant as a result of discrimination within the meaning of this Directive is the refusal to take his/her job application into consideration' (*Draehmpaehl*). Article 6(4)/Article 17 adds that the rules laid down in Article 6/Article 17 are 'without prejudice to national rules relating to time limits for bringing actions as regards the principle of equal treatment'. This is a restatement of the principle of national procedural autonomy and the Court's case law on time limits which is discussed further in chapter 10.

2.3. Victimization

While most cases on effective remedies concern compensation, *Coote*[279] is authority for the fact that the obligation to provide an effective remedy includes protection against victimization. In that case the Court said that the principle of effective judicial control laid down in Article 6 of the original Equal Treatment Directive would be deprived of an essential part of its effectiveness if the protection which it provided did not cover measures which an employer might take as a reaction to legal proceedings brought by an employee to enforce compliance with the principle of equal treatment. Therefore, it ruled that Article 6 required Member States to introduce into their national legal systems measures necessary to ensure judicial protection for workers whose employer refused to provide them with a reference as a result of victimization. Article 7 of the amended Equal Treatment Directive (Article 24 of the Consolidated Directive) now provides:

Member States shall introduce into their national legal systems such measures as are necessary to protect employees, including those who are employees' representatives provided for by national laws and/or practices, against dismissal or other adverse

---

[278] Introduced by Art. 18 of the Consolidated Directive. Art. 25 requires Member States to lay down the rules on penalties.

[279] Case C–185/97 [1998] ECR I–5199. See Dougan, 'The Equal Treatment Directive: Retaliation, Remedies and Direct Effect' (1999) 24 *ELRev.* 664.

treatment by the employer as a reaction to a complaint within the undertaking or to any legal proceedings aimed at enforcing compliance with the principle of equal treatment.

3. Burden of Proof

Normally, the burden of proof rests on the complainant. However, in a number of equal pay cases discussed in chapter 7 the Court indicated that the burden of proof should be reversed and this led to the adoption of Directive 97/80 on the burden of proof[280] which did just that. The Directive laid down minimum standards[281] which applied to situations covered by Article 141, the Directives on Equal Pay and Equal Treatment and, in so far as discrimination based on sex is concerned, the Directives on Pregnant Workers' and Parental Leave.[282] It has now been incorporated into the Consolidated Directive. The central provision (Article 4 of the Burden of Proof Directive, Article 19 of the Consolidated Directive) provides that Member States must take such measures as are necessary, in accordance with their national judicial systems, to ensure that:

... when persons who consider themselves wronged because the principle of equal treatment has not been applied to them establish, before a court or other competent authority, facts from which it may be presumed that there has been direct or indirect discrimination, it shall be for the respondent to prove that there has been no breach of the principle of equal treatment.

4. Representative Organizations

Some of the Court's most important decisions on equality have arisen in the context of cases referred by the British courts. In the early days, a disproportionate number of cases testing the limits of Article 141 on equal pay and the Equal Treatment Directive came from the United Kingdom. This was largely due to the fact that the British Sex Discrimination Act 1975 gave powers to the Equal Opportunities Commission (EOC), to fund individual cases which included support for Article 234 references to the European Court of Justice. Strategically selecting cases to fund to the Court of Justice eventually became part of the EOC's litigation strategy.[283]

---

[280] OJ [1998] L14/16, amended by Council Directive 98/52 (OJ [1998] L205/66). See Lanquetin, 'Discriminations à raison du sexe' (1998) 7/8 *Droit Social* 688.
[281] Art. 4(2).   [282] Art. 3(1)(a).
[283] Barnard, 'A European Litigation Strategy: the Case of the Equal Opportunities Commission', in Shaw and Moore (eds), *Dynamics of European Integration* (Clarendon, Oxford, 1996).

Inspired by this model, and tempering somewhat the problems faced by individual litigants bringing claims, the amended Equal Treatment Directive contains a provision to require other Member States to make similar provision. Article 6(3) of the Equal Treatment Directive/Article 17(2) of the Consolidated Directive now provides:

Member States shall ensure that associations, organisations or other legal entities which have, in accordance with the criteria laid down by their national law, a legitimate interest in ensuring that the provisions of this Directive are complied with, may engage, either on behalf or in support of the complainant, with his/her approval, in any judicial and/or administrative procedure provided for the enforcement of obligations under this Directive.

In addition, Article 8a/Article 20 of the Consolidated Directive requires Member States to designate a body or bodies for the promotion, analysis, monitoring and support of equal treatment of all persons without discrimination on the grounds of sex. These bodies may form part of agencies with responsibility at national level for the protection of human rights or the safeguard of individuals' rights. These bodies should be able to:

- provide independent assistance to victims of discrimination in pursuing their complaints about discrimination (without prejudice to the bodies laid down in Article 6(3)/Article 17(2));
- conduct independent surveys concerning discrimination;
- publish independent reports and make recommendations on any issue relating to such discrimination.
- exchange information with corresponding European bodies including the European Institute for Gender Equality.

Furthermore, Article 8c/Article 22 requires Member States to encourage dialogue with appropriate non-governmental organizations with a legitimate interest in contributing to the fight against discrimination on grounds of sex.

In addition, the Directives envisage a significant role for the Social Partners. Article 8b(1)/Article 21(1) provides that Member States must take adequate measures to promote social dialogue between the Social Partners with a view to fostering equal treatment, including through the monitoring of workplace practices, collective agreements, codes of conduct, research, or exchange of experiences and good practices. Article 8b(2)/Article 21(2) provides that Member States should also encourage the Social Partners, without prejudice to their autonomy, to promote equality between women and men and, according to the Consolidated Directive, flexible working arrangements, and to conclude, at the appropriate level, agreements laying down anti-discrimination rules in the fields coming within the material scope of the Directive which fall within the scope of collective bargaining.

Individual employers also have a role: Article 8b(3)/Article 21(3) provides that Member States must encourage employers to promote equal treatment for men and women in the workplace in a 'planned and systematic' way in access to employment, training and promotion. Employers must also be encouraged, according to Article 8b(4)/Article 21(4), to provide employees and/or their representatives with appropriate information on equal treatment for men and women in the undertaking at appropriate regular intervals. Such information may include:

- statistics on proportions of men and women at different levels of the organization;
- their pay and pay differentials; and
- possible measures to improve the situation in co-operation with employees' representatives.

These provisions (Articles 8a–c), introduced by the Equal Treatment Directive 2002/73, are intended to introduce a 'new governance' approach into what is broadly an 'old governance' measure. Thus, it encourages a wider range of actors to become involved in the process of securing equality, largely through mainstreaming and 'gender proofing' workplace practices and collective agreements.

5. Race and Ethnic Origin

The revisions to the Equal Treatment Directive draw extensively on the remedies provisions found in the Race Directive. The Race Directive envisages two rights: the right of victims to a personal remedy against the discriminator (Article 7) as well as the duty on each Member State to lay down rules on penalties for breach of the Directive (Article 15). As far as the first right is concerned, Member States must ensure that 'judicial and/ or administrative procedures, including where they deem it appropriate conciliation procedures, for the enforcement of obligations under this Directive are available to all persons who consider themselves wronged by failure to apply the principle of equal treatment to them, even after the relationship in which the discrimination is alleged to have occurred has ended' (Article 7(1)). As with Article 6(2)/Article 17(2) of the Equal Treatment Directive, Member States must ensure that relevant interest groups can bring a claim on the individual's behalf or support him in his claim.[284] National time limits will apply (Article 7(3)). Protection against victimization is found in Article 9; the burden of proof is reversed in Article 8.

Member States are under an obligation to ensure the elimination of dis-

---

[284] Provision is also made for Member States to encourage dialogue with appropriate NGOs (Art. 12).

crimination from any legal or administrative provisions, as well as from collective agreements or individual contracts of employment, rules of profit making and non-profit making associations, and workers' and employers' associations (Article 14). States must also disseminate information about the content of the Directive (Article 10). They must also take 'adequate measures to promote the social dialogue between the two sides of industry with a view to fostering equal treatment, including through the monitoring of workplace practices, collective agreements, codes of conduct, research or exchange of experiences and good practices' (Article 11). The European Social Partners have already concluded a Joint Declaration on Racism and Xenophobia in the Workplace adopted in Florence in 1995 and, at national level in certain states, have adopted framework agreements and codes of conduct on combating racial and ethnic discrimination in companies. States must also promote dialogue with NGOs (Article 12).

Perhaps the most striking feature of the Race Directive (not found in the Framework Directive) is the obligation for Member States to 'designate a body or bodies for the promotion of equal treatment of all persons without discrimination on the grounds of racial or ethnic origin' (Article 13). These bodies may form part of agencies charged at national level with the defence of human rights or the safeguard of individuals' rights. Not only must an agency be set up but, following the model of the British Commission for Racial Equality, these bodies must have among their functions: providing independent assistance to victims of discrimination in pursuing complaints about discrimination on grounds of racial or ethnic origin; conducting independent surveys concerning discrimination based on racial or ethnic origin; and publishing independent reports and making recommendations on issues relating to discrimination based on racial or ethnic origin.

6. Framework Directive

The remedies provisions also mirror those in the Race Directive: individuals or associations acting for them should have access to the judicial process (Article 9); the burden of proof is reversed (Article 10), there is protection against victimization (Article 11); states are under an obligation to disseminate information (Article 12); and states are encourage the social dialogue to foster equal treatment (Article 13) and dialogue with NGOs. States are, however, under no obligation to set up an independent agency to promote and enforce these rights.

J. CONCLUSIONS

Equality is a multi-layered, multi-faceted concept, and nowhere is this more clearly identified than in the field of equal treatment. The law in this area, through a combination of legislative and judicial intervention, has produced a sophisticated framework of rights for individuals which they can enforce in their national courts. The dialogue between the courts and the legislature has been productive, and the learning that has been gained in the field of sex equality has been extended to the other strands; and developments in respect of the other strands have spilled back into the field of sex discrimination. To date, the intervention has, however, been broadly confined to achieving the negative objective of prohibiting discrimination, and not the more positive approach of realizing equality. Some of the means of achieving equality, particularly in the field of gender, requires policy intervention rather than just legal rights. Such intervention may take the form of encouraging the provision of childcare and care for elderly relatives. This is one strand of what are now referred to as family friendly policies. This forms the subject of the next chapter.

9

Family Friendly Policies

A. INTRODUCTION

With women historically taking primary responsibility for childcare in most western societies, their flexibility to participate fully in work has often been limited. Since the first equality action programme the Commission has recognized that full equality of opportunity can be achieved only by taking measures which will 'enable men and women to reconcile their occupational and family obligations'.[1] The Community's approach to what is now generally referred to as 'family friendly policies' has three strands.[2] The first strand relates to pregnancy, birth, and maternity. The case law of the Court on Directive 76/207 and now the Consolidated Directive 2006/54, and Directive 92/85 on Pregnant Workers[3] are the principal instruments. It is this aspect of the work/life balance which is emphasized in Article 33(2) of the EU Charter of Fundamental Rights 2000 (Article II–93(2) of the Constitutional Treaty):

To reconcile family and professional life, everyone shall have the right to protection for dismissal for a reason connected with maternity and the right to paid maternity leave and to parental leave following the birth or adoption of a child.

The second strand concerns attempts at reconciling work and family life: on the one hand, Directive 96/34 on Parental Leave gives rights to working parents to take time off for domestic reasons while, on the other, Directive 97/81 on Part-time Work, Directive 99/70 on Fixed-term Work[4] and the Social Partners' agreement on telework[5] give some protection to atypical workers, the majority of whom are women seeking to balance work and caring commitments. To a limited extent, Directive 2003/88 on Working Time[6]

---

[1] Third para. of point 16 of the Social Charter of 1989. The 'family' in this context tends to be viewed as the 'traditional' family, cf. Caracciolo di Torella and Reid, 'The Changing Shape of the "European Family" and Fundamental Rights' (2002) 27 ELRev. 80.

[2] For a discussion of how the UK has approached the same agenda: Conaghan, 'Women. Work, and Family: A British Revolution' in Conaghan, Fischl and Klare (eds), Labour Law in an Era of Globalization: Transformative Practices and Possibilities (OUP, Oxford, 2002).

[3] Council Directive 92/85/EEC (OJ [1992] L348/1).

[4] OJ [1998] L14/9, as amended by Council Directive 98/23/EC (OJ [1998] L131/10) (consolidated OJ [1998] L131/13) and OJ [1999] L175/43, respectively.

[5] http://europa.eu.int/comm/employment_social/social_dialogue/docs/300_20020716_agreement_telework_en.pdf

[6] This is considered further in Ch. 12.

should also be considered as part of this strategy in that its aim of limiting working time is intended to enable workers to have sufficient time to spend with their families. However, since the Working Time Directive's principal aim is health and safety it is considered in detail in Part IV of this book (health, safety, and working conditions). The third, and least developed, strand concerns provision for childcare and, to a limited extent, care for other dependants. The adoption of a Council Recommendation on childcare represents one step in this direction.[7] The European Pact for Gender Equality launched by the Spring European Council in March 2006[8] is also significant for it recognizes clearly that in order to promote a better 'work–life balance for all' not only must there be provision of childcare facilities but also the 'provision of care facilities for other dependents' has to be improved.

The importance of these three policy strands have been recognized in the original equal opportunities pillar of the Luxembourg Employment Guidelines.[9] Under the heading 'Reconciling work and family life' the Council agreed:

Policies on career breaks, parental leave and part-time work, as well as flexible working arrangements which serve the interests of both employers and employees, are of particular importance to women and men. Implementation of the various Directives and social partner agreements in this area should be accelerated and monitored regularly. There must be an adequate provision of good quality care for children and other dependants in order to support women's and men's entry and continued participation in the labour market. An equal sharing of family responsibilities is crucial in this respect.

In order to strengthen equal opportunities the Member States and the Social Partners are to 'design, implement and promote family-friendly policies, including affordable, accessible and high quality care services for children and other dependants, as well as parental and other leave schemes'.

We begin by examining the rights given to women in respect of pregnancy and maternity before moving on to look at the question of parental leave and childcare. We conclude with an examination of atypical work.

B. PREGNANCY, MATERNITY, AND BEYOND

1. Introduction

The original version of the Equal Treatment Directive 76/207 made no specific provision for rights for pregnant workers. It merely allowed employers,

---

[7] 92/241/EEC OJ [1992] L123/16.

[8] Presidency Conclusions, Brussels European Council, 23–24 March 2006, Annex II. See further Ch. 6.

[9] Council Resolution of 15 December 1997 on the 1998 Employment Guidelines (OJ [1998] C30/1), as amended by Council Resolution of 22 February 1999 on the 1999 Employment Guidelines (OJ [1999] C69/2).

derogating from the principle of equal treatment, to take special provisions to protect pregnant workers and women on maternity leave, such as preventing them from working at night (Article 2(7) (formerly Article 2(3) of Directive 76/207 and Article 28(1) of the Consolidated Directive). In *Johnston*[10] the Court made clear that this provision was intended 'to protect a woman's biological condition and the special relationship which exists between a woman and her child'.

Nevertheless, cases started coming before the Court where pregnant women argued that they wanted to be treated in the *same way* as their (non-pregnant) colleagues. It is in this context that the discrimination model shows its limitations: since pregnancy is unique to women, trying to find a similarly situated male comparator 'suffering from an equivalent problem' for the purposes of arguing less favourable treatment has always been an artificial exercise.[11] In fact, the Court of Justice has shown some sense in addressing the problem. Its approach has been to make pregnancy discrimination per se unlawful thereby dropping the need to find a comparator.[12] Nevertheless, to shoehorn pregnancy and maternity into an anti-discrimination model has always proved difficult. The adoption of the Pregnant Workers' Directive 92/85, with its specific provisions dealing with pregnant workers not dependent on the anti-discrimination model, was a positive step forward. Nevertheless, the Pregnant Workers' Directive does not exhaustively regulate the whole area of the treatment of pregnant women and women on maternity leave. There is therefore still a role for the Equal Treatment Directive. For this reason, we begin by considering the position under the Equal Treatment Directive (primarily Directive 76/207 as amended and the Consolidated Directive, but also Article 141 on equal pay) before considering the position under the Pregnant Workers' Directive.

2. The Approach under the Equal Treatment Directive

2.1. The (Equal) Treatment of Pregnant Women

(a) Appointment and Dismissal

The leading case in which the Court first addressed the rights of pregnant workers is *Dekker*.[13] In that case, the employer decided not to appoint the applicant who was pregnant, even though she was considered the best person

---

[10] Case 222/84 [1986] ECR 1651.

[11] See e.g. the approach of the Court of Appeal in the English case of *Webb* v. *EMO Air Cargo* [1992] 1 CMLR 793. The Court in Case C–32/93 *Webb* [1994] ECR I–3567 said 'pregnancy is not in any way comparable with a pathological condition'.

[12] Cf. Wintemute, 'When is Pregnancy Discrimination Indirect Discrimination' (1998) 27 *ILJ*. 23.

[13] Case C–177/88 [1990] ECR I–3941.

for the job, on the grounds that the employer's insurers refused to cover the costs of her maternity leave. Despite the fact that all the other candidates for the job were women, the Court ruled that since employment could only be refused because of pregnancy to a woman, refusal to appoint a woman on the grounds of her pregnancy constituted direct discrimination on the grounds of sex, contrary to Articles 2(1) and 3(1) of the Equal Treatment Directive (Article 14 of the Consolidated Directive).[14] The Court also dismissed concerns about the cost implications of its decision: it said that a refusal to employ a woman on account of her pregnancy could not be justified on the grounds of the financial loss which an employer who appointed a pregnant woman would suffer for the duration of her maternity leave.[15]

Dekker concerned the refusal to appoint a woman on the grounds of her pregnancy; in *Hertz*[16] the Court ruled that the *dismissal* of a female worker on account of pregnancy also constituted direct discrimination on the grounds of sex contrary to the Equal Treatment Directive.[17] The Court also applied *Hertz* in the more difficult case of *Webb*.[18] Ms Webb was appointed by EMO Air Cargo Ltd, initially to replace another employee, Ms Stewart, who was about to go on maternity leave, but then to continue working on Ms Stewart's return. Shortly after starting work, Ms Webb announced that she too was pregnant. The employers dismissed her not, they said, because of her pregnancy but because of her unavailability, at least at first, to work during the period for which she was needed.

The Court rejected this argument and ruled that her dismissal was on the grounds of pregnancy and so contravened the Directive. Emphasizing the fact that Ms Webb was not employed on a fixed term contract, the Court ruled that 'dismissal of a pregnant woman recruited for an indefinite period *cannot be justified* on grounds relating to her inability to fulfil a fundamental condition of her employment contract'. This suggestion that direct discrimination due to pregnancy could in some circumstances be justified (e.g. the dismissal of a pregnant woman employed under a fixed term contract), in situations beyond those listed in Article 2(7) Article 28(1) of the Directive, set alarm bells ringing.[19]

---

[14] See also Case C–207/98 *Mahlburg* v. *Land Mecklenburg-Vorpommern* [2000] ECR I–549, para. 27.
[15] Para. 12. The same conclusion must be drawn as regards the financial loss caused by the fact that the woman appointed cannot be employed in the post for the duration of her pregnancy: Case C–207/98 *Mahlburg* v. *Land Mecklenburg-Vorpommern* [2000] ECR I–549, para. 29.
[16] Case C–179/88 *Handels- og Kontorfunktionaerernes Forbund i Danmark (Hertz)* v. *Dansk Arbejdsgiverforening* [1990] ECR I–3979.
[17] This view was confirmed in Case C–421/92 *Habermann-Beltermann* [1994] ECR I–1657. See also Art. 10 of Dir. 92/85/EC [1992] OJ L348/1 considered below. For an analysis of this line of case law, see Caracciolo di Torella and Maselot, 'Pregnancy, maternity and the organization of family life: an attempt to classify the case law of the Court of Justice' (2001) 26 *ELRev*. 239.
[18] Case C–32/93 [1994] ECR I–3567.   [19] See further Ch. 6.

However, in *Tele-Denmark*[20] the Court appeared to reject that possibility. It said that the ruling in *Webb* could not be 'altered by the fact that the contract of employment was concluded for a fixed-term'.[21] Therefore a woman who took a fixed-term job, knowing she was pregnant and so would not be able to do the job for some of the period of employment, but did not tell the employer of this fact, could claim discrimination on the grounds of pregnancy if she was dismissed.

The approach to pregnancy discrimination first laid down by the Court in *Dekker* has now been confirmed by Article 2(7) of Directive 76/207 (Article 2(2)(c) of the Consolidated Directive):

Less favourable treatment of a woman related to pregnancy or maternity leave within the meaning of Directive 92/85/EEC shall constitute discrimination within the meaning of this Directive.[22]

The advantage of this approach—deeming less favourable treatment on the grounds of pregnancy to be discrimination—is that it avoids doing such damage to the concept of direct discrimination since direct discrimination presupposes the existence of a comparator of the opposite sex.[23] However, the concept 'less favourable' does presuppose that there is someone being treated more favourably. It seems that that person can be either a male or female worker who is not pregnant.

(b) Terms and Conditions of Employment

The Court has extended the approach adopted in *Dekker* to discrimination against pregnant workers in respect of terms and conditions of employment. Thus, in *Thibault*[24] the Court ruled that a woman who continued to be bound to her employer by her contract of employment during maternity leave could not be deprived of the benefit of working conditions which applied to both men and women and were the result of that employment relationship. Therefore, the Court said, to deny a female employee the right to have her performance assessed annually would discriminate against her in her capacity as a worker because, had she not been pregnant and not taken the maternity leave, she would have been assessed for the year in question and could therefore have qualified for promotion. Such conduct constituted discrimination on grounds of sex within the meaning of the Directive.[25]

---

[20] Case C–109/00 *Tele Danmark A/S* v. *Kontorfunktionaerernes Forbund I Danmark* [2001] ECR I–6993.

[21] Para. 30.   [22] The structure of the prohibition is different in the Consolidated Directive.

[23] See Wintemute's criticisms 'When is Pregnancy Discrimination Direct Discrimination?' (1998) 27 *ILJ*. 23.

[24] Case C–136/95 *Thibault* [1998] ECR I–2011.

[25] See also Case C–333/97 *Lewen* [1999] ECR I–7243, para. 48, discussed below, where the Court ruled that Art. 141 precludes an employer taking periods of maternity leave into account when granting a Christmas bonus so as to reduce the benefit *pro rata*.

Similar issues arose in *Sarkatzis Herrero*,[26] this time in the context of a new appointment. Ms Sarkatzis Herrero was appointed to a permanent post in the Spanish health service, having previously been employed on a temporary post. She asked to defer taking up that post until the end of her maternity leave, which was granted, but her request that her seniority dated from the time of the appointment and not the time when she took up the post was not. The Court found that she had been discriminated against contrary to the Equal Treatment Directive. The Directive, it said, precluded a national law which did not afford a woman who was on maternity leave the same rights as other successful applicants from the same recruitment competition by deferring the start of her career to the end of that leave, without taking account of the duration of the leave, for the purpose of calculating her seniority of service.[27]

In *Busch*[28] the Court pushed the principle of non-discrimination to its outermost limits. After the birth of her first child in June 2000, Ms Busch, a nurse, took parental leave which was supposed to be for three years. In October 2000, she became pregnant again. In January 2001, she successfully requested permission to terminate her parental leave early and returned to full-time work as a nurse in April 2001. The day after she returned to work, she informed her employer that she was seven months' pregnant. Given that German law prohibited pregnant women from working in certain circumstances, the clinic which employed Ms Busch said that she was not able to carry out her duties effectively. It therefore rescinded its consent to her returning to work on grounds of fraudulent misrepresentation and mistake.

The Court disagreed. It said that where an employer took an employee's pregnancy into consideration when refusing to allow her to return to work before the end of her parental leave, that constituted direct discrimination on grounds of sex;[29] and since the employer could not take the employee's pregnancy into account in deciding whether she could return to work early, she was not obliged to inform the employer that she was pregnant.[30] The Court also said that the discrimination could not be justified by the fact that she was temporarily prevented, by a legislative prohibition imposed because of pregnancy, from performing all of her duties; and that discrimination on the grounds of sex could not be justified on grounds relating to the financial loss for an employer.[31] For good measure, the Court added that the fact that, in asking to return to work, Ms Busch intended to receive a maternity allowance higher than the parental leave allowance, as well as the supplementary allowance paid by the employer, did not legally justify sex discrimination over working conditions.

---

[26] Case C–294/04 *Sarkatzis Herrero v. Imsalud* [2006] ECR I–000.
[27] Para. 47.
[28] Case C–320/01 *Busch v. Klinikum Neustadt GmbH & Co.Betriebs-KG* [2003] ECR I–2041.
[29] Para. 39.   [30] Para. 40.   [31] Para. 44.

(c) Sick Leave

Despite the long line of case law beginning with *Dekker* which finds that less favourable treatment on the grounds of pregnancy is directly discriminatory, the Court has not provided women suffering from the problems of pregnancy or childbirth with absolute protection. This was shown by the case of *Hertz*.[32] Hertz suffered from a complicated pregnancy, causing her to take a lot of sick leave. When the maternity leave came to an end she returned to work but, shortly afterwards, had to take a further 100 days' sick leave due to an illness resulting from her pregnancy. As a result, she was dismissed.

The Court distinguished between two situations: first, the period of maternity leave, and, secondly, the period after the maternity leave. During the first period the Court said that a woman was protected from being dismissed due to her absence from work (the *per se* discriminatory approach). However, during the second period the Court said it saw no reason to distinguish an illness attributable to pregnancy or confinement from any other illness. It therefore applied a comparative test. It reasoned that although certain disorders were specific to one or other sex, the only question was whether a woman was dismissed on account of absence due to illness in the same circumstances as a man. If this was so, then there was no direct or indirect discrimination on the grounds of sex.

While this decision can be justified by reference to practical and economic necessity,[33] it cannot be defended in terms of logic: if the dismissal of a female worker on account of pregnancy constitutes direct discrimination, the dismissal of a woman on account of a pregnancy-related illness which arises after the end of her maternity leave should also constitute direct discrimination. Nevertheless, the Court reaffirmed this ruling in *Larsson*[34] and took it one stage further. It said that the Directive did not preclude dismissals which were the result of absences due to an illness attributable to pregnancy or confinement even where that illness arose during pregnancy and continued during and after maternity leave. This decision was much criticized and the Court reconsidered it in *Brown*.[35]

In *Brown* the employer had a policy of dismissing any employee who took more than 26 weeks' sick leave. Ms. Brown, who suffered from a pregnancy-related disorder, was dismissed after 26 weeks' absence in line with the policy. The Court said that although pregnancy was not in any way comparable to a pathological condition, pregnancy was a period during which disorders and

---

[32] Case C–179/88 [1990] ECR I–3979.

[33] See esp. Advocate General Darmon's discussion in his Joined Opinion in Cases C–177/88 *Dekker* ECR I–3941 and C–179/88 *Hertz* [1990] ECR I–3979, para. 43.

[34] Case C–400/95 *Larsson v. Føtex Supermarked* [1997] ECR I–2757. See Caracciolo di Torella, 'Maternity and Equal Treatment' (1998) 23 *ELRev*. 164.

[35] Case C–394/96 [1998] ECR I–4185. See Boch, 'Official: During Pregnancy, Females are Pregnant' (1998) 23 *ELRev*. 488.

complications might arise compelling a woman to undergo strict medical supervision and, in some cases, to rest absolutely for all or part of her pregnancy. The Court then said that the principle of non-discrimination required protection against dismissal 'throughout the period of pregnancy'[36] so that, reversing *Larsson*, periods of sick leave during pregnancy could not be taken into account for calculating the 26 weeks of sick leave. The clock would, however, start ticking in respect of periods of sick leave taken after the end of her maternity leave on the same terms as a man.

However, sometimes the requirement to find a comparator does spill over to the pre-maternity leave phase, despite the Court's professed attempts to cut the pre-maternity leave period free of such a requirement. This can be seen in *Høj Pedersen*.[37] The Court said that Article 141 required a woman taking sick leave due to a pathological condition connected with her pregnancy,[38] in a period prior to the start of her maternity leave, to receive full pay from her employer (and not, as in this case, part pay with additional benefits being paid by the local authority). The Court then added the comparator element. It said that a pregnant woman taking sick leave should receive full pay when, in the event of incapacity for work on grounds of illness, a worker is in principle entitled to receive full pay from his or her employer.[39]

2.2. Maternity Leave

Once a woman goes on maternity leave her situation changes. This was made clear by the Court in *Gillespie*[40] where it said that since the case concerned women taking maternity leave provided for by the national legislation they were in a special position requiring them to be afforded special protection.[41] This situation was not comparable either with that of a man or with a woman actually at work.[42] In respect of the payment during maternity leave, the

---

[36] For criticism of this approach, see Ellis (1999) 36 *CMLRev.* 625.

[37] Case C–66/96 *Høj Pedersen* v. *Kvickly Skive* [1998] ECR I–7327. See also Case C–284/02 *Land Brandenburg* v. *Sass* [2004] ECR I–11143, para. 37 cf. Case C–294/04 *Sarkatzis Herrero* v. *Imsalud*, judgment of 16 February 2006, para. 47.

[38] The position is different in respect of a woman's absence due to 'routine pregnancy-related minor complaints when there is no incapacity for work or of a medical recommendation intended to protect the unborn child but not based on any actual pathological condition or any special risks for the unborn child': para. 50.

[39] Para. 41.The only exception to this rule was where the sums received by employees by way of state benefits were equal to the amount of their pay. It would then be for the national court to ascertain whether the circumstance that the benefits were paid by a local authority was such as to bring about discrimination in breach of Art. 141.

[40] Case C–342/93 [1996] ECR I–475. See Conaghan, 'Pregnancy, Equality and the European Court of Justice: Interrogating *Gillespie*' (1998) 3 *IJLD*. 115.

[41] Para. 17. It said that 'discrimination involves the application of different rules to comparable situations or the application of the same rule to different situations'.

[42] See also Case C–218/98 *Abdoulaye* [1999] ECR I–5723 (women could be paid a maternity bonus not payable to new fathers).

Court said that, although maternity benefit constituted pay within the meaning of Article 141, neither Article 141 nor Article 1 of Directive 75/117 (Article 4 of the Consolidated Directive) required that women should continue to receive full pay during maternity leave,[43] nor did those provisions lay down any specific criteria for determining the amount of benefit to be paid to them during that period.

The Court did, however, add that the amount payable could not be so low as to undermine the purpose of the maternity leave, namely the protection of women before and after giving birth. In order to assess the adequacy of the amount payable, the national court had to take into account not only the length of the maternity leave but also the other forms of social protection afforded by the national law in the case of justified absence from work. On the facts of the case there was nothing to suggest that the amount of benefit granted was such as to undermine the objective of protecting maternity leave.

The Court also said in *Gillespie* that a woman on maternity leave should receive a pay rise awarded before or during that period. It said that the benefit paid during maternity leave was equivalent to a weekly payment calculated on the basis of the average pay received by the worker at the time when she was actually working and which was paid to her week by week, just like any other worker. The principle of non-discrimination therefore required that a woman who was still linked to her employer by a contract of employment or by an employment relationship during maternity leave had to benefit from any pay rise, even if backdated.[44] To deny her such an increase would discriminate against her purely in her capacity as a worker since, had she not been pregnant, she would have received the pay rise.

In *Gillespie*, the maternity pay was calculated on the basis of a woman's average earnings over an eight-week reference period which was taken between the fourth and sixth month of pregnancy when the woman was most likely to be well. The pay increase she benefited from occurred after the reference period but was backdated to the reference period. In *Alabaster*[45] the woman also benefited from a pay rise prior to her maternity leave but after the reference period, but this time the pay rise was not backdated. The Court extended its ruling in *Gillespie* to this situation so that 'any pay rise awarded after the beginning of the period covered by her reference pay must be included in the elements of pay used to determine the amount of pay owed to the worker during her maternity leave'.[46]

Directive 2002/73 amended Directive 76/207 by expressly giving a woman the right to return to her job after her maternity leave and to enjoy any

[43] Para. 20.   [44] Para. 22.
[45] Case C–147/02 *Alabaster v. Woolwich plc, Secretary of State for Social Security* [2004] ECR I–000.
[46] Para. 49.

improved terms and conditions of employment. Article 2(7), paragraph 2 (Article 15 of the Consolidated Directive) provides:

A woman on maternity leave shall be entitled, after the end of her period of maternity leave, to return to her job or to an equivalent post on terms and conditions which are no less favourable to her and to benefit from any improvement in working conditions to which she would [have been][47] entitled during her absence.

2.3. Express Derogation from the Principle of Equal Treatment

As we saw in the last chapter, different treatment on the grounds of pregnancy may be lawful if the employer's actions are caught within the derogation contained in Article 2(7), paragraph 1 of the Directive 76/207 (Article 28(1) of the Consolidated Directive) (protection of women, particularly on the grounds of pregnancy and maternity).[48] In *Habermann-Beltermann*[49] the Court held that the prohibition on night-time work by pregnant women was 'unquestionably compatible with Article [2(7)]'. However, since the prohibition on night-time work by pregnant women takes effect only for a limited period in relation to the total length of an indefinite contract 'the termination of a contract without a fixed term on account of the woman's pregnancy . . . cannot be justified on the ground that a statutory prohibition, imposed because of pregnancy, temporarily prevents the employee from performing night-work'.[50]

3. Directive 92/85 on Pregnant Workers

3.1. Introduction

The significance of the decisions of the Court under the Equal Treatment Directive in respect of dismissals[51] (but not in respect to other discriminatory treatment) have been reduced in the light of Directive 92/85/EC[52] which is designed to protect pregnant workers and workers who have recently given

---

[47] Words introduced by Art. 15 of the Consolidated Directive.

[48] Cf. Art. 5(3) of the Goods and Services Dir. 2004/113/EC (OJ [2004] L373/37): when considering actuarial factors, the Directive says that 'costs related to pregnancy and maternity shall not result in differences in individuals' premiums'.

[49] Case C–421/92 [1994] ECR I–1657.

[50] See also Art. 7 of Dir. 92/85 [1992] OJ L348/1. See also Case C–320/01 *Busch* v. *Klinikum Neustadt GmbH & Co.Betriebs-KG* [2003] ECR I–2041 considered above, n. 28.

[51] See Art. 2(7) of Dir. 76/207 (Art. 2(2)(c) of the Consolidated Directive).

[52] Council Dir. 92/85/EEC (OJ [1992] L348/1) (tenth individual Directive adopted within the meaning of Art. 16(1) of Dir. 89/391, considered further in Ch. 11) on the introduction of measures to encourage improvements in the safety and health at work of pregnant workers who have recently given birth or are breastfeeding. The Directive was based on Art. 118a (new Art. 137). See further Cromack, 'The EC Pregnancy Directive: Principle or Pragmatism?' (1993) 6 *JSWL*. 261. Commission Report on Implementation: COM(99)100 final.

birth or who are breastfeeding.[53] The Directive is intended to provide minimum requirements for encouraging improvements,[54] especially in the working environment, to protect the health and safety of pregnant workers.[55]

3.2. 'Employment' Rights

The Directive provides three specific forms of 'employment' protection[56] to pregnant workers and workers on maternity leave, which, with one exception relating to payment during maternity leave, exist from the first day of employment. First, they are entitled to time off, without loss of pay, in order to attend ante-natal examinations, if such examinations have to take place within working hours.[57] Secondly, they are entitled to a continuous period of at least 14 weeks' maternity leave, of which at least two weeks must be allocated before and/or after confinement.[58] The purpose of maternity leave is 'to protect a woman's biological condition and the special relationship between a women and her child over the period which follows pregnancy and childbirth, by preventing that relationship from being disturbed by the multiple burdens which would result from the simultaneous pursuit of employment'.[59] In *Boyle*[60] the Court said that the Pregnant Workers' Directive did not preclude a clause in an employment contract from requiring an employee who had expressed her intention to commence her maternity leave during the six weeks preceding the expected week of childbirth, and was on sick leave with a pregnancy-related illness immediately before that date and gave birth during the period of sick leave, to bring forward the date on which her paid maternity leave commenced either to the beginning of the sixth week preceding the expected week of childbirth or to the beginning of the period of sick leave, whichever was the later.

Taking maternity leave cannot affect the right to take any other period of leave guaranteed by Community law, such as annual leave under the Working Time Directive.[61] However, in *Boyle*[62] the Court said that the contract of employment could limit the period during which annual leave accrued to the minimum period of 14 weeks' maternity leave. Thus, annual leave would not

---

[53] These three terms are defined by reference to national law and practice and are dependent on the worker informing her employer of her condition (Art. 2). The term 'pregnant worker' will be used to apply to the three situations unless otherwise stated.

[54] Art. 1(3) provides that the Directive may not have the effect of reducing the level of protection afforded to pregnant workers.

[55] See further Ch. 11.

[56] The Directive was adopted under Art. 118a (now Art. 137) on health and safety.

[57] Art. 9, which applies only to pregnant workers. [58] Art. 8(1) and (2).

[59] Case C–519/03 *Commission v. Luxembourg* [2005] ECR I–000, para. 32.

[60] Case C–411/96 *Boyle v. EOC* [1998] ECR I–6401.

[61] Dir. 2003/88: Case C–342/01 *Merino Gómez* [2004] ECR I–000, para. 41 considered further in Ch. 12.

[62] Case C–411/96 *Boyle v. EOC* [1998] ECR I–6401.

accrue in respect of any period of supplementary maternity leave granted by the employer.

During her (minimum 14-week) maternity leave, a woman's rights connected with the contract of employment must be maintained.[63] To date, the Court has answered some very specific questions on this point. For example, in *Boyle*[64], the Court said that a clause in an employment contract which prohibited a woman from taking sick leave during the minimum period of 14 weeks' maternity leave to which a female worker was entitled pursuant to Article 8(1) of Directive 92/85, unless she elected to return to work and thus terminated her maternity leave, was not compatible with Directive 92/85. By contrast, a clause in an employment contract which prohibited a woman from taking sick leave during a period of supplementary maternity leave granted to her by the employer, unless she elected to return to work and thus terminated her maternity leave, was compatible with the Equal Treatment Directive and the Pregnant Workers' Directive 92/85. The Court also said that Directive 92/85 precluded a clause in an employment contract from limiting, in the context of an occupational scheme wholly financed by the employer, the accrual of pension rights during the period of maternity leave referred to by Article 8 to the period during which the woman received the pay provided for by that contract or national legislation.

The (major) exception to the rule that a woman's rights connected with the contract of employment must be maintained relates to pay. All the Directive requires is the maintenance of pay or the payment of an (unspecified) 'adequate' allowance,[65] but Member States may make entitlement to pay conditional upon the worker fulfilling the conditions of eligibility for such benefits laid down by national legislation. These conditions may not, however, provide for periods of previous employment in excess of 12 months immediately prior to the presumed date of confinement.[66] As far as the level of maternity pay is concerned, the Court ruled in *Gillespie*[67] that the allowance must not be paid at such a derisory level as to undermine the purpose of the maternity leave. However, if the employer pays maternity pay higher than the statutory

---

[63] Art. 11(2)(a). See Case C–342/93 *Gillespie* [1996] ECR I–475; Case C–284/02 *Land Brandenburg* v. *Sass* [2004] ECR I–11143, para. 44.

[64] Case C–411/96 *Boyle* v. *EOC* [1998] ECR I–6401.

[65] Art. 11(2)(b). An allowance is adequate (Art. 11(3)) if it guarantees income at least equivalent to that which the worker concerned would receive in the event of a break in her activities on grounds connected with her state of health, subject to any ceiling laid down by national legislation, in other words, sick pay. However, a statement of the Council and the Commission added to the Directive (OJ [1992] L348/8) states that the reference to the state of health is not 'intended in any way to imply that pregnancy and childbirth be equated with sickness'. The link with such allowance is intended to serve as a concrete fixed reference in all Member States for the determination of the minimum amount of maternity allowance. In Case C–66/96 *Høj Pedersen* [1998] ECR I–7327 the Court said that Art. 11(3) applied only to pay or benefits received in the context of *maternity* leave and did not apply to allowances which a woman could claim when pregnant.

[66] Art. 11(2)(b) and (4).   [67] Case C–342/93 [1996] ECR I–475.

payments in respect of maternity leave the Court ruled in *Boyle*[68] that Community law permitted the employer making those payments conditional on the worker undertaking to return to work after the birth of the child for at least one month, failing which she would be required to repay the difference between the statutory and the higher rate of pay.

The third employment right can be found in Article 10(1) which provides that pregnant workers cannot be dismissed during the period from the beginning of their pregnancy to the end of their maternity leave, save in exceptional cases not connected with their condition which are permitted under national law or practice.[69] Employers must provide pregnant workers who are dismissed within this period with duly substantiated written grounds for dismissal[70] and Member States must provide a remedy for pregnant workers who are dismissed.[71]

In *Jiménez Melgar*[72] the Court confirmed that Article 10 was directly effective.[73] It also made clear that the prohibition of dismissal laid down in Article 10 applied both to fixed-term contracts of employment and to those concluded for an indefinite duration.[74] In reaching this conclusion, the Court helped to lay to rest the suggestion made in *Webb*[75] (above), a case decided under the Equal Treatment Directive, that the dismissal of a worker employed on a fixed-term contract (as opposed to a contract of indefinite duration) could be justified if she was unable to do the job because she was pregnant. Thus, where an employer unilaterally terminates a contract—whether for a fixed term or an indefinite duration—this contravenes Article 10. As the Court made clear in *Jiménez Melgar*, and in *Tele Danmark*[76] which was decided the same day, had the Community legislature wished to exclude fixed-term contracts, which represent a substantial proportion of employment relationships, it would have done so expressly.[77]

Where, however, a fixed-term contract has expired, because it has come to the end of its stipulated term, and it is not subsequently renewed, the Court

---

[68] Case C–411/96 *Boyle* v. *EOC* [1998] ECR I–6401.

[69] Member States do not have to specify the particular grounds on which workers may be dismissed: Case C–438/99 *Jiménez Melgar* v. *Ayuntamiento de Los Barrios* [2001] ECR I–6915, para. 38. Member States are also not obliged to have a national authority in place which is required to give consent prior to the employer's dismissal of a pregnant worker (para. 52).

[70] Art. 10(2).

[71] Art. 10(3). In addition, Art. 12 provides more generally that Member States must allow those who consider themselves wronged by the failure to comply with the obligations of the Directive to pursue their claims by judicial process.

[72] Case C–438/99 *Jiménez Melgar* v. *Ayuntamiento de Los Barrios* [2001] ECR I–6915.

[73] Para. 34.

[74] Case C–438/99 *Jiménez Melgar* v. *Ayuntamiento de Los Barrios* [2001] ECR I–6915, para. 44.

[75] Case C–32/93 [1994] ECR I–3567.

[76] Case C–109/00 *Tele Danmark A/S* v. *Kontorfunktionaerernes Forbund I Danmark* [2001] ECR I–6993.

[77] See now the Fixed Term Work Dir. 99/70 considered below, nn. 210–19.

said in *Jiménez Melgar* that this could not be regarded as a dismissal;[78] and so its non-renewal did not contravene Article 10 of Directive 92/85.[79] However, the Court added that since the non-renewal of a fixed-term contract could be viewed as a refusal of employment then the Court's case law (*Dekker* and *Mahlburg*) on the Equal Treatment Directives would apply. Thus, if the non-renewal of a fixed-term contract was motivated by the worker's pregnancy this would constitute direct discrimination contrary to Articles 2(1) and 3(1) of Directive 76/207 (Article 14 of the Consolidated Directive).[80]

Jiménez Melgar makes clear that Article 10 of Directive 92/85 has largely replaced the Court's case law on pregnancy-related dismissals under the Equal Treatment Directive 76/207 (which in turn was developed against the backcloth of Article 10 of the Pregnant Workers' Directive[81]). However, given the limited scope of Directive 92/85, the Court's case law under Directive 76/207 continues to be important in respect of other forms of discrimination occurring during pregnancy (such as refusal to appoint or discriminatory terms and conditions).

3.3. Health and Safety Protection

Directive 92/85 also provides more specific rights to protect the health and safety of the pregnant worker.[82] The Directive makes a distinction between the risks contained in Annex I (certain physical, biological and chemical agents, certain industrial processes and underground mining) and those contained in Annex II (a more limited list of physical, biological and chemical agents and underground mining). In the case of the Annex I risks, the employer is obliged to examine the nature, degree and duration of exposure of the pregnant worker to these risks.[83] The pregnant worker and/or the worker's representatives are

---

[78] Cf. the position under British law, s. 95(1)(b) Employment Rights Act 1996, which provides that an employee is dismissed if . . . 'he is employed under a limited-term contract and that contract terminates by virtue of the limiting event without being renewed under the same contract'.

[79] Para. 45.   [80] Para. 46.

[81] As the Court said in Case C–394/96 *Brown* [1998] ECR I–2757, it was 'precisely in view of the harmful effects which the risk of dismissal may have on the physical and mental state of women who are pregnant, women who have recently given birth or women who are breastfeeding, including the particularly serious risk that pregnant women may be prompted voluntarily to terminate their pregnancy, that the Community legislature, pursuant to Article 10 of Council Directive 92/85/EEC of 19 October 1992 . . . provided for special protection to be given to women, by prohibiting dismissal during the period from the beginning of their pregnancy to the end of their maternity leave'. Therefore the Court took this 'general context' into account in construing the relevant provisions in *Brown*.

[82] Commission Communication on the guidelines on the assessment of the chemical, physical and biological agents and industrial processes considered hazardous for the safety or health of pregnant workers and workers who have recently given birth or are breast feeding : COM(2000) 466

[83] Art. 4(1). Technical adjustments to Annex I can be made according to the provisions in Art. 12. Art. 3 obliges the Commission to draw up guidelines in conjunction with the Advisory

to be informed of any risks and of the measures to be taken. These measures may include a temporary adjustment to the working conditions or working hours of the pregnant worker. If this is not technically or objectively feasible, or cannot reasonably be required on duly substantiated grounds, the employer must take the necessary measures to move the worker to another job. If this is not possible the worker concerned must be granted leave in accordance with the national legislation for the whole of the period necessary to protect her health and safety.[84] These rules apply equally to Annex II risks. In addition, Article 6 provides that neither pregnant workers nor workers who are breast-feeding may be obliged to perform duties for which the assessment has revealed a risk of exposure to the agents and working conditions listed in Annex II, section A, in the case of pregnant workers, and Annex II, section B in the case of workers who are breastfeeding.[85]

In *Høj Pedersen*[86] the Court has insisted that these provisions be strictly applied. The case concerned a Danish law allowing employers to send home a pregnant woman, although not unfit to work, without paying her salary in full, when they considered that they could not provide work for her. The Court said that this law did not comply with the requirements laid down in Directive 92/85 on the grounds that giving leave to the employee was based on the interest of the employer and that decision could be taken by the employer without first examining the possibility of adjusting the employee's working conditions and/or hours or even the possibility of moving her to another job.

Article 7 recognizes that pregnant workers have the right not to have to work at night during their pregnancy and for a period to be determined by the national authorities following childbirth. These rights are dependent on the production of a medical certificate stating that these arrangements are necessary for the safety or health of the worker. If this is the case then the pregnant worker must be transferred to day work or be granted leave from work or an extension of maternity leave where such a transfer is not possible.

Committee on Safety, Hygiene and Health Protection at work, on the assessment of the chemical, physical and biological agents and industrial processes considered hazardous for the health and safety of pregnant workers.

[84] Art. 5.

[85] Art. 6. Annex II may only be amended in accordance with the Art. 118a (new Art. 137) procedure.

[86] Case C–66/96 *Høj Pedersen v. Kvickly Skive* [1998] ECR I–7327.

C. DIVISION OF RESPONSIBILITIES IN THE FAMILY: THE BALANCE BETWEEN WORK AND CARING

1. Introduction

In the previous section we considered how European Community law regulated the position of women workers from the start of their pregnancy to the end of their maternity leave. We now turn to the question of how the law has responded to the ongoing challenge of the way parents combine raising a family with employment. Traditionally, once a child was born the woman gave up work either as a matter of choice or social expectation or because the law required it. Women have therefore always been associated with the role of principal childcarer and/or carer for elderly dependent relatives. However, for many families this is no longer an option, because of the economic need of having two salaries, particularly where the family unit has broken down, and/or because the woman wants to work. Yet, children (and increasingly, with an ageing society, elderly relatives) need caring for, school days are short and holidays long. The question for women and, increasingly men, is how to balance work and family life. For some families it has meant that one partner, often the woman, opts for working part time, doing a job share, or being employed under fixed term contracts or doing agency work which fits around school terms. For others it has meant working full time and paying for others to do the childcare or elderly care.

The Court has been at the frontline of fielding questions raising the issue of how the law balances the rights of those with families with the principle of equal treatment under both the Directives and Article 141. As we shall see in the next section, in the last 20 years the Court has moved quite a long way from supporting the traditional male breadwinner/female carer model towards recognizing a 'dual breadwinner/dual carer' model. In searching for a resolution of the work/life balance dilemma, the Court has sought to reconcile its desire not to deprive women of hard-won benefits that reward the childcare function[87] and its wish not to stereotype the woman as carer.[88]

The work/life balance issue has also become central to many western government agendas—for economic as well as moral reasons. Addressing work/life balance issues is seen as a way of attracting and retaining more people in employment, increasing the labour supply and modernizing social protection systems,[89] in other words to make 'full and effective use of the

---

[87] Case C–218/98 *Abdoulaye* v. *Régre Nationale des Usines Renault SA* [1999] ECR I–5723.

[88] Case C–476/99 *Lommers* v. *Mininster van Landbouw* [2002] ECR I–2891.

[89] This is the chapeau to Guidelines 18 ('Promote a lifecycle approach to work' which includes 'better reconciliation of work and private life and the provision of accessible and affordable childcare facilities and care for other dependants'), 19 ('Ensure inclusive labour markets') and 20 ('Improve Matching of Labour Market needs'): Co. Dec. 2005/600 (OJ [2005] L205/21).

productive capacities of all sections of the population'.[90] The European Employment Strategy recognized the need to reconcile 'work and family life' in its first set of guidelines in 1997.[91] In 2000 the Council issued a Resolution on the Balanced Participation of women and men in family and working life[92] which recognized that the principle of equality between men and women in relation to employment and labour 'implies equal sharing between working fathers and mothers, in particular of time off work to look after children or other dependants',[93] that the balanced participation of women and of men in both the labour market and in family life is 'an advantage to both men and women' and is an essential aspect of the development of society; and that maternity, paternity and the rights of children are 'eminent social values to be protected by society, the Member States and the European Community.'[94] The Preamble concludes with the radical statement that:

The beginning of the twenty-first century is a symbolic moment to give shape to the new social contract on gender, in which the de facto equality of men and women in the public and private domains will be socially accepted as a condition for democracy, a prerequisite for citizenship and a guarantee of individual autonomy and freedom, and will be reflected in all European Union policies.

By the 2001 Employment Guidelines, the EES' policy towards work/life balance issues had become more fully articulated. Under the heading of 'Reconciling work and family life', the guidelines provide:[95]

Policies on career breaks, parental leave and part-time work, as well as flexible working arrangements which serve the interests of both employers and employees, are of particular importance to women and men. Implementation of the various Directives and social-partner agreements in this area should be accelerated and monitored regularly. There must be an adequate provision of good quality care for children and other dependants in order to support the entry of women and men into, and their continued participation in, the labour market. An equal sharing of family responsibilities is crucial in this respect. Those returning to the labour market after an absence may also have outmoded skills, and experience difficulty in gaining access to training. Reintegration of women and men into the labour market after an absence must be facilitated.

The 'various Directives and social partner agreements' referred to include the

---

[90] Commission's own summary of the four pillars cited in Ashiagbor, 'European Employment Strategy and Regulation in Sciarra, Davies and Freedland (eds), *Employment Policy and the Regulation of Part-time Work in the European Union: A Comparative Analysis* (CUP, Cambridge, 2004) 53.

[91] Para. 16 of the Community Social Charter 1989 had already recognized that 'measures should also be developed enabling men and women to reconcile their occupational and family obligations'.

[92] OJ [2000] C218/5.   [93] 3rd Preambular paragraph.

[94] 4th Preambular paragraph.   [95] Co. Dec. 2001/63/EC (OJ [2001] L22/18).

Parental Leave Directive and the Part-time and Fixed Term Work Directives which we shall examine below. However, first, we shall look at the Court's approach to these issues.

2. Equal Treatment and the Changing Approach of the Court of Justice

As we have seen, the Court has been forced to address the issue of work/life balance through Article 234 references made in the context of the Equal Treatment Directives. Initially its response was to reinforce the traditional gender division of roles: women as childcarers; men as breadwinners. For example, *Commission* v. *Italy*[96] concerned an Italian law allowing a mother, but not a father, who adopted a child under six, compulsory maternity leave and the corresponding financial allowance. The Court said that the difference in treatment could not be regarded as discrimination within the meaning of the Directive.[97] Similarly, in *Hofman*[98] the Court's response to a complaint by a father that he was not allowed a maternity leave payment was that Directive 76/207 was not 'designed to settle questions concerning the organisation of the family or to alter the division of responsibility between parents'.[99]

Fifteen years later, in *Abdoulaye*[100] the Court upheld a benefit paid by Renault to women on maternity leave. This benefit was intended to offset the 'occupational disadvantages experienced by women on maternity leave'.[101]

[96] Case 163/82 [1983] ECR 3273.

[97] Para. 17. Once again, in this case the Court appears to suggest that direct discrimination can be justified. The Court said that the difference in treatment between the mother and the father was 'justified . . . by the legitimate concern to assimilate as far as possible the conditions of entry of the child into the adoptive family to those of the arrival of a newborn child in the family during the very delicate initial period' (para. 16).

[98] Case 184/83 *Hofman* v. *Barmer Ersatzkasse* [1984] ECR 3047. See Hervey and Shaw, 'Women, Work and Care: Women's Dual Role and Double Burden in EC Sex Equality Law' (1998) 8 *Journal of European Social Policy Law* 43.

[99] See also Case 170/84 *Bilka-Kaufhaus* v. *Weber von Hartz* [1986] ECR 1607 where the Court stopped short of imposing a positive requirement on companies to organize their occupational pension schemes in such a way as to accommodate the needs of their employees, and Case C–297/93 *Grau-Hupka* v. *Stadtgemeinde Bremen* [1994] ECR I–5535 where the Court said that since Community law on equal treatment did not oblige Member States to take into account in calculating the statutory pension years spent bringing up children, the national rules also did not breach Art. 119 (new Art. 141).

[100] Case C–218/98 *Abdoulaye* v. *Régre Nationale des Usines Renault SA* [1999] ECR I–5723.

[101] Renault listed these disadvantages as first, that a woman on maternity leave might not be proposed for promotion; second, that on her return, her period of service would be reduced by the length of her absence; third, that a pregnant woman could not claim performance-related salary increases; fourth, a female worker could not take part in training; lastly, since new technology was constantly changing the nature of jobs, the adaptation of a female worker returning from maternity leave becomes complicated (para. 19).

Certain male employees argued that since this benefit was payable only to women it contravened Article 141. The Court disagreed. It said that in respect of benefits intended to offset occupational disadvantages, male and female workers were 'in different situations, which excludes any breach of the principle of equal pay laid down in Article [141]'.[102]

Concern was expressed at the time that the ruling in *Abdoulaye* served only to reinforce the position of women as principal childcarers.[103] *Lommers*,[104] the positive action case considered in chapter eight, can also be criticized in this regard, where the Court upheld the female employees' preferential entitlement to nursery places. Yet the Court did itself note the paradox—that a measure whose purported aim was to abolish a *de facto* inequality, might nevertheless also help 'to perpetuate a traditional division of roles between men and women.'[105]

The Court showed itself increasingly sensitive to these issues in *Griesmar*[106] where it distinguished between benefits which were directly related to the maternity and post-maternity period from those which apply to child rearing more generally. The Court said that where a benefit was designed to offset the occupational disadvantages which 'arise for female workers as a result of being absent from work *during the period following childbirth*' the situation of a male worker was not comparable to that of a female worker and so Article 141 did not apply. By contrast, where a benefit was designed essentially to offset the occupational disadvantages which arise for female workers as a result of having brought up children, it was necessary to examine the question whether the situations of a male civil servant and a female civil servant were comparable. This was the situation in *Griesmar* itself which concerned a service credit applied to the calculation of pensions for female but not male civil servants in respect of each of their children. The Court said that the national law infringed Article 141 inasmuch as it excluded male civil servants who could prove that they assumed the task of bringing up their children from entitlement to the credit.

The new 'social contract' referred to in the Council's Resolution on balanced participation between men and women (considered above) had already been anticipated by the Court in *Hill*[107] where it noted that most of the women who choose to job share use that option 'in order to be able to combine work and family responsibilities which invariably involve caring for children'. The Court then added:

---

[102] Para. 20.
[103] McGlynn, 'Pregnancy, Parenthood and the Court of Justice in *Abdoulaye*' (2000) 6 *ELJ*. 39.
[104] Case C–476/99 *Lommers v. Mininster van Landbouw* [2002] ECR I–2891.
[105] Para. 41.
[106] Case C–366/99 *Griesmar v. Ministre de l'Économie, des Finances et de l'Industrie* [2001] ECR I–9383, para. 46.
[107] Case C–243/95 *Kathleen Hill and Ann Stapleton v. Revenue Commissioners* [1998] ECR I–3739, paras. 41–2.

Community policy in this area is to encourage and, if possible, adapt working conditions to family responsibilities. Protection of women within family life and in the course of their professional activities is, in the same way as for men, a principle which is widely regarded in the legal systems of the Member States as being the natural corollary of the equality between men and women, and which is recognised by Community law.

However, there are limits to what the Court can achieve when interpreting the Equality Directives. In _Grau-Hupka_[108] the woman complained that her state pension was reduced because it had been calculated without taking into account the five years she had spent looking after her child (and this had consequences for other payments she received). Under German law, as it then stood, a woman could claim only one year spent looking after her child to count towards her state pension. Because the case concerned the _state_ pension, Article 141 did not apply;[109] and the Social Security Directive 79/7 did not help her either because it does not require Member States to grant advantages in respect of old-age pension schemes to people who have brought up children, nor does it require states to provide benefit entitlements where employment has been interrupted to bring up children.[110]

3. Parental Leave Directive

The question of taking time off to care for young children was addressed for the first time by the legislature in the Parental Leave Directive 96/34/EC.[111] It gave effect to the first collective agreement concluded by the Social Partners under the collective route to legislation contained in the Social Policy Agreement.[112] It lays down minimum requirements designed to facilitate the reconciliation of parental and professional responsibilities for working parents.[113] It applies to all workers, both men and women who have an employment contract or an employment relationship.[114]

The Directive envisages two main rights. First, it entitles men and women

---

[108] Case C–297/93 _Grau-Hupka v. Stadtgemeinde Bremen_ [1994] ECR I–5535.

[109] See further Ch. 10.

[110] Para. 27. In a rather similar vein, see Case C–160/01 _Mau v. Bundesanstalt für Arbeit_ [2003] ECR I–4791, paras. 52–3 concerning the Insolvency Dir. 80/987 considered further in Ch. 14.

[111] OJ [1996] L145/4, amended by Council Directive 97/75/EC (OJ [1998] L10/24), consolidated 16 January 1998. A question was referred to the ECJ as to whether the right to parental leave should apply to all parents after 15 December 1999 or only to those whose children were born or adopted after 15 December 1999: _R v. Secretary of State, ex parte TUC_, 23 May 2000 but was subsequently withdrawn (OJ [2003] C184/28) because the UK amended its law: SI 2001/4010 the Maternity and Parental Leave (Amendment) Regulations 2001 to ensure that both groups of parents, with the necessary qualifying service benefit from the right.

[112] The draft agreement was concluded on 6 November 1995 by ETUC, CEEP and UNICE and formally agreed on 14 December 1995. The process for adopting this agreement and the subsequent litigation are considered in Ch. 2.

[113] Clause 1(1).   [114] Clause 1(2).

workers to parental leave on the birth or adoption of a child to enable them to take care of that child, for at least three months, until a given age up to 8 years, to be defined by the Member States or the Social Partners.[115] No requirement is imposed that the leave be paid. As the Court made clear in *Commission* v. *Luxembourg*,[116] parental leave and maternity leave are different: parental leave enables either parent to look after their child; maternity leave applies to mothers only immediately after childbirth. Therefore, each parent is entitled to parental leave of at least three months and that period cannot be reduced when it is interrupted by another period of leave such as maternity leave.

The Directive leaves a large number of issues to be resolved by the Member State and/or Social Partners.[117] In respect of parental leave, the Member States and/or the Social Partners may decide whether parental leave is granted on a full-time or part-time basis, in a fragmented way or in the form of a time credit system; whether entitlement to parental leave be subject to a period of work qualification and/or length of service qualification (which cannot exceed one year); whether to adjust conditions for access and the detailed rules for applying parental leave to the special circumstances of adoption; and whether notice periods be given by the worker to the employer specifying the beginning or the end of the parental leave.[118] In addition, the Member States, in consultation with the Social Partners, can define the circumstances in which the employer is allowed to postpone the granting of parental leave for justifiable reasons relating to the operation of the undertaking[119] and can authorize that special arrangements be made for small undertakings.[120] Member States and/or the Social Partners must define the status of the employment contract or employment relationship for the period of the parental leave.[121] All matters relating to social security in relation to the agreement are left to be determined by the Member States according to national law.[122]

In order to ensure that workers can exercise their right to parental leave, they must be protected against dismissal on the grounds of applying for, or taking parental leave, in accordance with national legislation, collective agreements or practice.[123] At the end of the parental leave workers have the right to return to the same job, or, if that is not possible, to an equivalent or similar job consistent with their employment contract or employment

---

[115] Clause 2(1). Clause 2(2) adds 'To promote equal opportunities and equal treatment between men and women, the parties to this agreement consider that the right to parental leave . . . should, in principle, be granted on a non-transferable basis'.

[116] Case C–519/03 *Commission* v. *Luxembourg* [2005] ECR I–000, para. 32.

[117] Clause 2(3).   [118] Clause 2(3)(a)–(d).

[119] E.g. where the work is of a seasonal nature, where a replacement cannot be found within the notice period, where a significant proportion of the workforce applies for parental leave at the same time, and where a specific function is of strategic importance.

[120] Clause 2(3)(e)–(f).   [121] Clause 2(7).   [122] Clause 2(8).   [123] Clause 2(4).

relationship.[124] In addition, rights acquired by the worker or in the process of being acquired on the date on which parental leave starts must be maintained as they stand until the end of the parental leave. These rights, including any changes arising from national law, agreements or practice, will apply to the worker.[125]

The second right given to workers by the agreement is to time off on the grounds of *force majeure* for urgent family reasons in cases of sickness or accident, making the immediate presence of the worker indispensable.[126] Member States and/or Social Partners may specify the conditions of access and the detailed rules for applying this rule and can limit the entitlement to a certain amount of time per year and/or per case.

As we have seen, the rights provided here are minima and Member States can maintain or introduce more favourable provisions than those set out in the Agreement.[127] Further, the implementation of the provisions of the collective agreement must not constitute grounds for reducing the general level of protection afforded to workers in the field of this agreement.[128] However, 'this does not prejudice the right of the Member States and/or Social Partners to develop different legislative, regulatory or contractual provisions, in the light of changing circumstances (including the introduction of non-transferability), as long as the minimum requirements provided for in this agreement are complied with'.[129]

While there have not yet been any comprehensive studies on the use made by parents to their right to leave under the Directive,[130] experience from the Nordic countries where parental leave already exists indicates that it is usually the woman who takes the parental leave.[131] This fact was recognized by the Court in *Lewen*[132] where it said that failure to pay a Christmas bonus to employees on parental leave was *prima facie* indirectly discriminatory against women. Such discrimination contravened Article 141 if the bonus was awarded retroactively for work performed in the course of the year and the woman did not receive an amount proportionate to the time worked. If, on the other hand, the bonus was paid as a way of encouraging those in active employment to work hard and to reward *future* loyalty to an employer then failure to pay such a bonus was not discriminatory since a woman on parental leave was in a 'special situation' which could not be 'assimilated to that of a man or woman at work since such leave involves suspension of the contract of employment and, therefore, of the respective obligations of the employer and the worker'. Thus, if the payment is made *prospectively* the Court treats those

---

[124] Clause 2(5).   [125] Clause 2(6).   [126] Clause 3(1).   [127] Clause 4(1).
[128] Clause 4(2): the standard non-regression clause.   [129] Clause 4(2), second sentence.
[130] A legal assessment on the implementation of the Directive can be found in COM(2003) 358.
[131] Bruning and Plontenga, 'Parental Leave and Equal Opportunities' (1999) 9 *JESP*. 195.
[132] Case C–333/97 *Lewen v. Lothar Denda* [1999] ECR I–7243, para. 35.

on parental leave, just like those on maternity leave,[133] as being in a 'special situation' and so Article 141 offers no protection. It also offers no protection against employers taking into account periods of parental leave (but not maternity leave) to reduce the benefit *pro rata*.[134]

4. The Relationship between the Parental Leave Directive and other Measures

The Parental Leave Directive is about just that: leave for parents (mothers *and* fathers). It is not to be confused with paternity leave (granted to fathers on the birth of their child) for which Community law makes no provision, nor is it about the right to request to work flexibly,[135] for which Community law also makes no provision. That said, Article 2(7), paragraph 4 of Directive 76/207 (Article 28(2) of the Consolidated Directive) makes clear that not only are the Equal Treatment Directives without prejudice to the provisions of Parental Leave Directive, but they are also without prejudice to the right of Member States to recognize distinct rights to paternity and/or adoption leave (Article 16 of the Consolidated Directive). Those Member States which recognize such rights must take the necessary measures to protect working men and women against dismissal due to exercising those rights and ensure that, at the end of such leave, they shall be entitled to return to their jobs or to equivalent posts on terms and conditions which are no less favourable to them, and to benefit from any improvement in working conditions to which they would have been entitled during their absence.

D. CHILDCARE

Parental leave enables workers to take some time off to look after young children but for the rest of the time they are dependent on childcare. The Community is conscious of this issue (but less so of care for elderly relatives). To date, it has issued a Recommendation 92/241 on Childcare Services[136] and the Barcelona European Council agreed that by 2010 Member States should provide childcare for at least 90 per cent of children between three years old and the mandatory school age and at least 33 per cent of children under three years of age.

According to the Commission, the rationale for a (non-binding) Recommendation on Childcare is both economic and social. Despite increasing

---

[133] See above, nn. 40–7.   [134] Case C–333/97 *Lewen* [1999] ECR I–7243, paras. 48–9.

[135] Cf. the possibility provided by the British statute to request flexible working: ERA 1996, ss. 80F–80I.

[136] Council Recommendation 92/241/EEC of 31 March 1992 on childcare (OJ [1992] L123/16).

numbers of women entering the labour force there has not been a correlative decrease in women's share of family responsibilities. According to the Commission, women will only be able to take advantage of the new jobs due to be created by the advent of the Single European Market if affordable support measures—including childcare—are available, enabling them time to train or retrain in order to be able to meet the demands of a restructured labour market.

Article 1 recommends that Member States, possibly in co-operation with national, regional or local authorities, management and labour, and other relevant organizations and private individuals, take and encourage initiatives in four areas:

* the provision of childcare services[137] while parents are working, following a course of education or training in order to obtain employment, or are seeking a job or a course of education or training in order to obtain employment;
* special leave for employed parents with responsibility for the care and upbringing of children;[138]
* adapting the environment, structure and organization of work to make them responsive to the needs of workers with children;[139]
* sharing of occupational, family, and upbringing responsibilities arising from the care of children between women and men. This includes, according to Article 6, encouraging increased participation by men in order to achieve a more equal sharing of parental responsibilities.

Because this measure is a recommendation, it lacks the legal force of a Directive.[140] Furthermore, the broad strategic nature of the policy—and the complexities created by the recognition of subsidiarity in the provision of the services—means that it will be very difficult for an individual to raise provisions of the Recommendation before a national court. Nevertheless, the Recommendation has a symbolic value in demonstrating the EC's commitment to childcare and Member States are obliged to inform the Commission of

---

[137] Childcare services, defined as any type of childcare whether public or private, individual or collective, should be affordable, flexible and diverse. They should combine reliable care, from the point of view of health and safety, with a general upbringing and a pedagogical approach. They should be available in all areas and regions of the Member States, and be accessible to parents and children, including children with special needs (Art. 3).

[138] These special leave initiatives apply to both men and women. They are intended to combine some flexibility as to how leave may be taken (Art. 4).

[139] This includes action, esp. within the framework of a collective agreement to create an environment which takes into account the needs of all working parents with childcare responsibilities, ensures that due recognition is given to persons engaged in childcare services and the social value of their work; and promotes action, especially in the public sector, which can serve as an example in developing initiatives in this area (Art. 5).

[140] The Court has not been prepared to extend Art. 141 to reinforce this Recommendation: Case C–249/97 *Gruber* [1999] ECR I–5295.

the measures taken to give effect to the Recommendation;[141] and in this respect, the Recommendation sits comfortably with the OMC techniques envisaged by the European Employment and Lisbon strategies.

E. ATYPICAL WORKERS: PART-TIME, FIXED TERM AND AGENCY WORK

1. Introduction

One way of balancing work and family life is to work part-time, or under a short fixed-term contract, or as an agency worker (temp). While these types of contract offer flexibility, they are also the most precarious types of contract. As far back as 1989, the Community Social Charter identified the need for action to ensure the improvement in living and working conditions as regards 'forms of employment other than open-ended contracts, such as fixed-term contracts, part-time working, temporary work and seasonal work'. The Action Programme noted that atypical workers constitute an 'important component in the organisation of the labour market', and said that the growth of atypical work, 'often in a quite anarchical manner' raised a 'danger of seeing the development of terms of employment such as to cause problems of social dumping, or even distortion of competition, at Community level' unless safeguards were introduced.

Although Directive 91/533/EEC on proof of the employment contract[142] provided some transparency in contracts of employment, the Commission proposed three specific directives concerning atypical workers, intended to improve the operation of the internal market and introduce greater transparency into the labour market, to improve living and working conditions of workers, and to protect the health and safety of workers at the workplace. The three Directives were proposed on three different legal bases. The first, and least radical, Directive 91/383/EEC, proposed on the basis of Article 118a (new Article 137), concerned health and safety and was the only measure successfully adopted. This is considered below. The second Directive, proposed on the basis of Article 100 (new Article 94),[143] applied the principle of non-discrimination to atypical workers,[144] in a limited set of circumstances,

---

[141] The Commission intends to follow up the Childcare Recommendation by assessing the implementation of the Recommendation and establishing baseline data on childcare infrastructure and services in the Member States (COM(94) 333, 43).

[142] OJ [1991] L288/32. See Ch. 12.   [143] COM(90) 228 final (OJ [1990] C224/90).

[144] Atypical work was defined in both the Arts. 100 and 100a (Arts. 94 and 95) Directives as including:

(i) part-time employment involving shorter working hours than statutory, collectively agreed or usual working hours;

subject to objective justification. This eventually formed the intellectual basis of Directive 97/81 on Part-time Work and Directive 99/70 on Fixed Term work considered below.

The third Directive, proposed on the basis of Article 100a (new Article 95), contained the more ambitious aim of creating a level playing field of indirect costs for employing atypical workers. As the Commission explained,[145] variations in wage costs relating to atypical employment are often due to factors unrelated to productivity—principally to national laws and collectively agreed regulations. Cost differences 'not justified by the workers' performance over time unit' are mainly related to costs arising from social protection and indirect costs associated with the duration of the contract, such as seniority. For example, costs to employers in some Member States arising from statutory social protection schemes, such as sickness, unemployment, insurance, and pensions, vary according to whether the worker concerned is employed full time or part time. As a result, some states can produce with lower labour costs than others for reasons unrelated to productivity, thus placing them at a competitive advantage.[146]

This draft Directive therefore proposed imposing three obligations on the Member States. First, Member States had to ensure that atypical employees were afforded, vis-à-vis full-time employees, social protection under statutory and occupational social security schemes underpinned by the same groundwork and the same criteria, taking into account the duration of work and/or pay.[147] Therefore, those employees working more than eight hours a week would be entitled to maternity protection, protection against unfair dismissal, redundancy payments, occupational pensions, sickness benefits, and survivor's benefits. Secondly, Member States had to ensure that part-time workers (but not the other classes of atypical worker) received the same entitlements

(ii) temporary employment relationships in the form of: (a) fixed term contracts, including seasonal work, concluded directly between the employer and the employee, where the end of the contract is established by objective conditions such as reaching a specific date, completing a specific task or the occurrence of a specific event; and (b) temporary employment covers any relationship between the temporary employment business (a temp agency), which is the employer, and its employees (the temps), where the employees have no contract with the user undertaking where they perform their activities. In other words, the employees have a contract with the temp agency who sends them to work as a temp for a company needing additional staff.

[145] Proposal for a Council Directive on the Approximation of Laws of the Member States Relating to Certain Employment Relationships with Regard to Distortions of Competition COM(90) 228 final (OJ [1990] C224/90); amended proposal in COM(90) 533 final (OJ [1990] C305/90).

[146] In Denmark e.g. complementary pensions scheme contributions amounting to about 2.5% of the gross wages of the employees concerned are not paid by employers in respect of employment of less than 10 hours per week. In Ireland, main social security contributions amounting to 15.95% of gross wages are not paid in respect of employment for less than 18 hours a week. 200 EIRR/13 (September 1990).

[147] Art. 2.

to annual holidays, dismissal allowances, and seniority allowances as full-time employees, in proportion to the total hours worked.[148] Thirdly, Member States had to ensure that national laws provided a limit on the renewal of temporary employment relationships of 12 months or less, so that the total period of employment did not exceed 36 months.[149] In addition, an equitable allowance had to be paid in the event of an unjustified break in the employment relationship before the end of the fixed term.[150] Neither this Directive, nor the Article 100 Directive, were adopted. It took two agreements by the Social Partners to apply the principle of non-discrimination (similar to the Article 100 Directive) to part-time and fixed term workers.[151] Elements of the Article 100a Directive were also included in the Fixed Term Work Directive.

In none of these proposals or the Directives themselves is any attempt made to challenge the need for these 'new' forms of employment. The Commission recognizes that the marked increase in the more flexible forms of work contract is 'not only because management wants to increase flexibility but also because the workers involved quite often prefer alternative work patterns'. Nevertheless, the Commission also recognizes that if these flexible forms of work are to be generally accepted there is a need to ensure that such workers are given broadly equivalent working conditions to standard workers.[152]

2. Directive 91/383/EEC on Health and Safety of Atypical Workers

Council Directive 91/383/EEC[153] encourages improvement in the health and safety of atypical workers who are defined as those on fixed term contracts and those in temporary employment relationships.[154] By applying the principle of equal treatment, the Directive requires atypical workers to be given the same level of health and safety protection as other workers in the user undertaking.[155] The Directive warns that the existence of an atypical employment relationship does not justify different treatment in respect of health and safety, especially as regards access to personal protective equipment.[156] Consequently, as a bare minimum,[157] the Framework Directive 89/391/EEC[158] on

---

[148] Art. 3.   [149] Art. 4(a).   [150] Art. 4(b).

[151] See now Dir. 97/81/EC (OJ [1998] L14/9) on part-time work and Dir. 99/70/EC (OJ [1999] L175/43). See further Ch. 4.

[152] COM(94) 333, 30.   [153] OJ [1991] L206/19. See also COM(90) 228 final.

[154] Art. 1. No reference is made to part-time workers.   [155] Art. 2(1).

[156] Art. 2(2).

[157] Art. 9 provides that the Directive is without prejudice to existing or future national or Community legislation which is more favourable to the health and safety protection of atypical workers.

[158] OJ [1989] L183/1. See further Ch. 11.

health and safety and all the individual daughter Directives apply equally to atypical workers.[159]

In addition, all atypical workers must be informed of the risks they face before taking up a particular activity, including any special occupational qualifications or skills they need or any special medical surveillance that is required.[160] In the case of temporary employment relationships (temps), the user undertaking must also specify to the temp agency, possibly in a contract of assignment, the occupational qualifications required and the specific features of the job to be filled, and these details must be conveyed by the temp agency to the workers concerned.[161] It is, however, the user undertaking which is responsible for the conditions in which the temp's work is performed. This is without prejudice to any responsibility imposed on the temp agency by national law.[162] This is perhaps the most controversial feature of the Directive. Although it is useful to identify one individual as being responsible for the temp, at times it may be preferable for the employer, usually the temp agency, to take responsibility, because usually it is the agency who has the ongoing relationship with the temp, and it is the agency which can monitor the individual's long-term exposure to, for example, radiation, over a variety of temporary jobs.

Atypical workers must also receive sufficient training appropriate to the job, taking into account the qualifications and experience[163] of the worker, who must be provided with special medical surveillance where the nature of the work demands it.[164] Member States have the option to extend that medical surveillance beyond the end of the employment relationship or to exclude atypical workers from work which is particularly dangerous to their health and safety.[165]

3. Part-time Work

3.1. The Equal Treatment Approach

In the days before the Part-time Work Directive,[166] indirect discrimination was a useful tool to address less favourable treatment of part-time workers on the grounds that considerably fewer men than women work part time.[167] Unless

---

[159] Art. 2(3).   [160] Art. 3.   [161] Art. 7.   [162] Art. 8.   [163] Art. 4.
[164] Art. 5. The existence of atypical workers at an undertaking must be notified to workers designated to protect and prevent occupational risks in accordance with Art. 7 of Dir. 89/391 (Art. 6).
[165] Art. 5.   [166] Dir. 97/81 (OJ [1998] L14/9).
[167] See Case 96/80 *Jenkins* [1981] ECR 911; Case 170/84 *Bilka-Kaufhaus* [1986] ECR 1607; Case 171/88 *Rinner-Kühn* [1989] ECR 2743; Case 33/89 *Kowalska v. Freie und Hansestadt Hamburg* [1990] ECR I–2591; Case C–360/90 *Arbeiterwohlfahrt der Stadt Berlin eV v. Bötel* [1992] ECR I–3589; Case C–184/89 *Nimz v. Freie und Hansestadt Hamburg* [1991] ECR I–297; Case C–1/95 *Gerster v. Freistadt Bremen* [1997] ECR I–5253, and Case C–100/95 *Kording v. Senator für Finanz* [1997] ECR I–5289. These cases are discussed by Traversa, 'Protection of Part-time Workers in the Case Law of the Court of Justice of the European Communities' (2003) 19 *IJCLLIR*. 219.

the differential treatment could be objectively justified, the part-time workers were entitled to have the same scheme applied to them as applied to other workers, on a basis proportional to their working time.[168]

The German works council cases provide a good example of how the principle of indirect discrimination has been used to assist part-time workers. German law provided that both full- and part-time workers attending training courses connected with their functions as staff representatives could be compensated up to the limit of their respective normal working hours. In *Bötel*[169] the Court found that this legislation discriminated against part-time workers, and thus against women, because, while both part-time and full-time employees participated in the same number of hours of training, part-timers received less compensation due to the lower number of hours worked. The Court said that this method of compensation acted as a disincentive to part-time workers from attending such training courses and acquiring further skills and knowledge.

This decision led to considerable concern in Germany since it interfered with the special status of works and staff councils in the organization of German employment policy and labour relations. In particular, it interfered with the principle that members of staff councils carry out their duties without loss of earnings and without any financial incentives to take on such a responsibility. As a result, in *Lewark*[170] the Court was asked to reconsider *Bötel*.[171] Once again the Court recognized that the application of the legislation discriminated against women contrary to Article 141 unless it could be objectively justified, which was a matter for the national court. However, the Court did note that such legislation was likely to deter part-time workers from performing staff council functions or from acquiring the knowledge necessary for performing them, which made it more difficult for part-time workers to be represented by qualified staff council members.[172]

In some cases, the Court has been unable to see the issue affecting part-time workers at all. For example, in *Helmig*[173] the Court ruled that there was no discrimination when part-timers, who were predominantly women, did not receive overtime rates for hours worked over their normal contractual hours but less than the full-time hours, even though the social consequences for part-timers to work one hour's overtime was likely to be

---

[168] Case C–102/88 *Ruzius Wilbrink v. Bestuur van de Bedrijfsvereniging voor Overheidsdiensten* [1989] ECR 4311.

[169] Case C–360/90 [1992] ECR I–3589. Cf. Case C–399/92 *Helmig* [1994] ECR I–5727, a case where part-timers did not receive the higher rate of overtime pay until they worked in excess of the normal working hours for full-timers.

[170] Case C–457/93 [1996] ECR I–243.   [171] Case C–360/90 [1992] ECR I–3589.

[172] See also Case C–278/93 *Freers and Speckmann v. Deutsche Bundespost* [1996] ECR I–1165 and see Shaw, 'Works Councils in German Enterprises and Article 119 EC' (1997) 22 *ELRev.* 256.

[173] Case C–399/92 *Stadt Lengerich v. Helmig* [1994] ECR I–5727. On the serious consequences of this decision, see the House of Lords' decision in *Barry v. Midland Bank* [1999] IRLR 581.

more disruptive than for full-timers.[174] However, 10 years later, in *Elsner-Lakeberg*[175] the Court had a change of heart, albeit without referring to *Helmig*.[176] Ms Elsner-Lakeberg worked part time as a secondary school teacher. Full-time teachers worked for 24.5 hours per week (98 hours per month) whereas Ms Elsner-Lakeberg taught for 15 hours per week (60 hours per month). In December 1999 she was required to teach 2.5 additional hours. Her request for remuneration of those hours was refused on the basis that the legislation provided that excess hours worked by a teacher would be remunerated only when the additional work exceeded three hours in a month. She therefore received no pay at all for the additional hours worked.

The Court said that although the pay appeared to be equal, inasmuch as the entitlement to remuneration for additional hours was triggered only after three additional hours had been worked by part-time and full-time teachers, three additional hours was in fact a greater burden for part-time teachers than it was for full-time teachers: a full-time teacher had to work an additional three hours over his regular monthly schedule of 98 hours (approximately 3 per cent extra) in order to be paid for his additional hours, while a part-time teacher had to work three hours more than his monthly 60 hours (5 per cent extra). Since the number of additional teaching hours giving entitlement to pay was not reduced for part-time teachers in a manner proportionate to their working hours, they received different treatment compared with full-time teachers as regards pay for additional teaching hours.[177] Having reached this conclusion, the Court said that it was for the national court to determine whether the different treatment affected considerably more women than men and, if so, whether the rule could be objectively justified.

The drawback with the indirect discrimination approach to dealing with less favourable treatment of part-time workers is that it is dependent on the part-timers showing that the rule actually[178] disadvantaged a considerably higher percentage of women than men.[179] Thus, female part-time workers have to show disparate impact; male part-time workers cannot make the claim at all. In this respect the Part-time Work Directive 97/81 represented an important step forward.

---

[174] See Rubinstein [1995] IRLR 183.
[175] Case C–285/02 *Elsner-Lakeberg v. Nordrhein-Westfalen* [2004] ECR I–000.
[176] AG Jacobs did discuss and distinguish *Helmig*.   [177] Para. 17.
[178] Cf. the statutory language of the amended Equal Treatment Directive (Article 2(1)(b) the Consolidated Directive) considered in Ch. 6.
[179] Case C–236/98 *Jämställdhetsombudsmannen v. Örebro läns landsting* [2000] ECR I–2189, para. 50.

3.2. The Part-time Work Directive 97/81

(a) Introduction

Given that the two proposals for the Directives based on Articles 100 and 100a were blocked in Council, the Commission decided to initiate the procedure under Article 3 (new Article 138) of the Social Policy Agreement. In June 1996 the Social Partners (UNICE, ETUC, and CEEP) announced their intention to begin negotiations.[180] On 6 June 1997 they agreed the 'European Framework Agreement on Part-time Work' which, following the procedure under Article 4(2) SPA (new Article 139(2)) was subsequently implemented by Council Directive 97/81/EC[181] and extended to the UK by Council Directive 98/23/EC.[182] The drafting of the Agreement was much influenced by the 1994 ILO Convention No. 175 establishing minimum standards on part-time work and the supplementary Recommendation 182.[183]

The purpose of the framework agreement is, first and foremost, 'to provide for the removal of discrimination against part-time workers and to improve the quality of part-time work'.[184] However, as the Preamble makes clear, the Directive applies the principle of non-discrimination to employment conditions and not to social security. Thus, an important aspect of the Article 100a proposal has disappeared.

The Directive has two other objectives:[185] 'to facilitate the development of part-time work on a voluntary basis *and* to contribute to the flexible organisation of working time in a manner which takes into account the needs of employers and workers'. Thus, the Part-Time Work Directive forms part of the EU's flexibility agenda aimed at encouraging adaptability of business and, in particular, modernizing work organization.[186] But what sort of flexibility— supply-side (where part-time work is encouraged to enable those with family commitments to combine work with family life) or demand-side (where flexible working arrangements such as part-time, fixed term, or temporary work is

---

[180] For a fuller description of the background, see Sciarra, 'New discourses in labour law: part-time work and the paradigm of flexibility' in Sciarra *et al.* (ed.), above n. 90, 21–6.

[181] OJ [1998] L14/9.

[182] OJ [1998] L131/10. Consolidated legislation OJ [1998] L131/13. On the background to the legislation, see Jeffery, 'Not Really Going to Work? Of the Directive on Part-time Work, "Atypical Work" and Attempts to Regulate It' (1998) 3 *ILJ*. 193.

[183] See further Jeffery, above, n. 182, 200, and Murray 'Social Justice for Women? The ILO's Convention on Part-time Work' (1999) 15 *IJCLLIR*. 3.

[184] Clause 1(a).   [185] Clause 1(b), emphasis added.

[186] See, e.g., Guideline 13 of the 2001 Employment Guidelines (OJ [2002] L22/18) which encourages the Social Partners to 'negotiate and implement at all appropriate levels agreements to modernise the organisation of work, including flexible working arrangements, with the aim of making undertakings productive and competitive, achieving the required balance between flexibility and security, and increasing the quality of jobs. Subjects to be covered may, for example, include the introduction of new technologies, new forms of work and working time issues such as . . . the development of part-time working, access to career breaks, and associated job security issues.'

used by management to adapt their staffing needs to market conditions)?[187] If the latter,[188] then, as Ashiagbor notes, the first objective of the Directive risks being undermined by the second and third objectives: the reason why atypical work has been promoted is to provide a way of circumventing the high levels of employment protection associated with typical work.[189]

Given the dualism of the Directive, this chapter focuses on its role as part of the Community's agenda on family friendly policies. However, comments made in this respect must be considered against the broader backcloth of the Directive's role in 'increasing the employment-intensiveness of growth, in particular by a more flexible organization of work in a way which fulfils both the wishes of the employees and the requirements of competition'.[190]

(b) Personal Scope

The Directive applies to part-time workers who have an employment contract or employment relationship as defined by the law, collective agreement, or practice in force in each Member State.[191] Thus, the self-employed cannot benefit from this Directive. Moreover, Member States can, after consultation with the Social Partners, or the Social Partners themselves can exclude wholly or partly from the agreement part-time workers who work on a casual basis. Such exclusions must be reviewed periodically to establish if the object-ive reasons for making them remain valid.[192] In *Wippel*[193] the Court said that a part-time worker employed under a 'framework contract' (like a zero-hours contract), working as and when the employer required it, was a worker for the purposes of the Directive provided that she satisfied the requirement of national law for the existence of an employment contract or relationship, and did not fall under any derogation by the Member States under Clause 2(2).

The term 'part-time worker' refers to 'an employee whose normal hours of work, calculated on a weekly basis or on average over a period of employment of up to one year, are less than the normal hours of work of a comparable full-time worker'.[194] Clause 3(2) explains that the term 'comparable full-time worker' means 'a full-time worker in the same establishment having the same type of employment contract or relationship, who is engaged in the same or a similar work/occupation, due regard being given to other consider-ations which may include seniority, qualification/skills'. Where there is no

---

[187] See generally, Deakin and Read, 'Between Social Policy and EMU: the New Employment Title of the EC Treaty' in Shaw (ed.), *Social Law and Policy in an Evolving European Union*, (Hart Publishing, Oxford, 2000).

[188] A perspective supported by Guideline 13.

[189] 'European Employment Strategy and Regulation' in Sciarra *et al.* above n. 90, 54–5.

[190] Fifth Preambular paragraph.   [191] Clause 2(1).   [192] Clause 2(2).

[193] Case C–313/02 *Nicole Wippel* v. *Peek & Cloppenburg GmbH & Co. KG* [2005] ECR I–000, para. 40.

[194] Clause 3(1). Cf. Case C–322/98 *Kachelmann* v. *Bankhaus Hermann Lampe KG* [2000] ECR I–7505, paras. 26 and 28 which suggests that part-time and full-time work are not comparable.

comparable full-time worker in the same establishment, the comparison must be made by reference to the applicable collective agreement or, where there is no applicable collective agreement, in accordance with national law, collective agreements, or practice.

The scope of the comparator may well prove to be the Achilles heel of the Directive.[195] Some of the problems it raises can be seen in *Wippel*.[196] The applicant was a casual worker employed on a 'work on demand' contract. She brought an action claiming the same treatment as a regular full-time worker. Her contract did not stipulate either weekly working hours or the manner in which her working time was to be organized, leaving it up to her whether to accept or reject the work offered by the employer. Her comparator, a full-time worker, worked under a contract with a fixed working week of 38.5 hours. The full-time worker had to work for the employer for the whole working week without being able to refuse to work if the worker could not or did not wish to do it. Because of these differences between the full-timers' and part-timers' contracts, the Court found that there was no full-time worker comparable to Ms Wippel.[197]

(c) The Principle of Non-discrimination

The essence of the Directive can be found in Clause 4. This provides that:

(1) In respect of *employment conditions*, part-time workers shall not be treated in a less favourable manner than comparable full-time workers solely because they work part-time unless different treatment is justified on objective grounds.

(2) Where appropriate, the principle of *pro rata temporis* shall apply.

Clause 4(3) concludes that 'The arrangements for the application of this clause shall be defined by the Member States and/or Social Partners, having regard to European legislation, national law, collective agreements and practice.'

Thus Clause 4(1) contains the principle of non-discrimination, a principle which is, however, subject to a defence that the difference in treatment can be justified on (unspecified) objective grounds.[198] In addition, Clause 4(4) provides that:

When justified by objective reasons, Member States, after consultation of the Social Partners in accordance with national law or practice and/or Social Partners may, where appropriate, make access to particular conditions of employment subject to a period of service, time worked or earnings qualification. Qualifications relating to

---

[195] For a discussion of the position under British law, see McColgan, 'Missing the Point? The Part-time Workers (Prevention of Less Favourable Treatment) Regulations 2000 (SI 2000/1551)' (2000) 29 *ILJ*. 260.

[196] See Case C–313/02 *Nicole Wippel v. Peek & Cloppenburg GmbH & Co. KG* [2005] ECR I–000.

[197] Para. 62.

[198] Case 170/84 *Bilka Kaufhaus v. Weber von Hartz* [1986] ECR 1607. See further Ch. 4.

access by part-time workers to particular conditions of employment should be reviewed periodically having regard to the principle of non-discrimination as expressed in clause 4.1.

The significant feature of this Directive is that part-time workers no longer have to rely on the difficult concepts of indirect discrimination to make their case to ensure that they are not treated less favourably than full-time workers in respect of working conditions.[199] The Part-time Workers' Directive will remove the need for two stages of the indirect discrimination analysis. First, the Directive removes the obligation to show that a full-time work requirement has an adverse impact on women in a particular pool: merely discriminating against the part-timer will be unlawful *per se* unless it can be justified. Secondly, it would seem that a worker will not have to show that he/she cannot comply with a full-time work requirement to seek to challenge it: treating full-time and part-time staff differently requires justification of itself. However, these advances come at a price: *direct* discrimination on the grounds of being a part-time worker can be objectively justified.

It is, however, remarkable that, despite the existence of the Part-time Workers' Directive, the Court continues to decide cases based on the existing Equal Treatment Directives. *Steinicke*[200] is one such case. Although the case largely predated the Directive, the Court was not prepared to consider Directive 97/81 at all because the scheme fell within the scope of Article 5(1) of Directive 76/207.

(d) Encouragement of Part-time Work

Much of the remainder of Directive 97/81 has the feel of an exhortatory resolution rather than a hard law measure.[201] It charges the Member States and, within their spheres of responsibility, the Social Partners, with responsibility for identifying and, where possible, removing obstacles (in legislation, administrative practice, and collective agreements) to part-time work.[202] This particular provision could be read as inviting the removal of protective legislation which, according to deregulatory thinking, might hinder opportunities for part-time work. Although it is too broadly phrased to amount to an instruction to deregulate, it could be prayed in aid by a Member State to justify the exclusion of part-time workers from protective measures.

[199] Case C–313/02 *Nicole Wippel* v. *Peek & Cloppenburg GmbH & Co. KG* [2005] ECR I–000, paras. 30–3 suggests that the phrase 'working conditions' has the same meaning as in Art. 5(1) of Dir. 76/207. It continues: 'The fact that that type of contract has financial consequences for the worker concerned is not, however, sufficient to bring such conditions within the scope of Art. 141 . . .'.

[200] Case C–77/02 *Steinicke* v. *Bundesanstalt für Arbeit* [2003] ECR I–9027, para. 52.

[201] Barnard and Hepple, 'Substantive Equality' (2000) 59 *CLJ*. 562, 582 cf. Kilpatrick and Freedland, 'The United Kingdom: How is EU Governance Transformative?' in Sciarra *et al.* (eds), above n. 90, 329.

[202] Clause 5.

However, the obligation to remove such obstacles is subject to the principle of non-discrimination and to the non-regression provision found in Clause 6(2).

The Directive also considers the question of the movement of workers from full-time to part-time work, and vice versa. A worker's refusal to transfer from the one form of work to the other is not to constitute, of itself, a valid ground for dismissal;[203] conversely, the employer must give consideration to requests by workers to transfer between full-time and part-time work[204] and must provide information about opportunities for transfers.[205] However, it is not required to accede to workers' requests. Finally, the least strong provision in clause 5 provides that employers should give consideration to measures to facilitate access to part-time work at all levels in the enterprise, including skilled and managerial positions, and, where appropriate, to facilitate access by part-time workers to vocational training to enhance career opportunities and occupational mobility.[206]

The Court has already considered the situation of a part-time worker, a job sharer, wishing to return to full-time work under Article 141. In *Hill*[207] two women who had shared a job found themselves at a disadvantage when they converted to full-time employment when compared with those who had worked on a full-time basis for the same number of years since, when converting, a job-sharing worker was placed on the full-time pay scale at a level below that which she had previously occupied on the pay scale applicable to job-sharing staff and, consequently, at a level lower than that of a full-time worker employed for the same period of time. The court noted that 99.2 per cent of clerical assistants who job-shared were women, as were 98 per cent of all civil servants employed under job-sharing contracts and so a provision which adversely affected the legal position of those workers had discriminatory effects based on sex.[208] Because the rule was indirectly discriminatory, the defendants had to establish before the national court that the rule could be objectively justified.[209]

4. Fixed Term Work

In the Preamble to the Part-Time Work Agreement the Social Partners announced their intention to consider the need for similar agreements relating to other forms of flexible work. On 23 March 1998 the European Social Partners said they would start negotiations on fixed term work. They

---

[203] Clause 5(2).   [204] Clause 5(3)(a) and (b).   [205] Clause 5(3)(c) and (e).

[206] Clause 5(3)(d).

[207] Case C–243/95 *Kathleen Hill and Ann Stapleton v. Revenue Commissioners* [1998] ECR I–3739, para. 42. Cf. McGlynn and Farrelly, 'Equal Pay and the "Protection of Women within Family Life" ' (1999) 24 *ELRev*. 202.

[208] Para. 25.   [209] Para. 43.

concluded a framework agreement on 18 March 1999 which the Council put into effect by Directive 99/70 on 28 June 1999.[210] They intended to negotiate a further agreement on temporary workers (temps)[211] but so far no such agreement has been forthcoming.

The purpose of the 1999 agreement is to 'improve the quality of fixed-term work by ensuring the application of the principle of non-discrimination; and to establish a framework to prevent abuse arising from the use of successive fixed term employment contracts or relationships'.[212] Thus, unlike the Part-time Work Directive the dual purpose of the Fixed Term Work Directive is not so stark. The Fixed Term Work Directive is more obviously about worker protection, albeit that the Preamble to both the Directive and the Framework Agreement refer to the EES and, in particular to the need to achieve a better balance between 'flexibility in working time and security for workers'.

The Directive applies to 'fixed-term workers who have an employment contract or employment relationship as defined in law, collective agreements or practice in each Member State'.[213] Clause 3 provides that 'fixed-term worker' means 'a person having an employment contract or relationship entered into directly between an employer and a worker where the end of the employment contract or relationship is determined by objective conditions such as reaching a specific date, completing a specific task, or the occurrence of a specific event'. The Preamble to the agreement makes clear that the 'agreement applies to fixed term workers with the exception of those placed by a temporary work agency at the disposition of a user enterprise', since the Social Partners intend to 'consider the need' for a similar agreement relating to temporary agency work. In addition, Member States, after consultation with the Social Partners, and/or the Social Partners themselves, may provide that the Directive does not apply to:[214]

(a) initial vocational training relationships and apprenticeship schemes;
(b) employment contracts and relationships which have been concluded within the framework of a specific public or publicly supported training, integration and vocational retraining programme.

The Directive contains three main rights for fixed term workers. First, as with the Part-time Work Directive, the principle of non-discrimination applies. Clause 4(1) provides that in respect of employment conditions, fixed term workers are not to be treated in a less favourable manner than comparable permanent workers solely because they have a fixed term contract or relationship unless justified on objective grounds. Where appropriate, the principle of

---

[210] OJ [1999] L175/143. For the original proposal, see COM(99) 203 final. The Member States have until 10 July 2001 to comply with the Directive (see Corrigendum OJ [1999] L244/64). For a discussion of the potential impact of the Directive see the contributions to the special issue of the (1999) 15/2 *IJCLLIR*.

[211] See below at nn. 220–8.   [212] Clause 1.   [213] Clause 2.   [214] Clause 2(2).

pro rata temporis applies.[215] The term 'comparable permanent worker' means a worker with an employment contract or relationship of indefinite duration, in the same establishment, engaged in the same or similar work/occupation, due regard being given to qualifications/skills.[216] Where there is no comparable permanent worker in the same establishment, the comparison is to be made by reference to the applicable collective agreement, or where there is no applicable collective agreement, in accordance with national law, collective agreements or practice.[217]

The arrangements for the application of Clause 4(1) are to be defined by the Member States after consultation with the Social Partners, and/or the Social Partners, having regard to Community law, national law, collective agreements and practice. Once again, the principle of non-discrimination is subject to objective justifications. Further, clause 4(4) provides that period of service qualifications relating to particular conditions of employment are to be the same for fixed term workers as for permanent workers except where different length of service qualifications are justified on objective grounds.

The second pillar of protection found in the Directive concerns the prevention of abuse of fixed term contracts. In countries such as the UK there were no limits on the number of occasions on which fixed term contracts could be renewed and in some sectors (notably the media and universities) misuse of fixed-term contracts was widespread. As a result, Clause 5(1) provides that:

... Member States, after consultation with social partners in accordance with national law, collective agreements or practice, and/or the social partners, shall, where there are no equivalent legal measures to prevent abuse, introduce in a manner which takes account of the needs of specific sectors and/or categories of workers, one or more of the following measures:

a) objective reasons justifying the renewal of such contracts or relationships;
b) the maximum total duration of successive fixed-term employment contracts or relationships;[218]
c) the number of renewals of such contracts or relationships.

In *Adeneler*[218A] the Court said that the concept of objective reasons required recourse to fixed-term work agreements to be justified 'by the presence of specific factors relating in particular to the activity in question and the conditions under which it is carried out'. The mere fact that the use of fixed term contracts was provided for in national law could not be an objective reason. The Court also said that a national rule, under which fixed term contracts

---

[215] Clause 4(2). [216] Clause 3(2). [217] Clause 3(2), second paragraph.

[218] Member States after consultation with the Social Partners, and/or the Social Partners, shall, where appropriate, determine under what conditions fixed-term employment contracts or relationships: a) shall be regarded as 'successive'; b) shall be deemed to be contracts or relationships of an indefinite duration (Clause 5(2)).

[218A] Case C–212/04 *Adeneler v. ELOG* [2006] ECR I–000.

that were separated from one another by a period of more than 20 working days could not be regarded as successive, was not compatible with the Fixed-Term Work Directive[218B]

The third right given by the Directive to fixed term workers relates to information. Clause 6(1) requires employers to inform fixed-term workers about vacancies which become available in the undertaking or establishment by, for example, displaying a general announcement at a suitable place in the undertaking, to ensure that fixed term workers have the same opportunity to secure permanent positions as other workers. Clause 6(2) adds that, as far as possible, employers should facilitate access by fixed term workers to appropriate training opportunities to enhance their skills, career development, and occupational mobility. Clause 7(1) requires that fixed term workers be taken into consideration in calculating the threshold above which workers' representative bodies provided for in national and Community law may be constituted in the undertaking as required by national provisions.[219] In addition, Clause 7(2) requires employers, as far as possible, to give consideration to the provision of appropriate information to existing workers' representative bodies about fixed term work in the undertaking.

5. Agency Work

Addressing the problems experienced by agency workers was always going to prove the hardest situation for the Community legislature to deal with due to the triangulation of the relationships involved. Agency workers (temps) are usually employed by an agency (a temping agency) which then offers their services to a user undertaking which controls the individual's day to day activities. Where the engagement with the user is for a short term, then it is likely that the agency remains the temp's employer. But where the engagement is for a longer term, the position is much less clear.[220]

As we saw from the Preamble to the Fixed Term Work Directive, it was certainly the intention that there was to be a Directive on Temporary Agency Work which would operate on the same principle as the other two Directives, with equal treatment at its core. Although negotiations between the *intersectoral* social partners on this subject started in May 2000, they

[218B] The Court also made clear that national courts are bound by Directives from the end of the transition period, not from the date the Directive enters into force as had been suggested by the Court in Case C–144/04 *Mangold* v. *Helm* [2006] ECR I–000.

[219] The arrangements for the application of Clause 7.1 are to be defined by Member States after consultation with the Social Partners and/or the Social Partners in accordance with national law, collective agreements or practice and having regard to clause 4.1.

[220] See, in the context of the UK, *Dacas* v. *Brook Street Bureau* [2004] IRLR 140; *Cable & Wireless plc* v. *Muscat* [2006] IRLR 354.

proved difficult because of the triangulation of the employment relationships. The negotiations eventually broke down a year later over the issue of the definition of a comparable worker for the purposes of equal treatment (the ETUC had insisted on a comparator being a worker in the user undertaking, UNICE rejected this). In October 2001 the *sectoral* Social Partners Euro-CIETT (the European Committee of the International Confederation of Temporary Work Businesses) and Uni-Europa (the European regional organization of Union Network International) issued a joint declaration on temporary agency work which, they hoped, would form the basis for a future European Directive. Indeed, in March 2002 the Commission put forward a proposal for a Directive on agency work[221] which built on the sectoral partners' joint declaration and on those areas where the intersectoral Social Partners had been able to agree.

Once again, the proposed Directive has a dual aim: on the one hand to improve the quality of temporary work by ensuring that the principle of non-discrimination is applied to temporary workers and, on the other, to establish a suitable framework for the use of temporary work to contribute to the smooth functioning of the labour and employment market.[222] On the crucial issue of equal treatment, the Directive provides that temporary workers shall, during their posting, receive at least as favourable treatment, in terms of basic working and employment conditions (including working time, rest periods, night work, paid holidays, public holidays, pay,[223] and seniority in the job), as a comparable worker in the user enterprise, unless the difference in treatment is justified for objective reasons.[224] Thus, to this extent, the Commission's proposal supported the ETUC's position: the comparable worker is the 'worker in the user undertaking occupying an identical or similar post to that occupied by the worker posted by the temporary agency, account being taken of seniority, qualifications and skills'.[225] The Directive then contains a number of important limitations to the general principle of equality. For example, Member States can decide not to apply the principle of equal treatment to temporary workers who have a permanent contract of employment with the temp agency and who continue to be paid between postings[226] or where the period of assignment is less than six weeks.[227] Member States may also allow the Social Partners to conclude collective agreements which derogate from the principle of equal treatment provided an adequate level of protection is given to temporary workers.[228]

Even though this Directive is much more limited in its objectives than the sectoral partners' declaration (e.g. it contains no reference to the fact that temp agencies should not make workers available to user undertakings in order to replace striking workers), the Council could not agree on key aspects

---

[221] COM(2002)149 final.
[222] Art. 3.   [223] Art. 3(1)(d).   [224] Art. 5(1).
[225] Art. 5(5) provides further details as to how comparability is to be determined.
[226] Art. 5(2).   [227] Art. 5(4).   [228] Art. 5(3).

of the proposal, in particular the question of a transitional period of five years during which an exemption to the principle of equal treatment could be granted in view of the specific conditions of Member States' labour markets. The proposal is currently stalled.

6. Telework

More successful from the perspective of Social Partner co-operation has been the conclusion of the telework agreement by the intersectoral Social Partners[229] and two sectoral agreements in commerce and telecommunications. The intersectoral agreement, one of the first 'autonomous agreements' to be implemented at national level by collective agreement rather than through legally binding measures derived from a Directive,[230] is intended to facilitate telework 'both as a way for companies and public service organisations to modernise work organisation, and as a way for workers to reconcile work and social life and giving them greater autonomy in the accomplishment of their tasks'. Thus, the telework agreement falls squarely within the Lisbon priorities. As the Social Partners put it, 'If Europe wants to make the most out of the information society, it must encourage this new form of work organisation in such a way, that flexibility and security go together and the quality of jobs is enhanced, and that the chances of disabled people on the labour market are increased.'

The agreement defines telework as 'a form of organising and/or performing work, using information technology, in the context of an employment contract/relationship, where work, which could also be performed at the employer's premises, is carried out away from those premises on a regular basis'. It also emphasizes that telework is voluntary for the worker and the employer and that a worker's refusal to opt for telework is not, as such, a reason for terminating the employment relationship or changing the terms and conditions of employment of that worker. Further, if telework is not part of the original job description the decision to move to telework is reversible by individual and/or collective agreement.

The agreement then details a number of substantive rights for teleworkers and obligations for employers. These include the requirement that:

• the employer is to provide teleworkers with the relevant written information as required by Directive 91/533[231] but supplemented by information connected with telework (e.g. the department to which the teleworkers is attached, his/her immediate superior);[232]

---

[229] http://europa.eu.int/comm/employment_social/social_dialogue/docs/300_20020716_agreement_telework_en.pdf.
[230] See further Ch. 2.   [231] OJ [1991] L288/32 considered further in Ch. 12.
[232] Clause 3.

- teleworkers benefit from the same rights, guaranteed by applicable legislation and collective agreements, as comparable workers at the employers' premises, although specific collective agreements may be needed to take into account the particularities of telework.[233] They also enjoy the same collective rights as workers at the employer's premises;[234]
- the employer is responsible for ensuring the protection of the data used and processed by the teleworkers and for respecting the teleworker's privacy;[235]
- generally the employer is responsible for providing, installing and maintaining the equipment necessary for regular telework unless the teleworker uses his/her own equipment. If telework is performed on a regular basis the employer compensates or covers the costs directly caused by the work, in particular those relating to communication;[236]
- the employer is responsible for the protection of the teleworker's health and safety in accordance with the Framework Directive on health and safety 89/391 and its daughters,[237] together with the teleworker's training.[238] Teleworkers can manage their own time but the workload and performance standards must be equivalent to those of comparable workers at the employer's premises.[239] The employer is also responsible for ensuring that the teleworker is not isolated from the rest of the working community in the company.[240]

This Directive is innovative in terms of its method of implementation, relying as it does solely on the Social Partners rather than the Member States for its implementation. However, the absence of a Directive, and thus an obligation for the Member States to guarantee the outcome, has meant that this agreement lacks the visibility of its predecessors.

7. Assessment

During the 1980s the Commission attempted to *limit* the use of temporary work.[241] In a proposed Directive of 1982[242] it listed limited grounds in which fixed term and temporary work provided by employment agencies could be used. In the intervening 15 years there has been a sea change in attitude and now the focus is on *encouraging* atypical work as part of the

---

[233] Clause 4.   [234] Clause 11.   [235] Clauses 5 and 6.   [236] Clause 7.
[237] Clause 8, considered further in Ch. 11.   [238] Clause 10.   [239] Clause 9.
[240] Ibid. See also Commission Recommendation 98/370/EC on the ratification of ILO Convention No. 177 on homework of 20 June 1996 (notified under Doc. No. C(1998)764) (OJ [1998] L165/32).
[241] See Murray, 'Normalising Temporary Work' (1999) 28 *ILJ*. 269.
[242] OJ [1982] C128/2.

agenda of modernizing 'the organisation of work, including flexible working arrangements, with the aim of making undertakings productive and competitive and achieving the required balance between flexibility and security'.[243] The two Directives on Part-time Work and Fixed Term Work do attempt to reconcile, on the one hand, demand-side needs for numerical flexibility, allowing the firm to modulate the numbers employed, and supply-side needs for family friendly policies. In respect of those working part time in the EU there may be a degree of coalescence of interests: from the employer's point of view part-time work provides the flexibility necessary to meet changing consumer demands. From the worker's point of view it provides the flexibility to make it easier to combine work with other family responsibilities.[244] Through the principle of non-discrimination the Directives provide a degree of protection for these workers.

Both the Part-time Work and Fixed Term Work Directives are drafted in a similar manner. However, they employ the same tool to address different problems. While part-time work may well represent a positive 'choice' for many workers, those engaged under fixed term contracts would usually choose, given the choice, contracts of indefinite duration,[245] since fixed term contracts, by their very nature are insecure and precarious. To a limited extent this is recognized in the two Directives: the Fixed Term Work Directive does not contain a clause requiring Member States and the Social Partners to remove obstacles to fixed term work. Further, the Preamble to the Directive expressly states that 'contracts of an indefinite duration are, and will continue to be, the general form of employment relationship'. Given the differences between the nature of fixed term and part-time work, Murray argues[246] the protection that temporary workers need is actually a fully fledged scheme of portability of entitlements which recognizes all relevant working experience, even if undertaken with different employers and with breaks in between, to qualify for employment rights. This, rather than the principle of non-discrimination, would provide security for fixed term workers which would balance the flexibility offered by fixed term contracts to employers.

---

[243] Council Resolution of 15 December 1997 on the 1998 Employment Guidelines (OJ [1998] C30/1). See also the Supiot report, *Transformation of Labour Law in Europe* (June 1998), para. 755, and Ashiagbor, 'Promoting Precariousness? The Response of the EU Employment Policies to Precarious Work', in Fudge (ed.), *Precarious Work, Women and the New Economy* (Hart Publishing, Oxford, 2006).

[244] Green Paper, *Partnership for a New Organisation of Work*, COM(97) 127 final, para. 52.

[245] See Delsen, 'Atypical Employment Relations and Government Policy in Europe' (1991) 5 *Labour* 123.

[246] Murray, 'Normalising Temporary Work' (1999) 28 *ILJ*. 269.

F. CONCLUSIONS

The European Union's approach to work/life balance issues has undergone a rapid evolution. There is now recognition at the highest level that work/life balance is a Community concern and that steps need to taken to address it. Yet, the rhetoric in the Council's radical resolution on the balanced participation of women and men in family life was undermined by the limited and carefully tailored language of Article 33(2) of the Charter (Article II–93(2) of the Constitutional Treaty). The original drafting of this provision, which referred to the 'right to reconciliation' was dropped before the Charter was finally adopted.[247] McGlynn says, 'rhetoric and reality could not be further apart'[248] but, as we have already seen, the law can only go so far and in this key *policy* domain, it is employers, the Social Partners, and workers themselves who need to make this work. This is now recognised in Article 21(2) of the Consolidated Directive 2006/54 which requires the Member States to encourage the social partners to promote 'equality between men and women, and flexible working arrangements, with the aim of facilitating the reconciliation of work and private life'. In this respect there is a clear role for softer policy coordination, perhaps underpinned by law, including the Charter rights. Until these various policy actors manage to work together, women will continue to suffer from the gender segregation of labour, 'wage disparities and extra workload (the "double working day")'.[249]

[247] McGlynn, 'Reclaiming a Feminist Vision: The Reconciliation of Paid Work and Family Life in European Union Law and Policy' (2001) 7 *Columbia Jo. E.L.* 241, 262.
[248] Ibid., 263.
[249] The Supiot report, *Beyond Employment: Changes in Work and the Future of Labour Law in Europe* (OUP, Oxford, 2001) 229.

10

Equal Treatment in Social Security and Pensions

A. INTRODUCTION

While the previous chapter looked at the position of those at an earlier stage of their careers seeking to juggle work and family life, this final chapter on equality considers how the non-discrimination principle applies to those coming out of the workforce either involuntarily—through sickness, invalidity, or unemployment—or through the effluxion of time, on retirement. This chapter focuses in particular on two issues. First, it examines Directive 79/7[1] on equal treatment in *state* social security systems which was intended to complement the sex equality Directives, Directive 75/117 on equal pay,[2] and Directive 76/207 on equal treatment.[3] In particular, it considers the derogation from the equality principle in respect of benefits based on a discriminatory state pension age. This aspect of the chapter provides the relevant legislative background to the second issue considered here: the controversial question of the discriminatory retirement age and the discriminatory age at which occupational pensions were payable. 'Retirement age' relates to the age at which a worker retires—the upper age at which the worker stops working. Pension age is the age at which a worker is entitled to receive a pension, from the state (state pension) or the employer (occupational pension). Originally, Directive 86/378/EEC[4] was adopted to ensure equal treatment in respect of *occupational* social security benefits. However, the contents of this Directive were largely superseded by the Court's case law on sex equality in respect of occupational pensions and survivors' benefits under Article 141. The Court's complex case law has now been incorporated into the Consolidated Directive. However, we begin by examining Directive 79/7 on Equal Treatment in Social Security.

---

[1] OJ [1979] L6/24.   [2] OJ [1975] L45/19.
[3] OJ [1976] L39/40. In addition, Dir. 92/85/EEC (OJ [1992] L348/1) makes specific provision for entitlement to maternity leave and maternity benefits. These three Directives are considered in Chs. 6–9.
[4] OJ [1986] L225/40 as amended by Council Dir. 96/97 (OJ [1997] L46/20).

B. DIRECTIVE 79/7: EQUAL TREATMENT IN SOCIAL SECURITY

1. Introduction

Directive 79/7,[5] adopted alongside Directive 75/117[6] on equal pay for men and women and Directive 76/207[7] on equal treatment, formed a package of measures put forward under the 1974 Social Action Programme designed to eliminate discrimination between men and women both in the workplace and in respect of social security schemes.[8] Directive 79/7 insures only against the main employment risks of sickness, invalidity, unemployment, and old age.

2. The Material and Personal Scope of the Directive

2.1. Material Scope

According to Article 1, the purpose of Directive 79/7 is the *progressive implementation*[9] of the principle of equal treatment in matters of social security and other areas of social protection provided for in Article 3(1). These areas are:

(a) statutory schemes which provide protection against:

- sickness;
- invalidity;
- old age;
- accidents at work and occupational diseases;
- unemployment;[10] and

(b) social assistance, in so far as it is intended to supplement or replace schemes referred to in (a).

Thus the principle of equal treatment, as defined in Article 4 (see below) will

[5] Council Dir. 79/7 of 19 December 1978 on the progressive implementation of the principle of equal treatment for men and women in matters of social security (OJ [1979] L6/1). It has been in force since 23 December 1984. Member States therefore had six years to implement the Directive, the longest period ever set for a Directive (see Hoskyns, *Integrating Gender* (Verso, London, 1996), 111). Art. 5 requires Member States to take the measures necessary to abolish any laws, regulations and administrative provisions contrary to the principle of equal treatment. See Luckhaus, 'Changing Rules Enduring Structures' (1990) 53 *MLR.* 655.

[6] OJ [1975] L45/19. See further Ch. 7.   [7] OJ [1976] L39/40. See further Ch. 8.

[8] The original draft of Dir. 79/7 referred to both statutory and occupational social security schemes. During negotiations the occupational dimension was postponed to a further Directive: Dir. 86/378/EEC (OJ [1986] L225/40) as amended by Council Dir. 96/97 (OJ [1997] L46/20).

[9] The significance of this point was reiterated by the Court in Case 150/85 *Drake v. Chief Adjudication Officer* [1986] ECR 1995.

[10] Cf. the eight risks covered by Art. 4(1) of Reg. 1408/71.

only apply if the benefit is intended to protect against one of the risks listed in Article 3(1).

At first the Court adopted a generous approach to the material scope of the Directive. In *Drake*[11] the Court expanded the scope of Article 3(1) to include benefits which constitute 'the whole *or part*' of a statutory scheme providing protection against one of the specified risks, including, on the facts of the case, invalidity.

However, *Drake* now appears to be a somewhat exceptional case and the Court has since shown signs of retrenchment.[12] In *ex parte Smithson*,[13] a case concerning housing benefit which was paid to people on a low income, the Court said that, since Article 3(1)(a) did not refer to statutory schemes relating to housing costs, the British legislation fell outside the scope of the Directive because the benefit was not 'directly and effectively linked to the protection provided against one of the risks specified in Article 3(1)',[14] even though the recipient of the benefit was in one of the circumstances listed in Article 3(1). Similarly, in *Jackson and Cresswell*[15] the Court said that benefits designed to supplement the income of claimants (supplementary allowance and income support) were excluded from the scope of Directive 79/7. The Court pointed out that because the national scheme exempted claimants from being available for work this showed that the benefits in question could not be regarded as being directly and effectively linked to protection against the risk of unemployment.[16]

Thus, for the benefit to fall within the material scope of the Directive it must provide direct and effective protection against one of the risks specified in Article 3(1), rather than merely 'incidental' protection against such a risk.[17] *Atkins*[18] is an example of a case which fell on the 'incidental' protection side of the line. It concerned a concessionary travel scheme which allowed men over the age of 65 and women aged over 60 reduced fares on public transport. The Court said that this benefit was not directly and effectively linked to the protection provided against one of the risks specified in Article 3(1). The purpose of concessionary travel was to facilitate access to public transport for certain classes of persons who, for various reasons, were recognized as having a particular need for public transport and who were, for the same reasons, less well-off financially and materially. It said that although old age and invalidity were among the categories covered by Directive 79/7 they were only two of

---

[11] Case 150/85 [1986] ECR 1995. This case is considered further below.
[12] Cousins, 'Equal Treatment and Social Security' (1994) 19 *ELRev.* 123.
[13] Case 243/90 R v. *Secretary of State for Social Security, ex parte Smithson* [1992] ECR I–467.
[14] Para. 12.
[15] Joined Cases C–63/91 and 64/91 [1992] ECR I–4737. This case concerned a challenge to the national legislation which prevented child-minding expenses from being taken into account in assessing entitlement to various means-tested payments on the grounds that it indirectly discriminated against women.
[16] Para. 21. [17] White, *EC Social Security Law* (Longman, Harlow, 1999) 121.
[18] Case C–228/94 *Atkins v. Wrekin DC and Department of Transport* [1996] ECR I–3633.

the criteria which might be applied to define the classes of beneficiaries of such a scheme of concessionary fares. The fact that the recipient of the benefit happened to fall within one of the categories envisaged by Article 3(1) was not sufficient to bring the benefit within the scope of EC law. A similar argument can be made to explain why benefits designed to supplement the income of claimants (*Jackson and Cresswell*) and a child-raising allowance (*Hoever and Zachow*)[19] fell outside the scope of the Directive.[20] Since most forms of cash benefit offer protection against unemployment, that is not sufficient to bring the benefit within the scope of the Directive.

By contrast, in *ex parte Richardson*[21] the Court ruled that exemption from prescription charges fell within the scope of Article 3(1) because it provided direct and effective protection against sickness; and in *ex parte Taylor*[22] the Court ruled that a winter fuel payment directly and effectively protected against the risk of old age.

2.2. Personal Scope

The potential beneficiaries of the Directive are widely drawn by Article 2. The Directive applies to the 'working population' which covers 'self-employed persons, workers and self-employed persons whose activity is interrupted by illness, accident or involuntary unemployment and persons seeking employment—and to retired or invalided workers and self-employed persons'. A person is still a member of the working population even if one of the risks mentioned in Article 3 happens not to the worker herself but to a relative of the worker, forcing the worker to interrupt her occupational activity. This was the situation in *Drake*.[23] Mrs Drake, who had given up work to care for her invalid mother, was regarded as being a member of the working population, because her employment had been interrupted, albeit by the invalidity of another. The Court justified this conclusion by reference to the objectives of the Treaty and the Directive. It emphasized that 'there is a *clear economic link* between the benefit and the disabled person, since the disabled person derives an advantage from the fact that an allowance is paid to the person caring for him . . . the fact that a benefit . . . is paid to a third party and not directly to the disabled person does not place it outside the scope of Directive 79/7'.[24]

A person is also a member of the working population where the risk

---

[19] Joined Cases C–245/94 and C–312/94 *Hoever and Zachow* [1996] ECR I–4895.

[20] Cf. Case C–139/95 *Livia Balestra v. Istituto Nazionale della Presidenza Sociale* [1997] ECR I–549 where early retirement benefits fell within Art. 3(1) because they provide protection against the 'risk' of old age.

[21] Case C–137/94 [1995] ECR I–3633.

[22] Case C–382/98 *R v. Secretary of State for Social Security, ex parte Taylor* [1999] ECR I–8955, para. 23.

[23] Case 150/85 [1986] ECR 1995.

[24] Case 150/85 *Drake* [1986] ECR 1995. This case was the subject of a well orchestrated

materializes while the person concerned is seeking employment immediately after a period without occupational activity,[25] or where the employment in question is regarded as minor since it consists of less than 15 hours' work a week and attracts remuneration of less than one-seventh of the average monthly salary[26] or where, as in *Verholen*,[27] the individual who is not within the Article 'bears the effect' of the discriminatory treatment directed at another who does fall within the scope of Article 2.

On the other hand, the Court said, the Directive does not apply to people who are not working and are not seeking work or to people whose occupation or efforts to find work were not interrupted by one of the risks referred to in Article 3 of the Directive.[28] Therefore, in *Achterberg-te Riele* the Court held that a person who has given up his or her occupational activity to bring up their children did not fall within the scope of the Directive.[29] This point was confirmed in *Züchner*[30] where the Court ruled that Article 2 of Directive 79/7/EEC did not cover a woman who was not 'economically active' (neither in paid employment, nor seeking work, nor whose employment was interrupted by one of the risks listed in Article 3 of the Directive) who undertook the unpaid care of her invalid husband, even though she had to undertake special training to care for him properly.

In the light of *Verholen*, *Züchner* seems particularly harsh. It also takes no account of the social circumstances in which women's relationship with the paid employment market and social security systems is constituted.[31] If Mrs Züchner's husband had had no relative to care for him, the caring work would have been remunerated, either privately or by the state through its social security provision. Yet it seems that the caring work carried out by

---

campaign led by the ICA. See further Luckhaus, 'Payment for Caring: A European Solution' [1986] *PL*. 526, who suggests that the Court was motivated by its desire to condemn such unabashed discrimination and so engaged in 'some well meaning subterfuge' in order to extend the reach of Community law into the realm of domestic unpaid work. See also Case C–343/92 *De Weerd, née Roks and Others* v. *Bestuur van de Bedrijfsverenigning voor de Gezondheid* [1994] ECR I–571.

[25] Case C–31/90 *Johnson (No. 1)* v. *Chief Adjudication Officer* [1991] ECR I–3723. The onus of proof is on the applicant to show that they were seeking work in these circumstances. This is a matter for the national court to decide, taking into account such factors as whether a person was registered with an employment organization, whether they had sent out job applications and whether they could produce certificates to show that they had attended interviews.

[26] Case C–317/93 *Nolte* v. *Landversicherungsanstalt Hannover* [1995] ECR I–4625 and Case C–444/93 *Megner and Scheffel* v. *Innungskrankenkasse Vorderpfalz* [1995] ECR I–4741. See also Case C–280/94 *Posthuma-van Damme* v. *Bestuur van de Bedrijfsvereniging voor Detailhandel* [1996] ECR I–179.

[27] Joined Cases C–87/90, 88/90 and 89/90 *Verholen* v. *Verzekeringsbank Amsterdam* [1991] ECR I–3757. Cf. Case C–77/95 *Bruna-Alessandra Züchner* v. *Handelskrankenkasse (Ersatzkasse) Bremen* [1996] ECR I–5689, and Waddington (1997) 22 *ELRev*. 587.

[28] Case 48/88 *Achterberg-te Riele and Others* v. *Sociale Verzekeringsbank* [1989] ECR 1963.

[29] Case C–31/90 *Johnson (No. 1)* [1991] ECR I–3723.

[30] Case C–77/95 [1996] ECR I–5689.

[31] Sohrab, *Sexing the Benefit: Women, Social Security and Financial Independence in EC Sex Equality Law* (Dartmouth, Aldershot, 1996).

women on a private basis is not characterized by EC law as 'work' and therefore falls outside the scope of EC sex equality provisions. In reaching its conclusion in *Züchner* the Court seems to have been concerned with limiting the scope of Directive 79/7. To have extended the application of the Directive to women such as Mrs Züchner would, as the Court put it, 'have the effect of infinitely extending the scope of the directive'.[32] Such an extension might threaten severe disruption of national social security systems, whose conceptual (and financial) basis is the protection of economically active persons, whose employment is interrupted by a risk against which the social security system provides protection.

3. The Principle of Equal Treatment

3.1. Direct and Indirect Discrimination

Article 4(1) gives concrete expression to the principle of equal treatment set out in Article 1.[33] It provides that:

... there shall be no discrimination whatsoever on the ground of sex either directly, or indirectly, by reference in particular to marital or family status,[34] in particular, as concerns:

— the scope of the schemes and the conditions of access thereto;
— the obligation to contribute and the calculation of the contributions;
— the calculations of benefits including increases[35] due in respect of a spouse[36] and for dependants[37] and the conditions governing the duration and retention of entitlements to benefits.[38]

The 'fundamental' principle of equal treatment was recognized in *Drake*.[39] Under British law an Invalid Care Allowance (ICA) was not payable to a married woman who lived with her husband although it was payable in

---

[32] Para. 15.   [33] Case 150/85 *Drake* [1986] ECR 1995.
[34] This definition closely mirrors that found in the Equal Treatment Directive 76/207. The reference to 'marital status' is particularly important because the national social security systems of the Member States are in general based on the model of the family unit, consisting of one breadwinner (male), one adult dependant (female) and dependent children. This model is prone to discrimination against the female sex.
[35] Member States are entitled to stipulate whatever increases they wish for entitlement to increases in social security benefits, provided they comply fully with the principle of equal treatment laid down in Art. 4(1): Case C–377/89 *Cotter and Others* v. *Minister for Social Welfare* [1991] ECR I–1155.
[36] Spouses do not need to be dependent (Case C–377/89 *Cotter and Others* [1991] ECR I–1155).
[37] No proof of their dependency is actually required under the Directive as a prior condition of the application of the principle of equal treatment (Case C–377/89 *Cotter and Others* [1991] ECR I–1155).
[38] Art. 4(1). Art. 4(2) contains an exclusion for provisions relating to the protection of women on the grounds of maternity.
[39] Case 150/85 [1986] ECR 1995.

corresponding circumstances to a man. The Court found that this legislation was directly discriminatory and contravened Articles 1 and 4(1).[40] In *FNV*[41] the Court said that Article 4(1) was sufficiently precise and unconditional to be directly effective.[42] Together, these decisions paved the way to challenge a wide variety of national legislation which discriminated either directly or indirectly, usually against women.

For example, in *Borrie Clarke*[43] the Court held that Article 4(1) did not permit Member States to make conditional or to limit the application of the principle of equal treatment, nor did it allow Member States to maintain beyond 22 December 1984 (the deadline for implementing the Directive) any inequalities of treatment which had their origin in the fact that conditions of entitlement to the benefit were those which applied before that date. *Borrie Clarke* concerned Severe Disablement Allowance (SDA), introduced to replace the discriminatory Non-Contributory Invalidity Pension (NCIP). In order to receive NCIP the household duties test was applied to women but not men. This test asked whether the woman was capable of performing 'normal household duties'. Under the transitional provisions, automatic entitlement to the SDA was subject to the same discriminatory criteria as for NCIP (i.e. the household duties test). The Court found that women were entitled to be treated in the same manner and to have the same rules applied to them as men.[44] Therefore, since a man was automatically entitled to the new SDA, a woman should also receive the new benefit automatically.

Relying on the decision in *Borrie Clarke*, Mrs Johnson also claimed SDA.[45] She gave up work to look after her daughter in 1970. By 1980 she wished to return to work but, since she was unable to do so due to a back condition, she received NCIP. However, this payment was stopped when Mrs Johnson began to cohabit because she was considered capable of performing normal household duties. Mrs Johnson applied for SDA on the basis that she would

[40] E.g. Case C–337/91 *A. M. van Gemert-Derks* v. *Bestuur van de Nieuwe Industri'le Bedrijfs-vereniging* [1993] ECR I–5435.

[41] Case 71/85 *Netherlands* v. *Federatie Nederlandse Vakbeweging* [1986] ECR 3855.

[42] The derogations contained in Arts. 5 and 7 of the Directive do not confer on the Member States the power to make conditional or limit the application of the principle of equal treatment and thus do not prevent Art. 4(1) from having direct effect. See Arnull (1987) 12 *ELRev.* 276. The fact that Art. 4(1) is directly effective (and has been since 23 December 1984) has been endorsed by the Court in numerous cases including Case 150/85 *Drake* [1986] ECR 1995, Case 286/85 *McDermott and Cotter* v. *Minister for Social Welfare and Attorney General* [1987] ECR 1453 and Case 384/85 *J. B. Clarke* v. *Chief Adjudication Officer* [1987] ECR 2865. Member States can belatedly introduce legislation and make it retroactive to the date when implementation was required, see Case 80/87 *Dik and Mencutos-Demirci* v. *College van Burgermeester en Wethouders Arnhem and Winterswijk* [1988] ECR 1601.

[43] Case C–384/85 [1987] ECR 2865.

[44] The Court applied *Borrie Clark* in another case concerning discriminatory transitional provisions, Case 80/87 *Dik and Mencutos-Demirci* [1988] ECR 1601, which in turn was applied in Case C–377/89 *Cotter and Others* [1991] ECR I–1155. See also Case 286/85 *McDermott and Cotter* [1987] ECR 1453 and Case C–154/92 *Van Cant* v. *Rijksdienst voor Pensionenen* [1993] ECR I–3811.

[45] Case C–31/90 *Johnson (No. 1)* [1991] ECR I–3723, noted by Laske (1992) *CMLRev.* 101.

have been entitled to the NCIP immediately prior to the abolition of the benefit, had the discriminatory household duties test not been applied to her in 1980. The Court supported her arguments, concluding that national legislation making entitlement to a benefit, such as the SDA, subject to an earlier claim for a benefit which incorporated a discriminatory requirement was incompatible with Article 4(1) of Directive 79/7. The national legislation therefore had to be set aside. Similarly, in *Cotter and Others*[46] the Court ruled that if married men have automatically received increases in social security benefits in respect of a spouse and children deemed to be dependants without having to prove actual dependency, married women without actual dependants were also entitled to those increases, even if in some circumstances that would result in double payment of the increases.

While many of the cases concern discrimination against women, *Integrity*[47] is an example of a case of discrimination against men. Belgian law provided a possibility for married women and widows to be exempted from having to make social security contributions without granting the same possibility to married men or widowers who otherwise satisfied the same conditions. The Court said this rule contravened Article 4(1).[48] *Richards*,[49] on the other hand, is a case about discrimination on the grounds of gender reassignment. Richards, born a man, underwent gender reassignment. In the UK, women receive their state pension at 60, men at 65. When Ms Richards applied for a pension at 60 she was turned down on the grounds that the law, at that time, considered her still to be a man and so she was not entitled to receive a pension until she was 65. The Court ruled that this unequal treatment arose from her gender reassignment and so was regarded as discrimination contrary to Article 4(1).[50]

The cases considered so far concern legislation which was directly discriminatory. *Teuling*[51] confirms that Article 4(1) also outlaws indirectly discriminatory measures, that is, measures which although formulated in neutral terms, work to the disadvantage of far more women than men,[52] unless they can be objectively justified. *Teuling* concerned a system of benefits where

---

[46] Case C–377/89 [1991] ECR I–1155. See also Case C–338/91 *Steenhorst-Neerings* v. *Bestuur van de Bedrijfsvereniging* [1993] ECR I–5475 where a national law deprived women of benefits which men continued to receive, even though the national court applied the law in a non-discriminatory manner; see also Case C–187/98 *Commission* v. *Greece* [1999] ECR I–7713.

[47] Case C–373/89 *Caisse d'assurances sociales pour travailleurs independents 'Integrity'* v. *Rouvroy* [1990] ECR I–4243.

[48] Para. 15.

[49] Case C–423/04 *Richards* v. *Secretary of State for Work and Pensions* [2006] ECR I–000. See also *Grant* v. *UK* (Application no.32570/03), judgment of 23 May 2006 where the European Court of Human Rights ruled that denying the state pension at age 60 from a male to female transsexual was a breach of the right to respect for private life contrary to Art. 8 ECHR.

[50] Para. 30.

[51] Case 30/85 *Teuling* v. *Bedrijfsvereniging voor de Chemische Industrie* [1987] ECR 2497.

[52] Case C–343/92 *De Weerd* [1994] ECR I–571, para. 33, and Case C–229/89 *Commission* v.

supplements were provided which, although not directly based on the sex of the beneficiaries, took account of their marital status or family situation. It became apparent that a considerably smaller number of women than men were entitled to such supplements and that the scheme was therefore indirectly discriminatory and contrary to Article 4(1), unless the system could be justified on grounds other than sex. The Court, however, accepted the justification that the system sought to ensure an adequate minimum subsistence income for beneficiaries who had a dependent spouse or dependent children, by means of a supplement to the social security benefit which compensated for the greater burdens they had to bear in comparison with single people.

This approach was confirmed in *Ruzius Wilbrink*.[53] This case concerned Dutch legislation providing disability allowances to workers which were lower for part-time workers than for full-time workers. The Court found, first, that such a provision was indirectly discriminatory against female workers, and secondly, that the discrimination could not be objectively justified. The Court therefore concluded that since in the case of direct discrimination women were entitled to be treated in the same manner as men, so part-time workers had to be treated in the same way as full-timers in the case of indirect discrimination (a levelling up of benefit), because such rules relating to full-timers remained the only valid point of reference so long as the Directive had not been implemented correctly.[54]

3.2. Objective Justification

The question of objective justification was considered further in *De Weerd*.[55] The case concerned national legislation making receipt of a benefit for incapacity for work subject to the requirement of having received a certain income from or in connection with work in the year preceding the commencement of the incapacity. That requirement was indirectly discriminatory because it affected more women than men and therefore breached Article 4(1), 'unless that measure is based on objectively justified factors unrelated to any discrimination on grounds of sex' (para. 33).[56] The Court continued, 'That is the case where the measures chosen reflect a legitimate social policy aim of the Member State whose legislation is at issue, are appropriate to achieve that aim and are necessary in order to do so' (para. 34).[57] Budgetary

---

Belgium [1991] ECR I–2205, para. 13. See generally Steiner, 'The Principle of Equal Treatment for Men and Women in Social Security', in Hervey and O'Keeffe (eds), *Sex Equality Law in the European Union* (Wiley, London, 1996).

[53] Case C–102/88 *Ruzius-Wilbrink* v. *Bedrijfsvereniging voor Overheidsdiensten* [1989] ECR 4311.

[54] Para. 16.   [55] Case C–343/92 [1994] ECR I–571.

[56] Para. 33, citing Case C–229/89 *Commission* v. *Belgium* [1991] ECR I–2205.

[57] This follows Case 171/88 *Rinner-Kühn* v. *FWW Spezial-Gebäudereinigung GmbH* [1989] ECR 2743, para. 14, concerning legislation which was prima facie indirectly discriminatory

considerations did not, however, justify a difference in treatment. As the Court said, '[A]lthough budgetary considerations may influence a Member State's choice of social policy and affect the nature or scope of the social protection measures it wishes to adopt, they cannot themselves constitute the aim pursued by that policy and cannot therefore justify discrimination against one of the sexes'. However, the Court did say that Community law did not prevent budgetary constraints being taken into account when making the continuance of entitlement to social security benefit dependent on certain conditions, the effect of which was to withdraw benefits from certain categories of people, provided that when they did so they did not infringe the rule of equal treatment laid down in Article 4(1).[58]

In *Nolte*[59] and *Megner and Scheffel*[60] the Court relaxed the rigorous test for objective justification laid down in *De Weerd*. These cases concerned a German social security law under which individuals working fewer than 15 hours per week and whose income did not exceed one-seventh of the monthly reference wage[61] ('minor' or 'marginal' part-time workers) were not subject to the statutory old-age insurance scheme and were also exempt from paying contributions for unemployment benefit. Although the legislation affected considerably more women that men, the German government argued that the exclusion of persons in minor employment corresponded to a structural principle of the German social security scheme. Having cited the test contained in paragraphs 33 and 34 of the judgment in *De Weerd* (see above), the Court then said that in the current state of Community law, social policy was a matter for the Member States.[62] Consequently, it was for the Member States to choose the measures capable of achieving the aim of their social and employment policy. In exercising that competence Member States had a broad margin of discretion. It then said:

It should be noted that the social and employment policy aim relied on by the German government is objectively unrelated to any discrimination on the grounds of sex and

contrary to Art. 141. In Case C–226/91 *Molenbroeck* v. *Sociale Verzekeringsbank* [1992] ECR I–5943 the Court emphasized 'the reasonable margin of discretion' allowed to Member States as to the nature of the social protection measures and the detailed arrangements for their implementation.

[58] Para. 29.

[59] Case C–317/93 [1995] ECR I–4625. See generally Hervey, 'Sex Equality in Social Protection: New Institutional Perspectives on Allocation of Competence' (1998) 4 *ELJ*. 196.

[60] Case C–444/93 [1995] ECR I–4741.

[61] The average monthly salary of persons insured under the statutory old-age insurance scheme during the previous calendar year.

[62] This point was made clearly by the Court in Case C–343/92 *De Weerd* [1994] ECR I–571, para. 28: 'Directive 79/7 leaves intact, however, the powers reserved by Articles 117 and 118 [new Arts. 136 and 140] of the Treaty to the Member States to define their social policy within the framework of close co-operation organised by the Commission, and consequently the nature and extent of the measures of social protection, including those relating to social security and the way in which they are implemented', citing Case C–229/89 *Commission* v. *Belgium* [1991] ECR I–2205. The point was again repeated in Case C–280/94 *Posthuma-van Damme* [1996] ECR I–179, para. 26.

that, in exercising its competence, the national legislature was *reasonably entitled* to consider that the legislation in question was necessary in order to achieve that aim. [Emphasis added]

It therefore said that the legislation could not be described as indirectly discriminatory within the meaning of Article 4(1).[63] Thus, in the context of social security at least, a weaker test of objective justification applies than is applied in respect of employment.[64]

The weaker test of justification was applied again in *Laperre*.[65] The case concerned the conditions of access (previous employment, age, and incapacity) to a non-means-tested social security benefit, the IOAW, which Mrs Laperre argued gave rise to indirect sex discrimination. Another scheme, the RWW, also provided a minimum income but was subject to a means test. The Netherlands government said that while the RWW aimed to bring the unemployed back to work by providing income for those of 'modest assets', the IOAW was not means-tested because the legislature sought to protect potential beneficiaries from having to break into their life savings given that they had little chance of rebuilding their assets by resuming gainful employment. The Court said that the aim relied on by the Dutch government was a matter of social policy, that it was objectively unrelated to any discrimination on the grounds of sex and that, in exercising their competence, the national legislature was reasonably entitled to consider that the legislation in question was necessary in order to achieve that aim.[66]

The Court showed the same deference to the national system in *Posthuma-van Damme*.[67] In that case the Court was asked to consider whether its judgment in *De Weerd* meant that the national law could not be justified at all or only that it could not be justified on budgetary grounds. The Court confirmed the latter interpretation. It also accepted the Dutch government's arguments that guaranteeing a minimum income to people who had given up work on the grounds of incapacity satisfied a legitimate aim of social policy. It also agreed that imposing conditions on access to the benefit constituted a measure appropriate to achieve the objective which the national legislature, in the exercise of its competence, was reasonably entitled to consider necessary. The

---

[63] Case C–317/93 *Nolte* [1995] ECR I–4625, paras. 34 and 35; Case C–444/93 *Megner and Scheffel* [1995] ECR I–571, paras. 30 and 31.

[64] See also the discussion of this subject in Ch. 7.

[65] Case C–8/94 *Laperre v. Bestuurcommissie beroepszaken in de provincie Zuid-Holland* [1996] ECR I–273.

[66] Although the Court was not provided with a detailed explanation of the employment conditions at issue, Advocate General Lenz was prepared to assume that the condition relating to employment operated to the disadvantage of women whose employment histories often had long gaps because of their need to fulfil their family obligations. Nevertheless, he accepted that the provisions were not contrary to Community law because Dutch law was entitled to offer specific protection to those who had maintained themselves from earned income over a long period.

[67] Case C–280/94 [1996] ECR I–179.

fact that the scheme replaced a scheme of pure national insurance and that the number of people who actually benefited was further reduced did not affect the finding. This case, more than any other, sounded the death knell to the rigorous approach adopted in *De Weerd*.

4. Exceptions and Derogations

Directive 79/7 contains permanent exceptions and temporary, 'permissive' derogations. Into the first category fall survivors' benefits, family benefits,[68] occupational pension schemes,[69] and provisions relating to the protection of women on the grounds of maternity.[70] Into the second category fall the derogations found in Article 7. Member States have the right to exclude from the scope of the Directive a long list of benefits,[71] the most significant of which is Article 7(1)(a), the determination of pensionable age for the purposes of granting old-age and retirement benefits, and the possible consequences for other benefits.[72] In respect of all derogations, the basic rule applies: that derogations are narrowly construed.[73]

4.1. Article 7(1)(a) on the Determination of Pensionable Age for Granting Old-age and Retirement Benefits

According to Article 7(1)(a), the Directive is without prejudice to the right of Member States to exclude from its scope the determination of pensionable age

---

[68] Art. 3(2).

[69] Art. 3(3). See now Dir. 86/378 (OJ [1986] L225/40) on equal treatment in occupational social security as amended by Council Dir. 96/97/EC (OJ [1997] L46/20).

[70] Art. 4(2).

[71] The other exclusions relate to entitlements granted to those who have brought up children, derived entitlements of a wife, and the exercise of a right of option not to acquire rights or incur obligations under a statutory scheme. See further Atkins, 'The EEC Directive on Equal Treatment in Social Security Benefits' (1978–79) 1 *JSWL*. 244.

[72] Art. 7(1), discussed further below. Member States must periodically examine matters excluded under Art. 7(1) in order to ascertain whether there is justification for maintaining the particular exclusion (Art. 7(2)). Art. 8(2) obliges the Member State to notify the Commission of the reasons for maintaining the derogation under Art. 7(2). A Directive on the Implementation of the Principle of Equal Treatment for Men and Women in Statutory and Occupational Social Security Schemes was proposed (OJ [1988] C95/4), designed to fill the gaps left by Directives 79/7 and 86/378, although its purpose may have been overtaken in part by decisions of the Court. It extends the principle of equal treatment to the areas previously excluded by the earlier Directives, esp. pensionable age in both statutory and occupational schemes. Art. 9 proposes two alternatives for achieving this objective: the first involves selecting a uniform age for men and women but with safeguards for those who have already reached a certain age close to retirement; the second envisages flexible retirement, allowing workers to choose their retirement age during a specified period, provided that the conditions, esp. with regard to the number of contribution years, are identical for both sexes.

[73] See e.g., Case C-423/04 *Richards v. Sereatry of State for Work and Pensions* [2006] ECR I-000, para. 36.

for the purposes of (1) granting old-age and retirement pensions, and (2) the possible consequences for other benefits which, the Court has added, are 'necessarily and objectively linked to the difference in pensionable age'. However, in view of the fundamental importance of the principle of equal treatment, the exception to the prohibition of discrimination on the grounds of sex has to be interpreted strictly.[74]

(a) Discrimination for the Purposes of Granting Old-age and Retirement Benefits

The first part of Article 7(1)(a) was at issue in *ex parte EOC*[75] where it was argued that the British state pension scheme, which allowed women to receive their state pension at 60, while men had to wait until 65, unlawfully discriminated against men in two ways. First, it required men to pay contributions for 44 years to qualify for the same basic retirement pension as women who had contributed for only 39 years. The corollary of this was that a man who had made contributions for 39 years received a lower basic pension than a woman who had contributed for 39 years. Secondly, men working between the ages of 60 and 64 had to pay contributions but women in the same situation did not.

According to the Court, the purpose of the Directive was to achieve *progressive* implementation of the principle of equal treatment in social security. The progressive nature of the implementation was reflected in the number of derogations. The purpose of the derogations, allowing Member States to maintain temporarily advantageous treatment of women in the field of state pensions, was to enable Member States 'progressively to adapt their pension systems [towards equality] without disrupting the complex financial equilibrium of those systems'. Therefore, the Court said that any derogation under Article 7(1)(a) would be rendered nugatory if it did not apply to contribution periods, such as those in *ex parte EOC*, as well as at the moment at which they become entitled to a pension. If the derogation did not apply, Member States would be obliged to alter the existing financial equilibrium substantially.

(b) Discrimination in respect of other Benefits Objectively Linked to Old-age and Retirement Benefits

The second part of Article 7(1)(a) provides that sex discrimination is still permitted in respect of other benefits which, the Court has added, are 'necessarily and objectively linked to the difference in pensionable age'. That will be the case where the discrimination is necessary (a) to avoid disturbing the

---

[74] Case C–328/91 *Secretary of State for Social Security* v. *Thomas and Others* [1993] ECR I–1247.
[75] Case C–9/91 R v. *Secretary of State for Social Security, ex parte Equal Opportunities Commission* [1992] ECR I–4297.

financial equilibrium of the social-security system or (b) to ensure coherence between the retirement pension scheme and other benefit schemes.[76]

Graham[77] illustrates how the Court will approach the question of whether the benefit is 'necessarily and objectively linked to the difference in pensionable age'. The case concerned two benefits, an invalidity pension and an invalidity allowance. The first part of Graham's claim related to the *invalidity pension*. Graham had to stop working before reaching pensionable age due to ill health. Initially she received sickness benefit and then invalidity pension at the full retirement pension rate. When she reached pensionable age (65 for men, 60 for women) she opted to continue receiving the invalidity pension, which was not taxable, rather than a retirement pension which was taxable. As she had not fulfilled the contribution conditions for the grant of a full retirement pension, the amount of her invalidity pension was reduced to the rate of the retirement pension which would have been paid to her. Had Graham been a man, she would have continued to receive the invalidity pension at the full retirement pension rate until she was 65 and only then would a reduction have been made to reflect the number of years that she had paid contributions.

Graham also complained about the discriminatory effect of the *invalidity allowance* which was paid in addition to the invalidity pension to a person who was more than five years below pensionable age on the first day of incapacity for work. Mrs Graham, who was aged over 55 when she became incapacitated for work, was refused invalidity allowance. Had she been a man she would have received the payment.

The Court found that the forms of discrimination at issue were objectively linked to the setting of different pensionable ages for men and women. It said that since invalidity benefit was designed to replace income from an occupational activity there was nothing to prevent a Member State from providing for its cessation and replacement by a retirement pension at the time when the recipients would have stopped work because they had reached pensionable age.[78] The Court continued that to prohibit a Member State which has set different pensionable ages from limiting, in the case of individuals becoming incapacitated for work before reaching pensionable age, the rate of invalidity benefit payable to them from that age to the actual rate of the retirement pension to which they were entitled under the retirement pension scheme would mean restricting the very right enjoyed by the UK under Article 7(1)(a) of Directive 79/7 to set different pensionable ages.

The Court added that such a prohibition would also undermine the

---

[76] Case C–92/94 *Secretary of State for Social Security and Chief Adjudication Officer* v. *Graham and Others* [1995] ECR I–2521, para. 11, and Case C–139/95 *Balestra* v. *INPS* [1997] ECR I–549, para. 33.
[77] Case C–92/94 *Secretary of State for Social Security* v. *Graham* [1995] ECR I–2521.
[78] Para. 14.

coherence between the retirement pension scheme and the invalidity benefit scheme because, first, the UK would be prevented from granting to men who became incapacitated for work before reaching pensionable age invalidity benefits greater than the retirement pensions which would actually have been payable to them if they had continued to work until reaching pensionable age unless it granted to women over pensionable age retirement pensions greater than those actually payable to them; and secondly, if women did not have their invalidity pension reduced to the level of their retirement pension until they reached the age of 65, as in the case of men, women aged between 60 and 65, thus over pensionable age, would receive an invalidity pension at the rate of a full retirement pension if their incapacity for work commenced before they reached pensionable age and a retirement pension corresponding to the rate actually payable if it did not. Consequently, the Court ruled that the derogation in Article 7(1)(a) applied to the differences between the rates of invalidity pension payable to men and women from the time when they reached pensionable age.

The Court added that, due to the link between invalidity pension and invalidity allowance, the same conclusion applied with regard to the difference between the qualifying dates for the grant of invalidity allowance.

The Court will check to see if the defendant state can make the necessary link. For example, in *Buchner*[79] the Court said that the Austrian government had failed to make out the case that the link between, in that case, the early old-age pension on account of incapacity for work and the old-age pension was necessary to preserve coherence between the two. The Court pointed out that there was no precise relationship between the minimum qualifying age for the early old-age pension on account of incapacity for work and the statutory retirement age (55 for women, five years before the statutory retirement age, and 57 for men, eight years before the statutory retirement age) and that this difference in the age condition was introduced essentially for budgetary reasons. Therefore the discrimination was not covered by Article 7(1)(a) of Directive 79/7.

Cases involving non-contributory benefits are unlikely to satisfy the requirement of the need to avoid disturbing the financial equilibrium of the social security system. For example, *Thomas*[80] concerned the refusal under British law to grant severe disablement allowance and invalid care allowance to those who had reached state pensionable age. The Court suggested that discrimination between men and women under such *non-contributory* schemes was unnecessary to preserve the financial equilibrium of the entire social security system and therefore Article 7(1)(a) could not be invoked. Similarly, in *ex parte Richardson*[81] a retired man of 64 claimed that he was discriminated

---

[79] Case C–104/98 *Buchner v. Soxialversicherungsanstalt der Bauern* [200] ECR I–3625.
[80] Case C–328/91 *Secretary of State for Social Security v. Thomas and Others* [1993] ECR I–1247.
[81] Case C–137/94 [1995] ECR I–3633.

against on the grounds of his sex by national legislation which exempted women, but not men, aged between 60 and 64 from paying prescription charges. The Court agreed. It said that Article 7(1)(a) did not apply to the rules on prescription charges since the removal of the discrimination would not affect the financial equilibrium of the pension scheme and that the discrimination was not objectively necessary to ensure coherence between the retirement pension system and regulations concerning prescription charges.[82] And again in *ex parte Taylor*[83] the Court said that arguments concerning financial equilibrium did not apply to other non-contributory benefits, such as a winter fuel payment. Consequently eliminating discrimination had no impact on the financial equilibrium of the social security scheme as a whole and so was not covered by the Article 7(1)(a) derogation.

In cases which do not involve non-contributory schemes, the Court will scrutinize any claim about the serious effect on the financial equilibrium of the scheme with care. Thus, in *Haackert*,[84] a case with rather similar facts to *Graham*, the Court said that the percentage of early old-age pensions on account of unemployment paid in relation to the total of old-age pensions represented barely 1.2 per cent. The Court therefore concluded that the removal of such discrimination could not have any serious effect on the financial equilibrium of social security system.[85] However, on the facts, the Court found that the discrimination could be justified on the grounds of preserving coherence between early old-age pensions on account of unemployment and the old-age pension.[86]

(c) Transitional Arrangements

Can Member States continue to rely on Article 7(1)(a) when they are in the process of removing discrimination in state pension ages? This was the issue in *Van Cant*.[87] From 1991 Belgian law allowed both men and women to receive their state pension from age 60, but it maintained a different method

---

[82] In Case C–228/94 *Atkins* [1996] ECR I–3633 (reduced fares on public transport) the Advocate General urged the Court to follow *ex parte Richardson* rather than *Graham*. He said that the scheme fell within the material scope of the Directive, and that the derogation contained in Art. 7(1)(a) did not apply since the travel concessions had no connection with the extent of entitlement to an old-age pension or with the overall financing of the pensions system. To remove the discrimination would not, he said, affect the financial equilibrium of the pensions scheme. However, as we saw above, the Court decided that the case fell outside the material scope of the Directive.

[83] Case C–382/98 [1999] ECR I–8955, paras. 30–1.

[84] See also Case C–303/02 *Haackert v. Pensionsversicherungsanstalt der Angestellten* [2004] ECR I–2195 concerning the discriminatory ages at which a Belgian early old-age pension on account of unemployment was paid which was 'objectively necessary in order to ensure coherence between early old-age pension on account of unemployment and the old-age pension' (para. 37).

[85] See also Case C–104/98 *Buchner v. Soxialversicherungsanstalt der Bauern* [200] ECR I–3625, para. 30.

[86] See also Case C–196/98 *Hepple v. Adjudication Officer* [2000] ECR I–3701.

[87] Case C–154/92 [1993] ECR I–3811.

of calculating the pension for each sex. The Court ruled that this was discriminatory contrary to Article 4(1) of the Directive and could not be justified
under Article 7(1)(a). It said that once the national system took the step
of abolishing the difference in state pensionable ages Article 7(1)(a) could
no longer be relied on to justify maintaining a difference in the method of
calculating the retirement pension which was linked to the difference in
retirement ages.

This decision in *Van Cant* seemed to allow no scope for (necessary) transitional arrangements which may incorporate the discriminatory features of
the earlier scheme. Paradoxically, had the Belgian government maintained
different state pension ages it could have continued to rely on Article 7(1)(a)
in respect of the method of calculating the pension.[88] There was some dispute
in *Van Cant* as to whether the national law had in fact maintained different
pensionable ages. The Court ruled that this was a matter for the national
court to decide, but because different Belgian courts had reached different
conclusions on this question, an interpretative law was passed which indicated that the different pensionable ages had not been removed.[89]

The consequences of these developments were at issue in *De Vriendt*[90] and
Wolfs.[91] The references in these cases concerned the new Belgian law establishing a flexible retirement age for men and women, which allows all workers
to retire 'early' at age 60 during a transitional period. The amount of pension
paid was accrued on an annual basis and calculated based on a proportion of
the worker's remuneration for that year. For men the highest number of years
taken into account to determine the pension was 45, but only 40 for women.
If a worker worked longer than this, the most advantageous 45 or 40 years
were used as the basis for the calculation of the pension. Even under the new
system, for men the relevant proportion of salary was one-forty-fifth, but for
women it was one-fortieth of salary. A number of Belgian men applied for
their pensions to be calculated on the basis of fortieths of salary, rather than
forty-fifths. Subsequent amendments to, and implementations of, Belgian law
were to the effect that for men, pensionable age was to be 65 and pension
calculated in forty-fifths; for women, pensionable age was to be progressively
raised to 65 over a transitional period of 13 years, and the rate of pension was
to be progressively raised over that period. The flexible retirement age was to
be maintained, allowing both men and women to take their pension 'early' at
60, if they met an employment-record entitlement. The employment-record
entitlement was to be 20 years in 1997, and to be progressively raised to
35 years in 2005. The question arose as to whether these provisions were
compatible with Community law.

---

[88] Rubinstein [1994] IRLR 1.   [89] White, above, n. 17, 125.
[90] Joined Cases C–377–384/96 *De Vriendt and Others* v. *Rijksdienst voor Pensioen* [1998] ECR
I–2105.
[91] Case C–154/96 *Wolfs* v. *Office national des pensions* [1998] ECR I–6173.

Once again, the Court repeated its test whether the rules in question were 'necessarily and objectively linked' to the difference in state pensionable age. The national court was to determine, as an issue of fact, whether the national legislation maintained a different pensionable age for men and women. If there was a difference, then 'the specification of the age for the award of a retirement pension effectively determines the length of the period during which persons can contribute to the pension scheme'.[92] In such a case, the method of calculating pensions would be necessarily and objectively linked to the pensionable age difference. Thus, if national legislation had maintained a different pensionable age for male and female workers, the Member State could calculate the amount of pension differently depending on the worker's sex. Differences in state pensionable ages could lawfully be maintained under Article 7(1)(a) to 'enable [Member States] progressively to adapt their pension systems in this respect without disrupting the complex financial equilibrium of those systems'.[93] Thus the principle established in *Van Cant* did not apply to transitional arrangements. The effect of these rulings was to leave it to the national court to decide whether the net effect of the Belgian legislation was to equalize state pensionable age. If it was not, then the different mechanisms for calculation were lawful, within Article 7(1)(a).

(d) Levelling Up or Down?

This litigation raises a variation on the long-standing debate about whether Community sex equality law requires 'levelling up' of benefits, or pay, or treatment, to the level of the better treated sex, or whether it is permissible to achieve formal equality between men and women by 'levelling down' benefits to those enjoyed by the worse treated sex.[94] The Court's case law makes it clear that nothing in Directive 79/7 requires equalization of state pensionable ages by levelling up. This of course leaves maximum discretion for Member States in this sensitive area of national social policy. The Court's rulings also make clear that Community law implies no specific duty on Member States to undertake the equalization process in any particular way. This conclusion is problematic, as the economics of the situation mean that any equalization is bound to take time. Provision must be made for interim or transitional period, often of several years or even decades. On the Court's interpretation in *De Vriendt* and *Wolfs*, Directive 79/7 seems to leave Member States with full discretion even during that period. This is, at the least, a rather minimalist approach to the duties imposed by Directive 79/7.[95]

---

[92] Joined Cases C–377–384/96 *De Vriendt* [1998] ECR I–2105, para. 29.
[93] Case C–154/96 *Wolfs* [1998] ECR I–6173, para. 25.   [94] See below, n. 211–16.
[95] Barnard and Hervey, 'European Union Employment and Social Policy Survey 1998' (1998) *YEL*. 613, 649–51.

4.2. Other Derogations

Article 7(1) provides other grounds for derogating from the Directive. For example, Article 7(1)(c) allows Member States to exclude from the scope of the Directive the granting of entitlement to old-age benefits by virtue of the derived entitlement of a spouse. Therefore, in *Van Munster*[96] the Court said Directive 79/7 permitted a Member State not to apply to a retired person's pension the 'household rate', which took account of the position of both the retired person and his dependent spouse, where the spouse was entitled to a retirement pension in his or her own right.[97]

Article 7(1)(d) allows Member States to exclude from the scope of the Directive the granting of increases of long-term invalidity benefits, old-age benefits, accidents at work and occupational disease benefits for a dependent wife. This exception was successfully relied on by the UK in *Bramhill*.[98] The UK had abolished discrimination in respect of the rules relating to increases in long-term old-age benefits but only for certain categories of women. The Court said that the retention of the discriminatory rules in respect of the women not benefiting from the changed rules fell within the scope of Article 7(1)(d).

5. Remedies

5.1. Adequacy of Compensation

Article 6 of Directive 79/7 repeats almost verbatim the requirement laid down in the original Article 6 of the Equal Treatment Directive 76/207 for complainants to have the right to pursue their claims by judicial process.[99] The parallels between the two Directives, and especially in the content of the remedies provisions, led many to think that the Court would interpret Article 6 similarly in both cases. Therefore, the decision in *ex parte Sutton*,[100] a Directive 79/7 case, delivered on the same day as *Draehmpaehl*,[101] a Directive 76/207 case, came as a surprise, and marked a departure from the emphasis on effective protection laid down in *Von Colson*[102] and *Marshall (No. 2)*[103] in the context of Directive 76/207. In *Sutton*, a question was raised concerning the payment of interest on arrears of a social security benefit, invalid care

---

[96] Case C–165/91 *Van Munster v. Rijksdienst voor Pensionen* [1994] ECR I–4661.
[97] Para. 17.   [98] Case C–420/92 *Bramhill v. Chief Adjudication Officer* [1994] ECR I–3191.
[99] The Burden of Proof Directive also applies to Dir. 79/7. See further Ch. 7.
[100] Case C–66/95 *The Queen v. Secretary of State for Social Security, ex parte Eunice Sutton* [1997] ECR I–2163.
[101] Case C–180/95 *Draehmpaehl v. Urania Immobilien Service* [1997] ECR I–2195, considered in Ch. 8.
[102] Case 14/83 *Von Colson and Kamann v. Land Nordrhein-Westfalen* [1984] ECR 1891.
[103] Case C–271/91 *Marshall (No. 2) v. Southampton and South West Area Health Authority* [1993] ECR I–4367.

allowance (ICA), when the delay in payment of the benefit was the result of discrimination prohibited by Directive 79/7 which had been declared unlawful by the Court in *Thomas*.[104] In the light of the Court's ruling in *Marshall (No. 2)* that interest was payable for an award under Directive 76/207, Mrs Sutton and the Commission argued that interest should also be paid under Directive 79/7. They pointed out, first, that the wording of Article 6 of Directive 79/7 was practically identical to that of Article 6 of Directive 76/207; secondly, that both Directives pursued the same objective, namely real equality of treatment for men and women; and thirdly, that Directive 79/7 gave effect to the legislative programme initiated by the adoption of Directive 76/207, which provided that subsequent instruments would be adopted with a view to ensuring the progressive implementation of the principle of equal treatment in matters of social security.

The Court, however, rejected these submissions. It said that the judgment in *Marshall (No. 2)* concerned the award of interest on amounts payable by way of reparation for loss and damage sustained as a result of discriminatory dismissal, where full compensation for the loss and damage sustained could not leave out of account factors such as the effluxion of time, which might have reduced its value. Therefore, in accordance with the applicable national rules, the award of interest had to be regarded as an essential component of compensation for the purposes of restoring real equality of treatment. By contrast, *Sutton* concerned the right to receive interest on amounts payable by way of social security benefits. Those benefits were paid to the person concerned by the competent bodies which had to examine whether the conditions laid down in the relevant legislation were fulfilled. Consequently, the Court said, the amounts paid by way of social security benefit were not compensatory in nature and in no way constituted reparation for loss or damage sustained. Therefore, it said its reasoning in *Marshall (No. 2)* could not be applied; and that Article 6 of Directive 79/7 merely required that the Member States adopt the measures necessary to enable all persons who consider themselves to have been wronged by discrimination prohibited under the Directive to establish the unlawfulness of such discrimination and to obtain the benefits to which they would have been entitled in the absence of discrimination. The payment of interest on arrears of benefits could not be regarded as an essential component of the right.

These arguments are not convincing: the purpose of any remedy by way of arrears of payment is to place complainants in the position they would have been in but for the discrimination. That must include interest on the money they would have otherwise received.[105] The Court did not, however, leave Mrs Sutton entirely without a remedy. It said (without having received a question on the point) that the state might be liable, following the cases of *Francovich*

---

[104] Case C–328/91 [1993] ECR I–1247.   [105] Rubinstein [1997] IRLR 487.

No. 1[106] and *ex parte Factortame (No. 3)*,[107] for loss and damage caused to individuals as a result of breaches of Community law for which the State could be held responsible. It said that a Member State's obligation to make reparation for the loss and damage was, however, subject to three conditions: the rule of law infringed had to be intended to confer rights on individuals; the breach had to be sufficiently serious; and there had to be a direct causal link between the breach of the obligation resting on the state and the damage sustained by the injured parties. It then added that, while the right to reparation was founded directly on Community law where the three conditions were fulfilled, the national law on liability provided the framework within which the state had to make reparation for the consequences of the loss and damage caused (the principle of national procedural autonomy).[108] It therefore said that it was for the national court to assess, in the light of this principle, whether Mrs Sutton was entitled to reparation for the loss which she claimed to have suffered as a result of the breach of Community law by the UK, and, if appropriate, to determine the amount of such reparation.

5.2. Time Limits

The principle of national procedural autonomy outlined in *Sutton* has been a long-established rule of Community law. In essence it means that national procedural rules apply provided that they satisfy the requirements of equivalence (i.e. the same rules apply for breaches of Community law as for breaches of domestic law) and effectiveness (i.e. the national rules must not make it virtually impossible to bring a claim). Generally, reasonable national rules about time limits for bringing a claim do satisfy these tests.

However, in one of the earliest Directive 79/7 cases on this issue, *Emmott*,[109] the Court appeared to interfere with the principle of national procedural autonomy by saying that a Member State was precluded from relying on national procedural rules relating to time limits for bringing proceedings so long as the state had not properly transposed the Directive into its domestic legal system. The facts of *Emmott* were striking. The applicant had relied on the Court's judgment in *McDermott and Cotter*[110] to claim entitlement to invalidity benefit under Article 4(1) of Directive 79/7. The administrative authorities declined to adjudicate on her claim since Directive 79/7 was the subject of proceedings before the national court. Once these proceedings were completed, Emmott's claim was out of time, even though

---

[106] Joined Cases C–6/90 and C–9/90 *Francovich (No. 1)* v. *Italy* [1990] ECR I–5357.
[107] Joined Cases C–46/93 *Brasserie du Pecheur* v. *Bundesrepublik Deutschland* and C–48/95 *R* v. *Secretary of State for Transport, ex parte Factortame (No. 3)* [1996] ECR I–1029.
[108] Case 199/82 *Amministrazione delle finanze dello Stato* v. *San Giorgio* [1983] ECR 3595.
[109] Case C–208/90 *Emmott* v. *Minister for Social Welfare* [1991] ECR I–4269.
[110] Case 286/85 [1987] ECR 1453.

Directive 79/7 had still not been correctly transposed into national law. The Court ruled that:[111]

... until such time as a Directive has been properly transposed, a defaulting Member State may not rely on an individual's delay in initiating proceedings against it in order to protect rights conferred upon him by the provisions of the directive and that a period laid down by national law within which proceedings must be initiated cannot begin to run before that time.

Given the potential implications of the ruling in *Emmott* it is not surprising that the Court began to backtrack. In *Steenhorst-Neerings*,[112] for example, the Court said that *Emmott* did not establish an automatic entitlement to *damages* backdated to the date on which an EC Directive should have been implemented into domestic law. This case concerned a national procedural rule limiting to one year the retroactive effect of claims made for the purpose of obtaining a particular benefit. The Court distinguished *Steenhorst-Neerings* from *Emmott* on the ground that while *Emmott* concerned a domestic rule fixing time limits for bringing actions, which had the effect of denying the right to rely on the Directive in order to claim, the rule in *Steenhorst* concerned only the amount of benefit. The limit in *Steenhorst* also served 'to ensure sound administration, most importantly so that it may be ascertained whether the claimant satisfied the conditions for eligibility, and so that the degree of incapacity which may vary over time, can be fixed'. The case also reflected 'the need to preserve financial balance in a scheme'.[113]

Similarly, in *Johnson (No. 2)*,[114] Mrs Johnson, who had been discriminated against in respect of her claim for NCIP and SDA,[115] was given SDA for a period of 12 months prior to her claim but was refused payments in respect of any period prior to that date. The Court said that the decision in *Emmott* was justified by the particular circumstance of the case. The national rule in *Johnson (No. 2)*, on the other hand, was similar to that in *Steenhorst-Neerings* where 'Neither rule constitutes a bar to proceedings; they merely limit the period prior to the bringing of the claim in respect of which arrears of benefit are payable'.[116]

In *Fantask*[117] the Court confirmed the limits to the rulings in *Emmott*. Having reasserted the principle of national procedural autonomy the Court pointed out that, in the interests of legal certainty, the setting of reasonable limitation periods for bringing proceedings was compatible with Community law. It said that such periods could not be regarded as rendering virtually impossible or excessively difficult the exercise of rights conferred by Community

---

[111] Para. 23.   [112] Case C–338/91 [1993] ECR I–5475.   [113] Para. 23.
[114] Case C–410/92 *Johnson (No. 2)* v. *Chief Adjudication Officer* [1994] ECR I–5483.
[115] Case C–31/90 *Johnson (No. 1)* [1991] ECR I–3723. See above, n. 45.
[116] Para. 30.
[117] Case C–188/95 *Fantask and Others* v. *Industriministeriet* [1997] ECR I–6783.

law, even if expiry of those periods necessarily entailed the dismissal, in whole or in part, of the action brought. The Court therefore ruled that the five-year limitation period at issue in *Fantask* had to be considered reasonable, especially since the period applied without distinction to actions based on Community law and those based on national law. The Court then referred to its decisions in *Johnson (No. 2)* and *Steenhorst-Neerings* and said that the solution adopted in *Emmott* was justified by the particular circumstances of the case, in which the time bar had the result of depriving the applicant of any opportunity whatever to rely on her right to equal treatment under a Community directive. Where the time bar did not have that effect, as in *Fantask* itself, Member States could rely on national time limits, provided that they were not less favourable for actions based on Community law than for actions based on national law, and did not render virtually impossible or excessively difficult the exercise of rights conferred by Community law (as was the case in *Emmott*),[118] even where a Member State had not properly transposed the Directive.

C. EQUALITY, RETIREMENT, AND PENSIONS

1. Introduction

The application of the principle of equality to the highly controversial field of retirement and pension ages demonstrates both the interface between Article 141 and the equality Directives, and the potential cost to employers and the state of granting equality to men and women. Some Member States have directly discriminated between men and women in respect of state pension age, allowing men to receive their *state pension* at 65, but women at 60. As we saw above, Article 7(1)(a) of Directive 79/7 allows Member States to derogate from the principle of equality when determining pensionable age for the granting of (state) old-age and retirement benefits. And because the state pension age has (lawfully) discriminated against men and women, employers and trustees of occupational pensions schemes followed suit and set their retirement ages and the consequential entitlement to occupational pension ages in line with the state pension age, with the result that, for decades these ages have also discriminated (against men). As we shall see, this was in fact not a wise decision.

---

[118] Coppel 'Domestic Law Limitations on Recovery for Breach of EC Law' (1998) 27 *ILJ.* 259, 260.

2. Retirement Age

Although the Court has now decided, in *Marshall (No. 1)*,[119] that men and women must not suffer discrimination in respect of retirement age, it had some difficulty reaching this conclusion. In the earliest case on this point, *Defrenne (No. 3)*,[120] the Court held that Article 141 did not apply to discriminatory retirement ages. In that case air hostesses, but not cabin stewards, had to retire when they reached the age of 40. The Court said that since retirement age related to working conditions, Article 141 could not be stretched to apply to this situation.

The next decision, *Burton*,[121] arose after the enactment of the Equal Treatment Directive 76/207. This case concerned a voluntary redundancy scheme under which male employees could take voluntary redundancy at 60, women at 55 (in each case five years earlier than the British state pension age). Burton, a man of 58 who was refused redundancy on the grounds that he was too young, claimed that he was a victim of discrimination: had he been a woman he could have taken voluntary redundancy at 58. The Court argued that the case concerned not the benefit itself—the same amount was paid to men and women—but *the conditions of access to the benefit*.[122] The matter therefore fell to be considered under the Equal Treatment Directive 76/207 and not under Article 141.[123] It then decided that although the term 'dismissal' in Article 5(1) of Directive 76/207 (now Article 3(1)(c) of the Directive, Article 14(1)(c) of the Consolidated Directive) had to be broadly construed to include the termination of an employment relationship even as part of a voluntary redundancy scheme,[124] it concluded that British Rail's redundancy scheme was not discriminatory because the only difference in treatment stemmed from the fact that the *state pension age* was not the same for both sexes. This difference in ages did not amount to discrimination prohibited by Community law because Article 7(1)(a) of *Directive 79/7* expressly excluded

---

[119] Case 152/84 *Marshall (No. 1)* v. *Southampton and South West Hampshire Area Health Authority* [1986] ECR 723. See also Art. 6(f) of Dir. 86/378/EEC as amended (OJ [1997] L46/13).

[120] Case 149/77 *Defrenne (No. 3)* v. *SABENA* [1978] ECR 1365.

[121] Case 19/81 *Burton* v. *British Railways Board* [1982] ECR 555. For criticism of this decision, see Lester, 'The Uncertain Trumpet, References to the Court of Justice from the United Kingdom: Equal Pay and Equal Treatment without Sex Discrimination', in Schermers, Timmermans, Kellermann and Watson (eds), *Article 177 EEC: Experiences and Problems* (The Asser Institute, The Hague, 1987).

[122] It is widely thought that *Burton* has been *sotto voce* overruled on this point. The distinction between access to payment as opposed to the amount of benefit was not maintained in Case 170/84 *Bilka-Kaufhaus* v. *Weber von Hartz* [1986] ECR 1607 where the Court recognized that access to benefits for part-timers fell within Art. 141, see Curtin (1990) 27 *CMLRev.* 475, 482.

[123] For a more recent reaffirmation of this point, see Case C–207/04 *Vergani* v. *Agenzia delle Entrate* [2005] ECR I–000, para. 26.

[124] Again this was confirmed in Case C–207/04 *Vergani* [2005] ECR I–000, para. 27.

the determination of pensionable age from the application of the equality principle.[125] Thus, to reach the conclusion that dismissal ages that were discriminatory under Directive 76/207 could be saved by a derogation from another Directive, Directive 79/7, was an extraordinary step to take and the Court was subject to much criticism as a result.[126]

The issue was finally resolved in *Marshall (No. 1)*.[127] Helen Marshall worked for an area health authority whose policy was that women should retire at 60 but men could carry on working until 65, ages which once again coincided with the state pension age. Miss Marshall wanted to work until she was 65 but was forced to retire at 62. She claimed that she had been discriminated against, again contrary to Article 5(1) of the Directive 76/207 (now Article 3(1)(c), Article 14(1)(c) of the draft Consolidated Directive). Her case was referred to the Court at the same time as *Roberts v. Tate & Lyle*.[128] Tate & Lyle's occupational pension scheme provided for compulsory retirement with a pension at 65 for men and 60 for women. When Tate & Lyle closed down one of their depots employees up to five years away from normal retirement age (60 for men and 55 for women) were entitled to receive an early pension. When the men complained that this was discriminatory, the company agreed that both men and women would receive the pension at 55. Miss Roberts, who was 53, then argued that the revised plan was also discriminatory since a male employee was entitled to receive a pension 10 years before the normal retirement age whereas women could receive the pension only five years before the normal retirement age.

Marshall (No. 1), *Roberts* and a third case, *Beets Proper*,[129] the facts of which were very similar to those in *Marshall (No. 1)*, presented the Court with a menu of options, forcing the Court to examine whether to require equality in respect of retirement ages and, if so, how. In the event, the Court opted for the formal equality model offered by *Marshall (No. 1)*. However, in order to achieve this, the Court had to address the problems caused by *Burton*. Its solution was to sever the link between retirement age and state pension age. It argued that *Marshall (No. 1)* was not about the conditions for paying an old-age pension; it actually concerned the fixing of an age limit in connection with the termination of employment pursuant to a general policy concerning

[125] It now seems that the exceptions to Directive 79/7 are confined exclusively to the field of social security benefits, see Case 152/84 *Marshall (No. 1)* [1986] ECR 723, 746.

[126] Without reference to *Burton* on this point, the Court reversed itself in Case C-207/04 *Vergani v. Agenzia delle Entrate* [2005] ECR I-000, para. 33: 'That exception [Art. 7(1)(a) of Dir. 79/7] to the prohibition of discrimination on grounds of sex is therefore not applicable in the case of a tax concession such as that at issue [to which Dir. 76/207 applies] . . ., which is not a social security benefit'.

[127] Case 152/84 [1986] ECR 723.

[128] Case 151/84 *Roberts v. Tate & Lyle* [1986] ECR 703.

[129] Case 262/84 *Beets Proper v. F. van Landschot Bankers NV* [1986] ECR 773. See also Millett, 'European Community Law: Sex Equality and Retirement Age' (1987) 36 *ICLQ*. 616.

dismissal. This situation was covered by Article 5(1) of Directive 76/207 (now Article 3(1)(c)). Consequently, Article 7(1)(a) of the Social Security Directive 79/7 did not apply since it covered only the determination of *pensionable* age for the purpose of granting old-age and retirement pensions. Therefore, since Article 5 was directly effective it could be invoked by Miss Marshall against her state employer to insist on equal treatment.[130] Similarly, in *Roberts* the Court concluded that the case concerned dismissal as a result of mass redundancy and not the granting of old-age or retirement pensions and so Article 5(1) of Directive 76/207 again applied. It then ruled that it was compatible with Article 5 to lay down a single age for the dismissal of men and women and the grant of an early retirement pension.

As a consequence of these decisions the Court has ensured formal equality in respect of retirement age but in so doing it has created an artificial distinction between retirement age and pension age. This presents a particular problem for men: while it may now be possible for men to retire at 60[131] with their female colleagues, the right to retire is of limited value if the men are dependent on a state pension which is not payable until they are 65. These inconsistencies are due to the maintenance of discriminatory state pension ages which are compatible with Community law.

3. State Pension Age

In *Defrenne (No. 1)*[132] the Court made it clear that differences in the state pension age would not fall within the ambit of Article 141. In the words of the Court:

Although payment in the nature of social security benefits is not excluded in principle from the concept of pay it is not possible to include in this concept as defined in Article [141] social security schemes and benefits especially retirement pensions which are directly settled by law without any reference to any element of consultation within the undertaking or industry concerned and which cover without exception all workers in general.[133]

The case concerned a pension scheme which applied to flight personnel of civil airlines with the exception of air hostesses. Miss Defrenne, an air hostess, argued that the scheme was discriminatory, contrary to Article 141. The Court disagreed, arguing first, that the scheme was determined less by the employment relationship between the employer and the worker than by

---

[130] In Case 262/84 *Beets Proper* [1986] ECR 773 the Court reiterated the principle laid down in *Marshall* but this time applied it to discriminatory retirement ages contained in a contract of employment based on a collective agreement. No reference to direct effect was made in that case.

[131] Subject now to the Age Discrimination provisions of the Framework Directive 2000/78 considered in detail in Ch. 8.

[132] Case 80/70 *Defrenne (No. 1)* v. *Belgian State* [1971] ECR 445.   [133] Para. 7.

considerations of social policy; and second, that the worker would receive the benefits not by reason of the employer's contributions but solely because the worker fulfilled the legal conditions for the grant of the benefits. Therefore, the Court said that the retirement pension did not constitute consideration which the workers received indirectly from their employer within the meaning of Article 141.

Since Article 141 cannot be used to eliminate a discriminatory state pension age then it is compatible with Community law to maintain this discrimination. As we saw in section B above and in *Burton*,[134] this is confirmed by Article 7(1)(a) of the Social Security Directive 79/7, and accepted by the Court in *ex parte EOC*.[135] Furthermore, measures taken by an employer to mitigate the consequences of a discriminatory pension age are also compatible with Community law. In *Roberts*[136] the employer reduced a woman's bridging pension by the amount of the state pension from the age of 60 but made no such reduction in respect of a man until the age of 65. While acknowledging that bridging pensions are 'pay' within the meaning of Article 141, the Court ruled that the difference in the 'objective premise'—that women receive a state pension at 60 but men do not—leading to differences in the amount of the bridging pension paid to men and women 'cannot be considered discriminatory'. This view can be contrasted with the approach adopted by the British House of Lords in *James*[137] where the Court ruled that gender-based criteria are discriminatory, *per se*, regardless of their purpose or justification. However, the Court's decision in *Roberts* is now confirmed by new Article 2(3) of Directive 86/378 (Article 8(2) of the Consolidated Directive).

4. Occupational Pensions

4.1. Introduction

Occupational pensions are offered by employers to their employees in connection with their employment. In defined contribution or money purchase schemes the employer and employee agree to a level of contributions, usually a fixed percentage of salary, and the resulting lump sum saved is used to purchase a pension at the time of retirement. In defined benefit or final salary schemes there is usually a fixed employee contribution (although in some schemes the employer funds the total cost) but the employer undertakes to

---

[134] Case 19/87 [1982] ECR 555.

[135] Case C–9/91 [1992] 3 ECR I–4297. In the UK from 2020 men and women will both receive their state pension at 65, which represents a levelling down of benefit for women, with the changes being introduced over a 10-year period from 2010.

[136] Case C–132/92 *Birds Eye Walls v. Roberts* [1993] ECR I–5579. See now Art. 2(3) of Dir. 86/378.

[137] *James v. Eastleigh Borough Council* [1990] 3 WLR 55.

provide a level of benefits according to a formula. Consequently the employer's contribution to the scheme will vary from year to year.[138] These occupational pensions can be a substitute for a state pension (such as a pension contracted-out from the state scheme) or a supplement to a state pension. Following the model of state schemes, the occupational pension age for many schemes was also discriminatory. For this reason Directive 86/378,[139] introduced to implement the principle of equal treatment in occupational social security schemes, allowed for derogations in respect of, *inter alia*, occupational pension age.

4.2. Directive 86/378 on Equal Treatment in Occupational Social Security (Articles 5–13 of the Consolidated Directive)

Directive 86/378 was intended to complement Directive 79/7,[140] and the beneficiaries of the principle of equal treatment[141] were almost identical in both. Occupational social security schemes are defined as those schemes not governed by Directive 79/7 whose purpose is to provide workers, whether employees or self-employed, in an 'undertaking or group of undertakings, area of economic activity, occupational sector or group of sectors with benefits intended to supplement the benefits provided by the statutory social schemes or to replace them, whether membership of such schemes is compulsory or optional'.[142] It applies to occupational social security schemes which provide protection against sickness, invalidity, old age, including early retirement, industrial accidents, occupational diseases, and unemployment. It also applies to occupational schemes which provide for other social benefits, in cash or in kind, and in particular survivors' benefits and family allowances, if such benefits constitute a consideration paid by the employer to the worker by reason of the worker's employment.[143]

Article 5 (of both Directive 86/378 and the Consolidated Directive) spells out the scope of the principle of equal treatment: without prejudice to the principle of equal pay, there is to be no direct or indirect discrimination on the grounds of sex in occupational social security schemes, in particular as regards:

- the scope of such schemes and the conditions of access to them;
- the obligation to contribute and the calculation of contributions;
- the calculation of benefits, including supplementary benefits due in respect of a spouse or dependants, and the conditions governing the duration and retention of entitlement to benefits.

---

[138] Nobles, *Pensions, Employment and the Law* (Clarendon Press, Oxford, 1993) 8.

[139] OJ [1986] L225/40.

[140] Art. 3(3) of Dir. 79/7 said that the Council will adopt provisions defining the principle of equal treatment in occupational pensions schemes.

[141] Art. 3.   [142] Art. 2(1) of Dir. 86/378 (Art. 2(1)(f) of the Consolidated Directive).

[143] Art. 4 of Dir. 86/378 (Art. 7 of the Consolidated Directive).

Article 6 of Directive 86/378 (Article 9 of the Consolidated Directive) gives examples of provisions which contravene the principle of equal treatment. The list includes determining people who can participate in occupational schemes, fixing the compulsory or optional nature of participation in an occupational scheme; laying down different rules as regards the age of entry into the scheme or minimum periods of employment or membership of the scheme required to obtain the benefits of the scheme; laying down different rules for the reimbursement of contributions when a worker leaves a scheme without having fulfilled the conditions guaranteeing a deferred right to long-term benefits; setting different conditions for granting of benefits or restricting the benefits to workers of one or other of the sexes; fixing different retirement ages, suspending the retention or acquisition of rights during periods of maternity leave or leave for family reasons which are granted by law or agreement and paid by the employer; setting different levels of benefit,[144] setting different levels of worker contribution[145] and employer's contribution,[146] laying down different standards applicable to workers of only one sex.[147]

As already mentioned, Article 9 of the original Directive 86/378 did, however, contain an extensive list of derogations. In particular, Member States could defer compulsory application of the principle of equal treatment with regard to (a) the determination of pensionable age for the purposes of granting old-age and retirement pensions, and the possible implications for other benefits, either until the date on which such equality is achieved in statutory schemes, or at the latest until such equality is required by a Directive; (b) survivors' pensions until a Directive requires the application of the principle of equal treatment, and (c) to setting the levels of worker contributions to take account of the different actuarial calculations factors, at least until the expiry of a thirteen-year period as from the 30 July 1986. As we shall see, considerable doubt was cast on the legality of most of these derogations, with the exception of the derogation relating to actuarial factors, by the Court's case law, in particular *Barber*[148] (occupational pensions age) which 'automatically invalidates certain provisions of Directive 86/378'[149] and *Ten Oever*[150] (survivors' benefits). In each case the benefit concerned was deemed to fall within the definition of 'pay' in Article 141 of the *Treaty* which took

---

[144] Special provision is made in respect of actuarial factors which is considered below.

[145] See also case C–152/91 *Neath v. Steeper* [1993] ECR I–6935 and Case C–200/91 *Coloroll* [1994] ECR I–4389 and 10th Preambular paragraph.

[146] Certain exceptions are provided here in the case of defined contribution and defined benefit schemes.

[147] Again certain exceptions are provided here too.

[148] Case C–262/88 *Barber v. Guardian Royal Exchange Assurance Group* [1990] ECR I–1889.

[149] Preamble to Council Directive 96/97/EC (OJ [1997] L46/20).

[150] Case C–109/91 *Ten Oever v. Stichting Bedrijfspensionenfonds voor het Glazenwassers—en Schoomaakbedrijf* [1993] ECR I–4879.

precedence over the Directive. As the Court said in *Moroni*,[151] the 'effects of the Directive do not matter, for its provisions cannot in any way restrict the scope of Article [141]'.[152] This led to the adoption of a new Directive 96/97/EC,[153] amending Directive 86/378 to 'adapt the provisions affected by the *Barber* case law',[154] which is now found in the Consolidated Directive. The derogations from the Directive now apply largely to the self-employed.[155]

4.3. Occupational Pensions, 'Pay', and Article 141

There had been hints in the early case law that occupational pensions could fall within the definition of pay in Article 141. For example, in *Garland*[156] the Court said that the concept of pay embraced both 'immediate and *future* benefits',[157] which in that case included free travel after retirement. Consequently, occupational pensions, although received after employment, could be construed as a type of remuneration received directly or indirectly from the employer. Advocate General Dutheillet de Lamothe in *Defrenne (No. 1)*[158] had also taken this view. He considered that pensions payable directly by the employer came within the scope of Article 141 since they could be regarded as a form of deferred pay. He also regarded *supplementary* pensions as falling within the scope of Article 141 if they could be regarded as being independent of the state scheme. On the facts of *Defrenne (No. 1)* the Court found that this was not the case.

Advocate General Dutheillet de Lamothe's approach in *Defrenne (No. 1)* was endorsed by the Court in *Bilka-Kaufhaus*.[159] The case concerned an occupational pension scheme which, although adopted in accordance with German legislation, was voluntary in origin and arose from an agreement between the employer and the works council.[160] It *supplemented* the social security legislation with benefits financed entirely by the employer. In the words of the Court, the scheme was contractual rather than statutory and formed an integral part of the contracts of employment. The scheme therefore

---

[151] Case C–110/91 *Moroni v. Collo* [1993] ECR I–6591, para. 24.
[152] Approved in Case C–7/93 *Bestuur van het Algemeen burgerlijk Pensioenfonds v. Beune* [1994] ECR I–4471 where the Court said that the same interpretation applied with regard to Art. 8(2) of the original Dir. 86/378.
[153] OJ [1996] L46/20.   [154] Preamble to Dir. 96/97.
[155] E.g. Art. 2(2)(a) and (b); Art. 9 of Dir. 86/378 as amended by Dir. 96/97 (Arts. 8(1)(a) and (b) and Art. 11 of the Consolidated Dir.). New Art. 8 of Dir. 86/378 (Art. 10 of the draft Consolidated Directive) requires Member States to take the necessary steps to ensure that the provisions of occupational schemes for self-employed workers contrary to the principle of equal treatment are revised with effect from 1 January 1993 (later for accession states).
[156] Case 12/81 *Garland v. British Rail Engineering* [1982] ECR 359.   [157] Para. 5.
[158] Case 80/70 [1971] ECR 445.   [159] Case 170/84 [1986] ECR 1607.
[160] The emphasis on agreement is important. It takes precedence over the criterion of statutory origin. However, the negotiations between the employer's and the employees' representatives must result in a formal agreement and not just consultation (Case C–7/93 *Beune* [1994] ECR I–4471, para. 32).

offered the necessary link between pay and the employment relationship which was absent from the scheme in *Defrenne (No. 1)*.[161]

However, Advocate General Warner in *Worringham*[162] did not feel the distinctions made by Advocate General Dutheillet de Lamothe in *Defrenne (No. 1)* were so easy to apply in the context of the British system of contracted-out schemes which were a *substitute for* the state scheme and not a *supplement to* the state scheme. Because he was worried that an unbalanced result would arise if equalization was required in the context of occupational schemes and not in the case of the state scheme, he argued that such contracted-out occupational schemes had to fall outside Article 141. *Worringham* concerned a pension scheme under which men were required to contribute to the bank's pension scheme from the date on which they started work but women could start making contributions only when they reached the age of 25. The contributions amounted to 5 per cent of an employee's salary. In order to make up for this difference men under 25 received a 5 per cent addition to their gross pay. If a man left the bank before he was 25 he was entitled to a refund on his contributions but women leaving before the age of 25 received nothing. Women also suffered other disadvantages: any redundancy pay, unemployment benefit, and credit facilities were calculated by reference to gross earnings which would be less for women than for men.

The bank argued that the case concerned a contracted-out scheme and so Article 141 did not apply; the women argued that the scheme was a supplementary scheme to which Article 141 did apply. The Court, by examining the discriminatory effects of the scheme rather than its legal nature, noted the way in which the contributions affected the calculation of gross pay. It concluded that contributions to a retirement benefits scheme, which were paid by the employer in the name of the employees by means of an addition to the gross salary, were 'pay' within the meaning of Article 141[163] and therefore no discrimination was permitted.

By contrast, in *Newstead*,[164] the Court found that because the deduction in question resulted in a reduction in *net* pay, due to a contribution paid to a social security scheme, and in no way affected gross pay, Article 141 did not apply. Newstead was a civil servant employed by the Department of Transport. He was required to contribute to an occupational pension scheme

---

[161] Case 80/70 [1971] ECR 445.

[162] Case 69/80 *Worringham* v. *Lloyds Bank* [1981] ECR 767. See Ellis and Morrell, 'Sex Discrimination in Pension Schemes: Has Community Law Changed the Rules?' (1992) 21 *ILJ*. 16.

[163] Cf. Case 23/83 *Liefting* v. *Academisch Zieckenhuis bij de Universiteit van Amsterdam* [1984] ECR 3225. Curtin concludes that the Court is prepared to look squarely at the nature of the pension scheme when confronted with questions relating to the payment of benefits (*Defrenne (No. 1)* and *Bilka-Kaufhaus*) but not when the questions can be confined to the effect of contributions to pensions schemes on gross pay (*Worringham* and *Lieftung*) ((1990) 27 *CMLRev*. 475). See also old Art. 6(c) of Dir. 86/378.

[164] Case 192/85 *Newstead* v. *Department of Transport* [1987] ECR 4753.

which made provision for a widow's pension fund. All male civil servants were obliged to contribute to this scheme at a rate of 1.5 per cent of their gross salary, irrespective of their marital status; female civil servants had the choice whether to contribute to the scheme or not. Civil servants who remained unmarried throughout the period during which they were covered by the scheme were entitled to a refund of their contributions plus interest at 4 per cent when they left the service. Newstead, a confirmed bachelor in his fifties, objected to making this payment, albeit temporarily, and claimed that he was the victim of unlawful discrimination. The Court decided that the pension scheme was a substitute for a social security scheme and consequently any contribution to such a scheme was 'considered to fall within the scope of Article 118 [new Article 140] of the Treaty and not Article [141]'. This decision was the subject of much criticism and it is difficult to reconcile it with the earlier cases.[165] It took the momentous decision by the Court in *Barber* to cut through this muddle and state authoritatively that occupational pensions, including contracted-out pension schemes,[166] constituted 'pay' within the meaning of Article 141.[167]

Mr Barber belonged to a non-contributory pension scheme (a scheme wholly financed by the employer). Since the scheme was contracted-out from the state pension scheme it was a substitute for the state scheme. Under the terms of the scheme the normal pensionable age was fixed at 62 for men and 57 for women—three years prior to the state pension age. In the event of redundancy, members of the pension fund were entitled to an immediate pension at 55 for men and 50 for women, seven years before the scheme's normal pensionable age. Staff who did not fulfil these conditions but who had been made redundant received cash benefits calculated on the basis of their years of service and a deferred pension payable at the normal pensionable age. Barber found himself in this position. Made redundant at 52, he received the cash benefits, statutory redundancy pay and an *ex gratia* payment but he was not entitled to his occupational pension until he was 62. A woman of 52 would have received the pension immediately, as well as the statutory redundancy payment, and the total value of those benefits would have been greater than the amount paid to him. Barber claimed that he had been discriminated against on the grounds of his sex.[168]

---

[165] See e.g. Arnull (1988) 13 *ELRev.* 136.

[166] In Case C–7/93 *Beune* [1994] ECR I–4471, para. 37, the Court said that benefits awarded under an occupational scheme which *partly or entirely* take the place of the benefits paid by a statutory social security scheme may also fall within the scope of Art. 141.

[167] Case C–262/88 *Barber* [1990] ECR I–1887. On the effect of *Barber* on the pensions industry see Moffat and Luckhaus, 'Occupational Pension Schemes, Equality and Europe: a Decade of Change' (1998) 20 *JSWL*. 1.

[168] A comparator is necessary. In Case C–200/91 *Coloroll Pension Trustees* v. *Russell* [1994] ECR I–4389 the Court ruled that Art. 141 did not apply to schemes whose members are all of one sex (para. 104).

The Court began by distinguishing contracted-out private *occupational* schemes from the state *social security* scheme at issue in *Defrenne (No. 1).*[169] First, it noted that contracted-out schemes resulted from either an agreement between workers and employers or a unilateral decision by the employer. The schemes were funded by the employer or by the employer and the workers, with no contribution from the public authorities. The Court therefore concluded that such occupational pension schemes formed part of the consideration offered to the workers by the employer. Secondly, the Court said that such schemes were not compulsorily applicable to general categories of workers: they applied only to workers employed in certain undertakings, with the result that affiliation to those schemes derived from the employment relationship with a given employer. In addition, such schemes were governed by their own rules, even if they were established in conformity with national legislation. Thirdly, the Court reasoned that even if such occupational schemes were substitutes for the general statutory scheme these schemes might grant their members benefits greater than those paid under the statutory scheme, with the result that their economic function was similar to that of supplementary schemes, which, as the Court had held in *Bilka-Kaufhaus,*[170] fell within the concept of pay within the meaning of Article 141. Therefore, a pension paid under a contracted-out scheme constituted consideration paid by an employer in respect of his employment and consequently fell within the scope of Article 141.

4.4. The Application of the Equality Principle to Occupational Pension Schemes

It is clear that the principle of non-discrimination laid down by Article 141 relates to the *quantum* of benefit[171] so that men and women receive the same amount. In *Barber*[172] the Court established that *each* benefit received under an occupational pension scheme was to be paid on a non-discriminatory basis:[173] it was not sufficient to make a comprehensive assessment of the total consideration paid to workers. The Court's justification for reaching this conclusion was pragmatic: it referred to the fundamental principle of transparency which would enable national courts to review schemes with a view to eliminating discrimination based on sex. The Court argued that such judicial review

---

[169] Case 80/70 [1971] ECR 445.   [170] Case 170/84 [1986] ECR 1607.

[171] Curtin suggests that *Barber* does not require that the total amount of a particular benefit be mathematically equal since neither the costs nor the value of the total pension benefits will ever be known in advance. She argues that *Barber* requires that the *rate* at which the benefit is enjoyed be equal ((1990) 27 *CMLRev.* 475, 484–85).

[172] Case C–262/88 [1990] ECR I–1889.

[173] This is also the approach which had been adopted by the House of Lords in *Haywards* v. *Cammell Laird* [1988] 2 WLR 1134 concerning the interpretation of the British Equal Pay Act 1970.

would be difficult and the effectiveness of Article 141 would be diminished if the national courts were required to make a comparative assessment of the package of consideration granted.

However, Article 141 does not only apply to the quantum of benefits. As Article 6 of Directive 86/378 (and Article 9 of the Consolidated Directive) indicated, it also applies to *access and conditions of access* to the scheme.[174] The question of *access* was first raised in *Bilka-Kaufhaus*[175] where the Court ruled that Article 141 covered not only entitlement to benefits paid by an occupational pensions scheme but also the right to be a member of such a scheme. In *Bilka-Kaufhaus* the employers refused to pay Mrs Weber, a part-time worker, an occupational pension since she had not worked full time for the minimum period of 15 years. She alleged that the exclusion of part-time workers from the occupational pension scheme constituted indirect discrimination, contrary to Article 141. As the Court had explained in *Jenkins*,[176] if a pay policy setting a lower hourly rate for part-time work than for full-time work entailed discrimination between men and women, then the same applied where part-time workers were refused access to a company pension. Since a pension fell within the definition of pay, it followed that hour for hour the total remuneration paid by the employer to full-time workers was higher than that paid to part-time workers. The Court followed this approach in *Vroege*.[177] It said that an occupational pension scheme which excluded part-time workers from membership contravened Article 141 if the exclusion affected a much greater number of women than men, and which the employer could not explain by objectively justified factors unrelated to any discrimination on grounds of sex. In *Vroege* the Court also recognized that the exclusion of married women from membership of an occupational pension scheme did entail discrimination directly based on sex and was contrary to Article 141.[178]

As far as *conditions of access* are concerned, the principle of equality in Article 141 also applies. As the Court ruled in *Barber*,[179] Article 141 prohibited any discrimination with regard to pay as between men and women, *whatever the system which gives rise to such inequality*. Thus, the Court said it

---

[174] See also Arts. 5(1) and 6(a) of Dir. 86/378 (Art. 5(9) and Art. 9(1)(a) of the Consolidated Directive).

[175] Case 170/84 [1986] ECR 1607. However, in Case C–256/01 *Allonby* v. *Accrington & Rosendale College* [2004] ECR I–000, para. 57 the Court said that a teacher employed by an agency could not rely on the principle of equal pay in order to secure entitlement to membership of an occupational pension scheme for teachers set up by state legislation of which only teachers with a contract of employment could become members, using as a basis for comparison the remuneration, including such a right of membership, received for equal work or work of the same value by a man employed by the woman's previous employer

[176] Case 96/80 *Jenkins* v. *Kingsgate* [1981] ECR 911.

[177] Case C–57/93 *Vroege* v. *NCIV* [1994] ECR I–4541.

[178] See also Case C–128/93 *Fisscher* v. *Voorhuis Hengelo BV* [1994] ECR I–4583.

[179] Case C–262/88 [1990] ECR I–1889. See also Art. 6(e) of Dir. 86/378 (Art. 9(1)(e) of the Consolidated Directive).

was contrary to Article 141 to impose an age condition which differed according to sex in respect of pensions paid under a contracted-out scheme, even if the difference between the pensionable age for men and women was based on the age laid down by the national statutory scheme.[180] The Court extended this ruling to supplementary (non-contracted-out) occupational pension schemes in *Moroni*[181] and *Coloroll*.[182]

Earlier cases, such as *Burton*,[183] *Marshall (No. 1)*[184] and *Roberts*,[185] had, however, suggested that the fixing of pensionable ages related to the *conditions of access* to the pension and consequently was governed by the Equal Treatment Directives, despite the consequences that such discrimination might have for the worker's pay.[186] On the other hand, Article 1 of the Equal Pay Directive 75/117, which was designed to facilitate the application of Article 141,[187] made clear that 'the principle of equal pay . . . means the elimination of all discrimination on the grounds of sex with regard to all aspects and *conditions of remuneration*' (emphasis added) and so in this respect the *Barber* judgment only serves to confirm the position under Directive 75/117.[188] Nevertheless, the distinction between the Equal Treatment Directive and Article 141 is no longer as clear as it once was.[189]

4.5. The Non-retrospective Effect of the *Barber* Judgment: the Temporal Limitation

The Court, aware of the potential financial consequences of any decision on equalization of benefits under an occupational pension scheme, decided to limit the retrospective effect of its judgment. It had already restricted the retrospective effect of its judgment in *Defrenne (No. 2)*[190] 'by way of exception, taking account of the serious difficulties which its judgment may create as regards events in the past'. Thus, the direct effect of Article 141 which was established in that case for the first time could not be invoked in respect of periods of service prior to 8 April 1976, the date of the judgment in *Defrenne (No. 2)*. In *Barber* the Court considered that, in the light of the exclusion of pensionable age from the scope of Directive 79/7 and the formal extension of this derogation by Article 9(a) of Directive 86/378/EEC to occupational pension schemes, Member States were reasonably entitled to consider that

[180] See also Case C–351/00 *Niemi* [2002] ECR I–7007, para. 53.
[181] Case C–110/91 [1993] ECR I–6591.   [182] Case C–200/91 [1994] ECR I–4389.
[183] Case 19/81 [1982] ECR 555.   [184] Case 152/84 [1986] ECR 723.
[185] Case 151/84 [1986] ECR 703.
[186] Art. 5 of Dir. 76/207 and Art. 6(f) of Dir. 86/378.
[187] Case 96/80 *Jenkins* [1981] ECR 911.
[188] See also Arts. 5(1) and 6(e) of Dir. 86/378 (Arts. 5(a) and Art. 9(1)(e) of the Consolidated Directive).
[189] Advocate General Van Gerven in *Barber* [1990] ECR I–1889 did suggest that the two are not mutually exclusive, a point now reinforced by the Consolidated Directive. See further Ch. 7.
[190] Case 43/75 [1976] ECR 455.

Article 141 did not apply to pensions paid under contracted-out schemes. Therefore, in the interests of legal certainty and out of a wish to avoid upsetting the financial balance of many contracted-out pension schemes, the Court concluded that:

... the direct effect of Article [141] of the Treaty may not be relied upon in order to claim entitlement to a pension with effect from a date prior to that of this judgment (17 May 1990), except in the case of workers or those claiming under them who have before that date initiated proceedings or raised an equivalent claim under the applicable national law.

The Court then added that 'no restriction on the effects of the aforesaid interpretation can be permitted as regards the acquisition of entitlement to a pension as from the date of this judgment'.

Such statements caused considerable uncertainty as to the precise meaning of the scope of the non-retrospectivity ruling. Advocate General Van Gerven discussed four possible interpretations:[191]

A *first interpretation* would be to apply the principle of equal treatment only to workers who became members of, and began to pay contributions to, an occupational pension scheme as from 17 May 1990. This view would deprive the *Barber* judgment of almost all retroactive effect. In practical terms, it would mean that the full effect of the judgment would be felt only after a period of about 40 years.

A *second interpretation* is that the principle of equal treatment should only be applied to benefits payable in respect of periods of service after 17 May 1990. Periods of service prior to that date would not be affected by the direct effect of Article [141].

According to a *third interpretation,* the principle of equal treatment must be applied to all pensions which are payable or paid for the first time after 17 May 1990, irrespective of the fact that all or some of the pension accrued during, and on the basis of, periods of service completed or contributions paid prior to that date. In other words, it is not the periods of service (before or after the judgment in *Barber*) which are decisive, but the date on which the pension falls to be paid.

A *fourth interpretation* would be to apply equal treatment to all pension payments made after 17 May 1990, including benefits or pensions which had already fallen due and, here again, as in the previous interpretation, irrespective of the date of the periods of service during which the pension accrued. This interpretation undoubtedly has the most far-reaching effect.

At the Intergovernmental Conference at Maastricht the heads of state added Protocol No. 2 (now called the Protocol concerning Article 141) to 'clarify' the temporal limitation of *Barber*. This provides:

For the purposes of Article [141] of the Treaty establishing the European Community, benefits under occupational social security schemes shall not be considered as

---

[191] Cases C–109/91, C–110/91, C–152/91, and C–200/91 *Ten Oever, Moroni, Neath,* and *Coloroll* [1993] ECR I–4879. See also Honeyball and Shaw, 'Sex and the Retiring Man' (1991) 16 *ELRev.* 56 and Curtin (1990) 27 *CMLRev.* 475, 487.

remuneration if and insofar as they are attributable to periods of employment prior to 17 May 1990, except in the case of workers or those claiming under them who have before that date initiated legal proceedings or introduced an equivalent claim under the applicable national law.

The Protocol favours the second approach identified by Advocate General Van Gerven that benefits need to be equal only in respect of periods of employment after 17 May 1990. The approach contained in the Protocol was followed by the Court in *Ten Oever*[192] (thereby avoiding a constitutional conflict with the European Council). The Court said that account had to be taken of the fact that in the case of pensions 'there is a time lag between the accrual of entitlement to the pension, which occurred gradually throughout the employee's working life and its actual payment, which is deferred until a particular age'.[193] It noted the way in which occupational pension funds are financed and the accounting links existing in each individual case between the periodic contributions and the future amounts paid. It continued that 'equality of treatment in the matter of occupational pensions may be claimed only in relation to benefits payable in respect of periods of employment subsequent to 17 May 1990, the date of the *Barber* judgment, subject to the exception prescribed therein for workers or those claiming under them who have, before that date, initiated legal proceedings or raised an equivalent claim under the applicable national law'. [194]

The Protocol concerning Article 141 made no distinction between contracted-out and supplementary occupational schemes, talking only in general terms of 'benefits under occupational social security schemes'. This suggested that the *Barber* time limit also applied to supplementary schemes. This was confirmed by *Moroni*[195] and *Coloroll*,[196] despite the fact that in the earlier case of *Bilka-Kaufhaus*,[197] which also concerned supplementary occupational schemes, no temporal limitation was imposed. This position is now confirmed in Article 2(1) of Directive 96/97 (Article 12(1) of the Consolidated Directive) which provides that any measure implementing the Chapter (on occupational social security) as regards workers must cover 'all benefits under occupational social security schemes derived from periods of employment subsequent to 17 May 1990[198] and shall apply retroactively to that date, without prejudice

---

[192] Case C–109/91 [1993] ECR I–4879 and applied in Case C–152/91 *Neath* v. *Steeper* [1993] ECR I–6935 and Case C–200/91 *Coloroll* [1994] ECR I–4389.

[193] See further Advocate General Van Gerven in Case C–109/91 *Ten Oever* [1993] ECR I–4879. The same justification was given by the Court to justify the application of the *Barber* limitation to transfer benefits and lump-sum options in Case C–152/91 *Neath* [1993] ECR I–6953.

[194] The Court has refused to permit any further exception to the rule: Joined Cases C–4/02 and C–5/02 *Schönheit* v. *Stadt Frankfurt am Main* [2003] ECR I–12575, para. 103.

[195] Case C–110/91 [1993] ECR I–6591, para. 33.

[196] Case C–200/91 [1994] ECR I–4389, para. 71.   [197] Case 170/84 [1986] ECR 1607.

[198] Art. 12(4) of the Consolidated Directive adds that for states that acceded to the EU after 17 May 1990, the date of 17 May 1990 is replaced by the date on which Art. 141 became

to workers or those claiming under them who have, before that date, initiated legal proceedings or raised an equivalent claim under national law'. In respect of this latter group the implementation measures apply retroactively to 8 April 1976 (the date of the judgment in *Defrenne (No. 2)*).[199]

It is now quite clear that Article 141 does not apply to any benefit or part of any benefit relating to service before 17 May 1990 (except for legal claims started before that date)[200] and true equality of pension *benefits* will not be achieved under Community law until all those employed prior to 17 May 1990 have retired. However, *Barber* does require all occupational schemes to allow men and women to receive their occupational pensions at the same age, as from 17 May 1990, albeit that the payments which relate to service prior to 17 May 1990 are of different amounts.

A simple example may serve to illustrate the application of the *Barber* principles.[201] In May 1984 ABC Ltd employs Mrs X and Mr Y, both aged 50. ABC Ltd runs an occupational pension scheme with a normal pension age of 60 for women and 65 for men. An actuarial reduction of 4 per cent per annum is made for each year by which retirement precedes the normal pension age. Mrs X and Mr Y both retire in May 1994 aged 60. Mr Y's pension is subject to a 20 per cent actuarial reduction (4% × 5 years). Therefore, if Mrs X receives an occupational pension of £1,000 per month, Mr Y will receive only £800 due to the 20 per cent actuarial reduction. As a result of the decision in *Barber* he will now be able to claim an additional £80 per month calculated as follows:

May 1984–May 1990
(period of service between date of commencement of
employment and date of *Barber* judgment)

6/10 of service	£600	
Minus 20% actuarial reduction	(£120)	
		£480

May 1990–May 1994
(period of service between date of *Barber* judgment and
date of retirement when no deduction can be made)

4/10 of service	£400	
		£400
Total		£880

applicable in their territory. Art. 12(3) provides that for states that were not members of the EU on 17 May 1990 but were members of the EEA on 1 January 1994, the date of 17 May 1990 is replaced by 1 January 1994. See, e.g., Case C–351/00 *Niemi* [2002] ECR I–7007, para. 54.

[199] For states that acceded to the EU after 8 April 1976, that date is replaced by the date on which Art. 141 became applicable on their territory.

[200] This was confirmed by Advocate General Ruiz-Jarabo Colomer in Case C–166/99 *Defreyne* v. *SABENA* [2000] ECR I–6155.

[201] I am grateful for Lorraine Fletcher of the EOC for help with this illustration.

The temporal limitation in *Barber* also applies to survivors' benefits[202] and to benefits not linked to actual service, such as a lump sum payment in the event of an employee's death, where the operative event (the death) occurred before 17 May 1990.[203] However, according to the Court in *Vroege*[204] and *Fisscher*,[205] the temporal limitation does not apply to conditions of membership of occupational schemes which are governed by the judgment in *Bilka-Kaufhaus*[206] where no temporal limitation was prescribed. This serves to emphasize the Court's ambivalence towards financial costs. While accepting that retrospective rights to equality in *benefits* might upset the financial balance of pension schemes, it did not seem aware of the costs of granting retrospective *access* to those benefits. Consequently, the direct effect of Article 141 can be relied on in order to claim equal treatment retroactively in relation to the right to join an occupational pension scheme and this may apply from 8 April 1976,[207] the date of the *Defrenne (No. 2)*.[208] This may mean that both the employer and the employee have to make contributions from 8 April 1976, although national time limits may preclude such extensive retrospective claims.[209] In the case of part-timers claiming access to a pension scheme, the employers may attempt to show that any indirect discrimination that occurred from 1976 could at any given moment be objectively justified and so no discrimination occurred, hence no contribution would be needed to be paid for that period. If national law allows retrospective claims before 8 April 1976, this is compatible with Community law, despite the risk of competition being distorted between economic operators in the different Member States.[210]

---

[202] Case C–109/91 *Ten Oever* [1993] ECR I–4879, considered below.

[203] Case C–200/91 *Coloroll* [1994] ECR I–4389.

[204] Case C–57/93 [1994] ECR I–4541, para. 32. In *Vroege* the Court pointed out that a limitation of the effects in time of an interpretative preliminary ruling can only be in the actual judgment ruling upon the interpretation sought. Consequently, if the Court had considered it necessary to impose a limit in time, it would have done so in *Bilka-Kaufhaus*. See also Case C–7/93 *Beune* [1994] ECR I–4471, paras. 61–2, and Case C–128/93 *Fisscher* [1994] ECR I–4583, para. 28.

[205] Case C–128/93 [1994] ECR I–4583.

[206] Case 170/84 [1986] ECR 1607. The Court has repeated this in Joined Cases C–270/97 and C–271/97 *Deutsche Post AG v. Sievers and Schrage* [2000] ECR I–929, paras. 34 and 35; Joined Cases C–234/96 and C–235/96 *Deutsche Telekom AG v. Vick and Conze* [2000] ECR I–799, para. 40; and Case C–50/96 *Deutsche Telekom v. Schröder* [2000] ECR I–743, para. 38.

[207] Case C–57/93 *Vroege* [1994] ECR I–4541.　　　　[208] Case 43/75 [1976] ECR 455.

[209] Case C–128/93 *Fisscher* [1994] ECR I–4583, but cf. Case C–246/96 *Mary Teresa Magorrian and Irene Patricia Cunningham v. Eastern Health and Social Services Board and Department of Health and Social Services* [1997] ECR I–7153. See also Case C–78/98 *Preston v. Wolverhampton Health Care NHS Trust* [2000] ECR I–3201. The requirement to bring a claim within 6 months from the end of the contract of employment struck out quite a lot of the 60,000 plus pension claims in those cases.

[210] Case C–50/96 *Schröder* [2000] ECR I–743, paras. 50 and 59; Joined Cases C–234/96 and C–235/96 *Vick and Conze* [2000] ECR I–799, para. 50; and Joined Cases C–270/97 and C–271/97 *Sievers and Schrage* [2000] ECR I–929, para. 59.

4.6. Levelling Up or Down?

The *Barber* judgment did not, however, make clear whether the equalization demanded by Article 141 required levelling the man's terms up to the more favourable terms enjoyed by the women or whether it permitted levelling the woman's terms down to the inferior terms 'enjoyed' by the man. A question was referred to the Court on this point in *Smith* v. *Avdel Systems*.[211] In that case the employer, in order to give effect to the *Barber* judgment in its own occupational pension scheme, decided that as from 1 July 1991 both men and women would receive their occupational pensions at 65 (levelling down of the women's conditions) rather than providing that the men would receive their occupational pensions at 60 at the same age as the women (levelling up). The Court was faced with a difficult choice: levelling down was more affordable for the pension schemes, particularly in the light of an ageing population, but levelling up was more consistent with the Treaty's aspiration of an improvement in working conditions and its earlier jurisprudence. In *Defrenne (No. 2)*[212] the Court said that in view of the connection between Article 141 and the harmonization of working conditions while the improvement is being maintained,[213] compliance with Article 141 could not be achieved in ways other than by raising the lowest salaries.[214] Similarly, in *Nimz*[215] the Court ruled that the national court was obliged to apply to the members who had been victims of discrimination 'the same arrangements as are applied to other employees, arrangements which, failing the correct application of Article [141] of the EEC Treaty in national law, remain the only valid system of reference' — in other words, levelling up.

In *Smith* v. *Avdel Systems* the Court reached a compromise solution. It identified three separate points of time: first, the period before 17 May 1990, the date of the *Barber* judgment; second, after 17 May 1990 but before any remedial action had been taken by the employer; and third, once remedial action had been taken. In respect of the first period (service prior to 17 May 1990), the *Barber* judgment excluded the application of Article141 to pension benefits payable in respect of those periods so that employers and trustees were not required to ensure equal treatment as far as those benefits were concerned. However, in respect of the second period (periods after 17 May

---

[211] Case C–408/92 *Smith* v. *Avdel Systems* [1994] ECR I–4435. The Court reached similar conclusions in Case C–28/93 *Van den Akker* v. *Stichting Shell Pensioenfonds* [1994] ECR I–4527 and Case C–200/91 *Coloroll* [1994] ECR I–4389, para. 36.

[212] Case 43/75 [1976] ECR 455.

[213] See Art. 117 (new Art. 136) and Case 126/86 *Zaera* v. *Instituto Nacional de la Seguridad Social* [1987] ECR 3697.

[214] Case 43/75 [1976] ECR 455. See also Case C–102/88 *Ruzius Wilbrink* [1989] ECR 4311 where the Court stated that part-timers are entitled to have the same system applied to them as other workers in proportion to their working hours, and the application of this in the case of collective agreements (Case 33/89 *Kowalska* v. *Freie und Hansestadt Hamburg* [1990] ECR I–2591).

[215] Case C–184/89 [1991] ECR I–297.

1990), when the Court found that discrimination in relation to pay existed, and so long as measures bringing about equal treatment had not been adopted by the scheme, the Court ruled that the only proper way of complying with Article 141 was to grant those in the disadvantaged class, the men, the same advantages as those enjoyed by the people in the favoured class, the women (levelling up).

As regards the third period (periods of service completed after the entry into force of rules designed to eliminate discrimination (1 July 1991)), the Court said that Article 141 did not preclude measures which achieve equal treatment by reducing the advantages of persons previously favoured (levelling down) since Article 141 merely required that men and women should receive the same pay for the same work without imposing any specific level of pay.[216] The Court added that since equal treatment was a fundamental principle of Community law its application by employers had to be 'immediate and full'. As a result, 'the achievement of equality cannot be made progressive on a basis that still maintains discrimination, even if only temporarily'. Therefore, it was not possible to phase in the process of levelling down.

If the principles laid down in *Smith* v. *Avdel* are applied to the example outlined above, with the modification that the employer equalized the occupational pension age to 65 for both men and women in May 1991, Mrs X will receive £940 a month, and Mr Y £820. This is calculated as follows:

Mrs X's position

1984–1990	6/10 of service	£600	
			£600
1990–1991	1/10 of service	£100	
			£100
1991–1994	(period of service for which levelling down is permitted)		
	3/10 of service	£300	
	Minus 20% of actuarial reduction for early retirement	(£60)	
			£240
	Total		£940

Mr Y's position

1984–1990	(no equality required)		
	6/10 of service	£600	
	Minus 20% of actuarial reduction for early retirement	(£120)	
			£480

---

[216] See also Preamble to amended Dir. 86/378.

1990–1991	(period of service between date of *Barber* judgment and date on which pension scheme adopts measures to achieve equality: levelling up required and no actuarial reduction can be made)		
	1/10 of service	£100	
			£100
1991–1994	(period of service for which levelling down is permitted)		
	3/10 of service	£300	
	Minus 20% of actuarial reduction for early retirement	(£60)	
			£240
	Total		£820

4.7. *Barber* and Beyond

In the light of the decision in *Barber* a series of other pension practices have been examined for unlawful discrimination.

(a) Survivors' Benefits

In *Ten Oever*[217] the Court established that the concept of pay in Article 141 included survivors' benefits. Mr Ten Oever's wife belonged to an occupational pension scheme which provided for a survivor's pension for widows only. It was not until 1 January 1989 that this entitlement was extended to widowers. Mrs Ten Oever died on 13 October 1988 and Mr Ten Oever unsuccessfully claimed entitlement to a survivor's pension. The Court ruled that since this scheme was a result of an agreement between both sides of industry and was funded wholly by the employees and the employers without any financial contribution from the public purse,[218] this survivors' pension fell within the scope of Article 141. The Court added that it was not relevant that a survivors' pension was paid, by definition, not to the employee but to the employee's survivor.[219] Entitlement to such a benefit was consideration deriving from the survivor's spouse's membership of the scheme, the pension being vested in the survivor by reason of the employment relationship that had existed between the employer and the survivor's spouse and being paid to him

---

[217] Case C–109/91 [1993] ECR I–4879.
[218] Cf. Case 80/70 *Defrenne (No. 1)* [1971] ECR 445.
[219] This is now recognized in Art. 3 of Dir. 86/378 as amended by Dir. 96/97 (which is now Art. 6 of the Consolidated Directive.

or her by reason of the spouse's employment.[220] In *Coloroll*[221] the Court confirmed that the survivor could rely on Article 141 to assert his rights since the right to payment of a survivors' pension arose at the time of the death of an employee affiliated to the scheme and the survivor was the only person in a position to assert the right. The Court also confirmed in *Coloroll* that the temporal limitation laid down in *Barber* applied to survivors' pensions.[222]

(b) Actuarial Factors

In *Neath*[223] the Court drew the line at expanding the definition of 'pay' in Article 141 to include the use of actuarial factors differing according to sex in funded and defined-benefit schemes. Mr Neath belonged to a contributory defined-benefit/final salary scheme where male and female employees' contributions were identical[224] but the employer's contributions varied over time to ensure that the pension scheme was properly funded to cover the cost of pensions promised. The employer's contributions were higher for female than for male employees, due to a variety of actuarial factors in the mechanism for funding the scheme, including the fact that women live, on average, longer than men. This meant that when part of the pension was converted into capital, the male employees received lower sums than the female employees.

While recognizing that the commitment by the employer to pay a periodic pension to the employees fell within the definition of pay in Article 141, the Court ruled that that 'commitment does not necessarily have to do with the funding arrangements (including the selection of actuarial factors) chosen to secure the periodic payment of the pension' which remained outside the scope of Article 141. Consequently, since the use of sex-based actuarial factors in funded defined-benefit schemes did not fall within Article 141, inequalities in the amounts of capital benefits 'whose value can only be determined on the basis of the arrangements chosen for funding the scheme are likewise not struck at by Article 141'.[225]

However, sex-based actuarial factors run directly contrary to the essence of

---

[220] Since survivors' pensions now fall in principle within Art. 141 the exclusion of survivors' pensions from the application of the principle of equal treatment in Art. 9(b) of Dir. 86/378 was *ultra vires*.

[221] Case C–200/91 [1994] ECR I–4389.

[222] See also Case C–50/99 *Podesta v. CRICA* [2000] ECR I–4039, para. 46 and 9th Preambular paragraph of Dir. 96/97.

[223] Case C–152/91 [1993] ECR I–6935 affirmed in Case C–200/91 *Coloroll* [1994] ECR I–4389, para. 85.

[224] The employees' contributions are an element of pay since they are deducted directly from an employee's salary which, according to the Court in Case 69/80 *Worringham* [1981] ECR 767, is pay. In Case C–200/91 *Coloroll* [1994] ECR I–4389 the Court added that whether contributions are payable by the employer or the employees has no bearing on the concept of pay (para. 88).

[225] Case C–152/91 *Neath* [1993] ECR I–6935, para. 33, and Case C–200/91 *Coloroll* [1994] ECR I–4389, para. 85.

anti-discrimination laws which require that workers be regarded on the basis of their individual characteristics and not on the basis of gender stereotypes.[226] As Advocate-General Van Gerven recognized, health, race, occupation, and social class provide better indicators of life expectancy, and other Community countries manage their occupation pension schemes without reference to sex-based actuarial factors. However, in the UK sex-based actuarial assumptions are used not only by employers but also by pension providers to whom it would be difficult to extend the application of Article 141.[227]

The rationale behind the decision in *Neath* focuses on the fact that the case concerns a defined benefit scheme where the employer knows the extent of the commitment. The same considerations may not apply to money purchase schemes. The Court has yet to rule on this point.

In the amendments to Directive 86/378 introduced by Directive 96/97 (Article 9(1)(h) of the Consolidated Directive) the Directive provides that setting different levels of benefit is unlawful 'except in so far as may be necessary to take account of actuarial calculation factors which differ according to sex in the case of defined-contribution schemes; in the case of funded defined-benefit schemes, certain elements may be unequal where the inequality of the amounts results form the effects of the use of actuarial factors differing according to sex at the time when the scheme's funding is implemented'.[228]

(c) Additional Voluntary Contributions

The Court also took a strict line in respect of Additional Voluntary Contributions (AVCs) paid by employees to secure additional benefits such as an additional tax-free lump sum.[229] Since the AVCs are paid into a separate fund merely administered by the occupational scheme, and since they secure benefits additional to those connected with their employment, the Court said in *Coloroll*[230] that AVCs were not pay within the meaning of Article 141 and this has now been confirmed by Article 2(2)(e) of the revised Directive 86/378 (Article 8(1)(e) of the Consolidated Directive).

---

[226] Cf. Art. 5(1) of the Goods and Services Dir. 2004/113/EC (OJ [2004] L373/37. However, Art. 5(2) does permit proportionate differences in individuals' premiums and benefits where the use of sex is a determining factor in the assessment of risk based on relevant and accurate actuarial and statistical data.

[227] Rubinstein, Editorial [1994] IRLR 51.

[228] The Directive also provides that setting different levels for employers' contributions contravenes the principle of equal treatment except:
- in the case of defined-contribution schemes if the aim is to equalize the amount of the final benefits to make them more nearly equal for both sexes;
- in the case of funded defined-benefit schemes where the employer's contributions are intended to ensure the adequacy of the funds necessary to cover the cost of the benefits defined.

[229] Case C–200/91 *Coloroll* [1994] ECR I–4389.

[230] Case C–200/91 [1994] ECR I–4389.

4.8. Remedies

The obligation to secure equality applies not only to employers but also to the trustees of a pension scheme. The Court made this clear in *Barber*.[231] The Court recognized that Article 141 applied to an occupational pension scheme set up in the form of a trust and administered by trustees who were technically independent of the employer because Article 141 applied to 'consideration received indirectly from the employer'.[232] In *Coloroll*[233] the Court added that the trustees were bound to do everything within the scope of their powers to ensure compliance with the principle of equal treatment, especially when a worker changes job, transferring pension rights from one occupational scheme to another. When the worker reaches retirement age, the *second* scheme is obliged to increase the benefits it undertook to pay him when accepting the transfer so as to eliminate the effects, contrary to Article 141, suffered by the worker due to the inadequacy of the capital transferred because of discrimination suffered under the first scheme.[234]

If securing the principle of equality is beyond the powers of trustees, employers and trustees are bound to use all means available under domestic law, such as having recourse to the national courts, especially where the involvement of the courts is necessary to amend the provisions of the pension scheme or trust deed.[235] The courts are bound to provide the legal protection which individuals derive from the direct effect of provisions of the Treaty,[236] and where necessary they must disapply any incompatible domestic provisions.

Given the long-term investment involved in accumulating a pension, the question of national time limits has become a major issue which has arisen in the context of remedies, particularly in respect of access to occupational pensions as a result of the decisions in *Vroege*[237] and *Fisscher*.[238] It will be recalled that the temporal limitation laid down in *Barber*[239] did not apply to

---

[231] Case C–262/88 [1990] ECR I–1889, paras. 28 and 29. See also new Art. 6(2) of Dir. 86/378 (Art. 9(2) of the Consolidated Directive).

[232] The Court has also said that Art. 141 applies to administrators of a pension scheme (Case C–128/93 *Fisscher* [1994] ECR I–4583, para. 32).

[233] Case C–200/91 [1994] ECR I–4389.

[234] This only applies to benefits payable in periods of service subsequent to 17 May 1990.

[235] Case C–200/91 *Coloroll* [1994] ECR I–4389, para. 39. The same applies to the administrators of an occupational pension scheme: Case C–128/93 *Fisscher* v. *Voorhuis Hengelo BV* [1994] ECR I–4583, para. 31; and insuring bodies responsible for administering occupational pension schemes in Germany: Case C–379/99 *Pensionskasse für die Angestellten der Barmer Ersatzkasse VVaG* v. *Hans Menauer* [2001] ECR I–7275, para. 24. If the funds held by the pension scheme are insufficient to meet the principle of equal pay, this is a matter for national law to resolve: Case C–200/91 *Coloroll* [1994] ECR I–4389, paras. 42 and 43.

[236] Case C–213/89 R v. *Secretary of State for Transport, ex parte Factortame* [1990] ECR I–2433, para. 19.

[237] Case C–57/93 [1994] ECR I–4541.   [238] Case C–128/93 [1994] ECR I–4583.

[239] Case 262/88 [1990] ECR I–1889.

the right of access to occupational pension schemes. Consequently, the direct effect of Article 141 could be relied on in order retroactively to claim equal treatment in relation to the right to join an occupational pension scheme and this may be done as from 8 April 1976. However, the Court said that in those cases national time limits might preclude such extensive retrospective claims.[240]

Doubt has been cast on that rule by *Magorrian*.[241] In that case the applicants began employment as full-time workers and then became part-time workers when they had children. When they retired they were not entitled to the more favourable pension benefits available to full-time workers. In response to their claim under Article 141, the UK government argued that under the relevant statute no award of arrears of pay could be made relating to a period earlier than two years before the date on which the proceedings were instituted. The Court, reaffirming its decisions in *Vroege* and *Fisscher*, said that the direct effect of Article 141 could be relied on, as from 8 April 1976, in order retroactively to claim equal treatment in relation to the *right to join* (access to) an occupational pension scheme. The UK, however, argued that this case concerned the amount of *benefits* payable under the scheme (to which the *Barber* temporal limitation would apply) and not the right to belong to the scheme. However, the Court referring to its decision in *Dietz*,[242] said that membership of a scheme would be of no interest to employees if it did not confer entitlement to the benefits provided by the scheme in question. Therefore, entitlement to a retirement pension under an occupational scheme was indissolubly linked to the right to join such a scheme. It continued that the same was true in *Magorrian* where the discrimination suffered by part-time workers stemmed from discrimination concerning access to a special scheme which conferred entitlement to additional benefits. While helpful to the applicants in *Magorrian*, this observation creates a problematic distinction because benefit claims can usually be defined in terms of claims for full access to that benefit and access claims can usually be described in terms of a claim for benefit which flows from the access.[243]

As far as the backdating was concerned, the Court said the fact that the right to be admitted to a scheme could take place no earlier than two years before the institution of proceedings deprived the applicants of the additional benefits under the scheme to which they were entitled to be affiliated. However, the UK argued that following *Johnson (No. 1)*[244] and *Steenhorst Neerings*[245] a restriction on backdating was valid under Community law. The Court disagreed. It said that in *Magorrian* the claim was not for the retroactive

[240] See 5th Preambular paragraph of Dir. 96/97. See also Art. 12(2) of the Consolidated Dir.
[241] Case C–246/96 [1997] ECR I–7153.
[242] Case C–435/93 *Dietz v. Stichting Thuiszorg Rotterdam* [1996] ECR I–5223.
[243] Rubinstein [1998] IRLR 55.   [244] Case C–31/90 [1991] ECR I–3723.
[245] Case C–338/91 [1993] ECR I–5475.

award of certain additional benefits but for recognition of entitlement to full membership of an occupational scheme. Whereas the rules at issue in *Johnson* merely limited the period, prior to commencement of proceedings, in respect of which backdated benefits could be obtained, the rule at issue in *Magorrian* prevented the entire record of service completed by those concerned after 8 April 1976 until 1990 from being taken into account for the purposes of calculating the additional benefits which would be payable even after the date of the claim. Consequently, the Court said that the UK rule rendered any action by individuals relying on Community law impossible in practice and limited the direct effect of Article 141 of the Treaty in cases in which no such limitation had been laid down either in the Court's case law or in Protocol No. 2 annexed to the Treaty on European Union.

The scope of this aspect of the ruling is not clear and sits uncomfortably with the earlier decisions in *Fisscher* and *Fantask*.[246] It seems that in the ordinary case of a limitation on the retroactive effect of such claims, the claim is limited in terms of periods which are prior to the date of institution of proceedings but the claimant is able to vindicate her rights for the future. The Court's view of the effect of the rule in *Magorrian* was that it prevented the applicants from claiming access to the scheme for the future as well: if each woman could count only two years of past part-time service towards the 20-year requirement, the applicants would have had to come out of retirement and seek to work for some considerable time into the future to vindicate their rights of access under Article 141.[247]

Nevertheless, in *Preston*[248] the Court repeated its approach in *Magorrian* (and thus continued to draw a distinction between arrears of benefits (time limited by *Barber*) and access to retroactive membership of the scheme (time limited back to April 1976[249]), thereby enabling the part-time workers, who formed part of 22 test cases co-ordinated by the TUC, to claim retrospective membership of occupational pension schemes in respect of periods of employment since April 1976, despite the fact that English law limited retrospective membership to two years, although these women would, if necessary, have to pay employee contributions relating to the period of membership.[250]

The other issue raised in *Preston* concerned time limits for bringing a claim. Under English law claimants had six months from the end of the contract of employment to lodge a claim. The Court said this was compatible with Community law provided that it did not contravene the principle of equivalence.[251] When the case returned to the House of Lords,[252] the Lords found that the six-month limit did not breach the principle of equivalence because it was not less favourable than the six-year limitation period for bringing a claim for

---

[246] Case C–188/95 [1997] ECR I–6783.   [247] Coppel (1998) 27 *ILJ*. 259, 261.
[248] Case C–78/98 *Preston v. Wolverhampton Healthcare NHS Trust* [2000] ECR I–3201.
[249] Para. 37.   [250] Para. 39.   [251] Para. 35.   [252] [2001] IRLR 237.

breach of contract.[253] This meant that some of the 60,000 test cases failed because the part-timers had not brought their claims in time, even though they could not reasonably have known of their right to bring claims. However, for those still in the same employment, the clock had yet to start ticking and they could claim back to the start of the employment relationship.

But what about those applicants who were employed on a series of fixed term contracts but with intervals in between those contracts? Should they have brought their claim at the end of each individual contract or at the end of the employment relationship as a whole? The Court of Justice, opting for the latter approach, said that the former approach made it excessively difficult to bring a claim.[254] The House of Lords followed this and said that fixed term employees did not have to bring their claim within six months of the end of each contract so long as there was a 'stable employment relationship'.[255] However, where there were intermittent contracts of service without a stable employment relationship, the period of six months ran from the end of each contract of service.

D. CONCLUSIONS

The Court's case law on pensions shows just how radical the application of the equality principle can be. It also demonstrates that the Court is prepared to disregard the views of the legislature to give full effect to the 'fundamental' principle of equality. While in some respects, women, especially women who work part time, have benefited from the Court's case law, in others their position may have deteriorated as a result of the employer's need to secure equality for men in occupational pension schemes.

The pensions issue will not go away. With an ageing population and considerable shortfalls in the funding of pensions[256] it may well be that the pension age will continue to rise, that there will be a move towards flexible retirement[257] and that there will be an increasing interest in the portability of pensions. Most interesting will be the interrelationship between pension provision and the age discrimination provisions in the Framework Directive on Equal Treatment.

---

[253] Lord Slynn refused to look merely at the limitation periods themselves but the whole context of the limitation periods: e.g. a claim under contract can only go back six years while a claim for equal pay brought within six months of the termination of employment can go back to the beginning of employment or 8 April 1976.

[254] Para. 72.   [255] On the meaning of this term see the EAT's decision: [2004] IRLR 96.

[256] Marshall and Butterworth, 'Pensions Reform in the EU: the Unexploded Time Bomb in the Single Market' (2000) 37 *CMLRev.* 739.

[257] Art. 9a of Dir. 86/378 (Art. 13 of the Consolidated Directive) provides that 'Where men and women may claim a flexible pensionable age under the same conditions, this shall not be deemed to be incompatible with this Chapter'.

PART IV

Health and Safety and Working Conditions

11

Health and Safety

A. INTRODUCTION

The Community has been concerned about health and safety issues since its inception. Article 117 EEC (now 136) calls for the improvement in working conditions and standards of living of workers[1] while Article 118 EC (now 140) empowers the Commission to promote close co-operation between Member States in the field of occupational hygiene. There is a two-fold justification for addressing health and safety. The first is personal, the second economic. Industrial accidents and work-related ill health represent not only a cost in terms of human suffering but also a financial cost estimated at between 1.5 and 4 per cent of GDP.[2] Four sectors (fishing, agriculture, construction, and health and social services) have an accident rate 30 per cent above average; four others (the extractive industries, manufacturing, hotels and restaurants, and transport) have an accident rate 15 per cent above average. The Commission therefore argues that higher health and safety standards, while initially imposing increased costs, should guarantee in the long term a reduction in the number of accidents and occupational diseases, thereby reducing costs to business and increasing competitiveness without reducing the number of jobs.[3]

The other main economic justification for EC action in the field of health and safety is to create a level playing field. Community rules deprive those countries with low health and safety standards of a perceived competitive advantage over those countries with higher standards and thus greater costs. This argument has particular resonance within the UK, which has always guaranteed relatively high levels of health and safety protection for its workforce, for which British industry has incurred a heavier financial burden.

This chapter looks at the Community measures traditionally regarded— certainly from a common law perspective—as health and safety matters: the Framework Directive 89/391 on health and safety and, in outline, its

---

[1] See also Art. 3 ECSC; Art. 2 Euratom refers to the establishment of uniform safety standards to protect the health of workers.

[2] See http://europa.eu.int/comm/dg05/h&s/intro/prog2000.htm. Even though the EU's record has improved, when the number of occupational accidents fell by just short of 10% between 1994 and 1998, the absolute figures remain high with approx. 5,500 deaths and 4.8 million accidents resulting in three days or more off work in 1998: COM(2002) 118, 3.

[3] COM(88) 74, Commission's Memorandum to the Framework Dir. 89/391/EEC.

daughters. Chapter 12 then examines those measures which fall within a rather broader—and more Scandinavian—definition of health and safety, which encompasses references to the working environment. In particular, it examines the Working Time Directive 2003/88 and the Young Workers Directive 94/33 as well as considering two measures which are traditionally considered labour law matters: proof of the contract of employment, and pay.

B. THE DEVELOPMENT OF A UNION POLICY IN RESPECT OF HEALTH AND SAFETY

1. Introduction

All Member States have traditionally regulated the health and safety of workers, through constitutional provisions (Greece, Portugal, Italy, and Luxembourg), codes or statutes (France, Netherlands, Germany, Spain, and the UK) or through implied terms in the contract of employment (for example, UK and Ireland).[4] Moreover, in all states employers are under a general duty to provide safe and healthy working conditions. This is variously described as the duty to ensure 'with the diligence of a good father' that work takes place in suitable conditions for health and safety and to observe the requirements of the law (Belgium), 'to take measures necessary in relation to the type of work and the state of technology to protect the physical and mental welfare for employees' and to observe the requirements of the law (Italy) and to ensure so far as reasonably practicable the health, safety and welfare of all employees (UK).

Individual Member States have also evolved a common pattern to the legislative control of occupational health and safety. This involves a basic framework of primary legislation establishing general principles and some specific requirements.[5] This framework may provide the basis for more detailed and specific secondary legislation which then sets out detailed requirements based on general principles established in the primary legislation. Finally, codes of practice and technical guidance may provide a third tier of control. While

---

[4] See generally *The Regulation of Working Conditions in the Member States of the European Community*, Vol. I, *Social Europe* 4/92, 108–11.

[5] See e.g. Denmark, the Working Environment Act 1975; Greece, Health and Safety of Workers Act 1985; Ireland, the Safety, Health and Welfare at Work Act 1989; Netherlands, the Working Environment Act 1980; UK, the Health and Safety at Work Act 1974.

breaches of codes and guidelines are not generally offences, evidence of compliance or non-compliance may be used in legal proceedings. In recent years this national approach has influenced the Commission's strategy to legislation. It has adopted framework Directives prescribing general duties and more specific daughter Directives.

2. Historical Perspective

2.1. The Early Days

Under the ECSC Treaty[6] various health and safety research programmes were carried out and attempts were made to reduce the number of explosions and fires in coal mines. Similarly, in the early stages of the evolution of a Community policy on health and safety under the Treaty of Rome the emphasis was on 'mapping' the area and identifying the problems.[7] The 1974 Social Action Programme[8] talked of establishing a programme for workers 'aimed at the humanisation of their living and working conditions . . . with particular reference to: . . . improvement in safety and health conditions at work.' This led to the Advisory Committee for Safety, Hygiene and Health Protection at Work,[9] designed to assist the Commission in preparing and implementing activities in the fields of health, safety and hygiene, and the adoption of the first two health and safety Directives, concerning signs at the workplace and protection against vinyl chloride monomers (VCMs). The safety signs Directive 77/576[10] was introduced at a time of increasing freedom of movement of persons[11] to reduce both the risk of accidents at work and occupational diseases due to language problems. The Directive provided a comprehensive set

---

[6] Art. 55(2) ECSC.

[7] For a detailed discussion of the development of a Community policy on health and safety, see Neal and Wright (eds), *The European Communities' Health and Safety Legislation* (Chapman & Hall, London, 1992) Preface.

[8] Council Resolution 74/C 13/1 of 21 January 1974.

[9] Council Decision 74/325/EEC (OJ [1975] C185/15). A year later the European Foundation for the Improvement of Living and Working Conditions (the Dublin Foundation) was established (Reg. 1365/75) (OJ [1975] C139/1), a body engaged in applied research in areas of social policy, including the improvement and protection of the environment. As a result of the Community Social Charter 1989 there is now a European Agency for Safety and Health at Work (in Bilbao) Council Reg. (EC) No. 2062/94 (OJ [1994] L216/1) amended by Council Reg. (EC) No. 1643/95 (OJ [1995] L156/1) COM(90) 564 final (OJ [1991] C27/3) which is intended to provide support for the implementation of programmes relating to the workplace, including technical and scientific assistance and co-ordination as well as assistance in the field of training. The Agency works closely with European Foundation.

[10] OJ [1977] L229/12.   [11] Considered further in Chs. 4 and 5.

of colour co-ordinated signs to draw workers' attention to specific hazards.[12] This Directive was superseded by Directive 92/58.[13]

The VCM Directive 78/610/EEC[14] provided the model which was to be applied in subsequent Directives. Employers were required to take technical preventive measures (reducing the concentration of VCM to which workers are exposed,[15] setting limits on the atmospheric concentration of VCM in the working area,[16] making provisions for monitoring the atmospheric concentration of VCM,[17] and, where necessary, making provision for personal protection measures[18]), to provide adequate information to the workers on the risks to which they are exposed and the precautions to be taken;[19] to keep a register of workers with particulars of the type and duration of their work and the exposure to which they have been subjected;[20] and to provide medical surveillance, ensuring that workers are examined by a competent doctor, both on recruitment or prior to taking up the activities and subsequently.

This period (1978–1982) also saw the adoption of the first action programme on safety and health at work,[21] focusing on the causes of occupational accidents and disease, the protection against dangerous substances, prevention of hazards caused by machinery and the improvement of human behaviour. The second action programme 1982–1986, added measures on training, information, statistics and research. The 1978–1982 action programme resulted in the enactment of the first Framework Directive on

---

[12] Art. 1(1): red means stop or prohibition and is also used to identify fire-fighting equipment; yellow, caution or possible danger and can be used to identify particular dangers, such as fire, radiation, and chemical hazards, as well as to identify steps and dangerous obstacles; green, no danger or first aid and can be used to identify emergency routes and exits, first aid stations and rescue points; and blue, a mandatory sign or conveys information and is used to demonstrate the obligation to wear individual safety equipment and the location of a telephone.

[13] Council Dir. 92/58/EEC of 24 June 1992 on the minimum requirements for the provision of safety and/or health signs at work (OJ [1992] L245/23) (ninth individual Directive within the meaning of Art. 16(1) of Dir. 89/391). The principles relating to Dir. 89/391 (see below), including information and consultation of workers, apply equally to this Directive.

[14] Council Dir. 78/610/EEC on the approximation of laws, regulations and administrative provisions of the Member States on the protection of the health of workers exposed to VCM (OJ [1978] L197/12). This Directive was repealed by Council Dir. 1999/38/EC on the protection of workers from the risks related to exposure to carcinogens at work and extending it to mutagens (OJ [1999] L138/66) which in turn was repealed and replaced by Dir. 2004/37/EC (OJ [2004] L 158/50) considered below.

[15] Art. 3(1).   [16] Arts. 2(b) and 4 and Annex I.   [17] Arts. 5 and 6.
[18] Art. 7.   [19] Art. 8.   [20] Art. 9.

[21] Council Resolution of 29 June 1978 (OJ [1978] C165/1), supplemented and revised by the second action programme—Council Resolution of 27 February 1984 (OJ [1984] C67/02). The first action programme focused principally on the causes of occupational accidents and diseases, protection against dangerous substances, prevention of the hazards and harmful effects associated with machinery and the improvement of human behaviour. The second action programme added training, information, statistics and research, and co-operation with other international bodies such as the ILO and WHO.

hazardous agents, 80/1107/EEC,[22] which was intended to protect workers against risks to their health and safety, including the prevention of such risks arising from exposure to harmful chemical, physical and biological agents.[23] The Directive said that exposure of workers to agents had to be avoided or kept at as low a level *as is reasonably practicable*.[24] This provided a margin of discretion in the application of the Directive, particularly for small companies, a discretion which has largely been removed in the Directives adopted under the subsequent Framework Directive, Directive 89/391/EEC,[25] despite strong arguments made to the contrary by the UK and the Commission.[26]

The 1980 Directive was followed by Directives designed to protect workers from lead[27] and asbestos,[28] and noise.[29] The Directives laid down limit values on the exposure to the agents and require risk assessment, risk reduction, medical surveillance, and the provision of workers with information, following the pattern of the parent Directive. The fourth daughter Directive 88/364 banned the use of certain specified substances altogether[30] because precautions were not sufficient to ensure a satisfactory level of worker protection. The parent Directive, as amended, and Directive 82/605/EEC on lead and Directive 88/364/EEC on banned substances have been reviewed and are now included in Directive 98/24/EC on chemical agents.[31]

---

[22] Council Dir. 80/1107/EEC of 27 November 1980 on the protection of workers from the risks related to exposure to chemical, physical and biological agents at work (OJ [1980] L327/8). This Directive was repealed by the Chemical Agents Dir. 98/24/EC (OJ [1998] L131/8).

[23] Art. 1(1).   [24] Art. 3(1).

[25] Although, as we shall see, certain Articles of the Directive make specific provisions for SMEs.

[26] See also Case C–5/00 *Commission v. Germany* [2002] ECR I–1305 where Germany was condemned for exempting businesses employing fewer than 10 workers from being in possession of an assessment in documentary form of the health and safety risks at work under Dir. 89/391.

[27] Council Dir. 82/605/EEC on the protection of workers from the risks related to the exposure to metallic lead and its ionic compounds at work (OJ [1982] L247/12), due to be implemented by 1 January 1986. See now Dir. 98/24 (OJ [1998] L131/11).

[28] Council Dir. 83/477/EEC of 19 September 1983 on the protection of workers from the risks relating to exposure to asbestos at work (OJ [1983] L263/25), amended by Council Dir. 91/382/EEC (OJ [1991] L 206/16; Council Dir. 98/24/EC (OJ [1998] L131/8) and Dir. 2003/18/EC (OJ [2003] L 097/48). Despite the adoption of the Carcinogens Dir. 2004/37 (see below), Dir. 83/477 continues to apply whenever its provisions are more favourable.

[29] Council Dir. 86/188/EEC on the protection of workers from the risks relating to exposure to noise at work (OJ [1983] L137/28). This Directive was repealed by the Physical Agents Dir. 2003/10 (OJ [2003] L42/38). See also Code of Good Practice implementing Dir. 86/188 on the protection of workers from the risks related to exposure to noise at work in underground workings of the extractive industries: http://europa.eu.int/comm/employment_social/health_safety/docs/good_practice_en.pdf

[30] Council Dir. 88/364/EEC on the protection of workers by the banning of certain specified agents and/or certain work activities (OJ [1988] L179/44) due to be implemented by 1 January 1990. See now Dir. 98/24/EC (OJ [1998] L131/11).

[31] OJ [1998] L131/11.

2.2. The Single European Act 1986 and Beyond

The Single European Act, passed to facilitate the completion of the internal market in goods, persons, services and capital by 31 December 1992,[32] also contained some recognition of the role of a social dimension to the internal market programme by means of the new Article 118a.[33] Article 118a(1) contained the commitment that:

Member States shall pay particular attention to encouraging improvements, especially in the working environment, as regards the health and safety of workers, and shall set as their objective the harmonisation of conditions in this area, while maintaining the improvements made.

In order to achieve this objective a new legal basis was introduced. Article 118a(2) provided that:

the Council, acting by a qualified majority on a proposal from the Commission, in co-operation with the European Parliament, . . . shall adopt, by means of directives, minimum requirements[34] for gradual implementation, having regard to the conditions and technical rules obtaining in each of the Member States.[35]

The introduction of qualified majority voting marked a significant departure from the unanimous vote required by Article 100 (new Article 94) for measures directly affecting the establishment or functioning of the Common Market. For the Commission this represented an ideal opportunity to push through social measures on the basis that they were health and safety matters, thereby circumventing any veto that the UK might wish to exercise. The only constraint imposed upon the Commission was that the Directives had to avoid imposing 'administrative, financial and legal constraints in a way which would hold back the creation and development of small and medium-sized undertakings'.[36]

In addition to the new legal basis on health and safety, the Single European Act also introduced Article 100a(2) (new Article 95(2)) which provided that measures relating to 'the rights and interests of employed persons' could not be adopted by qualified majority voting, as provided by Article 100a(1) (new Article 95(1)). This meant that the unanimous voting rules laid down by Article 100 (new Article 94) applied. As the UK government discovered in

---

[32] Art. 8a EEC, Art. 7a TEU.

[33] Art. 21 SEA. This provision is discussed in some detail in Ch. 2.

[34] The reference to minimum standards does not imply lowest common denominator standards. Instead it refers to the power granted by Art. 118a(3), introduced at the behest of the Danes in an attempt to avoid downward harmonization, enabling Member States to maintain or introduce more stringent conditions. This view was confirmed in Case C–84/96 *UK v. Council* [1996] ECR I–5755, para. 17, and again in Case C–2/97 *IP v. Borsana* [1998] ECR I–8597, para. 35.

[35] Art. G(33) TEU replaced the reference to qualified majority voting and the co-operation procedure with the requirement 'acting in accordance with the procedure laid down by Article 189C'.

[36] Art. 118a(2) (new Art. 137(2)), para. 2.

Working Time,[37] there is no clear line distinguishing Article 100a(2) from Article 118a. However, in that case the Court ruled that measures which had as their 'principal aim' the protection of health and safety, albeit with ancillary objectives such as employment rights, could be adopted under Article 118a.

The Treaty of Amsterdam revised the wording of Article 118a. What is now Article 137(1) provides that 'the Community shall support and complement the activities of the Member States' in the fields of, *inter alia*, 'improvement in particular of the working environment to protect workers' health and safety' and 'working conditions'. The inclusion of working conditions is significant for it recognizes that there is a blurring of the distinction between health and safety matters, which required qualified majority voting, and other issues affecting working conditions which, prior to Amsterdam, might have required unanimous voting under Article 100 (new Article 94) and Article 100a(2) (new Article 95(2)). The Treaty of Amsterdam also applied the co-decision procedure (Article 251) for the adoption of measures listed in Article 137(1), replacing the co-operation procedure.

Equipped with the new Article 118a, the Commission drew up a third action programme (1988–1992)[38] to outline ideas for applying Article 118a. The action programme took a broad approach to the meaning of health and safety, determined that workers should have adequate protection from accidents at work and occupational diseases and insisted that the 'competitive pressures of the single market did not jeopardize the safety and health protection of workers'.[39] This programme was therefore focused on legislation. This was emphasized by the 1989 Social Charter[40] and its related action programme.[41] Paragraph 19(1) of the Social Charter provides that:

Every worker must enjoy satisfactory health and safety conditions in his working environment. Appropriate measures must be taken in order to achieve further harmonisation of conditions in this area while maintaining the improvements made.

Article 19(3) adds that 'the provisions regarding implementation of the internal market shall help to ensure such protection'. Thus, the Social Charter Action Programme identified a two-pronged approach: first, the adoption of 'product' or 'trading' directives based on Article 100a(1) (now Article 95(1)) to ensure that equipment being used by workers was safe, and secondly, provisions concerning protection in the working environment based on Article 118a (now Article 137), including a new Framework Directive 89/391/EEC[42]

---

[37] Case C–84/94 *UK v. Council* [1996] ECR I–5755. See further Ch. 1.
[38] COM(87) 520 final and Council Resolution on Safety, Hygiene and Health at Work of 21 December 1987 (OJ [1987] C28/88).
[39] http://europa.eu.int/comm/employment_social/health_safety/strategies_en.htm
[40] COM(89) 471 final.   [41] COM(89) 568 final.   [42] OJ [1989] L183/1.

and its daughter Directives laying down minimum health and safety requirements for the workplace, the use of work equipment, personal protective
equipment, and chemical, physical and biological agents. The Commission
emphasized that priority would be given to new initiatives in areas where
safety caused significant problems, such as the building industry, and fisheries.
It also urged Member States to put forward ideas for a schedule of industrial
diseases. This led to a Commission Recommendation,[43] suggesting that Member States introduce into their national laws provisions concerning scientifi-
cally recognized occupational diseases liable to compensation and subject to
preventive measures. Although this Recommendation is only soft law, in
Grimaldi v. *Fonds des Maladies Professionnelles*[44] the Court ruled that recommendations had to be taken into account by national courts when deciding
disputes before them, in particular when Recommendations clarify the interpretation of national rules adopted in order to implement them or when they
are designed to supplement binding Community measures.

The fourth Community action programme (1996–2000)[45] was designed to
support the implementation and the application of the existing legislation. It
also put increased emphasis on non-legislative measures,[46] especially providing information. In particular, the Commission focused on making legislation
more effective, preparing for enlargement, strengthening the link with (what
was to become) the employability pillar of the Employment Guidelines, especially after the Amsterdam and Luxembourg Summits, and examining the
new health and safety risks faced by the changing structure of the working
population and employment patterns (an ageing workforce; a steady increase
in the proportion of female workers; an increase in casual and part-time work
and, in economic sectors other than agriculture, self-employment, with a
continuing increase in jobs in the service sector). Social dialogue was also
emphasized as central to successful action on health and safety.

2.3. The European Employment Strategy and the Commission's Strategy on Health and Safety at Work

At first, health and safety did not feature in the European Employment Strategy. It was not until the 2001 Employment Guidelines,[47] under the heading
'Modernisation of Work', that the Guidelines provided that Member States

---

[43] Commission Recommendation 90/326/EEC of 22 May 1990 to the Member States concerning the adoption of a European Schedule of Occupational Diseases (OJ [1990] L160/90). See
also the Commission's earlier Recommendations 2188/62 of 23 July 1962 and 66/462/CEE of
20 July 1966.
[44] Case C–222/88 [1989] ECR 4407.   [45] COM(95) 282 final (OJ [1995] C262/18).
[46] See esp. the proposed SAFE programme designed to finance guidance and information to
help small and medium-sized enterprises apply Community legislation correctly (COM(95) 282
and COM(96) 652). Much to the Commission's concern, this programme remains unadopted.
[47] Co. Dec. 2001/53 (OJ [2001] L22/18).

would, where appropriate in partnership with the Social Partners or drawing upon agreements negotiated by the Social Partners:[48]

Endeavour to ensure a better application at workplace level of existing health and safety legislation by stepping up and strengthening enforcement, by providing guidance to help enterprises, especially SMEs, to comply with existing legislation, by improving training on occupational health and safety, and by promoting measures for the reduction of occupational accidents and diseases in traditional high risk sectors.

In its Social Policy Agenda of 2000, the Commission had emphasized the importance of promoting health and safety at work as part of the quality agenda. Thus, it committed itself to codifying and simplifying health and safety legislation and adapting and improving existing legislation, taking into account Community case law and the changing world of work.[49] The Nice European Council's Social Agenda was more prescriptive.[50] It emphasized not only consolidation and simplification of the existing acquis but also required the Community to respond to new risks, such as work-related stress, by initiatives on standards and exchanges of good practice; to promote the application of legislation in SMEs, taking into account the special constraints to which they are exposed, to apply them by means of a specific programme, and to develop exchanges of good practice and collaboration between labour inspection institutions in order to satisfy the common essential requirements more effectively. This concern with health and safety also fed into the Charter of Fundamental Rights 2000. Under the heading 'Fair and Just Working Conditions', Article II–91(1) of the Constitutional Treaty (Article 31(1) of the Charter) provided that 'Every worker has the right to working conditions which respect his or her health, safety and dignity'.

Health and safety also formed one of the indicators of quality at work in the Commission's communication on quality.[51] Thus, it said that the key policy objective is to ensure that working conditions are safe, healthy, and supportive—in both physical and psychological terms. Indicators to be adopted include accidents at work (fatal and serious), rates of occupational disease including new risks (e.g. repetitive strain), stress levels, and other difficulties concerning working arrangements. This was followed up by the Commission's Strategy on Health and Safety at Work 2002–6[52] which has three 'novel' features.[53]

First, it adopts a 'global approach' to 'well being at work', taking account of (1) changes in the world of work (a changing profile of the workforce—an increasingly feminized society with a particular susceptibility to allergies, infectious diseases, neurological and skin complaints, and an increasingly

---

[48] Para. 14.   [49] COM(2000) 379, 18.

[50] Annexes to the Presidency Conclusions Nice European Council Meeting 7, 8 and 9 December 2000, II.

[51] COM(2001) 313.   [52] COM(2002) 118.   [53] Ibid., 3.

diverse active population, where older workers have an above average fatality rate and younger workers tend to suffer from more accidents at work; and changes in the forms of employment with strong growth in atypical employment relationships, where there is a higher risk of accidents at work especially in the construction industry and in health and social services); (2) the emergence of new 'social' risks, especially stress,[54] depression, anxiety, violence at work,[55] harassment and intimidation, and risks related to dependence on alcohol, drugs and medicines;[56] and (3) increasing flexibilization of work, with more work being done by SMEs,[57] very small businesses, the self-employed, and at home. The global approach has eight objectives including a continuing reduction in occupational accidents and illnesses at work, mainstreaming the gender dimension, prevention of social risks, enhanced prevention of occupational illnesses (especially illnesses due to asbestos, hearing loss and musculo-skeletal problems), and analysis of new or emerging risks with special reference to risks associated with the interaction between chemical, physical and biological agents and those associated with the general working environment (ergonomic, psychological, and social risks).[58]

The second aspect of the Commission's strategy is based on consolidating the culture of risk prevention. This, like the Lisbon strategy itself, is to be achieved through a variety of political instruments—legislation (adapting and update existing Directives, addressing new risks and consolidating existing Directives), the social dialogue (especially at the sectoral level where codes of conduct already exists and best practice has already been identified), progressive measures (benchmarking and identifying best practices), CSR (health at work has been used as a criterion in the choice of subcontractors, and it has been included in voluntary certification and labelling initiatives),[59] and economic incentives (such as through reduced insurance premiums for those with a low accident record). The Council, in endorsing the strategy, emphasized the importance of preparing non-binding instruments (technical handbooks, codes of good practice) to make it easier to implement legal provisions in businesses.[60] The Commission also calls upon a variety of actors to be involved. For

---

[54] The Commission has issued Guidance on work-related stress: http://europa.eu.int/comm/employment_social/health_safety/docs/g_05_guidance_stress_en.pdf

[55] The Commission has issued Guidance on the prevention of violence at work: http://europa.eu.int/comm/employment_social/health_safety/docs/violence_en.pdf

[56] These are responsible for 18% of all problems associated with health at work, with a quarter of them resulting in absence of two weeks or more: COM(2002) 118, 8.

[57] In the construction industry the mean accident rate is 41% above the average. It jumps to 124% for firms with between 1 and 9 workers and 130% for firms with between 10 and 49 workers.

[58] The European Agency for Health and Safety at Work is responsible for acting as the driving force in matters concerning awareness building and risk anticipation.

[59] See also the CSR Green Paper where health at work was identified as one of the ideal areas for 'voluntary good practices' on the part of firms that want to go beyond existing rules and standards: COM(2001) 366.

[60] Res. 2002/C 161/01 (OJ [2002] L161/1), para. 3.

example, a 'fundamental role' is given to the Senior Labour Inspectors Committee (SLIC) to encourage exchanges of information and experience and organizing mutual co-operation and assistance;[61] and the Social Partners are given an important role, especially at sectoral level, together with public authorities, companies, and public and private insurers. The Commission also wants to 'mainstream' health and safety at work: at the micro-level, in individual firms, and at the macro-level. In particular, it should be more prominent in the EES and there should be an improved linkage between health and safety and the Community rules on the manufacture and marketing of work equipment and chemical products and Community policies in the fields of public health, disability, transport, the environment, and fisheries.[62]

The third feature of the Community's strategy, again dovetailing with the Social Policy Agenda, is that 'an ambitious social policy is a factor in the competitiveness equation and that, on the other side of the coin, having a non-policy engenders costs which weigh heavily on economies and societies'.[63]

The Commission's 2002 Strategy—and its enthusiastic endorsement by the Council of Ministers[64]—fed into the 2003 Employment Guidelines.[65] Health and safety formed part of the second of the three 'overarching and interrelated objectives', quality and productivity at work,[66] and formed part of the third specific guideline (address change and promote adaptability and mobility in the labour market) which urged Member States to improve working conditions, including health and safety. Specifically, policies are to achieve 'a substantial reduction in the incidence rate of accidents at work and occupational disease' but, contrary to the Commission's hope,[67] no national quantified targets are set. Yet, by the time of the Lisbon relaunch and the 2005 Guidelines,[68] the prominence of health and safety was reduced to a brief reference in Guideline 21.

However, the Commission's 2005 Communication on the Social Agenda[69] proposes a new strategy for 2007–2012 based on the idea that prevention pays off: fewer work-related accidents and less disease push up productivity, contain costs, strengthen quality in work and hence improve the value of Europe's human capital. The new strategy is to focus on new and emerging risks and safeguarding minimum levels of protection in workplace situations and to workers not adequately covered. Specific attention is also to be given to

---

[61] COM(2002) 118, 10.

[62] This was also emphasized by the Council in its Res. 2002/C 161/01 (OJ [2002] L161/1), paras. 2(e)(a) and 5.

[63] COM(2002) 118, 3.

[64] Co. Res. 2002/C 161/01 on a new Community strategy on health and safety at work (2002–6) (OJ [2002] L161/1.

[65] Co. Dec. 2003/578/EC (OJ [2003] L197/13).

[66] For a full discussion of this approach, see Ch. 3.   [67] COM(2002) 118, 15.

[68] Co. Dec. 2005/600/EC (OJ [2005] L205/21).   [69] COM(2005) 33, 7.

the quality of prevention services, health and safety training, as well as other tools to ensure a better application of health and safety standards. Since the quality of implementation is of vital importance, the Commission is also committed to pursuing its efforts to monitor the transposition and implementation of legislation. Moreover, in order to ensure effective implementation, all the players concerned must have the capacity to take on their responsibilities. The ESF will play a key role in strengthening the capacity of national administrations and Social Partners.

2.4. The Social Partners' Agreement on Work-related Stress

In recognition of the 'new and emerging risks', and their own responsibilities, the Social Partners produced an agreement on work-related stress in October 2004.[70] Stress is defined as 'a state, which is accompanied by physical, psychological or social complaints or dysfunction and which results from individuals feeling unable to bridge a gap with the requirements or expectations placed on them'. It continues that '[s]tress is not a disease but prolonged exposure to it may reduce effectiveness at work and may cause ill health.' The agreement then outlines various anti-stress measures:

- management and communication measures such as clarifying the company's objectives and the role of individual workers, ensuring adequate management support for individuals and teams, matching responsibility and control over work, improving work organization and processes, working conditions and environment;
- training managers and workers to raise awareness and understanding of stress, its possible causes and how to deal with it, and/or to adapt to change;
- provision of information to and consultation with workers and/or their representatives in accordance with EU and national legislation, collective agreements, and practices.

The Social Partners agreed that the Directive to implement the agreement in accordance with the procedures and practices specific to management and labour in the Member States and in the EEA.[71]

The Stress Agreement makes express reference to the employer's legal obligation to protect the occupational safety and health of workers including from the problems of work-related stress. This obligation comes from the cornerstone of Community health and safety law, Framework Directive 89/391.

---

[70] http://europa.eu.int/comm/employment_social/news/2004/oct/stress_agreement_en.pdf
[71] See further Ch. 2.

C. FRAMEWORK DIRECTIVE 89/391 ON HEALTH AND SAFETY

1. Introduction

The most important legislative measure adopted under the Social Action Programme was the Framework Directive, Directive 89/391/EEC,[72] which marked the advent of a new approach to health and safety. While building on the principles laid down in the parent Directive 80/1107, Directive 89/391/ EEC and its more specific daughter Directives,[73] Directive 89/391 lacks the detailed technical requirements found in the earlier Directives and relies instead on broad general principles of prevention.[74] Article 1(1) makes clear that the object of Directive 89/391 is to introduce measures to encourage improvements in the health and safety of workers at work. To that end, it contains 'general principles concerning the prevention of occupational risks, the protection of safety and health, the elimination of risk and accident factors, the informing, consultation [and] balanced participation of workers and their representatives'.[75] Thus, as the Court put it in *Commission v. Netherlands*,[76] the aim of the Directive is not only to improve the protection of workers against accidents at work and the prevention of occupational risks but also to introduce specific measures to organize that protection and prevention. This approach, based on principles rather than detailed technical requirements, obviated the need for lengthy technical debates.[77] The specification of any relevant technical standards has been left to be resolved through a Technical Adaptation Procedure.[78]

Directive 89/391 lays down minimum standards but it does not justify any reduction in the levels of protection already achieved in Member States, since the states are committed to encouraging improvements in working conditions

---

[72] OJ [1989] L183/1.

[73] The enactment of these daughter Directives is provided for under Art. 16(1) of Dir. 89/391. See also Communication from the Commission on the practical implementation of the provisions of the Health and Safety at Work Dirs. 89/391 (Framework), 89/654 (Workplaces), 89/655 (Work Equipment), 89/656 (Personal Protective Equipment), 90/269 (Manual Handling of Loads) and 90/270 (Display Screen Equipment) COM (2004) 62.

[74] Art. 3(d) defines 'prevention' as 'all steps or measures taken or planned at all stages of work in the undertaking to prevent or reduce occupational risks'.

[75] Art. 1(2).

[76] Case C–441/01 *Commission v. Netherlands* [2003] ECR I–5463, para. 38.

[77] See James, *The European Community: A Positive Force in UK Health and Safety Law* (1993) IER 6.

[78] See e.g. Art. 17 of Dir. 89/391/EEC replaced by Reg. 1882/2003 of the European Parliament and of the Council adapting to Council Decision 1999/468/EC the provisions relating to committees which assist the Commission in the exercise of its implementing powers laid down in instruments subject to the procedure referred to in Art. 251 of the EC Treaty (OJ [2003] L284/1).

and harmonizing conditions while maintaining the improvements made.[79] This is specifically recognized in Article 1(3) which provides that the Directive is without prejudice to 'existing or future national and Community provisions which are more favourable to protection of safety and health of workers at work'. Article 4 makes clear that the responsibility for ensuring that employers, workers, and workers' representatives are subject to the legal provisions necessary for the implementation of the Directive lies with the Member States.

2. The Personal Scope of the Directive

The Directive applies to all sectors of activity, both public and private. This includes, in a non-exhaustive list, industrial activity, agricultural, commercial, administrative, service, educational and cultural activities, and leisure.[80] There are limited derogations in the case of 'certain specific *public sector* activities' (emphasis added), such as the armed forces or police, and 'certain specific activities in the civil protection services'.[81] The Directive recognizes that these occupations inevitably conflict with the principle of health and safety. Nevertheless, even in these situations, the health and safety of workers must be 'ensured as far as possible in the light of the objectives of the Directive'.[82] The Directive applies to 'workers', defined as meaning any person employed by an employer, including trainees and apprentices but excluding domestic servants.[83] Thus, by implication, the self-employed are excluded from the benefit of the Directives unless otherwise provided.[84] 'Employers' means natural or legal persons having an employment relationship with the worker and having responsibility for the undertaking and/or the establishment.[85]

3. Employers' Obligations

3.1. The Basic Requirements

Article 5(1) contains the demanding obligation that the employer has the duty 'to ensure the health and safety of workers in *every aspect* related to the work'.[86] This duty extends to taking responsibility for services provided by third parties[87] and is not diminished by the workers' own obligations for their health and safety.[88] Such a definitive statement, when read in conjunction

---

[79] Para. 5 of the Preamble.   [80] Art. 2(1).   [81] Art. 2(2).
[82] Art. 2(2).   [83] Art. 3(a).
[84] Cf. Council Rec. 2003/134/EC (OJ [2003] L53/45) which recognizes the precarious position of the self-employed and encourages Member States to promote health and safety for self-employed workers.
[85] Art. 3(b).   [86] Emphasis added.   [87] Arts. 5(2), 7(3).   [88] Art. 5(3).

with Article 1(1), clearly sets the tenor of the Directive: worker protection. Member States may, however,

provide for the exclusion or the limitation of employers' responsibility where occurrences are due to unusual *and* unforeseeable circumstances, beyond the employers' control, or to *exceptional* events, the consequence of which could not have been avoided despite the exercise of *all due care*.[89]

This derogation, being an exception to the basic principle of the Directive, will be narrowly construed[90] and is unlikely to permit broad defences based on financial considerations or arguments related to lack of time or effort to deal with the risk. The emphasis on the exceptional nature of the events also suggests that, on its face, a defence that the employer took all reasonably practicable steps to avoid the risk would not be acceptable. On the other hand, since the general principle of proportionality applies to the Directive as a whole, it may well be that a more general defence based on proportionality applies to all the provisions in the Directive.[91]

Article 6 fleshes out the wide-ranging general obligations on employers: not only must they take the measures *necessary* for safety and health protection of workers, but they must also prevent the occurrence of occupational risks, provide information and training and establish the necessary organization and means.[92] These measures must be further adjusted to take account of changing circumstances.[93]

Article 6(2) then details the following general principles of prevention[94] designed to guide the employer:

(a) avoiding risks;
(b) evaluating the risks which cannot be avoided;
(c) combating the risks at source;
(d) adapting the work to the individual, especially as regards the design of work places, the choice of work equipment and the choice of working and production methods, with a view, in particular, to alleviating monotonous work and work at a predetermined work rate, thus reducing the effects on health. This provision probably goes further than legislation in all Member States. It is a key requirement which addresses the well-being of workers in a comprehensive way rather than focusing on specific hazards;[95]

---

[89] Art. 5(4). Emphasis added.

[90] To see the application of two principles in the context of the free movement of workers, see Case 41/74 *Van Duyn* v. *Home Office* [1974] ECR 1337, para. 18.

[91] This issue is currently being challenged before the Court: Case C–127/05 *Commission* v. *UK*.

[92] Art. 6(1).   [93] Ibid.

[94] Defined in Art. 3(d) to mean all steps or measures taken or planned at all stages of work in the undertaking to prevent or reduce occupational risks.

[95] For a similar idea see the principle of the humanization of work contained in Art. 13 of the Working Time Dir. 2003/88/EC (OJ [2003] L299/9).

(e) adapting to technical progress;
(f) replacing the dangerous by the non-dangerous or the less dangerous (the principle of substitution);
(g) developing a coherent prevention policy which covers technology, organization of work, working conditions, social relationships, and the influence of factors related to the working environment;
(h) giving collective protective measures priority over individual protective measures;
(i) giving appropriate instructions to the workers.

Article 6(3) continues that the employer shall, taking into account the nature of the activities of the enterprise and/or establishment:

(a) evaluate the risks to the safety and health of workers, *inter alia*[96] in the choice of work equipment, the chemical substances or preparations used, and the fitting-out of work places. Subsequent to this evaluation and as necessary, the preventive measures and the working and production methods implemented by the employer must:

— assure an improvement in the level of protection afforded to workers with regard to safety and health,
— be integrated into all the activities of the undertaking and/or establishment and at all hierarchical levels;

(b) where he entrusts tasks to a worker, take into consideration the worker's capabilities as regards health and safety;
(c) ensure that the planning and introduction of new technologies are the subject of consultation with the workers and/or their representatives, as regards the consequences of the choice of equipment, the working conditions and the working environment for the safety and health of workers;
(d) take appropriate steps to ensure that only workers who have received adequate instructions may have access to areas where there is serious and specific danger.

The Directive also contains more specific employers' duties which can be subdivided into the following five categories:[97] duty of awareness and evaluation, duty to plan and take action, duty to train and direct the workforce, duty to inform and consult workers and their representatives, and duty to report. These will be considered in turn.

---

[96] This is a non-exhaustive list: Case C–49/00 *Commission v. Italy* [2001] ECR I–8575, para. 12.

[97] See also Neal and Wright, above, n. 7, 18, and Neal, 'The European Framework Directive on the Health and Safety of Workers: Challenges for the UK' (1990) 6 *IJCLLIR*. 80, 82.

3.2. Duty of Awareness and Evaluation

Article 9(1)(a) requires the employer to have conducted an assessment of health and safety risks and be aware of the situation of groups of workers who are exposed to particular risks. Respecting the principle of subsidiarity, the Directive prescribes the objectives but allows Member States to decide how these are to be achieved. There is thus no guidance as to how this risk assessment is to be carried out or any indication of the minimum enquiry necessary.

Employers must then evaluate both the risks to the safety and health of workers, *inter alia*, in the choice of work equipment, the chemical substances or preparations used and the fitting out of the workplace,[98] and decide on the protective measures and equipment needed.[99] The employer, when entrusting tasks to a worker, must take account of the capabilities of the individual workers as regards health and safety.[100] This is particularly relevant in the case of pregnant women or women who have recently given birth or who are breastfeeding.[101] Further, Article 14 requires that workers receive health surveillance appropriate to the risks they incur at work. These checks may be provided as part of the national health system. According to the Preamble, employers must also keep themselves informed of the latest advances in technology and scientific findings concerning workplace design.[102] This suggests that the review of health and safety measures should be a continuous process, requiring constant reassessment and evaluation.

3.3. Duty to Plan and Take Action

Having completed the assessment the employer must, where necessary, introduce preventive measures and changes to working and production to improve the health and safety of workers. Any steps taken must form part of a coherent prevention policy[103] and be integrated into all the activities of the undertaking and at all hierarchical levels.[104] In addition, particularly sensitive risk groups must be protected against the dangers which specifically affect them.[105]

The Framework Directive, when read in conjunction with the various daughter Directives, envisages a hierarchy of control measures as follows:[106]

- Elimination of risk from the workplace. While this is clearly advantageous from a health and safety perspective it may not be feasible in practice. Consequently, employers must consider means by which those risks can be reduced.

---

[98] Art. 6(3)(a).   [99] Art. 9(1)(b).   [100] Art. 6(3)(b).
[101] See also Dir. 92/85/EEC (OJ [1992] L348/1) which is considered in Ch. 9.
[102] See also Art. 6(2)(e).   [103] Art. 6(2)(g).   [104] Art. 6(3)(a), para. 2.
[105] Art. 15.   [106] *HSIB* 200, 5.

- The principle of substitution. This may involve replacing one chemical with another one which is less dangerous but is still capable of working as effectively. It may also involve the substitution of another form of the same substance which is likely to be less hazardous, for example, by replacing powdered ingredients with a less dusty form.[107]
- Engineering control. This may involve introducing ventilation, enclosing dangerous processes,[108] using mechanical handling aids,[109] or automation.
- Personal protective equipment (PPE).[110] From a health and safety perspective this is the least advantageous because much PPE is not 100 per cent effective[111] and its success is largely dependent on the correct selection of the most appropriate type of PPE. Its other drawback is that it protects only the individual rather than the workforce collectively. The disadvantages of this approach are reflected in Article 6(2)(h) of the Framework Directive which requires employers to give collective (as against individual) protective measures priority.

Where several undertakings share a workplace it is possible that the different employers may co-operate in implementing the health and safety provisions and co-ordinate their action in protecting and preventing occupational risks.[112] Nevertheless, whatever action is taken 'may in no circumstances involve the worker in financial cost'.[113] This refrain also appears in various daughter Directives.[114]

In order to carry out activities related to the protection and prevention of occupational risks, including the risks faced by young workers,[115] the employer must designate one or more workers to fulfil these tasks.[116] Where—and only where[117]—no appropriate workers exist then the employer can enlist 'competent external services or persons' who must be fully informed by the employer of the factors which may affect the health and safety of workers.[118] Delegating the tasks does not mean, however, that the employer is able to delegate responsibility.[119] Both the internal and external health and safety staff must have the necessary skills and be sufficient in number to deal with the organization of the health and safety measures, taking into account the size of the undertaking, the hazards to which the workers are exposed and

---

[107] See further *HSIB* 200, 5.
[108] See e.g. Art. 5 of Dir. 90/394/EEC (OJ [1990] L196/1). This Directive was repealed and replaced by Dir. 2004/37/EC (OJ [2004] L158/50).
[109] See Art. 3(1) of Dir. 90/269/EEC (OJ [1990] L156/9).
[110] See Dir. 89/656/EEC (OJ [1989] L393/181).
[111] E.g. the effectiveness of respiratory protective equipment can be reduced if the user wears glasses or has a beard.
[112] Art. 6(4).   [113] Art. 6(5).
[114] E.g. Dir. 90/270 on VDUs and Dir. 89/656 on PPE discussed below.
[115] Arts. 6(4) and 7(3) of Dir. 94/33/EEC (OJ [1994] L216/12).   [116] Art. 7(1).
[117] Case C–441/01 *Commission* v. *Netherlands* [2003] ECR I–5463, paras. 20–1; Case C–428/04 *Commission* v. *Austria* [2006] ECR I–000, para. 54.
[118] Art. 7(3) and (4).   [119] Art. 5(2).

their distribution throughout the entire undertaking or establishment.[120] This provision does allow a certain degree of flexibility, particularly for SMEs, as to the appointment of health and safety personnel. Finally, Article 7(2) provides that those workers to whom responsibility for health and safety has been designated must be given adequate time for the task[121] and must not be placed at a disadvantage in respect of their careers because of their health and safety role.[122]

In the specific context of first-aid, fire-fighting, and the evacuation of workers, Article 8(1) allows the employer to take the necessary measures, *adapted to the nature of the activities and the size of the undertaking*, while Article 8(2) provides that the employer can designate workers who are required to implement such measures.[123] However, the most significant feature of Article 8 is the right to stop work. Article 8(3) provides that the employer must also give instructions to enable workers in the event of serious, imminent and unavoidable danger to stop work and/or immediately leave the workplace and proceed to a place of safety. If, in these circumstances workers do leave their workplace under instruction from the employer, or at their own initiative when an immediate supervisor cannot be contacted, they must not be placed at 'any disadvantage because of their action and must be protected against any harmful and unjustified conduct'.[124] Therefore, they should be protected from dismissal or any lesser disciplinary measure. Furthermore, where workers have acted on their own initiative because a superior cannot be contacted and have taken appropriate steps in the face of serious and imminent danger, a subjective test is applied and account is taken of their knowledge and the technical means at their disposal. They are only liable to censure if they acted carelessly or negligently.[125]

The employer must also refrain from asking for workers to resume work where a serious and imminent danger still exists, save in exceptional cases for reasons duly substantiated.[126] This provision is principally designed to apply to safety and repair workers.

---

[120] Art. 7(5). Member States may specify the appropriate numbers, see Art. 7(8). Member States must lay down sufficiently clear and detailed rules relating to the capabilities required of the persons concerned with the organisation of protective and preventive measures: Case C–49/00 *Commission v. Italy* [2001] ECR I–8575

[121] There is no provision for time off without loss of pay in the case of designated workers. Cf. Art. 11(5) which does, expressly, provide for this. This might be explained by the fact that responsibility for health and safety may be part of a designated worker's job and therefore they will be paid for it.

[122] Art. 7(2).

[123] Art. 8(2), unlike Art. 8(1), is not subject to a caveat for SMEs: Case C–428/04 *Commission v. Austria* [2006] ECR I–000, para. 66.

[124] Art. 8(4) and (5).   [125] Art. 8(5).   [126] Art. 8(3)(c).

3.4. Duty to Train and Direct the Workforce

Article 12 provides that all workers must receive adequate health and safety training, particularly relating to the operation of their work stations. This training must be given on recruitment, if and when workers change jobs, if the work equipment is changed, or if new technology is introduced. The training must be adapted to take account of new or changed risks and repeated periodically where necessary.[127] Special training must be provided for workers' representatives with a specific role in the health and safety protection of workers.[128] In either case, training must not be at the workers' or workers' representatives' expense and must take place during working hours.[129]

In addition, the Directive recognizes the role of the responsible exercise of managerial prerogative. Article 6(2)(i) talks of an employer giving 'appropriate instructions to the workers' and where there are specific danger areas the employer must ensure that only workers who have received adequate instructions may have access to them.[130]

3.5. Duty to Inform Workers and Workers' Representatives, to Consult, and to Encourage the Participation of the Workforce

The EU has long had ambitions of incorporating contributions of both management and labour in decisions and initiatives in this field.[131] This was given further impetus by Article 138 providing for a social dialogue, and the Community Social Charter 1989 which required that health and safety measures to take account of the need for 'the training, information, consultation and balanced participation of workers as regards the risks incurred and the steps taken to eliminate or reduce them'.[132]

It is possible to identify three distinct approaches to workplace organization on health and safety.[133] In the first system, found in Germany, Luxembourg, Italy, and the Netherlands, works councils elected by employees occupy a central position, and safety delegates or committees play only a secondary role. Works councils have the right to approve or reject measures proposed by the employer, assist in planning, monitor compliance with the legislation, be informed of relevant information, and accompany inspectors on visits and

---

[127] Art. 12(1).   [128] Art. 12(3).   [129] Art. 12(4).

[130] Art. 6(3)(d). This provision may be read in conjunction with Art. 8(3)(c).

[131] See the Preambles to the 1978 and 1984 Action Programmes and the 1988 Action Programme which envisaged that the Advisory Committee on Safety, Health and Hygiene as a 'highly appropriate forum for consultation between two sides of industry'. See Neal and Wright, above, n. 7, 19–20.

[132] COM(89) 471 final, para. 19(2).

[133] See above, n. 7, 114, and COM(88) 073 final. See also Korostoff, Zimmermann and Ryan, 'Rethinking the OSHA Approach to Workplace Safety: A Look at Worker Participation in the Enforcement of Safety Regulations in Sweden, France and Great Britain' (1991) 13 *Comparative Labour Law Journal* 45.

consult with them. The second system sees joint safety committees as the main channel of participation. In Belgium a special committee must be established to act as a forum for consultation between the employer and employee in all undertakings with more than 50 employees. Similarly, health and safety committees must be set up in all establishments which employ over 50 people in France and Portugal. In Spain committees are compulsory for certain companies, depending on the number of employees and the nature of the risk. The third system, found in Denmark and the UK, involves the workers electing safety representatives who become members of safety committees and are entitled to be informed of all relevant information and to consult the relevant inspectorates.

Directive 89/391/EEC does impose onerous requirements on employers in respect of the provision of information to the workers themselves and/or to their representatives. The term 'workers' representatives with specific responsibility for the safety and health of workers' is defined by Article 3(c) as any person elected, chosen *or designated* in accordance with national laws and/or practices to represent workers where problems arise relating to safety and health protection of workers at work. In *Commission v. Portugal*[134] the Court confirmed that the Directive does not oblige Member States to provide for an election procedure for workers' representatives but envisages other possibilities for choosing or designating such representatives.[135] If the Member State does decide to hold an election, the Directive does not require the national legislation to state all the detailed rules applying to the procedure,[136] although the workers' representatives must be elected by workers in accordance with national law or practice.

The duty to inform extends to temporary and hired workers currently working in the enterprise or establishment[137] and workers from any outside undertakings working in the employer's establishment.[138] Depending on the size of the undertaking, and in accordance with national laws and/or practices, the employer must, according to Article 10, provide all necessary information concerning:

(a) the safety and health risks and protective and preventive measures and activities in respect of both of the undertakings and/or establishments in general, and each type of work station and job;
(b) the measures taken to deal with first-aid, fire-fighting and evacuation.[139]

In order to help workers or workers' representatives, they must be provided with the results of the risk assessment conducted by the employer and details of the necessary protective measures to be taken, as well as details about

---

[134] Case C–425/01 [2003] ECR I–6025.   [135] Para. 20.   [136] Para. 21.
[137] Art. 10(2). See also Arts. 3 and 7 of Dir. 91/383/EEC (OJ [1991] L206/19) on Atypical Workers considered in Ch. 9.
[138] Ibid.   [139] Art. 10(1).

occupational accidents and illnesses and any health and safety reports made to national authorities.[140]

Article 11(1) provides that employers must also consult workers and/or their representatives and allow them to take part in discussions on all questions including working conditions and the working environment, the planning and introduction of new technology,[141] and the consequences of the choice of equipment on the safety and health of workers.[142] The Article presupposes:[143]

- the consultation of workers;
- the right of workers and/or their representatives to make proposals, including making proposals which mitigate hazards for workers and/or remove sources of danger;[144]
- balanced participation in accordance with national laws and/or practices.[145]

The phrase 'balanced participation' is not defined.[146] It has been suggested that the qualification 'in accordance with national laws and practices' has caused particular problems of interpretation,[147] allowing a diversity of potentially inadequate implementation.

Workers or workers' representatives must be consulted in advance *and in good time*[148] with regard to any measure which may substantially affect health and safety, the appointment of designated workers, risk assessment and the provision of information, the enlistment of services or personnel, and the planning and organization of training.[149] If they consider that the measures taken and the means employed by the employer are inadequate they are entitled to appeal to the national authority responsible for health and safety protection.[150] They must also be given the opportunity to submit their observations during official inspection visits.[151]

As with designated workers, workers and their representatives entitled to be consulted about health and safety matters must be given adequate time off work without loss of pay to fulfil their duties. They must also be provided with the necessary means to enable them to exercise their rights and functions[152] and must not be placed at a disadvantage because of their activities.[153] In

---

[140] Art. 10(3).
[141] A study found that only 60% of firms in Europe satisfied this requirement, see Krieger, 'Employee Participation in Health and Safety Protection' (1990) 6 *IJCLLIR*. 217.
[142] Art. 6(3)(c).   [143] Art. 11(1).   [144] Art. 11(3).   [145] Art. 11(1).
[146] This issue is considered further in Ch. 15.
[147] Walters and Freeman, 'Employee Representation in Health and Safety in the Workplace: a Comparative Study in Five European Countries', OPEC, cited in *HSIB* 201, 6. See also Walters, *Worker Participation in Health and Safety: A European Comparison* (IER, London, 1990).
[148] Cf. Council Dir. 98/59/EC on Collective Redundancies (OJ [1998] L225/16), discussed in Ch. 14.
[149] Art. 11(2).   [150] Art. 11(6).   [151] Ibid.   [152] Art. 11(5).
[153] Art. 11(4).

other words, they cannot be dismissed or suffer any other detriment. The full requirements of the information and consultation provisions have been incorporated into the daughter Directives.

Research conducted for the Commission has revealed a picture of only partial implementation in the Member States of the provisions relating to worker representation, particularly in the case of small workplaces and those in the tertiary sector. The same report criticized the Directive's provisions on worker involvement and consultation in that they allow Member States to continue to exempt small workplaces from participative arrangements, they do little to stimulate the development of more general institutions of work-force representation and they fail to encourage state enforcement agencies to adopt a more interventionist role where such institutions are absent.[154]

3.6. Duty to Report

The employer must draw up a list of accidents which resulted in the worker being unfit for work for more than three working days[155] and provide these reports to the responsible national authorities.[156] The detail and scope of the reports may be determined by the Member States, taking into account the size of the undertaking and the nature of its activities.[157]

4. Workers' Responsibilities

Complementing the duties imposed on the employer, the Directive also places significant and detailed obligations on workers. We have already seen, in Article 7, that employers must designate one or more workers to carry out activities related to the protection and prevention of occupational risks. This, according to the Court,[158] is an 'organisational measure consistent with the aim of participation of workers in their own safety'. In addition, Article 13(1) lays down the general principle that:

It shall be the responsibility of each worker to take care as far as possible of his own safety and health and that of other persons affected by his acts or commissions at work in accordance with his training and the instructions given by his employer.

This is part of the Community's preventive policy bringing in all players, including the workers themselves, with a view to developing a genuine culture of risk prevention.[159]

---

[154] Walters and Freeman, above, n. 147.   [155] Art. 9(1)(b).   [156] Art. 9(1)(d).
[157] Art. 9(2).
[158] Case C–441/01 *Commission v. Netherlands* [2003] ECR I–5463, para. 40.
[159] COM(2002) 118, 9.

Article 13(2) fleshes out the workers' general obligation, with examples of three specific duties. The first requires the worker to make correct use of personal protective equipment,[160] machinery, apparatus, tools, dangerous substances, transport equipment, and other means of production.[161] This includes refraining from disconnecting, changing, or arbitrarily removing safety devices fitted to the machinery and equipment.[162]

The second obligation is for the worker to inform immediately the employer or workers with responsibility for health and safety whenever they have reasonable grounds for fearing a serious and immediate danger or highlight any shortcomings in the protection arrangements.[163] Thirdly, workers must co-operate with the implementation of health and safety measures[164] and ensure that the working environment and working conditions are safe.[165] Nevertheless, the final responsibility rests with the employer.[166]

5. Remedies

Article 4 of the Directive provides that Member States must take the necessary steps 'to ensure that the employers, workers and workers' representatives are subject to the legal provisions necessary for the implementation of [the] Directive' but the final responsibility rests with the Member States who must ensure 'adequate controls and supervision'. Although the Directive does not expressly state that Member States must provide workers with recourse to the judicial process if they are denied the rights conferred by the Directive, as a general principle of Community law[167] some remedy must be provided to secure full implementation of the Directive. In *Commission v. Greece*[168] the Court made clear that an infringement of Community law must be 'penalised under conditions, both procedural and substantive, which are analogous to those applicable to infringements of national law of similar nature and importance' and that the penalty must be 'effective, proportionate and dissuasive'.

D. THE DAUGHTER DIRECTIVES

1. Introduction

The Framework Directive provides that a series of individual Directives will be passed to cover specific risks.[169] The general principles contained in the parent

---

[160] Art. 13(2)(b).   [161] Art. 13(2)(a).   [162] Art. 13(2)(c).   [163] Art. 13(2)(d).
[164] Art. 13(2)(e).   [165] Art. 13(2)(f).   [166] Art. 5(3).
[167] See e.g. Case C–326/88 *Hansen* [1990] ECR I–2911.
[168] Case 68/88 *Commission v. Greece* [1989] ECR I–2965.   [169] Art. 16(1).

Directive apply to the daughter Directives, without prejudice to the more specific provisions of the daughter Directives.[170] These (19) daughter Directives can loosely be divided into three categories: those affecting the workplace, those laying down requirements relating to work equipment, and those relating to chemical, physical, and biological agents. They will be considered in outline under these headings.

2. The Workplace Directives

Community legislation on the workplace has adopted a twin-track approach: a general directive covering most industries running parallel with a number of complementary measures targeting specific sectors.

2.1. Directive 89/654/EEC on the Minimum Safety and Health Requirements for the Workplace [171]

The principal aim of this Directive is to protect the health and safety of workers through the proper layout of the workplace. A workplace is defined as 'the place intended to house workstations on the premises of undertakings and/or establishments and any other place within the area of the undertaking to which the worker has access in the course of his employment.'[172] Article 6 imposes general requirements on the employer to safeguard the health and safety of workers by ensuring that:

- traffic routes to emergency exits and the exits themselves are kept clear at all times;
- technical maintenance of the workplace and of the equipment and devices is carried out, and that any faults are rectified as quickly as possible;
- the workplace, the equipment and any devices are regularly cleaned to an adequate level of hygiene;
- safety equipment and devices intended to prevent or eliminate hazards are regularly maintained and checked.

Workers must be informed and consulted about any measures to be taken concerning health and safety at the workplace.[173] More detailed obligations imposed on employers in connection with their workplaces are found in the Annexes to the Directive. The nature of the obligations depends on whether

---

[170] See e.g. Art. 1(3) of Dir. 89/654.
[171] Council Dir. 89/654/EEC on the minimum health and safety requirements for the workplace (first individual Directive within the meaning of Art. 16(1) of Dir. 89/391/EEC) (OJ [1989] L393/1). See also COM(88) 74 final.
[172] Art. 2.   [173] Arts. 7 and 8.

the workplace was used for the first time after 31 December 1992 or was already in use. The obligations do not, however, apply to specific risk sectors, where there is a particularly high incidence of accidents[174] which are covered by specific directives.

2.2. Specific Risk Sectors

Developing and expanding the principles in Directive 89/654, specific Directives are intended to address the special problems relating to industries identified as creating a particular risk. Directive 92/57 concerns temporary or mobile construction sites.[175] It acknowledges that the work site[176] brings together the self-employed and a number of different undertakings working at the site simultaneously or in succession, and that the self-employed, as well as employed workers, must be bound by certain obligations to avoid exposing other workers to various risks.[177] The Directive aims at a 'global approach to accident prevention':[178] by establishing a chain of responsibility linking all the parties concerned—the clients, the project supervisors, the employers, the co-ordinators, and the self-employed—and by integrating health and safety requirements at all stages of the project, in particular by strengthening co-ordination between the parties.[179]

Two Directives concern the mineral extracting industry: Directive 92/91/EEC concerns the safety and health protection of workers in the mineral extracting industries through drilling,[180] which takes into account the findings of the Cullen inquiry into the Piper Alpha oil platform disaster,[181] and Directive 92/104/EEC[182] concerns the health and safety protection of workers in surface and underground mineral extracting industries. Both Directives follow a common format, obliging employers to ensure that:[183]

- workplaces are designed, constructed, equipped, commissioned, operated and maintained in such a way that workers can perform the work assigned

---

[174] Art. 1(2).

[175] Council Dir. 92/57/EEC on the implementation of minimum health and safety requirements at temporary or mobile construction sites (eighth individual Directive) (OJ [1992] L245/6).

[176] Defined to include any construction site at which building or civil engineering works are carried out (Art. 2(a)). A non-exhaustive list of building and civil engineering works is contained in Annex I.

[177] COM(90) 275 final.   [178] COM(90) 275 final.   [179] See esp. Art. 3.

[180] Council Dir. 92/91/EEC on the minimum requirements for improving the safety and health protection of workers in the mineral-extracting industries through drilling (eleventh individual Directive) (OJ [1992] L348/9).

[181] *HSIB* 196, 12, and *HSIB* 181, 2.

[182] Council Dir. 92/104/EEC on the minimum requirements for improving the safety and health protection of workers in surface and underground mineral-extracting industries (twelfth individual Directive) (OJ [1992] L404/10). See also COM(92) 14 final/2.

[183] Art. 3.

to them without endangering their safety and/or health and/or those of other workers;

- the operation of workplaces when workers are present takes place under the supervision of a person in charge;
- work involving special risk is entrusted only to competent staff and carried out in accordance with instructions given;
- safety instructions are comprehensible to all the workers concerned;
- appropriate first-aid facilities are provided;
- any relevant safety drills are performed at regular intervals;

Directive 93/103/EC[184] concerns the minimum health and safety requirements on board fishing vessels. The Directive imposes general duties relating to all vessels and specific obligations on vessels depending on their age and size. Owners must ensure that their boats are used without endangering the health and safety of workers, in particular in foreseeable meteorological conditions, without prejudice to the responsibility of the skipper.[185] Owners also have responsibility in respect of equipment and maintenance: they must ensure that the vessels and their fittings and equipment are technically maintained, that any defects are rectified as quickly as possible, and that the equipment is hygienic.[186] Moreover the vessel must be supplied with an adequate quantity of suitable emergency and survival equipment.[187]

Finally, Directive 99/92/EC on explosive atmospheres has been adopted.[188] This requires the establishment of a coherent strategy for the prevention of explosions.[189]

3. Equipment Used at Work

The Directives examined so far address the health and safety problems arising from the layout of the workplace. The next group of Directives concerns the rules relating to the equipment used by workers. The principal Directive,

---

[184] Council Dir. 93/103/EEC of 23 November 1993 (thirteenth individual Directive) (OJ [1993] L307/1). See also Council Dir. 92/29/EEC (OJ [1992] L113/19) on minimum health and safety requirements for improved medical treatment on board vessels. Art. 8 on the procedure to make purely technical adjustments to the Directive was amended by Reg. (EC) No. 1882/2003 (OJ [2003] L284/1).

[185] Art. 3(1)(a). The skipper is the person commanding the vessel or having responsibility for it (Art. 2(g)).

[186] Art. 7.   [187] Ibid.

[188] European Parliament and Council Dir. 99/52/EC on minimum requirements for improving safety and health protection of workers potentially at risk from explosive atmospheres (15th individual Directive) (OJ [2000] L23/57). See also European Parliament and Council Dir. 94/9/EC (OJ [1994] L100/1) on equipment and protective systems in potentially explosive atmospheres.

[189] Non-binding guide to good practice for implementing the European Parliament and Council Directive 1999/92/EC on minimum requirements for improving the safety and health protection of workers potentially at risk from explosive atmospheres: COM(2003)515.

Directive 89/655/EEC,[190] concerning the minimum health and safety requirements for the use of work equipment by workers, obliges employers to ensure
that the work equipment made available to workers is suitable for the work to
be carried out, or properly adapted for that purpose, and may be used by
workers without impairment to their health and safety.[191] Work equipment,
defined to include any machine, apparatus, tool or installation used at
work,[192] must be selected to take account of the specific working conditions
and hazards existing in the workplace.[193] The equipment provided must
satisfy the minimum requirements laid down in the Annex.[194]

Three Directives supplement Directive 89/655 providing individual, as
opposed to collective,[195] protection. First, Directive 89/656/EEC concerns the
use of personal protective equipment (PPE) in the workplace.[196] PPE can be
used only when the risks cannot be avoided or sufficiently limited by technical
means of collective protection or by measures, methods of procedures or work
organization. PPE means all equipment designed to be worn or held by workers to protect them against one or more hazards likely to endanger their
health and safety.[197] PPE must comply with the relevant Community provisions
in the design and manufacture of the equipment,[198] and must:[199]

---

[190] Council Dir. 89/655/EEC (second individual Directive) (OJ [1989] L393/13). This has been
amended by Council Dir. 95/63/EC (OJ [1995] L335/28) and by Dir. 2001/45/EC on working at
height (OJ [2001] L 195/46).

[191] Art. 3.

[192] Art. 2(a). This is much broader than the original draft which envisaged minimum
requirements for machinery only.

[193] Art. 3(1).

[194] Art. 4(1)(a)(ii). The equipment must satisfy these requirements by 31 December 1992 in
the case of equipment provided for the first time after that date or within four years in the case of
existing equipment. This delay in implementation is designed to lessen the immediate financial
burden, particularly on small businesses. Member States can set a shorter time limit provided that
the time limit is not so short that it does not enable employers to make the changes or it entails a
cost that is excessive compared with what they would have to meet if the time limit had been
longer, see Case C–2/97 *Borsana* [1998] ECR–8597, para. 53.

[195] Collective protection is considered more favourable: Art. 6(2)(b) of Dir. 89/391/EEC (OJ
[1989] L183/1). See also Art. 4 of Dir. 80/1107 (OJ [1980] L327/7).

[196] Dir. 89/656/EEC on the minimum health and safety requirements for the use by workers of
personal protective equipment at the workplace (third individual Directive) (OJ [1989] L393/18)
due to be implemented by 31 December 1992. See also the Commission Communication of 30
December 1989 (89/C 328/02) on the implementation of Council Dir. 89/656/EEC.

[197] Art. 2(1).

[198] Both Dir. 89/655/EEC on work equipment and Dir. 89/656/EEC on PPE provide a social
supplement to two specific, technical 'product' Directives setting minimum safety standards in
respect of machinery, Council Dir. 89/392/EEC (OJ [1989] L183/9), now Dir. 98/37/EC (OJ
1998] L 207/01) on the approximation of the laws of the Member States relating to machinery,
and PPE, Council Dir. 89/686/EEC on the approximation of the laws of the Member States
relating to PPE (OJ [1989] L399/19) as amended by Council Dir. 93/68/EEC (OJ [1993] L220/1)
and by Council Dir. 93/95/EEC (OJ [1993] L276/11), and European Parliament and Council Dir.
96/58/EC (OJ [1996] L236/44). See also Commission Communication 2000/C76/03 (OJ [2000]
C76/3); OJ [2000] C 159/03; OJ [2000] C 185 /04; OJ [2000] C 40/07; OJ C 40/08; OJ [2000] C
40/09; OJ C315/24.

[199] Art. 4(1).

- be appropriate for the risks involved, without itself leading to any increased risk;
- correspond to existing conditions in the workplace;
- take account of ergonomic requirements and the worker's state of health;
- fit the wearer correctly after any necessary adjustment.

Any PPE which is chosen must be provided free of charge by the employer,[200] who must ensure that it is in good working order and in a satisfactory and hygienic condition. The employer must also inform workers of the purpose of the PPE and arrange appropriate training and demonstrations.[201]

The second Directive, Directive 90/269/EEC, addresses the health and safety requirements involved in the manual handling of heavy loads.[202] Manual handling is defined to mean 'any transporting or supporting of a load, by one or more workers, including lifting, putting down, pushing, pulling, carrying or moving of a load, which by reason of its characteristics or of unfavourable ergonomic conditions involves a risk particularly of back injury to workers'.[203] The Directive envisages a hierarchy of measures which employers must consider. Primarily, they are obliged to take appropriate organizational measures, in particular by providing for the use of mechanical equipment, to avoid the need for manual handling of loads by workers.[204] Other steps might include redesigning the job to eliminate manual handling altogether or automating the process. If this is not possible, employers must strive to reduce the risk involved.[205]

The third Directive, Directive 90/270/EEC, lays down minimum health and safety requirements for work with display screen equipment (VDUs).[206] Article 2(a) defines display screen equipment as 'an alphanumeric or graphic display screen, regardless of the display process employed'. In *Dietrich*[207] the Court ruled that the phrase 'graphic display screen' included screens that displayed film recordings in analogue or digital form. Therefore, the applicant, a film cutter, could rely on the Directive against her employers, a German public broadcasting company.[208]

The Directive applies to any worker, as defined in Article 3(a) of Directive 89/391/EEC, 'who habitually uses display screen equipment as a significant

---

[200] Art. 4(b). The worker can be asked to make a contribution towards the cost of the PPE where its use is not exclusive to the workplace.

[201] Art. 4(7)–(8).

[202] Council Dir. 90/269/EEC on the minimum health and safety requirements for the manual handling of loads where there is a risk particularly of back injury to workers (fourth individual Directive) (OJ [1990] L156/9).

[203] Art. 2.   [204] Art. 3(1).   [205] Art. 3(2).

[206] Council Dir. 90/270/EEC (fifth individual Directive) (OJ [1990] L156/14), COM(88) 77.

[207] Case C–11/99 *Dietrich v. Westdeutscher Rundfunk* [2000] ECR I–5589.

[208] The case is also authority for the proposition that the exclusions form the Directive, found in Art. 1(3) should be narrowly construed (para. 50).

part of his normal work'.[209] Neither the term 'habitual' nor 'significant' is defined. In X[210] the Court ruled that Article 3(a) could not be defined in the abstract and that it was for the Member States who, given the vagueness of the phrase, had a broad discretion to specify its meaning when adopting national implementing measures.

The specific obligations imposed on employers are fivefold. First, they must analyse the workstations[211] to evaluate the health and safety conditions affecting their workers, particularly as regards possible risks to eyesight, physical problems, and mental stress, and to take measures to remedy the risks found.[212] Secondly, they must ensure that workstations comply with the minimum requirements set out in the Annex.[213] Thirdly, the employee must receive training on the use of the workstation before commencing work and further training whenever the organization of the workstation is substantially modified.[214] Fourthly, employers are obliged to keep themselves informed of the latest advances in technology and scientific findings concerning workstation design so that they can make any changes necessary to guarantee better levels of health and safety protection.[215] Fifthly, the employer must plan the worker's activities in such a way that daily work on a display screen is periodically interrupted by breaks or changes of activity reducing the workload at the display screen.[216] In addition, workers are entitled[217] to an appropriate eye and eyesight test carried out by a person with the necessary skills before commencing display screen work, at regular intervals thereafter, and whenever they experience visual difficulties which may be due to display screen work.[218] If, as a result of this examination, workers need further assistance they are entitled to an opthalmalogical examination[219] and, if need be, they must be provided with 'special corrective appliances appropriate for the work concerned' if normal appliances cannot be used.[220] Protection of workers'

---

[209] Art. 2(c).

[210] Joined Cases C–74/95 and C–129/95 *Criminal Proceedings* v. *X* [1996] ECR I–6609, para. 30.

[211] Workstation is defined to mean an assembly comprising display screen equipment, which may be provided with a keyboard or input device and/or software determining the operator/machine interface, optional accessories, peripherals including the diskette drive, telephone, modem, printer, document holder, work chair and work desk or work surface, and the immediate work environment (Art. 2(b)).

[212] Art. 3.

[213] Arts. 4 and 5 respectively. These requirements apply to all workstations and not just those used by 'habitual users' (Case C–74/95 *X* [1996] ECR I–6609, para. 41).

[214] Art. 6(2).   [215] Preamble to the Directive.   [216] Art. 7.

[217] Art. 9. Earlier drafts talked of workers being obliged to have an appropriate eyesight test but this was considered an invasion of workers' privacy.

[218] Art. 9(1). According to Case C–74/95 *X* [1996] ECR I–6609, para. 36, regular eye tests are carried out on all workers to whom the Directive applies and not just to certain categories of workers.

[219] Art. 9(2). The *X* case makes clear that this applies only to those for whom an Art. 9(1) test reveals that they need further assistance.

[220] Art. 9(3). See further Case C–455/00 *Commission* v. *Italy* [2002] ECR I–9231.

eyes and eyesight may be provided as part of the national health system[221] but in any case, measures taken pursuant to this Article may 'in no circumstances involve workers in additional financial cost'.[222]

4. Carcinogens, Chemical, Physical and Biological Agents

As we have already seen the four daughters under the original parent Directive 80/1107/EEC concerned specific agents (for example asbestos and lead). The new approach, adopted under the Framework Directive 89/391, is to address the problems of classes of agents—biological, physical and chemical agents, and carcinogens. The first of these new Directives, Directive 90/394/EEC,[223] originally one of the daughter Directives under Directive 80/1107/EEC, introduced general and specific measures for a list of occupational carcinogens[224] and reputedly carcinogenic processes.[225] This Directive was modified a number of times and has now been codified by Directive 2004/37/EC.[226] The Directive aims to protect workers against risks arising or likely to arise from exposure to carcinogens and mutagens at work. The Directive provides that where workers are, or are likely to be, exposed to carcinogens, employers must determine the nature, degree, and duration of workers' exposure in order to assess the risk posed to their health and safety.[227] Article 4 applies the principle of substitution, requiring employers to use non-carcinogenic substitutes which are not dangerous or are less dangerous to a worker's health and safety.[228] Where that is technically unfeasible, employers must ensure that production is carried out in a closed system. Where a closed system is not technically possible, the employer must ensure that the level of exposure of

---

[221] Art. 9(5). [222] Art. 9(4).

[223] Dir. 90/394/EEC on the protection of workers from the risks relating to exposure to carcinogens at work (sixth individual Directive) (OJ [1990] L196/1). Its adoption was also inspired by the 'Europe Against Cancer' campaign, see Decisions 88/351/EEC and 90/238/Euratom, EEC and ECSC.

[224] Defined as a process which may cause cancer and with reference to Dir. 67/548/EEC (OJ [1967] L196/1), Dir. 88/379/EEC (OJ [1988] L187/14) and Annex I of this Directive. An IARC (International Agreement for Research on Cancer) survey found that of 107 chemical substances examined, 38 were carcinogens and 68 were probably carcinogens COM(87) 641 final.

[225] The Directive does not apply to workers exposed to radiation (Art. 1(2)). This is covered by the Euratom Treaty and Directives adopted under that Treaty, in particular Dir. 80/836/Euratom (OJ [1980] L246/1) repealed by Dir. 96/29 (OJ [1996] L159/1) laying down the fundamental principles governing operational protection of exposed workers and Dir. 90/641/Euratom (OJ [1990] L349/21) on the operational protection of outside workers exposed to the risk of ionizing radiation during their activities in a controlled area. Council Dir. 96/29/Euratom laying down basic safety standards for the protection of the health of workers and the general public against the dangers arising from ionizing radiation (OJ [1996] L159/1).

[226] OJ [2004] L 158/50. [227] Art. 3.

[228] This is not contingent on the outcome of the assessment of risks under Art. 3: Case C–2/97 *Borsana* [1998] ECR I–8597.

workers is reduced to as low as is technically possible.[229] Exposure cannot exceed the limit values set out in the Annex.[230] Whenever a carcinogen or mutagen is used the employer must protect workers[231] by, for example, limiting the quantities of carcinogen in the workplace,[232] reducing the number of workers likely to be exposed,[233] designing work processes and engineering control measures to avoid or minimize the release of carcinogens and mutagens,[234] providing collective protection measures and/or individual protective equipment[235] and appropriate hygiene measures,[236] laying emergency plans,[237] providing for safe storage and disposal of the waste,[238] organizing continuous ad hoc training,[239] providing information to workers[240] and/or their representatives,[241] and, on request, to the appropriate competent authority, and arranging medical surveillance.[242] Whatever the cost of these measures, it must not be imposed on the workers.[243] Finally, the list of the persons exposed in the firm must always be accessible to the workers themselves and to their medical representatives.[244]

The scope of this Directive is potentially very broad, for Article 11 expressly recognizes that employers must inform workers of 'the potential risks to health, including the additional risk due to tobacco consumption'. Since there is a recognized link between cigarettes and cancer, the obligations imposed by this Directive on all employers are far-reaching. The Commission recognizes that this Directive will impose a financial burden particularly on industries such as those producing chemicals, fibre, sterilizing agents, crystal glass, and wood preservatives. It argues, however, that enterprises will benefit in the long term through reduced sickness absence and rehabilitation costs, and fewer retirements due to ill health.

The structure and approach adopted in what is now Directive 2004/37 on carcinogens is mirrored in what was Directive 90/679/EEC on biological agents[245] which has now been codified by Directive 2000/54/EC.[246] This Directive relates to those who work in laboratories, hospitals and veterinary clinics and those who are employed in the manufacturing industries, particularly those manufacturing vaccines, and those dealing with sewage and

---

[229] Art. 5(3).   [230] Art. 5(4).

[231] Art. 5(5). This is contingent on the outcome of the assessment of risks under Art. 3: Case C–2/97 *Borsana* [1998] ECR I–8597, para. 41.

[232] Art. 5(5)(a).   [233] Art. 5(5)(b).   [234] Art. 5(5)(c).   [235] Art. 5(5)(g).

[236] Art. 5(5)(h).   [237] Art. 5(5)(k).   [238] Art. 5(5)(m).   [239] Art. 11.

[240] Arts. 5(5)(i) and 12.

[241] Art. 12. There must also be consultation and participation of workers under Art. 13.

[242] Art. 14.   [243] Art. 10(2).   [244] Art. 12(d) and (e).

[245] Council Dir. 90/679/EEC of 26 November 1990 on the protection of workers from the risks related to exposure to biological agents at work (seventh individual Directive) (OJ [1990] L374/1), amended by Council Dir. 93/88/EEC of 12 October 1993 (OJ [1993] L268/71, corrected OJ [1994] L217/18), Council Dir. 95/30/EEC of 30 June 1995 (OJ [1995] L155/410); Commission Dir. 97/59/EC (OJ [1997] L282/33) and Commission Dir. 97/65/EC (OJ [1997] L335/17) which took particular account of the risks concerning the transmissibility of the BSE agent at work.

[246] OJ [2000] L262 /21.

breweries.[247] The Directive classes biological agents, defined as micro-organisms, including those which have been genetically modified,[248] cell cultures and human endo-parasites, which may be able to provoke any infection, allergy or toxicity,[249] into four categories according to their intrinsic danger,[250] and defines appropriate confinement measures. Once again the Directive requires the employer to assess the risks posed by the exposure to the biological agent,[251] replace the harmful agent where possible,[252] and, if not, reduce the risks connected with the exposure to the agents.[253] Detailed requirements as to worker training, information and consultation[254] and medical surveillance,[255] also apply.

Directive 98/24/EC on chemical agents,[256] replaces in a single Directive the first parent Directive 80/1107/EEC, as amended, the lead Directive 82/605/EEC and Directive 88/364/EEC banning specific agents at work. It is thus an example of 'simplified and rationalised legislation'. Chemical agents are defined as any chemical element or compound, on its own or admixed, as it occurs in the natural state or as produced by any work activity, whether produced intentionally and whether or not placed on the market. The Directive follows the pattern of its sister Directives: it requires a risk assessment to be made, it lays down occupational exposure levels and it provides for worker consultation, information and medical surveillance.

The Directives on physical agents also follow this pattern. They aim to harmonize the minimum health and safety requirements regarding exposure of workers to the risks arising from physical agents. The physical agents

---

[247] Arts. 15 and 16.

[248] Two further Directives have been passed concerning genetically modified organisms (GMOs). The first, Dir. 90/219/EEC of 23 April 1990 (OJ [1990] L117/1), amended by Commission Dir. 94/51/EC (OJ [1994] L297/29), and also by Council Dir. 98/81/EC (OJ [1998] L 330/13); Council Dec. 2001/204/EC (OJ [2001] L 73/32); Reg. (EC) No. 1882/2003 (OJ [2003] L 28/01). The first concerns the contained use of GMOs which refers to any work in conditions which are intended to prevent the escape of GMOs into the environment with a view to protecting human health and the environment. The Directive requires risk assessment, minimizing the level of risk, and drawing up emergency plans. The second, Dir. 90/220/EEC (OJ [1990] L117/15), now Dir. 2001/18/EC (OJ [2001] L 106/01) concerns the deliberate release of GMOs into the environment for research purposes and the marketing of products involving GMOs. Those enterprises proposing to undertake either of these activities must notify the competent authorities, assess and provide information on the risks, and may make specified information available to the public.

[249] Art. 2(a).   [250] Art. 2(d).   [251] Arts. 3 and 4.   [252] Art. 5.   [253] Art. 6.
[254] Arts. 7, 9, 10 and 12.   [255] Art. 14.

[256] Council Dir. 98/24/EC of 7 April 1998 on the protection of the health and safety of workers from the risks related to chemical agents at work (fourteenth individual Directive within the meaning of Art. 16(1) of Dir. 89/391/EEC) (OJ [1998] L131/11). The Scientific Committee on Occupational Exposure Limits advises the Commission on occupational exposure limits both in respect of this Directive and Dir. 2004/37.

covered to date are noise,[257] vibration,[258] electromagnetic fields,[259] and artificial optical radiation.[260] The Directives establishes threshold action and ceiling levels for exposure to the agents. In addition, employers are required to conduct exposure risk assessments, avoid risks where possible, failing which reduce any risks, provide personal protective equipment, conduct health surveillance depending on levels of exposure, and engage in worker information, consultation, participation, and training.

E. CONCLUSIONS

The volume of legislation in this field supports the Commission's claim that 'Health and safety at work represents today one of the most important [and] most advanced fields of the social policy of the Union.'[261] Less clear is the Commission's claim that the solid corpus of legislation covers 'the maximum number of risks with the minimum number of regulations'. That said, the EU's approach, based on prevention, is clearly the sensible one, albeit an approach which has yet to bear full fruit, especially in the new accession states.[262]

Despite its undoubted importance, health and safety has always been the Cinderella area of Community employment law, even though there is more regulation in this area than any other area of EC social law. Yet when the delicate issue of working time is thrown into the equation, the whole issue assumes a rather different complexion. It is to this subject that we now turn.

---

[257] Dir. 2003/10/EC of the European Parliament and of the Council on the minimum health and safety requirements regarding the exposure of workers to the risks arising from physical agents (noise) (seventeenth individual Directive within the meaning of Article 16(1) of Dir. 89/391/EEC), (OJ [2003] L 042/38).

[258] Dir. 2002/44/EC of the European Parliament and of the Council on the minimum health and safety requirements regarding the exposure of workers to the risks arising from physical agents (vibration) (sixteenth individual Directive within the meaning of Article 16(1) of Dir. 89/391/EEC) (OJ [2002] L 177/13).

[259] Dir. 2004/40/EC of the European Parliament and of the Council on the minimum health and safety requirements regarding the exposure of workers to the risks arising from physical agents (electromagnetic fields) (eighteenth individual Directive within the meaning of Art. 16(1) of Dir. 89/391/EEC) (OJ [2004] L 159/01).

[260] Dir. 2006/25/EC of the European Parliament and of the Council on the minimum health and safety requirements regarding the exposure of workers to the risks arising from physical agents (artificial optical radiation) (nineteenth individual Directive within the meaning of Art. 16(1) of Dir. 89/391/EEC) OJ [2006] L 114/38.

[261] http://europa.eu.int/comm/employment_social/health_safety/index_en.htm

[262] COM(2002) 118, 4.

12

Working Conditions

A. INTRODUCTION

In the last chapter we concentrated on those measures traditionally considered to concern health and safety in the narrow, common law sense. Since the introduction of Article 118a into the EC Treaty by the Single European Act 1986, all such measures have been adopted under this legal basis and its successor, Article 137. More controversially, Article 118a was also used to adopt other measures which, some considered, were less intimately connected with (an Anglo-Saxon conception of) health and safety, notably the Working Time Directive 93/104,[1] now Directive 2003/88.[2] This chapter will begin by examining this controversial measure, together with the Young Workers' Directive 94/33,[3] before moving on to look at measures which are more clearly linked to employment conditions, notably pay, as well as examining the Proof of Employment Contract Directive which aims at introducing transparency in respect of the terms and conditions of an employment relationship.

B. WORKING TIME

1. Introduction

The Working Time Directive clearly demonstrates the emerging grey area between traditional health and safety measures and the rights of employed persons. The Working Time Directive 93/104/EEC and the Young Workers' Directive 94/33/EC were both adopted under Article 118a EC (new Article 137) and formed key pillars of the EC's Social Charter Action Programme. Previously there existed only certain sectoral legislation[4] and some soft law measures on working time, such as a Council Recommendation of 1975 on

---

[1] OJ [1993] L307/18.   [2] OJ [2003] L299/9.   [3] OJ [1994] L216/12.

[4] See Reg. 561/2006 on the harmonization of certain social legislation relating to road transport (OJ [2006] L102/1) repealing Reg. (EEC) No. 3820/85 (OJ [1985] L370/1) on the harmonization of certain social legislation relating to road transport; Reg. (EEC) No. 3821/85 (OJ [1985] L207/1) on recording equipment in road transport was amended by Reg. 561/2006; Dir. 88/599/EEC (OJ [1988] L325/1) on standard checking procedures on recording equipment in road transport, repealed by Dir. 2006/22 (OJ [2006] L102/35).

the principle of the 40-hour week and four weeks' annual paid holiday,[5] and a Resolution of 1979 on the adaptation of working time.[6] Both the recommendation and the Resolution focused on the reduction in working time for the purposes of *job creation*.[7] The Community Social Charter 1989 marked a change in emphasis. Articles 7 and 8 advocated action on the duration and organization of working time so that the completion of the internal market would lead to an improvement in the living and working conditions of workers in the EC. This enabled the Commission to conceive a Directive on working time, not as a job creation measure, but a health and safety matter, enabling it to select Article 118a as the appropriate legal basis. To support its choice the Commission cited a variety of studies which variously showed that weekly working time of more than 50 hours could, in the long run, be harmful to health and safety, that working weeks of more than six days showed some correlation with health problems including fatigue and disturbed sleep, and that longer working hours substantially increased the probability of accidents at work.[8] This evidence was, however, disputed[9] and the UK challenged the choice of legal basis,[10] a challenge which, as we saw in chapter 2, was ultimately unsuccessful.

The health and safety legal basis of the Directive has subsequently proved influential in the interpretation of the Directive's provisions.[11] For example, in *Wippel*[12] the Court said that 'it is clear both from Article 118a of the EC Treaty . . . and from the first, fourth, seventh and eighth recitals in the preamble as well as the wording of Article 1(1) itself, that the purpose of the directive is to lay down minimum requirements intended to improve the living and working conditions of workers through approximation of national provisions concerning, in particular, the duration of working time'.[13] The Court continued that such harmonization at Community level in relation to the organization of working time is intended 'to guarantee better protection of the safety and health of workers' by ensuring that they are entitled to minimum rest periods and adequate breaks and by providing for a ceiling on the duration of the working week.[14] It concluded, 'That protection constitutes a

---

[5] Recommendation 75/457/EEC (OJ [1975] L199/32).

[6] OJ [1982] L357/27.

[7] See also Council Recommendation 82/857/EEC on the principles of a Community policy with regard to retirement age (OJ [1982] L357/27) which also has the objective of lower activity levels.

[8] COM(90) 317.

[9] See Bercusson, 'Working Time in Britain: Towards a European Model, Part I' (1993) *IER* 4.

[10] Case C–84/94 *UK v. Council* [1996] ECR I–5755, considered further in Ch. 2.

[11] As the Court emphasized in Case C–84/94 *UK v. Council* [1996] ECR I–5755 and again in Case C–151/02 *Landeshauptstadt Kiel v. Jaeger* [2003] ECR I–8389, para. 93, health and safety is interpreted widely, embracing all factors, physical or otherwise, capable of affecting the health and safety of workers in his working environment.

[12] Case C–313/02 *Wippel v. Peek & Cloppenburg GmbH & Co. KG* [2005] ECR I–000.

[13] Para. 46.   [14] Para. 47.

social right conferred on each worker as an essential minimum requirement in order to ensure the protection of his security and health'.[15] In a similar vein, the Court said in the earlier case of *BECTU*[16] that the objective of improving workers' health and safety could not be subjected to 'purely economic considerations'.[17] Therefore, increases in administrative costs in providing the rights laid down by the Directive (in this case annual leave to staff on short contracts) which would weigh more on small and medium-sized undertakings, could not be taken into account.

The Advocate General in *BECTU* went further, suggesting that the right to annual paid leave was a fundamental social right.[18] Citing various international instruments on human rights, including Article 8 of the Charter of Fundamental Rights 1989,[19] he noted that the Directive 'specifically upheld the right to paid leave as a manifestation of the right to fair and equitable working conditions'. He continued, 'Even more significant, it seems to me, is the fact that that right is now solemnly upheld in the Charter of Fundamental Rights [2000]'. Article 31(2) of the Charter declares that 'Every worker has the right to limitation of maximum working hours, to daily and weekly rest periods and to an annual period of paid leave.' That statement, which is inspired by Article 2 of the European Social Charter and by Article 8 of the Community Charter of Workers' Rights, also took account of the Working Time Directive 2003/88.[20] Advocate General Tizzano continued:

> Admittedly, like some of the instruments cited above, the Charter of Fundamental Rights of the European Union has not been recognised as having genuine legislative scope in the strict sense. In other words, formally, it is not in itself binding. However, . . . the fact remains that [the Charter] includes statements which appear in large measure to reaffirm rights which are enshrined in other instruments.[21]

He therefore concluded that 'in proceedings concerned with the nature and scope of a fundamental right, the relevant statement of the Charter cannot be ignored'.[22]

As the Court's remarks in *Wippel* emphasize, the Working Time Directive does not affect the right of Member States or the two sides of industry to conclude agreements which are more favourable to the health and safety protection of workers.[23] The Court recognized this possibility in *Dellas*[24]

---

[15] Ibid.

[16] Case C–173/99 *R v. Secretary of State for Trade and Industry, ex parte Broadcasting, Entertainment, Cinematographic and Theatre Union (BECTU)* [2001] ECR I–4881.

[17] Para. 59. See also Case C–151/02 *Landeshauptstadt Kiel v. Jaeger* [2003] ECR I–8389, paras. 66–7.

[18] See also his views in Case C–133/00 *BECTU* [2001] ECR I–7031, para. 31.

[19] This was expressly referred to by the Court in Case C–151/02 *Landeshauptstadt Kiel v. Jaeger* [2003] ECR I–8389.

[20] Para. 26   [21] Para. 27.   [22] Para. 28.   [23] Art. 15.

[24] Case C–14/04 *Abdelkader Dellas and Others v. Premier ministre and Others* [2006] ECR I–000, para. 51.

where it acknowledged that France had made use of this option by laying down a maximum weekly working time of 44 hours over 12 consecutive weeks, while the Directive imposes only a limit of 48 hours over four consecutive months.[25] However, the Court was at pains to point out that it will verify compliance with the rules laid down by the Directive by reference solely to the limits fixed by the Directive, to the exclusion of the national provisions that provide greater protection.[26] As we shall see below, in this respect the French rules were found wanting.

The original Working Time Directive contained a number of important exceptions, including doctors in training and the transport sector. Both mobile and non-mobile (office) transport staff[27] were excluded.[28] This led to various sectoral agreements being negotiated by the transport sector Social Partners which were given legal effect by Directive,[29] notably:

- Directive 99/63 on the organization of working time of seafarers;[30]
- Directive 2000/79 on the organization of mobile staff in civil aviation;[31]
- Directive 2005/47 on certain aspects of the working conditions of mobile workers engaged in interoperable cross-border services in the railway sector.[32]

A further sectoral Directive, Directive 2002/15,[33] this time concluded via the conventional legislative route, made provision for the working time of persons performing mobile road transport activities (commercial drivers and crew).[34]

---

[25] Para. 52.   [26] Ibid.
[27] Art. 1(3) of Dir. 93/104. See also Case C–133/00 *Bowden* v. *Tuffnells Parcels Express Ltd* [2001] ECR I–7031, para. 44.
[28] These exclusions were interpreted strictly: Case C–303/98 *Sindicato de Médicos de Asistencia Pública (Simap)* v. *Conselleria de Sanidad y Consumo de la Generalidad Valenciana* [2000] ECR I–7963, para. 35.
[29] See further Ch. 2.
[30] OJ [1999] L167/33. Dir. 99/63 implements the sectoral agreement on the organization of working time of seafarers concluded by the European Community Ship Owners Association (ECSA) and the Federation of Transport Workers in the European Union (FST). This agreement reflects the provision of the ILO Convention 180 on seafarers' hours of work. It provides for either a maximum number of working hours (14 hours in any 24-hour period and 72 hours in any seven-day period) or a minimum rest period regime (10 hours in any 24-hour period and 77 hours in any seven-day period). A second Directive (European Parliament and Council Directive 99/95/EC (OJ [2000] L14/29) concerns enforcement of seafarers' hours of work on board ships using Community ports. In addition, a Recommendation (Commission Recommendation 99/130/EC on ratification of ILO Convention 180) concerning seafarers' hours of work and the manning of ships, and ratification of the 1996 Protocol to the 1976 Merchant Shipping (minimum standards) Convention (OJ [1999] L43/9) were also adopted.
[31] OJ [2000] L302/57.   [32] OJ [2005] L195/15.   [33] OJ [2002] L80/35.
[34] This Directive applies to mobile workers employed by enterprises carrying out transport work on their own account. Self-employed drivers, when driving a bus, coach, or heavy goods vehicle, are also included from 2009. This Directive supplements the provisions of Reg. (EEC) 3820/85 now Reg. 561/2006 (OJ [2006] L102/1) on driving rest periods. The Directive is without prejudice to this Regulation, which remains applicable in its entirety as does the European agreement on international road transport (AETR). On whether to apply the Regulation and the Agreement, see Case C–439/01 *Cipra* v. *Bezirkshauptmannschaft Mistelbach* [2003] ECR I–745.

Directive 93/104 itself was amended by Directive 2000/34[35] to include the sectors previously excluded from the scope of the Directive that were not covered by the sectoral directives. Both Directives 93/104 and 2000/34 have now been consolidated and repealed by Directive 2003/88/EC.[36]

2. Personal and Material Scope of Directive 2003/88

Directive 2003/88 concerns all sectors of activity,[37] both public and private, as defined by Article 2 of the Framework Directive 89/391 on health and safety (industrial, agricultural, commercial, administrative, service, educational, cultural, leisure, etc).[38] In the original Directive, the transport sector (both mobile and non-mobile) was excluded, as were the activities of doctors in training. This exclusion has now been removed; the only express exception relates to seafarers, as defined in Directive 99/63.[39] In addition, the Directive does not apply to certain specific activities such as the armed forces or the police, or to certain specific activities in the civil protection services, but only where the characteristics of those activities inevitably conflict with the requirements of the Framework Directive 89/391.[40]

The Directive applies to 'workers' which are defined in Article 3 of Directive 89/391[41] as 'any person employed by an employer, including trainees and apprentices but excluding domestic servants'.[42] It does not apply to those normally regarded as self-employed.[43]

3. Entitlements and Limits

3.1. Introduction

The Directive makes a distinction between limits and entitlements. The provisions concerning working time and night work are *limits*. This means employers must not allow workers to exceed those limits, subject to derogations

---

[35] OJ [2000] L195/41.   [36] OJ [2003] L299/9.

[37] Art. 1(3). Given the health and safety objective of the Directive, the scope is interpreted broadly: Case C–303/98 *Simap* [2000] ECR I–7963, para. 34.

[38] OJ [1989] L183/1. Considered in detail in Ch. 11.

[39] Art. 1(3), para. 2. Similarly, the provisions of the Working Time Directive do not apply where other Community instruments exist relating to specific occupations: Art. 14.

[40] Art. 2(2) of Dir. 89/391. This exclusion is included due to the reference in Art. 1(3) of Dir. 89/391. See Ch. 11.

[41] Art. 1(3) and (4).

[42] The provisions of Framework Dir. 89/391 on health and safety are fully applicable to the Working Time Directive, without prejudice to the more stringent and/or specific provisions contained in the Working Time Directive: Art. 1(4).

[43] Although cf. Dir. 2002/15 (OJ [2002] L80/35) considered above n. 33.

and, where appropriate, the individual opt-out. By contrast, the rest provisions (in-work rest breaks and daily, weekly, and annual rest) all concern worker *entitlements*: the employer cannot lawfully require the worker to work during any such period. On the other hand, if workers choose to work in a way which means forgoing a rest period to which they are entitled this is not unlawful and workers are free to do so. At least, this is the British perspective of the Directive. As the DTI put it in its Guidance accompanying the implementing Regulations, 'Employers must make sure that workers *can* take their rest, but are not required to make sure that they *do* take their rest'. In the UK, the distinction between limits and entitlements is also reflected in the way in which the provisions are enforced: limits are enforced through criminal sanctions against the employer, entitlements through civil action in an Employment Tribunal.

However, in *Commission* v. *UK*[44] Advocate General Kokott has cast doubt on the validity of the distinction between limits and entitlements.[45] She argues that 'no qualitative distinction can be derived from the respective choice of wording between the requirements of Articles 6 and 8 [maximum working time and night work] of the Directive, on the one hand, and Articles 3 and 5 [daily and weekly rest periods] at issue here, on the other'. She continues that the eighth recital in the preamble to the Directive in particular militates against such a distinction, referring as it does to minimum rest periods and maximum working time in one breath and against the background of the same defined objective—both serve to ensure the safety and health of workers.[46]

On the facts of the case, the Commission criticized the DTI's Guidelines on entitlements which 'clearly endorse and encourage a practice of non-compliance with the requirements of the Directive.' The Advocate General agreed. She said that in order to secure effective protection of the safety and health of workers, it was necessary that workers are *actually granted* the minimum periods of rest provided for, and that presupposes that they are put

[44] Case C–484/04 *Commission* v. *UK*, Opinion of 9 March 2006.
[45] At para. 62 she examines the wording of the different provisions of the Directive which, she admits, is highly inconsistent. She says: 'Admittedly, for example, in its English version in Articles 3, 4, 5 and 7 the term "entitled to" is used throughout, which could be interpreted as meaning a mere entitlement. However, in the French, Italian and Portuguese language versions of those articles the terms "bénéficie" (French), "benefici" (Italian) and "beneficiem" (Portuguese) are used, which may be translated into German as "genießen" ("enjoy") or "zugute kommen" ("benefit") and therefore could also be interpreted as meaning an obligation of result. In other language versions again, the use of terminology is not even consistent within the various provisions on rest periods (Articles 3, 4, 5 and 7). Thus for example the German version of Articles 3, 4 and 5 contains the expression "gewährt wird", whereas Article 7 uses "erhält". Articles 3 and 5 of the Spanish version use the term "disfruten", whilst Article 4 reads "tengan derecho a disfrutar" and Article 7 simply "dispongan". In a similarly inconsistent manner the Dutch version uses the word "genieten" in Articles 3 and 5 but the word "hebben" in Article 4, and the expression "wordt toegekend" in Article 7.'
[46] Para. 64.

in a position by their employer actually to take the rest periods which are due to them and are not, for example, deterred from doing so by what she describes as 'factual constraints',[47] such as the risk of becoming unpopular within the business.[48] However, she did concede that it would normally be excessive, if not even impossible, to demand that employers *force* their workers to claim the rest periods due to them; the employer's responsibility concerning observance of rest periods cannot be without limits[49] but she added that an employer could not withdraw into a purely passive role and grant rest periods only to those workers who expressly request them and if necessary enforce them at law.[50]

The limits and entitlements must be read subject to the general organizing principle of the Directive, found in Article 13, of 'humanisation of work'.[51] This provides that an employer intending to organize work according to a certain pattern must take account of the:

general principle of adapting work to the worker, with a view, in particular, to alleviating monotonous work and work at a pre-determined work rate, depending on the type of activity, *and* of health and safety requirements, especially as regards breaks during working time. [Emphasis added]

This provision envisages not only implementing health and safety measures but also respecting the general principle of adapting the work to the worker, an idea which is not directly related to narrowly construed health and safety requirements. This principle is entirely consistent with the broader duty imposed on employers by some Continental systems. In Italy, for example, Article 1087 of the Civil Code provides that, in the organization of the enterprise, the employer must adopt all measures which, according to the nature of the work, experience, and technical possibilities, are required to protect the physical integrity and moral personality of the employees. From the common law perspective, this breaks down the distinction between, on the one hand, the duty of mutual trust and confidence and, on the other, health and safety and may help to explain the debate about the choice of legal basis.

3.2. Entitlements

(a) Daily Rest and In-work Rest Breaks (Articles 3 and 4)

Every worker is entitled to a minimum daily rest period of 11 *consecutive* hours per 24-hour period.[52] Although this implies a 13-hour working day

---

[47] Para. 66.   [48] Para. 68.   [49] Para. 67.   [50] Para. 68.

[51] See Bercusson, above, n. 9. Although Art. 13 is located at the end of Section III on night work there is no evidence that it is confined to this section, particularly since the Article makes express reference to breaks during working time which is found in Section II. Indeed, it would appear from the breadth of Art. 13 that all provisions must be interpreted in the light of the principle of humanization of work.

[52] Art. 3.

the principle of the 'humanisation of work', would prevent an employer from requiring an employee to work such long hours regularly.

If the working day is longer than six hours every worker is entitled to an in-work rest break, the details of which, including the duration of the break and the terms on which it is taken must, by preference, be laid down by collective agreement between the two sides of industry or, failing that, by national legislation.[53] In the British decision of *Gallagher* v. *Alpha Catering Services*[54] the Court of Appeal gave a purposive reading to the rest provisions. The claimants were responsible for delivering food to aircraft. Between loading assignments they were on downtime—they were not physically working but were required to remain in radio contact with their employers and at their disposal. The employers said that these periods of downtime constituted the workers' rest breaks. The Court of Appeal disagreed. Peter Gibson LJ said that a period of downtime could not retrospectively become a rest break only because it could be seen, after it was over, that it had been an uninterrupted period of at least 20 minutes. He said that the worker had to know, at the start of a rest break, that it was a rest break which he could use as he pleased.

(b) Weekly Rest (Article 5)

In addition to the daily rest period, workers are also entitled to weekly rest. Article 5 provides for a minimum uninterrupted rest period of 24 hours for each seven-day period worked plus the 11 hours' daily rest. Therefore, workers are entitled to 35 consecutive hours of rest (11 hours' daily rest plus 24 hours' weekly rest) at least once a week averaged over 14 days.[55] However, if objective, technical, or work organization conditions justify it, a minimum rest period of 24 hours (instead of 35 hours) may be applied.[56]

Article 5(2) originally provided that the minimum weekly rest period 'shall in principle include Sunday'. Although this provision was consistent with the Court's jurisprudence on Sunday trading,[57] the UK government successfully challenged its validity in the *Working Time*[58] case. The Court said that the 'Council has failed to explain why Sunday as a weekly rest day, is more closely connected with health and safety of workers than any other day of the week'. As a result, the provision 'which is severable from the other provisions of the Directive', had to be annulled.

---

[53] Art. 4.
[54] [2005] IRLR 102. See also *MacCartney* v. *Overley House Management*, UKEAT/0500/05/ MAA.
[55] Art. 16(1).   [56] Art. 5(3).
[57] See e.g. Case C–169/91 *Stoke on Trent* v. *B & Q* [1992] ECR I–6457.
[58] Case C–84/94 *UK* v. *Council* [1996] ECR I–5755.

(c) Annual Leave (Article 7)

The Basic Rules

According to the Directive, every worker is entitled to *paid* annual leave of at least four weeks,[59] in accordance with conditions for entitlement to, and granting of, such leave laid down by national legislation and/or practice.[60] This provision, says the Court, is a 'particularly important principle of Community social law' and is intended to enable the worker 'actually to take the leave to which he is entitled'.[61] The minimum period of paid annual leave cannot be replaced by an allowance in lieu, except where the employment relationship is terminated.[62] This point was emphasized in *Federatie Nederlandse Vakbeweging*[63] where the Court said that the employer could not buy out leave which was not taken in one year by paying an allowance in lieu in the following year.

Article 7 is the only substantive provision in the Directive from which there are no derogations.[64] It would therefore appear that the right to four weeks' paid annual leave applies to all workers falling within the scope of the Directive, including part-timers and those on other atypical contracts for whom, presumably, the entitlement will be provided on a pro-rata basis (although this is not expressly provided for in the Directive).[65] As the Court made clear in *BECTU*,[66] such workers often find themselves in a more precarious situation than those employed under longer-term contracts, so that 'it is all the more important to ensure that their health and safety are protected in a manner consonant with the purpose of Directive [2003/88]'.[67] For this reason the UK could not provide that a worker does not begin to accrue rights to paid annual leave until he has completed a minimum period of 13 weeks' uninterrupted employment with the same employer.[68] Member States did, however, have the option under Article 18(1)(b)(ii) (now Article 22(2)) of 'making use' of a transitional period of not more than three years from 23 November 1996

---

[59] It is not clear whether the public holidays are included in this entitlement.

[60] Art. 7(1). Thus, pre-existing national rules permitting workers to qualify for the minimum entitlement to annual leave after 12 months' service would continue to apply. The introduction of a service requirement where none existed previously might breach the non-regression clause found in Art. 18(3).

[61] Joined Cases C–131/04 and C–257/04 *Robinson–Steele* [2006] ECR I–000.

[62] Art. 7(2).

[63] Case C–124/05 *Federatie Nederlandse Vakbeweging v. Staat der Nederlanden* [2006] ECR I–000.

[64] According to Case C–173/99 *BECTU* [2001] ECR I–4881, para. 43, the absence of any derogations emphasizes Art. 7's importance as a principle of Community social law.

[65] Case C–313/02 *Wippel v. Peek & Cloppenburg GmbH & Co. KG* [2005] ECR I–000, para. 48.

[66] Case C–173/99 *R v. Secretary of State for Trade and Industry, ex parte Broadcasting, Entertainment, Cinematographic and Theatre Union (BECTU)* [2001] ECR I–4881.

[67] Para. 63.   [68] Para. 64.

(i.e. until 22 November 1999), during which every worker could receive *three* weeks' paid annual leave.[69]

The annual leave provisions have been more litigated than most. Two issues, in particular, have proved particularly problematic: rolled up holiday pay, and the relationship between sick leave/maternity leave and annual leave. It is these matters that we shall now consider.

Rolled up Holiday Pay

As we have seen, the Directive requires four weeks' annual leave which cannot be contracted out from, save on termination. But how do casual workers enjoy paid leave? Often employers argue that an element of the hourly pay includes an element for holiday pay ('a rolled up rate'). While some tribunals accepted this, provided that the situation was clear to the worker,[70] others were less sure,[71] expressing concern whether rolled up holiday pay was compatible with the health and safety basis of the Directive. In the light of this confused case law, the EAT tried to offer some guidance in *Marshalls Clay Products* v. *Caulfield*.[72] It identified five types of 'rolling-up' provisions, namely:

(1) contracts which are silent as to holiday pay;
(2) contracts which purport to exclude liability for holiday pay;
(3) contracts where rates are said to include an amount for holiday pay, but there is no indication or specification of an amount;
(4) contracts providing for a basic wage or rate topped up by a specific sum or percentage in respect of holiday pay;
(5) contracts where holiday pay is allocated to and paid during (or immediately before or after) specific periods of holiday.

The EAT said that (1), (2) and (3) offended the Working Time Directive but that categories (4) and (5) were permissible. Subsequently, in *Smith* v. *Morrisroes*[73] the EAT provided further general guidance as to the circumstances where a rolled up rate would be legitimate. It said that there had to be *mutual*

---

[69] Prior to the UK's implementation of the Directive, the EAT found in *Gibson* v. *East Riding of Yorkshire Council* [1999] IRLR 358 that, notwithstanding the derogations, Art. 7 was sufficiently clear and precise to have direct effect so that during the period from 23 November 1996 to 1 October 1998 an employee of an emanation of the state (such as Ms Gibson, a swimming instructor at a leisure centre) could take advantage of four weeks' paid leave and not three, since the UK had not enacted legislation to take advantage of the period of delayed implementation. The tribunal left the question open as to whether an individual in private sector employment would have an action for *Francovich* damages. However, in *R* v. *Attorney General for Northern Ireland, ex parte Burns* [1999] IRLR 315 Kerr J seemed to think that the UK's delayed implementation of the Directive in Northern Ireland was an actionable breach of Community law: it constituted a sufficiently serious breach and therefore the Member State was liable for an injury suffered by an individual who suffered loss and damage as a result.

[70] *College of North East London* v. *Leather*, EAT/0528/00 and *Blackburn* v. *Gridquest Ltd* [2002] IRLR 604.

[71] *MPB Structure Ltd* v. *Munro* [2002] IRLR 601 (EAT); Court of Session [2003] IRLR 350.

[72] [2003] IRLR 552.   [73] [2005] IRLR 72.

agreement for genuine payment for holidays, representing a *true addition* to the contractual rate of pay for time worked. The best way of evidencing this was for:

(a) the provision for rolled up holiday pay to be clearly incorporated into the contract of employment;
(b) the percentage or amount allocated to holiday pay (or particulars sufficient to enable it to be calculated) to be identified in the contract, and preferably also in the payslip;
(c) records to be kept of holidays taken (or of absences from work when holidays can be taken) and for reasonably practicable steps to be taken to ensure that workers take their holidays before the end of the relevant holiday year.

When *Marshalls Clay* reached the Court of Appeal,[74] a reference was made to the European Court of Justice. Before doing so, Laws LJ said that Article 7 laid down two requirements: (1) the worker's entitlement to annual leave of at least four weeks; and (2) he was to be paid as well for the period when he takes leave as for the period when he worked. Laws LJ added that Article 7 said nothing about the timing of the payment for the leave. He also dismissed the argument[75] that rolled up holiday pay arrangements would discourage workers from taking their holidays. He argued that a provision which discouraged individuals from taking their holidays was not antipathetical to Article 7 of the Directive. He also thought that workers were up to the task of planning their holiday arrangements. He added that the fact that the arrangements about rolled up holiday pay were the product of a collective agreement pointed to their legitimacy.

The Article 234 reference in *Marshalls Clay* was joined to another, earlier reference, *Robinson-Steele* v. *RF Retail Services Ltd*,[76] where an employment tribunal decided that it did not want to follow the EAT's decision in *Marshalls Clay*. In *Robinson-Steele* the employer provided in the applicant's contract that:

Entitlement to payment for leave accrues in proportion to the amount of time worked continuously by the temporary worker on assignment during the leave year. The temporary worker agrees that payment in respect of the entitlement to paid leave shall be made together with and in addition to the temporary worker's hourly rate at 8.33% of his hourly rate.

This sum reflected one week's pay after the worker had worked continuously for three months. The ET thought that only situation (5) of the EAT's catalogue of five types of rolled up holiday pay situations was compatible with the

---

[74] [2004] IRLR 564.
[75] See e.g. *MPB Structure Ltd* v. *Munro* [2002] IRLR 601 (EAT); [2003] IRLR 350 (the Court of Session).
[76] Case No. 1800174/2004.

Directive and so the employer's rolled up holiday pay practice contravened the Directive.

Having heard these references, the Court of Justice ruled out the possibility of rolled up holiday pay. It noted that the term 'paid annual leave' meant that, for the duration of annual leave, remuneration had to be maintained. In other words, 'workers must receive their normal remuneration for that period of rest'.[77] The Court continued that 'an agreement under which the amount payable to the worker, as both remuneration for work done and part payment for minimum annual leave, would be identical to the amount payable, prior to the entry into force of that agreement, as remuneration solely for work done, effectively negates, by means of a reduction in the amount of that remuneration, the worker's entitlement to paid annual leave under Article 7 of the directive'.[78] Thus, the Court of Justice ruled out the situation which arose in *Smith* v. *Morrisroes*. Smith was employed as a sub-contractor earning £150 per day; holiday pay was not paid. From the end of 2002, Smith was informed by his site manager that he would be receiving £138 per day, while the employer would retain £12 from the £150 and then pay it to Smith as and when he took holiday. He protested: 'I was not paying for my own holiday pay out of my wages and for them to give it back to us as holiday pay.' Even prior to *Robinson-Steele* the EAT had accepted that such an arrangement was not compatible with the Directive: there was no mutual agreement for genuine payment for holidays representing a true addition to the contractual rate of pay for time worked and the Court of Justice agreed.

The Court of Justice also ruled out the possibility, practised by many employers, of rolling up holiday pay in weekly or monthly pay cheques. It said that Article 7 of the Directive precluded the payment for minimum annual leave from being made in the form of part payments, staggered over the corresponding annual period of work and paid together with the remuneration for work done, rather than in the form of a payment in respect of a specific period during which the worker actually takes leave.[79] As the Court said, a regime of rolled up holiday pay could lead to situations in which 'the minimum period of paid annual leave is, in effect, replaced by an allowance in lieu'.[80] Advocate General Stix-Hackl in *Robinson-Steele* expressed a different concern, one which echoed the fears of the Scottish courts. She said that if rolled up holiday pay were allowed, low paid workers, in particular, could use most, if not all of their pay for subsistence, with the risk that holiday pay would be used up and so they would forgo leave in favour of carrying on working; the possibility of earning money was a substantial encouragement for forgoing leave.

Thus, it seems that employers must pay holiday pay during the specific period during which the worker takes leave; it is unlawful to stagger payment

---

[77] Para. 50.   [78] Para. 51.   [79] Para. 63.   [80] Para. 61.

over the year. However, given the implications of its rulings for many thousands of employers employing casual staff, the Court endorsed what is, in essence, a transitional regime. It allowed employers to set off part payments staggered over the corresponding annual period of work and paid together with the remuneration for work done (i.e. rolled up holiday pay) against the payment for specific leave which was actually taken by the worker,[81] provided that the sums paid were *additional* to remuneration which has been paid and that the sums were *transparent* and comprehensible.[82] In other words, provided that the rolled up holiday pay arrangements satisfied these conditions (essentially those of the EAT in *Marshall's Clay* and *Smith*), with the burden of proof on the employer,[83] they were lawful. However, Member States were under an obligation to rectify this illegality, ensuring that 'practices incompatible with Article 7 of the Directive are not continued'.[84] This, the DTI has done in its revised guidance which says:[85]

Following an ECJ Judgement on 16 March 2006, Rolled Up Holiday Pay (RHP) is considered unlawful and employers should renegotiate contracts involving RHP for existing employees/workers *as soon as possible* so that payment for statutory annual leave is made at the time when the leave is taken. Where an employer has already given RHP in relation to work undertaken, and the payments have been made in a transparent and comprehensible manner, they can be set off against any future leave payments made at the proper time.

The Effect of Sick Leave and Maternity Leave

The other question that frequently arises is whether the four weeks' paid leave will be added to any period of maternity leave or long-term sick leave. In respect of sick leave, the British courts have ruled that the four weeks' paid leave will not be added to any period of long-term sick leave.[86] In *Gómez*[87] the Court of Justice considered the issue, at least in part, in respect of maternity leave. Factory workers employed by Continental could only take leave during certain periods over the summer. Gomez was on maternity leave during those periods and was denied the right to take the leave after her maternity leave. The Court distinguished maternity leave from annual leave. Maternity leave, it noted, was intended to protect a woman's biological condition during and after pregnancy and to protect her special relationship with her child.[88] Therefore, the Court said that where the dates of a worker's maternity leave coincided with those of the entire workforce's annual leave, the requirements of the Directive relating to paid annual leave could not be met.[89] However, the

---

[81] Para. 69   [82] Para. 66.   [83] Para. 68.   [84] Para. 67.
[85] http://www.dti.gov.uk/employment/employment-legislation/employment-guidance/page14382.html#paid_annual
[86] *Inland Revenue v. Ainsworth* [2005] IRLR 465.
[87] Case C–342/01 *Gómez v. Continental Industrias del Caucho SA* [2004] ECR I–000.
[88] Para. 32. See further Ch. 9.   [89] Para. 33.

Court continued that the determination of *when* paid annual leave is to be taken falls within the scope of the Equal Treatment Directive (76/207 and the Consolidated Directive 2006/54) which required a worker to be able to take her annual leave during a period other than that of maternity leave.[90]

In *Federatie Nederlandse Vakbeweging*[91] the Court recognized that there may well be an aggregation of several periods of leave guaranteed by Community law at the end of a year, with the result that the carrying forward of annual leave or part thereof might be inevitable.[92] While the Court would prefer to see leave taken in the current year,[93] it recognized that 'the significance of that rest period remains if it is taken during a later period'.[94] That leave could be taken during the later year and could not be replaced by an allowance in lieu.[95]

3.3. Limits

(a) Working Time (Article 6)

The Basic Rule

Article 6 provides that although working hours should be regulated by laws, regulations or administrative provisions or by collective agreements or agreements between the two sides of industry, the average working time for each seven-day period, *including overtime*,[96] must not exceed 48 hours over a reference period of four months. Periods of paid annual leave under Article 7 or sick leave are not to be included or are neutral in the calculation.[97] In *Pfeiffer* the Court said that the 48-hour upper limit on working time constitutes a rule of Community social law of particular importance from which every worker must benefit.[98] The Court also ruled that Article 6(2) was sufficiently clear and precise to be directly effective.[99] The problem for the Court was that the case concerned two individuals (emergency workers working for the German Red Cross who argued that they were being required to work in excess of the 48-hour working week). The Court did not reverse its long-standing rule that

[90] Para. 38.
[91] Case C–124/05 *Federatie Nederlandse Vakbeweging v. Staat der Nederlanden*, judgment of 6 April 2006.
[92] Para. 24.   [93] Para. 30.   [94] Ibid. and para. 31.   [95] Para. 33.
[96] For a consideration of the meaning of the term overtime, albeit in the context of the proof of Employment Contract Dir. 91/533, considered below (nn. 225–55), see Case C–350/99 *Wolfgang Lange v. Georg Schünemann GmbH* [2001] ECR I–1061, paras. 16–19.
[97] Art. 16(2). By virtue of Art. 17 it is possible to derogate from this provision but any derogations must not result in the establishment of a reference period exceeding six months. However, Member States have the option, subject to compliance with the general principles relating to the protection of health and safety of workers, and allowing for objective or technical reasons or reasons concerning the organisation of work, to allow collective agreements to set reference periods which do not exceed 12 months (Art. 17(4)).
[98] Joined Cases C–397/01 to C–403/01 *Pfeiffer v. Deutsches Rotes Kreuz* [2004] ECR I–000, para. 69.
[99] Para. 73.

unimplemented Directives have only vertical direct effect. Instead, it imposed on the German courts a very broad interpretative obligation. It said:

[W]hen hearing a case between individuals, a national court is required, when applying the provisions of domestic law adopted for the purpose of transposing obligations laid down by a directive, to consider the whole body of rules of national law and to interpret them, so far as possible, in the light of the wording and purpose of the directive in order to achieve an outcome consistent with the objective pursued by the directive. In the main proceedings, the national court must thus do whatever lies within its jurisdiction to ensure that the maximum period of weekly working time, which is set at 48 hours by Article 6(2) of Directive [2003/88], is not exceeded.[100]

The Definition of Working Time

The key issue, then, is, what constitutes working time? Article 2(1) defines 'working time' as having three elements: (1) any period during which the worker is working, (2) at the employer's disposal, and (3) carrying out his activities or duties, in accordance with national laws and/or practices. The question is whether these three elements are cumulative or disjunctive, an issue of particular significance to 'on-call workers'. If read disjunctively then, for on-call workers waiting at home, this time constitutes working time. If read cumulatively, then this time may not represent working time since the worker is not 'working'. The Court of Justice, insisting on a Community definition of working time (and rest periods),[101] has supported the cumulative reading,[102] but with the lightest touch in respect of the third criteria.[103] This can be seen in various cases concerning the emergency services (*Simap* (doctors in primary care teams),[104] *CIG* (nursing staff in the emergency services),[105] and *Jaeger* (doctor in the surgical department of a hospital).[106] In these cases, the Court ruled that the time spent by these medical and emergency workers at their workplace on-call *and* on the premises of the employer (even where they could sleep in a bed provided by the employer[107]) constituted working time.[108] As the Court explained in *Jaeger*,[109] an on-call

---

[100] Para. 88.

[101] Case C–151/02 *Landeshauptstadt Kiel v. Jaeger* [2003] ECR I–8389, para. 58.

[102] See e.g., Case C–303/98 *Simap* [2000] ECR I–7963, para. 48.

[103] For a full discussion, see Kenner, 'Re-evaluating the concept of working time: an analysis of recent case law' (2004) 32 *IRJ*. 588, 594.

[104] Case C–303/98 *Simap* [2000] ECR I–7963.

[105] Case C–241/99 *CIG v. Sergas* [2001] ECR I–5139.

[106] Case C–151/02 *Landeshauptstadt Kiel v. Jaeger* [2003] ECR I–8389.

[107] Case C–151/02 *Jaeger* [2003] ECR I–8389, paras. 60–4.

[108] At para. 50 the Court added that the situation is different where doctors in primary care teams are on call by being contactable at all times without their having to be at the health centre. Even if they are at the disposal of the employer, in that it must be possible to contact them, doctors may manage their time with fewer constraints and pursue their own interests. In those circumstances, only time linked to the actual provision of primary care services must be regarded as working time.

[109] Case C–151/02 *Jaeger* [2003] ECR I–8389, para. 65.

doctor who is required to keep himself available to the employer at a place designated by the employer is subject to appreciably greater constraints than a doctor on standby (i.e. a doctor required to be permanently accessible but not present at the health centre) since he has 'to remain apart from his family and social environment and has less freedom to manage the time during which his professional services are not required'.

Furthermore, the time spent asleep or otherwise inactive on the employer's premises could not count towards the rest periods because the worker must be able 'to remove himself from the working environment . . . to enable him to relax and dispel the fatigue caused by the performance of his duties'.[110] As the Court put it in *Simap*, in the scheme of the Directive, working time is placed 'in opposition to rest periods, the two being mutually exclusive'.[111]

In *Dellas*[112] the Court confirmed that on-call duty was classified as working time (this time in the context of night duty carried out by a teacher in an establishment for handicapped persons) and had to be taken into account in its entirety for the purposes of calculating the 48-hour week. The case concerned a French law which provided a weighting mechanism to reflect periods of inactivity during on-call duty, when calculating pay and overtime. The decree established a 3 to 1 ratio for the first nine hours followed by a 2 to 1 ratio for subsequent hours between the hours of presence and the working hours actually counted. The Court said that while the Directive did not apply to the remuneration of workers, it did apply to working hours; and because the weighting mechanism took into account only in part the number of hours a worker was actually present, the total working time of a worker could amount to at least 60 hours a week contrary to the Directive. The Court noted that the Directive (unlike the Commission's proposal currently before Council) did not provide for any intermediate category between working time and rest periods. It also noted that the definition of working time did not include any reference to 'the intensity of work done by the employee and his output'.[113] It therefore said that 'The fact that on-call duty includes some period of inactivity is thus completely irrelevant in this connection'.[114]

The Consequences of a Broad Definition of Working Time

The decisions of the ECJ defining working time so broadly as to encompass time spent on the employer's premises, even when asleep, have caused many problems for employers, especially in the health care sector. This has led to far greater attention being given to the derogations from the Directive. As we shall see, a complex set of derogations apply to this provision. In the case of those with 'unmeasured working time', Member States can derogate both

---

[110] Para. 95.   [111] Para. 47.
[112] Case C–14/04 *Abdelkader Dellas and Others v. Premier ministre and Others* [2006] ECR I–000.
[113] Para. 43.   [114] Para. 47.

from Article 6 (48-hour week) *and* Article 16(b) (the reference period) provided due regard is paid to the general principles of the protection of the safety and health of workers. In the case of other workers (i.e. those considered to be special cases and those covered by a collective agreement) Member States can derogate, but only from Article 16(b) (reference period). Furthermore, according to Article 19(1), the option to derogate may not result in the establishment of a reference period exceeding six months. However, Member States have the option, subject to compliance with general health and safety principles, of allowing for objective or technical reasons concerning the organization of work, collective agreements, or agreements concluded between the two sides of industry to set longer reference periods but in no event exceeding 12 months.[115] But, perhaps more important than all the derogations is the highly controversial 'opt-out'.

The Opt-out

Article 22(1) (formerly Article 18(1)(b)(i)) provides that Member States need not apply Article 6 on the maximum 48-hour week provided certain conditions are satisfied. Member States must ensure that:

- the general principles of the protection of health and safety of workers is respected;
- no employer requires a worker to work more than 48 hours over a seven-day period unless the workers' consent has been obtained previously;
- any worker refusing to give this consent must not be subjected to any detriment by the employer as a result;
- the employer must keep up-to-date records of all workers who work more than 48 hours a week;
- records must be placed at the disposal of the competent authorities, who may, for reasons connected with the health and safety of workers, prohibit or restrict the possibility of exceeding the maximum weekly working hours;
- the employer provides the competent authorities at their request with information on cases in which agreement has been given by workers to perform work exceeding 48 hours over a period of seven days (calculated as an average for any reference period set down under the option available in Article 16(b).

The Court has considered the use of the opt-out in *Pfeiffer*,[116] where it said:

Any derogation from those minimum requirements must therefore be accompanied by all the safeguards necessary to ensure that, if the worker concerned is encouraged to

---

[115] Art. 19(2).
[116] Joined Cases C–397/01 to C–403/01 *Bernhard Pfeiffer (C–397/01), Wilhelm Roith (C–398/01), Albert SuB (C–399/01), Michael Winter (C–400/01), Klaus Nestvogel (C–401/01), Roswitha Zeller (C–402/01) and Matthias Dobele (C–403/01)* v. *Deutsches Rotes Kreuz, Kreisverband Waldshut eV* [2004] ECR I–000.

relinquish a social right which has been directly conferred on him by the directive, he must do so freely and with full knowledge of all the facts. Those requirements are all the more important given that the worker must be regarded as the weaker party to the employment contract and it is therefore necessary to prevent the employer being in a position to disregard the intentions of the other party to the contract or to impose on that party a restriction of his rights without him having expressly given his consent in that regard.

The Court added that, for a derogation to Article 6 to be valid, 'the worker's consent must be given not only individually but expressly and freely'.[117] Consent given by trade union representatives in the context of a collective or other agreement is not equivalent to that given by the worker himself.[118] Therefore, in *Pfeiffer* individual contracts of employment incorporating a collective agreement allowing working hours to be extended breached the Directive.

Originally, the UK (and Ireland) were the only countries to take advantage of the opt-out. Ireland abandoned the opt-out but the UK hung on to it tenaciously. The use of the opt-out by the UK was subject to review in 2003,[119] and the Commission then issued a Communication[120] which criticized the UK's implementation, noting that[121] legislation and practice do not appear to offer all the guarantees laid down by the Directive. In particular, the Commission was critical of the practice of employers giving new recruits the opt-out to sign at the same time as signing the contract of employment, thereby compromising the workers' freedom of choice. The Commission noted that this practice undermined the second intent of (what was) Article 18(1)(b)(i), which aims to guarantee the worker's free consent by ensuring that no worker may suffer harm due to the fact that he is not prepared to give his agreement. The Communication concludes with a general criticism of the UK's approach:

The only experience that is applicable here (in the United Kingdom . . .) has shown the existing difficulties in ensuring that the spirit and terms of the Directive are respected and that real guarantees are provided for workers. It also brings out an unexpected effect in that it is difficult to ensure (or at least check) that the other provisions in the Directive have been complied with, concerning whether workers have signed the opt-out agreement.

Despite the Commission's desire to remove the opt-out from a (health and safety) Directive, it discovered that, following the *Simap* line of case law, the use of the opt-out was becoming more widespread across other

---

[117] Para. 84.
[118] Para. 81. See also Case C–303/98 *Simap* [2000] ECR I–7963, para. 74.
[119] Barnard, Deakin and Hobbs, 'Opting Out of the 48 Hour Week: Employer Necessity or Individual Choice?' (2003) 32 *ILJ*. 223.
[120] COM(2003) 843.   [121] Para. 2.2.1.2.

Member States, particularly in the healthcare sector.[122] The UK Presidency in the second half of 2005 came close to securing a deal on revisions to the Working Time Directive according to which the opt-out would have been preserved but with its conditions tightened. However, the deal failed over another matter entirely: whether the 48-hour week (and all other limits) applied per worker (as in the UK, Germany, Italy, Ireland, and the Netherlands) or per contract (in a number of other Member States such as France, Portugal, and the Scandinavian countries). The Austrian Presidency had another go in June 2006, hoping to bridge the divide between those Member States wanting to see the opt-out phased out and those determined to keep it, by proposing that the opt-out be retained but with increased safeguards for workers. These included a 'cooling-off period' of one month within which new recruits could change their mind about the opt-out and a requirement that opt-outs be renewed annually, with a statement by the employer as to the reason why long hours are needed. These attempts also failed.[123]

(b) Night Work (Article 8)

Night time is any period of not less than seven hours, *as defined by national law*, which must include, in any case, the period between midnight and 5 a.m.[124] This gives the national systems a possible range of the hours between 10 p.m. and 7 a.m. to designate as night time. Night workers are defined in two ways by the Directive. First, 'night workers' are those who, during night time, work at least three hours of their daily working time as a normal course.[125] Secondly, the Directive defines night workers as those who are likely to work a certain proportion of their working time during night time, as defined by national legislation *or* collective agreements concluded by the two sides of industry at national or regional level.[126] The definition of night worker was considered by the High Court in Northern Ireland in *ex parte Burns*.[127] The applicant worked a rotating shift pattern during which she worked, one week in three from 9 p.m. to 7a.m. The government argued that she was not a night worker since night workers were those who worked night shifts exclusively or predominantly. Kerr J rejected this, arguing that it was sufficient that night working be a 'regular feature' of the employment. In *Simap*[128] Advocate General Saggio said that doctors working at night or who were contactable at night constituted night workers.

---

[122] See Barnard, 'The EU Agenda for Regulating Labour Markets: Lessons from the UK in the Field of Working Time' in Bermann and Pistor (eds), *Law and Governance in an Enlarged Europe* (Hart Publishing, Oxford, 2004).

[123] 2733rd Council Meeting, Employment, Social Policy, health and Consumer Affairs, EU Council press release, 1–2 June 2006.

[124] Art. 2(3).   [125] Art. 2(4)(a).   [126] Art. 2(4)(b).   [127] [1999] IRLR 315.

[128] Case C–303/98 [2000] ECR I–7963.

Normal working hours for night work must not exceed an average of eight hours in any 24-hour period.[129] The reference period is to be determined after consulting the two sides of industry or by collective agreements or agreements concluded between the two sides of industry at national or regional level.[130] Night workers whose work involves special hazards or mental strain—to be defined by national legislation or collective agreements or agreements concluded between the two sides of industry—must not work more than eight hours in any period of 24 hours during which they work at night.[131] Thus, no reference period exists in the case of such workers.

In addition, night workers are entitled to a free and confidential health assessment, possibly conducted within the national health system before their assignment and then at regular intervals thereafter.[132] If night workers are found to suffer from health problems related to night work they must be transferred wherever possible to suitable day work.[133] In addition, Member States can make the work of 'certain categories of night workers subject to certain guarantees, under the conditions laid down by national law and practice, in the case of workers who incur risks to their safety or health linked to night time working'.[134] However, any guarantees made must be careful not to offend the principle of equal treatment of men and women.[135] Employers who *regularly* use night workers must inform the competent authorities on request.[136] Finally, Article 12 provides that both night workers and shift workers must both enjoy health and safety protection appropriate to the nature of their work, and that such protection is equivalent to that applicable to other workers and is available at all times.

4. Derogations

The Directive contains a complex series of derogations which Member States can choose to apply. However, they can take advantage of the derogations only if they have implemented them.[137] As always, with derogations, they have to be interpreted in such a way that their scope is limited to what is strictly necessary in order to safeguard the interests which those derogations enable to be protected'.[138] In summary, the derogations fall into six categories, considered next.

---

[129] Art. 8(1).   [130] Art. 16(3).   [131] Art. 8(2).   [132] Art. 9(1)(a), (2) and (3).
[133] Art. 9(1)(b).   [134] Art. 10.
[135] See Case 312/86 *Commission* v. *France* [1988] ECR 3559, Case 345/89 *Criminal Proceedings Against Stoeckel* [1991] ECR I–4047 and Case C–158/91 *Ministère public and Direction du travail et de l'emploi* v. *Levy* [1993] ECR I–4287, discussed in Ch. 8.
[136] Art. 11.   [137] Case C–303/98 *Simap* [2000] ECR I–7963.
[138] Case C–151/02 *Jaeger* [2003] ECR I–8389, para. 89.

4.1. Unmeasured Working Time (Article 17(1))

With due regard for the general principles of the protection of the safety and health of workers, Member States may derogate from Articles 3, 4, 5, 6, 8, and 16 of the Directive (i.e. all limits and entitlements except annual leave) when 'on account of the specific characteristics of the activity concerned, the duration of the working time is not measured and/or predetermined or can be determined by the workers themselves', particularly in the case of managing executives, family workers, and 'religious' workers.[139] As the guidance notes accompanying the British implementation of the Directive explain,[140] this derogation essentially applies to workers who have complete control over the hours they work and whose time is not monitored or determined by their employer. Such a situation may occur if a worker can decide when the work is to be done, or may adjust the time worked as they see fit. An indicator may be if the worker has discretion over whether to work on a given day without needing to consult their employer. [141]

4.2. Other Special Cases (Article 17(3))

In the case of industries requiring 'continuity of service or production' (for example security, prisons, hospitals,[142] the utilities and the press),[143] or industries where there is a foreseeable surge of activity (for example, tourism, agriculture, postal industry),[144] or where the worker's home and work are distant,[145] or for people working in railway transport,[146] or where there is a dangerous situation,[147] derogations can be adopted from Articles 3, 4, 5, 8, and 16 of the Directive (i.e. from the entitlements, night work, and the reference period but not from the working time limit itself) by laws, regulations, administrative provisions, collective agreements, or agreements between the two sides of industry.[148] These derogations are subject to the requirement that

---

[139] Art. 17(1).

[140] Para. 2.2.2. of DTI, Regulatory Guidance on the Working Time Regulations 28 August 1998.

[141] SI 1999/3372 added a new clause in Reg. 20(2) which was intended to deal with workers whose working time was partly measured, predetermined or determined by the worker and partly not. The 48-hour limit applied to the work which was predetermined or measured. In respect of the part of the job which was not predetermined, the 48-hour limit did not apply. The trade union Amicus complained about this Regulation which was repealed, two days before the hearing in Case C–484/04 *Commission v. UK*: SI 2006/99 The Working Time (Amendment) Regulations 2006.

[142] See Case C–151/02 *Jaeger* [2003] ECR I–8389, para. 87: the organization of teams of on-call services in hospitals and similar establishments falls within this derogation.

[143] Art. 17(3)(b)–(c).   [144] Art. 17(3)(d).   [145] Art. 17(3)(a).

[146] Art. 17(3)(e) (i.e. where the activities are intermittent, where the people spend their time working on board trains or whose activities are linked to transport timetables and to ensuring the continuity and regulation of traffic).

[147] Defined as circumstances described in Art. 5(4) of Dir. 89/391 and in cases of accident or imminent risk of accident (Art. 17(3)(f) and (g)).

[148] Art. 17(3).

the workers concerned are afforded equivalent periods of compensatory rest. This rest must, according to *Jaeger*,[149] follow on immediately from the working time in order to prevent the worker from experiencing a state of fatigue or overload owing to the accumulation of consecutive periods of work. In exceptional cases in which it is not possible for objective reasons to grant such rest, the workers concerned must be afforded appropriate protection.[150] As far as the option to derogate from Article 16(b) is concerned (reference period of four months for calculating average weekly working time), the reference period may not exceed six months, or 12 months where there are objective, technical or work organization reasons and a collective agreement or agreement between the two sides of industry has been concluded.[151]

4.3. Shift Work (Article 17(4))

Shift work is defined as any method of organizing work in shifts, whereby workers succeed each other, at the same work stations, according to a *certain pattern*, including a rotating pattern, which may be continuous or discontinuous, entailing the need for workers to work at different times over a given period of days or weeks.[152] This period is not defined by the Directive. In *Simap*[153] the Court said that working time spent both on call where doctors in primary care teams are required to be present at health centres and on the actual provision of primary care services when doctors are on call by having merely to be contactable at all times, fulfilled all the requirements of the definition of shift work. It added that the work of doctors in primary care teams is organized in such a way that workers are assigned successively to the same work posts on a rotational basis, which makes it necessary for them to perform work at different hours over a given period of days or weeks.[154]

Articles 3 and 5 (daily rest and weekly rest) do not apply in relation to shift workers when they change shift and cannot take a daily and/or weekly rest period between the end of one shift and the start of the next one or in the case of activities involving periods of work split up over the day, as may be the case for cleaning staff.[155] As with 'Other Special Cases' (Article 17(3)) the derogation can be laid down by laws, regulations, administrative provisions, collective agreements, or agreements between the two sides of industry.[156] These derogations are subject to the requirement that the workers concerned are afforded equivalent periods of compensatory rest or appropriate protection.[157]

---

[149] C–151/02 *Landeshauptstadt Kiel* v. *Jaeger* [2003] ECR I–8389, paras. 94 and 97.
[150] Art. 17(2).   [151] Art. 19.   [152] Art. 2(5).
[153] Case C–303/98 *Simap* [2000] ECR I–7963, para. 61.   [154] Para. 62.
[155] Art. 17(4)   [156] Art. 17(2).   [157] Art. 17(2).

4.4. Collective Agreements or Agreements between the Two Sides of Industry (Article 18)

Derogations may be made from Articles 3, 4, 5, 8, and 16[158] (entitlements, night work limit and reference period) by means of collective agreements or agreements between the two sides of industry at national or regional level.[159] These derogations are allowed on condition that equivalent compensating rest periods are granted to the workers concerned or, in exceptional cases where it is not possible for objective reasons to grant such periods, the workers concerned are afforded appropriate protection.[160] Once again, as with Article 17(3), the option to derogate from the reference period in Article 16(b) (of four months for calculating average weekly working time) the reference period may not exceed six months, or 12 months where there are objective, technical, or work organization reasons and a collective agreement or agreement between the two sides of industry has been concluded.[161] Therefore, collective agreements are permitted to lower the standard of protection provided by the legislation subject to the provision on compensatory rest.

In the UK, one of the states envisaged by Article 18(4) in which there is no statutory system for ensuring the conclusion of collective agreements, the collective dimension of the Directive has posed considerable problems for a traditionally single channel system where worker representation has been performed by recognized trade unions.[162] With the decline in trade union membership and recognition, the approach adopted by the British Working Time Regulations 1998 is to give a role to elected worker representatives where there is no recognized trade union. While trade unions can enter collective agreements, worker representatives can enter workforce agreements. To be valid a 'workforce agreement' must:

- be in writing;
- have effect for a specified period not exceeding five years;
- apply either to all of the relevant members of the workforce (other than those covered by collective agreement—thus employers cannot by-pass a recognized trade union), or to all of the relevant members of the workforce who belong to a particular group;

---

[158] As far as derogations from Art. 16(2) are concerned, the same periods apply as for other special cases (see above, n. 150, and Art. 17(4)).

[159] Art. 18, para. 1. Where it is in conformity with the rules laid down by such agreements, derogations can be made by means of collective agreements or agreements between the two sides of industry at a lower level (Art. 18, para. 1). Member States where there is no statutory system for ensuring the conclusion of collective agreements or agreements between the two sides of industry or Member States where there is a specific legislative framework may allow derogations by collective agreement or agreement between the two sides of industry at the appropriate collective level (Art. 18, para. 2).

[160] Art. 18, para. 3.   [161] Art. 19.   [162] See further Ch. 15.

- be signed by the representatives of the workforce[163] or the representatives of the group where appropriate (excluding in either case any representative not a relevant member of the workforce on the date on which the agreement was first made available for signature). If the employer employs 20 or fewer workers on the date on which the agreement was first made available for signature, it must be signed either by the appropriate representatives *or* by the majority of workers. Thus, in a small workforce the British regulations envisage a form of direct representation to achieve a collective goal.

Thus, collective or workforce agreements can be used to secure so-called 'statutory bargained adjustments'[164] to the rules on working time.

4.5. Doctors in Training (Article 17(5))

The Directive applies to doctors in training from 2 August 2004 but it also makes provision for transitional arrangements in respect of the maximum working week and the reference period over which it is calculated.[165] In essence, derogations from the maximum working week are permitted for five years (or seven years in those states having difficulties in meeting the working time provision or eight years in those states having particular difficulties).[166] However, Member States must ensure that in no case will the number of weekly working hours exceed an average of:[167]

- 58 hours for the first three years which can be averaged over 12 months (i.e. until 31 July 2007);
- 56 hours for the following two years which can be averaged over a maximum of six months (i.e. until 31 July 2009);
- 52 hours for any remaining period which can be averaged over a maximum of six months.

The employer must consult the representatives of employees in good time

---

[163] Para. 2 of Sch. 1 provides that 'representatives of the workforce' are workers duly elected to represent the relevant members of the workforce; 'representatives of the group' are workers duly elected to represent the members of a particular group, and representatives are 'duly elected' if their election satisfies the requirements of para. 3 of the Schedule. The Working Time Regulations provide some details of the method of carrying out elections (Sch. 1, para. 3). The Working Time Regulations are, however, far less prescriptive than those contained in TULR(C)A 1992 for the election of trade union officials and, as the TUC has pointed out, employers have too much power in deciding how the representatives are to be elected and there are no controls on ballot-rigging (Research Paper 98/82, 25). This has prompted concern as to whether the elected worker representatives will pass the test of representativity laid down by the Court in Case T–135/96 *UEAPME* v. *Council of the European Union* [1998] ECR II–2335, considered in Ch. 2.

[164] Davies and Kilpatrick, 'UK Worker Representation after Single Channel' (2004) 33 *ILJ*. 121, 137.

[165] Art. 17(2) also applies to this provision.

[166] Art. 17(5), paras. 2–4   [167] Art. 17(5), para. 5.

with a view to reaching agreement on the arrangements applying to the transitional period.[168]

4.6. Transport Workers (Articles 20 and 21)

The provisions on daily rest, in work rest breaks, weekly rest and night work do not apply to mobile workers,[169] defined to mean any worker employed as a member of travelling or flying personnel by an undertaking which operates transport services for passengers or goods by road or air.[170] Member States must, however, take the necessary measures to ensure that such workers are entitled to adequate rest except in a dangerous situation or cases of accident or imminent risk of accident.[171] Member States can derogate from the reference period laid down in Article 16(b) in respect of offshore workers provided that there is compliance with the general principles of health and safety and provided that there is consultation of representatives of the employer and employees.[172]

The provisions on daily rest, in work rest breaks, weekly rest, the 48-hour working week and night work do not apply to any worker on board a seagoing fishing vessel flying the flag of a Member State[173] but states are required to take the necessary measures to ensure that any such worker is entitled to adequate rest and that they do not have to work more than 48 hours a week referenced over 12 months. Within these confines, the Directive then lays down details of maximum hours of work and minimum hours of rest.

5. Conclusions

The adaptability pillar of the Luxembourg Employment Guidelines saw the reform of working time as a key component of realizing demand-side flexibility. According to the 1998 Employment Guidelines,[174] the Social Partners are invited to negotiate, at the appropriate levels, agreements to 'modernise the organisation of work, including flexible working arrangements, with the aim of making undertakings productive and competitive and achieving the required balance between flexibility and security'. The 1999 Guidelines offered some further guidance: the Social Partners might negotiate agreements on the expression of working time as an annual figure, the reduction of

---

[168] Art. 17(5), para. 6.   [169] Art. 20.   [170] Art. 2(7).   [171] Art. 20(1), para. 2.
[172] 'Offshore work' means work that is performed 'mainly on or from offshore installations (including drilling rigs) directly or indirectly in connection with the exploration, extraction or exploitation of mineral resources, including hydrocarbons, and diving in connection with such activities, whether performed from an offshore installation or vessel (Art. 2(8)).
[173] Art. 21.   [174] Council Res. 98/C 30/01.

working hours, the reduction of overtime, the development of part-time working, lifelong training, and career breaks—issues which far exceed the scope of the Working Time Directive.[175] However, in subsequent guidelines, working time has featured less prominently. For example, the 2005 Guidelines[176] contain only two brief references to working time, the first under Guideline 21 (promoting flexibility); the second under Guideline 24 (adapt education and training systems).

Nevertheless, working time remains a key issue on the Community's flexibility agenda. The sectoral specific Directives, negotiated by the Social Partners, represent a step in this direction. However, many businesses viewed the Working Time Directive as a significant constraint on their ability to introduce flexible working arrangements, not least because its provisions were so prescriptive (especially when compared with the Framework Directives on, for example, Parental Leave 96/34[177]), and the content of the derogations unclear. This helps to explain why so many employers, in the UK at least, have taken advantage of the opt-out. In many cases they do not actually need it, but it provides them with a security blanket in case of breach. However, the negative effect of the use of the opt-out is that it has insulated employers from the need to consider whether organizational changes are necessary to reduce the length of the working week and improve productivity.[178]

C. YOUNG WORKERS

1. Introduction

The Court's decision in *UK* v. *Council* to uphold the choice of Article 118a (new Article 137) as the legal basis for the Working Time Directive saved three other Directives designed to protect specific groups of workers adopted in the same period—pregnant workers,[179] young workers,[180] and atypical workers[181]—all adopted under Article 118a but combining a mixture of health and safety with working conditions and employment rights.[182] This section will consider the Young Workers' Directive, where the same dilemmas emerge.

---

[175] Council Res. 99/C 69/02, para. 16.
[176] Council Dec. 2005/600/EC (OJ [2005] L205/21).
[177] OJ [1996] L145/9 considered further in Ch. 9.
[178] Barnard, Deakin and Hobbs, 'Opting Out of the 48 Hour Week: Employer Necessity or Individual Choice?' (2003) 32 *ILJ*. 223.
[179] Council Dir. 92/85/EEC (OJ [1992] L348/1). See further Ch. 9.
[180] Council Dir. 94/33/EC (OJ [1994] L216/12).
[181] Council Dir. 91/383/EC (OJ [1991] L206/19). See further Ch. 9.
[182] Art. 31 recognizes this bridge between health and safety and working conditions. It provides that 'Every worker has the right to working conditions which respect his or her health safety and dignity'.

The Young Workers' Directive[183] is intended to prevent abuse of young people's labour while allowing sufficient flexibility in schemes providing both work experience and training. The Directive requires Member States to ensure that employers guarantee that young people (any person under 18 'having an employment contract or employment relationship')[184] have working conditions which suit their age, and are protected against 'economic exploitation and against any work likely to harm their safety, health or physical, mental, moral or social development or to jeopardise their education'.[185] Since this is the purpose of the Directive, any subsequent provisions must be interpreted in the light of this objective. These points are now reinforced by Article 42 of the Charter of Fundamental Rights 2000 which provides:

The employment of children is prohibited. The minimum age of admission to employment may not be lower than the minimum school-leaving age, without prejudice to such rules as may be more favourable to young people and except for limited derogations.

Young people admitted to work must have working conditions appropriate to their age and be protected against economic exploitation and any work likely to harm their safety, health or physical, mental, moral or social development or to interfere with their education.

2. The Personal Scope of the Directive and Derogations

The Young Workers' Directive envisages two categories of young workers: first, children, defined as any young person less than 15 years old or who is still subject to compulsory full-time schooling under national law,[186] and second, adolescents, defined as any young person who is at least 15 years old but younger than 18, who is no longer subject to compulsory full-time schooling.[187] The basic premise of the Directive is that while work by adolescents

---

[183] Council Dir. 94/33/EC (OJ [1994] L216/12). See also Commission Recommendation 67/125/EEC (OJ [1967] 25/405: http://europa.eu.int/eur-lex/lex/LexUriServ/ LexUriServ.do?uri=CELEX:31967H0125:FR:HTML). Inspiration for the Directive came, in particular, from ILO Conventions 5, 6, 7, 10, 13, 15, 16, 33, 58, 59, 60, 77, 78, 79, 90, 112, 123, 124, 138, the European Social Charter 1961 Art. 7, and Art. 32 of the UN Convention on the Rights of the Child: COM(91) 543 final. Member States were required either to implement the Directive by 22 June 1996 or to ensure that the two sides of industry introduced the requisite provisions by means of collective agreements (Art. 17(1)(a)). The UK, however, did not need to implement certain provisions (Art. 8(1)(b,) limiting the working time of children to two hours a day on a school day and 12 hours a week; Art. 8(2), limiting the working time of adolescents to eight hours a day and 40 hours a week; and Art. 9(1)(b) and (2), relating to the night work of adolescents) of the Directive until 2000 (Art. 17(1)(b)). This is the first time in the social field that a named Member State has secured at least a significant delay in implementing a Directive.

[184] Arts. 3(a) and 2(1).   [185] Art. 1(3).   [186] Art. 3(b).

[187] Art. 3(c). Member States must ensure that the minimum working or employment age is not lower than the minimum age at which compulsory full-time schooling as imposed by national law ends or 15 years in any event.

must be strictly regulated under the conditions laid down by the Directive, work by children is prohibited.[188]

In the case of children, Member States do, however, have the option to derogate from this basic prohibition in three circumstances. First, children can perform cultural, artistic, sports or advertising work, subject to prior authorization by a competent authority,[189] provided that the activities are not harmful either to the safety, health and development of children or to their attendance at school or their participation in vocational training programmes.[190] The Member States must also prescribe the working conditions for children taking advantage of this exception. Secondly, children over 14 can work under a combined work/training scheme or an 'in-plant work experience scheme'.[191] Thirdly, children over 14 can perform light work, defined to mean all work, taking into account the inherent nature of the tasks involved and the particular conditions under which they are to be performed, which is not likely to harm the health and safety or development of young people nor harm their attendance at school, their participation in vocational guidance and training or their capacity to benefit from the instruction received.[192] This exception would appear to allow children over 14 to continue to do newspaper rounds and baby-sitting, provided in both cases the time taken does not jeopardize their health, safety, and schooling. Member States can also permit 13-year-olds to perform designated types of light work provided that the Member States specify the conditions in which the work is to be performed.[193]

In addition, Member States have the option not to apply the Directive to occasional work or short-term work involving either domestic service in a private household or to work in family undertakings provided the work is not regarded as being harmful, damaging, or dangerous to young people.[194] The accompanying memorandum explains that the Directive is not intended to apply to occasional or limited work in the family context, for example, work in the household or in the family business, whether agriculture (for example, grape picking or crop harvesting) or in a distributive or craft trade (for example, shelf filling or other light shop work).[195]

3. Health and Safety

As with the Framework Directive 89/391 on health and safety, the Young Workers' Directive imposes general obligations on employers to take the

---

[188] Arts. 1(1) and 4(1).

[189] However, in the case of children over 13 Member States can authorize the employment of children in cultural, artistic, sports or advertising agencies (Art. 5(3)). Member States with a specific authorization system for modelling agencies can retain that system (Art. 5(4)).

[190] Art. 5(2)(ii).   [191] Art. 4(2)(b).   [192] Art. 3(d).   [193] Art. 4(3).

[194] Art. 2(2).   [195] COM(91) 543, 10.

necessary measures to protect the safety and health of all young workers permitted to work by the Directive.[196] This requires the employer to conduct a risk assessment before young people begin work and when there is any major change in their working conditions.[197] In particular, employers must have regard to the fitting-out and layout of the workplace, the nature, degree and duration of exposure to physical, biological and chemical agents, the form, range and use of work equipment, the arrangement of the work process and the level of training and instruction given to young workers.[198] If this assessment reveals a risk to the physical or mental health, safety or development of young people 'an appropriate *free* assessment and monitoring of their health must be provided',[199] possibly as part of the national health system, and involving the protective and preventive services referred to in Article 7 of Directive 89/391/EEC.[200] In addition, employers must inform both the young workers and their legal representatives of possible risks and measures adopted to protect their health and safety.[201]

Given the 'vulnerability of young people', due to their 'absence of awareness of existing or potential risks' or because 'young people have not yet fully matured', Member States must ensure that young people are protected from any specific risks[202] to their health, safety, and development. Young workers are also prohibited from being employed in work which is beyond their physical or psychological capacity, work involving harmful radiation or exposure to agents which are toxic, carcinogenic, cause heritable genetic damage or chronically affect human health in any other way; work which puts them at risk of accidents; or work where their health may suffer from extreme cold, heat, noise, vibration, or from handling heavy loads. Exceptionally, derogations from these provisions can be made in the case of adolescents where it is indispensable for their vocational training, provided that their work is performed under the supervision of a 'designated worker'.[203]

4. Working Time Limits

In the case of children permitted to perform light work or engage in a training scheme, the Directive limits their working time to:[204]

---

[196] Art. 6(1).   [197] Art. 6(2).   [198] Art. 6(1) and (2).   [199] Art. 6(2).
[200] OJ [1989] L183/1. See Ch. 11.   [201] Art. 6(3).
[202] Art. 7(2). This includes work involving harmful exposure to the physical, biological and chemical agents referred to in point I of the Annex to the Young Workers' Directive and to the processes and work referred to in point II of the Annex. Changes to the Annex can be made in accordance with the procedure in Art. 17 of Dir. 89/391/EEC.
[203] See Art. 7 of Dir. 89/391/EEC.   [204] Art. 8(1).

- 8 hours a day and 40 hours a week for work performed under a combined work/training scheme or work experience scheme;[205]
- two hours on a school day and 12 hours a week for work performed outside the hours fixed for school attendance if this is permitted by national law; daily working time must not exceed seven hours, or eight hours in the case of children over the age of 15;
- seven hours a day and 35 hours a week for work performed during the school holiday period; eight hours a day and 40 hours a week in the case of the over 15s;
- seven hours a day and 35 hours a week for light work performed by children no longer subject to compulsory full-time schooling.

Adolescents can work up to eight hours a day and 40 hours a week.[206] Where daily working time is more than four and a half hours, young people are entitled to a break of at least 30 minutes.[207]

Children cannot work between 8.00 p.m. and 6.00 a.m.[208] and adolescents between 10.00 p.m. and 6.00 a.m. or between 11.00 p.m. and 7.00 a.m.,[209] although adolescents may work at night under the supervision of an adult if Member States so provide, but not between midnight and 4.00 a.m.[210] However, Member States may authorize adolescents to work between midnight and 4.00 a.m. in the shipping or fisheries sectors, the armed forces and the police, hospitals and similar establishments, in cultural, artistic, sports or advertising activities, where there are objective grounds for doing so and provided that adolescents are allowed suitable compensatory rest.[211]

5. Rest Periods

For each 24-hour period, children are entitled to a minimum rest period of 14 consecutive hours and adolescents to 12 consecutive hours.[212] Although it appears that children can therefore work 10 hours a day and adolescents 14 hours a day such an interpretation directly contradicts the requirements of Article 8 on working time. Further, for each seven-day period worked, both children and adolescents are entitled to a minimum rest period of two days,

---

[205] Art. 8(1)(a). Time spent training counts as working time (Art. 8(3)). Member States can derogate from Art. 8(1)(a) but must determine the conditions for such derogation (Art. 8(5)).

[206] Art. 8(2). Member States can derogate from this provision either by way of exception or where there are objective grounds for so doing provided the Member State determines the conditions, limits and procedure for implementing such derogations (Art. 8(5)).

[207] Art. 12.   [208] Art. 9(1)(a).   [209] Art. 9(1)(b).   [210] Art. 9(2).

[211] Art. 9(2). Adolescents are also entitled to a free health assessment prior to any assignment to night work and at regular intervals thereafter, unless their work is of 'an exceptional nature' (Art. 9(3)).

[212] Art. 10(1).

consecutive if possible, including in principle a Sunday.[213] Where justified by technical or organizational reasons, the minimum rest period may be reduced, but may in no circumstance be less than 36 consecutive hours.[214] However, extensive derogations are permitted to this rule, in the case of the shipping and fisheries sector, the armed forces or the police, work performed in hospitals or similar establishments, agriculture, tourism, hotels and catering and activities involving periods of work split up over the day.[215]

It is also possible, in the case of adolescents, to derogate from the provisions on working time, night work, and rest periods in the case of *force majeure*, provided that the work is temporary, must be performed immediately, that adult workers are not available and that the adolescents are allowed equivalent compensatory rest time in the following three weeks.[216] Finally, children are permitted to work on a combined work/training scheme and must have a period free from work including, as far as possible, in the school holidays.[217] No minimum period of leave is specified nor is the situation of adolescents addressed. It had been thought that the Working Time Directive 2003/88[218] would fill the gap but a decision of the British Employment Appeal Tribunal[219] suggested that while the Working Time Directive applied to adult workers and young workers it did not apply to children.[220] Therefore a 15-year-old paperboy who had delivered papers six days a week from the age of 13 was not entitled to four weeks' paid holiday.

6. Conclusions

The parallels between the Young Workers' Directive and Directive 2003/88 on Working Time are obvious, and concerns about its lack of flexibility and the burdens on small business apply to both. The Directive applies to all types of business regardless of size, in both the public and private sector.[221] Certain sectors of the economy are particularly affected, including the distributive trades, hotels and catering, services and events for the young. On the other hand, the ILO has criticized the Directive for not being compatible with the international conventions (a point strongly denied by the Commission).[222]

---

[213] Art. 10(2). The equivalent provision in the original Working Time Dir. 93/104 was annulled.
[214] Ibid.
[215] Art. 10(4). There must be objective grounds for derogation, workers must be granted compensatory rest time and the objectives set out in Art. 1 of the Directive must not be called into question.
[216] Art. 13.   [217] Art. 11.   [218] OJ [1993] L307/18.
[219] *Ashby* v. *Addison* [2003] IRLR 211.
[220] Under English law, children were covered by the Children and Young Persons Act 1933 which made no specific reference to annual leave entitlement but provided that a child was entitled to at least two consecutive weeks without employment during the school holidays.
[221] COM(91) 543 final—SYN 383, 51.   [222] WE/2/94, 20 January 1994.

Yet the Directive does not go as far as the Community Social Charter 1989 intended: Article 21 requires that young people who are in gainful employment must receive equitable remuneration in accordance with national practice, and Article 23 provides that following the end of compulsory education, young people must be entitled to receive initial vocational training of a sufficient duration to enable them to adapt to the requirements of their future working life. The choice of Article 118a (new Article 137) as the appropriate legal basis has prevented the development of a more ambitious programme for young workers. This has been left to the European Employment Strategy (EES) which places much emphasis on the need to improve employment prospects for young people, especially those who leave school without relevant skills. Since its inception, tackling youth unemployment has been a priority for the EES and it is one of the areas in which substantive targets are laid down. Thus, under the 'employability' pillar the 1998 Guidelines required that every unemployed young person be offered a new start before reaching six months of unemployment (e.g. training, retraining) within five years, that Member States improve the quality of school to reduce 'substantially' the number of young people who drop out from school early, to ensure that they equip young people with greater ability to adapt to technological and economic changes.[223] In 2001 the Council added that Member States should develop measures aimed at halving by 2010 the number of 18 to 24-year-olds with only lower secondary level education who are not in further education and training.[224] This is now reinforced by the European Youth Pact, adopted at the same time as the Lisbon relaunch in March 2005, which aims to improve the education, training, mobility, vocational integration, and social inclusion of 'young Europeans' while facilitating the reconciliation of work and family life.

D. WORKING CONDITIONS

Finally, this chapter considers two further measures adopted under the Social Charter Action Programme concerning working conditions: a Directive on the Proof of the Employment Contract 91/533/EEC[225] which is intended to harmonize the diverse national laws concerning the provision of information about working conditions,[226] and an Opinion on an Equitable Wage.

[223] Co. Res. 98/C 30/01. [224] Council Dec. 2001/63 (OJ [2001] L22/18).
[225] Council Dir. 91/533/EEC (OJ [1991] L288/32) on an employer's obligation to inform employees of the conditions applicable to the contract or employment relationship. See also COM(90) 563 final. Although the UK and Ireland were the only countries with pre-existing rules providing that most workers are entitled to a written statement of their terms and conditions, the UK abstained in the final vote.
[226] See also e.g. Dir. 96/71/EC concerning the posting of workers (OJ [1997] L18/1) adopted on the basis of Arts. 57(2) and 66 (new Arts. 47(2) and 55), discussed further in Ch. 5.

1. Proof of Employment Contract

1.1. Introduction

The Social Charter Action Programme recognized that the great diversity of terms of recruitment and multiplicity of types of employment contract might hinder the mobility of workers. It concluded that Community workers, particularly those covered by atypical contracts, must have their working conditions set out in writing, to ensure greater transparency in the respective rights and obligations of employers and employees throughout the Community market. The final text of Directive 91/533/EEC, inspired by British law, was rapidly adopted and is richer, more precise, and more demanding than the Commission's original proposal. In essence, the Directive obliges employers to provide all employees with a document containing information about the essential elements of their contract or employment relationship.

1.2. Material and Personal Scope of the Directive

The Directive applies to every paid employee having a contract *or* an employment relationship defined by the law in force in a Member State and/or governed by the law in force in a Member State.[227] These terms reflect a Continental distinction. For example, under German law the contract of employment (*Arbeitsvertrag*) is a contract of service by which the employee undertakes to perform work in accordance with instructions.[228] The contract of employment establishes an employment relationship (*Arbeitsverhältnis*). While the contract of employment consists only of the specific arrangements relating to work that are agreed between employer and employee, the employment relationship encompasses the entire legal relationship between the contracting parties. The rights and obligations concerned may be laid down either by the individual contract or by collective agreement or by law. If the contract of employment is invalid but the employee has already entered into employment, there still exists a valid employment relationship with retrospective effect, including all the rights and obligations between employer and employee in the form of a *de facto* employment relationship.[229] In a similar way, Italian law also recognizes a distinction between employment contract and employment relationship. An employment relationship (*rapporto di lavoro*) is the legal relationship in which the worker is obliged to work and the employer to remunerate this work. The employment relationship is brought

---

[227] Art. 1(1). It would appear that this definition does not apply to the self-employed.
[228] Civil Code 611.
[229] Weiss, *European Employment and Industrial Relations Glossary, Germany* (Sweet & Maxwell, London, 1992) paras. 82 and 85.

about by the conclusion of a contract of employment (*contratto di lavoro*) between the worker and the employer.[230]

In considering the term 'employment relationship' the Commission, in its memo accompanying the draft Directive, envisaged both wholly new forms of employment as well as variations on traditional forms, including distance work,[231] training schemes, work/training contracts, work outside the traditional workplace, job-sharing and on-call work. However, in order to 'maintain a certain degree of flexibility in employment relationships',[232] Member States can exclude two categories of employees from the Directive's scope. The first relates to those employees who have a contract or employment relationship not exceeding one month and/or with a working week not exceeding eight hours. It has been suggested[233] that such an exclusion may be indirectly discriminatory against women since a higher proportion of woman than men work part time. However, if the Court's reasoning in *Kirsammer*[234] is accepted, such discrimination may be objectively justified in order to secure flexibility.

The second category of employees who may be excluded from the scope of the Directive are those employees of a casual and/or specific nature, provided that the non-application of the Directive is justified by objective considerations.[235] This derogation might apply to casual workers or seasonal workers such as fruit pickers, cleaners, hotel staff and others on very short-term contracts for occasional days or for a fixed purpose. The burden of proof would rest on the employer to justify the failure to provide the employee with the relevant information.

1.3. The Employer's Obligations to Notify

Under Article 2(1) the employer must notify the employees of the *essential aspects* of the contract or employment relationship.[236] This must include—in a non-exhaustive list:[237]

(a) the identity of the parties;
(b) the place of work or, if there is no fixed or main place of work, a statement

---

[230] Treu, *European Employment and Industrial Relations Glossary* (Sweet & Maxwell, London, 1991) paras. 188 and 561.

[231] See now the Telework Agreement concluded between the European instersectoral social partners (http://europa.eu.int/comm/employment_social/social_dialogue/docs/300_20020716_agreement_telework_en.pdf) considered further in Ch. 9.

[232] Preamble to Dir. 91/533/EEC.

[233] See Clark and Hall, 'The Cinderella Directive? Employee Rights to Information about Conditions Applicable to their Contract or Employment Relationship' (1992) 21 *ILJ*. 106, 111.

[234] Case C–189/91 *Petra Kirsammer-Hack v. Sidal* [1993] ECR I–6185.

[235] Art. 1(2).

[236] Art. 2(1). 'Contract' will be used to refer to both contracts and employment relationships.

[237] Art. 2(2). The Court ruled in Case C–253/96 *Kampelmann and Others v. Landschaftsverband Westfalen-Lippe and Others* [1997] ECR I–6907 that Art. 2(2)(c) is sufficiently precise and unconditional to have direct effect.

to that effect and details of the registered place of business or, where appropriate, the domicile of the employer;

(c) the title, grade, nature or category of work, and a brief description of the work;

(d) the date of commencement of the contract and,

(e) in the case of a temporary contract, its duration;

(f) the amount of paid leave;[238]

(g) the length of the notice periods;

(h) the initial basic amount, the other component elements, and the frequency of payment of the employee's remuneration;

(i) the length of the employee's normal working day or working week;[239]

(j) where necessary the collective agreements governing the employee's conditions of work.

In *Lange*[240] the Court said that since Article 2(1) lays down the basic rule, Article 2(2) cannot reduce the scope of the general requirement.[241] Therefore, the Court ruled that, in addition to the elements listed in Article 2(2), any element which, in view of its importance, must be considered an essential element of the contract of employment of which it forms part must be notified to the employee.[242] On the facts of the case, the Court said that this applies in particular to a term under which an employee is obliged to work overtime whenever requested to do so by his employer.

Some Continental commentators suggest that the obligation to inform the employee of the essential aspects of the contract indicates that all these aspects must have been agreed for the relationship to have been formed correctly. However, the position under English law is different. As Parker LJ said in *Eagland*,[243] where no terms exist relating to, for example, holiday pay and sick pay, the requirement to have a written statement does not empower or require the Tribunal to impose on the parties terms which had not been agreed.

Article 3(1) provides that this information must be given to the employee 'not later than two months[244] after the commencement of employment' in the form of a written contract of employment and/or a letter of engagement and/or one or more other written documents, where one of these documents contains at least all the information required by (a)–(d), (h), and (i). Alternatively, the employer can provide the employee with a written declaration

---

[238] This information, together with the information in (g), (h) and (i) may be given by reference to the laws, regulations, administrative or statutory provisions or collective agreements governing those particular points: Art. 2(3). In Case C–350/99 *Lange* [2001] ECR I–1061, para. 24, the Court said that, by analogy, information about overtime could also be provided in this way.

[239] But not including overtime: Case C–350/99 *Lange* [2001] ECR I–1061, paras. 16–19.

[240] Case C–350/99 *Wolfgang Lange* v. *Georg Schünemann GmbH* [2001] ECR I–1061.

[241] Paras. 21–2.   [242] Para. 23.

[243] *Eagland* v. *British Telecommunications* [1992] IRLR 323.

[244] If the work comes to an end before the two months expires the information must be provided by the end of the contract at the latest.

signed by the employer containing the information listed in (a)–(j). The written declaration can either take the place of the written documents or can supplement these documents. Employees going to work abroad for more than a month must be provided with additional information, including details of the duration of the period abroad, the currency to be used for the payment of remuneration, benefits in cash or kind, and details of their repatriation.[245]

Article 5 provides that if the terms and conditions of employment are changed in the course of the contract, the employee must be notified in writing at the earliest opportunity, and not later than one month after the date of entry into force of the change. This rule does not apply if the contractual terms are altered as a result of a change in the laws, regulations, and administrative or statutory provisions or collective agreements.

1.4. The Probative Value of the Written Statement

According to Article 6, the rules laid down by the Directive do not prejudice national rules and practice concerning the form of the contract, proof of the existence and the content of the contract and any relevant procedural rules. In the UK the written statement of terms is merely evidence of the terms of the contract; it does not constitute the contract itself. However, as Browne-Wilkinson J said in *Systems Floors* v. *Daniel*,[246] the written particulars represent 'strong prima facie evidence' of the contract terms. The written terms do not, however, place a 'heavy burden on the employer to show that the actual terms of the contract are different from those which he has set out in the statutory statement'. This 'heavy burden' does not apply to the employee who wishes to show that the contract terms are different to those in the statement.[247]

The probative value of the written statement of terms was considered by the Court in *Kampelmann*.[248] It said that although under Article 6 of the Directive national rules concerning the burden of proof are not to be affected by the Directive, the employer's obligation to notify an employee of the essential aspects of the contract or employment relationship had to be given some meaning. Therefore, employees had to be able to use the information contained in the notification referred to in Article 2(1) as evidence before the national courts, particularly in disputes concerning essential aspects of the contract or employment relationship. The Court therefore ruled that national courts had to apply and interpret their national rules on the burden of proof in the light of the purpose of the Directive. Thus, they had to give the notification referred to in Article 2(1) such evidential weight as to allow it to serve as

---

[245] Art. 4.   [246] [1982] ICR 54, 58.
[247] *Robertson* v. *British Gas Corporation* [1983] ICR 351.
[248] Case C–253/96 *Kampelmann* v. *Landschaftsverband Westfalen-Lippe* [1997] ECR I–6907.

factual proof of the essential aspects of the contract of employment or employment relationship. The notification also had to enjoy the same presumption as to its correctness as would attach, in domestic law, to any similar document drawn up by the employer and communicated to the employee.[249]

The Court added that since the Directive did not itself lay down any rules of evidence, proof of the essential aspects of the contract or employment relationship could not depend solely on the employer's notification under Article 2(1). The employer therefore had to be allowed to bring any evidence to the contrary, by showing that the information in the notification was either inherently incorrect or has been shown to be so in fact.[250] Thus, the judgment in *Kampelmann* is compatible with the approach adopted by the British courts outlined above. Nevertheless, as Kenner concludes,[251] while the central thrust of *Kampelmann* has fortified Directive 91/533 as a means of transmitting contractual information in a transparent form, it has also helped to reveal its most serious limitation. Article 6 ensures that the employer retains a large measure of control over the contractual bargain. The precise content of the contract remains a matter for the parties. The Directive is concerned with how that information is conveyed. Where the framework of regulation at national level is stripped away and no longer offers a minimum level of protection in the enumerated areas there is no compulsion on the employer to include them in the contractual terms and the Directive offers no protection.

1.5. Implementation and Remedies

Member States may, of course, introduce rules which are more favourable to employees.[252] They must also ensure that employees who consider themselves wronged by failure to comply with the obligations arising from the Directive can pursue their claims by judicial process.[253] Thus, as usual, remedies are a matter for the Member States. The most effective remedy in the circumstances would be an order that the employer produce a written statement compatible with the provisions of the Directive. The Directive does not require this but clearly envisages it as a possibility: Article 15(2) provides that, with the exception of expatriate employees, workers on temporary contracts and employees not covered by collective agreements, prior to seeking a judicial remedy the employee must notify the employer who has 15 days to reply. In *Lange*[254] the Court made clear that no provision of the Directive requires an essential element of the contract of employment that has not been mentioned in a

---

[249] Para. 33.   [250] Para. 34.

[251] Kenner, 'Statement or Contract—Some Reflections on the EC Employee Information (Contract or Employment Relationship) Directive after *Kampelmann*' (1999) 28 *ILJ*. 205.

[252] Art. 7.   [253] Art. 8(1).

[254] Case C–350/99 *Wolfgang Lange v. Georg Schünemann GmbH* [2001] ECR I–1061, para. 29.

written document or has not been mentioned with sufficient precision to be regarded as inapplicable.[255]

2. Pay

2.1. Introduction

Article 5 of the Community Social Charter 1989 provides that 'all employment shall be fairly remunerated'. To this end, and in accordance with arrangements applying in each country, 'workers shall be assured of an equitable wage, i.e. a wage sufficient to enable them to have a decent standard of living'. The term 'equitable' wage is carefully selected. No reference is made to a 'minimum' wage. Respecting the principle of subsidiarity, the Commission states in its Action Programme that wage setting is a matter for the Member States and the two sides of industry alone. It recognizes that the majority of the Member States, either through their constitution, legislation or by means of international agreements to which they are party, guarantee the right of workers to sufficient remuneration to provide them and their families with a decent standard of living. As a result it recognizes that it is not the Community's task to set a decent reference wage. It argued that low pay gives a competitive advantage: minimum wage provision means that richer countries would deprive poorer countries of their competitive advantage.[256] Although the link between low pay and competitiveness has been disputed,[257] and the evidence suggesting that the introduction of a minimum wage would cause large-scale unemployment is not conclusive, the Commission has nevertheless exercised extreme caution in this area, being prepared only to 'outline certain basic principles on equitable wages' in a non-legally-binding opinion.[258] Otherwise its activities have concentrated on the reform of national systems of social protection to ensure that individuals are not discouraged by the operation of national social security systems from going back to work and therefore earning enough money to support themselves. We consider this issue in outline in the final part of this chapter; first we shall look at the Opinion on Equitable Wages.

2.2. The Opinion on Equitable Wages

Article 1 of the Opinion defines an equitable wage as meaning 'that all workers should receive a reward for work done which in the context of the

---

[255] Para. 29.   [256] House of Lords Evidence 1989, 16.

[257] Deakin and Wilkinson, *The Economics of Employment Rights* (IER, London, 1991), esp. at 32–3.

[258] COM(93) 388 final.

society in which they live and work is fair and sufficient to enable them to have a decent standard of living'. Four principles underpin the Commission's approach: the first involves the recognition of the role of investment and training in order to achieve high productivity and high quality employment; the second restates the proposition that the pursuit of equitable wages is to be seen as part of the Community's basic objectives of greater economic and social cohesion and more harmonious development; the third recognizes that discriminatory wage practices should be eliminated; and the fourth recommends that attitudes to traditionally low-paid groups should be reassessed. In the context of discrimination, the commitment to pay an equitable wage to all workers, 'irrespective of gender, disability, race, religion, ethnic origin or nationality', which, at the time, was an important step forward because it went further than the commitment contained elsewhere in Community law to equal pay without discrimination on the grounds of sex or nationality.

The Commission envisaged a three-pronged plan of action: first, improving transparency of the labour market by better collection and dissemination of comparable statistical information about wage structures in the Community; secondly, ensuring that the right to an equitable wage is respected, in particular by prohibiting discrimination, ensuring fair treatment for workers in all age groups and for home workers, and establishing the mechanisms for negotiated minima and the strengthening of collective bargaining arrangements. Member States should also ensure that 'the measures taken do not force low-paid workers into the informal economy and do not encourage unlawful employment practices'. In addition, they must check that wages agreed under the contract of employment are paid in full and that employees are 'correctly paid in respect of periods of leave and sickness'. Thirdly, action should be taken to improve the long-term productivity and earnings potential of the workforce. Finally, the Social Partners are invited to address all the issues raised in the Opinion, in particular to examine what contribution they can make to ensuring the right of every worker to an equitable wage. Indeed, the Social Partners have already considered questions relating to the adaptation of remuneration systems as part of the social dialogue.[259] However, little further action can be expected at Community level on matters relating to pay. Article 137(5) provides that the provisions of Article 137 do not apply to pay, and so the Community's competence is at best circumscribed.

2.3. Supporting Measures

(a) Recommendation 92/441

Accompanying the Commission's opinion on an equitable wage is the Council Recommendation 92/441/EEC on common criteria concerning sufficient

---

[259] Commission, *Adaptation of Remuneration Systems*, Luxembourg, 1993.

resources and social assistance in the social protection systems.[260] While the former concentrates on fair remuneration for work performed with particular attention paid to the more vulnerable members of the labour force, the latter concerns guaranteed minimum income from all sources, and contains a more resounding commitment to respect for human rights. Article 1 requires Member States to:

recognise the basic right of a person to sufficient resources and social assistance to live in a manner compatible with human dignity as part of a comprehensive and consistent drive to combat social exclusion, and to adapt their social protection systems.

It then lays down principles according to which this right must be assured. In particular, the resources should be provided on an individual basis,[261] should not be time limited,[262] and should be fixed at a level considered 'sufficient to cover essential needs with regard to respect for human dignity, taking account of living standards and price levels in the Member State concerned, for different types and sizes of household'.[263] Thus, the Recommendation guidance is carefully circumscribed by respect for the principle of subsidiarity and the divergence of national systems.[264]

(b) Recommendation 92/442

Recommendation 92/442,[265] by contrast, provides guidance on the co-ordination of national policies. Although still hemmed in by the principle of subsidiarity and respect for the autonomy of the national systems, it is more ambitious. It begins with four basic principles for social protection policies. First, it recommends that Member States give any person legally resident in its territory, regardless of resources, access to the state's health service.[266] It also recommends that states provide employed workers who retire or interrupt their careers with replacement income to maintain their standard of living.[267] Second, social benefits must be provided on a non-discriminatory basis without regard to 'nationality, race, sex, religion, customs or political opinion'[268] and must be granted according to the principles of fairness,[269] so that beneficiaries of social benefits receive their share from the improvements in the standard of living of the population as a whole. Third, it recommends that social policies should adapt to the development of behaviour and of family structures responsive to changes in the labour market; and fourth, that social protection should be administered with maximum efficiency. The

---

[260] COM(91) 161 final (OJ [1992] L245/46). See also Art. 10 of the Community Social Charter 1989 and Art. 34 of the Charter of Fundamental Rights 2000.

[261] Para. I.B.2.   [262] Para. I.B.4.   [263] Para. I.C.1(a).

[264] See also the emphasis on subsidiarity in COM(97) 102.

[265] OJ [1992] L245/46.   [266] Para. I.A.1(b).   [267] Para. I.A.1(d).

[268] Para. I.A.2(a).   [269] Para. I.A.2(b).

Recommendation then makes specific suggestions in respect of six policy areas including sickness, maternity, and unemployment.[270]

(c) Reform of the National Systems of Social Protection

Reform of the social protection systems has now become a major concern of the European Union. In its 1993 the White Paper on Growth, Competitiveness and Employment[271] the Commission argued that, due to inappropriate social protection schemes and employment services, there was insufficient motivation to work. It also expressed concerns about the funding of these schemes by high non-wage costs, particularly in the form of statutory levies and charges, through which an equivalent of 40 per cent of the Community's GDP was channelled. These concerns were picked up in the Commission's 1997 Communication on Modernising and Improving Social Protection in the European Union.[272] While recognizing that publicly funded social protection systems (social security and social assistance) established decades ago have played a 'fundamental role in ensuring income redistribution and cohesion, and in maintaining political stability and economic progress over the life of the Union', the systems were in need of modernization to ensure their continued effectiveness. Although it said that social protection could be a productive factor, it expressed concerns about the level of non-wage costs and the need for policies designed to improve flexibility and to provide security. This was reflected in the Entrepreneurship pillar of the Employment Guidelines which envisaged setting a target for gradually reducing the overall tax burden and, where appropriate, a target for gradually reducing the fiscal pressure on labour and non-wage labour costs, in particular on relatively unskilled and low-paid labour.[273] This theme has been carried through into the Integrated Guidelines of the Lisbon relaunch.[274] The tenor of these statements suggests that the results of future co-ordination of social protection may lead to the reduction in the level of benefits rather than their improvement, especially for those Member States participating in EMU which have agreed to limit public deficit to 3 per cent and have a maximum of 60 per cent of GDP in public debt.[275]

The Commission followed up its 1997 Communication with a Concerted strategy on Modernization of Social Protection[276] which argued for an agenda of deepened co-operation based on four key objectives within the overall challenge of modernization: (1) to make work pay and to provide secure income; (2) to make pensions safe and pension systems sustainable; (3) to

---

[270] See also Council Resolution on the role of social protection systems in the fight against unemployment (OJ [1996] C386/3).

[271] Bull. Supp. 6/93, 124, 136ff.   [272] COM(97) 102.

[273] Council Res. 98/128 on the 1998 Employment Guidelines (OJ [1998] 30/1).

[274] See, e.g., Council Dec. 2005/600 (OJ [2005] L205/21): Guideline No. 22.

[275] See Guild, 'How Can Social Protection Survive EMU? A United Kingdom Perspective' (1999) 24 *ELRev.* 22.

[276] COM(99) 347, 4.

promote social inclusion; and (4) to ensure high quality and sustainable health care.[277] This strategy was to be supported by 'enhanced mechanisms for exchanging information and monitoring policy developments in order to give the process more visibility and political profile'—in essence OMC-style techniques facilitated by the establishment of a Social Protection Committee.[278] This approach was endorsed by the Lisbon European Council,[279] which noted that developed social protection systems were a key pillar of the European Social model,[280] and confirmed by the Commission.[281] Member States now present National Action Plans for Inclusion and National Strategy reports on pensions, on the basis of which the Commission and Council agree a Joint Inclusion Report and a Joint Pensions report. The OMC processes have now been strengthened and streamlined with the Integrated Guidelines.[282]

E. CONCLUSIONS

With the discussion of social protection, we have come a long way from the health and safety Directives with which we started this chapter. The discussion does, however, emphasize that it is not possible easily to compartmentalize those areas of law in which the European Community has intervened. In its Green Paper on Social Policy 1993[283] the Commission advocated extending legislative action at Union level still further to include protection against individual dismissal,[284] the prohibition of discrimination against workers who wish to enforce their rights or who refuse to perform unlawful tasks, the right to payment of wages on public holidays and during illness, and the right of the worker to be heard in internal company matters which concern him or her personally. With the exception of worker information and consultation,[285]

---

[277] This was endorsed by the Council in its conclusions of 17 December 1999 on the strengthening of cooperation for modernizing and improving social protection (OJ [2000] C8/7.)

[278] Initially established by Council Dec. 2000/436/EC (OJ [2000] L172/26 which was repealed and replaced by Council Dec. 2004/689/EC (OJ [2004] L314/8) based on Art. 144 EC introduced by the Treaty of Nice.

[279] Lisbon European Council, Presidency Conclusions, 23–24 March 2000, para. 31.

[280] The objectives were defined by the Brussels European Council in November 2000 (http://europa.eu.int/comm/employment_social/social_inclusion/docs/approb_en.pdf), revised in 2002, (http://europa.eu.int/comm/employment_social/social_inclusion/docs/counciltext_en.pdf) and replaced by new objectives in March 2006 (http://europa.eu.int/comm/employment_social/social_inclusion/docs/2006/objectives_en.pdf) which in turn were based on the Commission's Communication Working together, working better: A new framework for the open coordination of social protection and inclusion policies in the European Union (COM(2005) 706).

[281] Communication, Strengthening the social dimension of the Lisbon strategy: streamlining open coordination in the field of social protection (COM(2003) 261).

[282] COM(2005) 706.   [283] COM(93) 551.

[284] See also Art. 30 of the Charter of Fundamental Rights 2000: 'Every worker has the right to protection against unjustified dismissal, in accordance with Community law and national laws and practices.'

[285] See further Ch. 15.

none of these plans for a 'European labour law' have come to fruition. Indeed, it is questionable whether the Community should be contemplating entering all (any?) of these policy areas, thereby replicating national attainments at Community level. As we have seen, in fact, the Lisbon strategy has diverted the Community's attention away from enacting an ever wider range of employment rights and focused more on different forms of regulation, especially OMC, aimed at co-ordinating national policies in a range of areas, including social protection. Where there has been legislation, it has concentrated on the EU's areas of specialism: equality, health and safety, information and consultation, and employees' rights on the restructuring of a business. It is to this latter subject that we now turn.

PART V

Employee Rights on Restructuring Enterprises

13

Transfers of Undertakings

A. INTRODUCTION

In the early 1970s there was much concern about the absence of a 'social face' to the then Common Market. In particular there was concern that, in the inevitable process of restructuring brought about by increased competition as barriers to trade were removed, individual employees would suffer. For example, they might see their part of the business transferred to another owner who would either want to dismiss extraneous employees or at least change their terms and conditions of employment. Alternatively, they might face redundancy when their employer decides to downsize and so make a large number of workers redundant, or they find that their employer cannot compete and so closes their business, resulting in arrears of salary outstanding.

As a result, three important Directives were adopted as part of the 1974–1976 Social Action Programme aimed at addressing the social consequences of economic change: Directive 77/187 concerned employees' rights on the transfer of undertakings,[1] Directive 75/129 concerned collective redundancies[2] and Directive 80/987 concerned insolvency.[3] Since these Directives were drafted to facilitate the restructuring of enterprises with a view to making them more competitive and efficient, they did not question the managerial prerogative to restructure and to dismiss employees. Instead, the Directives aimed to address the social consequences of these managerial decisions and mitigate their effects. In this respect the Directives were intended both to encourage a greater degree of industrial democracy and to provide an element of social protection.[4]

The three Directives, as originally conceived, focused on restructuring at *national* level. With the advent of the internal market programme in 1986 the

---

[1] Council Dir. 77/187/EEC on the approximation of the laws of the Member States relating to the safeguarding of employees' rights in the event of transfers of undertakings, businesses or parts of businesses (OJ [1977] L61/126).

[2] OJ [1975] L48/29.

[3] OJ [1980] L283/23, as amended by Dir. 87/164 (OJ [1987] L66/11) and substantially revised by Dir. 2002/74 (OJ [2002] L270/10).

[4] Blainpain, recalling the discussions held in a group of labour law experts from different Member States, *Labour Law and Industrial Relations of the European Community* (Kluwer, Deventer, 1991), 153.

Community shifted its focus towards the social consequences of *transnational* corporate restructuring, caused by the need of a market economy to establish, on the most appropriate sites, 'businesses capable of implementing the large-scale economic operations which a large market is likely to require'.[5] As a result, the Collective Redundancies Directive was revised by Directive 92/56[6] to give it a transnational dimension. It was subsequently consolidated in Directive 98/59.[7] Directive 77/187 on Transfers of Undertakings was also revised by Directive 98/50,[8] in the light of the Court's now extensive jurisprudence,[9] and was subsequently consolidated in Directive 2001/23.[10] The Insolvency Directive was amended by Directive 87/164[11] and was substantially revised by Directive 2002/74.[12]

We shall now examine these Directives in turn. In this chapter we consider the most litigated Directive, Directive 2001/23 on Transfers of Undertakings, sometimes referred to as the Acquired Rights Directive; in the next chapter we examine the Directives on Collective Redundancies and Insolvency.

B. TRANSFERS OF UNDERTAKINGS: OVERVIEW

Since 1928 French law has required that, if there is a change in the juridical situation of an employer, for example as a result of succession, sale, or fusion, all contracts of employment existing on the date of the transfer will continue between the new employer and the employees of the enterprise. This provision was introduced at the behest of employers to ensure that, on the date of the transfer, not only were the assets of the business transferred but so was the workforce, thereby ensuring that the new employer had the necessary skilled workers to operate the equipment. The French position can, however, be contrasted with the approach adopted by other states. For example, in the UK the employment contract was considered to be a personal contract which could not be transferred to another employer. The new employer could therefore not expect to receive a trained workforce in the event of a transfer, but neither could employees be guaranteed any job security.

Directive 77/187 (now Directive 2001/23) on transfers of undertakings

---

[5] COM(94) 300, 3.   [6] Council Dir. 92/56/EEC (OJ [1992] L245/3).
[7] OJ [1998] L225/16.
[8] OJ [1998] L201/88. See Hunt, 'Success at Last? The Amendment of the Acquired Rights Directive' (1999) 24 *ELRev.* 215; Painter and Hardy, 'Acquiring "Revised" Rights? Council Proposal to Revise the Acquired Rights Directive' (1996) 3 *Maastricht Journal* 35.
[9] Preambular para. 5 says that 'considerations of legal security and transparency require that the legal concept of transfer be clarified in the light of the case law of the Court', but that 'such clarification does not alter the scope of Directive 77/187 as interpreted by the Court of Justice'.
[10] OJ [2001] L82/16.   [11] OJ [1987] L66/11.   [12] OJ [2002] L270/10.

favoured the French position and altered the common law position.[13] The Preamble to the Directive recognized that 'economic trends are bringing in their wake, at both national and Community level, changes in the structure of undertakings, through transfers of undertakings'. The Preamble continued that it was 'necessary to provide for the protection of employees in the event of a change of employer, in particular, to ensure that their rights are safeguarded'.[14] The Court has been particularly influenced by this wording,[15] and has, at times, been prepared to give a purposive interpretation to the Directive to 'ensure as far as possible that the contract of employment or employment relationship continues unchanged with the transferee, in order to prevent the workers concerned from being placed in a less favourable position solely as a result of the transfer'.[16]

The Directive establishes three pillars of protection for employees. First, it provides for the automatic transfer of the employment relationship with all of its rights and obligations from the transferor (A, the natural or legal person who, by reason of the transfer, ceases to be the employer in the undertaking)[17] to the transferee (B, the natural or legal person who becomes the employer)[18] in the event of a transfer (see Figure 13.1).[19] Secondly, it protects workers against dismissal[20] by the transferor or transferee. This is, however, subject to the employer's right to dismiss employees for 'economic, technical or organisational reasons entailing changes in the workforce'.[21] Thirdly, the

---

[13] The original (1977) Directive was significantly watered down from earlier drafts: Elias, 'The Transfer of Undertakings: A Reluctantly Acquired Right' (1982) 3 *Company Lawyer* 147, 156, described the 'protections afforded to employees are now but a pale shadow of what might once have been anticipated'.

[14] For the interface between the need to transfer ownership and to save jobs in the context of Small and Medium Enterprises, see Commission, Communication from the Commission on the Transfer of Businesses (OJ [1994] C204/1).

[15] Case 135/83 *Abels v. Bedrijfsvereniging voor de Metaalindustrie en de Electrotechnische Industrie* [1985] ECR 469, para. 6; Case 179/83 *Industrie Bond FNV v. Netherlands* [1985] ECR 511, para. 4; Case 186/83 *Botzen v. Rotterdamse Drbogdok Maatschappij* [1985] ECR 519, para. 6; Case 19/83 *Wendelboe v. L J Music* [1985] ECR 457, para. 8; Case 105/84 *Foreningen af Arbejdsledere i Danmark v. Danmols Inventar* [1985] ECR 2639, para. 15; Case 24/85 *Spijkers v. Benedik* [1986] ECR 1119, para. 6; Case 237/84 *Commission v. Belgium* [1986] ECR 1247; Case 235/84 *Commission v. Italy* [1986] ECR 2291, para. 2; Case 287/86 *Landsorganisationen i Danmark for Tjenerforbundet i Danmark v. Ny Mølle Kro* [1987] ECR 5465, para. 11; Case 324/86 *Foreningen af Arbejdsledere i Danmark v. Daddy's Dance Hall* [1988] ECR 739, para. 9; Joined Cases 144 and 145/87 *Berg v. Besselsen* [1988] ECR 2559; Case 101/87 *Bork International v. Foreningen af Arbejdsledere i Danmark* [1988] ECR 3057, para. 13; Case C–362/89 *d'Urso v. Ercole Marelli Elettromeccanica Generale* [1991] ECR I–4105; Case C–29/91 *Sophie Redmond Stichting v. Bartol* [1992] ECR I–3189; Joined Cases C–132, 138 and 139/91 *Katsikas v. Konstantinidis and Skreb and Schroll v. PCO Stavereibetrieb Paetz & Co. Nachfolger GmbH* [1992] ECR I–6577 and Case C–209/91 *Watson Rask and Christensen v. ISS Kantineservice A/S* [1992] ECR I–5755; Case C–392/92 *Schmidt v. Spar und Leihkasse* [1994] ECR I–1311, para. 15; Case C–399/96 *Europièces v. Wilfried Sanders and Automotive Industries Holding Company SA* [1998] ECR I–6965, para. 37.

[16] Case 287/86 *Ny Mølle Kro* [1987] ECR 5465, para. 25; Case C–478/03 *Celtec Ltd v. John Astley and others* [2005] ECR I–000, para. 26.

[17] Art. 2(1)(a)   [18] Arts. 2(1)(b).   [19] Art. 3(1).   [20] Art. 4(1).

[21] Art. 4(1), second sentence.

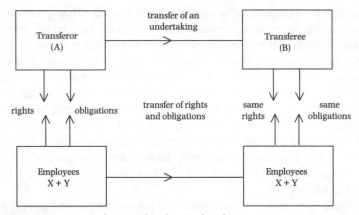

Figure 13.1 Consequences of a Transfer of an Undertaking

Directive requires the transferor and the transferee to inform and consult the representatives of the employees affected by the transfer.[22] These three pillars of protection are minimum requirements:[23] Member States are free either to apply laws, regulations or administrative provisions which are more favourable to employees or to promote or permit more favourable collective agreements or agreements between the Social Partners[24] which are more favourable to employees.

The Directive is intended as a means of only 'partial harmonisation'.[25] According to the Court in *Danmols Inventar*,[26] it is not intended to 'establish a uniform level of protection throughout the Community on the basis of common criteria'. Therefore national law still has a significant role to play, particularly in defining key terms such as 'employee'.[27] National law also prescribes the consequences of a refusal to be transferred[28] and the sanction in the case of the failure to inform and consult worker representatives and the dismissal of a worker in the event of a transfer.[29] The inevitable consequence of partial harmonization is a certain divergence in the level of employee protection across the European Union.

The Directive is not without its critics who argue that it interferes with free enterprise. They say that it severely restricts contractors in their ability to restructure their workforces, or to devise new, performance-related arrangements or to introduce innovative ways of doing the work, thus

---

[22] Art. 7.   [23] Art. 8   [24] Ibid.
[25] Case 105/84 *Danmols Inventar* [1985] ECR 2639, para. 26. See Garde, 'Partial harmonisation and European Social Policy: A Case Study on the Acquired Rights Directive' (2002–3) 5 *CYELS*. 173.
[26] Case 105/84 [1985] ECR 2639, para. 26.
[27] Case 105/84 *Danmols Inventar* [1985] ECR 2639, para. 16, and now Art. 2(1)(d) of Dir. 2001/23 considered below.
[28] Joined Cases C–132, 138 and 139/91 *Katsikas* [1992] ECR I–6577.   [29] Art. 9.

interfering with any anticipated increase in efficiency. They also say that it dissuades a potential transferee from acquiring the undertaking.[30] Not surprisingly, the Commission makes a different assessment. It says:

Generally speaking, as far as legislation is concerned, the effectiveness in social terms of the protection afforded by the Directive is beyond dispute. The Directive has proved to be an invaluable instrument for the protection of workers in the event of the reorganisation of an undertaking, by ensuring peaceful and consensual economic and technological restructuring and providing minimum standards for promoting fair competition in the context of such changes.[31]

C. THE PERSONAL SCOPE OF THE DIRECTIVE

1. 'Employees'

The rights laid down by the Directive are conferred, in the English language version, on 'employees'[32] who are defined by Directive 2001/23 as 'any person who, in the Member State concerned, is protected as an employee under national employment law'.[33] This definition of employees, which refers back to *national* law, confirms the Court's earlier jurisprudence[34] but stands in sharp contrast to the case law on Article 39 on free movement of workers[35]

---

[30] Earl Howe, Hansard, HL, Vol. 533, col. 148, in the context of a discussion as to whether the British rules which implement the Directive should be extended to all transfers of work from a local authority direct service organization to an external contractor, discussed in Napier, 'CCT, Marketing Testing and Employment Rights: The Effects of TUPE and the Acquired Rights Directive' (1993) *Institute of Employment Rights*, 12. See also the arguments of the Italian government in Case C–362/89 *d'Urso* [1991] ECR I–4105.

[31] Commission memorandum on Acquired Rights of Workers in Cases of Transfers of Undertakings (http://europa.eu.int/comm/dg05/soc-dial/labour/memo/memoen.htm). This memo provides guidelines on the application of Directive 2001/23 based on the Court's case law. See generally Hunt, 'The Court of Justice as a Policy Actor: the Acquired Rights Directive' (1998) 18 *Legal Studies* 336.

[32] Although the English version of the Directive uses the term 'employee', other language versions use 'worker' and the Court uses the terms interchangeably. See e.g. para. 15 in Case 19/83 *Wendelboe* [1985] ECR 457. See translator's note in Case 105/84 *Danmols Inventar* [1985] ECR 2639.

[33] Art. 2(1)(d). Public service employees are not covered by the Directive insofar as they are not subject to the labour law in force in the Member States: Case C–343/98 *Collino* v. *Telecom Italia SpA* [2000] ECR I–6659, paras. 39–40. See AG Poiares Maduro's criticisim of this in Case C–425/02 *Delahaye* [2004] ECR I–108273, para. 17.

[34] Case 19/83 *Wendelboe* [1985] ECR 457, para. 16; Case 105/84 *Danmols Inventar* [1985] ECR 2639, para. 16.

[35] Case 105/84 *Danmols Inventar* [1985] ECR 2639. In the same case Advocate General Slynn agreed (p. 2644) that the Directive did not envisage a Community definition of the term 'worker'. According to Hepple ('Community Measures for the Protection of Workers on Dismissal' (1977) 14 *CMLRev.* 489, 494), any definition would be based on the following—'an employee is one who, in return for remuneration, agrees to work for another and who can, as a matter of law, be directed as to what he does and how he does it, whether pursuant to a contract of employment or an employment relationship.'

where the Court has insisted on a *Community* definition of the term 'worker'.[36]

In English law, an 'employee' means an individual who has entered into or works under a 'contract of employment' and a contract of employment is defined as 'a contract of service or apprenticeship, whether express or implied, and (if it is express) whether oral or in writing'.[37] Article 2(2) of Directive 2001/23 provides that the Directive shall be 'without prejudice to national law as regards the definition of the contract of employment or employment relationship'.[38] However, Article 2(2) continues that Member States shall not exclude contracts of employment or employment relationships from the Directive solely because:

- of the number of working hours performed or to be performed;
- they are employment relationships governed by a fixed term contract as defined by Article 1(1) of Directive 91/383;[39]
- they are temporary employment relationships within the meaning of Article 1(2) of Directive 91/383 and the undertaking transferred is or is part of the temp agency which is the employer.

The Directive confers rights only on those employees[40] who, during their working hours, are *wholly* engaged in the part[41] of the business transferred. Advocate General Slynn in *Botzen*[42] suggested that in order to determine whether an employee was 'wholly engaged' in the part of the organization transferred it was necessary to consider whether the employee would have been employed by the owners of that part or by the owners of the remaining part, if that part of the business had been separately owned before the transfer. The only exception made by Advocate General Slynn to the requirement of being 'wholly engaged' was where an employee was required to perform other duties to an extent which could be described as *de minimis*. If, however, an employee was in fact engaged in the activities of the whole business or in several parts then he could not be regarded as an employee of the part of the business transferred for the purpose of the Directive. Thus, a person who works for several parts of a company, including the part transferred—for

---

[36] See e.g. Case 53/81 *Levin* [1982] ECR 1035. This is considered further in Ch. 4.

[37] S. 230(1)–(2) ERA 1996.

[38] The reference to the 'contract of employment or employment relationship' may embrace the German *Arbeitsvertrag* and *Arbeitsverhältnis* and the Italian *contratto di lavoro* and *rapporto di lavoro* where the employment relationship arises out of the contract of employment.

[39] OJ [1991] L206/19; see further Ch. 9.

[40] This will cover full-time and part-time workers: Advocate General Slynn in Case 186/83 *Botzen* [1985] ECR 519.

[41] The Court has also refused to define comprehensively what is meant by 'part of' a business. In Case 186/83 *Botzen* [1985] ECR 519, 521 Advocate General Slynn suggested that this was a question of fact but that 'it will usually involve the transfer of a department or a factory or facet of the business' or the sale of 'a fraction or a single unit of business'.

[42] Case 186/83 [1985] ECR 519, 521.

example, a sales representative or a personnel officer—cannot claim to be transferred to the new employer, for their jobs may be different in scope, a position which is not envisaged by the Directive.

This view was taken by the Court in *Botzen*. In that case the transferee took over the general engineering departments of the transferor and the relevant staff but not the departments containing the support staff. The Court ruled an employment relationship was essentially characterized by the link existing between the employee and the part of the undertaking or business to which he was assigned to carry out his duties.[43] As the Commission put it, a transfer takes place of the departments to which the employee was assigned and which formed the organizational framework within which their employment relationship took effect.[44] Therefore, the Directive would not apply to those employees who, although not employees in the transferred part of the undertaking, performed certain duties which involved the use of assets assigned to the part transferred or who, while being employed in an administration department of the undertaking which was not transferred, carried out certain duties for the benefit of the part transferred.[45]

As the Court made clear in *Wendelboe*,[46] the employees must be employed by the transferor undertaking on the date of transfer. The transferee is therefore not liable for holiday pay and compensation in respect of those employees who were not employed in the undertaking on the date of transfer.[47] Subsequent employees also cannot enjoy the benefits of the Directive;[48] nor can employees who have decided *of their own volition*[49] that they do not wish to continue the employment relationship with the new employer after transfer.[50]

2. 'Representatives of Employees'

The Directive also confers rights on employees' representatives who must be informed and consulted. They are defined in Article 2(1)(c) as the representatives of the employees provided for by the laws or practice of the Member

---

[43] Case 186/83 *Botzen* [1985] ECR 519 and Case C–392/92 *Schmidt* [1994] ECR I–1311.

[44] Para. 14.   [45] Para. 16.

[46] Case 19/83 *Wendleboe* [1985] ECR 457. The Court reached this conclusion after examining the various language versions of the Directive. In the Dutch, French, German, Greek, and Italian versions the phrase 'existing on the date of the transfer' relates unequivocally to the expression 'contract of employment . . . or employment relationship' and that the English and Danish versions were capable of bearing the same interpretation. Furthermore, Art. 3(4) distinguishes between 'employees' and 'persons no longer employed'. Art. 3(1) does not make that distinction.

[47] This is considered further below.

[48] Case 287/86 *Ny Mølle Kro* [1987] ECR 5465, para. 26.

[49] Advocate General Slynn in Case 105/84 *Danmols Inventar* [1985] ECR 2639, however, stressed that it was crucial for the national courts to ensure that any such agreement is 'genuine and not tainted by duress on the part of the transferor or the transferee'.

[50] Case 105/84 *Danmols Inventar* [1985] ECR 2639, para. 26.

States. These representatives may be trade unionists and/or works council-lors. The Continental European tradition has typically provided for this 'dual channel' approach. However, in the UK the information and consultation procedures laid down by the original national rules implementing the Directive applied only to recognized trade unions (with the decision to recognize being entirely a matter for the employer). This was in line with the British 'single channel' approach through which all worker representation was traditionally directed.

In *Commission* v. *UK*[51] the Court ruled that, by confining the information and consultation obligations to recognized trade unions only, the UK had failed to transpose the Directive fully because British law did not provide a mechanism for the designation of workers' representatives where an employer refused to recognize a trade union. The UK government argued that, as a Directive of partial harmonization,[52] the term employees' representatives referred to those representatives provided for by the laws and practices of the Member States which, in the UK, meant recognized trade unions only. The Court rejected this argument, saying that the Directive was not simply a *renvoi* to the rules in force in the Member States.[53] Focusing on the effective applica-tion of Community law rather than the concept of partial harmonization, the Court said that the duty to inform and consult would be deprived of its full effect if Member States allowed only recognized employee representatives to be informed and consulted,[54] leaving employees in a workplace without a recognized trade union without information and consultation rights.[55]

The UK gave effect to the ruling by expanding the scope of those who could be consulted.[56] Where a recognized trade union exists, it still needs to be consulted. In the absence of a recognized trade union, consultation takes place with elected representatives.[57] The creation of elected 'employee rep-resentatives' marked the first substantial inroad into the single channel in the UK. However, the Labour government's amendments ensured that consult-ation with employee representatives is considered very much a secondary

[51] Case C–382/92 *Commission* v. *UK* [1994] ECR I–2435.   [52] Para. 27.
[53] Para. 18. The Court cited Case 61/81 *Commission* v. *UK* [1982] ECR 2601 which held that national legislation making it possible to impede protection unconditionally granted to employees by a Directive is contrary to Community law.
[54] Para. 19.   [55] Para. 29.
[56] The initial implementation can be found in SI 1995/2587 The Collective Redundancies and Transfer of Undertakings (Protection of Employment) (Amendment) Regulations 1995, amending SI 1981/1794 Transfer of Undertakings (Protection of Employment) Regulations 1981, Reg. 10.
[57] Unsuccessful judicial review proceedings were brought in *R* v. *Secretary of State for Trade and Industry, ex parte Unison* [1996] IRLR 438, challenging the implementation; the DTI issued a consultation paper, *Employees' Information and Consultation Rights on Transfers of Undertakings and Collective Redundancies*, URN 97/988. The relevant Regulations are now found in SI 1999/1925 The Collective Redundancies and Transfer of Undertakings Regulations (Protection of Employ-ment) (Amendment) Regulations 1999. These Regulations also make some provision for the election of worker representatives.

channel, prompting Davies to describe the current British rules as 'a modified single channel'.[58]

D. THE MATERIAL SCOPE OF THE DIRECTIVE

1. Introduction

According to Article 1(1)(a), the Directive applies to 'any transfer of an undertaking, business or part of an undertaking or business to another employer as a result of a legal transfer or merger'.[59] Because this is the threshold requirement—the gateway to the protection conferred by the Directive—this provision has been the subject of considerable litigation, particularly regarding the meaning of the two key terms 'transfer of an undertaking' and 'legal transfer'. At first it seemed that the transfer of an undertaking had to occur as a direct consequence of a legal transfer or merger. This view was taken by the Court in *Abels*.[60] However, in subsequent cases a distinction seems to have emerged between the terms 'transfer of an undertaking' and 'legal transfer'.[61] Although the Court has not adopted a consistent stance on this point, the decision in *Sophie Redmond*[62] suggests that the two concepts are distinct and require the answer to two separate questions:

- is the transfer a legal transfer within the meaning of the Directive (sale, contracting-out, leasing, etc)?[63] If so,
- is there a transfer of an undertaking on the facts, applying the criteria laid down by the Court in *Spijkers*[64] (considered below). This decision is usually a matter for the national courts.

We shall examine these questions in turn.[65]

---

[58] Davies, 'A Challenge to Single Channel' (1994) 23 *ILJ*. 272, 279. This issue is considered further in Ch. 15.

[59] The Directive does not apply to sea-going vessels (Art. 1(3)). The Commission proposed that the rights conferred by the Directive, with the exception of rights relating to information and consultation, should also apply to sea-going vessels (Art. 1(4) of 94/C274/08) but this was not adopted in the final draft.

[60] Case 135/83 [1985] ECR 469.

[61] De Groot, 'The Council Directive on the Safeguarding of Employees Rights in the Event of Transfers of Undertakings: An Overview of the Case Law' (1993) 30 *CMLRev*. 331 who suggests that the reason why the Court has developed a distinction between these two questions depends on the nature of the questions posed by the national court.

[62] Case C–29/91 [1992] ECR I–3189, para. 9. See also Case C–392/92 *Schmidt* [1994] ECR I–1311.

[63] See below, nn. 66–111.   [64] Case 24/85 *Spijkers* [1986] ECR 1119.

[65] Joined Cases 144 and 145/87 *Berg* [1988] ECR 2559, Case 287/86 *Ny Mølle Kro* [1987] ECR 5465, and Case C–29/91 *Bartol* [1992] ECR I–3189, respectively.

2. Legal Transfer or Merger

2.1. Legal Transfer

(a) Introduction

Article 1(1)(a) provides that the Directive applies to the transfer of an undertaking as a result of a legal transfer or merger.[66] We begin by considering the meaning of the term 'legal transfer'; 'merger' is considered below. The notion of 'legal' transfer relates to the method of the transfer. At first the cases concerned contractual relations—the sale of a business being the paradigm example.[67] Subsequently, the Court had to consider more complex transactions, including leasing arrangements and contracting out of services where there was no direct contractual link between the transferor and transferee (see Figures 13.2 and 13.3 below). This raised the problem whether the Directive covered only transfers arising directly from a contract, as the Dutch, German, French, Greek, Italian, Spanish, and Portuguese language versions suggested,[68] or whether the scope of the Directive was wide enough to cover other types of transfer which did not necessarily result from a contract, as the English phrase ('legal transfer') and the Danish version (*overdragelse*)[69] suggested.

The Court adopted a broad purposive interpretation of the notion of a legal transfer[70] and it is now clear that the Directive can apply to all transfers, including those involving an administrative or legislative act,[71] a court decision[72] and those where there is no contract at all.[73] Thus, as the Court said in *Allen*,[74] the Directive covers 'any legal change in the person of the employer'. Therefore, it could apply to a transfer between two subsidiary companies in

---

[66] The Directive does not apply to sea-going vessels (Art. 1(3)). The Commission proposed that the rights conferred by the Directive, with the exception of rights relating to and consultation, should also apply to sea going vessels (Art. 1(4) of 94/C274/08) but this was not adopted in the final draft.

[67] See Case 287/86 *Ny Mølle Kro* [1987] ECR 5465, para. 12, discussed below.

[68] *Overdracht krachtens overeen kommst, vertrágliche Ubertrágung, cession conventionnelle, sumbatkij exphoorijsij, cessione contrattuale, cesion contractual, cesio contractual.*

[69] The Danish version includes transfers by way of gift as well as by contract, but not by court order or inheritance.

[70] Case 135/83 *Abels* [1985] ECR 469.

[71] See e.g., Case C–29/91 *Sophie Redmond* [1992] ECR I–3189; Case C–478/03 *Celtec* [2005] ECR I–000; E–3/01 *Alda Viggósdóttir* v. *Iceland Post Ltd*, judgment of the EFTA Court, 22 March 2002, para. 23 considered below.

[72] See e.g. Case 135/83 *Abels* [1985] ECR 469 (surséance van betaling proceedings); Case C–362/89 *d'Urso* [1991] ECR I–4105 (special administration for large companies in critical difficulties); Case C–319/94 *Dethier Equipement* v. *Dassy* [1998] ECR I–1061 (winding up by the Court where the undertaking continues to trade); and Case C–399/96 *Europièces* [1998] ECR I–6965 (voluntary liquidation of a company).

[73] See e.g., Joined Cases C–171/94 and C–172/94 *Merckx* v. *Ford Motor Company* and *Neuhuys* [1996] ECR I–1253 considered further below.

[74] Case C–234/98 *Allen* v. *Amalgamated Construction Co. Ltd* [1999] ECR I–8643, para. 17.

the same group, which were distinct legal persons, each with specific employment relationships with their employees,[75] albeit that the companies had the same ownership, management and premises and were engaged in the same work.[76] In a similar vein, the Court suggested in *Temco*[77] that the Directive could apply in respect of a transfer between a contractor and its subcontractor which was a subsidiary of the contractor.

We turn now to consider some of the more complex arrangements which are covered by the Directive.

(b) Leasing Arrangements

Several cases have concerned leasing arrangements and the rescission of leases (see Figure 13.2). *Ny Mølle Kro*,[78] provides a good example. A leased a restaurant to B. When B failed to comply with the terms of the agreement A rescinded the lease and ran the restaurant herself. The Court reasoned that 'employees of an undertaking whose employer changes without any change in ownership are in a situation *comparable to that of employees of an undertaking which is sold* and require equivalent protection.'[79] Consequently, it said that the Directive would apply to this type of situation. Similarly, in *Daddy's Dance Hall*[80] A leased a restaurant to B. A subsequently terminated the lease with B and agreed that C should take on the lease. Once again the Court found that this could constitute a legal transfer and so the Directive in principle applied. It added that the fact that the transfer was effected in two stages, in that the undertaking was first retransferred from the original lessee (B) to the owner (A) which then transferred it to the new lessee (C), did not prevent the Directive from applying, provided that the economic unit retained its identity.[81]

In *Bork*[82] the Court confirmed that the Directive applied to a two-stage transfer. A leased a factory to B. In the autumn of 1981 B gave notice terminating the lease with effect from 22 December 1981 and dismissed the factory's employees with the appropriate period of notice (stage 1). A then sold the factory to C on 30 December 1981 (stage 2) who took on more than half of B's staff. The Court said that the Directive would apply to this situation

---

[75] The Court expressly did not apply its case law on competition (Art. 81), esp. Case C–73/95P *Viho v. Commission* [1996] ECR I–5457.

[76] Case C–234/98 *Allen* [1999] ECR I–8643, para. 17.

[77] Case C–51/00 *Temco* [2002] ECR I–969. See also the emphasis placed by AG Geelhoed on the need for a contractual link and more generally his criticism of the Court's case law in this field.

[78] Case 287/86 [1987] ECR 5465. See also Joined Cases 144 and 145/87 *Berg* [1988] ECR 2559 where the Court found that the transfer of a bar-discotheque by means of a lease-purchase agreement and the restoration of the undertaking to its owner as a result of a judicial decision constituted a legal transfer.

[79] Para. 12, emphasis added.   [80] Case 324/86 [1988] ECR 739.

[81] Para. 10. See also Case C–340/01 *Abler v. Sodexho MM Catering Gesellschaft mbH* [2003] ECR I–14023, para. 39.

[82] Case 101/87 [1988] ECR 3057.

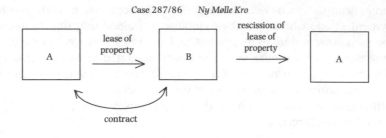

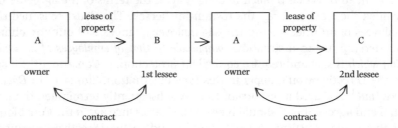

Figure 13.2 Leasing Arrangements

provided that the undertaking retained its identity (the transfer of undertaking question: see below).[83]

The are two common features of these cases: first, there is a change in the legal or natural person who is responsible for carrying out the business, regardless of whether or not ownership of the undertaking is transferred;[84] and second, that while there is a contract between the lessor and the lessee there is no contract between the successive lessees. As the Court made clear in *Merckx*,[85] a case concerning the termination of a motor vehicle dealership with one undertaking and its award to another dealership pursuing the same activities, for the Directive to apply, it was not necessary for there to be a direct contractual relationship between the transferor and the transferee.[86]

(c) Contracting Out

The absence of the need for a direct contractual relationship between the transferor and the transferee paved the way for the Directive to apply to contracting out. Contracting out is the process by which services previously

---

[83] The Directive would also apply to the transfer from B to A: this can be inferred from para. 19 of Joined Cases 144 and 145/87 *Berg* [1988] ECR 2559.

[84] Case C–478/03 *Celtec* [2005] ECR I–000, para. 33.

[85] Joined Cases C–171/94 and C–172/94 [1996] ECR I–1253.   [86] Para. 30.

provided in-house, and often ancillary to the main activity of the company (e.g. cleaning and catering), are offered out to tender to be performed by contractors which usually specialize in providing those specific services. This specialization should mean that the contractor can perform the work at lower costs,[87] in part due to economies of scale and in part through paying the staff less. If the Transfer of Undertakings Directive applied to contracting out then the contractor would be obliged to take on all of the staff previously employed by the company *and* on the same terms and conditions, therefore losing an important dimension of the cost saving. The question of whether contracting out constituted a legal transfer within the meaning of the Directive was therefore one of fundamental economic importance.[88]

Following the leasing cases, it was not surprising when the Court ruled in *Rask*[89] that contracting out fell within the scope of the Directive. *Rask* concerned an agreement between Philips and ISS that ISS would assume full responsibility for the running of Philips' canteens, in particular, for menu planning, purchasing and preparation of the food and for the recruitment and training of staff. In return, Philips agreed to pay ISS a fixed monthly sum and allowed ISS to use, free of charge, Philips' premises, including the canteens, equipment and utilities. The Court ruled that the Directive could apply to a situation in which the owner of an undertaking by contract assigns to the owner of another undertaking the responsibility for running a facility for staff, previously operated directly, in return for a fee and various other benefits the terms of which were determined by the agreement made between them.[90]

Therefore, the Directive can apply to the contracting out of services both in the private sector and, following *Sánchez Hidalgo*,[91] in the public sector. The Court said in *Rask* that it was irrelevant both that the activity transferred was only an ancillary activity[92] of the transferor undertaking,[93] not necessarily related to its main activities, and that the agreement between the transferor and the transferee related to the provision of services exclusively for the benefit of the transferor.[94] The Court repeated this conclusion in *Schmidt*[95] where it held that the fact that the activity concerned (cleaning) was performed, prior to the transfer, by a single employee was not sufficient to preclude the application of the Directive.

---

[87] See More, 'The Acquired Rights Directive: Frustrating or Facilitating Labour Market Flexibility', in Shaw and More (eds), *New Legal Dynamics of European Union* (Clarendon, Oxford, 1995).

[88] It was also of considerable political importance because in countries such as the UK with successive governments committed to cost-saving in the public sector, there was a statutory obligation on local authorities to put certain services out to tender.

[89] Case C–209/91 [1992] ECR I–5755.　　　[90] Para. 21.

[91] Joined Cases C–173/96 and C–247/96 *Sánchez Hidalgo and Others* [1998] ECR I–8237.

[92] This is confirmed by Art. 1(b) of Dir. 2001/23 introduced by Dir. 98/50.

[93] Para. 17.

[94] Ibid.　　　[95] Case C–392/92 [1994] ECR I–1311, para. 15.

First Round Contracting Out: *Rask, Schmidt*

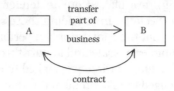

Second Round Contracting Out

1) Contracting out to Third Parties: *Süzen, Sanchez Hidalgo*

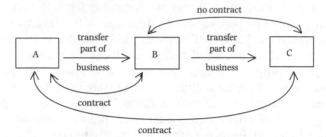

2) Contracting back in: *Hernández Vidal*

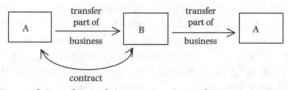

Figure 13.3 First and Second Round Contracting Out and Contracting In

The cases considered so far concern 'first round' contracting out (i.e. the first time the user undertaking contracts out part of its business to the contractor) where there was a contract between transferor and transferee (see Figure 13.3). The leasing cases, such as *Ny Mølle Kro*[96] and *Bork,*[97] suggested that the Directive would also apply, at least in principle, to second (and subsequent) round contracting out (i.e. after the expiry of the contract with the first contractor (B), the user undertaking (A) puts the work out to tender again and then enters into a contract with a second contractor (C)), as well as to contracting back in (i.e. after the expiry of the contract with the first contractor (B), the user undertaking (A) brings the work back in-house), where there is a contract between the user undertaking and the contractors but no

[96] Case 287/86 [1987] ECR 5456.   [97] Case 101/87 [1988] ECR 3057.

contract between the different contractors B and C (see Figure 13.3). *Süzen*[98] and *Hernández Vidal*[99] confirmed that the Directive applied to second round contracting out, while *Sánchez Hidalgo*[100] said the Directive applied to contracting back in. The Court also confirmed in these cases that there was no need for any direct contractual relationship between the transferor (B) and transferee (C);[101] and the transfer could take place in two stages (first-round contractor (B) to user undertaking (A) to second-round contractor (C)).[102]

(d) Transfer as a Result of a Legislative or Administrative Decision

Sophie Redmond[103] said that the approach adopted in the leasing and contracting out cases applied equally[104] to the situation where a municipal authority terminated the subsidy payable to one association which then closed and awarded the subsidy to another association with a similar aim. The Dr Sophie Redmond foundation provided assistance to drug addicts in the Netherlands, with funding provided by grants from the local authority. When the local authority decided to terminate the grant to the foundation the staff were dismissed and the foundation was closed. The local authority then switched the grant to another organization concerned with drug dependency, Sigma, which decided not to take on all of the former Redmond staff. The Court ruled that such a situation was capable of constituting a legal transfer and so the Directive could apply; it was irrelevant that the decision was taken unilaterally by the local authority rather than by agreement.[105]

In a similar vein, the Court has ruled that the Directive will also apply to privatization situations, as in *Beckmann*[106] concerning the transfer of a quantity surveyor from the National Health Service (NHS) to DWM, *Martin*[107] concerning the transfer of nursing lecturers from a college which was part of the NHS to South Bank University, and *Celtec*[108] concerning the transfer of training from the Department of Employment to private Training and Enterprise Councils (TECs).

---

[98] Case C–13/95 *Ayse Süzen v. Zehnacker Gebäudereinigung GmbH Krankenhausservice* [1997] ECR I–1259, considered further below.

[99] Joined Cases C–127/96, C–229/96 and C–74/97 *Hernández Vidal and Others* [1998] ECR I–8179.

[100] Joined Cases C–173/96 and C–247/96 [1998] ECR I–8237.

[101] Case C–13/95 *Süzen* [1997] ECR I–1259, para. 12.

[102] Joined Cases C–173/96 and C–247/96 *Sánchez Hidalgo* [1998] ECR I–8237, para. 23.

[103] Case C–29/91 [1992] ECR I–3189.

[104] See, e.g., Case C–51/00 *Temco* [2002] ECR I–969, para. 31.   [105] Paras. 15–17.

[106] Case C–164/00 *Beckmann v. Dynamco Whicheloe Macfarlane Ltd* [2002] ECR I–4893. In this case the applicability of the Directive was assumed. Cf. AG Alber's Opinion, para. 48. See also Case C–343/98 *Collino* [2000] ECR I–6659.

[107] Case C–4/01 *Martin v. South Bank University* [2003] ECR I–12859.

[108] Case C–478/03 *Celtec* [2005] ECR I–000.

(e) Conclusion

The Court's case law suggests that its interpretation of the phrase 'legal transfer' is now so broad that it is no longer a serious impediment to the application of the Directive. It has accepted that nearly all dispositions are covered by the phrase:[109] the Directive applies to contracting out (*Rask, Schmidt, Sánchez, Hidalgo*), subcontracting (*Allen, Temco*), privatization (*Beckmann, Martin, Celtec*) and transfers of undertakings to the state (*Mayeur, Delahaye*), as well as to the more usual transfer situations involving a contract. That said, the Court is not consistent and does, from time to time, resurrect the need for some form of contractual link, albeit of the broadest kind, before the Directive could apply. For example, in *Temco* the Court appeared to talk of the need for the transfer 'to be part of the web of contractual relations even if they are indirect'.[110] In order to clarify the situation the Commission proposed that all language versions of the Directive be revised to make clear that it covered any transfer effected by contract or by some other disposition or operation of law, judicial decision or administrative measure.[111] This proposal was not adopted in the final version of the Directive but does indicate how broadly the requirement of 'legal transfer' is now drawn.

2.2. Merger

According to Article 1(1)(a), the Directive applies to any transfer of an undertaking as a result not only of a legal transfer but also of a merger. The concept of a merger is not defined in Directive 2001/23, although it has always been assumed that the term refers to a merger within the meaning of Articles 3(1) and 4(1) of Council Directive 78/855/EEC.[112] Article 12 of this Directive makes express reference to the fact that employees' rights are to be protected in accordance with Directive 77/187 (now Directive 2001/23) in the event of a merger. Article 11 of Council Directive 82/891/EEC[113] contains similar

---

[109] See AG Poiares Maduro 's approach in Case C–478/03 *Celtec* [2005] ECR I–000. The Directive is therefore likely to apply, at least in principle, to other dispositions, such as gifts and transfers of ownership on the basis of succession.

[110] Para. 32. See also Joined Case C–232/04 and C–233/04 *Güney-Gorres* v. *Securicor Aviation* [2005] ECR I–000, para. 37 'whenever, in the context of contractual relations, there is a change in the legal or natural person who is responsible for carrying on the undertaking'; and Advocate General Van Gerven's Opinion in Case C–29/91 *Sophie Redmond* [1992] ECR I–3189 that a contract was an essential prerequisite to any transfer but he insisted that 'contract' be given an extremely broad interpretation, including any situation where there was an element of consensus between the parties. Such an interpretation is so broad that it significantly undermines the concept of a contract.

[111] Art. 1(1), para. 1, 94/C274/08.

[112] Third Council Directive concerning mergers of public limited companies (OJ [1978] L295/36). For an additional discussion of the definition of mergers in the context of taxation, see Art. 2(1)(a) of Council Dir. 90/434/EEC (OJ [1990] L225/1).

[113] OJ [1982] L378/47.

wording in the context of a division[114] of a public limited company. However, although the 45th recital of Council Regulation 139/2004 on the control of concentrations between undertakings[115] expressly states that it does not detract from 'the collective rights of employees as recognised in the undertakings concerned', it provides no machinery for ensuring these rights.

The crucial point is that the merger for the purposes of Directive 2001/23 must involve a change of identity of the employer. Consequently, the operation of the Directive is said to be confined to 'assets-mergers', for example by the sale of an undertaking by private contract, provided that the original employer is not retained in some nominal capacity, in which case the Directive does not apply. 'Share sales' or takeovers by the acquisition of share capital— where one company acquires the control of another without any change in the identity of the employer—are excluded from the scope of the Directive[116] because the rules relating to transfers are intended to deal with legal problems arising when the identity of the *employer* is changed. When a change of share ownership occurs legal theory considers that there is only a change in the identity of the proprietor of the share capital and not a change in the legal identity of the employer, albeit that, *in reality*, this change may be just as important to an employee as the change in identity of the employer following the transfer of the undertaking as recognized by the Directive. The majority shareholder may have plans for a major restructuring of the enterprise with a significant impact on the employees who are denied protection under the Directive. Earlier drafts of the original Directive (77/187) did extend its provisions to takeovers by acquisition of share capital but this was omitted from the final draft. This omission may be attributed to the difficult interface between labour law and company law and the corresponding overlap between the responsibilities of the different Directorates General of the Commission. Nevertheless, it is a serious omission for many employees because in states

---

[114] A division, or rather, using the language of the Directive, a 'division by acquisition', is defined in Art. 2(1) to mean the operation whereby, after being wound up without going into liquidation, a company transfers to more than one company all its assets and liabilities in exchange for the allocation to the shareholders of the company being divided of shares in the companies receiving contributions as a result of the division (hereinafter referred to as 'recipient companies') and possibly a cash payment not exceeding 10% of the nominal value of the shares allocated or, where they have no nominal value, of their accounting par value.

[115] OJ [2004] L24/1. This is considered further in Ch. 15.

[116] Hepple, above, n. 35 (1977) 14 *CMLRev.* 489, 493. However, doubt has been cast on this view by Advocate General Van Gerven in Case C–29/91 *Sophie Redmond* [1992] ECR I–3189. He argued that since the term merger had not been defined it should be given the usual commercial definition. In other words, it referred to a case where two or more undertakings which were formerly independent of each other unite or amalgamate giving rise to a merger in the broader sense of the term. He therefore invoked Art. 3(1) of what is now Council Reg. 139/2004 which provides that a merger occurs where: '(a) two or more previously independent undertakings merge, or (b) one or more persons already controlling at least one undertaking, or one or more undertakings acquire, *whether by purchase of securities or assets*, by contract or other means direct or indirect control of the whole or parts of one or more other undertakings' (emphasis added). The Court has yet to rule on this point.

such as the UK transfer by the sale of share capital is the most common form of transfer.

3. A Transfer of an Undertaking

3.1. The *Spijkers* Criteria

Having established that the transfer constitutes a legal transfer within the scope of the Directive, the next question is whether there is a transfer of the undertaking on the facts. *Spijkers*[117] provides the national courts with guidance on how to answer this question. Spijkers was employed by Colaris as an assistant manager of a slaughterhouse. By December 1982, when the business activities of Colaris had ceased and no goodwill remained, Benedik Abbatoir purchased the entire slaughterhouse, various rooms and offices, the land and certain specified goods. From February 1983 Benedik Abbatoir operated the slaughterhouse, having taken on all of Colaris' employees except Spijkers and one other. Spijkers contended that there had been a transfer of an undertaking within the meaning of the Directive.

The Court ruled that the decisive criterion for establishing the existence of a transfer of an undertaking for the purposes of the Directive was whether:

the business in question *retains its identity inasmuch as it is transferred as a going concern*, which may be indicated in particular by the fact that its operation is actually continued or resumed by the new employer with the same or similar activities.[118]

In order to decide whether the business is transferred as a going concern the Court ruled that 'it is necessary to consider all the facts characterising the transaction', including:

- the type of undertaking or business;
- whether the business' tangible assets,[119] such as buildings and moveable property, and intangible assets,[120] were transferred;[121]

---

[117] Case 24/85 [1986] ECR 1119.

[118] Wording actually taken from para. 18 of Case 287/86 *Ny Mølle Kro* [1987] ECR 5465 approving Case 24/85 *Spijkers* [1986] ECR 1119 and Case 29/91 *Dr Sophie Redmond v. Bartol* [1992] ECR I–3189, para. 23.

[119] It is clear that a transfer does *not* occur merely because the assets of a business are disposed of, see Case 24/85 *Spijkers* [1986] ECR 1119, para. 12. However, as Advocate General Slynn pointed out, the courts will identify any sham agreements for the disposal of assets designed to avoid the provisions of the Directive.

[120] Added by Case 101/87 *Bork* [1988] ECR 305. See also Case C–29/91 *Bartol* [1992] ECR I–3189.

[121] In Case 24/85 *Spijkers* [1986] ECR 1119 Advocate General Slynn suggested that the fact that at the date of transfer trading has ceased or has been substantially reduced does not prevent there from being a transfer of business if the wherewithal to carry on the business, such as plant, is available to be transferred. He also suggested that just because goodwill or existing contracts were not transferred was not conclusive against there being a transfer because the transferee might want to take over the activities of the business to supply existing customers.

- the value of intangible assets at the time of transfer;
- whether the majority of the business' employees are taken over by the new employer;
- whether its customers are transferred;
- the degree of similarity between the activities carried on before and after the transfer;[122]
- the period, if any, for which those activities were suspended.[123]

The Court said that no single factor was decisive;[124] national courts had to make an assessment of the overall position.[125]

However, the absence of any weighting of the *Spijkers* criteria caused a number of problems for national courts, albeit the very breadth of the formulation provided plenty of scope to national courts with long experience of working with the concept of transfer of undertaking to continue applying their own case law. Although the Court has subsequently reaffirmed the criteria in many cases,[126] in subsequent judgments it has focused on—and vacillated between—two elements of the *Spijkers* formula: 'activity' and 'economic entity'. These two elements are based on two contrasting conceptualizations of the undertaking which lie at the heart of the French debate over the scope of the transfer rule: that of the *entreprise-activité*, the labour law approach, and that of the *entreprise-organisation*, the commercial law approach.[127] Pre-*Süzen*[128] the Court tended to look at the labour law test focusing on 'activity': has the new employer taken over the running of the same or similar business

---

[122] Similarly, the fact that the business is carried on in a different way is not conclusive against there being a transfer—new methods, new types of machinery, and new customers are relevant factors but they do not prevent there being *in reality* a transfer. The activities before and after the transfer do not need to be the same for this would undermine the broad scope of the Directive (per Advocate General Van Gerven in Case C–29/91 *Bartol* [1992] ECR I–3189).

[123] In Case 24/85 *Spijkers* [1986] ECR 1119 Advocate General Slynn suggested that the transferee might want to spend time reorganizing or renovating the premises before reopening. If the employees were kept on and trading was resumed a national court was entitled to find that there was a transfer. In Case 287/86 *Ny Mølle Kro* [1987] ECR 5465 the undertaking, a restaurant, was regularly closed for part of the year. The transfer occurred when the undertaking was temporarily closed and the staff were absent. The Court decided that while this was a relevant factor it did not preclude the application of the Directive. The seasonal closure of a business did not mean that the undertaking has ceased to be a going concern. It was, however, for the national court to make the relevant factual appraisal. See also Case 101/87 *Bork* [1988] ECR 3057 where the closure coincided with the Christmas and New Year holiday.

[124] Case C–392/92 *Schmidt* [1994] ECR I–1311, para. 16; Case C–13/95 *Süzen* [1997] ECR I–1259, para. 14.

[125] Advocate General Slynn in Case 24/85 *Spijkers* [1986] ECR 119 argued for a 'realistic and robust view' to be taken of the facts. 'Technical rules are to be avoided and the substance matters more than the form'.

[126] See e.g. Case 287/86 *Ny Mølle Kro* [1987] ECR 5465, Case 101/87 *Bork* [1988] ECR 3057 and Case C–29/91 *Bartol* [1992] ECR I–3189; Case C–13/95 *Süzen* [1997] ECR I–1259; Joined Cases C–173/96 and 247/96 *Sánchez Hidalgo* [1998] ECR I–8237.

[127] Davies, 'Transfers of Undertakings' in Sciarra (ed.), *Labour Law in the Courts: National Judges and the European Court of Justice* (Hart Publishing, Oxford, 2001) 136.

[128] Case C–13/95 [1997] ECR I–1259.

activities as its predecessor? Post-*Süzen*, the Court emphasized the application of the more commercial test, focusing on whether the business had been transferred as an 'economic entity', dependent on the transfer of tangible or intangible assets. The labour law test was more likely to produce the result that there had been a transfer of an undertaking, which is consistent with the employment protection objectives of the Directive; but the commercial law approach had been preferred by the Italian and German courts and was increasingly being favoured by the French courts.[129]

3.2. The Labour Law Approach: Similarity of Activity

In the early cases concerning the transfer of leases, the Court focused on the question of whether one employer stepped into the shoes of another. This was a practical, rather than a legal, enquiry. As the Court said in *Ny Mølle Kro*:[130]

The Directive is therefore applicable where, following a legal transfer or a merger, there is a change in the legal or natural person who is responsible for carrying on the business and who by virtue of that fact incurs the obligations of an employer *vis-à-vis* employees of the undertaking, regardless of whether or not the ownership of the undertaking is transferred.[131]

Here the emphasis is on the question whether one employer has replaced another in respect of those employees; questions of ownership are not relevant.[132]

In subsequent cases the Court focused less on the employer and more on the similarity between the activity performed by the new employer compared with those carried out by its predecessor. This approach reached its zenith in the controversial case of *Schmidt*[133] which concerned the contracting out of cleaning services where the work was performed by a single employee. The Court emphasized that the decisive criterion for establishing whether there was a transfer of an undertaking was whether the business in question retained its identity which was indicated by actual continuation or resumption by the new employer of the same or similar activities (namely, cleaning work performed by the same employee). The Court therefore rejected the

---

[129] Davies, 'Transfers of Undertakings' in Sciarra (ed.), *Labour Law in the Courts* (Hart Publishing, Oxford, 2001), 136. For detailed consideration of the national rules, see Jeammaud and Le Friant, *La Directive 77/187 CEE, la Cour de Justice et le droit français*, EUI Working Paper 97/3; Körner, *The Impact of Community Law on German Labour Law—The Example of Transfer of Undertakings*, EUI Working Paper 96/8; Leccese, 'Italian Courts, the ECJ and Transfers of Undertakings: A Multi-Speed Dialogue?' (1999) 5 *EZW* 311.

[130] Case 287/86 [1987] ECR 5465.

[131] Para. 12. For similar wording see Case 101/87 *Bork* [1988] ECR 3057, para. 13 approving the decision in Joined Cases 144 and 145/87 *Berg* [1988] ECR 2559.

[132] See also Case 101/87 *Bork* [1988] ECR 3057 and Joined Cases 144 and 145/87 *Berg* [1988] ECR 2559.

[133] Case C–392/92 [1994] ECR I–1311, para. 16.

arguments made by the German and UK governments that the absence of any transfer of tangible assets precluded the existence of a transfer.[134]

This decision attracted a considerable amount of adverse comment. In its prescription of the *entreprise-activité* approach, the Court, contrary to the advice of its Advocate General, had abandoned the flexibility offered by the broad *Spijkers* formulation and offended the national courts (especially the German and Italian courts) which favoured the *entreprise-organisation* approach.[135] *Schmidt* also produced the surprising result noted famously by Rubinstein: that the *reductio ad absurdum* of the decision was that the Directive and its national implementing legislation would apply 'when I changed the contractor who cut my lawn. Absurd or not, there is nothing in *Schmidt* which provides a basis for concluding that that is not the law'.[136]

However, the decision in *Rygaard*[137] suggested that the Court was considering a change of approach. Rygaard was employed by Pedersen, a firm of carpenters, building SAS's canteen. Pedersen told SAS that it wanted part of the work to be carried out by Strø Mølle. Strø Mølle and SAS agreed that Strø Mølle would perform the contract, that some of Pedersen's workers would continue working for Strø Mølle, and that Strø Mølle would take over materials on the building site to complete the contracted work. Pedersen then wrote to Rygaard informing him that he would be dismissed, explaining that the firm was to be wound up and that the work would be taken over by Strø Mølle. The letter added that Rygaard would be transferred to Strø Mølle.

Following *Schmidt*, Rygaard argued that a transfer of an undertaking had occurred because the works taken over by Strø Mølle were the same as those entrusted to Pedersen, and that the duration of the works could not be decisive in determining whether a transfer of an undertaking had taken place. The Court rejected his arguments and said that the similarity between the activities of Pedersen and Strø Mølle was not sufficient. It said that the case law presupposed that 'the transfer relates to a *stable economic entity* whose activity is not limited to performing one specific works contract'.[138] On the facts of this case, the transfer did not relate to a stable economic entity because all that was transferred was one particular building project.[139] The Court continued that such a transfer could come within the terms of the Directive only if it included the transfer of a body of assets enabling the activities or certain activities of the transferor undertaking to be carried on in a stable way.[140]

---

[134] Para. 16.

[135] Davies, 'Transfers of Undertakings' in Sciarra (ed.), *Labour Law in the Courts* (Hart Publishing, Oxford, 2001) 137.

[136] Rubinstein [1994] ECR I–257. See also De Groot, 'The Council Directive on the Safeguarding of Employees' Rights in the Event of Transfers of Undertakings: an Overview of Recent Case Law' (1998) 35 *CMLRev.* 707, 714.

[137] Case C–48/94 *Ledernes Hovedorganisation, acting for Rygaard v. Dansk Arbejdsgiverforening, acting for Strø Mølle Akustik* [1995] ECR I–2745.

[138] Para. 20. Emphasis added.   [139] Para. 23.   [140] Para. 21.

That was not so where the transferor undertaking merely makes available to the new contractor certain workers and material.[141]

Rygaard therefore served to remind national courts of the relevance of the existence of a body of assets (even though this was not of paramount importance); and the requirement of a stable economic entity confirmed that there was a distinction between a one-off project of limited duration and contracting out of a continuing function.[142] And in concentrating on the need for a stable economic entity the Court's focus appeared to be shifting towards the conception of an *entreprise-organisation*.

However, *Rygaard* did not entirely bury the *Schmidt* 'same activity' approach which could still be detected in *Merckx*.[143] M and N were employed as salesmen by Anfo Motors, a Ford dealership in which Ford was the major shareholder. When Anfo Motors ceased its activities, the dealership was transferred to Novorabel which employed 14 of the 64 Anfo Motors employees on the same terms and conditions. Anfo Motors informed its customers of the situation and recommended the services of the new dealer. The Court, having cited the *Spijkers* criteria, considered that the transfer of the dealership was a transfer of an undertaking.[144] It reached this conclusion even though, as in *Schmidt*, there was no transfer of tangible assets, the business was carried on under a different name, from different premises with different facilities, and was situated in a different area of the same conurbation. For the Court it was sufficient that the contract territory remained the same.[145] Furthermore, the fact that a majority of the staff had been dismissed when the transfer occurred did not preclude the application of the Directive. The Court said that the dismissals might have taken place for economic, technical, or organizational reasons, in compliance with Article 4(1),[146] but failure to comply with Article 4(1) did not preclude the application of the Directive. The Court concluded that 'where a motor vehicle dealership concluded with one undertaking is terminated and a new dealership is awarded to another undertaking *pursuing the same activities*, the transfer of the undertaking is the result of a legal transfer'.[147]

---

[141] Cf. Case C–234/98 *Allen* [1999] ECR I–8643, para. 37 where the Court distinguished Case C–48/84 *Rygaard* [1995] ECR I–2745 on its facts, because in *Allen* a complete works project was transferred, probably along with some assets.

[142] Rubinstein [1996] IRLR 1. This was the view adopted by the British Employment Appeal Tribunal in *BSG Property Services* v. *Tuck* [1996] IRLR 134. The EAT considered that *Rygaard* did not alter the decision of the Court and that 'the requirement of "the stable economic entity" has to be read in the context of that case [*Rygaard*] and is apt to exclude economic activities under a short-term, one-off contract'. Continuing and recurrent maintenance activities in the present case could constitute a transfer of an undertaking.

[143] Joined Cases C–171/94 and C–172/94 [1996] ECR I–1253, esp. paras. 18, 23, and 30.

[144] Para. 19.   [145] Para. 21.   [146] See below, text attached to nn. 302–8.

[147] Para. 30. Emphasis added.

3.3. The Commercial Approach: Economic Entity

Despite *Merckx*, *Rygaard* essentially paved the way for the Court's new, tougher approach found in the seminal case of *Süzen*.[148] The case concerned second round contracting out: A, having entrusted the cleaning of its premises to B, terminated this contract and, for the performance of similar work, entered into a new contract with C without any concomitant transfer of tangible or intangible business assets from one undertaking to the other. The Court began in an orthodox manner, referring to the aim of the Directive (to ensure continuity of employment relationships within an economic entity, irrespective of any change of ownership[149]) and to the *Spijkers* test.[150] However, following *Rygaard*, the Court said that, for the Directive to be applicable, the transfer had to relate to a stable economic entity. It continued that the term entity referred to an 'organised grouping of persons and assets facilitating the exercise of an economic activity which pursues a specific objective'.[151] Having emphasized the importance of the 'economic entity' test, the Court then appeared to reject—or at least reduce the importance of—the labour law 'activity' test accepted in *Schmidt*.[152] It said that:

the mere fact that the service provided by the old and the new awardees of a contract is similar does not therefore support the conclusion that an economic entity has been transferred. An entity cannot be reduced to the activity entrusted to it. Its identity also emerged from other factors, such as its workforce, its management staff, the way in which its work is organised, its operating methods or indeed, where appropriate, the operational resources available to it.[153]

The Court continued that the mere loss of a service contract to a competitor could not, therefore, by itself indicate the existence of a transfer within the meaning of the Directive. In those circumstances, the service undertaking previously entrusted with the contract (B) did not, on losing a customer, thereby cease fully to exist, and a business or part of a business belonging to it could not be considered to have been transferred to the new awardee of the contract (C).

So how does a national court know whether an 'economic entity' has been transferred? The Court distinguished between two types of business: those which are assets-based and those which are not.[154] In the case of an *assets-based* business the Court said that there was a transfer of an undertaking only

---

[148] Case C–13/95 [1997] ECR I–1259 (noted Davies (1997) 26 *ILJ*. 193).
[149] Para. 10. [150] Ibid. [151] Para. 13. [152] Cf. para. 20. [153] Para. 15.
[154] The Commission suggested that in determining whether the entity has maintained its identity, situations can be categorized as three types: where the means of production are transferred, where non-material assets, such as knowledge and expertise, are transferred, and situations where no knowledge or expertise is required to do the job. The EFTA Court has made clear that if neither assets nor personnel are transferred then there is no transfer: see also Case E–3/96 *Tor Angeir Ask and Others* v. *ABD Offshore Technology AS and Aker Offshore Partner AS*, Advisory Opinion of the Court 14 March 1997 (OJ [1997] C136/7).

where there was a transfer of 'significant tangible or intangible assets'.[155] On the other hand, in the case of a *non-assets based* business (i.e. a business based essentially on manpower such as cleaning[156] or security[157]), the Court said that 'the maintenance of its identity following the transaction affecting it [could] not, logically, depend on the transfer of such assets'.[158] Therefore, the Court said in certain labour-intensive sectors (such as services) a group of workers engaged in a joint activity on a permanent basis could themselves constitute an economic entity.[159] The Court said it had to be recognized that such an entity was capable of maintaining its identity after it had been transferred where the new employer (C) did not merely pursue the activity in question but also took over a major part, in terms of their numbers and skills, of the employees specially assigned by its predecessor (B) to that task.[160] In those circumstances, the new employer took over a body of assets enabling him to carry on the activities or certain activities of the transferor undertaking on a regular basis.[161]

Thus, in the case of a *non-assets* business, there is only a transfer of an undertaking where the transferee takes over a majority of the transferor's staff, in terms of their numbers and skills.[162] As Davies points out, this test has a peculiar 'boot strap' quality to it. Since an adviser may need to know whether the Directive applies in order to determine whether the transferee ought to take the employees of the transferor into its employ, it is unhelpful to try to answer that question by application of the test whether the transferee has in fact done that very thing.[163] In *Hernández Vidal* Advocate General Cosmas made a similar point: the result achieved by the Directive (continuation of employment contracts by the transferee) 'becomes a condition determining whether [the Directive] is to apply'.[164] This test enables transferees to avoid their obligations under the Directive: if few assets are transferred the transferee can avoid the Directive by refusing to employ the 'major part' of the workforce. This test renders the Directive in many cases a 'voluntary obligation', contrary to the spirit of a Directive designed to give employment protection.

---

[155] Para. 23.

[156] Joined C–229/96 and C–74/97 *Hernández Vidal and Others* [1998] ECR I–8179.

[157] Or surveillance as the Court described it in C–247/96 *Sánchez Hidalgo and Others* [1998] ECR I–8237, para. 26.

[158] Para. 18. cf. AG La Pergola (p. 1266) who insisted that for a transfer of an undertaking to take place there had to be the actual transfer of tangible or intangible assets.

[159] Para. 21.   [160] Ibid.

[161] This was for the national court to establish: para. 21.

[162] Para. 21. See also Case C–51/00 *Temco* [2002] ECR I–969, para. 27 which makes clear that this rule applies even where a sectoral collective agreement obliges the transferee to take on, as far as possible, the transferor's staff. See also E–2/04 *Rasmussen* v. *Total E&P Norge AS*, judgment of the EFTA Court 10 December 2004, para. 43.

[163] Davies, above, n. 148, 196.

[164] Joined Cases C–229/96 and C–74/97 *Hernández Vidal and Others* [1998] ECR I–8179, para. 80.

A similar problem also arises in the case of an *assets-based* business. This can be seen in *Oy Liikenne*,[165] a case concerning second round contracting out of bus services in Helsinki. When the first contractor (B) lost the contract, it dismissed its 45 drivers. The second contractor (C) then took on 33 of those drivers (all those who applied) but none of B's buses since C had ordered new buses for use on the routes. The Court considered that bus transport could not be 'regarded as an activity based essentially on manpower, as it requires substantial plant and equipment'.[166] It continued that where the tangible assets contribute significantly to the performance of the activity, the absence of the transfer of such assets from the old to the new contractor meant that the entity did not retain its identity[167] and so the Directive did not apply.[168]

Thus, the classification of whether a transfer is assets or non-assets based is crucial. If it is non-assets based the transferee can circumvent the provisions of the Directive by refusing to take on the majority of the staff; if it is assets-based the transferee can circumvent the provisions of the Directive by refusing to take on the majority of the assets. The consequences of wrongly classifying the type of business can be seen in *Abler*,[169] a contracting out case concerning a transfer of the catering operation for a hospital. The transferee refused to take on the outgoing transferor's staff but did take on the equipment used by the transferor because it belonged to the hospital for whom the transferor, and now the transferee, was preparing meals. Somewhat surprisingly, the Court said that 'Catering cannot be regarded as an activity based essentially on manpower since it requires a significant amount of equipment.'[170] As this was therefore an assets transfer case and (use of)[171] the tangible assets needed— the premises, water and energy, the appliances, and the dishwashers—had been taken over by the transferee,[172] even though the tangible assets belonged to the contracting authority (the hospital) and not the transferor,[173] the Court found that there was a transfer of an economic entity. And because this case concerned an assets-based business, the transferee's failure to take over, in terms of numbers and skills, an essential part of the staff employed by its predecessor was not sufficient to preclude the existence of a transfer of an undertaking.[174]

---

[165] Case C–172/99 *Oy Liikenne Ab* v. *Liskojärvi* [2001] ECR I–745. See also Case C–234/98 *Allen* [1999] ECR I–8643, para. 30.

[166] Para. 39.   [167] Para. 42.   [168] Para. 43.

[169] Case C–340/01 *Abler* v. *Sodexho MM Catering Gesellschaft mbH* [2003] ECR I–14023.

[170] Para. 36.

[171] As opposed to ownership of the assets: Barrett, 'Light Acquired on Acquired Rights: Examining Developments in Employment Rights on Transfers of Undertakings' (2005) 42 *CMLRev.* 1053, 1063.

[172] Para. 36.

[173] Para. 42. See also Joined Cases C–232/04 and C–233/04 *Güney-Görres* [2005] ECR I–000, para. 42.

[174] Para. 37.

The *Süzen* 'economic entity' test is now the principal authority in determining whether there has been a transfer of an undertaking[175] which has been applied with more or less strictness in subsequent cases.[176] The Court has now favoured the commercial law, *entreprise-organisation*, approach over the labour law, *entreprise-activité*, approach, to the relief of the courts in some of the Continental jurisdictions.[177] And, in a move described as 'reverse codification',[178] the Court has *de facto* implemented the Commission's proposed definition of 'transfer of an undertaking' which had been successfully blocked by the European Parliament. The Commission defined a transfer of an undertaking as a 'transfer of an activity which is accompanied by the transfer of an economic entity which retains its identity'.[179] The proposal added that the 'transfer only of an activity of an undertaking . . . does not in itself constitute a transfer of an undertaking'.[180] Furthermore, the emphasis on 'economic entity' has now been picked up in what is now the Article 1(1)(b) definition of 'transfer' introduced by Directive 98/50. It defines transfer as 'the transfer of an economic entity which retains its identity, meaning an organised grouping of resources which has the objective of pursuing an economic activity whether or not that activity is central or ancillary'.[181]

3.4. Public Sector Reorganization

Given that the Directive requires a transfer of a stable economic entity, mere administrative reorganization in the public sector falls outside the scope of the Directive. This was the case in *Henke*.[182] Henke was employed as secretary to the mayor's office of the municipality of Schierke. When the municipality of Schierke and other municipalities formed an 'administrative collectivity', to which they transferred administrative functions, the municipality of Schierke

---

[175] Initially, there was some suggestion that *Süzen* might be confined to second-round contracting out (see Davies, above, n. 148, 194–5, and *Süzen*, paras. 8 and 9) but its extensive citation subsequently suggests that this is not the case: see e.g., Case C–172/99 *Oy Liikenne Ab* v. *Liskojärvi* [2001] ECR I–745; Case C–51/00 *Temco Service Industries SA* [2002] ECR I–969.

[176] Some commentators detected a slight relaxation of approach in, for example, Joined Cases C–173/96 and C–247/96 *Sánchez Hidalgo and Others* [1998] ECR I–8237 and Joined Cases C–127/96, Joined Cases C–229/96 and C–74/97 *Hernández Vidal and Others* [1998] ECR I–8179 but recognize that *Süzen* was applied with full rigour in Case C–172/99 *Oy Liikenne Ab* v. *Liskojärvi* [2001] ECR I–745. See, e.g., Deakin and Morris, *Labour Law* (Hart Publishing, Oxford, 2005) 222. There is also some evidence of greater flexibility shown by the EFTA Court which, in E–2/04 *Rasmussen* v. *Total E&P Norge AS*, judgment of the EFTA Court 10 December 2004, [2004] EFTA Court Reports 57, paras. 28 and 38 emphasized the need to take account of 'various factors'.

[177] On the French position, see Garde, 'Recent Developments in the Law Relating to Transfers of Undertakings' (2002) 39 *CMLRev.* 523, 524–5.

[178] Kenner, *EU Employment Law: From Rome to Amsterdam and Beyond* (Hart Publishing, Oxford, 2003), 347.

[179] Art. 1(1).   [180] COM(97) 60 final (OJ [1997] C124J).

[181] Art. 1(b) of Dir. 2001/23.

[182] Case C–298/94 *Annette Henke* v. *Gemeinde Schierke and Verwaltungsgemeinschaft* [1996] ECR I–4989.

dismissed Henke. The Court ruled that the reorganization of structures of the public administration or the transfer of administrative functions between public administrative authorities did not constitute a 'transfer of an undertaking' within the meaning of the Directive.[183] In a terse judgment in which no cases were cited, the Court said that the purpose of a number of municipalities grouping together was to improve the performance of those municipalities' administrative tasks.[184] The transfer carried out between the municipality and the administrative collectivity related only to activities involving 'the exercise of public authority'.[185] The Court said that even if it was assumed that those activities had aspects of an economic nature, they could only be ancillary.[186]

Therefore, in *Henke* the Court focused on the fact that the authority was not a business exercising an economic activity but was involved with public administration exercising public law powers. The Court, however, made no reference to its earlier decision in *Sophie Redmond*[187] where it had considered that the term 'legal transfer' covered the situation where a public authority decided to terminate the subsidy paid to one legal person, as a result of which the activities of that person were fully and definitively terminated, and to transfer it to another legal person with a similar aim. It also did not refer to *Commission v. UK*[188] where the Court found that the 'non-commercial venture' exclusion from the British Regulations implementing the Directive breached the Directive. Nevertheless, the Council of Ministers has followed the Court's approach. Article 1(1)(c) introduced by Directive 98/50 provides that 'An administrative reorganisation of public administrative authorities, or the transfer of administrative functions between public administrative authorities, is not a transfer within the meaning of this Directive'.[189]

However, in subsequent cases, the Court appears to have given a restrictive reading to its decision in *Henke*. For example, in *Sánchez Hidalgo*,[190] the Court said that where a public body, such as a municipality, contracted out a service (the provision of home help for disadvantaged people), this did not involve the exercise of public authority, and so the Directive still applied.[191] In *Collino*,[192] a case concerning the reorganization of the Italian telephone services and the transfer of the employees from a state body to a state owned company, the Court endorsed *Sánchez Hidalgo*, upheld *Sophie Redmond*, and concluded that the Italian reorganization fell within the scope of the Directive.[193]

---

[183] Para. 14.   [184] Para. 16.   [185] Para. 17.   [186] Ibid.

[187] Case C–29/91 [1992] ECR I–1311 considered above at nn. 103–5.

[188] Case C–382/92 [1994] ECR I–2435.

[189] This prompts De Groot, above, n. 136, 722, to observe that there exists a 'presumption of non-applicability of the Directive' as far as public administrative authorities are concerned.

[190] Joined Cases C–173/96 and 247/96 [1998] ECR I–8237, para. 24.

[191] Para. 24, distinguishing *Henke*.

[192] Case C–343/98 *Collino v. Telecom Italia SpA* [2000] ECR I–6659.

[193] Paras. 35 and 41. See also E–3/01 *Alda Viggósdóttir v. Iceland Post Ltd*, judgment of the EFTA Court, 22 March 2002, para. 23.

The (full) Court reached similar conclusions two weeks later in *Mayeur*.[194] It found that the transfer to the city of Metz of activities previously carried out by APIM, a non-profit making association set up as in independent entity by the city of Metz, funded by the city to promote the attractions of Metz, did constitute a transfer of an undertaking. By referring to the broad definition of undertaking,[195] to the fact that APIM was a distinct legal entity from the city of Metz,[196] and to the fact that APIM carried out an economic activity (publicity and information services on behalf of the city of Metz) the Court concluded that there was a transfer of an undertaking. It said that 'activity of this kind, consisting in the provision of services, is economic in nature and cannot be regarded as deriving from the exercise of public authority'.

Thus, the key feature distinguishing public sector reorganization cases to which the Directive does not apply (*Henke*) from those cases to which the Directive does apply (*Collino, Mayeur*) is the 'exercise of public authority'.[197] While the meaning of this phrase is not entirely clear, it would appear that the Directive will not apply only in cases with facts similar to those in *Henke* (i.e. those involving the reorganization of structures of the public administration or the transfer of administrative functions between public administrative authorities).[198] The Directive will, however, apply where the activity is non-profit making or carried out in the public interest. This is confirmed by Article 1(1)(c) of Directive 2001/23 which provides that the Directive applies to *public* or private undertakings engaged in economic activities, whether or not they are operating for gain.[199]

4. Territorial Scope

Article 1(2) provides that the Directive applies 'where and in so far as the undertaking, business or part of the undertaking or business to be transferred is situated in the territorial scope of the Treaty'.[200] It is the physical location of the business and not the location of the ownership that is the determinative feature. This may lead to a significant gap in the protection of workers

---

[194] Case C–175/99 *Mayeur* v. *Association Promotion de l'Information Meesine* [2000] ECR I–7755. See also Case C–425/02 *Delahaye* v. *Ministre de la Fonction publique et de la Réforme administrative* [2004] ECR I–10823 where the Court noted that the transfer of an economic activity from a legal person governed by private law to a legal person governed by public law was in principle within the scope of Directive.

[195] '[A]ny stable economic entity, that is to say, an organised grouping of persons and assets facilitating the exercise of an economic entity which pursues a specific objective. . . . Such a concept is independent of the legal status of that entity and the manner in which it is financed' (para. 32).

[196] Paras. 36–7.   [197] Para. 39.

[198] A view confirmed by Case C–425/02 *Delahaye* [2004] ECR I–10823, para. 30.

[199] Emphasis added.

[200] This includes a Member State of the EEA (Norway, Iceland, and Liechtenstein).

within the Union since, if the business transferred from outside the EU is transferred to a Community undertaking, workers in the acquiring Community enterprise may be adversely affected by the transfer. The Directive also does not apply to transfers of businesses located outside the Community but which belong to a company whose head office is in the territory of a Member State.

E. INSOLVENCY AND MEASURES FALLING SHORT OF A DECLARATION OF INSOLVENCY

1. The Basic Rules

Transfers on insolvency raise particular issues. Although the original Directive 77/187/EEC did not expressly exclude transfers on insolvency from its scope, in *Abels*[201] the Court achieved that result. It said that the Directive did not apply to transfers of undertakings 'taking place in the context of insolvency proceedings instituted with a view to the liquidation of assets of the transferor under the supervision of the competent judicial authority'.[202] The explanation of the Court's ruling lies in the special nature of the laws on insolvency[203] which are designed to weigh up the various interests involved, in particular, those of the creditors.[204] Consequently, insolvency rules derogate, at least in part, from the provisions of social law, both at national and Community level.[205] Therefore, the Court concluded, rather unusually, that an express provision in the Directive would have been *required* before it applied to an insolvency situation.[206]

In *Abels* the plaintiff was employed by Thole when, by successive decisions of the District Court, Thole was granted *surséance van betaling* (judicial leave to suspend payment of debts) in 1981 and then went into liquidation in 1982. During the liquidation proceedings Thole's business was transferred to TPP which continued to operate the undertaking and took over most of the

---

[201] The Court repeated its decision in Case 135/83 [1985] ECR 469 in three cases decided on the same day as *Abels*: Case 186/83 *Botzen* [1985] ECR 519, Case 19/83 *Wendelboe* [1985] ECR 457 and Case 179/83 *Industrie Bond FNV* [1985] ECR 511.

[202] Para. 23. This was deemed important by Advocate General Van Gerven in Case C–362/89 *d'Urso* [1991] ECR I–4105. He said it was insufficient that the preconditions to insolvency have been fulfilled.

[203] Para. 16. In the Community context, see Council Dir. 80/987/EEC (OJ [1980] L283/23). The Council did not take the opportunity of the enactment of Dir. 80/987 to apply the original Dir. 77/187/EEC to an insolvency situation.

[204] Para. 15.

[205] Para. 16. In the Community context, see Art. 1(2)(d) of Dir. 75/129/EEC (OJ L48/29) on collective redundancies which expressly excludes from its scope workers affected by termination of an establishment's activities 'where that is a result of a judicial decision'.

[206] Para. 17.

workforce, including the claimant. The claimant, however, complained that he had not received his wages or various other payments as required by the Directive.

It was argued by the Danish government that the transfer rules should apply to employees whose employer had become insolvent because this was the time when the workers were in most need of protection.[207] By contrast, the Dutch government and the Commission argued that if the Directive applied this might dissuade a potential transferee from acquiring an undertaking on conditions acceptable to the creditors, who might then prefer instead to sell the assets of the undertaking separately, thereby avoiding the scope of the Directive.[208] This, they argued, would entail the loss of all the jobs in the enterprise which would detract from the utility of the Directive.[209] As the Commission has subsequently recognized, the underlying problem here is the conflict between the acquired rights of employees and those of other creditors upon insolvency. If the employees of the insolvent transferor undertaking and all their rights and entitlements are transferred to the new solvent transferee, the effect is to treat those employees more favourably than other creditors of the insolvent undertaking. The creditors will assert that the transferee will pay less for the transferred undertaking, as a result of having to take over all liabilities to the new employees, and hence the pool of assets against which the creditors of the insolvent undertaking can claim will be reduced.[210]

The Court, while acknowledging that 'considerable uncertainty exists regarding the impact on the labour market of transfer of undertakings in the case of the employer's insolvency',[211] seemed to accept the Dutch government's view. It therefore decided that the interests of employees would be better served if the Directive did *not* apply 'otherwise a serious risk of general deterioration in living and working conditions of workers, contrary to the social objectives of the Treaty',[212] could not be ruled out.

The Court has, however, refused to extend the scope of its ruling in *Abels*. In *Sophie Redmond*,[213] for example, the Court rejected arguments that the Directive did not apply to situations comparable with insolvency, such as the closure of a foundation due to the withdrawal of its subsidy by the local authority. In *Merckx*,[214] the Court ruled that the application of the Directive could not be excluded merely because the transferor discontinued its activities when the transfer was made and was then put into liquidation. It added that if the business of that undertaking was carried on by another undertaking this tended to confirm that there had been a transfer for the purposes of the

---

[207] Para. 20.
[208] Assets only sales fall outside the scope of the Directive, see Case 24/85 *Spijkers* [1986] ECR 1119.
[209] Para. 21.   [210] Explanatory memorandum, COM(94) 300, para. 23.
[211] Para. 22.   [212] Para. 23.   [213] Case C–29/91 [1992] ECR I–3189.
[214] Joined Cases C–171/94 and C–172/94 [1996] ECR I–1253.

Directive. Even in *Abels*[215] the Court imposed two limits to its own ruling. First, it said that Member States could, if they wished, apply the provisions of the Directive to a transfer arising in the event of insolvency.[216] Secondly, it said that the Directive did apply to situations where an undertaking was transferred to another employer in the course of a pre-insolvency procedure, such as the Dutch 'surséance van betaling'.[217] This procedure allows a company, with the leave of the court, to suspend payment of its debts with a view to reaching a settlement. Such a settlement is intended to ensure that the undertaking is able to continue operating in the future.

The distinction drawn by the Court between insolvency and pre-insolvency proceedings may be based on a false premise. Although it acknowledged that the two types of proceedings share many common characteristics,[218] the Court failed to recognize that the reason why many companies go into pre-insolvent procedures is that there is a greater chance of selling off at least part of the company's business as a going concern, thereby securing at least some of the workers' jobs. This is precisely the situation which justified excluding insolvent companies from the operation of the Directive.[219] Nevertheless, the distinction between liquidation of insolvent companies and other ways of dealing with them has now been incorporated into the Directive by Directive 98/50/EEC.[220] Article 5(1) of what is now Directive 2001/23 provides that unless Member States provide otherwise, Articles 3 and 4 of the Directive (concerning transfer of the contract of employment and dismissals) do not apply to a transfer where the transferor is 'the subject of bankruptcy proceedings or any analogous insolvency proceedings which have been instituted with a view to the liquidation of the assets of the transferor and are under the supervision of a competent public authority'.[221]

If Member States do decide that Articles 3 and 4 are to apply to a transfer during insolvency proceedings which have been opened in relation to a transferor (whether or not those proceedings have been instituted with a view to the liquidation of the assets of the transferor), the Directive provides that a Member State may provide that:[222]

---

[215] Case 135/83 [1985] ECR 469.   [216] Para. 24.

[217] This point was confirmed in three cases decided on the same day as Case 135/83 *Abels* [1985] ECR 469, Case 186/83 *Botzen* [1985] ECR 519, Case 19/83 *Wendleboe* [1985] ECR 457, Case 179/83 *Industrie Bond FNV* [1985] ECR 511, and Case 105/84 *Danmols Inventar* [1985] ECR 2639.

[218] *Abels*, para. 28. See also Case C–362/89 *d'Urso* [1991] ECR I–4105, para. 24.

[219] Davies, 'Acquired Rights, Creditors' Rights, Freedom of Contract, and Industrial Democracy' (1989) 9 *YEL*. 21, 47.

[220] OJ [1998] L201/88.

[221] The supervision of a competent public authority may be an insolvency practitioner authorized by a competent public authority.

[222] Art. 5(2).

- the transferor's debts arising from any contracts of employment or employment relationships and payable before the transfer or before the opening of the insolvency proceedings are not transferred to the transferee, provided that the proceedings give rise to protection at least equivalent to that provided for by Council Directive 80/987/EEC on the protection of employees in the event of the insolvency of their employer; and/or
- the transferee or transferor on the one hand, and the representatives of the employees on the other hand may agree alterations, in so far as current law and practice permits,[223] to the employees' terms and conditions of employment designed to safeguard employment opportunities by ensuring the survival of the economic entity being transferred.[224]

Further, a Member State may apply this provision to *any* transfers where the transferor is in a situation of 'serious economic crisis'[225] and open to judicial supervision, on condition that such provisions already existed in national law by 17 July 1998.[226] Therefore worker representatives can agree collectively to the modification of terms and conditions of employment. Thus, the Directive, like the Working Time Directive 2003/88,[227] permits derogations from the legislative minima *in pejus*. In addition, new Article 6(1), paragraph 3 provides that where the transferor is the subject of bankruptcy proceedings or analogous proceedings, as described in Article 5(1), Member States 'may take the necessary measures to ensure that the transferred employees are properly represented until the new election or designation of representatives of the employees'. These new provisions are striking for their 'pick-and-mix' quality.[228] Member States are given a great deal of discretion which provisions to apply.

Finally, Article 5(4) requires Member States to take appropriate measures with a view to preventing misuse of insolvency proceedings in such a way as to deprive employees of their rights in the event of a transfer.

---

[223] Thus, the representatives cannot agree anything which the individual employee could not negotiate him or herself.

[224] Cf. Case C–362/89 *d'Urso* [1991] ECR I–4105.

[225] Art. 5(3). A situation of 'serious economic crisis' is to be defined by public law and declared by a competent public authority. In Italy an enterprise in crisis can go into *amministrazione controllata*, a procedure similar to the Dutch *surséance van betaling*, which allows the trade unions, as a derogation from Art. 2112 of the Civil Code, to agree to the reduction in protection for those workers transferred to the solvent transferee.

[226] Art. 5(3).   [227] OJ [2003] L299/9 considered in detail in Ch. 12.

[228] Hunt described these provisions as having an 'open-textured, framework nature' (above, n. 8, 228).

2. Distinguishing between Insolvency and Pre-insolvency Proceedings

Given that the Directive now distinguishes between insolvency proceedings, to which the Directive will (usually) not apply, and pre-insolvency proceedings such as *surséance* proceedings, to which the Directive will apply, how are these different types of procedure to be identified? Advocate General Van Gerven in *d'Urso*[229] offered some guidance. First, he distinguished between the two proceedings by reference to their purpose. He suggested that an inherent characteristic of *surséance* proceedings was that they were intended to resolve temporary cash-flow problems and not to liquidate the assets of the debtor— in other words, to *prevent* insolvency.[230] By contrast, he said, insolvency proceedings, were fundamentally different: their purpose was the liquidation of property by selling the assets with a view to offsetting the liabilities.

Secondly, Advocate General Van Gerven distinguished between the two proceedings, by reference to judicial control. In the case of *surséance* proceedings he noted that the supervision of the Court over the commencement and the course of the proceedings was much more limited than in the case of insolvency.[231] The judge's control extended only to ensuring that the debtor respected the obligations he had entered into. On the other hand, in insolvency the judge had more extensive control. This might be accompanied by the creation of an administration or a trust with special powers to determine the value of the undertaking, to sell off the assets and to meet the liabilities, which in turn is accompanied by the creation of a compulsory trust of the affairs of the debtor, who is deprived of any power to manage or to dispose of the assets. In *surséance* proceedings, there will be one or more designated receivers or administrators who will exercise control over the debtor, to whom they must give assistance or authorization before the debtor may carry out certain acts, but without ever depriving the debtor of the rights to manage or dispose of this property. In subsequent cases, the Court has placed less emphasis on the importance of judicial supervision than on the objective of the procedure at issue[232] as the distinguishing criteria.

The Court has been asked by various national courts to decide on which side of the line the national rules fall. For example, in *d'Urso* the Court said that the Directive did not apply to transfers of undertakings made as part of a creditor's settlement of the kind provided for in Italian legislation on 'compulsory administrative liquidation' whose effects were comparable to bankruptcy proceedings; while in *Spano*[233] the Court held that the Directive did apply to a

---

[229] Case C–362/89 [1991] ECR I–4105.
[230] See also the Court of Justice in *Abels*, para. 28.   [231] Ibid.
[232] Case C–362/89 *d'Urso* [1991] ECR I–4105.
[233] Case C–472/93 *Spano and Others v. Fiat Geotech and Fiat Hitachi* [1995] ECR I–4321.

transfer of an undertaking declared to be in critical difficulties pursuant to Italian Law No. 675 of 12 August 1977. It pointed out that the purpose of such a declaration was to enable the undertaking to retrieve its economic and financial situation and above all to preserve jobs, that the procedure in question was designed to promote the continuation of its business with a view to its subsequent recovery and that, by contrast with insolvency proceedings, it did not involve any judicial supervision or any measure whereby the assets of the undertaking were put under administration and did not provide for any suspension of payments.[234]

In *Dethier*[235] the Court was obliged to give more detailed guidance about the nature of the distinction between the two types of proceedings in the context of Belgian law on liquidation. In May 1991 the Tribunal de Commerce made an order putting Sovam into liquidation and appointing a liquidator. Three weeks later the liquidator dismissed Dassy and shortly afterwards transferred the assets of Sovam to Dethier under an agreement approved by the Tribunal de Commerce. In deciding whether the Directive applied to this Belgian winding up procedure, the Court said that the determining factor to be taken into consideration was the *purpose* of the procedure in question, but that account also had to be taken of the *form* of the procedure in question, in particular, in so far as it meant that the undertaking continues or ceases trading, and also of the Directive's objectives.[236] On the facts of the case, the Court said that it was apparent that although the objective of the Belgian procedure could sometimes be similar to those of insolvency proceedings, this was not necessarily the case, since liquidation proceedings could be used whenever it was wished to bring a company's activities to an end and whatever the reasons for that decision.[237]

Since the criterion relating to the *purpose* of the procedure for winding up was not conclusive, the Court examined the procedure in detail.[238] It pointed out that the liquidator, although appointed by the court, was an organ of the company who sells the assets under the supervision of the general meeting; that there was no special procedure for establishing liabilities under the supervision of the court; and that a creditor could enforce his debt against the company and obtain judgment against it. By contrast, in the case of an insolvency, the administrator was a third party vis-à-vis the company and realized the assets under the supervision of the court; that the liabilities of the company were established in accordance with a special procedure and individual enforcement actions were prohibited.[239] Therefore, the Court concluded that there was no insolvency situation where an undertaking continued to trade while it was being wound up by the court and so the Directive applied.[240]

In *Europièces*[241] the Court applied its ruling in *Dethier* to the case of voluntary

---

[234] Paras. 26, 28 and 29.   [235] Case C–319/94 [1998] ECR I–1061.
[236] Para. 25.   [237] Para. 27.   [238] Para. 28.   [239] Para. 29.   [240] Para. 32.
[241] Case C–399/96 [1998] ECR I–6965.

liquidation which, it noted, is 'essentially similar to winding up by the court, save for the fact that it falls to the shareholders in general meeting, and not to the court, to take the decision to wind up the company, appoint the liquidators and determine their powers'.[242] Since, at least in some procedural respects, voluntary liquidation had even less in common with insolvency than winding up by the court,[243] the Court said the Directive applied.

F. SAFEGUARDING INDIVIDUAL EMPLOYEES' RIGHTS

1. Introduction

If the transfer is a transfer of an undertaking within the meaning of Directive 2001/23, then according to the Court in *Wendelboe*:[244]

. . . the scheme and purposes of the Directive, . . . is intended to ensure, as far as possible, that the employment relationship continues unchanged with the transferee and by protecting workers against dismissals motivated solely by the fact of the transfer . . .[245]

In other words, the Directive is intended to protect those employees who are performing an identical job but under the orders of a different employer. The protection conferred has two pillars: first, the transfer of rights and obligations arising from the contract of employment or employment relationship[246] and collective agreements (Article 3) and, secondly, the protection against dismissal (Article 4). We shall consider these situations in turn.

2. Rights Arising from the Contract of Employment

2.1. Transfer of Rights and Obligations

(a) Basic Rules

Article 3(1) paragraph 1, as amended, requires the transferee to respect the transferor's rights and obligations towards the employees, thereby limiting the managerial autonomy of the transferee. It provides that:

---

[242] Para. 33. Only where a majority of the shareholders cannot be assembled must the company apply to the court for a declaration putting it into liquidation. The court then designates the liquidators in accordance with the company's articles of association or pursuant to the decision of the shareholders in general meeting, unless it is clear that disagreement between the shareholders will prevent them from taking a decision in general meeting, in which case the court itself appoints a liquidator.

[243] Para. 34.   [244] Case 19/83 [1985] ECR 457.

[245] Para. 15. Similar sentiments are expressed in Joined Cases C–132, 138 and 139/91 *Katsikas* [1992] ECR I–6577, para. 21, and Cases C–362/89 *d'Urso* [1991] ECR I–4105, para. 9.

[246] For the ease of reference 'contract of employment' will be used and should be interpreted as including 'employment relationship'.

The transferor's rights and obligations arising from a contract of employment or from an employment relationship existing on the date of a transfer shall, by reason of such transfer, be transferred to the transferee.

Therefore, the transferor's rights and obligations, a phrase which is broadly construed,[247] which exist at the time of transfer, the details of which are determined by national law, are *automatically* transferred to the transferee.[248]

The Court applies Article 3(1) strictly. For example, in *Rask*[249] the transferee changed the date of payment of the employee's salary from the last Thursday in the month to the last day in the month. The transferee also changed the composition of the payment: the claimants no longer received allowances for laundry or for shoes, although the total amount of their pay remained unchanged. Nevertheless, the Court ruled that Article 3(1) required that the terms of the contract of employment could not be varied on the transfer. Similarly, in *Collino*[250] the Court said that the transferee had to take into account the entire length of service of the employees transferred in calculating rights of a financial nature such as a termination payment or salary increases.[251] While the transferred employees' length of service with the transferor did not, as such, constitute a right which they could assert against their new employer, where length of service was used to determine financial rights, those rights would have to be maintained by the transferee in the same way as by the transferor.[252]

Berg[253] makes clear that the effect of Article 3(1) is to discharge the transferor from all its obligations arising under the contract of employment[254] from the date of transfer. In that case some employees objected to the transfer of certain contractual obligations which the transferor had, prior to the transfer contracted with them to observe, although they did not object to the transfer of their contract of employment. Nevertheless, the Court said that the transferor was released from his obligations as an employer solely by reason of the transfer and irrespective of the consent of the employees concerned.[255]

---

[247] See e.g. Case C–4/01 *Martin* [2003] ECR I–12859, para. 30 where the Court found that rights contingent on dismissal or the grant of early retirement by agreement with the employer were included within the definition.

[248] See e.g. Joined Cases 144 and 145/87 *Berg* [1988] ECR 2559, para. 13. In technical terms this means subrogating the rights and obligations of the transferor to the transferee.

[249] Case C–209/91 [1992] ECR I–5755.

[250] Case C–343/98 *Collino v. Telecom Italia SpA* [2000] ECR I–6659.   [251] Para. 51.

[252] Para. 50.   [253] Joined Cases 144 and 145/87 [1988] ECR 2559.

[254] The British EAT ruled in *Kerry Foods Ltd v. Kreber* [2000] IRLR 10 that the duty to consult was a right which arose from the individual contracts between each employee and the employer and therefore fell within Art. 3(1).

[255] Case C–305/94 *Rotsart* [1996] ECR I–5927.

(b) Date of Transfer

So when is the 'date of transfer'? According to *Celtec*,[256] it is the 'date on which responsibility as employer for carrying on the business of the unit in question moves from the transferor to the transferee'. Furthermore, according to the Court in *Rotsart*[257] the transfer of the contracts of employment 'necessarily takes place on the date of the transfer of the undertaking and cannot be postponed to another date at the will of the transferor or the transferee'.[258] If it were otherwise and the transferor or transferee could choose the date from which the contract of employment was transferred, this would amount to allowing employers to derogate, at least temporarily, from the provisions of the Directive which was not possible 'since the provisions are mandatory'.[259]

The importance of this ruling can be seen from the facts of *Celtec*. The British Department of Employment transferred responsibilities for vocational training to Training and Enterprise Councils (TECs) run by private sector employers. Civil servants who had been responsible for running the vocational training were initially seconded to the TECs for three years. At this point they resigned from the civil service and were employed by the TEC. Although the Advocate General suggested that the Directive did not require there to be a particular point in time at which all the aspects of the undertaking were transferred, thereby allowing the transfer of the contracts of employment to be transferred after the transfer of assets, the Court of Justice adopted the simple approach it had applied in *Rotsart*. It ruled that the date of transfer was the date on which responsibility as employer for carrying on the business moves from transferor (the government) to the transferee (Celtec). Thus, the contracts of employment existing on the date of transfer were deemed to be handed over on that date from the transferor to the transferee 'regardless of what has been agreed between the parties in that respect'.[260]

Although the basic principle is that the transferor is discharged from all obligations at the date of transfer, Member States can provide for joint liability for both the transferor and transferee after the date of the transfer in respect of obligations which arose before the transfer from a contract of employment existing on the date of transfer.[261] Various Member States (for example, Spain, France, Greece, Italy, the Netherlands, Portugal, and Germany) have adopted some form of co-liability rule so that the transferor continues to be liable for pre-transfer debts with the transferee. The period during which the transferor remains liable varies from six months (Portugal) to three years (Spain), while no time limit is fixed in France and Greece. Other Member States have adopted no co-liability rule so only the transferee is liable.[262]

---

[256] Case C–478/03 *Celtec* [2005] ECR I–000, para. 36.
[257] Case C–305/94 *Claude Rotsart de Hertaing v. J. Benoidt SA, in liquidation and Others* [1996] ECR I–5927.
[258] Para. 26.   [259] Paras. 17 and 25.   [260] Para. 44.   [261] Art. 3(1), para. 2.
[262] COM(94) 300.

New Article 3(2), added at the last minute by Directive 98/50, provides, in the interests of transparency, that Member States *may* adopt appropriate measures to ensure that the transferor notifies the transferee of all the rights and obligations which will be transferred to the transferee under Article 3, in so far as the transferor knew or ought to have known of the existence of those rights and obligations. However, a failure to notify will not affect the transfer of any of the rights or obligations nor will it affect the rights of any employees against the transferee and/or transferor in respect of that right or obligation.

(c) Contractual Variation

A question which has long troubled employers is whether the transferee (or even the transferor) can vary the contractual terms of the transferred employees to bring the transferred employees' terms and conditions into line with those of the staff already employed by the transferee. For the transferee this is important in terms of administrative convenience, good industrial relations and, probably, cost saving. However, as we saw in *Rask*, the Court appears to prohibit any changes to the terms and conditions of employment even where the changes are small and the employees consent to their variation. This point was made clearly in *Daddy's Dance Hall*,[263] where the Court said that since the protection conferred by the Directive was a 'matter of public policy, and therefore independent of the will of the parties to the contract of employment', the rules of the Directive had to be considered 'mandatory, so that it is not possible to derogate from them in a manner unfavourable to employees'.[264] The Court continued:[265]

It follows that employees are not entitled to waive the rights conferred on them by the Directive and that those rights cannot be restricted even with their consent. This interpretation is not affected by the fact that, as in this case, the employee obtains new benefits in compensation for the disadvantages resulting from an amendment to his contract of employment so that, taking the matter as a whole, he is not placed in a worse position than before.

---

[263] Case 324/86 [1988] ECR 739.

[264] Para. 14. See also Case 362/89 *d'Urso* [1991] ECR I–4105 where the Court said that the implementation of rights laid down by the Directive could not be made dependent on the agreement of the transferor, transferee, employees' representative, or employees themselves. For the problems experienced by the House of Lords in addressing the issue, see *Wilson* v. *St Helens B.C.*, *British Fuels* v. *Meade* [1999] IRLR 706. The Commission proposed that the Directive should contain a declaratory provision that, with the exception of insolvency situations, the transferee and the employees cannot by consent restrict any of the rights contained in the Directive, and that no provision should be made for waiver by collective agreements. This was not adopted in the final version.

[265] Para. 15.

However, the Court did suggest that the terms and conditions of employment could be amended, even in a manner unfavourable to employees,[266] in one situation: where national law allows such an amendment. The reasoning behind this is that because the Directive is a Directive of partial harmonization, it is only intended to prevent employees affected by a transfer of an undertaking from being placed in a less favourable position than had the transfer not occurred;[267] it is not intended to establish a uniform level of protection throughout the Community on the basis of common criteria. Therefore, if national law permits contractual variation then this law applies equally to transferees.

However, the case law makes clear that while contractual variation can occur if permitted by national law, 'the transfer of the undertaking itself may never constitute the reason for that amendment'.[268] While the principle is clear, its application is not. Is it necessary to wait for a certain period of time to elapse before any contractual variation is not related to the transfer of the undertaking?[269] Can a transferor cut the pay of the transferred staff so as to bring their pay into line with the remuneration received by the transferor's existing staff and, if so, would this be a variation due to a situation 'other than the transfer of an undertaking'? This issue arose in *Martin*[270] which concerned the transfer of a nursing college from the NHS to South Bank University (SBU). The college lecturers had enjoyed the benefits of the NHS Whitley Council terms and conditions, including those relating to early retirement. SBU sought to change those terms to bring them into line with those offered to its other employees. The Court said the alteration of the employment relationship had to be regarded as 'connected to the transfer'.[271] Thus the transferee had to offer the transferred employees early retirement on the same terms as had been offered by the transferor, including to those employees who had already accepted early retirement on the inferior terms.[272]

Given that the Court in *Martin* assumed that the change in terms was caused by the transfer it therefore did not answer the causation question referred: did the transfer have to be the sole or main reason for the change in

---

[266] Case C–392/92 *Schmidt* [1994] ECR I–1311, para. 19. On the facts, although the transferee offered to employ the transferred employee for a higher wage than she had received previously, she was not prepared to work on those terms because she thought that her hourly wage would, in fact, be lower due to the increase in the surface area to be cleaned. See also Case C–343/98 *Collino v. Telecom Italia SpA* [2000] ECR I–6659, para. 52.

[267] Case 324/86 *Daddy's Dance Hall* [1988] ECR 739, para. 16; AG Léger's Opinion in Case C–425/02 *Boor, neé Delahaye v. Ministre de la Fonction publique et de la Réforme admininstrative* [2004] ECR I–10823, para. 33.

[268] Case 324/86 *Daddy's Dance Hall* [1988] ECR 739, para. 17; Case C–343/98 *Collino* [2000] ECR I–6659, para. 52.

[269] See, by analogy, with the one-year period for collective agreements contained in Art. 3(3) considered below, n. 278.

[270] Case C–4/01 [2003] ECR I–12859.   [271] Para. 44.   [272] Para. 54.

terms, or was it sufficient that the transfer was only one of a number of reasons to explain the change in terms? If the former, then the transferee might enjoy some latitude to change terms; if the latter then it becomes very difficult for the transferee to change the employees' terms and conditions. However, this question may now be less important following Delahaye[273] where the Court suggested that even changes of contract *connected with* the transfer are permissible provided that they are not substantial.[274] The case concerned the transfer of training services in Luxembourg from the private sector to the public sector. Mrs Boor was duly transferred but her pay was cut by 37 per cent due to the fact that her years of service with the transferor had not been taken into account. In another terse judgment, the Court said the Directive had to be interpreted as 'not precluding in principle', in the event of a transfer, the new employer, 'from reducing the amount of the remuneration of the employees concerned for the purpose of complying with the national rules'.[275] However, the Court went on to say that the competent authorities responsible for applying and interpreting those rules were obliged to do so as far as possible in the light of the purpose of the Directive (namely to provide for protection of employees in the event of a change of employer). It continued that if the reduction in pay was substantial, such a reduction constituted a substantial change in working conditions to the detriment of the employees concerned by the transfer and this gave grounds for a claim of constructive dismissal against the transferee under Article 4(2). This claim is considered further below.

2.2. Rights Arising from a Collective Agreement

Article 3(3) provides that, following the transfer, the transferee is obliged to observe the terms and conditions of any collective agreement on the same terms as the transferor.[276] In many Member States this is merely a corollary of contractual subrogation, since in most systems the conditions of employment established by collective agreements are automatically incorporated in individual contracts.[277] This may well mean that different collective agreements regulate the employment conditions of different sections of the transferee's workforce which may interfere with the 'unité du personnel'. Consequently, in

---

[273] Case C–425/02 Delahaye [2004] ECR I–10823.

[274] See also AG Léger's opinion, paras. 54–6 which seems to have influenced the Court's judgment.

[275] Para. 35.

[276] The requirement that the transferee must respect 'customary industrial practice', which would include rules and practices governing the working environment which are not contractually binding, was removed from the final draft of the Directive (Hepple, above, n. 37, 495).

[277] Commission report to Council on progress with regard to the implementation of Dir. 77/187/EEC, SEC (92) 857 final, 2 June 1992, 29.

some states, such as Spain, the law provides that if the terms of the collective agreements enjoyed by the transferee's workers are superior to those of the transferor's workers, the transferor's workers enjoy the better terms.

However, the obligation on the transferee to respect the terms of pre-existing collective agreements is not indefinite: it lasts until the date of termination or expiry of the collective agreement or the entry into force or application of another collective agreement. Member States may also limit the period for observing the terms and conditions laid down in the agreement to one year.[278] Thus, if the transferor's obligations were contained in a collective agreement and the conditions set out in Article 3(3) are satisfied, then the collective agreement is no longer legally binding on the employees of the undertaking transferred and so the transferee is not obliged to respect those terms. This would be another way for the transferee to change the terms and conditions of employment, provided that they are contained in a collective agreement. As the Court explained in *Martin*,[279] if, at the time the transferred employees accepted early retirement on terms other than those laid down in the Whitley Council agreement, and the collective agreement giving rise to that provision had, as a matter of law, ceased to apply to them, the employees would lose their rights under the Whitley Council agreement.

The Court in *Werhof*[280] confirmed these points. It considered whether a transferee was bound by a collective agreement subsequent to the one in force at the time of the transfer of the business, when the transferee was not party to the collective agreement. The Court, using the case as an opportunity to discuss freedom of association,[281] favoured a 'static' interpretation of the Directive, making it possible to avoid a situation in which the transferee of a business, who was not party to a collective agreement, was bound by future changes to that agreement.[282] The Court said that this interpretation safeguarded the transferor's right not to join an association and thus not to be bound by a collective agreement subsequent to the agreement in force at the time of the transfer.[283]

2.3. Pension Rights, Invalidity and Survivors' Benefits

The final draft of the original version of Directive 77/187 excluded from the Directive employees' rights to 'old age, invalidity or survivor's benefits under supplementary company or inter-company schemes outside the statutory

---

[278] Art. 3(3), para. 2.   [279] Case C–4/01 *Martin* [2003] ECR I–12859, para. 48.
[280] Case C–499/04 *Werhof* v. *Freeway Traffic System GmbH & Co. KG* [2006] ECR I–000.
[281] Considered further in Ch.16.   [282] Para. 35.   [283] Para. 36.

social security schemes',[284] unless Member States provide otherwise.[285] This provision is now found in Article 3(4)(a) of Directive 2001/23. In *Eidesund*[286] the EFTA Court confirmed that the new contractor was not obliged under Article 3(4)(a) to maintain contributions to the employee's occupational pension scheme. From an employee's perspective, this is a grave omission from the protective scheme of the Directive. Since an occupational pension scheme may constitute an integral part of any remuneration package its loss would make any transfer considerably less attractive. The transferor, who may be insolvent, remains responsible under the terms of the scheme for any liabilities but neither the transferred employee nor the transferor would continue to make contributions.

The severity of this rule is, however, mitigated in two ways. First, Article 3(4)(b) provides that if the Directive does not apply to these benefits, the Member States must adopt the measures necessary to protect the interests of employees and persons no longer employed in the transferor's business at the time of transfer in respect of rights conferring on them immediate or prospective entitlement to old age benefits, including survivors' benefits, under supplementary schemes. Thus, the obligation falls on the Member State[287] and not the transferee, and it extends to persons no longer employed, as well as to employees.

Secondly, the Court of Justice ruled in *Beckmann*[288] that, since Article 3(4)(a) is an exception to the general rule found in Articles 3(1) and (3), it has to be interpreted strictly[289] so that the exception applies 'only to the benefits listed exhaustively in that provision and they must be construed in a narrow sense'. The case concerned an employee, a quantity surveyor, who was transferred from the NHS to a private sector employer, Dynamco Whicheloe Macfarlane Ltd (DWM). Under the terms of the NHS Whitley Council agreement, which was implemented by statutory instrument, employees over 50 and with more than five years' service in the NHS Superannuation Scheme were entitled to immediate payment of their retirement pension and compensation when they were dismissed for redundancy. Beckmann satisfied these conditions but still did not receive the benefits.

---

[284] The British Employment Appeal Tribunal confirmed in *Walden Engineering* v. *Warrener* [1993] IRLR 420 that contracted out occupational pension schemes fell within the definition of 'supplementary schemes' and consequently were excluded from the Directive.

[285] Added by Dir. 98/50. See further Hepple and Mumgaard, 'Pension Rights in Business Transfers' (1998) 27 *ILJ*. 309.

[286] Case E–2/95 [1996] IRLR 684. See also the British Court of Appeal's ruling to the same effect in *Adams* v. *Lancashire County Council* [1997] IRLR 436.

[287] Failure to implement may result in enforcement proceedings. See Case 235/84 *Commission* v. *Italy* [1986] ECR 2291 but the provision is unlikely to be directly effective, see e.g. the views of the British EAT in *Warrener* [1993] IRLR 420.

[288] Case C–164/00 *Beckmann* v. *Dynamco Whicheloe Macfarlane Ltd* [2002] ECR I–4893.

[289] Para. 29.

The (Full) Court ruled that DWM could not rely on the Article 3(4)(a) exception, declaring that 'it is only benefits paid from the time when an employee reaches the end of his normal working life as laid down by the general structure of the pension scheme in question, and not benefits paid in circumstances such as . . . [dismissal for redundancy] that can be classified as old-age benefits, even if they are calculated by reference to the rules for calculating normal pension benefits'.[290] Because these rights did not fall within the Article 3(4) exception, they were transferred under Article 3. It did not matter that the rights derived from a statutory instrument or were implemented by such instruments.[291] The effect of this judgment is that early retirement benefits payable on redundancy and all aspects of early retirement schemes are automatically transferred under Article 3; the exclusion applies only to pension benefits paid on or after normal retirement age.[292] In *Martin*[293] the Court extended the ruling in *Beckmann* to benefits applied for on early retirement agreed between the employer and the employee.

2.4. Consent to Transfer

The protection provided by the Directive is a matter of public policy and, as we have seen, operates independently of the will of the parties.[294] This approach contradicts the deep seated, particularly common law, notion that contract is based on a voluntary agreement between the parties. Thus, it is a principle of English law that contracts can be transferred only by novation, which requires the consent of both parties to the contract and of the substituting party. In a similar vein is the rule in the law of obligations that a debt may only be transferred with the creditor's consent. Nevertheless, the Court expressly rejected the common law approach in *Berg*, maintaining that the Directive overrode these principles[295] and did not permit derogations unfavourable to employees. Therefore, as we have seen in *Daddy's Dance Hall*,[296] the Court has said that employees could not waive the rights conferred on them by the Directive nor could these rights be restricted even with their consent.

Following *Daddy's Dance Hall* it was also thought that employees' consent was not relevant as to whether their contract as a whole could be transferred,[297] since it had always been assumed that continued employment by

---

[290] Para. 32.   [291] Para. 38.   [292] Rubinstein [2002] IRLR 509.
[293] Case C–4/01 *Martin* [2003] ECR I–000, para. 35.
[294] Case 324/86 *Daddy's Dance Hall* [1988] ECR 739.
[295] Joined Cases 144 and 145/87 *Berg* [1988] ECR 2559, para. 13.
[296] Case 324/86 *Daddy's Dance Hall* [1988] ECR 739 considered above, n. 80.
[297] See para. 11 of Joined Cases 144 and 145/87 *Berg* [1988] ECR 2559, Case C–362/89 *d'Urso* [1991] ECR I–4105, para. 12, and Case 101/87 *Bork* [1988] ECR 3057, para. 17.

the transferee would be the more attractive proposition for the employee. In fact, this might not always be the case. If the transferor is a public sector undertaking and the transferee a small private company of uncertain financial stability, with a doubtful commercial strategy or less favourable employment policies (including, perhaps, the policy relating to preservation and payment of pensions),[298] the employee may be well advised not to transfer. The Court opened up this possibility in *Katsikas* and *Skreb*,[299] where it made clear that employees could refuse to be transferred. In the first case, Katsikas, an employee in a restaurant run by Konstantinidis, refused to work for Mitossis to whom Konstantinidis had sub-let the restaurant. As a result, Konstantinidis dismissed Katsikas. In the second case, two employees were dismissed by their employers when they refused to accept the transfer of their employment relationship to another company to whom their employers had transferred their section of the business.

The Court reasoned that although the Directive permitted an employee to remain in employment with the new employer on the same terms and conditions as those agreed with the transferor, the Directive did not impose an *obligation* on the employee to continue the employment relationship with the transferee. Such an obligation would undermine the fundamental rights of employees who had to be free to choose their employer and could not be obliged to work for an employer whom they had not freely chosen.[300] This means that although employees can neither agree to waive their rights under the Directive nor contract for different terms since the provisions of the Directive are mandatory, they can decide not to be transferred.[301]

However, the judgment came with a sting in its tail: if the employee did voluntarily decide not to transfer, then it was for the Member States to determine the fate of the contract of employment. The Court made clear that the Directive did not oblige Member States to provide that the contract of employment or employment relationship be continued with the transferor. This is the approach adopted by the UK where the contract of employment is considered as terminated with no protection from the law of dismissal. This is a significant practical limitation to the fundamental rights recognized in the judgment.

[298] See further Advocate General Van Gerven's Opinion in Joined Cases C–132, 138 and 139/91 *Katsikas* [1992] ECR I–6577.

[299] Joined Cases C–132/91, C–138/91 and C–139/91 [1992] ECR I–6577. See also Case C–51/00 *Temco Service Industries SA* [2002] ECR I–969, para. 36.

[300] The decision accords with the English common law position, stated by Lord Atkin in *Noakes v. Doncaster Amalgamated Collieries* [1940] AC 1014, 1026: 'I had fancied that ingrained in the personal status of a citizen under our laws was the right to choose for himself whom he would serve and that this right of choice constituted the main difference between a servant and a serf'. See also Art. 4(2) of the European Convention on Human Rights concerning the prohibition of forced or compulsory labour and in the UK, s. 236 TULR(C)A 1992.

[301] The Court confirmed this ruling in Joined Cases C–171/94 and 172/94 *Merckx* [1996] ECR I–1253, Case C–399/96 *Europièces* [1998] ECR I–6965, para. 38.

3. Rights Relating to Dismissal

3.1. The Basic Rules

The second pillar of employment protection offered by the Directive relates to rights on dismissal. The first sentence of Article 4(1) provides that the transfer of the undertaking shall not *in itself* constitute grounds for dismissal by the transferor or the transferee. Article 4(2) concerns constructive dismissal. It provides that if the contract of employment is terminated because the transfer involves a substantial change in working conditions[302] to the detriment of the employee, the employer shall be regarded as having been responsible for termination of the contract. In *Merckx*[303] the Court ruled that a change in the level of remuneration awarded to an employee by the transferee constituted a substantial change in working conditions, even where the remuneration depended on the turnover achieved.[304] Similarly, in *Delahaye*[305] the Court ruled that a substantial reduction in the level of remuneration awarded to an employee (in this case a reduction of 37 per cent due to the fact that on the transfer the transferee took no account of the employee's length of service with the transferor) constituted a substantial change in working conditions.[306] In the UK such dismissals are automatically unfair[307] and the transferee is responsible.[308]

3.2. The Relationship between Articles 3 and 4

The Court has refused to allow a wedge to be driven between the two pillars of employment protection contained in Articles 3 and 4. As has already been seen, the employment protection provision applies only to those workers who have a contract of employment at the date of transfer,[309] which must be decided on the basis of national law.[310] Thus, in order to avoid the effect of Article 3 a transferor (possibly at the behest of the transferee), might dismiss the workforce shortly before the transfer and then the transferee subsequently re-engages the workforce after the transfer with inferior terms and conditions.

---

[302] This is a matter for the national court to decide, see Case C–399/96 *Europièces* [1998] ECR I–6965, para. 43.

[303] Joined Cases C–171/94 and 172/94 [1996] ECR I–1253.   [304] Para. 38.

[305] Case C–425/02 *Delahaye* [2004] ECR I–10823.   [306] Para. 33.

[307] Unlike other categories of unfair dismissal, the employee is required to satisfy the normal qualifying period to claim for unfair dismissal (one year), see TUPE Reg. 8(5)(b) inserted by SI 1995/2587 reversing *Milligan* v. *Securicor* [1995] IRLR 288. Such dismissals are, however, legally effective, according to the House of Lords in *Wilson* [1998] IRLR 706, and not a legal nullity, as the Court of Appeal had thought [1997] IRLR 505.

[308] AG Léger's Opinion in Case C–425/02 *Delahaye* [2004] ECR I–10823, para. 37.

[309] Case 19/83 *Wendleboe* [1985] ECR 457, para. 13.

[310] Case 101/87 *Bork* [1988] ECR 3057, para. 17.

In *Bork*[311] the Court tried to eliminate such practices. It said that it was for the national court to decide whether the reason for dismissal was the transfer itself. In reaching its decision the national court had to take account of the objective circumstances in which the dismissal occurred, noting, in particular, the fact that the dismissal took place on a date close to that of the transfer and that the workers concerned were re-engaged by the transferee.[312] If the national court decided that the dismissal occurred because of the transfer then those employees 'dismissed' in breach of Article 4(1), had to be considered as still employed by the undertaking on the date of the transfer with the result that the transferor's obligations towards the employees were automatically transferred to the transferee.[313]

Does this mean that an employee, dismissed by the transferor for a transfer-related reason before the transfer or by the transferee after the transfer, can enforce the primary obligation to continued employment or is his remedy confined to compensation enforceable against the transferee for loss of employment? The cases suggest that there is no right to continued employment. In *Dethier*[314] the Court said that the contract of employment of a person unlawfully dismissed shortly before the transfer had to be regarded as still extant as against the transferee even if the dismissed employee was not taken on by him after the undertaking was transferred.[315] This employee can claim that their dismissal was unlawful against the transferee. This suggests that the transferee is liable for all secondary contractual obligations, such as the right to claim unfair dismissal, but not the primary obligation to continued employment. This approach was adopted by the British House of Lords in *British Fuels and Wilson*[316] where Lord Slynn said the transferee had to meet all of the transferor's contractual and statutory obligations unless either the employee objected to being employed by the transferee or the reason or principal reason for dismissal was ETOR.[317]

3.3. The Limits to the Protection contained in Article 4(1)

The general rule contained in Article 4(1) that the transfer shall not constitute grounds for dismissal is subject to two limitations. First, Member States may exclude certain specific categories of employees who are not covered by the dismissal laws or practice of the Member States from the protection

---

[311] Case 101/87 [1988] ECR 3057. See also the decision of the British House of Lords in *Litster v. Forth Dry Dock & Engineering Co. Ltd* [1990] 1 AC 546 where it said that the Directive applied both to those who were employed immediately before the transfer and those who would have been so employed had they not been unfairly dismissed.

[312] Case 101/87 *Bork* [1988] ECR 3057, paras. 18 and 19.

[313] See also Case C–51/00 *Temco* [2002] ECR I–969, para. 28.

[314] Case C–319/94 [1998] ECR I–1061.   [315] Para. 41.

[316] *British Fuels Ltd v. Baxendale; Wilson v. St Helens Borough Council* [1998] 4 All ER 609.

[317] See below, nn. 320–4.

conferred by the first sentence of Article 4(1).[318] However, in *Commission* v. *Belgium*[319] the Court ruled that Member States cannot use this exception as a means of depriving rights from workers in the event of a transfer who already enjoy some protection, albeit limited, against dismissal under national law. Second, Article 4(1), second sentence, provides that:

This provision shall not stand in the way of dismissals that may take place for economic, technical or organisational reasons [ETOR] entailing changes in the workforce.[320]

The Court has offered surprisingly little guidance on the meaning of ETOR but seems merely to pay lip service to the existence of the provision.[321] The English courts, by contrast, have given the matter some attention. They have found that an 'economic' reason has to relate to the conduct of the business. Therefore, dismissals for reasons of redundancy fall within the ETOR[322] exception and so the transferee must make a redundancy payment. On the other hand, broader economic reasons, such as the desire on the part of the transferor to achieve a higher sale price or achieve a sale at all, did not constitute an economic reason.[323] Flexibility and cost-cutting measures also do not constitute an ETOR because the 'reason itself does not involve any change either in the number or the functions of the workforce'.[324]

The employer must be motivated by a genuine economic, technical or organizational reason and that reason must result in the dismissals. Therefore, any attempt by a transferee to rely on this provision to dismiss employees who are later re-engaged by the same transferee, usually on inferior terms, is regarded with suspicion. This view receives some support from Advocate General Van Gerven in *d'Urso*. He refused to countenance the argument that the Directive permits *any* dismissal for economic, technical, or organizational reasons. In fact, he says, the Directive expressly prohibits such dismissals when they occur as a result of the transfer of the undertaking. Only dismissals which would have been made in any case, for instance if the decision had been taken before there was any question of transferring the undertaking, fall within the exclusion. He therefore said that Article 4 could not be relied on as justification for dismissing some employees because the undertaking has been transferred.

---

[318] Art. 4(1), second para.   [319] Case 237/84 [1986] ECR 1247.

[320] This exception has received substantial criticism (Elias, above, n. 13, 153) and Davies (above, n. 219) has questioned the need for an exception in that form. He argues that Art. 4 risks creating a bigger exception than some national laws would have permitted. From the Court's perspective it reduces the impact of the decision in Case C–392/92 *Schmidt* [1994] ECR I–1311, para. 18.

[321] See, e.g., Case C–171/94 *Merckx* [1996] ECR I–1253.

[322] It was confirmed in Case C–319/94 *Dethier* [1998] ECR I–1061 that the ETOR exception applies to both the transferor and the transferee.

[323] *Wheeler* v. *Patel* [1987] IRLR 631.   [324] *Berriman* v. *Delabole Slate* [1990] ICR 85.

G. COLLECTIVE RIGHTS

The Directive envisages an important role for employee representatives[325] in respect of information and consultation. As far as information is concerned, Article 7(1) requires that the representatives of the employees be informed and consulted. As far as information is concerned, Article 6(1) requires the transferor *and* the transferee to inform the representatives of their respective employees affected by a transfer of the following:

*   the date or proposed date of the transfer;
*   the reasons for the transfer;
*   the legal, economic, and social implications of the transfer for the employees;
*   any measures envisaged in relation to the employees.

Both the transferor and the transferee are obliged to give the information to the employees' representatives in 'good time'. In the case of the transferor, the information must be given before the transfer is carried out but no specific time limit is set.[326] In the case of the transferee, it is under an obligation to provide its own employees' representatives with information before its employees are directly affected by the transfer as regards their conditions of work and employment.[327]

Employees' representatives have direct input only in respect of 'measures' envisaged by the transferor or transferee in relation to the employees (such as a reduction in the workforce, or the introduction of new working methods):[328] under Article 7(2) the transferor or the transferee must *consult* the employees' representatives,[329] again in good time, with a *view to seeking their agreement*. Thus, the Directive does provide for an element of employee participation, at least through their representatives, in commercial decisions but neither the employees nor their representatives have the right to veto any such decisions.

German law provides that the works council and the head of the undertaking may agree on a social plan intended to compensate for or mitigate the detrimental economic consequences which the worker might suffer as a result of the envisaged change. In the event of disagreement about the social plan, either of the two sides may bring the matter before the conciliation committee,

---

[325] Defined in Art. 2(1)(c) and discussed in the text accompanying nn. 51–8.

[326] Art. 7(1), para. 2.   [327] Art. 7(1), para. 3.

[328] European Works Councils may also have to be consulted in respect of these matters as well as transfers of production and mergers, see para. 2 of the Annex to Dir. 94/45/EC (OJ [1994] L254/64). Cf. Art. 9 of The Information and Consultation Dir. 2002/14 (OJ [2002] L80/29) which gives precedence to the specific information and consultation procedures set out in the Collective Redundancies and Transfers Directives.

[329] The first draft envisaged negotiations by the employees' representatives with the transferor or transferee with a view to seeking agreement and in default the matter could be referred to arbitration.

an arbitration body comprising an equal number of members appointed by the head of the firm and the works council with a Chair acceptable to both sides whose decision is binding.[330] This can continue: Article 7(3) provides that if the national system permits employees' representatives to have recourse to an arbitration board to obtain a decision on the 'measures to be taken in relation to employees', the duties of information and consultation may be limited to cases where the transfer is likely to entail 'serious disadvantages for a considerable number of employees'. Nevertheless, the information and consultations must concern the measures envisaged in relation to employees and must take place in good time before the transfer is effected.[331]

Article 7(4), introduced by Directive 98/50, addresses the situation of transnational companies where decisions may be taken by the parent in one state which affects a subsidiary in another state. In line with the amendments to the Directive on Collective Redundancies,[332] Article 7(4) provides that it is no 'excuse' for an employer subsidiary which is in breach of the information and consultation provisions to argue that the information was not provided by the controlling parent undertaking which took the decision. Article 7 applies irrespective of whether the decision resulting in the transfer is taken by the employer or an undertaking controlling the employer.[333]

Finally, Member States have the option of limiting the information and consultation rights to those businesses which in terms of the number of employees meet 'the conditions for the election or nomination of a collegiate body representing the employees'.[334] This provision addresses a situation such as that in the Netherlands where the statutory requirement of information and consultation of representatives of workers applies only to works councils,[335] and consequently to undertakings employing at least 100 people, or at least 35 people for more than one-third of the normal working hours, where the election of a works council is mandatory.[336] In the case of smaller undertakings where there are no employee representatives, Article 6(6) provides that the employees themselves must be given the same information 'in advance' (not 'in good time') as would have been given to the employee representatives.[337]

Given the importance of the information and consultation provisions to the Directive, Article 6 aims to safeguard and preserve 'the status and function of the 'representatives' or of the representation of the employees affected by the

---

[330] Commission Report to the Council, SEC (92) 857 final, 93.
[331] Art. 7(3), paras. 2 and 3.   [332] Council Directive 92/56/EEC (OJ [1992] L245/3).
[333] Art. 7(4), para. 1.   [334] Art. 7(5).   [335] Art. 25 of the Law on Works Councils.
[336] The proposed Directive (94/C274/08) provides that the Member States can limit the information and consultation requirements to undertakings or businesses which normally employ 50 or more employees. This was not included in the final version but reflects the Commission's thinking in the more general information and consultation proposal discussed in Ch. 8.
[337] Under Art. 6(5) of Dir. 77/187 the employees had only very limited information rights about when a transfer was to take place.

transfer, as laid down by the laws, regulations or administrative provisions of the Member States, on the same terms and subject to the same conditions as existed before the transfer. This protection is subject to two conditions. First, the business must preserve its autonomy.[338] Therefore, it must continue to be a unit capable of operating independently and not be absorbed into a larger unit. Secondly, if 'the conditions necessary for the re-appointment of the representatives of the employees or for the reconstitution of the representation of the employees are fulfilled the status and function of the original representatives will not be preserved'.[339] This may occur where the transfer results in an increase in the workforce necessitating a change in the number of representatives or in the structure of the representation.[340] Workers representatives whose term of office expires as a result of the transfer continue to enjoy the protection afforded by legislation in the Member States against action taken by employers which may be detrimental to workers' representatives.[341] Finally, Article 6(1) makes special provision for a transferor which is the subject of bankruptcy proceedings or any analogous insolvency proceedings. Article 6(1), paragraph 3 provides that Member States *may* take the necessary measures to ensure that the employees transferred who were represented before the transfer continue to be properly represented during the period necessary for the reconstitution or reappointment of the representation of employees in accordance with national law or practice.

H. IMPLEMENTATION AND REMEDIES

1. Implementation

Directive 2001/23 is a minimum standards Directive: states are free to enact provisions more favourable to employees or to promote or permit collective agreements more favourable to employees.[342] Even if Member States do not take advantage of improving upon the minimum protection laid down by the Directive, they do have to implement the Directive's minima either through laws, regulations or administrative provisions[343] or through collective agreements. This second possibility was introduced by Article 2(1) of Directive 98/50 which permitted employers and the employees' representatives to introduce

---

[338] Art. 6(1). If the business does not preserve its autonomy, the Member States must take the necessary measures to ensure that the employees transferred, who were represented before the transfer, continue to be properly represented during the period prior to the reconstitution or reappointment of the representatives of the employees (Art. 6(1), para. 4).

[339] Art. 6(1), para. 2.

[340] See Art. 6(1), para. 2, Commission Report to the Council, SEC (92) 857 final, Brussels 2 June 1992.

[341] Art. 6(2).   [342] Art. 8.   [343] Art. 8 of Dir. 77/187.

the required provisions 'by means of agreement',[344] albeit that the Member States retained responsibility for ensuring that all workers were afforded the full protection provided by the Directive.[345] In the words of the Court, 'the state guarantee must cover all cases where effective protection is not ensured by other means'.[346] Thus, in *Commission v. Italy*,[347] the Court accepted that collective agreements could be used as a means of laying down procedures for informing and consulting employees' representatives affected by a transfer.[348] However, since these agreements covered only specific economic sectors, the Italian government was obliged to enact appropriate laws, regulations or administrative measures to ensure full compliance with the Directive.

2. Remedies

While Directive 77/187 provided rights for employees and their representatives it made no provision for remedies in the event of the failure by a transferor or transferee to recognize those rights. However, in *Commission v. UK*[349] the Court said that where a Community Directive did not specifically provide any penalty for an infringement, or refers to national laws, regulations and administrative provisions, Article 10 EC required the Member States to take all measures necessary to guarantee the application and effectiveness of Community law. While the choice of penalties remained within their discretion (the principle of national procedural autonomy), Member States had to ensure, in particular, that infringements of Community law were penalized under conditions, both procedural and substantive, which were analogous to those applicable to infringements of national law of a similar nature and importance and which, in any event, made the penalty effective, proportionate and dissuasive.[350] Under UK law, an employer who failed to consult employee representatives at the time of the transfer could be ordered to pay a penalty of up to a maximum of four weeks' pay to employees affected by the transfer. However, any protective award made against the employer for failing to consult employees' representatives in the event of collective redundancies could be set off against any penalty payment received by the employee which, when

---

[344] As approved by the Court: Case 143/83 *Commission v. Denmark* [1985] ECR 427, and confirmed by Case 235/84 *Commission v. Italy* [1986] ECR 2291.

[345] Art. 2(1) of Dir. 98/50/EC. There is no equivalent provision in Dir. 2001/23 although Art. 12 refers to Annex I Part B which retains the deadline for implementation.

[346] Case 235/84 *Commission v. Italy* [1986] ECR 2291, para. 20.   [347] Ibid.

[348] Cf. Advocate General Slynn, in Case 235/84 *Commission v. Italy* [1986] ECR 2291 who doubted whether collective agreements could be used as a means of implementing a Directive.

[349] Case C–382/92 [1994] ECR I–2435.

[350] With regard to Community regulations see the judgments in Case 68/88 *Commission v. Greece* [1989] ECR 2965, paras. 23 and 24, and in Case C–7/90 *Criminal Proceedings against Vandevenne and Others* [1991] ECR I–4371, para. 11.

combined with the financial ceiling on the penalty, significantly weakened the initial financial penalty. In the eyes of the Court such a penalty was not a true deterrent and consequently the UK legislation did not comply with Article 10 EC.

The Directive has now been amended to introduce a standard remedies clause. Article 9 requires those employees and employee representatives who consider themselves wronged by failure to comply with the obligations arising from the Directive to pursue their claims by judicial process after possible recourse to other competent authorities.

I. CONCLUSIONS

Despite the overt recognition that the Directive on transfers of undertakings has a welfarist or market-correcting purpose (the protection of labour standards), it has become increasingly clear that the Court is also motivated by the desire to ensure a level playing field of costs so that the financial burden of restructuring an enterprise is the same in all Member States.[351] Express acknowledgement of this can be found in *Commission v. UK*[352] where the Court said:

By harmonising the rules applicable to collective redundancies,[353] the Community legislature intended both to ensure comparable protection of workers' rights in the different Member States and *to harmonise the costs which such protective rules entail for Community undertakings.*[354]

However, the effectiveness of this level playing field of costs is significantly reduced by the degree to which key matters are dictated by national legislation or practice. As we have seen in *Katsikas*,[355] while the Court recognized the worker's right to refuse to be transferred it allowed national law to prescribe the consequences for the worker of his or her refusal. As a result some Member States have said that the worker's contract of employment is treated as terminated while in others the contract with the transferor will usually continue. If the Court was genuinely committed to worker protection it could have provided that workers must not be prejudiced as a result of their decision not to be transferred.

[351] As a result, Art. 94, concerning the approximation of measures which directly affect the establishment and functioning of the Common Market, was chosen as the legal base for all three Directives.

[352] Case C–383/92 [1994] ECR I–2479.

[353] The Court used the same words in the context of the Directive on safeguarding employees' rights in the event of transfers of undertakings in Case C–382/92 *Commission v. UK* [1994] ECR I–2435.

[354] Emphasis added. See also Case C–55/02 *Commission v. Portugal* [2004] ECR I–9387, para. 48, citing the third, fourth and seventh recitals of the preamble to Dir. 98/59.

[355] Joined Case C–132, C–138 and 139/91 [1992] ECR I–6577.

It is perhaps concern about high levels of unemployment that has prompted the Court to re-orientate its case law, particularly in the context of transfers after *Süzen*,[356] in favour of the economic imperative to pursue the most cost-efficient forms of organizing such a contracting out. Concerns about unemployment are also reflected in the amendments to the Directives on Collective Redundancies and Transfers and show a shift towards an increasing flexibility and adaptability which, as we have seen,[357] form one of the four key pillars of the Community's employment policy. Yet, the lack of clarity and consistency in the Court's rulings carry their own cost and it is in this context that the criticism of the Court is most deserved. The next chapter considers how the Court has addressed the parallel issues raised by the Directives on collective redundancies and insolvency.

[356] Case C–13/95 [1997] ECR I–1259.
[357] See further Ch. 1. See also Hunt, above, n. 8, 229.

14

Collective Redundancies and Employees' Rights on the Employer's Insolvency

A. INTRODUCTION

In the last chapter we focused on the important and much-discussed Directives on Transfers of Undertakings. Now we consider the two other Directives adopted at around the same time as the original Transfers Directive: Directive 75/129 on Collective Redundancies,[1] revised by Directive 92/56[2] to give it a transnational dimension and subsequently consolidated in Directive 98/59,[3] and Directive 80/987 on insolvency,[4] also amended to take account of the transnational dimension of corporate activities. As with the Directive on Transfers, neither Directive interferes with the employer's decision to restructure; both focus instead on the consequences of restructuring.

B. THE COLLECTIVE REDUNDANCIES DIRECTIVE

1. Introduction

Council Directive 75/129/EEC[5] was agreed by the Council of Ministers as part of the 1974–6 Social Action Programme. According to Blanpain,[6] the Directive had its origins in the conduct of AKZO, a Dutch–German multinational enterprise which wanted to make 5,000 workers redundant as part of a programme of restructuring. AKZO compared the costs of dismissing workers in the various states where it had subsidiaries and chose to dismiss workers in the country where costs were lowest. This led to calls for action at European level to prevent this from happening again: Directive 75/129

---

[1] OJ [1975] L48/29.   [2] Council Directive 92/56/EEC (OJ [1992] L245/3).
[3] OJ [1998] L225/16.
[4] OJ [1980] L283/23, as amended by Dir. 87/164 (OJ [1987] L66/11) and substantially revised by Dir. 2002/74 (OJ [2002] L270/10).
[5] Council Directive 75/129/EEC of 17 February 1975 on the Approximation of the Laws of the Member States Relating to Collective Redundancies (OJ [1975] L48/29).
[6] See further, Blanpain, *Labour Law and Industrial Relations of the European Community* (Kluwer, Deventer, 1991) 153.

was the Community's response. The purpose of the Directive was two-fold:[7] first, that greater protection be afforded to workers in the event of collective redundancies,[8] while taking into account the need for balanced economic and social development within the Community';[9] and second, to promote 'approximation . . . while the improvement (in living and working conditions) is being maintained within the meaning of Article [136] of the Treaty'.[10]

The Directive set minimum standards[11] to ensure both that major redundancies were subjected to proper consultation with worker representatives and that the competent public authority was notified prior to dismissal.[12] The Directive was not, however, designed to harmonize national practices and procedures for actually making *individuals* redundant;[13] nor was it designed to affect the employer's freedom to effect, or refrain from effecting, collective dismissals.[14] This was confirmed in *Rockfon*[15] where the Court said that companies retained autonomy to manage their internal affairs, adding that 'the sole purpose of the Directive is the partial harmonisation of *collective* redundancy procedures and that its aim is not to restrict the freedom of undertakings to organise their activities and arrange their personnel departments in the way which they think best suits their needs'.

Directive 75/129 was amended by Directive 92/56/EEC[16] which was drafted against the backcloth of increasing transnationalization of companies, with decisions affecting employees in a subsidiary in State A being taken by controlling parent companies in State B. Directive 75/129 and Directive 92/56 were consolidated and repealed by Council Directive 98/59/EC[17] to which all subsequent references relate.

---

[7] Case 215/83 *Commission v. Belgium* [1985] ECR 103.

[8] Second recital in the preamble, cited in Case C–449/93 *Rockfon A/S v. Specialarbejderforbundet i Danmark, acting for Nielsen* [1995] ECR I–4291, para. 29; Case C–250/97 *Lauge v. Lønmodtagernes Garantifond* [1998] ECR I–8737, para. 19. See also the weight given to this recital by AG Tizzano in Case C–55/02 *Commission v. Portugal* [2004] ECR I–9387, para. 31 in influencing the interpretation given to the meaning of terms in the Directive.

[9] Second recital in the Preamble.

[10] Case 215/83 *Commission v. Belgium* [1985] ECR I–1039, para. 2.

[11] National laws, regulations, and administrative provisions can lay down laws more favourable to workers and, since Dir. 92/56, Member States can promote or allow the application of collective agreements more favourable to workers (Art. 5).

[12] Case 284/83 *Dansk Metalarbeiderforbund and special arbeiderforbundet i Danmark v. Nielsen & Son Maskin-fabrik A/S in liquidation* [1985] ECR 553, para. 10.

[13] Case 284/83 *Nielsen* [1985] ECR 553 and Case C–383/92 *Commission v. UK* [1994] ECR I–2435.

[14] Case 284/83 *Nielsen* [1985] ECR 553, para. 10.

[15] Case C–449/93 *Rockfon A/S v. Specialarbejderforbundet i Danmark, acting for Nielsen* [1995] ECR I–4291, para. 21, emphasis added.

[16] OJ [1992] L245/3.   [17] OJ [1998] L225/16.

2. The Material and Personal Scope of the Directive

2.1. The Meaning of Collective Redundancies

Article 1(1)(a) defines collective redundancies as 'dismissals effected by an employer for one or more reasons *not related to the individual* workers concerned'. In *Commission v. Portugal*[18] the Court insisted that the concept 'redundancy' be given a Community meaning,[19] namely 'any termination of [a] contract of employment not sought by[20] the worker, and therefore without his consent'.[21]

For the redundancies to be *collective*, the Directive adds a quantitative and temporal hurdle: it says that the number of redundancies must be:

(i)   either, over a period of 30 days:
— at least 10 redundancies in establishments normally employing more than 20 and less than 100 workers;
— at least 10 per cent of the number of workers in establishments normally employing at least 100 but less than 300 workers;
— at least 30 in establishments normally employing 300 workers or more;

(ii) or, over a period of 90 days, at least 20, irrespective of the number of workers normally employed in the establishments in question.

The choice between these alternatives is left to the Member State. Directive 92/56 added that for the purpose of calculating the number of redundancies 'terminations of an employment contract which occur on the employer's initiative for one or more reasons not related to the individual workers concerned' (so-called 'redundancies by assimilation')[22] are to be treated as redundancies, provided at least five redundancies occur.[23] Thus, other forms of termination, such as voluntary early retirement, or where the employment relationship is terminated on the employer's initiative but with the agreement of the worker, or where the worker is encouraged to give his agreement (for example in exchange for financial advantages),[24] are included within the scope of the Directive, but these must be taken to be, like the redundancies themselves, for a reason not related to the individual worker.[25]

From this we can see that the definition of collective redundancies contains both an *objective* element, concerning the scale of the redundancies (number or percentage of workers to be made redundant over a given period), and a

---

[18] Case C–55/02 [2004] ECR I–9387.   [19] Para. 49.
[20] Also translated as 'against the will of the worker' (para. 62).   [21] Para. 50.
[22] AG Tizzano in Case C–55/02 *Commission v. Portugal* [2004] ECR I–9387, para. 42.
[23] Art. 1(1), final para.
[24] AG Tizzano in Case C–55/02 *Commission v. Portugal* [2004] ECR I–9387, para. 46.
[25] Bourn, 'Amending the Collective Dismissals Directive: a Case of Rearranging the Deckchairs' (1993) 9 *Int. Jo. Comp. LLIR.* 227, 234.

subjective element concerning the reasons for the redundancies.[26] As far as the *objective* element is concerned, the Court gave some guidance in *Rockfon*[27] as to the definition of an establishment for the purposes of calculating the scale of redundancies. Rockfon, part of a multinational group, shared a joint personnel department responsible for recruitment and dismissals with three other companies in the group.[28] Internal rules required that any dismissal decision had to be taken in consultation with the personnel department. Between 10 and 28 November 1989 Rockfon dismissed 24 or 25 employees from its workforce of 162. Rockfon, considering itself to be part of the multinational group and not an independent establishment, did not consult the employees nor did it inform the relevant public authority. The question for the Court was whether Rockfon by itself constituted an establishment. If it did, then the dismissals were carried out in breach of the consultation requirements of the Directive since Danish law had chosen the first option provided by Article 1(1)(a) (over a period of 30 days, at least 10 dismissals in establishments normally employing between 20 and 100 workers, 10 per cent of the number of workers in establishments normally employing between 100 and 300 workers) to implement the Directive.

Although 'establishment' is not defined in the Directive, the Court said that the term had to be given a Community meaning.[29] The different language versions of the Directive use different terms:[30] 'establishment', 'undertaking', 'work centre', 'local unit', 'place of work'.[31] The Court said that a broad interpretation of the term establishment would allow companies belonging to the same group to try to make it more difficult for the Directive to apply to them by conferring on a separate decision-making body the power to take decisions concerning redundancies. They would thus be able to escape the obligation to follow the procedures provided by the Directive.[32] It therefore said that the term 'establishment' had to be interpreted as the unit to which the workers made redundant were assigned to carry out their duties.[33] It was not essential for the unit in question to be endowed with a management which could independently effect collective redundancies.[34] Since Danish law had chosen the first option provided for by Article 1(1)(a) the purposive construction set out in *Rockfon* defining 'establishment' *narrowly* was of benefit to Danish workers. The Court expressly said that the purpose of the Directive was to afford workers greater protection in the event of collective

---

[26] See Commission Report to Council, SEC(91) 1639 final, Brussels 13 September 1991, 11.
[27] Case C–449/93 [1995] ECR I–4291.   [28] Para. 17.   [29] Paras. 23 and 25.
[30] Danish *virksomhed*, Dutch *plaatselijke eenheid*, English 'establishment', Finnish *yritys*, German *Betrieb*, Italian *stabilemento*, Portugese *estabelecimento*, Spanish *centro de trabajo*, Swedish *arbetsplats*.
[31] Para. 27.   [32] Para. 30.
[33] Para. 31, citing Case 186/83 *Botzen* [1985] ECR 519, discussed in Ch. 13.
[34] Para. 32. This approach is supported by the fact that the Commission's initial proposal for the Directive used the term 'undertaking' and that term was defined as 'local employment unit'.

redundancies.[35] However, for countries such as the UK, which have chosen the second option provided for by Article 1(1)(a) (20 employees at one establishment within a period of 90 days), the decision in *Rockfon* threatens to undermine the position of those employees,[36] since for them the more *broadly* defined the establishment, the more likely the threshold of 20 employees will be met.

As far as the *subjective* element is concerned, the reasons for the redundancies must not be 'related to the individual workers concerned'. Therefore, dismissals for reasons relating to a worker's behaviour (e.g. disciplinary dismissals) are excluded from the scope of the Directive. Otherwise the scope of the Directive is broad,[37] as the Court made clear in two enforcement actions: first, in *Commission* v. *UK*[38] the Court found that the British definition of redundancy—the cessation of a business or cessation or diminution in the requirements of a business to carry out work of a particular kind—was too narrow since it did not cover cases where workers were dismissed as a result of new working arrangements which were unconnected with the volume of business.[39] Second, in *Commission* v. *Portugal*[40] the Court found that the Portuguese definition of redundancy which confined the concept of collective redundancies to redundancies for structural, technological or cyclical reasons (i.e. redundancies as a result of a 'willed' or 'voluntary' act of the employer) and excluded redundancies resulting from compulsory and other types of liquidation, compulsory purchase, fire, other *force majeure*, or death of the trader (i.e. redundancies not resulting from a voluntary act of the employer) also failed to correctly implement the Directive. The Court said that it was not necessary that the underlying reasons for the redundancies should 'reflect the will of the employer'.[41]

The Directive applies only when the *employer* dismisses the employees. The phrase employer is broadly construed, consistent with the worker protection aims of the Directive, and therefore applies to all employers.[42] Under Italian law, employers engaged in non-profit-making activities, such as trade unions, political parties, and NGOs, were excluded from the scope of the national rules implementing the Directive. In *Commission* v. *Italy*[43] the Court found that this exclusion contravened the Directive. In support of its arguments, the Commission referred to Article 1(1)(c) of Directive 2001/23 on transfer of

---

[35] Para. 29.   [36] Rubinstein [1996] IRLR 113.
[37] Case C–55/02 [2004] ECR I–9387, para. 58.
[38] Case C–383/92 [1994] ECR I–2435.
[39] S. 195 TULR(C)A 1992 was amended by s. 34 TURERA 1993 to bring British law in line with the Directive. This now provides that 'references to dismissal as redundant are references to dismissal for a reason not related to the individual concerned or for a number of reasons all of which are not so related'.
[40] Case C–55/02 [2004] ECR I–9387.   [41] Ibid.
[42] Case C–32/02 *Commission* v. *Italy* [2003] ECR I–12063, para. 26.
[43] Case C–32/02 [2003] ECR I–12063.

undertakings[44] which provides that the Directive applies to 'public and private undertakings engaged in economic activities whether or not they are operating for gain'. While the Court did not refer to Directive 2001/23 in its findings, its long reference to the Directive when summarizing the Commission's arguments, may suggest that the Court is prepared to see parallel developments in the two fields.[45]

The Directive does not apply to termination of employment by the employees themselves[46] since such resignations might be contrary to the employer's wishes. If the Directive did apply to voluntary resignations, the effect of an employee resigning would be to prevent the employer from discharging the obligations laid down by the Directive. This, according to the Court in *Nielsen*,[47] would lead to a result contrary to that sought by the Directive, namely to avoid or reduce collective redundancies.[48] The position may, however, be different if the employer is actively seeking to close the business and has forced the workers to give notice in order to escape the obligations imposed by the Directive.[49]

2.2. Where the Directive does not Apply

The Directive does not apply to:[50]

- collective redundancies resulting from the expiry of fixed term contracts or the completion of a particular task in the case of a contract to perform a particular task;[51]
- workers employed by public administrative bodies or by establishments governed by public law (or, in Member States where this concept is unknown, by equivalent bodies);[52]
- the crews of sea-going vessels.[53]

Since these instances are exceptions to the general rule they must be construed narrowly. Article 1(2)(d) of Directive 75/129 also excluded workers affected by the termination of an establishment's activities where that is the result of a judicial decision (e.g. an insolvency situation). Directive 92/56

---

[44] See Ch. 13.
[45] For further examples of cross-fertilization, this time with European Works' Councils Dir. 94/45 (OJ [1994] L 254/64) see AG Tizzano's Opinion in Case C–440/00 *Gesamtbetriebsrat der Kühne & Nagel AG & Co. KG* v. *Kühne & Nagel AG & Co. KG* [2004] ECR I–000, para. 32 in Ch. 15.
[46] AG Tizzano's Opinion in Case C–188/03 *Junk* [2005] ECR I–000, para. 49.
[47] Case 284/83 [1985] ECR 553.   [48] Para. 10.
[49] Advocate General Lenz, Case 284/83 *Nielsen* [1985] ECR 553.
[50] Art. 1(2). The Belgian government was condemned for failing to implement these provisions correctly in Case 215/83 *Commission* v. *Belgium* [1985] ECR 1039.
[51] Art. 1(2)(a). The Directive does, however, apply to redundancies which take place prior to the date of expiry of fixed term contracts or to the completion of the specific task.
[52] Art. 1(2)(b).   [53] Art. 1(2)(c).

removed this exception.[54] Nevertheless, the Directive still contains some specific provision for the termination of an establishment's activities as a result of judicial decision. Article 3(1), paragraph 2 says that Member States have the discretion whether to require dismissals arising in such circumstances to be notified to the competent public authority and Article 4(4) provides that Member States need not apply Article 4 (notification of collective redundancies to competent public authorities) to collective redundancies arising in these circumstances.

The most notable omission from this list of exceptions concerns cases of emergency or *force majeure*. The Court considered such a situation in *Nielsen*.[55] In February 1980 the employer, Nielsen, informed workers' representatives of its financial difficulties. On 14 March 1980 it informed the bankruptcy court that it was suspending payment of its debts, and, when it failed to provide a bank guarantee for the future payment of wages, the trade unions advised their members to stop work. On 25 March 1980 the employer was declared insolvent and the following day the workers were given notice of dismissal. The trade union argued that as soon as the employer experienced financial difficulties it ought to have contemplated collective redundancies and thus the application of the Directive. The Court disagreed. It argued that this interpretation would cause employers to incur penalties for failing to have foreseen the collective redundancies and consequently failing to implement the procedure required by the Directive. This would run counter to the wording of Article 1(2)(d) which excluded from the scope of the Directive collective redundancies caused by 'the termination of an establishment's activities where that is the result of a judicial decision'.[56] The logic of these arguments is undermined now that Article 1(2)(d) has been deleted from the Directive 92/56/EEC,[57] so the position in respect of *force majeure* is unclear.

3. The Employer's Obligations

An employer who is contemplating collective redundancies has two obligations: first, to consult with worker representatives under Article 2, and second, to notify the relevant public authority under Articles 3 and 4.

---

[54] Ninth recital to the Dir. and Case C–55/02 *Commission v. Portugal* [2004] ECR I–9387, para. 54.
[55] Case 284/83 [1985] ECR 553.   [56] Para. 16.
[57] See above, n. 54, although the Court still refers to it: Case C–55/02 *Commission v. Portugal* [2004] ECR I–9387, para. 55.

3.1. Consultation of Workers' Representatives

Article 2(1) provides that 'where an employer is contemplating collective redundancies, he shall begin consultations with the workers' representatives in good time *with a view to reaching an agreement*'.[58] There has been much writing and litigation over the meaning of each aspect of Article 2(1). We shall examine each limb in turn.

(a) 'Contemplating' Collective Redundancies

This entire consultation procedure is only triggered when the employer is *contemplating* redundancies and has drawn up a 'project' to that end.[59] At what moment in time does 'contemplation' occur? The Directive merely states that the consultations must be in good time,[60] but the Court in *Junk*[61] makes clear that the obligations to consult and to notify the competent public authority 'arise prior to any decision by the employer to terminate contracts of employment'.[62] The case concerned an employee who worked as a care assistant until her employer, AWO, went into liquidation. The liquidator gave notice to her and a number of other staff at the end of June that her contract would be terminated at the end of September 2002. At the end of August the liquidator notified the labour office of the collective redundancies. This went well beyond 'contemplating'. As the Court said, the case in which the employer 'is contemplating' collective redundancies corresponds to a situation in which 'no decision has yet been taken'[63] or, using Advocate General Tizzano's language, when the redundancies are still at the 'projection stage'.[64] By contrast, the notification to a worker that his or her contract of employment has been terminated (i.e. giving notice) is the expression of a decision to sever the employment relationship, and the actual cessation of that relationship on the expiry of the period of notice (i.e. the date when the dismissal takes effect) is no more than the effect of that decision.[65] As the Court explained,[66] given that the purpose of the Directive is to avoid terminations of contracts of employment or at least to reduce their number, the achievement of that purpose would be jeopardized if the consultation of worker representatives were to be subsequent to the employer's decision.

The Court therefore concluded that 'the event constituting redundancy consists in the declaration by an employer of his intention to terminate the

---

[58] Emphasis added. See also ILO Convention 158 and Art. 2(1)(b) of the Additional Protocol to the Social Charter.

[59] Case C–188/03 *Junk v. Kühnel* [2005] ECR I–000, para. 36.

[60] See the *obiter dicta* of Glidewell LJ in *R v. British Coal Corporation and Secretary of State for Trade and Industry, ex parte Vardy* [1993] IRLR 104 which envisages consultation at an early stage when the employer is first envisaging the possibility that he may have to make employees redundant.

[61] Ibid.   [62] Para. 37.   [63] Para. 36.   [64] Para. 47.   [65] Ibid.

[66] Para. 38.

contract of employment'[67] (i.e. giving notice of dismissal or *Kündigung* in German)[68] with the result that 'an employer cannot terminate contracts of employment before he has engaged in the consultation and notification process.[69] The effect of this decision is that the consultation process must take place before employees are given notice of dismissal, rather than after individual notices have been given but before they have taken effect. However, as Rubinstein points out,[70] the Court does not require that the full period for consultation provided under national law must elapse before the employees can be given notice of dismissal. The focus is on the substance of consultation.[71]

By implication the Directive does not apply when redundancies occur which have not been 'contemplated' since, as the Court recognized in *Nielsen*,[72] there is no implied obligation under the Directive to foresee collective redundancies. The Court said that the Directive did not stipulate the circumstances in which employers must contemplate collective redundancies and in no way affected their freedom to decide whether and when they must formulate plans for collective dismissals. This ruling favours the disorganized employer who would not have contemplated redundancies, to whom the Directive may not apply.

(b) Consultations with the Workers' Representatives

These consultations are with 'workers' representatives', defined as those representatives provided for by the laws or practices of the Member States.[73] This enables consultation to continue within established frameworks of the German and Dutch works councils, the French *comité d'entreprise* and collective bargaining in Britain, Ireland, and Denmark.[74] The UK's implementation of this provision (along with the equivalent term in Directive 77/187) was found by the Court to be defective since only recognized trade unions could be consulted.[75]

(c) The Subject-Matter of Consultation

The substance of these consultations must cover, as a minimum, two matters: first, ways and means of avoiding collective redundancies or reducing the number of employees affected; and secondly, ways of mitigating the consequences of the redundancies by recourse to 'social measures aimed, *inter*

---

[67] Para. 39.
[68] And not *Entlassung*, the word used in the German version of the Directive, which means the time when the redundancy becomes effective, i.e. when the employment relationship is actually at an end.
[69] Para. 41.   [70] [2005] IRLR 225.   [71] Para. 45.
[72] Case 284/83 [1985] ECR 553.   [73] Art. 1(1)(b).
[74] Hepple, 'Community Measures for the Protection of Workers on Dismissal' (1977) 14 *CMLRev.* 489.
[75] Case C–383/92 *Commission v. UK* [1994] ECR I–2479. See above, n. 38.

alia, at aid for redeploying or retraining workers made redundant'.[76] This is a pale reflection of the 'social plan' recognized by German law—a special form of redundancy programme drawn up by management and the works council in a legally binding agreement designed to 'compensate or reduce economic disadvantages for employees in the event of a substantial alteration to the establishment.[77] The fact that ways of avoiding collective redundancies appear as the first item on the list suggests that the drafters of the Directive did not presume that redundancies would occur[78] and considered that the avoidance of redundancies was at least as important as giving rights to those who will be made redundant.

Since the emphasis is on consultation and not just information the Directive also makes provision to ensure that the consultations are effective. To enable the workers' representatives to make constructive proposals the employer is obliged to supply the workers' representatives[79] in good time during the course of the consultations with all relevant information[80] *and* the employer must 'in any event' give in writing:[81]

- the reasons for the projected redundancies;
- the number of categories of workers to be made redundant[82] (Directive 75/129/EEC talked of the number of workers to be made redundant);
- the number of workers normally employed;
- the period over which the redundancies are to be effected;

Directive 92/56 added two further items to this list:

- the criteria proposed for the selection of workers to be made redundant in so far as national legislation and/or practice confers this power on the employer;
- the method for calculating any redundancy payments other than those arising out of national legislation and/or practice.

The most important addition made by Directive 92/56 is that the obligation to consult workers' representatives applies 'irrespective of whether the decision regarding collective redundancies is being taken by the employer *or by an*

---

[76] Art. 2(2). Furthermore, according to para. 2, Member States can provide that the workers' representatives can call upon the services of experts in accordance with national law or practice. Thus, there will still be a contrast between the position in France where employees may call upon the services of an accountant (*expert comptable*) and in Denmark and the UK where no such obligation exists (Bourn, above, n. 25, 236).

[77] Weiss, *European Employment and Industrial Relations Glossary: Germany* (Sweet & Maxwell, London, 1992), para. 657.

[78] On the importance of this, see Case C–188/03 *Junk* v. *Kühnel* [2005] ECR I–000, para. 38.

[79] The European Works Council will also need to be consulted, see para. 2 of Annex to Directive 94/45/EC (OJ [1994] L254/64).

[80] Art. 2(3)(a).   [81] Art. 2(3)(b).

[82] The tone of this section does suggest that the fact that redundancies will occur is a *fait accompli* which contradicts the tenor of Art. 2(1) and (2).

undertaking controlling the employer'.[83] It is no defence for an employer to argue that the parent or controlling undertaking had not provided the employer with the necessary information.[84] This provision was introduced in the light of the increasing 'transnationalization' of commercial ventures. As the Commission said, the dismantling of national barriers has led to major corporate reorganization, involving a significant increase in takeovers, mergers and joint ventures.[85] As a result, decisions affecting the workforce might be taken by a controlling undertaking which might not be situated in one of the Member States, or possibly not even in the Community. The obligation to acquire the information is, however, placed on the controlled undertaking to avoid the problem of extraterritoriality. The approach adopted by the Collective Redundancies Directive to complex corporate structures contrasts favourably with that adopted under the European Works Council Directive 94/45/EC[86] where rights are given against central management at a time when there is an increasing tendency towards decentralizing decision making in corporate groups.

(d) With a View to Reaching an Agreement

The reference to 'consultation' with a view to reaching an 'agreement'[87] blurs the distinction between consultation and collective bargaining. The Court confirms this in *Junk*,[88] where it said with stark simplicity: 'It thus appears that Article 2 of the Directive imposes an obligation to negotiate'.[89] The Court continued that the effectiveness of the obligation to negotiate would be compromised if an employer was entitled to terminate contracts of employment during the course of the procedure or even at the beginning of the procedure. It added that it would be significantly more difficult for workers' representatives to achieve the withdrawal of a decision that has been taken than to secure the abandonment of a decision that is being contemplated.[90] The Court therefore concluded that a contract of employment could be terminated only after the conclusion of the consultation procedure laid down by Article 2.[91]

---

[83] Art. 2(4), para. 1.   [84] Art. 2(4), para. 2.

[85] According to the Commission's figures, the number of mergers and acquisitions carried out by the top 1,000 European industrial enterprises doubled every three years during the 1980s, increasing from 208 in 1984–85 to 492 in 1988–89: Commission, XXth Report on Competition Policy, cited in COM(94) 300, 2.

[86] OJ [1994] L254/64. See also Bourn, above, n. 25, 237. Dir. 94/95 is considered further in Ch. 15.

[87] A concept absent from the UK legislation, see Case C–383/92 *Commission* v. *UK* [1994] ECR I–2479. Implemented by s. 34(2)(c) TURERA 1993 and included in s. 188 TULR(C)A 1992.

[88] Case C–188/03 *Junk* [2005] ECR I–000.

[89] Para. 44. See also AG Tizzano's Opinion in Case C–188/03 *Junk* [2005] ECR I–000, para. 59: '*At the least*, Article 2 therefore imposes an obligation to negotiate' (emphasis added).

[90] Para. 45.   [91] Para. 45.

3.2. Notification of the 'Competent Public Authority'

In France and the Netherlands the competent authorities have long-established powers to authorize or prohibit redundancies. In the Netherlands the procedure involves a system whereby the Dutch labour office issues a number of permits to dismiss.[92] Due to resistance from the UK, this principle was not included in the Directive.[93] Instead, Article 3(1) imposes an administrative obligation on employers to notify 'the competent public authority' in writing of 'any projected collective redundancies'.[94] The notification must contain all information relevant to the projected redundancies, the consultations with the workers' representatives provided for in Article 2,[95] and particularly the reasons for the redundancies, the number of workers to be made redundant, the number of workers normally employed, and the period over which the redundancies are to be effected.[96] In the case of planned collective redundancies arising from termination of the establishment's activities as a result of a judicial decision, the Member States can provide that the employer is obliged to notify the competent public authority on the request of the authority.[97] The employer must also send a copy of the Article 3(1) notification to the workers' representatives who may send any comments they have to the competent authority.[98]

In principle, the proposed redundancies cannot take place until at least 30 days after the Article 3(1) notification, 'without prejudice to any provisions governing individual rights with regard to notice of dismissal'.[99] The reference to national provisions with regard to 'notice of dismissal' safeguards the application of notice periods which are longer than the 30 days provided by the Directive.[100] The purpose of this delay is, according to Article 4(2), to enable the competent authority to seek solutions to 'the problems raised by the projected redundancies'. It is not clear whether this means that the authority should intervene in an attempt to stave off the redundancies or rather that it should make provision for coping with those employees facing

---

[92] In the Netherlands the employer wishing to terminate employment contracts unilaterally must apply to the District Labour Office for a permit. In 1980 98,387 permits were requested by employers of which 16% concerned 20 employees or more. In 1993 107,998 permits were requested of which 15% concerned 20 employees or more, based on figures for the Dutch Ministry for Social Affairs and Employment.

[93] Freedland, 'Employment Protection: Redundancy Procedures and the EEC' (1976) 5–6 *ILJ.* 24, 27.

[94] Advocate General Lenz argues that the employer must give notice to the competent authorities if he actually plans to make collective redundancies, whereas representatives of workers must be consulted at an earlier stage (Case 284/83 *Nielsen* [1985] ECR 553, 557).

[95] Art. 2(3), para. 2, obliges the employer to forward to the competent authority all written communications referred to in Art. 2(3)(b) except the method for calculating any redundancy payments.

[96] Art. 3(1), para. 2.   [97] Added by Dir. 92/56 as second sentence of para. 1 of Art. 3(1).
[98] Art. 3(2).   [99] Art. 4(1).
[100] AG Tizzano's Opinion in Case C–188/03 *Junk* [2005] ECR I–000, para. 66.

unemployment. Advocate General Tizzano's Opinion in *Junk*[101] suggests the latter. He saw the Article 2 consultation stage and the Article 3 notification stage as separate, consecutive stages,[102] serving different purposes: 'the notification stage, which, unlike the stage of consultation with workers' representatives, does not relate to the principle of redundancy but rather to its consequences, or "the *problems* raised by the . . . collective redundancies" '.[103] Thus, the consultation stage concerns 'managing' the effects of the redundancy[104] and for that reason, as the Court said in *Junk*,[105] it was possible for the contracts of employment to be terminated in the course of the notification procedure provided that such termination occurred after the projected collective redundancies have been notified to the competent public authority.[106]

The Member State can grant the competent authority the power to reduce or extend the 30-day period.[107] If, however, the initial period of delay is for less than 60 days Member States can grant the competent authority the power to extend the initial period to 60 days or longer[108] following notification, where the problems raised by the projected collective redundancies are not likely to be solved within the initial period.[109] The employer (but not the workers' representatives) must be informed of the extension and the reason why such an extension has been granted before the expiry of the initial 30-day period.[110]

4. Implementation and Remedies

As with the Transfer of Undertakings Directive 2001/23, the Collective Redundancies Directive is a minimum standards Directive.[111] So Member States could implement the Directive or promote collective agreements more favourable to employees. In any event, the Member States were obliged to implement both Directives 75/129 and 92/56 within two years of their notification.[112] The Court is strict about ensuring correct implementation, as the Belgian government found to its cost:

Member States must fulfil their obligations under Community Directives in every respect and may not plead provisions, practices or circumstances existing in their internal legal system in order to justify a failure to comply with those obligations.[113]

It said that the Belgian government could not plead that in practice very few workers were excluded from the benefits of the Directive, nor that the

---

[101] Case C–188/03 *Junk* [2005] ECR I–000.   [102] Para. 61.   [103] Para. 67.
[104] Ibid.   [105] Case C–188/03 *Junk* [2005] ECR I–000.   [106] Para. 53.
[107] Art. 4(1), para. 2.   [108] Art. 4(3), para. 2.   [109] Art. 4(3), para. 1.
[110] Art. 4(3), para. 3.   [111] Art. 5.
[112] Art. 6, 19 February 1977 and 24 June 1994, respectively.
[113] Case 215/83 *Commission v. Belgium* [1985] ECR 1039.

government's failure to comply fully with the Directive was justified by the fact that Belgian law provides the workers in question with other forms of security. The Italian government was equally unsuccessful in the arguments it raised in enforcement proceedings brought against it. Although it claimed that the Italian system as a whole created conditions and established procedures making it possible to attain the objectives of the Directive, it did concede that in certain sectors the legislation was not as comprehensive as the Directive required.[114] It was therefore found to be in breach of its obligations under the Directive.

Directive 75/129/EEC, like Directive 77/187, made no express provision for remedies in the event of employers' failure to comply with their obligations. However, in the case of the *Commission* v. *UK*[115] the Court insisted that Member States had to ensure that infringements of Community law were penalized under conditions, both procedural and substantive, which were analogous to those applicable to infringements of national law and which made the penalty effective, proportionate, and dissuasive. Consequently the Court ruled that a British law which allowed that a protective award, payable by an employer who had failed to consult workers' representatives to dismissed employees, could be set off in full or in part against any other amounts owed by the employer to the employees, deprived the sanction of its practical effect and deterrent value. In several Member States collective redundancies carried out in contravention of the Directive are null and void.[116] Originally this was also included in the new draft Directive but, faced with opposition from ECOSOC, the UK government and employers, it was deleted from the final version. Instead, Article 6, introduced by Directive 92/56, requires Member States to ensure 'that judicial and/or administrative procedures for the enforcement of obligations under this Directive are available to the workers' representatives or to the workers'.

C. THE INSOLVENCY DIRECTIVE 80/987/EEC

1. Introduction

The Insolvency Directive[117] is the third in the trilogy of measures designed to confer some protection on employees faced with their employers' insolvency

---

[114] Case 91/81 *Commission* v. *Italy* [1982] ECR 2133. Further enforcement proceedings were later brought for failing to implement the judgment in Case 91/81, see Case 131/84 *Commission* v. *Italy* [1985] ECR 3531.

[115] Case C–383/92 [1994] ECR I–2479.   [116] Bourn, above, n. 25.

[117] Council Dir. 80/987/EEC (OJ [1980] L283/23) on the approximation of the laws of the Member States relating to the protection of employees in the event of insolvency of their employer, as amended by Dir. 87/164 (OJ [1987] L66/11). See COM(96) 696 on the implementation of the Directive.

due to increased competition caused by the advent of the Common Market and, subsequently, Single Market. Also based on Article 94, the Directive has dual objectives: to promote the approximation of laws and to improve the living and working conditions by protecting employees in the event of the insolvency of their employer.[118] As with the Directives on Transfers of Undertakings and Collective Redundancies, Directive 80/987 does not interfere with any decision about the employer's insolvency; instead it provides employees with a minimum degree of protection under Community law in the event of their employer becoming insolvent, in particular by requiring Member States to put in place an institution guaranteeing employees the payment of their outstanding claims to remuneration for a specific period. The Directive has been the subject of much litigation and it was amended by Directive 2002/74.[119] This Directive retained the basic structure of Directive 80/987, whose results are 'beyond dispute',[120] but was adapted to reflect changes in insolvency law in the Member States.

2. The Material and Personal Scope of the Directive

According to Article 1(1), the Directive applies to employees' claims arising from contracts of employment or employment relationships[121] and existing against employers who are in a state of insolvency. This raises two questions: what is meant by insolvency and who are employees?

2.1. The Definition of Insolvency

According to Article 2(1), an employer is considered to be in a state of insolvency:

where a request has been made for the opening of collective proceedings based on insolvency of the employer, as provided for under the laws, regulations and administrative provisions of a Member State, and involving the partial or total divestment of the employer's assets and the appointment of a liquidator or a person performing a similar task, and the authority which is competent pursuant to national provisions has:

(a) either decided to open the proceedings, or
(b) established that the employer's undertaking or business has been definitively closed down and that the available assets are insufficient to warrant the opening of the proceedings.

---

[118] Fifth and sixth Preambular paras. See also Case 22/87 *Commission v. Italy* [1989] ECR 143.
[119] OJ [2002] L270/10.   [120] COM(2000) 832, 2.
[121] The term 'contract of employment' will be now be used to describe both the contract of employment and the employment relationship unless otherwise stated.

This new—and broader[122]—definition of insolvency was introduced by Directive 2002/74 and is based on the definition found in Article 1(1) of Regulation 1346/2000 on insolvency proceedings.[123] It covers bankruptcy (liquidation) proceedings as well as other collective insolvency proceedings.

Article 2(4) adds that the Directive allows Member States to extend workers' protection to other situations of insolvency (for example, where payments have been *de facto* stopped on a permanent basis) established by proceedings different from those laid down in Article 2(1).

2.2. Employees

'Insolvency' is the only term defined by the Directive; other terms used—employee, employer, pay and rights conferring immediate or prospective entitlement—are defined by reference to national law.[124] This measure is thus a further example of a partial harmonization Directive.

As far as 'employees' are concerned, the Court made clear in *Wagner-Miret*[125] that the Directive was intended to apply to all categories of employee defined as employees under national law. Therefore, the Spanish exclusion of higher management staff from the scope of the Directive was incompatible with Community law.

The Commission did, however, become increasingly concerned that the reference to national law for determining the definition of concepts such as 'employee' could limit the scope of the protection provided by the Directive.[126] Therefore, although Directive 2002/74 did not define 'employee', it followed the model used in the Transfers Directive 2001/23 and prohibited Member States from excluding part-time workers, within the meaning of Directive 97/81, workers with fixed term contracts within the meaning of Directive 99/70, and workers with a temporary employment relationship within the meaning of Directive 91/383/EEC.[127] Directive 2002/74 also provides that Member States may not set a minimum service requirement for workers to qualify for claims under the Directive.[128]

However, under Article 1(2) and (3), Member States may exclude two categories of employees from the scope of the Directive. First, certain categories of employees can be excluded where other forms of guarantee offer the employee protection equivalent to that conferred by the Directive.[129] In the original Directive an Annex provided further details[130] but the Annex was

---

[122] The original definition contained in the 1980 Directive was restricted to liquidation proceedings (collective settlement of creditors' claims). This definition was given a narrow interpretation by the Court in Case C–479/93 *Francovich (No. 2)* v. *Italy* [1995] ECR I–3843.

[123] OJ [2000] L160/1.   [124] Art. 2(2).

[125] Case C–334/92 *Wagner-Miret* v. *Fondo de Garant'a Salarial* [1993] ECR I–6911.

[126] COM(2000) 832, 5.   [127] Art. 2(2).   [128] Art. 2(3).   [129] Art. 1(2).

[130] E.g. the crews of sea-going vessels in Greece, Italy and the UK, and permanent and pensionable employees of local or other public authorities and certain groups of teachers in Ireland.

considered unnecessary and was removed by Directive 2002/74. Yet the principle identified by the Court in *Commission* v. *Greece*[131] remains valid: since the purpose of the Directive is to ensure a minimum degree of protection for all employees, these exclusions are possible only by way of exception and must be interpreted strictly.[132]

Secondly, the Directive allows Member States to 'continue to exclude' from the scope of the Directive (1) domestic servants employed by a natural person; and (2) share fisherman, where 'such provision already applies in their national legislation'.[133] The exclusion will apply only to those categories of workers which are expressly listed.[134]

2.3. The Application of the Provisions

The interrelationship between Articles 1 and 2 was considered in *Francovich (No. 1)* and *(No. 2)*. In *Francovich (No. 1)*[135] the applicants' employer went into liquidation leaving them with arrears of salary outstanding at a time when the Italian government had failed to implement the Directive. The Court ruled that in order to determine whether a person should be regarded as intended to benefit under the Directive a national court must verify, first, whether the person concerned was an employed person under national law and whether he was excluded from the scope of the Directive, and then ascertain whether a state of insolvency exists, as provided for in Article 2 of the Directive.

After the Court's decision in *Francovich (No. 1)* the Italian government adopted Decree-Law No. 80 (13 February 1992) transposing the Directive into national law. However, under this law, several categories of employer were excluded from proceedings to satisfy the claims of creditors collectively. In *Francovich (No. 2)*[136] the national court asked whether this was compatible with Article 2 of the Directive. Since the case concerned the definition of insolvency prior to the 2002 amendments the Court ruled that the Directive could not be relied on by employees whose contract of employment was with an employer who could not, under national law, be subject to proceedings to satisfy collectively the claims of creditors. The position is now different under the amendments.

---

[131] Case C–53/88 *Commission* v. *Greece* [1990] ECR I–3931.
[132] Case C–441/99 *Riksskatteverket* v. *Gharehveran* [2001] ECR I–7687, para. 26.
[133] Art. 1(3). Originally the excluded groups were listed in an Annex, and included, e.g. domestic servants in Spain and the Netherlands, outworkers, employees who are relatives of the employer, seasonal, casual or part-time workers in Ireland, and crews of fishing vessels in Greece and the UK. The rump of this list is now found in Art. 1(3) as a result of the amendments introduced by Dir. 2002/74.
[134] Case C–334/92 *Wagner-Miret* v. *Fondo de Garantía Salarial* [1993] ECR I–6911.
[135] Joined Cases C–6 and 9/90 [1991] ECR I–5357.
[136] Case C–479/93 *Francovich (No. 2)* v. *Italy* [1995] ECR I–3843.

3. The Protection Conferred by the Directive

The Directive provides three forms of protection for the worker: first, the payment of outstanding claims against the employer, including arrears of wages, by a specially established guarantee institution; secondly, the guarantee by the Member States that the insolvent employer's non-payment of state social security contributions does not adversely affect employees' benefit entitlement; and thirdly, in the case of former employees, the protection of their entitlement to old-age benefits under supplementary company or inter-company pension schemes. We shall examine these different types of protection in turn.

3.1. Payment by Guarantee Institutions of Employees' Claims

(a) The Content of the Right

The Directive obliges Member States to set up guarantee institutions to 'guarantee' the payment of employees' outstanding claims resulting from contracts of employment or employment relationships,[137] including, where provided for by national law, severance pay on termination of employment relationships.[138] The onus is on the Member State to lay down the detailed rules for the organization, financing (including by way of employer's contributions) and operation of the guarantee institution (Article 5).[139] By way of derogation,[140] Article 4 allows Member States to limit the liability of the guarantee institutions[141] subject to a minimum that the guarantee institution must cover the remuneration of the last three months of the employment relationship.[142] The original version of the Directive offered Member States a choice of three dates marking the beginning of the reference period within which the minimum period of guaranteed remuneration had to fall,[143] but this was considered too complicated. Directive 2002/74 simplified the rules by

---

[137] These terms are given Community meanings: Case C–160/01 *Mau v. Bundesanstalt für Arbeit* [2003] ECR I–4791, para. 41 where the Court ruled that periods during which the employment relationship is suspended on account of child raising are excluded from the period of three months because no remuneration is due in those periods.

[138] Art. 3, para. 1. Words which apply to the actual determination of the minimum guarantee must be given a uniform interpretation: Case C–160/01 *Mau v. Bundesanstalt für Arbeit* [2003] ECR I-4791, para. 41.

[139] The Member States must, however, take three principles into account: the assets of the guarantee institution must be independent of the employers' operating capital and be inaccessible to proceedings for insolvency; employers must contribute to the financing of the institution unless the costs are fully covered by the public authorities; and the guarantee institution's liabilities must not depend on whether obligations to contribute to the financing have been fulfilled.

[140] Case C–125/97 *Regeling v. Bestuur van de Bedrijfsvereniiging voor de Metaalnijverheid* [1998] ECR I–4493, para. 20.

[141] Art. 4(1).   [142] Art. 4(2), para. 1.   [143] Original Art. 3(2).

allowing the Member States to fix a date and reference period.[144] However, Article 4(2) provides that Member States may include this minimum period of three months in a reference period with a duration of not less than six months.[145] Member States having a reference period of not less than 18 months may limit the period for which outstanding claims are met by the guarantee institution to eight weeks. In this case, those periods which are most favourable to the employee are used for the calculation of the minimum period.[146]

Finally, in recognition that the Directive does not have solely welfarist objectives, Article 4(3) permits the Member States to set a ceiling for payment, so that the sums paid do not exceed 'the social objective of the Directive'. The Commission must be notified of the means of calculating this ceiling.[147] Even if the Commission has not been informed, Member States are still free to set a ceiling.[148] In *Barsotti*[149] the Court said while Member States are entitled to set a ceiling, they are bound to ensure, within the limit of that ceiling, the payment of all outstanding claims in question.[150] Any part payments received on account by employees had to be deducted from the total owed to employees[151] but they could not be deducted from the ceiling because this would undermine the social purpose of the Directive.[152]

The question of what constitutes payments that can be claimed was addressed in *Rodríguez Caballero*[153] which concerned unpaid unfair dismissal compensation (*salarios de tramitación*). The Court ruled that the Directive covers only employees' claims arising from contracts of employment or employment relationships where those claims relate to pay[154] and that pay is defined by national law.[155] This would suggest that unfair dismissal compensation could not be claimed. However, under Spanish law the guarantee institutions could meet claims relating to unfair dismissal compensation but only when the compensation had been awarded by judicial decision. In this case the compensation had been awarded as a result of conciliation and so the individual could not recover the money owed. This, the Court ruled, constituted unlawful discrimination contrary to the fundamental principle of equality which could not be objectively justified.[156]

The Spanish courts sought further clarification of this ruling in *Olaso Valero*.[157] Once again, the Court reiterated that the definition of pay was a matter for national law. However, it pointed out that Directive 2002/74 now

---

[144] Art. 3, para. 2.   [145] Art. 4(2), para. 1.   [146] Art. 4(2), para. 2.
[147] Art. 4(3), para. 2.
[148] Case C–235/95 *AGS Assedic Pas-de-Calais* v. *Dumon and Froment* [1998] ECR I–4531.
[149] Joined Cases C–19/01, C–50/01 and C–84/01 *INPS* v. *Barsotti* [2004] ECR I–000.
[150] Para. 36.   [151] Para. 37.   [152] Para. 38.
[153] Case C–442/00 *Rodríguez Caballero* v. *Fondo de Garantia Salarial* [2002] ECR I–11915.
[154] Para. 26.   [155] Art. 2(2) and para. 27.   [156] Para. 40.
[157] Case C–520/03 *José Vicente Olaso Valero* v. *Fondo de garantia Salarial* [2004] ECR I–000.

expressly referred to compensation for the termination of the employment relationship[158] as pay.

(b) Enforcement of the Rights

In *Francovich (No. 1)*[159] the Court considered Articles 3 and 4 (relating to the determination of the beneficiaries of the guarantee as well as those relating to the content of the guarantee) to be sufficiently precise and unconditional to be directly effective. The fact that the Member States had a choice as to the date from which payment of the claims were to be guaranteed (in what was old Article 3(2)) presented no obstacle.[160] However, the wide discretion conferred on the Member States by Article 5 in establishing the guarantee institution meant that Article 5 was not sufficiently precise to enable individuals to rely on it before the national court.[161] Nevertheless, in what became a seminal decision with ramifications extending far beyond the Insolvency Directive, the Court went on to say that the state would nevertheless be liable for failing to implement the Directive.[162]

Similarly in *Wagner-Miret*,[163] the Court said that the discretion given to the Member States by Article 5 of the Directive with regard to the organization, operation and financing of the guarantee institutions meant that higher management staff could not rely on the Directive to request payment of amounts owing by way of salary from the guarantee institution established for the other categories of employee. The Court then added that even when interpreted in the light of the Directive, in accordance with the principles laid down in *Marleasing*,[164] national law did not enable higher management staff to obtain the benefits provided by the guarantee institutions. However, such staff were entitled, as in *Francovich (No. 1)* itself, to request the state concerned to make good the loss and damage sustained as a result of the failure to implement the Directive.

The Directive does not lay down any time limit in which to lodge an application for insolvency compensation. Nevertheless, the Court said in *Pflücke*[165] that Member States were free to lay down such a time limit provided it was no less favourable than that governing similar domestic applications and was not framed in such as way as to render impossible in practice the exercise of rights conferred by Community law.[166]

---

[158] Para. 32.   [159] Joined Cases C–6 and C–9/90 [1991] ECR I–5357.
[160] Case 71/85 *Netherlands* v. *FNV* [1986] ECR 3855 and Case 286/85 *McDermott and Cotter* v. *Minister for Social Welfare and Attorney-General* [1987] ECR 1453.
[161] Joined Cases C–6 and 9/90 *Francovich (No. 1)* [1991] ECR I–5357.
[162] See below, nn. 190–1.
[163] Case C–334/92 [1993] ECR I–6911. Cf. Case C–441/99 *Gharehveran* [2001] ECR I–7687, para. 46 where the Member State has designated itself as liable to meet the claims under the Directive, an individual may rely on the direct effect of the provision against the states.
[164] Case 109/89 [1990] ECR I–4135.
[165] Case C–125/01 *Pflücke* v. *Bundesanstalt für Arbeit* [2003] ECR I–9375.
[166] Para. 46.

3.2. Provisions concerning Social Security Benefits

Article 6 says that Member States have the option to provide that the guarantee institution is not responsible for the contributions owed by the insolvent employer either to the national statutory social security scheme or to supplementary company or inter-company pension schemes.[167] Nevertheless, Article 7 provides that Member States *must* ensure that the non-payment by the insolvent employer of compulsory contributions to their insurance institutions under the state social security scheme does not adversely affect employees' benefit entitlement inasmuch as the employees' contributions were deducted at source from the remuneration paid.[168] In other words, as the Court explained in *Commission* v. *Italy*,[169] Member States had to choose another system for guaranteeing employees' entitlement to social security benefits.

3.3. Provisions concerning Old-age Benefits

Not only does the Directive provide some protection to workers employed at the time of employer's insolvency but it also requires Member States to protect 'the interests of employees and of persons having already left the employer's undertaking or business at the date of the onset of the employer's insolvency' in respect of rights conferring on them immediate or prospective entitlement to old-age benefits, including survivor's benefits, under occupational or supplementary schemes which fall outside the national statutory social security system.[170] However, these protective provisions do not prevent Member States from either taking measures to avoid abuses or refusing or reducing the liability of the guarantee institution if it appears that 'fulfilment of the obligation is unjustifiable because of the existence of special links between the employee and the employer and of common interests resulting in collusion between them'.[171]

4. Provisions concerning Transnational Situations

The original version of the Directive did not address the problems which inevitably arose in transnational companies where the parent in State A becomes insolvent and the guarantee institution in State B where the employee works refuses to make payments to the employees. The Court of Justice

---

[167] Art. 6. This view was confirmed by Case 22/87 *Commission* v. *Italy* [1989] ECR 143, para. 32.

[168] Art. 7. This does not explain the fate of an insolvent employer's unpaid contributions to an occupational scheme.

[169] Case 22/87 [1989] ECR 143.   [170] Art. 8.   [171] Art. 10.

considered this situation in two cases. First, *Mosbæk*[172] concerned a Danish woman working as an agent for a British company in Denmark. She was paid directly and no tax or social security contributions were deducted under Danish law. The British company was not established or registered in Denmark. The Court considered that proceedings were most often requested in the state in which the employer is established[173] and in which the employer contributed to the financing of the guarantee institution.[174] In *Mosbæk* the UK satisfied both criteria and so it was the UK's guarantee institution which had to pay. Thus, despite the apparent transnational dimension, in fact the case really concerned a single state. This can be contrasted with *Everson*[175] where there was a true transnational dimension. An Irish company was established and registered in the UK and paid its workers through its branch there, collecting the taxes and social security contributions under UK law. In this case the guarantee institution of the state of employment (the UK) was liable for payment of outstanding claims to the employees employed on that territory when the employer was placed in liquidation.

In the interests of clarity, Directive 2002/74 introduced new rules to deal with these transnational situations. Article 8a(1) provides that when an undertaking with activities in the territories of at least two Member States is in a state of insolvency 'the institution responsible for meeting employees' outstanding claims shall be that in the Member State in whose territory they work or habitually work'.[176] Article 8a(3) adds that Member States must take the measures necessary to ensure that decisions taken in the context of insolvency proceedings which have been requested in another Member State, are taken into account when determining the employer's state of insolvency. Article 8b makes provision for information sharing between the competent institutions of the Member States.

5. Abuse

Article 10 of Directive 80/987 allows Member States to take measures to prevent misuse of the Directive. As a derogation to the minimum guarantee laid down by the Directive, this provision is narrowly construed.[177] Article 10(a) provides that Member States can take measures necessary to avoid

---

[172] Case C–117/96 *Mosbæk v. Lønmodtagernes Garantifond* [1997] ECR I–5017.
[173] Para. 23.   [174] Para. 24.
[175] Case C–198/98 *Everson and Barrass v. Secretary of State for Trade and Industry* [1999] ECR I–8903, para. 19.
[176] Art. 8a(2) adds that 'The extent of employees' rights shall be determined by the law governing the competent guarantee institution.'
[177] Case C–201/01 *Walcher v. Bundesamt für Soziales und Behinderten wesen Steiermark* [2003] ECR I–8827, para. 38.

abuses.[178] According to *Walcher*,[179] the abuses referred to in Article 10(a) are 'abusive practices that adversely affect the guarantee institutions by artificially giving rise to a claim for salary, thereby illegally triggering a payment obligation on the part of those institutions'. The case concerned a husband and wife team running a company. She was an employee and a shareholder of the company. The company ran into difficulties in spring 1998. The following year the business was placed in judicial liquidation. Although Mrs Walcher had not been paid since September 1998 she was nevertheless refused a compensation payment. The Court said that while it was not abusive to try to enforce a claim against the employer who did not appear able to pay,[180] it might be abusive (although not in all cases)[181] to carry on in an employment relationship beyond the date on which an employee who was not a shareholder would have resigned (since such conduct sets up the preconditions for payment by the guarantee institution).[182]

Article 10 also provides that Member States can refuse or reduce the liability under Article 3 or the guarantee obligation under Article 7 if it appears that fulfilment of the obligation is either unjustifiable because of the existence of special links between the employee and the employer and of common interests resulting in collusion between them[183] or where the employee, on his or her own or together with his or her close relatives, is the owner of an essential part of the employer's undertaking or business and had a considerable influence on its activities.[184]

6. Implementation and Remedies

6.1. Implementation

The rules laid down are the minimum: Member States have the option of introducing laws, regulations or administrative provisions which are more favourable to employees.[185] Nevertheless, Member States were obliged at least to implement the minimum provisions of Directive 80/987 by 20 October 1983[186] and Directive 2002/74 by 8 October 2005. Furthermore, the implementation of the amendments to Directive 80/987 cannot be used as an excuse to lower the levels of protection already provided in the Member States.[187]

---

[178] Art. 10(a). Noted the careful scrutiny adopted by the Court to this (eventually unsuccessful) claim in Case C–442/00 *Rodríguez Caballero* v. *Fondo de Garantia Salarial* [2002] ECR I–11915, para. 36.

[179] Case C–201/01 [2003] ECR I-8827, para. 39.   [180] Para. 44.   [181] Para. 49.

[182] Paras. 47–8.   [183] Art. 10(b).   [184] Art. 10(c).   [185] Art. 9.

[186] Failure to implement the Directive has led to enforcement proceedings brought against Italy and Greece, see Case 22/87 *Commission* v. *Italy* [1989] ECR 143 and Case C–53/88 *Commission* v. *Greece* [1990] ECR I–3931.

[187] Art. 9, para. 2.

6.2. Remedies

Directive 80/987/EEC differs from the Directives on Transfers and Collective Redundancies in that it envisages a particular role for the state which cannot be fulfilled by any other body. Consequently, as the Court recognized in *Francovich (No. 1)*,[188] while Articles 1 and 2 were sufficiently precise and unconditional to be directly effective, the key provision of the Directive— Article 5 on the establishment of a guarantee institution—did not satisfy the requirements to be directly effective[189] and so could not be relied on by the applicants in the national court to claim arrears of salary. Instead, the Court ruled that Francovich and Bonifaci were obliged to sue the state for damages for the loss suffered due to the Italian government's failure to implement the Directive. Famously, the Court said that Member States were required to make good loss or damage caused to individuals by their failure to transpose a Directive since the principle of state liability was inherent in the system of the Treaty.[190] In *Francovich (No. 1)* the Court laid down three conditions for state liability, which it subsequently refined,[191] namely, that the rule of law infringed was intended to confer rights on individuals; the breach had to be sufficiently serious (always satisfied in the case of total failure to implement a Directive);[192] and there had to be a direct causal link between the breach of the obligation resting on the state and the damage sustained by the injured parties.[193] In *ex parte Factortame*,[194] the Court established that the reparation had to be commensurate with the loss or damage sustained, so as to ensure effective protection for the rights of the individuals harmed. Subject to this, it was on the basis of the rules of national law on liability that the state had to make reparation for the consequences of the loss or damage caused. However,

---

[188] Joined Cases C–6/90 and C–9/90 *Francovich (No. 1)* v. *Italy* [1991] ECR I–5357.

[189] In Joined Cases C–140/91, C–141/91, C–278/91 and C–279/91 *Suffritti* v. *INPS* [1992] ECR I–6337 the Court, however, held that the plaintiffs could not rely on the provisions of the Directive since both the declarations of insolvency and the termination of the employment relationships took place before the expiry of the time limit for the implementation of the Directive. The Court reminded the parties that it is only where a Member State has not correctly implemented a Directive within the period of implementation laid down that individuals can rely on rights which derive directly from provisions of the Directive before their national courts.

[190] Joined Cases C–6 and C–9/90 *Francovich (No. 1)* [1991] ECR I–5357.

[191] Joined Cases C–6 and C–9/90 [1991] ECR I–5357, para. 35; Joined Cases C–46/93 and C–48/93 *Brasserie du pêcheur and ex parte Factortame and Others* [1996] ECR I–1029, para. 31; Case C–392/93 *R* v. *Secretary of State for Trade and Industry, ex parte British Telecommunications* [1996] ECR I–1631, para. 38; and Case C–5/94 *R* v. *MAFF, ex parte Hedley Lomas* [1996] ECR I–2553, para. 24.

[192] Joined Cases C–178/94, C–179/94, C–188/94, C–189/94 and C–190/94 *Dillenkofer and Others* v. *Bundesrepublik Deutschland* [1996] ECR I–4845, para. 20.

[193] Joined Cases C–46/93 and C–48/93 *ex parte Factortame* [1996] ECR I–1029, para. 51; Case C–392/93 *ex parte British Telecommunications* [1996] ECR I–1631, para. 39; Case C–5/94 *ex parte Hedley Lomas* [1996] ECR I–2553, para. 25; and Joined Cases C–178/94, C–179/94, C–188/94, C–189/94 and C–190/94 *Dillenkofer and Others* [1996] ECR I–4845, para. 21.

[194] Para. 82.

the conditions for reparation of loss or damage laid down by national law could not be less favourable than those relating to similar domestic claims and could not be framed as to make it virtually impossible or excessively difficult to obtain reparation.

Finally, in *Maso*[195] and *Bonifaci*[196] the Court considered the extent of the reparation for the loss or damage arising from such failure. The Court said that in making good the loss or damage sustained by employees as a result of the belated transposition of the Directive, a Member State was entitled to apply retroactively the belated implementing measures to such employees, including rules against aggregation or other limitations on the liability of the guarantee institution, provided that the Directive had been properly transposed. However, it was for the national court to ensure that reparation of the loss or damage sustained by the beneficiaries was adequate. Retroactive and proper application in full of the measures implementing the Directive would suffice, unless the beneficiaries established the existence of complementary loss sustained on account of the fact that they were unable to benefit at the appropriate time from the financial advantages guaranteed by the Directive. If so, such loss also had to be made good.

Finally, in *Palmisani*[197] the Court ruled that Community law allowed Member States to require any action for reparation of the loss or damage sustained as a result of the belated transposition of Directive 80/987/EEC to be brought within a limitation period of one year from the date of its transposition into national law, provided that the limitation period was no less favourable than procedural requirements in respect of similar actions of a domestic nature.

D. CONCLUSIONS

Restructuring is currently the name of the game for the European Union. As the Commission put it in its Communication, *Restructuring and Employment*,[198] drafted in connection with the relaunched Lisbon strategy, restructuring must be well-managed to meet a two-fold economic and social requirement. *Enterprises* have to adapt to change and must do so rapidly to preserve and enhance their competitiveness; and *workers* have to be adaptable to be able to move from one job to another 'of equivalent quality'. This is, of course, not new, and the 1970s Directives on Employee Rights on Restructuring Enterprises, broadly aimed to achieve very similar objectives. What is new is that the Social Partners are now being used to achieve these objectives.

---

[195] Case C–373/95 [1997] ECR I–4051.
[196] Joined Cases C–94/95 and C–95/95 *Bonifaci v. INPS* [1997] ECR I–3969.
[197] Case C–261/95 *Palmisani v. INPS* [1997] ECR I–4025.
[198] Communication, *Restructuring and employment. Anticipating and accompanying restructuring in order to develop employment: the role of the European Union* COM(2005) 120.

The emphasis on a legal approach found in the 1970s is being replaced by softer methods, in particular OMC. For example, the Commission encourages the Social Partners to reach agreement on the requisite ways and means for implementing mechanisms for applying and monitoring existing guidelines on restructuring, and a discussion on the way forward and encouraging the adoption of best practices setting out existing guidelines on restructuring, promoting best practice. The role of the Social Partners—and other forms of worker representatives—in managing change is considered further in the next two chapters.

PART VI

Collective Labour Law

15

Worker Involvement in Decision-Making: Information, Consultation, and Worker Participation

A. INTRODUCTION

This chapter and the next concern the collective dimension of labour law in the EU. Collective labour law traditionally embraces the body of rules regulating the relationship between the collectivity of employees and employers/groups of employers. The diversity of collective labour law is reflected in the Community Charter of Fundamental Social Rights 1989 and the EU Charter of Fundamental Rights 2000. Both documents envisage a range of collective rights: rights of information, consultation and participation for workers,[1] freedom of association for employers and workers,[2] the right to 'negotiate and conclude collective agreements,[3] and the right to resort to collective action including strikes.[4] With the exception of the right to join or not to join a trade union, reference is made in all cases to national legislation and practice to clarify the substance and exercise of these rights. The reference to national law is explained in part by the absence of clear Community competence in the broad field of collective labour law. In particular, Article 137(5) excludes 'pay, the right of association, the right to strike or the right to impose lock-outs' from the Community's competence, or at least from its competence under Article 137. Because of this uncertainty about competence, only the rights to information, consultation and participation of workers' representatives, and collective bargaining have assumed any concrete form in the Community legal order.

In this chapter we shall consider the various steps taken by the Community to require employees—or more usually their representatives (union or non-union)—to be informed, consulted, and even to participate in the employer's

---

[1] Arts. 17–18 of the Social Charter 1989 and Arts. 27–28 of the EU Charter 2000 (Arts. II–87–88 of the Constitutional Treaty).

[2] Art. 11 of the Social Charter 1989 and Art. 12 of the EU Charter 2000 (Art. II–72 of the Constitutional Treaty).

[3] Art. 12 of the Social Charter 1989 and Art. 28 of the EU Charter 2000 (Art. II–88 of the Constitutional Treaty).

[4] Art. 13 of the Social Charter 1989 and Art. 28 of the EU Charter 2000 (Art. II–88 of the Constitutional Treaty). The internal orders of the Member States are free to determine the conditions and the extent of the application of the rights laid down in Arts. 11–13 of the Social Charter 1989 to the armed forces, police, and civil service.

decision-making. In the next chapter we consider the (limited) action taken by
the Community in the field of collective rights as they affect trade unions and
their members. In particular, we focus on the extent to which the Community
has encouraged the development of collective bargaining at EU, national, and
subnational levels.

B. INFORMATION, CONSULTATION, AND PARTICIPATION: SETTING THE SCENE

1. Introduction

In recent years, the Community has focused particular attention on
encouraging dialogue between workers/their representatives and their
employers. This is because the Community sees a clear link between dialogue
and greater productivity:[5]

> Regular, transparent, comprehensive dialogue creates trust . . . The systematic devel-
> opment of social dialogue within companies, nationally and at European level is
> fundamental to managing change and preventing negative social consequences and
> deterioration of the social fabric . . . Social dialogue ensures a balance is maintained
> between corporate flexibility and workers' [security].[6]

The argument runs that workers who participate in decisions which affect
them enjoy a greater degree of job satisfaction and should be more productive
than those who simply accept orders.[7] Social dialogue, replacing the more
traditional hierarchical management arrangements, is therefore seen as the
cornerstone of corporate governance designed to create a high skill, high
effort, high trust European labour market which now lies at the core of the
European Employment Strategy (EES).[8]

   Some have doubted the validity of these claims. Cheffins,[9] for example,
argues that employees are often cynical about worker participation measures
and so employers have little to gain by keeping in place whatever participative
measures they have introduced; that, over time, employees in high-effort workplaces have an incentive to free-ride off the efforts of fellow members; that
the *quid pro quo* for flexibility, job security, creates a cozy environment where
there is little likelihood of being fired which might hurt production levels, and
a low turnover of staff gives little chance for promotion. This, in turn, may
have a negative impact on flexibility, as would any formalized, bureaucratic

---

   [5] See COM(98) 592 discussed further below.
   [6] Final Report of the High Level Group on economic and social implications of industrial
change, November 1998, 9.
   [7] Cheffins, *Company Law: Theory, Structure and Operation* (OUP, Oxford, 1997).
   [8] See further Ch. 3.   [9] Cheffins, above, n. 7, 583–5, 588.

decision-making process[10] which might cause a company to postpone facing economic realities and defer changes which are required to foster the company's long-term growth and development.

Nevertheless, the Community documents continue to emphasize the value of social dialogue. For example, the Final Report of the High Level Group on the economic and social implications of industrial change,[11] published late in 1998, concluded that 'top-performing companies have a good social dialogue with their employees because motivated people are the vital component for commercial success'. The Group considered 'necessary the initiatives taken by the European Union, corporations, the social partners and governments to create a broader, high quality system of information and consultation'.[12]

Some of the inspiration for the Community's emphasis on the benefits of social dialogue comes from an examination of the success in the past of the German economy, which has been attributed in part to the well established system of co-determination (*Mitbestimmung*). Under this system workers are involved in decision-making not only at plant level through works councils,[13] but also at company level through the membership of workers' representatives on the supervisory board controlling the company.[14]

However, while a positive case can be made for social dialogue, the development of Community rules can also be considered defensive. A co-determination system is expensive and has inevitably raised fears about social dumping[15]—that in the absence of Community regulation companies will incorporate in countries which take a low-cost approach to employment relations.[16] Until recently this has not been a real problem in the EU since most countries operate the *siège réel* doctrine whereby a company's 'real seat'

---

[10] Citing Lane, *Management and Labour in Europe: The Industrial Enterprise in Germany, Britain and France* (E. Elgar Ltd, Aldershot, 1989) 232 and 236, and Hopt, 'Labor Representation on Corporate Boards: Impacts and Problems for Corporate Governance and Integration in Europe' (1994) 14 *Int. Rev. of Law and Econ.*, 203, 207–8, 210–11, 214.

[11] Commission, *Managing Change*, Gyllenhamer Report, November 1998, 5, http://europa.eu.int/comm/dg05/soc-dial/gyllenhamer/gyllen-en.pdf.

[12] Ibid. See also the Davignon Report, 'European System of Worker Involvement, with regard to the European Company Statute and other Pending proposals', and the Gyllenhammer Report, 'Interim Report of the High Level Expert Group on the Economic and Social Impact of Industrial Change'.

[13] Co-determination means employee representatives sharing responsibility with management for making decisions in areas such as organization of working time, methods of remuneration, leave arrangements, health and safety and bonus arrangements.

[14] See Adams, 'The Right to Participate' (1992) 5 *Employee Resp. and Rts J.*, 91, 94 and 97, and Thelan, *Union of Parts: Labor Politics in Postwar Germany* (Cornell University Press, Ithaca, NY, 1991) 1–5, 25–32, cited and discussed in Cheffins, above, n. 7, 582. Cf. Kraft, 'Empirical Studies on Codetermination: A Selective Survey and Research Design', in Nutzinger and Backhaus (eds), *Co-determination: A Discussion of Different Approaches* (Springer-Verlag, Berlin, 1989).

[15] These arguments are considered further in Ch. 1.

[16] See, e.g., Wiesmann, 'German Companies flee to the UK', *Financial Times*, 24 May 2006 which reports that Air Berlin, the low-cost airline, opted to become Germany's first UK plc, in part due to its desire to avoid the German system of co-determination.

is the country where its central administration or principal place of business is located. Therefore, a company incorporated in the UK, but with its plant and operations in Germany, will be considered under German law to have its real seat in Germany. The decision of the Court in *Centros*[17] has, however, cast doubt on the compatibility of the real seat doctrine with Community law. This, in turn, may create further pressure for the enactment of Community legislation on worker representation to protect existing worker participation structures.

2. Different Forms of Worker Involvement

What forms, then, can worker involvement take? *Participation* can be regarded as a generic term[18] embracing all types of industrial democracy,[19] ranging from the provision of information, consultation, and collective bargaining to more extensive involvement in the employer's decision-making process. The provision of *information*, the least intense form of worker involvement, is unilateral: the information is provided by management to workers or their representatives (trade unions or elected worker representatives). *Consultation*, on the other hand, is bilateral, giving workers' representatives the opportunity to make their views known. However, the final decision usually remains with the employers and that decision may or may not reflect the workers' views. This is the weak form of consultation.[20] A stronger approach to consultation brings consultation closer to collective bargaining because, as with Article 2 of Directive 98/59/EC[21] on collective redundancies, employers must consult with the workers' representatives 'with a view to reaching agreement'.[22]

---

[17] Case C–212/97 *Centros v. Erhvervs-og Selskabsstyrelsen* [1999] ECR I–1459. Deakin, 'Two Types of Regulatory Competition: Competitive Federalism Versus Reflexive Harmonisation. A Law and Economics Perspective on *Centros*' (1999) 2 *CYELS*. 231; Siems (2002) 27 *ELRev.* 47; Cabral and Cunha, ' "Presumed Innocent": Companies and the Exercise of the Right of Establishment under Community Law' (2000) 25 *ELRev.* 157.

[18] As we shall see below, in the context of certain Directives, 'participation' has a specific legal meaning.

[19] See generally Kahn-Freund, 'Industrial Democracy' (1977) 6 *ILJ*. 65; Davies and Wedderburn, 'The Land of Industrial Democracy' (1977) 6 *ILJ*. 197.

[20] See, e.g., Art. 2(g) of ECS Dir. 2003/72 (OJ [2003] L207/25); ' "consultation" means the establishment of dialogue and exchange of views between the body representative of the employees and/or the employees' representatives and the competent organ of the SCE, at a time, in a manner and with a content which allows the employees' representatives, on the basis of information provided, to express an opinion on measures envisaged by the competent organ which may be taken into account in the decision-making process within the SCE'.

[21] OJ [1999] L225/16.

[22] See also Case C–188/03 *Junk* [2005] ECR I–000, para. 44: 'It thus appears that Article 2 of the Directive imposes an obligation to negotiate'. See further Ch. 14.

At the other end of the spectrum, the most intense forms of worker involvement are, on the one hand participation on the company's board, a distinguishing feature of the German and Dutch systems, which is now a possibility also provided for by the European Company Statute,[23] and, on the other, collective bargaining. Traditionally, collective bargaining is a function carried out by trade unions and is usually linked to the right to strike: strike action is a union's principal sanction if the employer does not co-operate in the negotiations. This issue is considered further in chapter 16.

Participation (used in its generic sense) can be direct or indirect.[24] *Direct participation* permits *individual* employees to take part directly in decision-making or other company processes by, for example, participating in company finances through profit related pay or equity sharing. It can also include involvement in decision-making, particularly at workplace level. Such participation is designed primarily to promote motivation in order to achieve company goals such as increased productivity, better quality control and a greater sense of loyalty. However, it is also considered the least legitimate form of worker participation since workers, unlike trade unions, are not independent from their employers.

Indirect or *'representative' participation*, by contrast, involves procedures through which workers are *collectively* represented in the company's decision-making processes. The purpose of such participation is primarily the representation of interests. This participation can loosely be divided into three categories: first, collective bargaining; second, employee representatives sitting on the company's board (where their involvement is limited to structural matters at company level);[25] and thirdly, the establishment of works councils (or equivalent bodies) whose rights comprise the disclosure of information, consultation and co-determination over areas of concern at plant, company or group level. These types of indirect participation are designed to improve worker representation in the decision-making process. This, it is believed, will improve operational efficiency because problems are identified and resolved at an earlier stage, employers can put into practice employee's ideas to improve production processes, and workers feel a greater commitment to decisions in which they are involved or represented.[26] Further, it is thought that giving workers a voice discourages them from 'quitting', thereby reducing labour costs.

---

[23] See e.g. Art. 7(2) of Dir. 2003/72 (OJ [2003] L207/25).

[24] Gold and Hall, 'Legal Regulation and the Practice of Employee Participation in the European Community, European Foundation for the Improvement of Living and Working Conditions', EF/WP/90/41/EN, 26.

[25] Ibid.

[26] See, e.g. the British Labour Government's *Fairness at Work* White Paper, Cm. 3968 HMSO, London, 1998, 12.

3. Developments at Community Level

At Community level, the communiqué issued by the heads of state at the Paris summit in 1972 made reference to the importance of increasing the involvement of the Social Partners in the economic and social decisions of the Community,[27] a view endorsed by the 1974 Action Programme.[28]

At first the Community concentrated its efforts on the provision of information and the requirement to consult in specific fields, most notably health and safety,[29] collective redundancies[30] and transfer of undertakings.[31] However, there was continued resistance to the introduction of a more general, systematic and institutionalized right to employee participation in corporate decision-making for fear that it would cut across established national systems of worker involvement. The long and tortuous legislative history of various proposals over the last four decades bears testimony to this.[32] In particular, proposals for a European Company Statute date back to 1970, and for national level information and consultation to 1980 with the 'Vredling' proposal.[33] The difficulties created by radically different perceptions of worker representation in the Member States made it difficult to agree on a single approach. However, the Community Social Charter of 1989 and subsequently the EU Charter of Fundamental Rights 2000 recognized workers' rights to information and consultation as fundamental social rights. For example, Article 27 of the Charter of 2000 provides:

Workers or their representatives must, at the appropriate levels, be guaranteed information and consultation in good time in the cases and under the conditions provided for by Union law and national laws and practices.[34]

Article 21 of the revised European Social Charter 1996 of the Council of Europe is more prescriptive, encouraging workers or their representatives,

---

[27] Final declaration, EC Bull. 10/1972, 15–24.

[28] OJ [1974] C13/1, EC Bull. 2/1974. The Commission has also taken the view that the structure and activities of Community enterprises, esp. transnational enterprises, must be sufficiently transparent for the benefit of shareholders, creditors, employees, and the public interest in general. See Commission's Communication on *Multinational Undertakings and the Community*, EC Bull. Supp. 15/1973.

[29] The Framework Dir. 89/391/EEC on health and safety (OJ [1989] L183/1), discussed in Ch. 11.

[30] Council Dir. 75/129/EEC (OJ [1975] L48/29) as amended by Council Dir. 92/56/EC (OJ [1992] L245/3) and consolidated in Council Dir. 98/59/EC (OJ [1998] L225/16) considered in Ch. 14.

[31] See Council Dir. 77/187/EEC (OJ [1977] L61/126) as amended by Council Dir. 98/50/EC (OJ [1998] L201/88) and consolidated in Dir. 2001/23 considered in Ch. 13.

[32] See generally, Kolvenbach, 'EEC Company Law Harmonisation and Worker Participation' (1990) 11 *University of Pennsylvania Journal of International Business Law* 709.

[33] See below n. 184.   [34] Art. II–87 of the Constitutional Treaty.

again in accordance with national legislation and practice, to be informed regularly about the economic and financial situation of the undertaking employing them, and to be consulted in good time on proposed decisions which could substantially affect the interests of workers, particularly in respect of those decisions which could have an important impact on the employment situation of the undertaking. It is supplemented by Article 28 which requires states to support worker representatives by protecting them against detrimental treatment, including dismissal, and providing them with facilities to carry out their tasks.

As Davies points out, some rights theorists are sceptical about the value of the right to be informed and consulted, arguing that it is the 'second best' option to collective bargaining which offers a more effective form of participation because the presence of a trade union helps to equalize the bargaining power of workers and management. On the other hand, others argue that the right to be consulted sits closely alongside other procedural rights such as a right to a hearing, and, on this basis, the right to consultation is an important aspect of the more general right to a fair hearing at work.[35] This argument, together with the more general view that worker participation is good for productivity, have influenced the EU's approach to the need for legislation in this field. But how was the Community to push through the long-standing proposals on worker consultation provision? The answer lay in a new approach: a shift away from requiring consultation on specific issues (collective redundancies, health and safety, etc) and instead requiring employers to set up a mechanism, when asked to do so by their staff, in which to consult workers or their representatives on a regular basis. The adoption of the European Works Council Directive 94/45, based on encouraging workers and their employers to reach an agreement on what form worker participation should take in their workplace, with the sanction that the stricter subsidiary requirements found in the Annex would apply if they did not, paved the way for the adoption of a number of other Directives, notably the Directives on national-level information and consultation, Directive 2002/14[36] and Directive 2003/72[37] on worker participation in the European Company.

C. EUROPEAN WORKS COUNCILS

1. Background to the Adoption of the Directive

While the focus on developing Community rules on information and consultation at *national* level risked stepping on the toes of existing national

---

[35] Davies, *Perspectives on Labour Law* (CUP, Cambridge, 2004), 178.
[36] OJ [2002] L80/29.   [37] OJ [2003] L207/25.

structures, the Community realized that there might be a role for Community legislation dealing with the *transnational* provision of information. While the Directives on Collective Redundancies[38] and Transfer of Undertakings[39] did address the problem in part, their limited scope proved to be inadequate. A number of multinationals, mostly French and German (BSN, Bull, Elf-Aquitaine, Pechiney, Rhône-Poulenc, Saint Gobain, Thomson, Nestlé, Allianz, Volkswagen, and Mercedes-Benz), were already ahead of the game. They had established various types of jointly agreed European-level information and consultation arrangements.[40] These were influenced by the French basic model: a joint management/employee forum meeting annually, at the employer's expense, to discuss information provided by management about group-level matters relating to corporate strategy, finances, and employment.[41]

These precedents showed the Commission the way forward:[42] Community legislation could focus on the transnational dimension of employee information and consultation,[43] accommodating, but not cutting across, national practice in respect of employee representation,[44] in order to bridge the gap between increasingly transnational corporate decision-making and workers' nationally defined and nationally confined information and consultation rights.[45]

However, the UK remained implacably opposed to the principle of the proposed Directive,[46] arguing that such a Directive would undermine existing successful arrangements for consultation, particularly at local levels; that it would impose new statutory restrictions on a company's freedom to implement decisions and consequently would cause costly delays; and that the Directive would deter inward investment, rendering firms more prone to settle

---

[38] Council Dir. 75/129/EEC (OJ [1975] L48/29). This Directive was amended by Council Dir. 92/56/EEC (OJ [1992] L245/13) to reflect the increasing transnationalization of companies and consolidated by Council Dir. 98/59/EC (OJ [1998] L225/16). See further Ch. 14.

[39] Council Dir. 77/187/EEC (OJ [1977] L61/26). This Directive was revised by Dir. 98/50 (OJ [1998] L201/88) and was subsequently consolidated in Dir. 2001/23 (OJ [2001] L82/16). See further Ch. 13.

[40] Marginson, 'European Integration and Trans-national Management—Union Relations in the Enterprise' (1992) *BJIR*. 529, 540. The operation of these bodies is considered in Gold and Hall, *European Level Information and Consultation in Multi-National Companies: An Evaluation of Practice*, European Foundation for the Improvement of Living and Working Conditions (OPEC, Luxembourg, 1992).

[41] Hall, *Legislating for Employee Participation: A Case Study of the European Works Council Directive*, 1992, Warwick Papers in Industrial Relations, 4. An expanded version of this can be found in Hall, 'Behind the European Works Councils Directive: The European Commission's Legislative Strategy' (1992) 30 *BJIR*. 547.

[42] COM(90) 581, para. 17.

[43] See also the Opinion of the Economic and Social Committee on the social consequences of cross-frontier mergers (OJ [1989] C329/10).

[44] Commission Social Charter Action Programme, *Social Europe* (Special Edn) 1/90, 66.

[45] Gold and Hall, 'Statutory European Works Councils: the Final Countdown?' (1994) 25 *IRJ*. 177, 178.

[46] See COM(90) 581.

in only one Member State[47] or discourage them from expanding above the employee threshold set by the Directive. It also said that the EWCs would impose a form of collective arrangement which would undermine the many successful local employee involvement practices currently in place and weaken the important role played in them by individual employees.[48] Since the proposal was based on Article 94, the UK was able to block its adoption.

In October 1993 the Commission abandoned its attempt to secure unanimous agreement on the Directive and proposed reintroducing the measure under the Social Policy Agreement (SPA) instead, but this time providing for a choice between an EWC and an Information and Consultation Procedure (ICP). The Social Partners were consulted, as required by Article 3(2) (new Article 138(2)),[49] and then the Commission produced a revised draft where the term 'European Works Council' was dropped and replaced by 'information and consultation structure', albeit that the structure remained very similar to the EWC of earlier drafts.[50] This draft formed the basis for unsuccessful negotiations between the Social Partners. UNICE, the employers' association, considered that employee participation measures should not be regulated or harmonized by the Community but should be allowed to evolve naturally, to reflect local circumstances. It also considered that too much emphasis was placed by the Commission on regulated collective relationships between employers and trade unions or workers' representatives and not enough on direct employee contact and involvement with management.[51] Meanwhile, ETUC, the trade union body, strongly favoured the introduction of measures encouraging employee participation and called for a basic European legal framework to guarantee the information, consultation and participation rights of workers' representatives at all levels of decision-making within undertakings.[52]

With the breakdown of talks between the Social Partners, the Commission issued a further proposal aimed at establishing either a 'European Committee',[53] *or* a procedure for informing and consulting employees,[54] the more flexible alternative emphasized by the Belgian Presidency in 1993.[55] However,

---

[47] Cf. Visser, 'Works Councils and Trade Unions in the Netherlands: Rivals or Allies?' (1993) 29 *The Netherlands' Journal of Social Sciences* 64, esp. 86–7.

[48] Employment Department, *The United Kingdom in Europe: People, Jobs and Progress*, August 1993, 6–17.

[49] EIRR 241, 28.   [50] See further EIRR 242, 13.

[51] UNICE Press Release, 24 October 1989, cited in Gold and Hall, *Legal Regulation and the Practice of Employee Participation in the European Community*, European Foundation for the Improvement of Living and Working Conditions, Working Paper No. EF/WP/90/41/EN.

[52] Gold and Hall, above, n. 24, 46. Despite these disagreements a working party set up as a result of the Val Duchesse social dialogue did manage to identify some common ground as to the need for information and consultation on the introduction of new technology (6 March 1987).

[53] This term reflects the terminology used in voluntary information and consultation arrangements.

[54] COM(94) 134 final (OJ [1994] C199/10).   [55] Art. 1(2).

the term 'European Works Council' was reinstated in the final version of the Directive 94/45/EC[56] adopted in September 1994. Since the Directive was adopted under the SPA, the UK was initially excluded, but when the Labour government signed up to the Social Chapter in 1997, the Directive was extended to the UK.[57]

2. The Thresholds Laid Down by the Directive

The requirement to establish an EWC or a procedure for informing and consulting (ICP) employees applies only to Community-scale undertakings and Community-scale groups of undertakings[58] with more than 1,000 employees across the 28 Member States[59] and with at least two establishments[60] in different Member States each employing at least 150 people.[61] In *Bofrost*[62] the Court said that the employees' right to information in Article 11[63] existed even before it was ascertained whether there existed within the group a controlling undertaking.[64] This right to information enabled workers' representatives to obtain information about, for example, the structure or organization of a group of undertakings,[65] and the average total number of employees and their distribution across the Member States,[66] in order to establish whether the thresholds laid down by the Directive had been met to support a demand that negotiations for the establishment of an EWC/ICP be opened.[67]

The Directive also applies where Community-scale undertakings or groups of undertakings have their headquarters outside the territory of the Member

---

[56] OJ [1994] L254/64.   [57] Council Directive 97/74/EC (OJ [1997] L10/20).

[58] Art. 1(1) and (2). A group of undertakings means a controlling undertaking, defined to mean an undertaking which can exercise a dominant influence over another undertaking by virtue of ownership, financial participation or the rules which govern it (Art. 3(1) and (2)) and its controlled undertakings (Art. 2(1)(b)). These definitions are based on EP and Council Dir. 2004/18 (OJ [2004] L134/114), on the co-ordination of procedures for the award of public works contracts, public supply contracts and public service contracts.

[59] Art. 2(1)(a). The prescribed thresholds for the size of the workforce are to be based on the average number of employees, including part-time employees, employed during the previous two years calculated according to national legislation and/or practice (Art. 2(2)).

[60] In the case of Community scale groups of undertakings, read groups of undertakings in the place of establishments (Art. 2(1)(c)).

[61] Art. 2(1)(a) and (c). Member States may provide that this Directive does not apply to merchant navy crews (Art. 1(5)).

[62] Case C–62/99 *Betriebsrat de Bofrost* v. *Bofrost Josef H. Boquoi Deutschland West GmbH & Co. KG* [2001] ECR I–2579. See generally, Waas, 'The European Court of Justice and Directive 94/45/EC on the Establishment of European Works Councils' [2005] *European Company Law* 138.

[63] See below, n. 93.   [64] Para. 34.   [65] Para. 39.

[66] Case C–349/01 *Betriebsrat der Firma ADS Anker GmbH* v. *ADS Anker GmbH* [2004] ECR I–6803, para. 65. The Advocate General suggested that the provision of information on corporate structure and documentation should be subject to confidentiality requirements but the Court of Justice did not add this requirement.

[67] Para. 32. See also Case C–440/00 *Kühne* v. *Nagel* [2004] ECR I–787, para. 46.

States but meet the threshold requirements in the 28 Member States.[68] In this 'extra-territorial' situation, the Directive deems legal responsibility for carrying out the Directive's requirements: responsibility falls on either a representative agent of the undertaking or group of undertakings or the undertaking with the highest number of employees in the territory of the Member States.[69]

The importance of the deeming provisions have been highlighted by *Kühne* v. *Nagel*[70] and *Anker*.[71] In *Kühne* v. *Nagel* the Court said that the other undertakings belonging to the group and located in the Member States were under an obligation to assist the deemed central management in creating the conditions necessary for the establishment of an EWC or ICP, in particular by supplying it with the necessary information. *Anker* concerned the reverse situation: the obligation by the central management or deemed central management to supply information to workers' representatives. The Court said that not only must the information be supplied but also the Directive required that the information be supplied to employees' representatives through their undertaking in the group to which those representatives submitted a request in the first place.[72] The representatives were not required to submit requests for information directly to central management or deemed central management since this might discourage employees from exercising their rights.[73]

3. The Negotiating Procedure

The Directive envisages a two-stage approach to the establishment of an EWC or ICP (see Figure 15.1). The first stage involves voluntary negotiations. If there is no agreement or the parties so decide, then the mandatory ('subsidiary') provisions laid down in the annex of the Directive are triggered at the second stage.

3.1. Starting the Negotiations

The procedure for the first stage is activated at the initiative of central management of the undertaking or the controlling undertaking in a group of undertakings[74] or at the written request of at least 100 employees or their representatives[75] in at least two undertakings in at least two Member

---

[68] Art. 4(2).   [69] Art. 4(2).   [70] Case C–440/00 *Kühne* v. *Nagel* [2004] ECR I–787.
[71] Case C–349/01 *Betriebsrat der Firma ADS Anker GmbH* v. *ADS Anker GmbH* [2004] ECR I–6803, para. 49.
[72] Para. 56.   [73] Para. 59.   [74] Art. 2(1)(e).
[75] Employees' representatives means the employees' representatives provided for by national law or practice (Art. 2(1)(d)), a definition drawn from Council Dirs. 98/59 on collective redundancies and 2001/23 on transfers of undertakings.

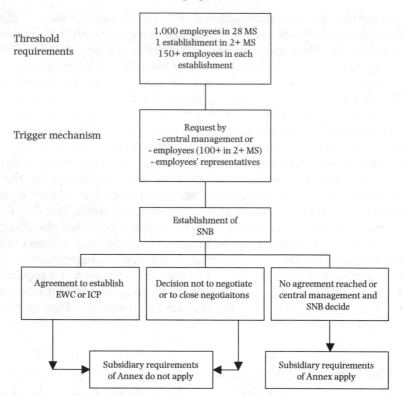

Figure 15.1 The Procedure under the EWC Directive 94/95

States.[76] This prevents an EWC from being imposed from the outside: the parties must actually want it. However, the onus is on central management to create the conditions and means necessary for the establishment of an EWC or ICP.[77]

3.2. The Outcome of the Negotiations

When a request has been received, a 'special negotiating body' (SNB)—essentially an employee representation body[78]—of between three and 17 members[79] must be set up. Individual Member States must determine the method to be used for the election or appointment of the members of

---

[76] Art. 5(1).   [77] Art. 4(1).
[78] Case C–349/01 *Betriebsrat der Firma ADS Anker GmbH* v. *ADS Anker GmbH* [2004] ECR I–6803, para. 49.
[79] Art. 5(2)(b).

the SNB.[80] Central management must then convene a meeting with the SNB.[81]

There are three possible outcomes of the meetings between the SNB and central management. First, they are able to conclude, possibly with the assistance of experts,[82] a written agreement on the scope, composition, functions and term of office of the EWC(s) or the arrangements for implementing an ICP.[83] If they succeed in reaching an agreement to establish an EWC, the agreement should include details of the undertakings covered by the agreement, the composition of the EWC, the number of members, the allocation of seats and the term of office, the function and procedure for informing and consulting the EWC, the venue, frequency and duration of meetings of the EWC, the financial and material resources to be allocated to the EWC, the duration of the agreement, and the procedure for its renegotiation.[84]

If central management and the SNB decide to establish an ICP instead, the agreement must specify the methods by which the employees' representatives have the right to meet to discuss the information conveyed to them.[85] The information supplied must relate, in particular, to transnational questions which significantly affect workers' interests.[86] Whether an EWC or ICP is established, the minimum requirements laid down in the Annex do not need to be incorporated into the agreement.[87]

The second possible outcome is that the SNB decides, by at least two-thirds of the votes, not to open negotiations or to terminate the negotiations already opened. In this case the provisions in the Annex again do not apply and a new request to convene the SNB cannot be made for at least two years, unless the parties lay down a shorter period.[88]

The third possible outcome is that, after three years of negotiations, the parties cannot reach an agreement on the nature, function or powers of the EWC, or if management fails to initiate negotiations within six months of the request being made, or if the two parties prefer, then the requirements laid down by the legislation of the Member State in which the central management is situated will apply, which must include the 'subsidiary' requirements set out in the annex.[89] Thus negotiators are fully aware that

---

[80] Art. 5(2)(a). The right to elect or appoint members of the SNB must apply equally to employees in those undertakings 'in which there are no employees' representatives through no fault of their own'. Special rules apply to ensure an even representation of employees (Art. 5(2)(c)). Central management and local management must be informed of the composition of the SNB (Art. 5(2)(d)).

[81] Art. 5(4). Expenses relating to the negotiations must be borne by the central management (Art. 5(6)).

[82] Art. 5(4), para. 2. Member States may limit funding to one expert only (Art. 5(6), para. 2).

[83] Art. 5(3).   [84] Art. 6(2).   [85] Art. 6(3), paras. 1 and 2.

[86] Art. 6(3), para. 3.

[87] Art. 6(4). Sixty-three agreements have been concluded under Article 6 (http://www.eurofound. ie/ewc/).

[88] Art. 5(5).   [89] Art. 7(1) and (2).

failure to reach an agreement will result in a mandatory procedure being imposed, or as Bercusson describes it, they bargain in the shadow of the law.[90] Putting it another way, law 'steers' negotiation: through the use of a 'penalty default' rule (the application of the subsidiary requirements), the more powerfully placed and better-informed party (the employer) is induced to enter into a bargaining process when it would otherwise lack an incentive to do so.[91]

4. The Subsidiary Requirements

So what do the subsidiary requirements provide? In fact, the Annex lays down fairly modest requirements regarding the composition[92] and operating methods of the EWC, requiring a minimum of one information and consultation meeting per year on the basis of a report drawn up by central management covering such issues as:

- the structure, economic and financial situation of the business;
- the probable development of the business and of production and sales;
- the employment situation and future trends;
- investments and substantial changes concerning the organization of the business;
- the introduction of new working methods or production processes;
- transfers of production;
- mergers and cut-backs or closures of undertakings or collective redundancies.[93]

In addition to the annual information and consultation meeting of the EWC, the annex requires that a 'select' committee,[94] a type of executive committee of the EWC, be informed of important decisions on matters such as relocation, closures, and collective redundancies. At its request, the select committee will have the right to meet central management or any other more appropriate level of management so as to be informed and consulted on measures significantly affecting employees' interests.[95]

---

[90] Bercusson, 'Maastricht: A Fundamental Change in European Labour Law' (1992) 23 *IRJ*. 177.

[91] I.Ayres and R.Gertner, 'Filling Gaps in Incomplete Contracts: a Theory of Default Rules' (1989) 99 *YLJ*. 87.

[92] The EWC shall be composed of employees of the Community scale undertaking or group of undertakings or appointed from their number by the employees' representatives or in their absence the entire body of employees. The EWC will have between 3 and 30 members.

[93] Annex, para. 2. According to Art. 12(1), the Directive does not affect measures taken pursuant to the Directives on collective redundancies (98/59) and transfer of undertakings (2001/23). In the event of collective redundancies both the EWC and the employees' representatives of the undertakings affected must be consulted. See further Chs. 13 and 14.

[94] Annex, para. 3. If there is no select committee the EWC must be informed.

[95] The members of the EWC who have been elected or appointed by undertakings which are directly affected have a right to participate in the meeting organized with the select committee.

The meeting with the select committee must take place as soon as possible. There must be a report drawn up by central management on which the select committee can give its opinion, either at a meeting or within a reasonable time. However, the Annex provides that this meeting will not affect the prerogatives of the central management.[96] This is a compromise between the employers, who were concerned about the disruptive effects of having too many consultation meetings every time an important decision was to be taken, and the Commission, which felt that the consultation of workers was an essential element in achieving the objectives of the proposed Directive.

Finally, the Annex provides that the operating expenses of the EWC must be borne by the Community-scale undertaking or group of undertakings, thereby reflecting the current practice of undertakings which have already set up information and consultation groups of this kind. According to the Commission,[97] given the substantial advantages that such EWCs can bring for the two parties, in particular by contributing to a better mutual flow of information and a constructive dialogue, it seems reasonable to suppose that these subsidiary requirements will not impose a significant additional burden on central management.

5. Related Provisions

The Directive contains three provisions designed to ensure that the EWCs/ICPs function smoothly. The first deals with confidentiality of the information received. While in principle the members of the EWC or ICP can inform the employees' representatives, or, in their absence, the employees themselves, of the content and outcome of the ICP, Member States can provide that members of the SNBs, or of the EWCs, or employee representatives in the ICPs, and any experts who assist them, are not authorized to reveal any information which has been expressly given to them in confidence,[98] even after the expiry

---

[96] Annex, para. 3, 3rd indent.   [97] COM(94) 134.

[98] Cf. Case C–384/02 *Grøngard* [2005] ECR I–000 concerning the prohibition under the Insider Dealing Dir. 384/02 (OJ [1989] L334/30) of disclosing information to third parties. The Court ruled that Dir. 89/592 precludes a person who receives inside information in his capacity as an employees' representative on a company's board of directors or in his capacity as a member of the liaison committee of a group of undertakings, from disclosing such information to the general secretary of the professional organization which organizes those employees and which appointed that person as a member of the liaison committee, unless (1) there is a close link between the disclosure and the exercise of his employment, profession or duties, and (2) that disclosure is strictly necessary for the exercise of that employment, profession or duties. The Court added that, as part of its examination, the national court must, in the light of the applicable national rules, take particular account of: (1) the fact that that exception to the prohibition of disclosure of inside information must be interpreted strictly; (2) the fact that each additional disclosure is liable to increase the risk of that information being exploited for a purpose contrary to Dir. 89/592, and (3) the sensitivity of the inside information. The same rules also apply to the general secretary wishing to disclose information to his colleagues.

of their terms of office.[99] In addition, Member States must provide that management can withhold any information which, according to objective criteria, would seriously harm the functioning of the undertakings concerned or would be prejudicial to them.[100] In response to a fear that these provisions could be abused by management, the Commission has said that the EWCs should be run by respecting the principles of transparency and mutual respect, particularly as prescribed by Article 9 (see below). The Directive also provides a practical solution to these concerns: Article 11(4) requires that complainants should have access to administrative or judicial appeal procedures where central management requires confidentiality or does not give information.

The second provision designed to ensure the smooth functioning of the EWC/ICP is Article 9 itself, which requires that 'The central management and the European Works Council shall work in a spirit of cooperation with due regard to their reciprocal rights and obligations'.[101] The same applies to co-operation between the central management and employees' representatives in the framework of an information and consultation procedure.[102] Such statements are designed to set the tenor of the Directive and it seems likely that the Directive will be interpreted in light of Article 9.

The third is Article 10 which provides that employees involved in the SNB, EWC or ICP should enjoy the same protection and guarantees provided for employees' representatives under national law and or practice, including the payment of wages.

6. Assessment

6.1. Flexibility

Despite the complex legislative history of this Directive its substance has remained remarkably intact from the earliest proposals. Its provisions draw heavily on the structure of the French and German works councils but lack the sophisticated co-determination principles found in the German system. Perhaps the most striking feature of the Directive, when contrasted with the earlier Vredling proposal, is its flexibility: the Directive now allows the Member States to determine practical matters, such as election methods, and encourages the Social Partners to negotiate the details of the operation of the

---

[99] Art. 8(1). Special provisions apply to 'entreprises de tendences' in Art. 8(3) i.e. undertakings which pursue 'directly and essentially the aim of ideological guidance with respect to information and the expression of opinions'.

[100] Art. 8(2). Member States can make such dispensation subject to prior administrative or judicial authorization.

[101] This draws on the joint opinion adopted by the two sides of industry in March 1987.

[102] Art. 9, second para. See also Art. 6(1).

agreement in order to accommodate local requirements. The result is what Streeck describes as convergence rather than harmonization[103] and what, for Weiss, amounts to a 'change of paradigm from substantial regulation to a merely procedural solution'.[104] In other words, the Directive takes effect not by imposing a uniform solution but by encouraging *both* Member States, through their laws, *and* companies themselves, through negotiations with employee representatives, to develop local-level solutions.

The greatest flexibility was provided by the so-called Article 13 voluntary agreements. Article 13 provides that where an agreement was already in existence on 22 September 1996,[105] and covered the entire workforce, the obligations contained in the Directive did not apply; and when these agreements expire the parties can decide jointly to renew them, failing which the provision of the Directive will apply. 386 such agreements were signed by the September 1996 deadline,[106] including 58 signed by British companies, even though the UK was not initially bound by the Directive. In addition, a further 350 multinationals have set up EWCs in accordance with the Directive.[107] Thus, about 13 million employees are covered by an EWC. That said, about 1,400 companies (and thus 7 million workers) covered by the Directive still do not have an EWC.[108]

6.2. The EWC's Success as a Model?

Commentators are divided as to whether the EWC Directive has been a successful experiment. For Ramsay, EWCs have a symbolic significance for industrial democracy:[109] the assertion of the right of labour to information and consultation provides some fetter on rights of ownership and management. Schulten, on the other hand, argues that the establishment of a new transnational micro-corporatism will not be free from tensions and contradictions because the Euro-company will also continue regime shopping to take advantage of the different national and local social standards, thereby playing

---

[103] Streeck, 'Citizenship under Regime Competition: The Case of European Works Councils', *MPIfG Working Paper* 97/3.

[104] 'The Future of Worker's Participation in the EU' in Barnard *et al.* (eds), *The Future of Labour Law: Liber Amicorum Sir Bob Hepple QC* (Hart Publishing, Oxford, 2004) 234.

[105] 15 December 1999 for the UK or earlier if the date of transposition in the UK is before then: Art. 3(1) of Dir. 97/74/EC (OJ [1998] L10/22).

[106] See Marginson, Gilman, Jacobi, and Krieger, *Negotiating European Works Councils: an Analysis of Agreements under Article 13*, European Foundation of Living and Working Conditions, EF9839. A particularly high incidence of such agreements can be found in Norway, see Knudsen and Bruun, 'European Works Councils in the Nordic Countries: An Opportunity and a Challenge for Trade Unionism' (1998) 4 *EJIR*. 131.

[107] http://www.eiro.eurofound.eu.int/2004/11/study/tn0411101s.html

[108] European Foundation for the improvement of Living and Working Conditions, *Industrial Relations Developments in Europe 2004* (OOPEC, Luxembourg, 2005), 77.

[109] Ramsay, below, n. 112, 320.

off its national personnel against each other.[110] He also suggests that the EWCs might exacerbate the trend towards decentralized, company-specific regulation by detaching an MNC's national subsidiaries from their national or sectoral systems.

Others express concerns that the lack of co-determination leads to the danger that EWCs will become a vehicle for 'Europeanised human resource management strategy';[111] and that they will subside into hearing management reports and offering some 'desultory discussion on the information offered but remaining insignificant to an employee relations still driven through local and national negotiations'.[112] In particular, Ramsay is concerned that MNCs, if they choose to take the initiative, may be able to increase management control by selling their own message convincingly, and by increasing enterprise consciousness by squeezing out external union representation.

The unions are generally more upbeat. Aided by generous EU funding for preparatory EWC meetings,[113] they have swiftly grasped the benefits of EWCs.[114] They are especially keen on sharing information and strategy and on exchanging ideas. They also think that EWCs help in countering perceived management attempts to misinform national workforces or 'play them off' against one another. Longer term, they think EWCs might lead to a more co-ordinated approach to collective bargaining among national unions—albeit restricted in the first instance to issues such as health and safety—although research by Gold and Hall found that management was implacably opposed to the development of European-level collective bargaining.[115]

However, TUC research has reported some problems in tailoring meetings of representatives to the complex business structures of multinationals where decision-making may well occur, not centrally, but at product division level or lower. This view was supported by a study conducted by the Multinational Business Forum[116] which argued that meaningful ICPs must follow company

[110] Schulten, 'European Works Councils: Prospects for a New System of European Industrial Relations' (1996) 2 *EJIR*. 303.

[111] Lecher and Rüb, 'The Constitution of European Works Councils: from Information Forum to Social Actor' (1999) 5 *EJIR*. 7, 8.

[112] Ramsay, 'Fool's Gold? European Works Councils and Workplace Democracy' (1997) 28 *IRJ*. 314.

[113] The budget was intended 'to finance transnational meetings of employees' representatives from undertakings operating on a transfrontier basis in the Community'. See EIRR 238 and 246. See also Roberts, 'Where are European Works Councils?—an Update' (1993) 24 *IRJ*. 178, 180. The budget was for 17 million ECU in 1993 and 1994, comprising about 30% of the Commission's entire 'social dialogue and employment budget'. This prompted criticism from the employers who argued that their organizations did not receive similar financial assistance, contrary to the requirements of what is now Art.138(1) EC which obliged the Commission to provide 'balanced support' to management and labour at Community level.

[114] *EIRR* 246, 16, and Gold and Hall, above, n. 24, 49.

[115] Gold and Hall, above, n. 24, 65.

[116] 'Thriving on Diversity: Informing and Consulting Employees in Multinational Enterprises' (September 1993) *EIRR* 238.

decision-making machinery: a statutory obligation to inform and consult at a level at which business decisions are not routinely taken is 'at best a waste of resources, and at worst necessitates the creation of a parallel and irrelevant organisation'.[117] Marginson also considers that the success of European industrial relations is dependent upon the structure of the multi-national enterprise. He argues that common management approaches across borders are less likely in companies which have expanded their access to markets in different European countries through licensing or franchise arrangements with local producers or joint ventures with enterprises based in other Member States. On the other hand, he suggests that in those transnationals that are organized to face the market on a European-wide basis, and where the primary axis of internal organization is around international product divisions, management is more likely to have an interest in developing common, cross-border approaches to the management of its workforce.

6.3. Looking Forward

In April 2004, the European Commission launched consultations with EU-level Social Partner bodies on measures to enhance the effectiveness of EWCs, including the possible revision of the Directive.[118] A year later the intersectoral Social Partners published a joint statement on the operation of EWCs following two seminars considering case studies of the operation of EWCs. According to the EIRO report,[119] the Social Partners concluded:

- EWCs 'can help management and workers to build a corporate culture and adapt to change in fast-evolving transnational companies';
- the establishment of 'a climate of mutual trust' between management and workers' representatives in the EWC is important for its effective functioning;
- investing in language as well as technical training helps to 'optimize' the functioning of the EWC;
- finding ways of reconciling different national industrial relations practices and addressing an increasingly diverse workforce is a 'constant challenge';
- ensuring a real sense of ownership of the EWC by the whole workforce was a 'considerable challenge';
- some companies seeking to enlarge their EWC have encountered difficulties in identifying workers' representatives in the new Member States;
- managing multiple layers of information and consultation can sometimes be very complex; and

---

[117] See also Marginson, Buitendam, Deutschmann and Perulli, 'The Emergence of the Euro-company: Towards a European Industrial Relations' (1993) 24 *IRJ.* 182.

[118] http://europa.eu.int/comm/employment_social/news/2004/apr/ewc_consultation_en.pdf

[119] http://www.eiro.eurofound.eu.int/2005/05/feature/eu0505204f.html

- that the effective functioning of EWCs is a 'learning and evolving process' requiring 'fine tuning over the years'.

These comments, while instructive, fall short of the 'best practice guidelines' on handling restructuring and on the operation of EWCs which the Commission had called for in its Communication, *Restructuring and Employment*.[120] This Communication was launched as part of the 'partnership for growth and jobs which lies at the heart of the reinvigorated Lisbon strategy'.

D. EUROPEAN COMPANY STATUTE

1. Introduction

The successful adoption of the EWC Directive has led to its basic model being adapted and applied to the worker participation provisions in other areas, notably the European company (Societas Europaea (SE)), which has now been established by Regulation 2157/2001 and the accompanying Directive 2001/86.[121] The conclusion of these two measures was the final chapter in 40 years of negotiations[122] about the creation of an SE, a free-standing, cross-frontier European Company which could be established independently from existing national laws. The Commission had long argued that the SE was the only way that European industry and services could take full advantage of the internal market, and pool their resources to be able to compete with Japan and the US.

The stumbling block in the creation of an SE has always been worker participation. This is because existing national systems vary so radically in this respect. For example, some Member States, notably the UK and Ireland, adopt a unitary or one-tiered system where the company is managed by a single administrative board which does not contain worker representation. Other Member States, notably Germany and the Netherlands, adopt a two-tier system under which the company is managed by a management board under the supervision of a supervisory board. Under German law, elected employees or trade unionists are members of the supervisory organ (*Aufsichsrat*) of the company.[123] While they constitute one-third of the members in companies employing between 500 and 2,000 employees, in companies employing 2,000 employees or more a system of quasi-parity operates where there are as many members representing the employees as representing the shareholders.

---

[120] COM(2005) 120, 11.   [121] OJ [2001] L294/1 and OJ [2001] L294/22 respectively.
[122] OJ [1970] C124/2, EC Bull. 8/1970 amended by COM(75) 150 final.
[123] See generally Weiss and Schmidt, *Labour Law and Industrial Relations in Germany* (Kluwer, The Hague, 2000).

However, the chair is always a representative of the shareholders and has a casting vote in the case of deadlock.

The Dutch system approaches the issue of worker participation from a different perspective from its German counterpart. It views the supervisory board as a genuinely non-executive body, reflecting as far as possible the views of the outside world and divorced from the internal power politics of the company; its role is to guide and supervise management on behalf of the shareholders and the employees. Consequently, it considers that there is no place on the supervisory board for either trade union representatives or employees. Whenever a vacancy on the board arises, the remaining members of the board co-opt a person from a list of candidates nominated separately by the shareholders, management and the works council. The new member must be independent and so cannot be an employee or a trade unionist. If one of the groups objects to the appointment it can pronounce a veto, in which case the matter is decided by the Enterprise Chamber Court.

How have these differences been accommodated by the EU? The original Commission proposal was for a regulation,[124] comprising 284 articles, which included provisions for an *obligatory* two-tier board with German style worker participation. This combined one-third to one-half employee representation on the supervisory board, charged with overseeing and appointing the management board, and the mandatory establishment of a works council. The amended proposal strengthened the original version by proposing that the supervisory board be made up of one-third employee representatives and one-third shareholder representatives, with the remainder being co-opted by these two groups.[125] The main area for disagreement in Council related to worker participation, particularly following the accession to the (then) EEC of the 'unitary' Member States (UK and Ireland), and negotiations ceased in 1982.

Over the next decade other proposals were put forward[126] offering various approaches to the seemingly intractable problem of worker participation in the European Company.[127] However, it took a combination of the determination of a number of presidencies in the late 1990s (including the British presidency in 1998) to push the matter forward. The final piece of the jigsaw was secured by the French presidency at Nice: Spain, which had been holding out against the proposal on board-level participation, agreed to the ECS when a quasi-exemption was granted authorizing the Member States not to implement the Directive on workers' participation in the case of European

---

[124] OJ [1970] C124/1, EC Bull. Supp. 8/1970. For a full discussion of the birth of the ECS, see Kenner, 'Worker Involvement on the *Societas Europaea*: Integrating Company and Labour Law in the European Union' (2005) 24 *YEL*. 223.

[125] Bull. Supp. 4/75. See also EIRR 223, 25.

[126] OJ [1989] C263/41; COM(89) final—SYN 218 and 219, 1. Later (p. 3) the Directive is described as an 'indispensable complement to the regulation'. Modified proposal COM(91) 174 Final—SYN 219.

[127] For more detailed discussion see the second edition of this book.

companies created by merger (the so-called Nice compromise). The Regulation establishing a European company (70 Articles) and the Directive (17 Articles) on employee involvement were finally adopted in October 2001 by the Belgian presidency, the 63rd presidency to deal with the statute.[128]

Adoption of the European Company Statute (ECS) was soon followed by the adoption of a Regulation establishing a European Co-operative Society (SCE)[129] and its Directive, Directive 2003/72,[130] concerning the involvement of employees in the SCE. The SCE is intended to provide co-operatives with the same opportunities for European level operation as the ECS provides for private limited companies. In addition, Directive 2005/56 on cross-border mergers of limited liability companies[131] takes the employee involvement provisions in the ECS Directive as its basis. Given the importance of the ECS model, it is this that we shall focus on. However, in order to understand the worker participation provisions of the Directive, it is first necessary to appreciate the key elements of the Regulation establishing a European company (SE).

2. The Key Features of the Regulation

According to the Regulation, an SE can be created in one of four ways. The first is by the merger of two or more *public* limited companies[132] formed under the laws of the Member States, provided at least two of the companies are governed by the laws of different Member States (the merger route).[133] The second and third options concern two or more public or private companies, formed under the law of a Member State. They can set up either (1) a holding *or* (2) a subsidiary SE, provided that at least two of the companies are governed by the law of different Member States or have, for at least two years, had a subsidiary governed by the law of another Member State or a branch situated in another Member State. (These two options will be referred to as

---

[128] Edwards, 'The European Company—Essential Tool or Eviscerated Dream?' (2003) 40 *CMLRev.* 443, 450. See also Villiers, 'The Directive on Employee Involvement in the European Company' (2006) 22 *IJCLLIR.* 183.

[129] The European Co-operative Society itself was set up by Reg. 1435/2003 (OJ [2003] L207/25). The choice of legal basis of this Reg (Art. 308) was unsuccessfully challenged in Case C–436/03 *Parliament v. Council* [2006] ECR I–000. See also Snaith, 'Employee Involvement in the European Cooperative Society' (2006) 22 *IJCLLIR.* 213.

[130] OJ [2003] L207/25.   [131] OJ [2005] L310/1.

[132] Groups involving subsidiaries incorporated as private companies will have to preface any consolidation as an SE by the conversion of such subsidiaries to public companies. This will make the process even more cumbersome: Edwards, above, n. 128, 463.

[133] Art. 2(1). However, as Edwards notes, above n. 128, 463 the adoption of the Cross-Border Mergers Dir. 2005/56 (OJ [2005] L310/1) means that mergers will be achievable without resorting to an SE. Using an SE for a cross-border merger gives no right to more favourable merger control review at either EU or national level.

(1) 'creating a holding company' or (2) 'forming a subsidiary' for short).[134] The fourth option involves the conversion of a public company, formed under the law of a Member State and with its registered office and head office within the Community, if, for at least two years, it has had a subsidiary company governed by the law of another Member State (the transformation route).[135] As we shall see, these different procedures for creating an SE affect the application of the employee involvement provisions.

To accommodate the different national approaches to the management body of the SE, the Regulation provides that an SE will comprise a general meeting of shareholders and *either* a supervisory organ and management organ (two-tier system) *or* an administrative organ (one-tier) depending on its statutes.

3. The Content of the Employee Involvement Provisions

3.1. Introduction

Central to the SE concept is the involvement of employee representatives. They can be involved in one, or possibly two, ways. At a minimum, employees must be informed and consulted through a representative body (RB). The rules on information and consultation are mandatory,[136] although they can be customized by the Social Partners.[137] In addition, the Directive envisages a role for employees in electing or appointing or otherwise influencing the selection of the members of the SE's (one-tier or two-tier) board.[138] This is the more controversial aspect of the Directive.

Article 12(2) of the Regulation makes clear that an SE may not be registered unless an agreement on arrangements for employee involvement has been concluded (which may include an explicit decision not to have special involvement provisions for the SE). And the employee involvement provisions draw heavily on the EWC model. As Keller notes, both the EWC and the ECS Directives give priority to voluntary negotiations between the Social Partners instead of binding legislation, both require the establishment of an SNB procedure to negotiate and agree with management, both specify the subject and scope of the employee involvement and both introduce binding fall back provision if the negotiations fail. However, there are notable differences between the two models and the ECS provisions are considerably more complex and detailed. The reason for this, as Davies explains,[139] is that the Community legislator was unwilling to give the employee representatives freedom to decide or agree that the system to operate in the SE would be less advanced

---

[134] Arts. 2(2) and 2(3).   [135] Art. 2(4).   [136] 6th Preambular recital to the Directive.
[137] Davies, 'Workers on the Board of the European Company?' (2003) 32 *ILJ*. 75, 81.
[138] Ibid.   [139] Davies, above n. 137, 80.

than that applying under national law in one of the founding companies and, where more than one system operated in the founding companies, the Directive also had to provide rules to determine which system was in fact the most advanced.

While much is made of the centrality of the employee involvement provisions to the Directive, in fact the so-called 'avant-après' or 'before and after' system identified in the Preamble[140] means that the Directive actually only requires employee participation where employee participation already existed in the companies involved in setting up the SE.[141] In other words, the Directive aims only to preserve existing rights unless the parties decide otherwise;[142] the aim of the Directive is not to promote board-level participation in all SEs. The Directive's approach is therefore negative rather than positive, a policy aimed at ensuring that the possibility of forming an SE is not used to circumvent national-level provisions on board-level participation.[143] Edwards summarizes the position in the following terms:

- there will be no participation in the management of the SE where there was none in the founding companies;
- where an SE is formed by the conversion of a public company, any existing participation must be continued in the SE;
- where an SE is formed by merger or the creation of a holding or subsidiary company and participation covered at least 25 per cent (in the case of formation by merger) or 50 per cent (in the case of SEs established by creating a holding company or a subsidiary) of the total employees involved, participation rights may be reduced only with the approval of two-thirds of the total employees.

We turn now to consider how the employee involvement provisions are negotiated.

3.2. Negotiating Procedure

According to Article 3(1), it is the management or administrative organs of the participating companies (not the employees or their representatives) which trigger the Directive's procedure for negotiating the arrangements for the involvement of the employees in the SE. When the management draws

---

[140] Particularly in the 3rd, 7th and 18th recitals.

[141] Cf. Worker participation provisions do not exist in Reg. 2137/85 (OJ [1995] L199/1) on European Economic Interest Groupings (EEIGs). The Preamble, however, states that national and EC law apply to matters not covered by the Regulation, including social and labour law. The Regulation provides that an EEIG must not employ more than 500 workers (Art. 3(2)(c)), a threshold inserted to avoid circumvention of the German employee participation provisions by German companies forming or joining an EEIG registered in another Member State with more lax worker participation rules.

[142] Edwards, above n. 128, 459.   [143] Davies, above n. 137, 84.

up a plan for the establishment of an SE it must, as soon as possible after publishing the draft terms of the mechanism for creating an SE (by any one of the four routes outlined above), take the necessary steps to start negotiations with the representatives of the companies' employees. This includes providing the employees' representatives with information about the identity of the participating companies/subsidiaries/establishments and the number of their employees affected.

To this end, an SNB must be set up, either by election or appointment, representative of the employees of the companies, subsidiaries and establishments involved, based on geographic and proportional criteria. In particular, the Directive provides for one seat per portion of employees employed in that Member State which equals 10 per cent, or a fraction thereof, of the number of employees employed by the participating companies and concerned subsidiaries or establishments in all the Member States taken together.[144] The Directive expressly states that these representatives can include representatives of trade unions.[145] The SNBs can be assisted by experts who,[146] unlike in the EWC Directive, can actually be present at negotiation meetings in an advisory capacity. These experts can also include representatives of appropriate Community level trade unions.[147] Any expenses relating to the functioning of the SNB and to the negotiations more generally are to be borne by the participating companies.[148] The legislation applicable to the negotiation procedure is that of the Member State in which the registered office of the SE is to be situated.[149]

As with the EWC Directive, the SNB's role, together with that of the competent organs of the participating companies is to determine, by written agreement, arrangements for the involvement of employees within the SE.[150] The SNB and management must start negotiations as soon as the SNB is established[151] and must negotiate in a spirit of co-operation with a view to reaching an agreement.[152] Normally, the SNB is to take decisions by absolute majority of members representing an absolute majority of employees. However, where the negotiations lead to a reduction of existing participation rights then a two-thirds majority is required representing at least two-thirds of the employees including the votes of members representing employees employed in at least two Member States (the so-called 'enhanced majority').[153]

3.3. The Possible Outcomes of the Negotiations

As with EWC Directive, there are three possible outcomes to the negotiations. The first possibility is that a voluntary agreement[154] is reached within six

---

[144] Art. 3(2)(a)(i).   [145] Art. 3(2)(b), para. 2.
[146] Member States can choose to limit the experts to one: Art. 3(7), para. 2.
[147] Art. 3(5).   [148] Art. 3(7), para. 1.   [149] Art. 6.   [150] Art. 3(5).
[151] Art. 5(1).   [152] Art. 4(1).   [153] Art. 3(4).   [154] Art. 4(1).

months (or a year if the parties agree to extend the period) to set up a representative body (RB). The RB is similar to an EWC or ICP. The agreement setting up the RB must cover:[155]

- the composition, number of members and allocation of seats on the representative body, which will be the discussion partner of the competent organ of the SE in connection with arrangements for informing[156] and consulting[157] the employees of the SE and its subsidiaries and establishments. This would also apply if the parties decide to establish an information and consultation procedure instead;
- the functions and the procedure for the information and consultation of the representative body;
- the frequency of meetings of the representative body;
- the financial and material resources to be allocated to the representative body;
- the date of the entry into force of the agreement, its duration, and any procedure for renegotiation.

For the purposes of the Directive, information means informing the body representative of the employees and/or employees' representatives by the competent organ of the SE on questions which concern the SE itself and any of its subsidiaries or establishments situated in another Member State or which exceed the powers of the decision-making organs in a single Member State at a time, in a manner and with a content which allows the employees' representatives to undertake an in-depth assessment of the possible impact and, where appropriate, prepare consultations with the competent organ of the SE.[158] The Directive envisages the soft form of 'consultation'. Article 2(j) defines 'consultation' as the establishment of dialogue and exchange of views between the body representative of the employees and/or the employees' representatives and the competent organ of the SE, at a time, in a manner and with a content which allows the employees' representatives, on the basis of information provided, to express an opinion on the measures envisaged by the competent organ. This opinion 'may be taken into account in the decision-making process within the SE'.

In addition, Article 4(2) permits the parties to agree details of arrangements for participation, if they so choose (although this is compulsory in some cases (considered above)). Participation means the influence of the body

---

[155] Art. 4(2).   [156] Defined in Art. 2(i).
[157] Defined in Art. 2(j). The definition of consultation is the weaker form: it means the establishment of a dialogue and exchange of views between the body representative of the employees or the employees' representatives and the competent organ of the SE in a manner which allows the employees' representatives to express an opinion on measures envisaged by the competent organ which may be taken into account in the decision-making process it the SE.
[158] Art. 2(i).

representative of the employees and/or employees representatives in the affairs of the company by way of either the right to elect or appoint some of the members of the company's supervisory or administrative organ or the right to recommend and/or oppose the appointment of some or all of the members of the company's supervisory or administrative organ.[159] The agreement must specify which, if any, of these options it wishes to take advantage of and whether the employees will be entitled to elect, appoint, recommend or oppose, and the procedures for putting this into effect.

Finally, Article 4(4) makes specific provision for an SE established by means of transformation: any voluntary agreement must provide for at least the same level of all elements of employee involvement as the ones already existing within the company to be transformed to an SE.

The second possible outcome (which is not available to SEs established by transformation)[160] is an agreement, by enhanced majority,[161] not to open negotiations or to terminate negotiations already opened and to rely on the rules on information and consultation of employees in force in the Member States where the SE has employees,[162] which will mean, as a minimum, complying with the information and consultation obligations under Directive 2002/14 (see below) and, more importantly given the transnational context of the ECS, the European Works Council Directive (otherwise excluded from the Directive).[163]

In neither the first nor the second possible outcome of the negotiations do the provisions of the standard rules found in the Annex apply.[164] By contrast, the standard rules (functionally equivalent to the 'subsidiary requirements' in the EWC Directive) will apply to the third situation. This is where no voluntary agreement is reached within six months (or a year if the parties agree to extend the period). The standard rules will also apply if the parties so choose[165] and if the SNB has not reached agreement under Article 3(6) in the case of an SE established by transformation. They will also apply, according to Article 7(2), if:

- in an SE established by transformation, the rules of a Member State relating to employee participation in the administrative or supervisory body applied to a company transformed into an SE;[166]
- in the case of an SE established by merger, one or more forms of participation applied in one or more of the companies covering at least 25 per cent of the total number of employees in all the participating companies or less than 25 per cent and the SNB decides to apply the participation rules;[167]

---

[159] Art. 2(k).   [160] Art. 3(6), para. 2.   [161] Art. 3(6), para. 2.
[162] Art. 3(6), para. 1. This decision can be revisited two years after the decision or earlier if the parties so agree: Art. 3(6), para. 4.
[163] Art. 13(1), para. 2.   [164] Art. 4(3) and Art. 3(6) respectively.
[165] Art. 7(1).   [166] Art. 7(2)(a).   [167] Art. 7(2)(b).

- in the case of an SE established as a holding or subsidiary company, if before registration of the SE, one or more forms of participation applied in one or more of the participating companies covering at least 50 per cent of the total number of employees in all the participating companies or less than 50 per cent and the SNB so decided.[168]

Therefore, the standard rules apply where all or most workers were covered by mandatory participation and here the 'highest level' principle (considered below) operates freely. By contrast, where large numbers of employees were not covered by mandatory participation (e.g. in an SE formed by merger 75 per cent of employees were not covered by participation rules, and in the case of a formation of a joint holding or subsidiary company 50 per cent of the employees are not covered by mandatory participation rules) then the standard rules do not automatically apply.[169]

The results of the Nice compromise can be found in Article 7(3) which says that Member States may provide that the standard participation provisions will not apply in the case of an SE established by merger. However, an SE established by merger of companies one or more of which was governed by participation rules may be registered in a Member State which has made use of the Article 7(3) option only where an agreement pursuant to Article 4 of the Directive has been concluded.[170]

3.4. The Standard Rules

So what do the standard rules say? Inevitably, like the rest of the Directive, they are complex. They are also more detailed than those found in the EWC Directive and cover a broader range of situations. In essence they provide for a standard RB, similar to the statutory EWC laid down in the EWC Directive's subsidiary requirements, and board-level participation where this existed in the participating companies.

The Standard rules are contained in three parts. The first part relates to the composition of the RB. It provides that the RB must be composed of employees of the SE and its subsidiaries and establishments elected or appointed (in accordance with national legislation and/or practice) from their number by the employees' representatives or, in the absence thereof, by the entire body of employees. The members of the representative body are elected or appointed in proportion to the number of employees employed in each Member State by the participating companies and concerned subsidiaries or establishments, by allocating one seat per portion of employees employed in that Member State which equals 10 per cent, or a fraction thereof, of the number of employees employed by the participating companies and

---

[168] Art. 7(2)(c).   [169] Davies, above n. 137, 88.   [170] Art. 12(3) of the Regulation.

concerned subsidiaries or establishments in all the Member States taken together. In other words, the membership of the RB reflects that of the SNB set up under Article 3. The competent organ of the SE must be informed of the composition of the RB. The RB must lay down its own rules of procedure. In addition, where its size so warrants, the RB must elect a select committee from among its members, comprising at the most three members. Four years after the RB is established, it must examine whether to open negotiations for the conclusion of an agreement referred to in Articles 4 and 7 or to continue to apply the standard rules adopted in accordance with the Annex.

The second part concerns the standard rules for information and consultation. These broadly map the subsidiary requirements in the EWC Directive. In essence, the RB has the right to be informed and consulted and, for that purpose, to meet with the competent organ of the SE at least once a year. On the basis of regular reports drawn up by the competent organ, the RB has the right to be informed and consulted on the progress of the business of the SE and its prospects. In addition, the competent organ of the SE must provide the RB with the agenda for meetings of the administrative, or, where appropriate, the management and supervisory organ, and with copies of all documents submitted to the general meeting of its shareholders. The meeting itself must relate to:

- the structure, economic and financial situation of the business;
- the probable development of the business and of production and sales;
- the situation and probable trend of employment, investments, and substantial changes concerning organization, introduction of new working methods or production processes, transfers of production, mergers, cutbacks or closures of undertakings, establishments or important parts thereof, and collective redundancies.

Where there are exceptional circumstances affecting the employees' interests to a considerable extent, particularly in the event of relocations, transfers, the closure of establishments or undertakings or collective redundancies, the RB has the right to be *informed*. The RB or, where it so decides, in particular for reasons of urgency, the select committee,[171] has the right to meet the competent organ of the SE or any more appropriate level of management within the SE, so as to be *informed and consulted* on measures significantly affecting employees' interests. However, unlike the EWC Directive, the ECS Directive provides that where the competent organ decides not to act in accordance with the opinion expressed by the representative body, the RB has the right to a further meeting with the competent organ of the SE *with a view to seeking agreement*. However, the standard rules then add: 'The meetings referred to

---

[171] In the case of a meeting organized with the select committee, those members of the representative body who represent employees who are directly concerned by the measures in question shall also have the right to participate.

above shall not affect the prerogatives of the competent organ.' Finally, the Standard rules expressly permit the members of the RB to inform the representatives of the employees of the SE and of its subsidiaries and establishments of the content and outcome of the information and consultation procedures.

As with the EWC Directive, the standard rules also contain provisions to ensure the smooth operation of the RB: the RB or the select committee can be assisted by experts of its choice, the members of the RB are entitled to time off for training without loss of wages (but no reference is made to paid time off for actual attendance at the meetings themselves), and the costs of the RB are to be borne by the SE which must provide the body's members with the financial and material resources needed to enable them to perform their duties in an appropriate manner.

Part Three of the standard rules concern participation. In essence these rules are premised on the 'no escape' principle: that forming an SE cannot be used as a means to escape from employee participation rules. The rules distinguish between SEs established by transformation and those formed in one of the three other ways outline above (merger, creating a holding company, or forming a subsidiary). In respect of SEs established by transformation, if the rules of a Member State relating to employee participation in the administrative or supervisory body applied before registration, all aspects of employee participation will continue to apply to the SE. In the other three cases establishing an SE, the employees of the SE, its subsidiaries, and establishments and/or their representative body have the right to elect, appoint, recommend or oppose the appointment of a number of members of the administrative or supervisory body of the SE equal to the *highest proportion* in force in the participating companies concerned before registration of the SE. Thus, the form of participation in principle to be adopted by the SE is the most advanced of the systems required by national laws applying to the founding companies.[172] The most advanced system is the one with the 'highest' proportion of members of the board subject to employee influence, irrespective of the form that influence might take. As Davies points out, there is no qualitative judgement among the various forms in which employee influence over board membership might express itself.[173] Once the highest level is determined, the most 'advanced' system will then be exported to the employees previously subject to less advanced systems. However, if none of the participating companies was governed by participation rules before registration of the SE (i.e. companies subject to the law of, for example, Belgium, France, Ireland, Italy, Portugal, Spain, and the UK)[174], the SE is not required to establish provisions for employee participation.

---

[172] Davies, above, n. 137, 84. For a fuller discussion of the 'highest-level' rules, see Davies, above, n. 137, 85.

[173] Ibid.   [174] Edwards, above n. 128, 462.

The RB must decide on the allocation of seats within the administrative or supervisory body among the members representing the employees from the various Member States or on the way in which the SE's employees may recommend or oppose the appointment of the members of these bodies according to the proportion of the SE's employees in each Member State. If the employees of one or more Member States are not covered by this proportional criterion, the representative body must appoint a member from one of those Member States, in particular the Member State of the SE's registered office, where that is appropriate. Each Member State may determine the allocation of the seats it is given within the administrative or supervisory body. The rules also provide that every member of the administrative body or, where appropriate, the supervisory body of the SE who has been elected, appointed or recommended by the representative body or, depending on the circumstances, by the employees is a full member, with the same rights and obligations as the members representing the shareholders, including the right to vote.

3.5. Supporting Provisions

In keeping with the Directive's aim of preventing the avoidance of national employee involvement rules, Article 11 of the Directive obliges Member States to take appropriate measures to prevent the misuse of an SE for the purpose of depriving employees of rights to employee involvement or withholding such rights.[175] More generally, Article 9 provides that the competent organ of the SE and the RB must work together in 'a spirit of cooperation with due regard for the reciprocal rights and obligations'.

As with the EWC Directive, the ECS Directive also lays down rules on issues such as confidentiality of information given to members of the SNB and RB or to experts which assist them,[176] on protection of employee representatives,[177] its relationship with other provisions (in essence the ECS Directive 2001/86 takes precedence over the EWC Directive unless the SNB decides not to open negotiations or terminate negotiations already opened), and compliance (each Member State must ensure that the management of establishments of an SE and the supervisory or administrative organs of subsidiaries and of participating companies which are situated within its territory and the employees' representatives or the employees themselves abide by the obligations laid down by the Directive, regardless of whether the SE has its registered office in its territory).[178] Member States must also provide for appropriate remedies.[179]

---

[175] Art. 11.   [176] Art. 8.   [177] Art. 10.   [178] Art. 12(1).   [179] Art. 12(2).

3.6. Assessment

It is not clear how much use will actually be made of the possibility of setting up an SE. As Edwards points out, while some view the possibility of creating an SE as beneficial in terms of administrative costs savings, others are concerned about the weaknesses of the ECS Regulation and Directive. In particular, they are critical of the absence of a genuine Community legal instrument, given that essentially 25 different statutes have been created, the absence of an agreed tax regime, the complexity of the rules on employee involvement, and the existence of too many options and references to national law. Davies describes the SE Regulation as 'but a shadow of its former self', with the disappearance of the goal of a non-national corporate law regime.[180]

That said, EIRO reported[181] that the German Insurance group Allianz merged with its Italian subsidiary RAS to create an SE. Allianz, and its subsidiary Dresdner Bank, have operations in Germany, France, the UK, Italy, Austria, Hungary, Slovakia, Spain, and Ireland. The legal seat of the company will be Germany. In terms of employee representation, the German legislation implementing the European Company Statute's employee involvement Directive was applied, because the seat of the new company is Germany. So the new company has a dual board structure, comprising a management board (*Vorstand*) and a supervisory board (*Aufsichtsrat*). Employee representation on the supervisory board is 50 per cent, which is in line with current practice at Allianz.[182]

E. NATIONAL-LEVEL INFORMATION AND CONSULTATION PROVISIONS

1. Background to the Adoption of the Measure

The adoption of Directive 2002/14 on national level information and consultation (I&C)[183] is probably of greater practical significance than the ECS. This Directive also had a long gestation period and, once again, came about partly as a result of the EWC Directive 94/45 which provided a model to help unblock long-standing proposals, in particular the ill-fated and highly

---

[180] Davies, above n. 137, 77–8.
[181] European Industrial Relations Observatory On-line: http://www.eiro.eurofound.eu.int/2005/11/inbrief/eu0511203n.html
[182] In June 2005 the Italian finance group UniCredito and the German group HypoVereins bank announced that they wished to set up a European Company.
[183] OJ [2002] L80/29.

controversial 'Vredling' Directive of 1980[184] and the substantially amended 'Richard' proposal in 1983.[185] These proposals were considered sisters to the Directives on collective redundancies (now 98/59), transfers of undertakings (now 2001/23), and the proposed Fifth Company Law Directive.[186] The 'Vredling' proposal contained two key rights: the right to periodic information and the right to be consulted in advance of important decisions in the life of the undertaking. Nevertheless, the various proposals prompted heated opposition and were accused firstly of being complicated and unfamiliar, secondly of interfering with information and consultation practices already in existence at national level (because the proposal covered large undertakings or groups of undertakings in a single state), and thirdly of disrupting voluntarist systems of industrial relations.[187] Allegations that the Commission was trying to harmonize diverse national industrial relations systems were not new,[188] but became an increasingly sensitive issue as the doctrine of subsidiarity gained in importance.

Various attempts were subsequently made to resurrect the various proposals[189] but these attempts assumed new importance with the launch of the EES where worker participation was seen as the key to achieving flexibility in the workplace. As the Green Paper on Partnership explained,[190] flexibility within organizations is to be encouraged by reinforcing mechanisms for employee participation at the level of the plant or enterprise; 'the role of workers in decision-making and the need to review and strengthen the existing arrangements for workers' involvement in their companies will . . . become essential issues'.[191]

The Commission hoped that the Social Partners would be able to negotiate a European-level collective agreement on national-level information and consultation, but, as with the EWC Directive, while the ETUC and CEEP were willing, UNICE was not, largely due to resistance from the British CBI. UNICE argued that any such agreement would not conform with the principle of subsidiarity; that there were adequate legal frameworks at national level; that

---

[184] OJ [1980] C297/3, Bull. Supp. 3/80, discussed by Vandamme, 'L'Information et la Consultation des Travailleurs dans la proposition de directive sur les entreprises a structure complexe, en particulier transnationale' [1982] *Revue du Marché Commun* 368 and Blanpain *et al.*, *The Vredling Proposal. Information and Consultation of Employees in Multinational Enterprises* (Kluwer, Deventer, 1983).

[185] OJ [1983] C217/3, Bull. Supp. 2/83, 3. Discussed by Blanquet, 'Amended Proposal for a Directive on Procedures for Informing and Consulting Employees—From the "Vredling Proposal" to the "Richard Proposal" ', *Social Europe* 9/83, 19.

[186] Pipkorn, 'The Draft Directive on Procedures for Informing and Consulting Employees' (1983) 20 *CMLRev.* 725, 726–7.

[187] Ibid., 281.

[188] See the Commission's concern expressed in its Green Paper on Employee Participation and Company Structures, EC Bull. Supp. 8/75.

[189] COM(95) 547.

[190] Green Paper on Partnership, COM(97) 127 final, Executive Summary.

[191] Ibid., para. 44.

there was no link between employee information and consultation and job security; and that labour management should be the exclusive preserve of the company's internal organization.

Indeed there was real concern that any EU initiative would cut across the very varied, culturally specific systems of worker involvement in the Member States. This was a particular issue for the UK where worker representation has traditionally been channelled through recognized unions.[192] This is known as the single-channel approach. The concept of works councils or their equivalents has been largely unfamiliar, albeit that larger firms often have joint consultative committees which comprise both union and non-union representatives.

The British 'single channel' can be contrasted with the 'dual channel' found in, for example, Germany[193] where unions and employers' associations are responsible for collective bargaining, usually at a *sectoral or regional* level, concerning quantitative matters (especially wages and hours). By contrast, works councils and management are responsible for relations in respect of essentially qualitative issues within a *company* (such as personnel planning and changes in work processes, the working environment, new technology, and job content). Works councils in Germany have wide powers ranging from information and consultation rights to co-determination rights, which include the right of veto over individual cases of hiring, grading, transfer, and dismissal.[194]

The German model thus has a clear 'space' in which works councils can operate, i.e. at firm level. Collective bargaining is mainly conducted at a higher (*sectoral or regional*) level. This is not the case in the UK, where collective bargaining is conducted largely at the enterprise/company or even plant/establishment level. Furthermore, while competition between unions is regulated by the so-called Bridlington principles, no such rules apply to 'competition' between trade unions and works councils/elected worker representatives. Therefore, in the UK any second channel might be perceived as a threat to established trade unions and might risk undermining collective bargaining, hence the concerns.

Regretting 'this lack of willingness to negotiate',[195] the Commission nevertheless decided to present a proposal,[196] even though it was faced with

---

[192] Traditionally, recognition has been entirely a matter for employers. This position has been changed in part by s. 1 and Sch. AI of the Employment Relations Act 1999, amending TULR(C)A 1992, introducing a statutory recognition procedure. See Wedderburn, 'Collective Bargaining or Legal Enactment: the 1999 Act and Union Recognition' (2000) 29 *ILJ*. 1; Gaal, 'The First Five Years of Britain's Third Statutory Recognition Procedure' (2005) 34 *ILJ*. 345.

[193] The following draws on Jacobi *et al.* 'Germany: Facing New Challenges', in Ferner and Hyman (eds), *Changing Industrial Relations in Europe* (Blackwell, Oxford, 1998).

[194] S. 87 BetrVG. If the parties cannot reach an agreement, either side may appeal to the conciliation board which would then rule on the matter.

[195] COM(98) 612, 2.   [196] OJ [1999] C2/3.

objections from the UK government.[197] The Renault affair gave new impetus to these proposals. In 1997 the French car manufacturer, Renault, closed its plant at Vilvoorde in Belgium without prior information and consultation of the workforce. As the Commission explained, 'Several events, which have given rise to enormous political and media attention, have illustrated the weakness of national and Community law. In fact, it has become clear that, even where information and consultation provisions existed, they were not effective as they were either only ritual in nature or effective only *a posteriori*'.[198]

The UK, with the initial support of Germany (and Denmark and Ireland), managed to block the proposal for a while but, once its blocking majority collapsed, the UK abandoned its hostility to the measure and focused instead on making the measure more UK-friendly.[199] The result, Directive 2002/14, is a measure which provides the minimum framework in which information and consultation (I&C) can take place: all the detail is left to be worked out by the Member States or the national or subnational Social Partners. The UK is now an enthusiastic supporter of the measure, seeing it as an important step in its partnership agenda.

2. The Directive

2.1. The Scope of the Directive

Article 1 says that the Directive's objective is to establish a general framework for informing and consulting employees in the EC. It refers to a 'right' to information and consultation.[200] Unlike the Collective Redundancies Directive where consultation is mandatory, employers do not have to inform and consult an unwilling workforce: employees need to request the right to be informed and consulted.

Information is defined in Article 2(e) as transmission by the employer to the employees' representatives of data in order to enable them to acquaint themselves with the subject-matter and to examine it. 'Employees' representatives' means 'the employees' representatives provided for by national laws and/or practices'.[201] This formulation allows Member States to use not only

---

[197] *Fairness at Work* White Paper, above, n.26, para. 4.5.

[198] See generally 'Employee Representatives in Europe and their Economic Prerogatives', Supp. *Social Europe* 3/96.

[199] Hall, 'Assessing the Information and Consultation of Employees Regulations (2005) 34 *ILJ*. 103, 108.

[200] Art. 1(1).

[201] Art. 2(e). For the difficulty this definition creates see Case C–382/92 *Commission v. UK* [1994] ECR I–2435 considered in Ch. 12. See also the Joint declaration of the European Parliament, the Council and the Commission on employee representation: 'With regard to employee representation, the European Parliament, the Council and the Commission recall the judgements of the European Court of Justice of 8 June 1994 in Cases C–382/92 (Safeguarding of employees rights in the event of transfers of undertakings) and C–383/92 (Collective redundancies).'

collegiate forms of employee representation, but also individual representatives (workforce delegates, trade union delegates, and others).[202] 'Consultation' means the exchange of views and establishment of dialogue between the employees' representatives and the employer. Finally, Article 2(d) defines 'employee' by reference to national law. It provides that 'employee' means any person who, in the Member State concerned, is protected as an employee under national employment law and in accordance with national practice.

The Member States have the choice to apply the Directive to:

(a) undertakings employing at least 50 employees in any one Member State,[203] or
(b) establishments employing at least 20 employees in any one Member State.

Article 2(a) defines 'undertaking' as a public or private undertaking carrying out an economic activity, whether or not operating for gain, which is located within the territory of the Member States. This definition draws on the revisions to the Transfer of Undertakings Directive 2001/23.[204] Article 2(b) defines 'establishment' as a unit of business defined in accordance with national law and practice, and located within the territory of a Member State, where an economic activity is carried out on an ongoing basis with human and material resources.

Member States are to determine the method for calculating the thresholds of employees employed. This is consistent with the overall aim of the Directive to ensure that it sits comfortably within the national industrial relations systems. This ethos is confirmed by Article 1(2) which provides that 'The practical arrangements for information and consultation shall be defined and implemented in accordance with national law and industrial relations practices in individual Member States in such a way as to ensure their effectiveness.' In much the same vein, the Directive permits Member States to lay down special rules applicable to so-called 'entreprises de tendences' i.e. undertakings or establishments which pursue 'directly and essentially political, professional organisational, religious, charitable, educational, scientific or artistic aims, as well as aims involving information and the expression of opinions', on condition that, at the date of entry into force of the Directive, provisions of that nature already exist in national legislation.[205]

---

[202] For the problems associated with this formula see Ch. 12.
[203] According to the Commission, this excludes 97% of companies in the EU with salaried employees.
[204] Art. 1 of Dir. 2001/23 considered in Ch. 12.
[205] Art. 3(2). According to Art. 3(3), Member States may derogate from this Directive through particular provisions applicable to the crews of vessels plying the high seas.

Article 10, introduced largely for the benefit of the UK,[206] contains the transitional provisions. It provides that the application of the national provisions implementing this Directive can be limited to undertakings employing at least 150 employees. Undertakings employing at least 100 employees have until 23 March 2007 to comply while the Directive does not apply to undertakings employing at least 50 employees until 23 March 2008.

2.2. Information and Consultation Agreements

Unlike the EWC and ECS Directives, Directive 2002/14 makes no provision for a special negotiating body to be set up to negotiate the content of the agreement. Instead, the Directive merely identifies three possible outcomes. These are referred to in the British implementation as pre-existing agreements (PEAs), negotiated agreements (NAs), and standard or fall back arrangements. PEAs are agreements existing on the date the Directive came into force (23 March 2005), as well as any subsequent renewals of such agreements. Negotiated agreements are those negotiated by management and labour, at the appropriate level including at undertaking or establishment level, setting out the practical arrangements for informing and consulting employees. Neither the PEAs nor the negotiated agreements are subject to the fall back provisions found in Article 4.

Article 4 contains the fall back position: it specifies the (minimal) rules which apply in the absence of the social partners entering a pre-existing or negotiated agreement. In essence, Article 4 is the I&C Directive's equivalent to the standard rules in the ECS Directive. Article 4(2) specifies that information and consultation must cover:

(a) *information* on the recent and probable development of the undertaking's or the establishment's activities and economic situation;
(b) *information and consultation* on the situation, structure and probable development of employment within the undertaking or establishment and on any anticipatory measures envisaged, in particular where there is a threat to employment;
(c) *information and consultation* on decisions likely to lead to substantial changes in work organization or in contractual relations, including those covered by the Community provisions referred to in Article 9(1).

Thus, the Directive covers three subject areas: economic or strategic matters (paragraph (a)), employment trends within the undertaking and associated measures (paragraph (b)) and specific decisions concerning work organization

---

[206] I.e. to a 'Member State in which there is, at the date of entry into force of this Directive, no general, permanent and statutory system of information and consultation of employees, nor a general, permanent and statutory system of employee representation at the workplace allowing employees to be represented for that purpose'.

or contractual relations (paragraph (c)). Since the matters referred to in paragraph (a) are generally outside the control of the employer, these are subject only to information. The Directive provides that 'Information shall be given at such time, in such fashion and with such content as are appropriate to enable, in particular, employees' representatives to conduct an adequate study and, where necessary, prepare for consultation'.[207] And Article 4(4) provides that consultation shall take place:

(a) while ensuring that the timing, method, and content thereof are appropriate;
(b) at the relevant level of management and representation, depending on the subject under discussion;
(c) on the basis of information supplied by the employer[208] in accordance with Article 2(f) and of the opinion which the employees' representatives are entitled to formulate;
(d) in such a way as to enable employees' representatives to meet the employer and obtain a response, and the reasons for that response, to any opinion they might formulate;
(e) with a view to reaching an agreement on decisions within the scope of the employer's powers referred to in paragraph 2(c).

Thus, the standard rules envisage the strong form of consultation; where there is a PEA or an NA the consultation is the weak form.

The only provisions which will apply regardless of whether it is the Member States or the social partners laying down the detail of the rules are those contained in Article 1. In particular Article 1(3) provides:

When defining or implementing practical arrangements for information and consultation, the employer and the employees' representatives shall work in a spirit of cooperation and with due regard for their reciprocal rights and obligations, taking into account the interests both of the undertaking or establishment and of the employees.

2.3. Related Provisions

Following the model of the EWC Directive, the Information and Consultation Directive lays down rules concerning the confidentiality of information,[209] the protection of employees' representatives[210] and a clause concerning the relation between this Directive and other Community and national measures,[211] which provides that Directive 2002/14 is without prejudice to the

---

[207] Art. 4(3).
[208] According to Art. 2(c), 'employer' means the natural or legal person party to employment contracts or employment relationships with employees, in accordance with national law and practice.
[209] Art. 6.   [210] Art. 7.   [211] Art. 9.

specific information and consultation procedures set out in the Collective Redundancies Directive 98/59/EC, the Transfer of Undertakings Directive 2001/23/EC, the European Works Council Directive 94/45/EC and to any other rights to information, consultation and participation under national law. The Directive also contains a non-regression clause.[212]

The remedies clause, found in Article 8(1), requires Member States to provide for appropriate measures in the event of non-compliance with the Directive by the employer or the employees' representatives. In particular, Member States must ensure that adequate administrative or judicial procedures are available to enable the obligations deriving from the Directive to be enforced. Article 8(2) adds that Member States must provide for adequate sanctions to be applicable in the event of infringement of this Directive by the employer or the employees' representatives. These sanctions must be effective, proportionate and dissuasive. The wording of the provision is broadly based on current Community law and the case law of the Court.[213]

The Commission had also proposed a provision that said that restructuring decisions taken by employers in serious breach of their information and consultation obligations would be suspended.[214] This ambitious provision was omitted from the final version of Directive 2002/14.

While the EWC, ECS, and I&C Directives are the principal Community measures on worker involvement, other Community instruments also require or permit varying forms of worker participation. In chapter 11 we have already examined the worker involvement provisions in the Framework Directive 89/391 on health and safety. In the next section we look at certain other measures which also envisage a degree of worker voice in the course of procedures leading to some form of restructuring.

---

[212] Art. 9(4).   [213] See further esp. Ch. 13.

[214] 'Member States shall provide that in case of serious breach by the employer of the information and consultation obligations in respect of the decisions referred to in Article 4(1)(c) of this Directive, where such decisions would have direct and immediate consequences in terms of substantial change or termination of the employment contracts or employment relations, these decisions shall *have no legal effect* on the employment contracts or employment relationships of the employees affected. The non production of legal effects will continue until such time as the employer has fulfilled his obligations or, if this is no longer possible, adequate redress has been established, in accordance with the arrangements and procedures to be determined by the Member States.

The provision of the previous paragraph also applies to corresponding obligations under the agreements referred to in Article 3.

Within the meaning of the previous paragraphs, serious breaches are:

a) the total absence of information and/or consultation of the employees' representatives prior to a decision being taken or the public announcement of that decision; or

b) the withholding of important information or provision of false information rendering ineffective the exercise of the right to information and consultation' [emphasis added].

F. WORKER PARTICIPATION UNDER OTHER COMMUNITY INSTRUMENTS

1. The Merger Regulation

Limited recognition of the collective interests of workers can also be found in the Merger Regulation, initially Regulation 4064/89[215] now replaced by Regulation 139/2004.[216] According to this Regulation, concentrations with a Community dimension, as defined by the Regulation,[217] must be notified to the Commission which must then consider whether the merger is compatible with the Common Market.[218] In making this appraisal the Commission may take into account considerations of a social nature.[219]

The Preamble also states that the 'Regulation in no way detracts from the collective rights of employees, as recognised in the undertakings concerned, notably with regard to any obligation to inform or consult their recognised representatives under Community and national law'.[220] Article 18(4) entitles the Commission to hear the views of 'Natural or legal persons showing a sufficient interest and especially . . . the recognised representatives[221] of their employees shall be entitled, upon application, to be heard'.[222] As the Court explained in the *Grandes Sources* case,[223] the primacy given in the Merger Regulation to the establishment of a system of free competition could be

---

[215] OJ [1989] L395/1, as corrected and amended.   [216] OJ [2004] L24/22.

[217] Arts. 1 and 3 of the Regulation.   [218] Art. 2.

[219] This is confirmed by the 23rd recital of the Preamble which says 'It is necessary to establish whether or not concentrations with a Community dimension are compatible with the common market in terms of the need to maintain and develop effective competition in the common market. In so doing, the Commission must place its appraisal within the general framework of the achievement of the fundamental objectives referred to in Article 2 of the Treaty establishing the European Community and Article 2 of the Treaty on European Union'. Cf. The thirteenth recital of the Preamble to Reg. 4064/89 which was more explicit about the social objectives. It provided that: 'The Commission must place its appraisal within the general framework of the achievement referred to in Article 2 of the Treaty, including that of strengthening the Community's economic and social cohesion, referred to in Article 130a.'

[220] Recitals, para. 45.

[221] In Case T–96/92 *Comité Central d'Entreprise de la Société General des Grandes Sources v. Commission* [1995] ECR II–1213, para. 34, the Court said that it is for the Member States to define which organizations are competent to represent the collective interest of the employees and to determine their rights and prerogatives, subject to the adoption of harmonization measures such as the European Works Council Directive 94/45/EC (OJ [1994] L254/64).

[222] See also para. 19 of the Preamble. For the difficulties involved in invoking these provisions see Case T–96/92R *Comité Central d'Entreprise v. Commission* [1992] ECR II–2579 and Case T–12/93R *Comité Central d'entreprise de la société Anonyme Vittel and Comité d'établissement de Pierval v. Commission* [1993] ECR II–449, Order of the President of the Court of First Instance [1993] ECR II–449. Anderman, 'European Community Merger and Social Policy' (1993) 22 *ILJ*. 318.

[223] Case T–96/92 *Comité Central d'Entreprise de la Société General des Grandes Sources v. Commission* [1995] ECR II–1213, para. 28. See also Case T–12/93 *Vittel v. Commission* [1995] ECR II–1247, para. 38.

reconciled, in the context of an assessment of whether a concentration is compatible with the Common Market, with the social effects of that operation if they are liable to affect adversely the social objectives referred to in Article 2 of the Treaty. The CFI continued that the Commission, therefore, might have to ascertain whether 'the concentration is liable to have consequences, even if only indirectly, for the position of the employees in the undertakings in question, such as to affect the level or conditions of employment in the Community or a substantial part of it'.

The *Grandes Sources* case concerned the Nestlé/Perrier merger.[224] Although the trade union representatives (CGT Perrier) had met with the Commission to express their concerns about the social consequences of the merger, the Commission nevertheless allowed the merger to proceed on condition that Nestlé complied with certain conditions, including selling the brand names and sources Vichy, Thonon, Pierval, and Saint-Yorre. This led to two sets of challenges. First, the trade union and the Perrier works council sought an Article 230 judicial review of the Commission's Decision allowing the merger.[225] Under Article 230 natural or legal persons can challenge a Decision addressed to another provided it is of direct and individual concern to them. In this case the Court ruled that while the employee representatives were individually concerned by the Commission's Decision they were not directly concerned because the Decision did not prejudice either the rights of the organizations or the employees affected. However, the Court did say that the employee representatives had standing to bring proceedings to ensure that the procedural guarantees which they were entitled to assert during the administrative procedure under the Merger Control Regulation were satisfied.

The second proceedings were brought by the Vittel and Pierval works councils, challenging the transfer of the Pierval source which was operated by Vittel. Interim relief was initially granted,[226] suspending the operation of the Commission Decision until certain obstacles relating to the transfer of the rights to exploit Vichy and Thonon had been removed and the Court had been informed of that fact by the Commission.[227] In the subsequent judicial review proceedings, the applicants, now supported by the Perrier trade union and works council, sought annulment of either the Commission's Decision as a whole or the imposition of conditions.[228] Once again the Court found that

---

[224] Case No. IV/M.190, *Nestlé/Perrier* (OJ [1992] L356/1).

[225] They also made a separate application of interim relief under Arts. 242 and 243, but this was dismissed (Case T–96/92R [1992] ECR I–2579).

[226] Case T–12/93R *Comité Central d'entreprise de la société Anonyme Vittel and Comité d'establissement de Pierval* v. *Commission* [1993] ECR II–449.

[227] Following the communication of that information the applications for interim measures were dismissed by order of the President of the CFI [1993] ECR II–785.

[228] Case T–12/93 *Vittel* [1995] ECR II–1247.

since the applicants were the recognized representatives of the employees
concerned by the concentration and they were expressly mentioned in the
Merger Regulation they were individually concerned. However, they were
not directly concerned and so had no *locus standi* because the transfer of
the Pierval plant 'did not in itself entail any direct consequences for the
rights which the employees derived from their contract of employment'.[229]
These rights were protected by Directive 2001/23 on transfers[230] and (now)
Directive 98/59 on collective redundancies.[231]

2. State Aid

While the Merger Regulation expressly grants procedural prerogatives to the
recognized representatives of employees, this is not the case with the state aid
provisions. Therefore, the Court of First Instance said in *SFP*[232] that
employees' representatives were not individually concerned for the purposes
of having locus to challenge a Commission decision declaring state aid to the
industry to be incompatible with the Common Market and ordering its
recovery. The Court of First Instance did, however, concede that bodies representing employees of the undertaking in receipt of aid might, *qua* parties
concerned within the meaning of Article 88(2), submit comments to the
Commission on considerations of a social nature which could be taken into
account by the Commission.[233]

    The Court of Justice upheld the CFI's decision.[234] It said that the employee
representatives' status as negotiators with regard to social aspects such as
staffing and salary structure within the company did not suffice to distinguish
them individually.[235] The Court admitted that when determining whether
state aid was compatible with the Common Market, social aspects were liable
to be taken into account by the Commission, 'but only as part of an overall
assessment which includes a large number of considerations of various kinds,
linked in particular to the protection of competition, regional development,
the promotion of culture or again to the protection of the environment'.[236]
However, on the facts, the status as negotiators with regard to the social
aspects within SFP constituted only a 'tenuous link' with the actual subject-
matter of that decision and so there was no locus.

---

[229] Para. 58.   [230] OJ [1977] L61/26 as amended.   [231] OJ [1998] L225/16.
[232] Case T–189/97 *Comité d'entreprise de la société française de production v. Commission* [1998]
ECR II–335.
[233] Para. 41.
[234] Case C–106/98 *Comité d'entreprise de la société française de production v. Commission* [2000]
ECR I–3659.
[235] Para. 51.   [236] Para. 52.

3. The Takeover Directive

Finally, the Directive on Takeover Bids 2004/25/EC[237] makes provision for 'appropriate' information[238] (that a bid has been made and the offer document) to be given to the 'representatives' of the offeree and offeror company's employees, of failing that, to the employees directly.[239] The board of the offeree company must draw up and make public a document setting out its opinion of the bid and the reasons on which it is based, including its views on the effect of the implementation of the bid on the company's interest 'and specifically employment'. The board of the offeree company must at the same time communicate that opinion to the representatives of its employees or, where there are no such representatives, to the employees themselves. Where the board of the offeree company receives in good time a separate opinion from the representatives of its employees on the effects of the bid on employment, that opinion must be appended to the document.[240] Article 14 adds that the Directive is without prejudice to the rules relating to information and to consultation of representatives of employees and, if Member States so provide, co-determination with the employees of the offeror and the offeree company governed by the relevant national provisions, and in particular those adopted pursuant to Directives 94/45/EC, 98/59/EC, 2001/86/EC and 2002/14/EC. The 23rd preambular paragraph goes further still. It says that 'The disclosure of information to and the consultation of representatives of the employees of the offeror and the offeree company should be governed by the relevant national provisions', in particular those adopted pursuant to the EWC Directive 94/45/EC, Council Directive 98/59/EC on collective redundancies, Council Directive 2001/86/EC of 8 October 2001 supplementing the statute for a European Company with regard to the involvement of employees and the I&C Directive 2002/14/EC. It continues that the employees of the companies concerned, or their representatives, should 'nevertheless be given an opportunity to state their views on the foreseeable effects of the bid on employment' and adds that Member States can always apply or introduce national provisions concerning the disclosure of information to and the consultation of representatives of the employees of the offeror before an offer is launched.

---

[237] OJ [2004] L142/12.   [238] Preambular para. 13.
[239] Art. 6(1) and (2).   [240] Art. 9(5).

G. FINANCIAL PARTICIPATION OF EMPLOYEES IN A COMPANY

1. Introduction

The discussion so far has focused primarily on industrial democracy: employee participation in the processes of management and decision-making within the firm. Economic democracy, on the other hand, has enjoyed a renaissance in recent years. It covers a variety of forms of direct participation by employees in the ownership of the enterprise and in the distribution of economic rewards.[241] While in the case of a wholly owned workers co-operative, economic democracy can go hand in hand with industrial democracy, more usually economic rewards are designed to encourage, in an indirect way, 'identification' of employees with employers and to produce incentives for employees to increase the profitability of their employing company by allowing them to reap some of the benefits of that increase (generally through share ownership or profit-sharing).[242] This form of financial flexibility offers both macroeconomic and microeconomic benefits. The macroeconomic effects relate to the flexibility of the job market: if workers accept a substantial proportion of their remuneration as a profit-related element, either in cash or shares in the company, then the company's wage bill increases only as it becomes more profitable. Consequently, the dangers of wage inflation are reduced. Companies can also deal with fluctuations in the economic cycle by reducing the profit-related pay element rather than dismissing workers.[243] At the microeconomic level profit-sharing can lead to increased effort and efficiency because employees with a financial stake in a company have an incentive to work more productively and co-operate more willingly with management.[244] This in turn leads to improved competitiveness and better industrial relations.

The Community has made various attempts to encourage the development of schemes for employee financial participation. For example, the Capital Directive on the formation of public limited liability companies and the maintenance and alteration of capital[245] permits Member States to derogate from

---

[241] McLean, *Fair Shares—The Future of Employee Financial Participation in the UK* (IER, London, 1994) 3.

[242] Ibid., 3.   [243] McLean, above, n. 241, 3 and 4, for a critique of this view.

[244] This model still allows room for 'free-riders' where an individual employee calculates that if other workers continue to perform optimally and he does not, the firm's productivity should be only marginally affected; the value of his ownership stake should not change and he can retain the gains from his self-serving behaviour. If most employees think this way the viability of the enterprise is threatened. Therefore managers are necessary to monitor the staff's performance. See Cheffins, above, n. 7, 559.

[245] Dir. 77/91/EEC (OJ [1977] L26/1) as amended by Council Dir. 92/101/EEC (OJ [1992] L347/64).

certain provisions of the Directive on the grounds of the need to adopt or apply provisions designed to encourage the participation of employees in the capital of companies.[246] In 1979 the Commission published a memorandum on employee participation on asset formation[247] but despite a resolution by the Parliament in 1983 calling on the Commission to draw up a Recommendation and to consider whether a Directive might be necessary, little progress was made. However, in the Social Charter Action Programme following the Social Charter 1989, the Commission said that employee participation in asset formation and productive capital formation helped bring about a fairer distribution of wealth and was a means of attaining an adequate level of non-inflationary growth. This, combined with the advantages of greater involvement of workers in the progress of their companies, precipitated the adoption of a non-legally-binding Recommendation concerning the promotion of employee participation in profits and enterprise results, known by the acronym PEPPER.[248]

2. PEPPER

The PEPPER Recommendation invites the Member States to acknowledge the potential benefits of a wider use of schemes to increase the participation of employees in the profits of the enterprise and to take account of the role and the responsibility of management and labour in this context. It recommends that the Member States ensure that legal structures are adequate to allow the introduction of such schemes, and to consider the possibility of financial advantages to encourage their introduction. The Recommendation also lists key points in the preparation of such schemes or in reviewing existing schemes, including the regularity of bonus payments and the formula for calculating the payment to each employee. However, the Commission suggests that the existence of financial participation schemes should not stand in the way of normal negotiations dealing with wages and conditions of employment. It also recommends that the risks inherent in participation schemes, particularly if their investments are relatively undiversified,[249] should be made clear to employees.

It seems that the Commission was not, at first, totally convinced by the benefits of these schemes. In the Preamble to the Recommendation, it said

---

[246] Art. 41(1). Moreover, Art. 41(2) provides that Member States may decide not to apply certain provisions of the Directive to companies incorporated under a special law which issue both capital shares and workers' shares, the latter being issued to the company's employees as a body, who are represented at general meetings of shareholders by delegates having the right to vote.

[247] Bull. Supp. 6/79.   [248] Council Recommendation 92/443/EEC (OJ [1992] L243/53).

[249] For developments in France, see *EIRR* 243, 28.

that the body of empirical research into the effects of PEPPER schemes 'does not yet provide overwhelming evidence of strong overall advantages'. This is because, although companies with extensive financial participation schemes do perform better on average than companies without them, this is as at least as likely to be due to the fact that they are better managed overall and have progressive employment policies. Research also suggests that employees tend to regard PEPPER schemes as a perk.[250] The Commission's view is now changing.[251] In its Communication on Modernizing the Organization of Work,[252] it considered that the financial participation of employees was an important way of promoting workers' motivation and adaptability. It argues that there is some evidence that a 'sense of ownership' is an important 'intervening variable' between actual ownership and attitudinal change, although it has been found that opportunities for participating in decision-making are more important than ownership *per se* in generating feelings of ownership.[253] By 2002 the Commission was so committed to the idea of employee financial participation that it issued a further Communication[254] aimed at promoting greater use of employee financial participation schemes across Europe.

H. CONCLUSIONS

This chapter has considered a wide range of mechanisms introduced by Community law to encourage worker participation in the workplace in an attempt to foster greater trust between workers and their employers. The principal model relied on by the Community is the provision of information to workers or their representatives, and consultation. This approach envisages a co-operative/partnership style of worker/employer relationship rather than the more antagonistic relationship sometimes found between trade unions and employers. In the next chapter we move on to consider freedom of association more generally in the Community legal order, together with the Community's approach to industrial action.

---

[250] McLean, above, n. 241, 4.
[251] See the Pepper II Report: COM(96) 697 which noted that financial participation schemes are associated with a number of important benefits, especially in terms of higher productivity levels, employment and workers' involvement.
[252] COM(98) 592, 5.
[253] Pendleton, Wilson and Wright, 'The Perception and Effects of Share Ownership: Empirical Evidence from Employee Buy-outs' (1998) 36 *BJIR*. 99 and Pendleton, 'Characteristics of Workplaces with Financial Participation: Evidence from the Workplace Industrial Relations Survey' (1997) 28 *IRJ*. 103.
[254] COM(2002) 364.

16

Freedom of Association, Collective Bargaining, and Collective Action

A. INTRODUCTION

So far we have considered the Community rights given to worker representatives. These representatives may well be trade unions or elected worker representatives. In this chapter we focus specifically on the limited way in which the European Community protects both trade union rights and the rights of employers and their associations. It will become apparent that the Community competence in this field is limited and the recognition of collective labour rights takes place largely through fundamental rights[1] which serve to limit any Community action (or Member State action in the Community sphere) impinging upon these rights. For this reason, this chapter will concentrate on the various sources that inform the shape of these fundamental rights as recognized by the Community. We begin by considering freedom of association—the right to form and join trade unions—and then examine the extent to which the Community recognizes the rights related to freedom of association—the right to bargain collectively and the right to take industrial action.

B. FREEDOM OF ASSOCIATION

1. The Meaning of Freedom of Association

1.1. Legal Sources of the Right

Freedom of association is recognized in a number of civil and political rights instruments as well as by economic and social rights documents as a fundamental right, in particular the International Labour Organization (ILO) Conventions 87 and 98, the United Nations Universal Declaration of Human

---

[1] See Ryan, 'The Charter and Collective Labour Law' in Hervey and Kenner (eds), *Economic and Social Rights under the EU Charter of Fundamental Rights* (Hart Publishing, Oxford, 2003) 67 on the paradox of the generous provision for collective rights at EU level in the Charter compared with the historical weakness of collective labour law at EU level.

Rights,[2] and the accompanying International Covenant on Economic, Social and Cultural Rights[3] and the International Covenant on Civil and Political Rights.[4] Most importantly, for the EU's purposes,[5] freedom of association is recognised in the European Convention on Human Rights (ECHR) and the complementary European Social Charter (ESC) 1961 (revised in 1996). Article 11(1) of the European Convention talks of workers having the rights of freedom of association with others, 'including the right to form and to join trade unions for the protection of their interests'. The contents of Article 11(1) are largely reiterated in Part I[6] of the European Social Charter 1961[7] but expanded in Part II, where Article 5 provides that 'with a view to ensuring or promoting the freedom of workers and employers to form local, national or international organisations for the protection of their economic and social interests and to join those organisations, the Contracting parties undertake that national law shall not be such as to impair, nor shall it be so applied as to impair, this freedom'.[8]

---

[2] Art. 23(4): 'everyone has the right to form and join trade unions for the protection of his interests' but it also provides that 'no one may be compelled to belong to any association' (Art. 20(2)).

[3] Art. 8(1). See generally Wedderburn, 'Freedom of Association or Right to Organise? The Common Law and International Sources', in Wedderburn, *Employment Rights in Britain and Europe: Selected Papers in Labour Law* (Lawrence & Wishart, London, 1991).

[4] Art. 22.

[5] The Preamble to the Single European Act 1986 recognized both the ECHR and the ESC 1961 as forming part of the foundations of the European Community. Art. 6 of the Treaty on European Union also provides that the Union must respect fundamental rights as guaranteed by the ECHR and Art. 136 as amended by the Treaty of Amsterdam refers to 'fundamental social rights such as those set out in the European Social Charter 1961 . . . and in the 1989 Community Charter . . .'. The Praesidium explanation accompanying the Charter of Fundamental Rights 2000 (drawn up as a way of providing guidance on the interpretation of the Charter and which has to be given due regard by the courts of the Union and of the Member States (Art. II–112(7)) expressly refers to Art. 11 ECHR. Furthermore, the case law of the European Court of Justice makes clear that when the Community institutions are legislating they must respect fundamental human rights, including those contained in the ECHR, as must the Member States when implementing or derogating from Community law or more broadly when acting in the field of Community law. For a full discussion, see Ryan, 'The Charter and Collective Labour Law' in Hervey and Kenner (eds), *Economic and Social Rights under the EU Charter of Fundamental Rights* (Hart Publishing, Oxford, 2003) 71.

[6] Part I of the Charter takes the form of a declaration which lists those social and economic rights which all Contracting Parties must accept as the aim of their policies. Part II consists of the breakdown of those rights into their component parts which it then elaborates. States are then obliged to consider themselves bound by such articles or paragraphs of articles as they choose subject to certain fundamental provisions and an overall minimum selection.

[7] A new Protocol to the Social Charter was concluded in 1991 designed to improve the machinery of the Charter.

[8] It has been suggested that while the Convention organs are prepared to look at the European Social Charter 1961 as an aid to interpretation, they have done so in a way that minimizes its impact on Art. 11: Lewis-Anthony, 'Case Law of Art. 11 of the European Convention on Human Rights', *Freedom of Association*, Council of Europe, citing *Swedish Engine Drivers* v. *Sweden*, Eur. Ct. H.R., judgment of 6 February 1976, Series A, No. 2.

The EU itself has also recognized the right of freedom of association. Article 11 of the Community Social Charter 1989 provides that:

Employers and workers of the European Community shall have the right of association in order to constitute professional organisations or trade unions of their choice for the defence of their economic and social interests. Every employer and every worker shall have the freedom to join or not to join such organisations without any personal or occupational damage being thereby suffered by him.

The Social Charter Action Programme talks only of responsibility for the implementation of such policies resting with the Member States 'in accordance with their national traditions and policies'. Certainly the right to freedom of association, that is 'to join, without interference by the state, in associations to attain various ends',[9] exists in all Member States of the Union. In a number of states the right of freedom of association is considered to be so fundamental that it is enshrined in the Constitution. Freedom of Association is also recognized in Article 12(1) of the EU's Charter of Fundamental Rights 2000 (Article II–72(1) of the Constitutional Treaty). This provides that: 'Everyone has the right to freedom of peaceful assembly and to freedom of association at all levels, in particular in political, trade union and civic matters, which implies the right of everyone to form and to join trade unions for the protection of his or her interests.'

1.2. The Content of the Right

(a) The Right to Establish Unions

Both the ECHR and the European Community Social Charter 1989 recognize two components to freedom of association. The first is the right to establish *unions*, which should be free to 'draw up their own rules, to administer their own affairs and to establish and join trade union federations'.[10] The use of the noun 'unions', in the plural, is important, because, as the Court of Human Rights indicated in *Young, James and Webster*,[11] it precludes the establishment of union monopolies and envisages the freedom to establish rival unions.

(b) The Right to Join or not to Join Trade Unions

The second right, and the corollary of the first, is for people to join—or not to join—those unions. The Community Social Charter 1989—but not the Charter of Fundamental Rights 2000—expressly recognizes the negative freedom, the right of an individual not to join a union. Consequently, a closed shop contravenes a worker's fundamental right. There is evidence that when

---

[9] Application 6094/73 *Association X v. Sweden* Dec.6.7.77, D.R. 9, 5, at 7 in the context of the European Convention on Human Rights.

[10] Application No. 10550/83 *Cheall v. United Kingdom*, Dec.13.5.85, D.R. 42, 178.

[11] *Young, James and Webster v. United Kingdom*, Eur. Ct. H.R, Series B, No. 39.

the ECHR was drafted the right not to join a trade union was expressly excluded.[12] Nevertheless, the organs of the ECHR have not been constrained by this and, in *Sigurjonsson*,[13] a case concerning a pre-entry closed shop, the Court of Human Rights pronounced conclusively that 'Article 11 must be viewed as encompassing a negative right of association' although it added that, 'It is not necessary for the Court to determine in this instance whether this right is to be considered on an equal footing with the positive right'. In *Sørensen*[14] the European Court of Human Rights referred to the Community's Social Charter 1989 and the Charter of Fundamental Rights 2000 to support its conclusion that 'there is little support in the contracting states for the maintenance of closed-shop agreements' and the EU instruments indicate that their use in the labour market is not an indispensable tool for the effective enjoyment of trade-union freedoms. Denmark has therefore failed to protect the applicant workers' 'negative right to trade union freedom'.[15]

These cases do, however, point to an individualist—as opposed to a collectivist—conception of the right to freedom of association. Individualists see freedom of association as a right for individuals to use as they choose. The collective wishes of the group—to force the individual to join a trade union on the ground that a powerful union is better placed than a weak one to bargain with the employer—are subordinated to the individual's choices. By contrast, the collectivist argues that groups are stronger if they are able to exercise some control over the individual: by forcing them to join a trade union or to go on strike. And a powerful union is better placed than a weak one to bargain with the employer.[16]

If an individual does decide to join a trade union, *Wilson and Palmer*[17]

---

[12] Report of 19 June 1950 of the Conference of Senior Officials, in Vol. 4 Collected Edition of Travaux Preparatoires, cited in Lewis-Anthony, above, n. 8, 45.

[13] *Sigurjonsson v. Ireland*, Eur. Ct. H.R, judgment of 30 June 1993, Series A, No. 264; see also *Sørensen and Rasmussen v. Denmark*, judgment of 11 January 2006, application nos. 52562/99 and 52620/99, para. 64 (pre-entry closed shop): the compulsion to join a trade union 'struck at the very substance of the freedom of association guaranteed by Article 11'. See too *Young, James and Webster* (post-entry closed shop), Eur. Ct. H.R., judgment of 13 August 1981, Series A, No. 44, 21, para. 52.

[14] See also *Sørensen and Rasmussen v. Denmark*, judgment of 11 January 2006, applications nos. 52562/99 and 52620/99, paras. 73–4.

[15] Paras. 75–6.

[16] See also the European Court of Human Rights' view in *Wilson and Palmer v. The United Kingdom*, Applications nos. 30668/96, 30671/96 and 30678/96, judgment of 2 July 2002: the 'essential object of Article 11 is to protect *the individual* against arbitrary interference by public authorities with the exercise of the rights protected' (para. 41). See also *Sørensen and Rasmussen v. Denmark*, judgment of 11 January 2006, application nos. 52562/99 and 52620/99, para. 58: 'although individual interests must on occasion be subordinated to those of a group, democracy does not simply mean that the views of the majority must always prevail: a balance must be achieved which ensures the fair and proper treatment of minorities and avoids any abuse of a dominant position'.

[17] *Wilson and Palmer v. The United Kingdom*, Application nos. 30668/96, 30671/96 and 30678/96, judgment of 2 July 2002.

makes clear that trade union membership means making use of the services offered by the trade union. The case concerned a decision by an employer to offer higher pay increases to employees who agreed to accept personal contracts in place of collectively agreed terms and conditions of employment. Employees who refused to agree, and consequently did not receive the increase, claimed that the employer had taken action short of dismissal against them on grounds of their union membership contrary to what is now section 146 TULR(C)A 1992. According to the Court of Appeal, the right of an employee under section 146 was not only a right to union membership itself: Dillon LJ said there was no genuine distinction between membership of the union and making use of essential services of the union. By contrast, the House of Lords held[18] that in the case of an omission (withholding from an employee a benefit which was conferred upon another employee) this could not amount to 'action', whatever the purpose of the omission, and hence the employers had not taken *action* short of dismissal against the employees. Consequently, the existing legal protection for trade members under section 146 meant no more than the right to carry a union card. It did not mean that members could call on the assistance of their union for help in dealing with their employer.[19]

However, the UK was subsequently condemned by the European Court of Human Rights.[20] At paragraph 46, it made clear that:

It is the essence of the right to join a trade union for the protection of their interests that employees should be free to instruct or permit the union to make representations to their employer or to take action in support of their interests on their behalf. If workers are prevented from so doing, their freedom to belong to a trade union, for the protection of their interests becomes illusory.

Ewing describes the paragraph 46 right as the 'weaker dimension' of the freedom of association right.[21] However, the Court then adds a stronger dimension: that it was the role of the state to ensure that trade union members are not prevented or restrained from using their union to represent them in attempts to regulate their relations with their employers.[22]

The Court therefore concluded in *Wilson and Palmer* that by permitting employers to use financial incentives to induce employees to surrender important union rights, the UK failed in its positive obligation to secure the enjoyment of the rights under Article 11 of the Convention, both in respect of the individual and, in a nod in the collectivist direction, to the applicant trade unions.[23]

---

[18] [1995] IRLR 258.
[19] Ewing, 'The Implications of *Wilson and Palmer*' (2003) 32 *ILJ*. 1.
[20] Applications nos. 30668/96, 30671/96 and 30678/96 *Wilson and NUJ v. UK*; *Palmer, Wyeth and National Union of Rail Maritime and Transport Workers v. UK*; *Doolan and others v. UK* [2002] IRLR 568.
[21] Above, n. 19, 6.   [22] Ibid.   [23] Para. 48.

(c) Legal Protection for those Exercising their Rights

The corollary of the rights to establish trade unions and to join a trade union is that, as the Community Social Charter expressly states, workers (or employers) must not suffer any 'personal or occupational damage' as a result of exercising their freedom of association.[24] This might include dismissal or action short of dismissal (the very protection that was at issue in *Wilson and Palmer*), or pressure by an employer on an employee to give up a position in the union. While such action is not expressly proscribed by the ECHR, the Convention provides practical recourse: Article 13 says that 'everyone whose rights and freedoms as set forth in this Convention are violated shall have an effective remedy before a national authority'.

1.3. Restrictions on the Right of Freedom of Association

There are, however, limits on the freedom of association. Most notably, Article 11(2) ECHR provides:

No restriction shall be placed on the exercise of these rights other than such as are prescribed by law and are necessary in a democratic society in the interests of national security or public safety, for the prevention of disorder or crime, for the protection of health or morals or for the protection of the rights and freedoms of others.[25] This article shall not prevent the imposition of lawful restrictions on the exercise of these rights by members of the armed forces, of the police or of the administration of the state.

The question of what constitutes 'lawful restrictions' was at issue in the *GCHQ* case.[26] Here the European Commission of Human Rights considered a ban on unions and union membership at a government intelligence-gathering centre to be lawful. However, the case fell at the admissibility stage and so did not get beyond the Commission to the Court. As Ewing points out, a more egregious form of anti-union activity is harder to contemplate, as both the Freedom of Association Committee[27] and the Committee of Experts of the ILO made abundantly clear, yet the *GCHQ* case provides a 'classic example of the failure of the Strasbourg system to protect trade union rights.[28] As we shall see below, the Court of Human Rights was somewhat more rigorous in its application of this derogation in the *UNISON* case.[29]

---

[24] No express prohibition is made by the Charter against unions exploiting their dominant position by e.g. expelling members contrary to union rules.

[25] Para. 14 of the Community Social Charter merely states that 'the internal legal order of the Member states shall determine under which conditions and to what extent the rights provided for in Arts. 11–13 apply to the armed forces, the police and the civil service'.

[26] Application no. 11603/85 *Council of Civil Servant Unions v. United Kingdom*, Dec. 20.1.87, D.R. 50, 228.

[27] ILO's Freedom of Association Committee, 234th Report of the Committee on Freedom of Association, Case no. 1261.

[28] Ewing, above, n. 19.

[29] *UNISON v. United Kingdom*, judgment of 10 January 2002, [2002] IRLR 497.

2. Freedom of Association and Community Law

What effect do these rules have on Community law? The first point to note is that Article 137(5) expressly excludes freedom of association from the Community's competence, at least under Article 137.[30] In other words, the Community has no power to legislate in the field of freedom of association under Article 137. However, the Court of Justice has recognized freedom of association to be a fundamental right which will bind (1) the Community institutions when they are legislating or adopting administrative measures, and (2) the Member States when they are implementing Community law, derogating from Community law or, more broadly, when acting in the field of Community law.[31] In this respect, the jurisprudence of the European Court of Human Rights interpreting this fundamental right is highly significant.

In respect of action by the *Community* institutions, the right to freedom of association was recognized in a staff case, *Kortner*,[32] where the Court said that 'Under the general principles of labour law the freedom of trade union activity recognised under Article 24a of the Staff Regulations means not only that officials and servants have the right to form associations of their own choosing, but also that these associations are free to do anything lawful to protect the interests of their members as employees.' Thus, as Advocate General Jacobs noted in *Albany*,[33] the Court recognized, first, the individual right to form and join an association and, second, the collective right to take action. In his view the fundamental nature of those two rights was confirmed in *Bosman*[34] with respect to freedom of association in general, and in *Maurissen* more specifically with regard to trade unions.[35] In the light of this line of case law, if the Community tried to legislate in a way which interferes with freedom of association, it is likely that any such measure could be successfully challenged as being incompatible with freedom of association. In respect of action by *Member States* when implementing or derogating from Community law, they will also be bound by the principle of freedom of association and the related right of freedom of assembly.

In addition, the Court has insisted that Community secondary legislation be interpreted in the light of freedom of association, as *Werhof*[36] demonstrates.

---

[30] For a discussion on this point, see Case C–14/04 *Abdelkader Dellas and Others* v. *Premier ministre and Others* [2006] ECR I–000, para. 39 considered in Ch. 2.

[31] Case C–260/89 *ERT* [1991] ECR I–2925 considered further in Ch. 1.

[32] Case 175/73 *Union Syndicale, Massa and Kortner* v. *Commission* [1974] ECR 917, para. 14.

[33] Case C–67/96 *Albany International BV* v. *Stichting Bedrijfspensioenfonds Textielindustrie* [1999] ECR I–5751.

[34] Case C–415/93 *Union Royale Belge des Sociétés de Football Association and Others* v. *Bosman and Others* [1995] ECR I–4921, paras. 79 and 80.

[35] Joined Cases C–193/87 and C–194/87 *Maurissen and European Public Service Union* v. *Court of Auditors* [1990] ECR I–95, paras. 11–16 and 21.

[36] Case C–499/04 *Werhof* v. *Freeway Traffic System GmbH & Co. KG* [2006] ECR I–000.

This was a case about the Transfer of Undertakings Directive 2001/88[37] where the question was raised whether a transferee was bound by a collective agreement subsequent to the one in force at the time of the transfer of the business, when the transferee was not party to the collective agreement. The Court began by recognizing 'Freedom of association, which also includes the right not to join an association or union[38] ... is one of the fundamental rights which, in accordance with the Court's settled case-law, are protected in the Community legal order'.[39] It then considered two approaches to the interpretation of the Directive. The first, the 'dynamic' interpretation, supported by the claimant employee, would mean that future collective agreements apply to a transferee who is not party to a collective agreement with the result that his fundamental right not to join an association could be affected.[40] The second, the 'static' interpretation, supported by the defendant transferee, makes it possible to avoid a situation in which the transferee of a business who is not party to a collective agreement is bound by future changes to that agreement.[41] This interpretation safeguards his right not to join an association and it is this approach that the Court chose.[42]

While fundamental rights are usually used to *limit* the powers of the Community or the Member States, they can also be used by the Member States to justify limiting other rights, in particular the free movement provisions. This can be seen most clearly in *Schmidberger*.[43] This case concerned not a trade union but an environmental association which organized a demonstration, blocking a stretch of the Brenner Motorway (the A13, the major transit route for trade between northern Europe and Italy) for 30 hours, to draw attention to the threat to the environment and public health posed by the constant increase in the movement of heavy goods vehicles on the motorway.[44] Schmidberger, a German transport company, sought damages for the losses it suffered from its lorries not being able to use this route. The Court said that the fact that the competent authorities of a Member State did not ban this demonstration was capable of restricting intra-Community trade in

[37] OJ [2001] L82/16 considered further in Ch. 13. See also the Consolidated Equality Dir. 2006/54 (OJ [2006] L 204/23), 20th preambular para.

[38] Citing Art. 11 of the European Convention and the ECtHR cases: Eur. Court of H.R., *Sigurjónsson* v. *Iceland*, judgment of 30 June 1993, Series A, No. 264, § 35, and *Gustafsson* v. *Sweden*, judgment of 25 April 1996, *Reports of Judgments and Decisions*, 1996-II, p. 637, § 45.

[39] Para. 33.   [40] Para. 34.   [41] Para. 35.   [42] Para. 36.

[43] Case C–112/00 *Eugen Schmidberger, Internationale Transporte und Planzüge* v. *Republic of Austria* [2003] ECR I–5659. See also *Viking* v. *The International Transport Workers' Federation and the Finnish Seamen's Union* [2005] EWHC 1222; [2005] EWCA Civ 1299; [2006] IRLR 58 where the Court will also have to address similar issues-discussed in detail in Ch. 5.

[44] This is a matter of serious concern for the Tyrolean authorities which tried to ban from the A12 Inntal motorway all heavy goods vehicles over 7.5 tonnes carrying certain goods (e.g. logs, cork, stone, vehicles) (IP/03/984) but were stopped by the Court: Case C–320/03 R *Commission* v. *Austria* [2003] ECR I–000.

goods and so breached Articles 28 and 29 EC on free movement of goods, read together with Article 10 on the duty of co-operation.[45]

However, the Austrian authorities justified their (in)action on the grounds of the fundamental rights of the demonstrators to freedom of expression and freedom of assembly guaranteed by the ECHR and the national constitution, principles which, the Court said, it recognized formed an integral part of the general principles of EC law.[46] It continued that 'since both the Community and its Member States are required to respect fundamental rights, the protection of those rights is a legitimate interest which, in principle, justifies a restriction of the obligations imposed by Community law, even under a fundamental freedom guaranteed by the Treaty such as the free movement of goods'.[47] Thus, the Court saw the fundamental rights—including freedom of association—as a free-standing justification or public interest requirement[48] which could in principle take precedence over the free movement of goods.

However, since the two human rights at stake, described by the Court as 'fundamental pillars of a democratic society',[49] were not absolute, the Court recognized that their exercise could be restricted, provided that 'the restrictions in fact correspond to objectives of general interest and do not, taking account of the aim of the restrictions, constitute disproportionate and unacceptable interference, impairing the very substance of the rights guaranteed'.[50] The Court then tried to determine whether a fair balance had been struck between the competing interests.[51] It noted that the demonstration took place following a request for authorization, as required by national law, and after the Austrian authorities had decided to allow it to go ahead;[52] the obstacle to free movement was limited (a single event, on a single route, lasting for 30 hours), the demonstrators were motivated by a desire to express their opinion on a matter of public importance and not by a desire to restrict trade in goods of a particular type or from a particular source;[53] and various administrative and supporting measures had been taken by the Austrian authorities to limit the disruption to road traffic, including an extensive publicity campaign launched well in advance by the media and the motoring organizations, both in Austria and in neighbouring countries,[54] as well as the designation of alternative routes. The Court therefore concluded that the fact that the authorities of a Member State did not ban the demonstration in these circumstances was compatible with Community law.[55]

Following the Court's ruling in an earlier case, *Commission v. France (Spanish Strawberries)*[56] which concerned a long history of violent attacks by

---

[45] Para. 64.   [46] Paras. 71–3.   [47] Para. 74.

[48] See further Barnard, *The Substantive Law of the EU: The Four Freedoms* (OUP, Oxford, 2004) Ch. 6.

[49] Para. 79.   [50] Para. 80.   [51] Para. 81.   [52] Para. 84.   [53] Para. 86.

[54] Para. 87.   [55] Para. 94.   [56] Case C–265/95 [1997] ECR I–6959.

French farmers directed against agricultural products from other Member States[57] to which the state had failed to respond, leading the Court to find France in breach of Article 28 on the free movement of goods and Article 10 on the duty of co-operation, the Council adopted Regulation 2679/98[58] which was designed to set up an intervention mechanism to safeguard free trade in the Single Market. This provides that State A can complain to the Commission about obstacles to the free movement of goods which are attributable to State B—either through action or inaction[59]—where the obstacles lead to serious disruption of the free movement of goods, cause serious loss to the individuals affected and require immediate action.[60] However, this complaints procedure is subject to the fundamental rights recognized in Article 2 of the Regulation:

This Regulation may not be interpreted as affecting in any way the exercise of fundamental rights, as recognised in Member States, including the right or freedom to strike. These rights may also include the right or freedom to take other actions covered by the specific industrial relations systems in Member States.

This Regulation demonstrates the importance of these fundamental rights as a defensive mechanism to claims against Member States for failing to prevent strikes and other forms of industrial action.

3. The Creation of a European-wide Trade Union Movement?

Will the EU's recognition of freedom of association lead to the creation of a European wide trade union movement? At present this seems unlikely. Industrial relations in the Member States are characterized by significant diversity within the trade union movement. In some Member States, such as the UK, Germany, Ireland, and Denmark, unions are 'unified'. In others, unions are politically ideological and confessional (i.e. religiously orientated).[61] In the Netherlands, for example, the three main trade union confederations comprise, firstly, a confederation (FNV) created from a merger between the socialist and most of the Catholic organizations, secondly, a Protestant Union

---

[57] Para. 2.

[58] OJ [1998] L337/8. See also the Resolution of the Council and of the Representatives of the Governments of the Member States meeting within the Council of 7 December 1998 (OJ [1998] L337/10) which encourages the Court to adopt an expedited procedure in respect of cases arising under Reg. 2679/98.

[59] 'Inaction' is defined in Art. 1(2) as covering the case when the competent authorities of a Member State, in the presence of an obstacle caused by actions taken by private individuals, fail to take all necessary and proportionate measures within their powers with a view to removing the obstacle and ensuring the free movement of goods in their territory.

[60] Art. 1(1).

[61] See Zachert, 'Trade Unions in Europe: Dusk or a New Dawn?' (1993) 9 *Int. Jo. Compar. LLIR* 15, 16.

federation (CNV) which includes some Catholic civil service unions who refused to join the socialists, and thirdly, a federation of white-collar organizations (MHP).[62] Similarly, in Italy industrial relations reflect that nation's divisions in politics and ideology: Catholic and anti-Catholic, Communist and anti-Communist, collectivist and individualist.[63] This pattern is echoed in Belgium where the three main ideological pillars of society—Catholicism, Protestantism, and socialism—are cross-cut in industrial relations by the differences: between employer and employee, Catholic and non-Catholic, and French-speaking and Dutch-speaking communities.[64] The existence of such differences, combined with the lack of significant transnational power resources, suggest that worker representation will continue to take place primarily within the national or subnational context but with co-operation through the European trade union confederation.

C. THE RIGHT TO ENGAGE IN COLLECTIVE BARGAINING

1. Introduction

As we saw in the previous chapter, Community legislation emphasizes information and consultation with worker representatives. This can be a far cry from collective bargaining since no agreement need be reached and ultimately the final decision rests with the employer. In the original Treaty of Rome the Social Partners had only a discreet presence—through the Economic and Social Committee (ECOSOC)[65] and as the subject of close co-operation which the Commission was obliged to promote between the Member States.[66] The situation has changed dramatically since 1957 and the Social Partners now have a potentially important role, as legislators and as partners of change in the European Employment Strategy. The Commission's discourse has changed dramatically too. It now focuses on the need to develop 'a strong partnership at all appropriate levels: at European, national, sectoral and enterprise level' to 'negotiate agreements to modernise the organisation of work'.[67]

---

[62] Visser, 'The End of an Era and the End of a System', in Ferner and Hyman (eds), *Industrial Relations in the New Europe* (Blackwell, Oxford, 1998) 328.

[63] Ferner and Hyman, 'Italy: Between Political Exchange and Micro-Corporatism', in Ferner and Hyman (eds), above, n. 62, 524.

[64] See Vilrokx and Van Leemput, 'Belgium: A New Ability in Industrial Relations?', in Ferner and Hyman (eds), above, n. 62, 363 and 367.

[65] Arts. 257–62.

[66] Art. 118 (now Art. 140) provides that subject-matter of close co-operation include 'the right of association, and collective bargaining between employers and workers'.

[67] COM(98) 592, 2. See also Art. I–48 of the Constitutional Treaty.

2. Collective Bargaining and Collective Agreements

2.1. The Meaning of Collective Bargaining

In its broad sense[68] collective bargaining is a process of interest accommodation which includes all sorts of bipartite or tripartite discussions relating to labour problems directly or indirectly affecting a group of workers. The discussions may take place in different fora, with or without the presence of governments, and aim at ascertaining the view of the other party, obtaining a concession or reaching a compromise. A narrower but more precise meaning of collective bargaining views it only in connection with the bipartite discussions leading to the conclusion of agreements. In this narrower sense, collective bargaining involves a process of negotiations between individual employers or representatives of employers' organizations and trade union representatives. As a rule, any agreement concluded is regarded as binding not only on its signatories but also on the groups they represent.

Collective bargaining offers a variety of benefits. As Advocate General Jacobs pointed out in *Albany*:[69]

It is widely accepted that collective agreements between management and labour prevent costly labour conflicts, reduce transaction costs through a collective and rule-based negotiation process and promote predictability and transparency. A measure of equilibrium between the bargaining power on both sides helps to ensure a balanced outcome for both sides and for society as a whole.

2.2. The Content of Collective Agreements

The content of collective agreements can be determined by the contracting parties but comprise principally of (1) normative clauses and (2) contractual or obligatory clauses. The normative stipulations refer to the terms and conditions of work which must be observed in all the individual employment contracts in the enterprise concerned. These include all aspects of working conditions, wages, fringe benefits, job classifications, working hours, time off, training, job security, and non-contributory benefit schemes. The collective agreement can also contain collective normative stipulations relating to informing and consulting workers, worker participation and procedural rules.[70]

---

[68] See Cordova, 'Collective Bargaining', in Blanpain (ed.), *Comparative Labour Law and Industrial Relations*, 3rd edn (Kluwer, Deventer, 1987). See now Blanpain (ed.), *Comparative Labour Law and Industrial Relations in Industrialised Market Economies*, 5th edn (Kluwer, Deventer, 1993). These definitions roughly correspond to what is called in France the informal and formal types of negotiation (*negociation officieuse* and *negociation officielle*).

[69] Case C–67/96 [1999] ECR I–5751, para. 181.

[70] Commission, *Comparative Study on Rules Governing Working Conditions in the Member States: a Synopsis*, SEC(89) 1137.

The contractual or obligatory clauses include all provisions spelling out the rights and duties of the parties. Often the main duty is the peace obligation which means that for the duration of the agreement neither of the parties is permitted to initiate industrial action against the other party with the intention of altering the conditions laid down in the collective agreement. Such an obligation is considered to be a natural consequence of collective bargaining, which is supposed to bring stability to labour relations. This obligation may be absolute, in which case the parties are obliged to refrain from all industrial action,[71] or relative, in which case neither of the parties is, for the duration of the collective agreement, permitted to initiate industrial action against the other party with the intention of altering conditions laid down in the agreement.[72] The relative peace obligation offers trade unions the advantage of safeguarding their right to formulate new demands if and when substantive changes in the socio-economic environment occur.[73]

Article 12(1) of the Community Social Charter 1989 provides that 'Employers or employers' organisations, on the one hand, and workers' organisations on the other, shall have the right to negotiate and conclude collective agreements under the conditions laid down by national legislation and practice'. In most Member States collective bargaining has been used as a means of setting standards or improving upon standards laid down by contract or statute. However, between the Member States attitudes and approaches to collective bargaining vary considerably. At one end of the spectrum lies Denmark where collective agreements form the cornerstone of labour standards. At the other stands the UK where there is a statutory presumption that collective agreements are not legally binding[74] between the parties. Collective agreements do have legal effect if incorporated into the contract of employment, but equally, since collective agreements do not constitute a floor of rights, the individual contract can be used to derogate from its provisions. In between lie Romano-Germanic countries such as Belgium, France, Germany, and Greece where collectively agreed norms can be given by law an *erga omnes* or 'extended' effect.[75] Thus, the law is used to ensure that the normative terms of collective agreements are applied more generally throughout the industry or sector. The original rationale for this procedure was the need to avoid unfair competition from non-unionized enterprises, but subsequently the

---

[71] Birk, 'Industrial Conflict: The Law of Strikes and Lock-outs', in Blanpain (ed.) above, n. 68, 413.

[72] Commission, above, n. 70, SEC (89) 1137.

[73] Cordova, 'Collective Bargaining', above, n. 68, 28.   [74] S. 179 TULR(C)A 1992.

[75] In Spain in branches with difficulties in reaching collective agreements, the Ministry of Labour may take the initiative for extension. This is also an option in France. In Greece an agreement which covers 60% of the workforce is normally eligible for extension. In the Netherlands the same applies to an agreement covering an 'important majority' of the workforce and in Germany one of the criteria for extension is that 50% of the employees in question are covered.

extension mechanism has been justified by the need to promote collective bargaining and to pursue more egalitarian goals.[76]

3. Collective Bargaining at Community Level

3.1. The Early Days

The Commission has long aspired to develop European level collective bargaining[77] from the weak legal basis provided by Article 118 (new Article 140). This provided that the Commission should have the task of promoting close co-operation between Member States in the social field, especially in matters relating to, *inter alia*, 'the right of association, and collective bargaining between employers and workers'.

The Commission's drive towards establishing a European industrial relations area has been frustrated by the fact that traditionally trade unions and employers' associations are national in scope and collective bargaining is usually conducted within a national framework and/or at regional, sectoral or enterprise level rather than at a centralized European level. Despite this, the two sides of industry—the intersectoral Social Partners—have long co-operated at Community level, for example, by participating in both formal and informal consultation. Formal consultation occurs in the Economic and Social Committee (ECOSOC),[78] in cross-industry advisory committees, such as the Tripartite Social Summit for Growth and Employment.[79] Consultation has also occurred informally, for example, where the Commission has sought the opinions of the EC-level Social Partners on its proposals for social legislation. This arrangement was placed on a formal footing by the Social Policy Agreement (SPA) of the Treaty on European Union.[80]

In addition, management and labour have been meeting at a sectoral level since the establishment of joint committees with the Commission's assistance in the 1960s. These committees, with equal numbers of employers and employee representatives, covered a range of sectors including agriculture (1963), road transport (1965), transport by inland waterway (1967), sea fishing (1968), rail transport (1971), and more recently civil aviation and telecommunications (1990).[81] They produced a number of joint opinions and recommendations on employment, working conditions and health and safety, but did not enter into European-wide collective agreements, largely due to

---

[76] Cordova, 'Collective Bargaining', in Blanpain (ed), above, n. 68, 329.
[77] See generally Bercussion, *European Labour Law* (Butterworths, London, 1996) Ch. 35.
[78] See above, n. 65.
[79] Co. Dec. 2003/174/EC (OJ [2003] L70/31) and Art. I–48 of the Constitutional Treaty.
[80] Art. 3(2) (new Art. 138). See further Ch. 2.
[81] For more details see *Social Europe* 2/95, 30.

opposition by the employers.[82] The Commission intended these bodies to 'contribute to the construction of a European system of industrial relations and foster free collective bargaining'[83] but the reality fell far short. Although some committees were successful, particularly those with Community-level issues to discuss (the agriculture, fisheries, and transport committees), many participants felt that the committees were formal and bureaucratic and doubted both the usefulness of their work and the Commission's real interest in their activities.[84] Consequently, the Commission initiated an informal dialogue between the sectoral Social Partners with the aim of encouraging exchanges of views, consultation on Community policies and the organization of studies and seminars, designed to 'create a climate of confidence between employers and workers'.[85] In the late 1980s this led to a new form of sectoral dialogue: informal working groups with the role of carrying out studies on employment in their sector and providing the Commission with a forum to consult on specific proposals. These contacts were formalized with the establishment of new sectoral dialogue committees.[86]

3.2. The SEA 1986 and the TEU 1992

Calls for increased dialogue between employers, trade unions, and the Community continued, not just at the sectoral level but at the intersectoral level, as a means of dealing with both economic recession and resolving the impasse which had been reached by the mid 1980s in passing social policy initiatives. Jacques Delors, then the Commission President, seized on the idea of the social dialogue as a vehicle for formulating social policy. He told the European Parliament: 'Collective bargaining must remain one of the cornerstones of our economy, and efforts must be made to secure some harmonisation at Community level. That is why I raised the idea . . . of European collective agreements to provide the framework which is essential for the achievement of a large market'.[87] This precipitated what has become known as the Val Duchesse intersectoral social dialogue in January 1985 between the European Trade Union Confederation (ETUC), representing employees, the Union of Industrial and Employers' Confederations of Europe (UNICE), representing private sector employers, and the European Centre of Public Enterprises[88] (CEEP), for public sector employers. Two working parties were established, one looking at the implications of new technology and work, the

---

[82] See *The Sectoral Social Dialogue* 224 EIRR 14 and Hepple, *European Social Dialogue—Alibi or Opportunity?* (Institute of Employment Rights, London, 1993) 13.
[83] *Social Europe* 2/85.   [84] 224 EIRR 16.   [85] Ibid.
[86] Commission Communication on Adapting and Promoting the Socail Dialogue at Community Level COM(98) 332 and Commission Decision 98/500/EC (OJ [1998] L225/27).
[87] Cited in *The Social Dialogue—Euro-Bargaining in the Making?* 220 EIRR 25, 27.
[88] Now known as the European Centre of Enterprises with Public Participation.

other dealing with employment and macroeconomic policies. Both groups issued 'Joint Opinions',[89] so called because the employers refused to countenance the notion of European-level collective agreements. However, the impetus was soon lost, in part because the exact purpose of the social dialogue had never been resolved.[90]

It was against this backcloth that Article 118b was introduced by the Single European Act 1986 (now the much amended Article 139). This provided that 'The Commission shall endeavour to develop the dialogue between management and labour at European level which could, if the two sides consider it desirable, lead to relations based on agreement'. This was reinforced by Article 12(2) of the Community Social Charter 1989 which provides that 'The dialogue between the two sides of industry at European level which *must* be developed, may, if the parties deem it desirable, result in contractual relations in particular at inter-occupational and sectoral level' (emphasis added). The Commission's view was that there should be 'complementarity between legislative initiatives on the part of the institutions and independent action by the two sides of industry'. The establishment of a balance between these two approaches would make it possible to manage 'the diversity of social practices and traditions specific to each Member State'.[91] However, since the Treaty prescribed no formal procedures for the organization of the dialogue under Article 118b and failed to specify the legal consequences of any such dialogue, it was difficult to regard Article 118b as more than a political gesture legitimating the Val Duchesse talks.[92] However, Article 118b did lead to a relaunch of the Val Duchesse dialogue, focusing this time on education and training and the problems surrounding the emergence of a European labour market.[93]

The Val Duchesse dialogue did send out the message that the two sides of industry could work together and this paved the way for consultation by the Social Partners in the drafting of the Community Social Charter 1989[94] and, more significantly the Social Partners concluded a joint agreement, on 31 October 1991, which was presented to the Maastricht intergovernmental conference and transposed almost verbatim into Articles 3 and 4 (new Articles 138 and 139) of the SPA by the Treaty on European

---

[89] E.g. 6 November 1986 for the macroeconomic committee, 6 March 1987 for the new technology committee.

[90] 220 EIRR 27.   [91] *Social Europe* 1/88, 67.   [92] Hepple, above, n. 82, 16.

[93] Ibid., 28. The relaunched dialogue was more productive. The education and training group produced three joint opinions and the working party on the labour market one further opinion, but these opinions lacked specific application and there was no requirement for the signatory parties to apply them.

[94] Their involvement is reflected in the numerous references to collective agreements, particularly as a means of guaranteeing the fundamental social rights in the Charter (Art. 27) and 'the active involvement of the two sides of industry' (Preamble). See generally, Guéry, 'European Collective Bargaining and the Maastricht Treaty' (1992) 131 *International Labour Review* 581.

Union. This Agreement entitled the Social Partners not only to be consulted about proposed legislation[95] but also to enter a dialogue which may lead to agreements[96] which can be implemented autonomously or by a Council 'decision'— in reality a Directive—on a proposal from the Commission.[97]

3.3. Assessment

For a while, the SPA, EMU and subsequently the EES revitalized the transnational role of the Social Partners both at the intersectoral and now at the sectoral level. From small beginnings, the Social Partners have the potential to enjoy significant influence at EU level and, in so doing, strengthened collective bargaining at national level. At EU level we see a form of tripartite or bipartite concertation—or Euro-corporatism—is emerging. The role now envisaged for the Social Partners is one of partnership[98] and co-operation rather than adversarialism, a shift from industrial pluralism[99] to a more managerialist perspective.[100] At national level we also see how European-level collective bargaining is helping to steer national collective bargaining. Social policy Directives, such as the Directives on proof of the employment contract,[101] working time[102] and young workers,[103] can now be implemented by collective bargaining. They contain a clause providing that the Member States must pass laws, regulations or administrative provisions to adopt the Directive by a particular date or shall ensure 'that the employers' and workers' representatives introduce the required provisions by way of agreement'. This method of implementation has now been confirmed by Article 139(2) (ex Article 4(2) SPA). Collective agreements or their equivalents can also be used to flesh out substantive standards in the Directives. For example, Article 4 of the Working

---

[95] Art. 138(2).   [96] Art. 139(1). See further Ch. 2.

[97] Art. 139(2). The English language version of the Treaty provides for a 'decision'. This has been interpreted to mean any legally binding instrument, including Directives. See further Ch. 2.

[98] See e.g. the Commission's Green Paper *Partnership for a New Organisation of Work* COM(97) 127. See also 'Developing a European Industrial Relations and Partnership Culture': COM(98) 322, 17; '. . . a process, based on partnership, represents the most promising way of modernising working life': COM(98) 592; 'a partnership-based working method aimed at identifying consistent solutions in all areas affected by the crisis': High Level Group, 'Managing Change', November 1998. See also the British Fairness at Work White Paper (http://www.dti.gov.ui/IR/fairness/ where the government talks of the principles of fairness of work and competitiveness providing a 'blueprint for the development of partnership in the longer term' (para. 1.11). At para. 4.7 it talks of trade unions as being 'a force for fair treatment, and a means of driving towards innovation and partnerships'.

[99] For a classic exposition of pluralism in labour law, see Kahn-Freund's *Labour and the Law* by Davies and Freedland, 3rd edn (Stevens, London, 1983).

[100] See the typology suggested in Terry, 'Systems of Collective Employee Representation in Non-union Firms in the UK' (1999) 30 *IRJ*. 16, 17.

[101] Council Dir. 91/533/EEC (OJ [1991] L288/32).

[102] Council Dir. 93/104/EC (OJ [1993] L307/18). See Scheuer, 'The Impact of Collective Agreements on Working Time in Denmark' (1999) 37 *BJIR*. 465.

[103] Council Dir. 94/33/EC (OJ [1994] L216/12). See generally Adinolfi, 'Implementation of Social Policy Directives through Collective Agreements' (1988) 25 *CMLRev*. 291.

Time Directive 2003/88[104] requires that rest breaks must be provided if the working day lasts longer than six hours but that details of breaks, 'including duration and the terms on which it is granted, shall be laid down in collective agreements or agreements between the two sides of industry or, *failing that*, by national legislation' (emphasis added). This is an example of what the Dutch and Germans call an opening clause, allowing greater flexibility of practices (notably over working time) at company level,[105] albeit that that flexibility comes at the price of allowing collective agreements to derogate from the legislative norms *in pejus*,[106] thereby allowing standards to deteriorate.

4. Is there a Fundamental Right to Bargain Collectively?

Do these developments mean that there is a fundamental right not only to freedom of association but also to bargain collectively? The answer seems to be no. In *Wilson and Palmer* the European Court of Human Rights said that 'although collective bargaining may be one of the ways by which trade unions may be enabled to protect their members' interests, it is not indispensable for the effective enjoyment of trade union freedom'. It continued that compulsory collective bargaining would impose on employers an obligation to conduct negotiations with trade unions. The Court has not yet been prepared to hold that the freedom of a trade union to make its voice heard extends to imposing on an employer an obligation to recognize a trade union.[107] As a result, the Court of Human Rights found that the absence under UK law of an obligation on employers to enter into collective bargaining, did not give rise to a violation of Article 11.[108]

Advocate General Jacobs, in the earlier EC case of *Albany*, also thought that there was no fundamental right to bargain collectively, even though it is the freedom most fully articulated in the Community legal order. He said that only Article 6 of the European Social Charter 1961 expressly recognized the existence of a fundamental right to bargain.[109] However, he then said, the mere fact that a right is included in the Charter does not mean that it is generally recognized as a fundamental right. The structure of the Charter is such that the rights set out represent policy goals rather than enforceable rights, and the states parties to it are required only to select which of the rights specified

---

[104] OJ [2003] L299/9 considered further in Ch. 12.

[105] Ferner and Hyman, above, n. 62, xvi.

[106] See generally Lord Wedderburn, 'Collective Bargaining at European Level: the Inderogability Problem' (1992) 21 *ILJ*. 245.

[107] Para. 44. See also *UNISON v. United Kingdom*, judgment of 10 January 2002, [2002] IRLR 497, para. 42 where the Court of Human Rights said that the Union could not claim under the Convention a 'requirement that an employer enter into, or remain in, any particular collective bargaining arrangement or accede to its requests on behalf of its members'.

[108] Para. 45.   [109] Case C–67/96 *Albany* [1999] ECR I–5751, para. 146.

they undertake to protect. He then pointed to Article 4 of 'the carefully drafted "Right to Organise and Collective Bargaining Convention" [which] imposes on the Contracting States an obligation to "encourage and promote" collective bargaining. No right is granted'.[110] He then considered the case law of the European Court of Human Rights where, he noted, 'there is a telling absence of any reference to the right to bargain collectively'. He concluded that:

... it cannot be said that there is sufficient convergence of national legal orders and international legal instruments on the recognition of a specific fundamental right to bargain collectively.[111]

Moreover, the collective bargaining process, like any other negotiation between economic actors, is in my view sufficiently protected by the general principle of freedom of contract. Therefore, a more specific fundamental right to protection is not needed. In any event the justified limitations on the alleged right to bargain collectively would arguably be identical to those on freedom of contract.[112]

Since *Albany* a new factor has entered the equation: the Charter of Fundamental Rights 2000. Article 28 (Article II–88 of the Constitutional Treaty) provides:

Workers and employers, or their respective organisations, have, in accordance with Community law and national laws and practices, the right to negotiate and conclude collective agreements at the appropriate levels and, in cases of conflicts of interests, to take collective action to defend their interests, including strike action.

The language of rights suggests a move towards a 'right' to collective bargaining. However, as we saw in chapter 1, some of the social rights are more akin to principles and so the Charter may not alter the view that there is no right to bargain collectively. This is particularly so in the case of collective bargaining whose voluntary nature has long been emphasized by the European Court of Human Rights.[113]

5. Collective Bargaining and Competition Law

The purpose of the discussion in *Albany* was to consider whether collective agreements on wages and conditions, as well as those implementing Community Directives, could be shielded from Community competition law (Article 81(1) and (2)). If collective bargaining had been a fundamental right then collective agreements might have been protected from Article 81,[114] although

---

[110] Para. 147.   [111] Para. 160.   [112] Para. 161.

[113] See also the views of the European Court of Human Rights to that effect in *Swedish Engine Drivers v. Sweden*, Application no. 5614/72, judgment of 6 February 1976, Eur. Ct HR Rep., Series A, No. 20 (1976), para. 39.

[114] See the arguments of the pension funds, the Dutch and French governments, and the Commission.

Advocate General Jacobs even doubted this.[115] However, since collective bargaining was not, according to Advocate General Jacobs, a fundamental right then in principle collective agreements risked being exposed to the full rigours of Article 81 because, according to the Commission's submissions, collective agreements are, by their very nature, restrictive of competition since generally employees cannot offer to work for a wage below the agreed minimum, and they affect trade between Member States.[116] Such agreements would thus be prohibited and void unless exempted by the Commission under Article 81(3).[117] The granting of such an exemption would be unlikely since that provision does not allow social objectives to be taken into account.[118] This result would occur despite the fact that 'there is international consensus on the legitimate and socially desirable character of collective bargaining'[119] which is to prevent employees from engaging in a 'race to the bottom' with regard to wages and working conditions.[120]

Collective agreements therefore present a conflict between the social and competition provisions of the Treaty. As Advocate General Jacobs pointed out,[121] the authors of the Treaty either were not aware of the problem or could not agree on a solution[122] and so the Treaty does not give clear guidance as to which policy should take priority. He said that since both sets of rules were Treaty provisions of the same rank, one set of rules should not take absolute precedence over the other and neither set of rules should be emptied

---

[115] Para. 163: 'The mere recognition of a fundamental right to bargain collectively would therefore not suffice to shelter collective bargaining from the applicability of the competition rules'.

[116] Para. 175. Advocate General Jacobs in *Albany* doubted this (para. 182). He said that collective agreements on wages, working time or other working conditions, although they may restrict competition between employees, probably do not have an appreciable restrictive effect on competition between employers. As regards competition on the demand side of the labour market, normally each employer remains free to offer more advantageous conditions to his employees. As regards competition on the product or services markets on which the employers operate, first, agreements on wages or working conditions harmonize merely one of many production cost factors. Therefore only one aspect of competition is affected. Secondly, proximity to the market of the factor in issue is an important criterion for assessing appreciability. In the case of collective agreements on wages and working conditions, the final price of the products or services in question is influenced by many other factors before they reach the market. Thirdly, and perhaps most importantly, production factor costs are only apparently harmonized, because in economic terms labour, in contrast to raw materials, is not a homogeneous commodity. The fact that employees earn nominally the same wage does not mean that the real costs for their respective employers are identical. Real costs can be determined only when the employees' productivity is taken into account. Productivity is determined by many factors, e.g. professional skills, motivation, technological environment, and work organization. All those factors can be and are influenced by employers. That is precisely the task of efficient management of human resources. Thus, competition on labour as a cost factor is in fact strong.

[117] This is increasingly unlikely: see Commission Notice, *Guidelines on the application of Article 81(3) of the Treaty* OJ [2004] C101/97 where no reference is made to social (or environmental) considerations. Only economic considerations can be taken into account when deciding whether an agreement fulfils the conditions of Art. 81(3).

[118] Para. 175. Cf. para. 193.   [119] Para. 164.   [120] Para. 178.   [121] Para. 179.
[122] Ibid.

of its entire content. He therefore suggested the following reconciliation: since the Treaty rules encouraging collective bargaining presuppose that collective agreements are in principle lawful, Article 81(1) could not have been intended to apply to collective agreements between management and labour on core subjects such as wages and other working conditions. Accordingly, such collective agreements should enjoy automatic immunity from antitrust scrutiny.

He then proposed three conditions for ipso facto immunity: first, the agreement must be made within the formal framework of collective bargaining between both sides of industry. Unilateral co-ordination between employers unconnected with the collective bargaining process should not be automatically sheltered, whatever the subject of the co-ordination may be.[123] Secondly, the agreement should be concluded in good faith. In that context account must be taken of agreements which apparently deal with core subjects of collective bargaining such as working time but which merely function as cover for a serious restriction of competition between employers on their product markets. In those exceptional cases, too, competition authorities should be able to examine the agreement in question.[124] Thirdly, the immunity extends only to those agreements for which it is truly justified, i.e. that the collective agreement deals with the core subjects of collective bargaining, such as wages and working conditions, and does not directly affect third parties or markets.

He suggested that the test should be 'whether the agreement merely modifies or establishes rights and obligations within the labour relationship between employers and employees or whether it goes beyond that and directly affects relations between employers and third parties, such as clients, suppliers, competing employers, or consumers'. Because the latter types of agreement have potentially harmful effects on the competitive process, they should be subject to antitrust scrutiny by the Commission or other competent authorities, which would examine whether there was in fact an appreciable restriction of competition. If so, the Commission should be able to balance the different interests involved and, where appropriate, grant an exemption according to Article 81(3). He pointed out that both the Court and the Commission have, on occasions, recognized the possibility of taking account of social grounds in particular by interpreting the conditions of Article 81(3) broadly so as to include concerns for employment.[125]

Thus, in Advocate General Jacobs' view, collective agreements concluded in

---

[123] Para. 191.   [124] Para. 192.

[125] Citing Case 26/76 *Metro v. Commission* [1977] ECR 1875, para. 43, Case 42/84 *Remia v. Commission* [1985] ECR 2545, para. 42; *Synthetic Fibres* (OJ [1984] L207/17), para. 37, and *Ford v. Volkswagen* (OJ [1993] L20/14), para. 23. However, cf. Commission Notice, *Guidelines on the application of Article 81(3) of the Treaty* OJ [2004] C101/97 considered above which refers only to economic considerations which can be taken into account when deciding whether an agreement satisfies Art. 81(3).

(1) good faith on (2) core subjects (such as wages and working conditions) which do not (3) directly affect third markets and third parties, are not caught by Article 81(1).[126] Agreements which do not satisfy one of these conditions are caught by Article 81(1) and will be subject to scrutiny by the Commission under Article 81(3) if notified. This is very much the perspective of a competition lawyer. The Court took a rather different, labour relations approach which offered greater respect to the autonomy of the Social Partners. It began by observing that the Community's activities include not only 'a system ensuring that competition in the internal market is not distorted'[127] but also 'a policy in the social sphere',[128] and that one of the Community's tasks is to promote a 'harmonious and balanced development of economic activities' and a 'high level of employment and social protection'.[129] It then pointed to the Commission's duties under Article 118 (new Article 140) and Article 118b (now amended Article 139) concerning collective bargaining and the role of the social dialogue under Article 1 SPA (now Article 136) and Articles 4(1) and (2) SPA (now Article 139(1) and (2)).[130] It continued:

59. It is beyond question that certain restrictions of competition are inherent in collective agreements between organisations representing employers and workers. However, the social policy objectives pursued by such agreements would be seriously undermined if management and labour were subject to Article [81(1)] of the Treaty when seeking jointly to adopt measures to improve conditions of work and employment.

60. It therefore follows from an interpretation of the provisions of the Treaty as a whole which is both effective and consistent that agreements concluded in the context of collective negotiations between management and labour in pursuit of such objectives must, by virtue of their nature and purpose, be regarded as falling outside the scope of Article [81(1)] of the Treaty.

Thus, while the Advocate General thought that competition law applied to collective agreements but they were immune subject to three strict conditions being satisfied conditions being applied, the Court took the view that competition law did not apply at all provided that the collective agreement was aimed at improving working conditions.[131]

Albany itself concerned a collective agreement negotiated by representative organizations of employers and workers setting up a supplementary pension scheme, managed by a pension fund, to which affiliation was compulsory. The Dutch Minister of Employment had, on request of the Social Partners, made affiliation to the scheme compulsory for all workers in the sector. The Court said this guaranteed a certain level of pension to all workers in the sector

---

[126] Para. 194.   [127] Art. 3(g).   [128] Art. 3(j).   [129] Para. 54.
[130] Paras. 55–8.
[131] AG Fennelly in Case C–222/98 *Van der Woude* v. *Stichting Beatrixoord* [2000] ECR I–7111, para. 26 said that '[A]s an exception to the general field of application of Article [81] of the EC Treaty, the scope of the *Albany* exception should be narrowly construed'.

which contributed directly to the improvement of one of the conditions of employment knowing their pay. Thus Article 81 did not apply.[132] As far as extending the collective agreement is concerned, as we have already seen, the possibility of giving *erga omnes* effect to a collective agreement exists in certain Member States[133] and in the Community itself (through a 'decision' of the Council of Ministers).[134] This was recognized by the Court in *Albany*.[135] It said that since the collective agreement itself was not caught by Article 81(1) the Member State was free to extend it to all workers in the sector.[136] Similarly, in *Van der Woude* the Court said that a collective agreement establishing a health care insurance scheme contributed to improving the working conditions of employees, not only by ensuring that they have the necessary means to meet medical expenses but also by reducing the costs which, in the absence of a collective agreement, would have to be borne by the employees.[137] By reason of its nature and purpose, the agreement did not therefore fall within the scope of Article 81(1).[138]

D. THE RIGHT TO TAKE COLLECTIVE ACTION

1. Introduction

Collective action can take a variety of forms. While strikes are the most obvious expression of conflict, industrial action can also include overtime bans, go-slows, a work to rule, withdrawal of co-operation, sit-ins, and picketing. Workers may also refuse to handle products made by a firm in a dispute (blacking) to support workers of that firm. Collective action is not necessarily one-sided: management can lock out workers, the reverse of a strike, dismiss workers or bring in others to do the strikers' jobs (blacklegging). These workers may be employed by a subsidiary or an agency located elsewhere in the Community and, exercising their right of free movement, drafted in to assist

---

[132] Paras. 63–4. See also Joined Cases C–115–7/97 *Brentjens Handelsonderneming BV* v. *Stichting Bedrijfspensioenfonds voor de Handel in Bouwmaterialen* [1999] ECR I–6025; Case C–219/97 *Maatschappij Drijvende Bokken BV* v. *Stichting Pensioenfonds voor de Vervoer- en Havenbedrijven* [1999] ECR I–6121. These cases are considered by Vousden, 'Albany, Market Law and Social Exclusion' (2000) 29 *ILJ*. 181. See also Case C–222/98 *Van der Woude* v. *Stichting Beatrixoord* [2000] ECR I–7111 considered by Evju, 'Collective Agreements and Competition Law. The *Albany* puzzle and *Van der Woude*' (2001) 17 *IJCLLIR* 165.

[133] See above, n. 75.   [134] See above, n. 97.   [135] Paras. 66 and 67.

[136] Although Art. 81 concerns only the behaviour of undertakings and not legislative or regulatory measures emanating from Member States, Member States are obliged under Art. 81 read in conjunction with Art. 10 not to take or maintain in force legislation capable of eliminating the useful effect of the competition rules which apply to undertakings. This is not the case here.

[137] Para. 25.   [138] Para. 26.

the employer. More drastically, the employer may decide to close the plant and/or relocate the business.

2. Recognizing the Right to Strike

The right to strike is recognized in a number of international economic and social rights instruments but not yet clearly by Article 11(1) of the European Convention on Human Rights.[139] In *National Union of Belgian Police*[140] the European Court of Human Rights relied on the phrase 'for the protection of his interests' in Article 11(1) to hold that freedom of association included the rights that were 'indispensable for the effective enjoyment' or 'necessarily inherent elements' of trade union freedom. It said that Article 11 therefore also 'safeguards the freedom to protect the occupational interests of trade union members by trade union action, the conduct and development of which the Contracting States must both permit and make possible'.[141] However, the scope of collective action that can be taken to protect those interests under the European Convention is far from clear. Given the Court of Human Rights' sensitivity to the social and political issues involved in achieving a proper balance between the respective interests of labour and management, and given the wide degree of divergence between the domestic systems in this field, it has given the Contracting States a wide margin of appreciation.[142] To date the only right expressly recognized by the Court of Human Rights has been to be 'heard' by the state.[143] On the other hand, a trade union has no right to be consulted by the state,[144] nor, as we saw above, is the state required to impose an obligation on employers to recognize a trade union or conclude collective agreements.[145] However, in *UNISON* v. *UK* the Court of Human Rights did expressly recognize the significance of strikes to trade unions,[146]

[139] *UNISON* v. *United Kingdom*, judgment of 10 January 2002, [2002] IRLR 497, para. 35: 'There is no express inclusion of a right to strike or an obligation on employers to engage in collective bargaining. At most, Article 11 may be regarded as safeguarding the freedom of trade union members to protect the occupational interests of their members.'

[140] *National Union of Belgian Police* v. *Belgium*, 27 October 1975, Eur. Ct HR Rep., Series A, No. 19 (1975), para. 39.

[141] Ibid., para. 40.

[142] See, e.g. *Schettini* v. *Italy*, Application no. 29529/95, judgment of 9 November 2000, under heading 2.

[143] Ibid., para. 39; *Swedish Engine Drivers' Union* v. *Sweden*, judgment of 6 February 1976, Eur. Ct HR Rep., Series A, No. 20 (1976), para. 40.

[144] *National Union of Belgian Police* v. *Belgium*, 27 October 1975, Eur. Ct HR Rep., Series A, No. 19 (1975), para. 38.

[145] *Swedish Engine Drivers' Union* v. *Sweden*, 6 February 1976, Eur. Ct HR Rep., Series A, No. 20 (1976), para. 39; *Wilson and Palmer* v. *The United Kingdom*, Applications nos. 30668/96, 30671/96 and 30678/96, judgment of 2 July 2002, para. 45.

[146] It expressed similar sentiments in *Schmidt and Dahlström*, judgment of 6 February 1976, Eur. Ct HR Rep., Series A, No. 21 (1976), para. 36.

albeit without actually declaring that Article 11 included a right to strike. It said that 'While the ability to strike represents one of the most important means by which trade unions can fulfil [the function of protecting the occupational interests of their members], there are others'.[147] However, when, in *Wilson and Palmer*, the Court repeated this phrase, the language had changed to become 'The grant of the *right* to strike, while it may be subject to regulation, represents one of the most important of the means by which the State may secure a trade union's freedom to protect its members' occupational interests'.[148] This comes close to the European Court of Human Rights recognizing the right to strike.

In *UNISON* the trade union had called a strike by its members working in University College London Hospital (UCLH) to protest about the fact that, with the transfer of the hospital's staff to a Private Finance Initiative consortium, the hospital would not enter into a contractual arrangement with the consortium guaranteeing the maintenance of the terms and conditions of employment of the transferred staff for 30 years on the same terms as the non-transferred staff. The employers successfully obtained an interlocutory injunction from the High Court restraining the strike, on the grounds that it was unlikely that the union would succeed at trial in establishing immunity from tort liability for the strike action. While the Court of Human Rights found that the prohibition on the strike was a restriction on UNISON's power to protect the occupational interests of its members and therefore disclosed a restriction the freedom of association guaranteed by Article 11(1),[149] the restriction could be justified under Article 11(2) (considered above). The restriction was prescribed by law,[150] pursued the legitimate aim of protecting the 'rights of others' (i.e. the employer, UCLH whose ability to carry out its functions effectively, including securing contracts with other bodies, would be interfered with),[151] and was proportionate (the union's members were not at any immediate risk of detriment or of being left defenceless against future attempts to downgrade pay or conditions).[152]

In some human rights instruments, such as Article 6 of the ESC 1961 and, more importantly for our purposes, Article 27 of the Charter of Fundamental Rights 2000, the right to strike is expressly linked to collective bargaining. Article 27 provides that workers and employers have the right to negotiate and conclude collective agreements 'and, in cases of conflicts of interests, to take collective action to defend their interests, including strike action'. Linking collective bargaining and strikes in this way emphasizes that the primary purpose of a strike is to put pressure on the employer in the course of negotiations over matters that can be collectively bargained, such as pay,[153] a link

---

[147] Ibid. [148] Para. 45. [149] Paras. 36–7. [150] Para. 38. [151] Para. 39.
[152] Para. 42.
[153] On the other hand, it also means that strikes not directly linked to collective bargaining, such as political strikes, are not permitted.

which was underlined in *Wilson and Palmer* where the Court of Human Rights said that 'the essence of a voluntary system of collective bargaining is that it must be possible for a trade union which is not recognised by an employer to "take steps including, if necessary industrial action, with a view to persuading the employer to enter into collective bargaining with it on those issues which the union believes are important for its members" interests'.[154] These observations highlight the structural imbalance in European-level collective bargaining where the ETUC cannot realistically threaten industrial action to persuade UNICE/UEAPME and CEEP to engage in collective bargaining.

3. The Meaning of the 'Right' to Strike

Article 13 of the Community Social Charter 1989 recognizes the 'right' to 'resort to *collective action* in the event of a conflict of interests' (emphasis added). This includes the '*right* to strike, subject to obligations arising under national regulations and collective agreements' (emphasis added).[155] In *Wilson and Palmer* the Court of Human Rights also emphasized the right to strike. It said that:

The grant of the right to strike, while it may be subject to regulation, represents one of the most important of the means by which the state may secure a trade union's freedom to protect its members' commercial interests.[156]

Consistent with the Romano-Germanic tradition, the 1989 Charter, and less clearly, the 2000 Charter, recognize the *right* to strike, as opposed to the Anglo-Saxon *freedom* to strike.[157] Freedom to strike means that the strike is legally permitted but no special privileges are granted: the strike is tolerated, but not privileged, and the legal limits of the strike are dictated by the general legal order. The right to strike, by contrast, means that the legal order of the state must take precautions to ensure the exercise of the right and so the strike is privileged. This demonstrates that the legal order evaluates the pursuit of collective interests more highly than the individual obligations arising from the contract of employment. The importance of this right, and the recognition of the inequality of bargaining power between workers and

---

[154] Para. 46.

[155] For a full discussion of this issue, see Novitz, *International and European Protection of the Right to Strike: a Comparative Study of Standards set by the International Labour Organization, the Council of Europe and the European Union* (OUP, Oxford, 2003).

[156] Para. 45.

[157] Birk, 'Industrial Conflict: The Law of Strikes and Lock-outs', in Blanpain (ed.), *Comparative Labour Law and Industrial Relations*, 3rd edn (Kluwer, Deventer, 1990) 406. The discussion that follows draws on this chapter. See also Wedderburn, 'The Right to Strike: Is There a European Standard?', in Wedderburn, above, n. 3.

employers, has meant that the right to strike is expressly recognized in the constitutions of many Member States.

In most countries the right to strike belongs to the employees who organize their interests collectively. Individual action is generally excluded. By contrast, in the UK the *right* to strike does not exist as such, but, subject to certain stringent conditions, trade unions are protected by immunities established by law when their members take certain forms of industrial action. These same immunities now do provide some protection for individual employees but they are likely to breach their individual employment contracts by taking any form of industrial action and can, in certain circumstances, be dismissed as a result. By contrast, in most Romano-Germanic countries, the contract of employment is merely suspended during the strike. By contrast, lock-outs do not enjoy the same protection as the right or freedom to strike.

The Community Social Charter recognizes that the right to strike is 'subject to the obligations arising under national regulations and collective agreements'. The equivalent right in the European Social Charter 1961 is expressed in similar terms.[158] These obligations relate to national rules concerning, for example, strike ballots, the need to announce a strike in advance, the requirement that any action taken must be proportionate[159] and a last resort, and the need to respect, where necessary, the peace obligation contained in the collective agreement and the obligation not to undertake political strikes (i.e. strikes designed to express a grievance against public policy) or sympathy/secondary strikes (i.e. strikes in support of primary strikes), at least if the interests of the sympathy strikers are not linked to those of the primary strikers.[160]

4. The Right to Strike and Community Law

Article 137(5) expressly excludes Community competence (at least under Article 137) in respect of the right to strike or the right to impose lock-outs. Thus, the Community will not be legislating on this basis. On the other hand, as we have seen, Advocate General Jacobs suggested in his opinion in *Albany*[161] that the collective right to take action was a fundamental right.[162] Later he added that 'In my view, the right to take collective action in order to

---

[158] Art. 6(4) recognizes 'the right of workers and employers to collective action in cases of conflicts of interest, including the right to strike, subject to obligations that may arise out of collective agreements previously entered into'.

[159] I.e. 'the use of the industrial action must be necessary, must be the suitable instrument to fulfil the intended purpose, and finally may not be an excessive instrument' (Weiss, *Labour Law and Industrial Relations in the Federal Republic of Germany* (Kluwer, Deventer, 1989) 135).

[160] See generally, Germanotta and Novitz, 'Globalisation and the Right to Strike: The Case for European-Level Protection of Secondary Action' (2002) 18 *IJCLLIR* 67.

[161] Case C–67/96 [1999] ECR I–5751.   [162] Para. 139.

protect occupational interests in so far as it is indispensable for the enjoyment of freedom of association is also protected by Community law.'[163] He said this was significant because any impairment of the substance of the right, even in the public interest, might be unlawful.[164]

This issue was acknowledged in Council Regulation No. 2679/98[165] which, as we saw above, provided that the intervention mechanism to safeguard free trade in the single market was not to be 'interpreted as affecting in any way the exercise of fundamental rights, as recognised in Member States, including the right or freedom to strike'.[166] This Regulation also provided the justification for the European Parliament to insert into its revised proposal for a Directive on services Article 2a which says:

This Directive may not be interpreted[167] as affecting in any way the exercise of fundamental rights as recognised in Member States, including the right or freedom to strike. These rights may also include the right to take other action covered by the specific industrial relations systems in Member States.

As the EP explains, 'This Directive deals with the provision of services and not with employees providing these services as such. It is important to state that this Directive should not be contrary to labour law related fundamental rights, such as the right to freedom of association, freedom of negotiation, to take industrial action and to conclude collective agreements.'[168] Thus, the recognition of the right to strike, as a fundamental right, serves to limit the activities of the Community institutions when legislating in this field. It also limits the actions that can be taken by the Member States which may impinge upon the right to strike. These issues will be fundamental in the Court's consideration of the *Viking* case[169] which was considered in detail in chapter 5.

5. Prevention and Settlement of Disputes

Most Member States, with the exception of the UK and Ireland, draw a distinction between disputes over conflicts of interests and disputes over conflicts

---

[163] Para. 159.

[164] Case C–280/93 *Germany* v. *Council* [1994] ECR I–4973, paras. 78 and 87; cf. paras. 162 and 163 in Case C–67/96 *Albany* [1999] ECR I–5751.

[165] OJ [1998] L337/8.

[166] Reg. 2679/98 was accompanied by a Resolution of the Council and representatives of the Member States of 7 December 1998 on the free movement of goods (OJ [1998] L337/10).

[167] Art. 2(3a) has already excluded 'the field of labour law, including collective agreements and industrial action, and social security law' from the Directive.

[168] A6–0409/2005.

[169] *Viking* v. *The International Transport Workers' Federation and the Finnish Seamen's Union* [2005] EWHC 1222; [2005] EWCA Civ 1299; [2006] IRLR 58.

of rights.[170] While disputes over conflicts of rights concern the interpretation and application of existing contractual clauses, disputes over conflicts of interests relate to changes in the establishment of collective rules and require the conflicting economic interest to be reconciled with a view to reaching a solution on the basis of legal or collective procedures. In principle, strikes are permitted to resolve conflicts of interests between labour and management, but the courts, especially the labour courts, usually decide disputes concerning conflicts of rights.

Article 13(2) of the Community Social Charter 1989 (but not the EU Charter of Fundamental Rights) encourages the use of alternative dispute resolution:

In order to facilitate the settlement of industrial disputes the establishment and utilisation at the appropriate levels of conciliation, mediation and arbitration procedures should be encouraged in accordance with national practice.

Member States recognize both judicial and non-judicial mechanisms for preventing and resolving collective disputes. Conciliation, mediation, and arbitration are the most common forms of non-judicial or third party intervention. Conciliation is where a third party encourages the parties to reach their own agreement. By contrast, in mediation a third party hears the dispute and makes formal but non-binding recommendations for resolving it. Finally, in arbitration a third party hears the dispute and makes a binding decision.

Conciliation and mediation may arise from, and have their legal base in, the obligatory part of the collective agreement. This suggests that the parties themselves are primarily responsible for finding a solution to their conflicts. This is closely related to the principles behind the peace obligation. Government mediation and conciliation services are available in most Member States, but in most cases they perform a secondary role.[171] Arbitration, by contrast, imposes a solution on the parties from outside and so interferes with the autonomy of the Social Partners. For this reason it is not permitted in some Member States.

E. CONCLUSIONS

The enormous difficulties faced by the EC in enacting measures relating to collective labour law bears testimony to Kahn-Freund's observation that 'individual labour law lends itself to transplantation very much more easily than . . . collective labour law. Standards of protection and rules on substantive terms of employment can be imitated—rules on collective bargaining, on

---

[170] See generally Blanpain, 'Prevention and Settlement of Collective Labour Disputes in the EEC Countries', Parts I and II (1972) 1 *ILJ.* 74 and 143.

[171] Commission, above, n. 70, SEC (89) 1137.

the closed shop, on trade unions, on strikes, cannot'.[172] The experience of the ILO and the European Social Charter is similar: according to Kahn-Freund, 'nothing could more clearly demonstrate the knowledge of the draftsman that collective bargaining institutions and rules are untransplantable'.[173] This, he attributes to a different 'habitat of industrial relations' where the relations between management and labour are organised under the influence of strong political traditions, traditions connected with the role played by organizations on both sides as political pressure groups promoting legislation, and as rule-making agencies through the procedures of collective bargaining.[174]

That said, at EU level, intersectoral and sectoral collective bargaining has enjoyed some success, and the recognition of freedom of association and the right to strike as fundamental rights has helped to protect the integrity of national systems of labour law from the full rigours of the internal market and competition law. Nevertheless, there remains a striking imbalance between the rhetoric of collective rights in the EU Charters and the Community's actual action in the field. Collective rights have long been the Cinderella area of European Union law; for the present they look destined to stay that way.

---

[172] 'Uses and Misuses of Comparative Law' (1974) 37 *MLR* 1, 21.
[173] Ibid, 22.   [174] Ibid, 20.

Index